PHILIP'S

07/22

LOCAL EXPLORER

LINCOLNSHIRE

www.philips-maps.co.uk

Published by Philip's a division of
Octopus Publishing Group Ltd
www.octopusbooks.co.uk
Carmelite House,
50 Victoria Embankment,
London EC4Y 0DZ
An Hachette UK Company
www.hachette.co.uk

First edition 2022
LINDA

ISBN 978-1-84907-604-3

© Philip's 2022

Map data This product includes
mapping data licensed from
Ordnance Survey® with the
permission of the Controller of
Her Majesty's Stationery Office.
© Crown copyright 2022. All rights reserved.
Licence number 100011710.

Photographic acknowledgements:
Alamy Stock Photo: /Matt Limb OBE front
cover. *Dreamstime.com:* /Chris Dorney II top
left; /Georgesixth II top right; /Nicola Pulham
II bottom; /Wellsie82 III top; /Stanislav Říha
III bottom.

Printed in China

CONTENTS

II	**Best places to visit**
IV	**Key to map pages**
VI	**Route planning**
X	**Key to map symbols**
1	**Street maps** at 1¾ inches to 1 mile
178	**Street maps** at 3½ inches to 1 mile
234	**Street map of Lincoln city centre** at 7 inches to 1 mile
235	**Index** of towns, villages, streets, hospitals, industrial estates, railway stations, schools, shopping centres, universities and places of interest

Best places to visit

◀ Lincoln Cathedral and Steep Hill (inset)

▶ Lancaster bomber statue at the International Bomber Command Centre

Lincoln Historic city, dramatically situated on a hill, where its most important sites are found. Its history began in the Bronze Age and it came to prominence when the Romans built a fortress on the hill, known as Lindum Colonia. **Lincoln Castle** is an impressive Norman castle, built under the orders of William I in the late 11th century, and housing original copies of both the Magna Carta (1215) and the revised Charter of the Forest (1217). Other castle highlights include the medieval stone curtain walls, with towers and dungeons, and the Victorian Prison. The spectacular **Lincoln Cathedral** is a vast Gothic cathedral, also built in the 11th century. As well as its sheer size, it is noted for intricate stone carvings, vaults, colourful stained glass windows, and the Christopher Wren-designed library. Adjacent to the cathedral is the partially ruined medieval **Bishops' Palace**. The 13th-century undercrofted East Hall can be visited and there are peaceful gardens within the ruins. Nearby, the cobbled **Steep Street** links the upper town to the lower, and dates from when the Romans expanded their settlement down towards the river. It is lined with attractive historic houses and shops. 🖥 www.visitlincoln.com **234**

Outdoors

Donna Nook Six-mile stretch of coastline, now a National Nature Reserve, where grey seals come to give birth to their pups. There is a viewing area during the winter when the seals are present. Large numbers of birds breed at the site, and rare migrant species are sometimes spotted. Interesting plant communities thrive on the inter-tidal areas, mudflats and saltings. *North Somercote* 🖥 www.lincstrust.org.uk **51 B7**

Far Ings Nature reserve on the south bank of the Humber Estuary, a popular site for bird-watching thanks to its position on a major migration route. The varied habitats, freshwater and saltwater environments allow microscopic and insect life to flourish, resulting in abundant fish and a large variety of birds. There are circular walks, a visitor centre and plenty of hides. It is an important breeding site for bitterns, whose distinctive booming call can be heard in the spring. *Barton-upon-Humber* 🖥 www.lincstrust.org.uk **3 D2**

Gibraltar Point Nature reserve that stretches from Skegness to the mouth of the Wash. The unspoilt coastline is home to a wide variety of wildlife year round and is particularly popular with birdwatchers. It is home to one of Britain's 19 official observatories, which monitor long-term bird populations and migration. There are hides, a visitor centre and marked paths. *Skegness* 🖥 www.lincstrust.org.uk **116 D4**

Lincolnshire Wolds Large area of unspoilt countryside covering about 216 square miles between the city of Lincoln and the coast, designated an Area of Outstanding Natural Beauty. Its hills, valleys, streams and villages have been shaped by thousands of years of agriculture, and today nearly 80% of the land is farmed. The varied habitats are important to numerous plant and animal species. The area is a magnet for walkers, cyclists and other outdoor enthusiasts; attractions range from the remains of deserted medieval villages and Bronze Age barrows to abandoned World War II airfields.
On the southern edge of the Wolds is the Snipe Dales country

▼ *Gibraltar Point*

park and nature reserve. Wet valleys and scrub characterise the nature reserve, whereas the adjoining country park is mainly woodland. Waymarked trails enable visitors to enjoy the varied wildlife, in particular birds, butterflies and dragonflies. *Lusby* 🖥 www.lincswolds.org.uk 🖥 www.lincstrust.org.uk **86 F3**

Normanby Hall Country Park Large estate surrounding a Regency mansion. Within the 300 acres are a Victorian Walled Garden, a woodland, with some unusual tree species, a deer park with red and fallow deer, and a fishing lake. Attractions include a Servants' Trail and Rural Life Museum, as well as a land train, miniature railway and family activities. The mansion dates from around 1825 and is furnished accordingly. 🖥 www.normanbyhall.co.uk **8 C3**

Saltfleetby and Theddlethorpe Dunes National Nature Reserve with over 900 hectares of sand dunes, mudflats, salt and freshwater marshes, which attract a wide variety of bird species. It is one of the few locations where the rare natterjack toad is found. There are walking trails and children's activities. 🖥 www.lincstrust.org.uk **51 E3**

Tetney Marshes RSPB reserve on the Humber Estuary, north Lincolnshire coast, a large area of mudflats, salt marsh, saline lagoons and low dunes. Vast numbers of waterfowl and waders are found here in the winter, and it is a breeding site for redshanks and other species in the spring. The reserve is also home to rare plant species. *Cleethorpes* 🖥 www.rspb.org.uk **37 C7**

Whisby Nature Park Former quarry, now a nature reserve with lakes, grassland, marsh, willows and scrub. It is popular with birdwatchers for the plentiful waterfowl in the winter, and nesting nightingales in the spring. There are waymarked trails, hides and viewpoints. The Natural World Centre has a café

and children's adventure play areas. *Thorpe on the Hill* 🖥 www.lincstrust.org.uk **79 F1**

Towns & villages

Boston Historic market town on the River Witham, just inland from the Wash. It was once a significant trading town and port, and a member of the Hanseatic League. **Boston Guildhall**, built in the 1390s for the Guild of St Mary, is now a museum, relating the town's history and its links with the Pilgrim Fathers. It has a notable medieval Banqueting Hall. The 14th-century **St Botolph's Church**, also known as Boston Stump, is one of the country's largest parish churches, its size reflecting the importance and wealth of Boston at the time. Visitors can climb the medieval tower, which is one of England's tallest. Other buildings of note include **Maud Foster Mill**, a working 200-year-old mill. Activities include boat trips on the river or seal-spotting in the Wash. Emigrants from the town named many settlements round the world, most famously Boston, Massachusetts. 🖥 www.mybostonuk.com **208-9**

Grantham Market town, important in the wool and leather trade in the Middle Ages, home to the Angel and Royal, believed to be the oldest coaching inn in the country. Of national significance is Grantham's medieval parish church, **St Wulfram**. It is cathedral-like in size and decoration, with an unusually tall early 14th-century tower and spire. Carved stone heads are found inside and out, some medieval and some more recent. Other highlights include the medieval Crypt Chapel, Victorian and contemporary stained glass, and the Chained Library, which was established in 1598 as the country's first public library. **211**

Louth Georgian market town, known for its specialist food shops and markets, and for the church of **St James**, which has

the tallest parish church spire in England, at 295 feet high. The church was largely built in the mid-15th century, although the spire was not completed until 1515. Much of the impressive stained glass dates from a restoration in the mid-19th century. **198**

Mablethorpe Traditional seaside resort with long sandy beach and family-friendly attractions. **See also** the **Mablethorpe Seal Sanctuary and Wildlife Centre 64 C3**

Skegness Traditional seaside resort, with long sandy beach, pier and numerous family activities, including go-karting, crazy golf and donkey rides. The **Skegness Aquarium** is home to many different species of fish, including sharks, stingrays, and other sea creatures. There are open-topped pools, large viewing windows and a tunnel through the display. Outdoor attractions include a dinosaur world, and there are interactive children's activities. Diving experiences can be arranged. 🖥 www.skegness-aquarium.uk **206**

Stamford Picturesque market town, known for its plethora of 17th- and 18th-century stone buildings, many of them listed, five medieval churches and variety of shops. It is a conservation area. The fine architecture reflects the wealth of Stamford at the time, which came about through the wool trade, in particular the production of haberget cloth, and its position on the coach route between London and York. Stamford is frequently used as a film location. **219**

Sutton on Sea Old-fashioned and quiet seaside town, with sandy beach. At very low tides, it is sometimes possible to see the remains of a forest lost to rising sea levels about 3000 years ago. **76 F8**

Buildings

See also Normanby Hall Country Park

St Paul and St Peter, Algakirk Large medieval parish church, dating from the 13th to 15th centuries, with some evidence of a Saxon church on the site, including a stone in the churchyard thought to mark the grave of the 9th-century Mercian earl, Algar. The church has nationally significant stained glass and decorations, particularly in the chancel, created during a major restoration in the 1850s. 🖥 www.algarkirkchurch.org.uk **136 B2**

Belton House Large estate, now owned by the National Trust, with a grand Carolean manor house, built in the 1680s, surrounded by ornamental gardens and a deer park. On display in the house are important collections of silver, ceramics, portraits and rare books. The large grounds contain a Pleasure Garden, open grassland and ancient woodland. Attractions include walking routes, children's activities, an adventure playground and punting. *Grantham* 🖥 www. nationaltrust.org.uk **130 B6**

Belvoir Castle Grand Regency castle owned by the Duke of Rutland, whose ancestors amassed a large collection of Old Masters, including works by Dürer, Rubens and Gainsborough, on display. Within the grounds are a Japanese Woodland, Rose, Hermit's and Statue gardens. There are walking trails and children's activities. *Grantham* 🖥 www. belvoircastle.com **138 B8**

Burghley House One of the largest surviving Tudor houses, conceived by William Cecil, one of Elizabeth I's most powerful courtiers, and built between 1555 and 1587. Much of its important art collection, which includes 17th-century paintings, Japanese porcelain and furniture, is on display in the grand state apartments. The substantial gardens and parkland were designed by Capability Brown in the 18th century. Highlights include a Garden of Surprises, with an Elizabethan water garden, and a Sculpture Garden. *Stamford* 🖥 www.burghley.co.uk **219 F3**

Cogglesford Watermill Fully restored watermill on the River Slea. The present mill dates from the early 18th century, but flour has been produced on the site for over 1,000 years. The mill is in full working order, operating on monthly milling days and producing stoneground flour for sale. *Sleaford* 🖥 www.heartof lincs.com/cogglesford **212 F5**

Crowland Abbey Former monastery of the Benedictine Order, now partially in ruins, with a parish church located in what was the north aisle. The monastery was founded in the 8th century but destroyed several times, and the buildings that remain date from the 12th century. Among the impressive ruins are arches from the Norman Nave and the elaborately decorated West Front. There is a small Visitor Centre. 🖥 www. crowlandabbey.org.uk **166 F1**

Doddington Hall and Gardens Elizabethan manor house with extensive gardens. The exterior of the house is largely unchanged since its construction; the interior reflects a major re-decoration in Georgian times. Interesting artefacts on display in the house include two sets of 17th-century Flemish tapestries. There are walking trails in the gardens and surrounding parkland. A cycle track links to the National Cycle Network. 🖥 www.doddingtonhall.com **79 D5**

Gainsborough Old Hall Well-preserved medieval manor house, with an unusual history of both business and residential use. Highlights include the large medieval kitchen and Great Hall, for a time used as a performance space, which date from the 15th century. There are interactive tours and activities, and visitors can climb the tower. 🖥 www. english-heritage.org.uk **197 C5**

Grimsthorpe Castle Magnificent castle set in extensive grounds. The imposing Baroque front was designed by Sir John Vanbrugh, architect of Blenheim Palace, in the early 18th century; much of the rest of the castle is Tudor. Rich collections of paintings, tapestries and furniture are on display in the state rooms. The formal gardens are noted for their topiary, and the 3,000 acres of parkland are home to red, fallow and muntjac deer. There are walking and cycling trails and an adventure playground. 🖥 www. grimsthorpe.co.uk **153 D5**

Gunby Hall National Trust-owned country house, dating from 1700, with a rather formal, red-brick exterior, often compared to that of a dolls' house. An interesting collection of portraits, furniture and books are on display inside the house. There are spacious lawns, colourful borders with unusual plants, and kitchen gardens that have hardly changed since the early 1800s. Towards the edge of the estate, near St Peter's Church, the remains of the medieval village of Gunby can be detected in the uneven contours of the ground. *Bratoft* 🖥 www.nationaltrust. org.uk **89 A1**

Harlaxton Manor Lavish manor house, dating from the 1830s and designed in an extravagant mixture of Gothic, Jacobean and Baroque styles. Within the grounds are colourful formal gardens, with French terraces and an Italian garden; a 6.5-acre walled garden; a 19th-century conservatory, with interesting tropical plants; and a large woodland famed for its bluebells in spring. *Grantham* 🖥 www.harlaxton.co.uk **139 D7**

Tattershall Castle Moated tower dating from the mid-15th century, and very unusual in being built of brick. It retains its original grand Gothic fireplaces and church-style windows. Visitors can see the largely unfurnished rooms and climb to the battlements for an impressive view over the flat Lincolnshire fens. 🖥 www. nationaltrust.org.uk **207 A4**

Woolsthorpe Manor 17th-century farmhouse, the family home and birthplace of Sir Isaac Newton, and the place where he developed his ground-breaking theories on optics and gravity. The tree from which the famous apple fell is said to be in the orchard still. There is a Science Centre, with interactive experiences and workshops, as well as displays on Newton's life and work. *Woolsthorpe-by-Colsterworth* 🖥 www. nationaltrust.org.uk **151 D7**

Museums & galleries

Alford Manor House Thatched manor house built in 1611, with Georgian and Victorian alterations. It is thought to be the largest thatched manor house in the country and has a very unusual structure, with a wooden frame encased in brick. Outside is an apothecary's garden and an orchard. Behind the house is the Museum of Rural Life, with collections relating to local businesses and trades. 🖥 www.alfordmanorhouse. co.uk **75 F3**

Cranwell Aviation Heritage Museum Relates the history of the Royal Air Force College Cranwell, the world's first military air academy, from its foundation in 1918 to the present day. Interactive exhibits include a Vampire T11 Cockpit and a Jet Provost flight simulator. There are changing exhibitions, events and a Jet Provost aircraft on display. *Sleaford* 🖥 www. heartoflincs.com/cranwell **120 D6**

Grimsby Fishing Heritage Centre Museum dedicated to Grimsby's history as one of the world's leading fishing ports. Preserved trawler interiors and realistic recreations allow visitors to experience life in the 1950s fishing industry. Permanently moored outside, and open for frequent tours to taste life aboard, is the diesel trawler Ross Tiger. 🖥 www.fishing heritage.com **191 D8**

International Bomber Command Centre Memorial and education centre, with a striking memorial spire surrounded by walls displaying the names of the almost 58,000 men and women who died serving or supporting Bomber Command in World War II. The Chadwick Centre uses interactive exhibits and recordings to tell the story of the Allied Bombing campaign, relating the experiences of those on all sides of the conflict, the impact of Bomber Command and the role of Lincolnshire in the war effort. There are two landscaped peace gardens. *Lincoln* 🖥 www.internationalbcc.co.uk **81 A4**

Lincoln Aviation Centre Museum that acts as a living memorial to the 55,500 men from Bomber Command who died during World War II. Exhibitions explore aviation heritage, and the collection of rare aircraft includes an Avro Lancaster Bomber. The museum is built on the old wartime airfield of RAF East Kirby and retains the original 1940s Control Tower. Special events include airshows and re-enactments. 🖥 www. lincsaviation.co.uk **99 F5**

Metheringham Airfield Visitor Centre Small museum in the former communal buildings of RAF Metheringham, home to 106 Bomber Squadron from 1943 until the end of World War II. Exhibitions display the history of the squadron, life and work on the airbase, with original equipment and aircraft parts. A Dakota KG651 transport aircraft is being restored on site. 🖥 www.metheringhamairfield. co.uk **96 A2**

Thorpe Camp Visitor Centre Museum on the site of the barracks for RAF Woodhall Spa during World War II. The Airmen's Mess, shower block and ration stores are preserved at the visitor centre, and there are displays about the squadrons stationed at the barracks, the history of the Air Training Corp and civilian life in Lincolnshire during the 1940s. Exhibits include the secret radio sets used by spies in occupied Europe and model aircraft. *Tattershall Thorpe* 🖥 www.thorpecamp.wixsite. com/visitorscentre **207 B8**

Family activities

Ark Wildlife Park Wildlife park and sanctuary, mainly caring for animals rescued from the exotic pet trade, including lemurs, macaques, lynx, wallabies and a variety of snakes, as well as many others. There are frequent talks and activities and a children's play area. *Stickney* 🖥 www. arkwildlifepark.co.uk **112 F8**

Hardy's Animal Farm Family farm offering opportunities to feed and handle a variety of animals, as well as learn about farming. There are indoor and outdoor play areas, tractor rides and daily family activities. *Ingoldmells* 🖥 www.hardys animalfarm.co.uk **90 D4**

Mablethorpe Seal Sanctuary and Wildlife Centre Wildlife centre, home to a wide variety of animals, many of them rescued, including seals, birds of prey, gibbons, lynx and iguanas among others, as well as an exhibition on prehistoric animals. The site occupies around two acres of sand dunes. Adjoining the wildlife centre is Mablethorpe Wildlife Rescue, which cares for injured seals and sea birds until they can be released back into the wild. 🖥 www.thesealsanctuary.co.uk **64 A5**

Natureland Seal Sanctuary Wildlife centre focussing on the rescue and rehabilitation of injured or orphaned seal pups, which are cared for in pools, where visitors can observe and feed them. There is also a breeding colony of Harbour Seals. Other animals include tropical butterflies, fish and reptiles, penguins and alpacas. There are children's activities and a pets corner. *Skegness* 🖥 www.skegnessnatureland. co.uk **206 E4**

North Sea Observatory Purpose-built marine observatory, known for the dramatic views from its huge windows overlooking the beach and the sea. It is a popular spot for birdwatching, and there are binoculars at the waterfront café. There is an art gallery on site. *Chapel Point, Chapel St Leonards* 🖥 www.lincsnaturalcoast.com/ north-sea-observatory **90 E7**

▶ *Burghley House*

IV

Key to map pages

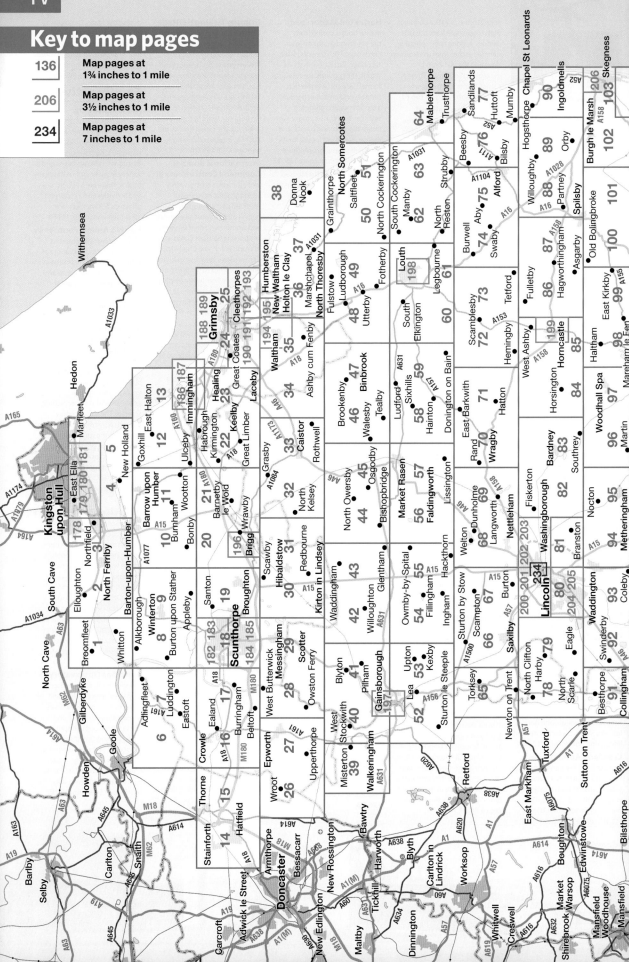

Hunstanton Heacham Snettisham Dersingham King's Lynn

Downham Market Littleport

March Chatteris Ramsey

116

Wainfleet All Saints Wainfleet St Mary **115** Wrangle **114**

Stickford New Leake Midville **113** Sibsey

Leverton **127** Butterwick
Hurn's End **126** Fishtoft
Scrane End

Holbeach St Matthew **149** Gedney Drove End
148 Gedney Dyke

161 Sutton Bridge Terrington St Clement

West Walton Leverington Wisbech

160 Sutton Bridge

Foul Anchor **170**

Stickney **112** Frithville
Coningsby Cowbridge **125** **208 209** Boston
Wyberton Kirton **136** Sutterton
137

Fosdyke **147**
Holbeach St Marks Moulton Seas End
148 **146** Moulton

215 Holbeach **159** Long Sutton
216 **160** Whaplode
158 Whaplode St Catherine Tydd St Giles **169** Gorefield
Whaplode Drove Gorefield **168**

Parson Drove **177** Guyhirn
176 Thorney

Chapel Hill **111** Gipsey Bridge Langrick **124**
Tattershall Bridge **110** **123** Swineshead Bridge Heckington
South Kyme **122** **134** Swineshead
Bicker **135**
Donington **145** Gosberton
144 Gosberton Clough Surfleet

Pinchbeck **157** Moulton Chapel
156 Moulton Deeping St Nicholas **167** Shepeau Stow
214 Spalding Crowland **166**

Newborough **175** Eye
Thorney Whittlesey Farcet

Timberland **207** Coningsby
Billinghay **109** Anwick Ruskington
Digby **108** **121** Sleaford **212**
Leadenham **107** Cranwell Leasingham **120** Ancaster **153**
Navenby **106** Wellingore
Boothby Graffoe

Helpringham **133** Horbling Folkingham Pointon **143**
Osbournby **132** **142** Dowsby Rippingale
Billingborough

Morton **155** Twenty
154 Bourne **213**
Baston **165**
Thurlby **164** Maxey
Market Deeping **217**
Uffington **173** Glinton Newark
Barnack **172** Castor

Bassingham Stapleford **105** Beckingham Fenton
Newark-on-Trent **104** Stubton **119** Honington Marston
Claypole **117** **118** Hough-on-the-Hill Caythorpe
Balderton Long Bennington **128** **129** Great Gonerby **210 211** Grantham
Bottesford **130** Barkston Culverthorpe **131** Londonthorpe **141** Great Ponton Ropsley Ingoldsby Irnham
Muston **138** Denton Harlaxton **139** South Witham
Knipton Croxton Kerrial Saltby **151** Colsterworth
Wymondham **150** Sproxton

Swinstead **153** Castle Bytham
152 Clipsham Corby Glen
Edenham **154** Swinstead Essendine **163** Ryhall
162 Essendine Stamford **218 219**
171

Empingham Oakham Easton on the Hill

Corby Oundle

Newark Peterborough Yaxley Morborne
226 227 **230 231** **232 233**
225 **229**
224 **228** Haddon
220 221 Castor
222 223 Water Newton

Sawtry

Desborough Market Harborough Lutterworth

Scale
0 5 10 15 20 km
0 5 10 15 miles

Nottingham West Bridgford Keyworth Cotgrave Bingham
Southwell Calverton Lowdham
Blidworth Ravenshead Hucknall
Rainworth

Loughborough Melton Mowbray Wymondham
Sileby Syston Leicester Mountsorrel
East Leake

Route planning

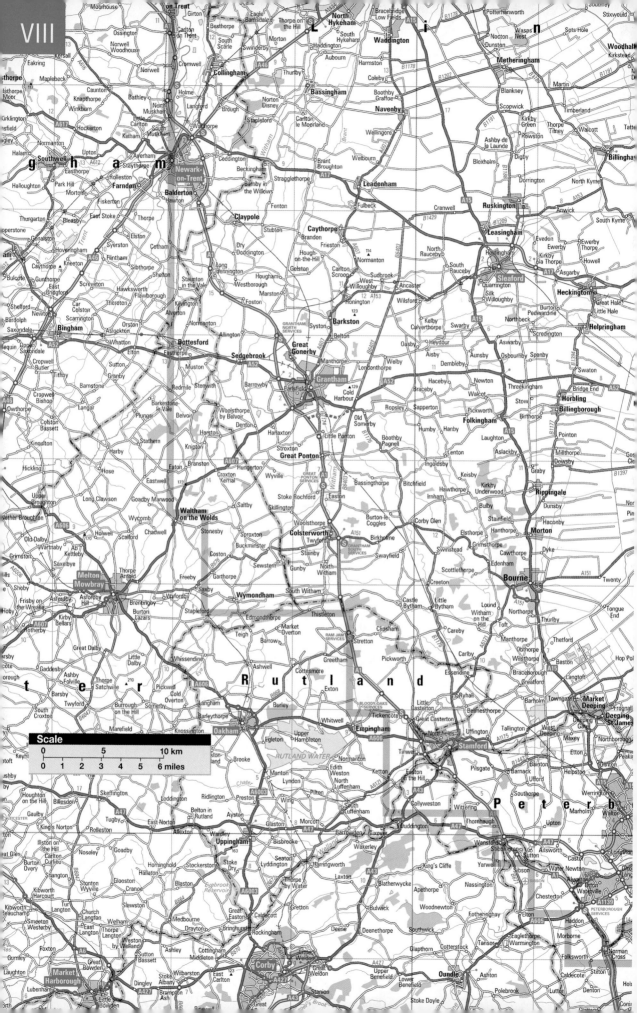

Key to map symbols

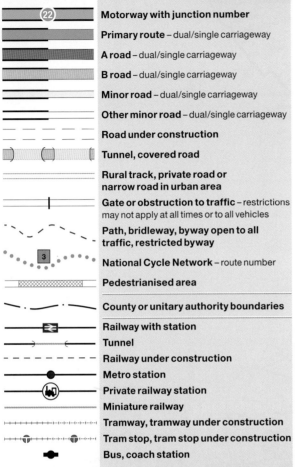

Motorway with junction number	
Primary route – dual/single carriageway	
A road – dual/single carriageway	
B road – dual/single carriageway	
Minor road – dual/single carriageway	
Other minor road – dual/single carriageway	
Road under construction	
Tunnel, covered road	
Rural track, private road or narrow road in urban area	
Gate or obstruction to traffic – restrictions may not apply at all times or to all vehicles	
Path, bridleway, byway open to all traffic, restricted byway	
National Cycle Network – route number	
Pedestrianised area	
County or unitary authority boundaries	
Railway with station	
Tunnel	
Railway under construction	
Metro station	
Private railway station	
Miniature railway	
Tramway, tramway under construction	
Tram stop, tram stop under construction	
Bus, coach station	

Ambulance station	
Coastguard station	
Fire station	
Police station	
Accident and Emergency entrance to hospital	
Hospital	
Place of worship	
Information centre	
Shopping centre, parking	
Park and Ride, Post Office	
Camping site, caravan site	
Golf course, picnic site	
Church ROMAN FORT Non-Roman antiquity, Roman antiquity	
Univ Important buildings, schools, colleges, universities and hospitals	
Woods, built-up area	
River Medway Water name	
River, weir	
Stream	
Canal, lock, tunnel	
Water	
Tidal water	

Adjoining page indicators and overlap bands – the colour of the arrow and band indicates the scale of the adjoining or overlapping page (see scales below)

The dark grey border on the inside edge of some pages indicates that the mapping does not continue onto the adjacent page

The small numbers around the edges of the maps identify the 1-kilometre National Grid lines

Abbreviations

Acad	Academy	Meml	Memorial
Allot Gdns	Allotments	Mon	Monument
Cemy	Cemetery	Mus	Museum
C Ctr	Civic centre	Obsy	Observatory
CH	Club house	Pal	Royal palace
Coll	College	PH	Public house
Crem	Crematorium	Recn Gd	Recreation ground
Ent	Enterprise	Resr	Reservoir
Ex H	Exhibition hall	Ret Pk	Retail park
Ind Est	Industrial Estate	Sch	School
IRB Sta	Inshore rescue boat station	Sh Ctr	Shopping centre
Inst	Institute	TH	Town hall / house
Ct	Law court	Trad Est	Trading estate
L Ctr	Leisure centre	Univ	University
LC	Level crossing	W Twr	Water tower
Liby	Library	Wks	Works
Mkt	Market	YH	Youth hostel

Enlarged maps only

Railway or bus station building	
Place of interest	
Parkland	

The map scale on the pages numbered in green is 1¾ inches to 1 mile
2.76 cm to 1 km • 1:36 206

The map scale on the pages numbered in blue is 3½ inches to 1 mile
5.52 cm to 1 km • 1:18 103

The map scale on the pages numbered in red is 7 inches to 1 mile
11.04 cm to 1 km • 1:9051

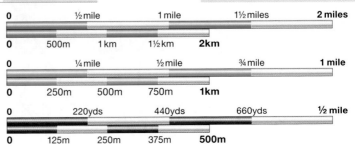

| 0 | ½ mile | 1 mile | 1½ miles | 2 miles |
| 0 | 500m | 1 km | 1½ km | 2km |

| 0 | ¼ mile | ½ mile | ¾ mile | 1 mile |
| 0 | 250m | 500m | 750m | 1km |

| 0 | 220yds | 440yds | 660yds | ½ mile |
| 0 | 125m | 250m | 375m | 500m |

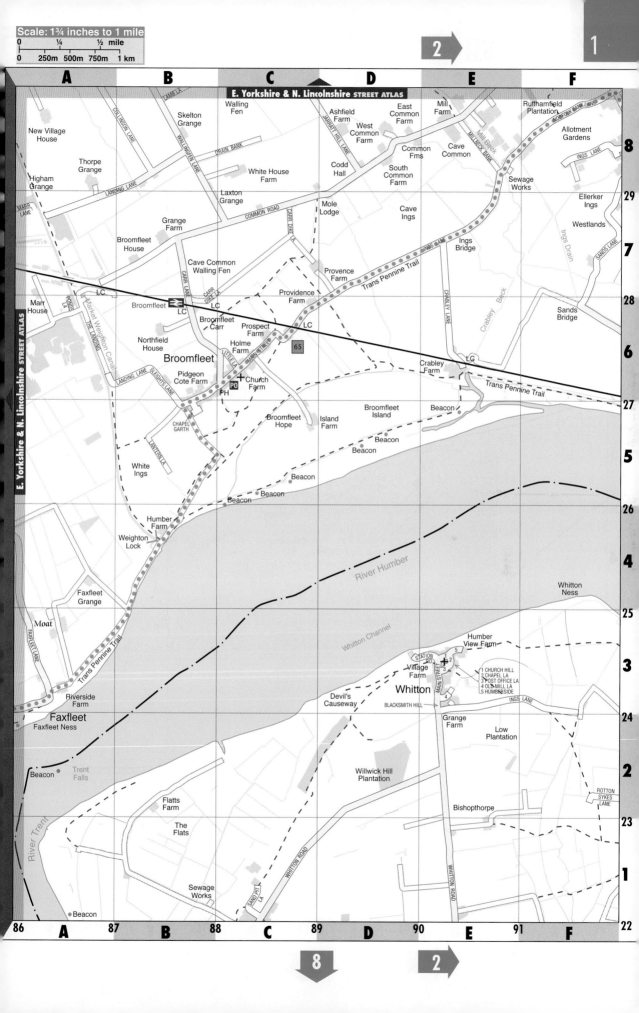

Scale: 1¾ inches to 1 mile

0   ¼   ½   mile
0   250m   500m   750m   1 km

1

2

8

2

E. Yorkshire & N. Lincolnshire STREET ATLAS

New Village House
Thorpe Grange
Higham Grange
Skelton Grange
Walling Fen
White House Farm
Laxton Grange
Grange Farm
Broomfleet House
Cave Common Walling Fen
Ashfield Farm
West Common Farm
East Common Farm
Codd Hall
South Common Farm
Common Fms
Cave Common
Mill Farm
Cave Ings
Mole Lodge
Provence Farm
Providence Farm
Ruffhamfield Plantation
Allotment Gardens
Ellerker Ings
Westlands
Sewage Works
Ings Bridge
Trans Pennine Trail
Sands Bridge
Marr House
Broomfleet
Broomfleet Carr
Northfield House
Prospect Farm
Holme Farm
Church Farm
Broomfleet Hope
Island Farm
Broomfleet Island
Crabley Farm
Beacon
Pidgeon Cote Farm
Chapel Garth
White Ings
Beacon
Beacon
Beacon
Beacon
Beacon
Humber Farm
Weighton Lock
River Humber
Whitton Ness
Faxfleet Grange
Moat
Whitton Channel
Humber View Farm
Riverside Farm
Faxfleet
Faxfleet Ness
Devil's Causeway
Station Rd
Village Farm
Whitton
Blacksmith Hill
Grange Farm
Low Plantation
1 CHURCH HILL
2 CHAPEL LA
3 POST OFFICE LA
4 OLD MILL LA
5 HUMBERSIDE
Beacon
Trent Falls
Willwick Hill Plantation
Bishopthorpe
Rotton Sykes Lane
Flatts Farm
The Flats
River Trent
Sewage Works
Beacon

Collinson Lane
Lamb La
Wallingfen Lane
Drain Bank
Jarratt Hill Lane
Carr Dike
Common Road
Carr Lane
Mill Beck
Millbeck Bank
Inghork Bank Lane
Ings Lane
Sands Lane
Ings Drain
Crabley Lane
Crabley Beck
Ings Lane
Landing Lane
Marr Lane
Ponds La
The Landing
Market Weighton Canal
Sleights Lane
Little La
Main Street
Lantern La
Faxfleet Lane
Trans Pennine Trail
Main Street
Ings Lane
Whitton Road
Sand Pit La
Whitton Road

LC
LC
LC
LC
LC
LC
65
PO
PH

86 A 87 B 88 C 89 D 90 E 91 F 22

A B C D E F

8 29 7 28 6 5 26 4 25 3 24 2 23 1

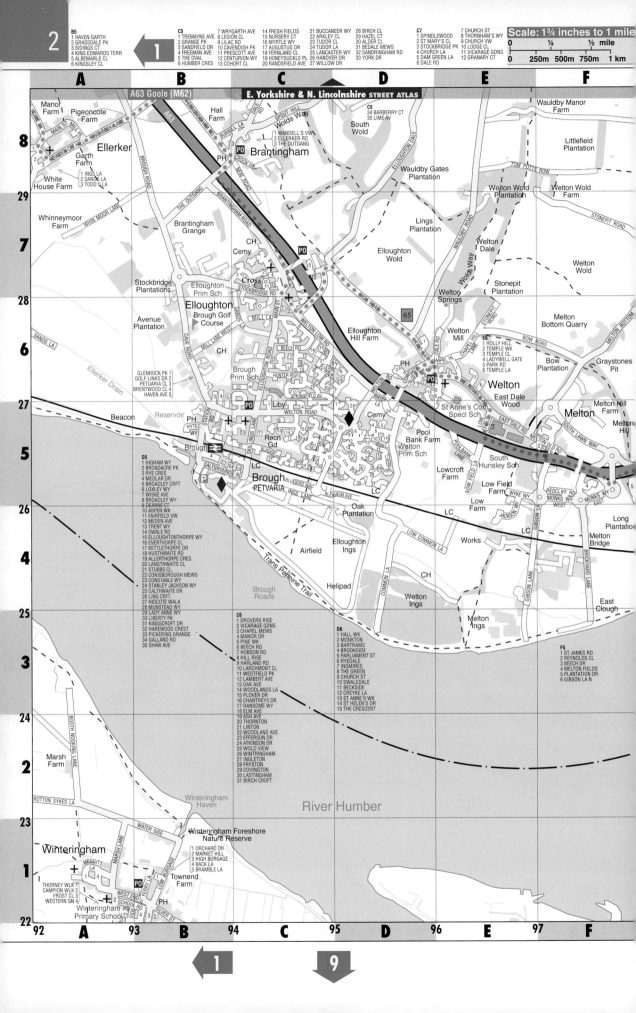

D8
1 ENDEAVOUR CRES
2 SPRINGDALE CL
3 BEWHOLME GR
4 MARFLEET AVE
5 CYPRUS ST
6 LITTLEFAIR RD

7 DELHI ST
8 FRODSHAM ST
9 CEYLON ST
10 CORPORATION RD

E8
1 GREAT FIELD LA
2 ASHWELL AVE
3 BOTHWELL GR
4 HEMSWELL AVE
5 CHURCH LA
6 ELBA ST

F8
1 BAMFORD AVE
2 SALTFORD AVE
3 SOUTHWELL AVE
4 FALKLAND RD
5 HALLIWELL CL
6 STOCKWELL GR

7 TOWER HOUSE LA

5

A1033 Market Weighton (A1079) | A165 Bridlington 181 **E. Yorkshire & N. Lincolnshire** STREET ATLAS

KINGSTON UPON HULL

River Humber

Marfleet

Stockwell Prim School

Salt End

Kingston International Bus Pk

King George Dock

Salt End Jetties

Goxhill Haven

Dawson City Claypits Nature Reserve

Skitter Ness

New Bank Farm

New Green Farm

Chimney

Neatgangs Farm

Regent House

Mast

NEATGANGS LANE

Salt Marsh Farm

Chimney

Ferry Farm

Chimney

East Marsh Farm

Wind Pump

Wind Pump

Fir Tree Farm

Horsegate Farm

Glebe Farm

Spring Farm

East Halton Skitter

North End Farm

Brook Hill Farm

Maydale Farm

Peartree Farm

Goxhill

Chimney

Meml

RUARDS LANE

RUARD ROAD

SYKES LANE

ELM LA

NORTH END

Chapel Farm

Langmere Covert

East Halton Beck

SKITTER ROAD

East Halton Skitter

For full street detail of the highlighted area see page 181.

A1
1 WINDSOR GR
2 THE CLOSE
3 FARROWS POND
4 MILL LA
5 MEADOW CL
6 WILLOW LA

12

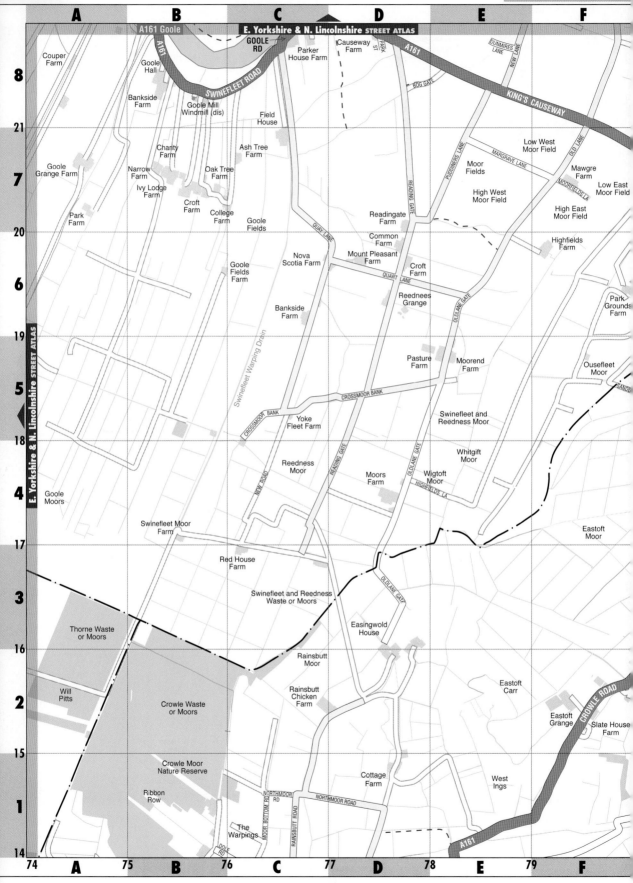

A   B   C   D   E   F

E. Yorkshire & N. Lincolnshire STREET ATLAS

A161 Goole

GOOLE RD

Couper Farm

Goole Hall

Bankside Farm

Goole Mill Windmill (dis)

Charity Farm

Ash Tree Farm

Field House

SWINEFLEET ROAD

Parker House Farm

Causeway Farm

PARK ST

A161

BOG GATE

DUNMIRES LANE

NEW LANE

KING'S CAUSEWAY

Goole Grange Farm

Narrow Farm

Ivy Lodge Farm

Croft Farm

Oak Tree Farm

College Farm

Goole Fields

Low West Moor Field

OLD LANE

Mawgre Farm

Low East Moor Field

PUDDIMERS LANE

MARGRAVE LANE

Moor Fields

High West Moor Field

MOORFIELDS LA

High East Moor Field

Park Farm

Readingate Farm

READING GATE

Common Farm

Nova Scotia Farm

Mount Pleasant Farm

Croft Farm

QUAY LANE

QUART LANE

Goole Fields Farm

Bankside Farm

Reednees Grange

OLDLANE GATE

Highfields Farm

Park Grounds Farm

Swineflet Warping Drain

Pasture Farm

Moorend Farm

Ousefleet Moor

SANDE

Crossmoor Bank

CROSSMOOR BANK

Yoke Fleet Farm

Swineflet and Reedness Moor

Goole Moors

NEW ROAD

Reedness Moor

READING GATE

Moors Farm

OLDLANE GATE

Wigtoft Moor

Whitgift Moor

HIGHFIELDS LA

Eastoft Moor

Swineflet Moor Farm

Red House Farm

Swineflet and Reedness Waste or Moors

OLDLANE GATE

Easingwold House

Thorne Waste or Moors

Rainsbutt Moor

Eastoft Carr

Will Pitts

Crowle Waste or Moors

Rainsbutt Chicken Farm

Eastoft Grange

Slate House Farm

CROWLE ROAD

Crowle Moor Nature Reserve

Ribbon Row

Cottage Farm

West Ings

The Warpings

NORTHMOOR RD

MOOR BOTTOM RD

RAINSBUTT ROAD

NORTHMOOR ROAD

A161

GOOLE RD

8   21   7   20   6   19   5   18   4   17   3   16   2   15   1   14

E. Yorkshire & N. Lincolnshire STREET ATLAS

74   A   75   B   76   C   77   D   78   E   79   F

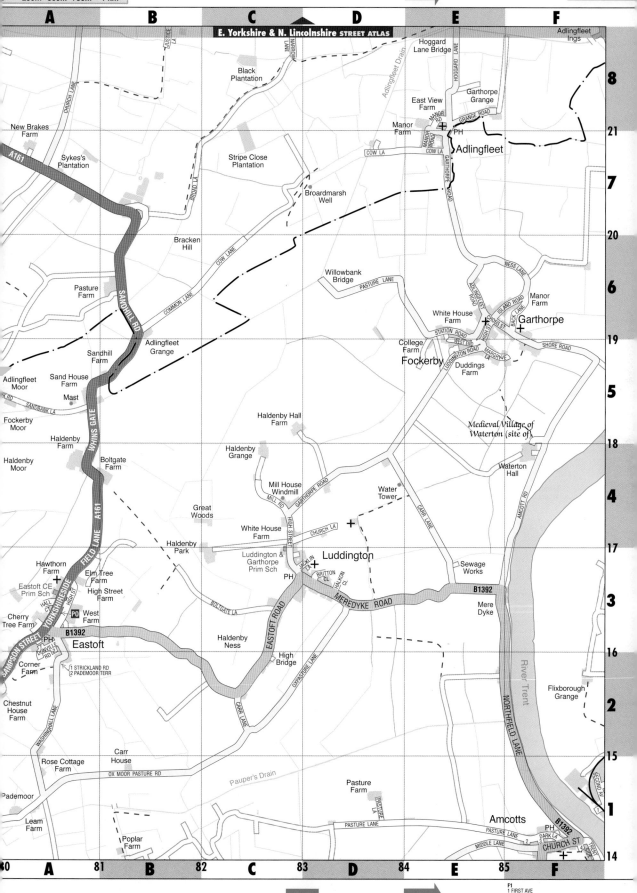

E. Yorkshire & N. Lincolnshire STREET ATLAS

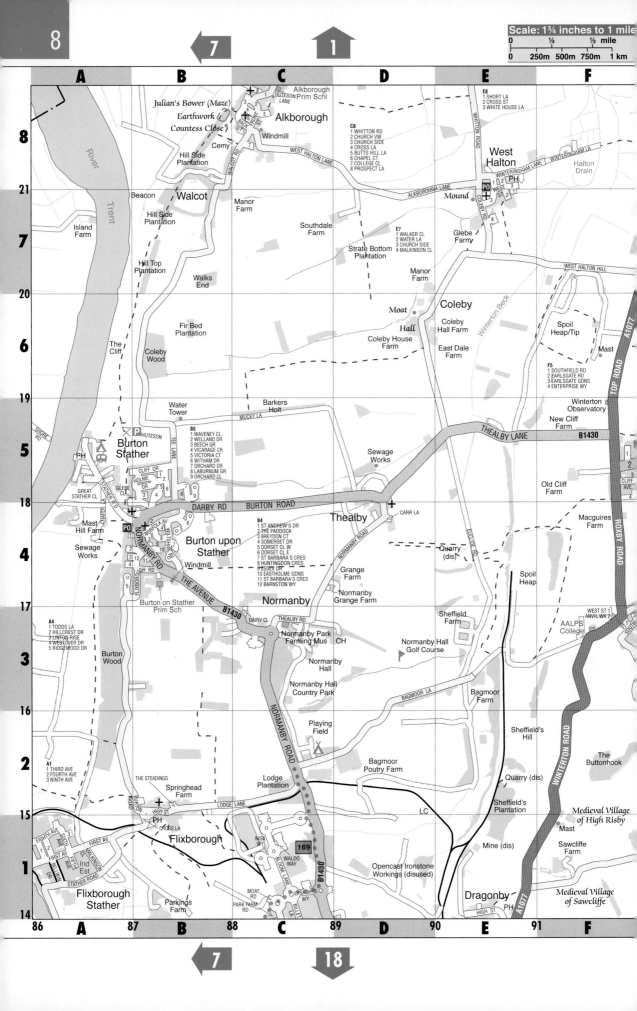

A   B   C   D   E   F

River
Trent

Julian's Bower (Maze)
Earthwork
Countess Close

Alkborough Prim Schl

Alkborough

HUTESON LANE

Windmill

WEST HALTON LANE

WHITTON ROAD

E8
1 SHORT LA
2 CROSS ST
3 WHITE HOUSE LA

West
Halton

WINTERINGHAM LANE

Halton
Drain

Cemy

Hill Side
Plantation

WALCOT RD

BACK ST

TRENT ST

C8
1 WHITTON RD
2 CHURCH VW
3 CHURCH SIDE
4 CROSS LA
5 BUTTS HILL LA
6 CHAPEL CT
7 COLLEGE CL
8 PROSPECT LA

PO

PH

WEST ST

8

21

Beacon

Walcot

Hill Side
Plantation

Manor
Farm

Southdale
Farm

ALKBOROUGH LANE

Mound

COLEBY RD

E7
1 WALKER CL
2 WATER LA
3 CHURCH SIDE
4 MALKINSON CL

Glebe
Farm

WEST HALTON HILL

7

Island
Farm

Hill Top
Plantation

Walks
End

Strate Bottom
Plantation

Manor
Farm

20

The
Cliff

Fir Bed
Plantation

Moat

Coleby

WINTERTON BECK

Spoil
Heap/Tip

TOP ROAD

A1077

6

Coleby
Wood

Hall

Coleby House
Farm

Coleby
Hall Farm

East Dale
Farm

Mast

F5
1 SOUTHFIELD RD
2 EARLSGATE RD
3 EARLSGATE GDNS
4 ENTERPRISE WY

19

SHORE RD

Water
Tower

MUCKY LA

Barkers
Holt

THEALBY LANE

B1430

Winterton
Observatory

New Cliff
Farm

5

PH

Burton
Stather

HUTESON

TEE LANE

B5
1 WAVENEY CL
2 WELLAND DR
3 BEECH GR
4 VICARAGE CR
5 VICTORIA CT
6 WITHAM DR
7 ORCHARD DR
8 LABURNUM GR
9 ORCHARD CL

Sewage
Works

Old Cliff
Farm

CLIFF AVE

1
2

3
4

18

GREAT
STATHER CL

GLEBE
CL

CLIFF DR

HOLME
DR

STATHER RD

CHAFER RD

DARBY RD

BURTON ROAD

Thealby

CARR LA

Macguires
Farm

ROXBY ROAD

Mast
Hill Farm

PO

NORMANBY RD

NORFOLK AV

WILTSHIRE

B4
1 ST ANDREW'S DR
2 THE PADDOCK
3 BREYDON CT
4 SOMERSET DR
5 DORSET CL W
6 DORSET CL E
7 ST BARBARA'S CRES
8 HUNTINGDON CRES
9 ESSEX DR
10 EASTHOLME GDNS
11 ST BARBARA'S CRES
12 BARNSTON WY

Quarry
(dis)

Spoil
Heap

4

Sewage
Works

Burton upon
Stather

Windmill

THOROLD RD

THE AVENUE

B1430

Normanby

EUCLIDE RD

NORMANBY ROAD

Grange
Farm

Normanby
Grange Farm

Sheffield
Farm

AALPS
College

WEST ST 1
ANVIL WK 2

17

A4
1 TODDS LA
2 HILLCREST DR
3 LINTON RISE
4 WESTOVER DR
5 RIDGEWOOD DR

Burton on Stather
Prim Sch

DAIRY CL

THEALBY RD

Normanby Park
Farming Mus

CH

Normanby Hall
Golf Course

SOUTH

3

Burton
Wood

Normanby
Hall

Normanby Hall
Country Park

BAGMOOR LA

Bagmoor
Farm

Sheffield's
Hill

The
Buttonhook

WINTERTON ROAD

16

NORMANBY ROAD

Playing
Field

Bagmoor
Poultry Farm

Quarry (dis)

2

A1
1 THIRD AVE
2 FOURTH AVE
3 NINTH AVE

THE STEADINGS

Springhead
Farm

Lodge
Plantation

Sheffield's
Plantation

Medieval Village
of High Risby

15

EIGHTH AVE

FIRST AV

THIRD AVE

MALKINSON CL

Ind
Est

HIGH ST

BURTON RD

LODGE LANE

CROSS LA

PH

Flixborough

NISA
WY

BLOOM LANE

169

WALDO
WAY

LC

Mast

Mine (dis)

Sawcliffe
Farm

1

FIFTH
AVE

BELWIN
DR

FIRST
AVE

STATHER ROAD

Flixborough
Stather

Parkings
Farm

MOAT
RD

PARK FARM
RD

ST ELYSABHTS
WY

BILLET
WY

B1430

Opencast Ironstone
Workings (disused)

Dragonby

PH

HIGH ST

A1077

Medieval Village
of Sawcliffe

14

86   A   87   B   88   C   89   D   90   E   91   F

A5
1 FARNDALE WY
2 WESLEY CL
3 NORTHLANDS AVE
4 WALKER DR
5 NEVILLE CRES
6 HILES AVE
7 MARMION DR
8 TEANBY DR
9 BOYNTON CRES
10 NORTHLANDS RD S
11 HIGH ST
12 MALKINSON CL
13 BLANKNEY CT
14 CHURCH SIDE
15 QUEEN ST
16 CHAPEL LA
17 SOUTH ST
18 LEEK HILL
19 WESTWINDS GDNS
20 HAWTHORNE CL
21 MALKINSON CL
22 WATERLOW DR
23 PLYMOUTH CL
24 LINCOLN DR
25 BOSTON CL
26 HILLSMERE GR
27 COATES AVE
28 BENNETT DR
29 DRIFFIL WAY
30 BAKER DR
31 MARKET ST
32 FOWLER CT

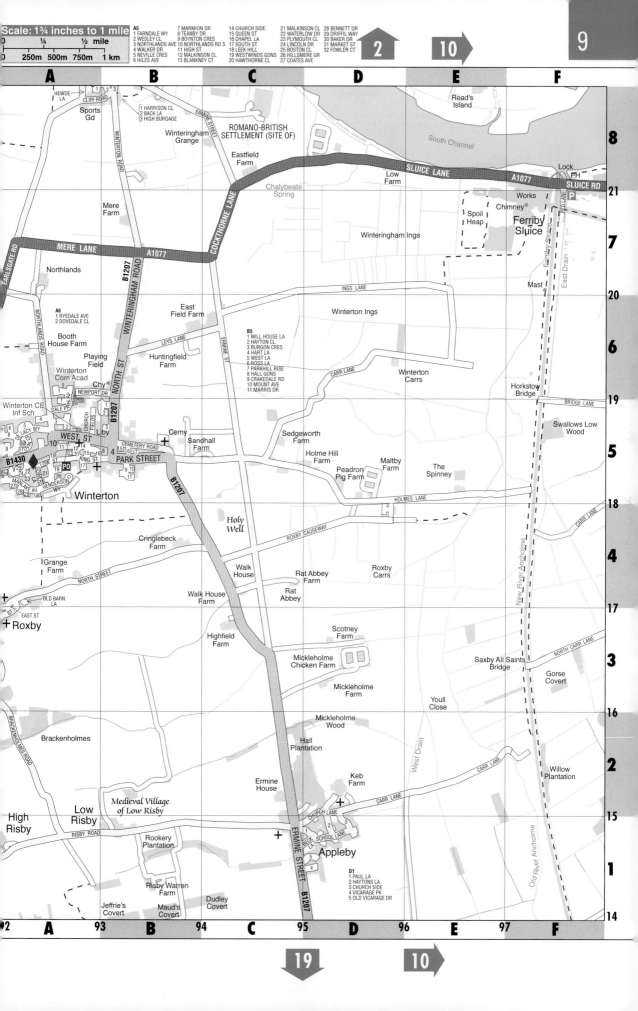

A **B** **C** **D** **E** **F**

HEWDE LA
Sports Gd

1 HARRISON CL
2 BACK LA
3 HIGH BURGAGE

CLIFF ROAD
ERMINE STREET

ROMANO-BRITISH
SETTLEMENT (SITE OF)

Winteringham
Grange

Eastfield
Farm

Read's
Island

South Channel

8

SLUICE LANE
A1077

Low
Farm

Lock
PH
SLUICE RD
P

21

Chalybeate
Spring

Mere
Farm

WINTERTON ROAD

COCKTHORNE LANE

Winteringham Ings

Works
Chimney

Ferriby
Sluice

7

MERE LANE
A1077

EARLSGATE RD
B1207

Northlands

INGS LANE

Mast

20

A6
1 RYEDALE AVE
2 DOVEDALE CL

East
Field Farm

Winterton Ings

East Drain

FERRIBY SLUICE

Booth
House Farm

NORTHLANDS ROAD

LEYS LANE
ERMINE ST

B5
1 MILL HOUSE LA
2 HAYTON CL
3 BURGON CRES
4 HART LA
5 WEST LA
6 ROSS LA
7 PARKHILL RISE
8 HALL GDNS
9 CRAKEDALE RD
10 MOUNT AVE
11 MARRIS DR

6

Playing
Field

Huntingfield
Farm

CARR LANE

Winterton
Carrs

Horkstow
Bridge

19

Winterton Com Acad

NORTH ST

Chy
Newport Dr

Winterton CE
Inf Sch

Dale Pk

CHURCH FIELDS

B1207

Liby

Cemy

Sandhall
Farm

Sedgeworth
Farm

Holme Hill
Farm

Maltby
Farm

The
Spinney

BRIDGE LANE

Swallows Low
Wood

5

WEST ST

PARK STREET
CEMETERY ROAD

Peadron
Pig Farm

B1430
PO

Winterton

B1207

HOLMES LANE

18

Holy
Well

ROXBY CAUSEWAY

New River Ancholme

CARR LANE

4

Cringlebeck
Farm

Walk
House

Rat Abbey
Farm

Roxby
Carrs

Grange
Farm

NORTH STREET

Walk House
Farm

Rat
Abbey

17

OLD BARN LA
EAST ST

Roxby

Highfield
Farm

Scotney
Farm

Saxby All Saints
Bridge

NORTH CARR LANE

Gorse
Covert

3

Mickleholme
Chicken Farm

Mickleholme
Farm

Youll
Close

16

Mickleholme
Wood

BRACKENHOLMES ROAD

Brackenholmes

Hall
Plantation

West Drain

CARR LANE

Willow
Plantation

2

Ermine
House

Keb
Farm

CARR LANE

Old River Ancholme

High
Risby

Low
Risby

Medieval Village
of Low Risby

CHURCH LANE

15

RISBY ROAD

Rookery
Plantation

BECK LA

1 2 3

SCHOOL LANE

ERMINE STREET

5
4

Appleby

D1
1 PAUL LA
2 HAYTONS LA
3 CHURCH SIDE
4 VICARAGE PK
5 OLD VICARAGE DR

1

Jeffrie's
Covert

Maud's
Covert

Dudley
Covert

Risby Warren
Farm

B1207

14

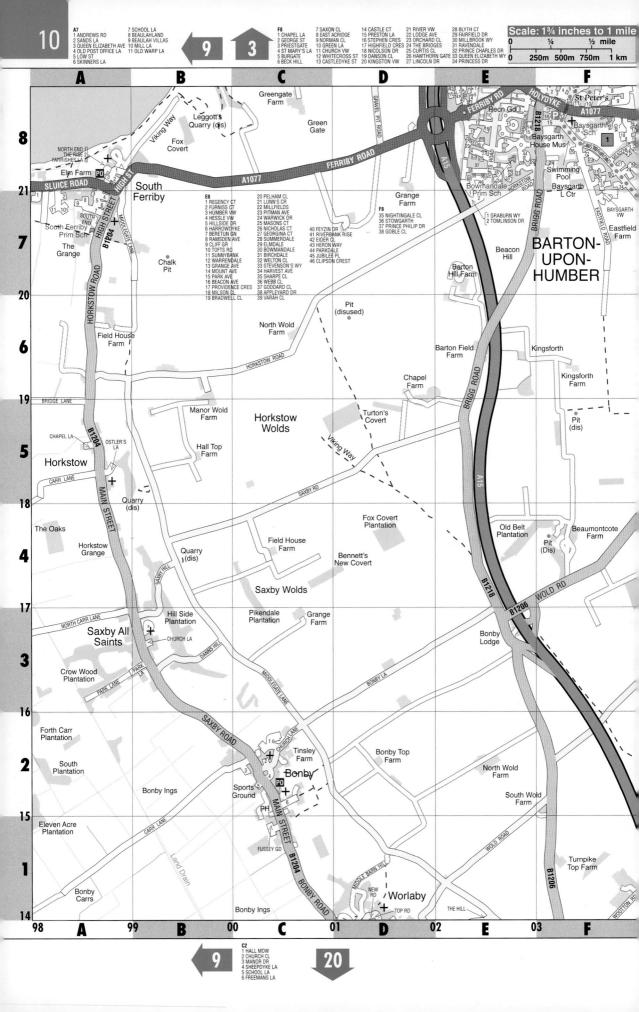

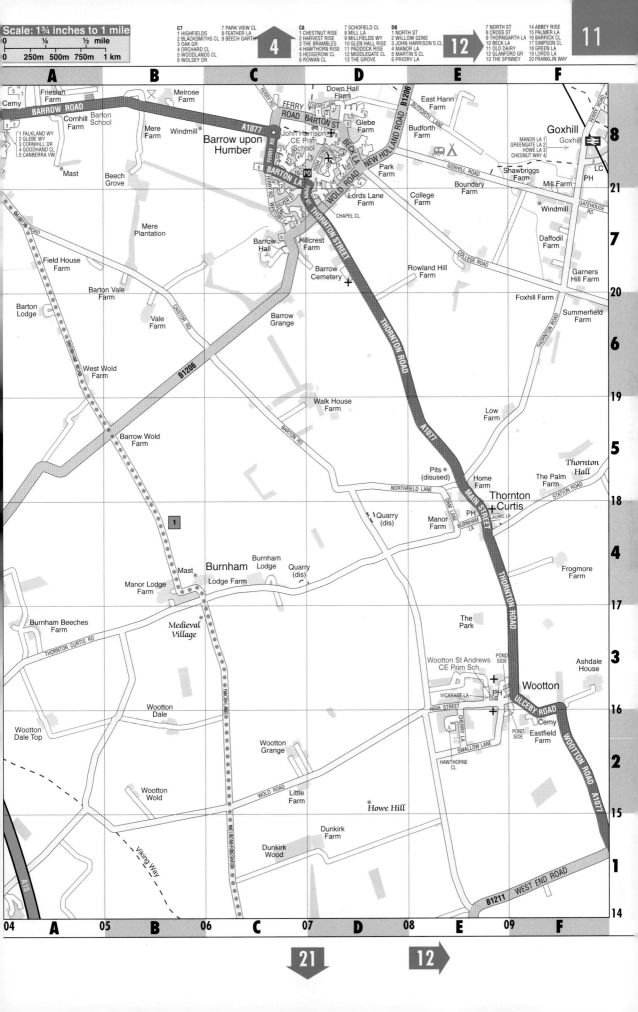

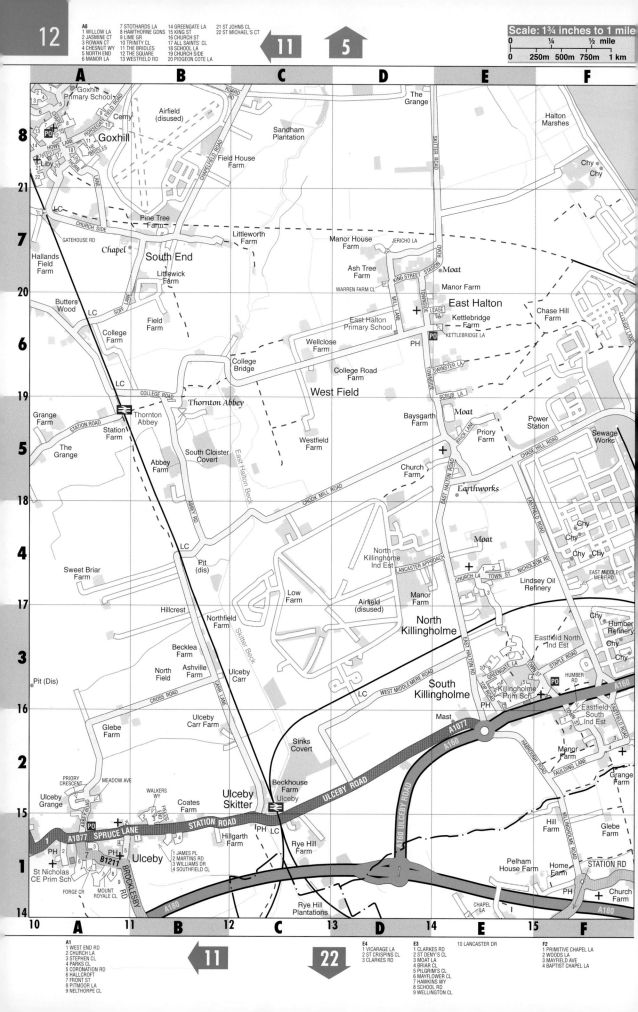

A8
1 WILLOW LA
2 JASMINE CT
3 ROWAN CT
4 CHESNUT WY
5 NORTH END
6 MANOR LA

7 STOTHARDS LA
8 HAWTHORNE GDNS
9 LIME GR
10 TRINITY CL
11 THE BRIDLES
12 THE SQUARE
13 WESTFIELD RD

14 GREENGATE LA
15 KING ST
16 CHURCH ST
17 ALL SAINTS' CL
18 SCHOOL LA
19 CHURCH SIDE
20 PIDGEON COTE LA

21 ST JOHNS CL
22 ST MICHAEL'S CT

Scale: 1¾ inches to 1 mile

0   ¼   ½ mile
0   250m 500m 750m 1 km

A1
1 WEST END RD
2 CHURCH LA
3 STEPHEN CL
4 PARKS CL
5 CORONATION RD
6 HALLCROFT
7 FRONT ST
8 PITMOOR LA
9 NELTHORPE CL

E4
1 VICARAGE LA
2 ST CRISPINS CL
3 CLARKES CL

E3
1 CLARKES RD
2 ST DENY'S CL
3 MOAT LA
4 BRIAR CL
5 PILGRIM'S CL
6 MAYFLOWER CL
7 HAWKINS WY
8 SCHOOL RD
9 WELLINGTON CL

10 LANCASTER DR

F2
1 PRIMITIVE CHAPEL LA
2 WOODS LA
3 MAYFIELD AVE
4 BAPTIST CHAPEL LA

Scale: 1¾ inches to 1 mile

0   ¼   ½ mile
0 250m 500m 750m 1 km

E. Yorkshire & N. Lincolnshire STREET ATLAS

Foulholme Sands

Cherry Cobb Sands

Cherry Cobb Sands

CHERRY COBB SANDS RD

Haven Rd

Oil Terminal

LC

C-OUNE LANE

HAVEN ROAD

Killingholme Haven Pits Nature Reserve

Killingholme Marshes

Mast

Sewage Works

Burkinshaw's Covert

STATION ROAD

LC

Killingholme High Lighthouse

LC

EAST MIDDLE MERE ROAD

ROSPER ROAD

Oil Refineries

MARSH LANE

LC

HUMBER RD

South Killingholme Haven

186

187

LC

Chy

A160

HUMBER ROAD

WEST HAVEN WY

LC

LC

Water Tower

WEST RIVERSIDE

Immingham Dock

A1173

MANBY ROAD

Houlton's Covert

SOUTHERN WY

SOUTHERN ROAD

SEVEN QUAY RD

ROBINSON ROAD

LC

East End Farm

186

Immingham Golf Course

MANBY ROAD BY PASS

GRESLEY WAY

LC

Chimney

LAPORTE ROAD

Cemy

CH

CHURCH LANE

WASHDYKE LANE

WOODLANDS

Football Gd

Sports Ground

Chimney

Humber Bank Factories

MILL LANE

STANSFIELD GDNS

Sch

PARK

BATTERY ST

MANBY RD

KINGS RD

KINGS RD

A1173

QUEENS RD

Chimney

Luxmore Farm

PILGRIMS WY

Recn Gd

BLUESTONE LANE

SONIA CREST

CLAYTON CL

WINSLOW RD

WORSLEY RD

SPRING ST

Liby

Acad

Immingham

A1173

Spoil Heap

NETHERLANDS WY

KILN LANE

KILN LANE IND EST

LC

HOBSON WAY

B1210

ROVAL DR

Sch

PH

PELHAM ROAD

PRINCESS ST

MARGARET ST

TALBOT RD

HADLEIGH RD

CORFE WALK

PILGRIM AVENUE

EUROPA WAY

HABROUGH RD

HUME BRAE

PO

Acad

For full street detail of the highlighted area see pages 186 & 187.

186   23   187   187

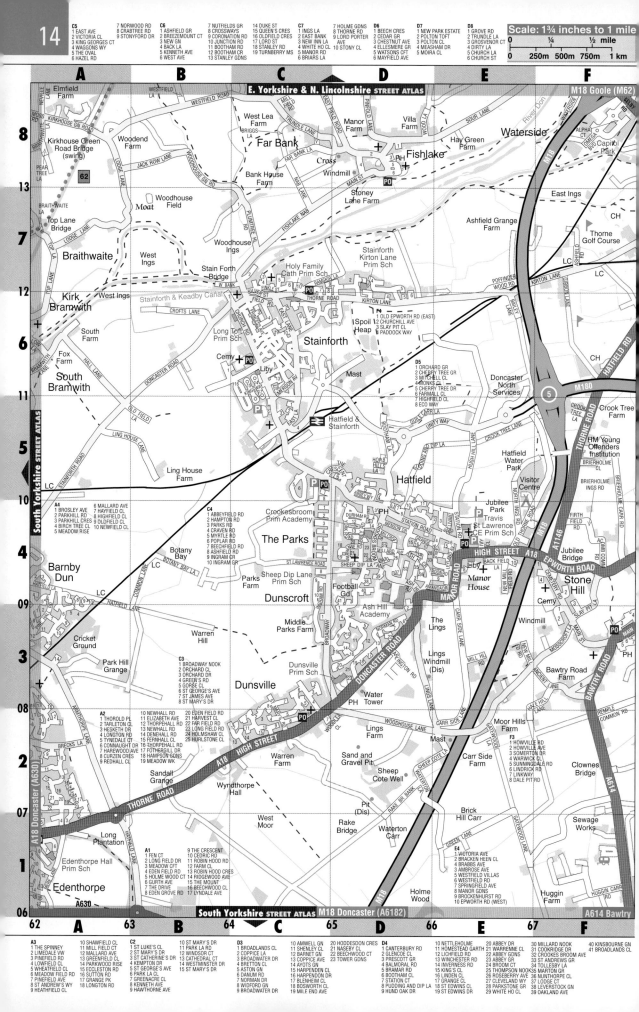

Scale: 1¾ inches to 1 mile

¼ ½ mile

250m 500m 750m 1 km

A7
1 MIDDLEBROOK LA
2 ASHFIELD AVE
3 QUANTOCK CL
4 MALVERN CL
5 COTSWOLD RD
6 CHEVIOT CL
7 PENNINE RD
8 MARINA VW
9 WENDAN RD
10 SOUTH WOOD DR
11 BURGAR RD
12 CANAL VW
13 PARK VW
14 WEST CT
15 PICKERING GR
16 ANCHOR CL

A8
1 CASSON'S RD
2 CLIFTON CT
3 CORONA DR
4 LIME TREE GR
5 BELLWOOD CR
6 BROOKFIELD CL
7 FOSTER RD
8 KENYON CL
9 UPR KENYON ST
10 LWR KENYON ST
11 GODFREY RD
12 FOUNDRY LA
13 BROWNS LA
14 CHAPEL LA
15 ROPE WK
16 WINDLASS CL
17 CAPSTAN WY
18 QUEEN'S CT
19 BOATING DYKE WY
20 ASHBURNHAM RD
21 BELLE VUE TERR
22 ORCHARD ST
23 THE GREEN
24 FAIRTREE WK
25 HORSE FAIR GREEN
26 CHURCH ST
27 BRIDGE ST
28 STONEGATE
29 PLANTATION RD
30 LOCK HILL
31 DUNSTAN WLK
32 OLD DAIRY CL
33 STATION CT

16

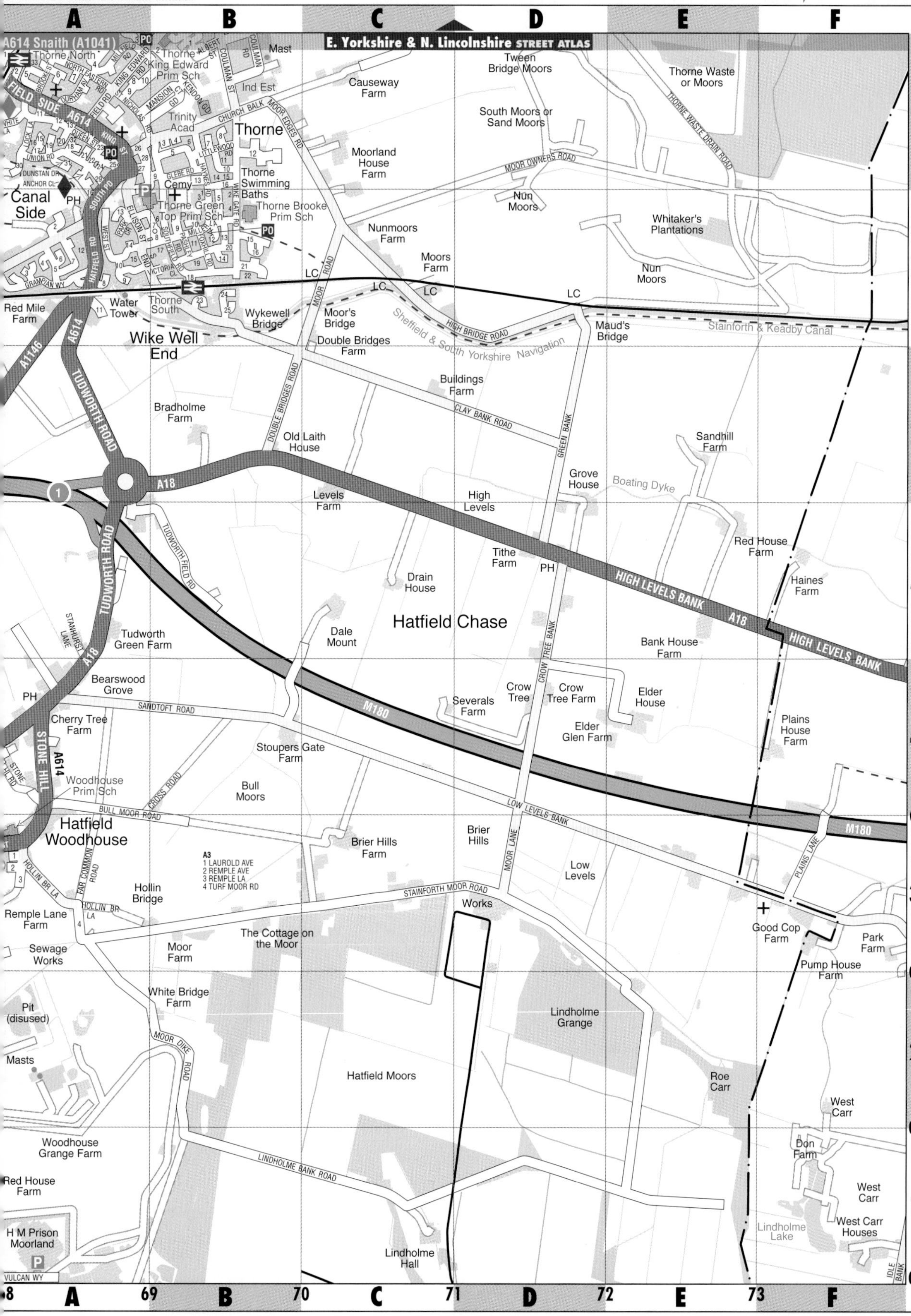

E. Yorkshire & N. Lincolnshire STREET ATLAS
A B C D E F
8 13 7 12 6 11 5 10 4 09 3 08 2 07 1 06
A614 Snaith (A1041)
Thorne North
Thorne
King Edward Prim Sch
Mast
Ind Est
Trinity Acad
Thorne Swimming Baths
Cemy
Thorne Green Top Prim Sch
Thorne Brooke Prim Sch
Canal Side
Causeway Farm
Tween Bridge Moors
Thorne Waste or Moors
South Moors or Sand Moors
Moorland House Farm
MOOR OWNERS ROAD
THORNE WASTE DRAIN ROAD
Nun Moors
Whitaker's Plantations
Nunmoors Farm
Moors Farm
Red Mile Farm
Water Tower
Thorne South
Wykewell Bridge
Moor's Bridge
Double Bridges Farm
HIGH BRIDGE ROAD
Sheffield & South Yorkshire Navigation
Maud's Bridge
Stainforth & Keadby Canal
Wike Well End
Bradholme Farm
Buildings Farm
CLAY BANK ROAD
Old Laith House
GREEN BANK
Sandhill Farm
Grove House
Boating Dyke
TUDWORTH ROAD
A18
Levels Farm
High Levels
Red House Farm
Tithe Farm
Drain House
Haines Farm
HIGH LEVELS BANK
Hatfield Chase
Dale Mount
Tudworth Green Farm
Bank House Farm
Bearswood Grove
SANDTOFT ROAD
Cherry Tree Farm
Severals Farm
Crow Tree
Crow Tree Farm
Elder House
Elder Glen Farm
Plains House Farm
M180
Stoupers Gate Farm
Woodhouse Prim Sch
Bull Moors
CROSS ROAD
BULL MOOR ROAD
LOW LEVELS BANK
Hatfield Woodhouse
Brier Hills Farm
Brier Hills
MOOR LANE
Low Levels
PLAINS LANE
A3
1 LAUROLD AVE
2 REMPLE AVE
3 REMPLE LA
4 TURF MOOR RD
Hollin Bridge
STAINFORTH MOOR ROAD
Works
Good Cop Farm
Park Farm
Remple Lane Farm
Sewage Works
The Cottage on the Moor
Moor Farm
Pump House Farm
White Bridge Farm
Lindholme Grange
Pit (disused)
MOOR DIKE ROAD
Masts
Hatfield Moors
Roe Carr
West Carr
Woodhouse Grange Farm
LINDHOLME BANK ROAD
Don Farm
Red House Farm
West Carr
H M Prison Moorland
West Carr Houses
Lindholme Lake
Lindholme Hall
VULCAN WY
IDLE BANK
68 69 70 71 72 73

B8
1 REDLAND CR
2 INGLENOOK DR
3 CHURCH CL
4 TENNYSON AVE
5 ELMHIRST RD
6 HAYNES GN
7 COVENTRY RD
8 HOUPS RD
9 TITHE BARN LA
10 ALWYNRD
11 DANUM CL
12 LOCKWOOD CL
13 HAYNES GD
14 TRAVIS CL
15 TRAVIS GR
16 TRAVIS GE

26

16

B7
1 HAYNES GR
2 WIKE GATE GR
3 HAYNES CL
4 WIKE GATE CL
5 WARREN RD
6 CHESTNUT AVE
7 ASHTREE RD
8 ELM TREE GR
9 PEEL HL RD
10 PEEL CASTLE RD
11 MARLBOROUGH RD
12 MILLER CL
13 FENLAND RD
14 MOWBRAY RD
15 STMICHAEL'S DR
16 ST MICHAEL'S CL
17 BEECH TREE AVE
18 SOUTHFIELD CL
19 AXHOLME GN
20 OLDFIELD RD
21 ST GEORGES RD
22 ST GEORGES CL
23 THE CROFT
24 SWANLAND CT
25 SWANLAND CL

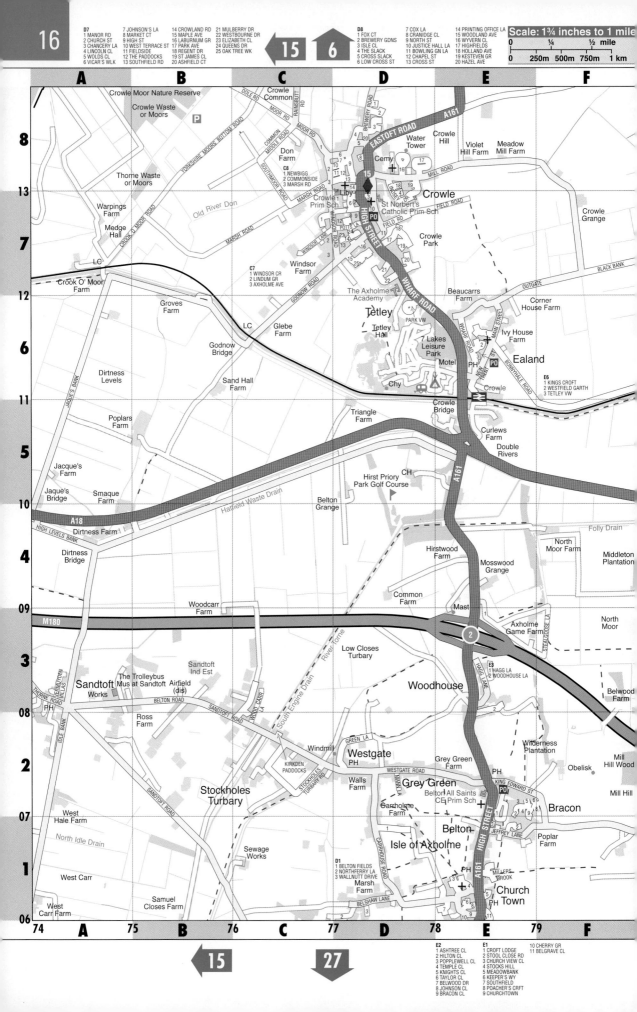

D5
1 MARGARET AVE
2 MILL RD
3 SANDS CL
4 GEORGE AVE
5 GEORGE ST

7

D6
1 WILLOW GR
2 MARINERS ARMS FLATS
3 SOUTH BANK
4 WOODGARR AVE
5 CORNWALL RD
6 DAY CL

18

E6
1 CAMPBELLS FARM AVE
2 FARM CL
3 ORCHARD DR
4 LABURNUM AVE
5 BEECH AVE
6 WHARFDALE CL

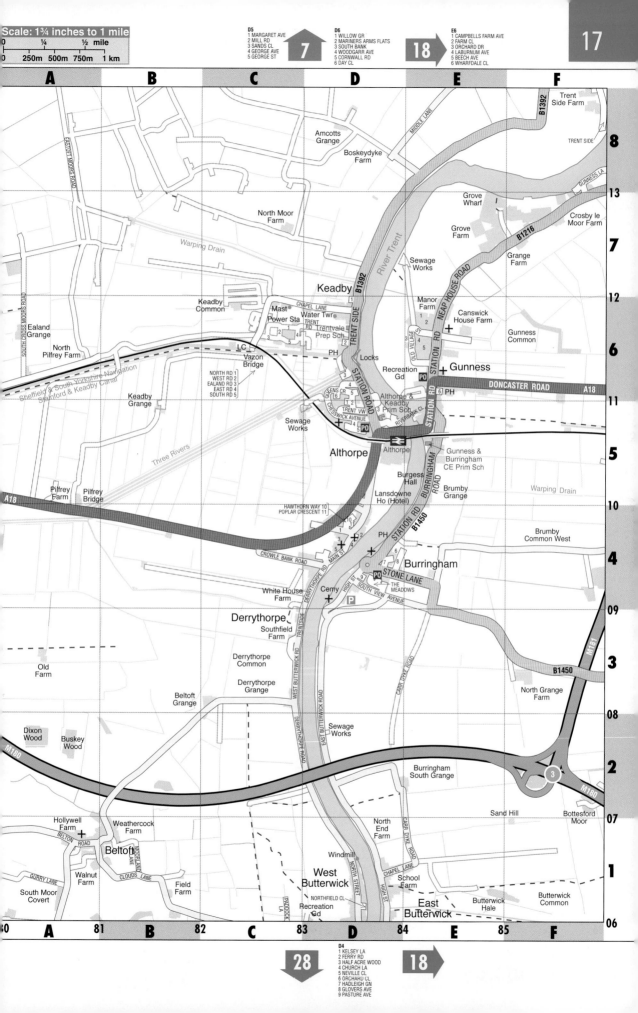

A   B   C   D   E   F

Trent Side Farm

TRENT SIDE

B1392

8

Amcotts Grange

Boskeydyke Farm

Grove Wharf

GUNNESS LA

13

Grove Farm

Crosby le Moor Farm

B1216

North Moor Farm

7

Sewage Works

Grange Farm

Warping Drain

Keadby

Manor Farm

Gunness Common

12

Keadby Common

Chapel Lane

Canswick House Farm

Mast Power Sta

Water Twr

NEAP HOUSE ROAD

Gunness

STATION RD

Ealand Grange

TRENT RD

Trentvale Prep Sch

OLD VILLAGE

6

South Cross Moors Road

North Pilfrey Farm

LC

Vazon Bridge

PH

Locks

Gunness

STATION RD

DONCASTER ROAD   A18

NORTH RD 1
WEST RD 2
EALAND RD 3
EAST RD 4
SOUTH RD 5

Recreation Gd

PO

PH

Sheffield & South Yorkshire Navigation
Stainforth & Keadby Canal

Keadby Grange

QUEENS CR

Althorpe & Keadby Prim Sch

PO

11

CRESSWICK AVENUE

STATION RD

RIVERBANK CL

5

Sewage Works

Althorpe

Althorpe

Gunness & Burringham CE Prim Sch

Three Rivers

BURRINGHAM ROAD

Warping Drain

Pilfrey Farm

Pilfrey Bridge

Burgess Hall

Brumby Grange

10

A18

Lansdowne Ho (Hotel)

STATION RD

B1450

Brumby Common West

HAWTHORN WAY 10
POPLAR CRESCENT 11

PH

4

CROWLE BANK ROAD

MAIN ST

Burringham

STONE LANE

White House Farm

DERRYTHORPE RD

Cemy

PO

THE MEADOWS

M181

Derrythorpe

P

SOUTH VIEW AVENUE

09

Southfield Farm

TRENTSIDE

HIGH ST

B1450

3

Old Farm

Derrythorpe Common

WEST BUTTERWICK RD

CARR DYKE ROAD

North Grange Farm

Derrythorpe Grange

Beltoft Grange

08

Dixon Wood

Buskey Wood

EAST BUTTERWICK ROAD

Sewage Works

Burringham South Grange

3

M180

2

DERRYTHORPE ROAD

M180

Sand Hill

Bottesford Moor

07

Hollywell Farm

Weathercock Farm

North End Farm

CARR DYKE ROAD

BELTON ROAD

Windmill

NORTH STREET

School Farm

CHAPEL LANE

1

Beltoft

MOORLANE LANE

CLOUDS LANE

West Butterwick

HIGH ST

GURRY LANE

Walnut Farm

Field Farm

PADDOCK LA

East Butterwick

Butterwick Hale

Butterwick Common

South Moor Covert

NORTHFIELD CL

Recreation Gd

06

A   B   C   D   E   F

80   81   82   83   84   85

28

D4
1 KELSEY LA
2 FERRY RD
3 HALF ACRE WOOD
4 CHURCH LA
5 NEVILLE CL
6 ORCHARD CL
7 HADLEIGH GN
8 GLOVERS AVE
9 PASTURE AVE

18

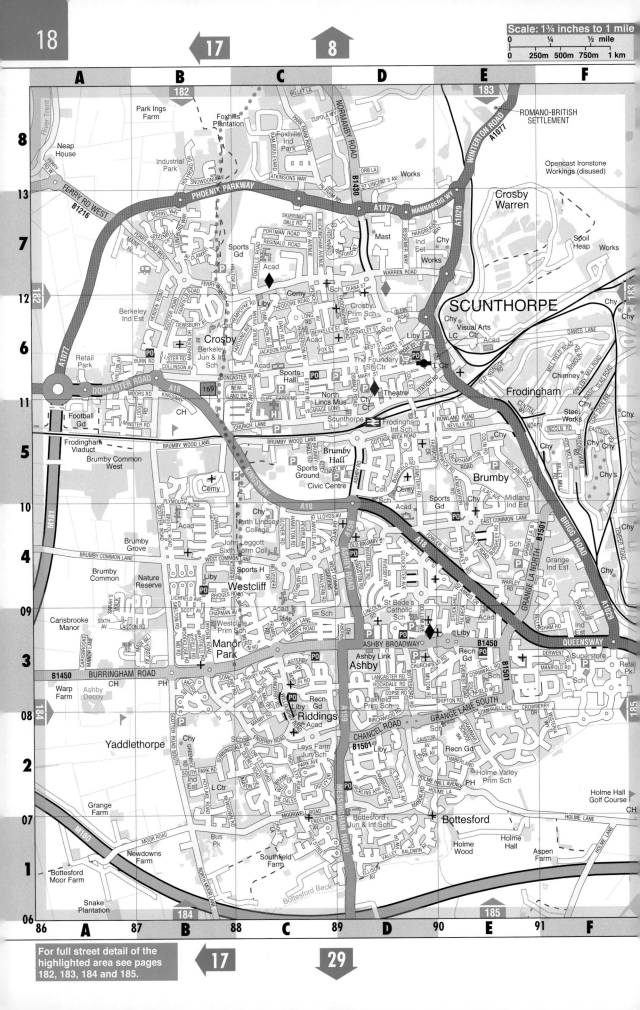

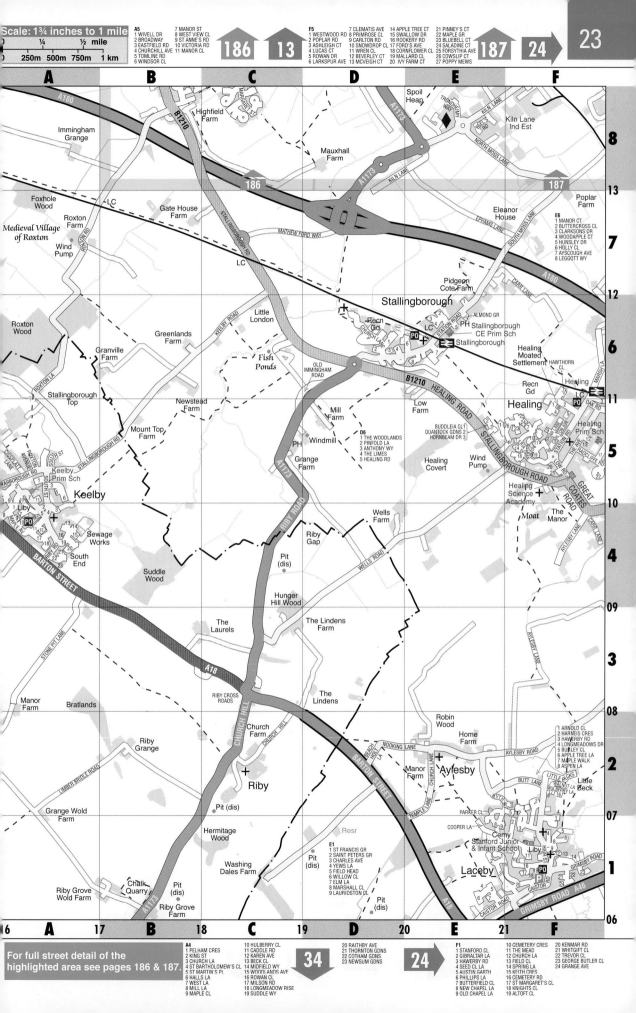

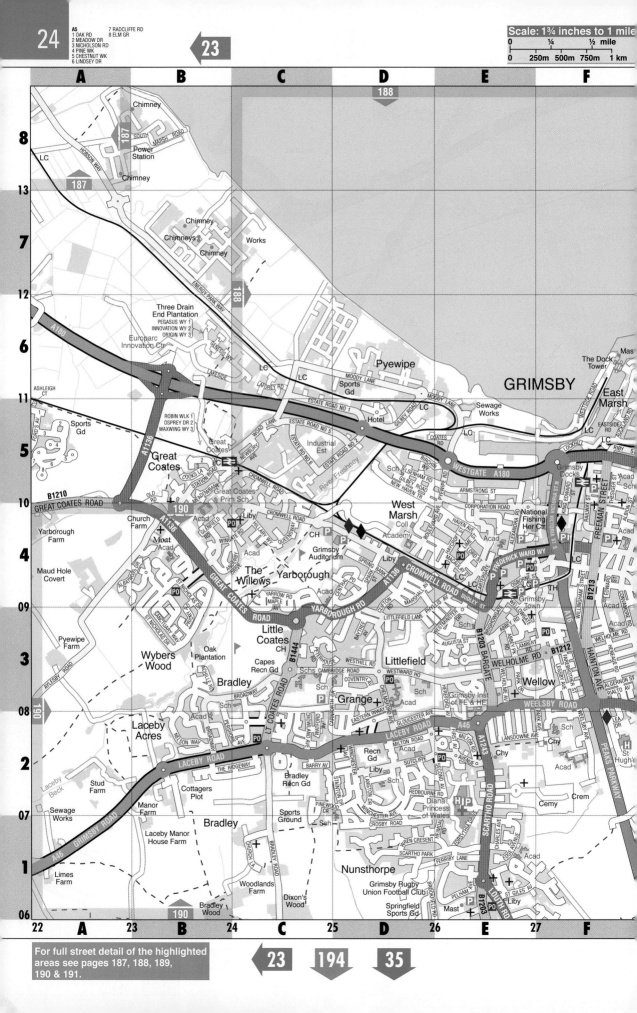

A   B   C   D   E   F

189

189

192

193

Grimsby Roads

CLEETHORPES

Cleethorpes

Water Twr

Cleethorpes Pier

SLIPWAY

Grant Thorold

Old Clee

Weelsby

Allotment Gardens

Cleethorpe Road

WEELSBY ROAD

A46

110

Kingsway

Cleethorpes Discovery Centre

The Jungle

Pumping Station

Villa Plantation

Taylor's Avenue

Mus

Lakeside

Miniature Railway

Carr Plantation

Old Hall Farm

Visitor Centre

Cleethorpes Country Park

Humberston

Cleethorpes

CH

Pleasure Island

Thorpe Park

Superstore

Humberston Rd

Grimsby Road

North Sea Lane

A1098

193

28   A   29   B   30   C   31   D   32   E   33   F

195

36

For full street detail of the highlighted areas see pages 189, 192 & 193.

8
13
7
12
6
11
5
10
4
09
3
08
2
07
1
06

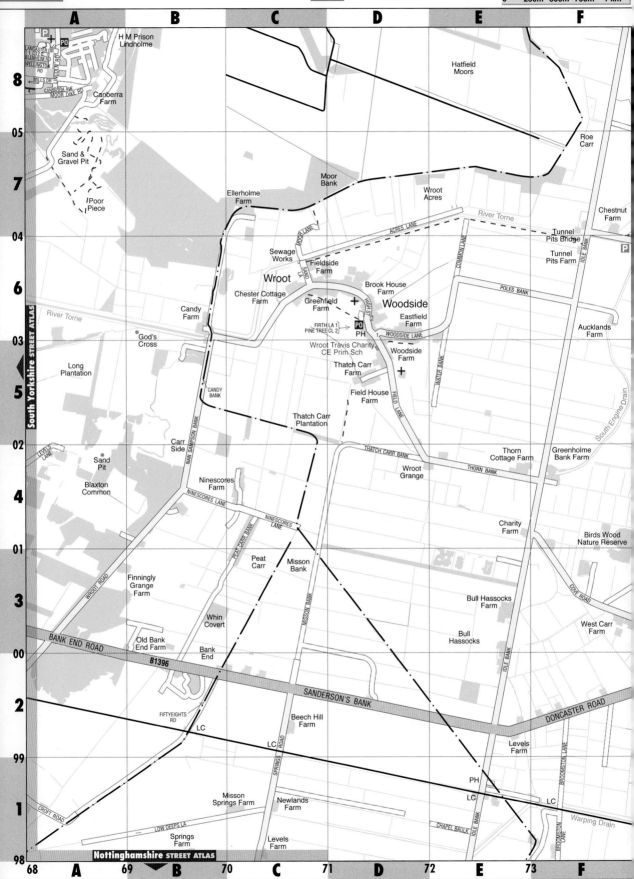

South Yorkshire STREET ATLAS

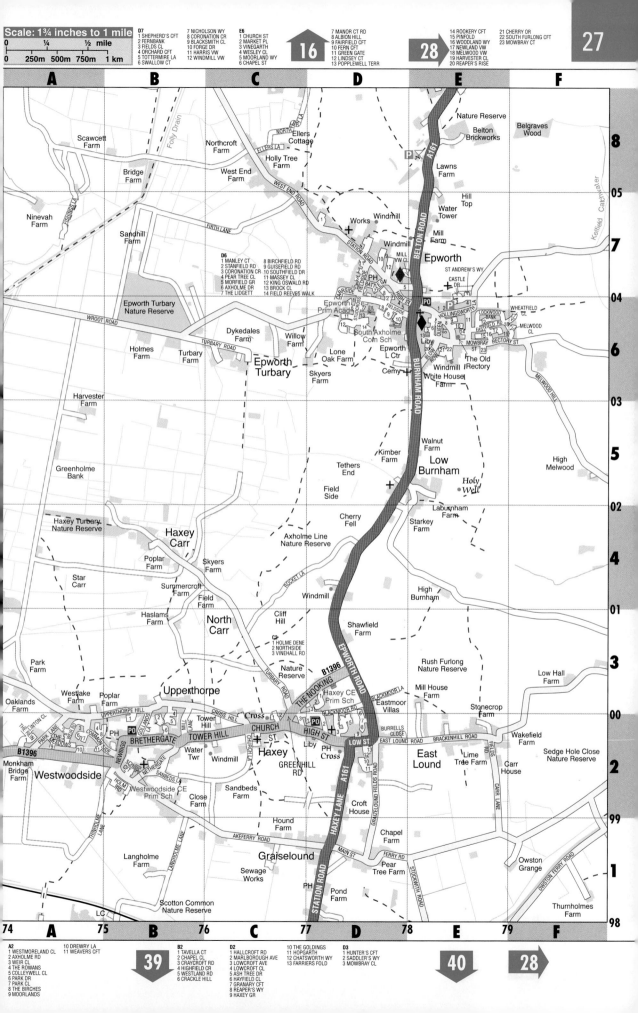

28

← 27

↑ 17

D8
1 FARM LA
2 THE CROFT
3 SCHOOL LA
4 PARKLANDS
5 CHRISTOPHERS MDW

Scale: 1¾ inches to 1 mile

0   ¼   ½ mile
0   250m 500m 750m 1 km

A B C D E F

Sealings Wood

Clouds Lane Farm

CLOUDS LA
WEST ST
CARR LANE

PARK VIEW TERR 1
ULYETT LA 2

West Butterwick CE Prim Sch

West Butterwick

East Butterwick

PH

SAND ROAD

Sewage Works

Messingham Road

Common Farm

Glebe Farm

Bonito Farm

Highfield Farm

Hollywood Farm

West Grange

Poplar Grove Farm

Sand House Farm

Newlands

NEWLANDS LANE

NARROW LANE

PADDOCK LANE

DARNHOLME CRESCENT

South Field Drain

Ings Farm

Messingham Ings

Trentings Farm

Black Bank Farm

Barlings Farm

Barlings House Farm

NORTH CARR ROAD

CARR DYKE BK

Newlands Farm

South Ewster Livery Farm

River Trent

Kelfield Grange

Priory (remains of)

Melwood Park

Low Melwood Farm

Moat

Walnut Tree Farm

Susworth

PH

Castle House Farm

Middlemoor Farm

BLACKDYKES ROAD

CARR DYKE BANK

Riverdale Farm

Cote House Farm

Glebe Farm

Kelfield

Drainhead Farm

Grove Farm

Tuetoes Hills

SUSWORTH ROAD

P

Mount Pleasant Farm

GAUTRY LANE

EPWORTH RD

MELWOOD VW

Owston Ferry

Cemy

St Martins CE Prim Sch

Windmill Farm

South Ings

South Carr

Warren Farm

New Farm

BURNHAM ROAD

BAGSBY ROAD

1 CROFT'S LA
2 MARKET PL
3 SANDARS CL

Ings Farm

Kelfield Grange

EAST FERRY ROAD

EAST LOUND RD CHURCH ST

War Meml

PH

NORTH STREET

HIGH ST

The Old Smithy & Heritage Centre

Ferry Barrier Bank

Hardwick Grange Farm

Castle Hill Motte & Bailey

STATION ROAD

PO

SILVER ST

SOUTH ST

East Ferry

South Ings

Hardwick Hill

Scotton Common

Laughton Woods

Chimney

Pin Hill

Windmill

Redgate Farm

Laughton Lodge

Lady Croft Farm

Jenny Hurn

Hornsey Hill

HORNSEY HILL ROAD

Jerry's Bog

Whitestone Farm

MEYNELL ST

EAST FERRY ROAD

80 A 81 B 82 C 83 D 84 E 85 F

A3
1 CHURCH WK
2 BURNHAM SQ
3 GASHOUSE LA
4 CHURCH CRES
5 TEMPERTON'S LA
6 SOMERBY DR
7 ST MARTINS PARK
8 BLUEBELL COURT

← 27

40

↓ 41

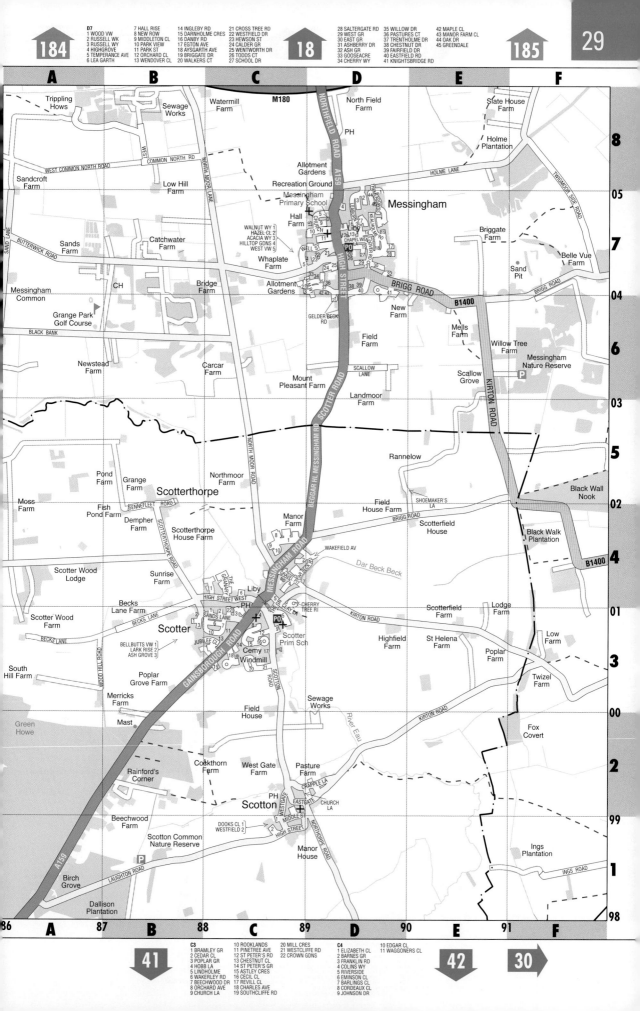

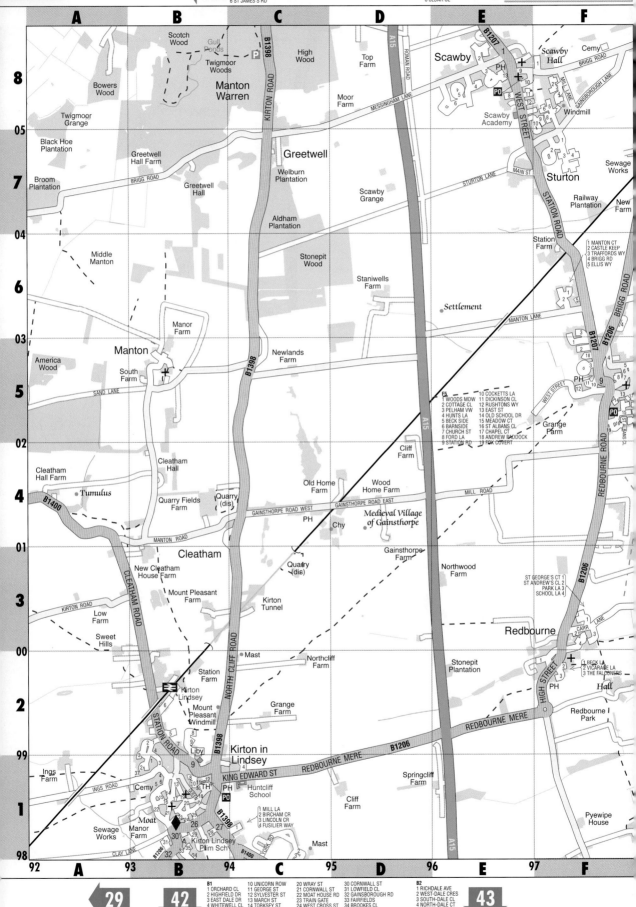

E8
1 VICARAGE LA
2 OLD VICARAGE PK
3 MANOR DR
4 ST MARTIN'S RD
5 ST JOAN'S DR
6 ST JAMES'S RD

8 COACH HOUSE GDNS
9 CHURCH ST
10 CHAPEL LA
11 INGRAM GDNS
12 BEECHWOOD DR
13 OLD MANOR DR

F7
1 WALNUT DR
2 ST HYBALD'S GR
3 SWANNACKS VW
4 SUTTON PL

F8
1 PARK LA
2 THE ROOKERY
3 MILL CROFT
4 MEADOW VALE
5 OAK AVE
6 CEDAR CL

7 WILLOW GR
8 LARCH GR
9 KINGS CT
10 LIDGETT CL

E5
1 WOODS MDW
2 COTTAGE CL
3 PELHAM VW
4 HUNTS LA
5 BECK SIDE
6 BARNSIDE
7 CHURCH ST
8 FORD LA
9 STATION RD

10 COCKETTS LA
11 DICKINSON CL
12 RUSHTONS WY
13 EAST ST
14 OLD SCHOOL DR
15 MEADOW CT
16 ST ALBANS CL
17 CHAPEL CT
18 ANDREW PADDOCK
19 FOX COVERT

1 MANTON CT
2 CASTLE KEEP
3 TRAFFORDS WY
4 BRIGG RD
5 ELLIS WY

St GEORGE'S CT 1
St ANDREW'S CL 2
PARK LA 3
SCHOOL LA 4

1 BECK LA
2 VICARAGE LA
3 THE FALCONERS

1 MILL LA
2 BIRCHAM CR
3 LINCOLN CR
4 FUSILIER WAY

B1
1 ORCHARD CL
2 HIGHFIELD DR
3 EAST DALE DR
4 WHITEWELL CL
5 GROVE ST
6 DARWIN ST
7 CHURCH ST
8 SUNNY HLL
9 SPA HLL

10 UNICORN ROW
11 GEORGE ST
12 SYLVESTER ST
13 MARCH ST
14 TORKSEY ST
15 TURNER ST
16 ST ANDREW'S ST
17 OLD SCHOOL YD
18 HIGH ST
19 WESLEY ST

20 WRAY ST
21 CORNWALL ST
22 MOAT HOUSE RD
23 TRAIN GATE
24 WEST CROSS ST
25 EAST CROSS ST
26 DUNSTAN HILL
27 SOUTH CLIFF RD
28 PARK HILL
29 DUNSTAN VILLAS

30 CORNWALL ST
31 LOWFIELD CL
32 GAINSBOROUGH RD
33 FAIRFIELDS
34 BROOKES CL
35 ENDELL DR
36 MARKET PL
37 LANES END

B2
1 RICHDALE AVE
2 WEST-DALE CRES
3 SOUTH-DALE CL
4 NORTH-DALE CT
5 BEECHCROFT DR
6 DARWIN ST
7 BOWLING GREEN GDNS
8 BARLEY CL
9 MILLSTONE CL

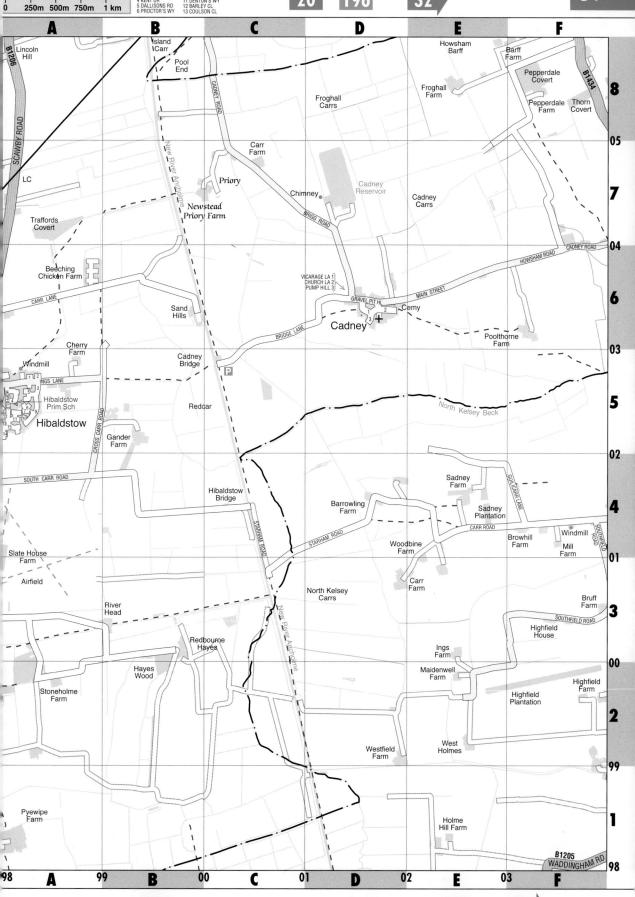

31

21

D8
1 BACK LA
2 HOWSHAM LA
3 MAIN ST
4 OWMBY RD

E7
1 MAIN ST
2 CHURCH HILL
3 CHURCH SIDE
4 FRONT ST
5 CANTY NOOK
6 BENTLEY LA

7 HOLLAND DR
8 THE OLD QUARRY

Scale: 1¾ inches to 1 mile

0 ¼ ½ mile
0 250m 500m 750m 1 km

Dawson's Covert
Oak Wood
Somerby Low Farm
Searby
Viking Way
Owmby Mount
A1084
OWMBY WOLD LANE
GRASBY WOLD LANE
Quarry
Park Wood
Bull House Farm
Hillside Farm
Manor Farm
VICARAGE LANE
PH
The Grasby All Saints CE Prim Sch
Grasby
CLIXBY LANE
PH
Clixby Manor Farm
B1434
MAIN ST
Fox Farm
Roseholme Farm
Owmby
LC
Low Farm
Owmby Vale
Pond Farm
MIDDLETONS LA
Grasby House Farm
A1084
Dale Farm
Brasted Farm
Howsham
HOWSHAM LANE
STATION LANE
Audleby Low Covert
Brandicar
Harding's Wood
White House Farm
GRASBY ROAD
Hill Farm
BRIGG ROAD
Stoneybridge Farm
Setcops Farm
FIR LANE
Moor Farm
Brook Farm
Twelve Month Hill Woods
CROSS LANE
Folly Farm
FOLLY LA
Landaum Farm
Wood Farm
Caistor Moor
Cemy
BRIGG ROAD
Fieldhouse Farm
North Kelsey Moor
Highfield Farm
CEMETERY LA
Steingrave Farm
STATION ROAD
Brickyard Farm
STATION ROAD
PH
North Kelsey
PO
Kelsey Prim Sch
Pit (dis)
Smithfield Farm
LC
CAISTOR ROAD
Far Farm
Moor Farm Nursery
Dairy Farm
PH
CARR RD
EASTHALL ROAD
STREET LANE
Drables Hill
Newlands Farm
Rochford Farm
LC
SMITHFIELD ROAD
SAND LANE
Nettleton Lodge Game Farm
West Moor Farm
Sheepcote Hill
Vicarage Farm
Drabble Hill Farm
Ellmore Farm
Big Wood
PH
Nettleton Lodge
SOUTHFIELD RD
B1434
B1205
Bruff Farm
South Barff Farm
GRANGE LANE
ELLMORE LANE
Moortown House Farm
Watermill Farm
Nettleton Manor
Manor Wood
Nettleton Moor
North End Farm
BRIGG ROAD
STATION ROAD
LC
PH
Long Wood
Black Wood
NORTH END LA
Mount Pleasant Farm
Moortown
KELSEY RD
HOLTON ROAD
Corner Farm
Holton Plantation
Noble's Wood
Nettleton Wood
South Kelsey
RASEN ROAD
Riverhead Farm
A6
Sands Plantation
1 FORGE CL
2 THORNTON RD
3 QUEENSFIELD
4 OLDE FARM CT
5 LAUREL GR
6 WESTERBY CT
Jervis Plantation
GIPSY LA
B1434
LC
Stope Hill Farm
WADDINGHAM ROAD
GIPSY LA
Daisy Hill Farm
GATEHOUSE RD
PH
B1205
CAISTOR ROAD

04 A 05 B 06 C 07 D 08 E 09 F

31

44

A4
1 LINDUM WK
2 OLD SCHOOL LA
3 MILL LA
4 SCHOOL LA
5 PATRICKS CL
6 OCCUPATION LA
7 CHAPEL ST
8 HIGH ST
9 HALLS LA
10 CHURCH LA
11 MAIDENWELL LA
12 CHURCH ST
13 GREEN LA
14 MIDDLE ST
15 SOUTH ST

45

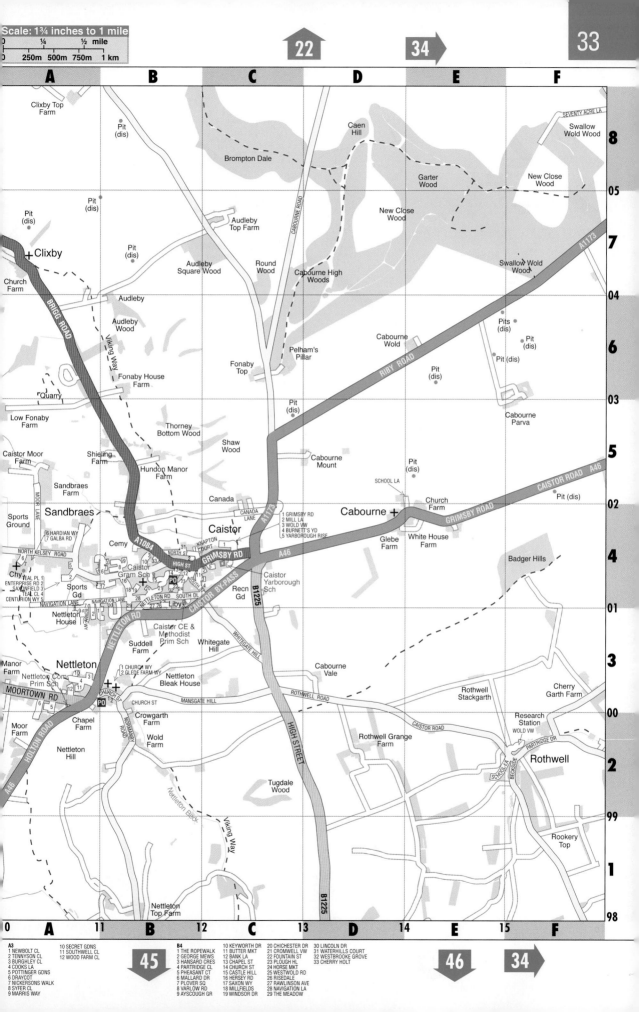

A   B   C   D   E   F

Clixby Top Farm
Pit (dis)
Caen Hill
Brompton Dale
SEVENTY ACRE LA
Swallow Wold Wood
8
Garter Wood
New Close Wood
05
Pit (dis)
Pit (dis)
Audleby Top Farm
New Close Wood
Pit (dis)
+ Clixby
A1173
7
Church Farm
Audleby Square Wood
Round Wood
Cabourne High Woods
Swallow Wold Wood
04
Pit (dis)
Audleby
CABOURNE ROAD
Pits (dis)
BRIGG ROAD
Audleby Wood
Fonaby Top
Pelham's Pillar
Cabourne Wold
RIBY ROAD
Pit (dis)
Pit (dis)
6
Viking Way
Fonaby House Farm
Pit (dis)
03
Quarry
Cabourne Parva
Low Fonaby Farm
Thorney Bottom Wood
Pit (dis)
Caistor Moor Farm
Shieling Farm
Shaw Wood
Cabourne Mount
Pit (dis)
CAISTOR ROAD A46
5
Sandbraes Farm
Hundon Manor Farm
SCHOOL LA
Pit (dis)
02
Sports Ground
Sandbraes
Canada
CANADA LANE
A1173
Cabourne +
Church Farm
GRIMSBY ROAD
Caistor
1 GRIMSBY RD
2 MILL LA
3 WOLD VW
4 BURNETT'S YD
5 YARBOROUGH RISE
Glebe Farm
White House Farm
Badger Hills
Pit (dis)
Cemy
A1084
KNAPTON COURT
NORTH ST
HIGH ST
GRIMSBY RD
A46
4
Chy+
TEAL PL
ENTERPRISE RD
SAXONFIELD
TEAL CL
CENTURION WY
Caistor Gram Sch
PO
SOUTH DL
Caistor Yarborough Sch
NAVIGATION LANE
NETTLETON RD
CAISTOR BY-PASS
Recn Gd
B1225
01
Sports Gd
Nettleton House
Caistor CE & Methodist Prim Sch
WHITEGATE HILL
Manor Farm
Suddell Farm
Whitegate Hill
Cabourne Vale
3
Nettleton Comm Prim Sch
1 CHURCH WY
2 GLEDE FARM WY
Nettleton Bleak House
Rothwell Stackgarth
Cherry Garth Farm
MOORTOWN RD
Nettleton
CHURCH ST
MANSGATE HILL
ROTHWELL ROAD
Research Station
WOLD VW
HOLTON ROAD
Chapel Farm
PO
CHURCH ST
Crowgarth Farm
HIGH STREET
Rothwell Grange Farm
CAISTOR ROAD
PARTRIDGE DR
Rothwell
00
Moor Farm
NORMANBY ROAD
Wold Farm
SCHOOL LA
BECKSIDE
2
A46
Nettleton Hill
Nettleton Beck
Tugdale Wood
99
Viking Way
Rookery Top
1
B1225
Nettleton Top Farm
98

0   A   11   B   12   C   13   D   14   E   15   F   98

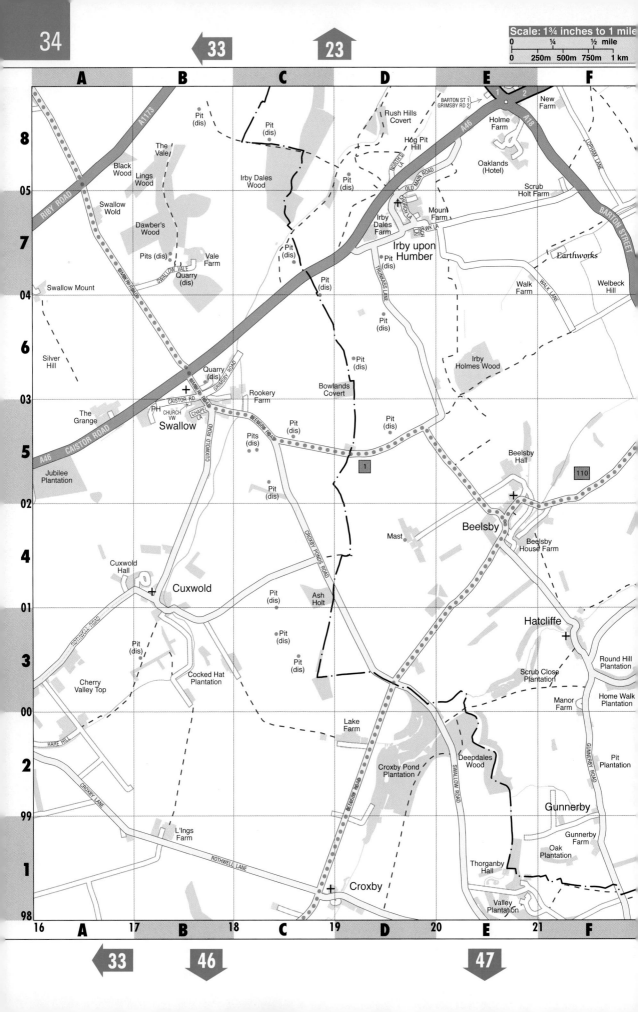

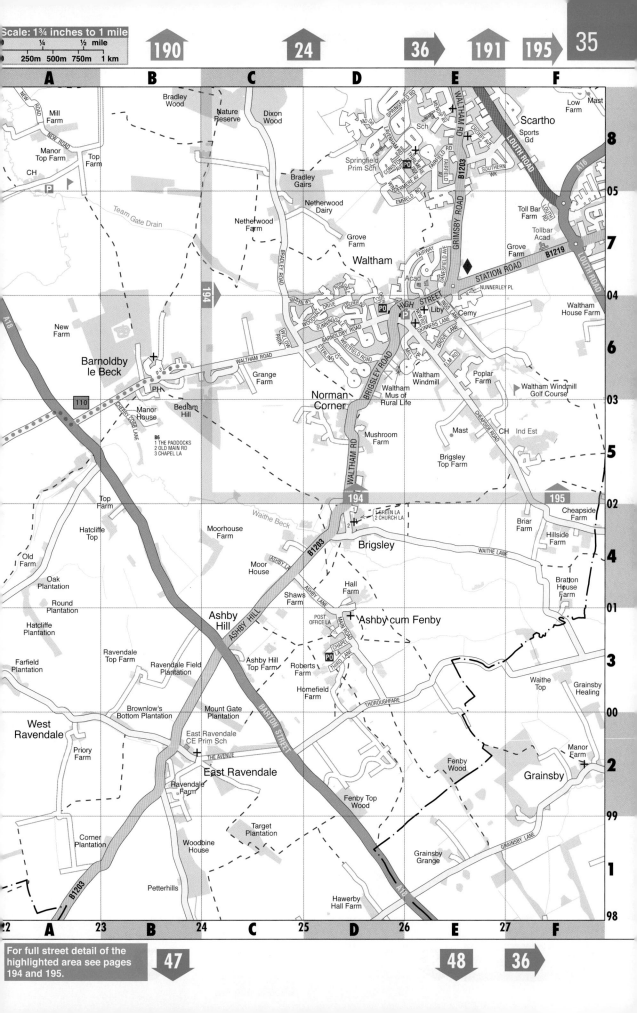

Scale: 1¾ inches to 1 mile

| A | B | C | D | E | F |

North Sea

8

05

7

04

6

03

5

02

4

01

3

Somercotes
Haven

DANGER
AREA

Donna Nook
National Nature Reserve

00

Seven Towns South Eau

P ⚔ Stonebridge

Porter's
Sluice

Donna
Nook

2

Pye's
Farm

Laramie

Sprakes
Farm

COASTGUARD RD

Wells
Farm

MARSH LANE

99

Marsh
Grange

Fivehundred
Acres

1

Porter's
Marsh

Sewage
Works

Holmes
Farm

Poplar
Farm

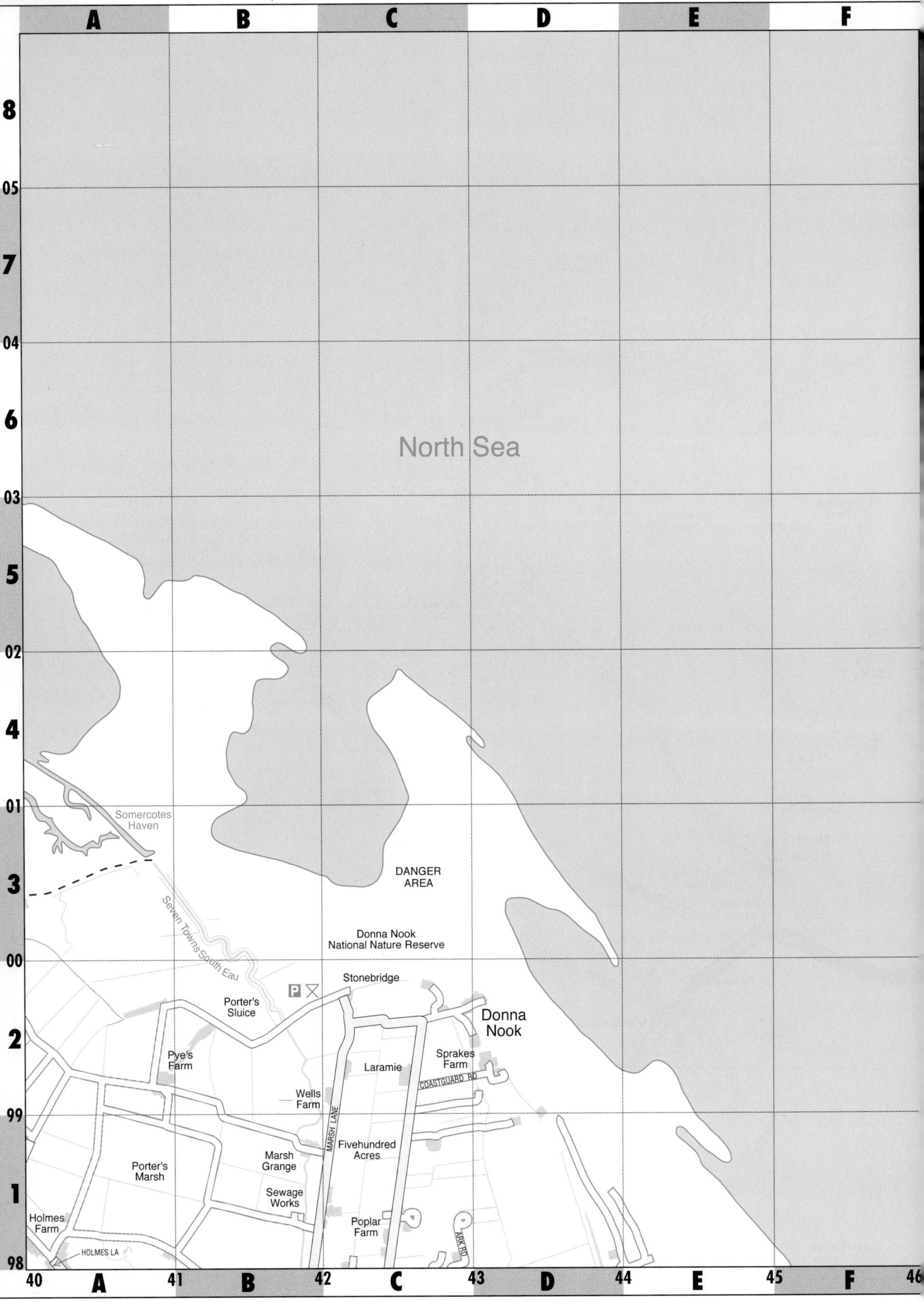

ARK RD

HOLMES LA

98

| 40 | A | 41 | B | 42 | C | 43 | D | 44 | E | 45 | F | 46 |

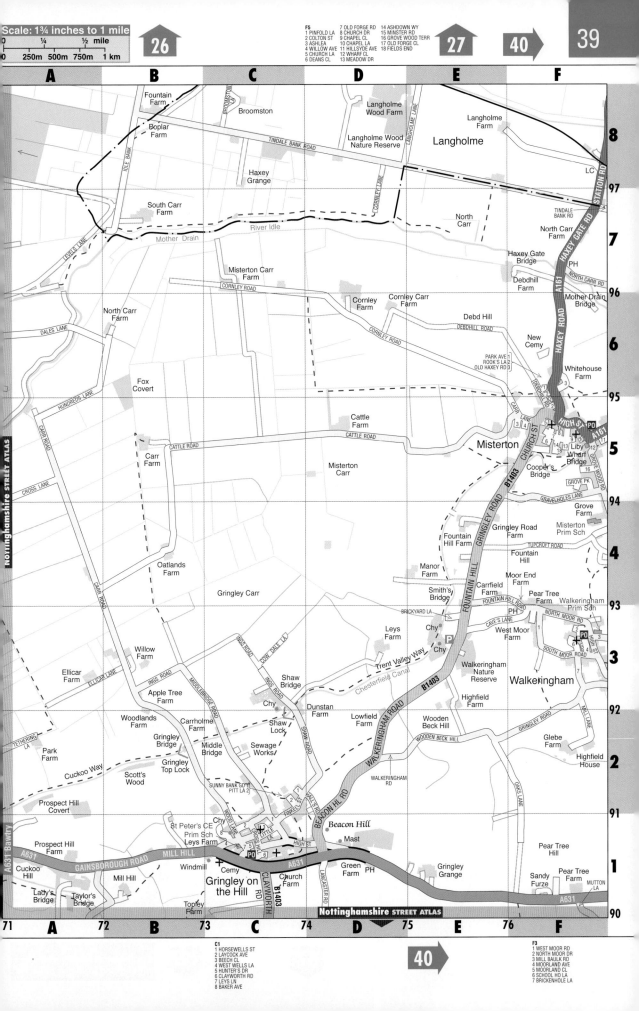

F5
1 PINFOLD LA
2 COLTON ST
3 ASHLEA
4 WILLOW AVE
5 CHURCH LA
6 DEANS CL
7 OLD FORGE RD
8 CHURCH DR
9 CHAPEL CL
10 CHAPEL LA
11 HILLSYDE AVE
12 WHARF CL
13 MEADOW DR
14 ASHDOWN WY
15 MINSTER RD
16 GROVE WOOD TERR
17 OLD FORGE CL
18 FIELDS END

Nottinghamshire STREET ATLAS

Fountain Farm
Poplar Farm
Broomston
Broomston
Langholme Wood Farm
Langholme Wood Nature Reserve
Langholme Farm
Langholme
TINDALE BANK ROAD
Haxey Grange
South Carr Farm
IDLE BANK
BROOMSTON LA
CORNLEY LANE
LANGHOLME LANE
LC
STATION RD
97
North Carr
North Carr Farm
TINDALE BANK RD
River Idle
Mother Drain
LEVELS LANE
Haxey Gate Bridge
PH
HAXEY GATE RD
A161
NORTH CARR RD
7
Misterton Carr Farm
CORNLEY ROAD
North Carr Farm
DALES LANE
Cornley Farm
Cornley Carr Farm
Debdhill Farm
A161
Mother Drain Bridge
96
HUNDREDS LANE
Fox Covert
CORNLEY ROAD
Debd Hill
DEBDHILL ROAD
HAXEY ROAD
New Cemy
PARK AVE 1
ROOK'S LA 2
OLD HAXEY RD 3
Whitehouse Farm
6
CARR ROAD
North Carr Farm
Cattle Farm
CATTLE ROAD
3 4
HIGH ST
PO
Misterton
95
CROSS LANE
Carr Farm
Misterton Carr
3 4
CHURCH ST
CARR LANE
14
18 13 12
Liby
GROVE WOOD RD
5
Cooper's Bridge
Wharf Bridge
16
CARR ROAD
Fox Covert
B1403
GRINGLEY ROAD
GRAVELHOLES LANE
GROVE PK
Grove Farm
94
Gringley Road Farm
Misterton Prim Sch
TUPCROFT ROAD
Fountain Hill Farm
Fountain Hill
4
Oatlands Farm
Gringley Carr
Manor Farm
Smith's Bridge
Carrfield Farm
Moor End Farm
Pear Tree Farm
FOUNTAIN HILL
FOUNTAIN HILL ROAD
PH
Walkeringham Prim Sch
NORTH MOOR RD
93
Willow Farm
INGS ROAD
COW DALE LA
BRICKYARD LA
Leys Farm
CAVE'S LANE
Chy
P
Chy
West Moor Farm
PO
SOUTH MOOR ROAD
HIGH ST
3
Ellicar Farm
ELLICAR LANE
Apple Tree Farm
MIDDLEBRIDGE ROAD
INGS ROAD
Shaw Bridge
Chy
Trent Valley Way
Chesterfield Canal
Walkeringham Nature Reserve
Walkeringham
Tethering La
Park Farm
Cuckoo Way
Scott's Wood
Woodlands Farm
Carrholme Farm
Gringley Bridge
Dunstan Farm
Shaw Lock
Lowfield Farm
B1403
WALKERINGHAM ROAD
Wooden Beck Hill
WOODEN BECK HILL
Highfield Farm
GRINGLEY ROAD
Glebe Farm
MILL LANE
92
Prospect Hill Covert
Gringley Top Lock
Middle Bridge
Sewage Works
SPAN ROAD
DALE FM RD
Walkeringham Rd
OAKS LANE
Highfield House
A631 Bawtry
Prospect Hill Farm
SUNNY BANK GDN
PITT LA 2
WOOD LANE
FINKELL ST
Pear Tree Hill
91
Cuckoo Hill
Lady's Bridge
Taylor's Bridge
GAINSBOROUGH ROAD
MILL HILL
Mill Hill
St Peter's CE Prim Sch
Leys Farm
Chy
CROSS HILL
HIGH ST
PO
Cemy
Windmill
LANCASTER RD
BEACON HILL RD
A631
Beacon Hill
Mast
Green Farm
PH
Gringley Grange
Sandy Furze
Pear Tree Farm
MUTTON LA
A631
90
Gringley on the Hill
Topley Farm
Church Farm
CLAYWORTH RD
B1403

C1
1 HORSEWELLS ST
2 LAYCOCK AVE
3 BEECH CL
4 WEST WELLS LA
5 HUNTER'S DR
6 CLAYWORTH RD
7 LEYS LN
8 BAKER AVE

F3
1 WEST MOOR RD
2 NORTH MOOR DR
3 MILL BAULK RD
4 MOORLAND AVE
5 MOORLAND CL
6 SCHOOL HO LA
7 BRICKENHOLE LA

A B C D E F

71 72 73 74 75 76

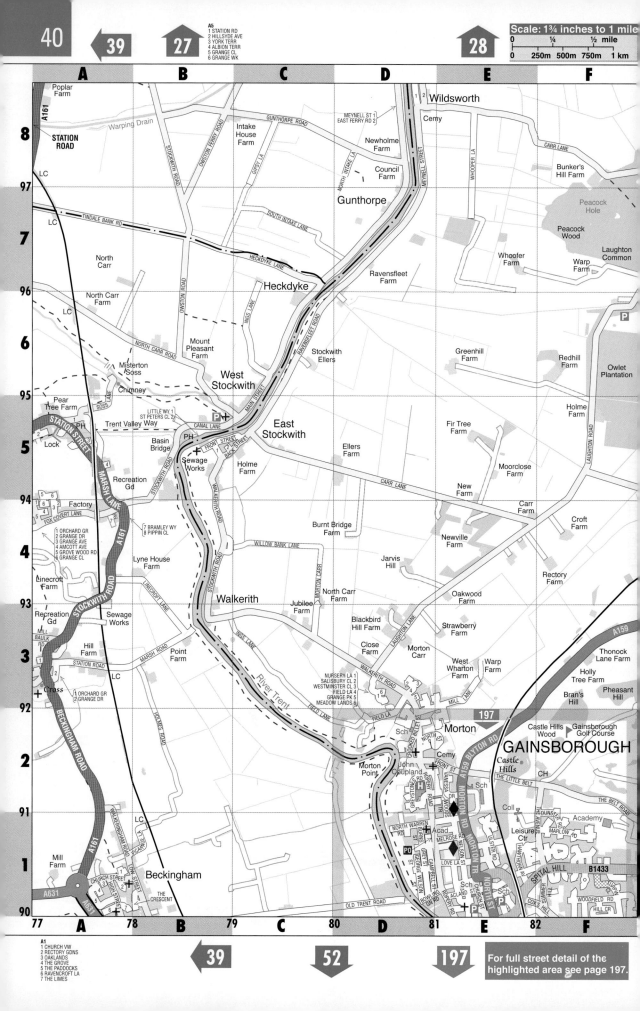

40

39

27

A5
1 STATION RD
2 HILLSYDE AVE
3 YORK TERR
4 ALBION TERR
5 GRANGE CL
6 GRANGE WK

28

Scale: 1¾ inches to 1 mile
0   ¼   ½   mile
0   250m 500m 750m 1 km

A   B   C   D   E   F

8

97

7

96

6

95

5

94

4

93

3

2

91

1

90

77   A   78   B   79   C   80   D   81   E   82   F

Poplar
Farm

STATION
ROAD

A161

Warping Drain

LC

LC

TINDALE BANK RD

North
Carr

North Carr
Farm

LC

NORTH CARR ROAD

Misterton
Soss

Chimney

Pear
Tree Farm

SOSS LANE

Station Street

PH

Lock

Recreation
Gd

Factory

FOX COVERT LANE

1 ORCHARD GR
2 GRANGE DR
3 GRANGE AVE
4 AMCOTT AVE
5 GROVE WOOD RD
6 GRANGE CL

Linecroft
Farm

A161

MARSH LANE

Recreation
Gd

Sewage
Works

MILL
BAULK
RD

Hill
Farm

STATION ROAD

LC

Cross

1 ORCHARD GR
2 GRANGE DR

STOCKWITH ROAD

LINECROFT LANE

Lyne House
Farm

Walkerith

Point
Farm

MARSH ROAD

HOLMES ROAD

River Trent

WALKERITH ROAD

INGS LANE

Mill
Farm

A161

BECKINGHAM ROAD

WALKINGHAM ROAD

LOW FARM

LC

Beckingham

A631

A61

CHURCH STREET

HIGH STREET

THE
CRESCENT

A1
1 CHURCH VW
2 RECTORY GDNS
3 OAKLANDS
4 THE GROVE
5 THE PADDOCKS
6 RAVENCROFT LA
7 THE LIMES

OWSTON FERRY ROAD

STOCKWITH ROAD

Intake
House
Farm

GIPSY LA

GUNTHORPE ROAD

SOUTH INTAKE LANE

HECKDYKE LANE

Heckdyke

INGS LANE

Mount
Pleasant
Farm

West
Stockwith

MAIN STREET

RAVENSFLEET ROAD

LITTLE WY 1
ST PETERS CL 2

CANAL LANE

Basin
Bridge

P

PH

FRONT STREET

BACK STREET

Sewage
Works

Holme
Farm

7 BRAMLEY WY
8 PIPPIN CL

WILLOW BANK LANE

Jubilee
Farm

MORTON CARR

NORTH INTAKE LA

MEYNELL STREET

WHOOPER LA

East Ferry Rd 2
MEYNELL ST 1

Wildsworth

Cemy

Newholme
Farm

Council
Farm

Gunthorpe

Ravensfleet
Farm

Stockwith
Ellers

Ellers
Farm

CARR LANE

Burnt Bridge
Farm

North Carr
Farm

Blackbird
Hill Farm

Close
Farm

LAUGHTON LANE

Greenhill
Farm

Fir Tree
Farm

New
Farm

Newville
Farm

Jarvis
Hill

Oakwood
Farm

Strawberry
Farm

Morton
Carr

West
Wharton
Farm

CARR LANE

Moorclose
Farm

Carr
Farm

Croft
Farm

Rectory
Farm

Warp
Farm

NURSERY LA 1
SALISBURY CL 2
WESTMINSTER CL 3
FIELD LA 4
GRANGE PK 5
MEADOW LANDS 6

FIELD LANE

Morton
Point

Sch

CROOKED BILLET RD

Morton

Cemy

John
Coupland
H

Castle
Hills

197

A159

Castle Hills
Wood

Gainsborough
Golf Course

THE LITTLE BELT

CH

GAINSBOROUGH

Thonock
Lane Farm

Holly
Tree Farm

Bran's
Hill

Pheasant
Hill

THE BELT ROAD

Academy

Coll

Leisure
Ctr

MORTON RD

MORTON TR

A159 BLYTON RD

NELSON ST

NORTH ST

MILL LANE

ULSTER RD

North Warren Rd

Acad

MELROSE

Love La 1

PO

GREY ST

GEORGE ST

BURNS ST

CAMPBELL ST

BOWLING GRN RD

RIPLEY ST

ACLAND

COX'S HILL

Sch

P

OLD TRENT ROAD

SPITAL HILL

B1433

WOODFIELD
RD

HILL CR

Peacock
Hole

Peacock
Wood

Bunker's
Hill Farm

CARR LANE

Whoofer
Farm

Laughton
Common

Warp
Farm

Holme
Farm

Redhill
Farm

Owlet
Plantation

P

P

Holme
Farm

LAUGHTON ROAD

39

52

197

For full street detail of the
highlighted area see page 197.

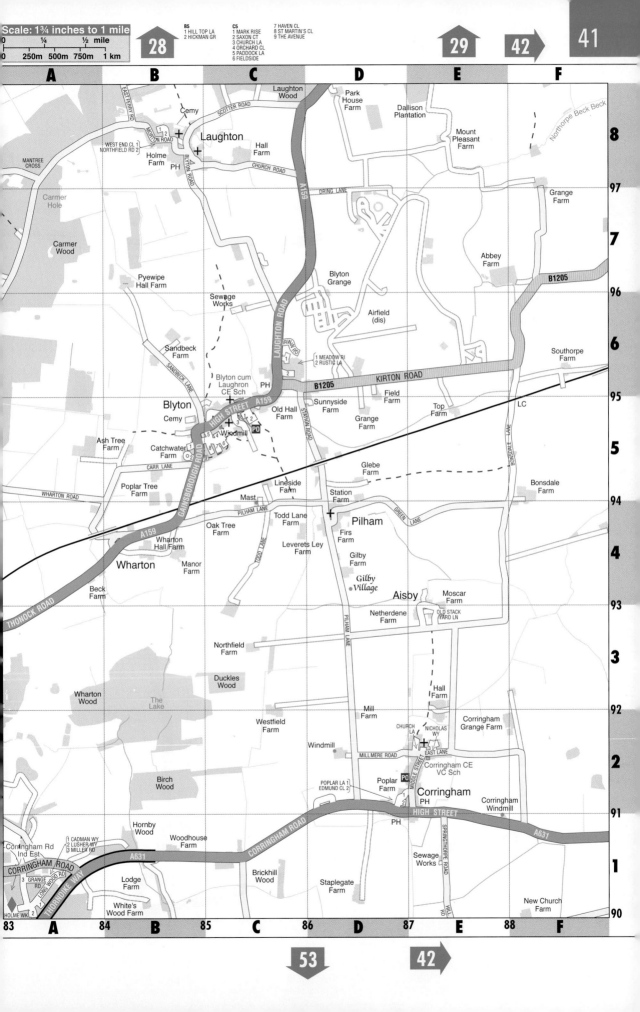

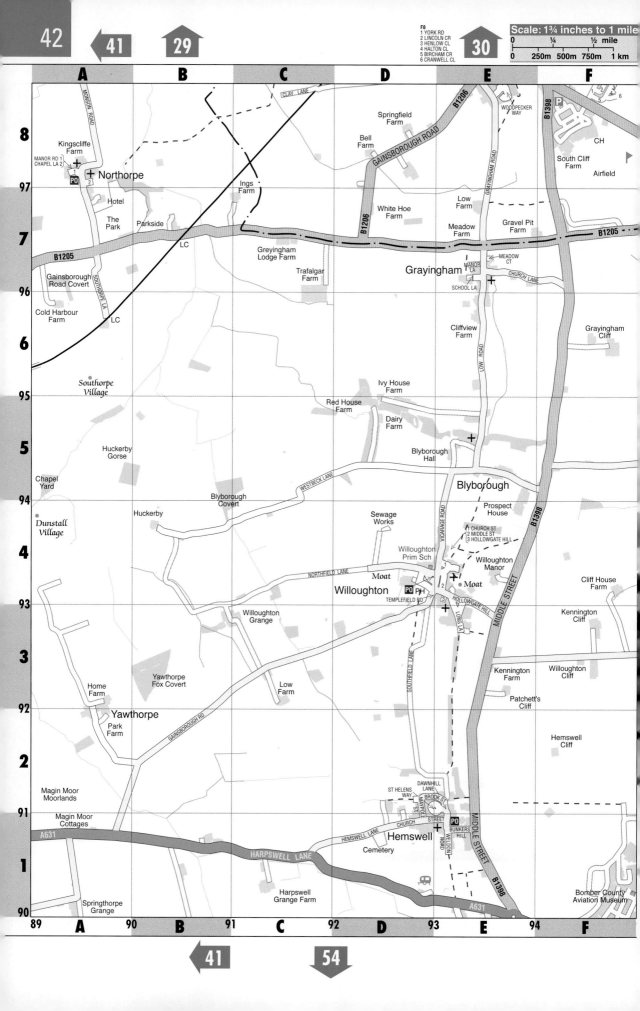

F8
1 YORK RD
2 LINCOLN CR
3 HENLOW CL
4 HALTON CL
5 BIRCHAM CR
6 CRANWELL CL

A   B   C   D   E   F

8

97

7

96

6

95

5

94

4

93

3

92

2

91

1

90

Northorpe
Kingscliffe Farm
MANOR RD 1
CHAPEL LA 2
Hotel
The Park
Parkside
MONSON ROAD
LC

Springfield Farm
Bell Farm
White Hoe Farm
GAINSBOROUGH ROAD
B1206
Ings Farm
CLAY LANE

WOODPECKER WAY
South Cliff Farm
CH
Airfield
B1398
P

B1205
Gainsborough Road Covert
SOUTHORPE LA
Cold Harbour Farm
LC

Greyingham Lodge Farm
Trafalgar Farm

Low Farm
Meadow Farm
Gravel Pit Farm
GRAYINGHAM ROAD
B1205

Grayingham
MANOR LA
MEADOW CT
CHURCH LANE
SCHOOL LA

Cliffview Farm
LOW ROAD
Grayingham Cliff

Southorpe Village

Huckerby Gorse

Ivy House Farm
Red House Farm
Dairy Farm
Blyborough Hall

Chapel Yard

Dunstall Village

Huckerby
Blyborough Covert
WESTBECK LANE

Sewage Works

Blyborough
Prospect House
1 CHURCH ST
2 MIDDLE ST
3 HOLLOWGATE HILL
B1398

Willoughton Prim Sch
NORTHFIELD LANE
Moat
Willoughton
PO PH
TEMPLEFIELD RD

Willoughton Manor
Moat
VICARAGE ROAD
HOLLOWGATE HILL
MIDDLE STREET
LONG LA
Cliff House Farm

Willoughton Grange

Home Farm
GAINSBOROUGH RD
Yawthorpe Fox Covert
Low Farm

Kennington Cliff
Kennington Farm
Willoughton Cliff
Patchett's Cliff

Yawthorpe
Park Farm

Hemswell Cliff

Magin Moor Moorlands

Magin Moor Cottages
A631

ST HELENS WAY
DAWNHILL LANE
BROOK ST
MAYPOLE ST
CHURCH STREET
Hemswell
Cemetery
HEMSWELL LANE
PO
BUNKERS HILL
WELTON ROAD
MIDDLE STREET
B1398

HARPSWELL LANE
Harpswell Grange Farm

Springthorpe Grange
A631

Bomber County Aviation Museum

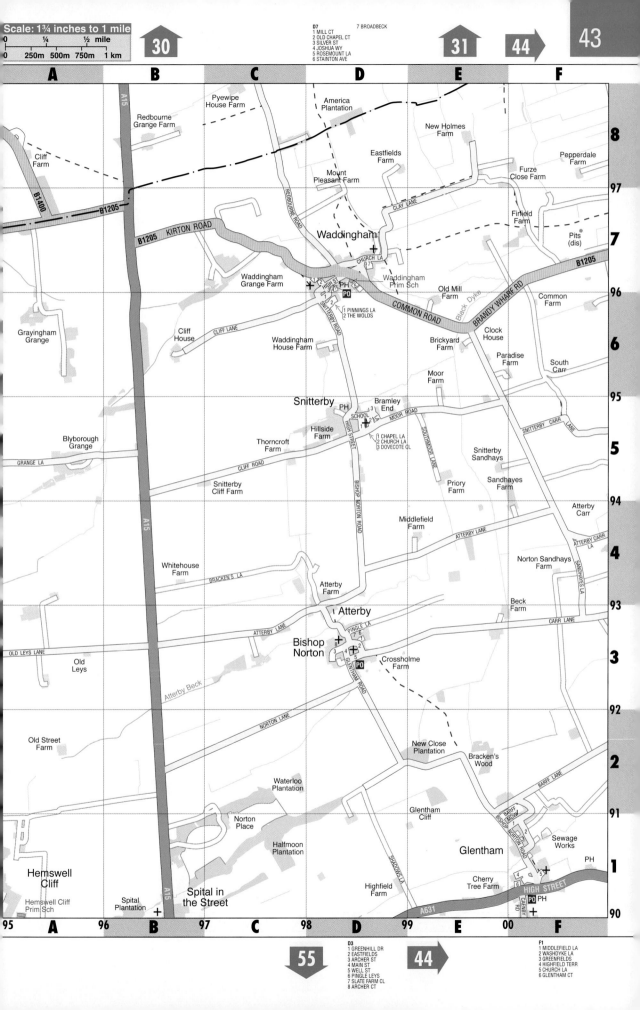

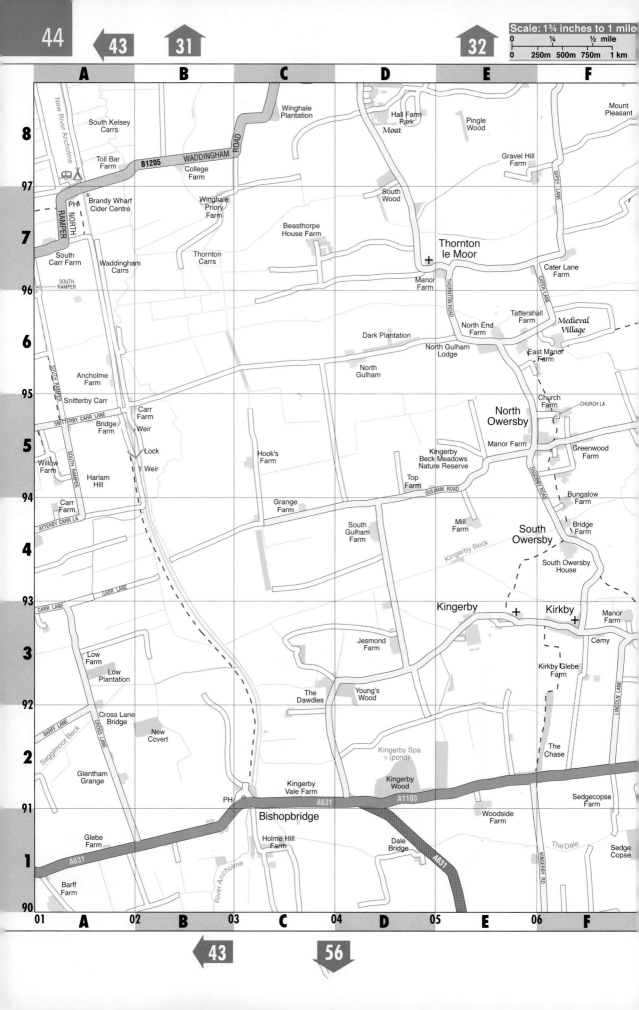

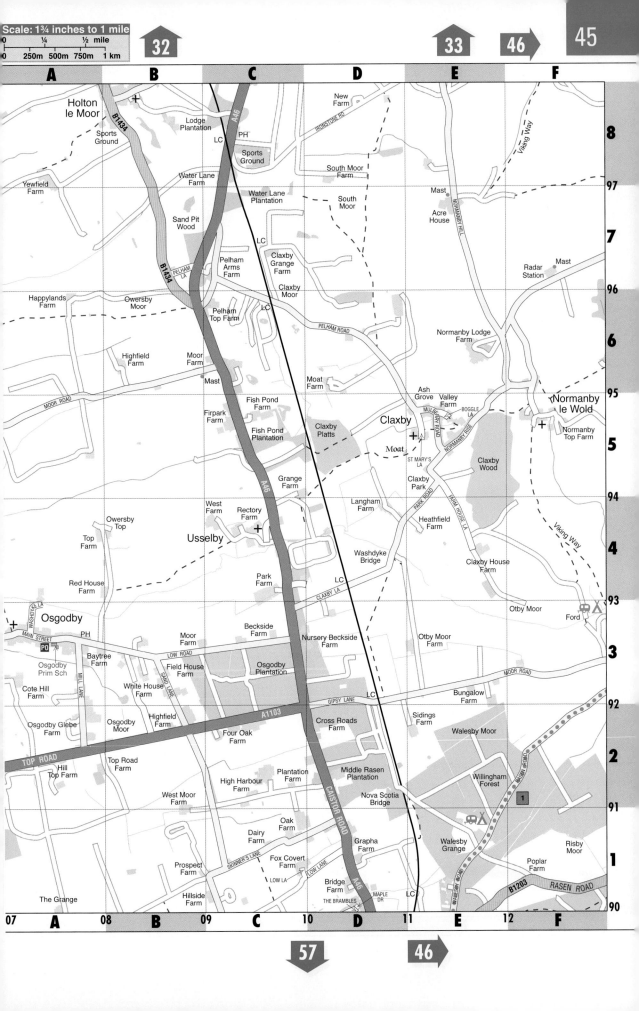

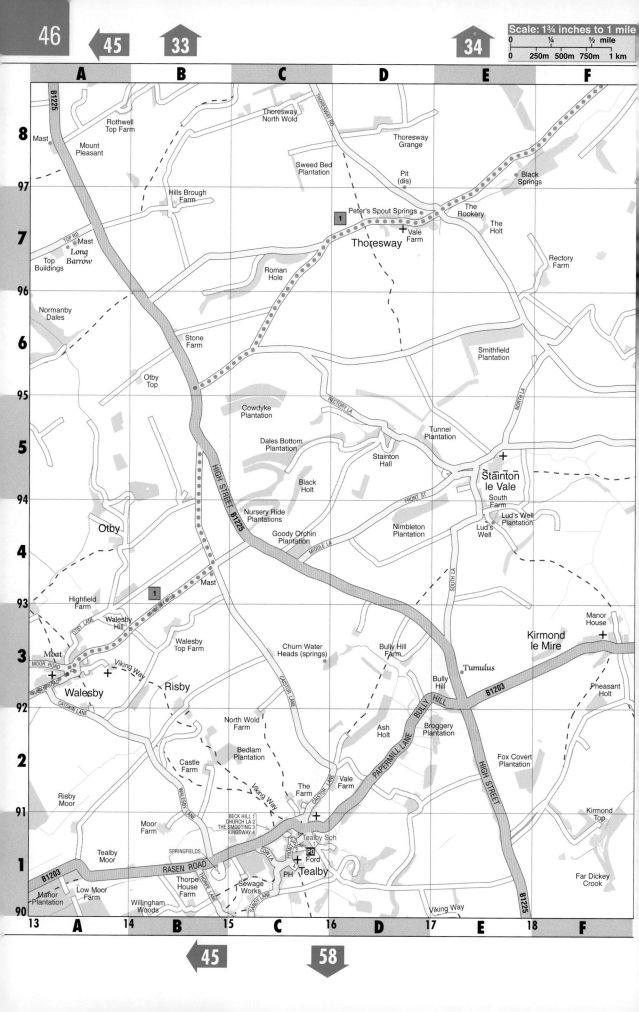

A   B   C   D   E   F

8
B1225
Mast
Rothwell Top Farm
Mount Pleasant
Thoresway North Wold
THORESWAY RD
Thoresway Grange

97
Hills Brough Farm
Sweed Bed Plantation
Pit (dis)
Black Springs

Peter's Spout Springs
1
The Rookery
The Holt

7
TOP RD
Mast
Long Barrow
Top Buildings
Vale Farm
Thoresway
Rectory Farm

Roman Hole

96
Normanby Dales
Stone Farm

Smithfield Plantation

6
Otby Top
RECTORY LA
NORTH LA

95
Cowdyke Plantation
Tunnel Plantation

Dales Bottom Plantation
Stainton Hall

5
HIGH STREET B1225
Black Holt
Stainton le Vale
South Farm
Lud's Well Plantation

Nursery Ride Plantations
FRONT ST
Nimbleton Plantation
Lud's Well

4
Otby
Goody Orchin Plantation
MIDDLE LA

Mast
SOUTH LA

93
Highfield Farm
Walesby Hill
1
Churn Water Heads (springs)
Bully Hill Farm
Kirmond le Mire
Manor House

3
Mast
MOOR ROAD
Walesby Top Farm
Risby
Viking Way
CASTOR LANE
Tumulus
BULLY HILL
B1203
Pheasant Holt

92
Walesby
RABBIT ROAD
CATSKIN LANE
North Wold Farm
Ash Holt
Broggery Plantation
HIGH STREET

2
Risby Moor
WALESBY LANE
Castle Farm
Bedlam Plantation
Viking Way
PAPERMILL LANE
CASTOR LANE
The Farm
Vale Farm
Fox Covert Plantation

91
Moor Farm
SPRINGFIELDS
BECK HILL 1
CHURCH LA 2
THE SMOOTING 3
KINGSWAY 4
Tealby Sch
Kirmond Top

1
B1203
Tealby Moor
RASEN ROAD
THORPE LANE
COW LA
FRONT ST
PO
PH
Ford
Tealby
Far Dickey Crook

Manor Plantation
Low Moor Farm
Thorpe House Farm
Willingham Woods
SANDY LANE
Sewage Works
Viking Way
B1225

90
13   A   14   B   15   C   16   D   17   E   18   F

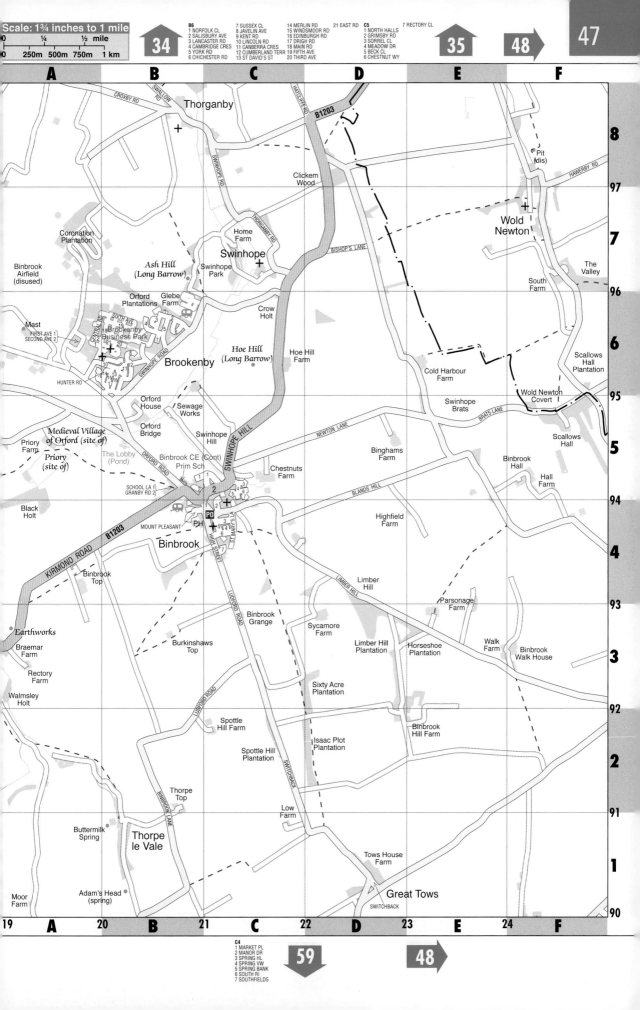

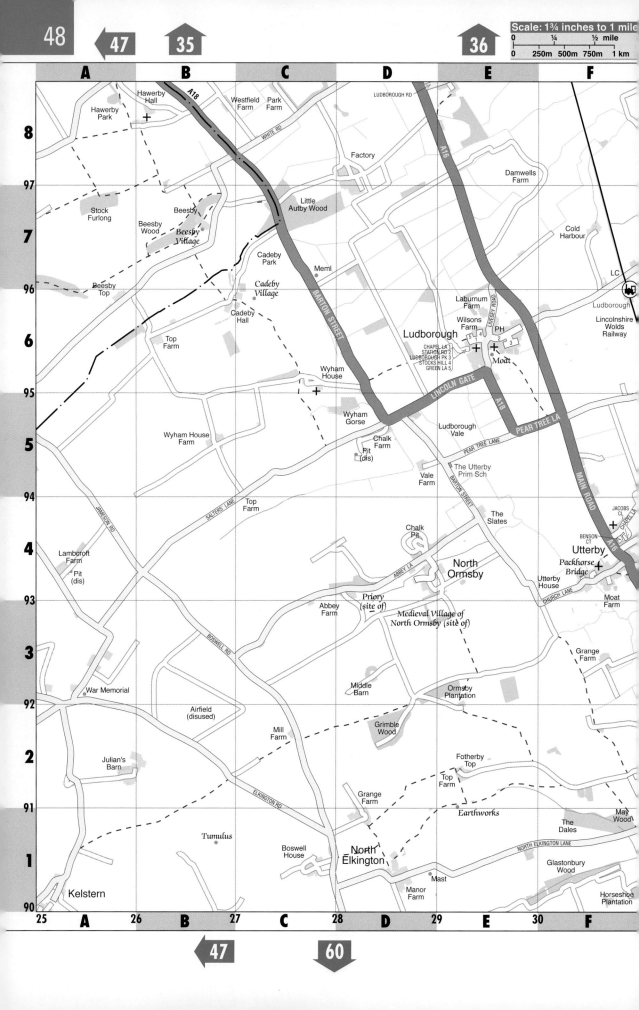

Scale: 1¾ inches to 1 mile
0   ¼   ½   mile
0   250m   500m   750m   1 km

A   B   C   D   E   F

8

Hawerby Hall
Hawerby Park
A18
Westfield Farm
Park Farm
LUDBOROUGH RD
WHITE RD
Factory
Damwells Farm

97

Stock Furlong
Beesby
Little Autby Wood
Cold Harbour

7

Beesby Wood
Beesby Village
Cadeby Park
Meml
LC

96

Beesby Top
Cadeby Village
Cadeby Hall
BARTON STREET
Ludborough
Laburnum Farm
LIVESEY ROAD
Wilsons Farm
Lincolnshire Wolds Railway
Ludborough

6

Top Farm
Wyham House
CHAPEL LA 1
STATION RD 2
LUDBOROUGH PK 3
STOCKS HILL 4
GREEN LA 5
PH
Moat

95

Wyham House Farm
Wyham Gorse
Chalk Farm
Pit (dis)
Ludborough Vale
LINCOLN GATE
PEAR TREE LA
A18
MAIN ROAD

5

SALTERS LANE
Top Farm
Vale Farm
PEAR TREE LANE
The Utterby Prim Sch
BARTON STREET

94

JAMESON RD
Top Farm
Chalk Pit
The Slates
JACOBS CL
BENSON CT
CHAPEL LA

4

Lamcroft Farm
Pit (dis)
ABBEY LA
North Ormsby
Utterby
Packhorse Bridge
Utterby House
CHURCH LANE
A16
Moat Farm

93

BOSWELL RD
Abbey Farm
Priory (site of)
Medieval Village of North Ormsby (site of)

3

War Memorial
Grange Farm

92

Airfield (disused)
Middle Barn
Ormsby Plantation

2

Julian's Barn
Mill Farm
Grimble Wood
Fotherby Top
Top Farm

91

ELKINGTON RD
Grange Farm
Earthworks
The Dales
May Wood

1

Tumulus
Boswell House
North Elkington
NORTH ELKINGTON LANE
Glastonbury Wood
Manor Farm
Mast
Horseshoe Plantation

90

Kelstern

25   A   26   B   27   C   28   D   29   E   30   F

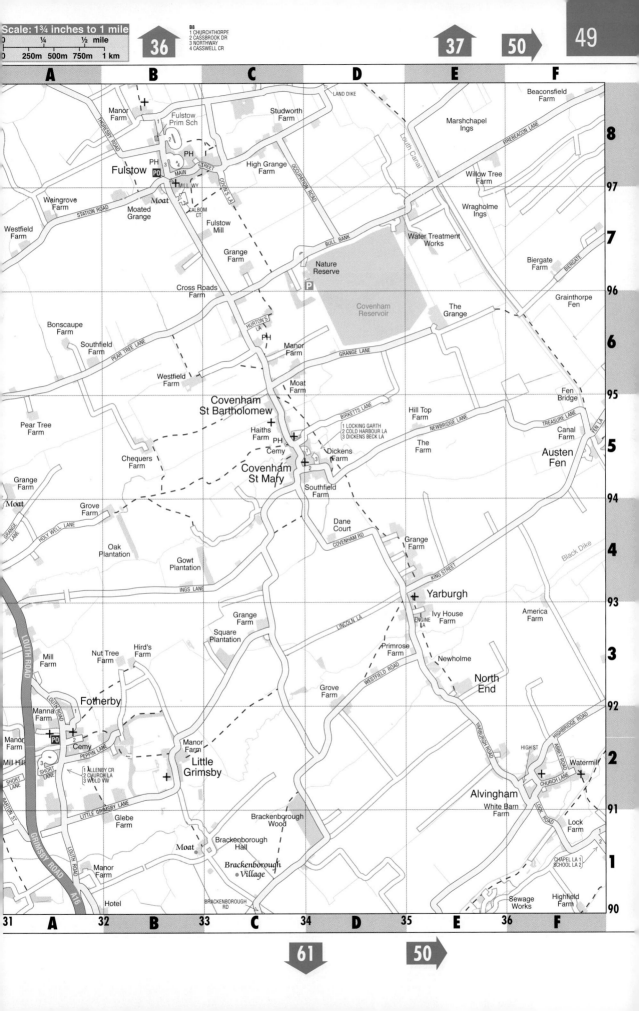

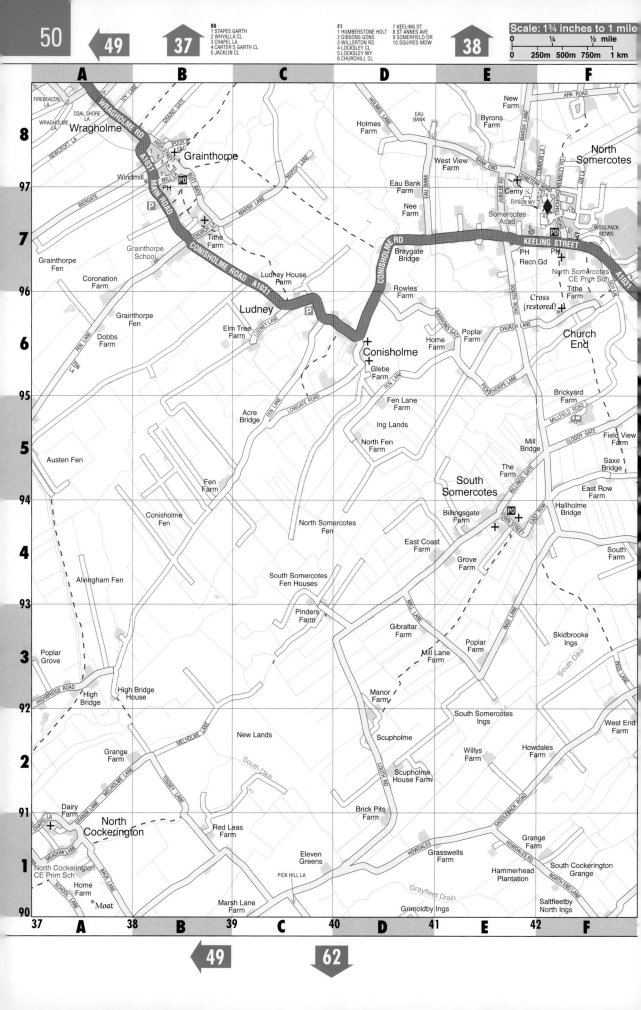

A   B   C   D   E   F

DANGER
AREA

New East
Marsh

Sand Haile
Flats

8

97

North Somercotes
Warren

Samphire
Bed

7

Jarvis's
Farm

Warren
Farm

Donna Nook
National Nature Reserve

96

WARREN ROAD

Salt Box
Farm

P

Dunes

6

Skidbrooke
Farm

Michaels
Farm

P

OWE'S LANE

Owes Lane
Farm

Skidbrooke
North End

95

SUNDERFLEET LANE

Buttons
Farm

Salt
Marsh

Toby's Hill
Nature
Reserve

5

WINE HILL LANE

MARSH LA

SEA VIEW

94

Grange
Farm

CHURCH LANE

Saltfleet

A1031 MAIN ROAD

1 2 3

5

PH

MILL
LA

6

Saltfleet Haven

P

4

LOUTH ROAD

Gowts
Farm

93

SOMERCOTES RD

TILLEY GATE

Bridge
Farm

Dunes

Skidbrooke Ings

INGS LA

SADDLEBACK ROAD

Weldon
House

THE BANK

White House
Farm

Skidbrooke

Saltfleetby - Theddlethorpe
Dunes National Nature
Reserve

3

P

SEA VIEW

Sea View
Farm

West View
Farm

WEST LANE

Ivy
Farm

Laburnum
Farm

Queen's
Bridge

Willow
Farm

Stone
Bridge

92

Lands End
Farm

SWALLOW GATE ROAD

Elm House
Farm

B1200

Great Eau

Viewpoint

P

Rimac

2

Saltfleetby
St Clement

RIMAC ROAD

Rimac
Farm

Dunes

Poplar
Farm

91

PH

A1031

Beulah
Farm

LONG GATES

SALTER GATE

FISHMERE GATE ROAD

Sturdys
Farm

MAIN ROAD

MILL LANE

Sphinx
Farm

BACK STREET

P

CRABTREE LANE

SALTFLEET RD

Cloves
Bridge

1

Saltfleetby
CE Prim Sch

B1200

White House
Farm

Saltfleetby
All Saints

CHURCHILL LA

P

Saltfleetby - Theddlethorpe
Dunes National Nature
Reserve

90

43   A   44   B   45   C   46   D   47   E   48   F

C4
1 BOTOLPH'S VW
2 HOLMES CL
3 JACKLIN DR
4 THE HILL
5 RUMP LA
6 HAVEN BANK
7 GREYFLEET BANK

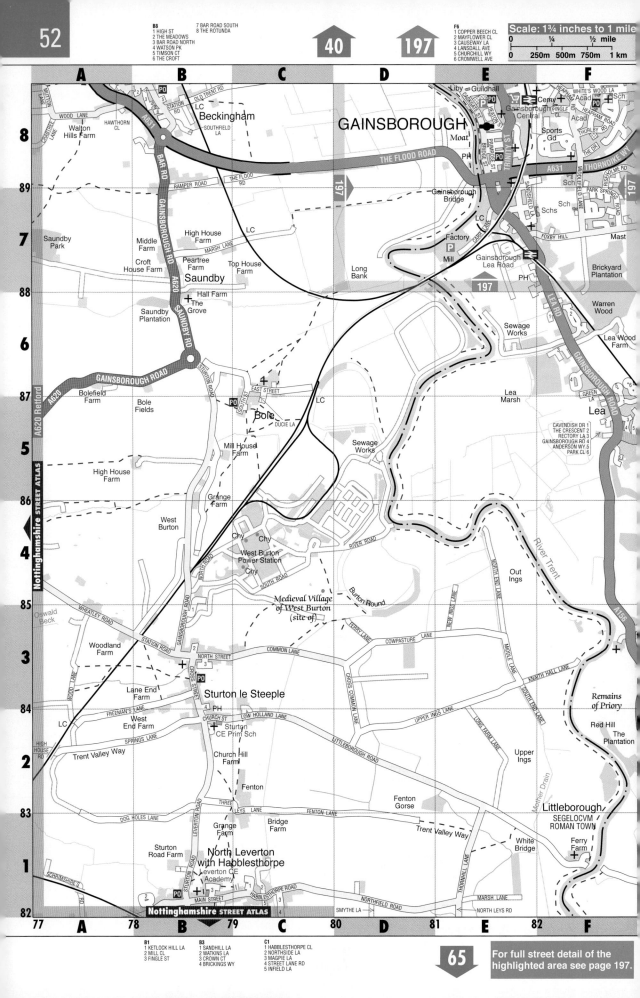

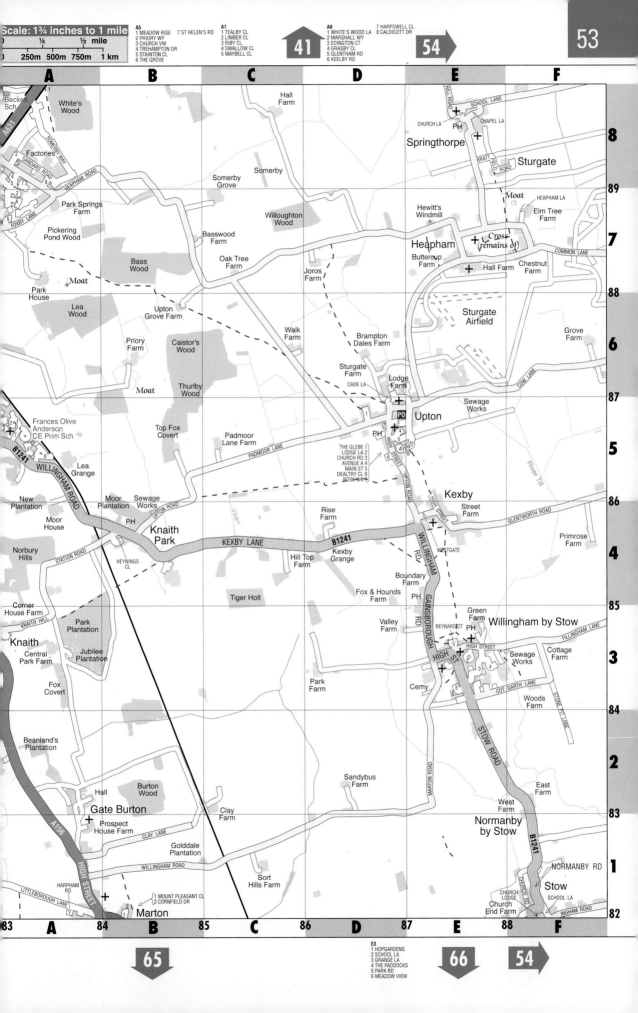

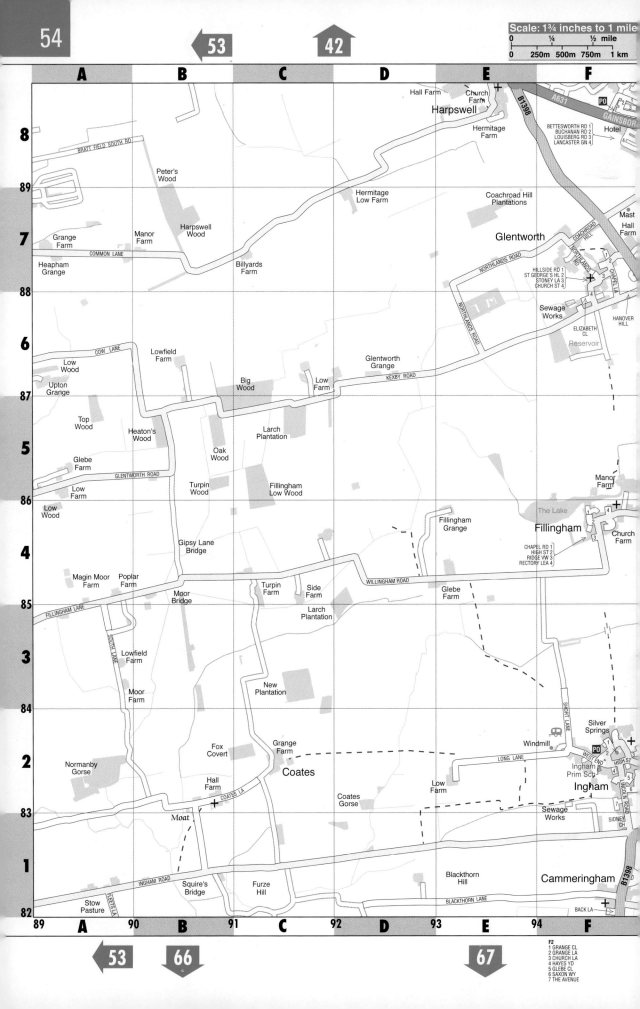

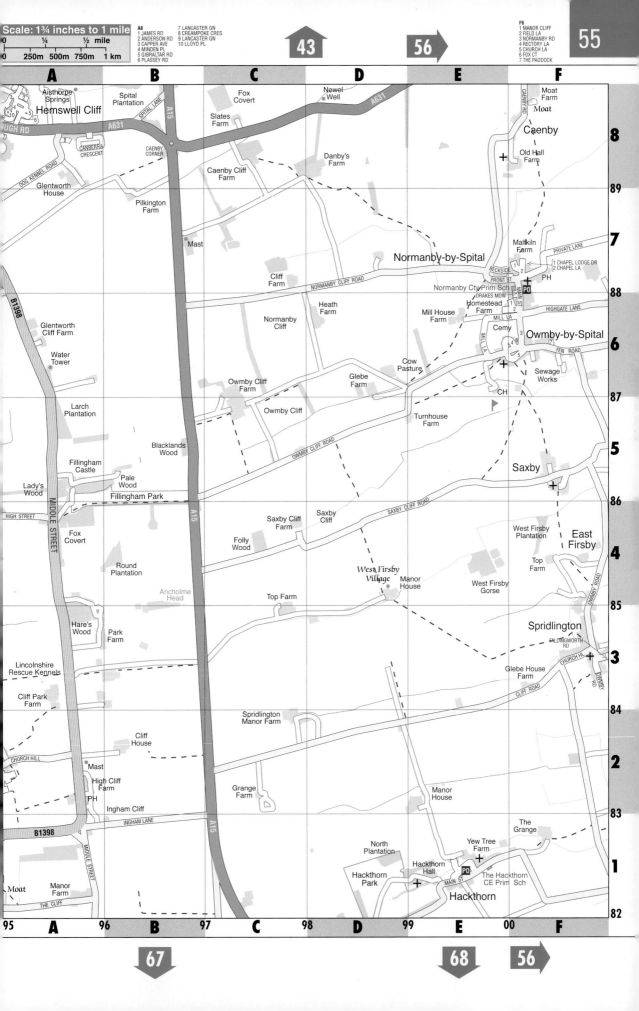

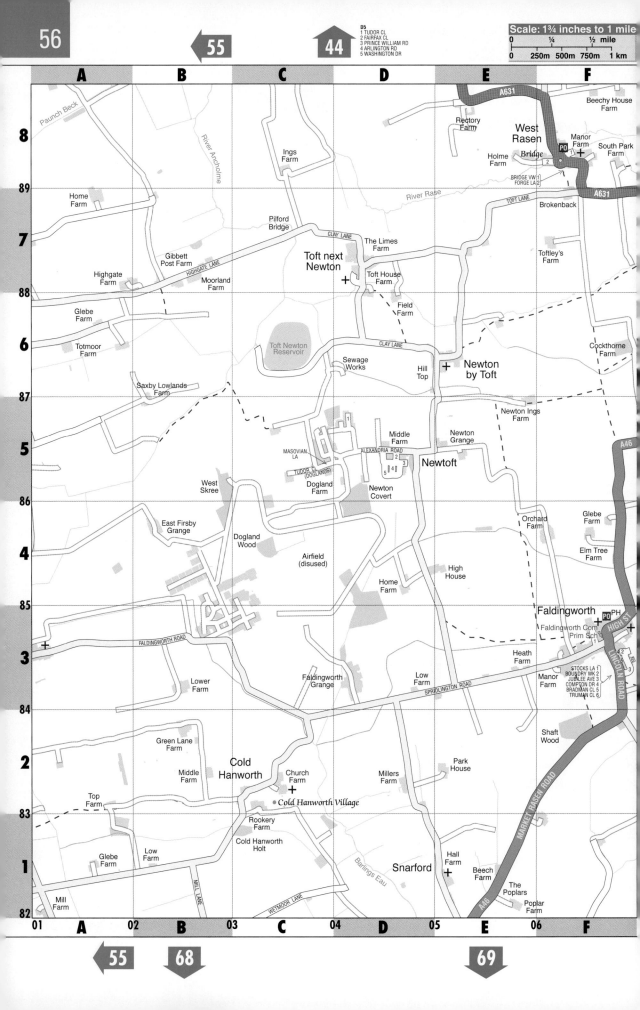

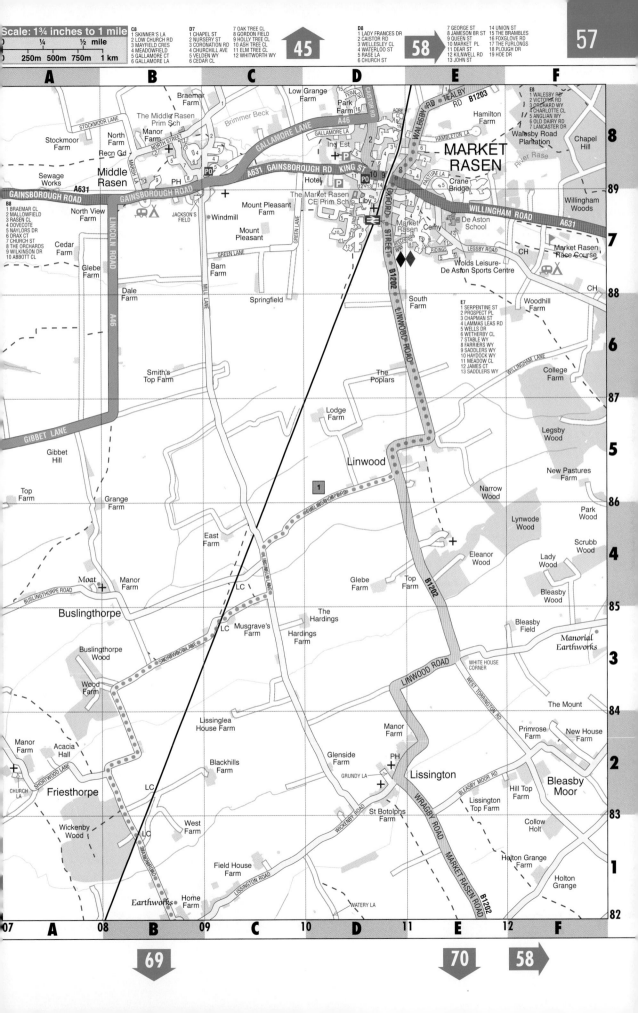

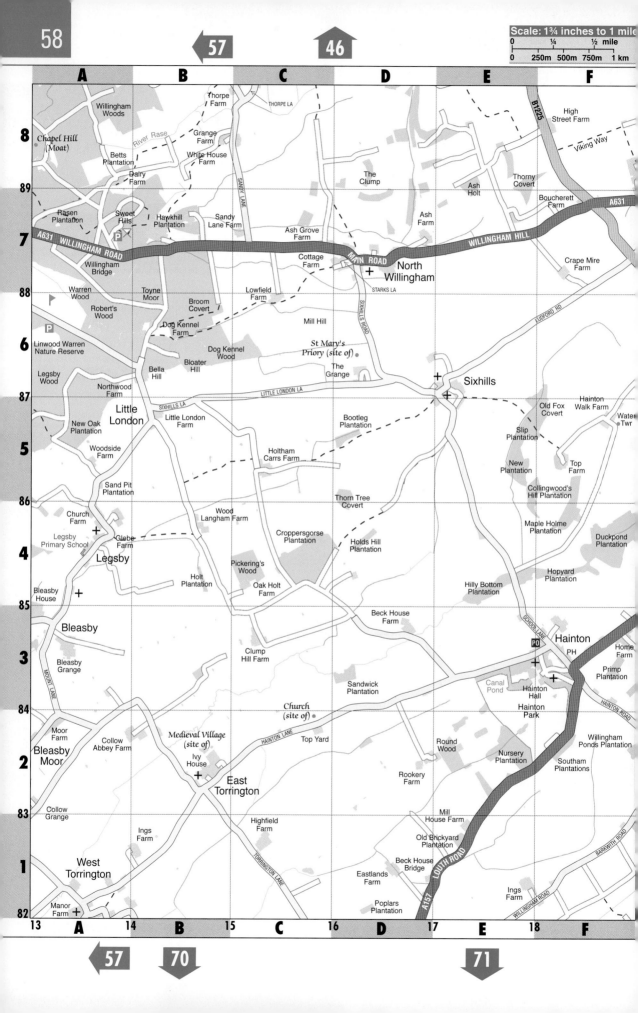

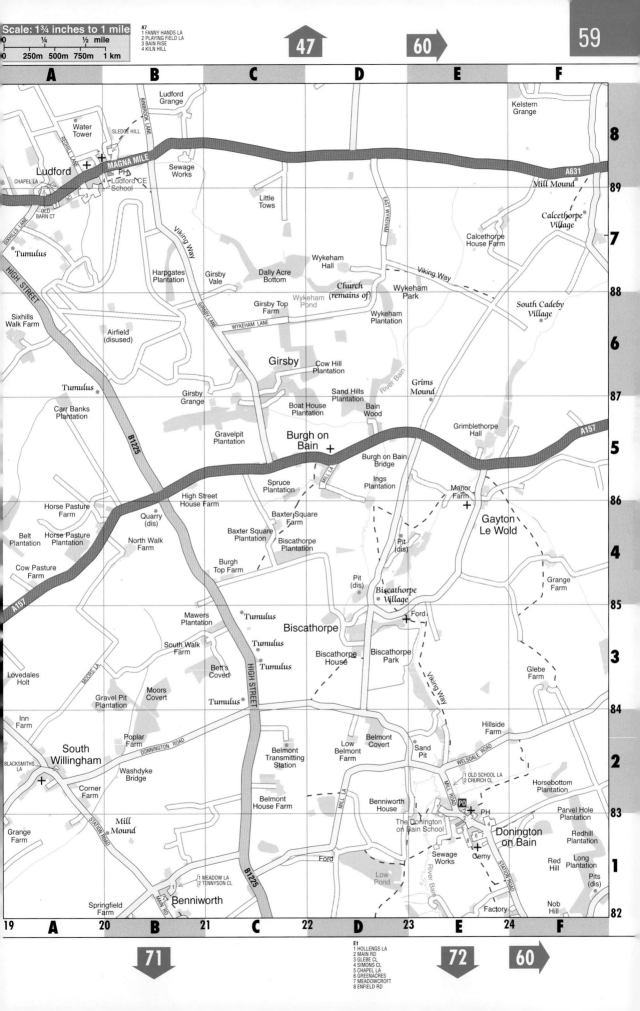

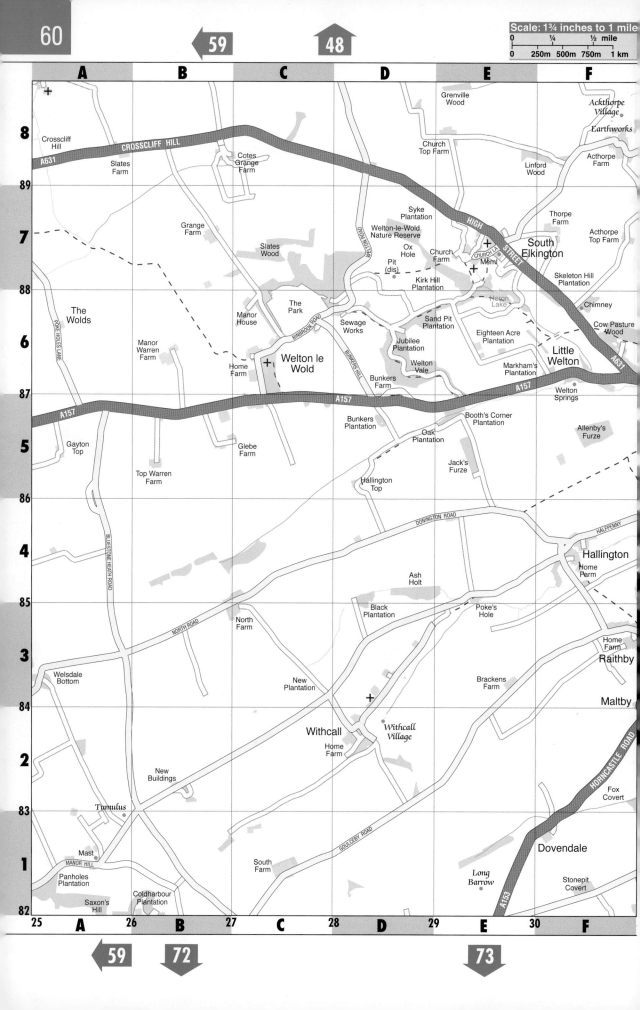

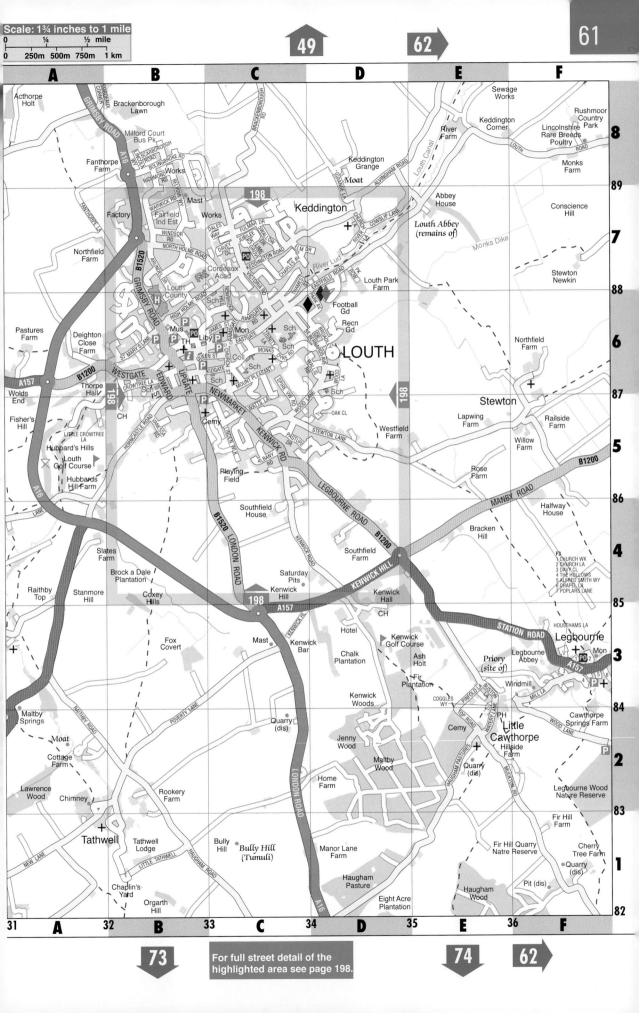

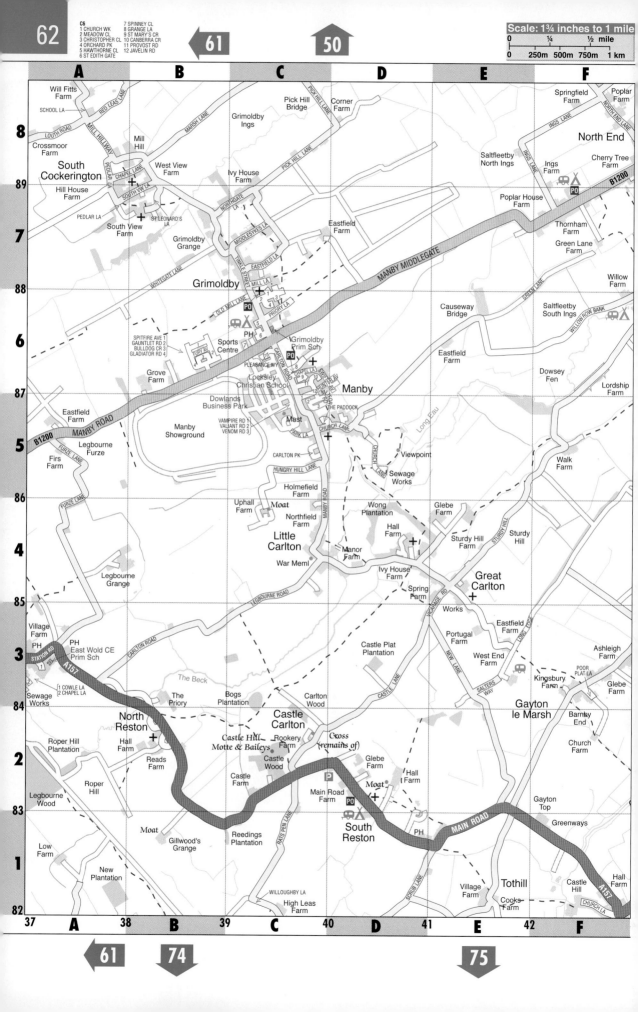

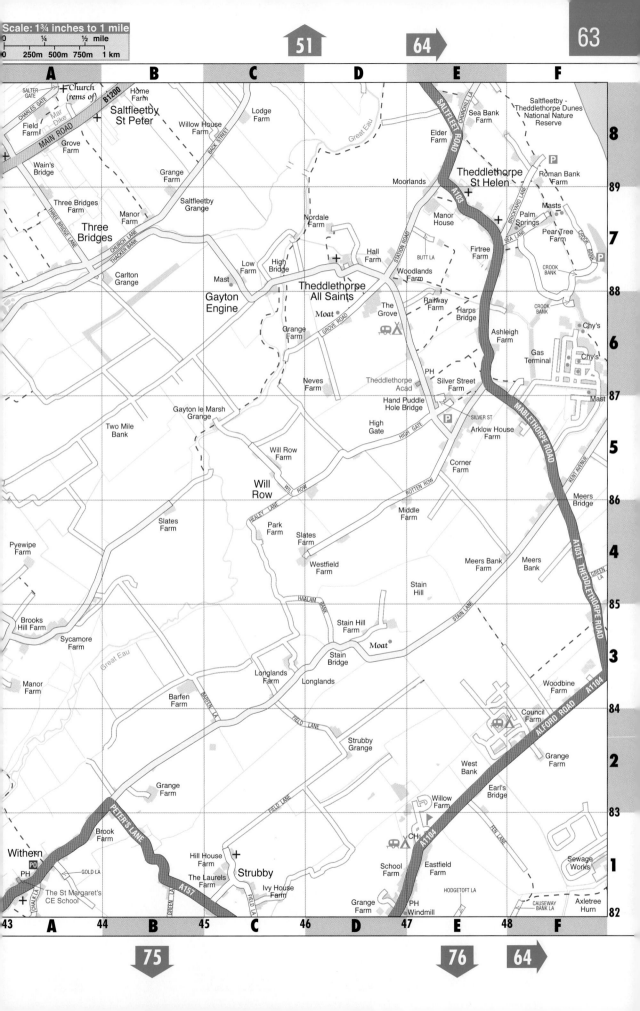

B5
1 CAMBRIDGE RD N
2 LINKS AVE
3 CAMBRIDGE RD S
4 IVEL GR
5 WHITEHEAD CL
6 IVEL CL

63

A **B** **C** **D** **E** **F**

8

89

7

88

6

87

Saltfleetby - Theddlethorpe Dunes National Nature Reserve

North End Farm

CROOK BANK

KENT AVE

MEERS BANK

PH

MEERS BANK

The Seal Sanctuary & Nature Centre

POPLAR AVE 1
CHALFONT AVE 2

5

86

GREEN LANE

GOLF ROAD

QUEBEC ROAD

A4
1 THE FAIRWAY
2 THE DRIVE
3 FALDOS WY
4 GOLF RD
5 LYLE CL
6 THE GREEN
7 EAGLE CL
8 PETER CHAMBERS WY
9
10 TUPLIN RD

The Dunes Family Entertainment Centre

Station Sports Ctr

Fun Fair

Mon

Liby

4

85

Mablethorpe Prim Acad

IRB Station

Olde Curiosity Mus

Mablethorpe Hall

Moat

ALFORD ROAD

A1104

PH

HIGH STREET

VICTORIA RD

SEAHOLME ROAD

MABLETHORPE

Art Gall

The Tennyson High School

CHURCH LANE

PH

SEAHOLME ROAD

Seahaven Springs

C3
1 QUEENS PK CL
2 NEWSTEAD RD
3 DYMOKE CL
4 BROOKE DR
5 DYMOKE RD
6 ARDEN CL

3

84

AQUA DR 1
MARIAN AVE 2
MEDINA GD 3
CHAMPION WY 4

Trusthorpe

Masts

Masts

SUTTON RD

Bourne Farm

C2
1 MILL FIELD
2 CAMPLING WY
3 BARTON CL
4 AUBREY PARKER CL
5 PARKINSON'S WY
6 JAMES AVE
7 ST PETER'S LA
8 BRAY AVE
9 ETON RD

2

83

Poplar Farm

MILE LANE

Bambers Farm

Bamber's Bridge

Elder Farm

NORTH ROAD

Crossing Farm

WHITELEYS CLOSE

ASHLY CLOSE

A52

TRUSTHORPE ROAD

Sewage Works

Bridge Farm

Thorpe Farm

Trusthorpe Hall

FEN LA

MAIN STREET

Boswell Farm

HIGH GATE

1 PARK RD E
2 CROMER AVE
3 HIGH ST
4 PROMENADE
5 YORK RD

1

82

Thorpe

63 76 77

A3
1 ORCHARD WY
2 ORCHARD CL
3 CHURCH RD
4 MALBOROUGH DR
5 OAKHAM AVE
6 WINCHESTER DR
7 CHELTENHAM WY

B3
1 HAWTHORN DR
2 MAYFLOWER WY
3 TRENCHARD RD
4 NELSON RD
5 STANLEY AVE
6 MAXWELL DR
7 KENSINGTON GDNS
8 STRAND CL
9 TOWER CL

10 HARLEQUIN DR
11 MARIAN AVE
12 HARRIS BOULEVARD
13 ELM AVE
14 KING ST
15 MARINA RD
16 ANCASTER RD
17 RIPON PL
18 VYNER CL
19 FOXE END

20 KNOWLE ST
21 PARK AVE
22 PARRY RD
23 THE BOULEVARD
24 GROSVENOR RD
25 RUTLAND ROAD

B4
1 LONG ACRE
2 ST ANDREWS RD
3 SHERWOOD RD
4 RUGBY RD
5 MALVERN RD
6 HARROW RD
7 REPTON RD
8 QUEENSWAY
9 SOMERSBY AVE

10 FITZWILLIAM ST
11 WELLINGTON AVE
12 CHAUCER AVE
13 RUSKIN RD
14 KINGSLEY RD
15 CHARLES WRIGHT CL
16 TENNYSON AVE
17 TENNYSON RD
18 HIGH ST
19 ADMIRALTY RD

20 STATION RD
21 ALEXANDRA RD
22 ALEXANDRA PK

C1
1 HALL LEAS DR
2 TRUSTHORPE RD
3 HIGHGATE CL
4 HIGHFIELD AVE
5 OUNDLE RD
6 UPPINGHAM RD
7 WILLOUGHBY RD
8 MARINE AVE
9 HARDING CL

C1
10 RICHMOND RD
11 ST JAMES CT
12 HIGHGATE LA

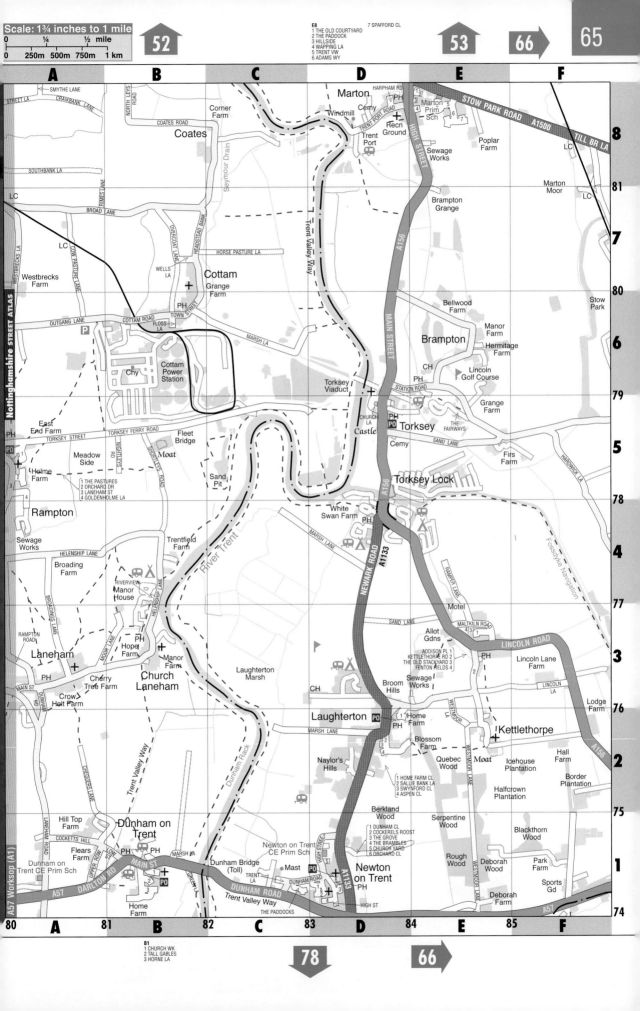

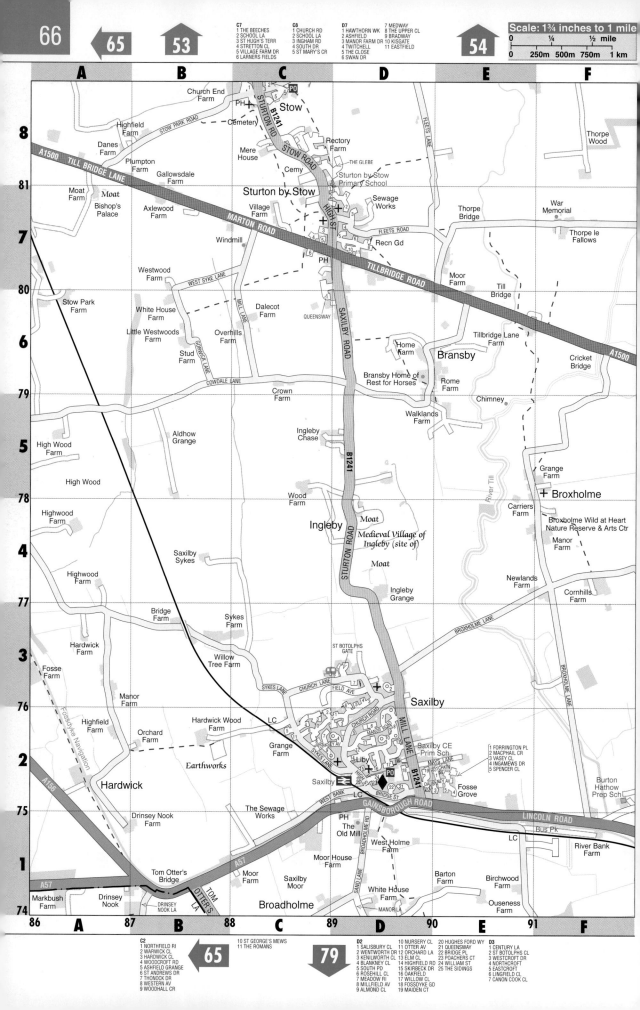

66

← 65

↑ 53

↑ 54

Scale: 1¾ inches to 1 mile
0   ¼   ½ mile
0   250m 500m 750m 1 km

C7
1 THE BEECHES
2 SCHOOL LA
3 ST HUGH'S TERR
4 STRETTON CL
5 VILLAGE FARM DR
6 LARNERS FIELDS

C8
1 CHURCH RD
2 SCHOOL LA
3 INGHAM RD
4 SOUTH DR
5 ST MARY'S CR

D7
1 HAWTHORN WK
2 ASHFIELD
3 MANOR FARM DR
4 TWITCHELL
5 THE CLOSE
6 SWAN DR

7 MEDWAY
8 THE UPPER CL
9 BRADWAY
10 KISGATE
11 EASTFIELD

Stow

Church End Farm

Cemetery

STURTON RD

B1241

PO

Highfield Farm

Stow Park Road

Danes Farm

A1500 TILL BRIDGE LANE

Plumpton Farm

Gallowsdale Farm

Moat Farm

Moat Bishop's Palace

Axlewood Farm

Mere House

Cemy

STOW ROAD

Rectory Farm

THE GLEBE

Sturton by Stow Primary School

Sturton by Stow

Village Farm

MARTON ROAD

HIGH ST

Sewage Works

Thorpe Bridge

War Memorial

Thorpe Wood

Windmill

PH

FLEETS ROAD

Recn Gd

Moor Farm

Till Bridge

Thorpe le Fallows

TILLBRIDGE ROAD

A1500

Westwood Farm

WEST SYKE LANE

MILL LANE

Dalecot Farm

QUEENSWAY

SAXILBY ROAD

Home Farm

Bransby

Tillbridge Lane Farm

Cricket Bridge

Stow Park Farm

White House Farm

Little Westwoods Farm

GORWICK LANE

Overhills Farm

Stud Farm

COWDALE LANE

Crown Farm

Bransby Home of Rest for Horses

Rome Farm

Chimney

River Till

High Wood Farm

Aldhow Grange

Ingleby Chase

Walklands Farm

Grange Farm

✠ Broxholme

High Wood

B1241

Wood Farm

Moat

Carriers Farm

Broxholme Wild at Heart Nature Reserve & Arts Ctr

Highwood Farm

Saxilby Sykes

Ingleby

Medieval Village of Ingleby (site of)

Moat

Manor Farm

Highwood Farm

Bridge Farm

Sykes Farm

STURTON ROAD

Ingleby Grange

BROXHOLME LANE

Newlands Farm

Cornhills Farm

Fosse Farm

Hardwick Farm

Willow Tree Farm

SYKES LANE

CHURCH LANE

St BOTOLPHS GATE

FIELD AVE

Saxilby

Fossdyke Navigation

Manor Farm

Highfield Farm

Orchard Farm

Hardwick Wood Farm

LC

CHURCH ROAD

MANOR ROAD

Saxilby CE Prim Sch

1 FORRINGTON PL
2 MACPHAIL CR
3 VASEY CL
4 INGAMEWS DR
5 SPENCER CL

A156

Hardwick

Earthworks

Grange Farm

SYKES LANE

Liby

MAYS LANE

MILL LANE

B1241

Fosse Grove

Burton Hathow Prep Sch

Drinsey Nook Farm

The Sewage Works

Saxilby

PO

WEST BANK

BRIDGE ST

GAINSBOROUGH ROAD

LC

LINCOLN ROAD

Bus Pk

LC

The Old Mill

PH

BROADHOLME RD

West Holme Farm

LC

River Bank Farm

A57

Tom Otter's Bridge

Moor Farm

Saxilby Moor

Moor House Farm

SAND LANE

White House Farm

Barton Farm

Birchwood Farm

Ouseness Farm

Markbush Farm

Drinsey Nook

TOM OTTER'S LA

DRINSEY NOOK LA

Broadholme

MANOR LA

86   87   88   89   90   91

A   B   C   D   E   F

C2
1 NORTHFIELD RI
2 WARWICK CL
3 HARDWICK CL
4 WOODCROFT RD
5 ASHFIELD GRANGE
6 ST ANDREWS DR
7 THONOCK DR
8 WESTERN AV
9 WOODHALL CR

10 ST GEORGE'S MEWS
11 THE ROMANS

← 65

↑ 79

D2
1 SALISBURY CL
2 WENTWORTH DR
3 KENILWORTH CL
4 BLANKNEY CL
5 SOUTH RD
6 ROSEHILL CL
7 MEADOW RI
8 MILLFIELD AV
9 ALMOND CL

10 NURSERY CL
11 OTTER AV
12 ORCHARD LA
13 ELM CL
14 HIGHFIELD RD
15 SKIRBECK DR
16 OAKFIELD
17 WILLOW CL
18 FOSSDYKE GD
19 MAIDEN CT

20 HUGHES FORD WY
21 QUEENSWAY
22 BRIDGE PL
23 POACHERS CT
24 WILLIAM ST
25 THE SIDINGS

D3
1 CENTURY LA
2 ST BOTOLPHS CL
3 WESTCROFT DR
4 NORTHCROFT
5 EASTCROFT
6 LINGFIELD CL
7 CANON COOK CL

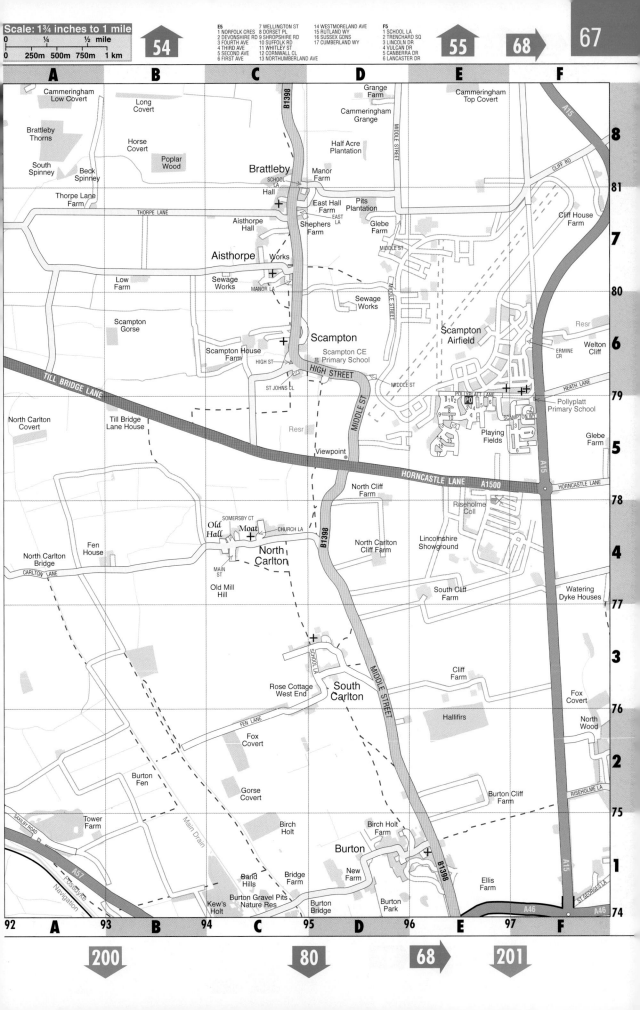

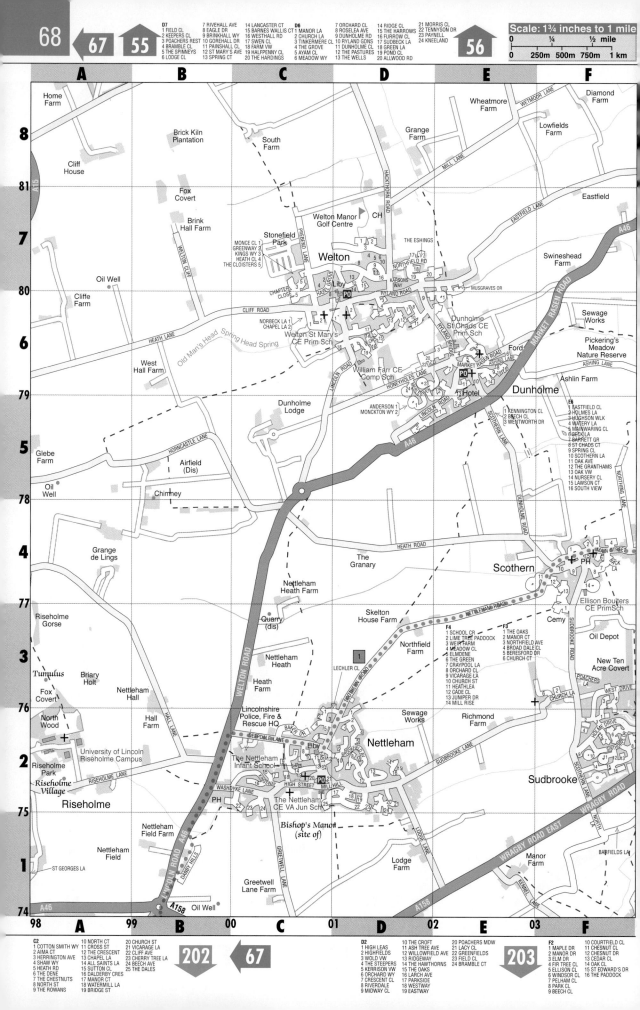

Home
Farm

Cliff
House

Brick Kiln
Plantation

South
Farm

Wheatmore
Farm

WETMOOR LANE

Diamond
Farm

Lowfields
Farm

Fox
Covert

Grange
Farm

Eastfield

EASTFIELD LANE

Oil Well

Brink
Hall Farm

WELTON CLIFF

MONCE CL 1
GREENWAY 2
KINGS WY 3
HEATH CL 4
THE CLOISTERS 5

Stonefield
Park

Welton Manor
Golf Centre

CH

THE ESHINGS

Welton

Swineshead
Farm

A46

Cliffe
Farm

Liby

PO

Dunholme
St Chads CE
Prim Sch

MARKET RASEN ROAD

Sewage
Works

CLIFF ROAD

NORBECK LA 1
CHAPEL LA 2

Welton St Mary's
CE Prim Sch

Dunholme

Ford

Pickering's
Meadow
Nature Reserve

HEATH LANE

Old Man's Head Spring Head Spring

William Farr CE
Comp Sch

RYLAND BRIDGE

Hotel

PO

ASHING LANE

Ashlin Farm

West
Hall Farm

Dunholme
Lodge

ANDERSON 1
MONCKTON WY 2

1 KENNINGTON CL
2 BEECH CL
3 WENTWORTH DR

E6
1 EASTFIELD CL
2 HOLMES LA
3 HUGHSON WLK
4 WATERY LA
5 MAINWARING CL
6 BECK LA
7 BARRETT GR
8 ST CHADS CT
9 SPRING CL
10 SCOTHERN LA
11 OAK AVE
12 THE GRANTHAMS
13 OAK VW
14 NURSERY CL
15 LAWSON CT
16 SOUTH VIEW

Glebe
Farm

HORNCASTLE LANE

Airfield
(Dis)

A46

NORTHING LANE

Oil
Well

Chimney

Grange
de Lings

HEATH ROAD

Scothern

MAIN STREET

PH

Ellison Boulters
CE PrimSch

Riseholme
Gorse

The
Granary

Nettleham
Heath Farm

Skelton
House Farm

NETTLEHAM ROAD

Cemy

SUDBROOKE ROAD

Oil Depot

F4
1 SCHOOL CR
2 LIME TREE PADDOCK
3 WEIR FARM
4 MEADOW CL
5 ELMDENE
6 THE GREEN
7 CRAYPOOL LA
8 ORCHARD CL
9 VICARAGE LA
10 CHURCH ST
11 HEATHLEA
12 CADE CL
13 JUNIPER DR
14 MILL RISE

F3
1 THE OAKS
2 MANOR CT
3 NORTHFIELD AVE
4 BROAD DALE CL
5 BERESFORD DR
6 CHURCH CT

New Ten
Acre Covert

Tumulus

Briary
Holt

Quarry
(dis)

Nettleham
Heath

Northfield
Farm

POACHERS LA

WEST DRIVE

Fox
Covert

Nettleham
Hall

Heath
Farm

LECHLER CL

CHURCH LA

North
Wood

Hall Farm

HALL LANE

Lincolnshire
Police, Fire &
Rescue HQ

DEEPDALE LANE

Sewage
Works

Richmond
Farm

University of Lincoln
Riseholme Campus

WELTON ROAD

The Nettleham
Infant School

Liby

BAKER DR

Nettleham

SUDBROOKE LANE

Sudbrooke

Riseholme
Park

RISEHOLME LANE

HIGH STREET

PO

MILL HILL

The Nettleham
CE VA Jun Sch

Riseholme
Village

Riseholme

WASHDYKE LANE

PH

Bishop's Manor
(site of)

GREETWELL LANE

Lodge
Farm

A46

DANBY HILLS

WRAGBY ROAD EAST

Manor
Farm

BARFIELDS LA

ST GEORGES LA

Nettleham
Field Farm

KENNEL LANE

Nettleham
Field

A46

A158

Oil Well

Greetwell
Lane Farm

A158

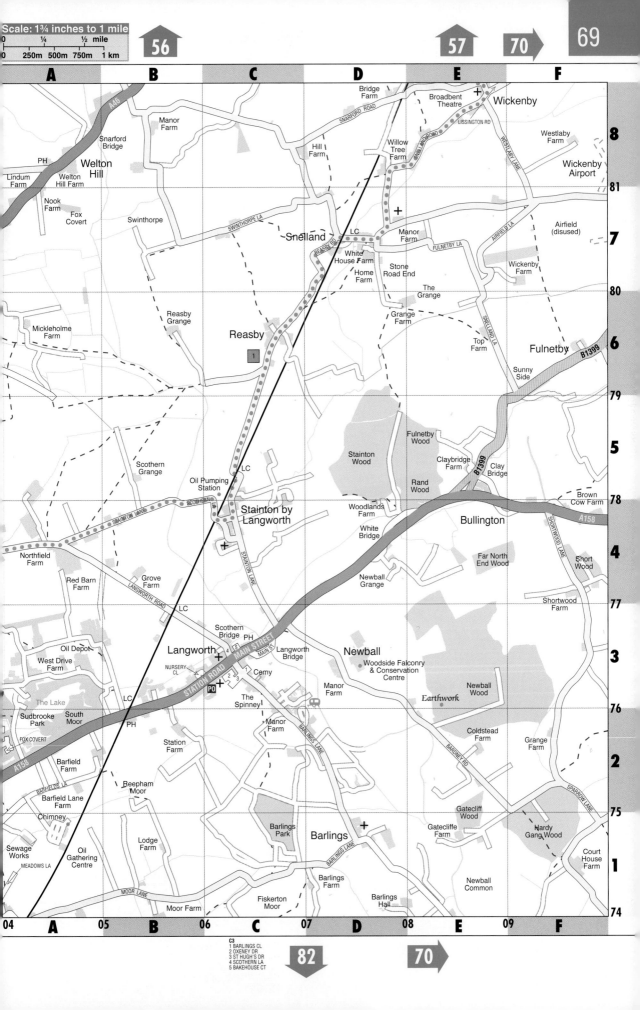

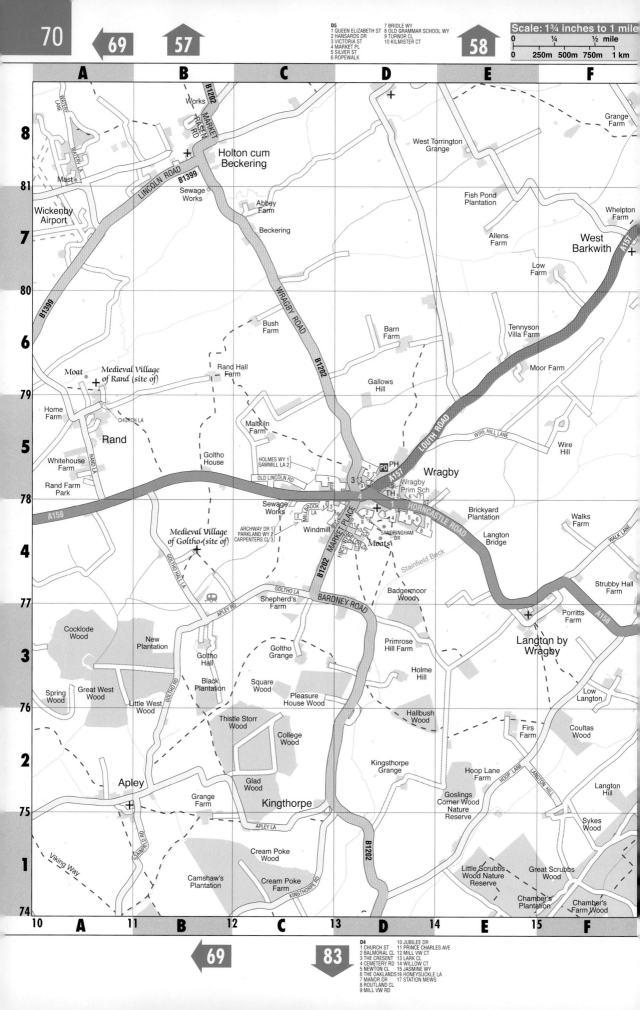

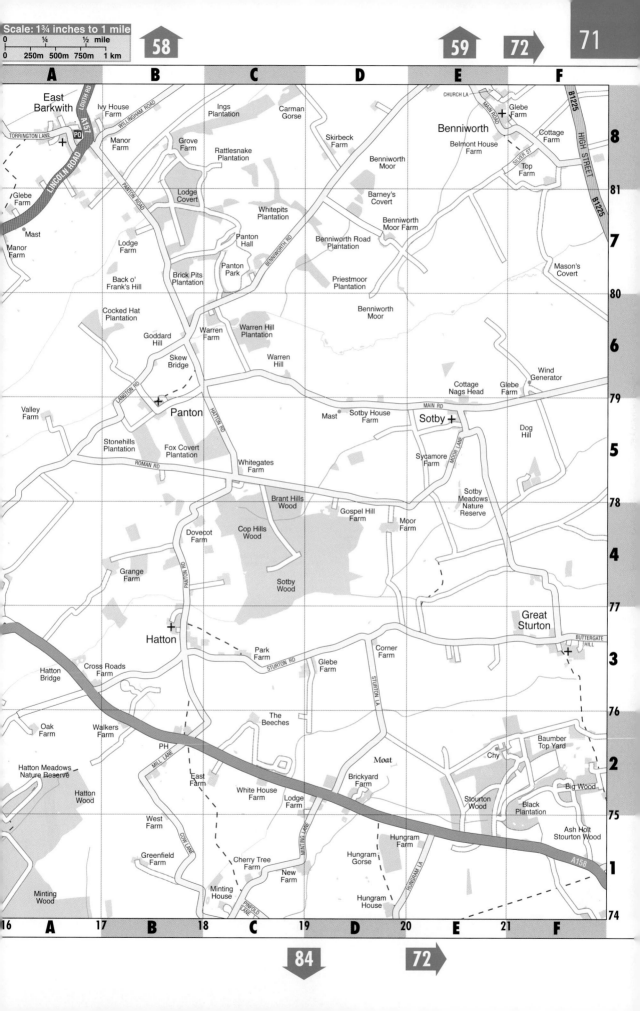

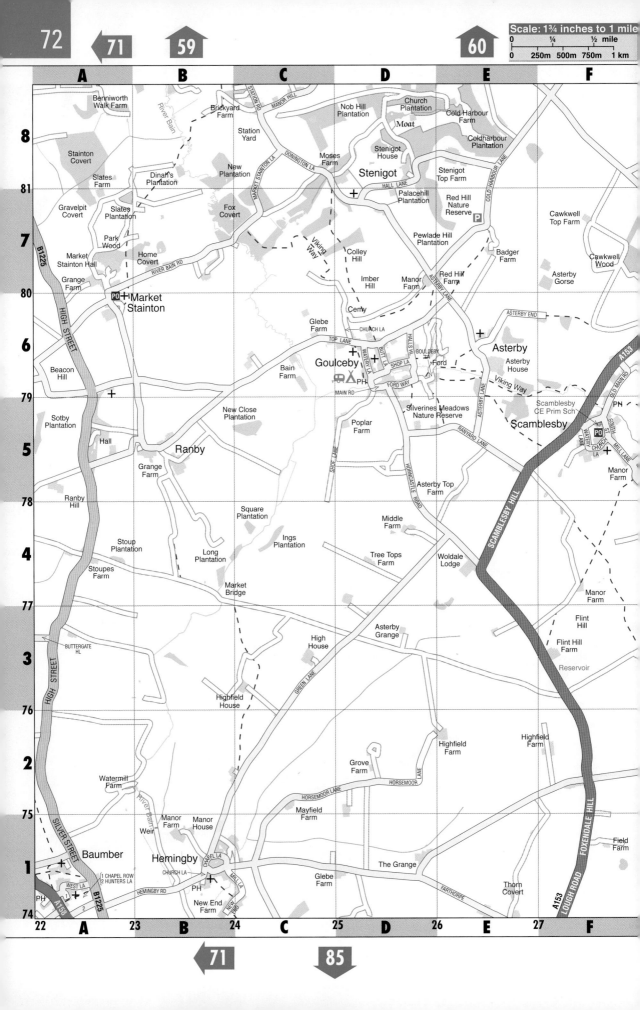

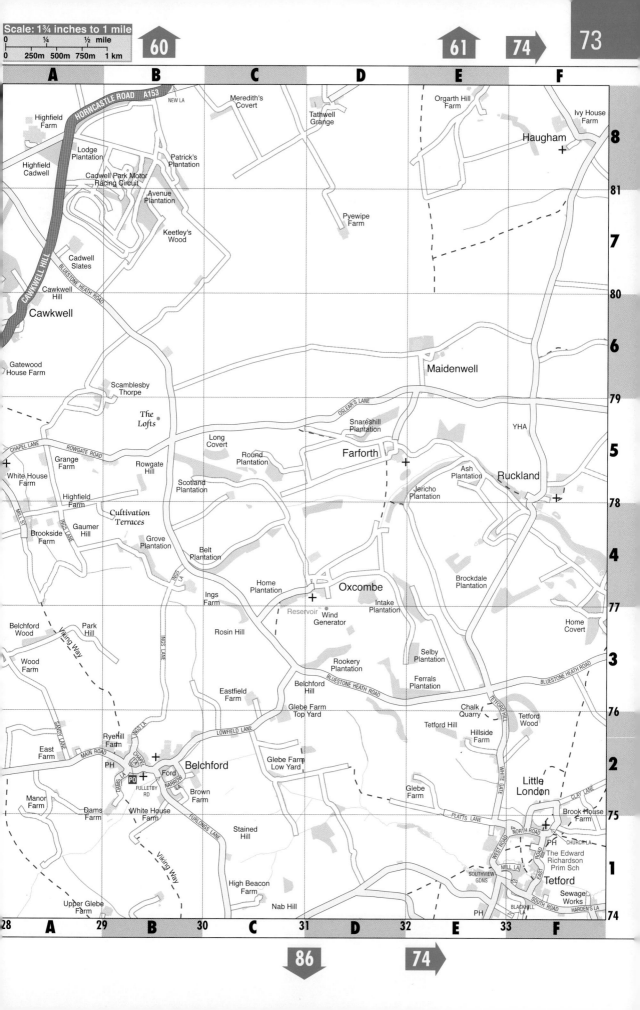

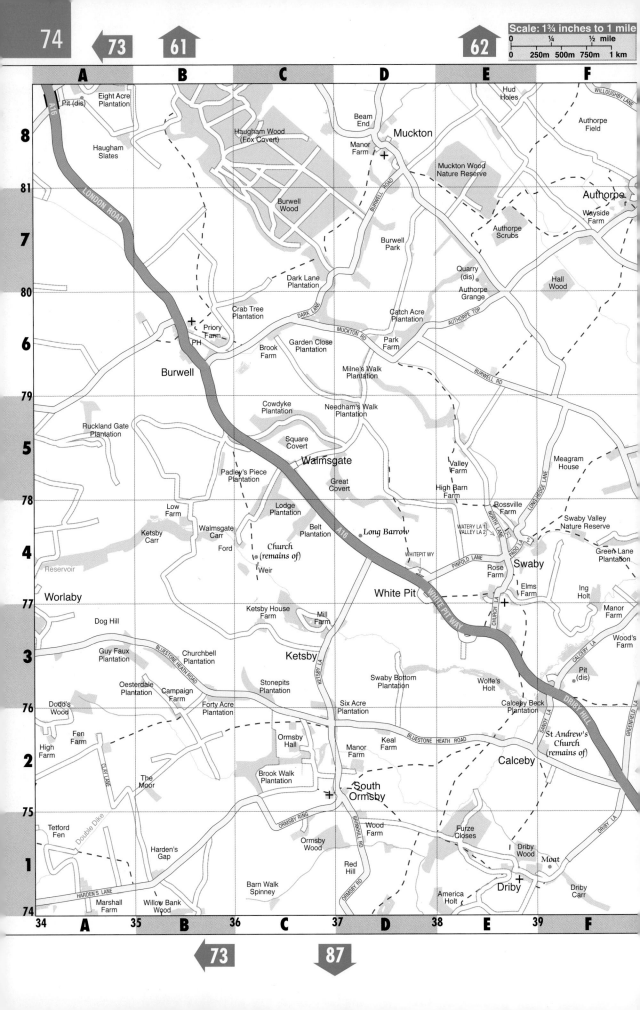

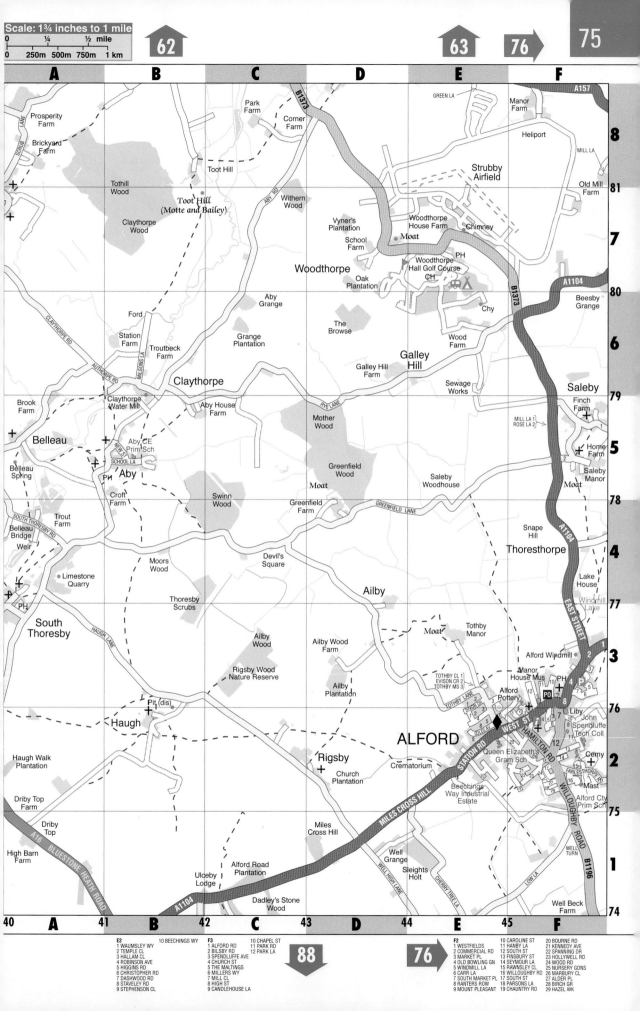

A   B   C   D   E   F

8

81

7

80

6

79

5

78

4

77

3

76

2

75

1

74

Prosperity Farm
Brickyard Farm
SCRUB LANE
Tothill Wood
Claythorpe Wood
Toot Hill
Toot Hill (Motte and Bailey)
ABY RD

Park Farm
Corner Farm
B1373
Withern Wood
Vyner's Plantation
School Farm
Woodthorpe House Farm
Woodthorpe Hall Golf Course
CH
PH
Chimney
Moat
Strubby Airfield
GREEN LA
Manor Farm
Heliport

A157
Old Mill Farm
MILL LA

A1104
Beesby Grange

Woodthorpe
Oak Plantation
The Browse
Aby Grange
Ford
Station Farm
Troutbeck Farm
Grange Plantation
CLAYTHORPE RD
AUTHORPE RD
MILSONS LA
Claythorpe
Claythorpe Water Mill
Aby House Farm
NEW ST
Aby CE Prim Sch
SCHOOL LA
PH
Aby
Croft Farm
Belleau
Belleau Spring
Brook Farm

Wood Farm
Galley Hill Farm
Galley Hill
RYE LANE
Mother Wood
Greenfield Wood
Moat
Swinn Wood
Greenfield Farm
Greenfield LANE

Sewage Works
Saleby Woodhouse
Saleby
Finch Farm
MILL LA 1
ROSE LA 2
2
Home Farm
Saleby Manor
Moat
Chy
A1104

SOUTH THORESBY RD
Trout Farm
Belleau Bridge
Weir
Limestone Quarry
PH
South Thoresby
HAUGH LANE
Moors Wood
Thoresby Scrubs
Devil's Square

Snape Hill
Thoresthorpe
Lake House
Windmill Lake
EAST STREET
A1104

Ailby
Ailby Wood
Ailby Wood Farm
Ailby Plantation
Rigsby Wood Nature Reserve
Moat
Tothby Manor
Alford Windmill
Manor House Mus
Alford Pottery
TOTHBY CL 1
EVISON CR 2
TOTHBY MS 3
TOTHBY LANE
DROVE DR
PH
PO
Liby
John Spendluffe Tech Coll

Haugh
Pit (dis)

Haugh Walk Plantation
Driby Top Farm
Driby Top
High Barn Farm
A16
BLUESTONE HEATH ROAD

Rigsby
Church Plantation
Crematorium
ALFORD
STATION RD
WEST ST
HAMILTON RD
Queen Elizabeth's Gram Sch
Beechings Way Industrial Estate
QUEENS RD
Cemy
Mast
Alford Cty Prim Sch
WILLOUGHBY ROAD
EARLESTHORPE RD

Ulceby Lodge
Dadley's Stone Wood
Alford Road Plantation
A1104
Miles Cross Hill
MILES CROSS HILL
Well Grange
Sleights Holt
WELL HIGH LANE
CHERRY TREE LA
LOW LA
Well Turn
Well Beck Farm
B1196

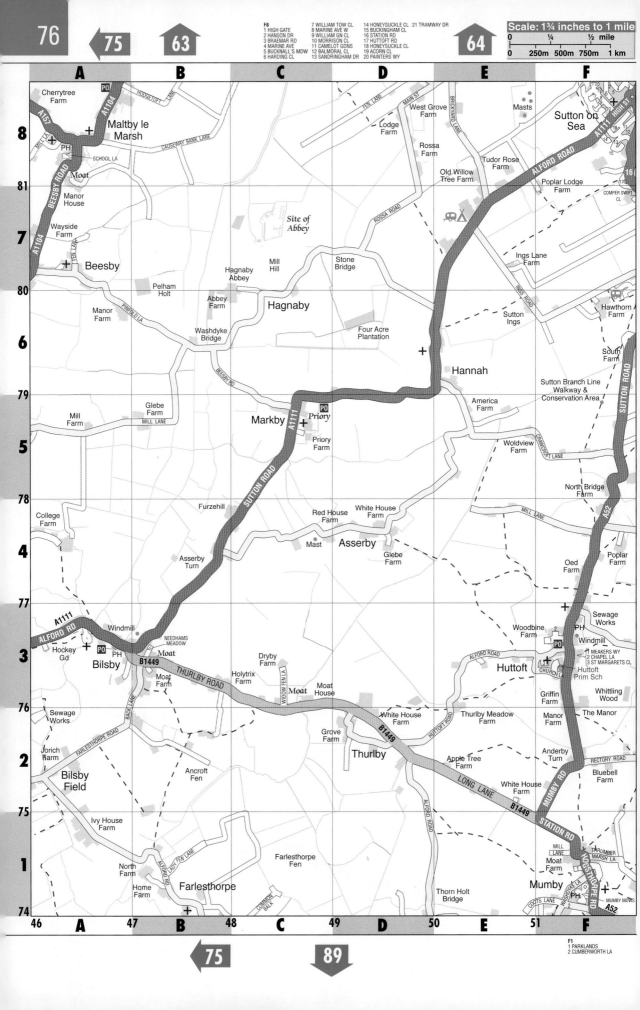

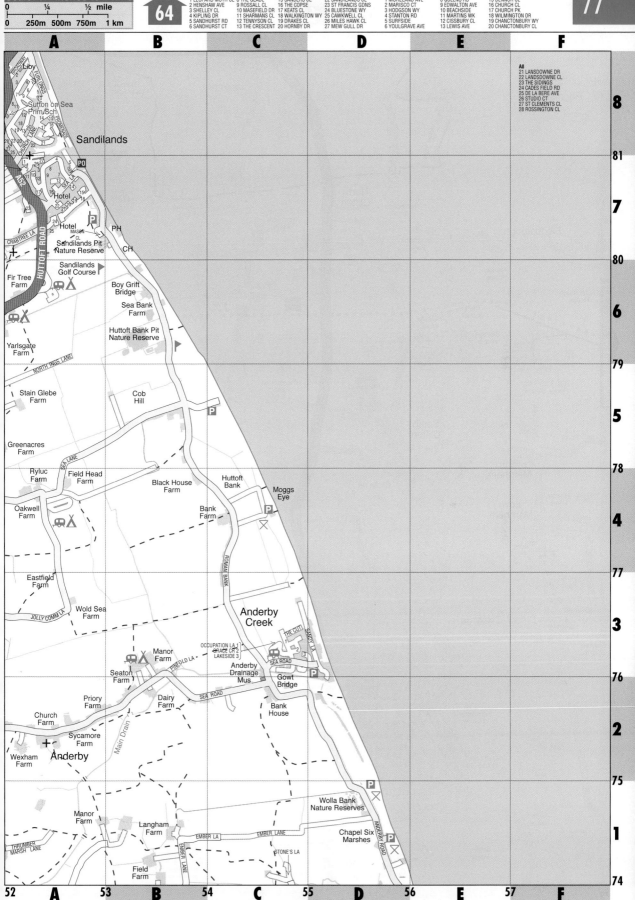

Scale: 1¾ inches to 1 mile

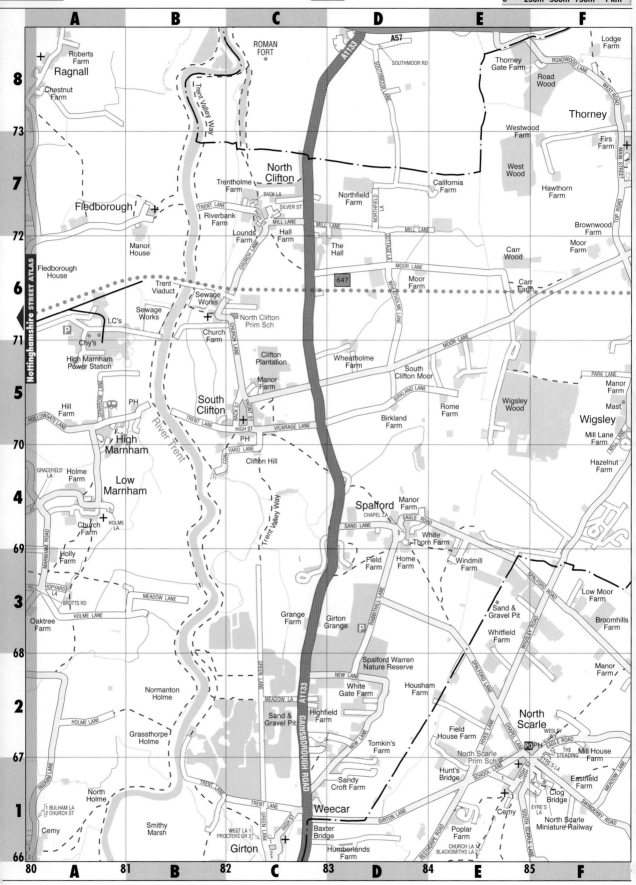

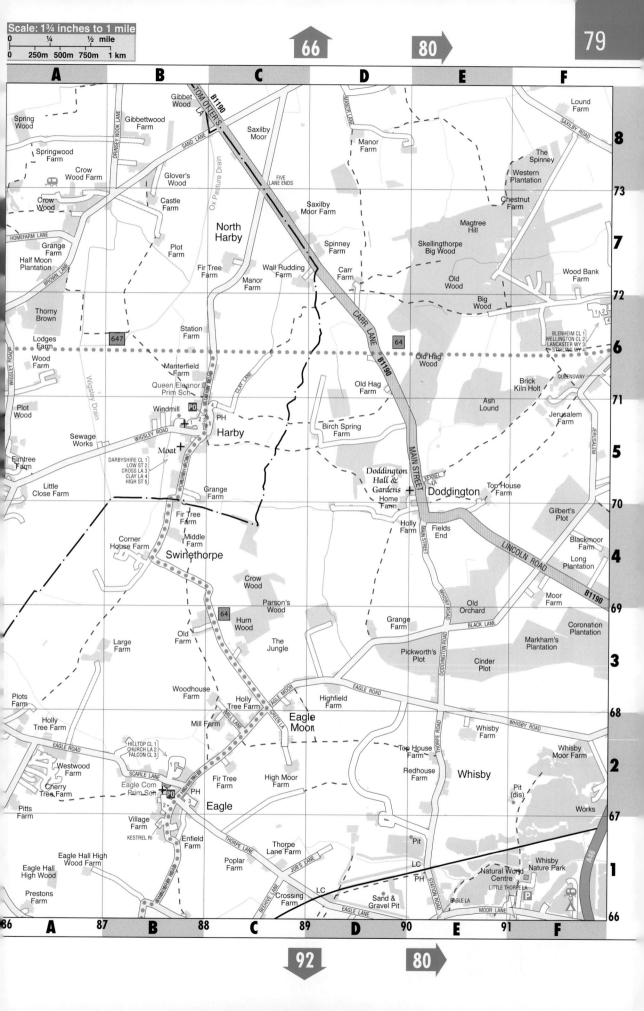

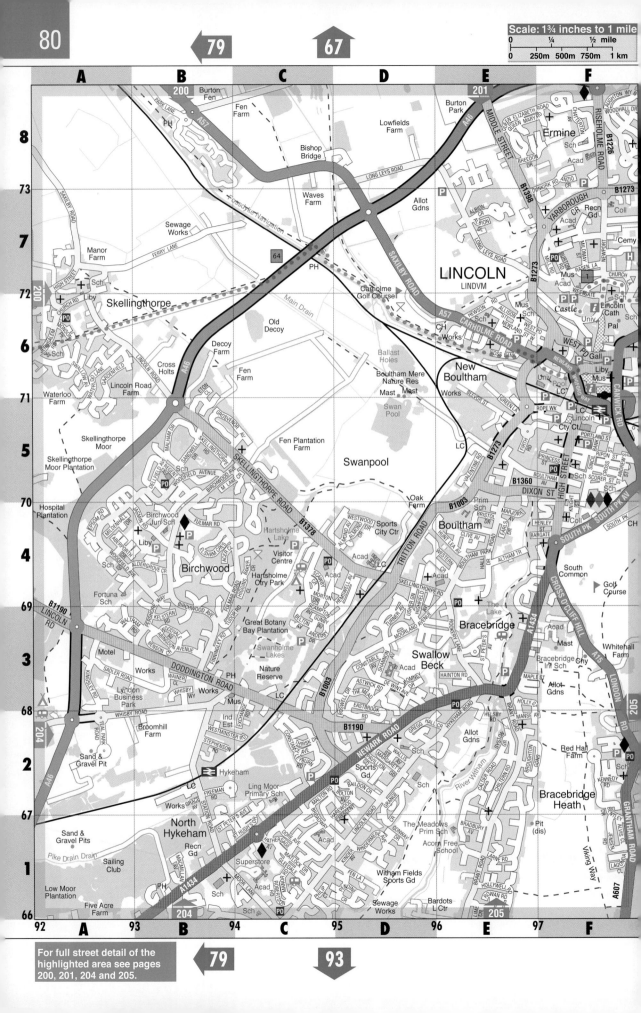

For full street detail of the highlighted area see pages 200, 201, 204 and 205.

79   93

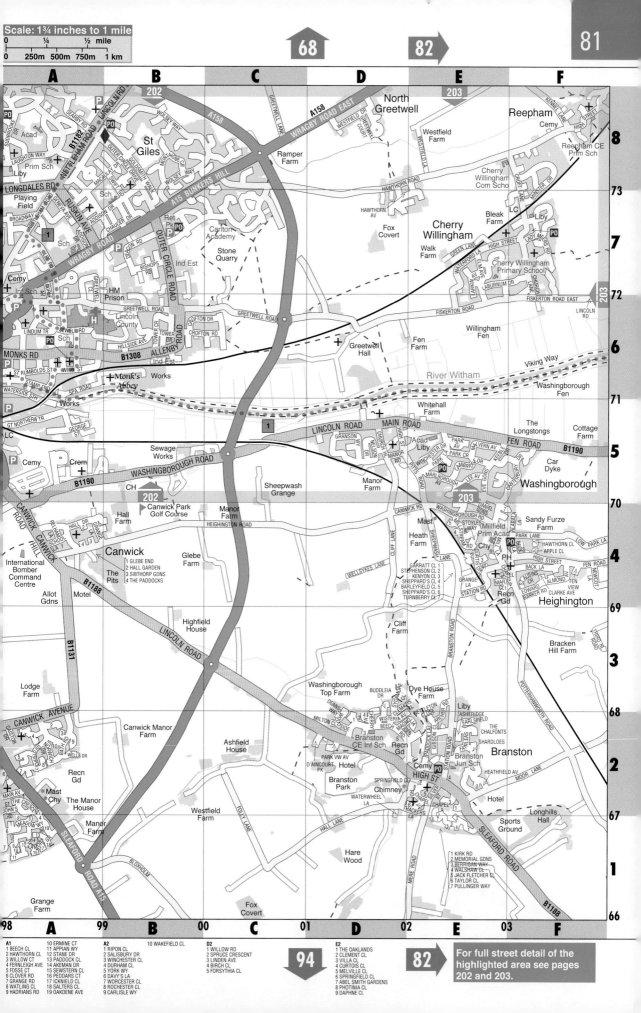

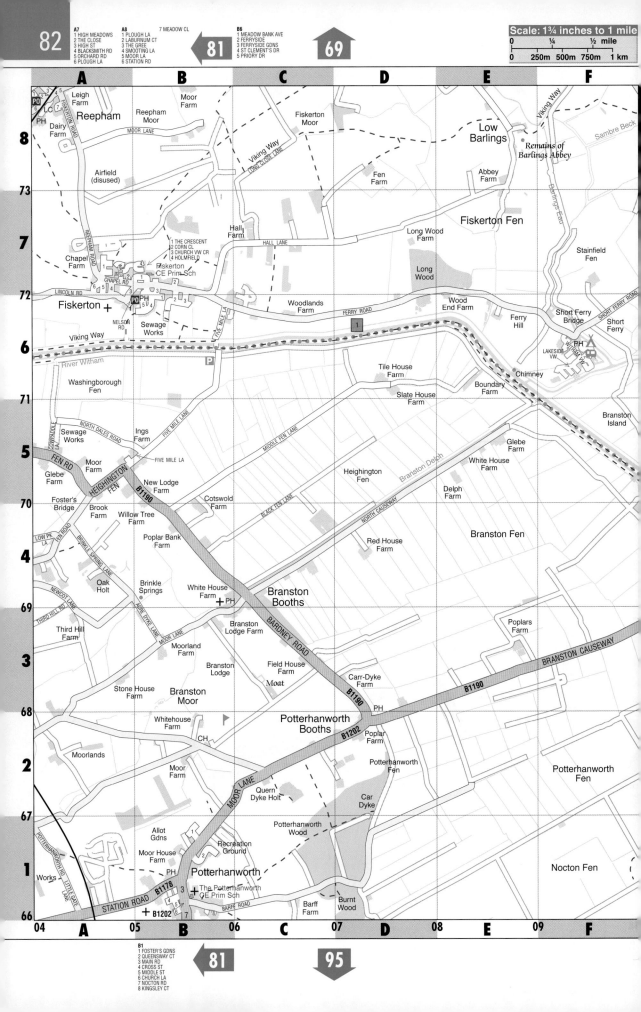

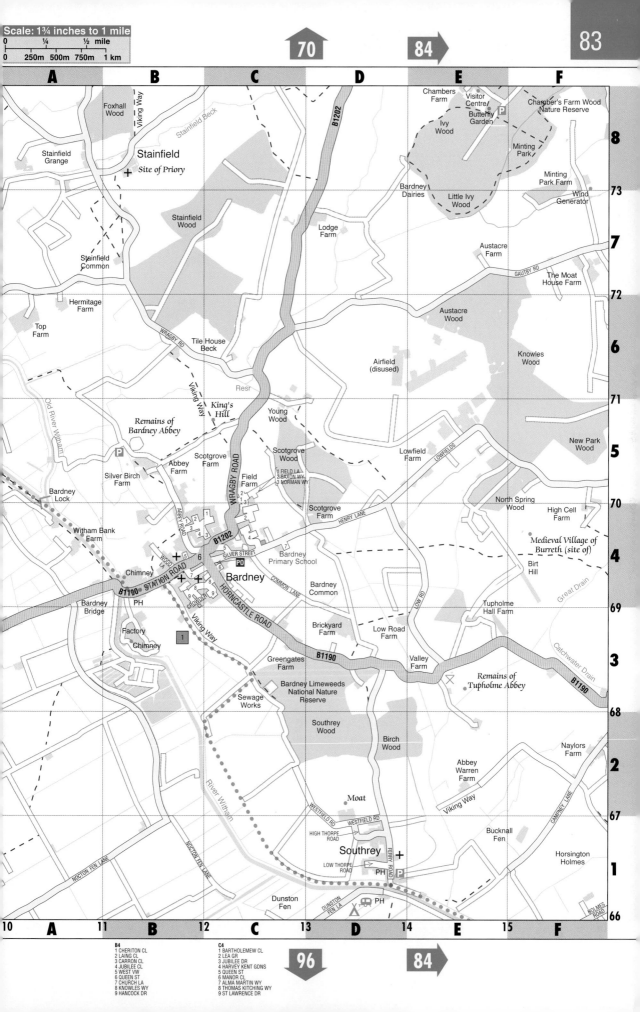

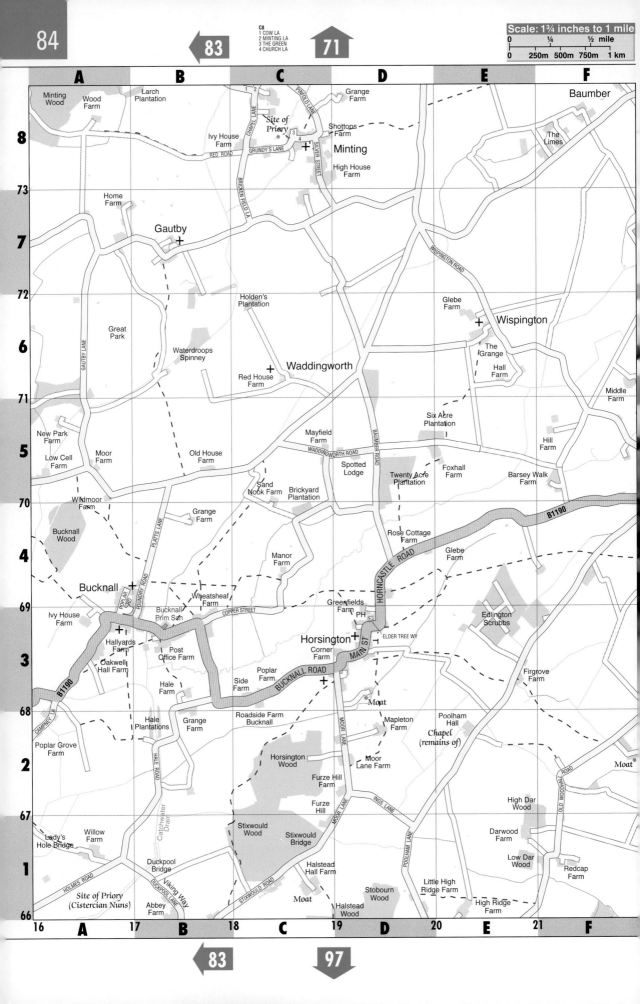

83
71

C8
1 COW LA
2 MINTING LA
3 THE GREEN
4 CHURCH LA

Scale: 1¾ inches to 1 mile

0   ¼   ½ mile
0   250m 500m 750m 1 km

Minting Wood
Wood Farm
Larch Plantation
Grange Farm
Baumber
The Limes

Ivy House Farm
Site of Priory
Shottons Farm
Minting
High House Farm

Home Farm
Gautby

Holden's Plantation
Glebe Farm
Wispington

Great Park
Waterdroops Spinney
Waddingworth
The Grange
Hall Farm

Red House Farm
Middle Farm

New Park Farm
Moor Farm
Old House Farm
Mayfield Farm
Six Acre Plantation
Hill Farm

Low Cell Farm
Spotted Lodge
Twenty Acre Plantation
Foxhall Farm
Barsey Walk Farm

Sand Nook Farm
Brickyard Plantation

Wildmoor Farm
Grange Farm
Bucknall Wood

Manor Farm
Rose Cottage Farm
Glebe Farm

Bucknall
Wheatsheaf Farm
Greenfields Farm
PH
Edlington Scrubbs

Ivy House Farm
Bucknall Prim Sch
Copper Street
Horsington
Corner Farm
ELDER TREE WY
Firgrove Farm

Hallyards Farm
Post Office Farm
Poplar Farm
MAIN ST.
BUCKNALL ROAD

Oakwell Hall Farm
Hale Farm
Side Farm
Moat

Poplar Grove Farm
Hale Plantations
Grange Farm
Roadside Farm Bucknall
Mapleton Farm
Poolham Hall
Chapel (remains of)
Moat

Horsington Wood
Furze Hill Farm
Moor Lane Farm
High Dar Wood

Willow Farm
Furze Hill
Darwood Farm

Lady's Hole Bridge
Stixwould Wood
Stixwould Bridge
Low Dar Wood

Duckpool Bridge
Viking Way
Halstead Hall Farm
Little High Ridge Farm
Redcap Farm

Site of Priory (Cistercian Nuns)
Abbey Farm
Moat
Stobourn Wood
High Ridge Farm

Halstead Wood

Minting Wood

83
97

GAUTBY LANE
BRICKEN FIELD LA
RED ROAD
GRUNDY'S LANE
CHAPEL LANE
PINFOLD LANE
SILVER STREET
WISPINGTON ROAD
WADDINGWORTH ROAD
BAUMBER ROAD
B1190
HORNCASTLE ROAD
PLATTS LANE
POPLAR YARD
FOUNDRY ROAD
CAMPNEY LA
B1190
HALE ROAD
Catchwater Drain
DUCKPOOL LANE
HOLMES ROAD
STIXWOULD ROAD
MOOR LANE
INGS LANE
POOLHAM LANE
OLD WOODHALL ROAD

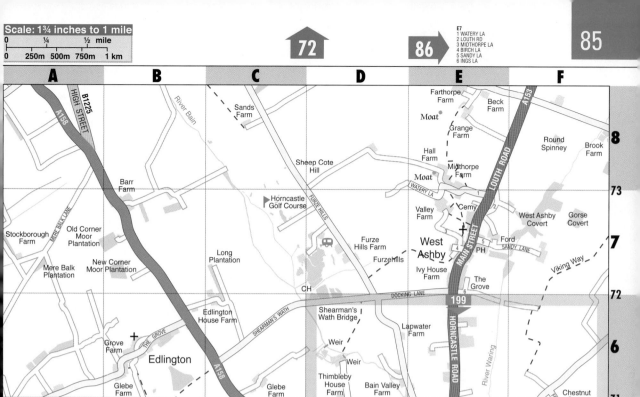

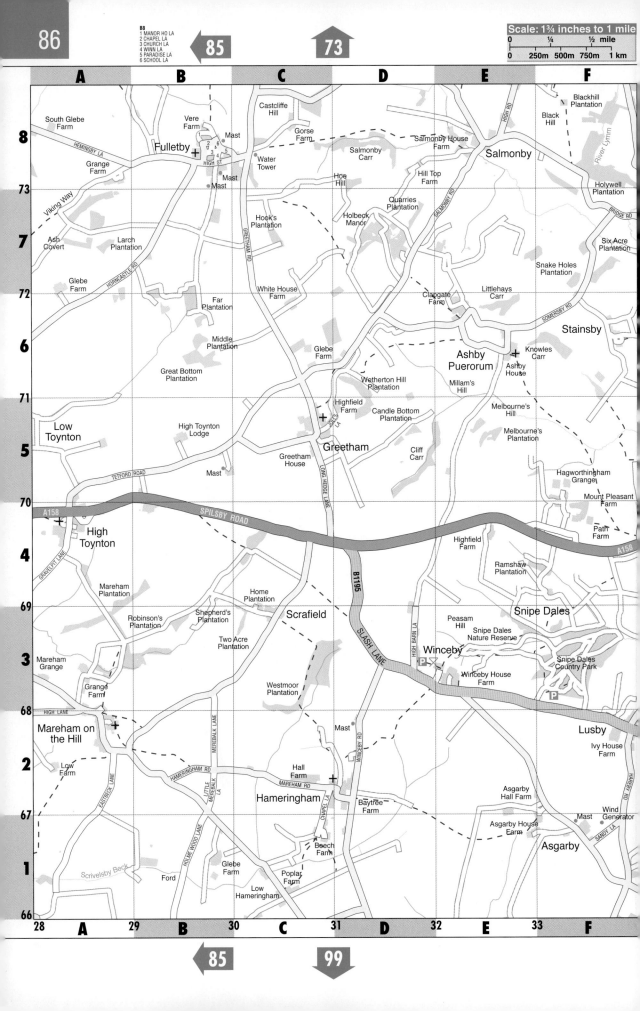

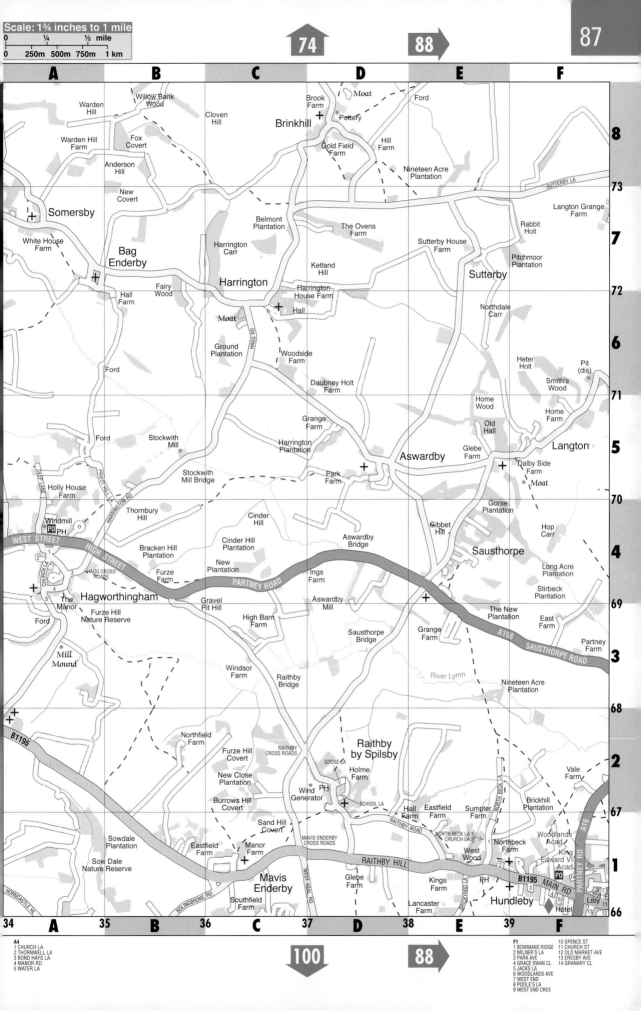

Scale: 1¾ inches to 1 mile

0   ¼   ½   mile
0   250m   500m   750m   1 km

A   B   C   D   E   F

8

ULCEBY CROSS
Motel
A16   A1104   A1028   MAIN ROAD

Dadley's Stone Wood

Well
WELL LA   HIGH LA
Grove Farm

Low Wood

Garth End

Well Vale

73

Ulceby Grange

Forest Wood

Badger Hill

Church Wood

Maypole House School

Mawthorpe

MAWTHORPE HILL RD
B1196

7

Scotland Farm

Ulceby
Church Farm
CHURCH LANE
PH   Glebe Farm

Fawn Wood

Fordington Wood

Rigge Wood

72

Spellow Hills (Long Barrow)

Deadmen's Graves (Long Barrows)

Mill Hill Quarry Nature Res

Cottage Farm

WILLOUGHBY RD

6

Dexthorpe
Earthworks
Dexthorpe Plantation

Pump Plantation

Fordington Village

Game Traps

PSALTER ROAD

Psalter Farm

Skendleby Psalter

Skendleby Nature Reserve

Claxby Spring Nature Res

Claxby Hall

Hopland's Wood Nature Res

SYCAMORE RD

Fordington

Earthwork

Grange Farm

CANDLESBY RD   SHADDY'S WALK

Dalby Grange

Low Plantation

71

FORDINGTON LA

Giant's Hills (Long Barrow)

Pit (dis)

BLUESTONE HEATH ROAD

Claxby St Andrew

Grange Farm

DANYER LANE

Bethlem Wood

Callow Carr

DALBY RD

Fordington Holt

Lodge Farm

SHADDY'S WALK

5

Helen's Fire

Dalby

Low Field Plantation

Short's Holt

Brackenbury Wood

Home Farm

A16

Hall

Thorpe Farm

A1028

Welton High Wood

70

The Park

PH

Skendleby

STONE PIT LANE

Minster Farm

Cottage Farm

Chalk Pit

Mill Farm

4

Dalby Hill

Sheepfold Plantation

Stripe Plantation

Highfield Farm

BASSINGHAM LANE

Moor Close Holt

Candlesby Hill Quarry Nature Res

69

1 MADDISON LA
2 HUDSON CL

Skendleby Holme Farm

Grebby Park

Sand Pit Plantation

The Grange

Partney CE (Aided) Prim Sch
Cemy

Home Plantation

Grebby
Windmill

GREENGATE ROAD   MILL LA

Mast

3

Sausthorpe Farm

SKEGNESS ROAD

Field Farm

DOWE LA

Fourteen Acre Plantation

Round Plantation

COOK'S LANE

Scremby Farm

CHALK PIT LANE

PH   PO
Partney

Long Plantation

Scremby Park

Hall Farm

Scremby

Candlesby

68

SAUSTHORPE ROAD   A16   A158

Mill Farm

HARDINGS LANE

LOWGATE ROAD

PH
A158

Partney Bridge

Model Farm

NORTHFIELD ROAD

Sweet Pits Plantation

Church Farm
Candlesby Park

College Farm

2

PARTNEY RD

Manor Farm

Moat

Hall Farm

67

Spilsby Prim Sch

Woodlands Trust Farm

Northorpe Farm

Northorpe Bridge

SCREMBY RD

Moat Farm

Beck Farm

MONKSTHORPE LANE

Glebe Farm

Fir Close Plantation

1

ASHBY ROAD   TASHBY RD

PO   P

SPILSBY

Ivy House Farm

Ashby by Partney

The Beck

SANDY LA

66

40   41   42   43   44   45

A   B   C   D   E   F

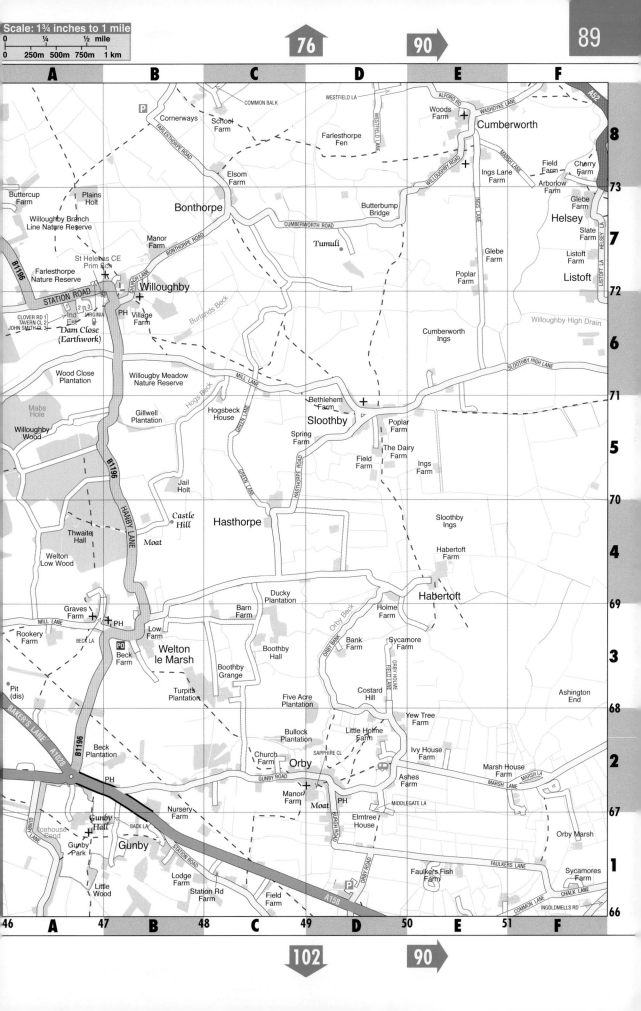

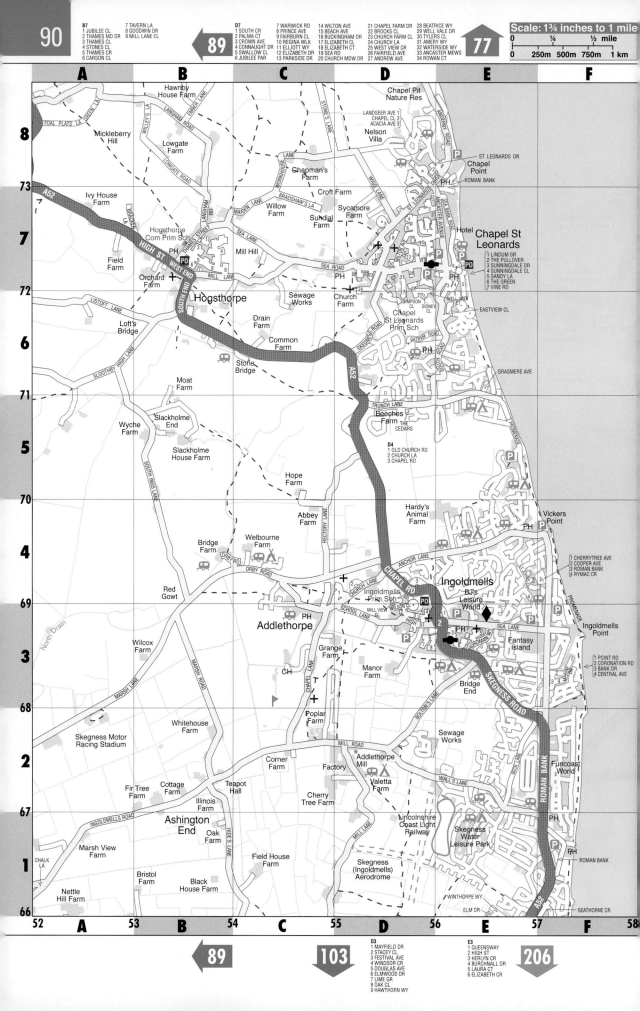

89
77

Scale: 1¾ inches to 1 mile

Mickleberry Hill

Hawnby House Farm

Lowgate Farm

Ivy House Farm

Field Farm

Orchard Farm

Hogsthorpe Com Prim Sch

Hogsthorpe

Mill Hill

Willow Farm

Chapman's Farm

Croft Farm

Sundial Farm

Sycamore Farm

Chapel Pit Nature Res

Nelson Villa

Chapel Point

St Leonards Dr

Roman Bank

Hotel

Chapel St Leonards

Church Farm

Chapel St Leonards Prim Sch

Sewage Works

Drain Farm

Common Farm

Stone Bridge

Loft's Bridge

Moat Farm

Slackholme End

Wyche Farm

Slackholme House Farm

Hope Farm

Abbey Farm

Beeches Farm

THE CEDARS

Trunch Lane

Grasmere Ave

Eastview Cl

Hardy's Animal Farm

Vickers Point

Bridge Farm

Welbourne Farm

Red Gowt

Ingoldmells Prim Sch

Church Lane

Ingoldmells

BJ's Leisure World

Addlethorpe

School Lane

Mill View Cl

Fantasy Island

Ingoldmells Point

Grange Farm

Manor Farm

Bridge End

CH

Wilcox Farm

Poplar Farm

Whitehouse Farm

Skegness Motor Racing Stadium

Corner Farm

Factory

Addlethorpe Mill

Valetta Farm

Sewage Works

Funcoast World

Fir Tree Farm

Cottage Farm

Teapot Hall

Cherry Tree Farm

Illinois Farm

Lincolnshire Coast Light Railway

Skegness Water Leisure Park

Marsh View Farm

Ashington End

Oak Farm

Field House Farm

Skegness (Ingoldmells) Aerodrome

Roman Bank

CHALK LA

Nettle Hill Farm

Bristol Farm

Black House Farm

Winthorpe Wy

Elm Dr

Seathorne Cr

89
103
206

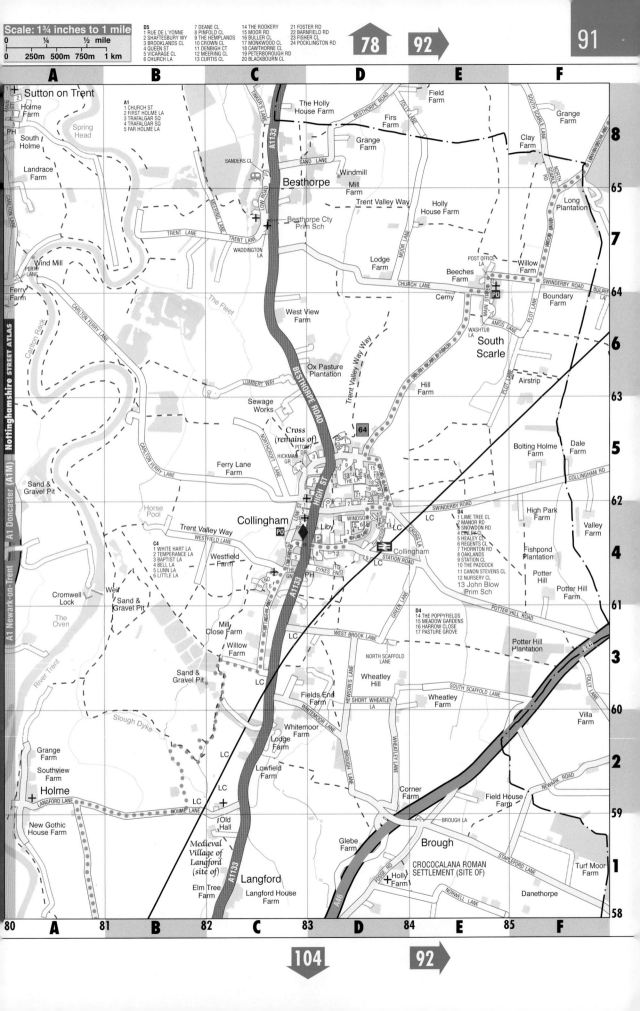

Scale: 1¾ inches to 1 mile

0   ¼   ½ mile
0   250m 500m 750m 1 km

A   B   C   D   E   F

8
Manor Farm
Eagle Hall Farm
64
Moat
Oaks Farm
LC
Birchwood Farm
Cocked Hat Plantation
Scotland Farm
Holly Tree Farm
St Michael's CE Primary School
1 LITTLE THORPE LA
2 HOLME CL
Thorpe on the Hill
SCHOOL LA 1
BLACKSMITH LA 2
WEST FIELD LA 3
SEMPERS CL 4
Motel

65
Eagle Hall Wood
Tunman Farm
Tunman Wood
Eagle Barnsdale
Jubilee Farm

7
Cottage Farm
BRACKEN RD
P
Morton Hall HM Prison
Housham Wood
Stocking Wood
Housham Grange
Sky Barn Farm
Thorpe Grange Farm
PH

64
Swinderby
LC
Ling Moor Farm
MORTON ROAD
PARK CRESENT
Morton
High Walks

6
LC
Kismul School
PACEY CL
PD
Park Farm
Ansons Farm
Mast
Fosse Way
A46
High Walks Farm
STONE LANE
High Walks
Haddington

63
Swinderby
HIGH STREET
MOOR LANE
PH
Halfway Lane Farm
Halfway House Lane
Green Lane Farm
Motel
PH
1 SQUIRREL GN
2 DOE CL
3 OWL CL
4 PARTRIDGE GN
5 CARAWAY DR
6 FOX HOLLOW
7 LEVERET CHASE
8 MEADOWSWEET LANE
9 POPPY RD
10 BUTTERCUP WY
Sheepwalks Farm
Sheepwalk
Corner Farm
DOVECOTE LA
BAILEYS LA
Moats

5
NEWTON CL 1
MEADOW VW 2
COLLINGHAM ROAD
COW LANE
GREEN LANE
Thurlby Moor
1 GIBSON GR
2 CHESHIRE LA
3 NETTLETON DR
4 HANNAH CRES
10 9
JUNIPER WAY
BLUEBELL WK
ELDER CL
Witham St. Hughs
Weir
MILL LANE
BASSINGHAM ROAD

62
Welbeck Farm
Newton's Farm
NEWARK ROAD
WARREN
Airfield (disused)
PATCH RD
SATTERLEY CL
OAK TREE DR
HEDGE LANE
Sewage Works
MOOR LANE
1 RAVEN'S VW
2 MOORHEN CL
3 PENDRED AVE
Thurlby
North Farm
New House North Farm
Moor Covert

4
Potterhill Farm
Oakhill Farm
NORTON LANE
South Farm
Greengate Farm
Northfield Farm
Witham Farm
LINCOLN ROAD

61
Birch Holt Farm
Stables Wood Farm
WOOD LANE
Thurlby Moor
Sand & Gravel Pit
Thurlby Moor
River Farm
THURLBY RD
CROFT
LINGA LANE

3
Hawdin's Wood
Gilbert's Wood
Norton Big Wood
Norton Low Wood
Killbuck Plantation
Church Farm
Thurlby Bridge
WATER LA
HIGH ST
ORCHARD CL
VILLAGE FARM
PD

60
Hill Holt Farm
Norton Disney Hall
Sand & Gravel Pit
Tonge's Plantation
Tonge's Farm
River Farm
Sewage Works
Recn Gd
Bassingham Prim Sch
MIDDLEGATE
Savages Farm
Bassingham

2
FOLLY LANE
Grove Farm
Lodge Farm
NEWARK ROAD
BLACKSMITH'S LANE
SWINDERBY ROAD
BUTT LA
DISNEY CT 1
CHURCH DR 2
Norton Disney
Twin Tree Farm
CLAY LANE
Manor Farm
BAKERS LA 1
WHITES LA 2
ASH TREE WAY 3
MANOR PADDOCKS 4
NEWARK RD
CARLTON ROAD
1 HIGH ST
2 EASTGATE
3 EAST FIELD
4 BROCKLEBANK CL
5 TORGATE AVE
6 LIME GR

59
Sand & Gravel Pit
Cold Harbour Farm
Witham Prospect Sch
Rose Farm
Village Farm
Vine Tree Farm PH
MAIN STREET
Scotwater Bridge
RINKS LANE
OLD BRICKKILN
QUEEN HEADLAND LA

1
NORTON ROAD
NORTON DISNEY ROAD
BASSINGHAM RD
BROUGHTON RD
SANDS LA
Carlton-le-Moorland

58
86 A 87 B 88 C 89 D 90 E 91 F

E1
1 WESTHALL CL
2 WHEATLEY LA
3 GRANGE CT
4 VICARAGE LA

F3
1 BLACKSMITH ROW
2 BADGERS OAK
3 CHESTNUT CRES
4 HAWTHORN WY
5 MAPLE DR
6 HOLMES FIELD
7 PINFOLD CL

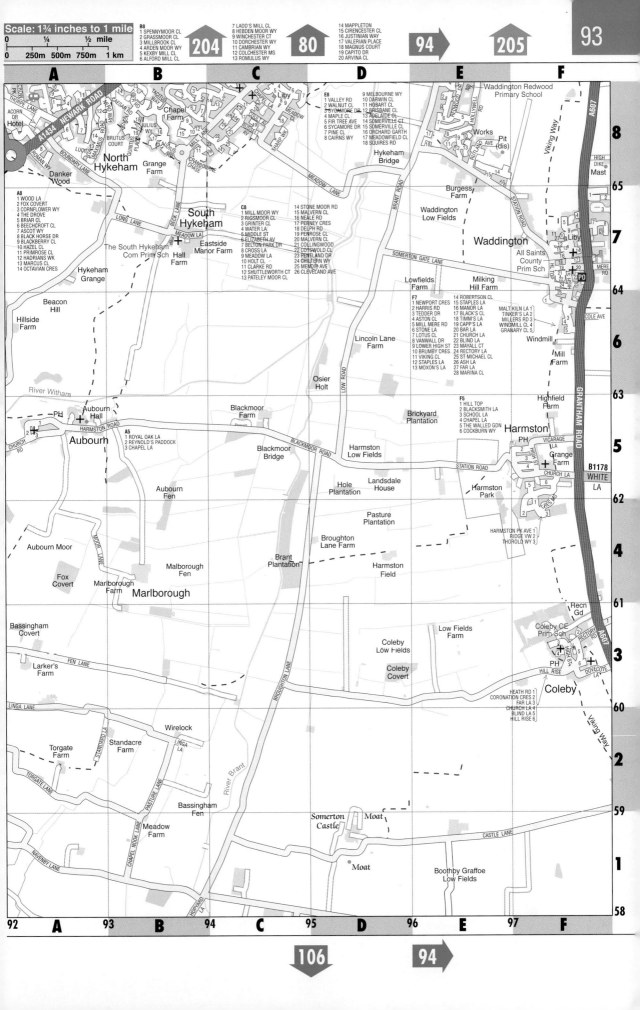

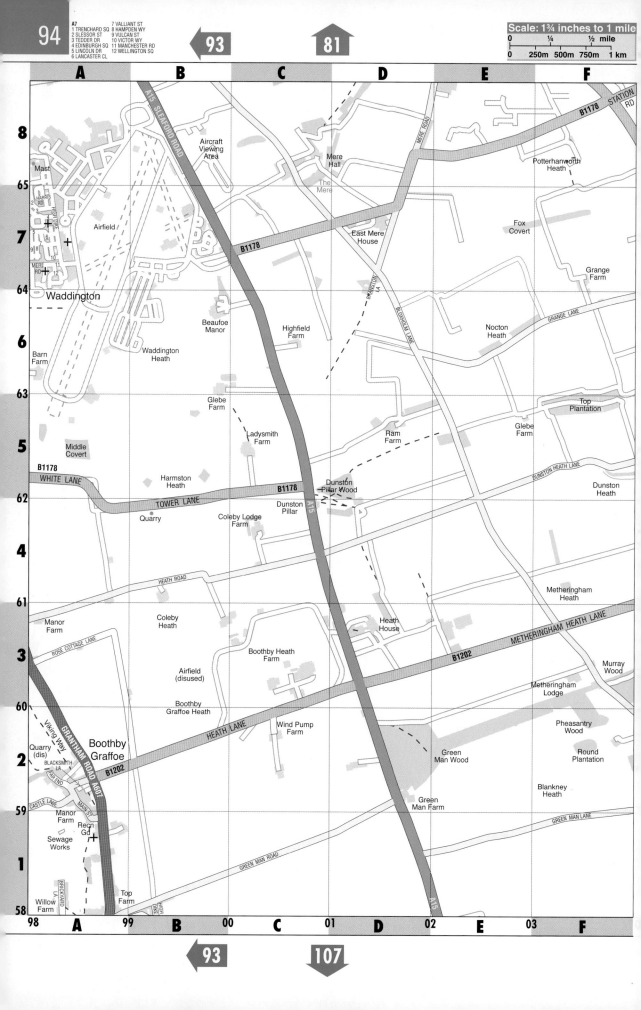

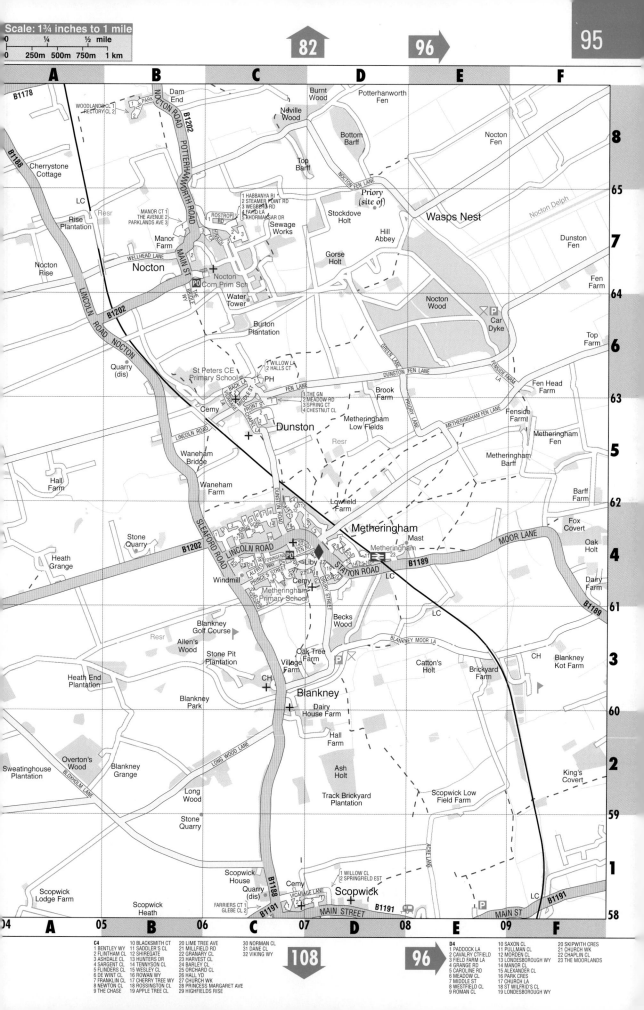

A **B** **C** **D** **E** **F**

8
65
7
64
6
63
5
62
4
61
3
60
2
59
1
58

B1178
B1202
B1188
B1202

Cherrystone Cottage
LC
Rise Plantation
Nocton Rise
Resr
WOODLAND CL 1
RECTORY CL 2
THE PARK
Dam End
Burnt Wood
Potterhanworth Fen
Neville Wood
Bottom Barff
Nocton Fen
Top Barff
Priory (site of)
Nocton Delph
Wasps Nest
Dunston Fen
Fen Farm
MANOR CT 1
THE AVENUE 2
PARKLANDS AVE 3
Manor Farm
Nocton
WELLHEAD LANE
MAIN ST
POTTERHANWORTH ROAD
NOCTON ROAD
ROSTROP RD
1 HABBANYA RI
2 STEAMER POINT RD
3 WEGBERG RD
4 FAYID LA
5 KHORMAKSAR DR
Sewage Works
Stockdove Holt
Hill Abbey
Nocton Wood
Top Farm
Fen Head Farm
PO
Nocton Com Prim Sch
Water Tower
Burton Plantation
Gorse Holt
Nocton Wood
Car Dyke
P
FENSIDE FARM LA
Quarry (dis)
LINCOLN ROAD NOCTON
St Peters CE Primary School
PH
1 WILLOW LA
2 HALLS CT
BACK LA
FEN LANE
FRONT ST
MIDDLE ST
CHAPEL LA
DUNSTON FEN LANE
Brook Farm
GREEN LANE
PRIORY LANE
Fenside Farm
Metheringham Fen
Cemy
1 THE GN
2 MEADOW RD
3 SPRING CT
4 CHESTNUT CL
Dunston
Metheringham Low Fields
METHERINGHAM FEN LANE
Metheringham Barff
Hall Farm
Waneham Bridge
LINCOLN ROAD
Waneham Farm
Resr
Barff Farm
Stone Quarry
SLEAFORD ROAD
B1202
DUNSTON ROAD
Lowfield Farm
Metheringham
Mast
MOOR LANE
Fox Covert
Oak Holt
Heath Grange
Heath End Plantation
LINCOLN ROAD
KINGS ROAD
FEN RD
PO
ALFRED ST
PRINCE'S STREET
TOWNSEND WAY
Liby
STATION ROAD
Metheringham
B1189
LC
Dairy Farm
B1189
Windmill
Cemy
Metheringham Primary School
DRURY STREET
Becks Wood
LC
Blankney Golf Course
Resr
Allen's Wood
Stone Pit Plantation
CH
Oak Tree Farm
Village Farm
P
Blankney Moor La
Catton's Holt
Brickyard Farm
CH
Blankney Kot Farm
Blankney Park
CH
Blankney
Dairy House Farm
Sweatinghouse Plantation
BLOXHOLM LANE
Overton's Wood
Blankney Grange
Long Wood
LONG WOOD LANE
Hall Farm
Ash Holt
Track Brickyard Plantation
Scopwick Low Field Farm
King's Covert
Long Wood
Stone Quarry
Scopwick House
ACRE LANE
Scopwick Lodge Farm
Scopwick Heath
Quarry (dis)
FARRIERS CT 1
GLEBE CL 2
B1188
B1191
Cemy
VICARAGE LANE
1 WILLOW CL
2 SPRINGFIELD EST
Scopwick
B1191
MAIN STREET
P
LC
B1191
MAIN ST

A 04   **B** 05   06   **C** 07   **D** 08   **E** 09   **F**

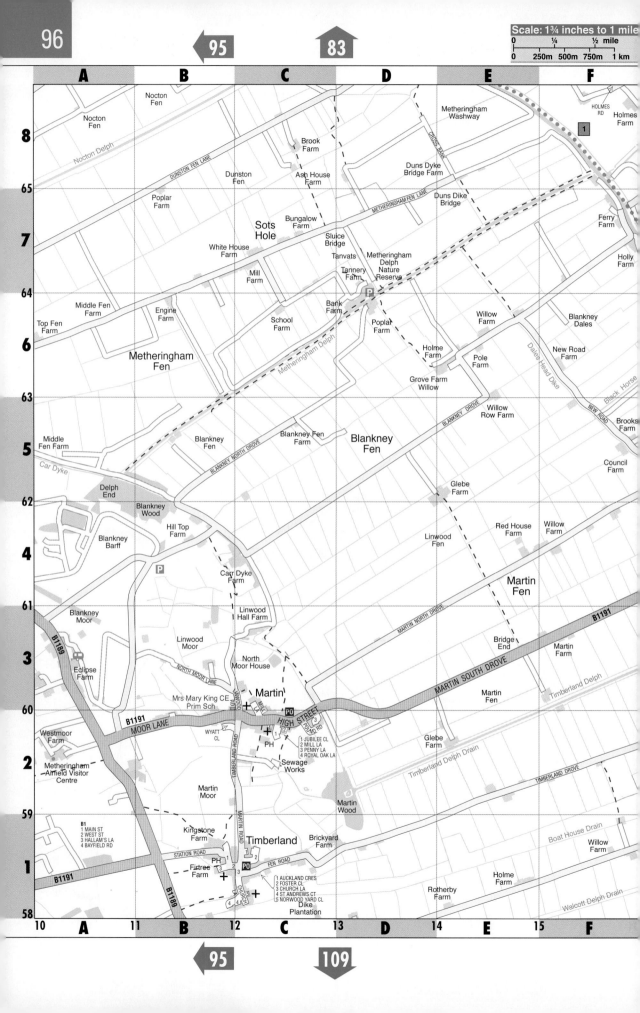

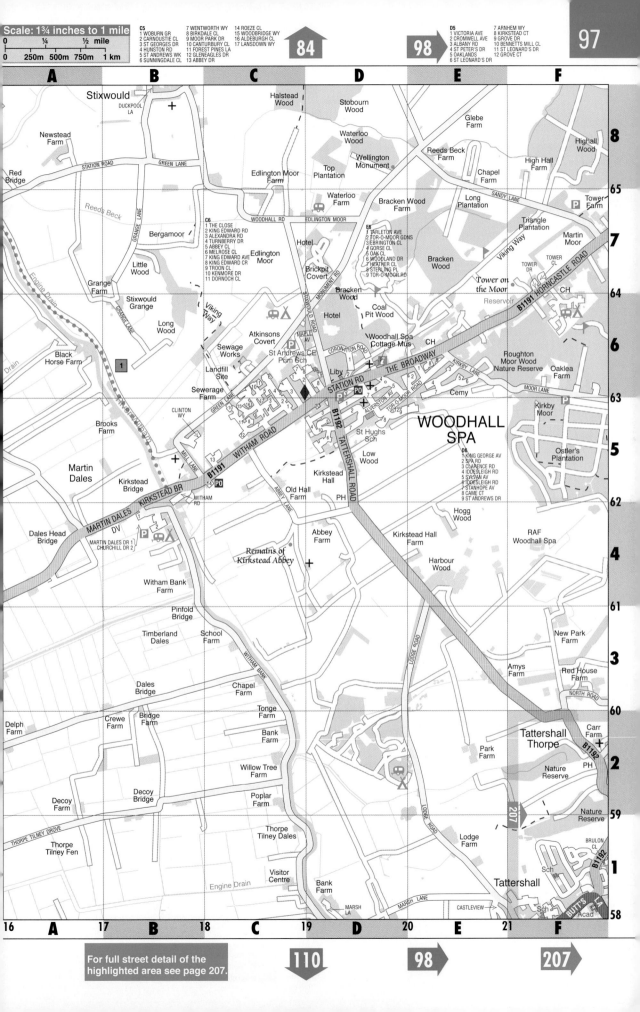

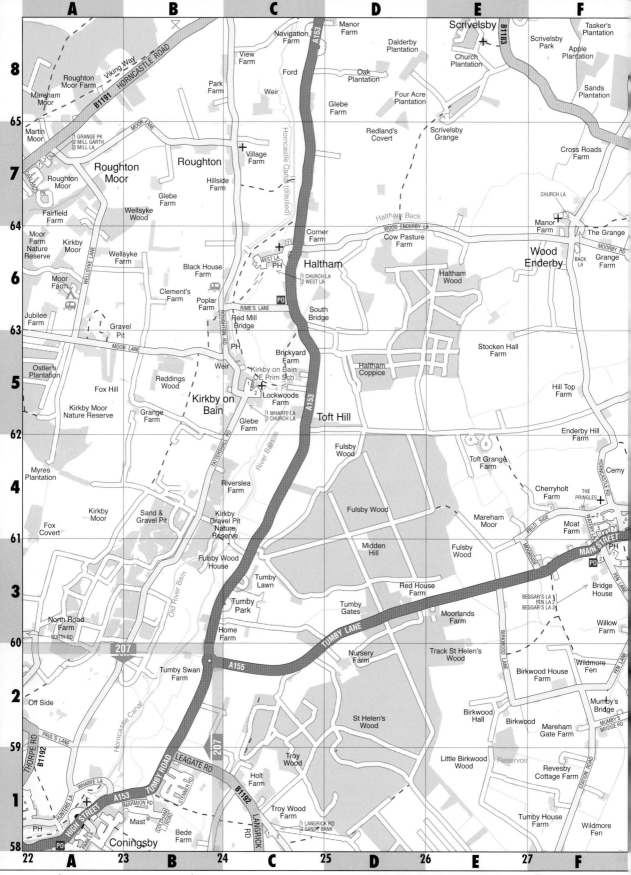

Scrivelsby
Tasker's Plantation
Manor Farm
Dalderby Plantation
Scrivelsby Park
Navigation Farm
View Farm
Apple Plantation
Church Plantation
Roughton Moor Farm
Mareham Moor
Park Farm
Ford
Weir
Oak Plantation
Four Acre Plantation
Sands Plantation
B1191
HORNCASTLE ROAD
Viking Way
MOOR LANE
Martin Moor
1 GRANGE PK
2 MILL GARTH
3 MILL LA
Village Farm
Glebe Farm
Redland's Covert
Scrivelsby Grange
Cross Roads Farm
Roughton Moor
Roughton
Hillside Farm
CHURCH LA
Roughton Moor
Fairfield Farm
Glebe Farm
Corner Farm
Cow Pasture Farm
Manor Farm
The Grange
Wellsyke Wood
Haltham Beck
WOOD ENDERBY LA
MOORBY LA
Moor Farm Nature Reserve
Kirkby Moor
Wellsyke Farm
Black House Farm
WEST LA
PH
Haltham
Haltham Wood
Wood Enderby
BACK LA
Grange Farm
WELLSYKE LANE
Moor Farm
Clement's Farm
Poplar Farm
1 CHURCH LA
2 WEST LA
Jubilee Farm
Gravel Pit
RIME'S LANE
Red Mill Bridge
PO
South Bridge
Stocken Hall Farm
ROUGHTON RD
PH
Brickyard Farm
Ostler's Plantation
MOOR LANE
Weir
Kirkby on Bain CE Prim Sch
Haltham Coppice
Hill Top Farm
Fox Hill
Reddings Wood
Kirkby on Bain
Lockwoods Farm
A153
1 WHARFE LA
2 CHURCH LA
Toft Hill
Enderby Hill Farm
Kirkby Moor Nature Reserve
Grange Farm
Glebe Farm
River Bain
Fulsby Wood
Toft Grange Farm
Cemy
Myres Plantation
Riverslea Farm
Cherryholt Farm
THE PRINGLES
Fox Covert
Kirkby Moor
Sand & Gravel Pit
Kirkby Gravel Pit Nature Reserve
Fulsby Wood
Mareham Moor
Moat Farm
Old River Bain
Fulsby Wood House
Midden Hill
Fulsby Wood
MOORSIDE
MAIN STREET
PH
PO
North Road Farm
NORTH RD
Tumby Lawn
Tumby Park
Tumby Gates
Red House Farm
BEGGAR'S LA
FEN LA 2
BEGGAR'S LA 3
Bridge House
207
Home Farm
Moorlands Farm
BIRKWOOD LANE
Willow Farm
TUMBY LANE
Off Side
Tumby Swan Farm
A155
207
Nursery Farm
Track St Helen's Wood
Birkwood House Farm
Wildmore Fen
FIELD SIDE
WATERY LA
HORNCASTLE RD
FEN LANE
PAUL'S LANE
Birkwood Hall
Birkwood
Mumby's Bridge
STATION ROAD
Horncastle Canal
LEAGATE RD
Troy Wood
Little Birkwood Wood
Reservoir
Mareham Gate Farm
MUMBY'S BRIDGE RD
THORPE RD
B1192
WHARFE LA
TUMBY ROAD
STEEPER RD
MARMION RD
Holt Farm
B1192
Revesby Cottage Farm
Coningsby
HIGH STREET
A153
COLDHAM RD
Mast
Bede Farm
Troy Wood Farm
LANGRICK RD
1 LANGRICK RD
2 SANDY BANK
Tumby House Farm
Wildmore Fen
HUNTERS LA
PARK LA
PO
PH

22   A   23   B   24   C   25   D   26   E   27   F

207

97

111

For full street detail of the highlighted area see page 207.

F4
1 TOFT HURN
2 RECTORY LA
3 CHURCH LA
4 WOODMAN'S CT
5 CHURCH RI
6 KIME'S LA
7 SHOP HL

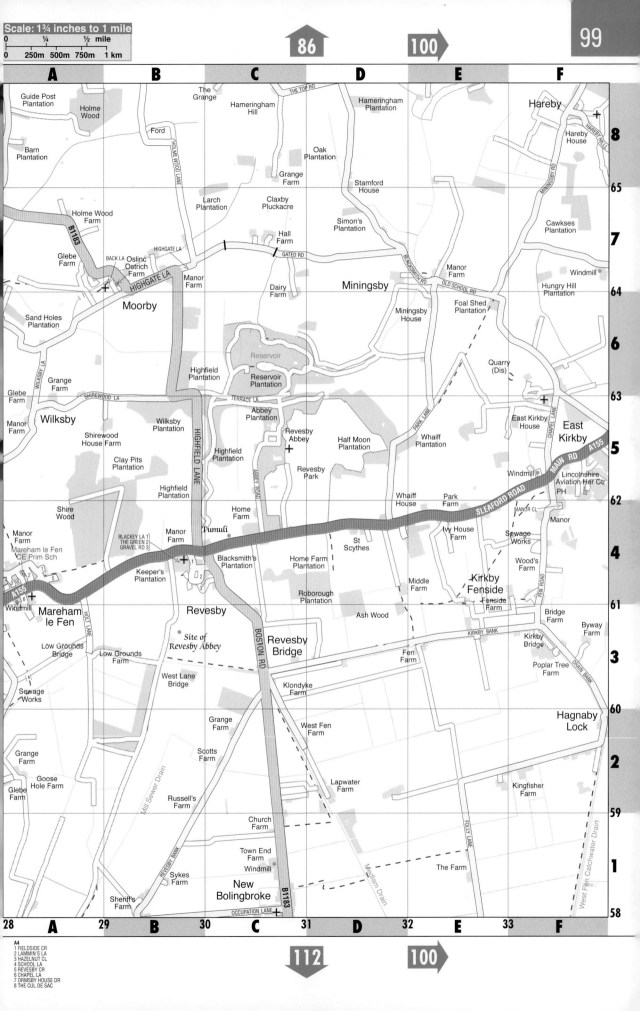

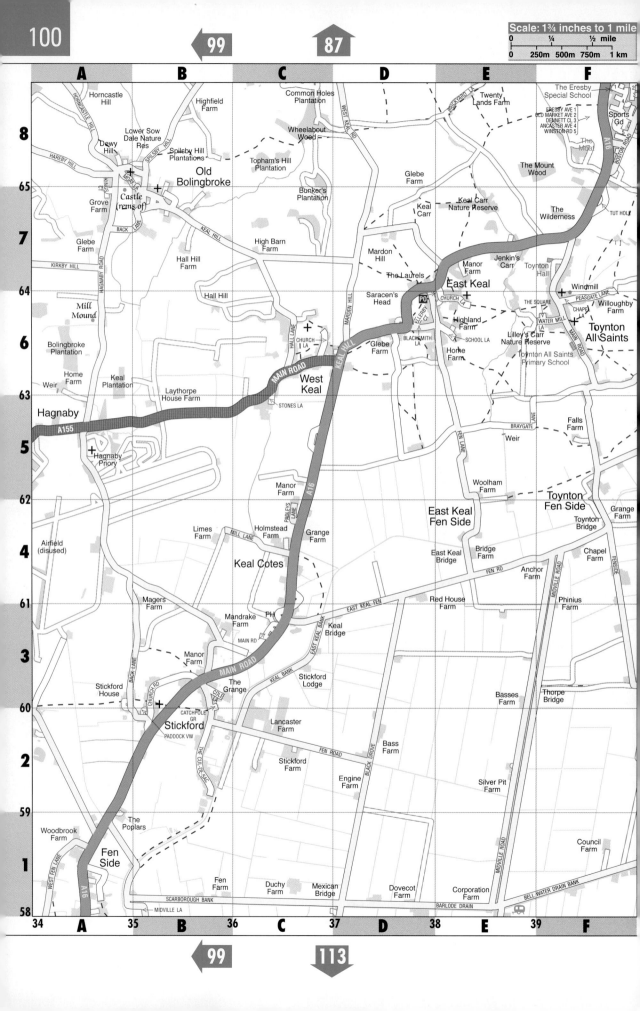

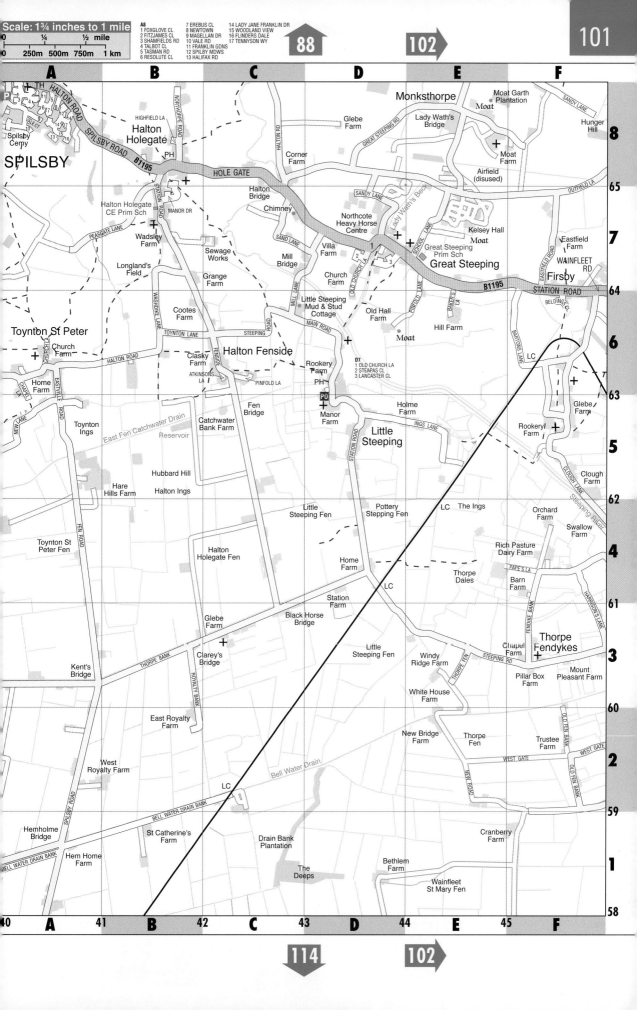

← 101   ↑ 89

Scale: 1¾ inches to 1 mile

0   ¼   ½ mile
0   250m 500m 750m 1 km

Map labels (north to south, west to east):

Grange Farm, Buttoncap Holt, Kirks Farm, Pear Tree Farm, Common Lane, Moat, Elmstead Farm, Gatrum Farm, Woody Nook Farm, Burgh Common, Motel, Willow Lodge, White Gate Farm, SANDY LA, GUNBY LANE, North Road, Orby Road, Ingoldmells Road, High Street, St Michaels Farm, Manor Farm, Bratoft, White House Farm, Gravel Pits Lane, Station Road, West End, DOUBLEDAYS LA 1 / WINDMILL DR 2 / ST PETER'S CL 3 / ELM CR 4, Windmill, Liby, Windmill, Moat Farm, Moat, Summergates La, Brambleberry Lane, Wongs Lane, Mill Hill Farm, St Peter & St Paul CE Prim School, ASH CL 2 / LINDEN DR 3 / LIME CL 4, St Pauls Cl 1, Burgh le Marsh, Hall Lane, Church Farm, Peartree Farm, B1195, Oxlands Lane, Green La, Ings, Ings Lane, Bratoft Corner, Long Plantation, Marsh Lane, Billgate Lane, Manor Farm, Irby in the Marsh, Wainfleet Road, End House Farm, Croft End, Low Lane, High Lane, Jock Hedge, Lloyds Farm, Blands Farm, Catchwater Drain, Lincoln Farm, Grove House Farm, Hollytrees Farm, The Hollies, Home Farm, Mast, New House Farm, The Ings, Low Road, Rivulet House, Millhill Bridge, Mill Hill Farm, The Hundreds, Church Lane, Pincheck Lane, Clough La, Lymn Bank, Washdike Lane, Meml, Croft, Clough Bridge, Lymn Bank Farm, Sycamore Cl, Church La, Firsby Clough, TIP LANE, White House Farm, Spilsby Road, Oak Bridge, Monson Farm, PH, Warth's Bridge, LC, Thorpe St Peter, PH, B1195, Wedland Lane, Florence Farm, Croft Road, Poplar Farm, Works, Bank House, Holly Farm, Corr Lane, LC, Station Road, Old Hall Farm, Moat, Thorpe Culvert, Wainfleet Road, Primrose Farm, Manor House Farm, Croft Bank, Thorpe Culvert, Culvert Road, PH, Thorpe Fen, Leader Gate, Brewster Lane, LC, Tower Tree Farm, Crown Farm, Havenhouse, Watson Farm, West Gate, Lady La, King Street, Wainfleet Common, Crow's Bridge, Collison Gate, Wainfleet All Saints, Waincroft Close, New England, Riverside Farm, Whiteheads Farm, Back La, Church Farm, Crow's Lane, LC, Wainfleet Magdalen CE/Meth Sch, Cemy, Spilsby Road, Skegness Road, Croft Bank, Green La, Wainfleet Bank, Magdalen Rd, Magdalen Mus, Liby, PO, White House Farm, Windsor Farm, Merrifield's Farm, Wainfleet St Mary Fen, Mill Lane, Wainfleet, Bateman's Brewery, High St, Dovecote La, Low Grounds, Church Lane, Low Road, Vicarage La, Station Rd, B1195, Boston Rd, A52, Low Farm, Hall Gate, Queen's Est

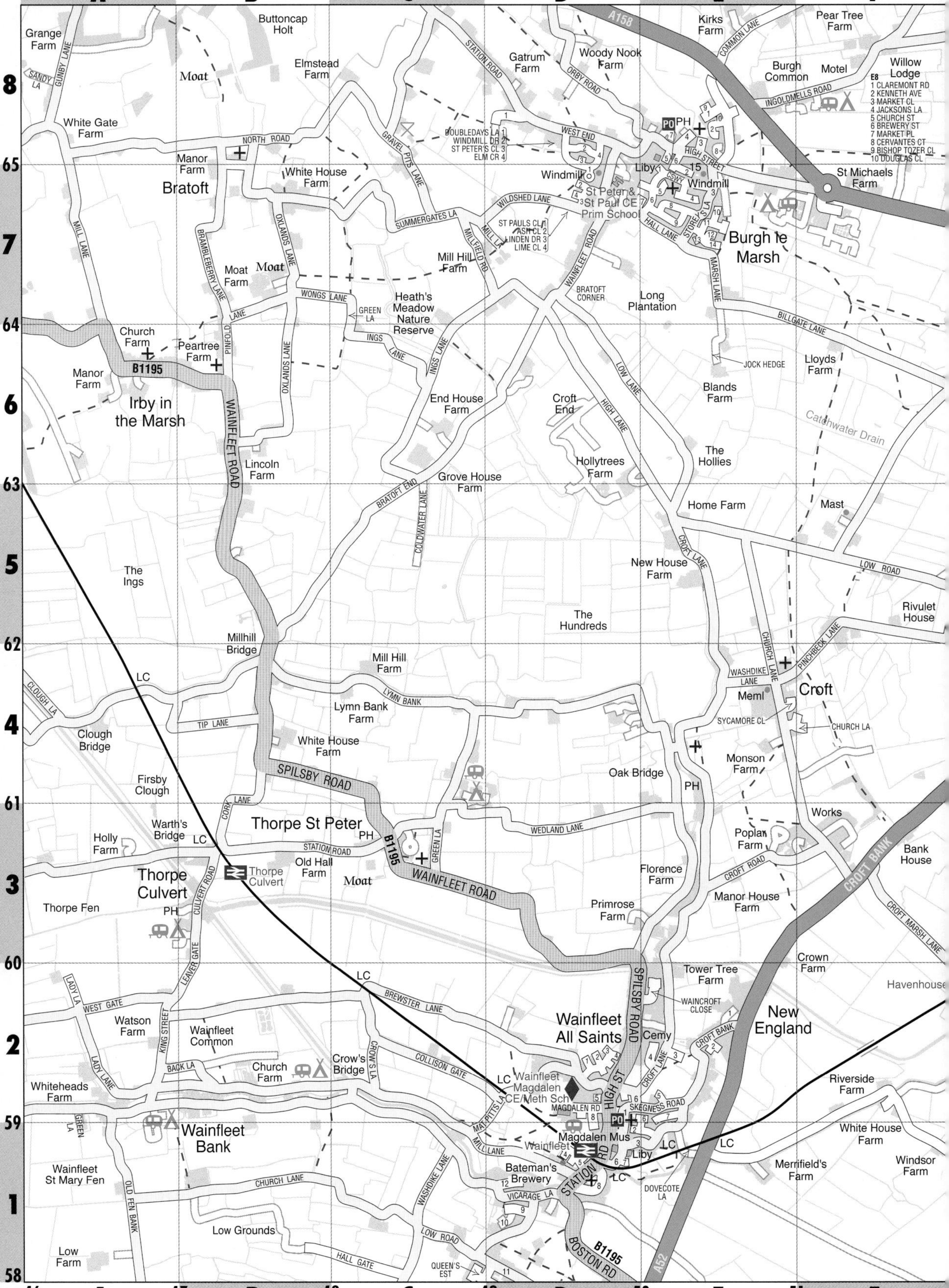

← 101   ↓ 115

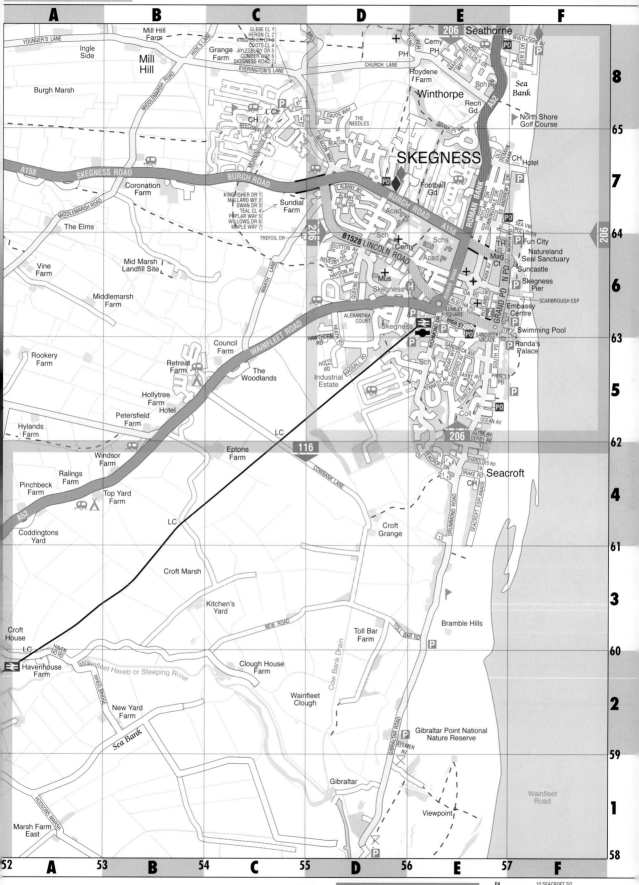

116

For full street detail of the highlighted area see page 206.

E4
1 ALBERT AVE
2 VINE RD
3 BUCKTHORN AVE
4 NORWOOD RD
5 PRECINCT CRES
6 BAYES RD
7 GREEN LA
8 LINKS CRES
9 SEA FRONT RD
10 SEACROFT SQ
11 HESKETH CRES
12 FREDERICA RD

B5
1 SWINDERBY CL
2 CRANWELL CL
3 NORMANTON RD
4 BLACKBROOK RD
5 SYERSTON W Y
6 AUTUMN CROFT RD
7 WINTERDALE CL
8 PHILLIPOT CL
9 MARLES CL
10 FARRAR CL
11 WHITTLE CL
12 BRUNEL CT

B7
1 THE DRIVE
2 CHAPEL LA
3 POCKLINGTON CRES
4 BRANSTON CL
5 SPEIGHT CL
6 GAINSBOROUGH RD

7 THE SPINNEY
8 WINTHORPE RD

C5
1 YEW TREE WY
2 ORDOYNO GR
3 BEACONSFIELD DR
4 PARKLANDS CL
5 OLD HALL GDNS
6 PENSWICK GR
7 HARVEY AVE
8 VALIANT RD
9 CLARICOATES DR
10 HAMPDENS CL
11 LANCASTER RD
12 STIRLING DR
13 HENTON CL
14 BRISTOL CL
15 NEWBURY RD
16 CANNON CL
17 BRYANS CL
18 YOUNGS CL
19 THOMPSON CL
20 ORCHARD PK

B2
1 HOWARD'S GDNS
2 CENTENARY CL
3 KINGSWAY
4 ALBERT AVE
5 LONDON RD
6 MOUNT CT
7 VESSEY CL
8 COGING CL
9 GIBSON CRES
10 BELVOIR PL
11 SMITHSON CL
12 LANSBURY RD
13 MOULTON CRES
14 HAYSIDE AVE
15 BAKEWELL CL
16 SHERIDAN CL
17 GLOVERS LA
18 PINFOLD LA
19 ORCHARD WAY
20 DERWENT ST
21 HADDON DR
22 CHURCH VIEW
23 GRANBY DR
24 MARQUIS AVE
25 THOROTON CL
26 MARSTON CL
27 DENTON CL
28 BARKSTON CL
29 HARBY CL
30 KNIPTON CL
31 LOVEDEN CL
32 WALTHAM CL
33 ELTON CL

A5
1 MALTKILN LA
2 KINGS SCONCE AVE
3 HATCHET'S LA
4 STRAWBERRY HALL LA
5 TRENT WAY
6 DERWENT WAY
7 WITHAM CL
8 CLARKS LA
9 WELLAND CL
10 PIPPIN CT
11 CLARKS LA
12 ROSEWOOD CL
13 STUKELEY CT
14 STANLEY ST
15 SUMMER'S RD
16 CURRIE RD
17 NEWNHAM RD
18 MEYRICK RD
19 WARBURTON ST
20 GEORGE ST
21 CLIFF NOOK LA
22 MUMBY CL
23 SYDNEY ST
24 NEWSTEAD AVE
25 LAWRENCE ST
26 CLIFF NOOK LA

A3
1 BYRON CL
2 BELVOIR CRES
3 RUTLAND AVE
4 CAVENDISH CL
5 GRANBY AVE
6 BROMLEY AVE
7 CARLTON RD
8 QUIBELL RD
9 STAUNTON RD
10 MARTON RD
11 BEESTON RD
12 FALSTONE AVE
13 SHAKESPEARE ST
14 GROVE ST
15 OLD DODHAMORCH
16 LINDEN AVE
17 ORCHID CL

A4
1 FRIARY RD
2 WELLINGTON RD
3 BEDE HOUSE LA
4 THE GATEWAY
5 OLIVER CL
6 JOHN GOLD AVE
7 HERCULES DR
8 THE AVE
9 MAGNUS ST
10 BALDERTON GATE
11 VICTORIA GDNS
12 LINDUM ST
13 EASTERN TERR
14 NEW ST
15 WILLIAM ST
16 PARKER ST
17 NICHOLSON ST
18 HATTON GDNS
19 WINCHILSEA AVE
20 MILNER ST
21 EARP AVE
22 WALKER CL
23 SYDNEY TERR
24 THE PARK
25 THE PADDOCKS
26 OLD SCHOOL LA
27 WOODSTOCK CL
28 SAWYERS CL

B5
13 LILY LA
14 CLOVER GDNS
15 GERBERA CL

C5
21 LAVENDER WAY
22 SNOWDROP AVE
23 SPEEDWELL CL

D5
1 THE GREEN
2 MORGANS CL
3 THORPE CL
4 PARKES CL
5 ROSS CL
6 HALL FARM
7 CHAPEL LA
8 VALLEY VW

B4
1 GOODWIN CL
2 HEATON CL
3 GILSTRAP CL
4 WHOMSLEY CL
5 APPLEBY CL
6 ASHWORTH CL
7 RANSOME CL

C2
1 BRANDON CL
2 SPRING LA
3 GAMAGE CL
4 WETSYKE LA
5 SIMPSON CL
6 WORTHINGTON RD
7 SOUTHFIELD
8 BYRON CL
9 MARSHALL CL
10 NIGHTINGALE CL
11 CHAUCER RD

B3
1 THE WOODWARDS
2 GLEBE PK
3 SAPLING CL
4 BLACKTHORNE CL
5 WILLOW RD
6 BIRCH RD
7 LONGFELLOW DR
8 GOLDSMITH RD
9 GOLDSWORTH CL
10 KEATS RD

B3
1 JERICHO RD
2 KIRTON CL
3 INGLEWOOD CL

Map labels:
Winthorpe Lake · Winthorpe · Winthorpe Bridge · Winthorpe Cricket Club · Winthorpe Prim Sch · Langford Hall · Hall Farm · High Wood · Danethorpe Hill · Danethorpe Hill Farm · Thorpe Field Farm · Quarry Plantation · Lingspot Farm · Langford Moor Farm · Langford Moor · Newark & Nottinghamshire Agricultural Society's Showground · Newark Air Museum · Drove Cott · Three Wood · Hilltop Farm · Stapleford Wood · Flawford Farm · South Airfield Farm · North Airfield Farm · Beaconsfield Farm · Sports Gd · Kelwick Wood · Sleaford Road · Newark Golf Course · Brown's Wood · Grove Farm · Redoubt · Sewage Works · Bishop Alexander L.E.A.D. Acad · Weir · North Gate · Allot Gdns · Beacon Hill · Beacon Hill Bridge · NEWARK-ON-TRENT · Manor Dairy Farm · Coddington · Coddington CE Prim Sch · Moat · Folly House · Coddington Plantation · Emu Lodge Farm · Slaney Lodge Farm · Plots Farm · Barnby in the Willows · Theatre · Highfields Sch · Corner Farm · Hope House School · Greenhill Farm · Windmill · Hill Farm · Hilltop Farm · Moor Farm · Grange Farm · Fen Farm · Cross Farm · Magnus CE Acad · Highfields Sch · The Newark Academy · Cricket Club · John Hunt Prim Sch · Chuter Ede Prim Sch · Field House Farm · Willow Farm · Bleak House Farm · Shire Dyke · New Balderton · Balderton · Bow Bridge · Quarry (Gypsum) · Sewage Works · Broad Fen Farm · Holme Barn Farm · Odd House Farm · Cross Lane Farm · The Suthers Sch

A2
1 NELSON RD
2 RICHMOND CL
3 KEW GDNS
4 COLEMAN AVE
5 ANDERSON CL
6 YARNSWORTH RD
7 COTTON DR
8 RADDLE WAY
9 CHARTERS DR

A6
1 WHEATSHEAF AVE
2 EMMENDINGEN AVE
3 BARROWS GATE
4 LINCOLN CT
5 SPIRE GDNS
6 CHESTNUT AVENUE
7 GAINSBOROUGH DRIVE
8 CEDAR AVENUE
9 MOUNTNEY PLACE
10 FLEMING DR
11 NORMAN AVE
12 PINE CL
13 PRIMROSE AVE
14 HOLLIES AVE
15 LINSEED AVE
16 EDWARD JERMYN DR
17 JOHN POPE WAY
18 HALLIWELL CL
19 BARLEY WAY
20 HATCHET'S LA
21 TERRY AVE

C1
1 DALE CRES
2 READ CL
3 BLACKBERRY WY
4 YOUNGS AVE
5 PINE CL
6 JOHNSONS RD
7 GARDINER AVE
8 CAMDALE CL
9 SPRING DR
10 THOMAS RD
11 EASTERN DR
12 SOUTHY RD
13 CAMERON LA
14 PINE CL
15 TOWNHILL SQ
16 CARNELL LA
17 DALE WY
18 GILMORES LA
19 COLLINSON LA
20 PHOENIX CL
21 DEEKE RD
22 SPRING DR
23 WISDOM CL
24 TOWNHILL SQ
25 BLACKBERRY RD
26 OAKFIELD RD
27 ROSEFIELD CL
28 GILBERT WAY
29 MARRON CL
30 PACH WAY
31 APPLE AVE
32 GOODWIN LA
33 WILLIAMS LA

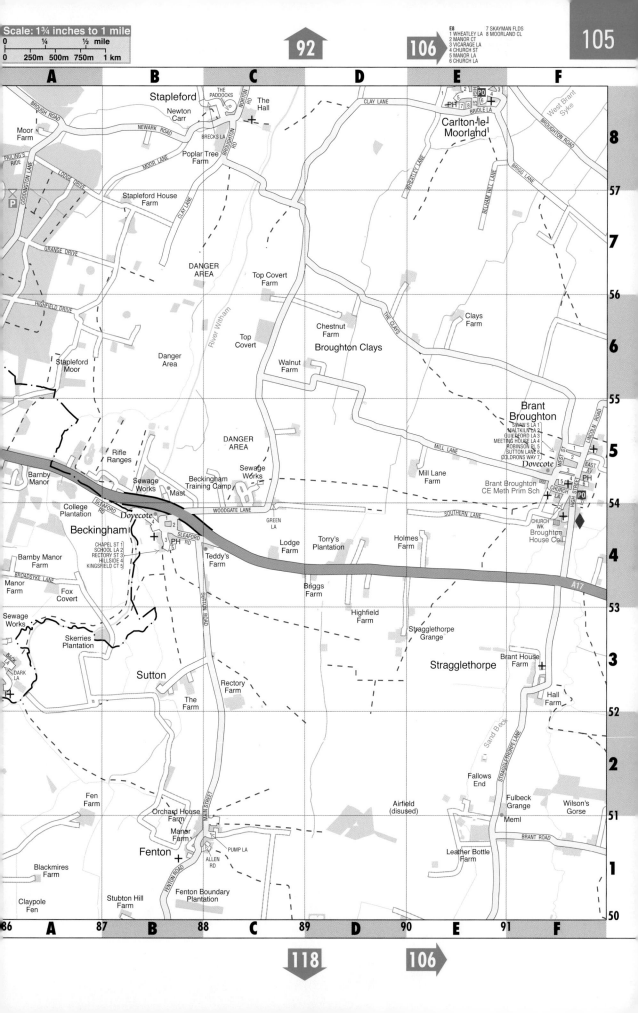

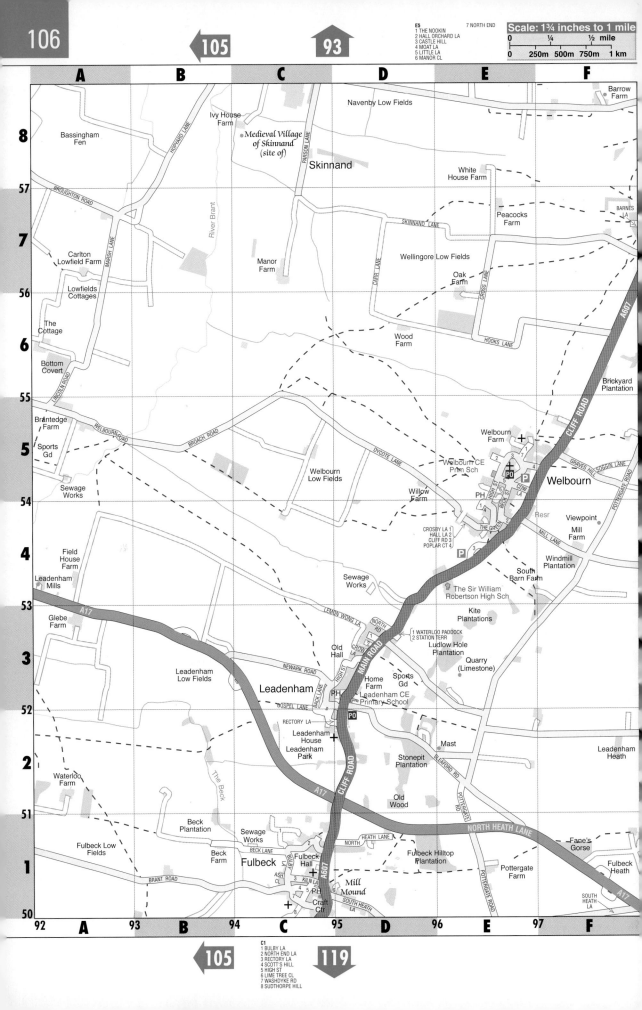

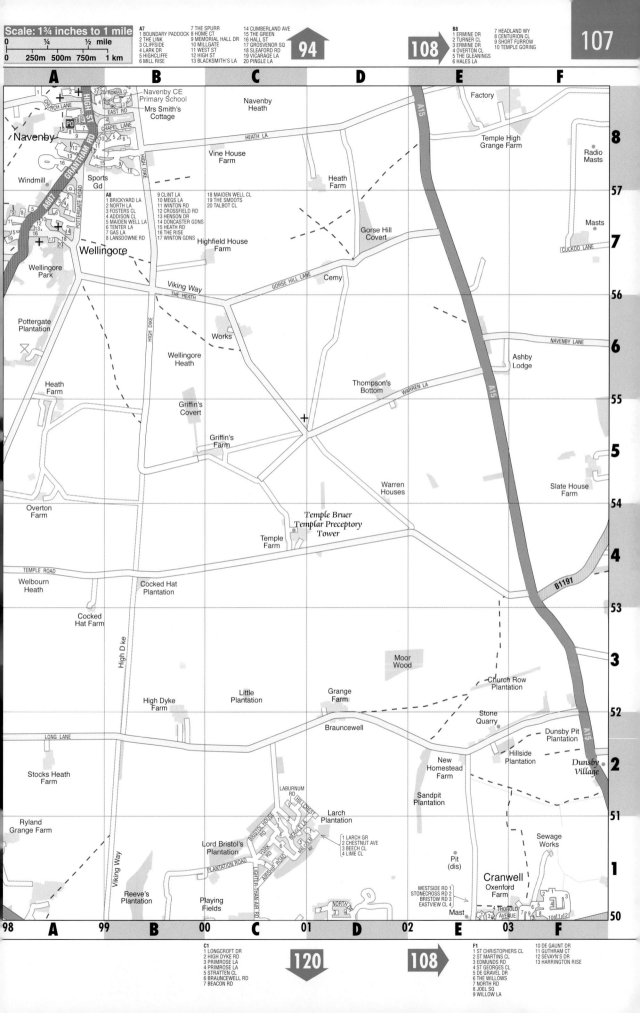

Scale: 1¾ inches to 1 mile

| 0 | ¼ | ½ mile |
| 0 | 250m | 500m | 750m | 1 km |

94
108

Navenby CE Primary School
Navenby Heath
Mrs Smith's Cottage
Factory
Temple High Grange Farm
Radio Masts

Navenby
Windmill
Sports Gd
Vine House Farm
Heath Farm
Masts

Wellingore
Highfield House Farm
Gorse Hill Covert
CUCKOO LANE

Wellingore Park
Pottergate Plantation
Viking Way
THE HEATH
Gorse Hill Lane
Cemy
Navenby Lane
Ashby Lodge

Works
Wellingore Heath
Thompson's Bottom
WARREN LA

Heath Farm
Griffin's Covert
Griffin's Farm
Warren Houses
Slate House Farm

Overton Farm
Temple Bruer Templar Preceptory Tower
Temple Farm

TEMPLE ROAD
Welbourn Heath
Cocked Hat Plantation
B1191

Cocked Hat Farm
High Dyke
Moor Wood
Church Row Plantation

High Dyke Farm
Little Plantation
Grange Farm
Stone Quarry
Dunsby Pit Plantation

LONG LANE
Brauncewell
Hillside Plantation
Dunsby Village

Stocks Heath Farm
New Homestead Farm
Sandpit Plantation

Ryland Grange Farm
Laburnum Rd
Larch Plantation
Sewage Works

Viking Way
Lord Bristol's Plantation
1 LARCH GR
2 CHESTNUT AVE
3 BEECH CL
4 LIME CL
Pit (dis)
Cranwell
Oxenford Farm

PLANTATION ROAD
Reeve's Plantation
Playing Fields
WESTSIDE RD 1
STONECROSS RD 2
BRISTOW RD 3
EASTVIEW CL 4
NORTH...
Mast

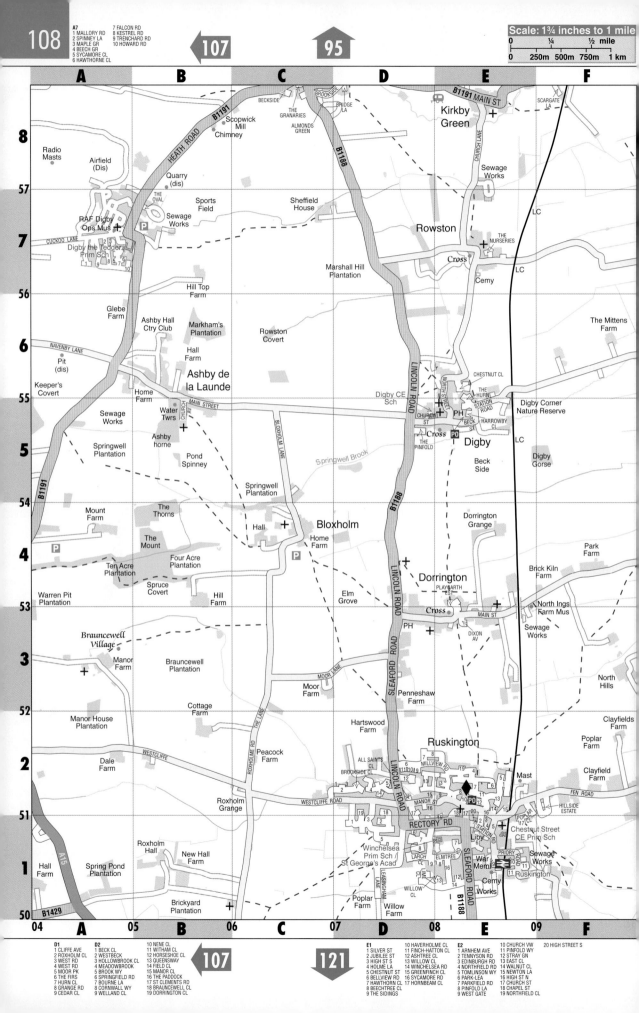

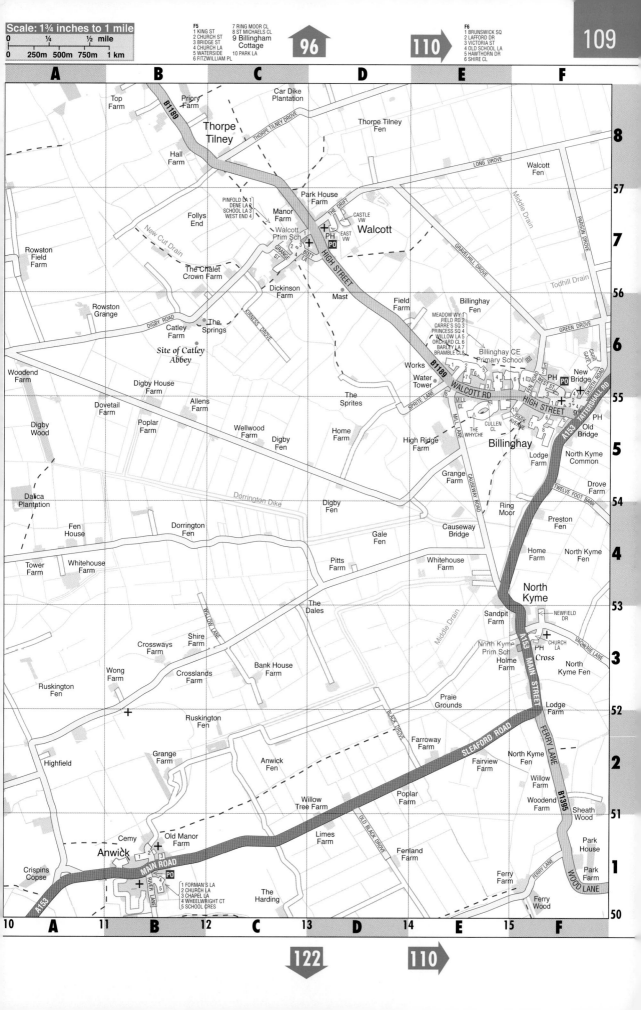

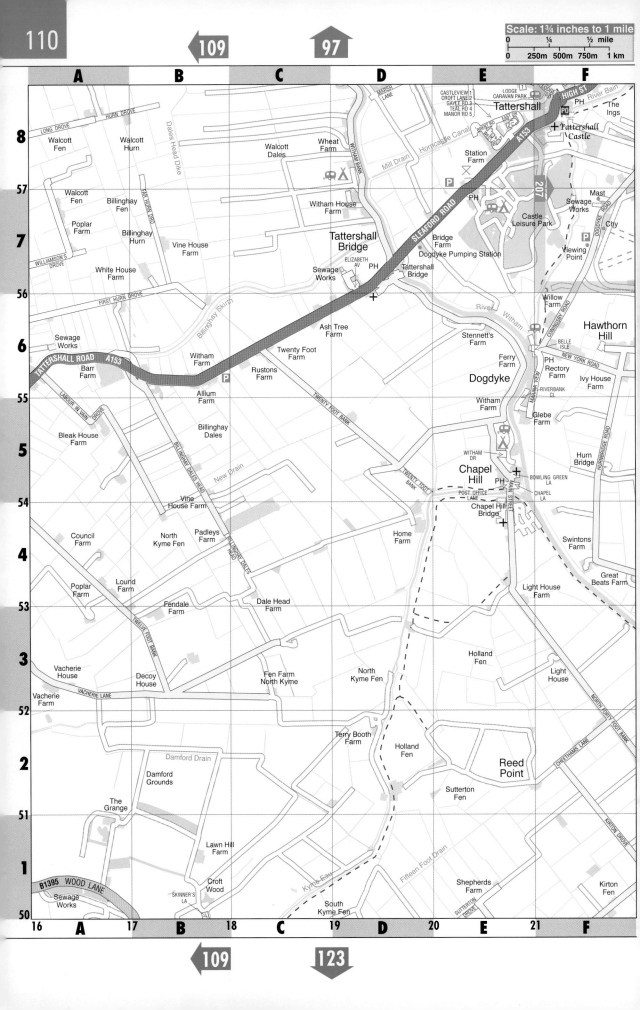

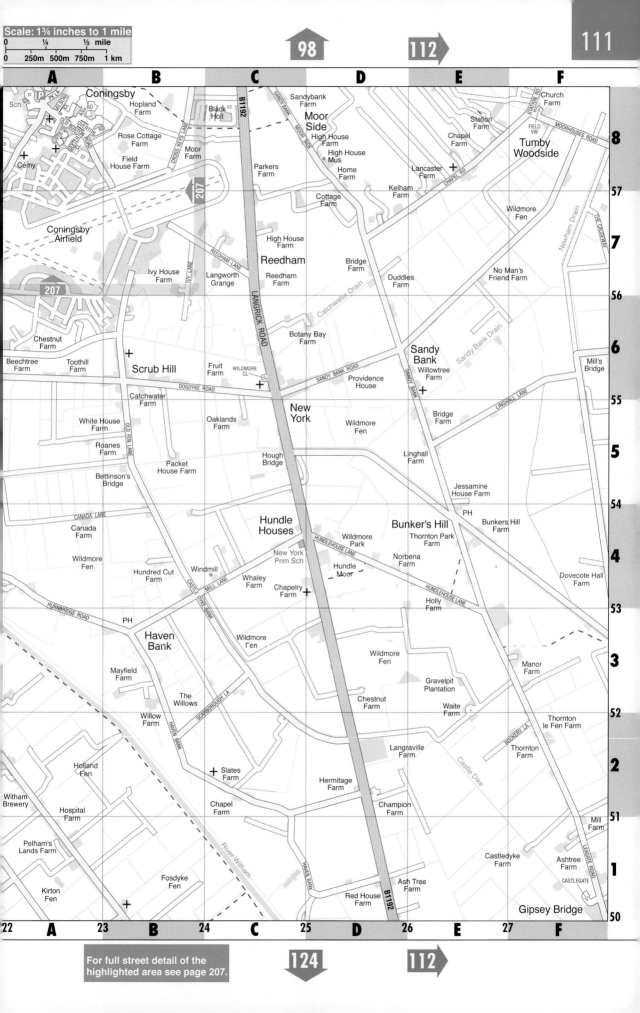

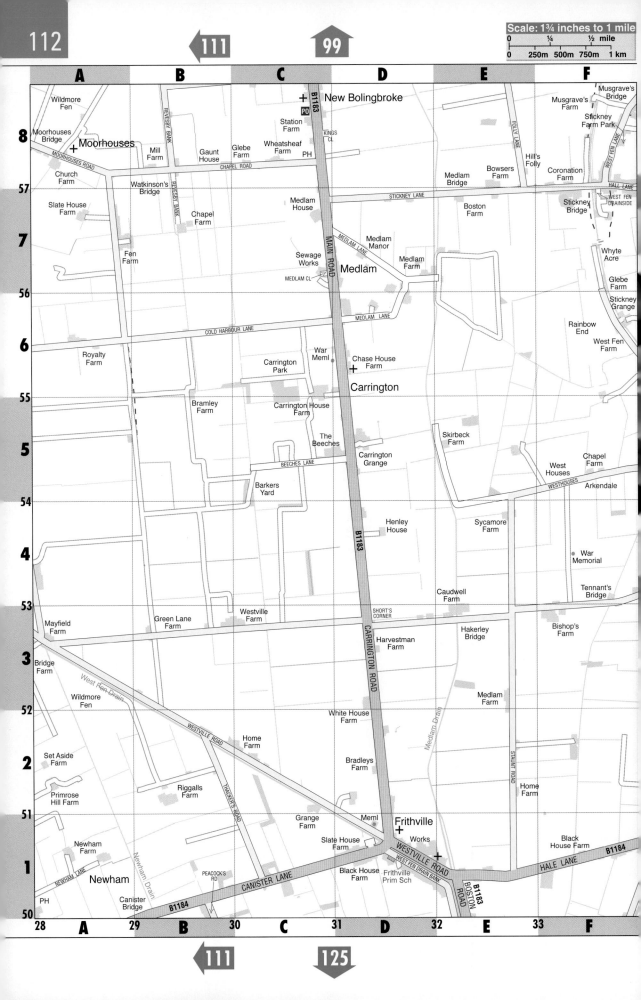

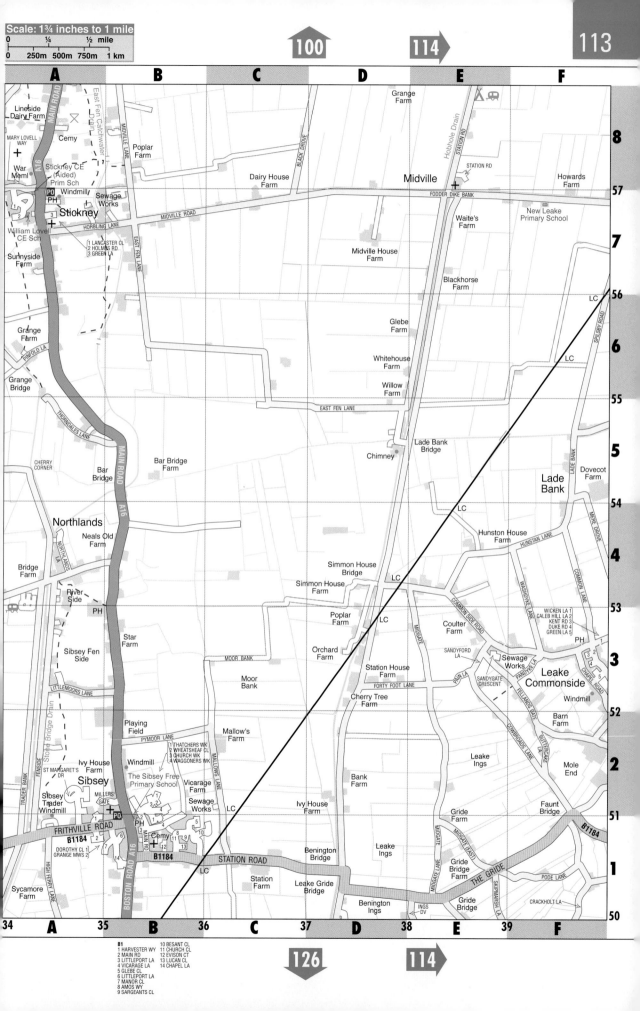

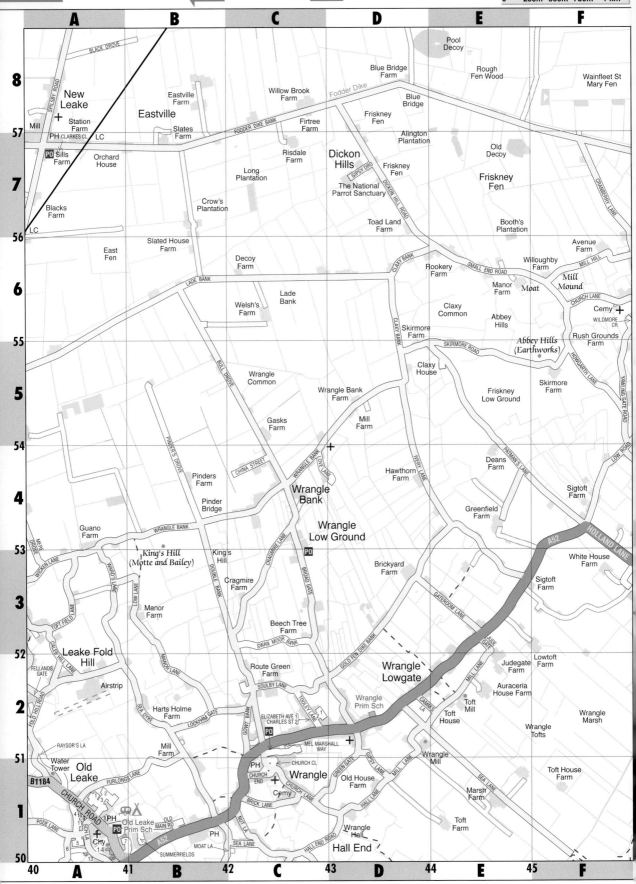

114

113

101

Scale: 1¾ inches to 1 mile

0   ¼   ½ mile
0   250m 500m 750m 1 km

A   B   C   D   E   F

8

BLACK DROVE

Pool
Decoy

Blue Bridge
Farm

Rough
Fen Wood

Wainfleet St
Mary Fen

New
Leake

Eastville
Farm

Willow Brook
Farm

Fodder Dike

Blue
Bridge

Eastville

Slates
Farm

57

Station
Farm

FODDER DIKE BANK

Firtree
Farm

Friskney
Fen

Alington
Plantation

Old
Decoy

PH CLARKES CL   LC

Risdale
Farm

Dickon
Hills

PO Sills
Farm

Orchard
House

Long
Plantation

GIPSY DRO

Friskney
Fen

Friskney
Fen

7

Crow's
Plantation

The National
Parrot Sanctuary

DICKON HILL ROAD

Booth's
Plantation

Blacks
Farm

Toad Land
Farm

Avenue
Farm

LC

56

East
Fen

Slated House
Farm

Decoy
Farm

CLAXY BANK

Rookery
Farm

SMALL END ROAD

Willoughby
Farm

MILL HILL

Mill
Mound

LADE BANK

Lade
Bank

Manor
Farm

Moat

CHURCH LANE

Cemy

6

Welsh's
Farm

Claxy
Common

Abbey
Hills

WILDMORE
CR

Rush Grounds
Farm

55

CLAXY BANK

Skirmore
Farm

SKIRMORE ROAD

Abbey Hills
(Earthworks)

Skirmore
Farm

HOWGARTH LANE

YAWLING GATE ROAD

BULL DROVE

Wrangle
Common

Wrangle Bank
Farm

Claxy
House

Friskney
Low Ground

5

Gasks
Farm

Mill
Farm

PINDER'S DROVE

CHINA STREET

Deans
Farm

PATMAN'S LANE

Sigtoft
Farm

54

Pinders
Farm

WRANGLE BANK

LOVE LANE

Hawthorn
Farm

IVERY LANE

LOW ROAD

Pinder
Bridge

Wrangle
Bank

4

Guano
Farm

WRANGLE BANK

Wrangle
Low Ground

Greenfield
Farm

A52

HOLLAND LANE

MERE DROVE

King's Hill
(Motte and Bailey)

King's
Hill

DOUBLE BANK

CRAGMIRE LANE

PO

Brickyard
Farm

White House
Farm

53

WICKEN LANE

WARD'S LANE

Cragmire
Farm

BROAD GATE

CATEROOM LANE

Sigtoft
Farm

3

TOFT FIELD LANE

LOW LANE

Manor
Farm

Beech Tree
Farm

JUDE GATE

MILL LANE

Lowtoft
Farm

52

Leake Fold
Hill

MANOR LANE

SWAN MOOR BANK

Route Green
Farm

SOULBY LANE

GOLD FEN DIKE BANK

Wrangle
Lowgate

Judegate
Farm

Auraceria
House Farm

FELLANDS
GATE

FOLD HILL ROAD

CALEB HILL LANE

Airstrip

Harts Holme
Farm

SEA DYKE

LOCKRAM GATE

GOWT BANK

TOOLEY LANE

Wrangle
Prim Sch

CAMMS LA

Toft
House

Toft
Mill

Wrangle
Marsh

2

RAYSOR'S LA

ELIZABETH AVE 1
CHARLES ST 2

PO

MEL MARSHALL
WAY

Wrangle
Tofts

Water
Tower

Old
Leake

Mill
Farm

FURLONGS LANE

PH

CHURCH CL

GREEN GATE

GIPSY LANE

MILL LANE

Wrangle
Mill

SEA LANE

Toft House
Farm

51

B1184

CHURCH
END

Wrangle

Old House
Farm

Marsh
Farm

CHURCH ROAD

PODE LANE

Cemy

CHURCH LANE

HALL LANE

Toft
Farm

Old Leake
Prim Sch

BRICK LANE

NUT LA

SEA LANE

Wrangle
Hall

Chy

PH

PH

MOAT LA

HALL END ROAD

Hall End

1

SUMMERFIELDS

A52

50

40   A   41   B   42   C   43   D   44   E   45   F

A1
1 BERT ALLEN DR
2 ST MARY'S WY
3 LIME CL
4 HAWTHORN RD
5 POPLAR CT
6 SOUTHFIELD LA
7 MEADOW WY
8 VICARAGE GDNS
9 LIME WALK
10 TILIA GR
11 HAWTHORN CRES
12 GILES CL
13 WOODLAND CL
14 The Giles Academy

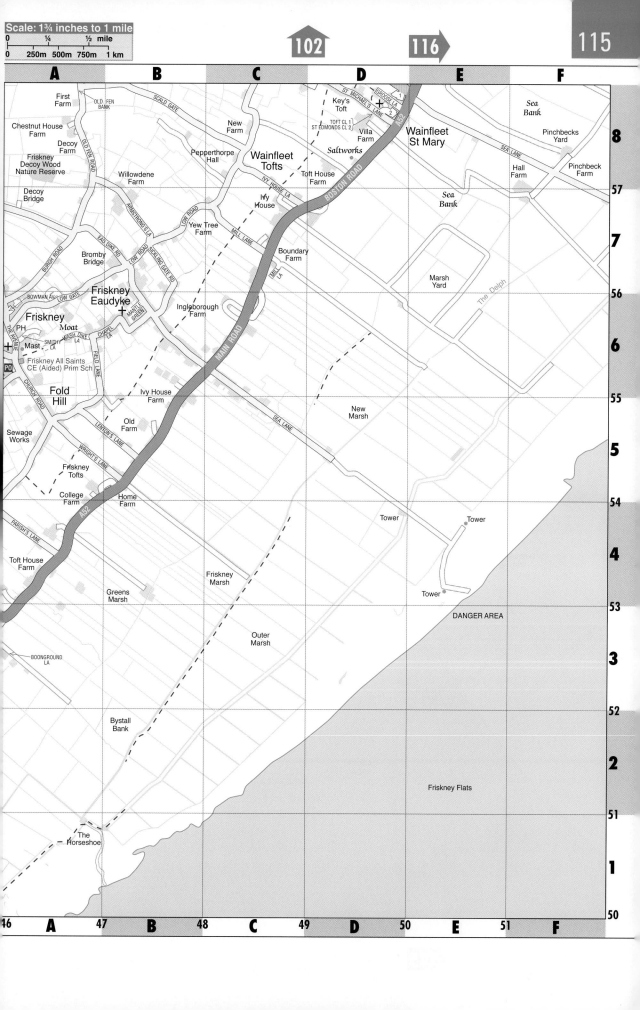

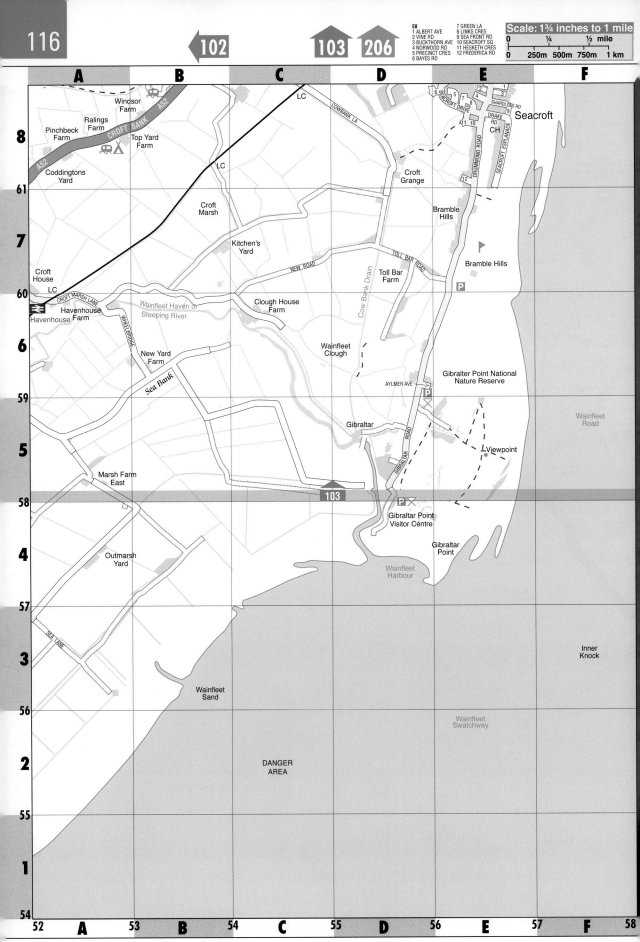

102

103 206

E8
1 ALBERT AVE
2 VINE RD
3 BUCKTHORN AVE
4 NORWOOD RD
5 PRECINCT CRES
6 BAYES RD
7 GREEN LA
8 LINKS CRES
9 SEA FRONT RD
10 SEACROFT SQ
11 HESKETH CRES
12 FREDERICA RD

Scale: 1¾ inches to 1 mile
0 ¼ ½ mile
0 250m 500m 750m 1 km

Windsor Farm
Pinchbeck Farm
Ralings Farm
CROFT BANK
A52
Top Yard Farm
Coddingtons Yard
A52
Croft House
LC
Havenhouse
Havenhouse Farm
CROFT MARSH LANE
WHEEL BRIDGE
New Yard Farm
Sea Bank
Marsh Farm East
Outmarsh Yard
SEA LANE

LC
COWBANK LA
LC
Croft Marsh
Kitchen's Yard
NEW ROAD
Clough House Farm
Wainfleet Haven or Steeping River
Wainfleet Clough
Cow Bank Drain
Gibraltar
103
Wainfleet Sand

Croft Grange
Bramble Hills
TOLL BAR ROAD
Toll Bar Farm
P
Gibralter Point National Nature Reserve
AYLMER AVE
P
GIBRALTAR ROAD
Viewpoint
103
P
Gibraltar Point Visitor Centre
Gibraltar Point
Wainfleet Harbour

SEACROFT DRIVE
SHARDLOES RD
DRUMMOND ROAD
DRAKE RD
CH
SEACROFT ESPLANADE
Seacroft
Bramble Hills

Wainfleet Road

Inner Knock

Wainfleet Swatchway

DANGER AREA

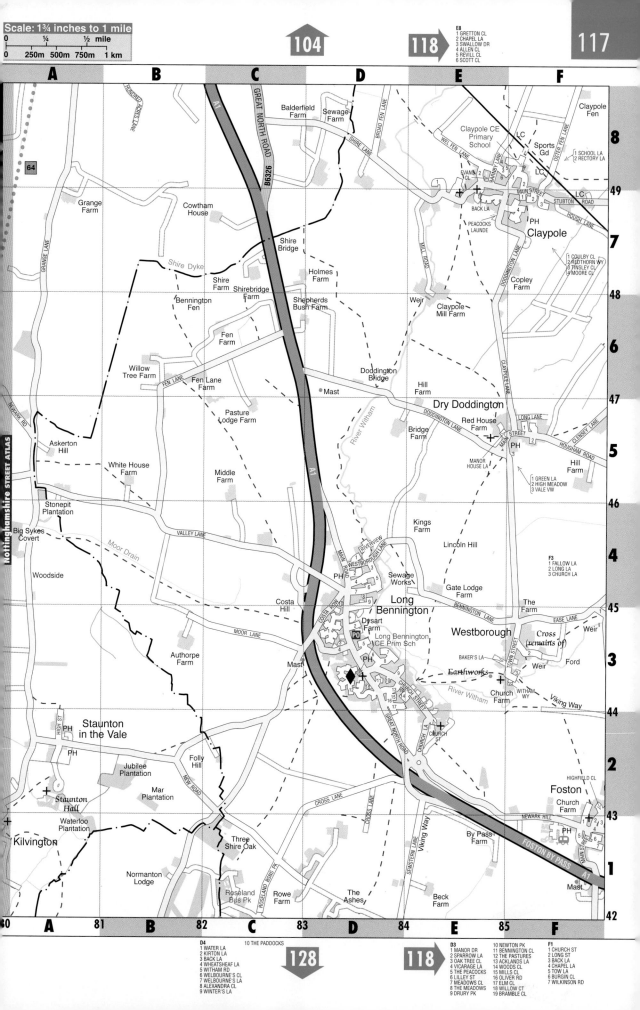

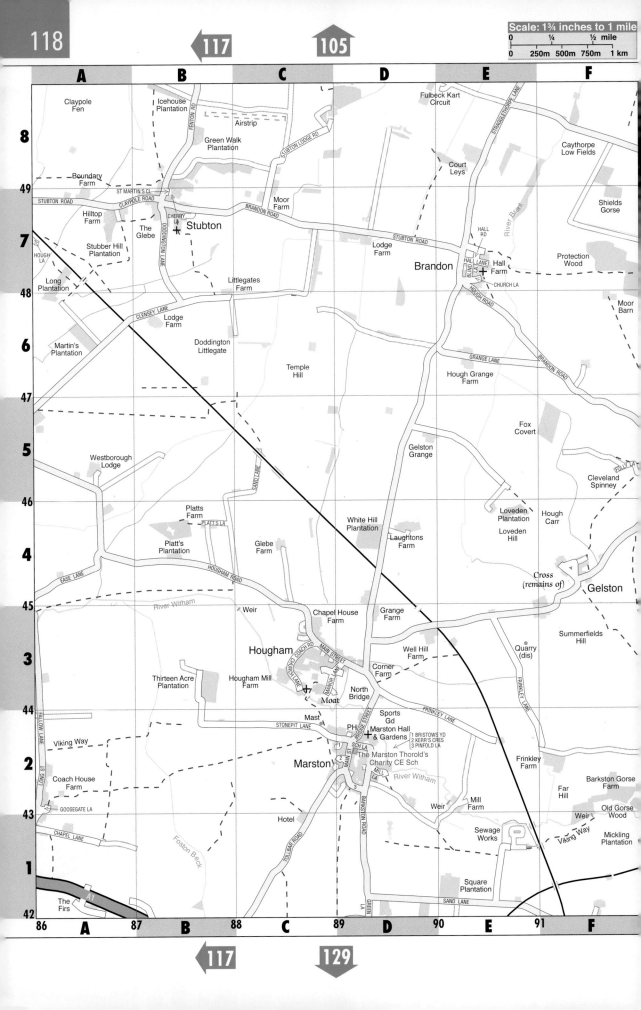

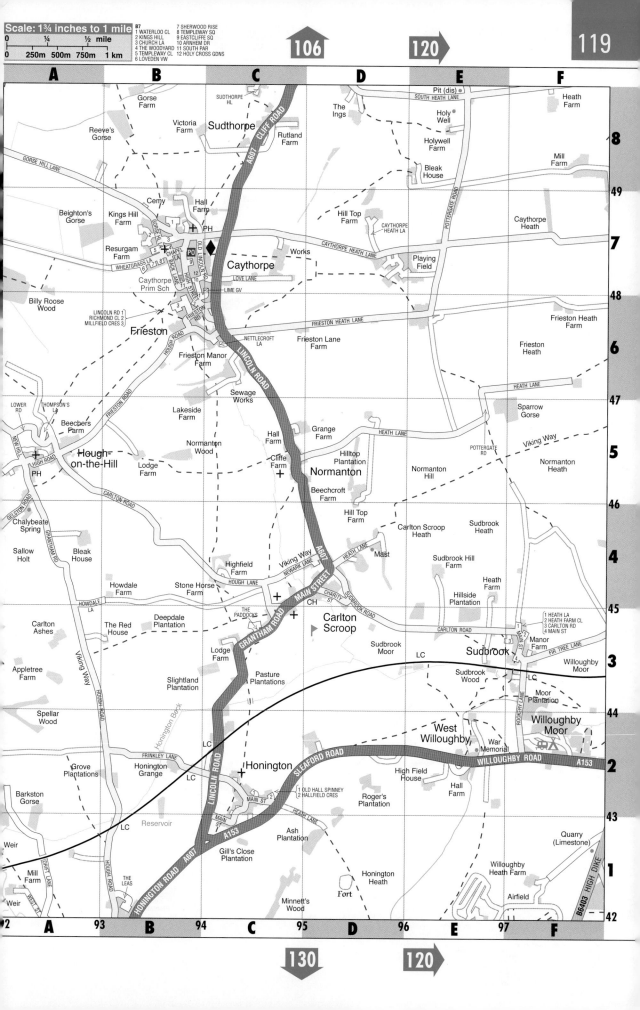

◄ 119
107

C8
1 ST MICHAEL'S WY
2 LIGHTER-THAN-AIR RD
3 LAWRENCE LA
4 ST ANDREW'S WY
5 HEADQUARTERS CR
6 YORK HOUSE RD

7 CENTRAL DR
8 EAST CAMP RD
9 WESTERN DR
10 SCHOOL RD
11 KINGS LA

D8
1 CHERRY TREE CL
2 BAGHDAD RD
3 DELHI SQ
4 EASTCHURCH RD
5 FLOWERDOWN AVE
6 WESTERN APPROACH

E8
1 FRANK WHITTLE CL
2 WESTSIDE RD
3 BRISTOW RD
4 ISON CL
5 THOROLD AVE

F8
1 CRANE CL
2 FARRIERS GATE
3 WILLOW LA
4 HOME PK
5 WYLSON CL
6 OLD SCHOOL LA

Scale: 1¾ inches to 1 mile

0   ¼   ½   mile
0 250m 500m 750m 1 km

A B C D E F

8

A17
High Dike
B1429
The Royal Air Force Coll
Wellesley Wy
Saddle Row
Byard's Leap Farm
Byard's Leap
Junior Cadets Rd
Airmanship Rd
Wellesley South Brick Lines
West Av
South Airfield Road
Paddock Road
Cranes Way
Trenchard Rd
Nursery Road
Mast
Cranwell Avenue B1429
College Road
Cross (restored)
PO Cranwell
The Sidings
Sleaford Rd

49

B6403
Home Park Plantation
Westfield Wood

7

Barns Farm
Viking Way
Cranwell Airfield
Chimney
Raueby La
Westfield Farm

48

Ermine Street Farm
Cranwell Aviation Heritage Centre
Heath Farm
A17
Windmill Plantation

6

Victory Plantation
Rauceby Grange
Burrow's Spinney
Windmill Hill Farm

47

North Rauceby Heath
Medieval Village (site of)
Main Street
North Rauceby

5

Sudbrook House
Woodside Farm
Nature Reserve
High Wood
Cross (restored)
Rauceby CE School
Tom Lane
Tank Plantations

46

Glebe Farm
Resrs
Century Plantation
Glebe Plantation
Lodge Farm
Church Lane
Glebe Farm
Mill Plantation
PH
Rauceby Park
Hall Farm

E4
1 CHAPEL CL
2 BEECH RI
3 SOUTHGATE SPINNEYS

4

Crowland Farm
Main Street
South Rauceby
Cliffe View
Pinfold La
Ash Holt

45

Waterwell Lane
The Moor
Cliff Hill
Rauceby Drive
Sewage Works

3

Pottergate Pit (dis)
PH
Ancaster
LC
Works
Allot Gdns
Sewage Works
Wilsford Moor
Stack Hill
Stackhill Plantation
Cliff Hill Plantation
Cliff Farm
Thorpe Drove
Beck Plantation
Rauceby
LC

44

Cemy
PH
PO
Ancaster CE Prim Sch
Norcliff Spring
Waterloo Farm
South Rauceby Lodge
Rauceby Warren Nature Reserve
Sleaford Golf Course
CH

2

Moor Closes Nature Reserve
A153
Sleaford Road
Ancaster ROMAN TOWN
Ermine Street
Wilsford La
Town End
Back Lane
Hill Top Farm
Main Street
PH
Airstrip (Private)
The Warren
LC
Welby's Holt
The Beck
Wilsford Warren
Grange Farm

KINROSS RD 1
BALMORAL DR 2
LOTHIAN 3

Wks
Lady Well (Spring)
Ancaster Valley Nature Reserve
Pitts Hill Farm
Castle Quarry (Limestone)
Slate House Farm
Medieval Village (site of)
Home Farm
Cemy
PO
P
Sewage Works
Kelby Farm

43

B6403
Pits Hills Plantation
Wilsford
Heath Lane
Kelby Rd
School
Wilsford Heath
1 ST MARY'S CL
2 MYERS CL
Kelby Plantation
Walks Road

1

King Street
High Dike
Duke's Covert Nature Reserve
Valley Farm
Willoughby Walks

42

98   99   00   01   02   03

A B C D E F

◄ 119
131

A2
1 WATER LA
2 SAXON WY
3 MERCIA DR
4 HILLSIDE
5 ANGEL CT
6 PADDOCK CL
7 ROMAN WY
8 FLAMINIAN WY
9 CHURCH LA

10 WILLOUGHBY RD

A3
1 FIR TREE LA
2 NORTH DR
3 WEST VW
4 ST MARTIN'S WY
5 ERMINE CL
6 STATION APP
7 BROOKSIDE CL
8 BROOKSIDE
9 MEADOWBROOK

10 ARNE CL
11 CHARLES AVE
12 CHARLESTOWN
13 MINERVA CL

F3
1 GLENEAGLES DR
2 TROON CT
3 MURRAYFIELD AVE
4 TURNBERRY CL

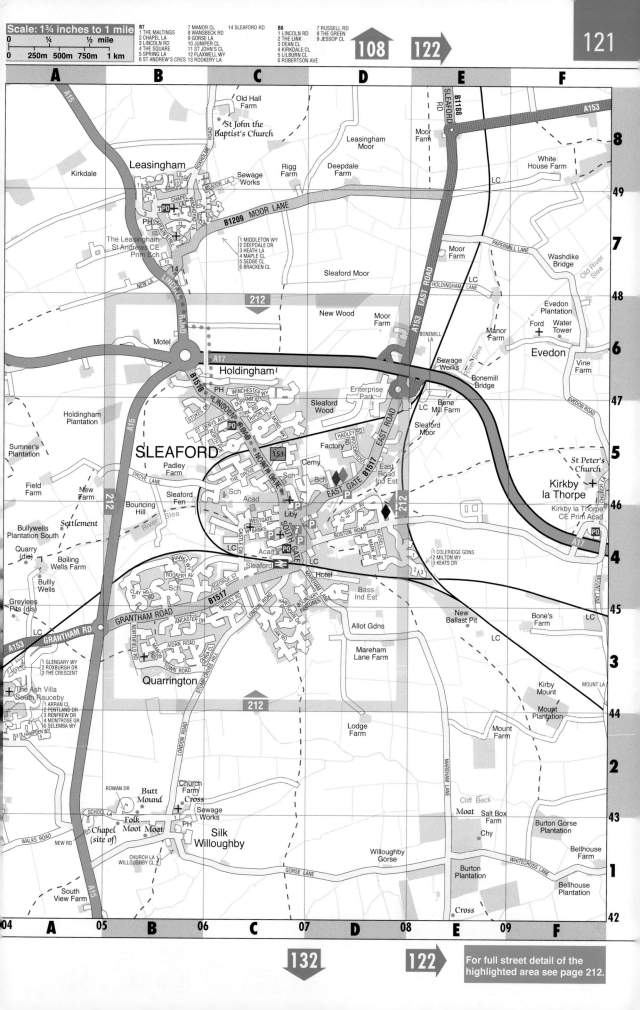

A17

A153

Row 8 area:
Haverholme Bridge
Sewage Works
Weir
Haverholme Park Farm
Haverholme Wood
Haverholme Priory
Site of St Mary's Priory
River Slea
Cobbler's Lock
Anwick Fen
Anwick Fen
Ewerby Pond Nature Reserve
Ewerby Waithe Common
Twelve Drain Bridge
Black Drove
South Kyme Fen

Haverholme Park
Evedon Wood

Evedon Mill
Mill Farm
Park Lane
Field La
Main St
Ewerby Thorpe
Ewerby Thorpe Farm
Ewerby
Church La
PH
Clay Pit La
Thorpe Road
Ewerby Fen
Fox Covert
Hodge Drain
Westmorelands

Kirkby Road
Ewerby Road
Church Lane
Bargate Hill
Fox Covert
Asgarby Road
Orchard Farm
New Wood
Howell Fen
Howell
Hall Farm
Cross
Boughton Plantation
Howell Fen Drove
Howell Fen
Walks Farm
Howell Fen Drove

Boughton
Grange Farm
Asgarby
Heckington Eau
Star Fen

A17
Fox Hall Farm
The Beck Beck
Red Roof Farm
Wash Dike
Washdike Bridge
Winkhill
Sewage Works
Court Row Farm
Littleworth Drove
Decoy Farm
Hall Farm

LC
Sewage Works
Sardesons Farm
Meeds Farm
Westfield Farm
LC
B1394
Heckington St Andrew's CE Sch
Heckington
Foster
Handle
Howell Road
Kyme Road
A17

Beacon Hill
Mount La
Grange Farm
Lodge Farm
Burton Road
Sleaford Road
Windmill
Churchill Wy
PO
High St
Boston Road
B1394
Cemy
Pea Room Craft Ctr & Heckington Village Trust Station Mus
Heckington
LC
South View Farm
Station Rd
Heckington Windmill
LC
LC
Rookery Farm
LC

Asgarby Road
Heckington Road
OATFIELD WY 1
MAYFLOWER DR 2
BARLEY CL 3
STIRLING CT 4
LAMBOURNE WY 5
Cottage Farm
Grove St
PO
Great Hale
Leas Road

Whitecross Lane
Burton Farm
Meadow Farm
HECKINGTON RD
PH
Church Farm
Cemy
Crow Lane
Beckstone Bridge
1 CHAPEL LA
2 HALL PK

Brackenbury Bridge
Scredington Road
Burton Pedwardine
Moat
Helpringham Road
Hercocks Farm
Reservoir
Highfields Farm
Hill Top Farm
Artesian Well (dis)
CHURCH ST 1
CHURCH LA 2
ORCHARD CL 3
THE PADDOCKS 4
Main Lt Hale Rd
B1394
Burton Road

D3
1 COLBY WY
2 HUBBARD CL
3 OAK WY
4 SCOGGINS WY
5 CHURCHVIEW CL
6 ALLISON RD
7 BEECH CL
8 POTESGRAVE WY
9 BECKETT CL
10 NORRIS CL
11 MULBERRY WK
12 MAPLE GR
13 RICHARDS CL
14 SKELTON CL
15 WOODMANS CL

E2
1 LIMETREE WK
2 BRAMLEY CL
3 SHRUBWOOD CL
4 BANKS LA
5 NEW ST
6 MILLERS WY
7 WELLINGTON CL
8 INGLEDEW CL
9 HARE CL
10 POCKLINGTON WY
11 MILLVIEW RD
12 ORCHARD DR
13 WINDMILL DR
14 QUEEN'S RD
15 MAGNA CRES
16 HIGH ST
17 OXBY CL
18 NASH CL

E3
1 HOULDEN WY
2 COWGATE
3 VICARAGE RD
4 CAMERON ST
5 CHRISTOPHER CL
6 CHURCH ST
7 MANOR ST
8 ST ANDREW'S ST
9 EASTGATE
10 WILLOW CL
11 COBHAM CL
12 LATIMER GDNS
13 ROYAL OAK CT

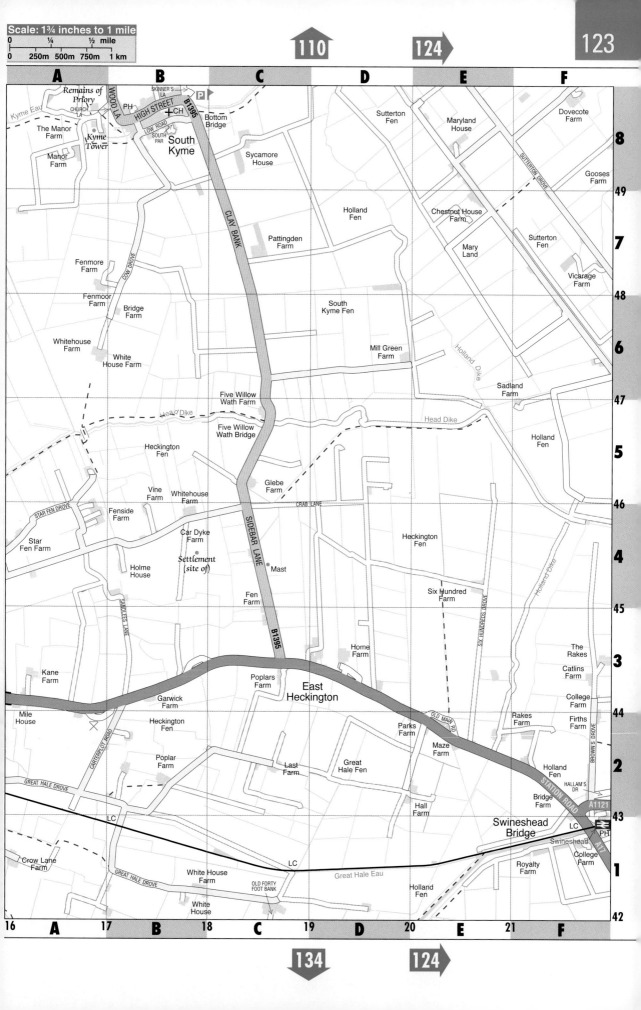

123
111

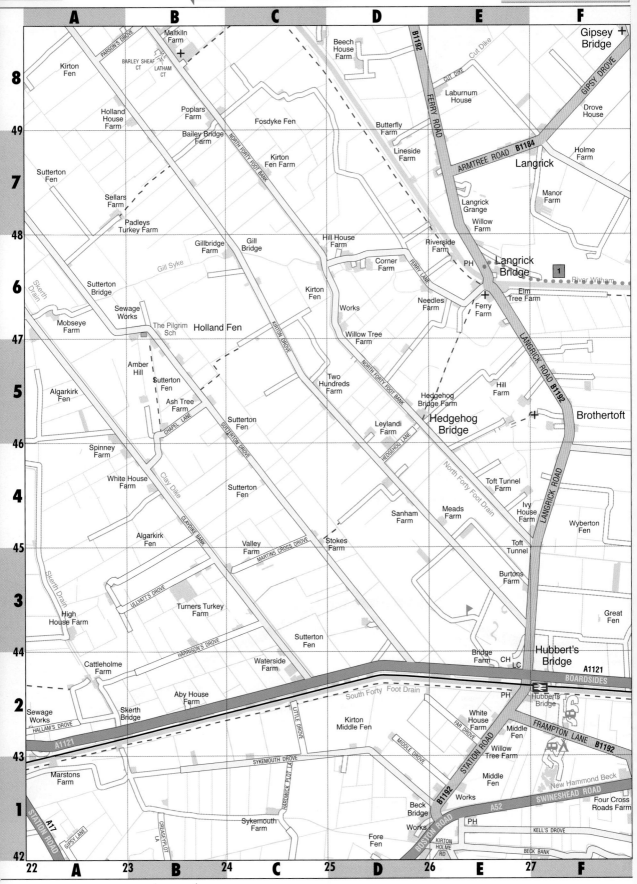

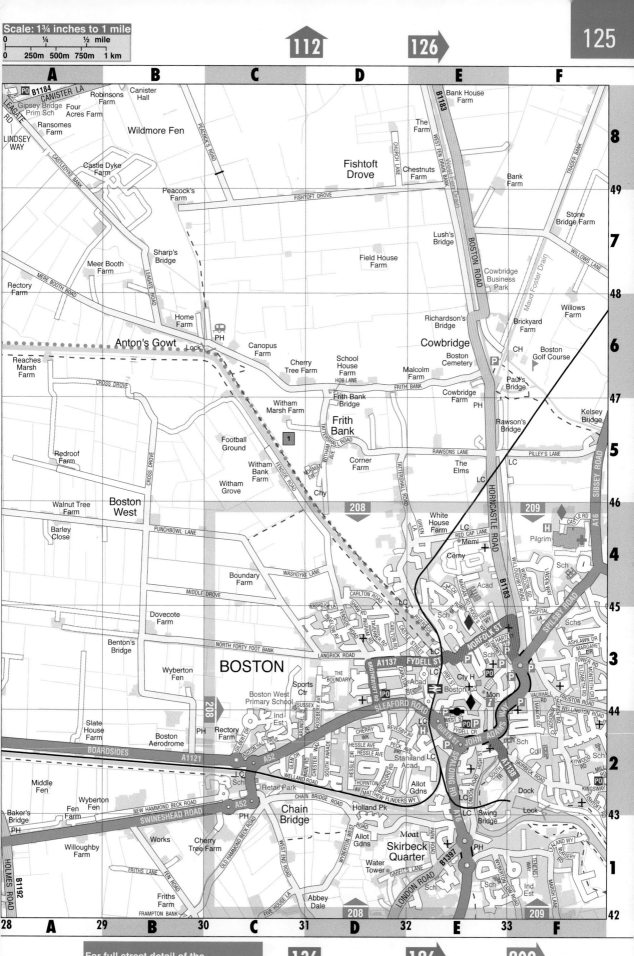

Scale: 1¾ inches to 1 mile

A · B · C · D · E · F

8 · 49 · 7 · 48 · 6 · 47 · 5 · 46 · 4 · 45 · 3 · 44 · 2 · 43 · 1 · 42

B1184
Canister La
Gipsey Bridge Prim Sch
Robinsons Farm
Canister Hall
Four Acres Farm
Ransomes Farm
Lindsey Way
Leagate Rd
Castledyke Bank
Castle Dyke Farm
Wildmore Fen
Peacock's Road
Peacock's Farm
Fishtoft Drove
Church Lane
Chestnuts Farm
The Farm
B1183
West Fen Drain Bank
Bank House Farm
Bank Farm
Trader Bank
Willows Lane
Sharp's Bridge
Meer Booth Farm
Mere Booth Road
Leagate Road
Home Farm
PH
Lush's Bridge
Field House Farm
Boston Road
Cowbridge Business Park
Stone Bridge Farm
Willows Farm
Maud Foster Drain
Rectory Farm
Reaches Marsh Farm
Anton's Gowt
Lock
Cross Drove
Canopus Farm
Cherry Tree Farm
School House Farm
HOB LANE
Malcolm Farm
Cowbridge
Boston Cemetery
P
CH
Boston Golf Course
Richardson's Bridge
Brickyard Farm
Kelsey Bridge
Redroof Farm
Witham Marsh Farm
Frith Bank
Frith Bank Bridge
Frith Bank
Cowbridge Farm
PH
Paul's Bridge
Rawson's Bridge
Football Ground
1
Frith Bank
Tattershall Ave
Witham Road
Corner Farm
Rawsons Lane
Pilley's Lane
Sibsey Road
Walnut Tree Farm
Boston West
Witham Bank Farm
Fenside Road
Norman Dr
Chy
Witham Grove
Tattershall Road
The Elms
LC
LC
Barley Close
Punchbowl Lane
208
White House Farm
209
A16
Castle Rd
Pilgrim
H
Boundary Farm
Washdyke Lane
Middle Drove
Carlton Road
LC
Green La
Meml
Cemy
Acad
B1183
Linden Wn
Willoughby Road
Sch
Dovecote Farm
Benton's Bridge
North Forty Foot Bank
Langrick Road
Washd'ke La
Sibsey Rd
Taverner Rd
Castle Street
Riverside
LC
Sch
Friar
Horncastle Road
Hospital
Spilsby Road
Schs
Ashlawn Dr
Margaret Dr
Wyberton Fen
BOSTON
Sports Ctr
THE BOUNDARY
Brothertoft Rd
A1137
FYDELL ST
Carlton Rd
Acad
Boston
Cty H
Mon
i
Norfolk St
Thanrey
Hartley
P
P
Tower Rd
Elizabeth Rd
Monteith Dr
Slate House Farm
Boston West Primary School
Ashton Drive
Gilbert Dr
Ind Est
Rectory Farm
PH
Sussex Av
Roseberry Ave
Acad
Boston
West St
P
PO
P
Sleaford Road
John Adams Wy
P
Vauxhall Rd
Wellington Road
Freiston Road
Middle Fen
Wyberton Fen Farm
New Hammond Beck Road
Glen Dr
Barn Rd
Chester Way
South Parade
Welland Road
Cherry Wk
Hessle Dr
Hessle Ave
Peck Av
Staniland Acad
Allot Gdns
Queen's Rd
LC
H
Spalding Rd
John Adams Wy
Skirbeck Road
Sch
Kitwood Rd
Makro Rd
Mill
Baker's Bridge
PH
Swineshead Road
Boston Aerodrome
A1121
BOARDSIDES
A52
A52
LC
Sch
Retail Park
Chain Bridge Road
Thornton Av
Matthew Flinders Wy
Holland Pk
London Road
A16
Kingsway
PO
Dock
Swing Bridge
Lock
Willoughby Farm
Works
Cherry Tree Farm
Friths Lane
Fen Road
Old Hammond Beck Road
West End Road
Wyberton West Road
Chain Bridge
Allot Gdns
Water Tower
Moat
Skirbeck Quarter
Garfit's Lane
B1397
Fydell Cr
PH
Wyberton Low Road
Marsh Lane
Lenland Wy
Nursery
Tenens Wy
Ind Est
209
Holmes Road
B1192
Friths Farm
Frampton Bank
Five House La
Abbey Dale

For full street detail of the highlighted area see pages 208 & 209.

Scale: 1¾ inches to 1 mile
0   ¼   ½ mile
0   250m 500m 750m 1 km

A B C D E F

8

High Ferry Lane
Holly Farm
Suttling Dales Lane
Highferry Farm
LC
Irelands Farm
Hobhole Bank
Benington Ings
Ings Road
Skipmarsh La
Crackholt Farm
Skipmarsh Farm
Gride Bank
Moulton Chantry House
Crack Holt La

49

Hurn Lane
LC
Boston Road
A16
Orchard Farm
Limes Farm
Freiston Ings
Hobhole Drain
Ivy House Farm
Leverton Ings
Rookery Farm
Ings Bank
Ings Lane
Cottage Farm
Ings Farm

7

Hilldyke Farm
Willows Lane
Pimlico House
LC
Bank House Farm
Ings Drive
Butterwick Ings
Peartree Farm
Mast
Sewage Works
Lenton's Lane
Leverton
Lacey's Dr 1
Lacey's Cl 2
Meadow Bank 3
Goldson's La 4
Middlemere Bank

48

LC
Sibsey Drain Bank
Freiston Ings Farm
Ings Bank
Ings Farm
Ings Bridge
Butterwick Ings Farm
Lacey's Lane
Willows Farm
A52
West End

6

Hurn House Farm
A16
Hilldyke
Boston Long Hedges
Boston Long Hedges
Long Hedges
Bridge Ings
Hobhole Farm
Double Bank
Lowfields Road
Fendyke End Lane
Bars Lane
Guide Post Farm

47

Sibsey Road
Mastins Farm
Cowbridge Drain
Baker's Bridge
Lowfields Lane
White House Farm
Shanks La
Starfleet's Lane
Bay Hall
Bede Cr
Benington

5

Mastin's Bridge
Bank House Farm
Round House
Dotam's Lane
Weirs Farm
Swanhole Lane
Weirs Lane
Lowfields Lane
Windmill
Guide Post Farm

46

209
Burton Corner
Shortfield Lane
Oak House Farm
Haltoft End
Homers Lane
Brand End
Windmill
Butterwick Road
Benington Farm

4

A52
Wainfleet Rd
Willoughby Hills
Baker's Lane
Acorn Cl
Oak House La
PH
Forge Cl
Spittal Hill Road
Foxhole Lane
Works
Old Post Office La
Peter Paine Cl
Butterwick

45

PH
Wainfleet Road
Haltoft End Bridge
Jolly Farmer La
Jolly Farmer Bank
Freiston Centre for Environmental Education
Haltoft End Est
The Butterwick Pinchbeck's Endowed CE Prim Sch
School Lane
Brand End Rd
PO
Benington Road
PH
Watery Lane
Vinters Wy
Sea Lane

3

Blackthorn La
Ings Road
Rochford Tower Lane
Rochford Tower
Campbell Cl
Sewage Works
Hobhole Drain
Playing Field
Girls School La
Doves Lane
Warren Lodge Farm

44

PO
Eastwood Road
Kenleigh Dr
Clifton Road
Ward Cr
Priory Ct
209
Priory Road
Freiston Bridge
Works PH
Park La
Freiston
PO
Church End Farm
White Loaf Hall

Meridian Rd
Churchill Drive
Smalley Rd
Sch
Church Green Road
Wytnes Lane
Bull Pasture
PH
Church Shore Road
VW

2

Wellington Road
Woodthorpe Ave
Winslow Rd
Kingsway
The Ch
Toot Lane
Bladon Estate
The Grange
Shore Road
Jail Lane
Cold Harbour Farm

Skirbeck
Toot Farm
White End Lane

43

River Wy
Mapl Rd
Powell's St
Fishtoft Road
Scotia Wy
Clamp Gate Bridge
Church End Rd
Coupledyke Hall
Windmill
Freiston Shore

1

The Haven
Works
Chy
Ivy Farm
Scott Rd
Playing Field
Campgate Road
Manor Grange
Fishtoft
Fishtoft Acad
Tamworth Green
Barneyfield Road
Broderfield Lane
Cropper's La
The Farm
Shore Road
Plummers Land Farm
P
Hotel

42

34   35   36   37   38   39

C1
1 ST GUTHLAC'S WY
2 RECTORY CL
3 MARSHALL CL
4 RIMINGTON RD
5 OLD SCHOOL LA
6 GAYSFIELD RD
7 SAXON GDNS

E3
1 BROUGHTON'S LA
2 TYLER CRES
3 CENTENARY CL
4 CHURCH RD
5 PINCHBECK RD
6 ST ANDREW'S RD
7 SPENCER GDNS
8 PRINCE WILLIAM DR
9 UPSALL RD

For full street detail of the highlighted area see page 209.

Scale: 1¾ inches to 1 mile

0   ¼   ½ mile
0 250m 500m 750m 1 km

A52

Sewage Works
Southfield La
Whitehouse Farm
Shaws Lane
Moat Lane
Home Farm
Market Lane
Sunnyville
Sea Lane
Sea Lane
Sea Bank
Toft Marsh
Heronshaw Hall
Moat House
Leake Hurn's End
Green Farm
Sailor's Home
8
Sports Ctr
Hampton House Farm
Hampton Lane
Moat
Bowsers Farm
49
PH
Works
Hurns End
Leverton L ctr
War Memorial
Beech Tree Farm
Leverton Outgate
Oldfield Lane
7
Old Lodge Farm
Highgate
Sycamore Farm
Lodge Farm
48
Leverton Highgate
Outgate
Burton Farm
Jenkins Lane
Leverton Prim Sch
Hall Farm
Oldfield Lane
6
Sheepgate
The Grange
Sea Lane
Dovecot La
Leverton Lucasgate
Sharp's Lane
Sea Lane
47
David's Lane
Spicer's Lane
Sea Lane
5
Ratten Row
Churchway
Tinkle Street
Benington Sea End
Glebe Farm
Sea Lane
Sea Lane
46
Lamb Lane
Sea End Road
Crowhall Lane
Maltbys Farm
4
Old House Farm
45
3
THE WASH
44
P
Butterwick Low
2
43
Freiston Shore Nature Reserve
1
40   A   41   B   42   C   43   D   44   E   45   F   42

Scale: 1¾ inches to 1 mile

0   ¼   ½ mile
0 250m 500m 750m 1 km

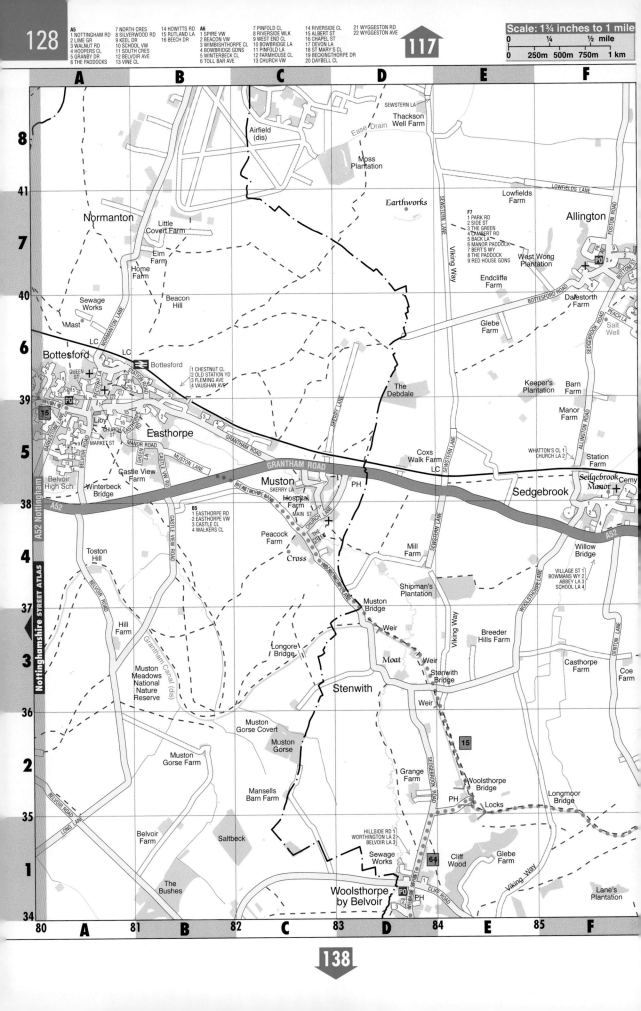

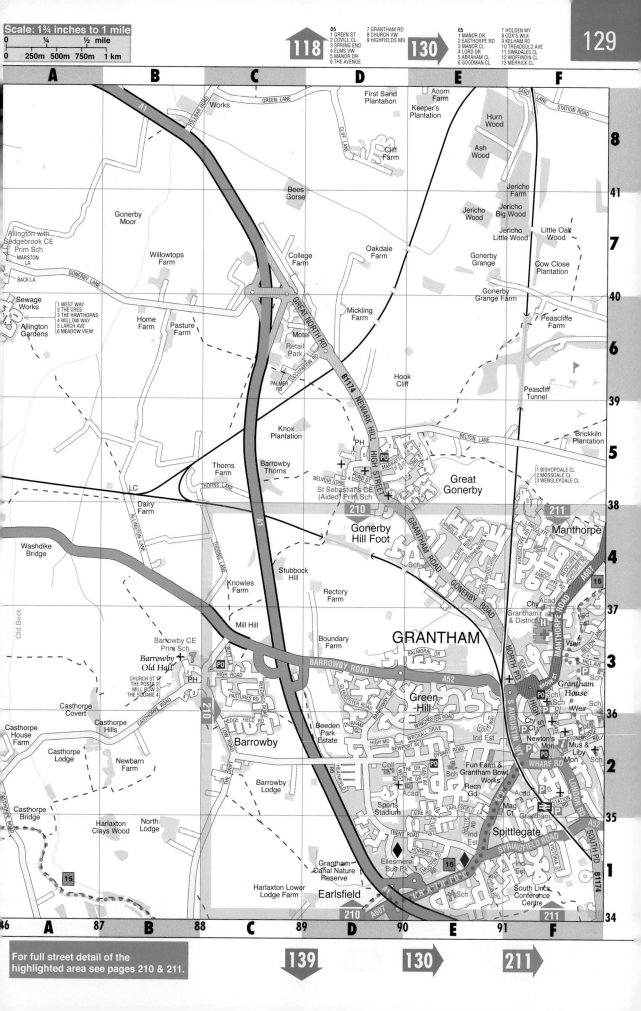

B8
1 THOROLD GDNS
2 HONINGTON RD
3 THE PADDOCK
4 ST NICHOLAS CL

← 129

119

West Street
The Close
THE CLOSE
STATION ROAD
Weir
Hambleton Hill
Hambleton Bridge
Syston
Weir
Dan's Plantation
Bridgewater House
Works
WASHDYKE LA
Hotel
CH
River Witham
Weir
Belton
Belton House
Towthorpe Hollow Ponds
Sewage Works
The Mill
Monument
Old Wood
Villa Pond
Manor Farm
LOW ROAD
Weir
Sch
Recn Gd
Harrowby Estate
Gorse Ri
SIGNAL RD
HILL AVE
NEW BEACON ROAD
Sandon Cl
Sch
BEACON LANE
Hall's Hill
Cemy
Chy
HARROWBY ROAD
St Vincent
ST VINCENT'S RD
SPRING RD
HILLSIDE CR
BRIDGE END RD
Dysart Park
Chy
Ind Estate
Recn Gd
MOUGHTON
BRIDGE END GROVE
SOMERBY HILL
Somerby Hill
A52

MAIN ROAD
Playing Field
Cemy
CHURCH
PO
PH
Barkston
Barkston & Syston CE Prim Sch
The Drift
The Lake
GREEN LANE
Works
Syston Park
Minnett's Hill
MINNETT'S HILL
Quarry (dis)
Quarry (dis)
Oak Wood
Boathouse Pond
Belton Park
CH
Works
LONDONTHORPE LANE
Green Lane
QUEENSWAY
PRINCESS DRIVE
CANBERRA CR
PO
SUNNINGDALE
SHARPE RD
GORSE RD
UPLANDS
BRITTAIN DR
Harrowby
SHAKESPEARE AV
TENNYSON AV
KENILWORTH RD
Sch
SECOND AV
PRUSTON RD
ALMA PARK ROAD
FIFTH AVE
Hall's Hill
HALL ROAD
Cold Harbour Lane
BELVOIR AVENUE
Radio Mast
Barracks
Somerby Hill

Minnett's Wood
Heath Farm
Minnett's Hill
Syston Park
Hundred Acres
Green Lane
Whippersall Hill
Bracken Plantation
Tar Lane Pond
Leg o'Mutton Pond
P
Bellmount Twr
Nature Reserve
P
Belton Park Golf Course
Londonthorpe Wood
Alma Park Industrial Estate
Alma Wood
Mast
Hill Top Farm
HARROWBY LANE
HEATH FARM ROAD
Heath Farm
TURNOR ROAD
Spitalgate Airfield (dis)
Ministry of Transport Testing Station

Heath Farm
Barkston Heath
HEATH LANE
Syston Grange
Syston Grange Farm
Mushroom Farm
Belton Ashes
Hanging Wood
The Belt
Sewage Works
Grange Farm
CHURCH LANE
High Road
PO
Manor Farm
Londonthorpe
NEWGATE LANE
Heath Farm
Mast
B6403
Welby Warren
HIGH DIKE
B6403
Cold Harbour
Rise Plot
B1176
Manor Farm
Moat

Airfield
Mast
Gipple Farm
HEATH LANE
Mast
HIGH DIKE
B6403
RED LANE
Welby
PH
Main Street
BLACKSMITHS LA
Swallowfield Farm
Welby Side Bar Farm
CHURCH LANE
Welby Heath
Quarry (dis)
Abney Wood
Ropsley Rise Wood
Nature Reserve
RISEWOOD LANE
RISEWOOD LANE

B6403
Mast
Wilsford Heath Farm
Pasture Farm
Pasture Farm

For full street detail of the highlighted area see page 211.

211   ← 129   ← 140

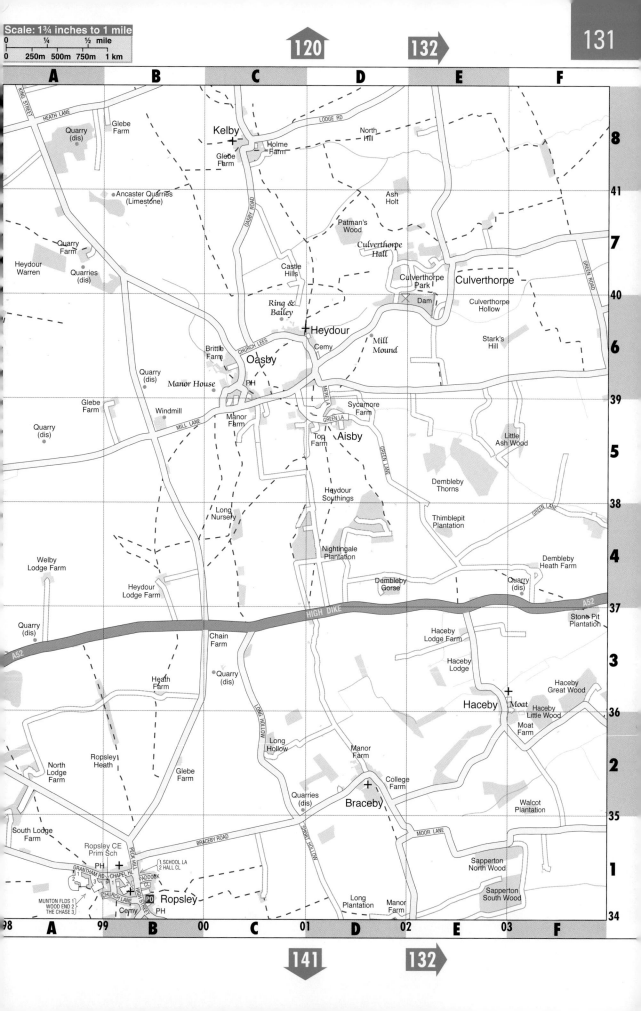

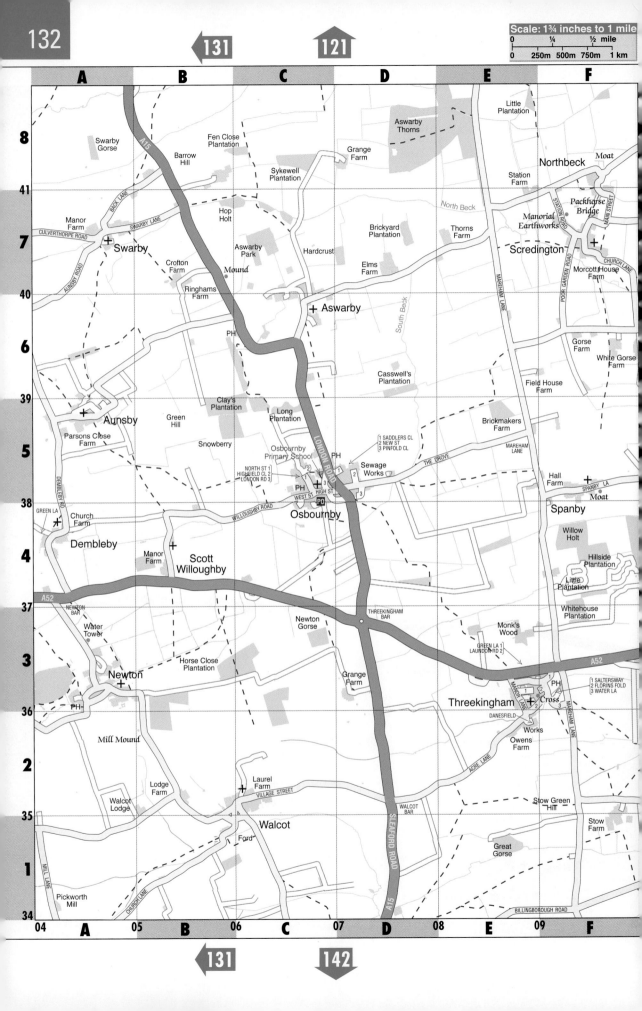

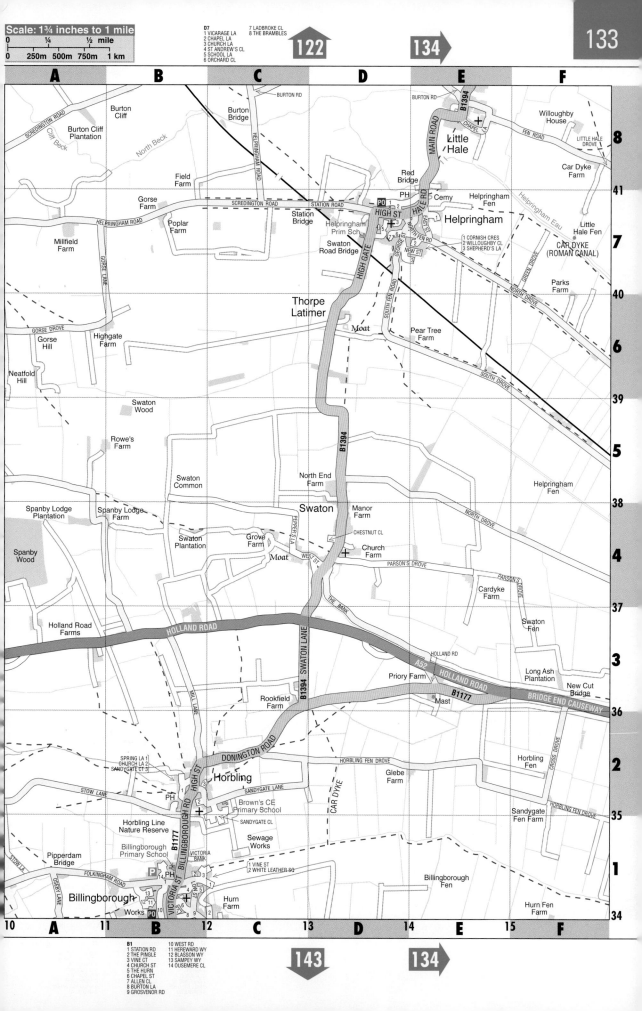

Scale: 1¾ inches to 1 mile

D7
1 VICARAGE LA
2 CHAPEL LA
3 CHURCH LA
4 ST ANDREW'S CL
5 SCHOOL LA
6 ORCHARD CL
7 LADBROKE CL
8 THE BRAMBLES

A B C D E F

8
41
7
40
6
39
5
38
4
37
3
36
2
35
1
34

Burton Cliff
Plantation

Scredington Road
Cliff Beck

Burton
Cliff

Burton
Bridge

BURTON RD

BURTON RD

B1394
CHAPEL LA

Little
Hale

MAIN ROAD

Willoughby
House

LITTLE HALE
DROVE

FEN ROAD

Car Dyke
Farm

North Beck

Field
Farm

Gorse Farm

Poplar
Farm

Millfield
Farm

HELPRINGHAM ROAD

GORSE LANE

SCREDINGTON ROAD

STATION ROAD

HELPRINGHAM ROAD

Station
Bridge

Helpringham
Prim Sch

Swaton
Road Bridge

HIGH ST

HIGH GATE

PO

PH

Red
Bridge

Cemy

HALE RD

EAST ST

NORTH FEN RD

GEORGE ST

NEW ST

Helpringham
Fen

Helpringham

1 CORNISH CRES
2 WILLOUGHBY CL
3 SHEPHERD'S LA

Helpringham Eau

Little
Hale Fen

CAR DYKE
(ROMAN CANAL)

Parks
Farm

GREEN DROVE

NORTH DROVE

Thorpe
Latimer

Moat

Pear Tree
Farm

SOUTH FEN ROAD

SOUTH DROVE

Gorse
Hill

GORSE DROVE

Highgate
Farm

Neatfold
Hill

Swaton
Wood

Rowe's
Farm

B1394

North End
Farm

Swaton

Manor
Farm

CHESTNUT CL

Helpringham
Fen

NORTH DROVE

Spanby Lodge
Plantation

Spanby Lodge
Farm

Swaton
Common

Swaton
Plantation

Grove
Farm

Moat

WEST ST

PEPPER'S LA

Church
Farm

PARSON'S DROVE

PARSON'S DROVE

Cardyke
Farm

Spanby
Wood

Swaton
Fen

THE BANK

HOLLAND ROAD

Holland Road
Farms

HOLLAND ROAD

SWATON LANE

B1394

Rookfield
Farm

HOLLAND RD

A52

HOLLAND ROAD

Priory Farm

B1177

Mast

BRIDGE END CAUSEWAY

Long Ash
Plantation

New Cut
Bridge

CROSS DROVE

DONINGTON ROAD

MILL LANE

SPRING LA 1
CHURCH LA 2
SANDYGATE CT 3

HIGH ST

Horbling

HORBLING FEN DROVE

Glebe
Farm

Horbling
Fen

STOW LANE

PH

SANDYGATE LANE

Brown's CE
Primary School

SANDYGATE CL

CAR DYKE

Sewage
Works

Horbling Line
Nature Reserve

B1177

BILLINGBOROUGH RD

VICTORIA ST

Billingborough
Primary School

VICTORIA
BANK

P

PH

1 VINE ST
2 WHITE LEATHER SQ

LOW ST

HORBLING FEN DROVE

Sandygate
Fen Farm

Billingborough
Fen

Pipperdam
Bridge

STOW LA

OSSERBY LANE

FOLKINGHAM ROAD

Billingborough

Works

13
12
11
10

PO

Hurn
Farm

Hurn Fen
Farm

B1
1 STATION RD
2 THE PINGLE
3 VINE CT
4 CHURCH ST
5 THE HURN
6 CHAPEL ST
7 ALLEN CL
8 BURTON LA
9 GROSVENOR RD
10 WEST RD
11 HEREWARD WY
12 BLASSON WY
13 SAMPEY WY
14 OUSEMERE CL

10 A 11 B 12 C 13 D 14 E 15 F

A **B** **C** **D** **E** **F**

8

Great Hale Fen

Holland Fen

Brand End Farm

Broadhurst Farm

TIMMS'S DROVE

West Low Grounds

OLD FORTY FOOT BANK

OLD SIXTEEN FOOT DRAIN

Ferry Farm

41

GREEN DROVE

LITTLE HALE DROVE

TILERBARN LANE

7

Fen Farm

Glebe Farm

Willow Farm

Little Hale Fen

OLD FORTY FOOT BANK

DOUBLETWELVES DROVE

Tile Barn Farm

40

LITTLE HALE DROVE

Lowgrounds Farm

NORTH DROVE

6

Drove Farm

Villa Farm

White House Farm

Crow Hall

Dovecote Farm

Bicker Gauntlet

SOUTH FORTY FOOT DRAIN

BICKER DROVE

Gauntlet Bridge

GAUNTLET DRO

BACK LANE

Gauntlet Farm

39

NORTH DROVE

Poplartree Farm

VICARAGE DROVE

LONGHEDGE DROVE

Walnut Tree Farm

Devonport Farm

Coot Hall Farm

Bicker Fen

Cow Bridge

COWBRIDGE ROAD

Cowbridge Farm

Mikinghill Field

5

Helpringham Fen

Eau End Farm

Hammond Beck

Strawberry Farm

OLD FORTY FOOT BANK

SOUTH DROVE

ING ROAD

Middle Fen

SOUTH DROVE

38

LC

ENGINE DROVE

River Farm

4

South Drove Farm

Middle Fen

Bicker Friest

Swaton Fen

Helpringham Fen

MIDDLE FEN DROVE

Cow Bridge

Beck Farm

NORTH FEN DRO

North Fen

37

Glebe Farm

Swaton Fen

North Ing

NORTH ING DROVE

North Fen

HOLYROOD CL

NORTHORPE RD

NORTHORPE ROAD

DAY'S LANE

NORTH DROVE

NORTH DROVE

3

Westdale Farm

Northorpe House

Northorpe

BICKER ROAD

NORTH DV

WESTDALE DROVE

Gibbet Fen

Cemetery

Donington Westdale

A52

CAYTHORPE RD

36

A52

The Thomas Cowley High Sch

BRIDGE END CAUSEWAY

Sixteen Foot Bridge

Donington High Bridge PH

Hammond Beck

GLEED AVE

P

PO

BARDGATE

Old Forty Foot Bridge

Park Farm

HIGH ST

A152

Liby

2

Chapel Bridge

Hammond Beck Bridge

Gibbet Fen

STATION STREET

MALTING LANE

BEECH GROVE

MILL LANE

TOWN DAM LANE

QUADRING RD

Fen End

Donington

MALLARD DROVE

Beck Farm

Donington Up Fen

Sewage Works

The Donington Cowley Endowed Prim Sch

HW'S LANE

35

Horbling Fen

HORBLING FEN DROVE

Mallard Hurn

Shoff Hills

SHOFF DROVE

Donington South Ing

ING DROVE

LC

SOUTH ING DROVE

SOUTH DRO

1

Fen Farm

Mallard House Farm

Donington South Ing

White House Farm

LC

SOUTH ING DRO

CHURCH END DRO 1

Mallard Farm

Donnington Shoff

COWDALE'S DROVE

MAIN RD 2

34

Billingborough Fen

SHOFF ROAD

BULL'S BANK

16 **A** **17** **B** **18** **C** **19** **D** **20** **E** **21** **F**

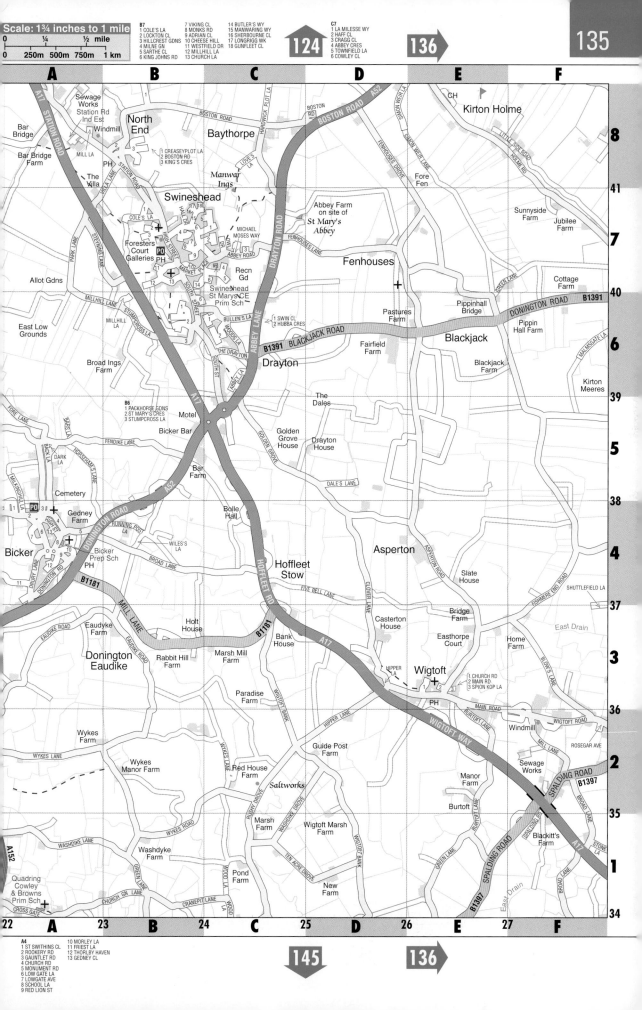

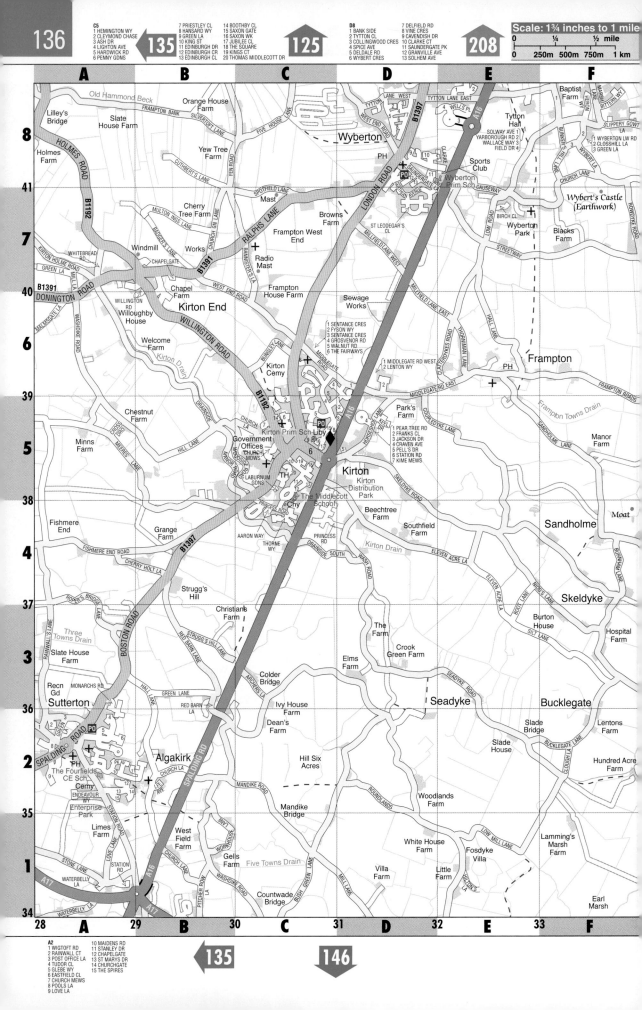

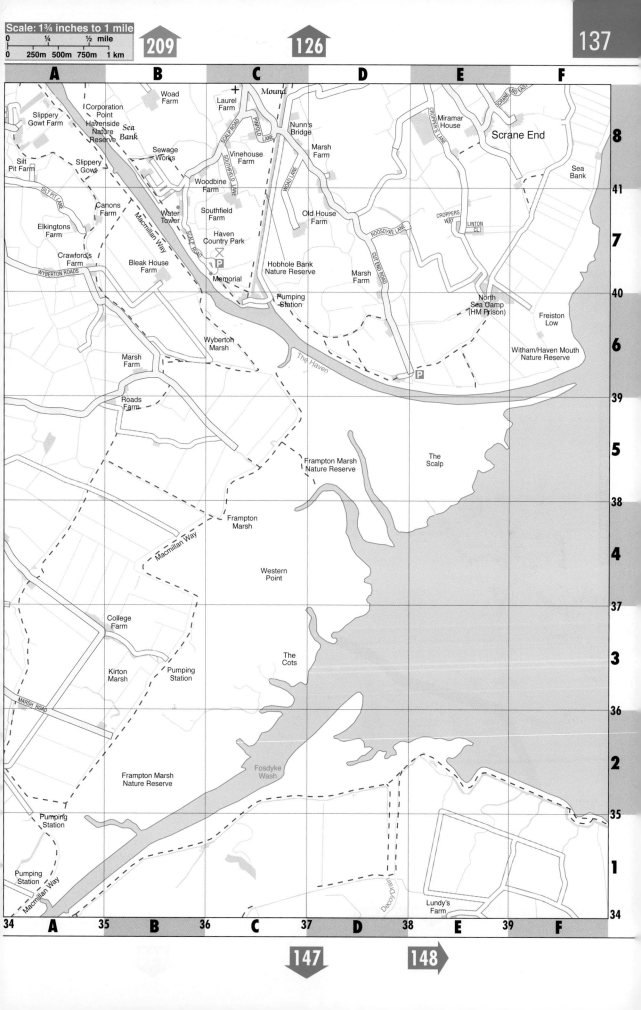

A   B   C   D   E   F

Slippery Gowt Farm
Corporation Point
Havenside Nature Reserve
Sea Bank
Woad Farm
Laurel Farm
Mound
Miramar House
Scrane End

8

Silt Pit Farm
Slippery Gowt
Sewage Works
Vinehouse Farm
Nunn's Bridge
Marsh Farm
Croppers Way

41

Canons Farm
Woodbine Farm
Southfield Farm
Old House Farm
Croppers Way
Sea Bank

7

Elkingtons Farm
Water Tower
Haven Country Park
Roosdyke Lane
Linton Cl

Crawford's Farm
Bleak House Farm
P
Memorial
Hobhole Bank Nature Reserve
Gut End Road
Marsh Farm

WYBERTON ROADS
SILT PIT LANE
Macmillan Way
SCALP ROAD

40

Pumping Station
North Sea Camp (HM Prison)

6

Marsh Farm
Wyberton Marsh
The Haven
P
Freiston Low

Roads Farm
Witham/Haven Mouth Nature Reserve

39

Frampton Marsh Nature Reserve
The Scalp

5

38

Frampton Marsh
Macmillan Way
Western Point

4

37

College Farm
The Cots

3

Kirton Marsh
Pumping Station

MARSH ROAD

36

Frampton Marsh Nature Reserve
Fosdyke Wash

2

Pumping Station

35

Pumping Station
Macmillan Way
Decoy Drain
Lundy's Farm

1

34

34   A   35   B   36   C   37   D   38   E   39   F

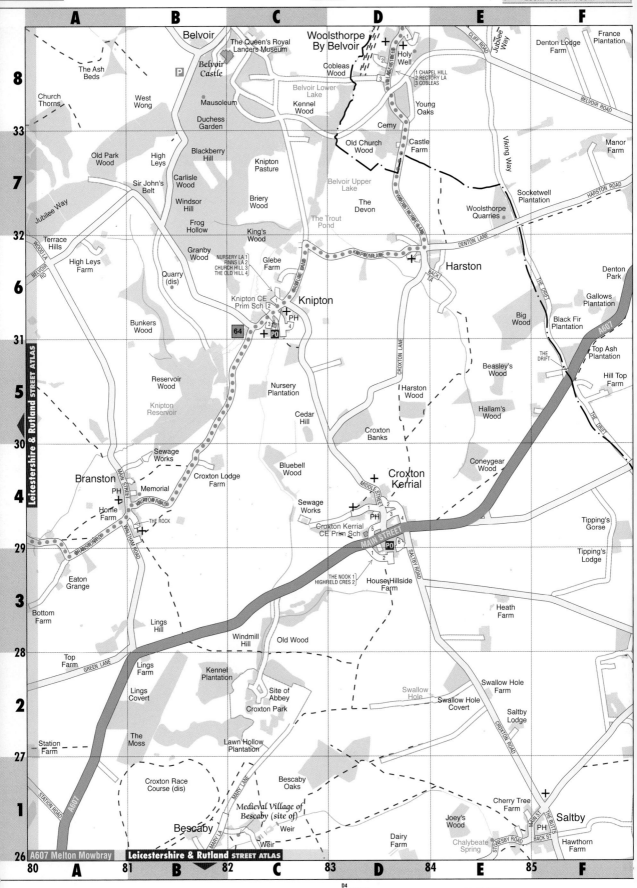

A   B   C   D   E   F

8

The Ash Beds

Church Thorns

West Wong

Belvoir

The Queen's Royal Lancers Museum

Belvoir Castle

Mausoleum

Woolsthorpe By Belvoir

Holy Well

Cobleas Wood

1 CHAPEL HILL
2 RECTORY LA
3 COBLEAS

France Plantation

Denton Lodge Farm

33

Duchess Garden

Belvoir Lower Lake

Kennel Wood

Young Oaks

Cemy

BELVOIR ROAD

Manor Farm

7

Old Park Wood

High Leys

Blackberry Hill

Knipton Pasture

Old Church Wood

Castle Farm

Viking Way

Socketwell Plantation

HARSTON ROAD

Sir John's Belt

Carlisle Wood

Briery Wood

Belvoir Upper Lake

The Devon

Woolsthorpe Quarries

Jubilee Way

Windsor Hill

Frog Hollow

32

Terrace Hills

High Leys Farm

Granby Wood

Frog Hollow

King's Wood

The Trout Pond

KNIPTON LANE

DENTON LANE

Harston

Denton Park

6

BELVOIR RD

WOOD LA

Quarry (dis)

NURSERY LA 1
FINNS LA 2
CHURCH HILL 3
THE OLD HILL 4

Glebe Farm

BARKESTONE DRAIN

CROXTON LANE THORPE LANE

BACK LA

Gallows Plantation

31

Bunkers Wood

Knipton CE Prim Sch

64

PH

PO

Knipton

Nursery Plantation

Harston Wood

Big Wood

Black Fir Plantation

THE DRIFT

Top Ash Plantation

Hill Top Farm

A607

5

Reservoir Wood

Knipton Reservoir

Cedar Hill

Croxton Banks

Beasley's Wood

Hallam's Wood

THE DRIFT

30

Sewage Works

Bluebell Wood

Coneygear Wood

4

Branston

Croxton Lodge Farm

Memorial

PH

Home Farm

BRANSTON RD

THE ROCK

MAIN STREET

WALTHAM ROAD

Sewage Works

Croxton Kerrial CE Prim Sch

MIDDLE STREET

PH

Croxton Kerrial

MAIN STREET

PO

SALTBY ROAD

Tipping's Gorse

Tipping's Lodge

29

Eaton Grange

Lings Hill

THE NOOK 1
HIGHFIELD CRES 2

House Hillside Farm

Heath Farm

3

Bottom Farm

Windmill Hill

Old Wood

28

Top Farm

GREEN LANE

Lings Farm

Kennel Plantation

Swallow Hole

Swallow Hole Farm

Swallow Hole Covert

Saltby Lodge

2

Lings Covert

STATION ROAD

WALTHAM ROAD

Site of Abbey

Croxton Park

CROXTON ROAD

Station Farm

The Moss

Lawn Hollow Plantation

27

A607

MARY LANE

Croxton Race Course (dis)

Bescaby Oaks

Joey's Wood

Cherry Tree Farm

PH

Saltby

1

Medieval Village of Bescaby (site of)

Weir

Bescaby

MARY LA

Weir

Dairy Farm

Chalybeate Spring

STONESBY ROAD

MAIN ST

BACK ST

THE BUTTS

Hawthorn Farm

26

80   A   81   B   82   C   83   D   84   E   85   F

D4
1 CHAPEL LA
2 CHURCH LA
3 THORPES LA
4 TOP RD
5 SCHOOL LA
6 SHIRES ORCH
7 MILL LA

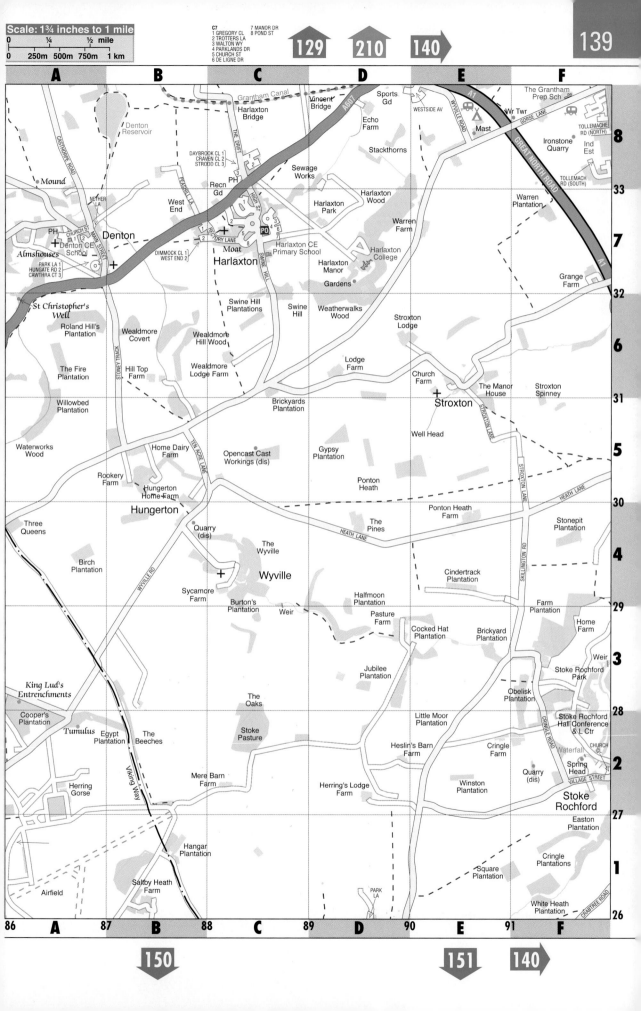

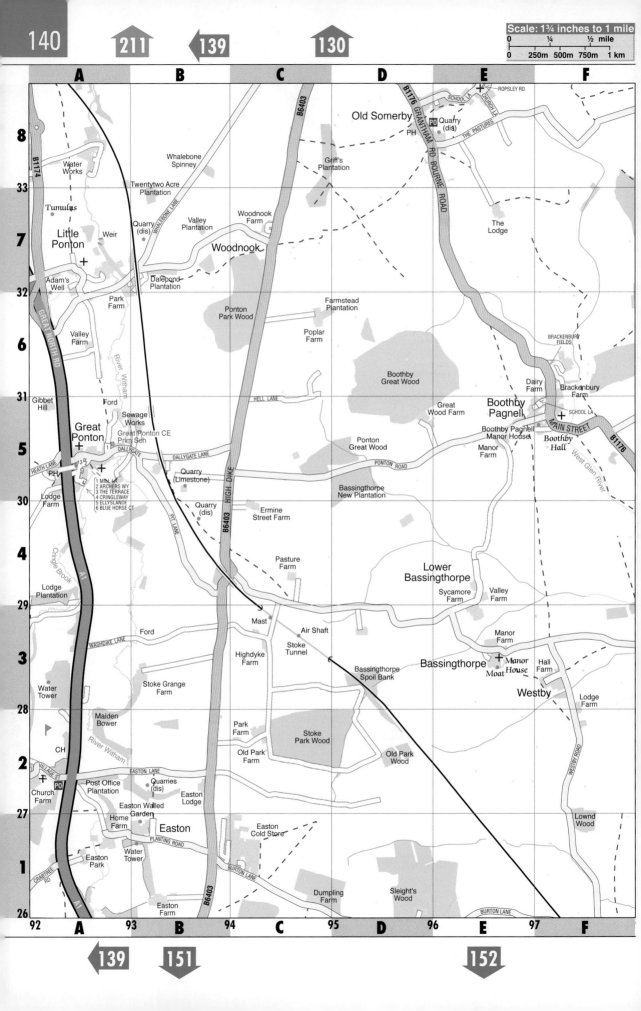

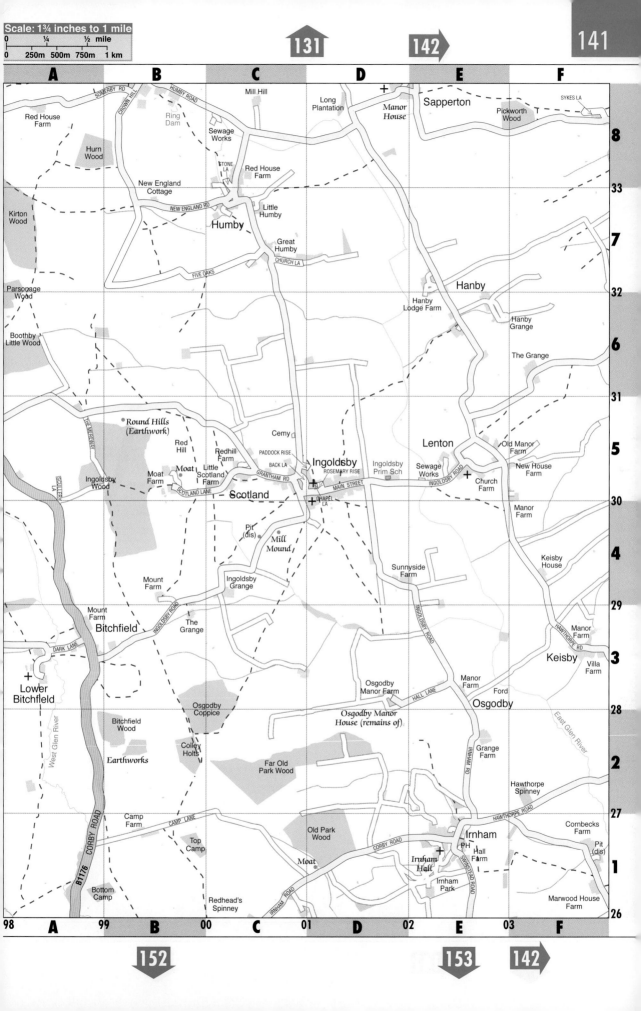

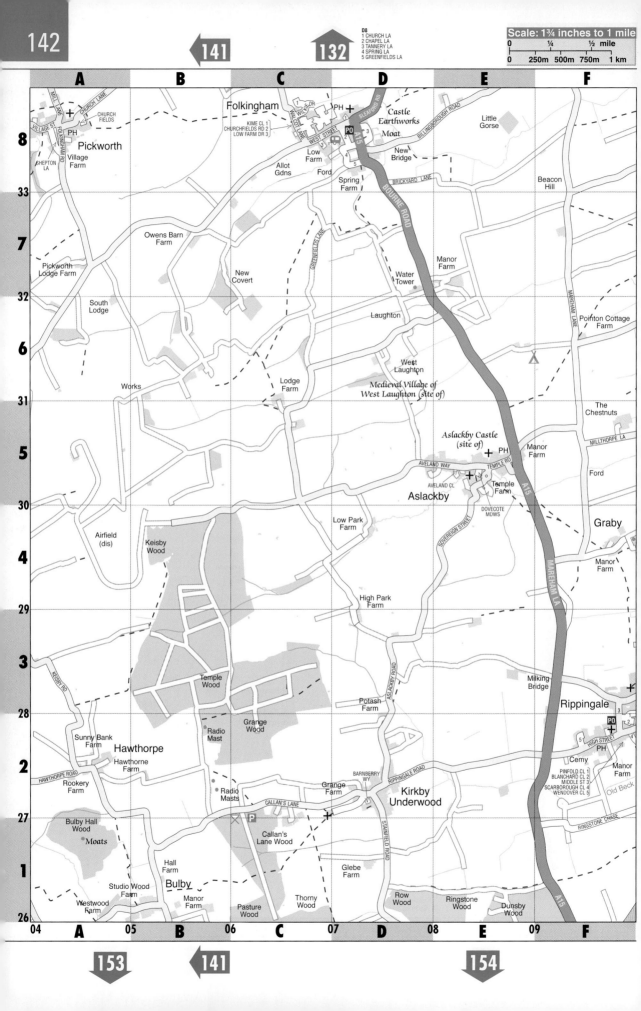

141
132

D8
1 CHURCH LA
2 CHAPEL LA
3 TANNERY LA
4 SPRING LA
5 GREENFIELDS LA

Scale: 1¾ inches to 1 mile
0   ¼   ½   mile
0   250m 500m 750m   1 km

A B C D E F

Folkingham

MILL LANE
CHURCH LANE
CHURCH FIELDS
VILLAGE ST
FOLKINGHAM RD
SHEPTON LA
PH

Pickworth
Village Farm

KIME CL 1
CHURCHFIELDS RD 2
LOW FARM DR 3
WALCOT LANE
WEST STREET
Low Farm
Allot Gdns
Ford

Castle Earthworks
Moat
New Bridge
SLEAFORD RD
BOURNE ROAD
A15
BILLINGBOROUGH ROAD
BRICKYARD LANE

Little Gorse

Beacon Hill

Spring Farm

8

33

Owens Barn Farm

New Covert

GREENFIELDS LANE

Water Tower

Manor Farm

7

32

Pickworth Lodge Farm

South Lodge

Laughton

West Laughton

MAREHAM LANE
Pointon Cottage Farm

6

31

Works

Lodge Farm

Medieval Village of West Laughton (site of)

Aslackby Castle (site of)
AVELAND WAY
AVELAND CL
Manor Farm

The Chestnuts

MILLTHORPE LA

5

30

Airfield (dis)

Keisby Wood

Low Park Farm

PH
Temple Farm
Temple RD
A15
Aslackby
DOVECOTE MDWS

Ford

Graby

Manor Farm

4

29

High Park Farm

SOVEREIGN STREET

KEISBY RD

3

28

Temple Wood

Radio Mast

Grange Wood

Potash Farm

ASLACKBY ROAD

Milking Bridge

Rippingale
PO
PH
HIGH STREET

Sunny Bank Farm
Hawthorpe
Hawthorne Farm
HAWTHORPE ROAD
Rookery Farm

Radio Masts

CALLAN'S LANE

Grange Farm

BARNBERRY WY

RIPPINGALE ROAD
Kirkby Underwood

Cemy
PINFOLD CL 1
BLANCHARD CL 2
MIDDLE ST 3
SCARBOROUGH CL 4
WENDOVER CL 5
Manor Farm
Old Beck

2

27

Bulby Hall Wood
Moats

Hall Farm

Callan's Lane Wood

P

STANFIELD ROAD

RINGSTONE CHASE

1

Westwood Farm
Studio Wood Farm
Bulby
Manor Farm
Pasture Wood
Thorny Wood
Glebe Farm
Row Wood
Ringstone Wood
Dunsby Wood
A15

26

04 A 05 B 06 C 07 D 08 E 09 F

153
141
154

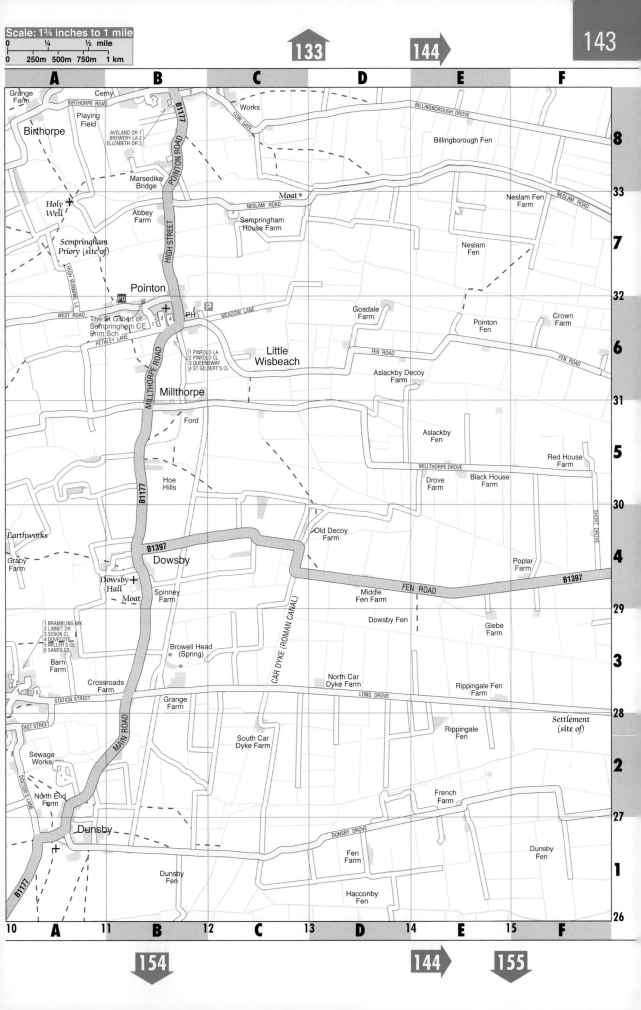

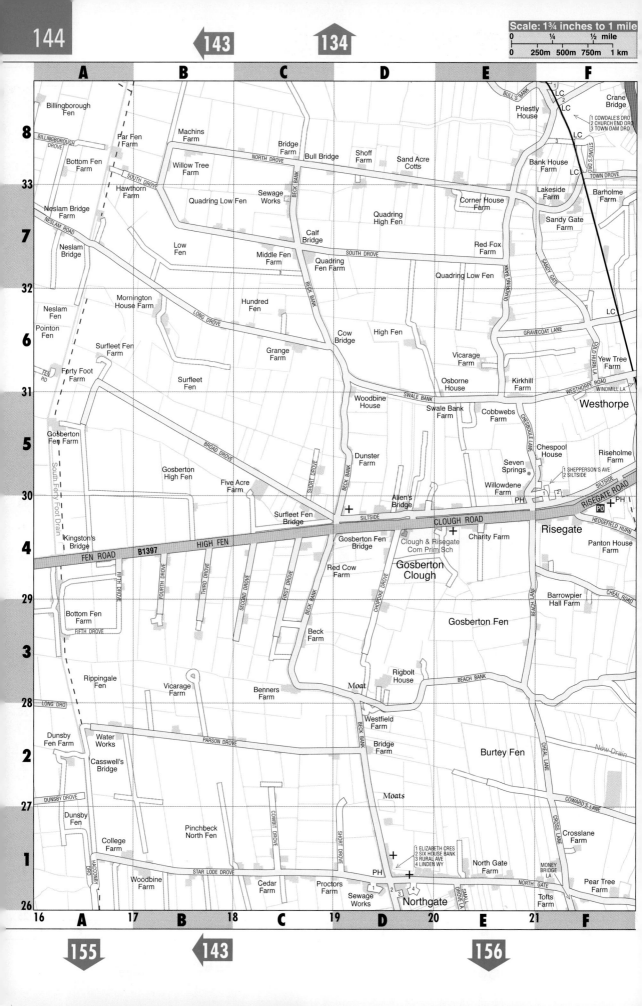

Scale: 1¾ inches to 1 mile
0 ¼ ½ mile
0 250m 500m 750m 1 km

A8
1 BOYFIELDS
2 ASHWIN GATE
3 DOVECOTES
4 LUDLOW GDNS
5 CHARLOTTE WK
6 ST MARGARET'S

B6
1 PARK CL
2 YORK GDNS
3 WELBY DR
4 CHURCH ST
5 SALEM ST
6 FIELD CL

B7
1 LILA DR
2 POACHERS HIDE
3 OAKTREE CL
4 CAMBRIDGE GDNS

C6
1 DAIRY CL
2 POPLAR DR
3 MEDWAY CL
4 LOWBRIDGE LA
5 WHITEHALL
6 GODFREY AVE

135   146

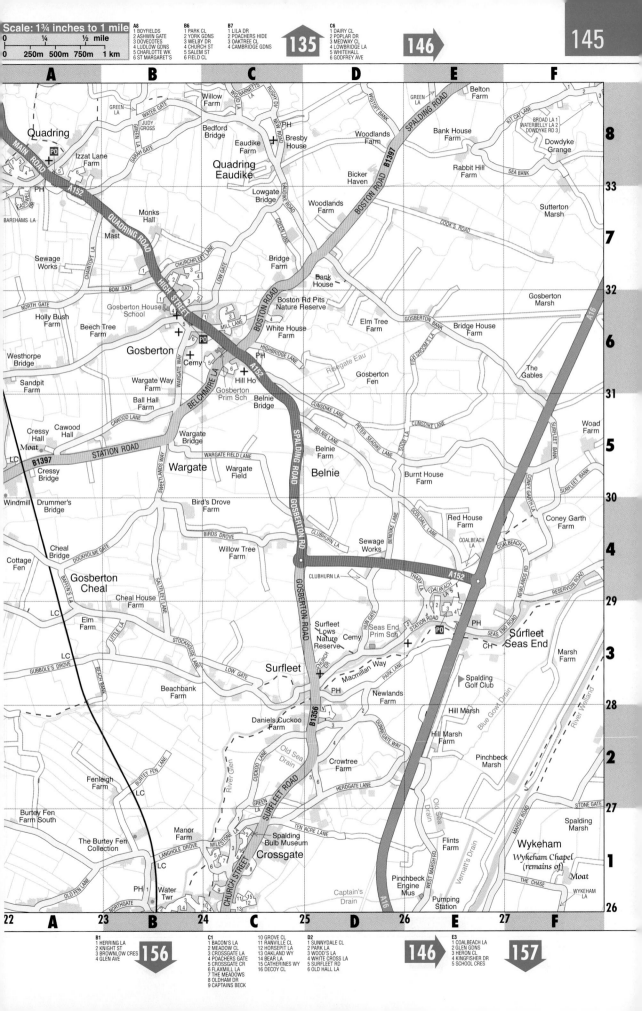

B1
1 HERRING LA
2 KNIGHT ST
3 BROWNLOW CRES
4 GLEN AVE

C1
1 BACON'S LA
2 MEADOW CL
3 CROSSGATE LA
4 POACHERS GATE
5 CROSSGATE CR
6 FLAXMILL LA
7 THE MEADOWS
8 OLDHAM DR
9 CAPTAINS BECK
10 GROVE CL
11 RANVILLE CL
12 HORSEPIT LA
13 OAKLAND WY
14 BEAR LA
15 CATHERINES WY
16 DECOY CL

D2
1 SUNNYDALE CL
2 PARK LA
3 WOOD'S LA
4 WHITE CROSS LA
5 SURFLEET RD
6 OLD HALL LA

E3
1 COALBEACH LA
2 GLEN GDNS
3 HERON CL
4 KINGFISHER DR
5 SCHOOL CRES

156   146   157

Scale: 1¾ inches to 1 mile

0   ¼   ½   mile
0   250m   500m   750m   1 km

A   B   C   D   E   F

8

Sutterton
Dowdyke

Willowtree
Farm

Walnut
Farm

PITCHER
ROW LA

BUSH GREEN LA

STATION ROAD

A17

Rose
Farm

PH

Fraglands
Farm

WASHDIKE RD

MILL
LANE

WHITECROSS GATE

WASH
ROAD

Macmillan Way

Firs
Farm

Sunset
Farm

BELL LANE

THOMPSON'S
LA

Grange
Farm

DOWDYKE
DROVE

Kenton
Farm

OLD MAIN ROAD

Cemy

Fosdyke

POT LANE

Moulton Marsh
Nature Reserve

33

DOWDYKE
RD

Bridgehouse
Bridge

COWHAMS LA

MARSH LANE

Graves
Farm

PUTTOCK GATE

CRAVEN'S LANE

Middle Marsh
Farm

DOWDYKE ROAD

MARSH ROAD

Three Towns Drain

Poplar
Farm

WASTE GREEN LANE

RANDOLPH RD 1
SNAITH AVE 2

1
2

P
Rec
Gnd

River Welland

7

Slate House
Farm

Irelands
Farm

Rose Place
Farm

SMEETON'S LANE

Heathley
Farm

Wilson
Place Farm

Lloyds
Farm

PULLOVER

WASH ROAD

Old Inn
La

MIDDLE MARSH ROAD

THIRD
DROVE

Main Drain

A16

Manor
House

Bank House
Farm

Pumping
Station

P

PH

Fosdyke
Bridge

32

Risegate Outfall

Welland House
Farm

WASHWAY RD

FIRST
DROVE

6

Algarkirk
Marsh

Marsh
Farm

Moulton
Marsh

Moulton River

RED COW DROVE

Welland House
Farm

Guys
Farm

31

Surfleet
Marsh

Macmillan Way

Pumping
Station

Wragg Marsh
Farm

Bank House
Farm

Three
Bridges

Charity
Farm

5

MARSH DROVE

Allot Gdns

Wragg Marsh
House

Scrimshaws
Farm

B1357

Whaplode
Marsh

Old Three
Tuns Farm

SURFLEET BANK

Wragg
Marsh

White House
Farm

Vickers
Farm

30

Pumping
Sta

RESERVOIR RD

PH

4

Vernatt's
Bridge

Crowtree
Farm

MARSH ROAD

COMMON ROAD

Moulton
Common

WASHWAY ROAD   A17

29

Welland House
Farm

CARRINGTON ROAD

3

Weston
Marsh

Crown
Farm

Moulton River

Yew Tree
Farm

28

GROCOCK CL

Mast

MANOR
HOUSE RD

2

Mill
Marsh

MILL MARSH ROAD

OAKWOOD PK

Moulton Seas
End

ROMAN BANK

Glebe
Farm

Hill Farm

Seas End
Hall

PO

MAWFORD CL

Crowhill
Farm

HALL LANE

B1357

Jack Bucks
Farm

GREEN LANE

PIPWELL GATE

Saracen's
Head

STONE GATE

SEAS END ROAD

Halesgate

GODDAM'S LANE

BROAD LANE

SALTNEY GATE

1

Shepherds
Farm

HALL GATE

Moulton Seas
End

WOODHOUSE LANE

Welland
House

26

28   A   29   B   30   C   31   D   32   E   33   F

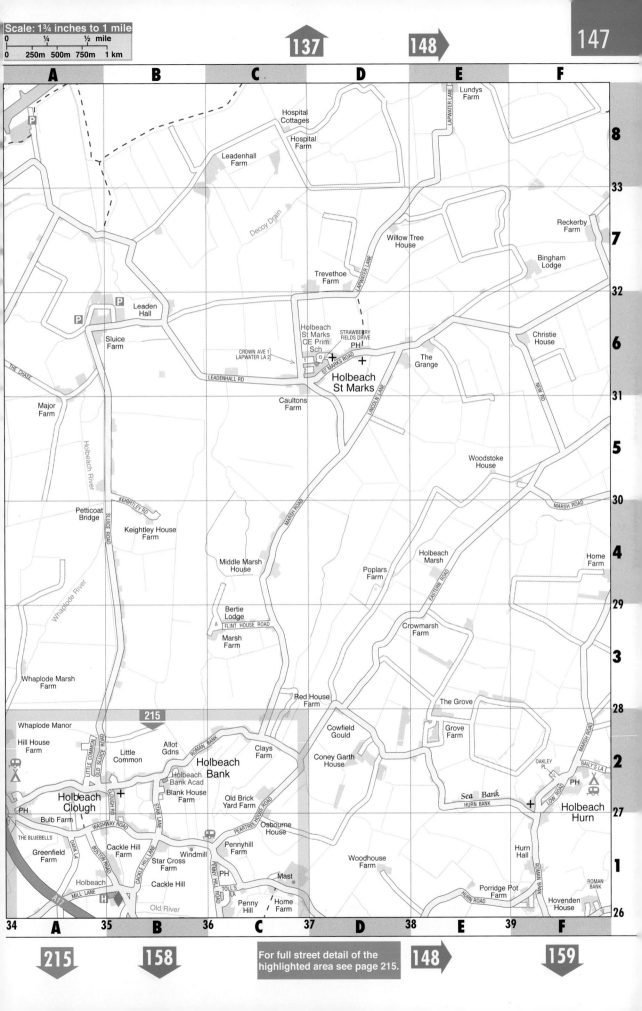

147

Scale: 1¾ inches to 1 mile

0   ¼   ½   mile
0   250m   500m   750m   1 km

A   B   C   D   E   F

8

33

DANGER AREA

Fleet Haven Outfall

Lawyers Farm

BARGE ROAD

Godfrey Farm

Thimbleby House

7

Bemrose Farm

Pumping Station

Acre House

Holbeach St Matthew

32

DANGER AREA

Acre Farm

Saltmarsh Farm

Wards Farm

EASTERN ROAD

6

Sot's Hole

Browns Farm

31

Hartley Farm

Red House Farm

Dawsmere House

DURHAMS ROAD

5

Wiles Farm

Dawsmere

Oldershaws Farm

MARSH ROAD

Cardwell Farm

30

Cemy

Bleak House Farm

Cardwell House

DAWSMERE ROAD

Fleet Haven

4

Gedney Marsh

GEORGE AVE 1
WILDFOWLERS WY 2

29

Marsh Farm

B1359

Gedney Drove End Prim Sch

Norfolk House Farm

3

Gable End Farm

Tylers Farm

Red House Farm

Manor Farm

Black Barn

28

Boat Mere Farm

Welby House

BLACKBARN ROAD

2

White House Farm

Middle Drove Farm

MARSH ROAD

Brook House Farm

Sutton Corner

27

MIDDLE DROVE

Smiths Farm

B1359

Green Woods

POPLAR LA

Allot Gnds

Fleet Marsh

LUTTON BANK

1

Gedney Dyke

ENGINE DYKE

Lutton Grange

Lutton Marsh

ROMAN BANK

MEMORIAL LA

PO

Windmill

GREEN DYKE

DEAR LOVE GATE

NORTH DROVE

Grange Farm

NORTH DROVE

Mill House Farm

26

Smiths Farm

MAIN STREET

ANVIL CL

Allot Gnds

40   A   41   B   42   C   43   D   44   E   45   F

Scale: 1¾ inches to 1 mile

0   ¼   ½   mile
0   250m 500m 750m 1 km

A   B   C   D   E   F

35
34
41   42   43   44

148

Outer
Westmark Knock

Dawsmere
Creek

Pumping
Station

DANGER
AREA

Cox's
Creek

Big
Annie

Inner
Westmark Knock

Norfolk STREET ATLAS

Gedney Drove
End

PIT LA

PH

Cherry
Farm

Deans
Farm

MARSH ROAD

NEW MARSH RD

Allot
Gnds

Manor
Farm

White House
Farm

Onslow
Farm

Crab's
Hole

The Wash
National Nature
Reserve

MARSH ROAD

Lodge
Farm

LITTON LODGE LA

SOUTH DROVE

LEAMLANDS LANE

GUY'S HEAD ROAD

Leamlands
Farm

Tychro Wing's Channel

Peter Scott Walk

46   A   47   B   48   C   49   D   50   E   51   F

160   161

8
33
7
32
6
31
5
30
4
29
3
28
2
27
1
26

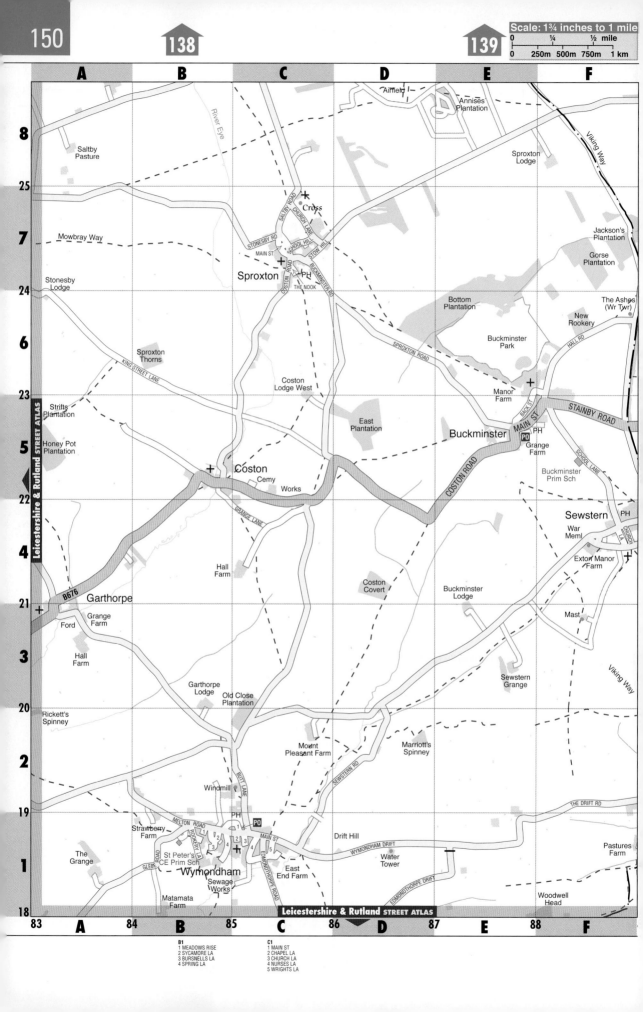

Scale: 1¾ inches to 1 mile

0   ¼   ½   mile
0   250m 500m 750m 1 km

A **B** **C** **D** **E** **F**

Leicestershire & Rutland STREET ATLAS

Saltby
Pasture

River Eye

Airfield

Annises
Plantation

Viking Way

Sproxton
Lodge

Cross

Mowbray Way

Saltby Road
Church Lane
Stonesby Rd
School Hill
Stow Hill
Main St

Sproxton

Jackson's
Plantation

Gorse
Plantation

Stonesby
Lodge

Coston Road
Buckminster Rd
PH
The Nook

Bottom
Plantation

The Ashes
(Wr Twr)

New
Rookery

Sproxton
Thorns

King Street Lane

Sproxton Road

Buckminster
Park

Hall Rd

Coston
Lodge West

Strifts
Plantation

Honey Pot
Plantation

East
Plantation

Manor
Farm

Buckminster

Main St
PO
PH

Back St

Stainby Road

Grange
Farm

Coston
Cemy

Works

Coston Road

School Lane

Buckminster
Prim Sch

Grange Lane

Sewstern
PH

War
Meml

Church La

Hall
Farm

Coston
Covert

Buckminster
Lodge

Exton Manor
Farm

B676

Garthorpe

Ford

Grange
Farm

Hall
Farm

Mast

Garthorpe
Lodge

Old Close
Plantation

Sewstern Rd

Sewstern
Grange

Viking Way

Rickett's
Spinney

Mount
Pleasant Farm

Marriott's
Spinney

Windmill

Butt Lane

The Drift Rd

Melton Road
PH
PO
Rookery La
Main St

Strawberry
Farm

Drift Hill

Wymondham Drift

Water
Tower

Pastures
Farm

The
Grange

Glebe Road

St Peter's
CE Prim Sch

Edmonthorpe Road

Wymondham

Sewage
Works

East
End Farm

Edmondthorpe Drift

Woodwell
Head

Matamata
Farm

A 83 **B** 84 **C** 85 **D** 86 **E** 87 **F** 88

B1
1 MEADOWS RISE
2 SYCAMORE LA
3 BURSNELLS LA
4 SPRING LA

C1
1 MAIN ST
2 CHAPEL LA
3 CHURCH LA
4 NURSES LA
5 WRIGHTS LA

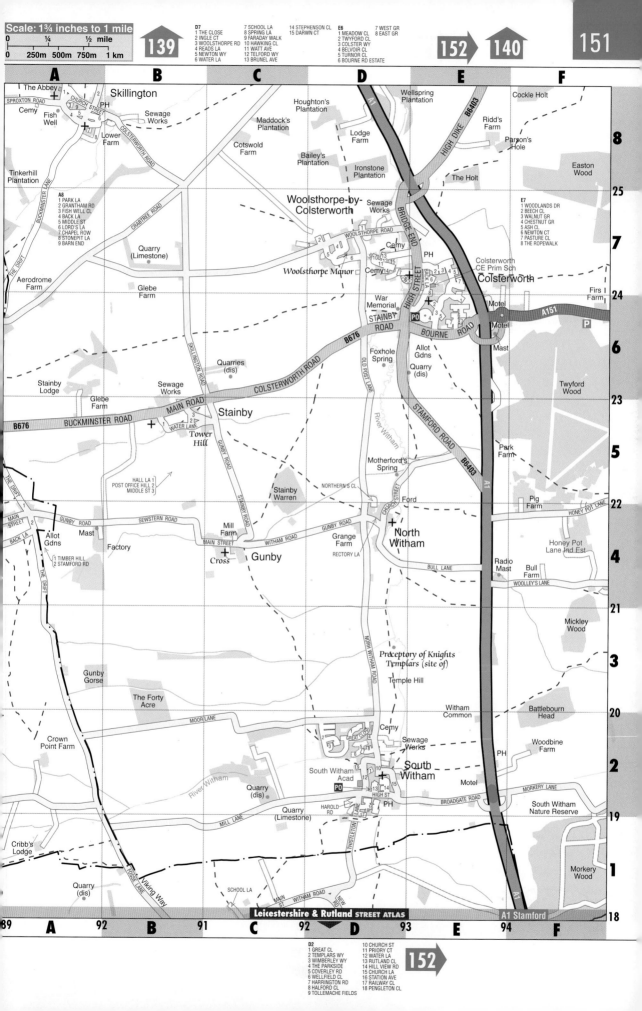

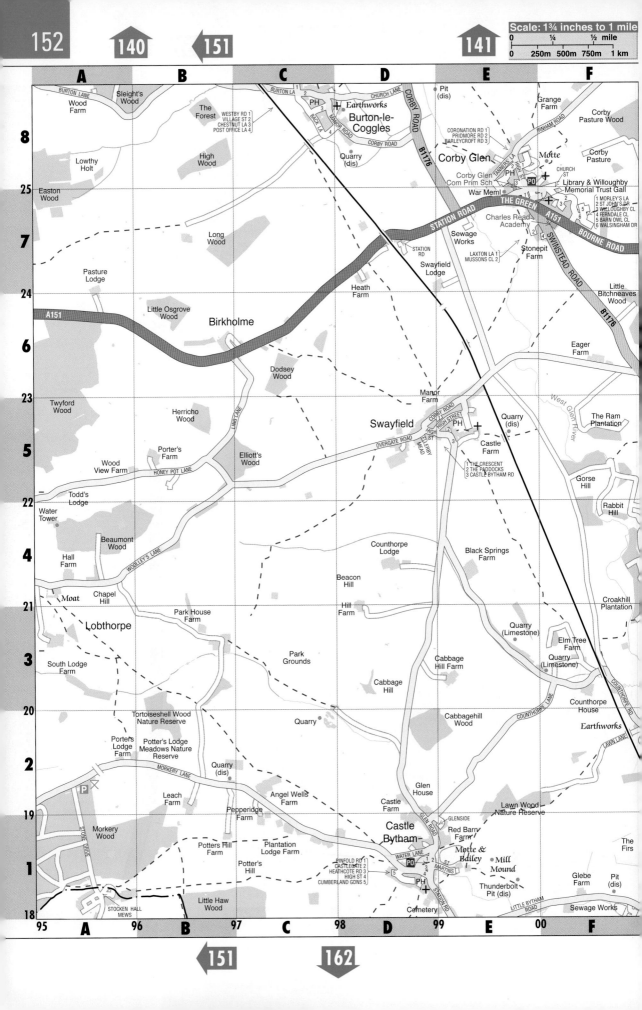

152
140
151
141

Scale: 1¾ inches to 1 mile
0   ¼   ½ mile
0   250m   500m   750m   1 km

A · B · C · D · E · F

Burton Lane
Wood Farm
Sleight's Wood
The Forest
Lowthy Holt
Easton Wood

Burton La
PH
Earthworks
Burton-le-Coggles
WESTBY RD 1
VILLAGE ST 2
CHESTNUT LA 3
POST OFFICE LA 4
BACK LA
MANOR ROAD
CORBY ROAD
Quarry (dis)

High Wood

Long Wood

Pit (dis)
CORBY ROAD
B1176
Grange Farm
Corby Pasture Wood
Corby Pasture
IRNHAM ROAD

CORONATION RD 1
PRIDMORE RD 2
BARLEYCROFT RD 3
Corby Glen
TANNERS LA
PH
Motte
CHURCH ST
PO
Corby Glen Com Prim Sch
War Meml
Library & Willoughby Memorial Trust Gall

1 MORLEY'S LA
2 ST JOHN'S DR
3 WILLOUGHBY CL
4 FERNDALE CL
5 BARN OWL CL
6 WALSINGHAM DR

STATION ROAD
THE GREEN
A151
BOURNE ROAD
SWINSTEAD ROAD
B1176

Pasture Lodge

A151

Birkholme
Little Osgrove Wood

STATION RD
Sewage Works
Swayfield Lodge
Heath Farm

LAXTON LA 1
MUSSONS CL 2
Stonepit Farm

Little Bitchneaves Wood

Twyford Wood
Herricho Wood
LING LANE
Dodsey Wood
Manor Farm
CORBY ROAD
Swayfield
HIGH STREET
PH
Quarry (dis)
Castle Farm

West Glen River
Eager Farm

The Ram Plantation

Porter's Farm
Elliott's Wood
Wood View Farm
HONEY POT LANE
OVERGATE ROAD
ELLERBY MEAD

1 THE CRESCENT
2 THE PADDOCKS
3 CASTLE BYTHAM RD

Gorse Hill
Rabbit Hill

Todd's Lodge
Water Tower
Beaumont Wood
WOOLLEY'S LANE
Hall Farm
Moat
Chapel Hill
Lobthorpe

Counthorpe Lodge
Beacon Hill
Hill Farm

Black Springs Farm

Croakhill Plantation

Park House Farm
Park Grounds
Cabbage Hill Farm
Cabbage Hill

Quarry (Limestone)
Elm Tree Farm
Quarry (Limestone)

South Lodge Farm

Tortoiseshell Wood Nature Reserve
Quarry
Cabbagehill Wood
COUNTHORPE LANE
Counthorpe House
Earthworks
COUNTHORPE RD

Porters Lodge Farm
Potter's Lodge Meadows Nature Reserve
MORKERY LANE
Quarry (dis)

Glen House
LAWN LANE

P
Leach Farm
Pepperidge Farm
Angel Wells Farm
Castle Farm
GLEN RD
Glenside
Red Barn Farm
Lawn Wood Nature Reserve

Morkery Wood
STONE DRIVE
Potters Hill Farm
Plantation Lodge Farm
Potter's Hill

Castle Bytham
WATER LANE
PO
BINFOLD RD 1
CASTLEGATE 2
HEATHCOTE RD 3
HIGH ST 4
CUMBERLAND GDNS 5

Motte & Bailey
ST MARTINS
Mill Mound
PH
Thunderbolt Pit (dis)

The Firs
Glebe Farm
Pit (dis)

STOCKEN HALL MEWS
Little Haw Wood
Cemetery
STAMORN RD
LITTLE BYTHAM ROAD
Sewage Works

A · B · C · D · E · F
95 · 96 · 97 · 98 · 99 · 00

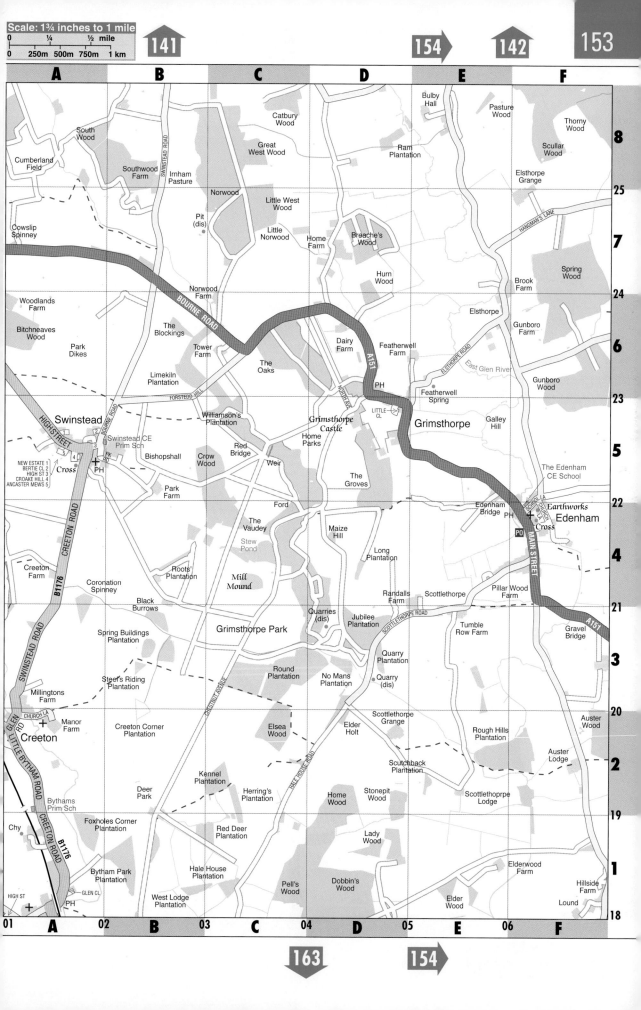

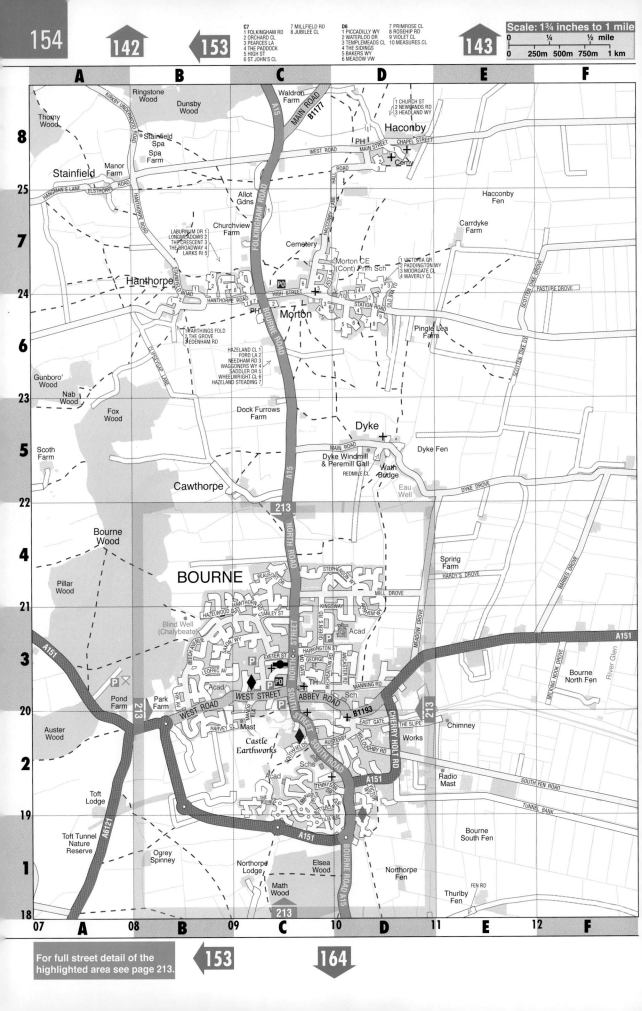

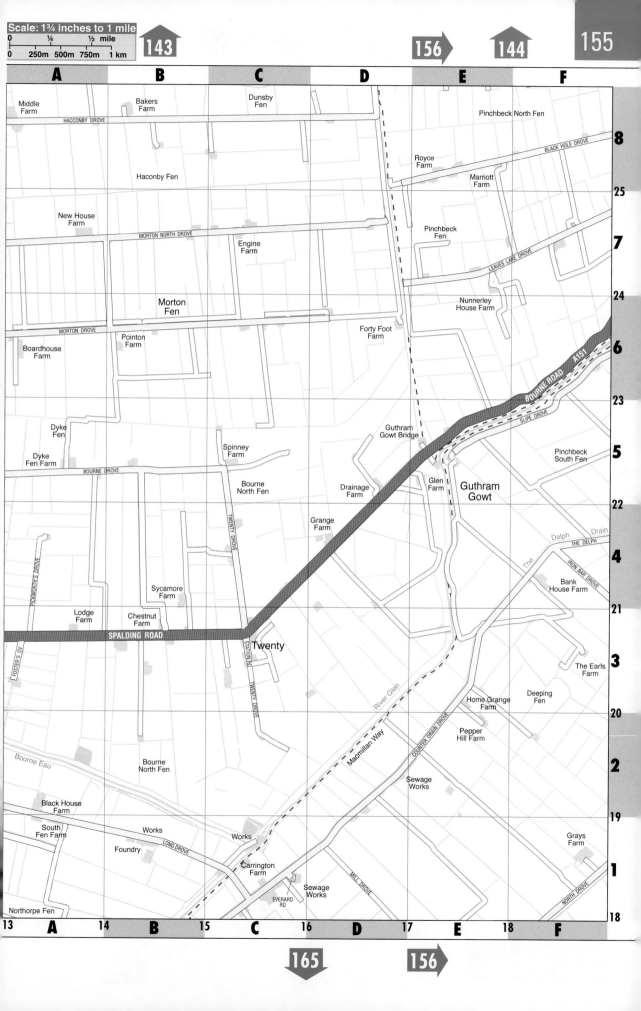

A   B   C   D   E   F

Middle
Farm

HACONBY DROVE

Bakers
Farm

Dunsby
Fen

Pinchbeck North Fen

BLACK HOLE DROVE

8

Haconby Fen

Royce
Farm

Marriott
Farm

25

New House
Farm

MORTON NORTH DROVE

Engine
Farm

Pinchbeck
Fen

LEAVES LAKE DROVE

7

Morton
Fen

Nunnerley
House Farm

24

Boardhouse
Farm

MORTON DROVE

Pointon
Farm

Forty Foot
Farm

A151

BOURNE ROAD

6

Dyke
Fen

SLIPE DROVE

23

Dyke
Fen Farm

BOURNE DROVE

Spinney
Farm

Guthram
Gowt Bridge

Pinchbeck
South Fen

5

Bourne
North Fen

Drainage
Farm

Glen
Farm

Guthram
Gowt

22

Grange
Farm

Delph   Drain

THE DELPH

The

4

PICKWORTH'S DROVE

TWENTY DROVE

Sycamore
Farm

IRON BAR DROVE

Bank
House Farm

Lodge
Farm

Chestnut
Farm

21

FOSTER'S DV

SPALDING ROAD

STATION RD

Twenty

The Earls
Farm

3

TWENTY DROVE

River Glen

Home Grange
Farm

Deeping
Fen

20

Macmillan Way

COUNTER DRAIN DROVE

Pepper
Hill Farm

Bourne
North Fen

Sewage
Works

2

Bourne Eau

Black House
Farm

19

South
Fen Farm

Works

LONG DROVE

Works

Grays
Farm

Foundry

Carrington
Farm

MILL DROVE

NORTH DROVE

1

Northorpe Fen

EVERARD
RD

Sewage
Works

18

13   A   14   B   15   C   16   D   17   E   18   F

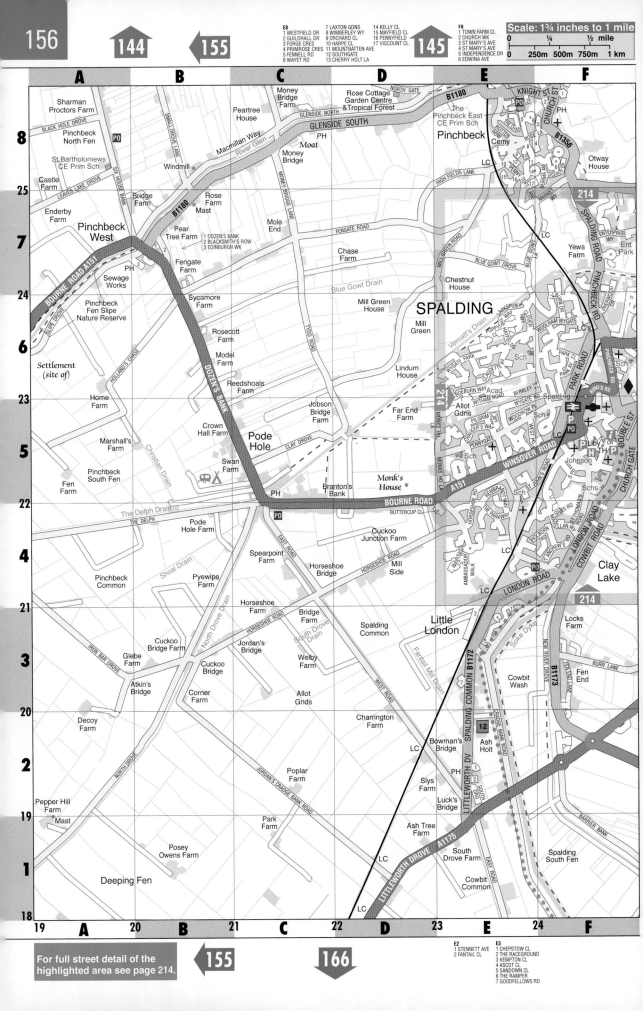

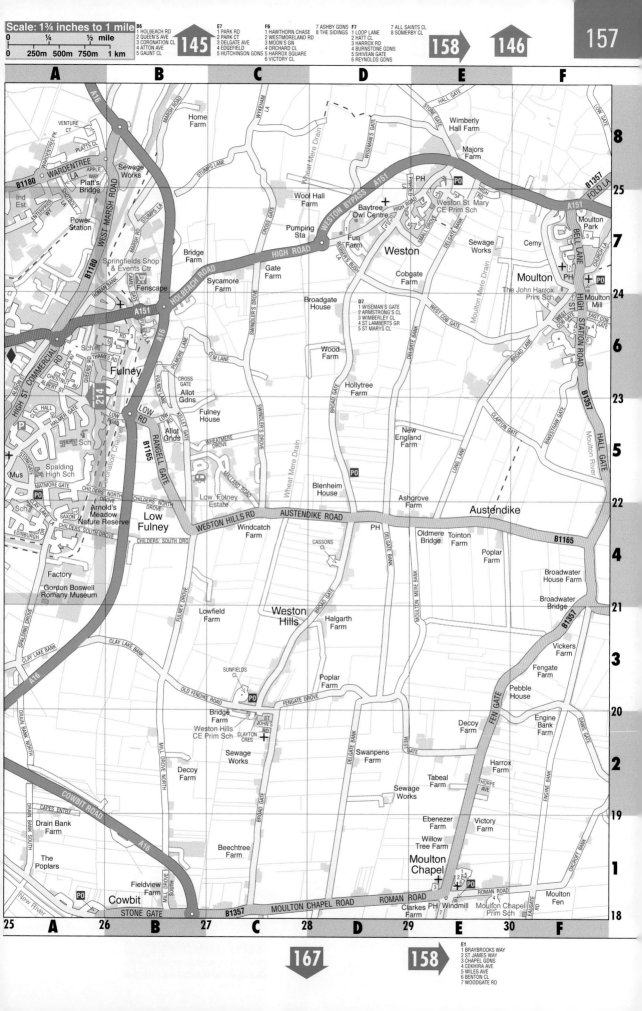

B6
1 ABBOTS GDNS
2 COBGATE CL
3 SANDRINGHAM CL
4 BUTTERCUP PADDOCK
5 FRANCKLIN WK
6 GOLDEN HARVEST WY

B7
1 WHEATFIELDS
2 CHAPEL GDNS
3 ST MARY'S GDNS
4 GREEN PASTURES
5 CROSS ST
6 KIRK GATE

7 MIDDLE RD
8 MALTEN LA
9 IRBY CRES
10 THE TILNEY

A | B | C | D | E | F

Loosegate

Woodhouse Lane
Seas End Rd
Field Farm
Distillery Farm
Sewage Works
Town Farm
Battle Fields

College Farm
Cragg's Hill House
Willow Tree Farm
Academy
Football Gd
Low La

Crown Farm
Craggs Hill Farm
Glebe Farm
Spalding Gate
Stockwell Gate

Whaplode Fields
Linden Farm
Tulip Fields

HOLBEACH

Roper's Bridge Cemy
Elloe Stone (restored)
Stock's Hill
High or Main Rd
Spalding Road
West End
High St
Fleet Street

Whaplode
Works
PH PO
Mill Lane
Whaplode CE Primary School

1 WALLISGATE
2 WESLEY RD
3 MILLERS REST

East Gate
East Cob Gate
Cob Gate
Cranesgate Farm
Crane's Gate House

Drings Farm
Bridge Farm
Hither Hold Farm
Halls Farm
Holbeach Fen
Pennington's Farm
Red House Farm
Millbank Farm

Little Lane
Eagle House
Holbeach Fen
Bridge Farm
Hurdletree House

Spark's Lane
Whaplode Fen
Barrington House Farm
New River

Moat
Oaklands Farm
Hurdle Tree Bank Farm
Highfield Farm

Home Farm
Broadwater La
B1165
Hurdletree Bank

Daisy Bank Farm
Crane's Gate House
Rose Cres
Little South Holland Drain

Bridge Farm
Ravens Bank
Saturday Bridge
B1165

St Catherine's Bridge
Whaplode St Catherine
PH
Allot Gdns
Red Lodge Farm
Turkey Farm

Sycamore Farm
Rookery Farm
Millgate House
Grange Farm
Ravensgate Farm
Snowdrop Farm
Sycamore Lodge

Daws Gate
Oxcroft House
Oxcroft Bank
Millgate Farm
Rookery Farm

Bees Farm
Poplars Farm
Vicarage Cl
PH
Ash Farm
Decoy Farm

Moulton Fen
Little Dog Drove
Jekil's Bank
Holbeach St Johns

31 | A | 32 | B | 33 | C | 34 | D | 35 | E | 36 | F

For full street detail of the highlighted area see page 215.

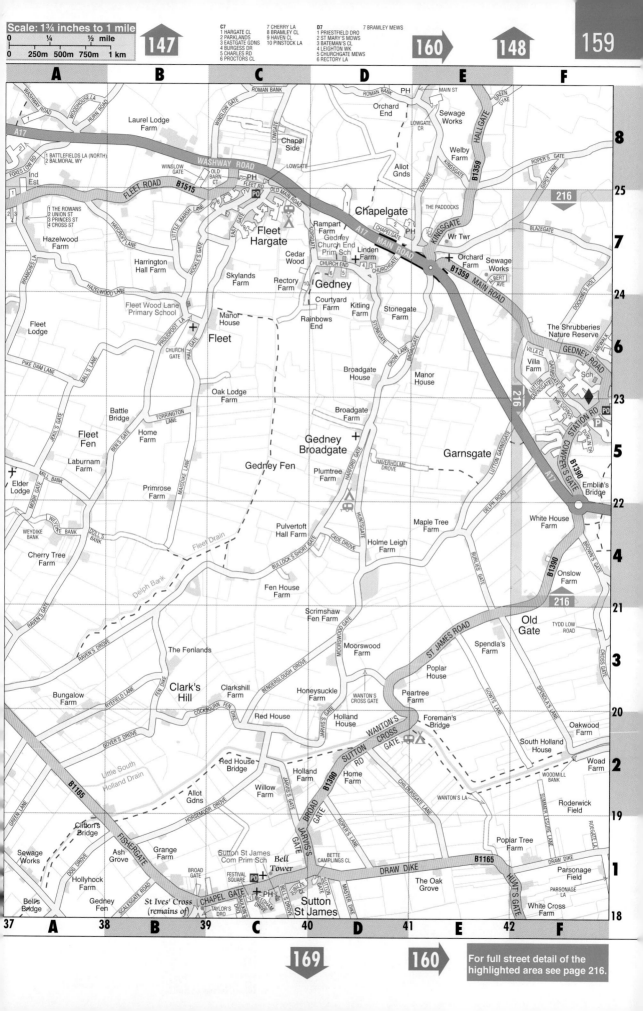

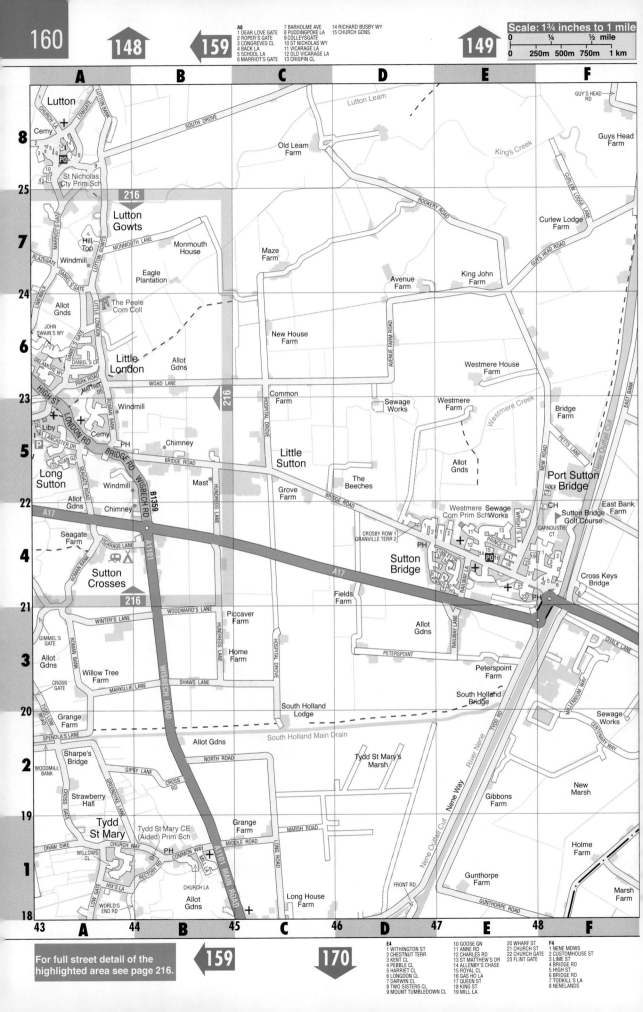

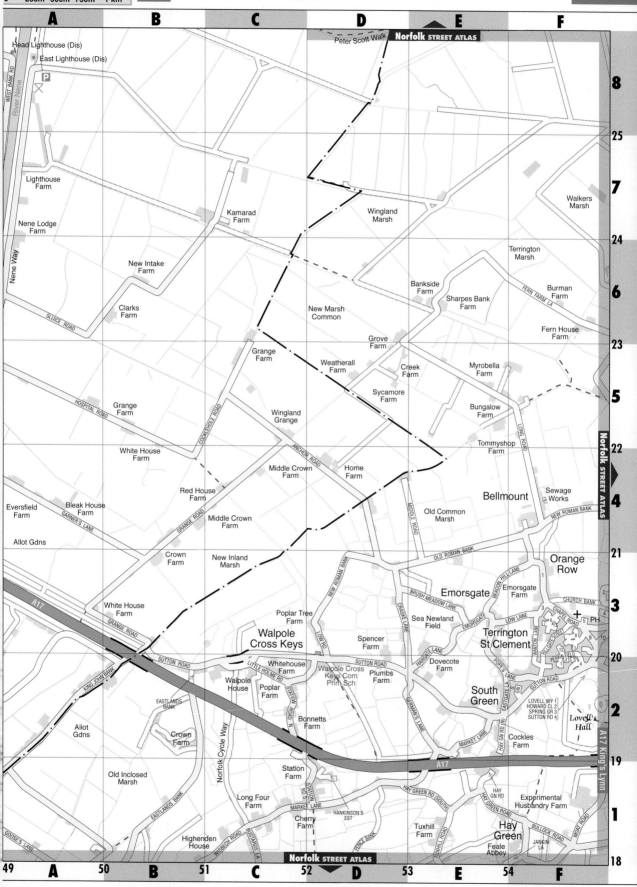

Norfolk STREET ATLAS

Head Lighthouse (Dis)
East Lighthouse (Dis)
WEST BANK RD
River Nene
Lighthouse Farm
Nene Lodge Farm
Nene Way
New Intake Farm
Kamarad Farm
Clarks Farm
SLUICE ROAD
Grange Farm
Grange Farm
HOSPITAL ROAD
White House Farm
COCKLEHOLE ROAD
Eversfield Farm
Bleak House Farm
GARNER'S LANE
Allot Gdns
Red House Farm
GRANGE ROAD
Middle Crown Farm
Crown Farm
New Inland Marsh
A17
White House Farm
GRANGE ROAD
King John Bank
Allot Gdns
EASTLANDS BANK
Crown Farm
SUTTON ROAD
Norfolk Cycle Way
LITTLE HOLME RD
Walpole House
Poplar Farm
STATION ROAD
Bonnetts Farm
Old Inclosed Marsh
EASTLANDS BANK
Station Farm
Long Four Farm
MARKET LANE
WISBECH ROAD S
BISTARDS LA
Highenden House
FENGE BANK
Cherry Farm
HANKINSON'S EST

Peter Scott Walk
Wingland Marsh
New Marsh Common
Grange Farm
Weatherall Farm
Wingland Grange
ANCHOR ROAD
Middle Crown Farm
Home Farm
MIDDLE ROAD
Old Common Marsh
OLD ROMAN BANK
NEW ROMAN BANK
Poplar Tree Farm
LOW RD
Walpole Cross Keys
Whitehouse Farm
Walpole Cross Keys Com Prim Sch
SUTTON ROAD
Plumbs Farm
Spencer Farm
CRASKE LANE
GERMAN'S LANE
Cherry Farm

Bankside Farm
Sharpes Bank Farm
Terrington Marsh
FERN FARM LA
Burman Farm
Fern House Farm
Grove Farm
Creek Farm
Myrobella Farm
Sycamore Farm
Bungalow Farm
LONG ROAD
Tommyshop Farm
Bellmount
Sewage Works
NEW ROMAN BANK
Orange Row
Emorsgate
BRUSH MEADOW LANE
BEACON HILL LANE
Emorsgate Farm
CHURCH BANK
Sea Newland Field
EMORSGATE
LOW LANE
Terrington St Clement
WATTON LANE
CHAPEL ROAD
PH
MARGATE LANE
Dovecote Farm
POPE'S LANE
EASTGATE LA
South Green
SUTTON ROAD
LOVELL WY 1
HOWARD CL 2
SPRING GR 3
SUTTON RD 4
Lovell's Hall
HAY GN RD (N)
MARKET LANE
Cockles Farm
A17
A17 King's Lynn
HAY GREEN RD (SOUTH)
HAY GN RD
HAY GREEN ROAD
Experimental Husbandry Farm
Tuxhill Farm
TUXHILL ROAD
BULLOCK ROAD
MOAT ROAD
Hay Green
JANKIN LA
Feale Abbey

Walkers Marsh

Norfolk STREET ATLAS

Norfolk STREET ATLAS

F3
1 ORANGE ROW RD
2 CHURCH BANK
3 ORANGE ROW
4 KING WILLIAM CL
5 WESLEY AVE
6 THE SALTINGS
7 BRELLOWS HILL
8 CAVE'S CL
9 WESLEY RD
10 MARSHLAND ST
11 WESLEY CL
12 FFOLKES DR
13 COBBS HILL

E8
1 LITTLE BYTHAM RD
2 REGAL GDNS
3 BYTHAM HEIGHTS

Scale: 1¾ inches to 1 mile

0   ¼   ½   mile

0   250m 500m 750m 1 km

A   B   C   D   E   F

8   Stocken Park
    HM Prison
    Lady Wood
    Little Haw Wood
    Quarry (dis)
    Glebe Farm
    Meadows End

    Addah Wood
    Chimney
    Cow Pasture Lane
    Clipsham Road

17 1 HESKETH CT
    2 FLEETWOOD CT
    3 WILSON CT
    4 STOVE CT
    Clipsham Park Wood
    School Farm

    Stretton Wood
    Belton Firs
    Lodge Farm

7   BRADLEY LA 1
    CHURCH LA 2
    NEW RD 3
    WEST ST 4
    Clipsham Park
    Quarry (dis)
    Pillowsyke Holt
    New Wood

    Moor Plantation
    Clipsham
    Castle Bytham Road
    Main St
    Holywell Hall
    Holy Well

16 Stockton Lane Plantation
    Stretton Road
    Clipsham Road
    Manor Farm
    Hill Top Farm
    The Quarries
    Holywell Quarry
    Careby Road
    Mill Farm

    PH
    Manor Rd
    New Quarry House
    Bidwell Lane
    Holywell Road

6   Bidwell Farm
    White's Plantation
    New Quarry Plantation
    Quarries (dis)
    Infield Holt

    Pettywood Farm
    Pattinson's Holt

15 Glebe Farm
    Osbonall Wood
    Clipsham Old Quarry (Limestone)
    Holywell Wood
    Lincolnshire Gate
    Robert's Field Nature Reserve

    Quarry (dis)
    Big Pits Wood
    Pickworth Great Wood
    Newell Wood
    Castle Dike

5   Greetham Wood Far
    Quarry (dis)
    The Grange
    Clay Pit
    Newell Lane

14 Quarry (dis)
    Woolfox Wood
    Church (remains of)
    Pickworth

4   Airfield (dis)
    The Plains
    Pit (dis)

    The Coppice
    Casterton Lane

13 Woolfox Depot
    Turnpole Wood

3   Hardwick Wood
    CH
    Pickworth Plain
    Taylor's Farm

    Rutland County Golf Course

12 North Road Spinney
    Pickworth Lane
    Exeter Gorse
    Woodhead
    East Wood

2   Medieval Village of Horn (site of)
    Little Oaks
    Bloody Oaks
    Warren Plantation
    Woodhead Castle (site of)

    Horn Farm
    Great North Road
    Tickencote Warren
    Pickworth Road

11 Pug's Park Spinney
    Mounts Lodge

    North Brook

1   Horn Lane
    Empingham Old Wood
    Wing Plantations
    Quarry (dis)

    Horn Mill Spinney
    Loves La
    Tickencote Laund
    A1

10
    95 A 96 B 97 C 98 D 99 E 00 F

A1 Grantham

Leicestershire & Rutland STREET ATLAS

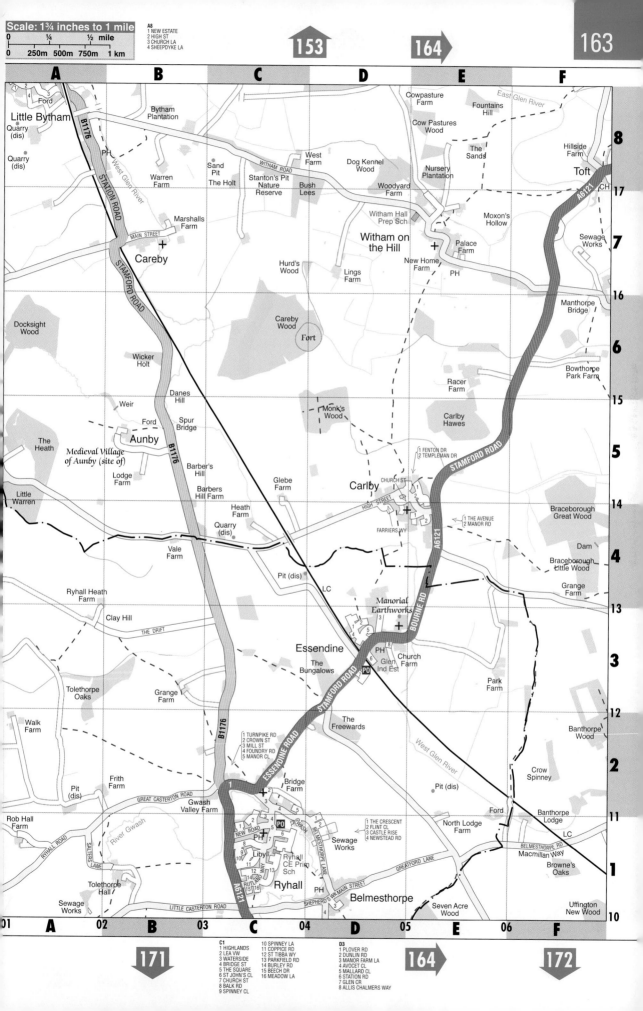

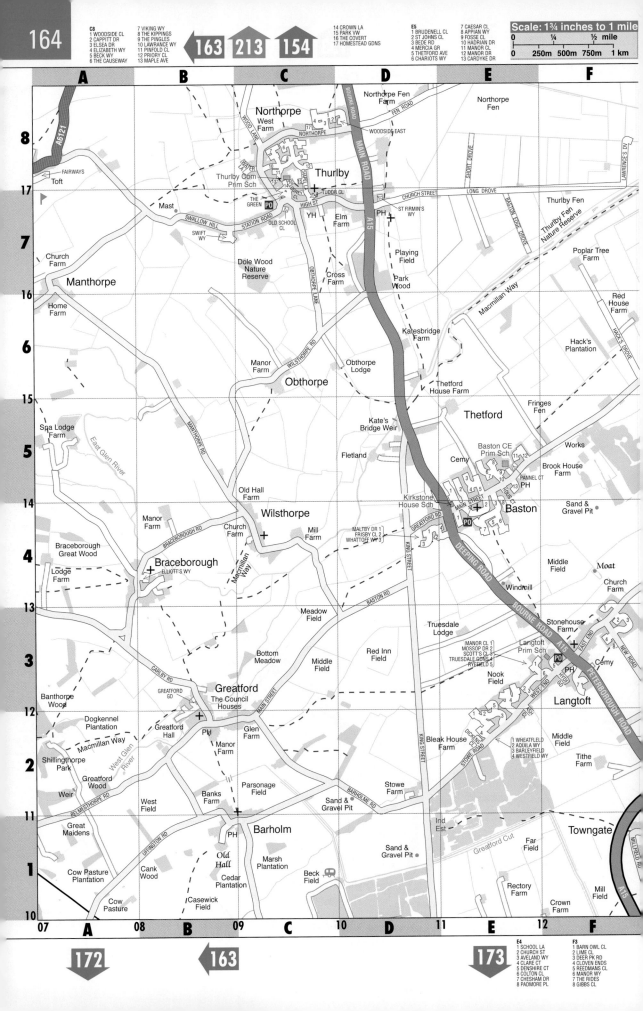

C8
1 WOODSIDE CL
2 CAPPITT DR
3 ELSEA DR
4 ELIZABETH WY
5 BECK WY
6 THE CAUSEWAY

7 VIKING WY
8 THE KIPPINGS
9 THE PINGLES
10 LAWRANCE WY
11 PINFOLD CL
12 PRIORY CL
13 MAPLE AVE

14 CROWN LA
15 PARK VW
16 THE COVERT
17 HOMESTEAD GDNS

E5
1 BRUDENELL CL
2 ST JOHNS CL
3 BEDE RD
4 MERCIA GR
5 THETFORD AVE
6 CHARIOTS WY

7 CAESAR CL
8 APPIAN WY
9 FOSSE CL
10 HADRIAN DR
11 MANOR CL
12 MANOR DR
13 CARDYKE DR

Scale: 1¾ inches to 1 mile
0   ¼   ½   mile
0   250m 500m 750m 1 km

163 213 154

A B C D E F

8 Fairways
Toft
Mast
Church Farm
Manthorpe

17 Thurlby Com Prim Sch
The Green PO
High St
YH
Elm Farm
St Firmin's Wy
PH
Northorpe Fen Farm
Woodside East
Northorpe Fen
West Farm
Northorpe
Thurlby
Tudor Cl
Church Street
Long Drove
Thurlby Fen Nature Reserve

7 Swallow Hill
Swift Wy
Station Road
Old School Cl
Cross Farm
Playing Field
Park Wood
Dole Wood Nature Reserve
Poplar Tree Farm

16 Home Farm
Manor Farm
Obthorpe
Obthorpe Lodge
Katesbridge Farm
Thetford House Farm
Hack's Plantation
Red House Farm

15 Spa Lodge Farm
Kate's Bridge Weir
Fletland
Thetford
Fringes Fen
Works

6 East Glen River
Manor Farm
Obthorpe Lodge
Cemy
Baston CE Prim Sch
Brook House Farm
Pannel Ct
PH

5 Spa Lodge Farm
Manthorpe Rd
Old Hall Farm
Wilsthorpe
Church Farm
Mill Farm
Kirkstone House Sch
Main Street
Baston
PO
Sand & Gravel Pit

14 Braceborough Great Wood
Manor Farm
Macmillan Way
Braceborough
Elliott's Wy
Maltby Dr 1
Frisby Cl 2
Whattoff Wy 3
Greatford Rd
King Street
Middle Field
Moat
Church Farm
Windmill

4 Lodge Farm
Braceborough Rd
Meadow Field
Truesdale Lodge
Deeping Road
Bourne Road
Stonehouse Farm
East End
New Road
Cemy

13 Banthorpe Wood
Carlby Rd
Bottom Meadow
Middle Field
Red Inn Field
Manor Cl 1
Mossop Dr 2
Scott's Cl 3
Truesdale Gdns 4
Ryefield 5
Langtoft Prim Sch
PO
PH

3 Greatford Gd
Greatford
The Council Houses
Nook Field
Langtoft

12 Shillingthorpe Park
Greatford Hall
PH
Macmillan Way
West Glen River
Manor Farm
Glen Farm
Bleak House Farm
King Street
Stowe Road
Dickens Cl
West End
1 Wheatfield
2 Aquila Wy
3 Barleyfield
4 Westfield Wy
Middle Field
Tithe Farm

2 Greatford Wood
Weir
Belmesthorpe Rd
West Field
Banks Farm
Parsonage Field
Sand & Gravel Pit
Barholme Rd
Stowe Farm
Ind Est

11 Great Maidens
Uftington Rd
Barholm
PH
Beck Field
Sand & Gravel Pit
Greatford Cut
Far Field
Towngate
Millford Rd

1 Cow Pasture Plantation
Cank Wood
Old Hall
Cedar Plantation
Casewick Field
Marsh Plantation
Rectory Farm
Crown Farm
Mill Field

10 Cow Pasture

07 08 09 10 11 12

A B C D E F

172 163 173

E4
1 SCHOOL LA
2 CHURCH ST
3 AVELAND WY
4 CLARE CT
5 DENSHIRE CT
6 COLTON CL
7 CHESHAM DR
8 PADMORE PL

F3
1 BARN OWL CL
2 LIME CL
3 DEER PK RD
4 CLOVEN ENDS
5 REEDMANS CL
6 MANOR WY
7 THE RIDES
8 GIBBS CL

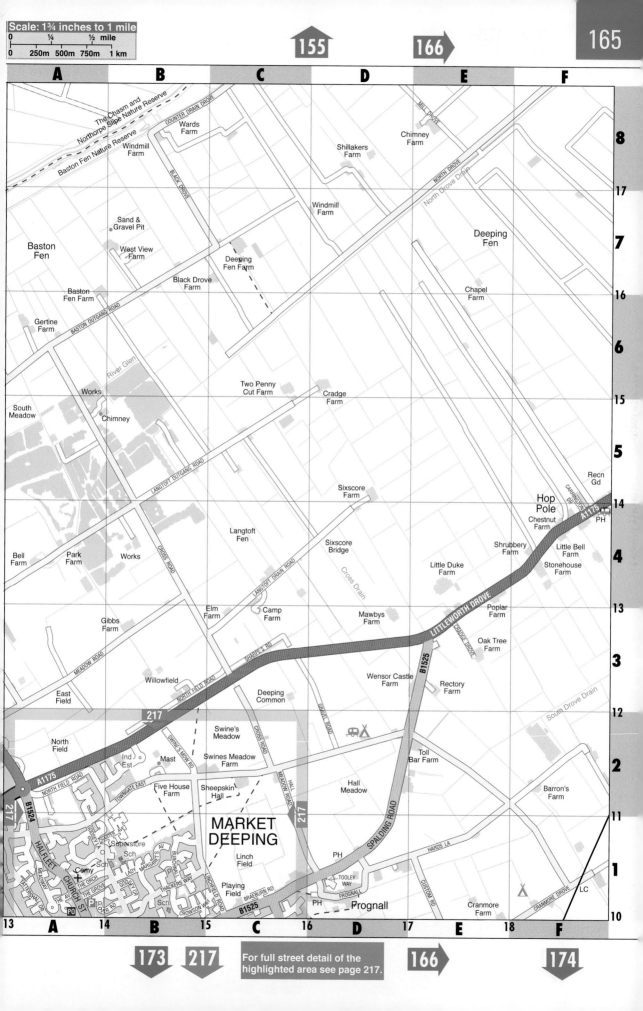

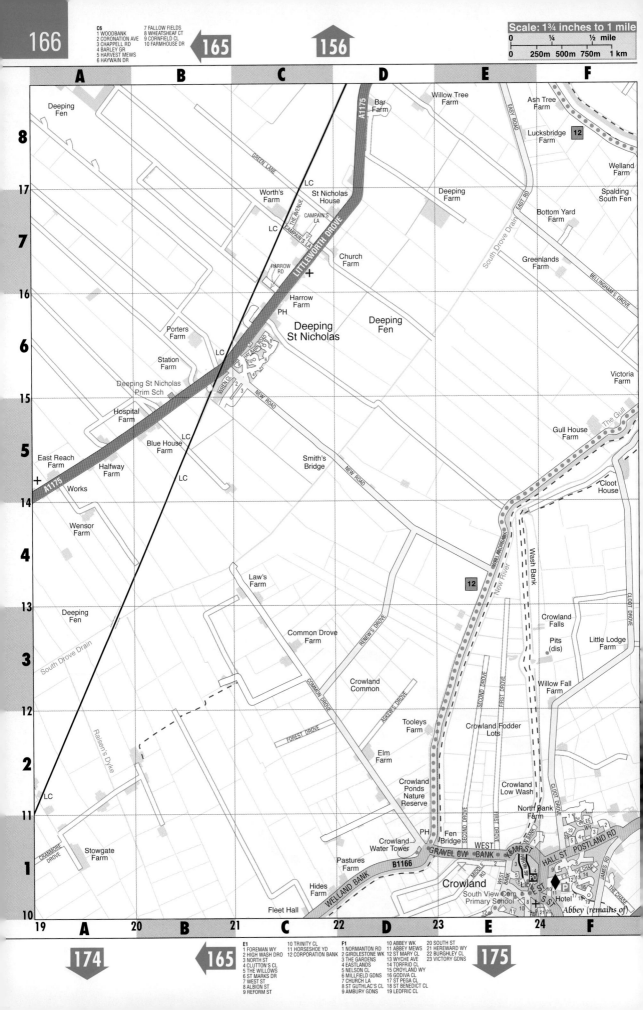

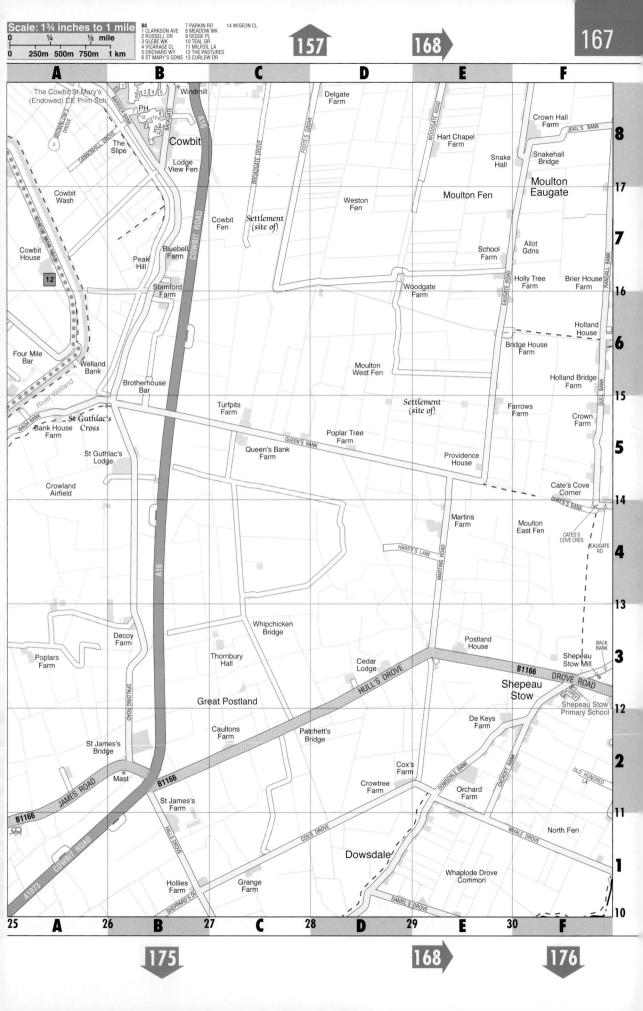

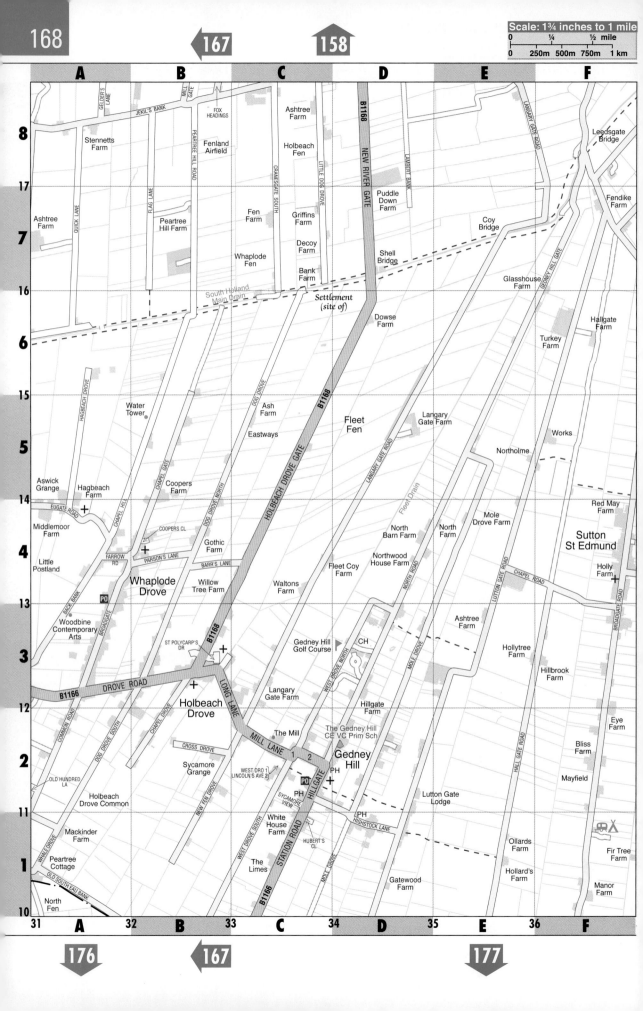

Scale: 1¾ inches to 1 mile

0   ¼   ½   mile

0   250m 500m 750m   1 km

Column A

GELDER'S LANE

Stennetts Farm

JEKIL'S BANK

Ashtree Farm

QUICK LANE

FLAG LANE

Middlemoor Farm

Aswick Grange

Hagbeach Farm

HAGBEACH DROVE

EUGATE ROAD

Little Postland

CHAPEL HILL

BACK BANK

FARROW RD

Woodbine Contemporary Arts

Whaplode Drove

PO

BROADGATE

B1166

COMMON ROAD

Old Hundred La

Holbeach Drove Common

Mackinder Farm

DOG DROVE SOUTH

WHALE DROVE

Peartree Cottage

OLD SOUTH EAU BANK

North Fen

Column B

MILL GATE

FOX HEADINGS

PEARTREE HILL ROAD

Fenland Airfield

Peartree Hill Farm

Coopers Farm

CHAPEL GATE

COOPERS CL

Gothic Farm

PARSON'S LANE

Willow Tree Farm

BARR'S LANE

DOG DROVE NORTH

St Polycarp's Dr

B1168

Holbeach Drove

CHAPEL DROVE

Sycamore Grange

CROSS DROVE

NEW FEN DROVE

Column C

Ashtree Farm

Holbeach Fen

CRANESGATE SOUTH

Fen Farm

Griffins Farm

Decoy Farm

Whaplode Fen

Bank Farm

LITTLE DOG DROVE

DOG DROVE

Water Tower

Ash Farm

Eastways

HOLBEACH DROVE GATE

Waltons Farm

Langary Gate Farm

LONG LANE

MILL LANE

The Mill

1 2

WEST DRO 1
LINCOLN'S AVE 2

STATION ROAD

WEST DROVE SOUTH

White House Farm

SYCAMORE VIEW

PH

The Limes

B1166

HUBERT'S CL

Column D

B1168

NEW RIVER GATE

Puddle Down Farm

LAMBERT BANK

Shell Bridge

Settlement (site of)

Dowse Farm

B1168

Fleet Fen

Fleet Coy Farm

Gedney Hill Golf Course

CH

WEST DROVE NORTH

Gedney Hill

PH

PO

PH

HIGHSTOCK LANE

PH

Gatewood Farm

MOLE DROVE

NORTH ROAD

North Barn Farm

North Farm

Northwood House Farm

The Gedney Hill CE VC Prim Sch

Hillgate Farm

HILLGATE

Column E

LANGARY GATE ROAD

Coy Bridge

GEDNEY HILL GATE

Glasshouse Farm

Turkey Farm

Langary Gate Farm

Northolme

LANGARY GATE ROAD

Fleet Drain

Mole Drove Farm

Ashtree Farm

LUTTON GATE ROAD

CHAPEL ROAD

Hollytree Farm

HALL GATE ROAD

Lutton Gate Lodge

Ollards Farm

Hollard's Farm

Column F

Leedsgate Bridge

Fendike Farm

Hallgate Farm

Works

Red May Farm

Sutton St Edmund

Holly Farm

BROADGATE ROAD

Hillbrook Farm

Eye Farm

Bliss Farm

Mayfield

Fir Tree Farm

Manor Farm

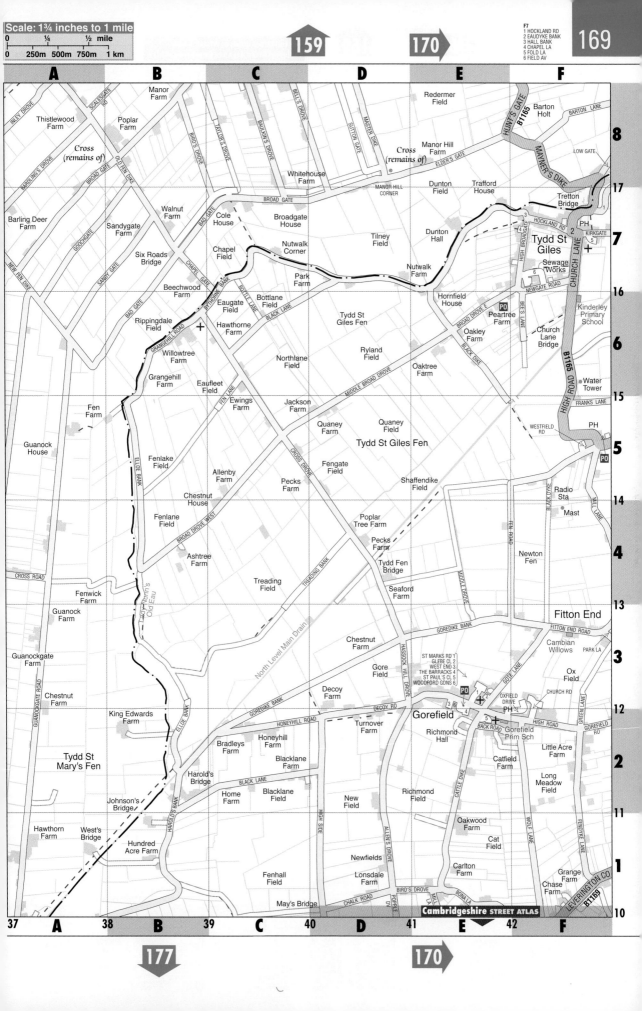

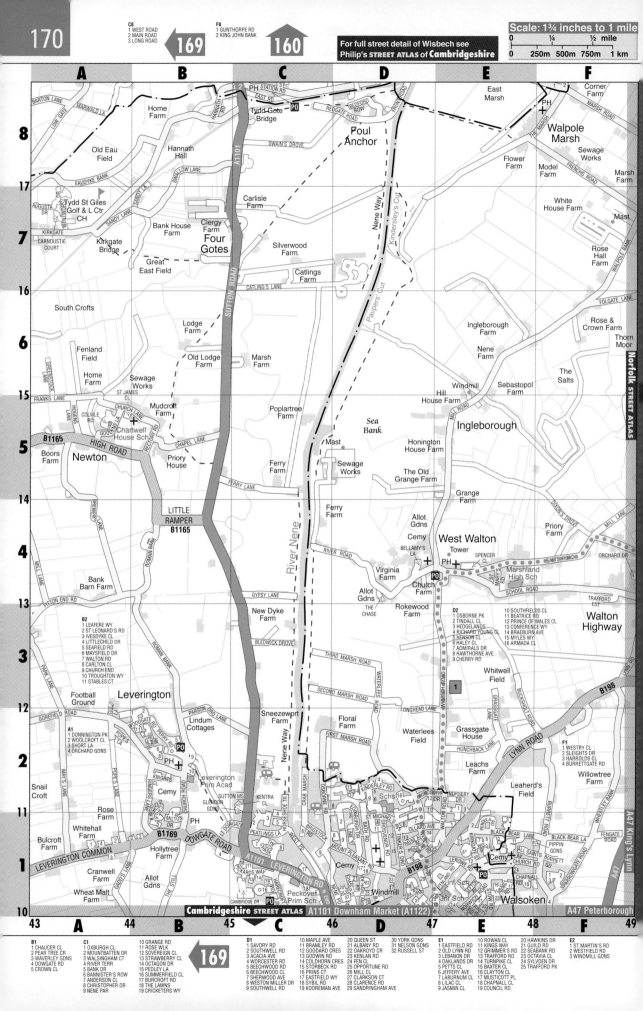

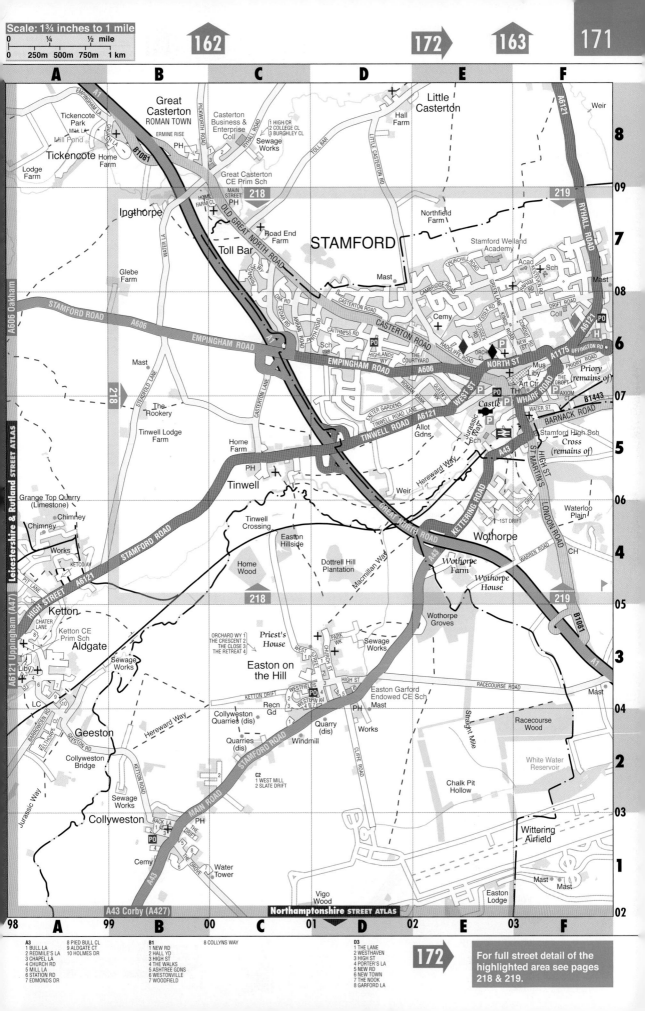

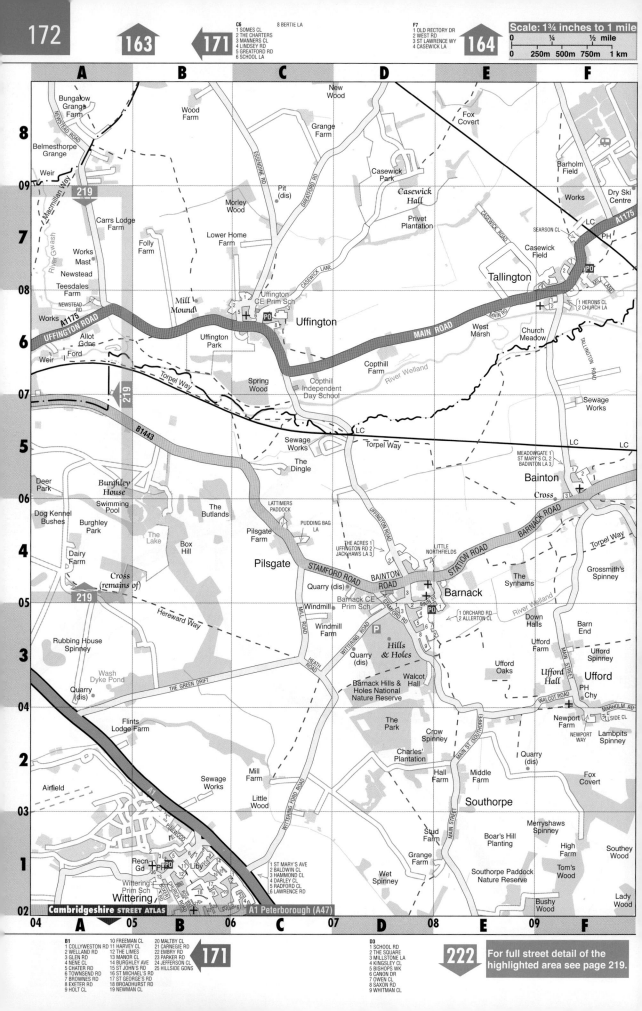

163
171
164

C6
1 SOMES CL
2 THE CHARTERS
3 MANNERS CL
4 LINDSEY RD
5 GREATFORD RD
6 SCHOOL LA

8 BERTIE LA

F7
1 OLD RECTORY DR
2 WEST RD
3 ST LAWRENCE WY
4 CASEWICK LA

Scale: 1¾ inches to 1 mile

0   ¼   ½ mile
0   250m 500m 750m 1 km

Column letters: A B C D E F

Row numbers: 8 09 7 08 6 07 5 06 4 05 3 04 2 03 1 02

Bungalow Grange Farm
Wood Farm
New Wood
Grange Farm
Fox Covert
Barholm Field
Dry Ski Centre

Belmesthorpe Grange
Weir
219
Essendine Rd
Pit (dis)
Casewick Park
Casewick Hall
Works
LC
A1175
Searson Cl
PH

Carrs Lodge Farm
Morley Wood
Privet Plantation
Casewick Road
Casewick Field
Mill La
PO
Macmillan Way

Works
Mast
Newstead
Folly Farm
Lower Home Farm
Casewick Lane
Tallington
1 HERONS CL
2 CHURCH LA

Teesdales Farm
NEWSTEAD RD
Mill Mound
Uffington CE Prim Sch
PO
Uffington
Main Rd
West Marsh
Church Meadow

Works
A1175
UFFINGTON ROAD
Allot Gdns
Uffington Park
Copthill Farm
River Welland
Tallington Road

Weir
Ford
Torpel Way
Spring Wood
Copthill Independent Day School
Sewage Works

River Gwash
219
B1443
Sewage Works
The Dingle
LC
Torpel Way
LC
LC

Deer Park
Burghley House
The Butlands
LATTIMERS PADDOCK
MEADOWGATE 1
ST MARY S CL 2
BADINTON LA 3
Bainton
Cross

Dog Kennel Bushes
Swimming Pool
Burghley Park
Pilsgate Farm
PUDDING BAG LA
THE ACRES 1
UFFINGTON RD 2
JACKHAWS LA 3
Station Road
BARNACK ROAD
Torpel Way

Dairy Farm
Box Hill
The Lake
Pilsgate
STAMFORD ROAD
BAINTON ROAD
LITTLE NORTHFIELDS
Barnack
Grossmith's Spinney
The Synhams

Cross (remains of)
219
Hereward Way
Quarry (dis)
Windmill
Barnack CE Prim Sch
PO
1 ORCHARD RD
2 ALLERTON CL
Down Halls
Barn End
Ufford Spinney

Rubbing House Spinney
Windmill Farm
MILL ROAD
P
WITTERING RD
Hills & Holes
Ufford Oaks
Ufford Hall
Ufford Farm
Ufford
PH
Chy

Wash Dyke Pond
THE GREEN DRIFT
HEATH ROAD
Quarry (dis)
Walcot Hall
Walcot Road
MARHOLM RD
HILLSIDE RD

Quarry (dis)
Barnack Hills & Holes National Nature Reserve
The Park
Crow Spinney
Newport Farm
NEWPORT WAY
Lambpits Spinney

Flints Lodge Farm
A1
Sewage Works
Mill Farm
WITTERING FORD ROAD
Charles' Plantation
MAIN ST ISOUTHORPE
Hall Farm
Middle Farm
Quarry (dis)
Fox Covert

Airfield
Little Wood
Southorpe
Merryshaws Spinney
High Farm
Southey Wood

PINEWOOD
Recn Gd
PH PO
Liby
1 ST MARY'S AVE
2 BALDWIN CL
3 HAMMOND CL
4 DARLEY CL
5 RADFORD CL
6 LAWRENCE RD
Stud Farm
Grange Farm
Boar's Hill Planting
Tom's Wood

Wittering Prim Sch
CHURCH ROAD
Wittering
A1 Peterborough (A47)
Wet Spinney
Southorpe Paddock Nature Reserve
Bushy Wood
Lady Wood

Cambridgeshire STREET ATLAS

B1
1 COLLYWESTON RD
2 WELLAND RD
3 GLEN RD
4 NENE CL
5 CHATER RD
6 TOWNSEND RD
7 BROWNES RD
8 EXETER RD
9 HOLT CL
10 FREEMAN CL
11 HARVEY CL
12 THE LIMES
13 MANOR CL
14 BURGHLEY AVE
15 ST JOHN'S RD
16 ST MICHAEL'S RD
17 ST GEORGE'S RD
18 BROADHURST RD
19 NEWMAN CL
20 MALTBY CL
21 CARNEGIE RD
22 EMBRY RD
23 PARKER RD
24 JEFFERSON CL
25 HILLSIDE GDNS

171

D3
1 SCHOOL RD
2 THE SQUARE
3 MILLSTONE LA
4 KINGSLEY CL
5 BISHOPS WK
6 CANON DR
7 OWEN CL
8 SAXON RD
9 WHITMAN CL

222   For full street detail of the highlighted area see page 219.

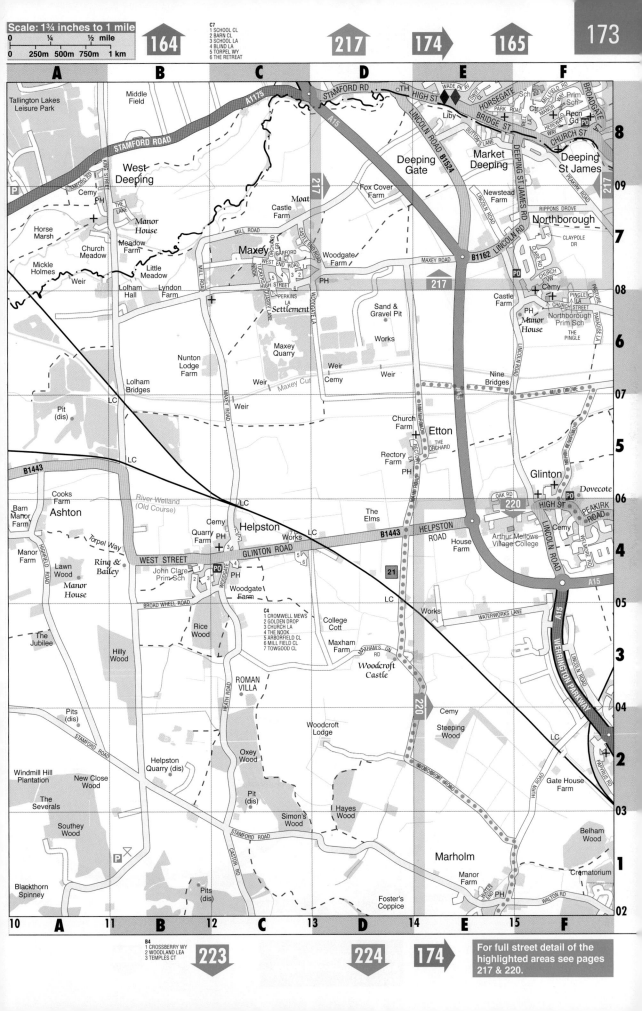

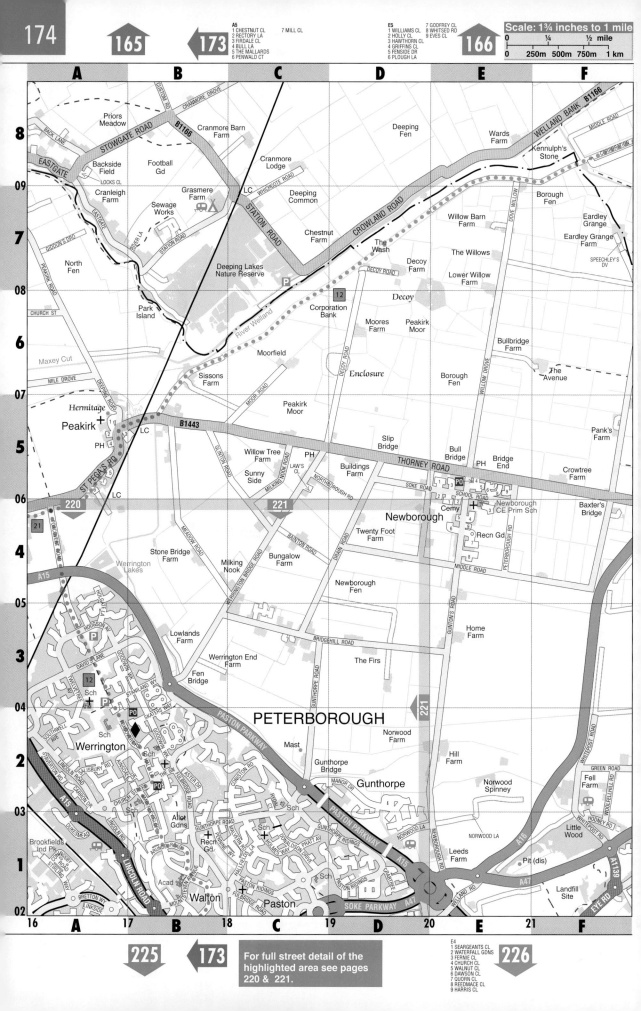

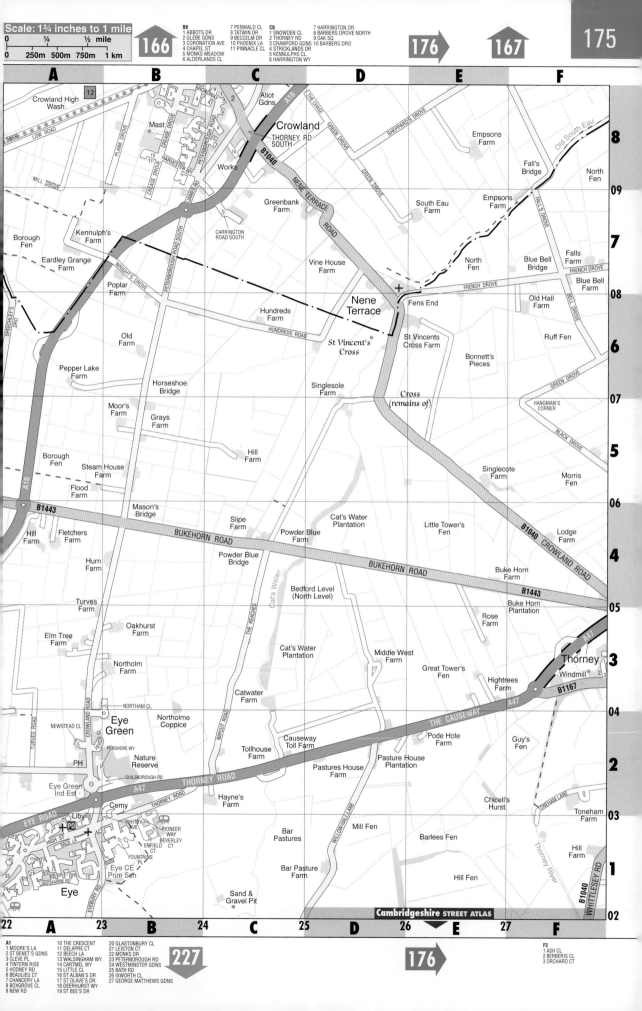

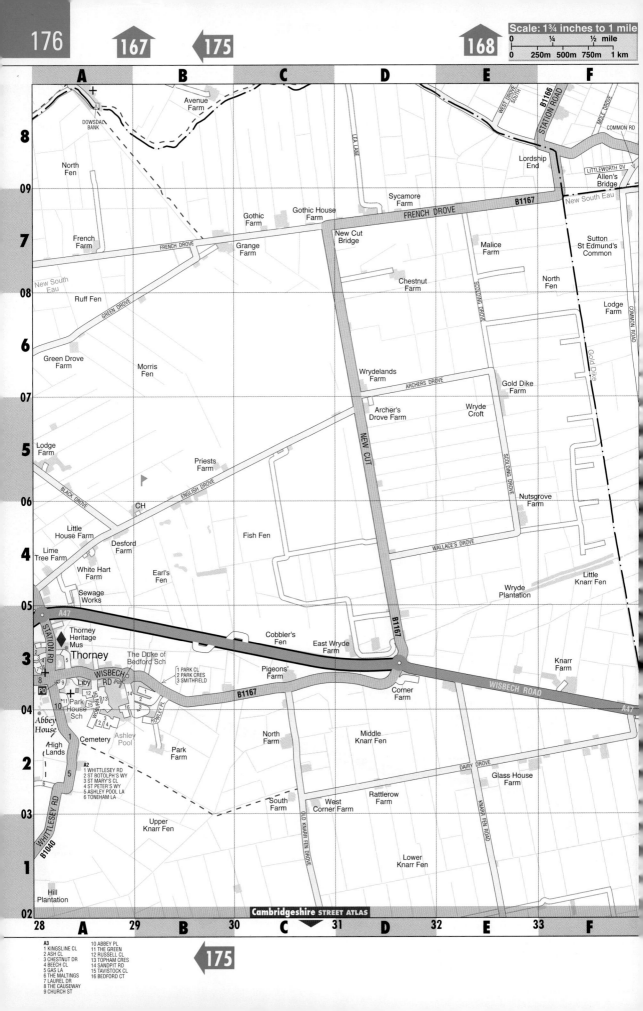

A   B   C   D   E   F

8
09
7
08
6
07
5
06
4
05
3
04
2
03
1
02

North Fen
DOWSDALE BANK
Avenue Farm
French Farm
French Drove
Gothic Farm
Gothic House Farm
Grange Farm
Sycamore Farm
New Cut Bridge
FRENCH DROVE
B1167
Malice Farm
Sutton St Edmund's Common
WEST DROVE SOUTH
STATION ROAD
B1166
COMMON RD
Lordship End
LITTLEWORTH DV
Allen's Bridge
New South Eau
North Fen
Lodge Farm

New South Eau
Ruff Fen
GREEN DROVE
Green Drove Farm
Morris Fen
LEA LANE
Chestnut Farm
Wrydelands Farm
ARCHERS DROVE
SCOLDING DROVE
Gold Dike Farm
Wryde Croft
GOLD DIKE
COMMON ROAD
Lodge Farm
Archer's Drove Farm
NEW CUT
Priests Farm
ENGLISH DROVE
BLACK DROVE
CH
Little House Farm
Desford Farm
Lime Tree Farm
White Hart Farm
Earl's Fen
Fish Fen
WALLACE'S DROVE
Nutsgrove Farm
Little Knarr Fen
Wryde Plantation
Sewage Works
A47
Thorney Heritage Mus
Thorney
The Duke of Bedford Sch
WISBECH RD
STATION RD
Cobbler's Fen
East Wryde Farm
B1167
Knarr Farm
Pigeons' Farm
1 PARK CL
2 PARK CRES
3 SMITHFIELD
Liby
PO
Park House Sch
B1167
Corner Farm
WISBECH ROAD
A47
Abbey House
Cemetery
Ashley Pool
High Lands
Park Farm
North Farm
Middle Knarr Fen
A2
1 WHITTLESEY RD
2 ST BOTOLPH'S WY
3 ST MARY'S CL
4 ST PETER'S WY
5 ASHLEY POOL LA
6 TONEHAM LA
DAIRY DROVE
Glass House Farm
WHITTLESEY RD
B1040
Upper Knarr Fen
South Farm
West Corner Farm
Rattlerow Farm
OLD KNARR FEN DROVE
KNARR FEN ROAD
Hill Plantation
Lower Knarr Fen

28   A   29   B   30   C   31   D   32   E   33   F

A3
1 KINGSLINE CL
2 ASH CL
3 CHESTNUT DR
4 BEECH CL
5 GAS LA
6 THE MALTINGS
7 LAUREL DR
8 THE CAUSEWAY
9 CHURCH ST
10 ABBEY PL
11 THE GREEN
12 RUSSELL CL
13 TOPHAM CRES
14 SANDPIT RD
15 TAVISTOCK CL
16 BEDFORD CT

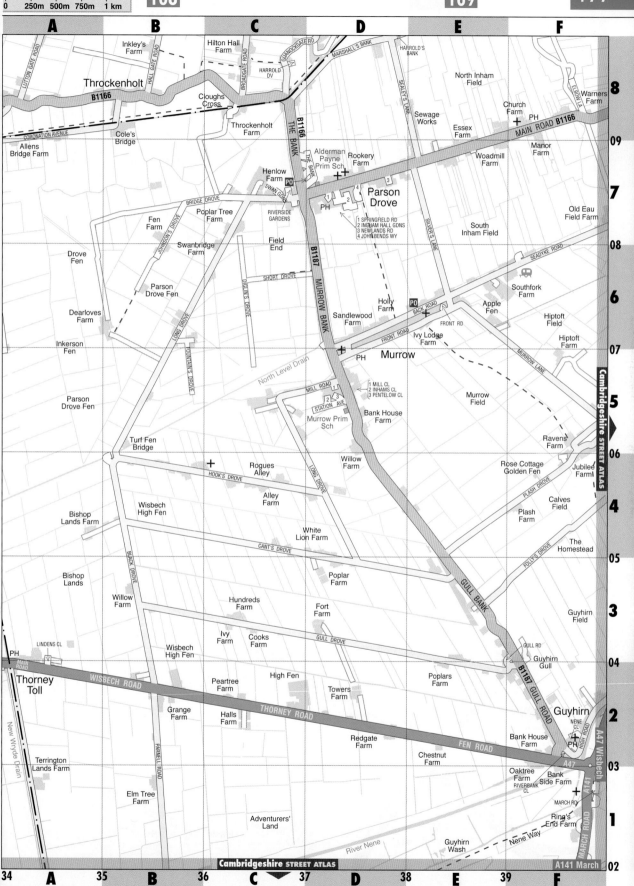

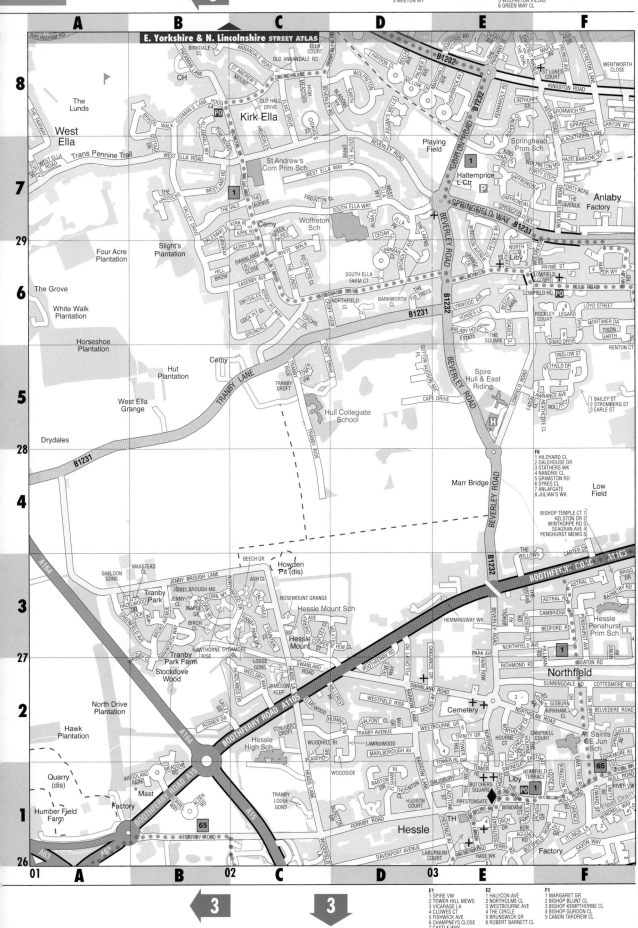

E6
1 NORTH DR
2 WILSON ST
3 WOLFRETON CT
4 RINGROSE LA

E7
1 CROMWELL CT
2 WOODHILL CL
3 NORWOOD CL
4 WAULDBY CL
5 WEETON WY

E8
1 COLLYNSON CL
2 SETTERWOOD GARTH
3 OAKDALE AV

F7
1 RAYWELL CL
2 PENWITH DR
3 ORCHARD CL
4 GLENHAM DR
5 WOLFRETON VILLAS
6 GREEN WAY CL

E. Yorkshire & N. Lincolnshire STREET ATLAS

E1
1 SPIRE VW
2 TOWER HILL MEWS
3 VICARAGE LA
4 CLOWES CT
5 FISHWICK AVE
6 CHAMPNEYS CLOSE
7 CASTLE WAY

E2
1 HALCYON AVE
2 NORTHOLME CL
3 WESTBOURNE AVE
4 THE CIRCLE
5 BRUNSWICK GR
6 ROBERT BARNETT CL

F1
1 MARGARET GR
2 BISHOP BLUNT CL
3 BISHOP KEMPTHORNE CL
4 BISHOP GURDON CL
5 CANON TARDREW CL

A3
1 BARNETBY RD
2 KELSTON DR
3 YARMOUTH AVE
4 WINTHORPE RD
5 BROCKLESBY CL
6 CORRAN GARTH
7 SEAGRAN AVE

B7
1 LANGFORD WK
2 HOLLYTREE AVE
3 LABURNUM DR
4 ROSEWOOD CL

C8
1 PRIMROSE DR
2 COUNTY RD S

D8
1 LOCKTON GR
2 HACKNESS GR
3 BARGATE GR
4 SNAINTON GR

E6
1 AIRMYN AVE
2 ST MARTINS AVE

F6
1 HAWTHORN CT

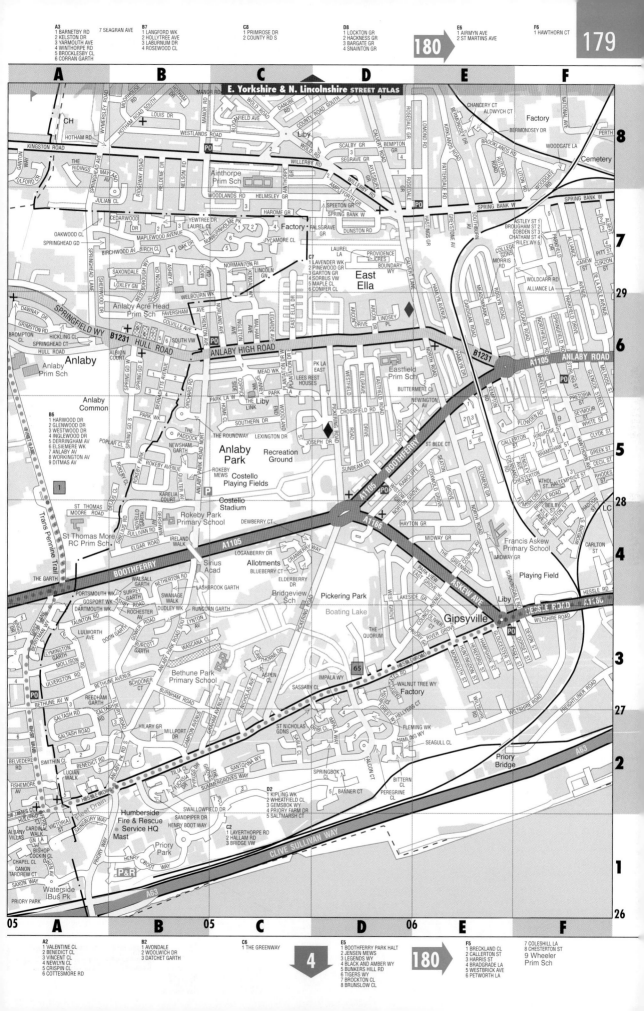

E. Yorkshire & N. Lincolnshire STREET ATLAS

A2
1 VALENTINE CL
2 BENEDICT CL
3 VINCENT CL
4 NEWLYN CL
5 CRISPIN CL
6 COTTESMORE RD

B2
1 AVONDALE
2 WOOLWICH DR
3 DATCHET GARTH

C6
1 THE GREENWAY

E5
1 BOOTHFERRY PARK HALT
2 JENSEN MEWS
3 LEGENDS WY
4 BLACK AND AMBER WY
5 BUNKERS HILL RD
6 TIGERS WY
7 BROCKTON CL
8 BRUNSLOW CL

F5
1 BRECKLAND CL
2 CALLERTON ST
3 HARRIS ST
4 BRADGRADE LA
5 WESTBRICK AVE
6 PETWORTH LA
7 COLESHILL LA
8 CHESTERTON ST
9 WHEELER PRIM SCH

E. Yorkshire & N. Lincolnshire STREET ATLAS

KINGSTON UPON HULL

River Humber

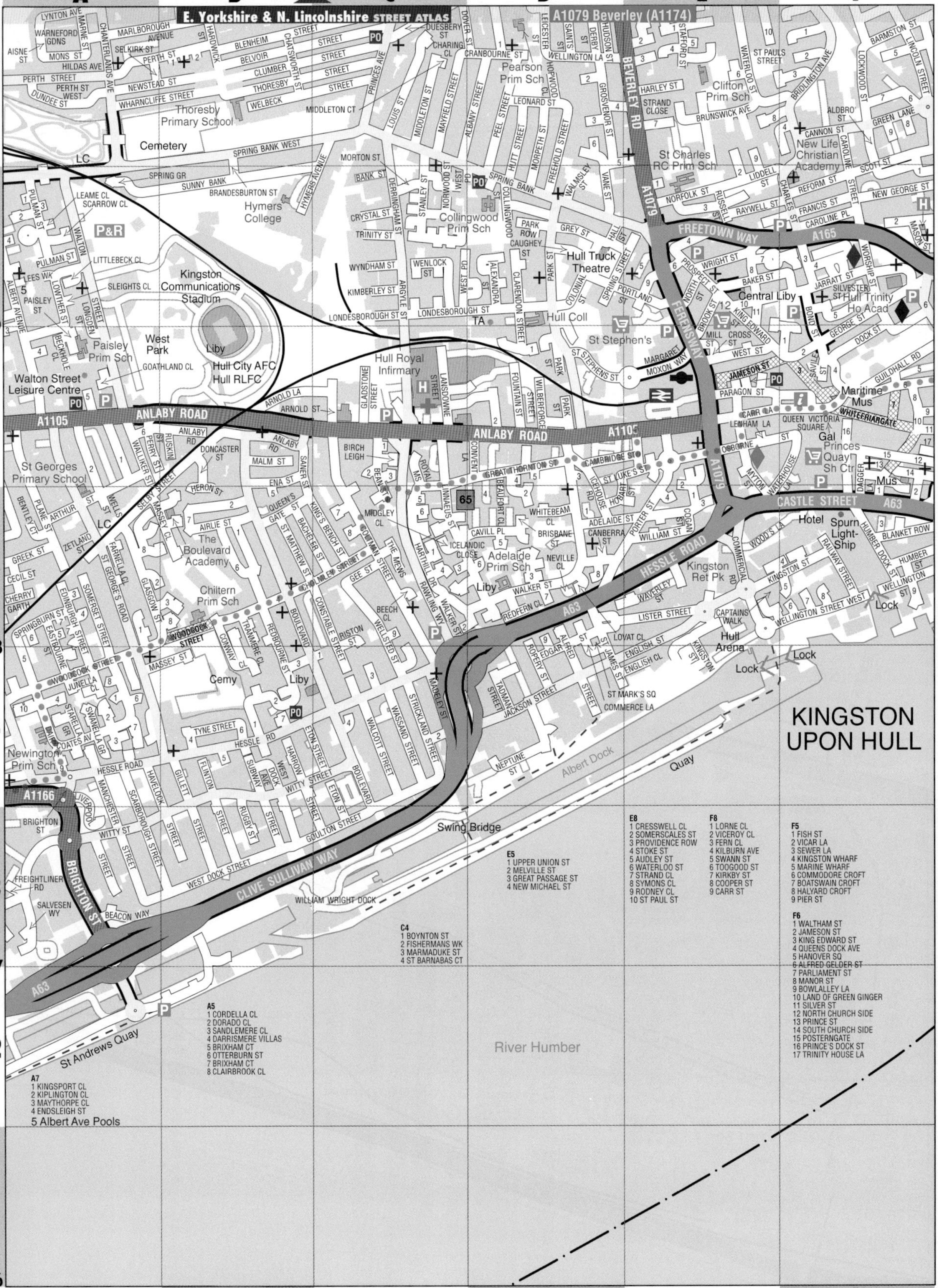

For full street detail of Hull see Philip's **STREET ATLAS** of **East Yorkshire**

A6	7 CHURCH LA STAITH	A7	B7	C7	7 DENMARK CT	C8	D7	E8
1 BLAIDES STAITHE	8 TRINITY WHARF	1 CHARTERHOUSE LA	1 PEMBERTON ST	1 PELHAM DR	8 EMILY ST	1 NORNABELL ST	1 BUTTERCUP CL	1 DOVEDALE GR
2 GUILDHALL RD	9 SCALE LA STAITH	2 APPLEGARTH RD	2 BLYTH ST	2 EDWARD COLLINS SQ		2 BALFOUR ST	2 PENISTONE CT	2 DEEPDALE GR
3 HANOVER SQ	10 CHAPEL LA STAITH	3 LITTLE MASON ST	3 NAYLOR'S ROW	3 HODGE CT		3 ARUNDEL ST	3 BEAUMONT CT	3 MIDDLEHAM CL
4 ALFRED GELDER ST		4 CARROLL PL	4 WILSON ST	4 ROSEY ROW		4 ST QUINTINS CL	4 BRUMBY'S TERR	4 BYLAND CT
5 GANDHI WY		5 CHARLOTTE PL	5 EAST ST	5 ALDERSON MEWS		5 BABINGTON ROW	5 EMPRINGHAM ST	
6 MARKET PL		6 DOCK OFFICE ROW	6 ALMA ST	6 BROADLEY CL				

181

C5
1 ACACIA AVE
2 MAPLE AVE
3 PIPPIN CT
4 RUSSET CL

C6
1 POPPY CL
2 WOODALE CL
3 FLETCHER CL
4 COLTSFOOT CL
5 ST MARY'S CT
6 HERON CL

17

8

B2
1 TANSLEY CT
2 ALFRETON CT
3 HATHERSAGE CT
4 GRASSMOOR CT
5 EASTWOOD CT
6 BELPER CT

B3
1 BAKEWELL CT
2 ILKESTON CT
3 DRONFIELD CT

E3
1 JACKSON RD
2 DE ASTON SQ
3 CONWAY SQ
4 TOMLINSON AVE
5 ASHDOWN AVE

E4
1 LOCKWOOD CT
2 MALLALIEU CT
3 MARY SUMNER WY
4 KIRK CLOSE

F2
1 ERYHOLME CR
2 FUCHSIA CRFT
3 PAVILION GDNS

F4
1 LONG RD
2 HENDERSON CRES
3 EDWARDS RD
4 SHEFFIELD ST
5 BUCKINGHAM ST
6 Comm Ctr

17

184

18

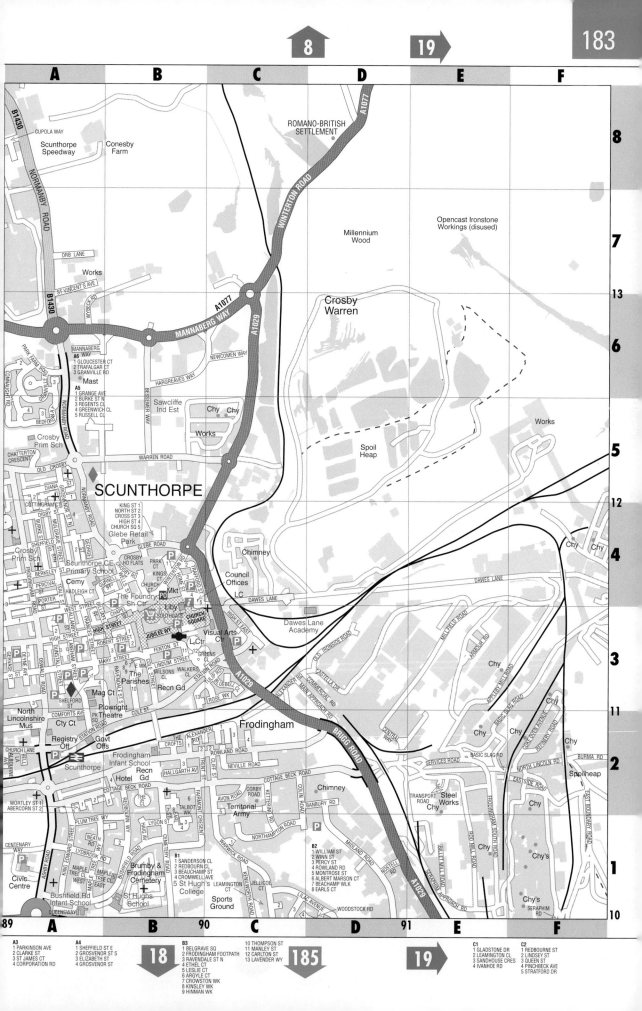

17

182

C5
1 BETULA WY
2 CONIFER CL
3 ACER GR

C6
1 FOURTH AVE
2 THIRD AVE
3 SECOND AVE
4 SHAKESPEARE AVE
5 SIDNEY RD

C7
1 ROCHESTER CL
2 SALISBURY CL
3 ST ALBANS CL

D7
1 CANTERBURY CL
2 NEWBOLT AVE
3 LANDOR AVE
4 KIPLING AVE
5 COVENTRY CL

D8
1 QUANTOCK CL
2 CLEVELAND CL
3 BARNSTAPLE RD

E6
1 BROWNING CL
2 MAVIS RD
3 MALLARD RD
4 KIPLING AVE
5 PHEASANT CL
6 SAXTON CL

F8
1 NORMAN CRES
2 GLANVILLE CRES
3 HAWTHORNE CRES
4 HAWTHORNE AVE

Column labels: A | B | C | D | E | F

Row labels: 8, 7, 09, 6, 5, 08, 4, 3, 07, 2, 1, 06

A18 KINGSWAY

M181
M180

Brumby Grove

BRIDPORT WK
HELSTON WK
TAMAR WK
HINDON WALK
LYNMOUTH DR
MELBURY WALK
EXMOOR RD
PADSTOW WK
BEAFORD COURT
TORRINGTON RD
WOOTTON CT
LULWORTH CT
DORCHESTER RD

Oasis Academy Parkwood

CHARLES LOVELL WY
BUCKFASTLEIGH
ALVESTON RD
BRIDGEWATER RD
SEATON RD
CLEVEDON RD
CHILTERN CR
STANIWELL LA

Cemy
Allotment Gardens

North Lindsey College
West Common Sports Hall
John Leggott College

BRUMBY COMMON LANE
WEST COMMON LANE

KINGSWAY
LLOYDS AVENUE
DANUM RD
ATLAS RD
HAMILTON RD
THOMAS RD
PEVERIL AVENUE
GLOVER RD
GLANVILLE AVE
WEST CL CRES
PEVERIL AV

Brumby Common Nature Reserve

Brumby Common

SARAH'S WALK
PAUL'S WK
CLARES WK
KERBLES WK
SIXTH AVE
FIFTH AVE
LAGOON RD

SELBY CT
SWINBURNE LA
SWINBURNE ROAD
COLERIDGE AVE
COWPER AVE
THE PRECINCT
BEVERLEY CT
KEATS
CLARE AVE
CHAUCER AVE
HARDY RD
HERRICK RD
CHAPMAN AVE

Liby
PO

Westcliff
169

BELVEDERE DR
WESTCLIFF GD
ROTHBURY RD
CLARENDON RD
WYNMOOR RD
CHELWOOD
CHANDOS
MALVERN ROAD

Melior Community Academy

LICHFIELD AVE
MARLOWE
SCOTT AV
NORTH CL
SKELTON ROAD
WORDSWORTH RD
GRAY AV
HOOD RD
SWIFT
MEREDITH AVE
WOODSCLOSE
BROOKDALE
BYFIELD RD
WHITFIELD RD
MEADOW RD
WHITESTONE RD
DRYDEN RD

Priory Lane Junior School

BLAKE AV
BYRON CL
BRIDGES RD
MERLIN RD
ORIOLE
DEAN
GREYFRIARS
PRIORY LA
TEMPLE RD
ABBEY RD
ABBOTS RD
CLOISTER CL
PRIORY LANE
MINNS RD
NUNS CT
HUMBER CR
DEVONSHIRE RD

Westcliffe Primary School

Manor Park

BURRINGHAM ROAD
B1450

Recreation Ground
PO
ROWAN WAY

Carisbrooke Manor

CARISBROOKE MANOR LANE
MAIN AVENUE
FIRST AVENUE
NEW ROAD
WESTFIELD RD

Ashfield Park

CH
PH
WOODSIDE DR

Warp Farm

Ashby Decoy

Ashby Decoy Golf Course

LAKESIDE DR
SANDFIELD CL
SILICA CR
THE DELL
ALBA
TATTERSALL CLOSE
ILCBY
WYBERB RD
ENDERBY ROAD

BEESBY ROAD
OXBY
GRASBY
FERRIBY ROAD
TEALBY RD
THORESBY RD
GUNBY
SOMERBY RD
SCAWBY
MALTBY RD
RIBY RD
RAINBY
SPILSBY ROAD
KINGERBY RD
AXHOLME
SALMONBY
KIRBY
MANBY ROAD
SCARBY ROAD
DRAGONBY
BIGBY
FOTHERBY RD

MORLEY
AYLESBY RD
ASTERBY RD
CLAXBY
PEACOCK ST
ANGERSTEIN ROAD
BARNETBY RD
APPLEBY CL
BONBY GR
PEACOCK RD

Recn Gd

Riddings
Liby
Willoughby Road Prim Acad
BROCKLESBY RD
WILLOUGHBY RD
POOL LA
DOLMAN
PARRIN RD

Riddings Swimming Pool
Melior Com Coll
Enderby Road Infant School

BOLINGBROKE RD
VANCOUVER CR
STAINTON DR
HAMMERTON RD
CRESTA
OVELL
ALBERT
QUEBEC ROAD
ONTARIO RD
OTTAWA
LOW LEYS RD
MASON DRIVE

Leys Farm Junior School
ETON CT
PARK AVENUE
SANDRINGHAM CRES
BALMORAL COURT
HIGH LEYS ROAD
ETON RD
OGILVY CR
THE DALES

Yaddlethorpe

Chy
P

GREENHOE
SUNNINGDALE ROAD
SUNNINGDALE RD
GOODWOOD
SOUTH PARK ROAD
BIRKDALE RD
HOYLAKE RD

South Park Industrial Estate

Bottesford Sports Ctr

South Park Ent Coll

NORTH FARM RD
NEWHOLME RD
WENTWORTH RD
MOORWELL ROAD
CROFT LA
ROSEDALE
KINGSDALE

Moorwell Business Park

Hillfoot Farm

BRANKWELL CR
WEST VW
ST ANNS
WEST VW
FENNELL
HILLFOOT AV
KENYA DR
SUTH GARTH
LOW GARTH
GREENGARTH
HIGH STREET
STUART RD
GRAVEL PIT LA
GARDENIA DR
ENDCLIFFE AVE
WINDSOR RD
GLANFORD RD
NURSERY

Southfield Farm

Grange Farm

M180

MOOR ROAD
GOLDEN CUP WAY

Bottesford Moor Farm
Newdowns Farm

Snake Plantation

Bottesford Beck

F2
1 LEE FAIR GDNS
2 ST ANDREWS AVE

17

29

E3
1 WADDINGTON DR
2 THE OVAL
3 EDGBASTON AVE
4 HEADINGLEY AVE
5 JESMOND AVE
6 LOW LEYS RD

F3
1 PRINCESS ALEXANDRA CT
2 SOUTH RIDGE CR
3 AUSTIN CR
4 THORNHILL CR
5 KIRMAN CR

F4
1 HARROW GDNS
2 KEDDINGTO CT

86 | 87 | 88

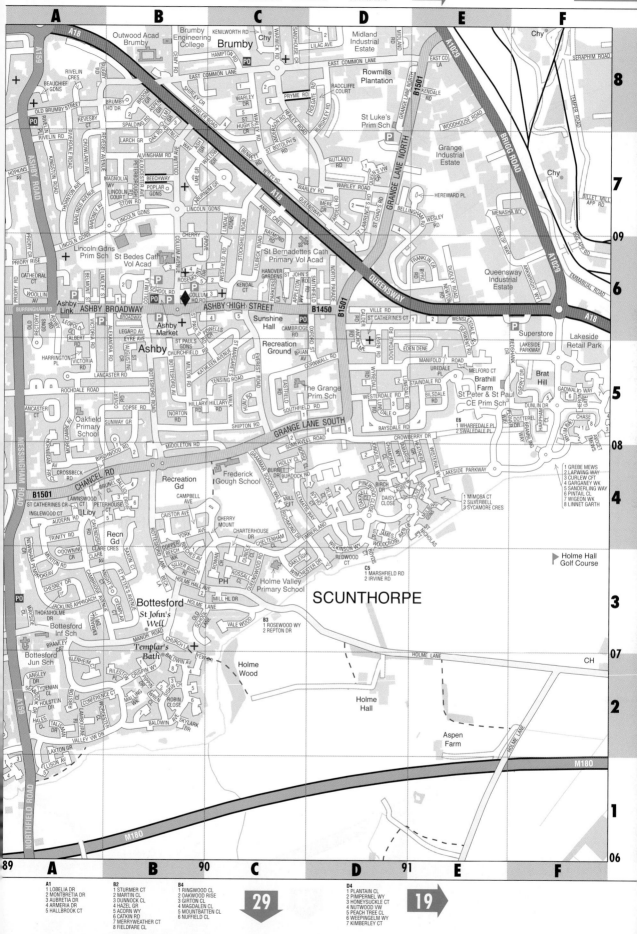

D5
1 HOYLAKE DR
2 COLLIER RD
3 BIRKDALE DR
4 SUNNINGDALE DR

Rosper Road Pools Nature Reserve

Houlton's Covert

Immingham Golf Course

Medieval Village of Immingham

Henderson Quay

Oil Storage Depot

Water Tower

West Haven Wy

West Riverside

Mineral Quay Road

Seven Quay Road

Alexandra Road South

South Osbourne Way

Gressley Way

Alexandra RD

Robinson RD

Works

Pelham Industrial Estate

Middleplatt Road

Sports Ground

Manby Hall Business Park

1 HUMBERVILLE RD
2 LARCH CL
3 TRENCHARD CL

HALL PARK RD

STANDISH LA 1
HINKLEY DR 2
WESTON GR 3
ATWOOD CL 4

Homestead Park

1 CEDAR DR
2 MAPLE GR
3 OAKLANDS RD

Football Ground

Allerton Primary School

Hotel

Immingham L Ctr

Washdyke Retail Park

Kennedy Way Shopping Ctr

Civic Ctr

Liby

Mkt

Cannon Peter Hall CE Prim Sch

IMMINGHAM

1 DEANE RD
2 SACKVILLE CL
3 WORSLEY CL
4 EATON RD

Swimming Pool

Oasis Academy

Immingham Business Units

Recreation Ground

Coomb Brigg's Prim Sch

ANCHOLME AVE 1
CALDER CL 2
STEEPING DR 3
AIRE CL 4

HABROUGH ROAD   B1210

THE ORCHARDS

Sports Gd

Highland Tarn

Immingham Museum

COLLIER RD 1
BREWSTER AV 2
THORNBURY RD 3

KISHORN CT 1
PERTH WY 2
TUMMEL CT 3

Eastfield Prim Academy

Highfield Farm

STALLINGBOROUGH ROAD

ORKNEY PL 1
FAIR ISLE RISE 2
LUNDY CT 3

Mauxhall Farm

A180   B1210

23   23

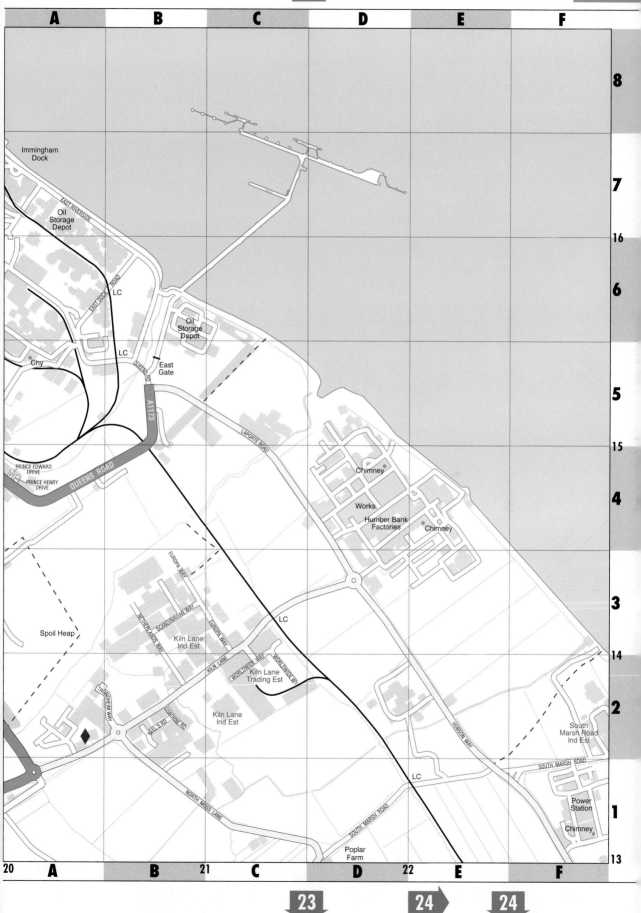

A B C D E F

8
7
13
6
5
12
4
3
11
2
1
10

River Humber

Works

Pyewipe

Chimney
Chimney
Works
Chimney

Water
Reclamation
Works

Sewage
Works

ENERGY PARK WAY

GENESIS WAY
LAKESIDE
LC
LC
LAFOREY ROAD

A180
Mast

NAVENSBY CL 1
ALLINGTON DR 2
RUSKINGTON CL 3

WOAD LANE

Sports
Ground

ESTATE RD NO 4
ESTATE RD NO 3
ESTATE ROAD NO 1

MOODY LANE

Sports
Ground

LC

Europa
Business
Park

ATHENA DR
APPIAN WY
Hotel

1 APIAN WY
2 SAXON CT

GILBEY ROAD

MOODY LANE

GATE WY

LC

ESTATE ROAD NO 5

SIBSEY
COURT

South Humberside
Industrial
Estate

ESTATE ROAD NO 7
ESTATE ROAD NO 6
ESTATE ROAD NO 2

Cherry Tree's
Business Park

Ventura
Business Park

ESTUARY WAY

WEST COATES RD

WESTSIDE ROAD

ALEXANDRA
DOCK NORTH

Alexandra Dock

NEWBURY AV
NEWBURY DR

PINE PL
TINTERN WALK
BYLAND GR
FOUNTAINS AV
MELROSE WY
BUCKFAST CL
SALTERGATE

CROMWELL RD
ST CHADS GATE
SOUTHLAND CT

CRANWELL DR
ESTATE RD NO 2

The Willows

West Marsh

HAVEN GDNS

Littlecoates
Prim Sch

NEW HAVEN TERRACE
HARLOW ST
GILBEY RD
ELSENHAM ROAD
HARGRAVE ST
SUMMON ST

Birch Way
Ind Est

BIRCHIN WAY

PYEWIPE ROAD

Pyewipe
Bungalows

BOULEVARD AV

BEESON GROVE
BEESON ST

WEST MARSH
IND EST

WESTGATE

ADAM SMITH ST
WATKIN ST NORTH

CHARLTON ST

ARMSTRONG ST

West Marsh
Ind Est

RENDEL ST
ALEXANDRA ROAD

Alexandra
Ret Pk

190 24 24 191

A1
1 FERNDOWN
2 SERVICE RD 12
3 SERVICE RD 14
4 SERVICE RD 13
5 RAVENSCAR RD
6 SERVICE RD 10
7 SERVICE RD 9
8 SERVICE RD 8
9 SERVICE RD 26

A3
1 ATHENIAN WY
2 FISKERTON GDNS
3 SARGON WY

D1
1 BRIDGE GDNS
2 CLEVELAND GDNS
3 CLEVELAND ST
4 CLAYDEN ST
5 STANSTED ST
6 CLAVERING ST
7 STORTFORD ST
8 SANDFORD ST

E1
1 CORPORATION RD
2 ARMSTRONG PL W
3 ARMSTRONG PL E
4 AYSCOUGH ST

F1
1 ANNESLEY ST
2 WATKIN ST STH

GRIMSBY

River Humber

The Dock Tower
Mast
Piers
Locks
Locks
Royal Dock
Fish Docks
BROWN ST
WHARNCLIFFE RD
KEMP ROAD
NORTH QUAY

Grimsby Marina

D1
1 CASSWELL CL
2 RUTLAND ST
3 MANSEL ST
4 SIDNEY ST

FARINGDON RD
HUMBER BRIDGE ROAD
WICKHAM ROAD
Works
WICKHAM ROAD
Works
MURRAY STREET
ROBINSON LA
RIBY STREET
ROSS ROAD
MARSDEN ROAD
New Clee
CLEETHORPE ROAD
SALVESEN RD
Grimsby Docks
The Caxton Theatre & Arts Ctr
Strand Com Sch
HARRINGTON STREET
BLUNDELL AVE
High Point Ret Pk
A180
VICTORIA ST N
A16
PRINCE ALBERT GARD
Victoria Retail Pk
CHURCH ST
NELSON STREET
DUNCOMBE GDNS
InShops Ctr
East Marsh
Ice House
GRIMSBY ROAD
A180
HAMILTON STREET
STIRLING ST
SPENCER ST
TAYLOR ST
MONTAGUE ST
GRANT ST
PHELPS ST
DAUBNEY ST
BARCROFT ST
LOVETT ST
TIVERTON ST

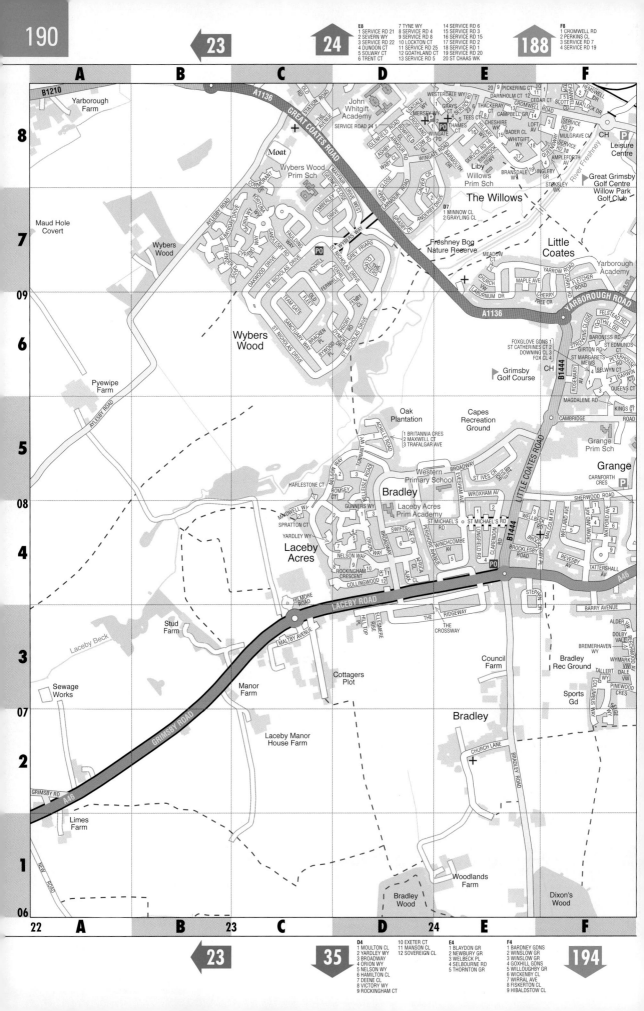

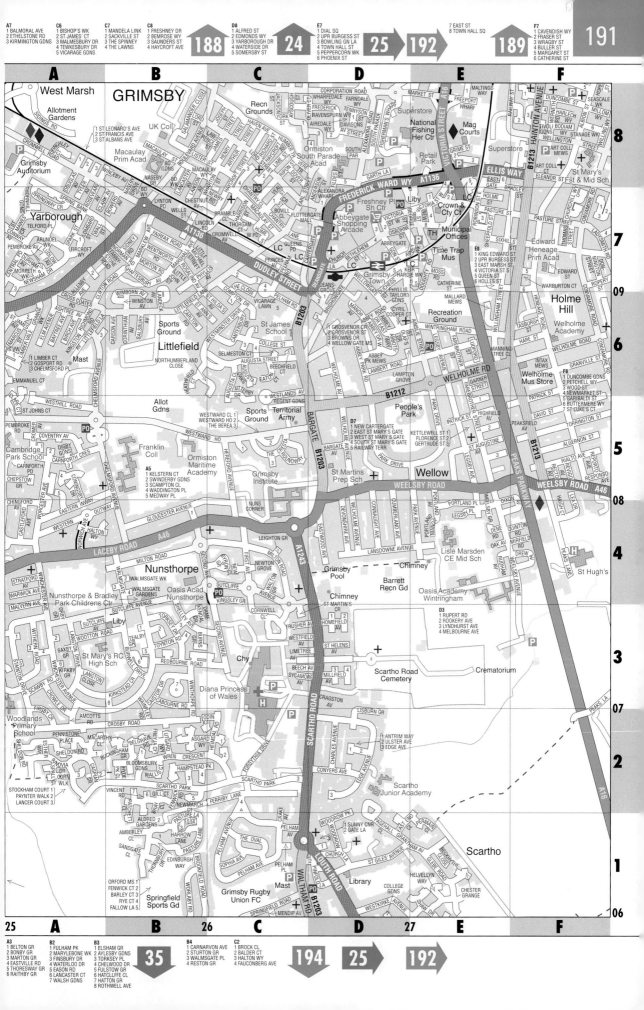

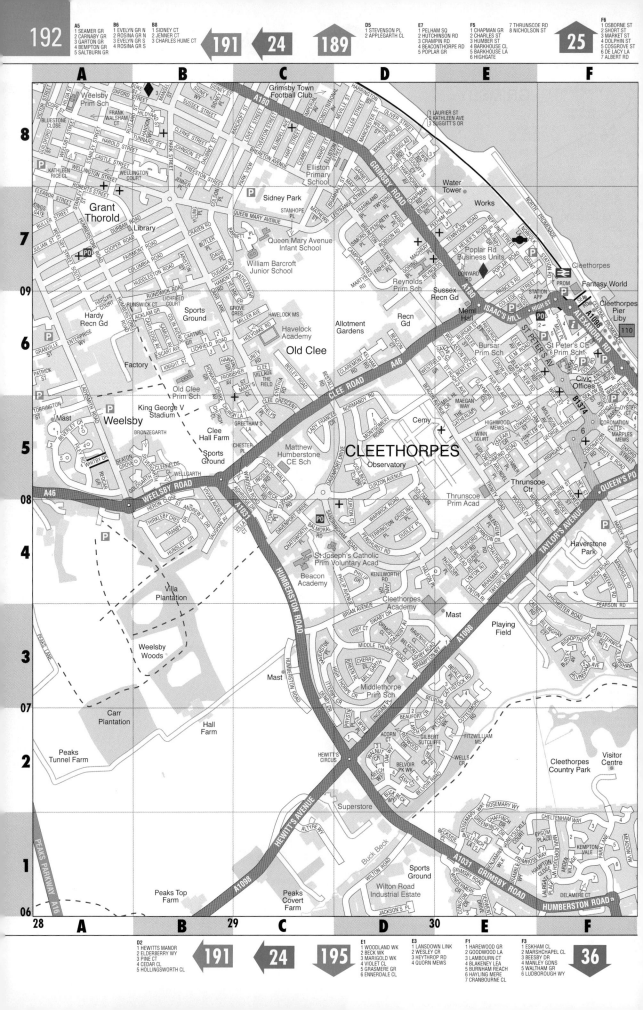

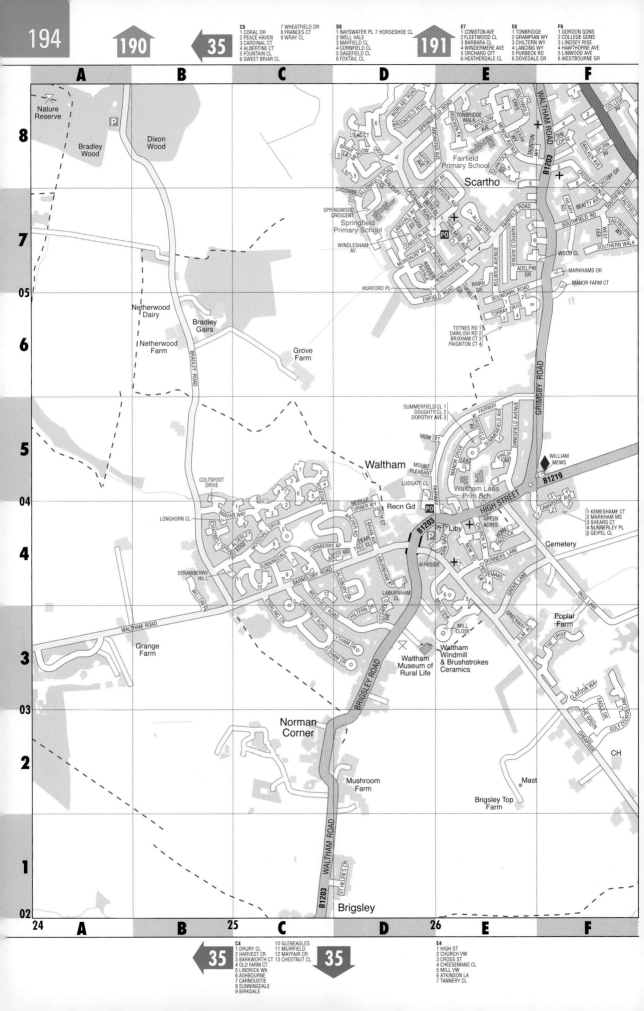

C5
1 CORAL DR
2 PEACE HAVEN
3 CARDINAL CT
4 ALBERTINE CT
5 FOUNTAIN CL
6 SWEET BRIAR CL
7 WHEATFIELD DR
8 FRANCES CT
9 WRAY CL

D8
1 BAYSWATER PL 7 HORSESHOE CL
2 WELL VALE
3 MAYFIELD CL
4 CORNFIELD CL
5 SAGEFIELD CL
6 FOXTAIL CL

E7
1 CONISTON AVE
2 FLEETWOOD CL
3 BARBARA CL
4 WINDERMERE AVE
5 ORCHARD CRFT
6 HEATHERDALE CL

E8
1 TONBRIDGE
2 GRAMPIAN WY
3 CHILTERN WY
4 LANCING WY
5 PURBECK RD
6 DOVEDALE DR

F8
1 GORDON GDNS
2 COLLEGE GDNS
3 LINDSEY RISE
4 HAWTHORNE AVE
5 LINWOOD AVE
6 WESTBOURNE GR

Nature Reserve

Bradley Wood

Dixon Wood

Worlaby Road
Brookfield Road
Springfield Road
LILAC CT
BRIAR LA
MEADOW DRIVE
Tonbridge Walk
Wicklow
Bracken Pk
Ainslaer Ave
Southwold
Perry Ave
Mendip Ave
Taunton Av

Fairfield Primary School

Scartho

The Copse
Crosby Ave
Crosby Gr
Walker Ave
Spurn Av

Oxcombe
Fallowfield Road
Walesby
Bayons Ave
Langdale Av
Amos
Elizabeth
Garden Ave
Allestree

WALTHAM ROAD
B1203

Hilary
Beaty Ave
Southfield Rd
West
Eastbourne
Lea
Eastfield
Southern Walk

Springwood Crescent
Springfield Primary School

Windlesham Av
Hurford Pl

Netherwood Dairy

Netherwood Farm

Bradley Gairs

Bradley Wood

BRADLEY ROAD

Grove Farm

Coniston Ave
Mordaunt Av
Rydal Avenue
Windermere Av
Kidderminster Ave
Rivan Gr
Emfield Road
Fairmere Ave
Bullwick Avenue
Fairfield Avenue
Fairfield Road
Adelphi Dr
Boundary Road
Torbay Drive

Wood Cl
Markhams Dr
Manor Farm Ct

GRIMSBY ROAD

TOTNES RD 1
DAWLISH RD 2
BRIXHAM CT 3
PAIGNTON CT 4

SUMMERFIELD CL 1
DOUGHTY CL 2
DOROTHY AVE 3
MDW CFT

Waltham

Coltsfoot Drive

Mount Pleasant
Ludgate Cl

Fairway
Norsefield Av
Summerfield Ave
Danesfield Avenue
Manor Drive
Leas Cl
Philip Av

William Mews
B1219

Longhorn Cl

Marian Way
Alderley
Channell
Spruce
Sedge
Woodhall Drive
Neville
Turner Wy
Archer Rd
Briar Ave
Pear Tree Cl
Ascot Rd
Turnberry Ap

Recn Gd
PO

1 KEMESHAME CT
2 MARKHAM MS
3 SHEARS CT
4 NUNNERLEY PL
5 GEIPEL CL

Cemetery

Strawberry Hill
Sunningdale
Barnoldby Road
Salisbury Rd
Westfield Road
Laburnham Ave
Laburnham Cl

WILLOW PK

B1203
P
PH
Liby
Kirk Gate Rd
New Rd
Church La
Kirkside
Mill View
Home Paddock
Green Acres
Skinners Lane
Cheesemans
Grove Lane

Poplar Farm

STIRLING CR
CHESTNUT CL
CHILTERN DR
COTSFORD DR
LYTHAM DR
ELSHAM DR

Mill Close

Greenway
Elm Rd

The Drive

Ings Lane

WALTHAM ROAD

Grange Farm

Waltham Museum of Rural Life

Waltham Windmill & Brushstrokes Ceramics

Claydon Way
The Green
Eagle Dr
Golf Course Lane
Cheapside
CH

BRIGSLEY ROAD

Norman Corner

Mushroom Farm

Brigsley Top Farm

Mast

B1203
ST HELEN'S CR

Brigsley

C4
1 DRURY CL
2 HARVEST CR
3 BARKWORTH CT
4 OLD FARM CT
5 LINDRICK WK
6 ASHBOURNE
7 CARNOUSTIE
8 SUNNINGDALE
9 BIRKDALE
10 GLENEAGLES
11 MUIRFIELD
12 MAYFAIR CR
13 CHESTNUT CL

E4
1 HIGH ST
2 CHURCH VW
3 CROSS ST
4 CHEESEMANS CL
5 MILL VW
6 ATKINSON LA
7 TANNERY CL

35   35

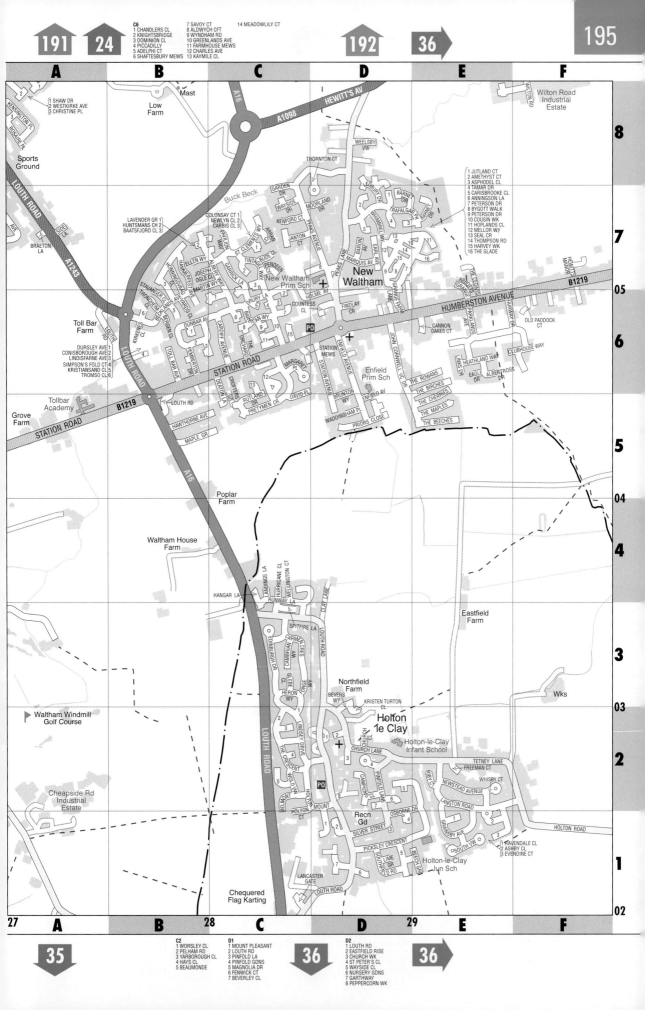

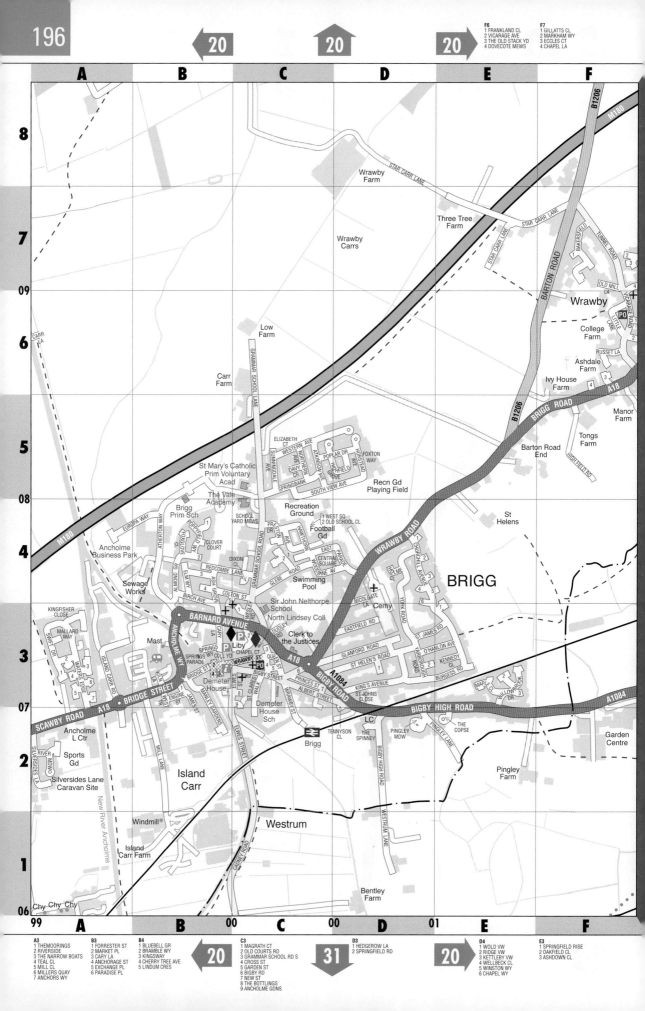

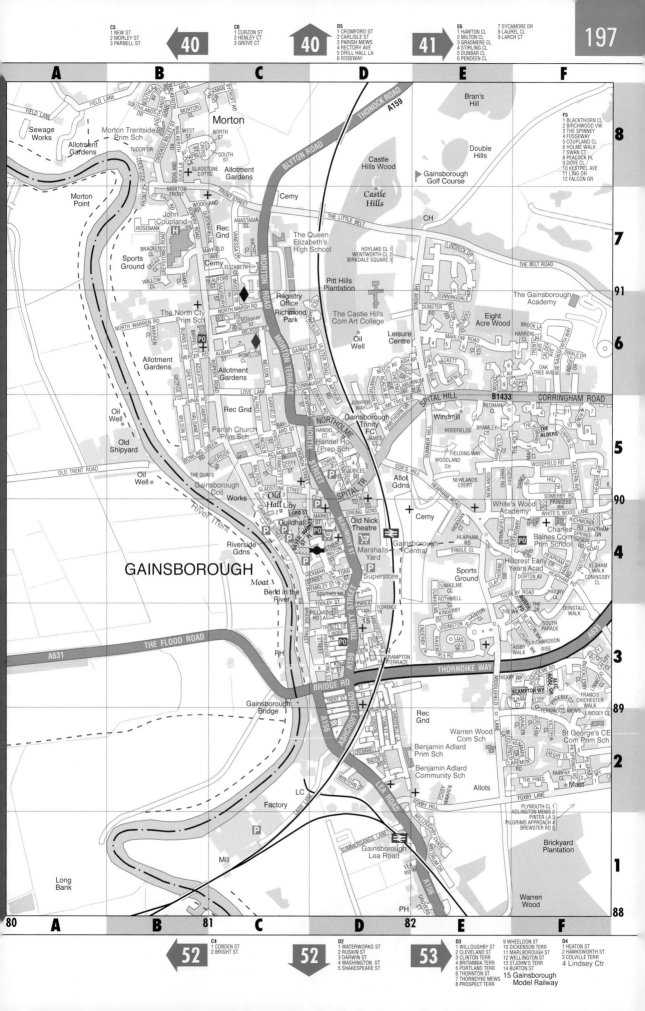

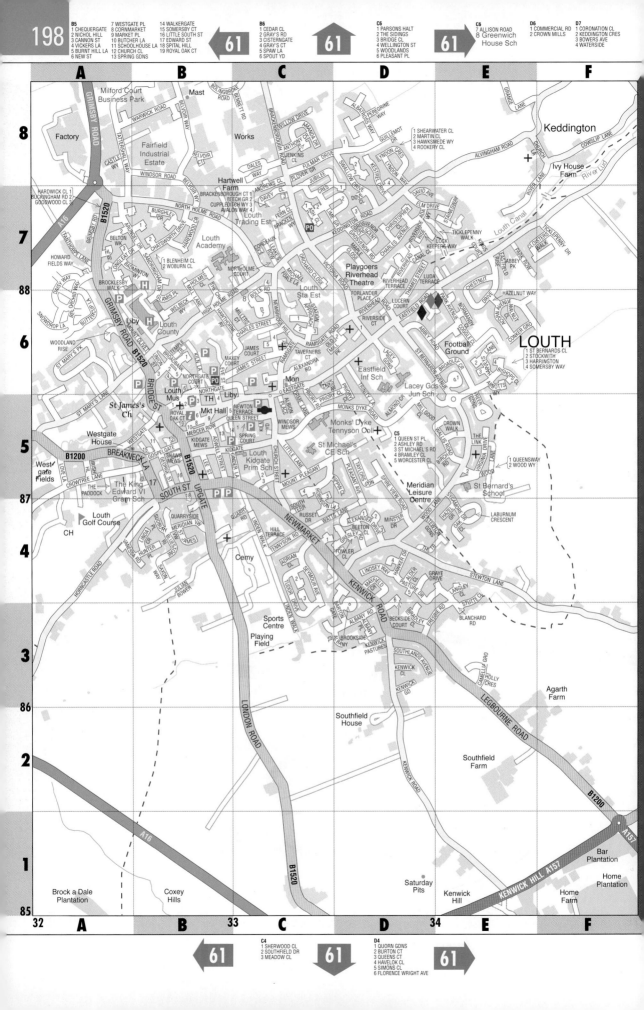

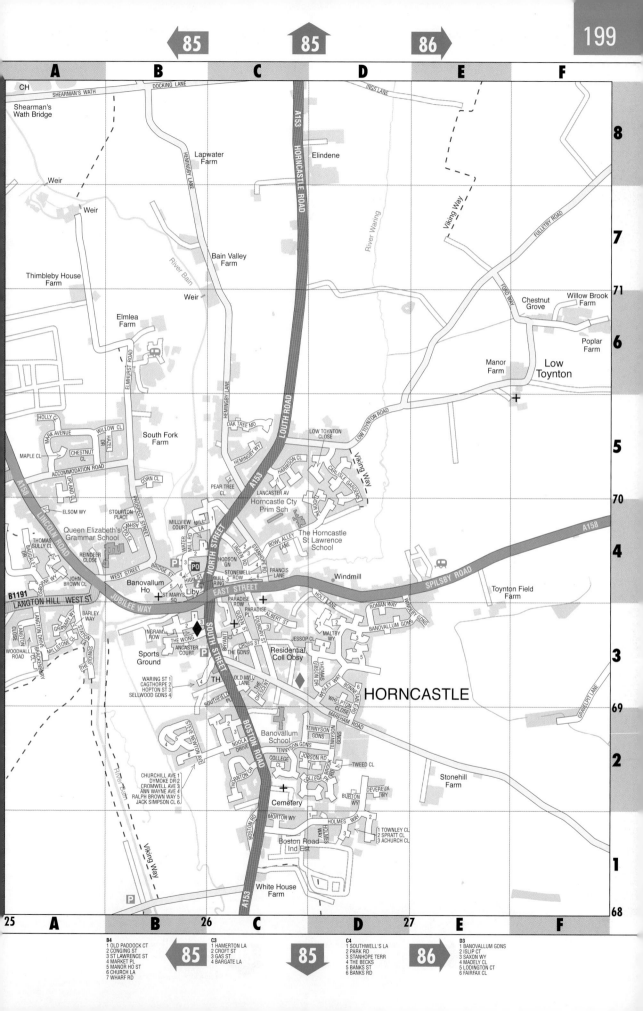

B4
1 OLD PADDOCK CT
2 CONGING ST
3 ST LAWRENCE ST
4 MARKET PL
5 MANOR HO ST
6 CHURCH LA
7 WHARF RD

C3
1 HAMERTON LA
2 CROFT ST
3 GAS ST
4 BARGATE LA

C4
1 SOUTHWELL'S LA
2 PARK RD
3 STANHOPE TERR
4 THE BECKS
5 BANKS ST
6 BANKS RD

D3
1 BANOVALLUM GDNS
2 ISLIP CT
3 SAXON WY
4 MADELY CL
5 LODINGTON CT
6 FAIRFAX CL

	A	B	C	D	E	F

8

Burton Fen

Fen Farm

A57

WOODCOCK LANE

BURTON LA END

PARK LANE

PH

BURTON LANE END

7

THE MOORINGS

PARK LANE

A57

Bishop Bridge

73

Fossdyke Navigation

Waves Farm

A46

6

Sewage Works

PH

SAXILBY ROAD

5

FOXFIELD
POACHERS BROOK
BEAVER CL
BROOKFIELD CL

Manor Farm

OAKFIELD RD

MARINE WALK

FERRY LANE

Main Drain

HIGH STONEY YD
LOWER CHURCH RD
HODSON CL

NURSES LA

72

WOODBANK
THE PADDOCK
ALMOND GR
CHURCH ROAD

Liby

St Lawrence CE (Cont) Prim Sch

64

Old Decoy

HIGH STREET
ATKSON CL
OLD CHAPEL RD

Skellingthorpe

4

JERUSALEM ROAD
MONSON PK
CANBERRA WY

PO

TOP LODGE CL

STATION FIELD

LINCOLN ROAD

The Holt Prim Sch
REDWING CL
MAGPIE
WOODPECKER
LAPWING
THE DENE
DENE RD
DENEFIELD
WILLOW
VICARAGE DR
GARDENFIELD

Decoy Farm

3

SWALLOW AVE
QUEENSWAY
MARTIN
MALLARD
GOLDFINCH CL
BIRDS HOLT CL
HAMILTON GR
WATERLOO LANE
GARDENFIELD

COOPERS
HOLT CL

Fen Farm

LIVERPOOL DR

71

WISEHOLME RD
WOODLAND AVE

Lincoln Road Farm

Cross Holts

FARRINGTON CR
ROCHESTER DRIVE
ELTON CL
CHELSEA
EUSTON
GROSVENOR AVE

Waterloo Farm

LINCOLN ROAD

2

Skellingthorpe Moor

MALHAM DRIVE
DENBY DL
ULDALE CL
DURHAM CL
RYDAL
SHELGRASMERE
WY
SKELLINGTHORPE ROAD
SHAFTESBURY AVE

SMALL GROVE
ROXBOROUGH
BELGRAVIA

Fen Farm

Birchwood

Skellingthorpe Moor Plantation

OLD WOOD
TESSDALE CL
DELLFIELD
CANWOOD DR
MALHAM CR
HICKORY RD
LANDMERE GR

BURGHLEY RD
HADDON CL
BURGHLEY

1

Monson Farm

Woodlands Inf Sch
PO
EASTLEIGH CL
EBONY
WHEATFIELD
REGENT CL
SUNFIELD CR
BIRCHWOOD AVENUE
MEADOWLANG CL
LARCHWOOD CR

SKELLINGTHORPE ROAD
B1378

SHEARWATER RD

Fen Plantation

Foal Close

70

A46

Hospital Plantation

STAVERTON CR
SYRINGA GREEN
SALIX
WOODFIELD AVENUE
HAZELWOOD CL

MALLARD
SHEARWATER RD

92	A	93	B	C	94	D	E	F

A4
1 HAMPDEN CL
2 LANCASTER WY
3 HALIFAX CL
4 STIRLING WY
5 WHITLEY CL
6 SUNDERLAND CL
7 MITCHELL CL

B1
1 LUTON CL
2 PRESTWICK CL
3 CHIVENOR CL

C1
1 OLD WOOD
2 WASDALE CL
3 BURNMOOR CL
4 BAYWOOD CL
5 HICKORY RD
6 BRIAR CL
7 WHITETHORN GR
8 DELLFIELD CT
9 WOODFIELD CL

10 SATINWOOD CL
11 TULIPWOOD AVE

D1
1 THIRLMERE WY
2 BUTTERMERE CL
3 ENNERDALE CL
4 RINGWOOD CL
5 PEARTREE CL
6 ELMWOOD CL
7 OLD POND CL

E1
1 STONES LA
2 GOLDCREST CL
3 SHEARWATER CL

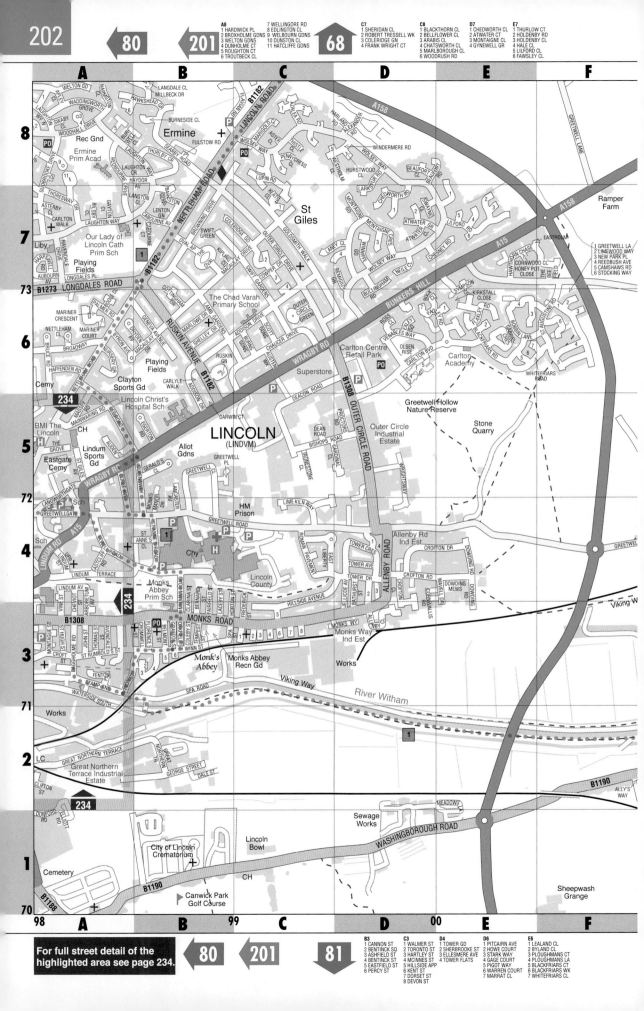

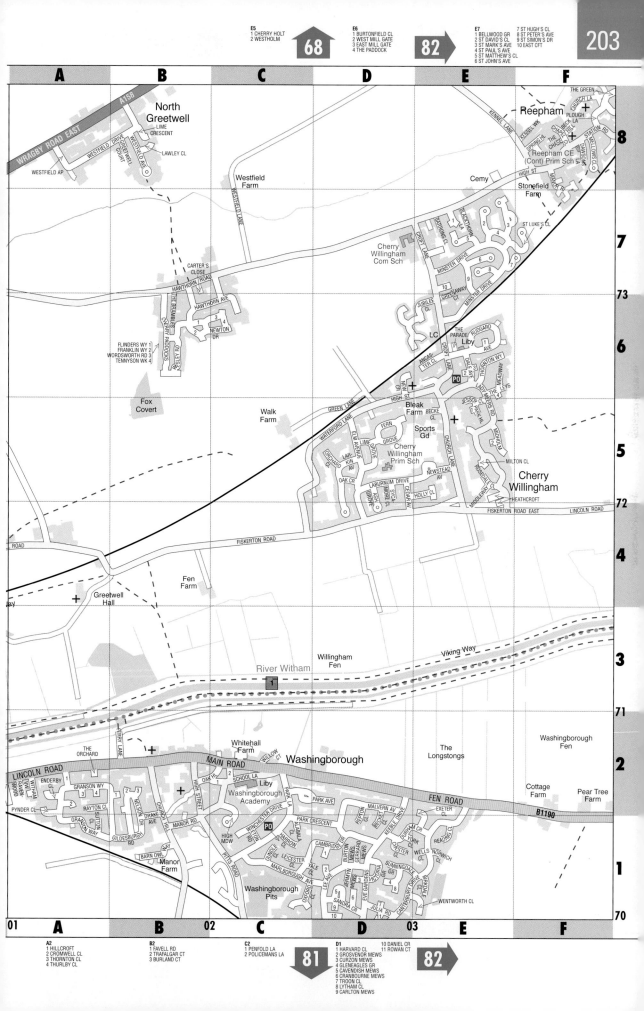

68 **82**

North Greetwell

Reepham

Cherry Willingham

Washingborough

81 **82**

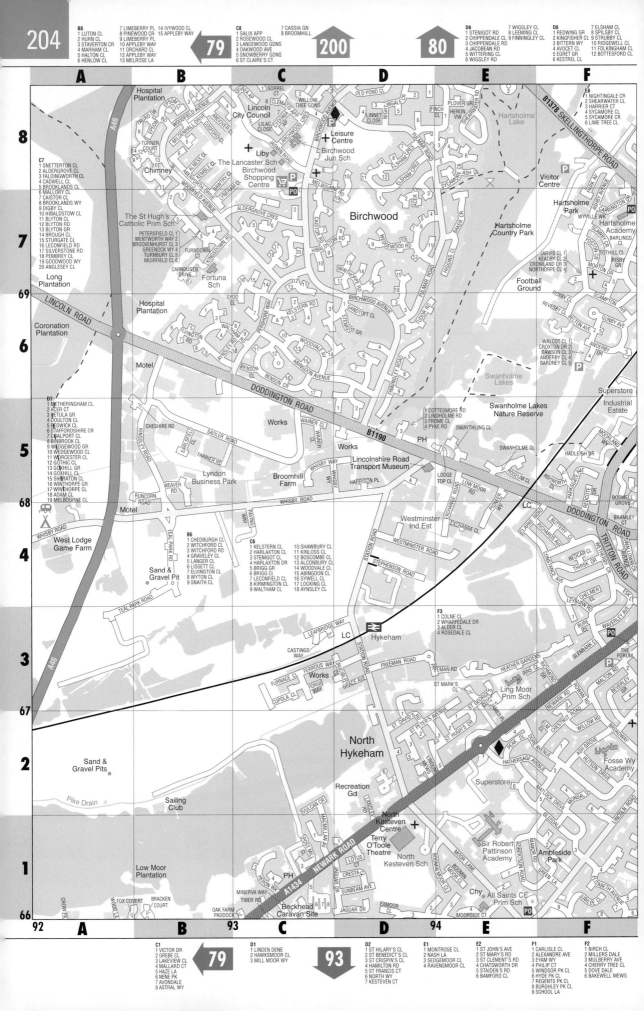

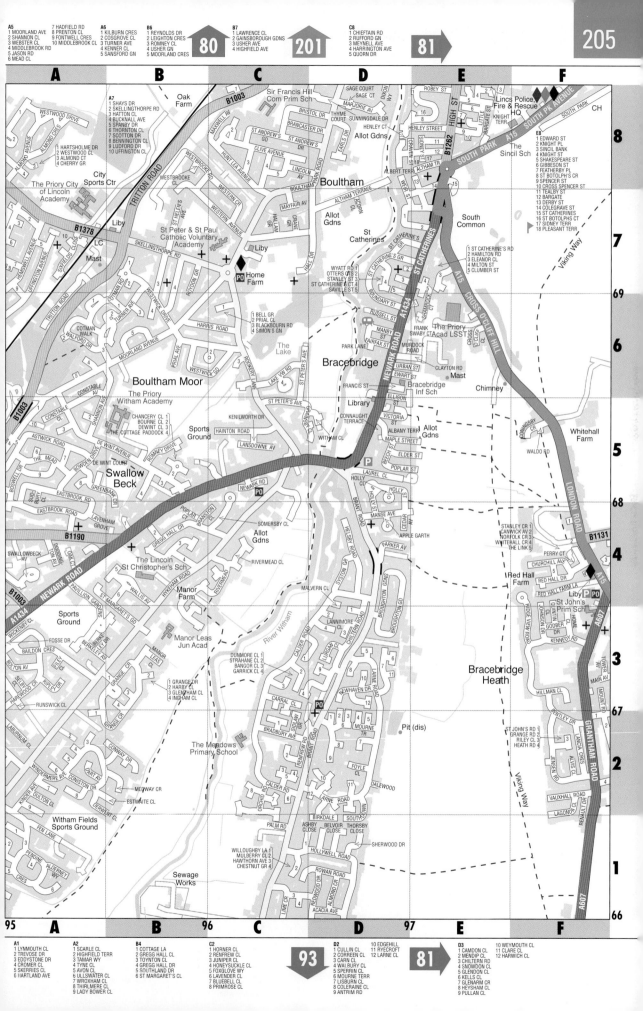

A5
1 MOORLAND AVE
2 SHANNON CL
3 WEBSTER CL
4 MIDDLEBROOK RD
5 JASON RD
6 MEAD CL

A7
1 SHAYS DR
2 SKELLINGTHORPE RD
3 HATTON CL
4 BUCKNALL AVE
5 SPANBY DR
6 THORNTON CL
7 SCOTTON DR
8 BENNINGTON CL
9 LUDFORD DR
10 UFFINGTON CL

A6
1 KILBURN CRES
2 COSGROVE CL
3 TURNER AVE
4 KENNER CL
5 SANSFORD GN

B6
1 REYNOLDS DR
2 LEIGHTON CRES
3 ROMNEY CL
4 USHER GN
5 MOORLAND CRES

B7
1 LAWRENCE CL
2 GAINSBOROUGH GDNS
3 USHER AVE
4 HIGHFIELD AVE

C8
1 CHIEFTAIN RD
2 RUFFORD GN
3 MEYNELL AVE
4 HARRINGTON AVE
5 QUORN DR

80   201   81

E8
1 EDWARD ST
2 KNIGHT PL
3 SINCIL BANK
4 KNIGHT ST
5 SHAKESPEARE ST
6 GIBBESON ST
7 FEATHERBY PL
8 ST BOTOLPH'S CR
9 SPENCER ST
10 CROSS SPENCER ST
11 TEALBY ST
12 BARGATE
13 DERBY ST
14 COLEGRAVE ST
15 ST CATHERINES
16 ST BOTOLPHS CT
17 SIDNEY TERR
18 PLEASANT TERR

A1
1 LYNMOUTH CL
2 TREVOSE DR
3 EDDYSTONE DR
4 CROMER CL
5 SKERRIES CL
6 HARTLAND AVE

A2
1 SCARLE CL
2 HIGHFIELD TERR
3 TAMAR WY
4 TYNE CL
5 AVON CL
6 ULLSWATER CL
7 WROXHAM CL
8 THIRLMERE CL
9 LADY BOWER CL

B4
1 COTTAGE LA
2 GREGG HALL CL
3 TOYNTON CL
4 GREGG HALL DR
5 SOUTHLAND CL
6 ST MARGARET'S CL

C2
1 HORNER CL
2 CORREEN CL
3 CARR CL
4 HONEYSUCKLE CL
5 FOXGLOVE WY
6 LAVENDER CL
7 BLUEBELL CL
8 PRIMROSE CL

D2
1 CULLIN CL
2 CARN CL
3 JUNIPER CL
4 WAI BURY CL
5 SPERRIN CL
6 MOURNE TERR
7 LISBURN CL
8 COLERAINE CL
9 ANTRIM RD
10 EDGEHILL
11 RYECROFT
12 LARNE CL

D3
1 CAMDON CL
2 MENDIP CL
3 CHILTERN RD
4 SNOWDON CL
5 GLENDON CL
6 KELLS CL
7 GLENARM CR
8 HEYSHAM CL
9 PULLAN CL
10 WEYMOUTH CL
11 CLARE CL
12 HARWICH CL

93   81

A6
1 BISCAY CL
2 ST VINCENT CL
3 TEAL CLOSE
4 BEACON PARK CL
5 THE HURST
6 FLAMBOROUGH CL

7 TAGGS DR
8 BURDETT CL
9 YARBOROUGH RD
10 BURGH RD
11 ST MATTHEWS CL
12 OLD BAKERY YARD

← **103**

A7
1 GLEBE CL
2 KINGFISHER DR
3 JOHNSON CL
4 NELSON CL
5 JENKINS CL
6 PORTLAND DR

7 THE HORN
8 THE NEEDLES
9 VERONICA CL

90

D8
1 ROMAN BANK
2 FAINLIGHT CL
3 NORTH FORELAND DR
4 GILBERTS GR

A5
1 WELLINGTON WY
2 CONINGSBY CL
3 BADER WY
4 CRANWELL CL
5 GIBSON PL
6 PERRIN AVE
7 CHESHIRE GR
8 PORTAL GN
9 PRIMROSE CL
10 GRUNNILL CL
11 HARRIS CL
12 HUDSON WY
13 SAMUEL JOHN WAY
14 WAGONERS WLK
15 HARVEST WAY
16 MOWBRAY CL

B6
1 HUCKLES WY
2 DAVID DR
3 SCOTTS CL
4 ST MARK'S CL
5 ST FRANCES CL
6 ST HUBERTS CL
7 CLEMENTINE CL
8 MANOR DR
9 BLENHEIM CL
10 MANOR DR
11 PARLIAMENT CL

D7
1 RANWORTH CL
2 CHURCHILL AV
3 SOUTHWELL DR
4 YORK WAY
5 WELLS CL
6 WINCHESTER CL
7 TRURO CL
8 CHESTER CL
9 SOUTHWELL DR
10 ELM WAY
11 RIPON CL

B5
1 LYNDHURST CT
2 MORRIS GDNS
3 ALMA CL
4 HALIFAX CL
5 LINDUM SQ

D6
1 BIRKDALE CL
2 ST DAVIDS CL
3 OLD ROMAN BANK
4 WENTWORTH CL

D5
1 ROSE GR
2 THE TOWERS

A4
1 BUTLIN BL
2 SWALLOWFIELDS CT
3 SYDNEY DR
4 MELBOURNE DR
5 BRISBANE CL
6 ABBEY CL
7 PERTH CL
8 THERESA CL
9 ADRIAN CL
10 ROBERTA CL

D4
1 SUNNINGDALE CL
2 SUNNINGDALE CRES
3 LUMLEY CRES
4 GLENTWORTH CRES

D3
1 PRINCE ALFRED AVE
2 EDINBURGH AVE

C1
1 COMPTON CL
2 BECKETT CL
3 TONGLET CL
4 REGENTS CL
5 ROYAL ARTHUR CL
6 EDEN CL
7 FAGANS WY
8 BURGHLEY RD
9 SEACROFT DR
10 SADLER CL

B3
1 OLD WAINFLEET RD
2 GRANTHAM DR
3 CROSS ST
4 CHURCH RD SOUTH
5 MAYFIELD GR
6 MARIAN WY
7 BEVERLEY GR

B4
1 CHARLES CL
2 ST CLEMENT'S RD
3 WESTFIELD DR
4 SWABY CR

C2
1 RICHMOND CT
2 DENHAM CL
3 TENNYSON GN
4 BERESFORD CL
5 BERESFORD CR
6 FORSYTH CR

← **103**

C3
1 DOROTHY CR
2 SUTTON CT
3 LINCOLN RD
4 LINCOLN RD
5 BERRY WY
6 ROMAN BANK
7 WAINFLEET RD
8 LUMLEY SQ
9 ALEXANDRA CT

103

C4
1 PELHAM RD
2 LANDSDOWNE RD
3 RONALD CL
4 THE CLOSE
5 GRANTHAM DR
6 SCHRIMSHAW CT
7 BRIAN AV
8 PEARL CL
9 The Children's Ctr

D1
1 LETTWELL CR
2 SOMERSBY GR
3 CLIFTON GR
4 MERRIEMEADE DR
5 SYNE AV

D2
1 LAWN CR
2 ARCADIA CR
3 WILLOUGHTON RD
4 SOUTH VIEW CL
5 SERENA RD
6 BARBARA RD
7 PEPPERMINT GR

SKEGNESS

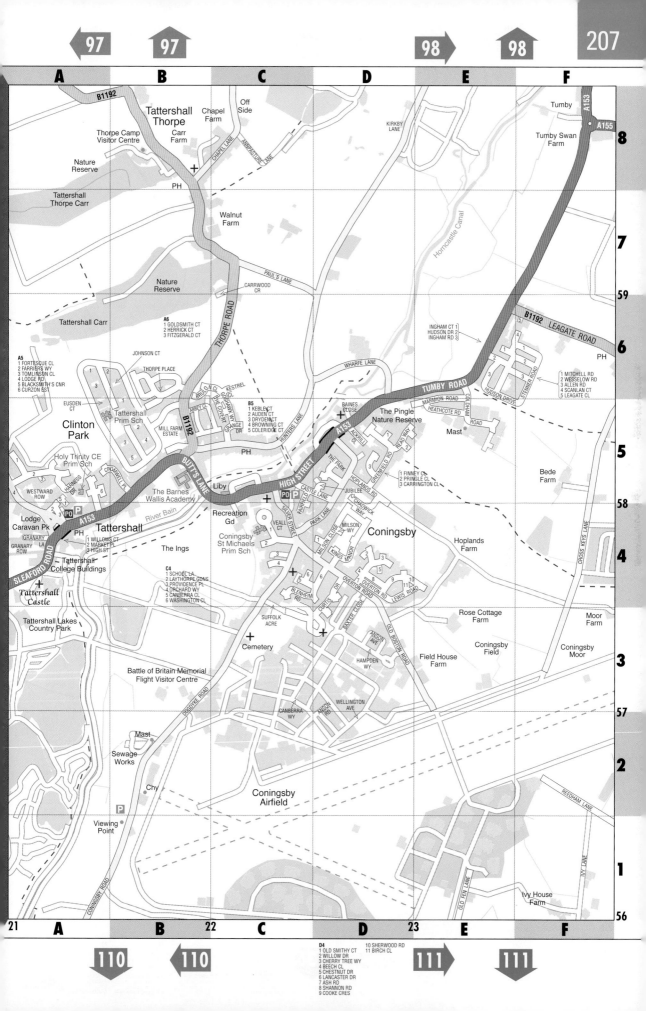

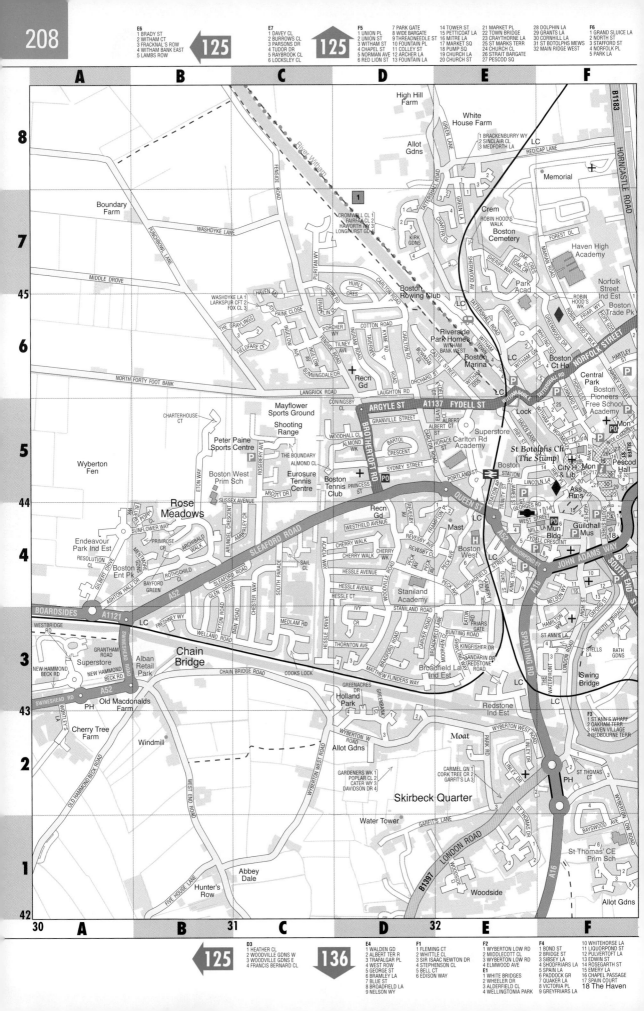

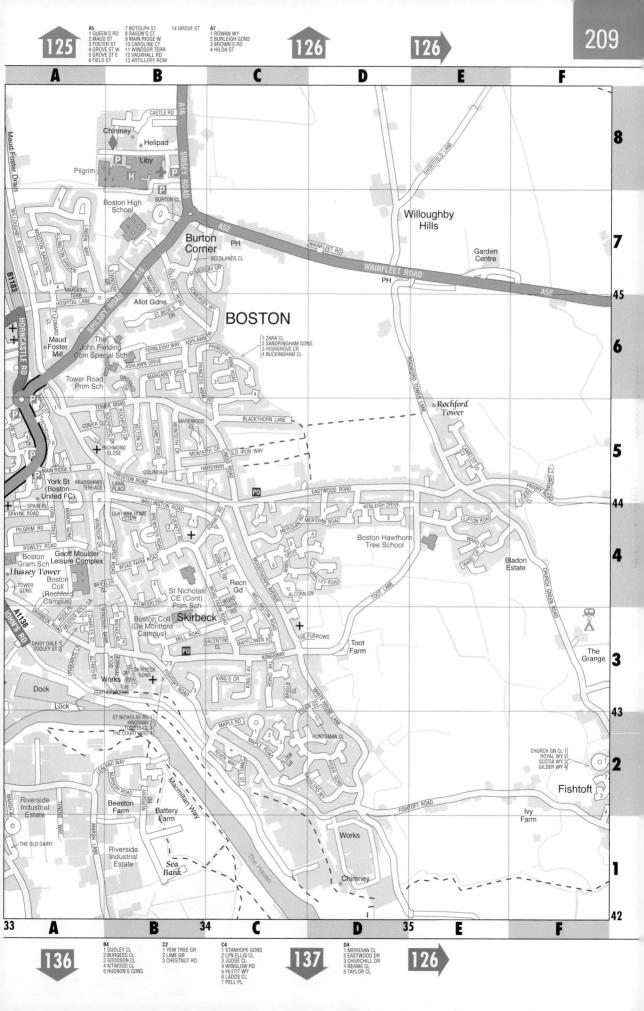

125

126

126

209

A	B	C	D	E	F

CASTLE RD

Chimney

Helipad

Pilgrim

Liby

Burton Corner

BOSTON

Willoughby Hills

Garden Centre

Rochford Tower

Boston Hawthorn Tree School

Bladon Estate

The Grange

Fishtoft

Ivy Farm

Riverside Industrial Estate

Beeston Farm

Battery Farm

Sea Bank

Riverside Industrial Estate

The Haven

Works

Chimney

E8
1 EMMINSON WY
2 KELHAM RD
3 THE HAVERLANDS
4 ORCHARD CL
5 MALVERN DR
6 MENDIP CL

F5
1 PORTSMOUTH CL
2 WESTMINSTER WY
3 ROBERTSON RD
4 CAMPBELL CL
5 ELY WY
6 RURO CL

F7
1 CEDARWOOD CL
2 BROOMWOOD CL
3 PALMWOOD CL
4 BIRCHWOOD CL
5 LILACWOOD CL
6 BRIARWOOD CL

7 ROWANWOOD DR
8 HOLLYWOOD DR

F8
1 VIVIAN CL
2 BEAUMONT DR
3 MALIM WY
4 PEACHWOOD DR
5 APPLEWOOD DR
6 BRAMBLEWOOD CL

7 ORANGAWOOD CL
8 OSTLER CL
9 COCHRAN CL

E5
1 CORFE CL
2 RIBER CL
3 TATTERSHALL CL
4 CAMARTHEN CL
5 BIRMINGHAM CL
6 CHICHESTER CL
7 NORWICH WY
8 HEREFORD WY
9 ROCHESTER DR
10 PETERBOROUGH CL
11 ROCHESTER DR

CHILTERN CL 1
CAMBRIAN CL 2
CHEVIOT CL 3
SWALLOW'S CL 4
KIMBERLEY TERR 5
LADYSMITH TERR 6

D5
1 SALISBURY CL
2 BLACKBURN CL
3 ST EDMUNDS CL
4 NEWCASTLE RD
5 ST ALBANS CL
6 CARLISLE CL
7 COVENTRY CL
8 CHESTER GDNS
9 WARWICK CL
10 BRADFORD CL

A5
1 RECTORY CL
2 CHURCH ST
3 CASTHORPE RD
4 CHAPEL LA
5 LAWSON LEAS
6 HIGHFIELDS
7 BERRYFIELD END
8 GRANGE PADDOCK

NEWARK VW 1
ST MAWES WAY 2
LEWES AVE 3
TAMWORTH CL 4
PEVERIL PL 5

1 GRIMSTHORPE CL
2 DOVER CL
3 OAKHAM CL
4 MONMOUTH WAY
5 JAMESTON CL
6 BAMBURGH CL
7 SCARBOROUGH CL
8 DALTON CL

1 THE NORTHINGS
2 ADAMSTILES

1 WALKERS WY
2 THE DRIFT

D2
1 CHESTNUT GR
2 LARCH CL
3 SYCAMORE CT
4 HAWTHORNE CT

E2
1 CLYDE CT
2 LYMN CT
3 WELLAND CT
4 NENE CT
5 TAMAR CT
6 COLNE CT
7 STOUR CT
8 GANNET CT
9 FALCON CT

10 MALLARD CT
11 GRESLEY CT
12 STURROCK CT
13 IVATT CT
14 STIRLING CT
15 HICKLING CT
16 KINOULTON CT

E4
1 DERBY CL
2 WESTBOURNE PL
3 SHORWELL CL

F3
1 HODDER CL
2 BARNWELL TERR
3 HARLAXTON RD

Map labels:
Gonerby Hill Foot
Gonerby Tunnel
Knowles Farm
Stubbock Hill
Rectory Farm
Mill Hill
Boundary Farm
Poplar Farm Sch
Gonerby Hill Foot CE Prim Sch
Royston Ford End
Recreation Gd
Barrowby
New Barn Farm
Green Hill
Recreation Gd
Autumn Park Ind Est
Fun Farm & Grantham Bowl
Beeden Park Estate
Ambergate Sports Coll
The West Grantham Academy St John's
Meres Leisure Centre & Swimming Pool
The West Grantham Acad St Hugh's Bluecoat Meres Acad
Grantham Town Football Club
Sports Stadium
Barrowby Lodge
Westry Corner
The Isaac Newton Prim Sch
Earlesfield
Recreation Ground
Harlaxton Road Ind Est
Old Wharf Ind Est
Mag Ct & County Ct
Ellesmere Business Park
The Walton Girls High Sch
Harlaxton Lower Lodge Farm
Grantham Canal Nature Reserve

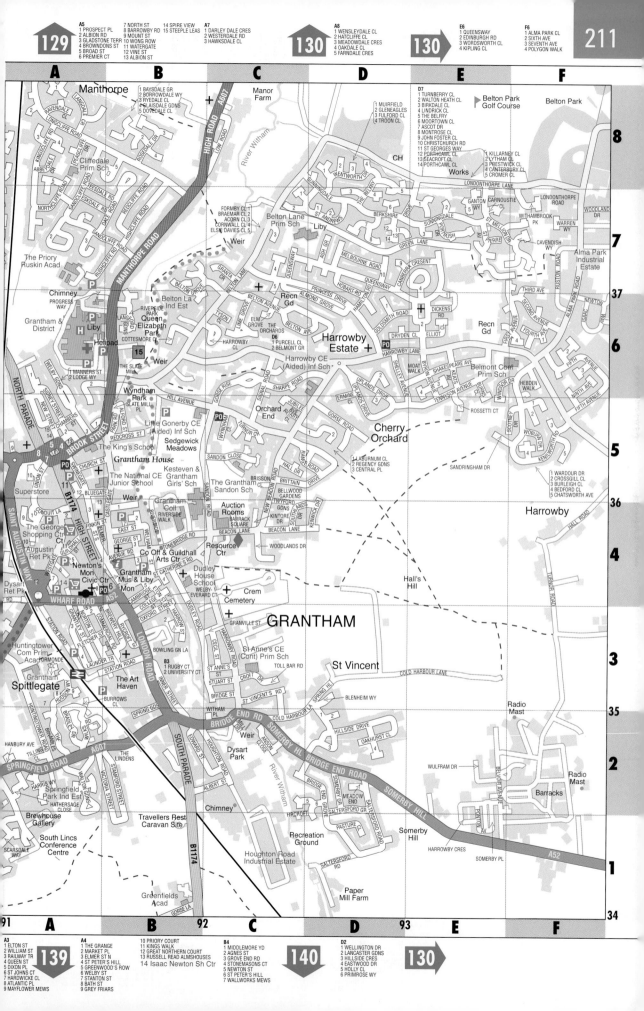

129

A5
1 PROSPECT PL
2 ALBION RD
3 GLADSTONE TERR
4 BROWNDONS ST
5 BROAD ST
6 PREMIER CT

7 NORTH ST
8 BARROWBY RD
9 MOUNT ST
10 WONG ROW
11 WATERGATE
12 VINE ST
13 ALBION ST

14 SPIRE VIEW
15 STEEPLE LEAS

A7
1 DARLEY DALE CRES
2 WESTERDALE RD
3 HAWKSDALE CL

130

A8
1 WENSLEYDALE CL
2 HATCLIFFE CL
3 MEADOWDALE CRES
4 OAKDALE CL
5 FARNDALE CRES

130

E6
1 QUEENSWAY
2 EDINBURGH RD
3 WORDSWORTH CL
4 KIPLING CL

F6
1 ALMA PARK CL
2 SIXTH AVE
3 SEVENTH AVE
4 POLYGON WALK

139

A3
1 ELTON ST
2 WILLIAM ST
3 RAILWAY TR
4 QUEEN ST
5 DIXON PL
6 ST JOHNS CT
7 HARDWICKE CL
8 ATLANTIC PL
9 MAYFLOWER MEWS

A4
1 THE GRANGE
2 MARKET PL
3 ELMER ST N
4 ST PETER'S HILL
5 BROWNLOW'S ROW
6 WELBY ST
7 STANTON ST
8 BATH ST
9 GREY FRIARS

10 PRIORY COURT
11 KINGS WALK
12 GREAT NORTHERN COURT
13 RUSSELL READ ALMSHOUSES
14 Isaac Newton Sh Ctr

140

B4
1 MIDDLEMORE YD
2 AGNES ST
3 GROVE END RD
4 STONEMASONS CT
5 NEWTON ST
6 ST PETER'S HILL
7 WALLWORKS MEWS

130

D2
1 WELLINGTON DR
2 LANCASTER GDNS
3 HILLSIDE CRES
4 EASTWOOD CL
5 HOLLY CL
6 PRIMROSE WY

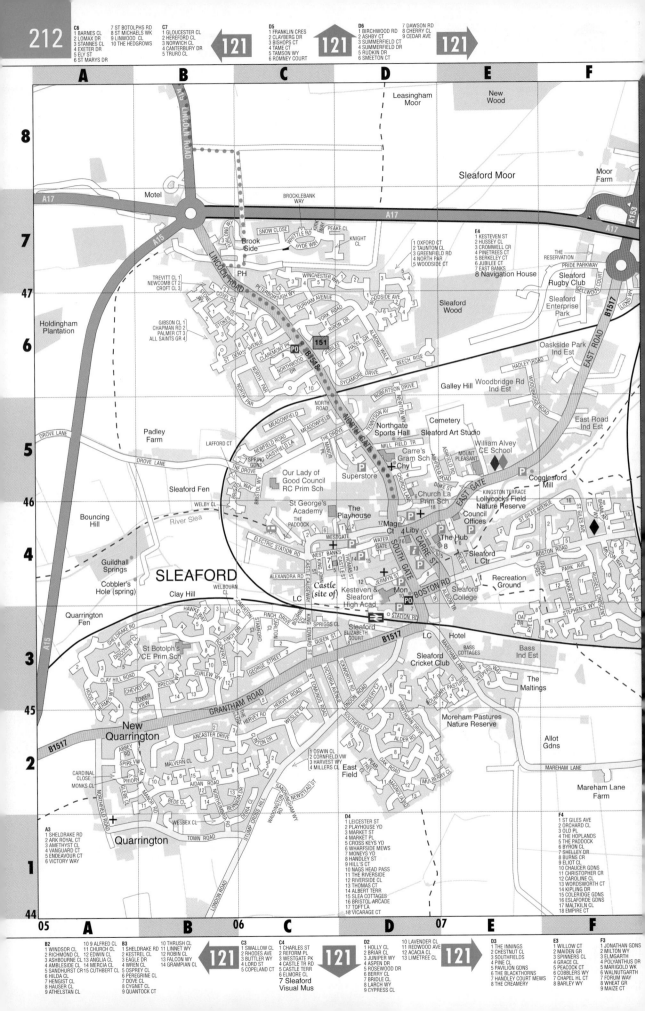

C6
1 BARNES CL
2 LOMAX DR
3 STANNES CL
4 EXETER DR
5 ELY ST
6 ST MARYS DR
7 ST BOTOLPHS RD
8 ST MICHAELS WK
9 LINWOOD CL
10 THE HEDGROWS

C7
1 GLOUCESTER CL
2 HEREFORD CL
3 NORWICH CL
4 CANTERBURY DR
5 TRURO CL

◀ 121

D5
1 FRANKLIN CRES
2 CLAYBERG DR
3 BISHOPS CT
4 TAME ST
5 TAMSON WY
6 ROMNEY COURT

◀ 121

D6
1 BIRCHWOOD RD
2 ASHBY CT
3 SUMMERFIELD CT
4 SUMMERFIELD DR
5 RUDKIN DR
6 SMEETON CT
7 DAWSON RD
8 CHERRY CL
9 CEDAR AVE

◀ 121

E4
1 KESTEVEN ST
2 HUSSEY CL
3 CROMWELL CR
4 PINETREES CT
5 BERKELEY CT
6 JUBILEE CT
7 EAST BANKS
8 Navigation House

Leasingham Moor
New Wood
Sleaford Moor
Moor Farm

Motel
Brook Side
PH
Holdingham Plantation

THE RESERVATION
PRIDE PARKWAY
Sleaford Rugby Club
Sleaford Enterprise Park

1 OXFORD CT
2 TAUNTON CL
3 GREENFIELD RD
4 NORTH PAR
5 WOODSIDE CT

TREVITT CL 1
NEWCOMB CT 2
CROFT CL 3

GIBSON CL 1
CHAPMAN RD 2
PALMER CT 3
ALL SAINTS GR 4

Sleaford Wood

Oaksside Park Ind Est

Galley Hill
Woodbridge Rd Ind Est
East Road Ind Est

Northgate Sports Hall
Sleaford Art Studio
Carre's Gram Sch
Cemetery
MOUNT PLEASANT
William Alvey CE School
Cogglesford Mill

Padley Farm
Lafford CT
Our Lady of Good Council RC Prim Sch
Superstore

Sleaford Fen
Bouncing Hill

Sleaford L Ctr
Church La Prim Sch
Kingston Terrace
Lollycocks Field Nature Reserve
Council Offices
The Hub

St George's Academy
The Playhouse
The Paddock
WESTGATE
Magd Ct
Liby

Guildhall Springs

SLEAFORD

Cobbler's Hole (spring)
Clay Hill
Castle (site of)
Kesteven & Sleaford High Acad
Sleaford College
Recreation Ground

Quarrington Fen
St Botolph's CE Prim Sch
Sleaford Elizabeth Court
Sleaford Cricket Club
Hotel
Bass Ind Est
Bass Cottages
The Maltings

New Quarrington

GRANTHAM ROAD

1 OSWIN CL
2 CORNFIELD VW
3 HARVEST WY
4 MILLERS CL
East Field

Moreham Pastures Nature Reserve

Allot Gdns
Mareham Lane Farm

A3
1 SHELDRAKE CL
2 ARK ROYAL CT
3 AMETHYST CL
4 VANGUARD CT
5 ENDEAVOUR CL
6 VICTORY WAY

Quarrington

D4
1 LEICESTER ST
2 PLAYHOUSE YD
3 MARKET ST
4 MARKET PL
5 CROSS KEYS YD
6 WHARFSIDE MEWS
7 MONEYS YD
8 HANDLEY ST
9 HILL'S CT
10 NAGS HEAD PASS
11 THE RIVERSIDE
12 RIVERSIDE CL
13 THOMAS CT
14 ALBERT TERR
15 SLEA COTTAGES
16 BRISTOL ARCADE
17 TOFT LA
18 VICARAGE CT

F4
1 ST GILES AVE
2 ORCHARD CL
3 OLD PL
4 THE HOPLANDS
5 BYRON CL
6 BYROAI CL
7 SHELLEY DR
8 BURNS CR
9 ELIOT CL
10 CHAUCER GDNS
11 CHRISTOPHER CR
12 CAROLINE CL
13 WORDSWORTH CT
14 KIPLING DR
15 COLERIDGE GDNS
16 ESLAFORDE GDNS
17 MALTKILN CL
18 EMPIRE CT

B2
1 WINDSOR CL
2 RICHMOND CL
3 ASHBOURNE CL
4 AMBLESIDE CL
5 SANDHURST CR
6 HILDA CL
7 HENGIST CL
8 HAUSER CL
9 ATHELSTAN CL
10 ALFRED CL
11 CHURCH CL
12 EDWIN CL
13 ANGLIA CL
14 MERCIA CL
15 CUTHBERT CL

B3
1 SHELDRAKE CL
2 RHODES AVE
3 EAGLE DR
4 WREN CL
5 OSPREY CL
6 PEREGRINE CL
7 DOVE CL
8 CYGNET CL
9 QUANTOCK CT
10 THRUSH CL
11 LINNET WY
12 ROBIN CL
13 FALCON WY
14 GRAMPIAN CL

◀ 121

C3
1 SWALLOW CL
2 RHODES AVE
3 BUTTLER WY
4 LORD ST
5 COPELAND CT

C4
1 CHARLES ST
2 REFORM PL
3 WESTGATE PK
4 CASTLE TR RD
5 CASTLE TERR
6 ELMORE CL
7 Sleaford Visual Mus

◀ 121

D2
1 HOLLY CL
2 BRIAR CL
3 JUNIPER WY
4 ASPEN DR
5 ROSEWOOD DR
6 BERRY CL
7 BRIDLE CL
8 LARCH WY
9 CYPRESS CL
10 LAVENDER CL
11 REDWOOD AVE
12 ACACIA CL
13 LIMETREE CL

◀ 121

D3
1 THE INNINGS
2 CHESTNUT CL
3 SOUTHFIELDS
4 PINE CL
5 PAVILION GDNS
6 THE BLACKTHORNS
7 HANDLEY COURT MEWS
8 THE CREAMERY

E3
1 WILLOW CT
2 MAIDEN GR
3 SPINNERS CL
4 GRACE CL
5 PEACOCK CT
6 COBBLERS WY
7 CHAPEL HL CT
8 BARLEY WY

F3
1 JONATHAN GDNS
2 MILTON CL
3 ELMGARTH
4 POLYANTHUS DR
5 MARIGOLD WK
6 WALNUTGARTH
7 FORUM WAY
8 WHEAT GR
9 MAIZE CT

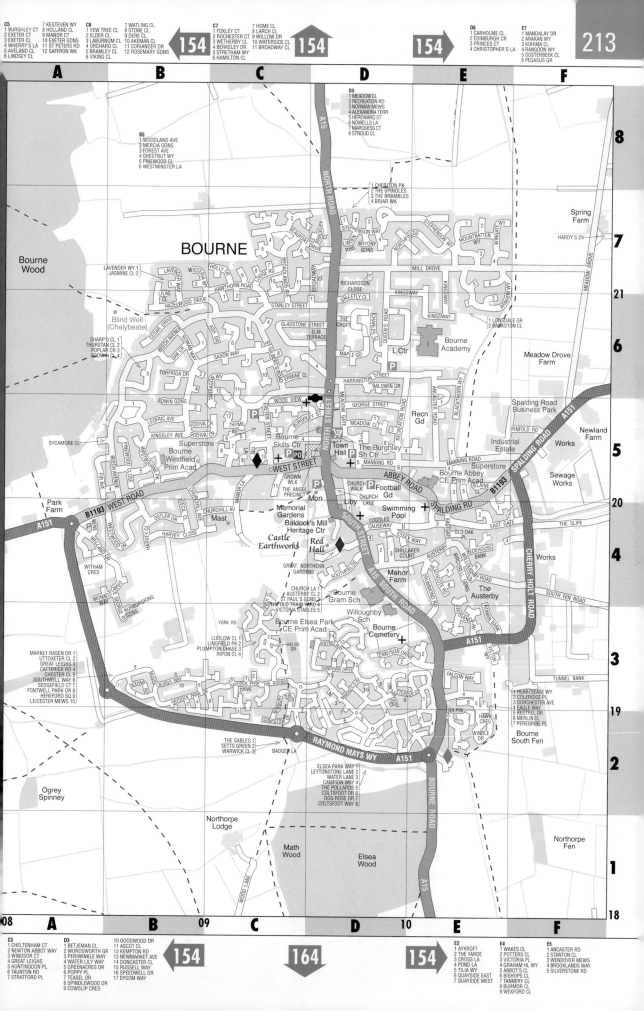

C5
1 BURGHLEY CT
2 EXETER CT
3 EXETER CL
4 WHERRY'S LA
5 AVELAND CL
6 LINDSEY CL

7 KESTEVEN WY
8 HOLLAND CL
9 MANOR CT
10 EXETER GDNS
11 ST PETERS RD
12 SAFFRON WK

C6
1 YEW TREE CL
2 ELDER CL
3 LABURNUM CL
4 ORCHARD CL
5 BRAMLEY CL
6 VIKING CL

7 WATLING CL
8 STONE CL
9 DERE CL
10 AKEMAN CL
11 CORIANDER DR
12 ROSEMARY GDNS

C7
1 FOXLEY CT
2 ROCHESTER CT
3 WETHERBY ST
4 BERKELEY DR
5 STRETHAM WY
6 HAMILTON CL

7 HOME CL
8 LARCH CL
9 WILLOW DR
10 WATERSIDE CL
11 BROADWAY CL

D6
1 CARHOLME CL
2 EDINBURGH CR
3 PRINCES CT
4 CHRISTOPHER'S LA

E7
1 MANDALAY DR
2 ARAKAN WY
3 KOHIMA CL
4 RANGOON WY
5 OOSTERBEEK CL
6 PEGASUS GR

213

BOURNE

Bourne Wood

D5
1 MEADOW CL
2 RECREATION RD
3 NORMAN MEWS
4 ALEXANDRA TERR
5 HEREWARD CL
6 NOWELLS LA
7 MARQUESS CT
8 STROUD CL

1 CHERITON PK
2 THE SPINDLES
3 THE BRAMBLES
4 BRIAR WK

Spring Farm

HARDY'S DV

1 LONSDALE GR
2 BARKSTON CL

Meadow Drove Farm

Spalding Road Business Park

Newland Farm

Works

Industrial Estate

Sewage Works

Works

LAVENDER WY 1
JASMINE CL 2

SHARP'S CL 1
THURSTAN CL 2
POPLAR CR 3
GODWIN CL 4

SYCAMORE CL

Blind Well (Chalybeate)

Bourne Westfield Prim Acad
Superstore

Bourne Skills Ctr

Town Hall

The Burghley Sh Ctr

Bourne Abbey CE Prim Acad

Superstore

CROWN WLK
THE ANGEL PRECINCT
Mon

CHURCH WALK
CHURCH LA
Football Gd

Park Farm

Mast

Memorial Gardens
Baldock's Mill Heritage Ctr

Castle Earthworks

Red Hall

Liby
Swimming Pool

WITHAM CRES

MARKET RASEN DR 1
UTTOXETER CL 2
GREAT LEIGHS 3
CATTERICK RD 4
CHESTER CL 5
SOUTHWELL WAY 6
SEDGEFIELD CT 7
FONTWELL PARK DR 8
HEREFORD SQ 9
LEICESTER MEWS 10

GREAT NORTHERN GARDENS
Manor Farm

CHURCH LA 1
AUSTERBY CL 2
ST PAUL'S GDNS 3
THE OLD TRAIN YARD 4
VICTORIA STABLES 5

Bourne Gram Sch

The Austerby

Willoughby Sch

Bourne Elsea Park CE Prim Acad

Bourne Cemetery

LUDLOW CL 1
LINGFIELD PK 2
PLUMPTON CHASE 3
RIPON CL 4

Bourne South Fen

1 HEARTSEASE WY
2 COLERIDGE PL
3 DORCHESTER AVE
4 EAGLE WAY
5 KESTREL DR
6 MERLIN CL
7 PEREGRINE PL

THE GABLES 1
SETTS GREEN 2
WARWICK CL 3

BADGER LA

ELSEA PARK WAY 1
LEYTONSTONE LANE 2
WATER LANE 3
CAMPION WAY 4
THE POLLARDS 5
COLTSFOOT DR 6
DOG ROSE DR 7
COLTSFOOT WAY 8

Ogrey Spinney

Northorpe Lodge

Math Wood

Elsea Wood

Northorpe Fen

C3
1 CHELTENHAM CT
2 NEWTON ABBOT WAY
3 WINDSOR CT
4 GREAT LEIGHS
5 HUNTINGDON PL
6 TAUNTON RD
7 STRATFORD PL

D3
1 BETJEMAN CL
2 WORDSWORTH GR
3 PERIWINKLE WAY
4 WATER LILY WAY
5 GREENACRES DR
6 POPPY PL
7 TEASEL DR
8 SPINDLEWOOD DR
9 COWSLIP CRES

10 GOODWOOD DR
11 ASCOT CL
12 KEMPTON RD
13 NEWMARKET AVE
14 DONCASTER CL
15 RUSSELL WAY
16 SPEEDWELL DR
17 EPSOM WAY

E2
1 AYKROFT
2 THE YARDE
3 CROSS LA
4 POND LA
5 TILIA WY
6 QUAYSIDE EAST
7 QUAYSIDE WEST

E4
1 WAKES CL
2 POTTERS CL
3 VICTORIA PL
4 GRAHAM HL WY
5 ABBOT'S CL
6 BISHOPS CL
7 TANNERY CL
8 BURMOR CL
9 WEXFORD CL

E5
1 ANCASTER RD
2 STANTON CL
3 WENDOVER MEWS
4 BROOKLANDS WAY
5 SILVERSTONE RD

← 154   ◆ 164   154 →

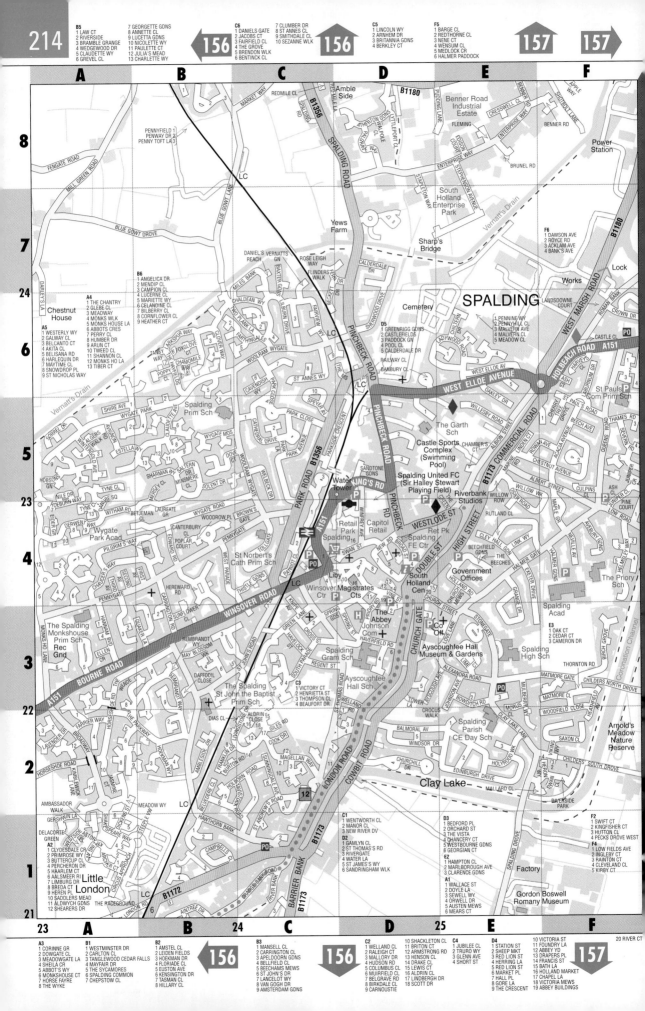

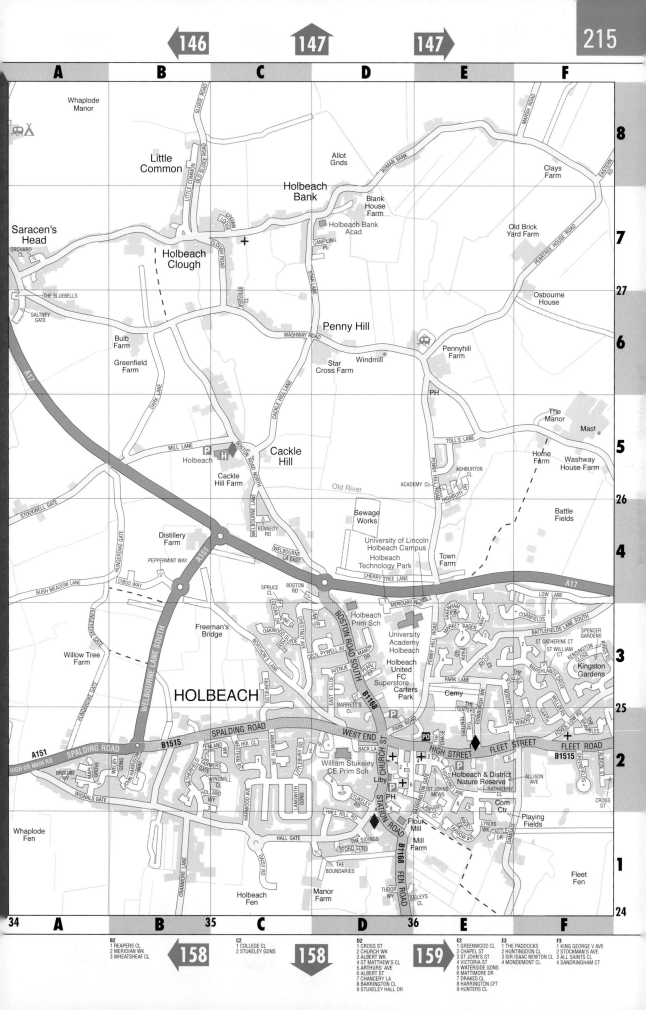

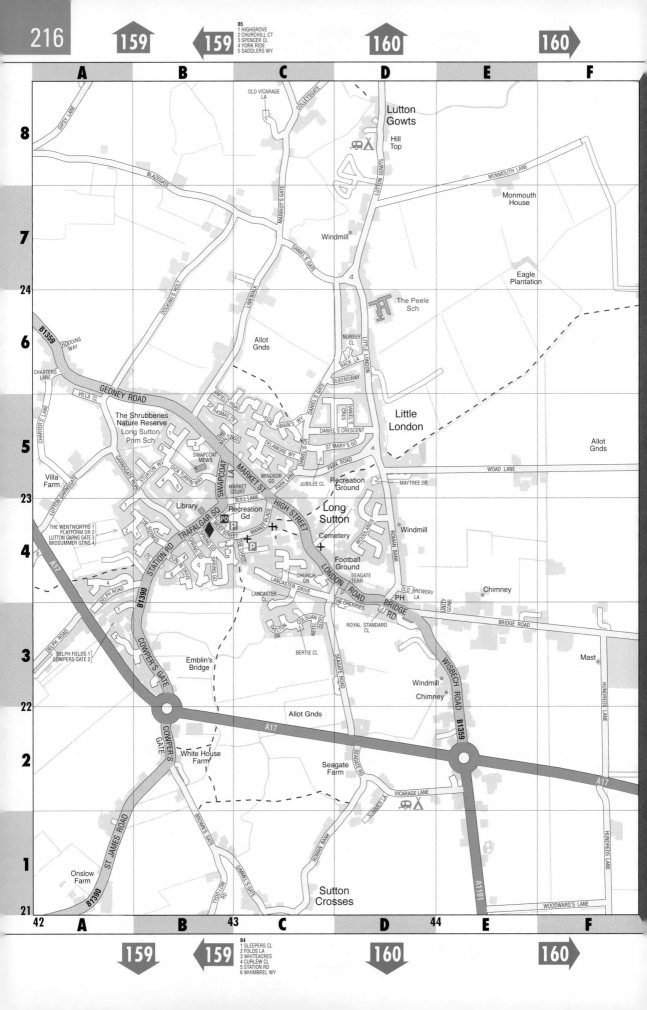

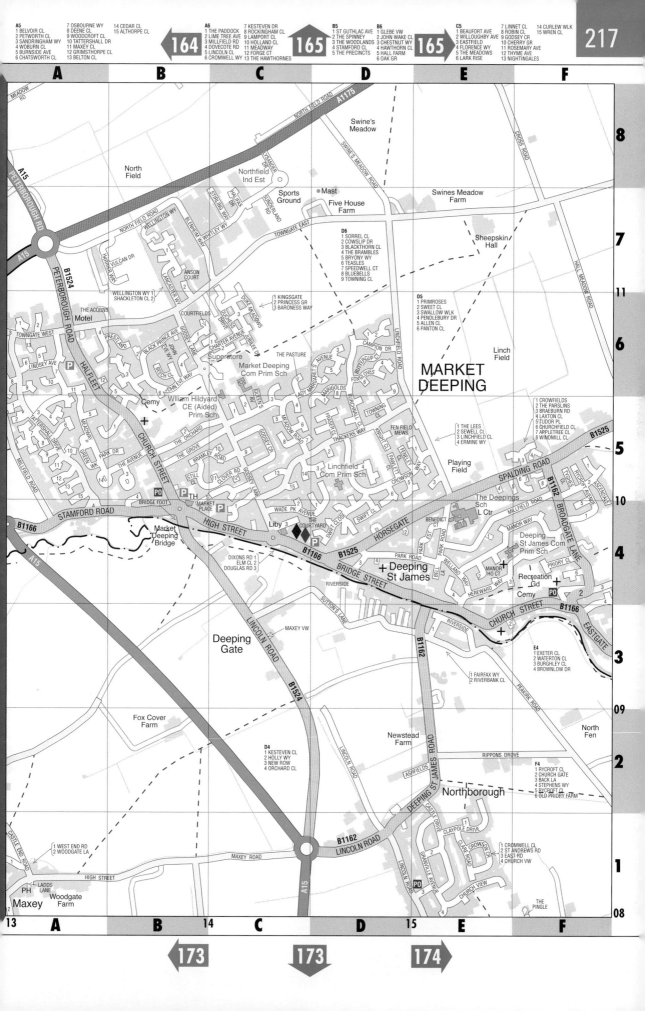

C7
1 FOXGLOVE RD
2 MEADOWSWEET
3 SWEETBRIAR
4 TOBIAS GR
5 BLACKTHORN
6 CLOVER GDNS

D6
1 FIR RD
2 BRAMBLE GR
3 ANGUS CL
4 SORREL CL
5 MORAY CL
6 ASH PL

D7
1 LAVENDER WY
2 BLUEBELL RD
3 BUTTERCUP CL
4 CAMPION GR
5 FOREST GDNS
6 BIRCH RD

E5
1 TENNYSON WY
2 KEATS GR
3 KIPLING CL
4 LUFFENHAM CL
5 COTTESMORE RD
6 EXTON CL

E6
1 BELVOIR CL
2 WALCOT WY
3 BARNWELL RD
4 ROCKINGHAM RD
5 GLENEAGLES CL
6 FALKIRK CL

7 OBAN CL
8 CROMARTY RD
9 MELROSE CL
10 MONTROSE CL
11 TROON CL
12 SHELLEY CL
13 AUDUS PL

14 LAUGHTON DR
15 BRADSHAW CL
16 CLAPTON CL

F6
1 HARDWICK RD
2 ELTON CL
3 WAVERLEY PL
4 CALEDONIAN RD
5 BURNS RD
6 MASON DRIVE
7 WINTERTON CL
8 JACKSON WAY

Ingthorpe
Ingthorpe Farm
Strawsons Farm
Great Casterton
MAIN STREET
HOME FARM CL
PH
Church Farm
Road End
Toll Bar
Road End Farm
Glebe Farm
WATER LANE
GAINSBOROUGH RD
Mast
PARKER CL
BURGESS RD
ROSS DR
COLLINS AVE
CHATSWORTH ROAD
HADDON RD
BANKS CRES
RAVEL CL
ELGAR WAY
WAVERLEY GD
CORNFLOWER CL 1
MARIGOLD CL 2
OAK WILLOW RD
OAK RD
PINE CL
FIFE CLOSE
CASTERTON ROAD
B1081
STAMFORD ROAD
A606
EMPINGHAM ROAD
CHARLOCK CTR
BEECH GR
CASTOR RD
ABERDEEN CL
HAZEL GR
ARRAN ROAD
AYR CL
CASTERTON ROAD
CAITHNESS ROAD
ROXBURGH RD
FOX DALE
PERTH RD
BRAEMAR CL
DEE DRIVE
GARDEN CLOSE
BYRON WY
CARISBROOKE GR
SUTHERLAND WY
STIRLING ROAD
PO
HIGHLANDS WAY
HIGHGROVE GDNS
EMPINGHAM ROAD
ERMINE WAY
Mast
The Rookery
CHESTNUT GDNS
ARRAN RD
Malcolm Sargent Prim Sch
BARNES CT
Rugby Club
ARGYLL WY 1
REFORM ST 2
ERMINE CL 3
SHERWOOD CL 4
WHEATSHEAF WAY
TILL PL
KINGSDOWN DR
LONSDALE CL
LYNDON WY
HOBBS GDNS
LONSDALE ROAD
HAMBLETON ROAD
BROOKE AVE
Sports Gd
EXETER GARDENS
TINWELL ROAD LANE
Tinwell Lodge Farm
BARROWFIELD DR 1
VANDERBANK TERR 2
FENNELL WAY 3
BOYFIELD CRES 4
LAUNDE GD 5
GROVES CRES
CULPEPPER WAY
TINWELL ROAD
GREAT NORTH ROAD
STEADFOLD LANE
CASTERTON LANE
HIGH CT LA
Home Farm
CROWN LA
PH
THE PADDOCKS
Tinwell
TINWELL ROAD A6121
MILL LA
South View Farm
Weir
STAMFORD ROAD
A6121
River Chato
Tinwell Crossing
Home Wood
Easton Hillside
Macmillan Way
Dottrell Hill Plantation
A1
LITTLE CASTERTON ROAD
OLD GREAT NORTH ROAD
GREAT NORTH ROAD

171
171
171
171

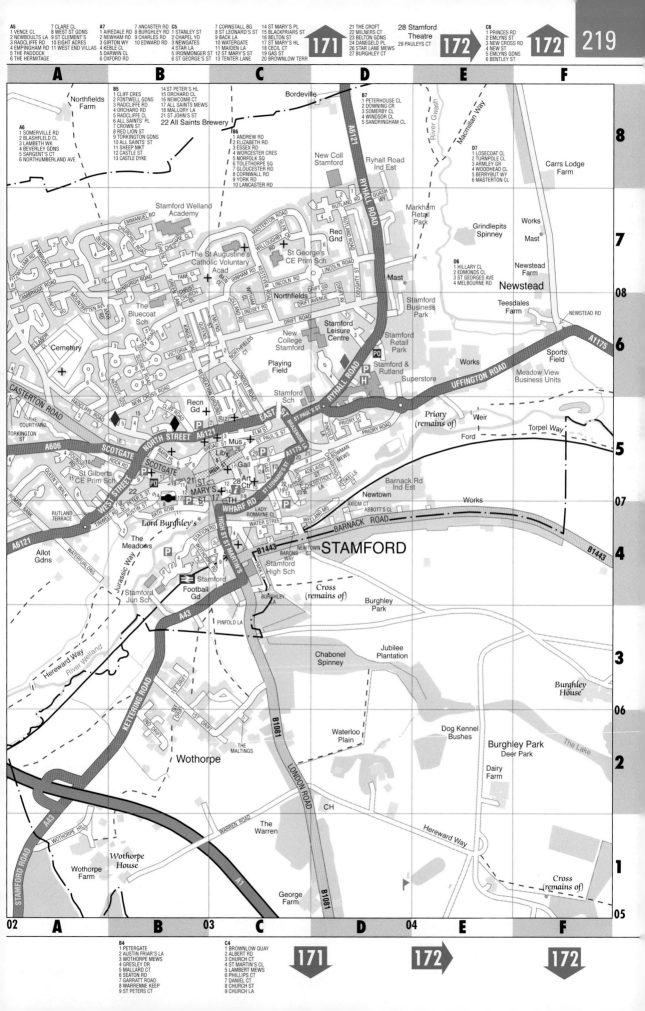

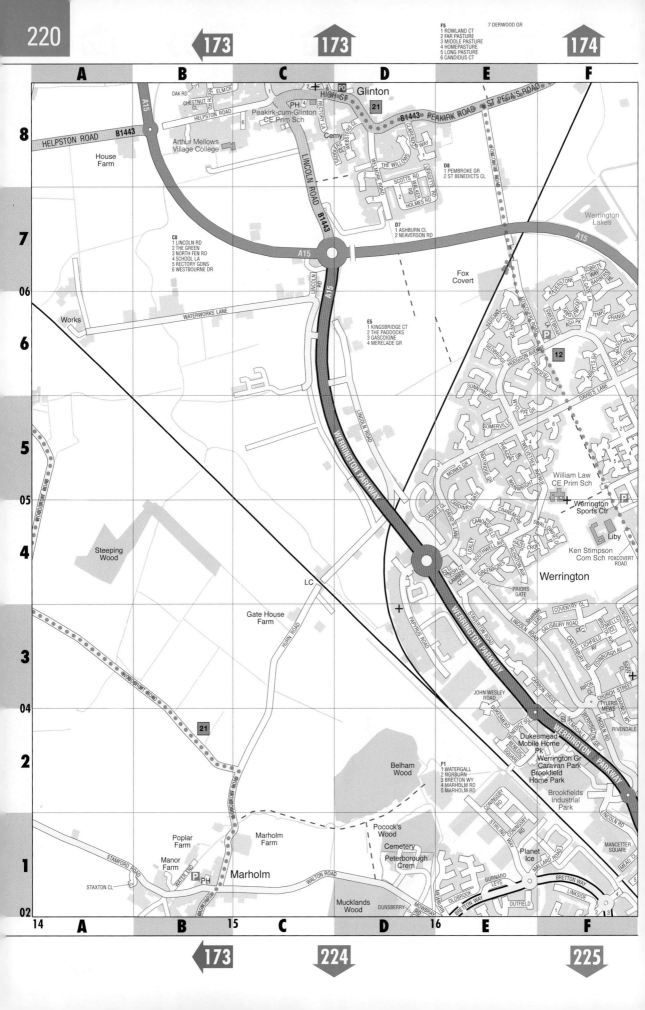

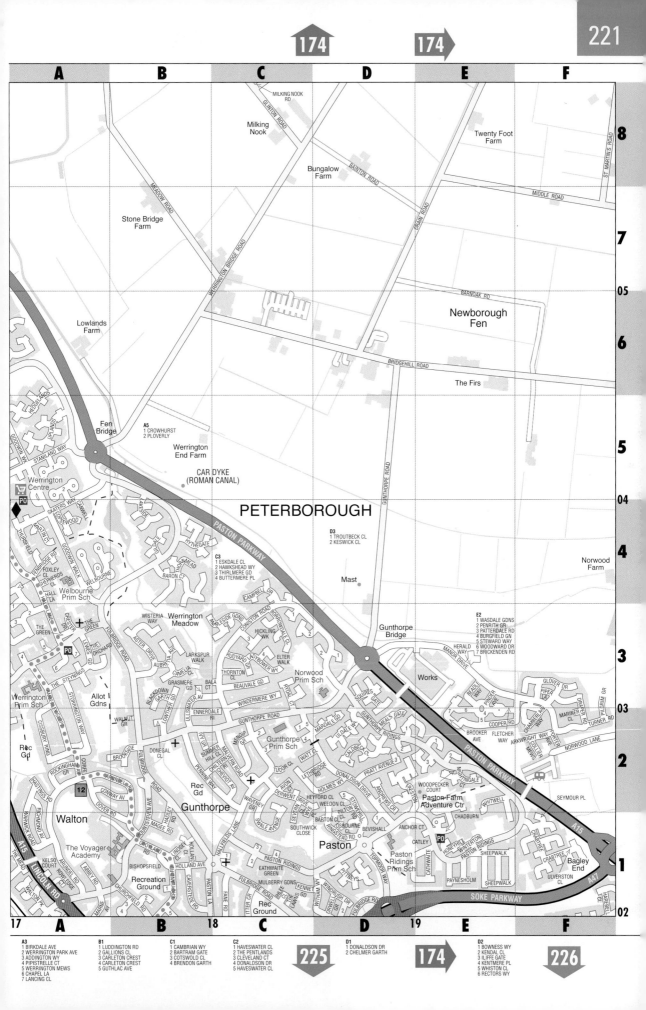

MILKING NOOK RD

Milking Nook

Bungalow Farm

Twenty Foot Farm

MIDDLE ROAD

Stone Bridge Farm

MEADOW ROAD

WERRINGTON BRIDGE ROAD

GLINTON ROAD

RAINTON ROAD

DRAIN ROAD

ST MARTIN'S ROAD

8

7

05

Newborough Fen

BARNOAK RD

6

Lowlands Farm

The Firs

BRIDGEHILL ROAD

Fen Bridge

A5
1 CROWHURST
2 PLOVERLY

Werrington End Farm

CAR DYKE (ROMAN CANAL)

GUNTHORPE ROAD

5

04

Werrington Centre

PO

PETERBOROUGH

PASTON PARKWAY

D3
1 TROUTBECK CL
2 KESWICK CL

Norwood Farm

4

C3
1 ESKDALE CL
2 HAWKSHEAD WY
3 THIRLMERE GD
4 BUTTERMERE PL

Mast

E2
1 WASDALE GDNS
2 PENRITH GR
3 PATTERDALE RD
4 BURGFIELD GN
5 STEWARD WAY
6 WOODWARD DR
7 BRICKENDEN RD

Welbourne Prim Sch

Wisteria Way

Werrington Meadow

Gunthorpe Bridge

HERALD WAY

MANOR DRIVE

GLOVER DR

PIPER LA

3

03

THE GREEN

PO

Norwood Prim Sch

Works

BEADLE WAY

PINKER LANE

MARINER CL

DRAPER RD

TURNER RD

PILGRIM GR

CHAMBERLAIN WAY

PORTER CL

Werrington Prim Sch

Allot Gdns

Gunthorpe Prim Sch

GUNTHORPE ROAD

COOPER RD

BROOKER AVE

FLETCHER WAY

ARKWRIGHT WAY

NORWOOD LANE

EXETER MEWS

PASTON PARKWAY

2

Rec Gd

Rec Gd

Gunthorpe

Gunthorpe Prim Sch

Paston Farm Adventure Ctr

WOODPECKER COURT

NIGHTINGALE

WHITWELL

CHADBURN

SEYMOUR PL

A15

Walton

The Voyager Academy

Paston

Paston Ridings Prim Sch

PO

WINTERTON

HONEY HILL

PAYNESHOLM

SHEEPWALK

Bagley End

CRABTREE

ULVERSTON CL

HAREBELL CL

A47

1

02

Recreation Ground

Rec Ground

SOKE PARKWAY

LINCOLN RD

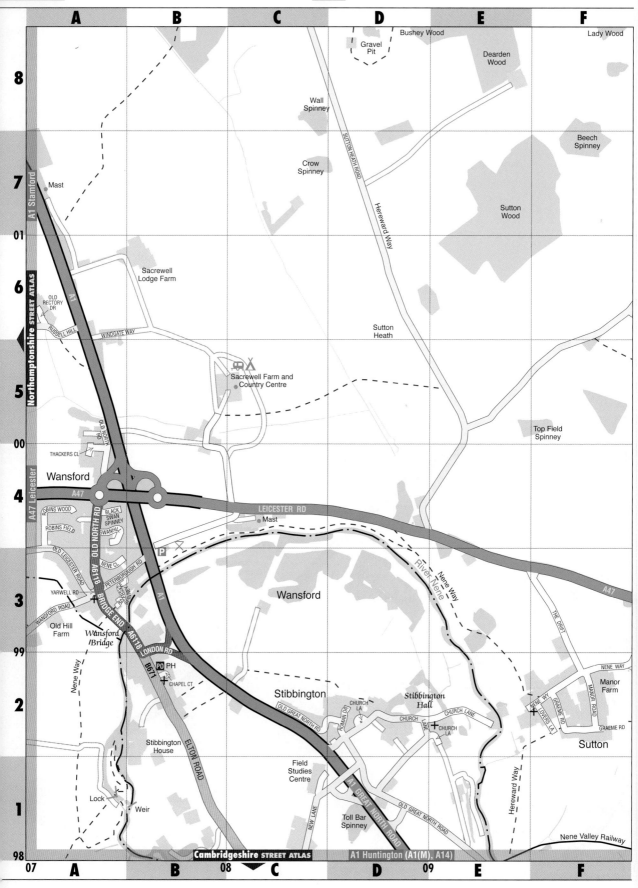

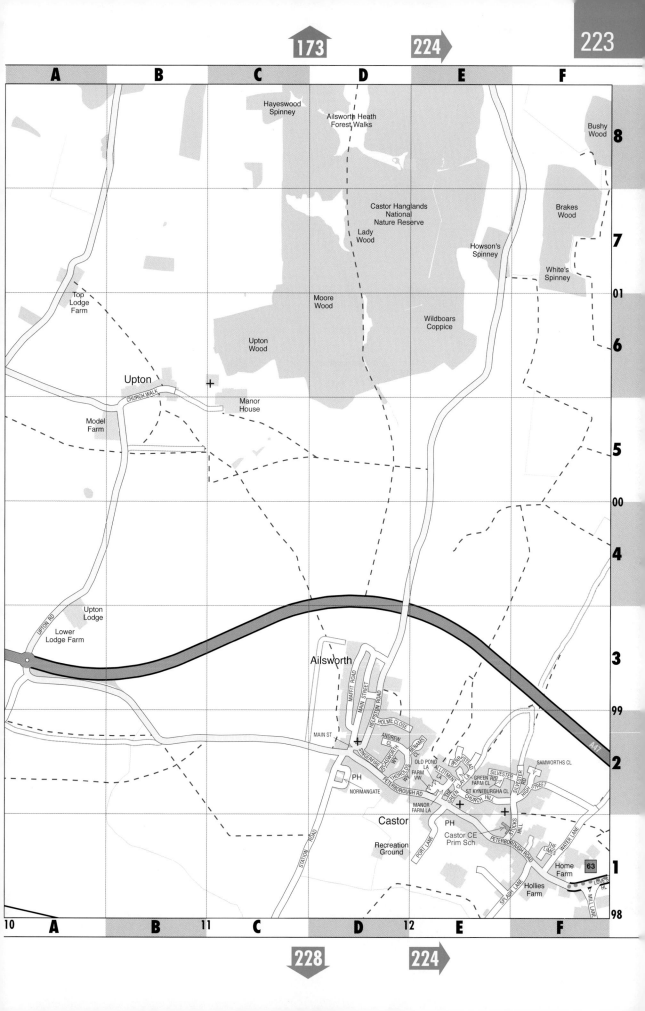

A B C D E F

8

Hayeswood
Spinney

Ailsworth Heath
Forest Walks

Bushy
Wood

Castor Hanglands
National
Nature Reserve

Brakes
Wood

7

Lady
Wood

Howson's
Spinney

Top
Lodge
Farm

White's
Spinney

01

Moore
Wood

Wildboars
Coppice

6

Upton
Wood

Upton

CHURCH WALK

Manor
House

5

Model
Farm

00

4

UPTON RD

Upton
Lodge

Lower
Lodge Farm

Ailsworth

3

99

MAFFIT ROAD

MAIN STREET

HELPSTON ROAD

HOLME CLOSE

A47

2

MAIN ST

ANDREW
CL

BENANS

Samworths Cl

OLD POND
LA
FARM
VW

ALLOTMENT
LA

GREEN CLAY CL

BERRSTEAD

SILVESTER
FARM CL

GREEN RD

SILVESTER ROW

HIGH STREET

PH

SINGERFIELD RD

AILSWORTH RD

HOROUS

PETERBOROUGH RD

NORMANGATE

ST KYNEBURGHA CL

CHURCH HILL

MANOR
FARM LA

Castor

PH

Castor CE
Prim Sch

STOCKS HILL

PETERBOROUGH ROAD

THE
LIMES

WATER LANE

Home
Farm

63

1

Recreation
Ground

PORT LANE

STATION ROAD

SPLASH LANE

Hollies
Farm

LOVE'S HL

MILL LANE

98

10 A 11 B C 12 D E F

8

Bushy
Wood

Foster's
Coppice

Home
Farm

Burmer
Wood

Mucklands
Wood

GULLYMORE

7

Marholm
Lodges

PARK FARM ROAD

WESTHAWE

01

Popple's Coppice

Belsize
Farm

Belsize
Wood

Thistlemoor
Wood

Park
Farm

Grimeshaw
Wood

6

Little
Thistlemoor Wood

21

5

Oldfield
Pond

Stamford
Plantations

Stamford
Lodge

STAMFORD LODGE ROAD

Deer Park

New Park
Farm

Ten Acre
Plantation

New
Plantation

00

Salter's
Wood

STAMFORD LODGE ROAD

Milton
Hall

MUSKHAM
SPRIGHILL

4

Recreation
Ground

NICHOLAS TAYLOR GDNS 1
STAMPER ST 2
BRAILSFORD CL 3
JOROSE WY 4
TEANBY CT 5
CARTERS CL 6
THOMAS CL 7
GOODWOOD RD 8
BARNARD WY 9
HARRISON CL 10
LONGTHORPE HOUSE MEWS 11

KENNEL'S ROAD

JORSE
WAY

Milton Park

WALKERS WY   HUNTSMAN'S GATE

RINGWOOD

3

Crickety Park

Sheep Park

LITTLE JOHNS
CL

MILTON WY

FERRY DRIVE

PETERBOROUGH DRIVE

BERTRAMS WY

99

Fitzwilliam

HERONRY DRIVE

EGAR WY

PELHAM

PEACOCK WY

LODGE
AVENUE

2

A47

MARHOLM ROAD

Ferry
House

Ferryhill
Plantation

PETERBOROUGH
DR

P

VIRGINIA CL 1
CYPRESS CL 2
LONGTHORPE CL 3

CH

P

63

River Nene

Bluebell Walk
Plantation

Mast

Thorpe
Wood

1

Love's
Hill

FERRY HILL

Little John
Robin Hood

Hereward Way

P

Playing
Fields

NENE WAY

Nene Way

98

Gunwade Lake

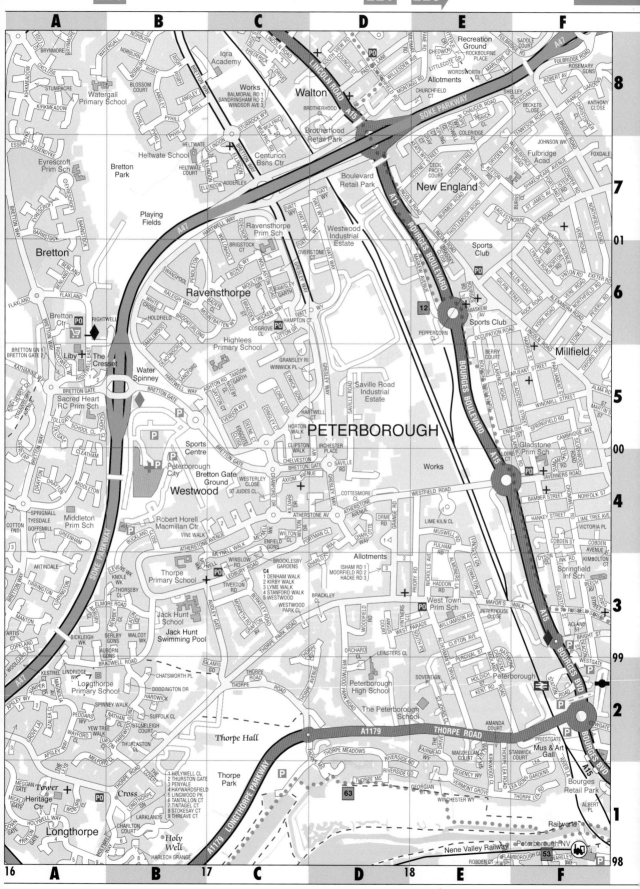

A B C D E F

8 01 7 6 5 00 4 3 99 2 1 98

D8
1 MEDBOURNE GDNS
2 WALTHAM CL
3 HUNGARTON CT
4 SOMERBY GARTH

E7
1 WHETSTONE CT
2 RAGDALE CL
3 ROTHERBY GR
4 ILLSTON PL
5 REDGATE CT
6 BLANDFORD GDNS
7 WIMBORNE DR

D7
1 RATCLIFFE CT
2 ALLEXTON GDNS
3 TWYFORD GDNS
4 BUCKMINSTER PL
5 REDMILE WLK
6 DORCHESTER CRES

A5
1 INGLEBOROUGH
2 DOGSTHORPE GR

C2
1 RUTLAND CT
2 SHROPSHIRE PL

D3
1 WETHERBY WY
2 RASEN CT
3 HEXHAM CT
4 NORTH BANK RD
5 VICARAGE FARM RD

A1
1 WENTWORTH ST
2 BRIDGE ST
3 RIVERGATE
4 EMBANKMENT RD

C1
1 RUDD CLOSE
2 BRADLEY WAY
3 HAMMONDS DRIVE

PETERBOROUGH

Dogsthorpe · Newark · Eastfield · Fengate · Eastgate

A2
1 KING ST
2 QUEEN ST
3 TRINITY ST
4 PRIESTGATE
5 BROADWAY CT
6 HEREWARD CROSS
7 CATTLE MARKET WAY
8 CATTLE MARKET RD
9 MINSTER PRECINCTS
10 CATHEDRAL SQ
11 DEAN'S CT

A3
1 BURGHLEY RD
2 BURGHLEY SQ
3 ST MARK'S CT
4 TOWNSEND CL

B2
1 FENGATE CL
2 HEREWARD CL
3 KESTEVEN WLK
4 WESTMORELAND GDNS
5 STEPHENSON CT
6 ST MARYS CT

B3
1 CRAWTHORNE ST
2 JORDAN MEWS

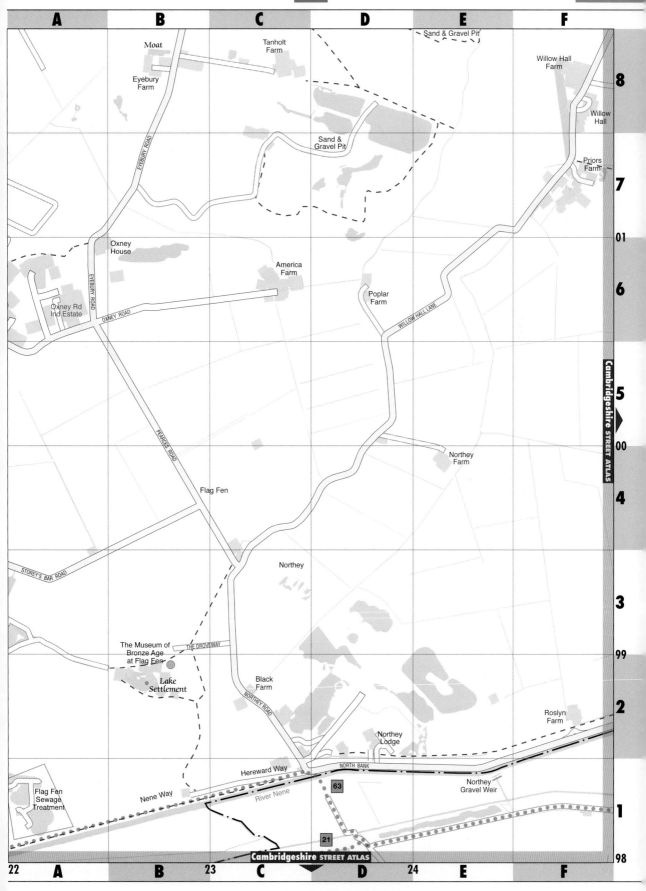

| A | B | C | D | E | F |

8

Moat

Tanholt Farm

Sand & Gravel Pit

Willow Hall Farm

Eyebury Farm

EYEBURY ROAD

Sand & Gravel Pit

Willow Hall

Priors Farm

7

01

Oxney House

EYEBURY ROAD

America Farm

Poplar Farm

WILLOW HALL LANE

6

Oxney Rd Ind Estate

OXNEY ROAD

5

00

Northey Farm

PEARCES ROAD

4

Flag Fen

STOREY'S BAR ROAD

Northey

3

99

The Museum of Bronze Age at Flag Fen

THE DROVEWAY

Lake Settlement

Black Farm

NORTHEY ROAD

Roslyn Farm

2

Northey Lodge

Flag Fen Sewage Treatment

Hereward Way

NORTH BANK

Northey Gravel Weir

Nene Way

River Nene

63

21

1

98

| 22 | A | B | 23 | C | D | 24 | E | F |

223

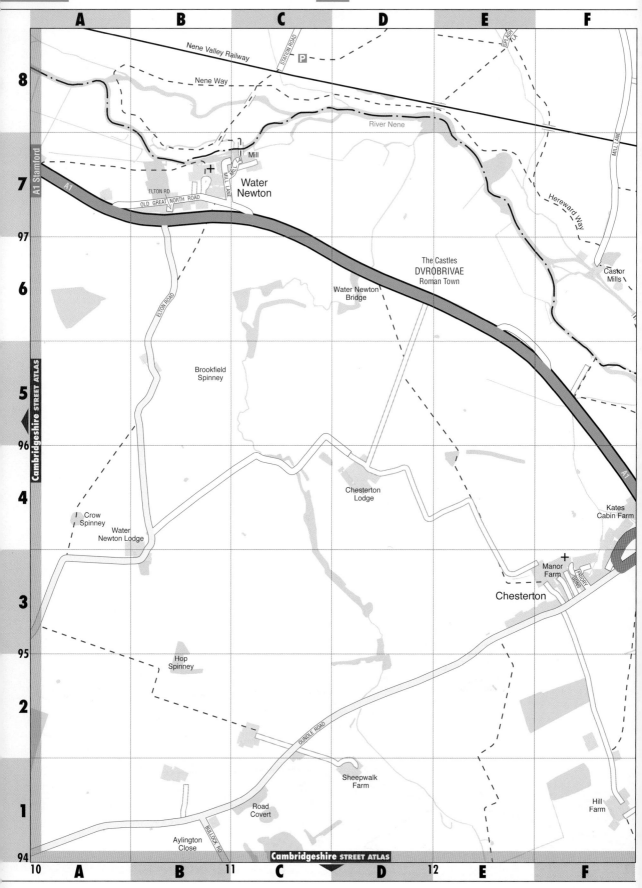

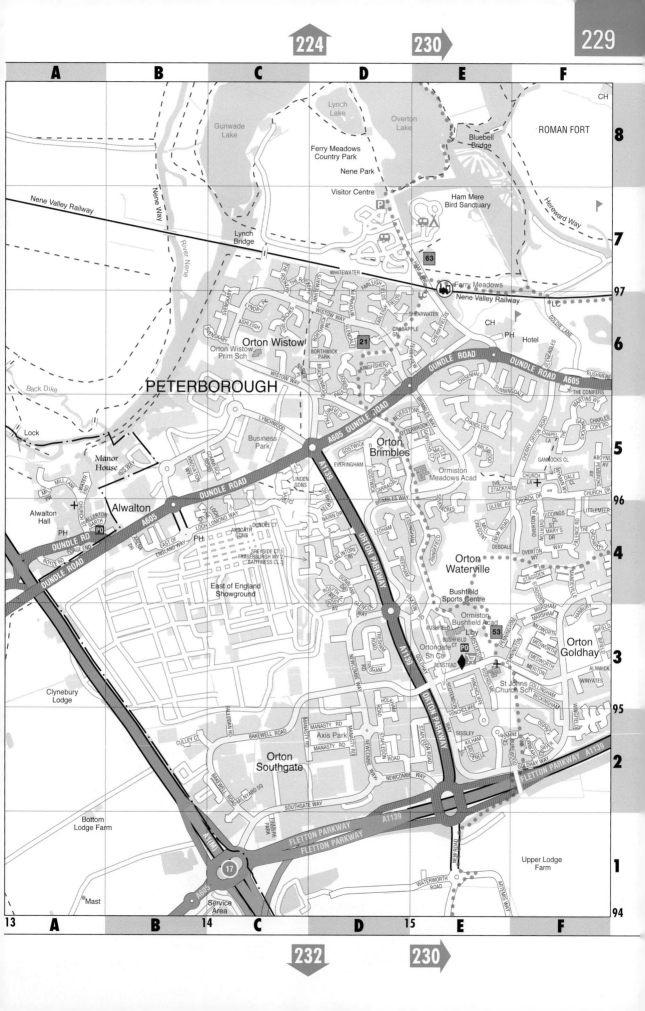

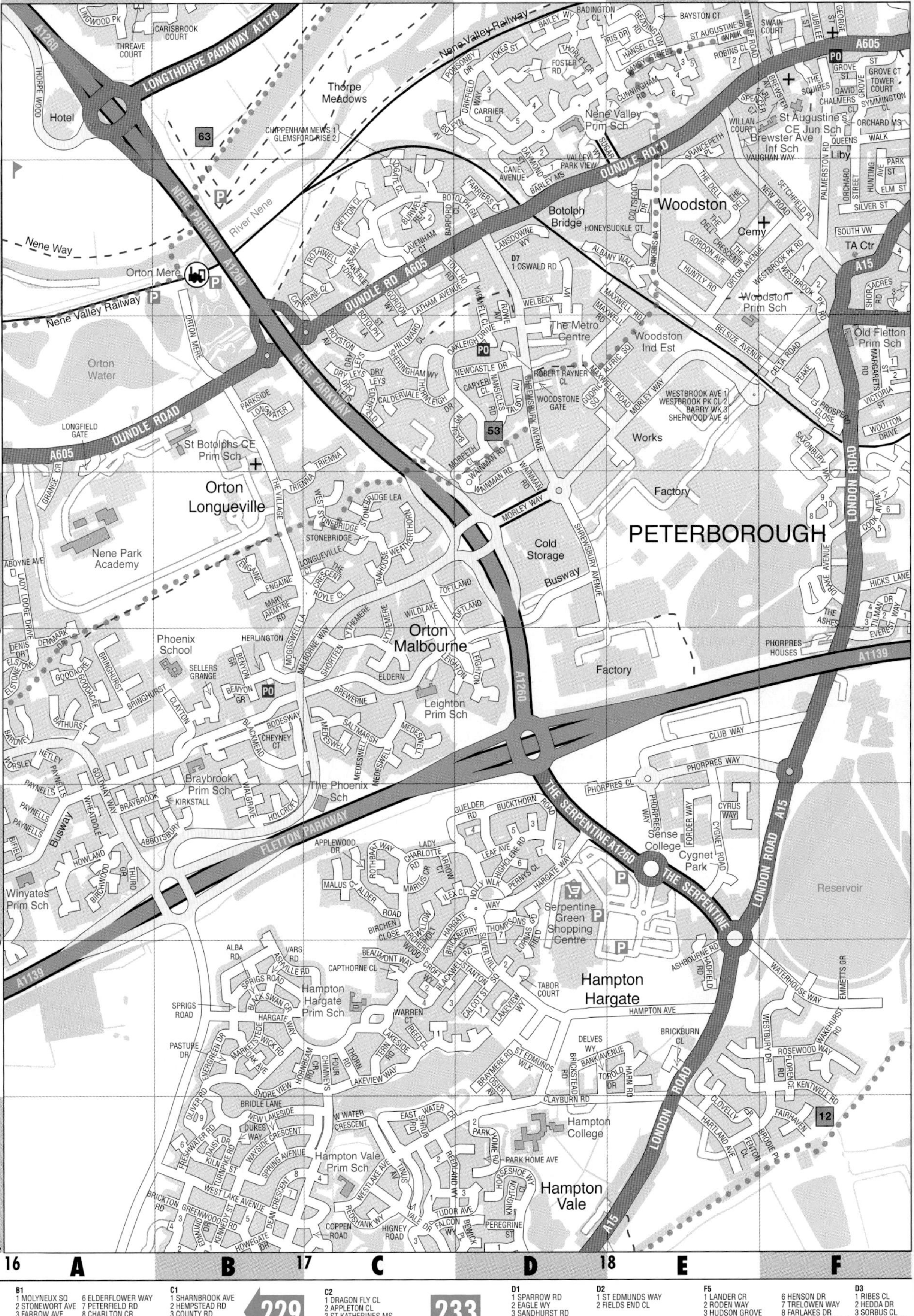

A B C D E F

8 7 97 6 5 96 4 3 95 2 1 94

Grid references (left margin): 8, 7, 97, 6, 5, 96, 4, 3, 95, 2, 1, 94
Grid references (bottom): 16, A, 17, B, C, 18, D, E, F

Major labels:

- Thorpe Wood
- Hotel
- Carisbrook Court
- Threave Court
- Longthorpe Parkway A1179
- Thorpe Meadows
- Nene Valley Railway
- River Nene
- Nene Way
- Nene Parkway A1260
- Orton Mere
- Orton Water
- Oundle Road A605
- Orton Longueville
- Nene Park Academy
- Phoenix School
- St Botolphs CE Prim Sch
- Orton Malbourne
- Leighton Prim Sch
- Braybrook Prim Sch
- The Phoenix Sch
- Winyates Prim Sch
- Fletton Parkway A1139
- Busway
- Woodston
- Woodston Prim Sch
- Nene Valley Prim Sch
- Botolph Bridge
- The Metro Centre
- Woodston Ind Est
- Works
- Factory
- **PETERBOROUGH**
- Cold Storage Busway
- The Serpentine A1260
- London Road A15
- Reservoir
- Serpentine Green Shopping Centre
- Hampton Hargate
- Hampton Hargate Prim Sch
- Hampton Vale
- Hampton Vale Prim Sch
- Hampton College
- Sense College
- Cygnet Park
- St Augustine's CE Jun Sch
- Brewster Ave Inf Sch
- Old Fletton Prim Sch
- Club Way
- Phorpres Way

D4	D3	E4
1 FORTUNA DR	1 TEMPESTES WAY	1 LIBERTAS DR
2 NEPTUNE CL	2 AUSTER RD	2 HERCULES WAY
3 LUNA WAY		3 SPIROS RD
4 VESTA CL		4 ELENA RD
		5 VIOLETA WAY

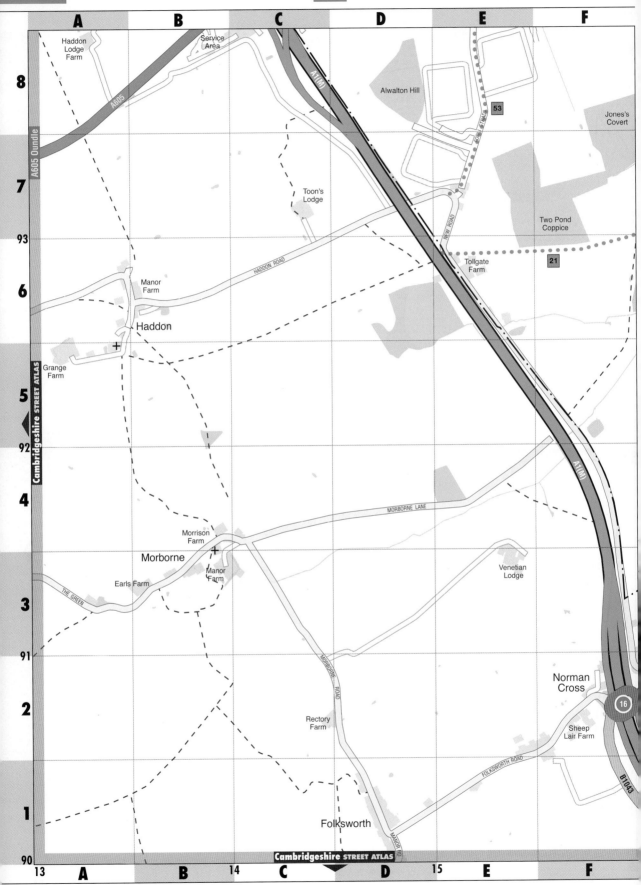

1 CORNFLOWER AVE
2 MID WATER CRES
3 LAKE FIELD RD
4 HOLLOWSIDE RD
5 COPPEN RD
6 STONEWORT AVE
7 WINDSOR CRES
8 SAFFRON DR

GAVEL ST 1
MAGISTRATES RD 2
EAGLE WY 3
BEWICK PL 4
HORSESHOE WY 5
HIGH CT WY 6

Orton Brick Works

Pit
(dis)

Madam
White's
Covert

Spendelows
Farm

Yaxley
Lodge Farm

Heye's Farm

1 STEPHENSON CL
2 PARTRIDGE CL
3 NIGHTINGALE DR
4 FARADAY CL

F6
1 AZALEA CT
2 LAVENDER CL

CROCUS
WAY

Fourfields
Prim Sch

Yaxley

The William
de Yaxley
CE Aided
Jun Sch

Liby

MALTING
SQUARE

Yaxley
Inf Sch

B1091

BROADWAY

D5
1 SCOTT DR
2 WESTFIELD CL
3 LIVINGSTONE RD
4 VICARAGE WY

Carysfort
CL

Church Street

Cemy

Yards End Dyke

Hod
Fen

A1(M) Huntingdon (A14)

A15

LONDON ROAD

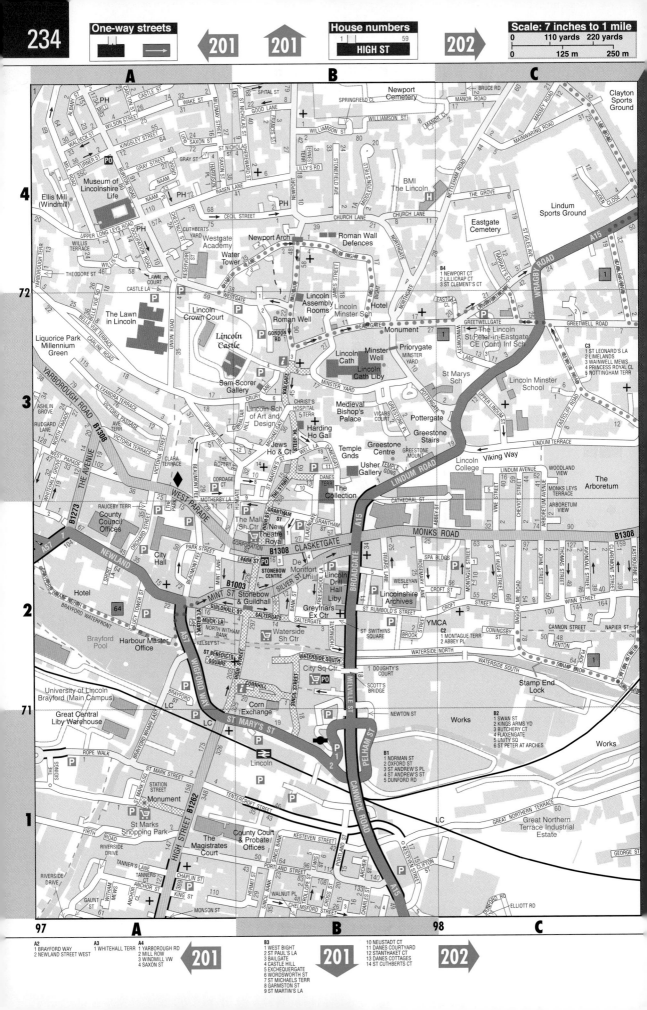

Index

Place name May be abbreviated on the map

Location number Present when a number indicates the place's position in a crowded area of mapping

Locality, town or village Shown when more than one place has the same name

Postcode district District for the indexed place

Page and grid square Page number and grid reference for the standard mapping

Church Rd **6** Beckenham BR2..........**53** C6

Cities, towns and villages are listed in CAPITAL LETTERS

Public and commercial buildings are highlighted in magenta   Places of interest are highlighted in blue with a star★

Abbreviations used in the index

Acad	Academy	Comm	Common	Gd	Ground	L	Leisure	Prom	Promenade
App	Approach	Cott	Cottage	Gdn	Garden	La	Lane	Rd	Road
Arc	Arcade	Cres	Crescent	Gn	Green	Liby	Library	Recn	Recreation
Ave	Avenue	Cswy	Causeway	Gr	Grove	Mdw	Meadow	Ret	Retail
Bglw	Bungalow	Ct	Court	H	Hall	Meml	Memorial	Sh	Shopping
Bldg	Building	Ctr	Centre	Ho	House	Mkt	Market	Sq	Square
Bsns, Bus	Business	Ctry	Country	Hospl	Hospital	Mus	Museum	St	Street
Bvd	Boulevard	Cty	County	HQ	Headquarters	Orch	Orchard	Sta	Station
Cath	Cathedral	Dr	Drive	Hts	Heights	Pal	Palace	Terr	Terrace
Cir	Circus	Dro	Drove	Ind	Industrial	Par	Parade	TH	Town Hall
Cl	Close	Ed	Education	Inst	Institute	Pas	Passage	Univ	University
Cnr	Corner	Emb	Embankment	Int	International	Pk	Park	Wk, Wlk	Walk
Coll	College	Est	Estate	Intc	Interchange	Pl	Place	Wr	Water
Com	Community	Ex	Exhibition	Junc	Junction	Prec	Precinct	Yd	Yard

Index of towns, villages, streets, hospitals, industrial estates, railway stations, schools, shopping centres, universities and places of interest

12th Ave DN36 . . . . 36 F8
1st Drift PE9 . . . . 219 B2
1st Main Rd DN36 . . . . 36 F8
2nd Ave DN36 . . . . 36 F8
2nd Drift PE9 . . . . 219 B2
4th Ave DN36 . . . . 36 F8
5th Ave DN36 . . . . 36 F8
6th Ave DN36 . . . . 36 F8
7th Ave DN36 . . . . 36 F8

A

AALPS Coll DN15 . . . . 8 F3
Aalsmeer Rise **6** PE11 . . 214 A2
Aaron Wy PE20 . . . . 136 C4
Abberton Mews PE7 . . . . . 233 E8
Abbey Bldgs **19** PE11 . . . . . 214 D4
Abbey Cl Coningsby LN4 . . . 207 B5
  6 Skegness PE25 . . . . . . 206 A4
  5 Woodhall Spa LN10 . . . 97 C6
Abbey Cres **3** PE20 . . . . . 135 C7
Abbeydale Cres NG31 . . . . 211 A8
Abbey Dr **20** Hatfield DN7 . . 14 D4
  13 Woodhall Spa LN10 . . . 97 C5
Abbey Dr E DN32 . . . . 191 D6
Abbey Dr W DN32 . . . . 191 D6
Abbeyfield Rd **1** DN7 . . . . 14 C4
Abbeyfields PE2 . . . . 231 A7
Abbeygate DN31 . . . . 191 D7
Abbey Gdns **2** DN7 . . . . . . 14 D4
Abbey Gr **23** DN7 . . . . 14 D4
Abbey La North Ormsby LN11 48 D4
  Sedgebrook NG32 . . . . . . 128 F4
  Swineshead PE20 . . . . 135 C6
  Woodhall Spa LN10 . . . . . . 97 C5
Abbey Mews **11** PE6 . . . . 166 F1
Abbey Park LN11 . . . . 198 E7
Abbey Pk Mews DN32 . . . . 191 D6
Abbey Pk Rd DN32 . . . . . . 191 D6
Abbey Pl **2** Lincoln LN2 . . 234 C2
  10 Thorney PE6 . . . . 176 A3
Abbey Rd Alvingham LN11 . . 49 F2
  Bardney LN3 . . . . 83 B4
  Bourne PE10 . . . . 213 D5
  Grimsby DN32 . . . . 191 D6
  Hatfield DN7 . . . . 14 D4
  Louth LN11 . . . . 198 D6
  North Killingholme DN39 . . . 12 B4
  Peterborough PE4 . . . . . . 221 A1
  Revesby PE22 . . . . 99 C5
  Scunthorpe DN17 . . . . 184 F6
  Sleaford NG34 . . . . 212 A2

Abbey Rd continued
  Swineshead PE20 . . . . 135 C7
  Ulceby DN39 . . . . 12 A1
Abbey Rise **14** DN19 . . . . . 11 D8
Abbey St
  Kingston upon Hull HU9 . . . 181 C7
  Lincoln LN2 . . . . 234 C2
Abbey Way DN7 . . . . 14 D5
Abbey Wlk
  10 Crowland PE6 . . . . . . 166 F1
  Grimsby DN32 . . . . 191 D7
Abbey Yd **12** PE11 . . . . . . 214 D4
Abbotsbury PE2 . . . . 230 A3
Abbot's Cl **5** PE10 . . . . . 213 E4
Abbots Cres **6** PE11 . . . . 214 A4
Abbots Dr **1** PE6 . . . . 175 B8
Abbots Gdns **1** PE12 . . . . 158 B6
Abbotsmede Prim Sch
  PE1 . . . . 226 C4
Abbots Rd DN17 . . . . 184 F6
Abbot St LN5 . . . . 201 E1
Abbotsway DN32 . . . . 191 D6
Abbot's Way **5** PE11 . . . . 214 A3
Abbott Cl **10** LN8 . . . . 57 B8
Abbott's Cl PE9 . . . . 219 D4
Abbotts Gr PE4 . . . . 220 F6
Abbotts Grange DN36 . . . . 195 E7
Abbotts Way LN11 . . . . 198 E6
Abbott's Wy NG24 . . . . . . 104 A5
Abbot Way PE7 . . . . 233 D4
Abel Cl PE6 . . . . 165 D1
Abel Smith Gdns **7** LN4 . . 81 E2
Abercorn St DN16 . . . . 183 A2
Aberdeen Cl PE9 . . . . 218 D6
Aberporth Dr LN6 . . . . 204 B8
Abingdon Ave LN6 . . . . . . 204 C6
Abingdon Cl **15** LN6 . . . . 204 C6
Aboyne Ave PE2 . . . . 229 F5
Abraham Cl **5** NG31 . . . . 129 E5
ABY LN13 . . . . 75 B5
Aby CE Prim Sch LN13 . . . . 75 B5
Aby Rd LN13 . . . . 75 C7
Acacia Ave
  Chapel St Leonard PE24 . . . . 90 D8
  Gainsborough DN21 . . . . . 197 D6
  Peterborough PE1 . . . . . . 226 B8
  Scunthorpe DN15 . . . . 182 C5
  Spalding PE11 . . . . 214 F5
  Waddington LN5 . . . . 205 D1
  3 Wisbech PE13 . . . . . . 170 C1
Acacia Cl **12** NG34 . . . . . 212 D2
Acacia Ct **3** DN16 . . . . . . 185 B6
Acacia Way Boston PE21 . . 208 C4

Acacia Way continued
  Messingham DN17 . . . . 29 C7
Acad PE11 . . . . 156 E6
Academy Cl PE12 . . . . 215 E5
Acadia Gr HU13 . . . . 178 F1
Acasta Wy HU9 . . . . 5 E8
Accommodation Rd LN9 . . 199 A5
Acer Cl LN6 . . . . 204 D7
Acer Ct **2** LN6 . . . . 204 D7
Acer Gr **3** DN17 . . . . 184 C5
Acer Rd PE1 . . . . 226 B6
Achille Rd DN34 . . . . 190 D5
Achurch Cl LN9 . . . . 199 D1
Acklam Ave **3** PE11 . . . . . 214 F6
Acklam Gr DN32 . . . . 192 B6
Acklands La **13** NG23 . . . . 117 D3
Ackrill Cl LN4 . . . . 207 D5
Acland St
  Gainsborough DN21 . . . . . 197 C5
  4 Kingston upon Hull HU3 . 180 A6
  Peterborough PE1 . . . . . . 225 F3
Acomb Comm Rd DN7 . . . . 14 F4
Acorn Avenue LN11 . . . . . 198 E6
Acorn Cl Freiston PE21 . . . 126 C4
  Grantham NG31 . . . . 211 C7
  Lincoln LN5 . . . . 205 D7
  19 Sutton on Sea LN12 . . . 76 F8
Acorn Ct DN35 . . . . 192 D2
Acorn Dr LN6 . . . . 93 A8
Acorns The PE6 . . . . 217 A6
Acorn Way
  5 Bottesford DN16 . . . . . 185 B2
  Hessle HU13 . . . . 178 B3
Acre Cl LN8 . . . . 57 D8
Acre Dyke La LN4 . . . . 82 B4
Acre La Scopwick LN4 . . . . . 95 E1
  Threekingham NG34 . . . . . 132 E2
Acres La DN9 . . . . 26 D7
Acres The **1** PE9 . . . . 172 C4
Acton Ct **12** DN32 . . . . . . 189 C1
Adam Cl **18** LN6 . . . . 204 D7
Adam Smith St DN31 . . . . 188 F1
Adamstiles **2** NG32 . . . . . 210 B4
Adams Way **6** DN21 . . . . . 65 E8
Ada Way LN11 . . . . 198 D7
Adderley PE3 . . . . 225 C7
Addington Way **3** PE4 . . . 221 A3
Addison Cl **4** LN5 . . . . . . 107 A8
Addison Dr LN2 . . . . 202 B6
Addison Pl LN1 . . . . 65 E3
ADDLETHORPE PE24 . . . . . 90 C3
Adelaide Cl
  Gainsborough DN21 . . . . . 197 F2

Adelaide Cl continued
  13 Waddington LN5 . . . . . 93 E8
Adelaide Prim Sch HU3 . . . 180 D5
Adelaide St
  Kingston upon Hull HU3 . . . 180 D5
  Stamford PE9 . . . . 219 D5
Adelphi Ct **5** DN36 . . . . . 195 C6
Adelphi Dr DN33 . . . . 194 E7
Adlard Gr DN36 . . . . 36 C7
ADLINGFLEET DN14 . . . . . . 7 E7
Adlingfleet Rd DN17 . . . . . . 7 E6
Adlington Mews DN21 . . . . 197 F2
Admirals Dr **7** PE13 . . . . . 170 D2
Admiralty Rd **19** LN12 . . . . 64 B4
Adrian Cl Louth LN11 . . . . 198 C4
  3 Skegness PE25 . . . . . . 206 A4
  9 Swineshead PE20 . . . . 135 B7
Advent Ct **2** DN39 . . . . . . 12 A1
Adwalton Cl **1** NG24 . . . . 104 C4
Aegir Cl DN21 . . . . 197 F2
Africa Cl DN34 . . . . 190 D4
Agard Ave DN15 . . . . 182 E3
Agnes St **2** NG31 . . . . . . 211 B4
Aidan Rd NG34 . . . . 212 B2
AILBY LN13 . . . . 75 D4
AILSWORTH PE5 . . . . 223 D3
Ainderby Gr HU5 . . . . 179 C7
Ainthorpe Prim Sch HU5 . . 179 C8
Aintree Dr PE11 . . . . 214 B1
Aintree Wy PE10 . . . . 213 D3
Aira Cl DN40 . . . . 186 A3
Airedale Cl
  12 Broughton DN20 . . . . . 19 E4
  Peterborough PE1 . . . . . . 226 A6
Airedale Way DN31 . . . . . 191 D8
Aire Rd NG31 . . . . 210 E3
Airfield La LN3 . . . . 69 E7
Airlie St HU3 . . . . 180 B5
Airmanship Rd NG34 . . . . 120 B8
Airmyn Ave **1** HU3 . . . . . 179 E6
Airship Rd NG34 . . . . 107 C1
AISBY Heydour NG32 . . . . . 131 D5
  Pilham DN21 . . . . 41 D4
Aisby Wlk DN21 . . . . 197 F3
Aisne Cl LN1 . . . . 201 E7
Aisne St HU5 . . . . 180 A8

12t–Alb

AISTHORPE LN1 . . . . 67 C7
Ajax Cl DN34 . . . . 190 D4
Ajax Ct DN15 . . . . 182 F5
Akeferry Rd DN9 . . . . 27 C1
Akeman Cl **10** PE10 . . . . . 213 C6
Akeman Dr **14** LN4 . . . . . . 81 A1
Akita Cl **4** PE11 . . . . 214 A5
Alabala Cl LN4 . . . . 203 C1
Alabala La LN4 . . . . 81 F4
Alan Cres DN15 . . . . 182 F2
Alba Cl DN17 . . . . 184 D5
Alban Ret Pk PE21 . . . . . . 208 B3
Albany Cl Louth LN11 . . . . 198 C5
  Skegness PE25 . . . . 206 A5
Albany Pl LN11 . . . . 198 D3
Albany Rd Louth LN11 . . . . 198 D3
  Skegness PE25 . . . . 206 A5
  21 Wisbech PE13 . . . . . . 170 D1
  3 Woodhall Spa LN10 . . . 97 D5
Albany St
  Gainsborough DN21 . . . . . 197 C6
  Kingston upon Hull HU3 . . . 180 D8
  Lincoln LN1 . . . . 234 A4
Albany Terr LN5 . . . . 205 D5
Albany Villas HU13 . . . . . . 179 A1
Albany Way PE25 . . . . 206 A5
Albany Wlk PE2 . . . . 230 D7
Alba Rd PE7 . . . . 230 B2
Albatross Dr DN37 . . . . . . 190 B7
Albatross Way LN11 . . . . . 198 D8
Albemarle Cl **5** HU15 . . . . 2 B5
Albemarle St **2** HU3 . . . . 180 B5
Alberta Cres DN17 . . . . . . 184 E3
Albert Ave
  Kingston upon Hull HU3 . . . 180 A7
  Long Sutton PE12 . . . . . . 159 E7
  4 Newark-on-Trent NG24 . 104 B2
  1 Skegness PE25 . . . . . . 103 E4
Albert Ave Pools **5** HU3 . . 180 A7
Albert Cl **7** DN32 . . . . . . 189 B1
Albert Cres Lincoln LN1 . . . 201 D4
  Yaxley PE7 . . . . 233 B8
Albert Ct PE21 . . . . 208 E5
Albertine Ct **4** DN37 . . . . 194 C5
Albert Marson Ct **6** DN16 183 B2
Albert Pl Grimsby DN32 . . . 189 B1
  Peterborough PE3 . . . . . . 225 F1
Albert Rd
  7 Cleethorpes DN35 . . . 192 F6
  Scunthorpe DN16 . . . . . . 185 A5

Albert Rd continued
Skegness PE25 . . . . .206 B3
2 Stamford PE9 . . . . .219 C4
Albertross Dr DN36 . . . . . . .195 E6
Albert St E DN32 . . . . .189 B1
Albert St W **5** DN32 . . . . . . .189 B1
Albert St Boston PE21 . . . . . . .208 D5
15 Bottesford NG13 . . . . . . .128 A6
Brigg DN20 . . . . .196 C3
Grantham NG31 . . . . .211 C2
6 Holbeach PE12 . . . . .215 D2
Horncastle LN9 . . . . .199 C3
7 New Holland DN19 . . . . . . 4 E2
Spalding PE11 . . . . .214 E5
Thorne/Moorends DN8 . . . . . 15 B8
Albert Terr **2** Boston PE21 208 E4
Boultham LN5 . . . . .205 D8
14 Sleaford NG34 . . . . .212 D4
Albert Wlk **3** PE12 . . . . . . .215 D2
Albery Way DN36 . . . . .195 C7
Albion Cl LN1 . . . . .201 C6
Albion Cres LN1 . . . . .201 C6
Albion Ct HU4 . . . . .179 B6
Albion Hill **8** DN9 . . . . 27 C6
Albion Pl LN11 . . . . .198 C5
Albion Rd **2** NG31 . . . . .211 A5
Albion St **8** Crowland PE6 . .166 E1
13 Grantham NG31 . . . . . . .211 A5
Grimsby DN32 . . . . .189 B1
Holbeach PE12 . . . . .215 F2
10 Kingston upon Hull HU1 . .180 E7
Spalding PE11 . . . . .214 E5
Albion Terr
4 Misterton DN10 . . . . 40 A5
Sleaford NG34 . . . . .212 E4
Albourne Ave DN15 . . . . . . .183 A2
Alconbury Cl
13 Birchwood LN6 . . . . .204 C6
Peterborough PE2 . . . . .231 E5
Alcorn Gn PE21 . . . . .209 C4
Aldbro' St HU2 . . . . .180 F8
Aldburgh Cl **16** LN10 . . . . . . 97 C5
Alden Cl DN40 . . . . .186 C4
Alder Ave **18** DN36 . . . . 36 C8
Alder Cl **30** Brough HU15 . . . 2 C5
3 Lincoln LN6 . . . . .204 F3
Louth LN11 . . . . .198 D4
Alderfield Cl **3** PE21 . . . . .208 E1
Alder Gr PE21 . . . . .209 C2
Aldergrove Cl **2** LN6 . . . . .204 C7
Aldergrove Cres LN6 . . . . . .204 C7
Alderlands Cl **6** PE6 . . . . .175 B8
Alderley Edge DN37 . . . . . .194 C4
Alderman Payne Prim Sch
PE13 . . . . .177 D2
Alderman's Dr PE3 . . . . . . .225 E3
Alderney Way
Immingham DN40 . . . . .186 C2
Lincoln LN6 . . . . .205 A1
Alder Pl **27** LN13 . . . . 75 F2
Alder Rd Hessle HU13 . . . . .178 B1
Peterborough PE7 . . . . .230 D4
Sleaford NG34 . . . . .212 D2
Alderson Mews **5** HU9 . . . .181 C7
Alders The DN21 . . . . .197 F5
Alder View DN33 . . . . .190 F3
ALDGATE PE9 . . . . .171 A3
Aldgate Ct **9** PE9 . . . . .171 A3
Aldred Gdns DN33 . . . . .191 B1
Aldrich Rd DN35 . . . . .192 F4
Aldrin Cl Spalding PE11 . . . . .214 C2
16 Spalding PE11 . . . . .214 C2
Aldsworth Cl **1** PE1 . . . . . .226 D6
Aldwych Croft **8** DN36 . . . .195 C6
Aldwych Ct HU5 . . . . .179 E8
Aldwych Gdns **11** PE11 . . . .214 A4
Alec Rose Gr DN21 . . . . .197 F3
Alexander Ave NG24 . . . . . .104 A6
Alexander Cl **15** LN4 . . . . . . 95 D4
Alexander Dr LN11 . . . . .198 D4
Alexander Rd Lincoln LN2 . . .202 D8
Scunthorpe DN16 . . . . .183 C3
Alexandra Cl **8** NG23 . . . . .117 D4
Alexandra Ct **9** PE25 . . . . .206 C3
Alexandra Dock N DN31 . . . .188 F2
Alexandra Pk **22** LN12 . . . . 64 B4
Alexandra Rd
Cleethorpes DN35 . . . . .192 F6
Grantham NG31 . . . . .210 F3
Grimsby DN31 . . . . .188 F1
Immingham DN40 . . . . .186 F6
Louth LN11 . . . . .198 C6
21 Mablethorpe/Sutton on Sea
LN12 . . . . 64 B4
Peterborough PE1 . . . . .225 F6
Scunthorpe DN16 . . . . .185 B6
Skegness PE25 . . . . .206 B3
Sleaford NG34 . . . . .212 C4
Spalding PE11 . . . . .214 E3
3 Woodhall Spa LN10 . . . . . 97 C6
Alexandra Rd S DN40 . . . . . .186 E6
Alexandra Ret Pk DN31 . . . .188 F1
Alexandra St HU3 . . . . .180 D7
Alexandra Terr LN1 . . . . . . .234 A3
Alexandra Terraces **4**
PE10 . . . . .213 D5
Alexandra Wharf DN31 . . . . .191 D7
Alexandre Ave **2** LN6 . . . . .204 F1
Alexandria Rd LN8 . . . . 56 D5
Alfonso St **5** HU3 . . . . .180 B5
ALFORD LN13 . . . . 75 E2
Alford Mill Cl LN6 . . . . 93 B8
Alford Pottery ★ LN13 . . . . . .75 E3
Alford Prim Sch LN13 . . . . . . 75 F2
Alford Rd **1** Alford LN13 . . . . 75 F3

Alford Rd continued
Bilsby LN13 . . . . 76 A3
Farlesthorpe LN13 . . . . 76 B1
Mablethorpe/Sutton on Sea
LN12 . . . . 64 A3
Alford St NG31 . . . . .211 B5
Alford Windmill ★ LN13 . . . . .75 F3
Alfred Ave LN4 . . . . 95 C4
Alfred Cl **10** NG34 . . . . .212 B2
Alfred Gelder St **6** HU1 . . . .180 C6
Alfred Smith Way **5** LN11 . . 61 F3
Alfred St Boston PE21 . . . . . .209 A3
Gainsborough DN21 . . . . . . .197 C5
Grimsby DN31 . . . . .191 D8
Kingston upon Hull HU3 . . . .180 D5
Lincoln LN5 . . . . .201 E1
Alfreton Ct **2** DN15 . . . . . . .182 B2
Alfric Sq PE2 . . . . .230 D6
ALGARKIRK PE20 . . . . .136 B2
Algernon St DN32 . . . . .191 F5
Algers Wlk PE11 . . . . .214 A5
Algitha Rd PE25 . . . . .206 C3
ALKBOROUGH DN15 . . . . 8 C8
Alkborough La DN15 . . . . 8 D7
Alkborough Prim Sch DN15 . 8 C8
Allan Ave PE2 . . . . .231 E5
Allanby St DN15 . . . . .183 A3
Allandale Cl LN1 . . . . .201 D8
Allandale View **11** LN1 . . . . .201 D8
Allanhall Way HU10 . . . . . . .178 B8
Allard Cl PE7 . . . . .233 D6
Allenby Ave DN34 . . . . .191 A6
Allenby Cl LN2 . . . . .202 D3
Allenby Cres LN11 . . . . 49 A2
Allenby Rd LN2 . . . . .202 D4
Allenby Rd Ind Est LN2 . . . .202 D4
Allenby's Chase **14** PE12 . . .160 E4
Allenby Way PE25 . . . . .206 D8
Allen Cl
7 Billingborough NG34 . . . .133 B1
4 Claypole NG23 . . . . .117 E8
5 Market Deeping PE6 . . . .217 D5
Fenton NG23 . . . . .105 C1
Peterborough PE2 . . . . .225 E6
Allens Bsns Pk LN1 . . . . 66 F1
Allen's Dro PE13 . . . . .169 D1
Allerthorpe Cres **15** HU15 . . 2 D5
Allerton Cl PE9 . . . . .172 D3
Allerton Dr DN40 . . . . .186 B4
Allerton Garth PE7 . . . . .229 A4
Allerton St DN34 . . . . .186 B4
Allestree Dr DN33 . . . . .194 E7
Allexton Gdns **2** PE1 . . . . . .226 D7
Alliance Ave HU3 . . . . .179 F7
Alliance La HU3 . . . . .179 F7
ALLINGTON NG32 . . . . .128 F7
Allington Dr DN37 . . . . .188 A2
Allington Gdn PE21 . . . . . . .209 A7
Allington La NG32 . . . . .129 B4
Allington Rd NG32 . . . . .128 F5
Allington with Sedgebrook CE
Prim Sch NG32 . . . . .129 A7
Allis Chalmers Way **8**
PE9 . . . . .163 D3
Allison Ave PE12 . . . . .215 E2
Allison Cl **3** DN17 . . . . 29 C7
Allison Pl **5** LN1 . . . . .201 D4
Allison Rd
6 Heckington NG34 . . . . . .122 D3
7 Louth LN11 . . . . .198 C6
Allison St LN1 . . . . .201 D4
Allotment La PE5 . . . . .223 E2
All Saints Ave PE13 . . . . . . .170 E1
All Saints Brewery ★ **22**
PE9 . . . . .219 B5
All Saints CE Jun Sch
HU13 . . . . .178 F2
All Saints CE Prim Sch
PE1 . . . . .226 A6
All Saints Cl **4** Hessle HU13 . 3 F4
3 Holbeach PE12 . . . . .215 F3
7 Moulton NG34 . . . . .157 F7
Ruskington NG34 . . . . .108 D2
4 Wainfleet All Saints
PE24 . . . . .102 D1
All Saints' Cl **17** DN19 . . . . .12 A8
All Saints Cty Prim Sch
LN5 . . . . 93 F7
All Saints Gr **4** NG34 . . . . . .212 B6
All Saints La **14** LN2 . . . . . . 68 C2
All Saints Mews **17** PE9 . . . .219 B5
All Saints' Pl **6** PE9 . . . . . . .219 B5
All Saints Rd LN2 . . . . .202 F6
All Saints' Rd PE1 . . . . .226 A5
All Saints' St
Kingston upon Hull HU3 . . . .180 D8
10 Stamford PE9 . . . . .219 B5
Allwood Rd **2** LN2 . . . . 68 D6
Ally's Wy LN4 . . . . .202 F2
Alma Ave PE25 . . . . .206 B5
Alma Cl
Kingston upon Hull HU10 . . .178 D7
3 Skegness PE25 . . . . .206 B5
Alma Martin Way **7** LN3 . . . .83 C4
Alma Pk Ind Est
Grantham NG31 . . . . .211 F7
Londonthorpe & Harrowby Without
NG31 . . . . .130 C4
Alma Pk Rd NG31 . . . . .211 F6
Alma Rd PE1 . . . . .225 F5
Alma St **6** HU9 . . . . .181 B7
Almond Ave Heighington LN4 81 F4
Lincoln LN6 . . . . .205 A8
Almond Cl Boston PE21 . . . . .208 C5

Almond Cl continued
9 Saxilby LN1 . . . . 66 D2
Almond Cres Lincoln LN6 . . . .205 A8
Louth LN11 . . . . .198 D5
Waddington LN5 . . . . .205 D1
Almond Ct LN6 . . . . .205 A8
Almond Gr Brigg DN20 . . . . . .196 B4
Grantham NG31 . . . . .211 C6
3 Kingston upon Hull HU3 . .180 D6
3 Scunthorpe DN16 . . . . . .185 B8
Skellingthorpe LN6 . . . . .200 A4
Stallingborough DN41 . . . . . . 23 E6
Almond Rd PE1 . . . . .226 B7
Almonds Gn LN4 . . . . .108 C8
Almond Wlk Boston PE21 . . . .208 D5
Sleaford NG34 . . . . .212 D6
Almoners La PE3 . . . . .225 E3
Alness Cl LN6 . . . . .204 B8
Alnwick Pl 229 F3
Alnwick Way NG31 . . . . .210 E6
Altham Terr LN5 . . . . .205 D7
ALTHORPE DN17 . . . . 17 D5
Althorpe Cl **15** PE6 . . . . . . .217 A5
Althorpe & Keadby Prim Sch
DN17 . . . . 17 D5
Althorpe Sta DN17 . . . . 17 D5
Altoft Cl **19** DN37 . . . . 23 F1
Altyre Way DN36 . . . . .192 C1
Alverston Ave LN10 . . . . 97 C5
Alveston Rd DN17 . . . . .184 D8
Alvey Rd NG24 . . . . .104 C2
ALVINGHAM LN11 . . . . 49 E2
Alvingham Ave DN35 . . . . . . .192 F3
Alvingham Rd
Keddington LN11 . . . . .198 E8
Scunthorpe DN16 . . . . .185 B7
Alvis Cl LN4 . . . . .205 F2
Alvis Dr PE7 . . . . .233 D6
ALWALTON PE2 . . . . .229 B4
Alwyn Rd **10** DN8 . . . . 15 B8
Amanda Cl PE3 . . . . .225 E2
Amanda Dr Hatfield DN7 . . . . 14 D4
Louth LN11 . . . . .198 C8
Ambassador Wlk PE11 . . . . .214 A1
Ambergate Sports Coll
NG31 . . . . .210 D3
Ambergate Wlk NG31 . . . . . .210 E3
Amberley Cl DN33 . . . . .191 B1
Amberley Cres PE21 . . . . . . .208 C4
Amberley Slope PE4 . . . . . . .221 A3
Amble Cl LN1 . . . . .201 E8
Ambleside Cl **4** DN34 . . . . . .212 B2
Ambleside Dr PE11 . . . . .214 B2
Ambleside Gdns PE4 . . . . . . .221 B3
Ambleside Pk LN6 . . . . .204 F1
Ambrose Ave **3** DN7 . . . . . . 14 E4
Ambury Gdns **9** PE6 . . . . . .166 F1
Amcott Ave DN10 . . . . 40 A4
Amcott Rd DN17 . . . . 7 F4
AMCOTTS DN17 . . . . 7 F1
Amcotts Rd DN33 . . . . .191 A2
Amelia Ct DN36 . . . . 36 D8
Amery Way **31** PE24 . . . . 90 D7
Amesbury Ave DN33 . . . . . . .194 D7
Amethyst Cl **3** NG34 . . . . . .212 A3
Amethyst Ct DN36 . . . . .195 D7
Amman Sq **1** NG34 . . . . . . .120 D8
Amos Cl DN33 . . . . .194 D7
Amos Cres **3** DN16 . . . . .185 D7
Amos La NG23 . . . . 91 E6
Amos Way **8** PE22 . . . . .113 B1
Ampleforth Ave DN32 . . . . . .190 F8
Ampleforth Gr HU5 . . . . .179 D8
Amstel Ct **1** PE11 . . . . .214 B2
Amsterdam Gdns **9** PE11 214 B3
Amwell Gn **10** DN7 . . . . 14 D3
Anastasia Cl DN21 . . . . .197 C7
ANCASTER NG32 . . . . .120 B2
Ancaster Ave
Chapel St Leonard PE24 . . . . 90 D7
Grimsby DN33 . . . . .194 D8
Lincoln LN2 . . . . .202 B5
Spilsby PE23 . . . . .100 F8
Ancaster CE Prim Sch
NG32 . . . . .120 A3
Ancaster Cl LN3 . . . . .203 E6
Ancaster Ct Horncastle LN9 .199 B3
Scunthorpe DN16 . . . . .185 A5
Ancaster Dr NG34 . . . . .212 B2
Ancaster Mews **33** PE24 . . . . 90 D7
Ancaster Rd
1 Bourne PE10 . . . . .213 E5
16 Mablethorpe/Sutton on Sea
LN12 . . . . 64 B3
7 Stamford PE9 . . . . .219 A7
Ancaster Sta NG32 . . . . .120 A3
Ancaster Valley Nature
Reserve ★ NG32 . . . . .120 A2
Ancholme Ave DN16 . . . . . . .186 A3
Ancholme Bsns Pk DN20 . . . .196 A4
Ancholme Cl LN1 . . . . .201 D8
Ancholme Gdns **9** DN20 . . . .196 C3
Ancholme Leisure Ctr
DN20 . . . . .196 A3
Ancholme Rd DN16 . . . . .185 D6
Ancholme Way DN20 . . . . . . .196 B3
Anchorage St **4** DN20 . . . . . .196 B3
Anchor Cl Canal Side DN8 . . . 15 A8
Lincoln LN5 . . . . .234 A1
Anchor Ct PE4 . . . . .221 D1
Anchor La PE25 . . . . 90 D4
Anchor Rd Scunthorpe DN16 . 19 B4
Sutton Bridge PE34 . . . . . . .161 C4
Anchor St LN5 . . . . .234 A1
Anchors Way **7** DN20 . . . . . .196 A3
Ancient La DN7 . . . . 14 E3
ANDERBY PE24 . . . . 77 A2
Anderby Cl LN6 . . . . .204 F6

ANDERBY CREEK PE24 . . . . . . 77 C3
Anderby Dr Grimsby DN37 . .190 D7
Anderby LN6 . . . . .204 F6
Anderby Drainage Mus ★
PE24 . . . . 77 C2
Anderby Rd PE24 . . . . .77 D1
Anderson LN2 . . . . 68 D5
Anderson Cl
5 Newark-on-Trent
NG24 . . . . .104 A2
7 Wisbech PE13 . . . . .170 C1
Anderson La **2** LN1 . . . . . . .201 F6
Anderson Rd
2 Hemswell Cliff DN21 . . . . 55 A8
Scunthorpe DN16 . . . . .185 C7
Anderson St DN31 . . . . .191 D7
Anderson Way NG21 . . . . 52 F5
Andover Cl LN6 . . . . .204 B8
Andrea Cl PE2 . . . . .231 C6
Andrew Ave **27** PE24 . . . . 90 D7
Andrew Cl PE5 . . . . .223 D2
Andrewe's Cl PE7 . . . . .231 B1
Andrew Paddock **18** DN20 . . 30 F7
Andrew Rd
9 Humberston DN36 . . . . . . 36 D8
1 Stamford PE9 . . . . .219 B6
Andrews Cl LN11 . . . . .198 C7
Andrews Cres PE4 . . . . .221 D2
Andrews Rd **1** DN16 . . . . . . .10 A7
Andrews Way **7** DN40 . . . . . .186 A4
Anfield Rd PE12 . . . . .216 B5
Angel Ct **5** NG32 . . . . .120 A2
Angelica Dr **2** PE11 . . . . . . .214 B6
Angell La PE12 . . . . .215 E1
Angel Prec The PE10 . . . . . .213 C5
Angerstein Rd DN17 . . . . . . .184 F5
Anglesey Cl **20** LN6 . . . . . . .204 C7
Anglesey Dr DN40 . . . . .186 C2
Anglia Cl **13** NG34 . . . . .212 B2
Anglian Cl PE2 . . . . .231 D6
Anglian Way **5** LN8 . . . . 57 E8
Angus Cl **3** PE9 . . . . .218 D6
Angus Ct PE3 . . . . .225 D3
ANLABY HU10 . . . . .179 A6
Anlaby Acre Head Prim Sch
HU4 . . . . .179 B7
Anlaby Ave **1** HU4 . . . . .179 B6
Anlaby High Rd HU4 . . . . . . .179 C6
Anlaby House Estate
HU10 . . . . .178 E6
ANLABY PARK HU4 . . . . .179 C5
Anlaby Pk Rd N HU4 . . . . . . .179 B5
Anlaby Pk Rd S HU4 . . . . . . .179 B2
Anlaby Prim Sch HU4 . . . . . .179 A6
Anlaby Rd HU3 . . . . .179 E6
Anlafgate **7** HU10 . . . . .178 F6
Annandale Rd HU10 . . . . .178 C8
Anne Rd Stamford PE9 . . . . . .219 A6
11 Sutton Bridge PE12 . . . .160 E4
Annes Cres DN16 . . . . .185 C7
Annesley St **1** DN31 . . . . . . .188 F1
Annette Cl **8** PE11 . . . . .214 B5
Anningson La DN36 . . . . .195 D7
Annpasture La LN4 . . . . .207 C8
Ann Wayne Ave **4** LN9 . . . . .199 B2
Anson Ave LN4 . . . . .207 D3
Anson Cl Grantham NG31 . . . .211 C2
Skellingthorpe LN6 . . . . .200 A4
Anson Ct PE6 . . . . .217 B7
Anson Rd LN4 . . . . .207 D2
Antelope Rd DN18 . . . . 4 A1
Anthony Cl PE1 . . . . .225 F8
Anthony Cres LN11 . . . . .198 C8
Anthony's Bank Rd DN36 . . .193 D1
Anthony Way **3** DN41 . . . . . . 23 D6
ANTON'S GOWT PE22 . . . . . .125 B6
Antrim Rd **9** LN5 . . . . .205 D2
Antrim Way DN33 . . . . .191 D2
Anvil Cl **1** PE2 . . . . .148 B1
Anvil Wlk **2** DN15 . . . . 8 F3
ANWICK NG34 . . . . .109 B1
Anzio Cres LN1 . . . . .201 E7
Anzio Terr LN1 . . . . .201 E7
Anzio Wlk LN1 . . . . .201 E7
Apeldoorn Gdns **3** PE11 . . . .214 B3
APLEY LN8 . . . . 70 A2
Apley Cl
Gainsborough DN21 . . . . . . .197 F3
Lincoln LN2 . . . . .202 A8
Apley La LN8 . . . . 70 C1
Apley Rd LN8 . . . . 70 B3
Apollo Ave
Peterborough PE2 . . . . .231 D4
Stanground PE7 . . . . .231 C4
Appian Way **8** Baston PE6 164 E5
11 Bracebridge Heath LN4 . .81 A1
West Marsh DN31 . . . . .188 C2
Apple Ave **31** NG24 . . . . .104 C1
APPLEBY DN15 . . . . .9 D1
Appleby Cl
5 Beacon Hill NG24 . . . . . .104 B4
Scunthorpe DN17 . . . . .184 F5
Appleby Ct **17** DN32 . . . . . . .189 C1
Appleby Gdns DN20 . . . . .19 C4
Appleby La DN20 . . . . .19 C4
Appleby Mill Rd DN16 . . . . . .183 E3
Appleby Wy
15 Birchwood LN6 . . . . . . .204 B8
12 Birchwood LN6 . . . . . . .204 B8
10 Birchwood LN6 . . . . . . .204 B8
Apple Cl LN4 . . . . 81 F4
Appledore Cl HU9 . . . . .181 C6
Apple Garth LN5 . . . . .205 D4
Applegarth Cl DN35 . . . . . . .192 D5
Applegarth Rd **2** HU8 . . . . . .181 A4
Appleton Cl **2** PE7 . . . . .230 C2
Appleton Gate NG24 . . . . . . .104 A5

Appleton Way DN16 . . . . . . .185 C6
Appletree Cl PE6 . . . . .217 F5
Apple Tree Cl **19** LN4 . . . . . . 95 C4
Apple Tree Ct **14** DN41 . . . . . 23 F5
Apple Tree La DN37 . . . . 23 F2
Applewood Dr
5 Gonerby Hill Foot
NG31 . . . . .210 F8
Hampton Hargate PE7 . . . . .230 C3
Apple Wy Pinchbeck PE11 . . .157 A8
Pinchbeck PE11 . . . . .214 F8
Appleyard PE2 . . . . .231 C7
Appleyard Dr **38** DN18 . . . . . .10 E8
Apricot Cl PE1 . . . . .226 C8
Apsley Way PE3 . . . . .225 A2
Aqua Dr LN12 . . . . 64 B2
Aqua Drive PE7 . . . . .233 E8
Aquila Way PE6 . . . . .164 C2
Arabis Cl **3** LN2 . . . . .202 C8
Arakan Way **2** PE10 . . . . . . .213 E7
Arbella Rd PE21 . . . . .209 C4
Arboath Gdns PE2 . . . . .229 C4
Arboretum Ave LN2 . . . . .234 C2
Arboretum The ★ LN2 . . . . . .234 C3
Arboretum View LN2 . . . . . . .234 C2
Arborfield Cl **5** PE6 . . . . . . .173 C4
Arbury Cl PE3 . . . . .225 A3
Arcadia Cres **2** PE25 . . . . . .206 D2
Arcadia Rd PE25 . . . . .206 D3
Archer Ct
8 Bishop Norton LN8 . . . . . 43 D3
Little London PE21 . . . . .214 A1
Archer La PE21 . . . . .208 B4
Archer Rd Branston LN4 . . . . . 81 E2
Waltham DN37 . . . . .194 D4
Archers Dro PE6 . . . . .176 D6
Archers La PE20 . . . . .136 C3
Archer St
3 Bishop Norton LN8 . . . . . 43 D3
Lincoln LN5 . . . . .234 B1
Archers Way NG33 . . . . .140 A5
Archibald Wlk PE21 . . . . . . .208 B4
Archway Dr LN8 . . . . 70 C4
Arcon Dr HU4 . . . . .179 D6
Arcott Dr PE21 . . . . .208 C5
Arden Cl **6** LN12 . . . . 64 C3
Arden Moor Way **4** LN6 . . . . 93 B8
Ardent Rd DN18 . . . . 4 A1
Arden Village DN35 . . . . .192 F1
Arena Dr PE2 . . . . .229 B4
Argyle Ct **6** DN15 . . . . .183 B3
Argyle St Boston PE21 . . . . . .208 D5
Kingston upon Hull HU3 . . . .180 C7
Argyll Way PE9 . . . . .218 F5
Ariston St DN32 . . . . .192 B7
Arkley Cl **22** HU15 . . . . 2 C5
Ark Rd LN11 . . . . 50 F8
Ark Royal Ct **2** NG34 . . . . . .212 A3
Arkwright St DN21 . . . . .197 C5
Arkwright Way
Peterborough PE4 . . . . .221 F2
Scunthorpe DN16 . . . . .185 C6
Arlington Rd Dunscroft DN7 14 D3
4 Toft Newton LN8 . . . . 56 D5
Arlington St **2** HU3 . . . . .180 D6
Armada Cl **3** PE13 . . . . .170 D2
Armeria Dr **4** DN17 . . . . .185 A1
Armley Gr **3** PE9 . . . . .219 D7
Armour Rd DN16 . . . . .183 E3
Armstrong Pl E **3** DN31 . . . .188 F1
Armstrong Pl W **7** DN31 . . . .188 E1
Armstrong Rd **12** PE11 . . . . .214 C2
Armstrong's Cl **2** PE12 . . . . .157 F7
Armstrong's La PE22 . . . . . . .115 B7
Armstrong St DN31 . . . . .188 E1
Armthorpe La DN3 . . . . 14 A3
Armtree Rd PE22 . . . . .124 E7
Arne Cl NG32 . . . . .120 A3
Arnhem Ave **1** NG34 . . . . . . .108 D2
Arnhem Cl LN1 . . . . .201 E7
Arnhem Dr
10 Caythorpe NG32 . . . . . . .119 B7
2 Spalding PE11 . . . . .214 C5
Arnhem Way Bourne PE10 . .213 E6
9 Woodhall Spa LN10 . . . . . 97 C5
Arnold Ave NG31 . . . . .210 E8
Arnold Cl DN37 . . . . .23 F2
Arnold Ct **11** DN32 . . . . .189 C1
Arnold La HU3 . . . . .180 B6
Arnold's Mdw Nature
Reserve ★ PE12 . . . . .214 F2
Arnold St HU3 . . . . .180 B6
Arran Cl Immingham DN40 . . .186 D2
New Waltham DN36 . . . . . . .195 C7
Sleaford NG34 . . . . .121 A2
Arran Rd PE9 . . . . .218 D5
Arras Cl LN1 . . . . .201 E6
Arrow Ct PE7 . . . . .230 C3
Art Coll Ct DN32 . . . . .191 F8
Art Coll Mews DN32 . . . . . . .191 F8
Artemis Way Haddon PE7 . . .232 F8
Orton Southgate PE2 . . . . . .228 E1
Art Haven The ★ NG31 . . . . .211 B3
Arthur Mellows Village Coll
PE6 . . . . .220 B8
Arthur Rd DN21 . . . . .197 D6
Arthurs' Ave **5** PE12 . . . . . .215 D2
Arthur St Grimsby DN31 . . . .191 C8
Kingston upon Hull HU3 . . . .180 A5
6 Lincoln LN5 . . . . .201 F1
Arthur Taylor St **1** LN1 . . . . .201 D4
Artillery Row **13** PE21 . . . . . .209 A5
Artindale St PE3 . . . . .225 A3
Artis Ct PE3 . . . . .225 A3
Arun Cl **9** PE11 . . . . .214 A4
Arundel Cl
Gainsborough DN21 . . . . . . .197 E6
Kingston upon Hull HU9 . . . .181 C8

Arundel Cres PE21........208 B4
Arundel Dr Green Hill NG31 210 E6
Louth LN11............198 A2
Arundel Pl DN35.........192 C5
Arundel Rd PE4..........221 A1
Arundel St 3 HU9........181 C8
Arundel Wlk DN34........191 A7
Arvina Cl DN6...........93 B8
Ascendale PE6...........217 F5
Ascot Cl 11 Bourne PE10..213 D3
4 Spalding PE11........156 E3
Ascot Dr
7 Grantham NG31.......211 D7
Peterborough PE1......226 B6
Ascot Rd DN37..........194 D4
Ascott Cl HU4..........179 D5
Ascot Way 7 LN6........93 A8
ASGARBY
Asgarby and Howell NG34..122 B4
Lusby with Winceby LN9...86 F1
Asgarby Rd NG34........122 B2
Asgard Way DN33........191 B2
Ash Ave 19 HU15........2 C6
Ashberry Dr
31 Messingham DN17.....29 D7
4 Scunthorpe DN16.....185 B6
Ashbourne 6 DN37.......194 C4
Ashbourne Cl 3 NG34....212 B2
Ashbourne Ct DN15......182 B3
Ashbourne Rd PE7.......230 E2
Ash Buckingham Studio*
LN9..................85 C5
Ashburn Cl 1 HU15......220 D7
Ashburnham Rd 20 DN8...15 A4
Ashburton Cl PE12......215 E5
ASHBY DN16.............185 B5
Ashby Ave LN6..........204 F7
Ashby Broadway DN16....185 A6
ASHBY BY PARTNEY PE23...88 D1
Ashby Cl Bracebridge LN5 205 D1
Grimsby DN37..........190 D8
Holton le Clay DN36....195 E1
Kingston upon Hull HU4..179 B7
Ashby Ct 2 NG34........212 B3
ASHBY CUM FENBY DN37....35 D3
ASHBY DE LA LAUNDE
LN4..................108 B6
Ashby Gdns 7 PE12......157 E6
Ashby High St DN16.....185 B6
ASHBY HILL DN37........35 C3
Ashby Hill DN37........35 C3
Ashby La DN37..........35 D4
Ashby Mdws PE23........88 A1
ASHBY PUERORUM LN9.....86 E6
Ashby Rd
Cleethorpes DN35.......192 D3
Kingston upon Hull HU4..179 B4
Scunthorpe DN16........183 A1
Spilsby PE23..........88 D1
Ash Cl Burgh le Marsh PE24 102 C1
5 Colsterworth NG33....151 E7
Fulbeck NG32..........106 C1
Hessle HU13...........178 C3
Holbeach PE12.........215 C3
Langtoft PE6..........164 E2
Lincoln LN6...........204 E8
Louth LN11............198 C7
Peterborough PE1......226 C7
Spalding PE11.........214 F5
1 Thorney PE6.........175 F3
Ashcroft Gdns PE1......226 C5
Ashcroft Rd DN21.......197 D2
Ash Ct Cleethorpes DN35..192 D2
5 Donington PE11......134 E2
Peterborough PE1......226 C7
Spalding PE11.........214 F6
Ashdale Cl 3 LN4.......95 C4
Ashdale Pk 18 HU14.....3 A5
Ashdene Cl DN15........182 E3
Ashdown Ave 5 DN15.....182 E3
Ashdown Cl 3 DN20......196 B3
Ash Dr
Kingston upon Hull HU10..178 E8
3 Kirton PE20.........136 C5
Asheridge LN4..........81 E2
Ashes The PE7..........230 F5
Ashfield 2 LN1.........66 D7
Ashfield Ave 2 DN8.....15 A4
Ashfield Ct 20 DN17....16 D7
Ashfield Gr 1 DN7......14 C4
Ashfield Grange 5 LN1...66 C2
Ashfield Pk DN17.......184 C5
Ashfield Rd 8 Hatfield DN7..14 C4
Sleaford NG34.........212 D5
Thorne DN8............14 F7
Ashfields PE6..........217 D2
Ashfield St 3 LN2......202 B3
Ash Gr Bourne PE10.....213 C6
Brigg DN20............196 B4
Cherry Willingham/Reepham
LN3..................203 D5
Gainsborough DN21.....197 D6
Grantham NG31.........211 D7
Lincoln LN6...........204 F2
32 Messingham DN17....29 D7
Scunthorpe DN16.......185 B7
Ash Hill Adacemy DN7...14 D4
Ash Hill Cres DN7......14 D4
Ash Hill Rd DN7........14 D4
Ashing La LN2..........68 F6
ASHINGTON END PE24.....90 B1
Ash La 26 LN5..........93 E6
Ashlawn Dr PE21........209 B6
Ashlea 3 DN10..........39 F5
Ashleigh 2 PE9.........229 C6
Ashleigh Ct 3 DN41.....23 F5
Ashley Cl LN12.........64 C1
Ashley Dr NG31.........210 E8

Ashley Pool La 5 PE6....176 A2
Ashley Rd 2 LN11.......198 C5
Ashlin Gr LN1..........234 A3
Ash Pk PE4.............220 F6
Ash Pl 6 PE9...........218 D6
Ash Rd 7 Coningsby LN4..207 D4
Peterborough PE1......226 C7
Ashridge Dr DN32.......192 C5
Ash Tree Ave 11 LN2....68 D2
Ash Tree Cl
Immingham DN40.........186 C5
10 Market Rasen LN8....57 D7
Ash Tree Dr 5 DN9......27 D2
Ashtree Gdns 5 PE9.....171 B1
Ash Tree Rd 7 DN8......15 B7
Ash Tree Wy LN5........92 E7
Ash Villa South Rauceby The
NG34.................121 A3
Ashville Cl PE12.......215 C6
Ashville Rd PE7........230 D2
Ashwell Ave 2 HU9......5 E8
Ashwin Gate 2 PE11.....145 A8
Ashwood Cl LN9.........199 B4
Ashwood Dr 10 DN36.....36 D8
Ashworth Cl
6 Beacon Hill NG24.....104 B4
Lincoln LN6...........204 F5
Askew Ave HU4..........179 E4
Askew's Dro PE6........166 D2
Askew's La PE7.........233 C5
ASLACKBY NG34..........142 D5
Aslackby Rd NG34.......142 D3
Aspen Cl Kettlethorpe LN1..65 D2
Kingston upon Hull HU4..179 C3
Aspen Ct Cleethorpes DN35 192 D2
Gainsborough DN21.....197 F6
Aspen Dr 4 NG34........212 D2
Aspen Gr DN16..........185 B8
Aspen La DN37..........23 F2
Aspen Wlk 10 HU15......2 D5
ASPERTON DN36..........135 D4
Asperton Rd PE20.......135 E4
Asphodel Cl DN36.......195 D7
Asquith St DN21........197 B6
ASSERBY LN13...........76 D4
Asterby Cl LN2.........202 A7
Asterby End LN11.......72 E6
Asterby La LN11........72 E5
Asterby Rd 2 DN17......184 F5
Aster Cl LN2...........202 C8
Aster Dr PE4...........221 B3
Astley Cres 15 DN21....29 C3
Astley St HU3..........179 F7
Aston Cl 4 Waddington LN5..93 F7
Yaxley PE7............233 E6
Aston Gn 5 DN7.........14 D3
Aston Hall Dr 12 HU14..3 A5
Aston Rd HU10..........178 F8
Astore Pk PE1..........226 E3
Astor Pl PE11..........214 A1
Astral Cl HU13.........178 F3
Astral Rd HU13.........178 F3
Astral Way 8 LN6.......204 C1
Astwick Rd LN6.........205 A5
ASWARBY NG34...........132 D6
ASWARDBY PE23..........87 E5
Aswell St LN11.........198 B5
Athelstan Cl 9 NG34....212 B2
Athena Cl PE7..........231 C4
Athena Dr DN31.........188 C2
Athenian Way 1 DN31....188 A3
Atherstone Ave PE25....225 B4
Atherton Gdns PE11.....214 D8
Atherton Way DN20......196 B4
Atholl Ave HU13........178 E3
Atholl St HU3..........179 F4
Atkinson Dr 24 HU15....2 C6
Atkinson La 6 DN37.....194 E4
Atkinsons La PE23......101 C6
Atkinson St PE1........226 C2
Atkinsons Warren Nature
Reserve* DN15.........182 D5
Atkinsons Way DN15.....182 F7
Atlantic Pl 8 NG31.....211 A3
Atlas Rd DN17..........184 F8
ATTERBY LN8............43 D3
Atterby Carr La DN21...43 F4
Atterby La LN8.........43 C3
Atton Ave 4 PE11.......157 B6
Atwater Cl LN2.........202 D7
Atwater Ct 2 LN2.......202 D7
Atwater Gr LN2.........202 D7
Atwood Cl DN40.........186 B5
Auborn Gdns PE3........225 B3
AUBOURN LN5............93 A5
Aubourn Ave LN2........201 F7
Aubourn Hall* LN5......93 A5
Aubretia Ave PE4.......221 B3
Aubretia Dr 3 DN17.....16 D7
Aubrey Parker Cl 4 LN12..64 C2
Auckland Cres 1 LN4....96 C1
Auckland Dr HU5........179 D8
AYLESBY DN37...........23 E2
Aylesby Gdns 2 DN33....191 B3
Aylesby La DN37........23 E2
Aylesby Rd Aylesby DN37..190 B6
Scunthorpe DN17.......184 F5
Aylesford St 7 HU3.....180 B5
Aylmer Ave PE24........103 D7
Aynsley Cl 18 LN6......204 C6
Aynsley Rd LN6.........204 B6
Ayots Gn 14 DN7........14 D3
Ayr Cl PE9.............218 E6

Audus Pl 13 PE9........218 E6
Augusta Cl Grimsby DN34..191 C5
Peterborough PE1......226 E6
Augusta Dr PE13........170 A7
Augusta Oaks DN34......191 C6
Augusta St DN34........191 C6
Augustin Ret Pk NG31...211 A4
Augustus Dr 17 HU15....2 C1
AUNBY PE9..............163 B5
AUNSBY NG34............132 A5
Aunsby Rd NG34.........132 A7
Aurora Wy PE2..........231 D4
Austacre Way LN2.......202 F6
AUSTENDIKE PE12........157 E4
Austendike Rd PE12.....157 C4
AUSTEN FEN LN11........49 F5
Austen Mews 5 PE11.....214 A1
Austen Wlk LN2.........202 C6
Austerby PE10..........213 E4
Austerby Cl PE10.......213 D4
Austerby The PE10......213 E4
Auster Rd 2 PE2........231 D3
Austin Cres 3 DN17.....184 F3
Austin Ct PE7..........233 D6
Austin Friar's La 2 PE9..219 B4
Austin Garth 5 DN37....23 F1
Austin St PE9..........219 B4
AUTHORPE LN11..........74 F7
Authorpe Top LN11......74 E6
Autumn Croft Rd 6 NG24..104 B5
Autumn Pk Ind Est NG31..210 F4
Avalon Wy LN1..........198 C7
Av Clumber NG24........104 A3
Avebury Gdns PE11......214 A5
Aveland Cl
Aslackby & Laughton
NG34.................142 E5
5 Baston PE6..........164 E4
Aveland Dr NG34........143 B8
Aveland Way
Aslackby & Laughton
NG34.................142 D5
3 Baston PE6..........164 E4
5 Foston NG32.........117 F1
Garthorpe & Fockerby DN17..7 F6
Heighington/Washingborough
LN4..................81 F4
Holbeach PE12.........215 D2
Ingoldsby NG33........141 C5
Leadenham LN5.........106 C3
Long Bennington NG23...128 D8
Long Sutton PE12......216 D6
North Clifton NG23....78 C7
North Cockerington LN11..50 A1
Scothern LN2..........68 F4
1 Searby cum Owmby DN38 32 D8
3 Skillington NG33....151 A8
4 Stainforth DN7......14 C6
9 Stamford PE9........219 C5
Stickford PE22........100 A3
Wainfleet All Saints PE24..102 A2
Wilsford NG32.........120 C2
Winteringham DN15.....2 B1
Yaxley PE7............233 E5
Back Rd Gorefield PE13..169 E2
Murrow PE13...........177 E6
Back St Alkborough DN15...8 C8
Buckminster NG33......150 E5
East Stockwith DN21...40 B5
Saltfleetby LN11......51 C1
South Clifton NG23....78 C5
Sproxton LE14.........138 F1
Bacon's La 1 PE11......145 C1
Bacon St DN21..........197 D2
Bader Cl Peterborough PE3 225 B6
The Willows DN37......190 E8
Bader Way 3 PE25.......206 A5
Badgate PE11...........134 F2
Badger La PE12.........169 B6
Badger's La 2 PE20.....136 B7
Badgers Oak 2 LN5......92 F3
Badger Way 1 DN20......19 E4
Badington Cl PE2.......230 D8
Badinton La PE3........172 F5
Badminton Way LN11.....198 A7
Baffen's La PE11.......145 A4
Baggaley St DN9........199 A4
Baggholme Rd LN2.......234 B2
Baghdad Rd 2 NG34.....120 D8
Bagmoor La DN15........8 D3
Bagsby Rd DN9..........28 B3
Baildon Cres LN6.......205 A3
Baildon Rd DN15........182 D4
Bailey Cl PE12.........215 D1
Baileys La PE11........92 F5
Bailey St HU10.........178 F5
Bailey Way PE2.........230 D8
Bailgate 3 LN2.........234 B3
Baily's La PE12........147 F2
Bain Cl 7 PE9..........219 C7
Baines Ave NG24........104 B2
Baines Rd DN21.........197 F4
Bain Rd PE21...........208 C3
Bain Rise 3 LN8........59 A7
Bain St LN1............201 D8
BAINTON PE9............172 F5
Bainton Rd Barnack PE9..172 C4
Newborough PE6........221 D8
Baird Cl PE7...........233 D6

Ayres Dr PE2...........231 C6
Ayscough Ave
7 Spalding DN11........214 D3
7 Stallingborough DN41...23 E4
Ayscoughfee Hall Mus &
Gdns* PE11...........214 D3
Ayscoughfee Hall Sch
PE11.................214 D3
Ayscough Gr 9 LN7......33 B4
Ayscough St 4 DN31.....188 E1
Aysgarth Ave 18 DN17...29 D7
Azalea Cl PE3..........225 A2
Azalea Ct 1 PE7........233 D6
Azalea Rd LN2..........202 C8

Baatsfjord Cl 3 DN36...195 B7
Babington Row HU9......181 C8
Bacheler St HU3........180 B5
Back Bank Crowland PE12..167 F3
Whaplode PE12.........168 A3
Back Field La DN7......14 E4
Backgate PE12..........167 B8
Back La 5 Allington NG32..128 F2
Aswarby & Swarby NG34...132 A7
Barnby in the Willows NG24 105 A3
Belvoir NG32..........138 D6
Bicker PE20...........134 F6
Bilsby LN13...........76 A2
Bolingbroke PE23......100 A7
Buckminster NG33......151 A4
Burton Coggles NG33...152 C8
Cammeringham LN1......54 F1
Candlesby with Gunby PE23..89 B1
Claxby with Moorby PE22..99 B7
Claypole NG23.........117 E7
Collyweston PE9.......171 B1
Colsterworth NG33.....151 E7
3 Deeping St James PE6..217 C6
Dunston LN4...........95 C6
Eye PE6...............175 A1
Foston NG32...........117 F1
Garthorpe & Fockerby DN17..7 F6
Heighington/Washingborough
LN4..................81 F4
Holbeach PE12.........215 D2
Ingoldsby NG33........141 C5
Leadenham LN5.........106 C3
Long Bennington NG23...128 D8
Long Sutton PE12......216 D6
North Clifton NG23....78 C7
North Cockerington LN11..50 A1
Scothern LN2..........68 F4
1 Searby cum Owmby DN38 32 D8
3 Skillington NG33....151 A8
4 Stainforth DN7......14 C6
9 Stamford PE9........219 C5
Stickford PE22........100 A3
Wainfleet All Saints PE24..102 A2
Wilsford NG32.........120 C2
Winteringham DN15.....2 B1
Wood Enderby PE22.....98 F6
Yaxley PE7............233 E5

Aru – Bar 237

Bakehouse Ct 5 LN3.....69 C3
Baker Ave 8 DN10.......39 C1
Baker Cres LN6.........204 E7
Baker Dr Nettleham LN2..68 C2
30 Winterton DN15.....9 A5
Bakers Cl DN38.........21 B5
Bakersfield............196 F7
Peterborough PE2......230 E7
Baker's La
Candlesby with Gunby PE23..89 A2
Fishtoft PE21.........126 C4
Great Steeping PE23...101 E6
Westborough & Dry Doddington
NG23.................117 E3
Baker St HU2...........180 E7
Bakers Way 5 PE10......154 D6
Bakestraw Gate PE12....157 F5
Bakewell Cl 13 NG34....104 B2
Bakewell Ct 1 DN15.....182 B3
Bakewell Mews 6 LN6....204 F1
Bakewell Rd PE2........229 C2
Bala Ct PE4............221 B3
Balder Ct 2 DN33.......191 C2
BALDERTON NG24.........104 C2
Balderton Gate 10 NG24..104 A4
Balderton La NG24......104 D3
Baldock's Mill Heritage Ctr*
.....................213 D4
Baldwin Cl DN16........185 B3
Baldwin Cl PE8.........172 C1
Baldwin Dr 1 PE2.......230 E8
Baldwin Gr PE10........213 D6
Balfour Pl 3 DN40......186 B4
Balfour St
Gainsborough DN21.....197 C5
2 Kingston upon Hull HU9..181 C8
Balintore Rise PE2.....229 D4
Balk Rd 8 PE9..........163 C1
Balliol Dr DN16........185 B4
Ball's La PE12.........159 A6
Balmoral Ave
1 Grimsby DN34........191 A7
Spalding PE11.........214 D2
Balmoral Cl
12 Mablethorpe/Sutton on Sea
LN12.................76 F8
2 Wragby LN8..........70 D4
Balmoral Ct DN17.......184 F4
Balmoral Dr
7 Beacon Hill NG24....104 C4
Grantham NG31.........210 E6
Sleaford NG34.........120 F2
Balmoral Rd
Cleethorpes DN35......192 C4
1 Hatfield DN7........14 D4
1 Peterborough PE4....225 C8
Balmoral Way PE12......159 A8
Bamber St PE1..........225 F4
Bamburgh Cl NG31......210 E6
Bamford Ave 1 HU9.....5 F8
Bamford Cl 6 LN6......204 E2
Banbury Cl PE21.......214 D6
Banbury Ct 9 DN31.....189 C1
Banbury Rd DN16.......183 D2
Bancroft Rd NG24......104 A3
Bangor Cl LN5.........205 C3
Bank Ave PE7..........230 D2
Bank Dr Ingoldmells PE25..90 F3
5 Wisbech PE13.......170 C1
Bank End LN11.........50 E8
Bank End Rd DN9.......26 A3
Bank La 12 LN7........33 B4
Bank's Ave 4 PE11.....214 F6
Banks Cres PE9........218 F6
Bank Side 1 PE21......136 D8
Banks La 6 NG34.......122 E2
Banks Rd 6 LN9........199 C4
Banks St 5 LN9........199 C4
Bank St Boston PE21...208 F5
Kingston upon Hull HU3..180 C7
Lincoln LN2...........234 B2
Bank The
Parson Drove PE13.....177 C7
Skidbrooke LN11.......51 B3
Swaton NG34...........133 D4
Banner Ct HU4.........179 D2
Bannister Cl 3 HU13...3 F4
Bannister Dr HU9......181 C7
Bannister's La PE20...136 C7
Bannister's Row 6 PE13..170 C1
Banovallum Gdns 1 LN9..199 D3
Banovallum Sch LN9....199 C2
Baptist Chapel La 4 DN40..12 F2
Baptist La 3 NG23.....91 C4
Barbara Cl 3 LN4......194 E7
Barbara Rd 6 PE25.....206 D2
Barber Cl PE2.........231 C7
Barberry Ct 3 HU3.....180 C5
Barbers Dro 10 PE6....175 C8
Barbers Dro North 8
.....................175 C8
Barbers Hill PE4......220 F7
Barbican Way DN36.....195 C6
Barcroft St DN35......189 E1
Bardling's Dro PE12...169 A7
BARDNEY LN3...........83 C4
Bardney PE2...........230 A4
Bardney Ave DN16......185 A7
Bardney Cl LN6........204 F6
Bardney Gdns 1 DN34...190 F4
Bardney Linewood National
Nature Reserve* LN3...83 C3
Bardney Primary School
LN3..................83 C4

Bardney Rd Barlings LN3....69 E2
  Branston & Mere LN4......82 C3
  Wragby LN8...........70 C4
Bardots Leisure Ctr LN5..205 C1
Barehams La PE11........145 A7
Barfen La LN13.........63 B3
Barff La LN8..........43 F2
Barff Mdw LN8.........43 B1
Barff Rd LN4..........82 B1
Barfields La LN3........68 F1
Bargate Grimsby DN34....191 C5
  12 Lincoln LN5........205 E8
Bargate Ave DN32.......191 C5
Bargate Gr **3** HU5.....179 D8
Bargate La **4** LN9......199 C3
Barge Cl **1** PE11......214 F5
Barge Rd PE12.........148 A7
Barham Ct PE2.........231 F5
BARHOLM PE9...........164 C1
Barholme Ave **7** PE12...160 A8
Barholme Rd PE9........164 D2
Barkestone La NG13......128 A5
Barkham St **7** PE24....102 D2
Barkhouse Cl **4** DN35...192 F5
Barkhouse La **5** DN35...192 F5
Bark St DN35..........192 F5
BARKSTON...........130 B8
Barkston Cl Bourne PE10..213 E6
  29 Newark-on-Trent NG24..104 B2
Barkston Dr PE1........226 B6
Barkston Gdns LN2.......202 B7
Barkston Rd NG32.......118 D2
Barkston & Syston CE Prim
  Sch NG32...........130 B8
Barkwith Rd LN8........58 F1
Barkworth Cl HU10......178 D6
Barkworth Ct **3** DN37...194 C4
Barkworth Way HU13.....178 B3
Bar La **20** LN5........93 F7
Barley Cl Heckington NG34..122 D2
  12 Hibaldstow DN20.....31 A5
  Kirton in Lindsey DN21...30 B2
  24 Metheringham LN4....95 C4
Barleycroft Rd NG33.....152 E8
Barley Ct DN33.........191 B1
Barleyfield PE6.........164 E2
Barleyfield Cl LN4......81 E4
Barley Gr **4** PE11.....166 C6
Barley La LN4..........109 E6
Barley Mews PE2........230 D7
Barley Sheaf PE20......124 B8
Barley Way LN9........199 A3
Barley Wy **19** NG24....104 A6
BARLINGS LN3..........69 D1
Barlings Ave DN16......185 A7
Barlings Cl **1** Barlings LN3..69 C3
  Hartsholme LN6........204 F7
  7 Scotter DN21......29 C4
Barlings La LN3........69 C2
Barlode Drain PE22......100 E1
Barmouth Dr DN37.......190 E8
Barmston St HU2.......180 F8
BARNACK PE9..........172 E4
Barnack CE Prim Sch
  PE9..............172 D4
Barnack Est **4** PE24....102 E7
Barnack Hill & Holes National
  Nature Reserve★ PE9..172 D3
Barnack Rd Bainton PE9..172 E4
  St Martin's without PE9..219 D4
Barnack Rd Ind Est PE9..219 D5
Barnard Ave DN20......196 B3
Barnard Way **9** PE3....224 F3
Barnard Wlk DN40......186 D3
Barnberry Way PE10.....142 D2
BARNBY DUN DN3.......14 A4
Barnby Gate NG24......104 A4
BARNBY IN THE WILLOWS
  NG24............104 F3
Barnby La NG23........104 F1
Barnby Rd NG24........104 B3
Barnby Road Acad Prim Sch
  NG24............104 A4
Barn Cl **2** Maxey PE6....173 C7
  Peterborough PE4.......220 F3
Barn End **9** NG33......151 A8
Barnes Cl **1** NG34.....212 C6
Barnes Cres
  Scunthorpe DN15.......182 E4
  Skegness PE25.........206 A5
Barnes Ct PE9.........218 E5
Barnes Dro PE10........154 F4
Barnes Gn **2** DN21.....29 C4
Barnes La LN5.........106 F7
Barnes Rd
  9 Donington PE11.....134 E2
  Skegness PE25.........206 A5
Barnes Wallis Acad The
  LN4..............207 B5
Barnes Way PE4........220 F3
Barnetby La DN20.......20 F7
BARNETBY LE WOLD DN38..21 C4
Barnetby Rd
  1 Kingston upon Hull
    HU1............179 A3
  Scunthorpe DN17.......184 F5
Barnetby Road DN38.....21 B2
Barnetby Sta DN38......21 A4
Barnet Dr DN36........195 E7
Barnet Gn **12** DN7.....14 D3
Barnett Pl DN35........192 B7
Barnetts La PE11.......145 D4
Barneyfield Rd PE22.....126 E1
Barnfield Rd **22** NG23...91 D5

Barn Hill PE9..........219 B5
BARNOLDBY LE BECK
  DN37............35 B6
Barnoldby Rd DN37......194 C4
Barn Owl Cl
  Corby Glen NG33.......152 F7
  23 Humberston DN36....36 D8
  1 Langtoft PE6.......164 F3
Barn Owl Wy LN4.......203 B1
Barnside **6** DN20.....30 F5
Barnstaple Rd **3** DN17..184 D8
Barnstock PE3.........225 A7
Barnston Way **12** DN15..8 B4
Barnswallace Ct **15** LN2..68 D7
Barnwell Rd **3** PE9.....218 E6
Barnwell Terr **2** NG31...210 F3
Baron Ave DN36........195 D7
Baron Ct PE4..........221 B4
Baroness Rd DN34......190 F6
Baroness Wy PE6.......217 C6
Barons Way PE9........219 C4
Barrack Sq NG31.......211 C4
Barracks The PE13......169 E2
Barraclough's La
  1 Barton-upon-Humber
    DN18...........3 E1
  Barton-upon-Humber DN18..3 E2
Barratt's Cl LN2........234 C4
Bar Rd DN10..........52 B8
Bar Rd N **3** DN10.....52 B8
Bar Rd S **7** DN10.....52 B8
Barrett Gr **7** LN2......68 E6
Barrett's Ct PE12.......215 D3
Barrick Cl **16** DN19....11 D8
Barrier Bank Cowbit PE12..156 F2
  Spalding PE12.........214 C1
Barrington Cl **8** PE12...215 D2
Barrington Gate PE12....215 E1
Barrons Cl LN3........203 E7
Barrow Blow Wells Nature
  Reserve★ DN19.......4 D1
BARROWBY NG32.......210 A5
Barrowby CE Prim Sch
  NG32............129 B3
Barrowby Gate NG31.....210 D4
Barrowby Rd **8** NG31...211 A5
Barrowden Rd PE9......171 A2
Barrowfield PE1........226 E7
Barrowfield Dr **1** PE9...218 E4
BARROW HANN DN19....4 E1
BARROW HAVEN DN19...4 B2
Barrow Haven Reedbed
  Nature Reserve★ DN19..4 B2
Barrow Haven Sta DN19...4 C2
Barrow La HU13........178 D2
Barrow Rd
  Barton-upon-Humber DN18..11 A8
  New Holland DN19......4 E1
Barrows Gate
  3 Beacon Hill NG24....104 A6
  North Somercotes LN11...50 D6
BARROW UPON HUMBER
  DN19............11 C8
Barr's La PE12.........168 B4
Barry Ave DN34........190 F3
Barry Wlk **3** PE2......230 F7
Bars La Benington PE22...126 E5
  Bicker PE20..........135 A5
Bartholemew Cl **1** LN3..83 C4
Bartol Cres PE21.......208 D5
Barton Cl
  3 Mablethorpe LN12...64 C2
  Paston PE4..........221 D1
Barton Dr HU13........178 D1
Barton Gate LN11.......198 D4
Barton La
  Barrow upon Humber DN19..11 C8
  Tydd St Mary PE13......169 F8
Barton-on-Humber Sta
  DN18............3 F1
Barton Outdoor Pursuits Ctr★
  DN18............3 D2
Barton Rd Burnham DN19..11 C5
  5 Wainfleet All Saints
    PE24...........102 D1
  Wrawby DN20.........196 F6
Barton St Peters CE Prim Sch
  22 DN18..........3 F1
Barton Sch DN18.......11 A8
Bartons La PE23........101 F6
Barton St
  Aylesby DN37.........23 D2
  Barrow upon Humber DN19..11 C8
  Fotherby LN11........49 A2
  Irby DN37...........34 F7
  Keelby DN41.........23 A4
  Ludborough DN36......48 C6
BARTON-UPON-HUMBER
  DN18............10 F7
BARTON WATERSIDE DN18..3 F2
Bartram Gate **2** PE4....221 C1
Bartrams **3** HU15.....2 D6
Basic Slag Rd DN16.....183 E2
Basil Gn PE2..........230 D6
Baslow Rd DN15........182 B2
Bass Cotts NG34.......212 E3
Bassett Cl **2** DN20.....19 E3
Bassett Rd DN35........193 A4
BASSINGHAM LN5.......92 F2
Bassingham Cres LN2....201 F7
Bassingham La PE23.....88 E3
Bassingham Prim Sch LN5..92 F2
Bassingham Rd LN5.....92 F5
BASSINGTHORPE NG33...140 F4
BASTON PE6..........164 E4
Baston CE Prim Sch PE6..164 E5
Baston Edge Dro PE10...164 E7

Baston Fen Nature Reserve★
  PE6.............165 A8
Baston Outgang Rd PE6..165 A6
Baston Rd PE6.........164 D4
Bateman's Cl **3** PE12...159 D7
Batemans Ct **2** PE24...102 E2
Bates La **4** PE7.......230 F5
Bath Gdns PE21........208 F3
Bath La **15** PE11......214 D4
Bath Rd
  Bracebridge Heath LN4..81 A2
  25 Peterborough PE6....175 A1
  Wisbech PE13.........170 D1
Bath Row PE9.........219 B4
Bath St **8** Grantham NG31..211 A4
  Grimsby DN32.........189 C1
Bathurst PE2..........230 A4
Bathurst St
  8 Kingston upon Hull
    HU3...........180 D5
  Lincoln LN2..........202 D3
Battery St DN40........186 D4
Battlefields La N PE12....159 A8
Battlefields La S PE12....215 F3
Battle Gn DN9.........27 D7
Battle of Britain Meml Flight
  Visitor Ctr★ LN4.....207 B3
Baulkin's Dro PE12......159 C1
BAUMBER LN9.........72 A1
Baumber Prim Sch LN9...72 A1
Baumber Road LN10.....84 D5
Bawtry Cl LN6.........204 C8
Bawtry Rd DN7.........14 F3
Baxter Cl Coningsby LN4..207 D3
  15 Wisbech PE13......170 E1
Baxter Gdns PE11.......214 C7
Bayard St DN21........197 C5
Bayes Rd **6** PE25.....103 E4
Bayfield Rd **4** LN4.....96 E5
Bayford Dr **8** NG24....104 C4
Bayford Gn PE21........208 B4
Bayleaf Ave PE7........233 A8
Bayleaf La **4** DN18....4 A1
Bayons Ave DN33.......194 D8
Baysdale Gr NG31.......211 B8
Baysdale Rd DN16......185 D5
Bayswater Pl **1** DN18...194 D8
Bayswood Ave PE21.....208 F1
BAYTHORPE PE20.......135 C8
Baytree Ave DN34......191 A6
Baytree Owl Ctr★ PE12..157 D7
Baywood Cl **4** LN6.....200 C1
Beach Ave **15** PE24....90 D7
Beach Bank
  Pinchbeck PE11........144 E3
  Surfleet PE11.........145 A3
Beach Holt La DN37.....23 D2
Beach La PE21.........144 F3
Beachside **10** LN12....77 A8
Beacon Acad LN35......192 C5
Beacon Ave
  16 Barton-upon-Humber
    DN18...........10 E8
  Cleethorpes DN35......192 C6
Beacon Cl **7** HU13.....3 F4
Beacon Ct DN35........192 D6
BEACON HILL NG24......104 B5
Beacon Hill La PE34.....161 E3
Beacon Hill Rd
  Gringley on the Hill DN10..39 D1
  Newark-on-Trent NG24...104 B4
Beacon Hts NG24.......104 B4
Beacon La NG31........211 C4
Beacon Pk Cl **4** PE25...206 A6
Beacon Pk Dr PE25......206 A6
Beacon Primary Acad
  PE25............206 C5
Beacon Rd **7** NG34....107 C1
Beaconsfield Dr **3** NG24..104 C5
Beaconthorpe Rd **4**
  DN35............192 E7
Beacon View **2** NG13...128 A6
Beacon Way PE25......206 A6
Beacon Wy HU3........180 A3
Beadle Way PE4........221 E3
Beadle Wy PE6.........221 E3
Beaford Cl **7** DN17....184 C8
Beagle Cl **16** DN20....19 E4
Beagle La NG34........107 C1
Bean St HU3..........180 C6
Bear La **14** PE11......145 C1
Beatrice Rd **11** PE13...170 D2
Beatrice Way **28** PE24..90 D7
Beatty Ave DN31.......190 C3
Beaubridge Bsns Pk PE25..206 B3
Beauchamp St **3** DN15..17 E6
Beauchamp Wlk **7** DN16..183 B2
Beauchief Gdns DN16....185 A8
Beaufort Ave **1** PE6....217 C6
Beaufort Cl
  Kingston upon Hull HU3..180 C6
  Lincoln LN2..........202 D8
Beaufort Cres DN35.....192 D2
Beaufort Dr Bourne PE10..213 C7
  4 Spalding PE11......214 C3
Beaufort Rd LN2.......202 D8
Beaufort St DN21.......197 B7
Beaulahland **3** DN18...10 A7
Beaulah Villas **9** DN18..10 A7
Beaulieu Ct **6** PE6.....175 A1
Beaumaris Way NG31....210 E6

Beaumonde **5** DN36....195 C2
Beaumont Cl **11** PE24...102 E7
Beaumont Ct **3** HU9....181 D7
Beaumont Dr **2** NG31...210 F8
Beaumont Fee LN1......234 A2
Beaumont St DN21......197 D5
Beaumont Way PE7.....230 C2
Beauvale PE4..........221 C3
Beauvoir Pl PE7........233 D5
Beaver Cl LN8.........200 A5
Beccelm Dr **9** PE6.....175 B8
Beck Bank Gosberton PE11..144 C3
  Kirton PE20..........124 E1
Beck Cl **5** Binbrook LN8..47 C5
  13 Keelby DN41......23 A4
  1 Ruskington NG34...108 D2
Becke Cl LN3..........203 E5
Becket Cl LN4.........203 D1
Beckets Ct Grantham NG31..210 F4
  New England PE1......225 F8
Beckett Ave DN21.......197 E6
Beckett Cl
  9 Heckington NG34....122 D3
  2 Skegness PE25......206 C1
Beckett Dr PE11........214 C6
Beckett St DN21........53 A8
Beckhall LN2..........68 D6
Beckhead Cvn Site LN6...204 C1
Beck Hill
  5 Barton-upon-Humber
    DN18...........10 F8
  Cherry Willingham/Reepham
    LN3............203 F8
  Tealby LN8..........46 C1
Beckhole Cl HU3.......180 A6
Beckhythe Cl DN33......191 E1
BECKINGHAM
  Barnby in the Willows
    NG24...........105 A4
  Beckingham DN10......40 B1
Beckingham PE2........229 F3
Beckingham Rd
  Coddington NG24......104 C5
  Walkeringham DN10....40 A2
Beckingthorpe Dr **19**
  NG13............128 A6
Beck La Appleby DN15....9 D1
  Aubourn Haddington & South
    Hykeham LN6.......93 B7
  10 Barrow upon Humber
    DN19...........11 D8
  7 Broughton DN20....19 E3
  Fulbeck NG32.........106 C1
  Heighington/Washingborough
    LN4............81 F4
  Ingoldmells PE25......90 E2
  Redbourne DN21.......30 F2
  Scunthorpe DN16......185 B3
  6 Welton/Dunholme LN2..68 E6
  Welton le Marsh PE23...89 A3
Becklands Ave DN16.....195 B6
Beckside **11** Brough HU15..2 D6
  Normanby by Spital LN8...55 E7
  Rothwell LN7.........33 F2
  Scopwick LN4........108 C8
Beck Side **5** DN20....30 F5
Beckside Cl DN36.......192 E1
Beckside Ct LN11.......198 D3
Becks La DN21.........29 A3
Beck St Digby LN4......108 E5
Beck Way **5** PE10.....164 C8
Beck Wlk **2** DN35.....192 E1
Bedale Mews **31** HU15..2 C5
Bedale Rd **3** DN16.....185 D5
Bedale Pl DN35.........192 E3
Bede Cl **8** NG34......212 B2
Bede Cres PE22........126 F5
Bedehouse Bank PE10...213 E4
Bede House La **3** NG24..104 A4
Bede Pl PE1..........226 A6
Bede Rd **3** PE6.......164 E5
Bedford Cl NG31.......211 F5
Bedford Ct **16** PE6....176 A3
Bedford Pl **1** PE11.....214 C3
Bedford Rd
  Humberston DN35......193 A1
  Kingston upon Hull HU13..178 F3
Bedford Row PE13......170 D8
Bedford St Grimsby DN32..189 C1
  2 Lincoln LN1.......201 D4
  Peterborough PE1......226 B4
Bedford Wy DN15.......183 A5
Beebys Way PE7........233 E8
Beechams Mews **5** PE11..214 B3
Beech Ave Bourne PE10...213 B5
  Gainsborough DN21.....197 D6
  Grimsby DN33.........191 C3
  5 Gunness DN15......17 E6
  Kingston upon Hull HU10..178 D8
  24 Nettleham LN2......68 C2
  Peterborough PE1......225 F3
  Scunthorpe DN15......182 B6
  Spalding PE11.........214 F5
Beech Cl
  1 Bracebridge Heath LN4..81 A1
  5 Broughton DN20....19 D3
  4 Colsterworth NG33...151 E2
  4 Coningsby LN4......207 D4
  Dunholme LN2........68 E5
  3 Gringley on the Hill DN10..39 D1
  4 Heckington NG34....122 D3
  Kingston upon Hull HU3..180 D5
  Market Deeping PE6....217 B6
  RAF Cranwell NG34.....107 D1
  9 Sudbrooke LN2......68 D3
  4 Thorney PE6.......176 A3

Beech Cres **1** DN7....14 D6
Beechcroft **6** LN6.....93 A8
Beechcroft Dr **5** DN21..30 B2
Beechcroft Rd NG31.....210 D3
Beech Dr
  18 Bottesford NG13...128 A5
  6 North Ferriby HU14...3 A4
  15 Ryhall PE9.......163 C1
  3 Welton HU14.......2 F5
Beeches Ave DN16......185 B4
Beeches Independent Sch The
  PE1.............226 A6
Beeches La PE22........112 C5
Beeches The
  New Waltham DN36.....195 E5
  Spalding PE11........214 E4
  1 Sturton by Stow LN1...66 C7
Beechfield Ct DN34......191 C6
Beechfield Rd **7** DN7...14 C4
Beech Garth **9** DN19...11 C7
Beech Gr
  Anlaby with Anlaby Common
    HU13...........178 C3
  3 Burton upon Stather DN15..8 B5
  Donington PE11.......134 E2
  Holton le Clay DN36....195 E1
  Louth LN11..........198 C7
  4 Scopwick Heath LN4..108 A7
  Stamford PE9.........218 D6
  4 Swanland HU14......3 C7
Beech Hill Rd HU14.....3 C7
Beechings Way **10** LN13..75 E2
Beechings Way Ind Est
  LN13............75 E2
Beech La **3** Eye PE6....175 A1
  20 New Waltham DN36...36 C8
Beech Lawn HU10......178 E8
Beech Rd Branston LN4...81 D2
  2 Brough HU15......2 C6
  Glinton PE6..........220 B8
Beech Rise Sleaford NG34..212 D6
  2 South Rauceby NG34..120 E4
Beech St LN5..........205 D5
Beech Tree Ave **17** DN8..15 B7
Beechtree Cl **8** NG34...108 E1
Beechway DN16........185 B7
Beech Way DN35.......192 D2
Beechwood Ave
  Grimsby DN33.........190 F3
  Immingham DN40......186 C4
Beechwood Cl
  16 Kirk Sandall DN3....14 A1
  Peterborough PE1......226 C7
  6 Wisbech PE13......170 D1
Beechwood Cres **4** DN20..19 E4
Beechwood Ct **22** DN7..14 D3
Beechwood Dr
  12 Scawby DN20......30 F8
  7 Scotter DN21......29 C3
Beechwood Rd **5** PE13..170 D1
BeechWy PE25.........103 C8
Beeden Pk Est NG31.....210 C4
Bee Field The LN2.......202 F7
Beehive La LN6........79 C1
Beeley Rd DN32........192 C6
BEELSBY DN37.........34 E4
Beelsby Rd LN7........34 C5
Beelsby Road DN37.....34 D2
Beel's Rd DN41.........187 B2
Bee Orchid Way LN11...198 A6
BEESBY LN13..........76 A7
Beesby Dr **3** DN35.....192 F3
Beesby Rd
  Maltby le Marsh LN13....76 A7
  Markby LN13.........76 B6
  Scunthorpe DN17......184 E5
Bees Cnr **1** PE24.....102 D2
Bee's La PE13.........169 F6
Beeson Gr DN31........188 E1
Beeson St DN31........188 E1
Beeston Dr PE7........231 F5
Beeston Rd **11** NG24...104 A3
Beeton Cl LN11........198 D4
Beetons Cl PE7........233 E5
Beevor St LN6.........201 C2
Beggar Hill Messingham Rd
  DN21............29 D4
Beggar's La PE22.......98 F3
Begger's Bush La PE12...157 D7
Beilby St HU3.........179 F4
Belcanto Ct **3** PE11....214 A5
BELCHFORD LN9........73 B2
Belchford Rd LN9......72 C1
Belchmire La PE11......145 B5
Beldings Ct PE23.......101 F6
Belfry The **5** NG31.....211 D7
Belgic Sq PE1.........226 E3
Belgrave Ct **11** DN9....16 E1
Belgrave Dr HU4.......179 D5
Belgrave Rd Grimsby DN33..191 B2
  7 Spalding PE11......214 C2
Belgrave Sq **1** DN15....183 B3
Belgravia Cl LN6.......200 C1
Belham Hill Lane LN5....105 E7
Belisana Rd **5** PE11....214 A5
Bellamy Ct HU9........181 C7
Bellamy's La PE14......170 D4
Bellbutts View DN21....29 B3
Bell Cl NG31..........210 E7
Bell Ct **5** PE21.......208 F1
Bell Dro **5** PE6.......175 F6
BELLEAU LN13.........75 A5
Belle Isle LN4.........110 F6
Belleisle Rd DN34......190 D4
Belle Vue PE2.........231 C6
Belle Vue Rd LN1......234 A3

Belle Vue Terr Lincoln LN1 234 A3
21 Thorne/Moorends DN8 15 A8
Bellfield Cl 4 PE11 214 B3
Bellflower Cl 2 LN2 202 C8
Bell Gr LN6 205 C6
Bellingham Rd DN16 185 D7
Bellingham's Dro PE11 166 F7
Bell La 4 Collingham NG23 91 C4
Fosdyke PE20 146 D8
Market Deeping PE6 217 E4
Moulton PE12 157 F7
Scunthorpe DN15 183 A2
BELLMOUNT PE34 161 E4
Bellona Dr PE2 231 E4
Bell's Dro PE12 159 C1
Bell's Pl PE1 226 A2
Bellview Rd 6 NG34 108 E1
Bellwin Dr DN15 8 A1
Bellwood Cres 5 DN8 15 A8
Bellwood Gdns NG31 211 C5
Bellwood Grange 1 LN3 203 E7
Bell Wr Drain Bank
Eastville PE22 101 B1
New Leake PE22 100 E1
BELMESTHORPE PE9 163 D1
Belmesthorpe La PE9 163 D1
Belmesthorpe Rd
Belmesthorpe PE9 163 F1
Greatford PE9 164 A2
Belmont DN36 195 C1
Belmont Cl DN35 192 D3
Belmont Com Prim Sch
NG31 211 E6
Belmont Gr 2 NG31 211 D6
Belmont St
Kingston upon Hull HU9 181 D8
Lincoln LN2 202 B3
Scunthorpe DN16 185 A6
BELNIE PE11 145 D5
Belnie La PE11 145 D5
Belper Ct 6 Crosby DN15 182 B2
Grimsby DN32 189 C1
Belsay Dr PE2 231 F5
Belshaw La DN9 16 D1
Belsize Ave PE2 230 E6
Belthorn Rd 2 DN17 7 F2
BELTOFT DN9 17 B1
Beltoft Road DN9 28 A7
BELTON Belton DN9 16 E1
Belton and Manthorpe NG32 130 B6
Belton All Saints CE Prim Sch
DN9 16 E2
Belton Ave Grantham NG31 211 C6
Lincoln LN6 204 F6
Belton Cl Boston PE21 209 B5
13 Market Deeping PE6 217 A5
Belton Fields 1 DN9 16 D1
Belton Gdns 23 PE9 219 C5
Belton Gr Grantham NG31 211 B7
1 Grimsby DN33 191 A3
Belton House★ NG32 130 B6
Belton La Grantham NG31 211 C6
Great Gonerby NG31 129 E5
Belton Lane Prim Sch
NG31 211 D7
Belton Park Rd PE25 206 B6
Belton Pk★ NG32 211 F8
Belton Pk Dr 7 LN6 93 C8
Belton Rd Belton DN9 17 A1
Epworth DN9 27 E7
Peterborough PE7 231 F5
Sandtoft DN9 16 B3
Belton St 16 PE9 219 C5
Belton Wlk LN11 198 A7
Belt Rd The DN21 197 F7
Beluga Cl PE2 231 B8
Belvedere Cl PE11 214 B2
Belvedere Dr DN17 184 E7
Belvedere Rd HU13 178 F2
BELVOIR NG32 138 B8
Belvoir Ave
12 Bottesford NG13 128 A5
Grantham NG31 210 F1
Spitalgate NG31 211 E2
Belvoir Castle★ NG32 138 B8
Belvoir Cl Bracebridge LN5 205 D1
4 Colsterworth NG33 151 E6
1 Market Deeping PE6 217 A5
1 Stamford PE9 218 E6
Belvoir Cres 2 NG24 104 A3
Belvoir Ct LN11 198 B8
Belvoir Gdns NG31 129 D5
Belvoir High Sch NG13 128 A5
Belvoir La NG32 128 D1
Belvoir Pk Wlk DN35 192 D2
Belvoir Pl 10 NG24 104 B2
Belvoir Rd Bottesford NG13 128 A4
Cleethorpes DN35 192 D2
Croxton Kerrial NG32 138 A6
Belvoir St HU5 180 C8
Belvoir Way Eye PE1 226 D8
Louth LN11 198 B8
Peterborough PE1 226 C8
Belwood Dr 7 DN9 16 E2
Bempton Gr
4 Grimsby DN32 192 A5
Kingston upon Hull HU5 179 D8
Bemrose Way 2 DN31 191 C8
Benams Cl PE5 223 E2
Benbow Way LN1 201 C6
Benderslough Dro PE12 159 C3
Bendike La PE11 145 D4
Benedict Cl 2 HU4 179 A2
Benedict Ct PE6 217 E5
Benedict Rd HU4 179 A2
Benedict Sq PE4 220 E2
BENINGTON PE22 126 F5
Benington Rd PE22 126 E3
Benjamin Adlard Com Sch
DN21 197 E2
Benjamin Adlard Prim Sch
DN21 197 E2
Benjamins Wlk DN35 192 E1
Benland PE3 225 A6
Benner Rd PE11 214 E8
Benner Rd Ind Est PE11 214 E8
Bennett Dr 28 DN15 9 A5
Bennett Rd
Cleethorpes DN35 192 D7
Louth LN11 198 C8
Scunthorpe DN16 185 C7
Bennetts Mill Cl 10 LN10 97 D5
Bennington Cl
8 Lincoln LN6 205 A7
11 Long Bennington NG23 117 D3
Bennington La NG23 117 E4
BENNIWORTH LN8 59 B1
Benniworth Rd LN8 71 C7
Ben's Gate PE12 159 B5
Benson Cl LN6 204 C6
Benson Cres LN6 204 C6
Benson Ct LN11 48 F4
Benstead PE2 229 E3
Bentinck Cl 6 PE11 214 C6
Bentinck Sq 2 LN2 202 B3
Bentinck St 4 LN2 202 B3
Bentley Ave PE7 233 E6
Bentley Ct HU3 180 A5
Bentley Dr LN4 205 F3
Bentley La 6 DN38 32 E7
Bentley St
Cleethorpes DN35 192 E6
6 Stamford PE9 219 C6
Bentley Way 1 LN4 95 C4
Benton Cl 6 PE12 157 E1
Benyon Gr PE2 230 B4
Berberis Cl 2 PE6 175 F3
Berea The DN34 191 C5
Beresford Ave PE25 206 C2
Beresford Cl 4 PE25 206 C2
Beresford Cres 5 PE25 206 C2
Beresford Dr 5 LN2 68 F3
Beretun Gn 7 DN18 10 E8
Bergen Cl DN36 195 B6
Berilldon Dr LN1 201 C7
Berkeley Ave
Green Hill NG31 210 E6
Lincoln LN6 205 A3
Berkeley Ct 5 NG34 212 E4
Berkeley Dr
4 Bourne PE10 213 C7
Lincoln LN6 205 A3
Berkeley Ind Est DN15 182 C4
Berkeley Inf & Jun Sch
DN15 182 D4
Berkeley Rd
Humberston DN35 193 A2
Peterborough PE3 225 C3
Berkeley St
1 Kingston upon Hull
HU3 180 D8
Scunthorpe DN15 183 A4
Berkley Ct 4 PE11 214 C5
Berkshire Dr NG31 211 D7
Bermondsey Dr HU5 179 E8
Bernadette Ave HU4 179 B5
Bernard St LN2 202 B4
Berners Rd DN35 193 B1
Bernicia Dr NG34 212 B2
Berrigan Way LN4 81 E1
Berrybut Way 5 PE9 219 D7
Berry Cl 6 NG34 212 D2
Berry Ct PE1 225 E5
Berryfield End 7 NG32 210 A5
Berryman Way HU13 179 A3
Berrystead PE5 223 E2
Berry Way 5 PE25 206 C3
Bert Allen Dr 1 PE22 114 A1
Bertie Cl Long Sutton PE12 216 C3
Swinstead NG33 153 A5
Bertie La 8 PE9 172 C6
Bert's Way 7 NG32 128 F7
Berwick Ct DN40 186 C4
Besant Cl 10 PE22 113 B1
BESCABY LE14 138 B1
Bessemer Way DN15 183 B6
Bess Wrights Dro PE7 233 E2
Bestall Rd DN32 192 C6
BESTHORPE NG23 91 C7
Besthorpe Cty Prim Sch
NG23 91 C7
Besthorpe Rd
Besthorpe NG23 91 C6
North Scarle NG23 78 D1
Beswick Cl 5 LN6 204 D7
Bethlehem St DN32 191 D7
Bethlem Cres 9 PE24 102 D1
Bethune Ave HU4 179 A3
Bethune Ave W HU13 179 A3
Bethune Pk Prim Sch
HU4 179 B3
Betjeman Cl
1 Bourne PE10 213 D3
Spalding PE11 214 B4
Betony Cl DN15 182 C6
Bette Camplings Cl PE12 159 D1
Bettesworth Rd DN21 54 F8
Bettles Cl PE1 226 A6
Betton Lane Ind Est NG31 211 B6
Betula Gr 3 LN6 204 D7
Betula Way 1 DN17 184 C5
Beverley Cl 7 DN36 195 D1
Beverley Cres DN32 192 A5
Beverley Ct Eye PE6 175 B1
12 Healing DN41 23 F5
Westcliffe DN17 184 D7
Beverley Gdns 4 PE9 219 A6
Beverley Gr Lincoln LN6 204 F3
7 Skegness PE25 206 B3
Beverley Rd HU3 180 D8
Beverstone PE2 229 D5
Bevers Wy DN36 195 D3
Bevishall PE4 221 D1
Bew Cl PE2 231 D4
Bewholme Gr 3 HU9 5 D8
Bewick Pl PE7 233 D8
Bexley Ct 10 DN32 189 C1
BICKER PE20 135 A4
Bicker Dro PE20 134 D6
BICKER GAUNTLET PE20 134 F6
Bicker Prep Sch PE30 135 A4
Bicker Rd PE11 134 F3
Bickleigh Wlk PE3 225 A3
Bidwell La LE15 162 B6
Biergate LN11 49 F7
Bifield PE2 229 F3
BIGBY DN38 21 C2
Bigby Gn DN38 21 B2
Bigby Gr DN17 184 F4
Bigby High Rd DN20 196 D2
Bigby Hill DN38 21 C1
Bigby Rd 6 DN20 196 C3
Bigby Road DN38 21 C4
Bigby St DN20 196 C3
Bilberry Cl 7 PE11 214 B6
Billet La DN15 182 F8
Billet Mill App Rd DN16 19 A4
Billet Mill Rd DN16 183 E1
Billgate La PE24 102 E7
BILLINGBOROUGH NG34 133 A1
Billingborough Dro NG34 143 E8
Billingborough Prim Sch
NG34 133 B1
Billingborough Rd
Billingborough NG34 133 B1
Folkingham NG34 132 E1
BILLINGHAY LN4 109 F5
Billinghay CE Prim Sch
LN4 109 F6
Billinghay Cottage★ 9
LN4 109 F5
Billinghay Ct DN35 192 F3
Billinghay Dales Head
LN4 110 B4
Billings Gate LN11 50 E5
BILSBY LN13 76 A3
Bilsby Cl LN2 202 A7
BILSBY FIELD LN13 76 A2
Bilsby Rd 2 LN13 75 F3
Bilsdale Gr HU9 181 F8
Bilsdale Rd DN16 185 E5
BINBROOK LN8 47 B4
Binbrook Cl 8 LN6 204 D7
Binbrook (Controlled) Prim
Sch LN8 47 B5
Binbrook La LN8 47 B2
Binbrook Road LN11 60 C6
Binbrook Way DN37 190 E8
Bircham Cres DN21 30 C1
Birch Ave Brigg DN20 196 B4
Grimsby DN34 191 A6
Birch Cl 4 Branston LN4 81 D2
28 Brough HU15 2 C5
11 Coningsby LN4 207 D4
Hessle HU13 178 B3
Kingston upon Hull HU5 179 B7
1 Lincoln LN6 204 F2
Wyberton PE21 136 E7
Birch Croft 31 HU15 2 C6
Birchdale 31 DN18 10 E8
Birch Dr DN17 185 D4
Birchen Cl PE7 230 C3
Birches The
New Waltham DN36 195 E6
8 Westwoodside DN9 27 A2
Birchfield Rd 8 DN9 27 D6
Birch Gdns 26 DN18 3 E1
Birch Gr 28 Alford LN13 75 F2
Gainsborough DN21 197 D6
Spalding PE11 214 F3
Birchin Way DN31 188 D1
Birch La 4 LN9 85 E7
Birch Leigh HU3 180 C6
Birchnell Gdns PE10 213 E4
Birch Rd Louth LN11 198 E5
6 Newark-on-Trent NG24 104 B3
6 Stamford PE9 218 D7
Birchtree Ave PE1 226 A7
Birch Tree Cl 4 DN3 14 A4
Birch Way DN38 21 C5
Birch Way Ind Est DN31 188 D1
BIRCHWOOD LN6 204 D7
Birchwood PE2 230 A3
Birchwood Ave
Birchwood LN6 200 D1
Kingston upon Hull HU5 179 A7
Birchwood Cl 4 NG31 210 F7
Birch Wood Cl 14 DN18 3 E1
Birchwood Jun Sch LN6 204 C8
Birchwood Rd
Scunthorpe DN16 185 A4
1 Sleaford NG34 212 D6
Birchwood Sh Ctr LN6 204 C8
Birchwood View 2 DN21 197 F5
Birdcroft La DN10 40 A3
Birds Dro PE11 145 C4
Bird's Dro Gorefield PE13 169 D1
Sutton St James PE12 169 B8
Birds Holt Cl LN6 200 A3
Birds Wood Nature Reserve★
DN9 26 F4
Birkbeck Sch & Com Arts Coll
LN11 50 E7
Birkdale Lincoln LN5 205 D1
Birkdale *continued*
9 Waltham DN37 194 C4
Birkdale Ave 1 PE4 221 A3
Birkdale Cl
3 Grantham NG31 211 D7
Heighington/Washingborough
LN4 203 E1
Kingston upon Hull HU10 178 B8
1 Skegness PE25 206 D6
8 Spalding PE11 214 C2
8 Woodhall Spa LN10 97 C5
Birkdale Dr 3 DN40 186 D5
Birkdale Rd DN17 184 D3
Birkdale Square DN21 197 E6
Birkdale Way HU9 181 D8
Birketts La LN11 49 D5
BIRKHOLME NG33 152 B6
Birkland La NG23 78 D5
Birkwood PE22 98 E2
Birkwood La PE22 98 E3
Birmingham Cl 5 NG31 210 E5
Birrel St DN21 197 B6
BIRTHORPE NG34 143 A8
Birthorpe Rd NG34 143 A8
BISCATHORPE LN11 59 D3
Biscay Cl 1 PE25 206 A6
Bishop Alexander L.E.A.D.
Acad NG24 104 A6
Bishop Blunt Cl 2 HU13 178 F1
BISHOPBRIDGE LN8 44 C1
Bishop Cockin Cl HU13 179 A1
Bishop Creighton Prim Sch
PE1 226 B2
Bishopdale Cl NG31 129 F5
Bishop Grosseteste Univ Coll
Lincoln LN1 201 F6
Bishop Gurdon Cl 4
HU13 178 F1
Bishop Kempthorne Cl 3
HU13 178 F1
Bishop King Ct 7 LN5 201 F1
Bishop La HU1 181 A6
Bishop La Staithe HU2 181 A6
BISHOP NORTON LN8 43 D3
Bishop Norton Rd LN8 43 E1
Bishops Cl
6 Bourne PE10 213 E4
Louth LN11 198 E6
Peterborough PE1 226 D5
Bishops Ct 3 NG34 212 D5
Bishopsfield PE4 221 B1
Bishops Gate LN1 201 E8
Bishop's La LN8 47 D7
Bishop's Pal The★ LN2 234 B3
Bishop's Pl 5 LN2 68 C6
Bishops Rd
Leasingham NG34 121 B7
Lincoln LN2 202 C5
Bishop's Rd PE1 226 A1
Bishops Wlk 5 PE9 172 D3
Bishop's Wlk 1 DN34 191 C6
Bishop Temple Ct HU13 178 F3
Bishopthorpe Rd DN35 192 F3
Bishop Tozer Cl 9 PE24 102 E8
BITCHFIELD NG33 141 B3
Bittern Cl
23 Barton-upon-Humber
DN18 3 E1
Kingston upon Hull HU4 179 D2
Bittern Way
3 Birchwood LN6 204 D8
Wyberton PE21 136 F8
BJ's Leisure Ctr PE25 90 E3
Black And Amber Wy 4
HU4 179 E5
Black Bank Ealand DN17 16 F7
Messingham DN17 29 A6
Blackbarn Road PE12 148 D2
Black Bear La PE13 170 F1
Blackberry Cl 9 LN6 93 A8
Blackberry Way 3 NG24 104 C1
Blackberry Wy 25 NG24 104 C1
Blackbourn Cl 20 NG23 91 D5
Blackbourn Rd LN6 205 C6
Blackbrook Rd 4 NG24 104 B5
Blackburn Ave HU15 2 C5
Blackburn Cl 2 NG31 210 D5
Black Dike PE13 169 E6
Blackdown Garth PE4 221 B3
Black Dro Anwick LN4 109 D2
Baston PE6 165 B8
Ewerby & Evedon NG34 122 E8
Midville PE22 100 D2
Thorney PE6 175 F5
Wisbech St Mary PE13 177 B4
Black Drove PE22 114 A8
Black Dyke PE13 169 F4
Blackdykes Rd DN9 28 B4
Blackey La PE22 99 B4
Black Fen La LN4 82 C4
Blackfriargate HU1 181 A5
Blackfriars Ct 5 LN2 202 E6
Blackfriars Rd LN2 202 E6
Blackfriars St 15 PE9 219 C5
Blackfriars Wlk 6 LN2 202 E6
Blackhill La LN9 73 F1
Black Hole Dro PE11 155 F8
Black Horse Dr 8 LN6 93 A8
BLACKJACK PE20 135 E6
Blackjack Rd PE20 135 C6
Black La
Doddington & Whisby LN6 79 E3
Gorefield PE13 169 C2
Blackmead PE2 230 B4
Blackmoor La DN9 27 D3
Blackmoor Rd
Aubourn Haddington & South
Hykeham LN5 93 C5
Blackmoor Rd *continued*
Haxey DN9 27 D2
Black Prince Ave PE6 217 B6
Black's Cl 17 LN5 93 F7
Blacksmith Cl 9 DN9 27 D7
Blacksmith Hill DN15 1 E3
Blacksmith La
Boothby Graffoe LN5 94 A2
East Keal PE23 100 D6
2 Harmston LN5 93 F5
Thorpe on the Hill LN6 92 E8
Blacksmith Rd
4 Fiskerton LN3 82 A7
Miningsby PE22 99 E7
Blacksmith Row 1 LN5 92 F3
Blacksmiths Cl 2 DN19 11 C7
Blacksmith's Cnr 5 LN4 207 A5
Blacksmiths Ct 10 LN4 95 C4
Blacksmiths La
North Scarle LN6 78 E1
South Willingham LN8 59 A2
17 Spilsby PE23 88 A1
Welby NG32 130 F5
Blacksmith's La
13 Navenby/Wellingore
LN5 107 A7
Norton Disney LN6 92 B2
Blacksmith's Row PE11 156 B7
Black Swan Cr PE7 230 B2
Black Swan Spinney PE8 222 A4
Blackthorn 5 PE9 218 C7
Blackthorn Ave 15 DN36 36 C8
Blackthorn Cl
1 Gainsborough DN21 197 F5
1 Lincoln LN2 202 C8
3 Market Deeping PE6 217 D6
13 Ruskington NG34 108 E1
Scunthorpe DN15 182 C6
Blackthorn Ct 4 HU3 180 D6
Blackthorne Cl 4 NG24 104 B3
Blackthorn La
Boston PE21 209 C5
Cammeringham LN1 54 E1
Cherry Willingham/Reepham
LN3 203 E7
Kingston upon Hull HU10 178 F7
Blackthorns The
4 Broughton DN20 19 D4
6 Sleaford NG34 212 D3
Blackthorn Way PE10 213 E5
Blackwell Rd PE7 230 C2
Bladon Est PE21 209 F4
Bladons Wlk HU10 178 D8
Blaides Staithe 1 HU1 181 A6
Blair Wlk DN40 186 E3
Blake Ave DN17 184 E7
Blake Cl 2 HU2 180 E7
Blakeney Lea 4 DN35 192 F1
Blanchard Cl PE10 142 F2
Blanchard Rd LN11 198 E3
Blandford Gdns 6 PE1 226 E7
Blands Hill LN8 47 D5
Blanket Row HU1 180 F5
BLANKNEY LN4 95 D3
Blankney Cl 4 LN1 66 D2
Blankney Cres LN2 201 F8
Blankney Ct 13 DN15 9 A5
Blankney Dro LN10 96 E5
Blankney Moor La LN4 95 E3
Blankney N Dro LN4 96 B5
Blashfield Cl 2 PE9 219 A6
Blasket Rd HU14 3 B4
Blasson Way 12 NG34 133 B1
Blatherwick Rd NG24 104 B4
Blaydon Gr 1 DN34 190 E4
Blazegate PE12 216 B8
BLEASBY LN8 58 A3
BLEASBY MOOR LN3 57 F2
Bleasby Moor Road LN3 57 E2
Bledwick Dro PE13 170 C3
Blenheim Ave HU15 2 C5
Blenheim Cl
17 Hatfield DN7 14 D3
Louth LN11 198 B7
9 Skegness PE25 206 B6
Skellingthorpe LN6 79 F6
Blenheim Ct DN16 185 A2
Blenheim Pl DN35 192 E4
Blenheim Rd
Coningsby LN4 207 C4
Lincoln LN1 201 D4
Moorland Prison DN7 26 A8
Blenheim Square LN1 201 E7
Blenheim St HU5 180 B8
Blenheim Way
Londonthorpe & Harrowby
Without NG31 211 D3
Market Deeping PE6 217 B7
Yaxley PE7 233 E5
Blenkin St HU9 181 B7
Blind La Coleby LN5 93 F3
Hough-on-the-Hill NG32 118 E7
4 Maxey PE6 173 C7
22 Waddington LN5 93 F7
Blithfield PE7 233 E8
Bloomfield Ave HU5 179 C8
Bloom La DN15 8 C1
Bloomsbury Ct 1 HU3 180 D6
Bloomsbury Gdns DN33 191 B2
Blossom Ct PE3 225 B8
Blossom Way 1 DN40 186 B3
Blow Row DN9 27 E6
Blow's La PE20 135 F3
BLOXHOLM LN4 108 C4
Bloxholm La Blankney LN4 95 A2

Bloxholm La continued
Bracebridge Heath LN4 . . . . . .81 B1
Nocton LN4 . . . . .94 D6
Bloxholm Lane LN4 . . . . .108 C5
Bluebell Ave PE1 . . . . .226 A8
Bluebell Cl 7 Lincoln LN5 . .205 C2
Scunthorpe DN15 . . . . .183 C3
Bluebell Cl 23 Healing DN41 . 23 C5
8 Owston Ferry DN9 . . . . . .28 A3
Bluebell Gdns HU13 . . . . . . 3 E4
Bluebell Gr 1 DN20 . . . . . . .196 B4
Bluebell Rd 2 PE9 . . . . .218 D7
Bluebells 8 PE6 . . . . .217 D6
Bluebells The PE12 . . . . . . .215 A6
Bluebell Wk LN6 . . . . .92 D5
Bluebell Wlk PE21 . . . . .208 B4
Blueberry Cl HU4 . . . . .179 C4
Bluebird Way HU15 . . . . 2 C5
Bluecoat Meres Acad
NG31 . . . . .210 E3
Bluecoat St The PE9 . . . . . . .219 B6
Bluegate NG32 . . . . .211 A5
Blue Gowt Dro PE11 . . . . . . .214 A7
Blue Gowt La PE11 . . . . .214 B7
Blue Horse Ct NG33 . . . . . . .140 A5
Blue St 7 PE21 . . . . .208 E4
Bluestone Cl DN32 . . . . .192 A8
Bluestone Heath Rd
Scambleby LN11 . . . . .73 A7
Skendleby PE23 . . . . .88 D5
South Ormsby cum Ketsby
LN11 . . . . .74 B3
South Thoresby LN13 . . . . . .75 A1
Tetford LN11 . . . . .73 F3
Ulceby with Fordington LN13 . 88 B8
Welton le Wold LN11 . . . . . . .60 A4
Bluestone La DN40 . . . . .186 B4
Bluestone Rise LN11 . . . . . . .198 B4
Bluestone Way 24 LN12 . . . . .77 A7
Blundell Ave DN35 . . . . .189 E1
Blundell Pk (Grimsby Town
FC) DN35 . . . . .192 C8
BLYBOROUGH DN21 . . . . . . .42 E5
Blyth Ct 28 DN18 . . . . .10 F8
Blyth St 2 HU9 . . . . .181 B7
Blyth Way DN37 . . . . .23 E2
BLYTON DN21 . . . . .41 C5
Blyton Cl 11 LN6 . . . . .204 C7
Blyton cum Laughton CE Sch
DN21 . . . . .41 C5
Blyton Gr 13 LN6 . . . . .204 C7
Blyton Rd
12 Birchwood LN6 . . . . . . .204 C7
Laughton DN21 . . . . .41 B8
Skegness PE25 . . . . .206 C6
Thonock DN21 . . . . .197 C8
BMI The Lincoln Hospl
LN2 . . . . .234 B4
Boardsides Frampton PE20 124 F2
Wyberton PE21 . . . . .208 A3
Boating Dyke Way 19 DN8 . 15 A8
Boatswain Croft 7 HU1 . . .180 F7
Bobbin La LN2 . . . . .202 E6
Bob Rainsforth Way DN21 197 F6
Bodiam Way DN32 . . . . .191 F8
Bodmin Cl DN17 . . . . .184 D8
Bodmin Moor Cl LN6 . . . . . .204 D1
Bog Gate DN14 . . . . 6 D8
Boggle La LN8 . . . . .45 E5
BOLE DN22 . . . . .52 C5
Boleyn Ave PE2 . . . . .230 C8
Bolingbroke Castle (remains
of) ★ PE23 . . . . .100 A7
Bolingbroke Rd
Cleethorpes DN35 . . . . .193 A3
Louth LN11 . . . . .198 B8
Mavis Enderby PE23 . . . . . . .87 B1
Scunthorpe DN17 . . . . .184 E4
Bolle Rd LN11 . . . . .198 C6
Bolsover Rd
Earlsfield NG31 . . . . .210 F1
Scunthorpe DN31 . . . . .182 B2
Boltgate La DN17 . . . . 7 C3
Bolton Ave LN6 . . . . .205 A3
Bolton's La PE25 . . . . .90 D2
Bomber Cty Aviation Mus ★
DN21 . . . . .42 F1
Bon Accord Rd HU13 . . . . . .178 E1
Bona La PE13 . . . . .169 E1
BONBY DN20 . . . . .10 C2
Bonby Gr 2 Grimsby DN33 191 A3
Scunthorpe DN17 . . . . .184 F5
Bonby La DN20 . . . . .10 D3
Bonby Rd DN20 . . . . .10 C1
Bond Hays La 3 PE23 . . . . . .87 A4
Bond St 1 Boston PE21 . . . .208 F4
Kingston upon Hull HU1 . . . .180 F7
Bonemill La NG34 . . . . .121 E6
Bonnetable Rd LN9 . . . . .199 D3
Bonnyhale Rd DN17 . . . . .16 E6
Bonsdale Lane DN21 . . . . . . .41 F5
BONTHORPE LN13 . . . . .89 B7
Bonthorpe Rd LN13 . . . . .89 B7
Boole Cl LN2 . . . . .202 A6
Boongate PE1 . . . . .226 C3
Boonground La PE22 . . . . . .115 A3
Bootham Cl 6 DN7 . . . . .14 D4
Bootham Cres 12 DN7 . . . . . .14 D5
Bootham La DN7 . . . . .14 D5
Bootham Rd 11 DN7 . . . . . . .14 D5
Boothby Cl 14 PE20 . . . . . . .136 C6
BOOTHBY GRAFFOE LN5 . . . .94 A2
BOOTHBY PAGNELL NG33 . .140 E5
Boothby Pagnell Manor
House ★ NG33 . . . . .140 E5

Boothferry Park Halt 1
HU4 . . . . .179 E5
Boothferry Rd HU13 . . . . . . .178 B2
Booth Nooking La DN15 . . . . 2 A2
Boot La PE20 . . . . .136 E3
Borman's La 7 DN36 . . . . . . .36 B1
Boroughfield Rd 8 PE2 . . . .230 F5
Borrowdale Cl PE4 . . . . .221 C3
Borrowdale Way NG31 . . . . .211 B8
Borthwick Pl PE2 . . . . .229 D6
Bos App Rd DN16 . . . . .185 F7
Boscombe Cl 12 LN6 . . . . . .204 C6
BOSTON PE21 . . . . .209 C6
Boston Aerodrome PE21 . . .125 B2
Boston Coll (De Montfort
Campus) PE21 . . . . .209 B3
Boston Coll (Rochford
Campus) PE21 . . . . .209 A4
Boston Ent Pk PE21 . . . . . . .208 A4
Boston Gram Sch PE21 . . . . .209 A4
Boston Hawthorn Tree Sch
PE21 . . . . .209 D4
Boston High Sch PE21 . . . . .209 B7
BOSTON LONG HEDGES
PE22 . . . . .126 B6
Boston Long Hedges
PE22 . . . . .126 C6
Boston Pioneers Free Sch
Acad PE21 . . . . .208 F5
Boston Rd
Algarkirk PE20 . . . . .136 A3
Frithville PE22 . . . . .125 E7
Gosberton PE11 . . . . .145 C6
Heckington NG34 . . . . .122 E2
Holbeach PE12 . . . . .215 C4
Horncastle LN9 . . . . .199 C1
Revesby PE22 . . . . .99 C3
Sleaford NG34 . . . . .212 D4
14 Spilsby PE23 . . . . .88 A1
Swineshead PE20 . . . . .124 D1
Wainfleet St Mary PE24 . . . .102 D1
Boston Rd N PE12 . . . . .215 C5
Boston Rd Pits Nature
Reserve ★ PE11 . . . . .145 C6
Boston Rd S PE12 . . . . .215 D3
Boston Road Ind Est LN9 . . .199 C1
Boston Sta PE21 . . . . .208 E5
Boston Stump (St Botolph's
Church) ★ PE21 . . . . .208 F5
Boston Trade Pk PE21 . . . . .208 F6
BOSTON WEST PE20 . . . . . . .125 B4
Boston West Hospl PE21 . . .208 E4
Boston W Prim Sch PE21 . . .208 B5
Boswell Cl PE1 . . . . .225 E8
Boswell Dr LN6 . . . . .205 A5
Boswell Gr LN6 . . . . .204 F5
Boswell Rd LN11 . . . . .48 B3
Bosworth Cl 18 DN7 . . . . . . .14 D3
Botany Bay La DN3 . . . . .14 B4
Bothwell Gr 3 HU9 . . . . 5 E8
Botolph Gn PE2 . . . . .230 C7
Botolph St 7 PE21 . . . . .209 A5
Botolph's View 1 LN11 . . . . .51 C4
Botteford Jun & Inf Schools
DN16 . . . . .185 A2
BOTTESFORD
Bottesford NG13 . . . . .128 A6
Scunthorpe DN16 . . . . .185 B3
Bottesford Ave DN16 . . . . . .185 B5
Bottesford Cl 12 LN6 . . . . . .204 D8
Bottesford La DN16 . . . . . . .185 B4
Bottesford Rd
Allington NG32 . . . . .128 E6
Scunthorpe DN16 . . . . .185 B5
Bottesford Sports Ctr
DN17 . . . . .184 C3
Bottesford Sta NG13 . . . . . .128 B6
Bottle La PE13 . . . . .169 C7
Bottlings The 8 DN20 . . . . .196 C3
Bottom St NG32 . . . . .128 F7
BOUGHTON NG34 . . . . .122 C4
Boughton Ave DN15 . . . . . . .182 F4
Boulevard HU3 . . . . .180 B5
Boulevard Acad The HU3 . . .180 B5
Boulevard Ave DN31 . . . . . . .188 E1
Boulevard Gdns DN31 . . . . . .191 B8
Boulevard Ret Pk PE1 . . . . . .225 D7
Boulevard The 28 LN12 . . . . .64 B3
Boulevard Way DN31 . . . . . . .191 B7
Boulevard Wlk DN31 . . . . . . .191 B8
BOULTHAM LN5 . . . . .205 D8
Boultham Ave LN5 . . . . .201 D1
Boultham Mere Nature
Reserve ★ LN6 . . . . .201 B3
BOULTHAM MOOR LN6 . . . . .205 B6
Boultham Pk Rd LN6 . . . . . . .201 D1
Boundaries The PE12 . . . . . .215 D1
Boundary La
Auburn Haddington & South
Hykeham LN6 . . . . .93 A8
Yaxley PE7 . . . . .233 D8
Boundary Paddock 1
LN5 . . . . .107 A7
Boundary Pastures NG34 . . .212 D3
Boundary Rd DN33 . . . . .194 E6
Boundary St LN5 . . . . .205 D7
Boundary The PE21 . . . . . . .208 C5
Boundary Wy HU5 . . . . .179 D7
Boundry Wlk LN8 . . . . .56 F3
Bourges Bvd PE1 . . . . .225 D7
Bourgess Ret Pk PE3 . . . . . .225 F1
BOURNE PE10 . . . . .213 C7
Bourne Abbey CE Prim Acad
PE10 . . . . .213 D5
Bourne Acad PE10 . . . . .213 E6
Bourne Cl Lincoln LN6 . . . . .205 B6
Sleaford NG34 . . . . .212 C3
Bourne Dro PE10 . . . . .155 A5

Bourne Elsea Pk CE Prim
Acad PE10 . . . . .213 C3
Bourne Gram Sch PE10 . . . .213 D4
Bourne La 2 NG34 . . . . .108 C2
Bourne Outdoor Swimming
Pool PE10 . . . . .213 D4
Bourne Rd 20
Alford LN13 . . . . .75 F2
Baston PE6 . . . . .164 E3
Bourne PE10 . . . . .213 E2
Colsterworth NG33 . . . . . . .151 E6
Essendine PE9 . . . . .163 E3
Folkingham NG34 . . . . .142 D8
Morton PE10 . . . . .154 C6
Old Somerby NG33 . . . . . . .140 D8
Pinchbeck PE11 . . . . .155 F5
Spalding PE11 . . . . .214 A3
Swinstead NG33 . . . . .153 A5
Thurlby PE10 . . . . .164 D8
Bourne Rd Est 6 NG33 . . . .151 E6
Bourne Skills Ctr PE10 . . . .213 D5
Bourne St HU2 . . . . .181 A7
Bourne Westfield Prim Acad
PE10 . . . . .213 B5
Bourne Westfield Prim Sch
PE10 . . . . .213 B5
Bovill Cl DN31 . . . . .191 C7
Bowbridge Gdns 4 NG13 128 A6
Bowbridge La
10 Bottesford NG13 . . . . . .128 A6
Hawton NG24 . . . . .104 A1
Bowbridge Rd NG24 . . . . . . .104 A2
Bowden Dr LN6 . . . . .205 A5
Bowditch Rd PE11 . . . . .214 E3
Bower Cl PE1 . . . . .226 C5
Bowers Ave Grimsby DN31 . .191 B7
3 Louth LN11 . . . . .198 D7
Bowfield Cl DN37 . . . . .190 D8
Bow Gate PE11 . . . . .145 B6
Bowlalley La 9 HU1 . . . . . . .180 F6
Bowl Alley La LN9 . . . . .199 C4
Bowling Gn La
Chapel Hill LN4 . . . . .110 E5
11 Crowle DN17 . . . . .16 D8
Grantham NG31 . . . . .211 B3
3 Grimsby DN32 . . . . .191 E7
Bowling Gn Rd DN21 . . . . . .197 B5
Bowling Green Gdns 7
DN21 . . . . .30 B2
Bowling La DN35 . . . . .192 E6
Bowman Ave PE22 . . . . .115 A6
Bowman Cl PE21 . . . . .208 D6
Bowmandale Prim Sch
DN18 . . . . .10 E8
Bowman Mews PE9 . . . . . . .219 D5
Bowmans Ridge 1 PE23 . . . .87 F1
Bowmans Way NG32 . . . . . .128 F4
Bowman Way 7 DN40 . . . . . .186 B3
Bowness Way 1 PE4 . . . . . .221 D2
Bow Rd HU15 . . . . 2 E6
Boxer Rd PE8 . . . . .172 B1
Boxgrove Cl 8 PE6 . . . . .175 A1
Boyfield Cres 4 PE9 . . . . . . .218 E4
Boyfields 1 PE11 . . . . .145 A8
Boynton Cres 9 DN15 . . . . . . 9 A5
Boynton St 1 HU3 . . . . .180 C4
Bozeat Way PE3 . . . . .225 C6
Brabbs Ave 4 DN7 . . . . .14 E4
BRACEBOROUGH PE9 . . . . . .164 B4
Braceborough Rd PE9 . . . . . .164 B4
BRACEBRIDGE LN5 . . . . .205 D6
BRACEBRIDGE HEATH
LN4 . . . . .205 E3
Bracebridge Inf Sch LN5 . . .205 D8
BRACEBY NG34 . . . . .131 D2
Braceby Rd
Ropsley & Humby NG33 . . . .131 B1
Skegness PE25 . . . . .206 B7
Brackenborough Ct LN11 198 C1
Brackenborough Rd
Brackenborough with Little
Grimsby LN11 . . . . .49 C1
Keddington LN11 . . . . .61 C8
Louth LN11 . . . . .198 C8
Brackenbury Way PE21 . . . .208 E8
Brackenbury La LN11 . . . . . .199 A3
Brackenbury Fields NG33 140 F6
Bracken Cl
Gainsborough DN21 . . . . . .197 B7
Leasingham NG34 . . . . .121 C7
Bracken Ct LN6 . . . . .204 B1
Bracken Heen Cl 2 DN7 . . . .14 E4
Brackenhill Rd DN9 . . . . .27 E2
Brackenholmes Rd DN15 . . . 9 A2
Bracken La PE24 . . . . .90 A7
Bracken Pk DN33 . . . . .194 E8
Bracken Pl DN37 . . . . .190 C6
Bracken's La LN8 . . . . .43 C4
Bracken Way LN11 . . . . .198 C7
Brackley Cl Bourne PE10 . . .213 D7
Peterborough PE3 . . . . .225 D3
Brackwood PE2 . . . . .229 D6
BRACON DN9 . . . . .16 F2
Bracon Cl 9 DN9 . . . . .16 E2
Bradbury Ave LN5 . . . . .205 C2
Bradden St PE3 . . . . .225 C6
Bradegate Dr PE1 . . . . .226 E7
Bradford Ave DN35 . . . . .193 A5
Bradford Cl 10 NG31 . . . . . .210 D5
Bradford Rd
Boston PE21 . . . . .208 D3
Immingham DN40 . . . . .186 B4
Bradgrade La 4 HU3 . . . . . . .179 F5
Brading Ave NG31 . . . . .210 E4
BRADLEY DN37 . . . . .190 E2
Bradley Cl LN11 . . . . .198 D3

Bradley & Dixon Woods
Nature Reserve ★ DN37 . .194 A8
Bradley Dr NG31 . . . . .211 A2
Bradley La LE15 . . . . .162 B7
Bradley Rd Bradley DN37 . . .194 B6
Grimsby DN37 . . . . .190 E2
Bradley St DN32 . . . . .191 F7
Bradley Wy PE1 . . . . .226 C1
Bradman Cl LN8 . . . . .56 F7
Bradman Ct 17 DN32 . . . . . .189 C1
Bradshaw Cl 15 PE9 . . . . . . .218 E6
Bradshaw's La PE24 . . . . .90 C7
Bradshaws Terr PE21 . . . . . .209 A5
Bradway 9 LN1 . . . . .66 D7
Bradwell Cl 10 DN18 . . . . . . .10 E8
Brady St 1 PE21 . . . . .208 E6
Braeburn Ave 14 PE13 . . . . .170 D2
Braeburn Rd PE6 . . . . .217 F5
Braemar Cl
Grantham NG31 . . . . .211 C7
1 Middle Rasen LN8 . . . . . .57 B8
Stamford PE9 . . . . .218 E6
Braemar Rd
Cleethorpes DN35 . . . . .192 E4
3 Mablethorpe/Sutton on Sea
LN12 . . . . .76 F8
Braemar Rd NG23 . . . . .91 D4
Braeton La DN33 . . . . .195 A7
Braids Wlk HU10 . . . . .178 B8
Brailsford Cl 3 PE3 . . . . .225 A4
Bramar Rd 5 DN7 . . . . .14 A8
Brambleberry La PE24 . . . . .102 D2
Bramble Cl Billingham LN4 . .109 E6
Grimsby DN31 . . . . .191 C7
19 Long Bennington NG23 . .117 D3
4 Welton/Dunholme LN2 . . .68 D7
Bramble Ct 24 LN2 . . . . .68 D2
Bramble Gr 2 PE9 . . . . .218 C6
Bramble Grange 3 PE11 . . . .214 B5
Bramble Hills PE25 . . . . .103 E3
Bramble La DN15 . . . . 2 B1
Brambles The
3 Barrow upon Humber
DN19 . . . . .11 C8
Bourne PE10 . . . . .213 D7
Cherry Willingham LN3 . . . .203 B7
Grantham NG31 . . . . .211 A2
8 Helpringham NG34 . . . . .133 D7
Holbeach PE12 . . . . .215 F2
4 Market Deeping PE6 . . . .217 D6
Market Rasen LN8 . . . . .45 D1
15 Market Rasen LN8 . . . . . .57 D8
Newton on Trent LN1 . . . . . .65 D1
Bramble Way
2 Brigg DN20 . . . . .196 B4
Humberston DN36 . . . . .192 E1
Bramblewood Cl 6 NG31 210 F8
Brambling Wlk PE10 . . . . . . .143 A3
Brambling Wy DN16 . . . . . . .185 F5
Bramhall St DN35 . . . . .192 C7
Bramley Cl
1 Barton-upon-Humber
DN18 . . . . 3 F1
5 Bourne PE10 . . . . .213 C6
6 Fleet PE12 . . . . .159 C7
3 Heckington NG34 . . . . . .122 E2
4 Louth LN11 . . . . .198 C5
Bramley Cres DN16 . . . . . . .185 A3
Bramley Ct
Gainsborough DN21 . . . . . .197 F5
Lincoln LN6 . . . . .204 F4
Bramley Gr 1 DN21 . . . . .29 C3
Bramley La 6 PE21 . . . . .208 E4
Bramley Mdws 7 PE12 . . . . .159 D7
Bramley Rd
Market Deeping PE6 . . . . . .217 B5
11 Wisbech PE13 . . . . .170 C1
Bramley Wlk PE25 . . . . .206 C6
Bramley Wy DN10 . . . . .40 A4
Bramling Way NG34 . . . . . . .212 F4
BRAMPTON LN1 . . . . .65 E6
Brampton Ct PE2 . . . . .231 D6
Brampton Way DN35 . . . . . .192 D3
Bramwith La DN7 . . . . .14 A6
Brancaster Dr Lincoln LN6 .205 C8
Skegness PE25 . . . . .206 D5
Brancepeth Pl PE2 . . . . .230 E7
Branches La PE22 . . . . .159 A7
BRAND END PE22 . . . . .126 D4
Brand End Rd PE22 . . . . . . .126 E4
Brandesburton St HU3 . . . . .180 B7
BRANDON NG32 . . . . .118 D7
Brandon Cl 1 NG34 . . . . . . .104 C2
Brandon Rd
Hough-on-the-Hill NG32 . . .118 E6
Scunthorpe DN15 . . . . .182 C6
Stubton NG23 . . . . .118 C7
Brandy Wharf Cider Ctr ★
DN21 . . . . .44 A7
Brandy Wharf Rd DN21 . . . . .43 E6
Brankwell Cres DN17 . . . . . .184 E3
BRANSBY LN1 . . . . .66 E6
Bransby Home of Rest for
Horses ★ LN1 . . . . .66 D6
Bransdale Gr HU9 . . . . .181 F8
Bransdale Rd 5 DN16 . . . . . .185 D5
Bransdale Way DN37 . . . . . .190 E8
BRANSTON
Branston and Mere LN4 . . . . .81 E2
Croxton Kerrial NG32 . . . . . .138 A4
BRANSTON BOOTHS LN4 . . . .82 C4
Branston CE Inf Sch LN4 . . . .81 D2
Branston Cl Lincoln LN6 . . . .205 B4
4 Winthorpe NG24 . . . . . .104 B7
Branston Cswy LN3 . . . . .82 F3

Branston Jun Sch LN4 . . . . . .81 E2
Branston La LN4 . . . . .94 D7
Branston Rd
Branston NG32 . . . . .138 A4
4 Lincoln LN4 . . . . .81 E3
BRANT BROUGHTON LN5 . . .105 F5
Brant Broughton CE
Methodist Prim Sch
LN5 . . . . .105 F5
BRANTINGHAM HU15 . . . . 2 C8
Brantingham Rd HU15 . . . . . . 2 B7
Brant Rd Fulbeck NG32 . . . . .105 F1
Lincoln LN5 . . . . .205 D2
Scunthorpe DN15 . . . . .182 E2
Waddington LN5 . . . . .93 D7
Brassey Cl PE1 . . . . .225 E6
BRATOFT PE24 . . . . .102 B7
Bratoft Cnr PE24 . . . . .102 D7
Bratoft End PE24 . . . . .102 C5
Brats La LN8 . . . . .47 E5
Bratt Field Rd DN21 . . . . . . .53 F8
Bratt Field South Rd DN21 . 54 A8
BRATTLEBY LN1 . . . . .67 C8
Brattleby Cres LN2 . . . . .201 F7
Brauncewell Cl 18 NG34 . . .108 C2
Brauncewell Rd 6 NG34 . . . .107 C1
Bray Ave 8 LN12 . . . . .64 C2
Braybrook PE2 . . . . .230 A3
Braybrook Prim Sch PE2 . . .230 B4
Braybrooks Way 1 PE12 . . . .157 E1
Bray Cl DN33 . . . . .191 B2
Brayfields 3 PE11 . . . . .156 F8
Brayford St LN5 . . . . .234 A2
Brayford Waterfront LN1 . . .234 B2
Brayford Way 1 LN1 . . . . . . .234 A2
Brayford Wharf E LN5 . . . . . .234 A1
Brayford Wharf N LN1 . . . . .234 A2
Braygate La PE23 . . . . .100 E5
Braymere Rd PE7 . . . . .230 D2
Brazenose La PE9 . . . . .219 C5
Brazil St HU9 . . . . .181 C4
Breakneck La LN11 . . . . .198 A5
Breckland Cl 1 HU3 . . . . . . .179 F5
Brecks La Kirk Sandall DN3 . 14 A2
Stapleford LN6 . . . . .105 C8
Brecon Cl NG31 . . . . .210 D8
Brecon Way NG34 . . . . .212 B3
Breda Ct 8 PE11 . . . . .214 A2
Bredon Dr LN1 . . . . .201 D7
Breezemount Ct 2 DN7 . . . .14 C6
Brellows Hill 7 PE34 . . . . . .161 F3
Bremerhaven Way DN33 . . .190 F3
Brendon Cl NG31 . . . . .210 D8
Brendon Garth 4 PE4 . . . . . .221 C1
Brendon Wlk 5 PE11 . . . . . .214 C6
Brent Rd LN4 . . . . .110 E8
Brentwood Cl HU15 . . . . 2 B6
Brereton Ave DN35 . . . . .192 C8
Brethergate DN9 . . . . .27 B2
BRETTON PE3 . . . . .225 A6
Bretton Cl 4 DN7 . . . . .14 D3
Bretton Ctr PE3 . . . . .225 A5
Bretton Gate 2 PE3 . . . . . . .225 A5
Bretton Gn 3 PE3 . . . . .225 A5
Bretton Way Bretton PE3 . . .225 A7
3 Peterborough PE3 . . . . . .220 F1
Brewerne PE2 . . . . .230 B4
Brewers La PE13 . . . . .170 A5
Brewery Gdns 2 DN17 . . . . . .16 D8
Brewery Hill NG31 . . . . .211 B3
Brewery La NG34 . . . . .143 B8
Brewery Rd DN17 . . . . .16 D8
Brewery St 6 PE24 . . . . .102 E8
Brewhouse Gall ★ NG31 . . . .211 A1
Brewster Ave
Immingham DN40 . . . . .186 D3
Peterborough PE2 . . . . .230 F8
Brewster Ave Inf Sch PE2 . .230 F8
Brewster La PE24 . . . . .102 C2
Brewster Rd Boston PE21 . . .209 B4
Gainsborough DN21 . . . . . .197 F2
Breydon Ct 3 DN15 . . . . 8 B4
Brian Ave
Cleethorpes DN35 . . . . .192 C3
Lincoln LN6 . . . . .185 C4
7 Skegness PE25 . . . . .206 C4
Waltham DN37 . . . . .194 D4
Briar Cl 6 Birchwood LN6 . . .200 C1
5 Lincoln LN6 . . . . .93 A8
Skegness PE25 . . . . .206 C3
2 Sleaford NG34 . . . . .212 D2
4 South Killingholme DN40 . .12 E3
Briar La Grimsby DN33 . . . . .194 D8
Healing DN41 . . . . .23 F5
Briars La 6 DN7 . . . . .14 C7
Briars The HU13 . . . . .178 E3
Briar Way
Peterborough PE1 . . . . .226 C5
Scunthorpe DN16 . . . . .182 C6
Skegness PE25 . . . . .206 C2
Briar Wlk PE10 . . . . .213 D7
Briarwood Cl 6 NG31 . . . . . .210 F7
Brickberry Cl PE7 . . . . .230 C2
Brickburn Cl PE7 . . . . .230 E2
Brickenden Rd 7 PE4 . . . . . .221 E2
Bricken Field La LN9 . . . . . . .84 C8
Brickings Way 4 DN22 . . . . .52 B3
Brick La
North Killingholme DN40 . . . .12 E5
Wrangle PE22 . . . . .114 C1
Brickstead Rd PE7 . . . . .230 D2
Brickton Rd PE7 . . . . .230 B1
Brickyard La Brigg DN20 . . . .20 C3
Folkingham NG34 . . . . .142 D8
Hundleby PE23 . . . . .87 D1
Mablethorpe & Sutton LN12 . 76 E8
Melton HU14 . . . . 2 F4

Brickyard La *continued*
Navenby LN5 . . . . .94 A1
Theddlethorpe St Helen LN12. 63 F7
Walkeringham DN10 . . . . .39 E3
Bridge Cl
Kingston upon Hull HU9 . . . .181 D6
3 Louth LN11 . . . . .198 C6
Bridge Dro PE13 . . . . .177 B7
Bridge End
Colsterworth NG33 . . . . .151 D7
Wansford PE8 . . . . .222 A4
Bridge End Cswy NG34 . . .133 F3
Bridge End Gr NG31 . . . . .211 D2
Bridge End Rd NG31 . . . . .211 C2
Bridge Foot PE6 . . . . .217 B4
Bridgegate Dr HU9 . . . . . .181 C6
Bridge Gdns 1 DN31 . . . . .188 D1
Bridgehill Rd PE6 . . . . .221 D6
Bridge La Cadney DN20 . . . .31 C6
Horkstow DN18 . . . . 9 F5
Scopwick LN4 . . . . .108 D8
Bridge Pl 22 LN1 . . . . .66 D2
Bridge Rd
Aubourn Haddington & South
  Hykeham LN5 . . . . .92 F5
Gainsborough DN21 . . . . . . .197 D3
Greetham with Somersby LN9 86 F7
Long Sutton PE12 . . . . .216 D3
4 Sutton Bridge PE12 . . . . .160 F4
Bridge St N 1 DN32 . . . . . .189 B1
Bridges Rd DN17 . . . . .184 E7
Bridge St 3 Billinghay LN4 .109 F5
2 Boston PE21 . . . . .208 F4
Brigg DN20 . . . . .196 A3
Gainsborough DN21 . . . . . . .197 C3
Grantham NG31 . . . . .211 C3
Horncastle LN9 . . . . .199 B4
Louth LN11 . . . . .198 B6
Market Deeping PE6 . . . . . . .217 D4
Marston NG32 . . . . .118 D2
19 Nettleham LN2 . . . . .68 C2
2 Peterborough PE1 . . . . . .226 A1
4 Ryhall PE9 . . . . .163 C1
Saxilby LN1 . . . . .66 D2
27 Thorne/Moorends DN8 . . .15 A8
Bridges The 24 DN18 . . . . . .10 F8
Bridge View LN8 . . . . .56 F8
Bridgeview Sch HU4 . . . . .179 C4
Bridge Vw 3 HU4 . . . . .179 C4
Bridgewater Rd DN17 . . . .184 D8
Bridle Cl Fishtoft PE21 . . . .209 C3
7 Sleaford NG34 . . . . .212 D2
Bridle La
Carlton-le-Moorland LN5 . . . .105 E8
Hampton Vale PE7 . . . . .230 B1
Bridles The 11 DN19 . . . . . .12 A8
Bridle Way 7 LN8 . . . . .70 D5
Bridle Way The LN4 . . . . . .95 B7
Bridlington Ave HU2 . . . . .180 F8
Bridport Wlk DN17 . . . . . . .184 D8
Brierholme Carr Rd DN7 . . .14 F5
Brierholme Cl DN7 . . . . .14 F5
Brierholme Ings Rd DN7 . . .14 F5
BRIGG DN20 . . . . .196 A4
Briggate Dr 19 DN17 . . . . . .29 D7
Brigg Cl 6 LN6 . . . . .204 C6
Brigg Dr HU13 . . . . .178 F3
Brigg Gr 5 LN6 . . . . .204 C6
Brigg La LN5 . . . . .105 F8
Brigg Prim Sch DN20 . . . . .196 B4
Brigg Rd
Barton-upon-Humber DN18 . . .10 E5
Broughton DN20 . . . . .19 E3
Cadney DN20 . . . . .31 D7
Grasby LN7 . . . . .33 A6
Hibaldstow DN20 . . . . .30 F6
North Kelsey LN7 . . . . .32 A5
Scawby DN20 . . . . .30 F8
Scunthorpe DN16 . . . . .183 D2
South Kelsey LN7 . . . . .32 A1
Wrawby DN20 . . . . .196 F5
Brigg Road DN21 . . . . .29 D4
Briggs La DN7 . . . . .14 C8
Brigg Sta DN20 . . . . .196 C2
Brighowgate DN32 . . . . . . .191 D6
Brighton St
2 Cleethorpes DN35 . . . . .193 A5
Kingston upon Hull HU3 . . . .180 A3
Bright St
2 Gainsborough DN21 . . . .197 C4
Kingston upon Hull HU8 . . . .181 B8
Peterborough PE1 . . . . .225 F3
BRIGSLEY DN37 . . . . .35 D4
Brigsley Rd DN37 . . . . .194 D2
Brigstock Ct PE3 . . . . .225 C6
Brigstock Rd PE13 . . . . . . .170 C1
Brimbles Way PE2 . . . . . . .229 E5
Brindle Road HU3 . . . . .179 F4
Bringhurst PE2 . . . . .230 A4
Brinkhall Way 9 LN2 . . . . . .68 D7
BRINKHILL LN11 . . . . .87 D8
Brinkhill Pottery★ LN11 . . .87 D8
Brinkhill Rd LN9 . . . . .74 D1
Brinkle Spring La LN4 . . . . .82 A4
Brisbane Cl
5 Skegness PE25 . . . . . . .206 A4
12 Waddington LN5 . . . . . .93 E8
Brisbane St HU3 . . . . .180 D5
Brisson Cl NG31 . . . . .211 C5
Bristol Arc 16 NG34 . . . . . .212 D4
Bristol Ave PE4 . . . . .220 E4
Bristol Cl
14 Beacon Hill NG24 . . . . .104 C5
Grantham NG31 . . . . .210 E4
Bristol Dr LN6 . . . . .205 C8
Bristol House Rd NG34 . . . .107 C1
Bristol Rd
Kingston upon Hull HU5 . . . .179 C8

Bristol Rd *continued*
Scunthorpe DN17 . . . . .182 C1
Bristol Way NG34 . . . . .212 D4
Bristow Rd Cranwell NG34 .107 E1
3 Cranwell & Byard's Leap
  NG34 . . . . .120 E8
Bristows Yd NG32 . . . . .118 D2
Britannia Cres DN34 . . . . . .190 D5
Britannia Gdns 3 PE11 . . . .214 C5
Britannia Terr 4 DN21 . . . .197 D3
Briton Ct 11 PE11 . . . . .214 C2
Britton Cl DN17 . . . . .7 D3
Brixham Ct Grimsby DN33 . .194 E6
7 Kingston upon Hull HU3 .180 A5
5 Kingston upon Hull HU3 .180 A5
Broach Rd NG32 . . . . .106 B5
Broadacre Pk 2 HU15 . . . . . .2 D5
Broad Avenue HU13 . . . . . .178 B3
Broadbank LN11 . . . . .198 B6
Broadbeck 7 DN21 . . . . .43 D7
Broad Cl PE1 . . . . .226 D5
Broad Dale Cl 8 LN2 . . . . . .68 F3
Broad Dro PE11 . . . . .144 B5
Broad Dro E PE13 . . . . .169 E6
Broad Dro W PE13 . . . . . . .169 B4
Broad Fen La NG23 . . . . . . .104 C1
Broadfield La 8 PE21 . . . . .208 E4
Broadfield La Ind Est
  PE21 . . . . .208 E3
Broadfield St PE21 . . . . . . .208 E3
Broadgate Gedney PE12 . . . .159 D6
Lincoln LN2 . . . . .234 B2
Whaplode PE12 . . . . .168 A3
Broad Gate
Sutton St James PE12 . . . . .169 A8
Weston PE12 . . . . .157 C1
Wrangle PE22 . . . . .114 C3
Broadgate Dro PE12 . . . . . .167 C8
Broadgate La PE6 . . . . .217 F4
Broadgate Rd
South Witham NG33 . . . . . . .151 E2
Sutton St Edmund PE12 . . . .168 F3
BROADHOLME LN1 . . . . .66 C1
Broadholme Rd LN1 . . . . . . .66 D1
Broadhurst Rd 18 PE8 . . . .172 B1
Broadings La DN22 . . . . .65 A4
Broad La Adlingfleet DN14 . . .7 B7
Bicker PE20 . . . . .135 B4
Moulton PE12 . . . . .157 F6
South Leverton DN22 . . . . . . .65 A7
Sutterton PE20 . . . . .135 F1
Whaplode PE12 . . . . .146 F1
Broadlands Ave PE10 . . . . .213 C7
Broadlands Cl 1 DN7 . . . . . .14 D3
Broadlands The PE1 . . . . . .226 E5
Broadley Ave HU10 . . . . . . .178 D6
Broadley Cl 6 HU9 . . . . . . .181 C7
Broadley Cres LN11 . . . . . .198 E6
Broadley Croft 5 HU15 . . . . .2 D5
Broadley Way 8 HU15 . . . . . .2 D5
Broad St
5 Grantham NG31 . . . . . . .211 A5
Spalding PE11 . . . . .214 D4
Stamford PE9 . . . . .219 B5
Broadstone Dr PE7 . . . . . . .233 E8
Broadsyke La NG24 . . . . . . .105 A4
Broadwater Dr 3 DN7 . . . . .14 D3
Broadwater La PE12 . . . . . .158 A4
Broadway Ashby DN16 . . . . .185 B6
Crowland PE6 . . . . .175 B8
Farcet PE7 . . . . .231 C1
3 Grimsby DN34 . . . . .190 D4
Hatfield DN7 . . . . .14 C3
2 Keelby DN41 . . . . .23 A5
Lincoln LN2 . . . . .201 F6
Mablethorpe/Sutton on Sea
  LN12 . . . . .77 A8
Peterborough PE1 . . . . .226 A3
Spalding PE11 . . . . .214 A2
Yaxley PE7 . . . . .233 D2
Broadway Cl
11 Bourne PE10 . . . . .213 C7
4 Lincoln LN2 . . . . .201 F6
Broadway Ct 5 PE1 . . . . . . .226 A2
Broadway Gdns PE1 . . . . . .226 B5
Broadway Nook 1 DN7 . . . . .14 C3
Broadway The
Morton PE10 . . . . .154 B7
Woodhall Spa LN10★ 97 D6
Broadway Theatre★ PE1 .226 A3
Broad Wheel Rd PE6 . . . . . .173 B3
Brock Cl 13 Epworth DN9 . . .27 D6
1 Grimsby DN33 . . . . .191 C2
Brockenhurst Cl LN4 . . . . .204 B7
Brockenhurst Rd 9 DN7 . . .14 E4
Brocklebank Cl LN5 . . . . . . .92 F2
Brocklebank Way NG24 . . .212 C7
BROCKLESBY DN41 . . . . .22 E6
Brocklesby Ave DN40 . . . . .186 A4
Brocklesby Cl
Gainsborough DN21 . . . . . . .197 F3
5 Kingston upon Hull
  HU13 . . . . .179 A3
Brocklesby Gdns DN35 . . . .225 C3
Brocklesby Pk Prim Sch
  DN37 . . . . .22 D4
Brocklesby Pl DN34 . . . . . . .190 E4
Brocklesby Rd
Brocklesby DN37 . . . . .22 E4
Brocklesby DN41 . . . . .22 E5
Grimsby DN34 . . . . .190 E4
Habrough DN40 . . . . .22 E8
Scunthorpe DN17 . . . . .184 F4
Ulceby DN39 . . . . .12 A1
Brocklesby Wlk LN11 . . . . .198 A7
Brocks Cl 22 PE24 . . . . .90 D7

Brockton Cl 7 HU3 . . . . . . .179 F5
Brodie Pl PE7 . . . . .230 F1
Brodsworth Rd PE7 . . . . . . .231 F5
Bromley Ave 6 NG24 . . . . .104 A3
Brompton Cl HU10 . . . . .179 A6
Bromwich Rd HU10 . . . . . . .178 F8
Bronzegarth DN32 . . . . . . .192 B5
Brookdale Rd DN17 . . . . . . .184 D6
Brook Dr 4 LN12 . . . . .64 C3
Brooke Ave PE9 . . . . .218 E4
Brooke Cl NG24 . . . . .104 B3
Brookfield Cl
Skellingthorpe LN6 . . . . .200 A5
6 Thorne/Moorends DN8 . . .15 A8
Brookfield Home Pk PE4. . .220 E2
Brookfield Rd DN33 . . . . . . .191 B1
Brookfields Ind Pk PE4 . . .220 F2
Brookfurlong PE3 . . . . .225 B6
Brook La Farcet PE7 . . . . . . .231 B2
Morton DN21 . . . . .197 F6
Scawby DN20 . . . . .20 A1
Brooklands 1 DN20 . . . . . . .19 E3
Brooklands Ave
Broughton DN20 . . . . .19 D4
Cleethorpes DN35 . . . . .193 A5
Brooklands Cl
5 Birchwood LN6 . . . . . . .204 C7
3 Collingham NG23 . . . . . .91 C5
Brooklands Rd HU5 . . . . . . .179 E8
Brooklands Wy 4 PE10 . . . .213 C5
Brooklyn Dr DN36 . . . . .193 B1
Brook Rd LN9 . . . . .199 D2
Brookside
8 Ancaster NG32 . . . . . . .120 A3
4 Brough HU15 . . . . .2 D6
Louth LN11 . . . . .198 D3
Peterborough PE4 . . . . .221 B2
Scopwick LN4 . . . . .108 C8
Brookside Cl
7 Ancaster NG32 . . . . . . .120 A3
Ruskington NG34 . . . . .108 D2
Brook St Grantham NG31 . . .211 A5
Hemswell DN21 . . . . .42 D2
Kingston upon Hull HU2 . . . .180 E7
Lincoln LN2 . . . . .234 B2
Peterborough PE1 . . . . .226 A2
Brook Way 5 NG34 . . . . . . .108 D2
Broom Cl PE1 . . . . .226 A8
Broom Ct 24 DN7 . . . . .14 D4
Broome Way PE12 . . . . .215 A2
BROOMFLEET HU15 . . . . .1 B6
Broomfleet Sta HU15 . . . . . .1 B6
Broom Gr DN16 . . . . .185 B8
Broomhill 8 LN6 . . . . .204 C8
Broomston La DN9 . . . . .26 F1
Broomwood Cl 2 NG31 . . . .210 F7
Brosley Ave 1 DN5 . . . . .14 A4
Brotherhood Cl PE4 . . . . . . .225 D8
Brotherhood Ret Pk PE4 . . .225 D8
BROTHERTOFT PE20 . . . . . . .124 F5
Brothertoft Rd PE21 . . . . . .208 D5
Brotts Rd NG23 . . . . .78 A3
BROUGH Brough HU15 . . . . . .2 C5
Collingham NG23 . . . . .91 E1
Brougham St HU3 . . . . .179 F7
Brough Cl 4 LN6 . . . . .204 C7
Brough La NG23 . . . . .91 D2
Brough Prim Sch HU15 . . . . .2 C6
Brough Rd LN6 . . . . .105 A8
Brough Road HU15 . . . . .2 B8
Brough Sta HU15 . . . . .2 B5
BROUGHTON DN20 . . . . .19 D3
BROUGHTON COMMON
  DN20 . . . . .19 F5
Broughton Gdns LN5 . . . . .205 D3
Broughton House Coll
  LN5 . . . . .105 F4
Broughton Jun Sch DN20 . .19 E3
Broughton La LN5 . . . . .93 C3
Broughton Rd
Carlton-le-Moorland LN5 . . . .92 A1
Stapleford LN6 . . . . .105 C8
Broughton's La 1 PE22 . . . .126 E3
Browndons St 4 NG31 . . . .211 A5
Brownes Rd 7 PE8 . . . . . . .172 B1
Browning Cl
3 Kingston upon Hull
  HU3 . . . . .180 D8
1 Scunthorpe DN17 . . . . . .184 E6
Browning Ct 4 LN4 . . . . . . .207 B5
Browning Dr LN2 . . . . .202 B7
Browning Rd NG24 . . . . . . .104 C3
Brown La NG23 . . . . .79 A7
Brownlow Cres 3 PE11 . . . .145 B1
Brownlow Dr 4 PE6 . . . . . . .217 E4
Brownlow Quay 1 PE9 . . . .219 C4
Brownlow Rd PE1 . . . . .226 A6
Brownlow's Dro PE12 . . . . .167 A8
Brownlow's Hill NG24 . . . . .104 D5
Brownlow Terr 20 PE9 . . . .219 C5
Brown's Church of England
  Prim Sch NG34 . . . . .133 C2
Brown's Dro PE20 . . . . .123 F2
Brown's Gate
Long Sutton PE12 . . . . .216 B1
Spalding PE11 . . . . .214 C4
Browns La 13 DN8 . . . . .15 A8
Browns Orch DN22 . . . . . . .191 D6
Brown's Rd 3 PE21 . . . . . . .209 A4
Brown St DN31 . . . . .189 C3
Browntoft La 2 PE11 . . . . . .134 F2

BROXHOLME LN1 . . . . .66 F5
Broxholme Gdns 2 LN2 . .201 E6
Broxholme La LN1 . . . . .66 F3
Broxholme Wild at Heart
Nature Reserve & Arts Ctr★
  . . . . .67 F4
Bruce Cl 7 Broughton DN20 .19 D3
Lincoln LN2 . . . . .234 C4
Bruce St DN15 . . . . .182 F3
Brudenell PE2 . . . . .229 E2
Brudenell Cl 1 PE6 . . . . . . .164 E5
Brulon Cl LN4 . . . . .207 B6
BRUMBY DN17 . . . . .185 C8
Brumby Comm La DN17. . .184 B7
Brumby Comm Nature
Reserve★ DN17 . . . . .184 C7
Brumby Cres 3 LN5 . . . . . . .93 F7
Brumby Engineering Coll
  DN16 . . . . .185 B8
Brumby Hall Gdns DN17 . .182 F2
Brumby House Dr DN16 . . .185 A8
Brumby's Terr 4 HU9 . . . . .181 D7
Brumby Wood La DN15 . . . .182 C2
Brumby Wood Nature
Reserve★ DN17 . . . . .182 D1
Brunel Ave 13 NG33 . . . . . .151 D7
Brunel Cl DN16 . . . . .185 B4
Brunel Ct 12 NG24 . . . . . . .104 B5
Brunel Dr Newark NG24. . . .104 B5
Yaxley PE7 . . . . .233 D6
Brunel Rd PE11 . . . . .214 E8
Brunslow Cl 8 HU3 . . . . . . .179 E5
Brunswick Ave HU2 . . . . . . .180 E8
Brunswick Dr PE25 . . . . . . .206 C4
Brunswick Gr 5 HU13 . . . . .178 E2
Brunswick Sq 1 LN4 . . . . . .109 F6
Brunton Way DN36 . . . . . . .195 D5
Brush Mdw La PE13 . . . . . .161 E3
Brustrokes Ceramics★
  DN37 . . . . .194 E3
Brutus Ct LN6 . . . . .93 B8
Bryans St 17 NG24 . . . . . . .104 C5
Bryant Cl LN9 . . . . .199 C3
Brynmore PE3 . . . . .225 A8
Bryony Gdns PE10 . . . . . . .213 D7
Bryony Way 5 PE6 . . . . . . .217 D6
Buccaneer Way 21 HU15 . . .2 C5
Buchanan Cl LN1 . . . . .201 D8
Buchanan Rd DN21 . . . . . . .54 F3
Buchanan St LN1 . . . . .201 D8
Buckfast Cl DN37 . . . . .188 A1
Buckfast Ct DN17 . . . . .184 D8
Buckingham Ave DN15 . . . .182 F5
Buckingham Dr 18 PE24 . . .90 D7
Buckingham Dr DN31 . . . . .182 B2
Buckingham Rd LN11 . . . . .198 A7
Buckingham St N DN15 . . . .182 F5
Buckingham St S DN15 . . . .182 F4
Buckland Cl PE3 . . . . .225 C8
BUCKLEGATE PE20 . . . . .136 F3
Bucklegate La PE20 . . . . . . .136 F2
Buckle St PE1 . . . . .226 C3
BUCKMINSTER NG33 . . . . . .150 E5
Buckminster Gdns NG31 . . .210 F2
Buckminster La NG33 . . . . .151 A7
Buckminster Pl 4 PE1 . . . .226 D7
Buckminster Prim Sch
  NG33 . . . . .150 F5
BUCKNALL LN10 . . . . .84 A4
Bucknall Ave 4 LN6 . . . . . .205 A7
Bucknall Prim Sch LN10 . . .84 B3
Bucknall's Mdw 5 LN12 . . .76 F8
Buckshot Rd PE14 . . . . .170 E3
Buckthorn Ave
3 Skegness PE25 . . . . . . .103 E4
8 Skegness PE25 . . . . . . .103 E4
Buckthorn Rd PE7 . . . . .230 D3
Buddleia Cl DN41 . . . . .23 E5
Buddleia Dr LN4 . . . . .81 D3
Bude Cl DN36 . . . . .195 C7
Bukehorn Rd PE6 . . . . .175 D4
BULBY PE10 . . . . .142 B1
Bulby La NG32 . . . . .106 C1
Bulham La NG23 . . . . .78 A1
Bull Bank LN11 . . . . .49 D7
Bull Dro PE22 . . . . .114 B5
Bullen's La PE20 . . . . .135 C4
Buller Cl 16 NG23 . . . . .91 D5
Buller St 4 DN32 . . . . .191 F7
Bullfinch La DN35 . . . . .192 E1
BULLINGTON LN8 . . . . .69 E4
Bullivant Rd DN7 . . . . .14 E4
Bull La 1 Ketton PE9 . . . . . .171 A3
Long Sutton PE12 . . . . .216 C4
North Witham NG33 . . . . . . .151 A4
4 Peakirk PE6 . . . . .174 A5
Bull Moor Rd DN7 . . . . .15 A4
Bullock Rd
Terrington St Clement
  PE34 . . . . .161 F1
Thorney PE8 . . . . .228 B1
Bullock's Short Gate
  PE12 . . . . .159 C4
Bull Pasture PE22 . . . . .126 D2

Bullpit Rd NG24 . . . . .104 C3
Bull Ring LN9 . . . . .199 B4
Bull's Bank PE11 . . . . .144 E8
Bully Hill LN8 . . . . .46 D2
Bulpit La LN6 . . . . .91 F7
Bulwick Ave DN33 . . . . .194 E7
Bungley La PE20 . . . . .136 C6
Bunkers Hill Hemswell DN21 42 E1
Lincoln LN2 . . . . .202 D6
Welton le Wold LN11 . . . . . . .60 C6
BUNKER'S HILL LN4 . . . . . . .111 E4
Bunkers Hill Cl 2 DN36 . . . .36 D4
Bunker's Hill La PE21 . . . . .136 C6
Bunkers Hill Rd 5 HU4 . . . .179 E5
Bunting Road PE21 . . . . . . .208 E3
Burchnall Cl PE6 . . . . .217 D6
Burchnall Dr 4 PE25 . . . . . .90 E3
Burcom Ave DN36 . . . . .36 D8
Burcott Garth HU4 . . . . .179 B3
Burcroft 17 PE13 . . . . .170 C1
Burdett Cl 8 PE25 . . . . .206 A6
Burdock Rd DN16 . . . . .185 C4
Bure Cl LN6 . . . . .204 F3
Burford Way PE1 . . . . .226 D6
Burgar Rd 11 DN8 . . . . .15 A7
Burgate 5 DN18 . . . . .10 F8
Burgess Cl 2 PE21 . . . . . . .209 B4
Burgess Dr 4 PE12 . . . . . . .159 C7
Burgess Rd Brigg DN20 . . . .196 B5
Little Casterton PE9 . . . . . . .218 F7
Burgfield Gn 4 PE4 . . . . . . .221 E2
BURGH LE MARSH PE24 . . . .102 E7
Burgh le Marsh Mus★ **15**
  PE24 . . . . .102 E7
Burghley Ave 14 PE8 . . . . .172 B1
Burghley Cl Birchwood LN6 .200 E1
22 Crowland PE6 . . . . .166 F1
Great Casterton PE9 . . . . . . .171 C8
3 Market Deeping PE6 . . . .217 E4
3 Nettleton LN7 . . . . .33 A3
Burghley Cres LN11 . . . . . .198 B7
Burghley Ct
1 Bourne PE10 . . . . .213 C5
27 Stamford PE9 . . . . .219 C5
Burghley House★ PE9 .219 F3
Burghley La PE9 . . . . .219 C4
Burghley Pk Cl 8 LN6 . . . . .204 F1
Burghley Rd
Birchwood LN6 . . . . .200 E1
1 Peterborough PE1 . . . . .226 A3
Scunthorpe DN16 . . . . .185 D7
8 Skegness PE25 . . . . . . .206 C1
8 Stamford PE9 . . . . .219 A7
Burghley Sh Ctr The
  PE10 . . . . .213 D5
Burghley Sq 2 PE1 . . . . . . .226 A3
Burghley St PE10 . . . . .213 C5
Burgh Old Rd PE25 . . . . . . .206 A6
BURGH ON BAIN LN8 . . . . . . .59 D5
Burgh Rd Friskney PE22 . . . .115 A7
Orby PE24 . . . . .89 C1
Skegness PE25 . . . . .103 C7
Burgin Cl NG32 . . . . .117 F1
Burgon Cres 3 DN15 . . . . . . .9 B5
Burke St (North) 2 DN15 . .183 A5
Burke St DN15 . . . . .183 A4
Burland Ct 3 LN4 . . . . .203 B2
Burleigh NG31 . . . . .211 F5
Burleigh Gdns 2 PE21 . . . .209 A7
Burleigh St HU8 . . . . .181 C8
Burley Ave DN35 . . . . .192 F3
Burley Cl DN37 . . . . .23 F2
Burley Rd 14 PE9 . . . . .163 C1
Burlies' Gate PE12 . . . . . . .159 E4
Burlington Rd PE25 . . . . . . .206 B3
Burma Dr HU9 . . . . .5 D8
Burma Rd DN16 . . . . .183 F2
Burmer Rd PE1 . . . . .225 E7
Burmor Cl 8 PE10 . . . . .213 C4
Burneside Cl LN2 . . . . .202 B8
Burnet Dr DN16 . . . . .185 C4
Burnett's Yd LN4 . . . . .33 C4
BURNHAM DN18 . . . . .11 C4
Burnham La Kirton DN20 . . .136 F4
Thornton Curtis DN39 . . . . . . .11 E4
Burnham Rd
Barton-upon-Humber DN18 . . .11 A6
Epworth DN9 . . . . .27 E6
Kingston upon Hull HU4 . . . .179 B3
New Barnetby DN38 . . . . .21 C7
Owston Ferry DN9 . . . . .28 A3
Scunthorpe DN15 . . . . .182 D2
Burnham Reach 5 DN35 . . .192 F1
Burnham Sq 2 DN9 . . . . . . .28 A3
Burnmoor Cl 3 LN6 . . . . . . .200 C1
Burn Rd DN15 . . . . .182 C3
Burns Cl Grantham NG31 . . .211 E6
Peterborough PE1 . . . . .225 F7
Burns Cres 8 NG34 . . . . . . .212 F4
Burns Gdns LN2 . . . . .202 C6
Burns Gr DN33 . . . . .191 B3
Burnside DN20 . . . . .19 D3
Burnside Ave 5 PE6 . . . . . .217 A5
Burns Rd PE9 . . . . .218 F6
Burns St DN21 . . . . .197 B6
Burnstone Gdns 4 PE12 . . .157 F7
Burnt Hill La 5 LN11 . . . . .198 B5
Burrells Cl DN17 . . . . .27 D2
Burrettgate Rd 4 PE13 . . . .170 F1
Burrett Gdns PE13 . . . . .170 F1
Burrett Rd PE13 . . . . .170 F2
Burrill La HU15 . . . . .2 B8
BURRINGHAM DN17 . . . . .17 E2
Burringham Rd
Burringham DN17 . . . . .17 E5

Burringham Rd *continued*
  Scunthorpe DN17 . . . . **184** D5
Burr La PE12 . . . . **156** F3
Burrows Cl 2 Boston PE21 **208** E7
  Grantham NG31 . . . . **211** A3
Burrows Ct PE1 . . . . **226** A5
Burrs The HU15 . . . . **2** B5
Bursar Prim Sch DN35 . . . **192** E6
Bursar St DN35 . . . . **192** E6
Bursnells La 3 LE14 . . . . . . **150** B1
Burswood PE2 . . . . **229** F2
Burtey Fen Collection The*
  PE11 . . . . **145** B1
Burtey Fen La PE11 . . . . **145** B2
Burtoft La PE20 . . . . **135** E2
BURTON LN1 . . . . **67** D1
Burton Cl PE21 . . . . **209** B7
BURTON CORNER PE21 . . . **209** B7
Burton Ct 2 Louth LN11 . . . **198** D4
  Peterborough PE1 . . . . **226** C3
Burtonfield Cl LN3 . . . . **203** E6
Burton Gravel Pits Nature
* Reserve** LN1 . . . . **67** C1
Burton Hathow Prep Sch
  LN1 . . . . **66** F1
Burton La
  8 Billingborough NG34 . . . **133** B1
  Burton Coggles NG33 . . . . . **140** E1
Burton La End LN1 . . . . **200** C8
BURTON-LE-COGGLES
  NG33 . . . . **152** D8
Burton Mews
  Heighington/Washingborough
    LN4 . . . . **203** D1
  5 Lincoln LN1 . . . . **201** E6
Burton on Stather Prim Sch
  DN15 . . . . **8** B4
BURTON PEDWARDINE
  NG34 . . . . **122** B1
Burton Rd
  Burton upon Stather DN15 . . . **8** C4
  Heckington NG34 . . . . **122** C2
  Lincoln LN1 . . . . **234** A4
  Spalding PE11 . . . . **214** B2
Burton Ridge 2 LN1 . . . . . . **201** D7
Burton St
  14 Gainsborough DN21 . . . **197** D3
  Peterborough PE1 . . . . **226** C3
BURTON STATHER DN15 . . . **8** B5
BURTON UPON STATHER
  DN15 . . . . **8** B4
Burton Way LN9 . . . . **199** D2
BURWELL LN11 . . . . **74** E6
Burwell Cl LN2 . . . . **202** A8
Burwell Dr DN33 . . . . **191** B3
Burwell Rd Belleau LN11 . . . **74** E6
  Burwell LN11 . . . . **74** D7
Burwell Reach PE2 . . . . **230** C7
Burystead PE2 . . . . **231** B8
Bush Cl HU4 . . . . **179** D3
Bushfield PE2 . . . . **229** E3
Bushfield Ct PE2 . . . . **229** E3
Bushfield Rd DN16 . . . . **183** B1
Bushfield Rd Inf Sch
  DN16 . . . . **183** A1
Bushfield Sports Ctr PE2 **229** E4
Bush Gn La Algarkirk PE20 **146** C8
  Fosdyke PE20 . . . . **136** C1
Bush Mdw La PE12 . . . . **215** A4
Bushy Cl 5 PE7 . . . . **230** D3
BUSLINGTHORPE LN8 . . . . **57** A4
Buslingthorpe Rd
  Faldingworth LN8 . . . . **57** A4
  Linwood LN8 . . . . **57** D5
Bustards' La PE14 . . . . **161** C1
Buston La LN11 . . . . **61** E3
Butcher La LN11 . . . . **198** B5
Butchers Sq HU13 . . . . **178** E1
Butchery Ct 3 LN2 . . . . **234** B2
Butforth La DN19 . . . . **11** E8
Butler Pl DN35 . . . . **192** B4
Butler's Way 14 PE20 . . . . . **135** B7
Butlin Cl 1 PE25 . . . . **206** A4
Buttercake La PE22 . . . . . . **113** F2
Buttercross Cl 2 DN41 . . . . **23** E6
Buttercup Cl
  1 Kingston upon Hull
    HU9 . . . . **181** D7
  3 Spalding PE11 . . . . **214** A2
  3 Stamford PE9 . . . . **218** C7
Buttercup Ct PE10 . . . . **217** D6
Buttercup Dr PE10 . . . . **213** D3
Buttercup La LN11 . . . . **198** A6
Buttercup Paddock 4
  PE2 . . . . **158** B6
Buttercup Wy LN6 . . . . **92** D5
Butterfield Cl 7 DN37 . . . . **23** F1
Buttergate Hill LN9 . . . . **71** F3
Buttermere Cl
  2 Birchwood LN6 . . . . **200** D1
  East Ella HU4 . . . . **179** E6
Buttermere Cres 2 DN36 . . **36** C8
Buttermere Pl 4 PE4 . . . . . **221** F3
Buttermere Way 6 DN32 . **191** B8
Butter Mkt 11 LN7 . . . . **33** B4
BUTTERWICK PE22 . . . . **126** F4
Butterwick Cl DN35 . . . . . . **192** F3
Butterwick Pinchbeck's
* Endowed CE Prim Sch The*
  PE22 . . . . **126** E3
Butterwick Rd
  Benington PE22 . . . . **126** F4
  Messingham DN17 . . . . **29** A7
Buttery Cl LN6 . . . . **204** F4
Buttfield Rd HU13 . . . . **178** E1

Butt Gate LN11 . . . . **50** B8
Butt La Barrowby NG32 . . . . **210** A6
  Goulceby LN11 . . . . **72** D6
  Laceby DN37 . . . . **23** F2
  Norton Disney LN6 . . . . **92** C2
  Theddlethorpe All Saints
    LN12 . . . . **63** E7
  Walcott LN4 . . . . **109** C7
  Wymondham LE14 . . . . **150** C2
Buttler Way 3 NG34 . . . . . . **212** C3
Butts Hill La 5 DN15 . . . . **8** C8
Butts La LN5 . . . . **92** F6
Butt's La HU4 . . . . **207** B5
Butts Rd DN18 . . . . **3** F1
Butts The LE14 . . . . **138** F1
Buxton Ct DN15 . . . . **182** B2
Bycroft Rd DN21 . . . . **197** C8
Byfield Rd DN17 . . . . **184** D6
Bygott Wlk DN36 . . . . **195** D7
Byland Cl 3 LN2 . . . . **202** E6
Byland Ct 4 HU9 . . . . **181** E8
Byland Gr DN37 . . . . **188** A1
Byrd Rd DN16 . . . . **185** E6
Byron Ave Grantham NG31 **211** E6
  Lincoln LN2 . . . . **202** A6
Byron Cl
  1 Newark-on-Trent
    NG24 . . . . **104** A3
  Peterborough PE2 . . . . **231** D6
  Scunthorpe DN17 . . . . **184** E6
  6 Sleaford NG34 . . . . **212** F4
Byron Ct 8 NG24 . . . . **104** C2
Byron Gr DN33 . . . . **191** C4
Byron Rd LN12 . . . . **64** B4
Byron Way PE9 . . . . **218** E5
Bytham Hts 3 NG33 . . . . . . **162** E8
Bythams Prim Sch The
  NG33 . . . . **153** A2
Bythorne Bank PE13 . . . . . . **169** B6
Bythorn Rd PE2 . . . . **231** C6
Bythorn Way PE2 . . . . **231** C6
Bywood Pl DN37 . . . . **190** C6

C

CABOURNE LN7 . . . . **33** D4
Cabourne Ave LN2 . . . . **202** B7
Cabourne Ct LN2 . . . . **202** B7
Cabourne Rd DN33 . . . . **191** B3
Cabourne Road LN7 . . . . **33** C7
CACKLE HILL PE12 . . . . **215** C5
Cackle Hill La PE12 . . . . **215** C5
Caddle Rd 11 DN41 . . . . **23** A4
Cade Cl 12 LN2 . . . . **68** F4
Cade Dro PE12 . . . . **159** D4
Cade La DN11 . . . . **53** D6
Cades Field Rd 24 LN12 . . . **77** A8
Cadman Way DN21 . . . . **41** A1
CADNEY DN20 . . . . **31** D6
Cadney Rd DN20 . . . . **196** C1
Cadwell Cl 4 LN6 . . . . **204** C7
Cadwell Pk Motor Racing
* Circuit** LN11 . . . . **73** B8
CAENBY LN8 . . . . **55** F8
Caenby Cl DN21 . . . . **197** F3
Caenby Cnr LN8 . . . . **55** B8
Caenby Rd Caenby LN8 . . . . **43** F1
  Cleethorpes DN35 . . . . **192** E4
  Scunthorpe DN17 . . . . **184** E5
Caenby St LN1 . . . . **201** D6
Caesar Cl 7 PE6 . . . . **164** E5
Caesar Rd LN6 . . . . **93** E8
Cagthorpe LN9 . . . . **199** B3
Cairns Way 8 LN5 . . . . **93** E8
CAISTOR LN7 . . . . **33** B4
Caistor Ave DN16 . . . . **185** B4
Caistor By-pass LN7 . . . . . . **33** B3
Caistor Cl 7 LN6 . . . . **204** C7
Caistor CofE and Methodist
* Prim Sch* LN7 . . . . **33** B3
Caistor Dr
  Bracebridge Heath LN4 . . . . **81** A2
  Grimsby DN33 . . . . **191** B3
Caistor Gram Sch LN7 . . . . **33** B4
Caistor La LN8 . . . . **46** C3
Caistor Rd
  Barrow upon Humber DN19 . . **11** B6
  Barton-upon-Humber DN18 . **11** A7
  Birchwood LN6 . . . . **204** C2
  Cabourne LN7 . . . . **33** F5
  Caistor LN7 . . . . **32** E4
  Laceby DN37 . . . . **23** E1
  2 Market Rasen LN8 . . . . . . **57** D8
  Middle Rasen LN8 . . . . **45** D2
  Rothwell LN7 . . . . **33** E2
  South Kelsey LN7 . . . . **32** A1
  Swallow LN7 . . . . **34** A5
Caistor Yarborough Acad
  LN7 . . . . **33** C4
Caithness Cl PE2 . . . . **229** D4
Caithness Rd PE9 . . . . **218** E6
Calbom Ct LN11 . . . . **49** B7
CALCEBY LN13 . . . . **74** E2
Calceby La LN13 . . . . **74** F3
Calcot St PE7 . . . . **230** D2
Caldbeck Cl PE4 . . . . **221** D2
Caldecote Cl PE2 . . . . **231** E6
Calder Ave DN21 . . . . **197** F6
Calder Cl Grantham NG31 . . **210** E3
  Immingham DN40 . . . . **186** A3
Calderdale Dr
  5 Spalding PE11 . . . . **214** D5
  Spalding PE11 . . . . **214** D7
Calder Gn 24 DN17 . . . . **29** D7
Calder Rd Lincoln LN5 . . . . . **205** C2
  Scunthorpe DN16 . . . . **185** D6
Caldervale PE2 . . . . **230** C6

Caldicot Gdns NG31 . . . . . . **210** E6
Caldicott Dr 8 DN21 . . . . . . **53** A8
Caleb Hill La
  Leake Commonside PE22 . . **113** F3
  Old Leake PE22 . . . . **114** A3
Caledonian Rd 4 PE9 . . . . **218** F6
Caledonia Pk HU9 . . . . **181** B5
Callan's La PE10 . . . . **142** C2
Callerton St East Ella HU3 . **179** F5
  2 Kingston upon Hull HU3 . **179** F5
Calthwaite Dr 25 HU15 . . . . . **2** D5
Calver Cres DN37 . . . . **190** D7
Calvert La HU4 . . . . **179** D7
Calvert Rd HU5 . . . . **179** D8
Camargue Ave DN37 . . . . . **194** F4
Camarthen Cl 4 NG31 . . . . **210** E5
Cambian Willows PE13 . . . **169** F3
Cambrai Cl LN1 . . . . **201** E7
Cambrian Cl NG31 . . . . **210** E5
Cambrian Way
  Holton le Clay DN36 . . . . . . **195** C3
  11 North Hykeham LN6 . . . **93** B8
  1 Peterborough PE4 . . . . . **221** C1
Cambridge Ave
  Lincoln LN1 . . . . **201** D4
  Peterborough PE1 . . . . **225** F5
  Scunthorpe DN16 . . . . **185** A3
Cambridge Cres 4 LN8 . . . **47** B6
Cambridge Dr
  Heighington/Washingborough
    LN4 . . . . **203** D1
  Wisbech PE13 . . . . **170** C1
Cambridge Gdns 4 PE11 **145** B7
Cambridge Mdws 6
  NG24 . . . . **104** C4
Cambridge Pk Sch DN34 . . **191** A5
Cambridge Rd
  Grimsby DN34 . . . . **190** F5
  Kingston upon Hull HU3 . . . **178** F3
  Scunthorpe DN16 . . . . **185** C6
  Stamford PE9 . . . . **219** A6
Cambridge Rd N 1 LN12 . . **64** B5
Cambridge Rd S 3 LN12 . . **64** B5
Cambridge St
  Cleethorpes DN35 . . . . **192** F6
  Grantham NG31 . . . . **211** B3
  Kingston upon Hull HU3 . . . **180** D6
Camdale La 8 NG24 . . . . . . **104** C1
Camden St 1 HU3 . . . . **180** B5
Camdon Cl 1 LN5 . . . . **205** D3
Came Ct 8 LN10 . . . . **97** D6
Camel Gate PE12 . . . . **157** B7
Camelia Cl PE4 . . . . **221** B3
Camellia Gdns LN11 . . . . . . **198** E3
Camelot Gdns Boston PE21 **209** E5
  11 Mablethorpe/Sutton on Sea
    LN12 . . . . **76** F8
Cameron Dr 3 PE11 . . . . . . **214** C3
Cameron La 3 NG24 . . . . . **104** C1
Cameron St 4 NG34 . . . . . **122** E3
Camilla Cl HU9 . . . . **181** A5
CAMMERINGHAM LN1 . . . . **54** F1
Camm's La PE22 . . . . **114** D2
Campain's La PE11 . . . . . . **166** C7
Campbell Ave DN16 . . . . . . **185** B4
Campbell Cl 4 NG31 . . . . . **210** F5
Campbell Ct HU13 . . . . **178** E2
Campbell Dr PE4 . . . . **221** C4
Campbell Gr DN37 . . . . **190** E8
Campbells Cl PE11 . . . . **214** B1
Campbells Farm Ave 1
  DN15 . . . . **17** E6
Campbell St DN21 . . . . **197** B5
Campden Cres DN35 . . . . . **192** D7
Campion Ave HU4 . . . . **179** B2
Campion Cl 3 PE11 . . . . . . **214** B6
Campion Dr PE6 . . . . **217** D6
Campion Gr 4 PE9 . . . . **218** D7
Campion Rd PE1 . . . . **226** B8
Campions Cl DN36 . . . . **195** D2
Campions' La 11 DN36 . . . . **36** B1
Campion Way PE10 . . . . . . **213** D2
Camp La NG33 . . . . **141** B1
Campling Pl PE12 . . . . **215** D7
Campling Way 2 LN12 . . . . **64** C4
Campney La LN10 . . . . **83** F1
Campus Way LN6 . . . . **201** D3
Camshaws Rd 5 LN2 . . . . **202** F6
Camwood Cres LN6 . . . . . . **200** C1
Canada La Caistor LN7 . . . . **33** C4
  Wildmore LN4 . . . . **111** A4
Canal Cl LN11 . . . . **198** D7
Canal La DN10 . . . . **40** B5
CANAL SIDE DN8 . . . . **15** A7
Canal View 12 DN8 . . . . **15** A7
Canberra Ave DN7 . . . . **26** A8
Canberra Cl 5 LN4 . . . . **207** C4
Canberra Cres
  11 Binbrook Tech Pk LN8 . . **47** B6
  Grantham NG31 . . . . **211** D7
  10 Manby LN11 . . . . **62** C6
Canberra Dr 5 LN1 . . . . **67** F5
Canberra St HU3 . . . . **180** D5
Canberra Vw
  Barrow Haven DN18 . . . . **4** A1
  Barton-upon-Humber DN18 . **11** A8
Canberra Way LN6 . . . . **200** A4
Canberra Wy LN4 . . . . **207** C3
Candidus Cl 6 PE4 . . . . . . **220** F5
Candlehouse La 9 LN13 . . **75** F3
CANDLESBY PE23 . . . . **88** F2
Candlesby Hill Quarry Nature
* Reserve** PE23 . . . . **88** F2
Candlesby Rd
  Claxby St Andrew LN13 . . . . **88** A4
  Grimsby DN37 . . . . **190** C7
Candy Bank DN9 . . . . **26** B5
Candy St PE2 . . . . **230** E8

Cane Ave PE2 . . . . **230** D7
Canister La Frithville PE22 . **112** C1
  Langrville PE22 . . . . **124** F8
Cannon Cl 16 NG24 . . . . . . **104** C5
Cannonhill Dro PE12 . . . . . **167** A8
Cannon Oakes Cl DN36 . . . **195** C6
Cannon Peter Hall CE Prim
* Sch* DN40 . . . . **186** D4
Cannon St
  Kingston upon Hull HU2 . . . **180** F8
  1 Lincoln LN2 . . . . **202** B3
  3 Louth LN11 . . . . **198** B5
Canon Cook Cl LN1 . . . . **66** D3
Canon Dr 6 PE9 . . . . **172** C3
Canon Peter Hall CE Prim Sch
  The DN40 . . . . **186** D4
Canonsfield PE4 . . . . **220** E4
Canon Stevens Cl 11 NG23 **91** D4
Canon Tardrew Cl 5
  HU13 . . . . **178** F1
Canon Tardrew Ct HU13 . . . **179** A1
Canterbury Cl
  Grantham NG31 . . . . **211** E7
  1 Scunthorpe DN17 . . . . . . **184** D7
  Spalding PE11 . . . . **214** B4
Canterbury Dr
  Grimsby DN34 . . . . **191** C6
  Heighington/Washingborough
    LN4 . . . . **203** D1
  Skegness PE25 . . . . **206** D7
  4 Sleaford NG34 . . . . **212** C7
Canterbury Rd
  1 Hatfield DN7 . . . . **14** D4
  Peterborough PE4 . . . . **220** F3
Cant's Dro PE13 . . . . **177** C4
Canturbury Cl 10 HU15 . . . . **97** C5
Canty Nook DN38 . . . . **32** E7
Canwell PE4 . . . . **221** A4
Canwick Ave LN4 . . . . **205** F4
Canwick Hill LN4 . . . . **81** A4
CANWICK LN4 . . . . **81** A4
Canwick Rd Canwick LN5 . . **81** A4
  Lincoln LN5 . . . . **234** B1
  Washingborough LN4 . . . . . . **81** A4
Cape Drive HU10 . . . . **178** D5
Capes Entry PE12 . . . . **157** A2
Capito Cl 19 LN6 . . . . **93** B8
Capitol Pk DN8 . . . . **14** F8
Capper Ave 3 DN21 . . . . . . **55** A8
Cappitt Dr 2 PE10 . . . . **164** C8
Capp's La 19 LN5 . . . . **93** F7
Capstan Way 17 DN8 . . . . . **15** A8
Captains Beck 9 PE11 . . . **145** C1
Captain's Hill NG34 . . . . . . **121** B7
Captains Wlk HU1 . . . . **180** E5
Capthorne Cl PE7 . . . . **230** C2
Caravan Pk LN6 . . . . **204** C1
CaraWy Dr LN6 . . . . **92** D5
Carbis Cl DN36 . . . . **195** C7
Cardiff Ave DN36 . . . . **195** C6
Cardigan Rd HU3 . . . . **179** E6
Cardinal Cl Lincoln LN2 . . . **202** D5
  New Quarrington NG34 . . . **212** A2
Cardinal Ct 3 DN37 . . . . . . **194** C5
Cardinals Gate PE4 . . . . . . **220** E4
Cardinal Wlk HU3 . . . . **179** A1
Cardyke Dr 13 PE6 . . . . . . **164** E5
CAREBY PE9 . . . . **163** B7
Careby Road PE9 . . . . **162** F6
Carew St HU3 . . . . **179** F7
Carholme Cl 4 PE10 . . . . . **213** D6
Carholme Rd LN1 . . . . **201** C4
Carisbrook Ct PE3 . . . . **230** B8
Carisbrooke Cl
  2 Lincoln LN1 . . . . **201** E6
  New Waltham DN36 . . . . . . **195** D7
Carisbrooke Gr PE9 . . . . . **218** E5
Carisbrooke Manor La
  DN17 . . . . **184** A5
Carisbrooke Wlk DN40 . . . **186** D3
CARLBY PE9 . . . . **163** D5
Carlby Rd PE9 . . . . **164** B3
Carleton Crest 3 PE4 . . . . **221** B1
Carline Rd LN1 . . . . **234** A3
Carlisle Cl
  6 Grantham NG31 . . . . . . **210** C5
  1 Lincoln LN6 . . . . **204** F1
Carlisle Gdns LN9 . . . . **199** D5
Carlisle St 3 DN21 . . . . **197** D5
Carlisle Way 9 LN4 . . . . **81** A2
Carlton Acad LN2 . . . . **202** E6
Carlton Ave DN41 . . . . **23** F5
Carlton Bvd LN2 . . . . **202** D5
Carlton Cl
  Humberston DN35 . . . . **193** B5
  8 Leverington PE13 . . . . . **170** B2
  Sleaford NG34 . . . . **212** C3
  2 Spalding PE11 . . . . **214** B1
Carlton Ctr Ret Pk LN2 . . . **202** D6
Carlton Ferry La NG23 . . . . **91** A6
Carlton Gr LN2 . . . . **201** F7
Carlton La Broxholme LN1 . . **67** A4
  Sutton-on-Trent NG23 . . . . . **91** A7
CARLTON-LE-MOORLAND
  LN5 . . . . **105** E8
Carlton Mews 9 LN4 . . . . . **203** D1
Carlton Pk LN11 . . . . **62** C5
Carlton Rd Ancaster NG32 . **119** E3
  Bassingham LN5 . . . . **92** E2
  Boston PE21 . . . . **208** D5
  Grimsby DN34 . . . . **191** B6
  9 Healing DN41 . . . . **23** F5
  Hough-on-the-Hill NG32 . . **119** B5
  Manby LN11 . . . . **62** C6
  7 Newark-on-Trent NG24 **104** A3
Carlton Rd Acad PE21 . . . . **208** E5
Carlton Road LN11 . . . . **62** B3
CARLTON SCROOP NG32 . . **119** D3

Carlton St
  Kingston upon Hull HU3 . . . **179** F4
  1 Lincoln LN2 . . . . **234** A4
  12 Scunthorpe DN15 . . . . . **183** B3
Carlton Wlk LN2 . . . . **202** A7
Carlyle Cl DN35 . . . . **193** A2
Carlyle Wlk LN2 . . . . **202** B6
Carmel Ave 5 PE2 . . . . **230** E8
Carmel Gn PE21 . . . . **208** E2
Carmen Cres DN36 . . . . . . **195** C3
Carnaby Gr 2 DN32 . . . . . . **192** A5
Carnarvon Ave 1 DN34 . . . **191** B4
Carn Cl 3 LN5 . . . . **205** D2
Carnegie Rd 21 PE8 . . . . . **172** B1
Carnegie St 6 HU3 . . . . **180** A6
Carnell La 16 NG24 . . . . . . **104** C1
Carnforth Cres DN34 . . . . . **191** A5
Carnforth Parade DN34 . . . **191** A5
Carnoustie
  Spalding PE11 . . . . **214** C2
  7 Waltham DN37 . . . . **194** C4
Carnoustie Cl
  Harrowby Est NG31 . . . . . . **211** E7
  2 Woodhall Spa LN10 . . . . **97** C5
Carnoustie Ct
  Port Sutton Bridge PE12 . . **160** F4
  Tydd St Giles PE13 . . . . **170** A7
Carnoustie Dr LN6 . . . . **204** B3
Carol Dickson Ct 3 HU3 . . **180** C5
Caroline Cl 12 NG34 . . . . . **212** F4
Caroline Ct 10 PE21 . . . . . **209** A5
Caroline Pl HU2 . . . . **180** F7
Caroline Rd 5 LN4 . . . . **95** D4
Caroline St 10 Alford LN13 . . **75** F2
  Kingston upon Hull HU3 . . . **180** F8
Carpenters Cl LN8 . . . . **70** C4
Carradale PE2 . . . . **229** D5
Carral Cl LN5 . . . . **205** C3
Carram Way LN1 . . . . **201** C2
Carr Dike La HU15 . . . . **1** C7
Carr Dyke Bank
  Kelfield DN17 . . . . **28** C5
  West Butterwick DN17 . . . . . **28** D5
Carr Dyke Rd DN17 . . . . **17** D3
Carre's Gram Sch NG34 . . **212** D5
Carre's Sq LN4 . . . . **109** A8
Carre St NG34 . . . . **212** D4
Carr Gate LN4 . . . . **109** F6
Carrhouse Rd DN9 . . . . **16** D1
Carrier Cl 5 PE3 . . . . **230** D8
CARRINGTON PE22 . . . . **112** C6
Carrington Cl
  Coningsby LN4 . . . . **207** D5
  2 Spalding PE11 . . . . **214** B3
Carrington Dr
  Deeping St Nicholas PE11 . **165** F5
  8 Humberston DN36 . . . . . **36** D8
  Lincoln LN6 . . . . **204** F7
Carrington Rd
  Carrington PE22 . . . . **112** D3
  Moulton PE12 . . . . **146** C3
  Spalding PE11 . . . . **214** B4
Carrington Rd South PE6 . **175** C7
Carrington St 6 HU3 . . . . . . **180** B5
Carr La 6 Alford LN13 . . . . . **75** F2
  Appleby DN15 . . . . **9** D2
  Bishop Norton LN8 . . . . **43** F3
  Blyton DN21 . . . . **41** B5
  Bonby DN20 . . . . **10** B1
  Broomfleet HU15 . . . . **1** B7
  Broughton DN20 . . . . **196** A6
  Burton upon Stather DN15 . . . **8** D4
  Doddington & Whisby LN6 . . **79** D6
  Gainsborough DN21 . . . . . . **197** C1
  Garthorpe & Fockerby DN17 . . **7** E4
  Grimsby DN32 . . . . **192** B7
  Haxey DN9 . . . . **27** E2
  Healing DN41 . . . . **23** F4
  Hibaldstow DN20 . . . . **31** A6
  Horkstow DN18 . . . . **9** F4
  Kingston upon Hull HU1 . . . **180** E6
  Luddington & Haldenby DN17 . **7** C1
  Misterton DN10 . . . . **39** F5
  Redbourne DN21 . . . . **30** F3
  Skinnand LN5 . . . . **106** D7
  Stallingborough DN41 . . . . . . **23** F7
  Ulceby DN39 . . . . **12** B3
  West Butterwick DN17 . . . . . **28** C8
  Wildsworth DN21 . . . . **40** F8
  Winterton DN15 . . . . **9** D6
  Worlaby DN20 . . . . **20** B7
Carroll Pl 4 HU1 . . . . **181** A7
Carron Cl 3 LN3 . . . . **83** B4
Carron Dr PE4 . . . . **220** E3
Carr Rd
  Gringley on the Hill DN10 . . **39** A4
  North Kelsey LN7 . . . . **31** E4
  Peterborough PE1 . . . . **226** D3
Carrside DN9 . . . . **27** D6
Carr Side La DN7 . . . . **14** E2
Carr St
  9 Kingston upon Hull
    HU2 . . . . **180** F8
  Lincoln LN1 . . . . **201** C4
Carrwood Cres LN4 . . . . . . **207** C7
Carson Ave DN34 . . . . **191** B6
Carson Gr PE24 . . . . **90** B7
Carson Rd DN21 . . . . **197** C6
Carter Dr HU13 . . . . **178** F4
Cartergate DN32 . . . . **191** C7
Carterplot Rd NG34 . . . . . . **123** A2
Carters Cl 6 PE3 . . . . **224** F3
Carters Cl 1 LN3 . . . . **203** B7
Carter's Garth Cl 4 LN11 . . **50** B8
Cartledge Ave DN32 . . . . . **192** B6
Cartmel Gr DN32 . . . . **192** B6
Cartmel Way 14 PE6 . . . . . **175** A1
Carver Rd Boston PE21 . . . . **208** D3

Carver Rd continued
Immingham DN40 . . . . 186 D3
Caryer Cl PE2 . . . . 230 D6
Cary La 3 DN20 . . . . 196 B3
Carysfort Cl PE7 . . . . 233 D4
Casewick La 4 PE9 . . . . 172 F7
Casewick Rd PE9 . . . . 172 E7
Caskgate St DN21 . . . . 197 C4
Caspian Cres DN33 . . . . 191 A2
Cassbrook Dr 2 LN11 . . . . . 49 B8
Cassia Gn 7 LN6 . . . . 204 C8
Cassons Cl PE12 . . . . 157 D4
Casson's Rd 1 DN8 . . . . 15 A8
Casswell Cl 1 DN32 . . . . 189 D1
Casswell Cres 4 LN11 . . . . . 49 B8
Casswell Dr PE11 . . . . 145 A7
Castella Dr DN16 . . . . 183 D3
Casterton Bus & Enterprise
Coll PE9 . . . . 171 C8
Casterton La PE9 . . . . 218 C4
Casterton Lane PE9 . . . . . . 162 E4
Casterton Rd PE9 . . . . 218 E6
Casthorpe Rd
3 Barrowby NG32 . . . . . . 210 A5
Denton NG32 . . . . 139 A4
Castings Way LN6 . . . . 204 C3
CASTLE BYTHAM NG33 . . . 152 D1
Castle Bytham Rd
Clipsham LE15 . . . . 162 C7
Swayfield NG33 . . . . 152 E5
Castle Bytham Road PE9 . . 162 F7
CASTLE CARLTON LN11 . . 62 C2
Castle Cl
3 Bottesford NG13 . . . . . 128 B5
Spalding PE11 . . . . 214 F6
Castle Cswy NG34 . . . . 212 C4
Castle Ct 14 DN18 . . . . 10 F8
Castle Dr Epworth DN9 . . . . 27 E7
Holbeach PE12 . . . . 215 E1
Northborough PE6 . . . . . . 217 E2
Castle Dyke 13 PE9 . . . . 219 B5
Castledyke Bank PE9 . . . . . 125 A8
Castle Dyke Bank LN4 . . . . 111 B4
Castledyke Prim Sch 27
DN18 . . . . 3 E1
Castledyke S 13 DN18 . . . . . 10 F8
Castledyke W 7 DN18 . . . . . 3 E1
Castle End Rd PE6 . . . . 217 A1
Castlefields 2 PE11 . . . . 214 D5
Castleford Ave DN34 . . . . . 191 A4
Castlegate
Castle Bytham NG33 . . . . 152 D1
Grantham NG31 . . . . 211 B4
Thornton le Fen PE22 . . . . 111 F1
Castle Hill 15 Caistor LN7 . . 33 B4
4 Lincoln LN1 . . . . 234 B3
3 Welbourn LN5 . . . . 106 E5
Castle Hills Com Art Coll
DN21 . . . . 197 D7
Castle Keep DN20 . . . . 30 F6
Castle La
Boothby Graffoe LN5 . . . . 93 E1
Coningsby LN4 . . . . 207 C5
Lincoln LN1 . . . . 234 A4
Castle Lane LN11 . . . . 62 D3
Castle Rd PE21 . . . . 209 B8
Castle Rise PE9 . . . . 163 D1
Castle Sports Complex
PE11 . . . . 214 E5
Castle St Boston PE21 . . . . . 208 D6
Grimsby DN32 . . . . 192 A8
Kingston upon Hull HU1 . . 180 E5
Lincoln LN1 . . . . 234 A4
Sleaford NG34 . . . . 212 D4
12 Stamford PE9 . . . . 219 B5
Castle Terr 5 NG34 . . . . 212 C4
Castle Terr N 6 NG34 . . . . . 212 C4
CASTLETHORPE DN20 . . . . 20 A1
Castleton Bvd PE25 . . . . . . 206 D4
Castleton Cres PE25 . . . . . . 206 D4
Castleton Rd DN15 . . . . 182 B2
Castleview Coningsby LN4 . . 110 E8
Tattershall LN4 . . . . 97 C1
Castle View LN4 . . . . 109 D7
Castle View Rd NG13 . . . . . 128 B4
Castle Wy 7 Hessle HU13 . . 3 F4
7 Hessle HU13 . . . . 178 E1
CASTOR PE5 . . . . 223 D1
Castor Rd Marholm PE6 . . . 173 C1
Marholm PE6 . . . . 220 B1
Peterborough PE6 . . . . . . 224 C6
Casworth Way PE5 . . . . 223 D2
Catchpole Gr PE22 . . . . 100 B2
Cater La LN7 . . . . 44 F7
Cater Way PE21 . . . . 208 D2
Cates's Cove Cnr PE6 . . . . . 167 F4
Cathedral Ct
13 Hatfield DN7 . . . . 14 C2
Scunthorpe DN17 . . . . . . 185 A6
Cathedral Dr PE11 . . . . 214 C5
Cathedral Sq 10 PE1 . . . . . . 226 A2
Cathedral St LN2 . . . . 234 B2
Catherine Cl PE2 . . . . 230 B7
Catherine Gr 8 DN20 . . . . . 19 E3
Catherine St
6 Grimsby DN32 . . . . 191 F7
1 Kingston upon Hull HU2 . 180 F7
Catherines Way 15 PE11 . . 145 C1
Cathwaite PE4 . . . . 221 E1
Catkin Rd 6 DN16 . . . . 185 B2
Catkin Wy NG24 . . . . 104 A2
Catley PE4 . . . . 221 E1
Catling's La PE13 . . . . 170 C7
Catskin La LN8 . . . . 46 A3

Catterick Rd PE10 . . . . 213 B3
Cattistock Rd DN35 . . . . . . 192 E3
Cattle Dike PE13 . . . . 169 E2
Cattle Mkt Rd 8 PE1 . . . . . 226 A2
Cattle Mkt Way 7 PE1 . . . . 226 A1
Cattle Rd DN10 . . . . 39 B5
Caughey St HU3 . . . . 180 D7
Causeway
Burgh le Marsh PE24 . . . . 102 E7
Wyberton PE21 . . . . 136 E7
Causeway Bank La NL13 . . 63 F1
Causeway La 3 DN21 . . . . . 192 F6
Causeway Rd LN4 . . . . 109 E5
Causeway The
6 Northorpe PE10 . . . . . . 164 C8
Revesby PE22 . . . . 111 F7
Thorney PE6 . . . . 175 E2
Cavalry Ct 2 LN4 . . . . 95 D4
Cave La HU15 . . . . 2 A8
Cavell Cl PE3 . . . . 225 B4
Cavendish Ave 4 NG24 . . . . 104 A5
Cavendish Cl DN35 . . . . 193 B1
Cavendish Dr
8 Boston PE21 . . . . 136 D8
Gainsborough DN21 . . . . . 52 F5
Cavendish Mews 5 LN4 . . . 203 D1
Cavendish Pk 10 HU15 . . . . 2 C5
Cavendish Rd
Scunthorpe DN16 . . . . . . 185 A4
Skegness PE25 . . . . 206 C4
Cavendish St PE1 . . . . 226 B3
Cavendish Way
1 Birchwood LN6 . . . . . . 191 F7
Harrowby Est NG31 . . . . . 211 F7
Spalding PE11 . . . . 214 C6
Cave Rd HU15 . . . . 2 B6
Caverstede Rd PE4 . . . . 221 B1
Cave's Cl 8 PE34 . . . . 161 F3
Cave's La DN10 . . . . 39 E3
Cavill Pl HU3 . . . . 180 D5
CAWKWELL LN11 . . . . 73 A6
Cawkwell 25 LN12 . . . . 77 A7
Cawkwell Hill LN11 . . . . . . 73 A6
Cawood La PE11 . . . . 145 B5
Cawthorne 18 NG23 . . . . . . 91 D5
Cawthorne Dr HU4 . . . . 179 C3
CAWTHORPE PE10 . . . . 154 B5
Cawthra Ct NG32 . . . . 139 A7
Caxton Theatre & Arts Ctr
The ★ DN32 . . . . 189 B1
Cayley Rd HU10 . . . . 178 F6
CAYTHORPE NG32 . . . . 119 D7
Caythorpe Heath La NG32 119 D7
Caythorpe Prim Sch
NG32 . . . . 119 B7
Caythorpe Rd PE11 . . . . 134 F2
Cecil Ave PE25 . . . . 206 C4
Cecil Cl Bourne PE10 . . . . . 213 B4
16 Scotter DN21 . . . . 29 C3
Cecil Ct 18 PE9 . . . . 219 C5
Cecile Cres DN35 . . . . 182 E3
Cecil Pacey Ct PE3 . . . . 225 E7
Cecil Pywell Ave PE12 . . . . 215 C3
Cecil Rd PE1 . . . . 226 A6
Cecil St Gainsborough DN21 197 C5
Grantham NG31 . . . . 211 C3
Kingston upon Hull HU3 . . 179 F5
Lincoln LN1 . . . . 234 A4
Cedar Ave
Cherry Willingham/Reepham
LN3 . . . . 203 D5
Lincoln LN5 . . . . 205 D4
8 Newark-on-Trent NG24 . 104 A6
Scunthorpe DN15 . . . . . . 182 B6
5 Sleaford NG34 . . . . 212 D6
2 Stainforth DN7 . . . . 14 D6
Cedar Cl
4 Cleethorpes DN35 . . . . 192 D2
Gainsborough DN21 . . . . . 197 B7
Kingston upon Hull HU10 . 178 F7
1 Louth LN11 . . . . 198 B6
14 Market Deeping PE6 . . 217 A5
6 Market Rasen LN8 . . . . 57 D7
6 Ruskington NG34 . . . . 108 D1
6 Scawby DN20 . . . . 30 F8
2 Scotter DN21 . . . . 29 C3
13 Sudbrooke LN2 . . . . . . 68 F2
Cedar Ct 2 Spalding PE11 . 214 E3
The Willows DN37 . . . . . . 190 E8
Cedar Dr Bourne PE10 . . . . 213 B6
Holbeach PE12 . . . . 215 C4
Immingham DN40 . . . . 186 C5
Cedar Gr PE1 . . . . 226 B8
Cedar Rd PE2 . . . . 231 D7
Cedars The
Chapel St Leonard PE24 . . 90 D5
New Waltham DN36 . . . . . 195 E7
Cedarwood Cl 1 NG31 . . . . 210 F7
Cedarwood Dr HU5 . . . . 179 B7
Cedric Rd 10 DN3 . . . . 14 A1
Cekhira Ave 4 PE21 . . . . . . 157 E1
Celandine Cl 6 PE11 . . . . . . 214 B6
Celta Rd PE2 . . . . 230 F6
Celtic Cl PE2 . . . . 231 D7
Cemetery Cres 10 DN37 . . . 23 F1
Cemetery La LN7 . . . . 32 A5
Cemetery Rd Hatfield DN7 . 14 F4
18 Laceby DN37 . . . . 23 F1
North Somercotes LN11 . . 50 E8
Scunthorpe DN16 . . . . . . 185 B8
Winterton DN15 . . . . 9 B5
4 Wragby LN8 . . . . 70 D4
Centaur Rd LN6 . . . . 201 D2
Centenary Cl
1 Butterwick PE22 . . . . . 126 E3
2 Newark-on-Trent NG24 . 104 B2
Centenary Way PE12 . . . . . 160 F2
Centenary Wy DN16 . . . . . . 183 A1

Central Ave
Ingoldmells PE25 . . . . 90 F3
Peterborough PE1 . . . . . . 226 C7
Central Dr 7 NG34 . . . . 120 C8
Central Parade DN34 . . . . . 191 A7
Central Pl NG31 . . . . 211 D5
Central Prom DN35 . . . . . . 192 F6
Central Rd LN8 . . . . 47 A6
Central Sq Brigg DN20 . . . . 196 C4
Peterborough PE2 . . . . . . 231 D5
Central Way DN16 . . . . 183 D2
Centurion Bsns Ctr PE2 . . . 225 C7
Centurion Cl 8 LN5 . . . . . . 107 B8
Centurion Way 12 HU15 . . . 2 C5
Centurion Wy LN7 . . . . 33 A4
Century La 1 LN1 . . . . 66 D3
Century Square PE1 . . . . . . 226 A5
Cerris Rd PE2 . . . . 226 B7
Cervantes Ct 8 PE24 . . . . . 102 E8
Ceylon St 9 HU9 . . . . 5 D8
Chadburn PE4 . . . . 221 E1
Chad Varah Prim Sch The
LN2 . . . . 202 B6
Chadwell Springs DN37 . . . 194 B4
Chadwick Way LN4 . . . . 207 D4
Chafer La DN15 . . . . 8 A4
Chaffinch Cl DN15 . . . . 182 D5
Chaffinch Dr DN35 . . . . 192 E1
Chaffinch La PE7 . . . . 233 D8
CHAIN BRIDGE PE21 . . . . . 208 B3
Chain Bridge Rd PE21 . . . . 208 B3
Chain Cl PE1 . . . . 226 B6
Chaintoft La PE11 . . . . 145 A7
Chaldean Way PE11 . . . . . . 214 B6
Chalfont Ave LN12 . . . . 64 A5
Chalfont Cl HU13 . . . . 178 D2
Chalfonts The LN4 . . . . 81 E2
Chalgrove Way LN6 . . . . . . 200 E2
Chalk La
Burgh le Marsh PE24 . . . . 89 F1
Sutton Bridge PE12 . . . . . 160 F1
Withern with Stain LN13 . . 63 A1
Chalk Pit La PE13 . . . . 88 F2
Chalk Rd PE13 . . . . 169 D1
Chamberlain Way PE4 . . . . 221 F2
Chamber's Ct PE11 . . . . 214 E5
Chamber's Farm Wood Nature
Reserve ★ LN8 . . . . 83 F8
Chambers St NG31 . . . . 211 A5
Chamomile Cl DN16 . . . . . . 185 D5
Chamomile Wy PE11 . . . . . 214 B6
Champion Way LN12 . . . . . . 64 B2
Champneys Cl 6 HU13 . . . . 178 E1
Chancel Rd DN16 . . . . 185 A4
Chancel Wlk 13 DN20 . . . . . 19 E3
Chancery Cl LN6 . . . . 205 B5
Chancery Ct
Kingston upon Hull HU5 . . 179 E8
4 Spalding PE11 . . . . 214 D3
Chancery La
3 Crowle DN17 . . . . 16 D7
7 Eye PE6 . . . . 175 A1
7 Holbeach PE12 . . . . . . 215 D2
Chanctonbury Cl 20 LN11 . . 77 A8
Chanctonbury Way 19
LN12 . . . . 77 A8
Chandlers PE2 . . . . 229 E5
Chandlers Cl 1 DN36 . . . . . 195 C6
Chandlers Ct HU9 . . . . 181 C6
Chandos Rd DN17 . . . . 184 F7
Chanterlands Ave HU5 . . . . 180 A8
Chantreys Dr 18 HU15 . . . . 2 C6
Chantry Cl Grimsby DN31 . . 191 C7
Peterborough PE1 . . . . . . 226 A5
Chantry La DN31 . . . . 191 C7
Chantry The 1 PE11 . . . . . . 214 A4
Chantry Way 16 HU14 . . . . 3 B7
Chantry Way E 14 HU14 . . . 3 B7
Chapel Baulk DN9 . . . . 26 E1
Chapel Cl
Barrow upon Humber DN19 . 11 D7
Chapel St Leonard PE24 . . 90 D8
Cherry Willingham/Reepham
LN3 . . . . 203 F8
9 Misterton DN10 . . . . . . 39 F5
Northfield HU13 . . . . 179 A1
1 South Rauceby NG34 . . 120 E4
2 Westwoodside DN9 . . . . 27 B2
Chapel Ct
6 Alkborough DN15 . . . . . 8 C8
Brigg DN20 . . . . 196 C3
17 Hibaldstow DN20 . . . . 30 F5
Scunthorpe DN15 . . . . . . 183 B4
Wansford PE8 . . . . 222 B2
Chapel Dro PE12 . . . . 168 B2
Chapel Farm Dr 21 PE24 . . 90 D5
Chapelfield Rd DN19 . . . . . 5 C1
Chapel Garth
Broomfleet HU15 . . . . 1 B5
18 Tetney DN36 . . . . 36 D4
CHAPELGATE PE12 . . . . . . 159 D7
Chapelgate Gedney PE12 . . 159 D7
Kirton End PE20 . . . . 136 B7
12 Sutterton PE20 . . . . . . 136 A2
Chapel Gate
Sutton St James PE12 . . . 159 B1
Whaplode PE12 . . . . 168 B5
Chapel Gdns
3 Moulton PE12 . . . . 157 E1
2 Whaplode PE12 . . . . . . 158 B7
CHAPEL HILL LN4 . . . . 110 E5
Chapel Hill Brough HU15 . . 2 D6
Ropsley NG33 . . . . 131 B1
Whaplode PE12 . . . . 168 A4
Chapel Hill Ct 7 NG34 . . . . 212 E4
Chapel Hill La HU15 . . . . . . 2 E6

Chapel La Addlethorpe PE24 . 90 C3
Amber Hill PE20 . . . . 124 B5
Anwick NG34 . . . . 109 B1
3 Aubourn Haddington & South
Hykeham LN5 . . . . 93 A5
4 Barnetby le Beck DN37 . 35 B6
4 Barrowby NG32 . . . . . . 210 A5
Barton-upon-Humber
DN18 . . . . 10 F8
Belchford LN9 . . . . 73 B2
Branston & Mere LN4 . . . . 81 E2
Caythorpe NG34 . . . . 119 B7
Chapel Hill LN4 . . . . 110 E5
2 Claypole NG23 . . . . 117 E8
3 Croxton Kerrial NG32 . . 138 D4
5 Donington on Bain LN11 . 59 E1
Dunston LN4 . . . . 95 C5
East Kirkby PE23 . . . . 99 F5
4 Elsham DN20 . . . . 20 F7
2 Folkingham NG34 . . . . . 142 D8
4 Foston NG32 . . . . 117 F1
Friskney Eaudike PE22 . . . 115 A6
2 Fulletby LN9 . . . . 86 B8
Gainsborough DN21 . . . . . 197 B8
Glentworth DN21 . . . . 54 F7
3 Grainthorpe LN11 . . . . . 50 B8
Habrough DN40 . . . . 12 E1
Hameringham LN9 . . . . . . 86 C2
4 Harmston LN5 . . . . 93 F5
Heckington NG34 . . . . . . 122 F1
Heighington/Washingborough
LN4 . . . . 81 E4
2 Helpringham NG34 . . . . 133 D7
Hemingby LN9 . . . . 72 B1
Horkstow DN18 . . . . 10 A5
Huttoft LN13 . . . . 76 F3
Ingoldmells PE25 . . . . 90 D4
2 Keadby with Althorpe DN17 . 17 C6
3 Ketton PE9 . . . . 171 A3
Kingston upon Hull HU1 . . 181 A6
2 Leasingham NG34 . . . . . 121 B7
2 Legbourne LN11 . . . . . . 61 F3
Lincoln LN1 . . . . 234 A4
Little Hale NG34 . . . . 133 E8
Ludborough DN36 . . . . . . 48 E6
Ludford LN8 . . . . 59 A8
Manby LN11 . . . . 62 C6
6 Mareham le Fen PE22 . . 99 A4
Messingham DN17 . . . . . . 29 D7
10 Minting LN9 . . . . 84 C8
10 Misterton DN10 . . . . . 39 F5
Navenby/Wellingore LN5 . . 107 A8
18 Nettleham LN2 . . . . . . 68 C2
7 Newark-on-Trent NG24 . 104 D5
Newton PE13 . . . . 170 B5
Normanby by Spital LN8 . . 55 F7
North Cockerington LN11 . 49 F1
Northorpe PE10 . . . . 164 C8
North Scarle LN6 . . . . 78 E2
6 Peterborough PE4 . . . . . 221 A3
Scamblesby LN11 . . . . . . 73 A5
4 Scawby DN20 . . . . 30 E8
14 Sibsey PE22 . . . . 113 B1
Snitterby DN21 . . . . 43 D5
South Cockerington LN11 . 62 A8
17 Spalding PE11 . . . . 214 D4
Spalford NG23 . . . . 78 C4
Springthorpe DN21 . . . . . 53 E8
Swallow LN7 . . . . 34 B5
Tattershall Thorpe LN4 . . . 207 C8
Thimbleby LN9 . . . . 85 B4
14 Thorne/Moorends DN8 . 15 A8
Toynton All Saints PE23 . . 100 F6
Toynton St Peter PE23 . . . 101 A6
4 Tydd St Giles PE13 . . . . 169 F7
Utterby LN11 . . . . 48 F4
Welton/Dunholme LN2 . . . 68 C6
West/East Butterwick DN17 . 17 D1
Whitton DN15 . . . . 1 E3
16 Winterton DN15 . . . . . . 9 A5
2 Winthorpe NG24 . . . . . . 104 B7
Wrawby DN20 . . . . 20 E4
2 Wymondham LE14 . . . . 150 C1
Chapel La Staith 1 HU1 . . . 181 A6
Chapel Lodge Dr LN8 . . . . . 55 F7
Chapel Mews 3 HU15 . . . . . 2 C6
Chapel Nook La LN5 . . . . . . 93 B1
Chapel Pas 16 PE21 . . . . . . 208 F4
Chapel Pit Nature Reserve ★
PE24 . . . . 90 D8
Chapel Rd Branston LN4 . . . 81 E2
4 Broughton DN20 . . . . . 19 E3
Carrington PE22 . . . . 112 B8
Fillingham DN21 . . . . 54 F4
Fiskerton LN3 . . . . 82 A7
4 Habrough DN40 . . . . . . 22 E8
Ingoldmells PE25 . . . . 90 D4
Leake Commonside PE22 . 113 F3
Sutton St Edmund PE12 . . 168 E4
Terrington St Clement PE34 161 F3
Tumby Woodside PE22 . . . 111 E8
Chapel Row Baumber LN9 . 72 A1
7 Skillington NG33 . . . . . . 151 A8
CHAPEL ST LEONARDS
PE24 . . . . 90 E7
Chapel St Leonards Prim
Sch
Chapel St Leonard PE24 . . 90 D6
Collingham NG23 . . . . 91 A4
Chapel St 10 Alford LN13 . . 75 F3
3 Amcotts DN17 . . . . 7 F1
Beckingham LN5 . . . . 105 B4
2 Billingborough NG34 . . 133 B1
4 Boston PE21 . . . . 208 F5
16 Bottesford NG13 . . . . . 128 A6
13 Caistor LN7 . . . . 33 B4

Chapel St continued
4 Crowland PE6 . . . . 175 B8
12 Crowle DN17 . . . . 16 D8
6 Epworth DN9 . . . . 27 E6
Goxhill DN19 . . . . 12 A8
Haconby PE10 . . . . 154 D8
2 Holbeach PE12 . . . . 215 E2
1 Market Rasen LN8 . . . . . 57 D7
3 North Kelsey LN7 . . . . . 32 A4
Peterborough PE1 . . . . . . 226 B2
18 Ruskington NG34 . . . . . 108 E2
Scunthorpe DN15 . . . . . . 183 B3
Yaxley PE7 . . . . 233 D5
Chapel Way 6 DN20 . . . . . . 196 B3
Chapel Yd 7 PE9 . . . . 219 C5
Chaplin Cl 22 LN4 . . . . 95 D4
Chaplin St LN5 . . . . 234 A1
Chapman Ave
6 Burgh le Marsh PE24 . . 102 E7
Scunthorpe DN17 . . . . . . 184 D6
Chapman Cres DN36 . . . . . . 36 D8
Chapman Gr 1 DN35 . . . . . 192 F5
Chapman Rd
Cleethorpes DN35 . . . . . . 192 D7
2 Sleaford NG34 . . . . 212 B6
Chapman St
Kingston upon Hull HU8 . . 181 A8
3 Market Rasen LN8 . . . . 57 E7
Chapnall Cl 18 PE13 . . . . . . 170 E1
Chapnall Rd PE13 . . . . 170 E1
Chappell Rd 3 PE11 . . . . . . 166 C6
Chapter Cl LN2 . . . . 68 C7
Chapter Wk 12 DN20 . . . . . 19 E3
Charing Cl HU3 . . . . 180 C8
Chariots Way 6 PE6 . . . . . . 164 E5
Charity St NG32 . . . . 119 D4
Charles Ave
11 Ancaster NG32 . . . . . . 120 A2
Grimsby DN33 . . . . 191 D2
3 Laceby DN37 . . . . 23 E1
Louth LN11 . . . . 198 D7
12 New Waltham DN36 . . . 195 C6
18 Scotter DN21 . . . . 29 C3
Charles Baines Com Prim Sch
DN21 . . . . 197 C4
Charles Cl Bourne PE10 . . . 213 D6
1 Skegness PE25 . . . . 206 B4
Charles Cope Rd PE2 . . . . . 229 F5
Charles Gate LN11 . . . . 198 C6
Charles Hume Ct 3 DN32 . . 192 B8
Charles Lovell Way DN17 . . 184 D8
Charles Rd
5 Fleet Hargate PE12 . . . 159 C7
2 Stamford PE9 . . . . 219 A7
12 Sutton Bridge PE12 . . . 160 E4
Charles Read Acad NG33 . . 132 F7
Charles St WN1 . . . . 201 D4
Charles St Boston PE21 . . . 209 A3
2 Cleethorpes DN35 . . . . 192 F5
3 Kingston upon Hull HU2 . 180 F7
Lincoln LN5 . . . . 234 B1
Louth LN11 . . . . 198 C6
Newark-on-Trent NG24 . . 104 A4
Peterborough PE1 . . . . . . 226 B3
1 Sleaford NG34 . . . . 212 C4
Wrangle PE22 . . . . 114 C2
Charleston 12 NG32 . . . . . . 120 A3
Charlestown Way HU9 . . . . 181 C6
Charlesworth St 2 LN1 . . . . 201 D3
Charles Wright Cl 15 LN12 . 64 B4
Charlette Way 13 PE11 . . . . 214 B5
Charlock Dr PE9 . . . . 218 D6
Charlotte Cl 4 LN8 . . . . 57 E8
Charlotte St 5 HU1 . . . . 181 A7
Charlotte Wlk 5 PE11 . . . . . 145 A8
Charlotte Wy PE3 . . . . 225 D3
Charlton Cr 8 PE7 . . . . 230 B1
Charlton Ct PE3 . . . . 225 B1
Charlton St DN31 . . . . 188 E1
Charnwood Cl PE2 . . . . 231 A7
Charter Ave PE6 . . . . 217 C6
Charter Cl PE21 . . . . 208 E7
Charterhouse Ct PE21 . . . . 208 B5
Charterhouse Dr DN16 . . . . 185 C4
Charterhouse La 1 PE21 . . . 181 A7
Charters Dr 9 NG24 . . . . . . 104 A2
Charter's La PE12 . . . . 216 A6
Charter's La PE12 . . . . 216 A5
Charters The 2 PE9 . . . . . . 172 C6
Chartwell Cl PE2 . . . . 231 A7
Chartwell House Sch
PE13 . . . . 170 A5
Chase Hill Rd DN40 . . . . . . 12 E5
Chase St PE13 . . . . 170 D1
Chase The Boston PE21 . . . 209 C3
Cherry Willingham/Reepham
LN3 . . . . 203 F8
Crowland PE6 . . . . 166 F1
Holbeach PE12 . . . . 215 E2
Long Sutton PE12 . . . . . . 216 C4
9 Metheringham LN4 . . . . 95 C4
Pinchbeck PE11 . . . . 156 E8
Ropsley NG33 . . . . 131 A1
Weston PE12 . . . . 145 F1
West Walton PE14 . . . . . . 170 D4
Whaplode PE12 . . . . 147 A6
Wisbech PE13 . . . . 170 C1
Chasm & Northrope Slipe
Nature Reserve The ★
PE10 . . . . 165 B8
Chater La PE9 . . . . 171 A3
Chater Rd 5 PE8 . . . . 172 B1
Chatham St HU3 . . . . 179 F7
Chatsfield PE4 . . . . 220 E6
Chatsworth Ave NG31 . . . . 211 F5

Chatsworth Cl
4 Lincoln LN2 . . . . .202 C8
6 Market Deeping PE6 . . .217 A5
Chatsworth Dr
4 Lincoln LN6 . . . . .204 E2
Louth LN11 . . . . .198 B7
Chatsworth Pl
Cleethorpes DN35 . . . . . .192 C4
Peterborough PE3 . . . . . .225 B2
Chatsworth Rd PE9 . . . . .218 E6
Chatsworth St HU5 . . . . .180 B8
Chatsworth Way 12 DN9 . . .27 D2
Chatterton Ave LN1 . . . . .201 E8
Chatterton Cres DN15 . . .183 A5
Chaucer Ave
12 Mablethorpe/Sutton on Sea
LN12 . . . . .64 B4
Scunthorpe DN17 . . . . . . .184 D7
Chaucer Cl 1 PE13 . . . . . .170 B1
Chaucer Dr LN2 . . . . .202 C6
Chaucer Gdns 10 NG34 . . .212 F4
Chaucer Rd
11 Balderton NG24 . . . . . . .104 C2
Peterborough PE1 . . . . . .225 E8
Chaucer's Way PE11 . . . . .214 A4
Chauntry Rd 19 LN13 . . . . .75 D7
Cheal La PE11 . . . . .144 F2
Cheal Rd PE11 . . . . .144 F4
Cheapside
Kingston upon Hull HU8 . .181 A8
Waltham DN37 . . . . .194 F2
Cheapside Rd DN36 . . . . . .36 A4
Cheapside Road Ind Est
DN37 . . . . .195 A2
Chedburgh Cl 1 LN6 . . . .204 B6
Chedworth Cl
1 Lincoln LN2 . . . . .202 D7
Peterborough PE4 . . . . . .225 E8
Chedworth Rd LN12 . . . . .202 D7
Cheese Hill 10 PE20 . . . . .135 B7
Cheesemans Cl 4 DN37 . .194 E4
Cheesemans La DN37 . . . .194 E4
Cheethams La LN4 . . . . . .110 F2
Chelmer Cl LN6 . . . . .204 F4
Chelmer Garth 2 PE4 . . . .221 D1
Chelmsford Ave DN34 . . .191 A6
Chelmsford Dr NG31 . . . .210 F4
Chelmsford Pl DN34 . . . . .191 A6
Chelmsford St LN5 . . . . . .234 B1
Chelsea Cl LN6 . . . . .200 D2
Chelsea Wlk DN35 . . . . . .193 A1
Cheltenham Cl
Peterborough PE1 . . . . . .226 B6
Scunthorpe DN16 . . . . . . .185 C4
Cheltenham Ct 1 PE10 . . .213 C3
Cheltenham Way
Humberston DN35 . . . . . .192 F1
7 Mablethorpe/Sutton on Sea
LN12 . . . . .64 A3
Chelveston Way PE3 . . . . .225 C4
Chelwood Dr 4 DN33 . . . .191 B3
Chelwood Rd DN17 . . . . . .184 F7
Chepstow Cl 1 PE11 . . . . .156 E3
Chepstow Dr PE10 . . . . . .213 C2
Chepstow Way DN34 . . . .191 A5
Chequered Flag Karting★
DN36 . . . . .195 C1
Chequergate 1 LN11 . . . .198 B5
Chequers La DN22 . . . . . . .65 A2
Chequers The DN35 . . . . .182 D3
Cheriton Cl 1 LN3 . . . . . . .83 B4
Cheriton Pk PE10 . . . . . . .213 D7
Cherries The PE12 . . . . . . .216 D4
Cherry Ave Branston LN4 . . .81 D2
Hessle HU13 . . . . .178 C3
Cherry Cl Humberston DN36 . .36 D8
8 Sleaford NG34 . . . . .212 D6
Cherry Cnr PE22 . . . . .113 A5
Cherry Cobb Lane DN37 . .35 B5
Cherry Cobb Sands Rd
HU12 . . . . .13 F8
Cherry Dale DN35 . . . . . . .192 C4
Cherryfields PE2 . . . . .229 E6
Cherry Garth HU3 . . . . . . .180 A8
Cherry Gr 10 Belton DN9 . . .16 E1
Lincoln LN6 . . . . .205 A8
10 Market Deeping PE6 . . .217 C5
Scunthorpe DN16 . . . . . .185 B6
Cherry Holt 33 Caistor LN7 . .33 B4
1 Cherry Willingham/Reepham
LN3 . . . . .203 E5
Cherryholt La PE9 . . . . . . .219 D5
Cherry Holt La
13 Pinchbeck PE11 . . . . . .156 E8
Sutterton PE20 . . . . .136 A4
Cherryholt Rd PE9 . . . . . .219 D5
Cherry Holt Rd PE10 . . . . .213 F4
Cherry La
Barrow upon Humber DN19 . .11 D8
7 Fleet PE12 . . . . .159 C7
21 New Waltham DN36 . . . .36 A4
Stubton NG23 . . . . .118 B7
Wootton DN39 . . . . .11 E2
Cherry Mount DN16 . . . . .185 C4
Cherry Orch
21 Epworth DN9 . . . . .27 E6
Grantham NG31 . . . . . . .211 D5
Cherry Orton Rd PE2 . . . .229 F5
Cherry Paddocks LN3 . . . .203 B6
Cherry Rd 9 PE13 . . . . . . .170 C2
Cherrytree Ave PE25 . . . . .90 E4
Cherry Tree Ave 4 DN20 . .16 B4
Cherry Tree Cl 4 LN6 . . . .204 F2
Cherry Tree Cres DN34 . . .190 F6
Cherry Tree Dr 5 DN7 . . . .14 D5

Cherrytree Gr PE1 . . . . . .226 C6
Cherry Tree Gr
2 Hatfield DN7 . . . . .14 D5
Spalding PE11 . . . . .214 F5
Cherry Tree La
Holbeach PE12 . . . . .215 D4
23 Nettleham LN2 . . . . .68 C2
Rigsby LN13 . . . . .75 E1
Cherry Tree Rd DN21 . . . .197 E5
Cherry Tree Rise DN21 . . . .29 C4
CherryTree's Bsns Pk
DN31 . . . . .188 C2
Cherry Tree Way
3 Coningsby LN4 . . . . . . .207 D4
17 Metheringham LN4 . . . . .95 C4
Cherry Way 34 DN17 . . . . .29 D7
CHERRY WILLINGHAM
LN3 . . . . .203 E5
Cherry Willingham Com Sch
LN3 . . . . .203 D7
Cherry Willingham Prim Sch
LN3 . . . . .203 D5
Cherry Wlk PE21 . . . . .208 D4
Cherrywood Rd NG31 . . . .210 F8
Chesboule La PE11 . . . . . .144 E5
Chesham Dr 7 PE6 . . . . . .164 E4
Cheshire Cl PE9 . . . . .219 B7
Cheshire Gr 7 PE25 . . . . .206 A5
Cheshire Rd LN6 . . . . .92 E5
Cheshire Rd LN6 . . . . . . .204 D5
Cheshire Wlk DN37 . . . . . .190 E8
Chesney Dr DN16 . . . . . . .185 A3
Chesney Rd LN4 . . . . .202 D7
Chesnut Cl 11 LN2 . . . . . . .68 F2
Chesnut Dr 12 LN2 . . . . . . .68 F2
Chesnut Way 4 DN19 . . . . .12 A8
Chesswick Ave DN17 . . . . .17 D5
Chester Cl Bourne PE10 . .213 B3
Heighington/Washingborough
LN4 . . . . .203 D1
8 Skegness PE25 . . . . . . .206 D7
Chesterfield Rd LN5 . . . . .182 B2
Chester Gdns 8 NG31 . . . .210 E5
Chester Grange DN33 . . . .191 E1
Chester Pl DN32 . . . . .192 C5
Chester Rd PE1 . . . . .226 C3
CHESTERTON PE7 . . . . . . .228 F3
Chesterton Gr PE2 . . . . . .231 D6
Chesterton St
East Ella HU3 . . . . .179 F5
8 Kingston upon Hull HU3 .179 F5
Chester Way PE21 . . . . . .208 C3
Chestnut Ave
7 Donington PE11 . . . . . . .134 E2
Edenham PE10 . . . . .153 C2
Gainsborough DN21 . . . .197 D6
Grimsby DN31 . . . . .191 B7
Immingham DN40 . . . . . .186 E5
Kingston upon Hull HU13 .178 E1
6 Newark-on-Trent NG24 . .104 A6
Peterborough PE1 . . . . . .226 B7
RAF Cranwell NG34 . . . .107 D1
8 Spalding PE11 . . . . .214 E5
3 Stainforth DN7 . . . . .14 D6
6 Thorne/Moorends DN8 . . .15 B7
Chestnut Cl
Bottesford NG13 . . . . . . .128 B6
Digby LN4 . . . . .108 E6
Glinton PE6 . . . . .220 B8
Horncastle LN9 . . . . .199 A5
4 Metheringham LN4 . . . . .95 C4
1 Peakirk PE6 . . . . .174 A5
13 Scotter DN21 . . . . .29 C3
2 Sleaford NG34 . . . . .212 D3
Swaton NG34 . . . . .133 D4
13 Waltham DN37 . . . . .194 C4
Chestnut Cres 3 LN5 . . . . .92 F3
Chestnut Dr
5 Coningsby LN4 . . . . . . .207 D4
Louth LN11 . . . . .198 E6
38 Messingham DN17 . . . . .29 D7
3 Thorney PE6 . . . . .176 A3
Chestnut Gdns PE9 . . . . . .218 D5
Chestnut Gr
11 Barnetby le Wold DN38 . .21 B4
8 Broughton DN20 . . . . . . .19 E4
4 Colsterworth NG33 . . . . .151 E7
1 Grantham NG31 . . . . . . .210 D2
Waddington LN5 . . . . . . .205 C1
Chestnut La NG33 . . . . . . .152 C8
Chestnut Rd
3 Boston PE21 . . . . .209 C2
Lincoln LN6 . . . . .204 F2
Waltham DN37 . . . . .194 C4
Chestnut Rise 1 DN19 . . . .11 C8
Chestnut St CE Prim Sch
NG34 . . . . .108 F1
5 Ruskington NG34 . . . . . .108 E1
Chestnuts The 7 LN2 . . . . .68 C2
Chestnut Terr 2 PE12 . . . .160 E4
Chestnut Way
5 Binbrook LN8 . . . . .47 C5
4 Bourne PE10 . . . . .213 B5
3 Market Deeping PE6 . . .217 B6
Scunthorpe DN16 . . . . . .185 B8
Chestnut Wlk 9 DN41 . . . . .24 A5
Cheviot Ave PE4 . . . . .221 C2
Cheviot Cl
Gonerby Hill Foot NG31 . .210 E7
Sleaford NG34 . . . . .212 A3
6 Thorne/Moorends DN8 . . .15 A7
Cheviot St LN2 . . . . .234 C2
Chichester Cl 6 NG31 . . . .210 E5
Chichester Dr 20 LN7 . . . . .33 B4
Chichester Rd
6 Binbrook Tech Pk LN8 . . .47 B6

Chichester Rd continued
4 Bracebridge Heath LN4 . . .81 A4
Cleethorpes DN35 . . . . . .192 F4
Chieftain Rd 1 LN6 . . . . . .205 C8
Chieftain Way 1 LN6 . . . . .205 C8
Childersgate La PE12 . . . .159 D2
Childers' N Dro
Cowbit PE12 . . . . .157 B5
Spalding PE11 . . . . .214 F3
Childers' S Dro
Cowbit PE12 . . . . .157 B4
Pinchbeck PE11 . . . . . . .214 F2
Chiltern Cl NG31 . . . . .210 E7
Chiltern Cres DN17 . . . . . .184 D8
Chiltern Dr Spalding PE11 .214 E6
Waltham DN37 . . . . .194 D3
Chiltern Prim Sch HU3 . . .180 B5
Chiltern Rd 3 LN5 . . . . . . .205 D3
Chiltern Rise PE4 . . . . . . .221 B2
Chiltern Way
3 Grimsby DN33 . . . . .194 E8
24 North Hykeham LN6 . . . .93 C8
Chilton Cl 7 DN40 . . . . . . .186 B4
China St PE22 . . . . .114 C4
Chingford Ave DN34 . . . . .191 A4
Chippendale Cl
2 Birchwood LN6 . . . . . . .204 D6
2 Humberston DN36 . . . . . .36 D8
Chippendale Rd 3 LN6 . . .204 D6
Chippenham Mews 1
PE2 . . . . .230 C7
Chisenhale PE2 . . . . .229 E6
Chivenor Cl 3 LN6 . . . . . . .200 B1
Cholmley St HU3 . . . . .180 B5
Chopdike Dro PE11 . . . . . .144 D3
Christ Church Cl PE9 . . . . .219 B7
Christchurch Rd 10 NG31 .211 D7
Christine Pl DN33 . . . . . . .195 A8
Christopher Cl
5 Heckington NG34 . . . . .122 E3
Louth LN11 . . . . .198 D7
Peterborough PE1 . . . . . .225 F8
Christopher Cres 11 NG34 212 F4
Christopher Dr 8 PE13 . . .170 C1
Christopher Rd 6 LN13 . . . .75 E2
Christopher's La 4 PE10 . .213 D6
Christ's Hospl Terr LN2 . . .234 B3
Church Ave
Ashby de la Launde & Bloxholm
LN4 . . . . .108 B5
Humberston DN36 . . . . . .36 C8
7 North Ferriby HU14 . . . . .3 A4
Church Balk DN8 . . . . .15 B8
Church Bank 2 PE34 . . . . .161 F3
Church Cl 2 Bonby DN20 . . .10 C2
24 Boston PE21 . . . . .208 F5
Donington on Bain LN11 . .59 E2
Grimsby DN32 . . . . .192 B5
Holton le Clay DN36 . . . .195 D2
12 Louth LN11 . . . . .198 B5
16 Mablethorpe/Sutton on Sea
LN12 . . . . .77 A8
4 Newborough PE6 . . . . . .174 E4
11 Sibsey PE22 . . . . .113 B1
11 Sleaford NG34 . . . . . . .212 B2
Stoke Rochford NG33 . . .139 F2
3 Thorne/Moorends DN8 . . .15 B8
Wrangle PE22 . . . . .114 C1
Church Cres 4 DN9 . . . . . .28 A3
Church Ct
Scunthorpe DN15 . . . . . .183 B4
3 Stamford PE9 . . . . .219 C4
6 Sudbrooke LN2 . . . . . . .68 F3
Church Dr Lincoln LN6 . . . .201 D1
8 Misterton DN10 . . . . .39 F5
Norton Disney LN6 . . . . . .92 C1
Peterborough PE2 . . . . . .229 F4
Surfleet PE11 . . . . .145 D3
CHURCH END LN11 . . . . . .50 F6
Church End Gedney PE12 .159 D7
9 Leverington PE13 . . . . . .170 D2
Skegness PE25 . . . . .206 B8
Wrangle PE22 . . . . .114 C1
Church End Dro PE11 . . . .134 F1
Church Farm Cl 23 PE24 . .90 D7
Church Farm Mus★ PE25 206 B4
Churchfield Cl PE6 . . . . . .217 F5
Churchfield Ct PE4 . . . . . .225 E8
Churchfield Rd
Peterborough PE4 . . . . . .221 B1
Scunthorpe DN16 . . . . . .185 B5
Church Fields
Pickworth NG34 . . . . . . .142 A8
Winterton DN15 . . . . .9 A5
Churchfields Rd NG34 . . . .142 C8
Churchfleet La PE11 . . . . .145 B7
Churchgate Gedney PE12 .159 D7
14 Sutterton PE20 . . . . . . .136 A2
Church Gate Fleet PE12 . .159 B6
2 Market Deeping PE6 . . .217 F4
Spalding PE11 . . . . .214 D3
22 Sutton Bridge PE12 . . .160 E4
Whaplode PE12 . . . . .158 B6
Churchgate Mews 5
PE12 . . . . .159 D7
Church Gdns 15 PE12 . . . .160 A8
Church Gn PE12 . . . . .216 C4
Church Gn Cl PE21 . . . . . .209 F2
Church Gn La
Frampton PE20 . . . . .136 B7
Quadring PE11 . . . . .135 A1
Church Gn Rd PE20 . . . . . .209 F4
Church Hill Belvoir NG32 . .138 C6
1 Burgh le Marsh PE24 . . .102 E7
Castor PE5 . . . . .223 E2
1 Grasby DN38 . . . . .32 E7
Heighington/Washingborough
LN4 . . . . .203 B2

Church Hill continued
Ingham LN1 . . . . .55 A2
Riby DN37 . . . . .23 C2
Spridlington LN8 . . . . .55 F3
Whitton DN15 . . . . .1 E3
Church Hill Cl PE7 . . . . . .231 C1
Churchill Ave Bourne PE10 213 B4
Bracebridge Heath LN4 . .205 F4
Brigg DN20 . . . . .196 D4
2 Hatfield DN7 . . . . .14 F4
Horncastle LN9 . . . . .199 C3
4 Keelby DN41 . . . . .23 A5
4 Market Rasen LN8 . . . . . .57 D7
Skegness PE25 . . . . .206 B6
2 Skegness PE25 . . . . . . .206 D7
Churchill Cl 6 LN11 . . . . . .50 F7
Churchill Ct 2 PE12 . . . . .216 B5
Churchill Dr
3 Boston PE21 . . . . .209 D4
2 Martin LN10 . . . . .97 B4
Spalding PE11 . . . . .214 D2
Churchill La LN12 . . . . .63 E8
Churchill Rd
Gorefield PE13 . . . . .169 F3
Gorefield PE13 . . . . .169 F3
North Somercotes LN11 . .50 F7
Stamford PE9 . . . . .219 B7
Churchill St HU9 . . . . .181 D7
Churchill Way
Grimsby DN32 . . . . .191 F7
Heckington NG34 . . . . . .122 D3
5 Lea DN21 . . . . .52 F6
Church La Addlethorpe PE24 90 D4
Algarkirk PE20 . . . . .136 B2
Alvingham LN11 . . . . .49 F2
9 Ancaster NG32 . . . . . . .120 A2
Appleby DN15 . . . . .9 D1
Aylesby DN37 . . . . .23 E2
4 Bardney LN3 . . . . .83 B4
Baumber LN9 . . . . .72 B1
Benniworth LN8 . . . . .71 E8
4 Billinghay LN4 . . . . .109 F5
Blyton DN21 . . . . .41 C5
Bonby DN20 . . . . .10 C2
19 Boston PE21 . . . . .208 F5
Bottesford NG13 . . . . . . .128 C4
Bourne PE10 . . . . .213 D4
Bourne PE10 . . . . .213 D5
Brant Broughton LN5 . . . .105 F5
Brigsley DN37 . . . . .35 D4
4 Brough HU15 . . . . .2 C7
15 Broughton DN20 . . . . . . .19 E3
Buckminster NG33 . . . . .150 F4
Burton Coggles NG33 . . .152 D8
Cadney DN20 . . . . .31 D6
6 Carlton-le-Moorland LN5 105 E8
4 Caythorpe NG32 . . . . . .119 B7
24 Chapel St Leonard PE24 . .90 D7
Cherry Willingham/Reepham
LN3 . . . . .203 E5
Clipsham LE15 . . . . .162 B7
Coleby LN5 . . . . .93 F3
6 Collingham NG23 . . . . . .91 D5
Corringham DN21 . . . . . . .41 C2
Counthorpe & Creeton
NG33 . . . . .153 A2
Croft PE24 . . . . .102 E5
7 Crowland PE6 . . . . .166 F1
3 Croxton Kerrial NG32 . . .138 D4
1 Donington PE11 . . . . . . .134 F2
Eagle & Swinethorpe LN6 . .79 B2
East Keal PE23 . . . . .100 E6
Edenham PE10 . . . . .153 F4
Elkington LN11 . . . . .60 E7
Ewerby & Evedon NG34 .122 C6
5 Fishlake DN7 . . . . .14 D8
1 Folkingham NG34 . . . . .142 D8
Fotherby LN11 . . . . .49 A2
Friesthorpe LN3 . . . . .57 A2
Friskney PE22 . . . . .114 F6
Frithville PE22 . . . . .125 D8
3 Fulletby LN9 . . . . .86 B8
5 Glentham LN8 . . . . .43 F1
Goulceby LN11 . . . . .72 D6
Grainthorpe LN11 . . . . . . .50 B7
Grayingham DN21 . . . . . .42 E7
Great Casterton PE9 . . . .171 B8
Great Gonerby NG31 . . . .210 C8
Great Limber DN37 . . . . . .22 D3
Grimsby DN37 . . . . .190 E2
1 Hagworthingham PE23 . . .87 A4
Harmston LN5 . . . . .93 F5
Haxey DN9 . . . . .27 C2
3 Helpringham NG34 . . . . .133 D7
3 Helpston PE6 . . . . .173 C4
Holton le Clay DN36 . . . .195 D2
Horbling NG34 . . . . .133 B2
6 Horncastle LN9 . . . . . . .199 B4
Hougham NG32 . . . . .118 C3
Humberston DN36 . . . . . .36 D8
Huttoft LN13 . . . . .76 E3
Immingham DN40 . . . . . .186 B5
3 Ingham LN1 . . . . .54 F2
Ingoldmells PE25 . . . . . .206 C8
4 Keadby with Althorpe
DN17 . . . . .17 D4
Keddington LN11 . . . . . . .198 E8
3 Keelby DN41 . . . . .23 A4
Kingston upon Hull HU10 .178 C8
Kirkby la Thorpe NG34 . .121 F4
Kirkby on Bain LN10 . . . . .98 C5
Kirton PE20 . . . . .136 C5
12 Laceby DN37 . . . . .23 F1
2 Legbourne LN11 . . . . . . .61 F3
Lincoln LN2 . . . . .234 A4

Church La continued
3 Little Bytham NG33 . . . .163 A8
Londonthorpe & Harrowby Without
NG31 . . . . .130 D5
Long Bennington NG23 . .117 E2
Luddington & Haldenby DN17 . .7 D1
Lutton PE12 . . . . .160 A8
14 Mablethorpe/Sutton on Sea
LN12 . . . . .77 A8
3 Mareham le Fen PE22 . . .98 F4
Marshchapel DN36 . . . . . .37 B1
17 Metheringham LN4 . . . . .95 D4
Minting LN9 . . . . .84 C8
5 Misterton DN10 . . . . .39 F5
Misterton LN13 . . . . .89 B6
Moulton PE12 . . . . .157 F7
Navenby LN5 . . . . .107 A8
Newton PE13 . . . . .170 A6
North Carlton LN1 . . . . . . .67 C4
10 North Kelsey LN7 . . . . . .32 A4
North Kyme LN4 . . . . . . .109 F3
North Scarle LN6 . . . . . . .78 E1
North Somercotes LN11 . .50 E6
Old Somerby NG33 . . . . .140 E8
Owersby LN8 . . . . .44 F5
5 Owmby LN8 . . . . .55 F6
Peterborough PE2 . . . . . .229 F5
Pickworth NG34 . . . . . . .132 A1
6 Potterhanworth LN4 . . . .82 B1
Rand LN8 . . . . .70 A5
Ropsley & Humby NG33 . .131 B1
Roughton LN9 . . . . .85 B1
Saltfleetby LN12 . . . . .63 B7
Saxby All Saints DN20 . . .10 B3
Saxilby with Ingleby LN1 . .66 C3
Scamblesby LN11 . . . . . . .72 F5
Scawby DN20 . . . . .20 A1
Scopwick LN4 . . . . .108 E4
9 Scotter DN21 . . . . .29 C3
Scredington NG34 . . . . . .132 F7
Scunthorpe DN15 . . . . . .182 E2
Sedgebrook NG32 . . . . . .128 E4
Silk Willoughby NG34 . . .121 D1
Skegness PE25 . . . . .206 B8
Skidbrooke with Saltfleet Haven
LN11 . . . . .51 B4
Sleaford NG34 . . . . .212 D5
Snitterby DN21 . . . . .43 D5
South Clifton LN23 . . . . . .78 C6
South Kyme LN4 . . . . . . .123 A8
15 South Witham NG33 . . .151 D2
Spilsby PE23 . . . . .87 E1
Springthorpe DN21 . . . . . .53 E8
Sproxton LE14 . . . . .150 C7
Stallingborough DN41 . . . .23 D6
9 Stamford PE9 . . . . .219 C4
Sudbrooke LN2 . . . . .68 F3
Swaby LN13 . . . . .74 E3
Swineshead PE20 . . . . . .135 B2
Tallington PE9 . . . . .172 F6
Tealby LN8 . . . . .46 C1
Tetford LN9 . . . . .73 F1
Tetney DN36 . . . . .36 D3
3 Timberland LN4 . . . . .96 C1
Torksey LN1 . . . . .65 D5
Toynton St Peter PE23 . .101 A6
Twin Rivers DN14 . . . . .7 A8
Tydd St Giles PE13 . . . . .169 F7
Tydd St Mary PE13 . . . . .160 B1
2 Ulceby DN39 . . . . .12 A1
Ulceby with Fordington LN13 88 C7
Utterby LN11 . . . . .48 F3
Waddingham DN21 . . . . . .43 D7
21 Waddington LN5 . . . . . . .93 F7
Wainfleet St Mary PE24 . .102 B1
Waithe DN36 . . . . .36 A3
Waltham DN37 . . . . .194 E4
Wansford PE8 . . . . .222 D2
Welby NG32 . . . . .130 F3
2 Welton/Dunholme LN2 . . .68 D6
3 Westborough & Dry
Doddington NG23 . . . . . .117 F3
West Keal PE23 . . . . .100 C6
Withern with Stain LN13 . . .62 F1
Wood Enderby LN9 . . . . . .98 F7
Wrangle PE22 . . . . .114 C1
3 Wyberton PE21 . . . . . . .136 F8
3 Wymondham LE14 . . . . .150 C1
CHURCH LANEHAM DN22 . .65 B3
Church La Prim Sch
NG34 . . . . .212 D5
Church La Staith 7 HU1 . .181 A6
Church Lees NG32 . . . . . . .131 C6
Church Lodge DN21 . . . . . .53 F1
Church Mdw Dr 20 PE24 . . .90 D7
Church Mdws PE20 . . . . . .136 C5
Church Mews
Spalding PE11 . . . . .214 E4
7 Sutterton PE20 . . . . . . .136 A2
Church Pk 17 LN12 . . . . . . .77 A8
Church Rd
Aubourn Haddington & South
Hykeham LN5 . . . . .93 A3
4 Bicker PE20 . . . . .135 A4
Boston PE21 . . . . .209 B4
4 Butterwick PE22 . . . . . . .126 E3
Friskney PE22 . . . . .115 A6
Harby NG23 . . . . .79 B5
4 Ketton PE9 . . . . .171 A3
Laughton DN21 . . . . .41 C8
Leverington PE13 . . . . . .170 E1
4 Mablethorpe/Sutton on Sea
LN12 . . . . .64 A3
North Ferriby HU14 . . . . . .3 A4
Old Leake PE22 . . . . .114 A1
Saxilby LN1 . . . . .66 D2
Skellingthorpe LN6 . . . . .200 A4

Church Rd *continued*
Stainforth DN7 . . . . 14 C6
Stickford PE22 . . . . .100 B3
1 Stow LN1 . . . . .66 C8
Upton DN21 . . . . .53 D5
Wigtoft PE20 . . . . .135 E3
Wisbech PE13 . . . . .170 B1
Wittering PE8 . . . . .172 B1
Church Rd N PE25 . . . . . . .206 B4
Church Rd S **4** PE25 . . . . .206 B3
Church Rise **5** PE22 . . . . .98 F4
Church Row HU8 . . . . .181 A8
Church Side
3 Alkborough DN15 . . . . . . 8 C8
3 Appleby DN15 . . . . 9 D1
16 Goxhill DN19 . . . . 12 A8
3 Grasby DN38 . . . . 32 E7
3 West Halton DN15 . . . . . .8 E7
14 Winterton DN15 . . . . 9 A5
Church Sq DN15 . . . . .183 B3
Church St **4** Alford LN13 . . 75 F3
Amcotts DN17 . . . . 7 F1
Barkston NG32 . . . . .130 B8
2 Barrowby NG32 . . . . . . .210 A5
2 Baston PE6 . . . . .164 E4
Beckingham DN10 . . . . .40 A1
4 Billingborough NG34 . . .133 B1
2 Billinghay LN4 . . . . .109 F5
20 Boston PE21 . . . . .208 F5
1 Brough HU15 . . . . 2 C7
5 Burgh le Marsh PE24 . . .102 E8
Caistor LN7 . . . . .33 B3
14 Caistor LN7 . . . . 33 B4
Candlesby PE23 . . . . .88 F2
Carlby PE9 . . . . .163 D5
4 Carlton-le-Moorland LN5 105 E8
Collingham NG23 . . . . .91 C4
Corby Glen NG33 . . . . .152 F8
2 Crowle DN17 . . . . 16 D7
Denton NG32 . . . . .139 A7
Digby LN4 . . . . .108 D5
3 Donington PE11 . . . . . . .134 E2
Easton on the Hill PE9 . . . .171 D3
Elsham DN20 . . . . .20 F7
1 Epworth DN9 . . . . .27 E6
1 Fishlake DN7 . . . . .14 D8
1 Foston NG32 . . . . .117 F1
Gainsborough DN21 . . . . . .197 C5
Glentworth DN21 . . . . .54 F6
4 Gosberton PE11 . . . . . . .145 B6
16 Goxhill DN19 . . . . 12 A8
Grantham NG31 . . . . .211 A5
Grimsby DN32 . . . . .189 B1
1 Haconby PE10 . . . . .154 D8
5 Harlaxton NG32 . . . . . . .139 C7
Haxey DN9 . . . . .27 C2
6 Heckington NG34 . . . . . .122 E3
Hemswell DN21 . . . . .42 D1
7 Hibaldstow DN20 . . . . . . 30 F5
Holbeach PE12 . . . . .215 D2
Kingston upon Hull HU10 . .178 E6
7 Kirton in Lindsey DN21 . . 30 B1
Long Bennington NG23 . . . .117 D3
Louth LN11 . . . . .198 C5
Market Deeping PE6 . . . . . .217 B5
6 Market Rasen LN8 . . . . . 57 D8
Messingham DN17 . . . . .29 D7
7 Middle Rasen LN8 . . . . . 57 B8
Misterton DN10 . . . . .39 F5
20 Nettleham LN2 . . . . 68 C2
Nettleton LN7 . . . . 33 B3
Northborough PE6 . . . . . . .173 F6
12 North Kelsey LN7 . . . . . 32 A4
North Witham NG33 . . . . . .151 D4
Owston Ferry DN9 . . . . .28 A3
Peterborough PE2 . . . . .231 C7
Peterborough PE4 . . . . .220 F3
Peterborough PE7 . . . . .229 A4
Pinchbeck PE11 . . . . .145 C1
17 Ruskington NG34 . . . . .108 E2
Ryhall PE9 . . . . .163 C1
9 Scawby DN20 . . . . 30 E8
10 Scothern LN2 . . . . .68 F4
Skillington NG33 . . . . .151 A4
10 South Witham NG33 . . .151 D2
Spalding PE11 . . . . .214 D4
11 Spilsby PE23 . . . . .87 F1
8 Stamford PE9 . . . . .219 C4
Sturton le Steeple DN22 . . . .52 B2
2 Sutton Bridge PE12 . . . .160 E4
1 Sutton on Trent NG23 . . . 91 A8
28 Thorne/Moorends DN8 . . 15 A8
1 Thorney PE6 . . . . .176 A3
Thurlby PE10 . . . . .164 D7
Willoughton DN21 . . . . .42 E4
1 Wragby LN8 . . . . .70 D4
Yaxley PE7 . . . . .233 D4
Churchthorpe **1** LN11 . . . .49 B8
Churchtown **9** DN9 . . . . . .16 E1
CHURCH TOWN DN9 . . . . .16 E1
Church View
2 Alkborough DN15 . . . . . . 8 C8
11 Barton-upon-Humber
DN18 . . . . 10 F8
13 Beckingham DN10 . . . . . 40 A1
13 Bottesford NG13 . . . . . .128 A6
1 Brough HU15 . . . . 2 C7
Freiston PE22 . . . . .126 D2
3 Gainsborough DN21 . . . . .53 A5
8 Great Gonerby NG31 . . . .129 D5
Grimsby DN34 . . . . .190 E2
23 Newark-on-Trent NG24 . .104 B2
Northborough PE6 . . . . . . .217 E1
Swallow LN7 . . . . .34 B5
2 Waltham DN37 . . . . . . .194 E4
Churchview Cl **5** NG34 . . .122 D3

Church View Cl
3 Belton DN9 . . . . 16 E1
3 Donington PE11 . . . . . . .134 E2
Peterborough PE2 . . . . .231 B7
Church View Cres LN3 . . . .82 B7
Churchway PE22 . . . . .127 A5
Church Way PE13 . . . . . . .160 A1
Church Wlk Bourne PE10 . .213 D5
Brant Broughton & Stragglethorpe
LN5 . . . . .105 F4
1 Dunham-on-Trent NG22 . .65 B1
2 Holbeach PE12 . . . . . . .215 D2
3 Holton le Clay DN36 . . . .195 D2
1 Legbourne LN11 . . . . . . .61 F3
1 Manby LN11 . . . . .62 C6
21 Metheringham LN4 . . . . 95 D4
1 Owston Ferry DN9 . . . . . .28 A3
Peterborough PE1 . . . . .226 A3
2 Pinchbeck PE11 . . . . . . .156 F8
Sibsey PE22 . . . . .113 B2
Upton PE6 . . . . .223 B5
Yaxley PE7 . . . . .233 D4
Church Wy LN7 . . . . .33 B3
Church Yd LN1 . . . . .65 D1
Chuter Ede Prim Sch
NG24 . . . . .104 C2
Cibus Way PE12 . . . . .215 D6
Cinder La LN11 . . . . .198 B5
Circle The **4** HU13 . . . . . .178 E2
Circus Approach PE11 . . . .214 A1
Cirencester Cl **15** LN6 . . . .93 B8
Cissbury Cl **12** LN12 . . . . . .77 A8
Cissbury Ring PE4 . . . . . . .221 A2
Cissplatt La Brocklesby DN41 22 F5
Keelby DN41 . . . . .23 A5
Cisterngate **3** LN11 . . . . .198 B6
Citadel Way HU9 . . . . .181 A6
City Rd PE1 . . . . .226 A2
City Sports Ctr LN6 . . . . . .205 A8
City Sq Ctr LN1 . . . . .234 B2
Clairbrook Cl **8** HU3 . . . . .180 A5
Claires Wlk DN17 . . . . . . .184 C7
Clampgate Rd PE21 . . . . . .126 C1
**Clapgate Pits Nature
Reserve** ★ DN15 . . . . .19 E5
Clapson's La **32** DN18 . . . . . 3 E1
Clapton Cl **16** PE9 . . . . . . .218 E6
Clapton Gate PE12 . . . . . . .157 E6
Clara Terr LN1 . . . . .234 A3
Clare Ave DN17 . . . . .184 D7
Clare Cl **11** Lincoln LN5 . . .205 D3
7 Stamford PE9 . . . . .219 A5
Clare Cres DN16 . . . . .185 A3
Clare Ct **3** Baston PE6 . . . .164 E4
Grimsby DN34 . . . . .191 A6
Claremont Park NG34 . . . .212 C6
Claremont Rd
1 Burgh le Marsh PE24 . . .102 E8
Gainsborough DN21 . . . . . .197 C2
Grimsby DN32 . . . . .192 D6
Claremont St LN2 . . . . . . .234 C2
Clarence Cl **2** DN40 . . . . .186 B3
Clarence Gdns **3** PE11 . . . .214 E2
Clarence Rd
Peterborough PE1 . . . . .225 E5
28 Wisbech PE13 . . . . . . .170 D1
3 Woodhall Spa LN10 . . . . .97 D6
Clarence St
Kingston upon Hull HU1 . . .181 A6
1 Lincoln LN1 . . . . .201 E6
Clarendon Gdns **1** LN1 . . .201 E8
Clarendon Rd
Grimsby DN34 . . . . .190 E4
Scunthorpe DN17 . . . . .184 F7
Skegness PE25 . . . . .206 A4
Clarendon St HU3 . . . . . . .180 D7
Clarendon View LN1 . . . . .201 E8
Clarendon Way PE6 . . . . . .220 D8
Clare Rd Northborough PE6 217 E1
Peterborough PE1 . . . . .225 F6
Claricoates Dr **9** NG24 . . .104 C8
Clarina St LN2 . . . . .202 B4
Clark Ave DN31 . . . . .191 A7
Clarke Ave LN4 . . . . .81 F4
Clarke Ct **10** PE21 . . . . . .136 D8
Clarke Rd **11** LN6 . . . . . . .93 C8
Clarkes Cl PE22 . . . . .114 A7
Clarke Rd **3** DN40 . . . . . .12 E4
Clarke St **3** DN15 . . . . . .183 A3
Clarke Way PE25 . . . . . . .206 A4
CLARK'S HILL PE12 . . . . . .159 B3
Clarks La
11 Beacon Hill NG24 . . . . .104 A5
8 Beacon Hill NG24 . . . . .104 A5
Clarkson Ave **1** PE12 . . . .167 B8
Clarkson Ct **27** PE13 . . . . .170 D1
Clarkson Infants Sch The
PE13 . . . . .170 E1
Clarksons Dr **3** DN41 . . . . 23 E6
Clasketgate LN2 . . . . .234 B2
Clatterdykes Rd PE20 . . . .136 E6
Claudette Ave PE11 . . . . . .214 B5
Claudette Way **5** PE11 . . .214 B5
Claudius Rd LN6 . . . . .93 B8
Clavering St **6** DN31 . . . . .188 D1
CLAXBY LN8 . . . . .45 D5
Claxby Rd DN17 . . . . .184 F5
CLAXBY ST ANDREW LN13 . 88 E6
**Claxby Springs Nature
Reserve** ★ LN13 . . . . .88 E6
Claxy Bank PE22 . . . . .114 D6
Clay Bank LN4 . . . . .123 C7
Clay Bank Rd DN8 . . . . . . .15 C6
Clayberg Dr **2** NG34 . . . . .212 D5
Clayburn Rd PE7 . . . . .230 D1
Clayden St **4** DN31 . . . . . .188 D1
Claydike Bank PE20 . . . . . .124 B4
Claydon Way DN37 . . . . . .194 F3

Clay Dro PE11 . . . . .156 C5
Clayfield Rd DN15 . . . . . . .182 F6
Clay Hill Rd NG34 . . . . . . .212 A3
Clay La
Carlton-le-Moorland LN5 . . .105 D8
Castor PE5 . . . . .223 D2
Gate Burton DN21 . . . . .53 B1
Harby NG23 . . . . .79 C5
Holton le Clay DN36 . . . . . .195 D3
Kirton in Lindsey DN21 . . . . .30 A1
Newark NG24 . . . . .104 B4
Norton Disney LN5 . . . . .92 D2
Scotter DN21 . . . . .29 C4
Stapleford LN6 . . . . .105 B7
Tetford LN9 . . . . .73 F2
Toft Newton LN8 . . . . .56 C7
Waddingham DN21 . . . . .43 D7
CLAY LAKE PE11 . . . . .214 E2
Clay Lake Bank PE12 . . . . .157 A3
Clay Lake La PE11 . . . . . . .214 E2
Claymore Cl DN35 . . . . . . .192 E6
Clay Pit La NG34 . . . . .122 C6
CLAYPOLE NG23 . . . . .117 F7
Claypole CE Prim Sch
NG23 . . . . .117 F8
Claypole Dr PE6 . . . . .217 E1
Claypole La NG23 . . . . . . .117 E6
Claypole Rd NG23 . . . . . . .118 A7
Clayside Wy **10** PE7 . . . . .230 F5
Clays The LN5 . . . . .105 D6
Claythorne Dr DN21 . . . . .197 E4
CLAYTHORPE LN13 . . . . . . .75 B6
Claythorpe Rd LN13 . . . . . .75 A6
Claythorpe Wr Mill ★ LN13 . 75 B5
Clayton PE2 . . . . .230 B4
Clayton Cl **16** PE13 . . . . . .170 E1
Clayton Cres PE12 . . . . . . .157 C2
Clayton Rd LN5 . . . . .205 E6
Clayworth Rd **6** DN10 . . . .39 C1
CLEATHAM DN21 . . . . .30 B3
Cleatham PE3 . . . . .225 A4
Cleatham Rd DN21 . . . . . . .30 B3
Clee Cres DN32 . . . . .192 C5
Clee Ness Dr DN36 . . . . . .193 A1
Cleefields Cl DN32 . . . . . . .192 B5
Clee Rd DN35 . . . . .192 C5
Cleethorpe Rd DN32 . . . . .189 B1
CLEETHORPES DN35 . . . . . .192 D5
Cleethorpes Acad DN35 . . .192 D4
**Cleethorpes Coast Light Rly &
Mus** ★ DN35 . . . . .193 B3
Cleethorpes Ctry Pk ★
DN35 . . . . .192 F2
Cleethorpes Discovery Ctr ★
DN35 . . . . .193 B3
Cleethorpes Leisure Ctr
DN35 . . . . .193 A4
Cleethorpes Nature Reserve ★
DN35 . . . . .193 D2
Cleethorpes Showground ★
DN35 . . . . .193 C3
Cleethorpes Sta DN35 . . . .192 F7
Clee Village DN32 . . . . . . .192 C6
Clematis App LN6 . . . . . . .204 C8
Clematis Ave **7** DN41 . . . .23 F5
Clematis Cl LN4 . . . . .81 D2
Clematis Way DN16 . . . . . .185 C4
Clement Ave NG24 . . . . . .104 C2
Clement Cl **2** LN4 . . . . . . .81 E2
Clementine Cl **7** PE25 . . . .206 B6
Clensey La NG23 . . . . .117 F5
Clerke St DN35 . . . . .192 B8
Clevedon Rd DN17 . . . . . . .184 D8
Cleveland Ave **28** LN6 . . . .93 C8
Cleveland Cl
2 Immingham DN40 . . . . .186 A4
2 Scunthorpe DN17 . . . . .184 D8
4 Spalding PE11 . . . . .214 F4
Cleveland Ct **3** PE4 . . . . . .221 C2
Cleveland Gdns **2** DN31 . .188 D1
Cleveland St
2 Gainsborough DN21 . . . .197 D3
3 Grimsby DN31 . . . . .188 D1
Kingston upon Hull HU8 . . .181 A8
Cleveland Way **27** DN7 . . . .14 D4
Cleve Pl **3** PE6 . . . . .175 A1
Cley Hall Gdns PE11 . . . . .214 A4
Cleymond Chase **2** PE20 . .136 C5
Cliff Ave **2** Nettleham LN2 . .68 C2
Winterton DN15 . . . . .8 F5
Cliff Closes Rd DN15 . . . . .182 D3
Cliff Cres **1** PE9 . . . . .219 B5
Cliff Dr
Burton upon Stather DN15 . . .8 B5
3 Kingston upon Hull HU13 . .3 E4
Cliffe Ave **1** NG34 . . . . . .108 D1
Cliffedale Prim Sch NG31 211 A8
Cliffe Rd
Easton on the Hill PE9 . . . .171 D2
Gonerby Hill Foot NG31 . . . .210 E7
Cliffe View NG34 . . . . .120 E4
Cliff Gdns DN15 . . . . .182 F2
Cliff Gr **2** DN18 . . . . .10 E8
Cliff La Marston NG32 . . . .129 D8
Waddingham DN21 . . . . .43 C6
Washingborough LN4 . . . . . .81 D4
Cliff Nook La
21 Beacon Hill NG24 . . . . .104 A5
26 Beacon Hill NG24 . . . . .104 A5
Clifford Rd PE25 . . . . .206 B4
Clifford's Cl DN20 . . . . . . .20 A1
Cliff Rd Fulbeck NG32 . . . .119 C8
Hessle HU13 . . . . 3 E4
Leadenham LN5 . . . . .106 D2
Scampton LN2 . . . . .67 F8
Snitterby DN21 . . . . .43 C5
Spridlington LN8 . . . . .55 F3
Stamford PE9 . . . . .219 B5

Cliff Rd *continued*
Welbourn LN5 . . . . .106 E4
Welton LN2 . . . . .68 C6
Winteringham DN15 . . . . .9 A8
Woolsthorpe by Belvoir
NG32 . . . . .128 D1
Cliffside **3** LN5 . . . . .107 A7
Cliff St DN16 . . . . .183 C2
Cliff The DN15 . . . . .182 D3
Cliff Top La **2** HU13 . . . . . . 3 E4
Clifton Ave PE3 . . . . .225 E3
Clifton Ct **2** DN8 . . . . .15 A8
Clifton Gr **3** PE25 . . . . . . .206 D1
Clifton Prim Sch HU2 . . . .180 E8
Clifton Rd Boston PE21 . . .209 E4
Grimsby DN34 . . . . .191 A6
Clifton St LN5 . . . . .234 B1
Clint La **9** LN5 . . . . .107 A8
Clinton Dr NG34 . . . . .212 C2
CLINTON PARK LN4 . . . . . .207 A5
Clinton Terr **3** DN21 . . . . .197 D3
Clinton Way LN10 . . . . .97 B5
Clipseygap La PE10 . . . . . .154 B6
CLIPSHAM LE15 . . . . .162 B7
Clipsham Rd PE9 . . . . .162 D8
Clipsham Road PE9 . . . . . .162 E6
Clipson Crest **46** DN18 . . . .10 E8
Clipston Wlk PE3 . . . . .225 C5
Clive Ave LN6 . . . . .205 C8
Clive Sullivan Way
Barton-upon-Humber DN19 . . 4 A4
Kingston upon Hull HU4 . . .179 C1
CLIXBY DN38 . . . . .32 E7
Clixby Cl DN35 . . . . .193 A3
Clixby La DN38 . . . . .32 E7
Cloddy Gate LN11 . . . . .50 F5
Cloister Cl DN17 . . . . .184 E6
Cloisters The
Grimsby DN37 . . . . .190 D7
17 Humberston DN36 . . . . 36 D8
Welton LN2 . . . . .68 C7
Cloister Wk **14** DN20 . . . . .19 E3
Cloot Dro PE6 . . . . .166 F2
Close The
Barkston NG32 . . . . .130 A8
1 Colsterworth NG33 . . . .151 D7
Easton on the Hill PE9 . . . .171 C3
2 Fiskerton LN3 . . . . .82 A7
2 Goxhill DN19 . . . . 5 A1
Grimsby DN34 . . . . .191 C7
Scunthorpe DN16 . . . . .183 B2
4 Skegness PE25 . . . . . . .206 C4
Sleaford NG34 . . . . .212 B2
1 Sturton by Stow LN1 . . . .66 D7
Woodhall Spa LN10 . . . . . . .97 C6
Closshill La PE21 . . . . .136 F8
Clouds La Belton DN9 . . . . .17 B1
West Butterwick DN17 . . . . .28 C8
Clough La East Halton DN40 . 12 F6
Firsby PE23 . . . . .101 F5
Kirton PE20 . . . . .136 F2
Clough Rd Gosberton PE11 144 D4
Holbeach PE12 . . . . .215 B7
**Clough & Risegate Com Prim
Sch** PE11 . . . . .144 D4
Clovelly Dr PE7 . . . . .230 E1
Cloven Ends **4** PE6 . . . . . .164 F3
Clover Ct DN20 . . . . .196 B4
Clover Gdns
14 Newark-on-Trent
NG24 . . . . .104 B5
6 Stamford PE9 . . . . .218 C7
Clover La PE20 . . . . .135 D4
Clover Rd
6 Bracebridge Heath LN4 . .81 A1
Market Deeping PE6 . . . . . .217 C5
Misterton LN13 . . . . .89 A6
Clover Road Ind Est LN13 . .89 A6
Clover Way PE11 . . . . .214 B6
Clowes Ct **4** HU13 . . . . . . .178 E1
Club Ct NG24 . . . . .104 B2
Clubhouse Way DN36 . . . . .195 F6
Clubhurn La PE11 . . . . .145 D4
Club Way PE7 . . . . .230 E4
Cludd Ave **5** NG24 . . . . . .104 C4
Clumber Ave NG24 . . . . . .104 A3
Clumber Dr **7** PE21 . . . . . .214 C6
Clumber Pl DN35 . . . . .192 E5
Clumber Rd PE2 . . . . .231 E6
Clumber St
Kingston upon Hull HU5 . . .180 C8
Lincoln LN5 . . . . .205 E2
Clutton's Cl **4** PE6 . . . . . .166 E1
Clyde Ct **1** NG31 . . . . . . .210 E2
Clydesdale Cres **1** PE11 . .214 A2
Clyde St HU3 . . . . .179 F5
Clyfton Cres DN40 . . . . . . .186 B4
Coach House Gdns **8**
DN20 . . . . .30 E8
Coachings The HU13 . . . . . . 3 E4
Coach Rd NG32 . . . . .118 C3
Coachroad Hill DN21 . . . . . .54 F7
Coalbeach La **1** PE11 . . . .145 E3
Coalbeach La S PE11 . . . . .145 E4
Coalport Cl **7** LN6 . . . . . . .204 D7
Coal Shore La LN11 . . . . . .37 D1
Coal Yd La NG23 . . . . .78 C4
Coastguard Rd LN11 . . . . . .38 C2
COATES
North Leverton with
Habblesthorpe DN22 . . . . . .65 B8
Stow LN1 . . . . .54 C2
Coates Ave **27** DN15 . . . . . . 9 A5
Coates La LN1 . . . . .54 B2
Coates Rd DN22 . . . . .65 B8
Cobbet Pl PE1 . . . . .226 B3
Cobblers Way **6** NG34 . . . .212 E3
Cobbs Hill **13** PE34 . . . . . .161 F3

Cobden Ave PE1 . . . . .225 F4
Cobden St
1 Gainsborough DN21 . . . .197 C4
Kingston upon Hull HU3 . . .179 F7
Peterborough PE1 . . . . .225 F4
Cob Gate PE12 . . . . .158 A6
Cobgate Cl **2** PE12 . . . . . .158 B6
Cobham Cl **11** NG34 . . . . . .122 E3
Cobleas NG32 . . . . .138 C8
Cochran Cl **9** NG31 . . . . . .210 F8
Cockbourn Fen Dike
PE12 . . . . .159 B2
Cockburn Way **6** LN5 . . . . .93 F5
Cockerels Roost LN1 . . . . . .65 D1
Cocketts Hill NG22 . . . . . . .65 A1
Cocketts La **10** DN20 . . . . . .30 F5
Cocklehole Rd PE34 . . . . . .161 B5
Cock Pit Cl HU10 . . . . .178 C6
Cockthorne La LN15 . . . . 9 C7
CODDINGTON NG24 . . . . . .104 D5
Coddington CE Prim Sch
NG24 . . . . .104 D5
Coddington La LN6 . . . . . . .105 A7
Coddington Rd NG24 . . . . .104 C3
Coelus St HU9 . . . . .181 A7
Cogan St HU1 . . . . .180 E5
Coggle Cl LN11 . . . . .198 E6
Coggles Cswy PE10 . . . . . .213 D4
Cogglesford Mill ★ NG34 . .212 F5
Coggles Way LN11 . . . . . . .61 E3
Coging Cl **8** NG24 . . . . . . .104 B2
Cohort Cl **13** HU15 . . . . . . .2 C5
Coke Oven Ave DN16 . . . . .183 F2
Colchester Mews **12** LN6 . . .93 B8
Coldham Rd LN4 . . . . .207 E6
COLD HANWORTH LN2 . . . . .56 C2
COLD HARBOUR NG33 . . . .130 D1
Cold Harbour La
Carrington PE22 . . . . .112 B6
Covenham St Mary LN11 . . . .49 D5
Grantham NG31 . . . . .211 C2
Cold Harbour Lane LN11 . . .72 F7
Coldhorn Cres **14** PE13 . . . .170 D1
Cold Hurn La PE11 . . . . . . .144 F6
Coldrons Wy LN5 . . . . .105 F5
Coldwater Lane PE24 . . . . .102 C5
Cole Ave LN5 . . . . .93 F6
COLEBY Coleby LN5 . . . . . .93 F3
West Halton DN15 . . . . 8 E6
Coleby CE Prim Sch LN5 . . .93 F3
Coleby Rd DN15 . . . . 8 E7
Coleby St LN2 . . . . .202 B3
Colegrave St **14** LN5 . . . . .205 E8
Cole La PE22 . . . . .100 B3
Coleman Ave **4** NG24 . . . .104 A2
Colenso Terr **3** LN1 . . . . . .201 D4
Coleraine Cl **8** LN5 . . . . . .205 D2
Coleridge Ave DN17 . . . . . .184 D7
Coleridge Ct **5** LN4 . . . . . .207 B5
Coleridge Gdns
Lincoln LN2 . . . . .202 B7
15 Sleaford NG34 . . . . . . .212 F4
Coleridge Gn **3** LN2 . . . . . .202 C7
Coleridge Pl Bourne PE10 . .213 E3
Peterborough PE1 . . . . .225 E8
Coleridge Rd NG24 . . . . . .104 C3
Coles Ave LN13 . . . . .75 E2
Coles Cl PE12 . . . . .215 E3
Coleshill La **7** HU3 . . . . . . .179 F5
Cole's La **1** PE20 . . . . .135 B7
Cole St DN15 . . . . .183 B3
Coles Wy NG31 . . . . .210 F4
Colin Ave DN32 . . . . .192 B6
Colindale PE21 . . . . .209 B5
Colin Rd DN16 . . . . .183 C2
Colins Wy **4** DN21 . . . . . . .29 C4
College Ave DN33 . . . . . . .194 F8
College Cl
7 Alkborough DN15 . . . . . .8 C8
1 Holbeach PE12 . . . . . . .215 C2
Horncastle LN9 . . . . .199 C2
Lincoln LN1 . . . . .201 F6
Stamford PE9 . . . . .171 C8
7 Wainfleet All Saints
PE24 . . . . .102 D1
College Gdns
East Ella HU3 . . . . .179 F7
2 Grimsby DN33 . . . . .194 F8
College Pk Horncastle LN9 .199 C2
Peterborough PE1 . . . . .226 C5
College Rd
Barrow upon Humber DN19 . .11 E7
Cranwell & Byard's Leap
NG34 . . . . .120 E8
Thornton Curtis DN39 . . . . .12 B6
College St
Cleethorpes DN35 . . . . .192 E6
Grantham NG31 . . . . .211 B3
Grimsby DN34 . . . . .191 C6
1 Kingston upon Hull HU2 . .180 E7
College Yd DN20 . . . . .196 B3
Colleysgate PE12 . . . . .216 C8
Colley St **11** PE21 . . . . . . .208 F5
Colleywell Cl **5** DN9 . . . . . .27 A2
Collier Cl **1** HU14 . . . . 3 A4
Collier Rd **2** DN40 . . . . . . .186 D5
COLLINGHAM NG23 . . . . . . .91 C4
Collingham PE2 . . . . .229 F3
Collingham Rd LN6 . . . . . . .91 F5
Collingham Sta NG23 . . . . .91 D4
Collingwood LN6 . . . . .93 C8
Collingwood Cres
3 Boston PE21 . . . . .136 D8
Grimsby DN34 . . . . .190 D4

Collingwood Prim Sch
HU3. . . . . .180 C7
Collingwood St HU3. . . . . . .180 D7
Collins Ave PE9. . . . . .218 F6
Collinson Ave DN15 . . . . . . .182 C3
Collinson La
19 Balderton NG24 . . . . . . .104 C1
Newport HU15. . . . . 1 A8
Collison Gate PE24 . . . . .102 C2
Collum Ave DN16. . . . . .185 B6
Collum Gdns **2** DN16. . . . . .185 B6
Collum House Rd DN16 . . . . .185 B6
Collum La DN16. . . . . .185 B6
Collynson Cl **1** HU10 . . . . . .178 E8
Collyns Wy **8** PE9. . . . . . . .171 B1
COLLYWESTON PE9 . . . . . . .171 B1
Collyweston Rd **1** PE8. . . . .172 B1
Colne Cl **1** LN6. . . . . .204 F3
Colne Ct **6** NG31. . . . . .210 E2
Colne Valley Visitor Ctr★
PE6 . . . . .227 B2
Colonial St HU2. . . . . .180 D7
Colonsay Ct DN36 . . . . .195 C7
Colson Pl DN35. . . . . .192 B7
Colster Way **3** NG33. . . . . .151 E6
COLSTERWORTH NG33 . . . . .151 E7
Colsterworth CE Prim Sch
NG33. . . . . .151 E7
Colsterworth Rd NG33. . . . . .151 C6
Colsuan St HU3. . . . . .180 C5
Coltman St HU3. . . . . .180 D7
Colton Cl **6** PE6 . . . . .164 E4
Colton St Brigg DN20. . . . . .196 B4
2 Misterton DN10. . . . . 39 F5
Coltsfoot Cl **4** DN35. . . . . .182 C6
Coltsfoot Dr Bourne PE10. . .213 D2
Bradley DN37. . . . . .194 B5
Peterborough PE2 . . . . .230 E7
Coltsfoot Way PE10. . . . . . . .213 D2
Columbia Rd DN32. . . . . .192 A7
Columbus Cl **5** PE11. . . . . .214 C2
Columbus Way DN33. . . . . . .190 F3
Colvile Rd PE13. . . . . .170 A5
Colville Ave HU4. . . . . .179 B6
Colville Terr **3** DN21. . . . . .197 D4
Colwyn Ave PE1. . . . . .226 E6
Comber Pl DN32 . . . . .189 B1
Combe St DN35 . . . . .192 C8
Comer Cl PE21 . . . . .209 A5
Comforts Ave DN15 . . . . . . .183 A2
Commerce La HU1. . . . . .180 D4
Commerce Rd PE2 . . . . .229 C5
Commercial Rd
2 Alford LN13 . . . . 75 F2
Grantham NG31. . . . . .211 A3
Kingston upon Hull HU1. . . . . .180 E5
1 Louth LN11. . . . . .198 D6
Scunthorpe DN16. . . . . .183 D3
Spalding PE11. . . . . .214 E5
Commodore Croft **6** HU1 180 F5
Common Balk LN13 . . . . 76 C1
Common Dro PE6 . . . . .166 C3
Common La Bardney LN3 . . . 83 C4
Barnby Dun with Kirk Sandall
DN3. . . . . 14 B4
Burgh le Marsh PE24 . . . . 89 F1
Heapham DN21 . . . . 53 F7
North Somercotes LN11. . . . . . 50 F8
Old Leake PE22 . . . . .113 F4
Sturton le Steeple DN22. . . . . . 52 C3
Twin Rivers DN14. . . . . 7 B6
Welton HU15 . . . . 2 D4
Woodside DN9. . . . . 26 E6
Common Mid Rd DN17. . . . . . 16 C8
Common Rd
Broughton DN20 . . . . 19 E4
Gedney Hill PE12 . . . . .176 F8
Moulton PE12. . . . . .146 E3
Parson Drove PE12 . . . . .176 F6
South Cave HU15. . . . . 1 C7
Waddingham DN21 . . . . 43 D6
Whaplode PE12 . . . . .168 A2
Wrangle PE22 . . . . .114 A4
Commons Dr PE7 . . . . .233 D8
Commonside
2 Crowle DN17. . . . . 16 C8
Westwoodside DN9. . . . . 27 A2
Common Side Rd PE22 . . . . .113 E4
Common Way PE13. . . . . .160 B1
Comper Swift Cl
1 Mablethorpe/Sutton on Sea
LN12. . . . . 77 A7
Sandilands LN12 . . . . 77 A7
Compton Cl **1** PE25. . . . . . .206 C1
Compton Dr
Faldingworth LN8. . . . . 56 F3
Grimsby DN34. . . . . .191 C7
Concast Rd DN16. . . . . 19 A3
Conduit La PE9 . . . . .219 C6
Conduit Rd PE9 . . . . .219 C5
Coney Garth La PE11. . . . . . .145 F5
Coneygree Rd PE2 . . . . .231 D6
Conference Ct DN16. . . . . . .185 A2
Conference Way **13** PE13 .170 D2
Conging St **2** LN9. . . . . . . .199 B4
Congreves Cl **3** PE12. . . . . .160 A8
Conifer Cl
6 Kingston upon Hull
HU5. . . . . .179 C7
2 Scunthorpe DN17. . . . . .184 C4
Conifers The PE2 . . . . .229 F6
Conifer Wy PE25 . . . . .103 C8
CONINGSBY LN4. . . . . .207 D4
Coningsby Airfield LN4. . . . .207 C2
Coningsby Cl Boston PE21 .208 D5

Coningsby Cl continued
Gainsborough DN21. . . . . . . .197 F4
2 Skegness PE25 . . . . .206 A5
Coningsby Cres LN4. . . . . . . .205 F5
Coningsby Dr DN34. . . . . . . .191 A5
Coningsby Rd
Coningsby LN4. . . . . .207 A1
Peterborough PE3 . . . . .220 E1
Scunthorpe DN17. . . . . .184 D5
Coningsby St Michaels Prim
Sch LN4. . . . . .207 C4
Coningsby St LN2. . . . . .234 C2
Conisborough Ave DN36. . . .195 B6
Conisborough Mews **22**
HU15. . . . . 2 D5
Conisbro Croft HU13. . . . . . .178 C2
CONISHOLME LN11. . . . . 50 D6
Conisholme Rd LN11. . . . . . . 50 B7
Coniston Ave **1** DN33 . . . . .194 E7
Coniston Cres DN36. . . . . . . .192 E1
Coniston Dr LN6 . . . . .205 A2
Coniston Rd PE4 . . . . .221 C3
Conker Gro LN11. . . . . .198 E6
Connaught Ave DN32. . . . . . .191 D4
Connaught Dr
4 Chapel St Leonard PE24 . 90 D7
6 Kirk Sandall DN3 . . . . . . 14 A2
Connaught Rd
Gainsborough DN21. . . . . . . .197 C6
Scunthorpe DN15. . . . . .183 A6
Connaught Terr LN5. . . . . . . .205 D5
Conquest Dro PE7. . . . . .231 D1
Consort Ct HU9. . . . . .181 B5
Constable Ave LN6. . . . . .205 A6
Constable Cl LN6. . . . . .205 A5
Constable St HU3. . . . . .180 C5
Constable Way **23** HU15. . . . 2 D5
Constance Ave LN6. . . . . . . .204 F4
Constantine Dr PE2. . . . . . . .231 E4
Constitutional Ave DN35. . . .192 C8
Convamore Rd DN32. . . . . . .191 F6
Convent La DN6. . . . . .180 D6
Conway Ave Grimsby DN34 191 A4
Peterborough PE4 . . . . .221 A2
Conway Cl HU3. . . . . .180 B5
Conway Dr LN6 . . . . .205 B2
Conway Sq **3** DN35 . . . . . . .182 E3
Conworth Cl PE1 . . . . .226 D5
Conyard Rd DN35. . . . . .192 E7
Conyers Ave DN33. . . . . .191 D2
Cook Ave PE7 . . . . .230 F5
Cook Cl Rd PE7 . . . . .233 D6
Cook Dr PE11 . . . . .214 C2
Cooke Cres **9** LN4 . . . . . . .207 D4
Cookridge Dr **51** DN7. . . . . . 14 C4
Cooks La Grimsby DN37. . . . . 24 B5
4 Nettleton LN7. . . . . 33 A3
Cook's La PE23 . . . . 88 E3
Cooks Lock PE21. . . . . .208 C3
Cookson Cl PE7. . . . . .233 D4
Cookson Wlk PE7 . . . . .233 E4
Cook's Rd PE11 . . . . .145 E2
Coomb Brigg's Prim Sch
DN40. . . . . .186 A3
Cooper Ave PE25 . . . . 90 E4
Cooper La DN37. . . . . .23 E1
Cooper Rd Grimsby DN32 . . .192 A7
Paston PE4. . . . . .221 E2
Coopers Cl PE12. . . . . .168 B4
Coopers Holt Cl LN6. . . . . . .200 A3
Cooper St Hessle HU13 . . . . .178 C3
8 Kingston upon Hull HU2. .180 F8
Coots Cl PE25 . . . . .103 C8
Coots La LN13 . . . . 76 E1
Copeland PE3. . . . . .225 A3
Copeland Ct **5** NG34 . . . . . .212 C3
Cope St DN32 . . . . .192 A8
Coppen Rd PE7 . . . . .233 C8
Copper Beech Cl
1 Gainsborough DN21 . . . . 52 F6
6 Swanland HU14. . . . . 3 B6
Copper Beech Way PE2 . . . . .231 B2
Copper Beech Wlk DN16. . . .185 B3
Copper St LN10 . . . . 84 B3
Coppice Ave **13** DN7 . . . . . . 14 D3
Coppice La **2** DN7 . . . . 14 D3
Coppice Rd **11** PE6 . . . . . . .163 C1
Coppice Side HU4. . . . . .179 C6
Coppingford Cl PE2 . . . . .231 D6
Copse Cl DN40 . . . . .186 C5
Copse Rd DN16 . . . . .185 B5
Copse The Brigg DN20. . . . . .196 E2
Grimsby DN33 . . . . .194 F8
16 Mablethorpe/Sutton on Sea
LN12. . . . . 77 A7
Copsewood PE4 . . . . .221 A4
Copthilll Independent Day Sch
PE9 . . . . .172 C6
Coral Dr **1** DN37. . . . . .194 C5
CORBY GLEN NG33. . . . . . . .152 E8
Corby Glen Com Prim Sch
NG33. . . . . .152 E8
Corby Pk HU14. . . . . 3 A5
Corby Rd
Burton Coggles NG33. . . . . . .141 A1
Scunthorpe DN16. . . . . .183 C2
Swayfield NG33. . . . . .152 D5
Cordage Ct LN1. . . . . .234 A3
Cordeaux Cl Louth LN11. . . .198 C7
8 Scotter DN21. . . . . 29 C4
Cordeaux Corner LN11. . . . . . 61 A8
Cordella Cl **1** HU3. . . . . . . .180 A5
Corden Cl PE25. . . . . .206 C1
Corfe Ave PE4 . . . . .221 A2
Corfe Cl **1** HU3. . . . . .210 E5
Corfe Wlk DN40 . . . . .186 D3
Coriander Dr
11 Bourne PE10. . . . . .213 C6

Coriander Dr continued
Yaxley PE7. . . . . .233 B8
Corinne Cres **3** PE25. . . . . .206 C3
Corinne Gr **1** PE11. . . . . . . .214 A3
Corinthian Ave DN34 . . . . . . .191 B6
Corinthian Way HU9. . . . . . . .181 D6
Cork La PE24 . . . . .102 B3
Cork Tree Cres PE21. . . . . . .208 E2
Cormack La **15** NG24 . . . . . .104 C1
Cormorant Dr DN37 . . . . . . .190 C8
Corn Cl Fiskerton LN3. . . . . . . 82 B7
Horncastle LN9. . . . . .199 B5
Cornfield Cl
9 Deeping St Nicholas
PE11. . . . . .166 C6
4 Grimsby DN33. . . . . .194 D8
Cornfield Dr DN21. . . . . 53 B1
Cornfields PE12. . . . . .215 F3
Cornfield View **4** NG34. . . .212 C2
Cornflower Ave PE7. . . . . . . .233 B8
Cornflower Cl
18 Healing DN41. . . . . 23 F5
8 Spalding PE11. . . . . .214 B6
Stamford PE9. . . . . .218 C7
Cornflower Way **3** LN6. . . . . 93 A8
Cornhill LN5. . . . . .234 B2
Cornhill Dr DN18. . . . . 11 A8
Cornhill La **30** PE21. . . . . . .208 F5
Cornish Cres NG34. . . . . . . .133 E7
Cornley Lane DN9. . . . . 39 D2
Cornley Rd DN10. . . . . 39 C7
Cornmarket **8** LN11. . . . . . .198 B5
Cornstall Bldgs **7** PE9. . . . .219 C5
Cornwall Cl
Grantham NG31. . . . . .211 C7
12 Scampton LN1. . . . . 67 E5
Cornwallis Rd LN2. . . . . .202 D4
Cornwall Rd
5 Keadby DN17 . . . . 17 D6
Scunthorpe DN16. . . . . .185 C5
8 Stamford PE9 . . . . .219 B6
Cornwall St **21** DN21. . . . . . 30 B1
Cornwall Way **8** NG34. . . . .108 D2
Cornwell Cl DN21. . . . . .191 C3
Corn Wlk DN35. . . . . .191 A2
Corona Dr **3** DN8. . . . . 15 A8
Coronation Ave
3 Crowland PE6. . . . . .175 B8
2 Deeping St Nicholas
PE11. . . . . .166 C6
Parson Drove PE12 . . . . .177 A7
Coronation Cl
1 Louth LN11. . . . . .198 D7
1 Spalding PE11. . . . . .157 B6
Coronation Cotts DN35 . . . . .192 F5
Coronation Cres Coleby LN5 93 F3
1 Epworth DN9. . . . . 27 D6
Coronation Rd
Cleethorpes DN35 . . . . .192 F5
Corby Glen NG33 . . . . .152 E8
Ingoldmells PE25. . . . . 90 F3
3 Market Rasen LN8. . . . . . 57 D7
9 Stainforth DN7 . . . . 14 C6
5 Ulceby DN39. . . . . 12 A1
Woodhall Spa LN10 . . . . 97 D6
Corporation Bank **12** PE6 .166 E1
Corporation Rd
1 Grimsby DN31. . . . . .188 E1
Grimsby DN31. . . . . .191 D8
10 Kingston upon Hull HU9. . . 5 D8
4 Scunthorpe DN15. . . . . . .183 A3
Corran Garth **6** HU4 . . . . . .179 A3
Correen Cl **2** LN5. . . . . .205 D2
CORRINGHAM DN21. . . . . 41 E2
Corringham CE Prim Sch
DN21. . . . . 41 E2
Corringham Rd DN21. . . . . . .197 F5
Corringham Rd Ind Est
DN21. . . . . 41 A1
Corsair Gr **4** HU3. . . . . .180 A4
Corwood Cl LN2. . . . . .202 E4
Cosford Cl LN6. . . . . .204 B8
Cosgrove Cl
2 Lincoln LN6. . . . . .205 A6
Peterborough PE3 . . . . .225 C6
Cosgrove St **5** DN35. . . . . .192 F6
Costa Row NG23 . . . . .117 D3
Costello Stadium★ HU4. . . .179 C4
COSTON LE14. . . . . .150 C5
Coston Rd NG33. . . . . .150 E5
Cot Garth La DN21. . . . . 53 E3
Cotham Gdns **22** DN41. . . . . 23 A4
Cotman Rd LN6. . . . . .205 B6
Cotman Wlk LN6. . . . . 46 C1
Cotswold Cl **22** Lincoln LN6 . 93 C8
3 Peterborough PE4. . . . . .221 C1
Cotswold Dr
Great Gonerby NG31 . . . . . . .210 E7
Waltham DN37. . . . . .194 D4
Cotswold Rd **5** DN8. . . . . . . 15 A7
Cottage Beck Rd DN16. . . . .183 B2
Cottage Cl **2** DN20. . . . . 30 F5
Cottage Dr HU10. . . . . .178 B8
Cottage La Collingham NG23 91 C3
1 Lincoln LN6. . . . . .205 B4
North Clifton NG23. . . . . 78 D7
Cottage Paddock The
LN6. . . . . .205 B5
Cottage Yd La DN36. . . . . 36 C7
COTTAM DN22. . . . . 65 C7
Cottesmore Cl
Grantham NG31. . . . . .211 B6
Peterborough PE3. . . . . .225 D4
Skegness PE25. . . . . .206 B6
Cottesmore Rd
Birchwood LN6. . . . . .204 D5
Cleethorpes DN35 . . . . .192 E2
Kingston upon Hull HU13 . . .178 F2

Cottesmore Rd continued
5 Stamford PE9 . . . . .218 E5
Cottingham Ct
35 Barton-upon-Humber
DN18. . . . . 3 E1
Scunthorpe DN15. . . . . .183 A4
Cottingham Rd LN2. . . . . . . .202 B7
Cotton Dr **7** NG24 . . . . .104 A2
Cotton End PE3 . . . . .225 A4
Cotton Rd PE21 . . . . .208 D6
Cotton Smith Way **1** LN2. . 68 C2
Coulam PE1 **11** DN36. . . . . . . 36 D8
Coulbeck Dr DN35. . . . . .192 D5
Coulby Cl NG23 . . . . .117 F7
Coulman Rd DN8. . . . . 15 B8
Coulman St DN8 . . . . 15 B8
Coulman Street Ind Est
DN8 . . . . 15 B8
Coulson Cl **13** DN20 . . . . 31 A5
Coulson Dr HU13. . . . . .178 F2
Coulson Rd LN6. . . . . .201 D1
Coultas Ct **3** HU3 . . . . .180 A6
Coult Ave LN6. . . . . 93 C8
Council Ave HU4. . . . . .179 E3
Council Rd **19** HU15 . . . . . . .170 E1
Council St PE4 . . . . .225 D8
Council Terr **6** DN18. . . . . . . 3 E1
Count Alan Rd PE25 . . . . . . .206 D8
Counter Drain Dro PE11 . . . .155 E2
Counthorpe La NG33 . . . . . . .152 E2
Counthorpe Rd NG33. . . . . . .152 F3
County Rd
3 Hampton Vale PE7. . . . .230 C1
Yaxley PE7. . . . . .233 C8
County Rd S **2** HU5 . . . . . . .179 C8
Coupland Cl **5** DN21. . . . . . .197 F5
Coupledyke La PE20. . . . . . . .136 D5
Courtfield Cl **10** LN2. . . . . . . 68 F2
Courtfields PE6. . . . . .217 B6
Courtney St HU8. . . . . .181 B8
Court The PE24 . . . . 77 C3
Courtyard The
Boston PE21. . . . . .209 B3
Market Deeping PE6. . . . . . . .217 C4
Stamford PE9. . . . . .219 A5
Cousin Wk DN36 . . . . .195 D7
Covel Rd NG34 . . . . .212 B6
Covenham Rd LN11. . . . . 49 D4
COVENHAM ST
BARTHOLOMEW LN11. . . . . .49 C5
COVENHAM ST MARY
LN11. . . . . .49 C5
Coventry Ave DN34. . . . . . . .191 A5
Coventry Cl
7 Grantham NG31 . . . . . . .210 D5
Peterborough PE4 . . . . .220 F3
5 Scunthorpe DN17. . . . . .184 D7
Coventry Rd **7** DN8 . . . . 15 B8
Cove Rd DN9. . . . . 26 F3
Coverley Rd **5** NG33 . . . . . .151 D2
Covert Rd DN16. . . . . .185 B5
Covert The
Clinton Park LN4. . . . . .207 C5
Peterborough PE3 . . . . .225 B1
16 Thurlby PE10 . . . . .164 C8
Covill Cl **2** NG31. . . . . .129 D5
Covington **29** HU15 . . . . 2 C6
Covin's La LN11. . . . . 49 C8
Coward's La PE11. . . . . .144 F2
Cowbank La PE24 . . . . .116 D8
Cowbank Lane PE24. . . . . . . .103 D4
COWBIT PE12 . . . . .157 B1
Cowbit Dro PE11. . . . . .144 C1
Cowbit Rd PE12. . . . . .214 D2
Cowbit St Mary's (Endowed)
CE Prim Sch The PE12 . . . .167 A8
COWBRIDGE DN22. . . . . .125 E6
Cowbridge Bsns Pk PE22 . . .125 E7
Cowbridge Rd PE20 . . . . . . .134 E5
Cowbroads La PE22 . . . . . . .113 E2
Cowdale La LN1. . . . . 66 B6
Cow Dale La DN10. . . . . 39 C3
Cowdale's Dro PE11. . . . . . . .134 F1
Cow Dro LN4 . . . . .123 B7
Cowes Rd NG31 . . . . .210 E4
Cowgate Brough HU15. . . . . . . 2 D6
2 Heckington NG34. . . . . . .122 E3
Peterborough PE1 . . . . .225 F2
Cow Gate NG34. . . . . .143 C8
Cowhams La PE20. . . . . .146 C8
Cow La Minting LN8 . . . . 71 B1
Swinderby LN6. . . . . 92 B5
Tealby LN8. . . . . 46 C1
Twin Rivers DN17. . . . . 7 C6
Upton DN21. . . . . 53 F6
Welbourn LN5. . . . . .106 C5
Cowle La **1** LN11. . . . . 62 A3
Cowley Cl **6** PE20. . . . . .135 C7
Cowley's Rd **10** PE11. . . . . .134 E2
Cow Marsh La DN36. . . . . 36 E5
Cowpaddle La LN4. . . . . 82 A5
Cowpasture La DN22. . . . . 52 D3
Cow Pasture La PE22 . . . . 65 A7
Cow Pasture Lane LE15. . . . .162 C8
Cowper Ave DN17. . . . . .184 D7
Cowper Cl DN36. . . . . 37 B2
Cowper Dr LN2. . . . . .202 C7
Cowper Rd PE1 . . . . .225 F2
Cowpers Gate PE12 . . . . . . .216 A3
Cowslip Cres **9** PE10. . . . . .213 D3
Cowslip Ct **26** DN41. . . . . . . 23 F5
Cowslip Dr **2** PE6. . . . . .217 D6
Cowslip La LN11. . . . . .198 F8
Cow La **7** LN7. . . . . 16 D8
Cox's Ct **7** DN20 . . . . 31 A5
Cox's Dro PE6. . . . . .167 C1
Cox's Hill DN21. . . . . .197 D5

Cox's Wlk **8** NG31. . . . . . . .129 E5
Coxwold Gr HU4 . . . . .179 E5
Crabapple Gn PE2. . . . . .229 D6
Crab La PE20 . . . . .123 C4
Crabley La HU15 . . . . 1 E7
Crab Marsh PE13. . . . . .170 C2
Crabtree PE4 . . . . .221 F1
Crabtree La
Beckingham DN10 . . . . 52 A8
Mablethorpe & Sutton LN12. . 77 A7
Saltfleetby LN12. . . . . 51 D1
Crabtree Rd
Colsterworth NG33. . . . . .151 B7
Easton NG33. . . . . .140 A1
8 Hatfield DN7 . . . . 14 C5
Skillington NG33. . . . . .139 F1
Crack Holt La PE22. . . . . . . .126 F8
Cradge Bank PE6. . . . . .217 C6
Cradge Bank Rd
Deeping St Nicholas PE11. . . .167 A7
Spalding PE11. . . . . .214 C1
Cradge Dro PE11. . . . . .165 E3
Cragg Cl **3** PE20. . . . . .135 C7
Cragmire La PE22. . . . . .114 C3
Cragston Ave DN33. . . . . . . .191 D3
Craig Cl **3** DN20 . . . . 19 D3
Craig St PE1 . . . . .225 F3
Craikbank La DN22. . . . . 65 A8
Craikhill Ave DN40. . . . . .186 C4
Craithie Rd DN35. . . . . .192 E4
Crake Ave DN33. . . . . .191 C1
Crakedale Rd **9** DN15 . . . . . . 9 B5
Crampin Rd **3** DN35. . . . . . .192 E7
Cranberry La PE22. . . . . .114 F7
Cranberry Way HU4. . . . . . . .179 C4
Cranbourne Chase LN6 . . . . . 93 B8
Cranbourne Cl **7** DN35. . . . .192 F1
Cranbourne Mews **6**
LN4. . . . . .203 D1
Cranbrook St HU3. . . . . .180 C8
Crane Ave PE7 . . . . .233 F6
Crane Cl **1** NG34. . . . . .120 F8
Crane Gr LN6. . . . . .205 C2
Cranemore PE4 . . . . .220 E4
Cranepit La PE11. . . . . .135 B1
Crane Rd HU9. . . . . .181 C6
Crane's Gate PE12. . . . . .158 C1
Cranesgate S PE12 . . . . .168 C8
Cranford Dr PE3 . . . . .225 C4
Cranidge Cl **8** DN17. . . . . . . 16 D8
Cranmore Dro PE6. . . . . .165 F1
Cranmore La PE12. . . . . .215 B1
CRANWELL NG34. . . . . .120 F8
Cranwell Airfield NG34 . . . . .120 D7
Cranwell Ave NG34 . . . . .120 D6
Cranwell Aviation Heritage
Cantre★ NG34. . . . . .120 D6
Cranwell Cl
2 Beacon Hill NG24. . . . . .104 B5
6 Kirton in Lindsey DN21 . . . 42 F8
4 Skegness PE25 . . . . .206 A5
Cranwell Dr DN37. . . . . .190 F8
Cranwell Prim Sch NG34. . . .120 D8
Cranwell St LN5. . . . . .201 C1
Crapple La DN21. . . . . 29 C2
Craske La PE24 . . . . .161 D3
Craven Ave **4** PE20 . . . . . . .136 C5
Craven Cl NG32. . . . . .139 C8
Craven Prim Acad HU9 . . . . .181 C3
Craven Rd
Cleethorpes DN35 . . . . .192 B7
4 Hatfield DN7 . . . . 14 C4
Craven St N HU9 . . . . .181 C8
Craven St S HU9 . . . . .181 D7
Craven's La PE20. . . . . .146 E2
Craven St LN5 . . . . .205 D8
Crawcroft La LN13 . . . . 76 E5
Crawford Gdns **3** PE6. . . . . .175 C8
Crawthorne Rd PE1. . . . . . . .226 A3
Crawthorne St **1** PE1 . . . . . .226 B3
Craycroft Rd **3** DN9. . . . . . . 27 B2
Craypool La **7** LN2. . . . . 68 F4
Craythorne La **23** PE21. . . . .208 F5
Creamery The **8** NG34. . . . .212 D3
Creampoke Cres **8**
DN21. . . . . 55 A8
Crease Dro PE6 . . . . .175 B7
Creaseyplot La PE20. . . . . . .124 B1
CREETON NG33. . . . . .153 A2
Creeton Rd NG33. . . . . .153 A1
Crescent Ct **7** LN2 . . . . 68 D2
Crescent Mews LN5. . . . . 93 F4
Crescent St DN31 . . . . .191 C7
Crescent The
Beckingham DN10 . . . . 40 B1
Bracebridge Heath LN4 . . . . . . 81 A2
15 Brough HU15. . . . . 2 D5
Easton on the Hill PE9 . . . . . .171 C3
10 Eye PE6. . . . . .175 A1
Fiskerton LN3. . . . . 82 B7
Gainsborough DN21. . . . . 52 F5
Hatfield DN7 . . . . 14 C5
Holton le Clay DN36 . . . . .195 C2
Horncastle LN9. . . . . .199 C3
9 Kirk Sandall DN3 . . . . . . 14 A2
Louth LN11. . . . . .198 B7
13 Mablethorpe/Sutton on Sea
LN12. . . . . 77 A7
Morton PE10. . . . . .154 B7
12 Nettleham LN2 . . . . 68 C2
Peterborough PE2. . . . . .230 C5
Ryhall PE9. . . . . .163 D1
Sleaford NG34. . . . . .121 A3
9 Spalding PE11. . . . . .214 D4
Swayfield NG33. . . . . .152 E5
Cresent The **3** LN8. . . . . 70 D4
Cresset The★ PE3 . . . . .225 A5
Cressey St **2** DN31. . . . . . .189 A1

Cresswell Cl
1 Kingston upon Hull
HU2..........................180 E8
Pinchbeck PE11............214 E8
Cresta Cl LN6................204 D1
Cresta Dr DN17..............184 E4
Cresta The DN34.............191 C5
Crester Dr PE4...............221 A3
Cres The NG32...............128 F6
Crew Rd NG23..................91 D5
Creyke La **12** HU15.........2 D6
Cricketers Way **19** PE13...170 C1
Cridling Pl DN35.............192 D4
Cringle Rd..................139 F2
Cringleway NG33.............140 A5
Crispin Cl
5 Kingston upon Hull
HU4...........................179 A2
13 Lutton PE12............160 A8
Crispin Way DN16............185 B2
Croake Hill NG33.............153 A5
Crocus Cl PE7...............233 F6
Crocus Gr PE1...............226 A8
Crocus Wlk PE11.............214 D2
CROFT PE24..................102 F4
Croft Bank **1** PE24........102 E2
Croft Cl **3** Croft PE24.....102 E2
Sleaford NG34...............195 C5
Croft Dr Grantham NG31.....211 C3
Kingston upon Hull HU10....178 C6
Crofters Gr DN36.............95 C5
Croft La Bassingham LN5......92 F3
Cherry Willingham LN3......203 E7
Coningsby LN4..............110 E8
Croft PE24..................102 E2
Scunthorpe DN17.............184 E2
Croft Lodge **1** DN9.........16 E1
Croft Marsh La PE24.........102 F3
Crofton Cl LN2...............202 D4
Crofton Dr LN2..............202 D4
Crofton Rd LN2..............202 D4
Croft Pk **4** HU14............3 A5
Croft Rd Croft PE24..........102 E2
Finningley DN10..............26 A1
Crofts La DN7................14 B6
Croft St **2** Horncastle LN9..199 C3
Lincoln LN2.................234 C1
Crofts The
7 Humberston DN36.......36 C8
Scunthorpe DN16............183 B2
Croft The
6 Beckingham DN10.......52 B8
Bourne PE10................213 D6
10 Nettleham LN2..........68 D2
21 Stamford PE9..........219 C5
23 Thorne/Moorends DN8...15 B7
2 West/East Butterwick
DN17.........................28 D8
Croft View HU10.............178 C6
Croft Way PE7...............230 C2
Cromarty Rd **8** PE9.........218 E6
Cromer Ave Grimsby DN34...191 A5
Mablethorpe/Sutton on Sea
LN12..........................64 D1
Cromer Cl
Harrowby Est NG31.........211 E7
4 Lincoln LN6.............205 A1
Cromford St **1** DN21.......197 D5
Cromwell Ave
6 Gainsborough DN21......52 F6
Grimsby DN31................191 C7
Horncastle LN9.............199 C2
4 Scunthorpe DN16........183 B1
2 Woodhall Spa LN10.......97 D5
Cromwell Cl Boston PE21....208 D7
2 Heighington/Washingborough
LN4..........................203 A2
2 Kingston upon Hull HU3..180 D8
Northborough PE6...........217 E1
Cromwell Cres **3** NG34....212 E4
Cromwell Ct **11** HU4.......178 E7
Cromwell Mews **1** PE6......173 C4
Cromwell Pl LN4.............207 A5
Cromwell Rd
Cleethorpes DN35...........193 A4
Grimsby DN37................188 A1
Peterborough PE1...........225 F4
Cromwell St
Gainsborough DN21.........197 D2
Lincoln LN2.................234 C1
Cromwell View **21** LN7......33 B4
Cromwell Way **6** PE6......217 A6
Crook Bank LN12..............63 F6
Crooked Billet St DN21......197 B8
Crookes Broom Ave **32**
DN7...........................14 D4
Crookes Broom La DN7.......14 D4
Crookesbroom Prim Acad
DN7...........................14 C4
Crook Hill HU15...............2 C8
Crook Mill Rd DN40...........12 C4
Crook O Moor Road DN8......15 D7
Crook Tree La DN7............14 F5
Crook Tree Lane DN7........14 E4
Cropper's La PE22............126 E1
Croppers Way PE22..........137 E7
Cropston Rd PE1.............226 E7
CROSBY DN15.................182 D4
Crosby Ave DN33.............182 D4
Crosby House Flats DN15....183 B4
Crosby La **1** LN5...........106 E4
Crosby Prim Sch
Scunthorpe DN15............183 A4
Scunthorpe DN15............183 A5
Crosby Rd Grimsby DN33....191 B2
Scunthorpe DN15............183 B4
Crosby Row PE12.............160 D4

CROSBY WARREN DN15.......183 D6
Crosland Rd DN37............190 D8
Cross Bank LN4................96 D8
Crossbeck Rd DN16..........185 A4
Crossberry Way **1** PE6.....173 B4
Cross Carr Rd DN20...........31 B5
Crosscliff Hill LN11...........60 A8
Cross Coates Rd DN34........191 A6
Cross Comm La DN22.........52 D3
Cross Dro Fleet PE12.........168 B2
Holland Fen with Brothertoft
PE20.........................125 B5
Horbling NG34..............133 F2
Kirton PE20.................136 A5
Tydd St Giles PE13..........169 C5
Crossfield Rd
Kingston upon Hull HU13....178 E3
12 Navenby/Wellingore
LN5..........................107 A8
CROSSGATE PE11.............145 C1
Cross Gate
Long Sutton PE12............159 F3
Quadring PE12..............135 A1
Spalding PE12...............157 B6
Tydd St Mary PE13..........160 A2
Weston PE12................157 C7
Crossgate Cres **5** PE11....145 C1
Crossgate La **7** PE11......145 C1
Crossgill Cl NG31............211 F5
Cross Hill
Gringley on the Hill DN10.....39 C1
Haxey DN9....................27 C3
Cross Keys La LN4...........207 F4
Cross Keys Yd **5** NG34....212 C4
Cross La **1** Alkborough DN15..8 C8
4 Amcotts DN17.............7 F1
Balderton NG24.............104 B1
3 Bourne PE10............213 E2
Butterwick PE22.............126 F3
Collingham NG23.............91 D5
Flixborough DN15.............8 B1
Glentham LN8................44 A2
Gringley on the Hill DN10.....39 A5
Harby NG23...................79 B5
8 Lincoln LN6..............93 C8
Long Bennington NG23......117 D1
North Kelsey LN7.............32 B5
Pinchbeck PE11.............144 F1
Wellingore LN5..............106 A6
Crosslands **5** PE11.........134 F2
Crossmoor Bank DN14..........6 C5
Cross O'Cliff Cl LN5.........205 E6
Cross O'Cliff Hill LN5.......205 E6
Cross Rd Hatfield DN7........15 B4
Langtoft PE6................165 B4
Market Deeping PE6.........217 F8
Sutton St Edmund PE12.....169 A4
Tydd St Mary PE13..........160 B2
Ulceby DN39...................12 B3
Cross Slack **5** DN17.......16 D8
Cross Spencer St **10** LN5..205 E8
Cross St
Barnby in the Willows
NG24........................104 A3
8 Barrow upon Humber
DN19..........................11 D8
4 Brigg DN20.............196 C3
Cleethorpes DN35...........192 E6
13 Crowle DN17...........16 D8
Gainsborough DN21........197 B8
Garthorpe & Fockerby DN17..7 E6
Grimsby DN31...............189 B2
1 Holbeach PE12.........215 D2
Horncastle LN9.............199 C3
Kingston upon Hull HU1....180 E6
Lincoln LN5.................234 B1
11 Nettleham LN2.........68 C2
Peterborough PE1...........226 A2
4 Potter Hanworth LN4....82 B1
Scunthorpe DN15............183 B4
3 Skegness PE25.........206 B3
Spalding PE11...............214 C3
Sturton le Steeple DN22......52 B3
2 Waltham DN37..........194 E4
2 West Halton DN15........8 E8
2 Whaplode PE12..........158 B7
Cross Tree Rd **21** DN17....29 D7
Crossways **8** DN7...........14 C6
Crossway The DN34..........190 E3
Crowberry Dr DN16..........185 D5
Crowder Cl LN3................83 B4
Crowdyke Gate PE12.........158 B5
Crowfields PE6...............217 F5
Crowhall La PE22............127 A4
Crowhurst **1** PE4..........221 A5
Crow La Gedney PE12.........159 D6
Great Hale NG34............122 F1
Leadenham LN5.............106 D3
CROWLAND PE6...............166 C1
Crowland Ave
Grimsby DN34...............190 F4
Scunthorpe DN16............185 A7
Crowland Dr LN6............204 F7
Crowland Ponds Nature
Reserve ★ PE6.............166 D2
Crowland Rd
14 Crowle DN17..........16 D7
Deeping St James PE6.....174 D7
Eye PE6....................175 A3
CROWLE DN17................16 D7
Crowle Bank Rd DN17........17 C4
Crowle Dr DN33.............191 A3
Crowle Moor Nature
Reserve ★ DN17............6 B1
Crowle Prim Sch DN17.......16 C7
Crowle Rd DN17...............6 F2
Crowle St HU9...............181 D7

Crowle Sta DN17.............16 E5
Crown Ave
3 Chapel St Leonard PE24..90 D7
Holbeach PE12..............147 C6
Crown Cl
10 Collingham NG23......91 D5
5 Leverington PE13.......170 B1
Crown Ct **3** DN22...........52 B3
Crown Dr PE11...............214 F6
Crown Gdns **2** DN21........29 C3
Crown Hill NG33.............141 B8
Crown La
14 Northorpe PE10.......164 C8
Tinwell PE9.................218 D3
Crown Lakes Ctry Pk ★
PE7..........................231 B2
Crown Lodge PE12...........215 C7
Crown Mills **2** LN11.......198 D3
Crown St Peterborough PE1.225 E7
Ryhall PE9..................163 C2
7 Stamford PE9..........219 B5
Crown Wlk Bourne PE10.....213 C6
Louth LN11.................198 E5
Crow Pk LN6................204 A1
Crow's La PE24..............102 C2
Crowson Cres PE6...........217 E1
Crowson Way PE6...........217 D5
Crowston Wlk **7** DN15.....183 B3
Crowther Way **8** HU14......3 B7
Crow Tree Bank DN8..........15 D4
Crowtree La LN11...........198 A5
CROXBY DN37.................34 D1
Croxby Ave DN33.............194 F8
Croxby Gr DN33.............194 F7
Croxby Lane LN7..............34 A2
Croxby Ponds Road DN37.....34 C4
Croxby Rd DN37..............47 B8
CROXTON DN39................21 F7
Croxton Dr LN6.............204 D3
CROXTON KERRIAL NG32...138 D4
Croxton Kerrial CE Prim Sch
NG32........................138 D4
Croxton La NG32.............138 D5
Croxton Rd Croxton DN39....21 F7
Kirmington DN39.............22 A5
Sproxton LE14..............138 E2
Croyland Rd PE4.............221 B1
Croyland Way **15** PE6......166 F1
Crucible Cl LN6.............204 D3
Crusader Rd LN6.............201 C1
Crystal Dr **1** PE2..........230 D8
Crystal St HU3..............180 C7
Cubitt Way PE2.............231 A8
Cuckoo La
Ashby de la Launde & Bloxholm
LN4..........................107 F7
Hatfield DN7..................14 E6
Pinchbeck PE11.............145 C2
Cul De Sac The **8** PE2......99 A4
Cul-de-sac The PE22.........100 B3
Cullen Cl LN4...............109 E5
Culley Ct PE2...............229 B2
Cullin Cl **1** LN5...........205 D2
Culpins Cl PE11..............214 F5
CULVERTHORPE NG32.......131 E7
Culverthorpe Hall ★ NG32.131 D7
Culverthorpe Rd NG34.......132 A7
Culvert Rd PE24.............102 B3
Cumberland Ave
14 Navenby/Wellingore
LN5..........................107 A7
Cumberland Gdns NG33.....152 D1
Cumberland Rd DN35........193 A2
Cumberland St HU2.........181 A8
Cumberland Way **11** LN1...67 E5
Cumberland Terr **12** LN8...47 B6
Cumberlidge Cl **10** PE24...102 C7
CUMBERWORTH LN13.........89 F8
Cumberworth La **2** LN13....76 F1
Cumberworth Rd LN13........89 C7
Cunningham Rd
1 Moorland Prison DN7...26 A8
Woodston PE2...............230 E8
Cunsdike La PE11...........145 D5
Cupola Cl LN6..............204 C3
Cupola Way DN15............183 A8
Cuppleditch Wy LN11........198 C7
Curle Ave LN2...............234 C4
Curlew Cft DN16.............185 F5
Curlew Cl **4** PE12.........216 B4
Curlew Dr **8** PE12.........167 B8
Curlew Pl PE2...............231 D7
Curlew Lodge La PE12.......160 F8
Curlew Way NG34...........212 B3
Curlew Wlk **14** PE6.......217 C5
Currie Rd **16** NG24.......104 A5
Curry Rd DN34...............190 F7
Curtis Cl **13** NG23.........91 D5
Curtis Dr Coningsby LN4.....207 D4
Heighington LN4.............81 E4
Curtois Cl **4** LN4..........81 E2
Curzen Cres **8** DN3........14 A2
Curzon Ave DN35.............192 D5
Curzon Ct DN35.............192 D5
Curzon Est **6** LN4..........207 A5
Curzon Mews **3** LN4.......203 D1
Curzon St
1 Gainsborough DN21....197 C6
Kingston upon Hull HU3......179 F7
Cushman Cres DN40..........186 C3
Customhouse St **2** PE12....160 F4
Custom Rd Frognall PE6.....165 E1
Newborough PE6............174 B8
Cut Dike PE22...............124 D8
Cut End Rd PE22............137 D7
Cuthbert Ave **6** DN38.......21 B4
Cuthbert Cl **15** NG34......212 B2

Cuthbert's La PE20..........136 B8
Cuthberts Yd LN1............234 A4
CUXWOLD LN7................34 B4
Cuxwold Rd
3 Scunthorpe DN16......185 C8
Swallow LN7.................34 B5
Cydonia App LN6............204 C8
Cygnet Cl **3** NG34.........212 B3
Cygnet Pk PE7...............230 E3
Cygnet Rd PE7..............230 E3
Cynthia Rd DN32............192 C5
Cypress Cl
2 Peterborough PE3......225 A2
9 Sleaford NG34..........212 D2
Cyprus St **5** HU9.............5 D8
Cyrano Way DN37............190 C7
Cyril Cooper Ct DN32........191 D6
Cyrus Wy PE7...............230 E3

D

Daffodil Cl PE11.............214 B3
Daffodil Gr PE2..............231 C7
Dagger La HU1...............180 F6
Daggett Rd DN35............193 A4
Daimler Ave PE7............233 E6
D'aincourt Pk LN4............81 D2
Dairy Cl **1** Gosberton PE11..145 C2
Normanby DN15................8 C3
Dairycoates Ave HU3........180 A4
Dairycoates Rd HU4.........179 C3
Dairy Dro PE6...............176 E2
Daisy Cl DN16..............185 D4
Daisy Ct PE13...............213 D3
Daisy Dale PE21.............209 A3
Daisy Dr PE2................230 B1
Daisyfield La NG34..........212 C5
Daisy Rd PE12...............215 C1
Daisy Way LN11.............198 A7
DALBY PE23...................88 B5
Dalby Ct PE1................226 D5
Dalby Rd LN13................88 C5
DALDERBY LN9................85 D1
Dalderby Cres **16** LN2......68 C2
Dale Ave LN3................203 E6
Dale Cl Peterborough PE2...229 F5
10 Swanland HU14.........3 B7
Dale Cres **1** LN4..........104 C1
Dalehouse Dr **2** HU10.....178 F6
Dale Pit Rd **8** DN7.........14 F3
Dale Pk Ave DN15.............9 A5
Dale Rd **6** Brough HU15....2 C7
Grantham NG31.............211 A7
Swanland HU14...............3 B7
Welton HU15.................2 E6
Dale St N DN15.............182 F5
Dales La DN10................39 A6
Dale's La PE20..............135 D5
Dale St Lincoln LN5.........202 B4
Scunthorpe DN17............184 E3
Dalesway HU10..............178 B6
Dales Wy LN11..............198 C8
Dales The **25** Nettleham LN2 68 C2
Daleswood **1** LN4...........81 E2
Dale Way **17** NG24........104 C1
Dalewood LN1...............205 D2
Dallisons Rd **5** DN20.......31 A5
Dallygate NG33.............140 A5
Dallygate La NG33...........140 B5
Dalmatian Way **14** DN20...19 E4
Dalton Cl NG31.............210 E6
Dame Kendal Gr DN33.......191 B3
Damgate PE12...............215 E1
Dam Gn La **5** HU15.........2 C7
Dam La DN39.................11 E5
Dam Rd DN18..................3 D1
Dams La LN9.................73 B2
Danby Hills LN2..............68 B1
Danby Rd **16** DN17.........29 D7
Dane Cl **15** Broughton DN20..19 E4
31 Metheringham LN4.....95 C4
Danegeld Pl **24** PE9.......219 C5
Danes Cl PE1................226 C4
Danes Cotts **3** LN2.........234 B3
Danes Ctyd **11** LN2........234 B3
Danes Dr **2** HU13...........3 F4
Danes Terr LN2..............234 B3
Danesfield Ave DN37........194 E5
Danesgate Lincoln LN2......234 B3
11 New Holland DN19......4 E2
Danes Rd DN21..............197 F5
Danes Terr LN2..............234 B3
Danethorpe La NG24........104 D8
Danial Cl PE25..............206 C8
Daniel Cres **10** LN4.......203 D1
Daniel Ct **7** PE9...........219 C4
Daniel's Cres PE12..........216 C5
Daniel's Dro PE6.............167 D1
Daniels Gate **1** PE11......214 C6
Daniel's Gate PE12...........216 C7
Daniel's Reach PE11.........214 C7
Danish Ct PE4...............220 E4
Danns Hill DN20...............10 B3
Dansom La S HU8...........181 B8
Danson Cl DN18.............10 F8
Danube Cl HU5..............179 C8
Danube Sq PE11.............214 A4
Danum Cl **11** DN16.........18 B8
Danum Rd **6** Hatfield DN7...14 D3
Scunthorpe DN17............184 F8
Daphne Cl **9** LN4...........81 E2
Dar Beck Rd DN21...........29 C4
Darby Rd DN15...............8 B4
Darbyshire Cl NG23..........79 B5
Dark La Amcotts DN17........7 F1
Barnby in the Willows NG24 105 A3

Cuthbert's La PE20..........136 B8
Cre–Dee 247

Dark La continued
Bicker PE20................135 A5
Bitchfield & Bassingthorpe
NG33........................141 A3
Burwell LN11.................74 A3
Holbeach PE12.............215 B5
Darley Cl DN35.............192 C5
Darley Dale Cres **1** NG31..211 A7
Darley's La PE11............214 A6
Darlton Rd NG22..............65 A1
Darnholme Cl DN16..........190 E8
Darnholme Cres **15** HU3...29 D7
Darrismere Villas **4** HU3..180 A5
Dart Ave LN6...............205 A2
Dartmouth Rd DN17.........182 D1
Dartmouth Wlk HU4.........179 A3
Darwin Cl
5 Stamford PE9..........219 A7
7 Sutton Bridge PE12....160 A8
10 Waddington LN5.......93 E8
Darwin Ct Lincoln LN2......202 B5
Little Coates DN34..........190 F6
Darwin St
3 Gainsborough DN21....197 D2
5 Kirton in Lindsey DN21..30 B1
6 Kirton in Lindsey DN21..30 A1
Dashwood Rd **7** LN13......75 E2
Datchet Garth **3** HU4......179 B2
Daubeney Ave LN1...........66 D2
Daubney St DN35............189 E1
Davenport Ave HU13........178 D1
Davenport Dr DN35..........192 C4
Davey Cl **1** Boston PE21...208 E7
Louth LN11.................198 C7
David Ave Lincoln LN1......201 D8
Louth LN11.................198 D7
David Chalmers Cl PE2......230 F8
David Dr PE25...............206 B6
David Pl DN36...............195 C5
David's Cl PE4..............220 D4
David's La Benington PE22...127 A5
Peterborough PE4..........220 F5
Davidson Dr PE21...........208 D2
David St DN32..............191 F5
Davie Pl DN35...............192 B7
Davisons Ave DN31..........191 D8
Davis's Cl HU10.............178 C8
Davos Way PE25.............206 A7
Davy Ave DN15..............182 E4
Davy Cl **3** LN1..............61 F3
Davy Cres DN20.............196 C5
Davy's La **6** LN4............81 A2
Dawber La
Claxby St Andrew LN13......88 F5
Thimbleby LN9................85 C5
Dawes La DN16.............183 D4
Dawes Lane Acad DN15.....183 D3
Dawlish Rd DN33............194 E6
Dawnay Dr HU10............179 A6
Dawnhill La DN21............42 A3
Daws Gate Moulton PE12...157 F2
Whaplode PE12.............158 A2
Dawson Ave **1** PE11.......214 F6
Dawson City Claypits Nature
Reserve ★ DN19.............5 C4
Dawson Cl Lincoln LN6.....204 F6
6 Newborough PE6........174 E4
Dawson Dr **8** PE24........102 E7
Dawson Rd **7** NG34.......212 D6
Dawsons La LN3.............203 F8
Daybell Cl **20** NG13........128 A6
Daybrook Cl NG32...........139 C8
Day Cl **6** Keadby DN17.....17 D6
Wrawby DN20................20 E4
Daymond St PE2............230 D8
Day's La PE20...............134 F3
Deacon Dr DN15.............182 B2
Deacon Rd LN2.............202 C5
Deaconscroft PE3...........225 B5
Deacon St PE1.............225 F3
Dealtry Cl DN21..............53 D5
Dean Cl **3** NG34..........121 B8
Dean Cres PE7..............230 B1
Deane Cl **7** NG23..........91 D5
Deane Rd DN40.............186 D4
Dean Rd Lincoln LN2........202 C5
Scunthorpe DN17............184 E6
Deans Cl **6** DN10...........39 F5
Dean's Ct **11** PE1..........226 A2
Deansgate DN32............191 C6
Deansgrove DN32...........191 D7
Deansleigh LN1.............201 E8
Deansway LN4................81 D3
Dear Love Gate
1 Gedney PE12..........160 A8
Lutton PE12................148 D1
Dearne St **9** HU15..........2 D5
Dear St **11** LN8.............57 D8
De Aston Sch LN8.............57 E7
De Aston Sq **2** DN15......182 E3
Deaton La DN36.............195 C6
Debdale PE2................229 E4
Debdale Rd NG32...........210 A5
Debdhill Rd DN10............39 F6
De Bec Cl PE1..............226 C3
Decoy Cl **16** PE11.........215 C1
Decoy Rd Borough Fen PE6..174 D6
Gorefield PE13..............169 D2
Deeke Rd **21** NG24.......104 C1
Deene Cl **7** Grimsby DN34.190 D4
8 Market Deeping PE6...217 A5
Deene Ct PE3...............225 C5

Deep (Aquarium & Marine
Research Centre) The★
HU1.....................181 A5
Deepdale Dr NG34......121 C7
Deepdale Gr 2 HU9.....181 E8
Deepdale La LN2.........68 C2
DEEPING GATE PE6.....217 C3
Deeping Lakes Nature
Reserve★ PE6...........174 C7
Deeping Rd Baston PE6...164 E4
Glinton PE6..............174 A6
DEEPING ST JAMES PE6..217 D4
Deeping St James Com Prim
Sch PE6................217 F4
Deeping St James Rd
PE6...................217 D2
DEEPING ST NICHOLAS
PE11..................166 C6
Deeping St Nicholas Prim Sch
PE11..................166 B6
Deepings Leisure Ctr PE6 217 E4
Deepings Sch The PE6...217 E5
Deep La PE23............87 A5
Deerhurst Way 18 PE6..175 A1
Deerleap PE3............225 A5
Deer Pk Rd 3 PE6......164 F3
Deer Valley Rd 4 PE2...230 E8
Dee St 6 HU3...........180 B4
Defender Dr DN37.......190 B7
De Gaunt Dr 10 NG34...107 F1
De Gravel Dr 5 NG34...107 F1
De Havilland Rd PE13...170 D1
Deira Cl NG34...........212 C1
De la Bere Ave 25 LN12..77 A8
Delacorte Gn PE11......214 A1
De Lacy Ave PE25.......206 C8
De Lacy La 6 DN35.....192 F6
De Lacy Way DN15........9 A5
Delaine Cl PE10........213 E5
Delamere Cl PE1........226 C5
Delamere Dr DN36......192 F1
Delamore Way PE12.....216 C5
De la Pole Ave HU3.....179 F7
Delapre Ct 11 PE6......175 A1
Deldale Rd PE21........136 D8
Delfield Rd PE21........136 D8
Delgate Ave 3 PE12....157 E7
Delgate Bank PE12......157 D2
Delhi Sq 3 NG34........120 D8
Delhi St 7 HU9...........5 D8
De Ligne Dr 6 NG32....139 C7
Delius Cl HU4...........179 B4
Dellfield Ave LN6.......200 C1
Dellfield Cl LN6.........200 C2
Dellfield Ct 8 LN6......200 C3
Dell The 1 Broughton DN20 .19 E3
Peterborough PE2.......230 E7
Scunthorpe DN17........184 D5
Delph Ct PE2...........231 F6
Delph Fields PE12.......216 A3
Delph Rd 18 Lincoln LN6..93 C8
Long Sutton PE12........216 A3
Delph The PE11.........155 F4
Delves Way PE7.........230 D2
DEMBLEBY NG34........132 A4
Dembleby Rd NG34.....132 A5
Demeter House Dr DN20 .196 B3
Demeter House Sch
DN20..................196 C3
De Montfort Univ LN2...234 B2
Denbigh Ct 11 NG23.....91 D5
Denby Cl DN15.........182 D5
Denby Dale Cl LN6......200 C2
Denby Dr DN35..........192 C3
Dene Cl LN6............200 B3
Denefield LN6...........200 B3
Denehall Rd 14 DN3.....14 A2
Dene La LN4............109 C7
Dene Rd Grimsby DN32..191 E4
Skellingthorpe LN6......200 B3
Denesway HU13.........178 D2
Dene The 6 Nettleham LN2 .68 C2
Skellingthorpe LN6......200 B3
Denham Cl 2 PE25.....206 C2
Denham Wlk 1 PE3.....225 C4
Denis Dr PE2...........230 A4
Denmark Ct 7 HU9.....181 C7
Denmark Dr PE2........230 A4
Dennett Ct PE23........100 F8
Dennor Cl 15 LN12......77 A8
Denshire St 5 PE6......164 E4
DENTON NG32..........139 B7
Denton Ave NG31.......210 F1
Denton CE Sch NG32...139 A7
Denton Cl Grantham NG31 .210 F1
28 Newark-on-Trent NG24 .104 B2
Denton La Barrowby NG32 .128 F3
Belvoir NG32............138 E6
Denton Rd PE2..........231 C6
Denton's Way 11 DN20...31 A5
Depot St LN1...........201 D3
Derby Ave PE25.........206 D3
Derby Cl
1 Grantham NG31......210 E4
23 Grimsby DN32.......189 C1
Derby Dr PE1...........226 C5
Derby Rd DN15.........182 B2
Derby St
Kingston upon Hull HU3 ...180 D8
13 Lincoln LN5..........205 E8
Dere Cl 9 PE10..........92 D5
Derringham Ave 5 HU4 .179 B6
Derringham St HU3......180 C7
DERRYTHORPE DN17....17 C3
Derrythorpe Rd DN17....17 D4

Derrythorpe Road DN17...17 C2
Derry Way DN33........194 E8
Derwent Ave 18 HU14....3 A4
Derwent Cl LN6.........205 A2
Derwent Ct 20 NG24...104 B2
Derwent Dr
1 Humberston DN36....36 C8
Peterborough PE4.......221 C2
Derwent Rd
Grantham NG31.........210 F3
Scunthorpe DN16.......185 E6
Derwent St LN1.........201 C4
Derwent Wy
6 Beacon Hill NG24....104 A5
Spalding PE11...........214 A4
Derwood Gr 7 PE4.....220 F5
Desborough Ave PE2....231 D5
Detuyll St W DN15......182 F5
Detuyll St DN15.........182 F5
Devereux Way LN9......199 D2
Devon La 17 NG13......128 A6
Devonshire Ave DN32...191 D4
Devonshire Rd
2 Scampton Airfield LN1...67 E5
Scunthorpe DN17........184 F6
Devon St
Kingston upon Hull HU4 ...179 F3
8 Lincoln LN1..........202 C3
Dewberry Ct HU4........179 C4
Dewey Cl PE7...........233 B8
De Wint Ave LN6........205 A5
De Wint Cl Lincoln LN6 .205 B5
6 Metheringham LN4....95 C4
De Wint Ct LN6.........205 A5
Dewsbury Ave DN15....182 C4
Dexter Ave NG31.......210 F3
Deyne Ave DN15.......183 A3
Dial Sq 1 DN7..........191 E7
Diana Princess of Wales Hospl
DN33..................191 C3
Diana St DN15.........183 A5
Dias Cl PE11...........214 B2
Dickens Beck La LN11....49 D5
Dickens Cl PE6.........164 E2
Dickens Dr PE9.........218 E5
Dickenson Terr 10 DN21 .197 D3
Dickens Rd NG31.......211 E6
Dickens St
Little London PE11......214 A1
Peterborough PE1.......226 B3
Dickinson Cl 11 DN20....30 F5
Dickinson's La 6 DN36....36 B1
Dickon Hill Rd PE22....114 D7
DICKON HILLS PE22....114 D7
Dick Turpin Way PE12..216 B5
DIGBY LN4.............108 E5
Digby CE Sch LN4......108 D6
Digby Cl 9 LN6.........204 C7
Digby Cnr Nature Reserve★
LN4...................108 F5
Digby Gdns DN34.......191 A5
Digby Rd LN4...........109 B6
Digby St DN15.........182 F4
Digby the Tedder Prim Sch
LN4...................108 B7
Dimmock Ct NG32......139 B7
Dingley Ct PE3.........225 C5
Dinna Nook National Nature
Reserve★ LN11.........51 B7
Dirty La 4 DN7...........14 D8
Discovery Cl NG34......212 A3
Disney Ct LN6...........92 C2
Ditmas Ave 9 HU4......179 B6
Division Rd 1 HU3......180 B4
Dixon Ave
14 Broughton DN20.....19 D3
Dorrington LN4.........108 E3
Grimsby DN32..........191 E4
Dixon Cl Brigg DN20....196 C4
Lincoln LN6............201 D1
12 Tetney DN36.........36 D4
Dixon Dr LN13...........75 E2
Dixon Pl 5 NG31.......211 A3
Dixon's Dro PE14.......170 F4
Dixons Rd PE6.........217 C4
Dixon St LN5...........201 D1
Dixon Way LN6.........201 D1
Dockholme Gate PE11...145 A4
Docking La LN9.........199 B8
Docking's Holt PE12....216 B6
Dock Office Row 6 HU1 .181 A7
Dock St HU1...........180 F6
Dock Terr PE1..........209 B3
Dock Twr The★ DN31...189 B3
Doctor's La PE10.......143 A2
DODDINGTON LN6.......79 E5
Doddington Ave LN6....205 A4
Doddington Dr PE3.....225 B2
Doddington Hall & Gdns★
LN6....................79 D5
Doddington La
Claypole NG23.........117 E7
Stubton NG23..........118 B7
Westborough & Dry Doddington
NG23.................117 E5
Doddington Rd
Birchwood LN6.........204 C6
Doddington & Whisby LN6 .79 E3
Lincoln LN6............204 D1
Dodswell Gr HU9.........5 F8
Doe Cl LN6.............92 D5
Dog and Duck La PE21 .197 B8
Dog Dro Holbeach PE12 .158 C5
Sutton St James PE12...159 A1
Dog Dro N PE12........168 B4
Dog Dro (Nutts Lane)
PE12..................158 D2
Dog Dro S PE12........168 A2

DOGDYKE LN4..........110 E6
Dogdyke Ppg Sta★ LN4 .110 D7
Dogdyke Rd Coningsby LN4 207 B2
Wildmore LN4...........111 B6
Dog Holes La DN22......52 A1
Dog Kennel Rd DN21....55 A8
Dog Rose Dr PE10......213 D2
DOGSTHORPE PE1.......226 C7
Dogsthorpe Gr 2 PE1...226 A5
Dogsthorpe Jun Sch PE1 .226 B7
Dogsthorpe Rd PE1.....226 A5
Dolby Vale DN33........190 F3
Dole Rd DN17............6 B1
Dole Wood Nature Reserve★
PE10..................164 C7
Doll La 1 DN20.........20 F7
Doll's Bank PE12.......159 A4
Dolman Cres DN17.....184 F4
Dolphin La 28 PE21....208 F5
Dolphin St 4 DN35.....192 F6
Dominion Cl 3 DN20...195 C6
Donaldson Dr 4 PE4...221 C2
Doncaster Cl 14 PE10..213 D3
Doncaster Gdns 14 LN5 .107 A8
Doncaster Rd
Gunness DN15..........17 E6
Hatfield DN7.............14 D3
Haxey DN9..............26 F2
Scunthorpe DN15.......182 B3
Stainforth DN7..........14 B6
Doncaster St HU3......180 B6
Donegal Cl PE4.........221 B2
DONINGTON PE11......134 F1
Donington Cowley Endowed
Prim Sch The PE11.....134 E2
DONINGTON EAUDIKE
PE20..................135 A3
Donington La LN11.......72 C8
DONINGTON ON BAIN
LN11....................59 E1
Donington on Bain Sch The
LN11....................59 E1
Donington Rd Bicker PE20 .135 A4
Horbling NG34..........133 C2
Kirton PE20............135 A4
Donington Road LN11....60 D4
DONNA NOOK LN11......38 D2
Donna Nook National Nature
Reserve★ LN11.........38 C2
Donna Nook Road LN11...38 C1
Donnington Gdns DN15 .182 F3
Donnington Pk 1 PE13..176 A1
Donnington Rd LN8......59 B2
Donnington St DN31....191 F7
Donville Rd DN17.........7 A2
Dooks Cl DN21..........29 C1
Doon Garth HU4.........179 A3
Dorado Cl 2 HU3.......180 A5
Dorchester Ave PE10...213 E3
Dorchester Cres 6 PE1..226 D7
Dorchester Rd DN17.....184 C8
Dorchester Way 10 LN6...93 B8
Dore Ave LN6............204 E2
Dormy Ave PE25........206 D8
Dornoch Cl 11 LN10.....97 C6
Dorothy Ave
Skegness PE25..........206 C3
Waltham DN37...........194 E5
Dorothy Cl PE22........113 A1
Dorothy Cres 1 PE25...206 C3
Dorrigan Cl LN1........201 C7
DORRINGTON LN4......108 E4
Dorrington Cl 19 NG34...108 D2
Dorset Cl E 6 DN15......8 B4
Dorset Cl W 5 DN15.....8 B4
Dorset Pl 8 LN1.........67 E5
Dorset St
Kingston upon Hull HU4 ...179 F3
Lincoln LN2............202 C3
Dorton Ave DN21.......197 F4
Dotam's La PE22.......126 D4
Dotterel Dr DN16.......185 F5
Double Bank PE22......126 D6
Double Bridges Rd DN8...15 B6
Doubledays La PE24....102 D8
Double St PE11.........214 B4
Doubletwelves Dro PE20 .134 D6
Doughty Cl DN37.......194 E5
Doughty Rd DN32......191 E7
Doughty's Ct LN5.......234 B2
Doughty St PE9.........219 D6
Douglas Ave Grimsby DN31 191 A8
5 Ingoldmells PE25.....90 D3
Douglas Cl 10 PE24....102 E8
Douglas Rd
Cleethorpes DN35......192 D8
Market Deeping PE6....217 C4
Doulton Cl 4 LN6......204 D7
Dove Cl
9 Gainsborough DN21..197 F5
Louth LN11.............198 D7
7 Sleaford NG34.......212 B3
Dovecote
4 Middle Rasen LN8.....57 B8
Rippingale PE10........143 A4
Dovecote Cl
Peterborough PE1.......226 B7
Snitterby DN21..........43 D5
Dovecote La
Auburn Haddington & South
Hykeham LN5...........92 F5
Coleby LN5..............93 F3
Wainfleet St Mary PE24 .102 E1
Yaxley PE7.............233 C5
Dovecote Mdws NG34..142 E5
Dovecote Mews 4 DN20 .196 F6
Dovecote Rd 4 PE6.....217 A6
Dovecotes 3 PE11......145 A8

Dovecot La PE22........127 D6
Dove Ct PE11...........214 B5
Dove Dale 5 LN6.......204 F2
Dovedale Cl
Grantham NG31.........211 B8
2 Winterton DN15.......9 A6
Dovedale Dr 6 DN33...194 E8
Dovedale Gr 1 HU9.....181 E8
Dovedale Rd DN16......185 D5
Dove Gdns 2 PE2......230 E8
DOVEDALE LN11.........60 F1
Dover Cl NG31..........210 E6
Dover Rd PE4...........221 A2
Dover St Grimsby DN31..191 C8
Kingston upon Hull HU3 .180 C8
Doves' La PE22.........126 E3
Dove Willow PE6........174 E6
Dowding Mews LN2.....202 E4
Dowding Rd LN2........202 E4
Dowdyke Dro PE20.....146 B8
Dowdyke Rd PE20......145 F8
Dower Rise 11 HU14......3 B7
Dowgate Cl 2 PE11....214 A3
Dowgate Rd 4 PE13....170 B1
Dowlands Bsns Pk LN11...62 C5
Down Gate PE3.........225 A1
Downing Cl DN34.......190 F6
Downing Cres
Scunthorpe DN16.......185 A3
2 Stamford PE9........219 B7
DOWSBY PE10..........143 B4
DOWSDALE PE6.........167 D1
Dowsdale Bank
Thorney PE6............176 A8
Whaplode PE12.........167 E2
Dowse Ave DN15.......182 E3
Dowsing Way PE25.....206 A6
Doyle La 2 PE11........214 A1
Dozen's Bank PE11......156 B6
DRAGONBY DN15........8 E1
Dragonby Rd DN17.....184 E4
Dragon Fly Cl 1 NG7...230 C2
Drain Bank East Kirkby PE23 .99 F3
Newport HU15............1 B8
Drain Bank North PE12..157 A2
Drain Bank South PE12..157 A1
Drain Rd PE6...........221 E7
Drainside PE20.........136 B5
Drainside S PE20.......136 C4
Drakards La PE21.......209 A3
Drake Ave Grimsby DN32 .192 B6
Heighington/Washingborough
LN4...................203 B1
Peterborough PE7......230 F5
Drake Cl 14 PE11......214 C2
Drake Rd PE25..........103 E4
Drakes Cl
7 Holbeach PE12......215 E2
19 Mablethorpe & Sutton
LN12....................77 A7
Drakes Mdw LN8........55 E6
Drake St
Gainsborough DN21....197 D2
Lincoln LN1............201 C4
Draper Rd PE4..........221 F2
Drapers Pl 13 PE11.....214 D4
Draw Dike PE12........159 D1
Drax Ct 6 LN8...........57 B8
Draycott Cl 6 LN7.......33 A3
DRAYTON PE20.........135 C6
Drayton PE3............225 A4
Drayton Rd PE20.......135 C7
Drayton The PE20......135 C6
Drew Ave DN32.........191 F4
Drewry La 10 DN9.......27 A2
DRIBY LN13.............74 E1
Driby Hill LN13...........75 F2
Driby La LN13...........74 F1
Driffield Way PE2.......230 D8
Driffil Way 29 DN15.....9 A5
Drift Ave PE9...........219 C6
Drift Gdns PE9.........219 C6
Drift La NG32...........119 A1
Drift Rd PE9............219 C6
Drift Rd The LE14......150 F2
Drift The Barrowby NG32 .210 A3
Belvoir NG32............138 F5
Buckminster NG33......151 A4
Collyweston PE9........171 B1
Croxton Kerrial NG32...138 F5
Harlaxton NG32........139 C8
Ryhall PE9.............163 B3
Skillington NG33........151 A7
Syston NG32...........130 A7
Walcott LN4............109 D7
Wansford PE8..........222 F3
Drigh Rd 17 LN8........47 B6
Drill Hall La 5 DN21....197 D5
Dring La DN21...........41 D7
Drinsey Nook La NG23...66 B1
Drive The
Brocklesby DN41.......22 E6
Gainsborough DN21....197 E3
Grantham NG31.........210 D3
Ingoldmells PE25.......206 E8
7 Kirk Sandall DN3......14 A1
2 Mablethorpe/Sutton on Sea
LN12....................64 A4
Peterborough PE3......225 E2
Waltham DN37.........194 F3
1 Winthorpe NG24....104 B7
Dronfield Ct 3 DN15...182 B3
Drove La Coddington NG24 .104 D7
Sleaford NG34..........212 A5
Drove Rd Crowland PE12 .167 F3
Whaplode PE12.........168 A3
Drovers Ct DN21........197 E1
Drovers Rise 1 HU15....2 C6

Drove The
4 Auburn Haddington & South
Hykeham LN5...........93 A8
Collyweston PE9........171 B1
Osbournby NG34.......132 D5
Sleaford NG34..........212 B5
Droveway The PE6......227 B3
Drummond Rd
Bourne PE10...........213 E4
Skegness PE25.........206 D1
Drury Cl 1 DN37........194 C4
Drury La Bicker PE20...135 A4
Lincoln LN1............234 B3
New Waltham DN36....195 C6
Drury Pk 9 NG23.......117 D3
Drury St LN4............95 D4
Drydales HU10.........178 C6
Dryden Ave
Balderton NG24........104 C3
Lincoln LN2............202 B6
Dryden Cl 3 DN15.....211 D6
Dryden Ct 3 LN4.......207 B5
Dryden Rd
Peterborough PE1.......225 E7
Scunthorpe DN17......184 D6
DRY DODDINGTON NG23..117 E5
Dry Leys PE2...........230 C6
Drypool Way HU9.......181 B6
Duchess Dr PE6........217 C6
Duchess St DN32.......191 D6
Ducie La DN22...........52 C5
Duckpool La LN10.......84 B1
Duckthorpe La DN36.....37 B2
Dudley Cl 1 PE21......209 B4
Dudley House Sch NG31 .211 B4
Dudley Pl DN35.........192 C4
Dudley Rd Brigg DN20..196 C3
Grantham NG31.........211 B4
Scunthorpe DN16.......185 E6
Dudley St DN31.........191 C7
Dudley Wlk HU4.........179 B3
Duesbery St HU3.......180 C8
Dugard Rd DN32........192 B7
Duke Mdws PE6........217 C6
Duke of Bedford Prim Sch
PE6...................176 A3
Duke Rd PE22..........113 C3
Duke's Covert Nature
Reserve★ NG32.......120 A1
Dukesmead PE4........220 E2
Dukesmead Mobile Home Pk
PE4...................220 E2
Duke St Boston PE21...208 E4
22 Grimsby DN32.......189 C1
Grimsby DN32..........192 B8
Peterborough PE2......231 A2
Sleaford NG34..........212 B5
14 Stainforth DN7......14 C6
Dukes Wy PE7..........230 B1
Dunbar Ave DN36......195 B6
Dunbar Cl 5 DN21......197 E6
Dunblane Dr PE2.......229 C4
Duncan Dr 34 DN18......3 E1
Duncombe Gdns 1 DN32 191 F8
Duncombe St DN32.....191 F8
Dundee Ct PE2.........229 C4
Dundee Dr PE9.........218 E6
Dundee St HU5.........180 A8
Dunes Family Entertainment
Ctr The★ LN12..........64 C4
Dunford Rd 5 LN5......234 B1
Dunham Cl LN1..........65 D1
DUNHAM ON TRENT NG22...65 B1
Dunham on Trent CE Prim
Sch NG22...............65 A1
Dunham Rd DN22........65 A3
DUNHOLME LN2..........68 E6
Dunholme Cl
Gainsborough DN21....197 E4
11 Welton/Dunholme LN2 .68 C5
Dunholme Ct 4 LN2....202 A8
Dunholme Rd
Gainsborough DN21....197 E4
6 Welton/Dunholme LN2 .68 C6
Dunholme St Chads CE Prim
Sch LN2................68 E6
Dunkirk Rd LN1.........201 D6
Dunlin Dr
Long Sutton PE12......216 B4
Scunthorpe DN16.......185 F5
Dunlin Rd 2 PE9........163 D3
Dunlop St LN5..........201 F1
Dunlop Way DN16......185 E7
Dunmires La DN14.......6 E3
Dunmore Cl LN5........205 C3
Dunmow St DN31.......188 D1
Dunnegate Way PE11...145 D2
Dunnock Cl 3 DN16....185 B2
Dunns Paddock 3 DN20 .20 F7
Dunoon Ct 4 DN37.....190 E8
Dunsberry
Marholm PE6...........220 D1
Peterborough PE3......224 F8
DUNSBY PE10..........143 A4
Dunsby Dro PE10.......143 D1
DUNSCROFT DN7........14 C4
Dunstall St DN15.......183 A3
Dunstall Wlk DN21......197 F3
Dunstan Dr DN8..........15 A4
Dunstan Hill 26 DN21...30 B1
Dunstan Villas 29 DN21..30 B1
Dunster Cl NG31.......210 F6
Dunster Rd DN21.......197 E6
DUNSTON LN4...........95 C5
Dunston Cl 10 LN2.....202 A8
Dunston Dr HU13.......178 D1
Dunston Fen La LN4.....83 D1
Dunston Heath La LN4...94 E5

Dunston Rd
Kingston upon Hull HU5 . . . . . .179 D7
Metheringham LN4 . . . . .95 C5
DUNSVILLE DN7 . . . . .14 C3
Dunsville Prim Sch DN7 . . . .14 C3
Durban Rd DN32 . . . . .192 A7
Durham Ave Grimsby DN34 .191 A7
Sleaford NG34 . . . . .212 C6
Thorne/Moorends DN8 . . . . . .15 A8
Durham Cl Birchwood LN6. .200 D2
Grantham NG31 . . . . .210 C4
Durham Cres LN4 . . . . .203 D1
Durham Rd
Cleethorpes DN35 . . . . .192 C4
Hatfield DN7 . . . . .14 C4
Peterborough PE1 . . . . .226 C3
Durham's Rd PE12 . . . . .148 D5
Dursley Ave DN36 . . . . .195 B6
Dutton Ave PE25 . . . . .206 A4
Dycote La LN5 . . . . .106 D5
DYKE PE10. . . . . .154 D5
Dyke Dro PE10 . . . . .154 E5
Dyke Rd 5 DN36 . . . . .37 C5
Dykes Cl 6 HU13. . . . . .3 F4
Dykes End NG23 . . . . .91 D4
Dyke Windmill & Peremill
  Galery ★ PE10 . . . . .154 D5
Dymoke Cl 3 LN11. . . . . .64 C3
Dymoke Dr Grimsby DN37. .190 C6
Horncastle LN9 . . . . .199 C2
Dymoke Rd 5 LN12 . . . . .64 C3
Dysart Rd NG31 . . . . .210 E4
Dysart Ret Pk NG31. . . . . . . .211 A4
Dyson Cl PE1 . . . . .225 F3

E

EAGLE LN6 . . . . .79 C2
EAGLE BARNSDALE LN6. . . . .92 C7
Eagle Cl 7 LN12 . . . . .64 A4
Eagle Com Prim Sch LN6 . .79 B2
Eagle Dr
New Waltham DN36 . . . . . . .195 E6
3 Sleaford NG34. . . . . .212 B8
Waltham DN37. . . . . .194 F3
8 Welton/Dunholme LN2 . . .68 D7
Eagle La LN6. . . . . .79 D1
EAGLE MOOR LN6 . . . . .79 C2
Eagle Moor LN6 . . . . .79 C3
Eagle Rd
Doddington & Whisby LN6 . . .79 D3
North Scarle LN6 . . . . .78 C2
Spalford NG23 . . . . .78 D4
Eagle Road LN6 . . . . .92 B6
Eaglesthorpe PE1 . . . . .225 E7
Eagle Way Bourne PE10. . . . .213 C3
2 Hampton Vale PE7 . . . . . .230 D1
Yaxley PE7 . . . . .233 D8
EALAND DN17 . . . . .16 E6
Ealand Rd 3 DN17 . . . . .17 C6
Eames Gdns PE1 . . . . .226 B6
Earl Ave DN36. . . . . .195 D7
EARLESFIELD NG31 . . . . .210 E3
Earlesfield La NG31 . . . . .210 F3
Earle's Rd HU9. . . . . .181 D7
Earle St HU10. . . . . .178 E6
Earls Cl PE2 . . . . .231 B6
Earlsfield Ind Est NG31 . . .139 F8
Earls Dr LN5 . . . . .205 D8
Earlsgate Gdns 3 DN15 . . . . .8 F5
Earlsgate Rd DN15 . . . . .8 F5
Earl Spencer Ct PE2 . . . . . . .230 E4
Earl St Grimsby DN31 . . . . . .191 C7
Scunthorpe DN16. . . . . .183 B5
Earls Wlk 8 DN16 . . . . .183 B2
Earlswood PE2. . . . . .229 C5
Earp Ave 21 NG24 . . . . .104 A4
Earth Cl PE2 . . . . .231 E5
Ease La NG23 . . . . .117 F3
Easenby Ave HU10 . . . . .178 C6
Easenby Cl 3 HU14 . . . . .3 C7
Eason Rd 5 DN36 . . . . .191 B2
East Acridge 15 DN18. . . . . . . .3 F1
East Ave
Brant Broughton LN5 . . . . . .105 F5
Grantham NG31 . . . . .210 E3
1 Stainforth DN7 . . . . .14 C5
East Bank 2 Stainforth DN7 .14 C7
Sutton Bridge PE12 . . . . . . .160 F5
East Banks 7 NG34 . . . . .212 C4
Eastbeck La LN9 . . . . .86 A2
East Bight LN2 . . . . .234 B3
East Boundary Rd DN16. .183 F2
Eastbourne St
Kingston upon Hull HU3 . . . .180 A5
Lincoln LN2 . . . . .234 C2
Eastbourne Way DN33 . . . .194 F7
Eastbrook Rd LN6. . . . . .205 A5
EAST BUTTERWICK DN17 . . .28 E8
East Butterwick Road
DN17. .17 D2
East Camp Rd 3 NG34. . . . . .120 C8
Eastchurch Rd 4 NG34 . . . .120 D8
East Cl 13 NG34 . . . . .108 E2
Eastcliffe Sq 9 NG32. . . . . . .119 B7
Eastcliff Rd LN2. . . . . .234 C3
East Cob Gate PE12 . . . . . . .157 F6
East Comm La DN16 . . . . . . .185 B8
Eastcroft 1 LN1 . . . . .66 D3
East Croft 10 LN3. . . . . .203 E7
East Cross St 25 DN21 . . . . .30 B1
East Dale Dr 3 DN21 . . . . . . .30 B2
East Dale Rd HU14. . . . . .2 E5
East Dr LN4 . . . . .110 E8
EAST ELLA HU5. . . . . .179 D7

East Ella Dr HU4 . . . . .179 C6
East Elloe Ave PE12 . . . . . . .215 D3
East End
3 Burgh le Marsh PE24. . . .102 E7
Humberside Airport DN39 . . .22 A6
Langtoft PE6. . . . . .164 F3
East End Cl DN33 . . . . .191 D1
Eastern Ave
Gainsborough DN21. . . . . . . .197 F5
Peterborough PE1 . . . . .226 C8
Eastern Cl PE1 . . . . .226 D7
Eastern Dr
11 Balderton NG24 . . . . .104 C1
RAF Cranwell NG34 . . . . . . .120 D8
Eastern Ind Est PE1 . . . . . . .226 E3
Eastern Inway DN34 . . . . . . .191 A4
Eastern Rd PE12 . . . . .215 F8
Eastern Terr LN5. . . . . .201 D1
Eastern Terr La 13 NG24 . . .104 A4
East Fen La PE22. . . . . .113 B7
EAST FERRY DN21 . . . . .28 B2
East Ferry Rd
East Ferry DN21 . . . . .28 E3
Laughton DN21 . . . . .41 B8
Wildsworth DN21. . . . . .40 D8
EASTFIELD PE1 . . . . .226 D4
Eastfield
14 Humberston DN36 . . . . . . .36 D8
3 Market Deeping PE6 . . . .217 C5
11 Sturton by Stow LN1 . . . . .66 D7
East Field LN5 . . . . .92 F2
Eastfield Ave DN33 . . . . .195 A7
Eastfield Cl
1 Dunholme LN2 . . . . .68 E6
6 Sutterton PE20 . . . . .136 A2
Eastfield Gr PE1 . . . . .226 B4
Eastfield Inf Sch LN11 . . . . .198 D6
Eastfield Prim Acad DN40 .186 C4
Eastfield Prim Sch HU4. . .179 D6
Eastfield Rd
Barton-upon-Humber DN18 . . .10 F7
Brigg DN20. . . . . .196 D3
Epworth DN9 . . . . .27 E6
Firsby PE23 . . . . .101 F7
Immingham DN40 . . . . .12 F3
3 Keelby DN41 . . . . .23 A5
Kingston upon Hull HU5 . . . .179 D6
Louth LN11. . . . . .198 D6
40 Messingham DN17 . . . . . .29 D7
North Killingholme DN40 . . . .12 E5
Peterborough PE1 . . . . .226 C4
Scunthorpe DN16. . . . . .185 C5
1 Wisbech PE13 . . . . .170 E1
East Field Rd DN7 . . . . .14 C8
Eastfield Rise
3 Holton le Clay DN36 . . . .195 D2
Louth LN11. . . . . .198 E7
Eastfields 8. . . . . .43 D3
Eastfield S Ind Est DN40 . . .12 F3
Eastfield St 5 LN1 . . . . .202 B3
Eastfield Way 17 PE13 . . . . .170 D1
East FIRSBY LN8 . . . . .55 F4
EASTGATE PE1 . . . . .226 D7
Eastgate Bassingham LN5 . . .92 F2
Bourne PE10 . . . . .213 E4
Grimsby DN32. . . . . .191 E8
Heckington NG34 . . . . .122 D6
Kingston upon Hull HU13 . . .178 E2
Lincoln LN2 . . . . .234 B3
Louth LN11. . . . . .198 C6
Market Deeping PE6. . . . . . .217 C3
Peterborough PE1 . . . . .226 B2
Scotton DN21. . . . . .29 C2
East Gate Bourne PE10. . . . .213 E4
Fleet PE12 . . . . .159 C7
Moulton PE12. . . . . .158 A7
Sleaford NG34 . . . . .212 E4
Whaplode PE12. . . . . .158 C7
Eastgate Cl LN2 . . . . .234 C3
Eastgate Gdns 3 PE12 . . . .159 C7
Eastgate La PE34. . . . . .161 E2
East Gn 30 DN17. . . . . .29 D7
East Gr
12 Barton-upon-Humber
  DN18. .3 F1
8 Colsterworth DN35. . . . . .151 E6
Kingston upon Hull HU4 . . . .179 D4
Easthall Rd LN7. . . . . .32 B4
EAST HALTON DN40 . . . . .12 E6
East Halton Prim Sch
DN40. .12 D6
East Halton Rd DN40 . . . . . . .12 E3
East Hann La DN19 . . . . .4 E1
EAST HECKINGTON PE20. . .123 D3
Eastholm LN2. . . . . .202 E7
Eastholm Cl PE1 . . . . .226 C6
Eastholme Gdns 10 DN15 . . .8 B4
EASTHORPE NG13 . . . . .128 B5
Easthorpe La NG13. . . . . .128 C5
Easthorpe Rd
1 Bottesford NG13. . . . . . . .128 B5
2 Great Gonerby NG31. . . .129 E5
Easthorpe View 9 NG13 . . .128 B5
East Hull Pools ★ HU9. . . . . .181 C8
EAST KEAL PE23 . . . . .100 E7
East Keal Bank PE23. . . . . . .100 C3
East Keal Fen PE23. . . . . .100 D3
EAST KEAL FEN SIDE
PE23. .100 E4
EAST KIRKBY PE23 . . . . .99 F5
East La Brattleby LN1. . . . . . . .67 C7
Corringham DN21 . . . . .41 E2
Morton PE10 . . . . .154 C7
Stainforth DN7 . . . . .14 C6
Eastlands 4 PE6 . . . . .166 F1

Eastlands Bank PE14 . . . . .161 B1
Eastleigh Cl LN6 . . . . .200 B1
Eastleigh Rd PE1. . . . . .226 C3
East Liberty LN2 . . . . .202 C4
EAST LOUND DN9 . . . . .27 E2
East Lound Rd Haxey DN9 . . .27 D2
Owston Ferry DN9 . . . . .28 A3
EAST MARSH DN32. . . . . .189 B1
East Marsh Rd DN19 . . . . .5 C3
East Marsh St 3 DN31. . . . . .191 E8
East Mid Mere Rd DN40. . . . .12 F4
East Mill Gate 3 LN3 . . . . . .203 E6
Eastmoor Villas DN9 . . . . . . .27 D3
East Mount 12 HU14 . . . . .3 A4
East of England
Showground ★ PE2. . . . . . .229 C4
East of England Way PE2 .229 B4
EASTOFT DN17 . . . . .7 A3
Eastoft CE Prim Sch DN17 . .7 A3
Eastoft Moors Road DN17. .17 A8
Eastoft Rd Crowle DN17. . . . . .16 D8
Luddington & Haldenby DN17. .7 C3
EASTON NG33 . . . . .140 B1
Easton Garford Endowed CE
Sch PE9 . . . . .171 D3
Easton La NG33 . . . . .140 A2
EASTON ON THE HILL
PE9 . . . . .171 C3
Easton Walled Gdn ★
NG33. .140 B2
East Parade DN20 . . . . .196 C4
EAST RAVENDALE DN37 . . . . .35 C2
East Ravendale CE Prim Sch
DN37. . . . . .35 C2
East Rd 21 Binbrook LN8 . . . .47 B6
Deeping St Nicholas PE11 . .156 C4
4 Keadby with Althorpe
  DN17. .17 C6
Navenby/Wellingore LN5. . .107 B8
Northborough PE6 . . . . .217 E1
Sleaford NG34 . . . . .212 F6
Tetford LN9 . . . . .73 F1
Tydd St Mary PE13 . . . . .170 C8
East Rd Ind Est NG34 . . . . . .212 F5
Eastrea 2 PE6 . . . . .231 E6
East Row LN11 . . . . .50 E4
East St Mary's Gate 2
DN31. .191 D7
Eastside Rd Grimsby DN31 .189 B1
Scunthorpe DN16. . . . . .183 F2
East St Alford LN13 . . . . .75 F4
Bole DN22 . . . . .52 C6
Crowland PE6. . . . . .166 E1
Grantham NG31 . . . . .211 B4
Grimsby DN32. . . . . .191 E7
Helpringham NG34. . . . . . . .133 E7
13 Hibaldstow DN20 . . . . . . .30 F5
Horncastle LN9 . . . . .199 C4
5 Kingston upon Hull HU9. .181 B7
Nettleham LN2. . . . . .68 C2
Rippingale PE10. . . . . .143 A2
Roxby cum Risby DN15. . . . . . .9 A3
Stamford PE9 . . . . .219 C5
East Sta Rd PE2. . . . . .231 B8
EAST STOCKWITH DN21 . . . . .40 C5
EAST TORRINGTON LN8. . . . . .58 C2
East View LN4 . . . . .109 D7
Eastview
Chapel St Leonard PE24. . . . .90 E4
Cranwell NG34. . . . . .107 E1
EASTVILLE PE22 . . . . .114 B8
Eastville Rd
4 Grimsby DN33. . . . . .191 A3
Toynton St Peter PE23 . . . . .101 A4
Eastway 19 LN2 . . . . .68 D2
East Wlk DN15 . . . . .183 B3
East Wold CE Prim Sch
LN11. . . . . .62 A3
Eastwood Ave DN32 . . . . . . .191 D4
Eastwood Ct 5 DN15 . . . . . . .182 B2
Eastwood Dr
2 Boston PE21 . . . . .209 D4
10 Broughton DN20 . . . . .19 E4
4 Grantham NG31 . . . . .211 D2
Eastwood Rd PE21 . . . . .209 D5
East Wr Cres PE7. . . . . .230 C1
East Wykeham LN8. . . . . .59 D7
Easy Rd PE11 . . . . .156 E1
Eathwaite Gn PE4 . . . . .221 C1
Eaton Cl HU10 . . . . .178 E5
Eaton Ct DN34 . . . . .191 C6
Eaton Rd Boston PE21 . . . . . .208 E3
Immingham DN40 . . . . .186 D4
Eau Bank LN11. . . . . .50 D7
Eaudike Rd
Donington PE20 . . . . .135 A3
Quadring PE11 . . . . .145 C8
Eau Dike Rd PE22 . . . . .115 A7
Eaugate Rd PE12 . . . . .157 F1
Ebony Gr LN6 . . . . .200 C1
Ebrington Cl 3 LN10 . . . . .97 E6
Eccles Ct 3 DN20 . . . . .196 F7
Eccleston Rd 15 DN3 . . . . . . .14 A3
Eco Wy 8 DN7. . . . . .14 D5
Eddystone Dr 3 LN6. . . . . . . .205 C1
Eden Cl 6 PE25 . . . . .206 C1
Edendale Gdns 3 LN1. . . . . .201 E8
Edendale View LN1. . . . . .201 E8
Eden Dene DN16 . . . . .185 D5
Edenfield PE2 . . . . .230 C6
Eden Field Rd 4 DN3. . . . . . . .14 A1
Eden Gr Rd 8 DN3. . . . . .14 A1
EDENHAM PE10. . . . . .153 F4
Edenham Church of England
Sch The PE10 . . . . .153 F5
Edenham Rd PE10. . . . . .154 B6
Edensand Rd HU3 . . . . .179 E5

EDENTHORPE DN3 . . . . .14 A1
Edenthorpe Hall Prim Sch
DN3. . . . . .14 A1
Edgar Cl 10 DN21. . . . . .29 C4
Edgar St HU3 . . . . .180 D5
Edgbaston Ave 3 DN17. . . . .184 E3
Edgcote Cl PE3 . . . . .225 C5
Edge Ave DN33. . . . . .191 D2
Edgefield 4 PE12 . . . . .157 E7
Edgehill St LN5. . . . . .205 D2
Edgehill Dr 4 NG24 . . . . .104 C4
Edgemere DN35 . . . . .182 B3
Edgerley Drain Rd PE1 . . . .226 F5
Edinburgh Ave
Peterborough PE4 . . . . .220 F3
2 Skegness PE25 . . . . .206 D3
Edinburgh Cl 13 PE20. . . . . .136 C5
Edinburgh Cres
2 Bourne PE10 . . . . .213 D6
12 Kirton PE20. . . . . .136 C5
Edinburgh Dr
Holton le Clay DN36 . . . . . .195 C3
11 Kirton PE20. . . . . .136 C5
Spalding PE11 . . . . .214 E2
Wisbech PE13 . . . . .170 D2
Edinburgh Rd
16 Binbrook Tech Pk LN8 . . .47 B6
3 Grantham NG31 . . . . .211 E6
3 Ruskington NG34 . . . . . . .108 E2
Stamford PE9 . . . . .219 B6
Edinburgh Sq 4 LN5 . . . . .94 A7
Edinburgh St HU3. . . . . .180 A5
Edinburgh Wlk
Holbeach PE12. . . . . .215 E2
Pinchbeck PE11 . . . . .156 B7
Edinburgh Wy DN33 . . . . . . .191 B1
Edington Ct 3 DN21. . . . . .53 A8
Edis Ct PE2 . . . . .231 B6
Edison Dr PE7 . . . . .233 D6
Edison Way 6 PE21 . . . . .208 F1
EDLINGTON LN9 . . . . .85 B6
Edlington Cl 6 LN2 . . . . .201 F8
Edlington Moor LN10 . . . . . . .97 D7
Edmonds Cl 2 PE9 . . . . .219 D6
Edmonds Dr 7 PE9 . . . . .171 A3
Edmonds Way 2 DN31 . . . . .191 D8
Edmondthorpe Drift LE14 .150 D1
Edmondthorpe Rd LE14. . . .150 C1
Edmund Cl DN21 . . . . .41 D2
Edmund Dr PE7 . . . . .230 B1
Edmunds Rd 3 NG34. . . . . . .107 F1
Edna St LN5 . . . . .201 F1
Edwalton Ave
9 Mablethorpe/Sutton on Sea
  LN12 .77 A8
Peterborough PE3 . . . . .225 E3
Edward Barker Rd LN4 . . . . .81 F4
Edward Collins Sq 2
HU9 . . . . .181 C7
Edward Cres PE25 . . . . .206 B3
Edward Heneage Prim Acad
DN32. .191 F7
Edward Jermyn Dr 16
NG24 .104 A6
Edward Rd
Gainsborough DN21. . . . . . . .197 D6
Spalding PE11 . . . . .214 B4
10 Stamford PE9 . . . . .219 A7
Edward Richardson Prim Sch
The LN9 . . . . .73 F1
Edwards Rd 3 DN15 . . . . . . .182 F4
Edward St
Cleethorpes DN35 . . . . .192 E5
Grantham NG31 . . . . .211 B2
Grimsby DN32. . . . . .191 F7
Kingston upon Hull HU13 . . .178 F1
1 Lincoln LN5 . . . . .205 E8
17 Louth LN11. . . . . .198 B5
Edwina Dr 6 PE11 . . . . .156 F8
Edwin Cl 12 NG34 . . . . .212 B2
Edwin St 13 PE21. . . . . .208 F4
Edwin Gdns PE10 . . . . .213 B5
Egar Way PE3. . . . . .224 F2
Egerton Rd LN2. . . . . .202 B5
Egginton Cl HU10 . . . . .178 C7
Egginton St 4 HU2. . . . . .180 F7
Egret Gr 5 LN6 . . . . .204 D8
Egton Ave 17 DN17 . . . . .29 D7
Egton St HU8 . . . . .181 A8
Eider Cl 42 DN18 . . . . .10 E8
Eider Gr PE11. . . . . .214 A4
Eight Acres 10 PE9 . . . . .219 A5
Eighth Ave DN15 . . . . .8 A1
Elan Cl PE21 . . . . .208 E5
Elba St 6 HU9 . . . . .177 F8
Elbow La PE21 . . . . .209 A4
Elderberry Dr HU4 . . . . .179 C4
Elderberry Way 2 DN35 . . .192 D2
Elder Cl
2 Bourne PE10 . . . . .213 C6
Skegness PE25. . . . . .206 A5
Witham St Hughs LN6. . . . . . .92 D5
Elderflower Wy 6 PE7 . . . . .230 B1
Eldern PE2 . . . . .230 C4
Elder's Gate PE12 . . . . .169 E8
Elder St LN5 . . . . .205 D5
Elder Tree Way LN10 . . . . . . .84 D3
Elderwood Cl 8 HU3. . . . . . . .180 D5
Eleanor Cl Lincoln LN5. . . . . .205 E7
Stamford PE9 . . . . .219 A6
Eleanor St DN32 . . . . .191 F8
Electric Sta Rd NG34 . . . . . .212 C4
Elena Rd 4 PE2 . . . . .231 E4
Eleven Acre La PE20. . . . . . .136 D4
Elgar Rd HU4 . . . . .179 B4
Elgar Way PE9 . . . . .218 D2
Eliot Cl Gainsborough DN21 .197 F3
5 Sleaford NG34. . . . . .212 F4

Elizabeth Ave
Dogdyke LN4 . . . . .110 D7
11 Kirk Sandall DN3. . . . . . . .14 A2
6 Lincoln LN6 . . . . .93 C8
Lincoln LN6 . . . . .204 F1
Wrange PE22 . . . . .114 C2
Elizabeth Cl
17 Chapel St Leonard PE24 . .90 D7
23 Crowe DN17 . . . . .16 D7
Gainsborough DN21. . . . . . . .197 C7
Glentworth DN21 . . . . .54 F6
Grimsby DN33 . . . . .194 D7
1 Scotter DN21 . . . . .29 C4
Elizabeth Cres
6 Ingoldmells PE25 . . . . . . .90 E3
Pinchbeck PE11 . . . . .144 D1
Elizabeth Ct Brigg DN20 . . . .196 C5
18 Chapel St Leonard PE24 . .90 D7
Dogsthorpe PE1 . . . . .226 A5
Sleaford NG34 . . . . .212 D3
Elizabeth Dr
Billingborough NG34 . . . . . .143 B8
12 Chapel St Leonard PE24 . .90 D7
Elizabeth Gr PE25 . . . . .206 C5
Elizabeth Rd Boston PE21. .209 B5
2 Stamford PE9 . . . . .219 B6
Elizabeth St 3 DN15 . . . . . . .183 A4
Elizabeth Way 6 HU10 . . . . .164 C8
Elkington Rd LN11 . . . . .48 C2
Ella Cl HU10 . . . . .178 C8
Ella Pk HU10 . . . . .178 D7
Ellen Cres PE11 . . . . .214 A3
Ellen Way DN36 . . . . .195 B7
Ellerby Ct PE23 . . . . .100 D6
Ellerby Mead NG33 . . . . .152 D5
ELLERKER HU15 . . . . .2 A8
Ellerker Rd HU15 . . . . .2 B8
Ellers La DN9 . . . . .27 C8
Ellesmere Ave DN31 . . . . . . .202 D4
Ellesmere Bsns Pk NG31 .210 E2
Ellesmere Gr 4 DN7 . . . . .14 D6
Ellesmere Rise DN34 . . . . . .190 D3
Ellicar La DN10 . . . . .39 A3
Ellindon PE3. . . . . .225 B7
Elliot Ave PE3. . . . . .224 F2
Elliot Cl NG31 . . . . .211 E6
Elliott Rd LN5. . . . . .234 C1
Elliott's Way PE9 . . . . .164 B4
Elliott Way 11 PE24. . . . . .90 D7
Ellis Mill ★ LN1. . . . . .234 A4
Ellison Ave DN16 . . . . .185 A4
Ellison Boulters CE Prim Sch
LN2 . . . . .68 F4
Ellison Cl 5 LN2 . . . . .68 F2
Ellison St Lincoln LN5. . . . . . .205 D5
Thorne/Moorends DN8 . . . . .15 A7
Elliston Prim Sch DN35 . . . .192 C8
Elliston St DN35. . . . . .192 C8
Ellis Way DN32. . . . . .191 E8
Ellis Wy DN20 . . . . .30 F6
Ellmore La LN7 . . . . .32 C3
Elloe Bank PE13. . . . . .169 B2
ELLOUGHTON HU15 . . . . .2 B6
Elloughton Dale HU15 . . . . . . .2 D8
Elloughton Prim Sch HU15. .2 B7
Elloughton Rd HU15 . . . . .2 C6
Elloughtonthorpe Way 13
HU15. . . . . .2 D5
Ellwood Ave PE2 . . . . .231 E6
Ellyslande NG33. . . . . .140 A5
Elm Ave 18 Brough HU15 . . . . .2 C6
Cherry Willingham/Reepham
  LN3 . . . . .203 D5
Cleethorpes DN35 . . . . .192 E6
Grimsby DN34 . . . . .191 A6
13 Mablethorpe/Sutton on Sea
  LN12 .64 B3
Newark-on-Trent NG24 . . . .104 A3
Elm Cl Lincoln LN6. . . . . .204 F2
17 Long Bennington NG23 . .117 D3
Market Deeping PE6. . . . . . .217 C4
13 Saxilby LN1. . . . . .66 D2
Yaxley PE7 . . . . .233 F7
Elm Cres
Burgh le Marsh PE24 . . . . . .102 D8
Glinton PE6 . . . . .220 B8
Elmdale 28 DN18 . . . . .10 E8
Elmdene 5 LN2. . . . . .68 F4
Elm Dr Ingoldmells PE25 . . . .206 D8
Louth LN11. . . . . .198 D7
Skegness PE25. . . . . .90 E1
3 Sudbrooke LN2 . . . . .68 F2
Elmer St N 3 NG31 . . . . .211 A4
Elmer St S NG31. . . . . .211 A4
Elmfield Rd PE1. . . . . .226 A7
Elmgarth 8 NG34 . . . . .212 F3
Elm Gdns DN35 . . . . .192 E6
Elm Gr Grantham NG31. . . . . .211 C6
8 Healing DN41 . . . . .24 A5
Scunthorpe DN16. . . . . .185 B8
Elmhirst Ave PE25. . . . . .206 D6
Elmhirst Rd 5 DN8. . . . . .15 B8
Elmhurst La LN9 . . . . .199 B6
Elm La Goxhill DN19 . . . . .5 A1
7 Laceby DN37. . . . . .23 E1
Low Fulney PE12 . . . . .157 C6
Elmore Cl 6 NG34 . . . . .212 C4
Elmore Rd PE3. . . . . .225 B7
Elm Rd Cleethorpes DN35. .192 E6
Waltham DN37. . . . . .194 E3
Elms Dr HU10. . . . . .178 C8
Elm St Peterborough PE2 . . .230 F7
Stamford PE9 . . . . .219 C5
Elms View 4 NG31 . . . . .129 D5

Elmswood HU13 . . . . .178 C2
Elm Terr PE10 . . . . .213 B6
Elmtree Ave **10** HU14 . . . . . 3 A4
Elm Tree Cl **11** LN8 . . . . . . .57 D7
Elm Tree Gr **8** DN8 . . . . . . 15 B7
Elmtree Rd NG34 . . . . .108 D1
Elm Way Brigg DN20 . . . . . .196 B4
  Messingham DN17 . . . . .29 C7
Elmwood Ave **4** PE21 . . . . .208 F2
Elmwood Cl **6** LN6 . . . . . . .200 D1
Elmwood Dr **6** PE25 . . . . . .90 D3
Elm Wy **10** PE25 . . . . .206 D7
Elsea Dr **3** PE10 . . . . .164 C8
Elsea Pk Way PE10 . . . . . . .213 D2
Elsenham Rd DN31 . . . . . . .188 D1
ELSHAM DN20 . . . . .20 F7
Elsham Cl **7** LN6 . . . . .204 D8
Elsham Cres LN6 . . . . .204 D8
Elsham Dr DN37 . . . . .194 C3
Elsham Gr **1** DN33 . . . . . . .191 B3
Elsham Hall Ctry & Wildlife
  Pk ★ DN20 . . . . .20 F6
Elsham Rd DN20 . . . . .20 D7
Elsham Rise HU13 . . . . .178 D1
Elsham Wlk DN21 . . . . .197 F4
Elsham Wold Ind Est DN20 . .21 A8
Elsie Davies Cl NG31 . . . . . .211 C7
Elsiemere Wlk **6** HU4 . . . . .179 B6
Elsom Way LN9 . . . . .199 A4
Elsthorpe Rd
  Edenham PE10 . . . . .153 D6
  Haconby PE10 . . . . .154 A7
Elstone PE2 . . . . .230 A4
Elter Wlk **1** LN1 . . . . .201 D6
Elton Cl Ermine LN1 . . . . . . .201 D6
  34 Newark-on-Trent NG24 . . .104 B2
  2 Stamford PE9 . . . . .218 F6
Elton Rd Thorney PE8 . . . . . .228 B6
  Wansford PE8 . . . . .222 B2
Elton St **1** NG31 . . . . .211 A3
Elveley Dr HU10 . . . . .178 A7
Elvin Cl **3** LN2 . . . . .201 F6
Elvington Cl **7** LN6 . . . . . . .204 B6
Elvington Rd LN6 . . . . .204 B6
Elwes St DN20 . . . . .196 C2
Elwyn Pl DN35 . . . . .192 D2
Ely Cl PE4 . . . . .220 F3
Ely St Lincoln LN1 . . . . .201 D4
  5 Sleaford NG34 . . . . .212 C6
Ely Way **5** NG31 . . . . .210 F5
Embankment Rd **4** PE1 . . .226 A1
Embassy Ctr ★ PE25 . . . . . 206 E3
Ember La
  Chapel St Leonard PE24 . . . . .77 B1
  Hogsthorpe PE24 . . . . .90 B8
Embry Rd **22** PE8 . . . . .172 B1
Emerald Gr **8** HU3 . . . . . . .180 A4
Emerson Ave DN7 . . . . .14 C5
Emery La **15** PE21 . . . . . . .208 F4
Emfield Gr DN33 . . . . .194 E7
Emfield Rd DN33 . . . . .194 D6
Emily St **8** HU9 . . . . .181 C7
Eminson Cl **6** DN21 . . . . . . .29 C4
Emlyns Gdns **5** PE9 . . . . . .219 C6
Emlyns St **2** PE9 . . . . .219 C6
Emmanual Rd DN16 . . . . . . .185 F6
Emmanuel Ct
  3 Scunthorpe DN16 . . . . . .185 C6
  Yarborough DN34 . . . . .191 A6
Emmanuel Dr DN16 . . . . . . .185 A3
Emmanuel Rd PE9 . . . . .219 B7
Emmendingen Ave **2**
  NG24 . . . . .104 A4
Emmery Cl **2** DN20 . . . . . . .19 D4
Emmetts Gr PE7 . . . . .230 F2
Emminson Way **1** NG31 . . .210 E3
EMORSGATE PE34 . . . . .161 E3
Emorsgate PE34 . . . . .161 E3
Emperor Wy PE2 . . . . .231 A6
Empingham La PE9 . . . . . . .171 A8
Empingham Rd
  4 Stamford PE9 . . . . .219 A5
  Tinwell PE9 . . . . .218 B6
Empire Ct **18** NG34 . . . . . .212 F4
Empringham St **5** HU9 . . . .181 D7
Empson Rd PE1 . . . . .226 F5
Ena St HU3 . . . . .180 B6
Endcliffe Ave DN17 . . . . . . .184 F2
Endeavour Cres **1** HU9 . . . .5 D8
Endeavour Ct **5** NG34 . . . .212 A3
Endeavour Pk Ind Est
  PE21 . . . . .208 A4
Endeavour Way PE20 . . . . . .136 A2
Endell Dr **35** DN21 . . . . . . .30 B1
Enderby Cl LN4 . . . . .203 A2
Enderby Cres DN21 . . . . . . .197 E3
Enderby Rd DN17 . . . . .184 D4
Enderby Rd Inf Sch DN17 . . .184 D4
Endsleigh St **4** HU3 . . . . . .180 A7
Energy Park Way
  Grimsby DN31 . . . . .24 B7
  Pyewipe DN37 . . . . .188 A4
Enfield Ave DN36 . . . . .195 D5
Enfield Cl PE6 . . . . .175 B1
Enfield Gdns PE3 . . . . .225 C4
Enfield Prim Sch DN36 . . . . .195 D6
Enfield Rd **8** LN11 . . . . . . .59 C1
Engaine PE2 . . . . .230 B5
Engine Bank PE12 . . . . .157 F2
Engine Dro NG34 . . . . .134 B4
Engine Dyke PE12 . . . . .148 B1
Engine La LN11 . . . . .49 E3
Engine St DN20 . . . . .196 B3
English Cl HU3 . . . . .180 E4
English Rd PE6 . . . . .176 B5

English St
  Kingston upon Hull HU3 . . . .180 E4
  Peterborough PE1 . . . . .225 E5
Ennerdale Cl
  3 Birchwood LN6 . . . . . . .200 D1
  10 Humberston DN36 . . . . .192 E1
Ennerdale Rise PE4 . . . . . . .221 B2
Enterprise Rd Caistor LN7 . . .33 A4
  Mablethorpe/Sutton on Sea
  LN12 . . . . .64 A4
Enterprise Way
  Grimsby DN32 . . . . .192 A6
  Pinchbeck PE11 . . . . .214 E8
  4 Winterton DN15 . . . . 8 F5
Ephams La DN41 . . . . .23 E7
Epperstone Residential Cvn
  Pk DN36 . . . . .193 C1
Epsom Cl LN6 . . . . .204 B8
Epsom Pl DN35 . . . . .192 F1
Epsom Rd LN6 . . . . .204 B8
Epsom Wy **17** PE10 . . . . . .213 D3
EPWORTH DN9 . . . . .27 E7
Epworth Leisure Ctr DN9 . . .27 D6
Epworth Prim Acad DN9 . . . .27 D6
Epworth Rd Epworth DN9 . . .28 A8
  Hatfield DN7 . . . . .14 F4
  Haxey DN9 . . . . .27 D3
  Owston Ferry DN9 . . . . .40 D4
Epworth Rd (West) **10** DN7 .14 E4
EPWORTH TURBARY DN9 . . .27 C6
Epworth Turbary Nature
  Reserve ★ DN9 . . . . .27 B6
Epworth View LN1 . . . . .201 E8
Erebus Cl **7** PE23 . . . . .101 A8
Eresbie Rd LN11 . . . . .198 D3
Eresby Ave **13** PE23 . . . . . .87 F1
Eresby Specl Sch The
  PE23 . . . . .100 F8
ERMINE LN2 . . . . .202 B8
Ermine Cl
  5 Ancaster NG32 . . . . . . .120 A3
  Bourne PE10 . . . . .213 C6
  Grantham NG31 . . . . .211 D5
  8 Lincoln LN1 . . . . .201 E8
  Stamford PE9 . . . . .218 F5
Ermine Cres LN1 . . . . .67 F6
Ermine Ct **10** LN4 . . . . .81 A1
Ermine Dr **3** LN5 . . . . .107 B8
Ermine Prim Acad LN2 . . . . .202 A8
Ermine Rise PE9 . . . . .171 B8
Ermine St Ancaster NG32 . . .120 A2
  Appleby DN15 . . . . .9 C1
  Winteringham DN15 . . . . . . .9 B8
  Winterton DN15 . . . . .9 C6
Ermine Way
  Market Deeping PE6 . . . . . .217 E5
  Stamford PE9 . . . . .218 F5
Ernest Terr LN2 . . . . .234 B4
Eryholme Cres **1** DN15 . . . .182 F2
Escart Ave DN32 . . . . .192 B6
Escombe View LN1 . . . . . . .201 D8
Eshings The LN2 . . . . .68 D7
Esk Cl LN6 . . . . .204 F4
Eskdale Cl **1** PE4 . . . . .221 C3
Eskdale Rd NG31 . . . . .211 A2
Eskdale Way DN37 . . . . .190 D8
ESKHAM DN36 . . . . .37 C1
Eskham Cl **1** DN35 . . . . . . .192 F3
Eslaforde Gdns **16** NG34 . .212 F4
ESSENDINE PE9 . . . . .163 D3
Essendine Rd Ryhall PE9 . . . .163 C2
  Uffington PE9 . . . . .172 C8
Essendyke PE3 . . . . .225 A7
Essex Dr **9** DN15 . . . . 8 B4
Essex Rd **3** PE9 . . . . .219 B6
Essex St HU4 . . . . .179 E3
Essex Way PE10 . . . . .213 D4
Estate Ave DN20 . . . . .19 D3
Estate Rd No 1 DN31 . . . . . .188 B1
Estate Rd No 2 DN31 . . . . . .188 B1
Estate Rd No 3 DN31 . . . . . .188 B1
Estate Rd No 4 DN31 . . . . . .188 B3
Estate Rd No 5 DN31 . . . . . .188 B1
Estate Rd No 6 DN31 . . . . . .188 B1
Estate Rd No 7 DN31 . . . . . .188 B1
Estate Rd No 8 DN31 . . . . . .188 B1
Estcourt Prim Sch HU9 . . . . .181 D8
Estcourt St HU9 . . . . .181 D8
Estella Way PE11 . . . . .214 A5
Esther Wy DN33 . . . . .191 A2
Estuary Way DN31 . . . . .188 D2
Estwaite Cl LN6 . . . . .205 B2
Ethel Ct **4** DN15 . . . . .183 B3
Ethelstone Rd **2** DN34 . . . .191 A7
Etherington St DN21 . . . . . .197 D4
Eton Cl LN6 . . . . .200 D3
Eton Ct DN17 . . . . .184 F4
Eton Dr DN17 . . . . .184 F3
Eton Rd
  Heighington/Washingborough
  LN4 . . . . .203 C1
  9 Mablethorpe/Sutton on Sea
  LN12 . . . . .64 C2
Eton St Grantham NG31 . . . .211 B4
  Kingston upon Hull HU3 . . . .180 C4
Eton Way PE21 . . . . .208 B5
ETTON PE6 . . . . .173 E5
Euclide Rd DN15 . . . . 8 E4
Eudo Rd PE25 . . . . .206 D7
Eugate Rd PE6 . . . . .167 F4
Europa Bsns Pk DN31 . . . . . .188 C2
Europarc Innovation Ctr
  DN37 . . . . .24 B6
Europa Way Brigg DN20 . . . .196 A4
  Immingham DN41 . . . . .187 B3
Eusden Ct LN4 . . . . .207 A5
Euston Ave **5** PE11 . . . . . .214 B2
Euston Cl LN6 . . . . .200 D2

Evans Cl NG23 . . . . .117 E8
EVEDON NG34 . . . . .121 F6
Evedon Rd NG34 . . . . .121 F5
Eve Gdns LN4 . . . . .203 D1
Evelyn Gr N **1** DN32 . . . . . .192 B6
Evelyn Gr S **3** DN32 . . . . . .192 B6
Evendine Ct DN36 . . . . .195 E1
Everard Rd PE11 . . . . .155 C1
Everdon Way PE3 . . . . .225 C5
Everest Rd DN16 . . . . .185 C5
Everest Wy PE7 . . . . .230 F4
EverGn Dr PE7 . . . . .230 B2
Everingham PE2 . . . . .229 D5
Everington's La PE25 . . . . . .103 C8
Everthorpe Cl **16** HU15 . . . . 2 D5
Ever Thorpe Cl **5** HU3 . . . .180 C5
Eves Cl **9** PE6 . . . . .174 E5
Evesham Ave DN34 . . . . . . .190 E5
Eve St LN11 . . . . .198 B6
Evison Cres **2** LN13 . . . . . .75 E3
Evison Ct **12** PE22 . . . . . . .113 B1
Evison Way LN11 . . . . .50 E7
Ewart St LN5 . . . . .205 D6
EWERBY NG34 . . . . .122 B6
Ewerby Pond Nature
  Reserve ★ NG34 . . . . .122 E8
Ewerby Rd NG34 . . . . .122 A5
EWERBY THORPE NG34 . . . .122 D6
Exchange Cl LN6 . . . . .204 E4
Exchange Pl **5** DN20 . . . . .196 B3
Exchange Rd LN6 . . . . .204 E4
Exchange St PE1 . . . . .226 A2
Exchequergate **5** LN2 . . . .234 B3
Exeter Cl **3** Bourne PE10 . . .213 C5
  Grantham NG31 . . . . .210 C5
  Heighington/Washingborough
  LN4 . . . . .203 E2
  1 Market Deeping PE6 . . . .217 E4
Exeter Ct **2** Bourne PE10 . . .213 C5
  10 Lincoln LN6 . . . . .190 D4
Exeter Dr **4** Sleaford NG34 .212 C6
  Spalding PE11 . . . . .214 E4
Exeter Gdns
  10 Bourne PE10 . . . . .213 C5
  Stamford PE9 . . . . .218 F4
Exeter Rd
  Peterborough PE1 . . . . .225 F5
  Scunthorpe DN15 . . . . .182 F3
  8 Wittering PE8 . . . . .172 B1
Exeter St PE10 . . . . .213 C5
Exley Sq LN2 . . . . .202 D6
Exmoor Ave DN15 . . . . .182 D7
Exmoor Cl LN6 . . . . .204 D1
Exmoor Rd DN17 . . . . .184 C8
Exton Cl **6** PE9 . . . . .218 E5
Eyam Way **3** LN6 . . . . .204 F1
EYE PE6 . . . . .175 A1
Eyebury Rd Eye PE6 . . . . . . .175 A1
  Peterborough PE6 . . . . .227 A6
Eye CE Prim Sch PE6 . . . . . .175 B1
EYE GREEN PE6 . . . . .175 B2
Eye Green Ind Est PE6 . . . . .175 A2
Eye Rd PE1 . . . . .174 F1
Eyre Ave NG16 . . . . .185 B5
Eyrescroft PE3 . . . . .225 A7
Eyrescroft Prim Sch PE3 . . .225 A7
Eyre's La LN6 . . . . .78 F1

F

Fabian Gr PE2 . . . . .231 E4
Fagans Way **7** PE25 . . . . . .206 C1
Fainlight Cl **2** PE25 . . . . . .206 D8
Fairburn Cl **9** PE24 . . . . . . .90 D7
Fairchild Way PE1 . . . . .226 A7
Fairfax Cl Boston PE21 . . . . .208 D7
  Gainsborough DN21 . . . . . . .197 F2
  6 Horncastle LN9 . . . . . . .199 D3
  2 Toft Newton LN8 . . . . . .56 D5
Fairfax Rd DN31 . . . . .191 B7
Fairfax St LN5 . . . . .205 D6
Fairfax Way PE6 . . . . .217 E3
Fairfield LN4 . . . . .207 C4
Fairfield Ave
  28 Chapel St Leonard PE24 . .90 D7
  Grimsby DN33 . . . . .194 E7
Fairfield Cl
  8 Broughton DN20 . . . . . .19 E3
  3 Spalding PE11 . . . . .214 C6
Fairfield Croft **3** DN9 . . . . .27 E6
Fairfield Ct **3** DN35 . . . . . .193 A1
Fairfield Dr
  29 Barton-upon-Humber
  DN18 . . . . .10 F8
  39 Messingham DN17 . . . . .29 D7
Fairfield Ind Est LN11 . . . . . .198 B8
Fairfield Pit Nature Reserve ★
  DN19 . . . . .4 D3
Fairfield Prim Sch DN33 . . . .194 E8
Fairfield Rd Grimsby DN33 . . .194 E7
  Peterborough PE2 . . . . .231 A8
  Scunthorpe DN15 . . . . .182 C4
Fairfields Holbeach PE12 . . . .215 C3
  33 Kirton in Lindsey DN21 . . .30 B1
Fairfield St LN2 . . . . .202 B4
Fairfield View **11** HU15 . . . . 2 D5
Fairhaven PE7 . . . . .230 F1
Fair Isle Rise DN40 . . . . .186 C2
Fairleas LN4 . . . . .81 E2
Fairmead Way PE3 . . . . .225 E2
Fairmont Cres DN16 . . . . . . .183 B2
Fairmont Rd DN32 . . . . .192 A7
Fairtree Wlk **24** DN8 . . . . . 15 A8
Fair View Ave DN35 . . . . . . .192 E6
Fairview Way PE11 . . . . .214 C6
Fairway DN37 . . . . .194 D5
Fairway Rd DN35 . . . . .193 C1

Fairways PE10 . . . . .164 A8
Fairways The Kirton PE20 . . .136 C6
  Scunthorpe DN15 . . . . .182 B2
  Torksey LN1 . . . . .65 E5
Fairway The
  Kingston upon Hull HU10 . . .178 A8
  1 Mablethorpe/Sutton on Sea
  LN12 . . . . .64 A3
Fairweather Ct PE1 . . . . . . .226 E3
Fakenham Chase PE12 . . . . .215 E3
Falcon Ct
  9 Grantham NG31 . . . . . .210 E2
  Kingston upon Hull HU4 . . . .179 D2
Falconers The DN21 . . . . . . .30 F2
Falcon Gr **12** DN21 . . . . . . .197 F5
Falcon Rd **7** LN4 . . . . .108 A7
Falcon Way
  Hampton Vale PE2 . . . . .230 C1
  13 Sleaford NG34 . . . . . . .212 B3
Falcon Wy PE10 . . . . .213 E3
FALDINGWORTH LN8 . . . . . .56 F3
Faldingworth Cl **3** LN6 . . . .204 C7
Faldingworth Com Prim Sch
  LN8 . . . . .56 F3
Faldingworth Rd LN8 . . . . . .55 F3
Faldos Way **3** LN12 . . . . . . .64 A3
Falkirk Cl **6** PE9 . . . . .218 E6
Falkland Rd **4** HU9 . . . . 5 F8
Falklands Cl LN1 . . . . .201 E8
Falklands Rd PE12 . . . . .160 C4
Falkland Way DN18 . . . . 3 F1
Fallodan Rd PE2 . . . . .229 C3
Fallowfield PE2 . . . . .229 D5
Fallowfield Rd DN33 . . . . . . .194 D7
Fallow Fields **7** PE11 . . . . .166 C6
Fallow La Foston NG32 . . . . .118 A2
  Nunsthorpe DN33 . . . . .191 B1
  1 Westborough & Dry
  Doddington NG23 . . . . .117 F3
Fall's Dro PE6 . . . . .175 F7
Falls Drove PE6 . . . . .167 B1
Falsgrave Gr HU5 . . . . .179 D7
Falstone Ave **12** NG24 . . . .104 A3
Fane Cl PE9 . . . . .219 B7
Fane Rd PE4 . . . . .221 C1
Fanny Hands La **1** LN8 . . . .59 A7
Fannystone Rd DN34 . . . . . .191 B7
Fantail Cl **2** PE11 . . . . .156 E2
Fantasy Island ★ PE25 . . . . .90 E3
Fantasy World ★ DN35 . . . . .192 F7
Fanthorpe La LN11 . . . . .198 A7
Faraday Cl PE7 . . . . .233 D6
Faraday Wlk **9** NG33 . . . . . .151 D7
FAR BANK DN7 . . . . .14 C8
Far Bank La DN7 . . . . .14 C8
FARCET PE7 . . . . .231 C2
Farcet CE Prim Sch PE7 . . . .231 C2
Far Comm Rd DN7 . . . . .15 A3
Fardell Rd DN16 . . . . .185 D7
Far Dro PE20 . . . . .124 E2
Farebrother St DN32 . . . . . .191 E6
Far End LN5 . . . . .94 A2
Far Field Rd **22** DN3 . . . . . .14 A2
FARFORTH LN11 . . . . .73 D5
Far Holme La **5** NG23 . . . . .91 A8
Far Hurn Dro LN4 . . . . .110 B7
Faringdon Rd DN31 . . . . . . .189 C2
Far Ings La DN18 . . . . .3 C1
Far Ings Nature Reserve ★
  DN18 . . . . .3 D2
Far Ings Rd DN18 . . . . .3 D1
Far La Coleby LN5 . . . . .93 F3
  27 Waddington LN5 . . . . . .93 F7
Farlakes Dr **8** PE2 . . . . . . .230 F5
Farleigh Fields PE2 . . . . . . .229 D6
FARLESTHORPE LN13 . . . . . .76 B1
Farlesthorpe Rd
  Alford LN13 . . . . .75 F2
  Bilsby LN13 . . . . .76 A2
  Willoughby with Sloothby
  LN13 . . . . .89 B8
Farmall Cl **6** DN7 . . . . .14 D5
Farm Cl **2** Gunness DN15 . . .17 E6
  12 Kirk Sandall DN3 . . . . . .14 A1
Farmers Gate PE12 . . . . . . .215 D2
Farmhouse Cl **12** NG3 . . . .128 A6
Farmhouse Dr **10** PE11 . . .166 C6
Farm House La LN8 . . . . .45 E4
Farmhouse Mews **11**
  DN36 . . . . .195 C6
Farm La **1** DN17 . . . . .28 D8
Farm View Castor PE5 . . . . . .223 D4
  18 Welton LN2 . . . . .68 D7
Farndale Cres **5** NG31 . . . .211 A8
Farndale Way
  Grimsby DN31 . . . . .191 D8
  1 Winterton DN15 . . . . .9 A5
Farnella Cl HU3 . . . . .180 A5
Far Pasture **2** PE4 . . . . . . .220 F5
Farrar Cl **10** NG24 . . . . . . .104 B5
Farrier Rd LN6 . . . . .204 B5
Farriers Ct
  Peterborough PE2 . . . . .230 D7
  Scopwick LN4 . . . . .95 C1
Farriers Fold **13** DN9 . . . . . .27 D2
Farriers Gate **2** NG34 . . . . .120 E3
Farriers Way Carlby NG3 . . . .163 D4
  8 Market Rasen LN8 . . . . . .57 C8
  2 Tattershall LN4 . . . . .207 A5
Farrier Way PE11 . . . . .214 A2
Farrington Cl **2** PE1 . . . . . .226 D6
Farrington Cres LN6 . . . . . . .200 D2
Farrishes La DN18 . . . . .10 A8
Farrow Ave
  3 Hampton Vale PE7 . . . . .230 B1

Farrow Ave continued
  Holbeach PE12 . . . . .215 E1
  Yaxley PE7 . . . . .233 B8
Farrow Rd PE12 . . . . .168 A4
Farrows Pond **3** DN19 . . . . .5 A1
Farthingales PE11 . . . . .214 C6
Farthing Ave PE3 . . . . .182 E4
Farthings Fold PE10 . . . . . . .154 B6
Farthorpe LN9 . . . . .72 D1
Far Wharf LN6 . . . . .201 D3
Fauconberg Ave **4** DN33 . .191 C2
Faulding La DN40 . . . . .12 F2
Faulding Way DN37 . . . . . . .190 C7
Faulkers La PE24 . . . . .89 E1
Fauna Wy PE7 . . . . .231 C3
Favell Rd **1** LN4 . . . . .203 B2
Faversham Ave HU4 . . . . . . .179 B6
Fawcett St DN21 . . . . .197 C5
Fawsley Cl **6** LN2 . . . . .202 E7
Fawsley Garth PE3 . . . . .225 C6
FAXFLEET DN14 . . . . 1 A2
Faxfleet La DN14 . . . . 1 A3
Fayid La LN4 . . . . .95 C7
Feale Abbey PE34 . . . . .161 E1
Featherby Pl **7** LN5 . . . . . .205 E8
Feather La **8** DN19 . . . . 11 C7
Featherworks The ★ PE21 209 B3
Felbrigg Wlk PE2 . . . . .231 F6
Fellands Gate PE22 . . . . . . .113 F3
Fellowes Gdns PE2 . . . . .231 A7
Fellowes Rd PE2 . . . . .231 A7
Felstead Rd DN34 . . . . .190 F6
Fenbridge Rd PE4 . . . . .221 A4
Fenby Cl DN37 . . . . .190 D6
Fence Bank PE34 . . . . .161 D1
Fen Cl **24** PE13 . . . . .170 D1
Fen Ct **1** DN3 . . . . .14 A1
Fen Dike PE22 . . . . .159 B3
Fendike Bank PE24 . . . . .101 F3
Fendike La PE20 . . . . .135 B5
Fen Dro PE7 . . . . .233 D1
Fendyke End La PE22 . . . . . .126 E5
Fendyke La PE13 . . . . .169 F1
Feneley Cl PE6 . . . . .217 D5
Fen End La PE12 . . . . .156 F3
Fen Field Mews PE6 . . . . . . .217 D5
FENGATE PE1 . . . . .226 D2
Fengate PE1 . . . . .226 D1
Fen Gate PE12 . . . . .157 E2
Fengate Cl **1** PE1 . . . . .226 E2
Fengate Dro PE12 . . . . .157 C3
Fengate Mobile Home Pk
  PE1 . . . . .226 D1
Fengate Rd
  Pinchbeck PE11 . . . . .214 A8
  Walsoken PE14 . . . . .170 F1
Fengate Trad Est PE1 . . . . . .226 D2
FENHOUSES PE20 . . . . .135 D7
Fenhouses Dro PE20 . . . . . .135 D8
Fenhouses La PE20 . . . . . . .135 C7
Fen La Balderton NG24 . . . . .104 D2
  Bassingham LN5 . . . . .93 A3
  Beesby with Saleby LN13 . . . .76 A7
  Conisholme LN11 . . . . .50 C5
  Dunston LN4 . . . . .95 C6
  East Keal PE23 . . . . .100 C5
  Grainthorpe LN11 . . . . .49 F5
  Lincoln LN6 . . . . .205 A1
  Long Bennington NG23 . . . . .117 B6
  Mablethorpe & Sutton LN12 . .64 A1
  Maltby le Marsh LN13 . . . . . .63 E1
  Mareham le Fen PE22 . . . . . .98 F2
  North Somercotes LN11 . . . . .50 D6
  North Thoresby DN36 . . . . . .36 C1
  South Carlton LN1 . . . . .67 C2
  Tydd St Giles PE13 . . . . . . .169 B5
Fenland Airfield PE12 . . . . . .168 B8
Fenland Ct **19** DN18 . . . . . . 3 F1
Fenland Rd
  13 Thorne/Moorends DN8 . . .15 B7
  Wisbech PE13 . . . . .170 E1
Fenland Wlk PE12 . . . . .215 B2
Fennell Rd **5** PE11 . . . . . . .156 E8
Fennell Way **3** PE9 . . . . . . .218 E4
Fenners Ave DN17 . . . . .184 E3
Fen Rd
  Billinghay LN4 . . . . .109 F6
  Dowsby PE10 . . . . .143 D4
  East Kirkby PE23 . . . . .99 F4
  Frampton PE20 . . . . .125 B1
  Gosberton PE11 . . . . .144 A4
  Heighington LN4 . . . . .82 A4
  Heighington/Washingborough
  LN4 . . . . .203 E2
  Holbeach PE12 . . . . .215 D1
  Little Hale NG34 . . . . .133 F8
  Metheringham LN4 . . . . .95 C4
  Newton LN13 . . . . .169 E4
  Owmby LN8 . . . . .55 F6
  Pointon & Sempringham
  NG34 . . . . .143 D6
  Ruskington NG34 . . . . .108 F2
  Stickford PE22 . . . . .100 C2
  Thurlby PE10 . . . . .154 E1
  Timberland LN4 . . . . .96 C1
  Toynton Fen Side PE23 . . . . .100 F4
  Toynton St Peter PE23 . . . . .101 A4
  Wisbech St Mary PE13 . . . . .177 E2
Fenscape ★ PE12 . . . . .157 B7
Fen Sch NG34 . . . . .123 C3
Fenside
  Halton Holegate PE23 . . . . .101 C6
  Sibsey PE22 . . . . .113 A2
  Toynton All Saints PE23 . . . .100 F4
FEN SIDE PE22 . . . . .100 A1
Fenside Dr **5** PE6 . . . . .174 E5
Fenside Farm La LN4 . . . . . . .95 D6
Fenside Boston PE21 . . . . . .208 C6

Fenside Rd continued
Holland Fen with Brothertoft
PE21.............................125 C5
FENTON Fenton LN1.........65 E3
Fenton NG23......................105 B1
Fenton CI PE7....................230 E1
Fenton Dr PE9...................163 E5
Fenton Fields LN1............65 E3
Fenton La DN22..................52 C1
Fenton PI LN2....................234 C2
Fenton Rd Fenton NG23....105 B1
Stubton NG23...................118 B8
Fenton St DN15................183 B3
Fen View Heighington LN4...81 F4
Peterborough PE2.............231 F6
Fenwick Ct
6 Holton le Clay DN36....195 D1
Nunsthorpe DN33..............191 B1
Fenwick Rd DN33..............191 B2
Fen Wlk DN36.....................37 C5
Ferens Art Gall★ HU2....180 F6
Ferensway HU2..................180 E7
Fernbank 2 DN9...............27 D7
Fern CI
3 Kingston upon Hull
HU2............................180 F8
Louth LN11.......................198 C2
Fern Croft 10 DN9...........27 E6
Fern Ct HU13....................179 A1
Ferndale PE7....................233 D6
Ferndale CI NG33.............152 F7
Ferndown 1 DN37...........188 A1
Ferndown Dr DN40...........186 D4
Fern Dr Market Rasen LN8..57 D8
Pinchbeck PE11................214 C7
Ferneries La 3 DN38........21 B4
Fern Farm La PE34..........161 F6
Fern Gr LN3......................203 D5
Fernhall CI 15 DN3............14 A2
Fernhill DN37....................190 C7
Fernie CI 3 PE6................174 E4
Fernland CI 18 HU15..........2 C5
Fernleigh Ave 4 LN4........81 A1
Fernleigh Way DN21.........209 B6
Fernwood Mews DN21......197 F2
Ferriby High Rd HU14........3 B5
Ferriby La DN33................191 C2
Ferriby Rd
Barton-upon-Humber DN18..10 E8
Hessle HU13....................178 B1
Scunthorpe DN17.............184 E5
FERRIBY SLUICE DN18......9 F7
Ferriby Sta HU14...............3 A4
Ferries St HU9...................181 D7
Ferrous Way LN6..............204 C3
Ferry Dr PE6......................224 C3
Ferry Hill PE5...................224 B1
Ferry La
Holland Fen with Brothertoft
PE20............................124 D6
Newton PE13....................170 B5
North Kyme LN4.................109 F2
Skellingthorpe LN6...........200 C5
South Kyme LN4................109 F1
Sturton le Steeple DN22.....52 D3
Washingborough LN4.........203 B2
Winteringham DN15............2 B1
Ferry Mdws Ctry Pk★
PE2...............................229 D8
Ferry Mdws Sta PE2........229 E7
Ferry Rd Bardney LN3.......83 D1
Barrow upon Humber DN19..4 C1
Fiskerton LN3....................82 D6
Haxey DN9........................27 D1
2 Keadby with Althorpe
DN17.............................17 D4
Kingston upon Hull HU13..178 E1
Langriville PE22................124 D8
Scunthorpe DN15.............182 E5
Ferry Rd W DN15.............182 A6
Ferryside 2 LN3...............82 B6
Ferryside Gdns 3 LN3.....82 B6
Ferryview PE2...................229 E6
Festival Ave 3 PE25.........90 D3
Festival Square PE12........159 C1
Feyzin Dr 40 DN18.............10 E8
Ffolkes Dr 12 PE34..........161 F3
Field Ave Saxilby LN1.........66 D3
8 Tydd St Giles PE13.....169 F7
Field CI 6 Gosberton PE11..145 B6
13 Laceby DN37................23 F1
23 Nettleham LN2..............68 D2
14 Ruskington NG34.......108 D2
1 Welton LN2....................68 D7
Field Dr 4 PE21...............136 E8
Fieldfare CI 8 DN16.........185 B2
Fieldfare Croft PE21.........208 C6
Field Farm La 3 LN4.........95 D4
Field Head 5 DN37...........23 E1
Fieldhouse Rd DN36.........193 A1
Fielding Way DN21...........197 E5
Field La Bardney LN3.........83 C5
Eastoft DN17......................7 A3
Ewerby & Evedon NG34....122 C6
Friskney PE22..................115 A6
Morton DN21....................197 A8
2 Normanby by Spital LN8..55 F6
Strubby with Woodthorpe
LN13..............................63 C1
Wroot DN9........................26 D5
Field Rd Billinghay LN4....109 E6
Crowle DN17......................16 D7
Stainforth DN7..................14 C6
Thorne/Moorends DN8......15 A8
Field Reeves Wlk 14 DN9..27 D6
Field Rise PE7..................233 D5
Fields CI 3 DN9................27 D7

Fields End
14 Misterton DN10............39 F5
Ulceby Skitter DN39..........12 B2
Fields End CI 2 PE7.........230 D2
Fieldside 6 Blyton DN21....41 C5
11 Crowle DN17................16 D7
Epworth DN9.....................27 D6
Field Side
Mareham le Fen PE22........98 F4
Thorne DN8........................15 A8
Fieldside Cres 1 PE22.......99 A4
Fields Rd DN9....................27 E2
Field St 6 Boston PE21....209 A5
Kingston upon Hull HU9....181 B7
Field Terr PE7...................231 C2
Field The DN32.................192 C6
Field View PE22................111 F8
Field Wlk PE1...................226 B2
Fife CI PE9.......................218 D6
Fifth Ave 18 Brookenby LN8..47 B6
Fixborough Ind Est DN15....8 A1
Grantham NG31...............211 F6
Scunthorpe DN17.............184 B6
Fifth Dro PE11..................144 A4
Fiftyeights Rd DN10...........26 B2
Figtree Wlk PE1................226 A7
Fildes St DN31..................191 D7
Filey CI LN6......................205 A3
Filey Rd DN32...................192 A5
FILLINGHAM DN21.............54 F4
Fillingham Cres
Cleethorpes DN35............192 F3
Scunthorpe DN15.............182 B3
Fillingham La DN21............53 F3
Finch CI LN6.....................204 D8
Finch Dr NG34..................212 B3
Finchfield PE1...................226 F7
Finchley Ct DN31..............191 A8
Finchley Gn PE3...............225 E4
Finch Wy LN8.....................70 D4
Findlay Cres DN36............195 D6
Fingle St 3 DN22...............52 B1
Finisterre Ave PE25..........206 A6
Finkell St DN10..................39 C1
Finkin St LN2....................211 A4
Finkle La 11 DN18...............3 F1
Finkle St Benington PE22..127 A5
Stainforth DN7...................14 C7
Finmere Park PE2.............229 C1
Finney CI LN4...................207 D5
Finningley CI 9 LN6.........204 D6
Finningley Rd LN6............204 D6
Finns La NG32..................138 C6
Finsbury Dr 3 DN33.........191 B2
Finsbury St 13 LN13..........75 F2
Fir Ave PE10......................213 A5
Firbeck Ave PE25..............206 D1
Fir CI DN16......................185 A4
Fircroft NG31...................211 C1
Firdale CI 3 PE6...............174 A5
Firebeacon La
Graintree LN11...................49 E8
Marshchapel LN11.............37 D1
Firecrest PE7...................233 AD8
Firethorn CI 3 HU3..........180 D5
**Fir Hill Quarry Nature
Reserve★** LN11................61 E1
Fir Lane LN7......................32 C5
Fir Rd 1 PE9....................218 D6
FIRSBY PE23....................101 F7
Firsby Cres DN33.............191 A2
First Ave Brookenby LN8...47 A6
1 Fixborough Ind Est DN15..7 F1
Grantham NG31...............211 E6
Grimsby DN33..................191 C4
6 Scampton Airfield LN1....67 E5
Scunthorpe DN17.............184 C6
Spalding PE11..................214 B4
First Dro Crowland PE6....166 C2
Gosberton PE11................144 C3
Moulton PE12...................146 E6
Peterborough PE1.............226 D1
Firs The 6 NG34..............108 D1
First Holme La 2 NG23.....91 A8
First Hurn Dro LN4...........110 A6
First La HU10...................179 A5
First Marsh Rd PE13.........170 C2
Firth Field Rd DN7.............14 F4
Firth La DN9......................26 D6
Firth Lane DN9...................27 C7
Firth Rd LN6.....................234 A1
Firtree Ave LN6................200 C1
Fir Tree CI 4 LN2...............68 C1
Firtree Dr 8 DN20..............20 F7
Fir Tree La NG32..............119 F3
Fir Trees The HU10...........178 D6
Fish Dock Rd DN31...........189 B2
Fishemore Ave HU13........178 F2
Fisher CI 28 NG23..............91 D5
Fishergate PE12...............159 B8
Fisherman's Wharf DN31..191 D8
Fishermans Wlk 2 HU3....180 E7
Fisher PI DN35..................192 D7
Fish Groom's La PE11.......145 E6
Fishings La DN9..................26 A7
FISHLAKE DN7....................14 D8
Fishlake Nab DN7...............14 C7
Fishmere End Rd
Sutterton PE20.................136 A4
Wigtoft PE20....................135 F3
Fishpond La PE12.............215 E2
Fish St 1 HU1...................180 F5
FISHTOFT PE21.................126 C1
Fishtoft Acad PE21...........126 C1
Fishtoft Dro PE22.............125 C7
FISHTOFT DROVE PE22....125 D8

Fishtoft Rd PE21............209 B3
Fish Well CI 3 NG33.........151 A8
Fishwick Ave 5 HU13.......178 E1
FISKERTON LN3.................82 A6
Fiskerton CE Prim Sch LN3..82 B7
Fiskerton CI 3 DN34.........190 F4
Fiskerton Dr LN2..............201 F8
Fiskerton Rd
Cherry Willingham LN3.....203 C4
Cherry Willingham/Reepham
LN3................................82 A6
Fiskerton Rd E LN3..........203 E4
Fiskerton Way 2 DN31....188 A3
Fitties La DN36..................37 C5
FITTON END PE13.............169 F3
Fitton End Rd PE13..........169 F3
Fitzgerald Ct 3 LN4..........207 A6
Fitzjames CI PE23............101 A8
Fitzwilliam Hospl PE6......224 E2
Fitzwilliam Mews DN35....192 E2
Fitzwilliam PI 6 LN4........109 F5
Fitzwilliam Rd PE9...........219 A7
Fitzwilliam St
10 Mablethorpe/Sutton on Sea
LN12..............................64 B4
Peterborough PE1.............226 A3
Five Arches PE7................229 C6
Five Bell La PE20..............135 C4
Five House La
Frampton PE20.................136 C8
Wyberton PE21................208 B1
Five La Ends NG23.............79 C8
Five Mile La Fiskerton LN3..83 B6
Washingborough LN4.........82 B5
Five Oaks NG33................141 C7
Flag Bsns Exchange PE1..226 E1
Flag Fen Bronze Age Mus★
PE6...............................227 B3
Flag Fen Rd PE1...............226 C4
Flag La PE12....................168 B7
Flamborough CI
Peterborough PE2.............225 E1
6 Skegness PE25.............206 A6
Flaminian Way 8 NG32....120 A2
Flarepath The DN20...........21 A8
Flavian Rd LN2................202 C8
Flaxengate 4 LN2.............234 B2
Flaxland PE3....................225 A6
Flaxley La NG24................104 A2
Flaxley Rd
Peterborough PE7.............231 A4
St Giles LN2....................202 E6
Flaxmill La 6 PE11...........145 C1
Flaxwell Way 12 NG34....121 F7
FLEDBOROUGH NG22........78 A7
FLEET PE12......................159 C6
Fleet CI HU13...................178 C3
Fleetgate 8 DN18................3 E1
FLEET HARGATE PE12......159 C7
Fleet Rd Fleet PE12..........159 B7
Holbeach PE12.................215 F2
Fleet Road Ind Est PE12..159 A8
Fleets La LN1.....................54 A1
Fleets Rd LN1....................66 D7
Fleet St Holbeach PE12....215 E2
Lincoln LN1......................201 C4
Fleetway DN36...................37 A3
Fleet Way PE2..................231 B6
Fleetwood CI 2 DN33......194 E7
Fleetwood Ct LE15...........162 A8
Fleet Wood La Prim Sch
PE12..............................159 B6
Fleming Ave NG13............128 B6
Fleming CI PE7.................233 D6
Fleming Ct 1 Boston PE21..208 F1
3 Woodston PE2..............230 D8
Fleming Dr 10 NG24.........104 A6
Fleming Rd PE11..............214 E8
Fleming Wlk HU4..............179 D2
Flemish Cres HU3............179 F5
Fletcher CI
Kingston upon Hull HU13..178 E2
3 Scunthorpe DN15.........182 C6
Fletcher Rd DN34.............190 F7
Fletcher St NG31..............211 A3
Fletcher Wy PE4..............221 E2
Fletton Ave PE2................231 A8
Fletton Fields PE2.............231 A7
Fletton Parkway PE2.........229 F2
Flinders CI 5 LN4...............95 C4
Flinders Dale 16 PE23......101 A8
Flinders Dr PE7................231 A5
Flinders Rd 13 PE11.........134 E2
Flinders Way LN3.............203 B6
Flinders Wlk PE11............214 C7
Flint CI PE9......................163 D1
Flint Gate 23 PE12...........160 E4
Flintham CI 2 LN4..............95 C4
Flint House Rd PE12.........147 C3
Flinton St HU3..................180 B3
FLIXBOROUGH DN15...........8 B1
Flixborough Rd DN15..........8 B4
FLIXBOROUGH STATHER
DN15...............................8 A1
Flood Rd The DN21...........197 B3
Flora CI PE7.....................231 D3
Flore CI PE3.....................225 C5
Florence Ave HU13...........178 F1
Florence Rd PE7...............230 F2
Florence St Grimsby DN32..191 E5
Lincoln LN5......................202 B3
Florence Way 4 PE6.........217 C5
Florence Wright Ave 6
LN11..............................198 D4
Floriade CI 4 PE11...........214 B2
Florins Fold NG34............132 F3
Floss La DN22....................65 B6
Flottergate Mall DN31......191 D7

Flour Sq DN31...............189 A1
Flowerdown Ave 5 NG34..120 D8
Foal Plats La LN13.............90 A8
FOCKERBY DN17...............7 E5
Fodder Dike Bank
Eastville PE22..................114 C7
Midville PE22...................113 E7
FOLD HILL PE22...............115 A6
Fold Hill Rd PE22.............114 A2
Fold La Moulton PE12.......157 F7
5 Tydd St Giles PE13......169 F7
Folds La PE12..................216 B4
Folgate La PE14...............170 F6
Folkingham CI 11 LN6......204 D8
Folkingham Rd
Billingborough NG34.........153 A1
1 Morton PE10................154 C7
Pickworth NG34...............142 A8
FOLKSWORTH PE7...........232 D1
Folksworth Rd PE7...........232 E1
Folly CI PE7.....................233 C5
Folly La
Branston & Mere LN4.........81 C2
Hough-on-the-Hill NG32...118 F5
North Kelsey LN7...............32 C5
North Scarle NG23.............91 D8
West Fen PE22..................99 E1
Folly's Dro PE13...............177 F3
Fontwell Cres 9 LN6.........205 A5
Fontwell Gdns 2 PE9.......219 B5
Fontwell Park Dr PE10.....213 B3
Foote's Dro PE12..............167 C8
Forbes Dr PE2..................231 A6
Forbes Rd PE21...............209 C4
Ford CI PE7......................233 E6
Ford Wy PE7....................230 E3
Fordham Dr LN1...............201 C7
FORDINGTON LN13...........88 C5
Fordington La PE23............88 A5
Ford La Hibaldstow DN20...30 F5
Morton PE10....................154 C6
Ford's Ave DN41................23 F5
Ford Way Asterby LN11....72 D6
Horncastle LN9..................85 F5
Low Toynton LN9..............199 E7
Foredyke Prim Sch HU9...5 D8
Fore La PE20....................135 A5
Foreman Way 1 PE6.........166 E1
Forest Ave 3 PE10............213 B5
Forest CE Prim Sch PE7..231 C2
Forest Dale PE1................208 F7
Forest Dro PE6.................166 C2
Forest Gdns 3 DN9...........27 D7
Forest Pines La 11 LN10...97 C5
Forest Way 7 DN36............36 B8
Forest Wy DN36...............193 B1
Forge CI Freiston PE22....126 C4
South Kelsey LN7..............32 A1
Forge Cres
3 Pinchbeck PE11............156 E8
Ulceby DN39.....................12 A1
Forge Ct 12 PE25.............217 A6
Forge Dr 10 DN9...............27 D7
Forge End PE7.................229 A4
Forge La LN8.....................56 F8
Forge Way Hartsholme LN6..204 D3
Holton le Clay DN36.........195 C3
Forkedale DN18.................10 E8
Forlander PI LN11.............198 D6
Forli Strada Haddon PE7..232 E7
Orton Southgate PE2........229 E1
Forman's La NG34...........109 B1
Formby CI NG31...............211 C7
Forrest Dr 5 PE7..............230 F5
Forrester St 1 DN20.........196 B3
Forrington PI LN11.............66 E2
Forstedd Hill NG33...........153 B5
Forster St DN21................197 C5
Forsyth Cres DN35...........206 C2
Forsythia Ave 28 DN41......23 F5
Forsythia CI 5 LN4.............81 D2
Forsythia Dr DN33............191 C2
Fortescue LE15................204 A7
Fortuna Dr 1 PE2.............231 D4
Fortuna Sch LN6...............204 B7
Fortuna Way DN37...........190 F8
Forty Acre HU10.............178 F7
Forty Acre Rd PE1............226 D2
Forty Foot La
Humberside Airport DN39...21 F6
Old Leake PE22................113 D3
Forty Stps HU10...............178 F7
Forum The LN6.................204 F3
Forum Way 7 NG34..........212 F3
FOSDYKE PE20.................146 D8
FOSDYKE BRIDGE PE12...146 E7
Foss Bank LN1.................201 D3
Fossdyke Gdns 18 LN1......66 D2
Fosse CI 9 PE6.................164 E5
Fosse Ct 5 LN4..................81 A1
Fosse Dr LN6...................205 A3
Fosse La Thistleton LE15..151 B1
Thorpe on the Hill LN6.......92 E7
Fosseway LN2..................197 F5
Fosse Way Acad LN6........204 F2
Foss St LN1......................201 D3
Foster CI 2 LN4..................96 C1
Foster Rd
27 Collingham NG23..........91 D5
7 Thorne/Moorends DN8...15 A8
Woodston PE2..................230 D8
Fosters CI 3 LN5...............107 A8
Foster's Dro PE10.............155 A3
Foster's Gdns 1 LN4..........82 B1

Fen–Fra 251

Foster St 3 Boston PE21..209 A5
Heckington NG34..............122 E3
Lincoln LN5......................201 E1
FOSTON NG32..................117 F2
Foston by Pass NG32........117 F1
Foston Cres LN6...............204 F7
Foston La NG32................128 F7
Foston Rd NG31...............210 E3
FOTHERBY LN11................49 A3
Fotherby Rd DN37............184 F4
Fotherby St 3 DN31.........189 A1
Fothergill Dr 17 DN37........14 A2
FOUL ANCHOR PE13.......170 D8
Foundary Sh Ctr The
DN15..............................183 B4
Foundry La
11 Spalding PE11.............214 D4
12 Thorne/Moorends DN8..15 A8
Foundry Rd Bucknall LN10..84 C6
Ryhall PE9.......................163 C2
Stamford PE9...................219 A5
Foundry St LN9.................199 C4
Fountain CI
Kingston upon Hull HU13..178 C3
5 Waltham DN37.............194 C5
Fountain Hill DN10.............39 E3
Fountain Hill Rd DN10........39 E4
Fountain La 13 PE21.........208 F5
Fountain PI 10 PE21.........208 F5
Fountains Ave DN37.........188 A1
Fountains PI PE6..............175 B1
Fountain St 22 Caistor LN7..33 B4
Kingston upon Hull HU3...180 D6
Four Acre CI HU10..........178 C6
Four Chimneys Cres
Hampton Hargate PE7.......230 C2
Yaxley PE7......................233 B8
Fourfields CE Sch The
PE20..............................136 A2
Fourfields Com Prim Sch
PE7...............................233 E6
FOUR GOTES PE13...........170 B7
Fourth Ave
2 Fixborough Ind Est DN15..8 A1
Grantham NG31...............211 F6
3 Scampton Airfield LN1...67 E5
1 Scunthorpe DN17.........184 C6
Fourth Dro Gosberton PE11..144 B4
Peterborough PE1.............226 F3
Fourways 6 DN36...............36 D4
Fowler CI LN11.................198 D4
Fowler Ct 32 DN15..............9 A5
Fowler Rd DN16................185 B8
Foxby Hill DN21................197 E2
Foxby La DN21.................197 F2
Foxby Warren DN21..........197 E2
Fox CI Boston PE21.........208 C6
Little Coates DN34............190 F6
Fox Covert
2 Aubourn Haddington & South
Hykeham LN6....................93 A8
19 Hibaldstow DN20...........30 F5
Lincoln LN6......................204 A1
North Hykeham LN6..........204 B1
Sudbrooke LN2..................69 A2
Fox Covert La DN10...........40 A4
Foxcovert Rd PE6.............220 E8
Fox Ct 1 Crowle DN17........16 D8
6 Owmby LN8....................55 F6
Foxdale PE1.....................225 F7
Fox Dale PE9....................218 F6
Foxe End 19 LN12..............64 B3
Foxendale Hill LN9.............72 F1
Foxes Low Rd PE12..........215 F2
Foxfield CI LN5.................200 A5
Foxglove CI
Brigg DN20......................196 B4
1 Spilsby PE23................101 A8
Foxglove Ct PE11.............214 B6
Foxglove Gdns DN34........190 F6
Foxglove Rd
16 Market Rasen LN8.........57 D8
1 Stamford PE9...............218 C7
Foxgloves PE2..................217 D6
Foxglove Way 5 LN5.........205 D2
Fox Headings PE12...........158 C1
Foxhill DN37.....................190 C7
Foxhill Rd DN8....................15 B7
Foxhills Ind Pk DN15........182 F7
Foxhills Rd DN15..............182 E5
Foxhole La PE22...............126 D3
Fox Hollow LN6..................92 D5
Foxley CI PE4...................221 A4
Foxley Ct 1 PE10..............213 C7
Fox St DN15.....................182 F3
Foxtail CI 6 DN33.............194 D8
Foxton Wy DN20...............196 D5
Foyle CI LN5.....................205 D2
Fracknal's Row 3 PE21...208 E6
Framlingham Rd PE7........231 F5
FRAMPTON PE20...............136 F6
Frampton Bank PE20.........136 B8
Frampton La PE20.............124 C2
**Frampton Marsh Nature
Reserve★** PE21................137 D5
Frampton PI PE21.............208 E4
Frampton Roads PE20......136 F6
Frances Askew Prim Sch
HU4...............................179 F4
Frances Ct 8 DN37...........194 C5
**Frances Olive Anderson CE
Prim Sch** DN21................53 A5
Frances St DN15...............183 A3
Francis Bernard CI 4
PE21..............................208 D3

Francis Chichester Wlk
DN21 . . . .**197** F3
Francis Gdns PE1 . . . . . . **225** F8
Francis La LN9 . . . . **199** C4
Francis St
Kingston upon Hull HU2 . . . .**180** F7
Lincoln LN1 . . . .**234** B4
14 Spalding PE11 . . . .**214** D4
Francklin Wlk 5 PE12 . . .**158** B6
Frankland Cl 1 DN20 . . .**196** F6
Frankland Pl DN35 . . . . . .**192** D7
Franklin Ave PE25 . . . .**206** D1
7 Metheringham LN4 . . . . . .**95** C4
Franklin Cl Boston PE21 . . .**208** C6
Franklin Cres
Peterborough PE1 . . . .**226** E6
Scunthorpe DN16 . . . .**185** E6
1 Sleaford NG34 . . . .**212** D5
Franklin Dr PE11 . . . .**214** B2
Franklin Gdns 11 PE23 . . .**101** A8
Franklin Mews 17 DN18 . . . .**3** F1
Franklin Rd 3 DN21 . . . . . .**29** C4
Franklin St HU9 . . . .**181** C8
Franklin Way
Humberside Airport DN39 . . . **21** F5
North Greetwell LN3 . . . . . .**203** B6
Franklin Wy 20 DN19 . . . . .**11** D8
Frank Perkins Parkway
PE1 . . . .**226** E6
Frank Perkins Way PE1 . . .**226** D3
Franks Cl 2 PE20 . . . .**136** D5
Franks La PE13 . . . .**169** F5
Frank Swaby Ct LN5 . . . . .**205** C6
Frank Walsham Ct DN32 . .**192** A8
Frank Whittle Cl 1 NG34 . .**120** E8
Frank Wright Ct 4 LN2 . . .**202** C7
Fraserburgh Way 2 PE2. .**229** D4
Fraser Cl PE6 . . . .**217** D5
Fraser St 2 DN32 . . . .**191** F7
Frederica Rd 12 PE25 . . . .**103** E4
Frederick Dr PE3 . . . .**225** C8
Frederick Gough Sch
DN16 . . . .**185** C4
Frederick St
Cleethorpes DN35 . . . .**192** E6
Grimsby DN31 . . . .**191** D8
Lincoln LN2 . . . .**202** C3
Frederick Ward Way
DN31 . . . .**191** D7
Freehold St HU3 . . . .**180** D7
Freeman Ave 4 HU15 . . . . . .**2** C5
Freeman Cl 10 PE8 . . . .**172** B1
Freeman Ct DN36 . . . .**195** E2
Freeman Dr LN6 . . . .**204** D3
Freemans La 6 DN20. . . . . .**10** C2
Freeman's La PE2 . . . .**52** A2
Freeman St DN32 . . . .**189** B1
Freeman Way DN32 . . . . . .**189** B1
Freeport Wharf DN31 . . . . .**191** E8
Freer Gdns LN11 . . . .**198** E6
Freeschool La LN2 . . . .**234** B2
Freesia Way PE7 . . . .**233** F6
Freeston St DN35 . . . .**192** B8
Freetown Way HU2. . . . . . .**180** E7
Freightliner Rd
Kingston upon Hull HU3 . . . .**179** F2
Kingston upon Hull HU3 . . . .**180** A3
FREISTON PE22 . . . .**126** D2
Freiston Ctr for
Environmental Ed★
PE22 . . . .**126** D3
Freiston Rd PE21 . . . .**209** B5
FREISTON SHORE PE22 . . . .**126** F1
French Dro PE6 . . . .**175** E7
French's Rd PE14 . . . .**170** F8
Fresh Fields 14 HU15 . . . . . .**2** C5
Freshney Bog Nature
Reserve★ DN37 . . . .**190** E7
Freshney Dr 1 DN31 . . . . .**191** C8
Freshney Pl Sh Ctr DN32 . .**191** D7
Freshney Way PE21 . . . . . .**208** B3
Freshwater Rd PE7 . . . .**230** B1
Freston PE4 . . . .**221** D2
Freyja Croft DN33 . . . .**191** B2
Friars Gate PE21 . . . .**208** E4
Friars La LN2 . . . .**234** B2
Friars Rd DN17 . . . .**184** E6
Friar Way PE21 . . . .**208** F6
Friary Rd 1 NG24 . . . .**104** A4
FRIESTHORPE LN3 . . . .**57** A2
Friest La 11 PE20 . . . .**135** A4
FRIESTON NG32 . . . .**119** B6
Frieston Heath La NG32. . .**119** C6
Frieston Rd NG32 . . . .**119** B6
Frieston Shore Nature
Reserve★ PE22 . . . .**127** A1
Frinkley La
Honington NG32 . . . .**119** B2
Hougham NG32 . . . .**118** D2
Frisby Cl PE6 . . . .**164** D4
FRISKNEY PE22 . . . .**115** A6
Friskney All Saints CE (Aided)
Prim Sch PE22 . . . .**115** A6
Friskney Decoy Wood Nature
Reserve★ PE22 . . . .**115** A8
FRISKNEY EAUDYKE
PE22. . . . .**115** B7
FRITH BANK PE21 . . . .**125** D5
Frith Bank PE21 . . . .**125** D6
Friths La PE20 . . . .**125** B1
FRITHVILLE PE22 . . . .**112** D1
Frithville Prim Sch PE22 . .**112** D1
Frithville Rd PE22 . . . .**113** A1
Frobisher Ave DN32 . . . . . .**192** B6

FRODINGHAM DN16 . . . . . .**183** C2
Frodingham Footpath 2
DN15 . . . .**183** B3
Frodingham Inf Sch DN16 **183** B2
Frodingham Rd DN15. . . . . .**183** A4
Frodingham S Rd DN16. . . .**183** E2
Frodsham St 8 HU9 . . . .**5** D8
FROGNALL PE6 . . . .**165** C1
Frognall PE6. . . . .**165** D1
Frog's Abbey Gate PE12 . .**158** E4
Front Rd
Tydd St Mary PE13 . . . .**160** D1
Wisbech St Mary PE13. . . . .**177** D6
Front St Alkborough DN15 . . . .**8** C8
Barnby in the Willows NG24 .**104** F3
Dunston LN4 . . . .**95** C5
East Stockwith DN21 . . . . . .**40** B5
Elsham DN20 . . . .**20** F7
Gainsborough DN21. . . . . . .**197** B7
4 Grasby DN38 . . . .**32** E7
Normanby by Spital LN8 . . . .**55** E7
South Clifton NG23 . . . .**78** C5
Stainton le Vale LN8 . . . .**46** C1
Tealby LN8 . . . .**46** C1
Ulceby DN39 . . . .**12** A1
Frost Cl DN15 . . . .**2** A1
Frostley Gate PE12 . . . . . .**158** F3
Frow Cl Bar DN33 . . . .**191** C3
Fryston 28 HU15 . . . .**2** C6
Fuchsia Croft 2 DN15 . . . .**182** F2
Fuchsia Dr HU4 . . . .**179** B2
FULBECK NG32 . . . .**106** C1
Fulbeck Rd DN16. . . . .**185** C6
Fulbridge Acad PE1 . . . . . .**225** F7
Fulbridge Rd PE4 . . . .**221** A3
Fulford Cl NG31 . . . .**211** D8
Fulford Cres
Kingston upon Hull HU10 . . .**179** A8
3 New Holland DN19 . . . .**4** E2
Fulford Way PE25 . . . .**206** C6
Fulham Pk 1 DN33. . . . . . .**191** B2
Fulham Rd PE3 . . . .**225** E4
Fuller St DN35 . . . .**192** D8
FULLETBY LN9 . . . .**86** B8
Fulletby Rd LN9 . . . .**73** B2
Fulletby Road LN9 . . . . . .**199** F7
Fulmar Dr LN11 . . . .**198** C8
Fulmar Rd LN6 . . . .**204** D8
Fulmen Cl LN11 . . . .**201** C7
FULNETBY LN8 . . . .**69** F6
Fulnetby La LN3. . . . .**69** E7
Fulney Dro PE12 . . . .**157** B6
Fulney La PE12 . . . .**157** B6
FULSTOW LN11 . . . .**49** B8
Fulstow Gr 5 DN33 . . . . . .**191** B3
Fulstow Prim Sch LN11 . . . .**49** B8
Fulstow Rd LN2 . . . .**202** B8
Fundrey Rd PE13 . . . .**170** E1
Fun Farm★ PE12 . . . .**157** D7
Furlongs La Belchford LN9 . .**73** B1
Old Leake PE22 . . . .**114** A1
Furlongs Rd 2 LN1 . . . .**77** A8
Furlongs The 17 LN8 . . . . . .**57** D8
Furlong Wy NG34 . . . .**212** B7
Furnace Cl Hartsholme LN6 **204** C3
Hartsholme LN6 . . . .**204** C3
Furndown Ct LN6 . . . .**204** B7
Furniss Ct 2 DN18 . . . .**10** E8
Furrow Cl 18 LN2 . . . .**68** D6
Furrows The PE21 . . . .**209** C3
Further Old Gate PE12 . . . .**158** D5
Fury Ave LN11 . . . .**62** B6
Furze Hill Nature Reserve★
PE23 . . . .**87** A3
Furze Hills LN9 . . . .**85** D7
Furze La LN11 . . . .**62** A5
Furze Ride PE1 . . . .**226** B8
Fusilier Wy DN31 . . . .**30** C1
Fussey Gdns DN20 . . . .**10** C1
Fydell Cres PE21 . . . .**208** E4
Fydell Ct PE21. . . . .**208** E6
Fydell St PE21 . . . .**208** E5
Fyson Way PE20. . . . .**136** C6

G

Gables The PE10 . . . .**213** C2
Gabriel Cres LN2 . . . .**202** E6
Gadd's La PE13 . . . .**170** A1
Gadwall Wy DN16. . . . .**185** F5
Gage Ct 4 LN2 . . . .**202** D6
Gainas Ave DN21. . . . .**197** C6
GAINSBOROUGH DN21. . . .**197** B4
Gainsborough Acad The
DN21. . . . .**197** F6
Gainsborough Central Sta
DN21. . . . .**197** E4
Gainsborough Coll DN21. . .**197** C5
Gainsborough Dr 7
NG24 . . . .**104** A6
Gainsborough Gdns 2
LN6 . . . .**205** B7
Gainsborough La DN20 . . . .**30** F8
Gainsborough Lea Rd Sta
DN21. . . . .**197** D1
Gainsborough Leisure Ctr
DN21. . . . .**197** D6
Gainsborough Model
Railway★ **15** DN21. . . . . .**197** D3
Gainsborough Old Hall★
DN21. . . . .**197** C5
Gainsborough Rd
Blyton DN21. . . . .**41** B4
Bole DN22 . . . .**52** A6
Girton NG23. . . . .**78** C2

Gainsborough Rd *continued*
Hemswell Cliff DN21 . . . .**54** F8
32 Kirton in Lindsey DN21 . . .**30** B1
Kirton in Lindsey DN21. . . . . .**42** D8
Little Casterton PE9 . . . .**218** F7
Middle Rasen LN8 . . . .**57** B7
Saundby DN22 . . . .**52** B7
Saxilby with Ingleby LN1 . . . .**66** D2
Scotter DN21. . . . .**29** B3
Sturton le Steeple DN22. . . . .**52** B3
West Rasen LN8. . . . .**57** A7
Willingham DN21. . . . .**53** E4
6 Winthorpe NG24 . . . .**104** B7
Wiseton DN10. . . . .**39** A1
Yawthorpe DN21. . . . .**43** B2
Gainsthorpe Rd E DN21. . . .**30** D4
Gainsthorpe Rd W DN21 . . .**30** D4
Galba Rd LN7 . . . .**33** A4
Gallagher Ret Pk DN15 . . .**182** A3
Gallamore Ct 5 LN8. . . . . . .**57** C8
Gallamore La
Market Rasen LN8 . . . .**57** D8
6 Middle Rasen LN8 . . . .**57** C8
Gallamore Lane Ind Est
LN8 . . . .**57** D8
Galland Rd 34 HU15 . . . .**2** D5
Gallands Cl 15 HU14 . . . .**3** B7
Galletly Cl PE10 . . . .**213** D6
Galley Ct HU3 . . . .**181** C6
GALLEY HILL LN13 . . . .**75** E6
Gallions Cl 2 PE4. . . . .**221** B1
Galway Cl 2 PE11. . . . .**214** A5
Gamage Cl DN34 . . . .**104** C2
Gamlyn Cl 1 PE11 . . . .**214** D2
Gannet Ct 8 NG31 . . . .**210** E2
Gannocks Cl PE2 . . . .**229** F5
Gannocks The PE2 . . . .**229** F5
Ganton Way
Harrowby Est NG31 . . . .**211** E7
Kingston upon Hull HU10 . . .**178** F8
Garbutt Pl DN35. . . . .**193** A4
Garcia Rd DN36 . . . .**36** C4
Garden Cl PE9 . . . .**218** E6
Garden Dr DN36. . . . .**195** C7
Garden End Rd PE1. . . . . . .**226** B6
Gardeners Wlk PE21. . . . . .**208** D2
Gardenfield LN6 . . . .**200** B3
Gardenia Dr DN17. . . . .**184** F1
Garden St 5 Brigg DN20 . . .**196** C3
Grimsby DN31 . . . .**191** D7
Gardens The
3 Crowland PE6 . . . .**166** F1
Horncastle LN9. . . . .**199** C3
Gardiner Ave 1 NG24 . . . . .**104** C1
Garfield Cl 2 DN21 . . . . . .**201** D8
Garfield St DN21 . . . .**197** C5
Garfield View LN1. . . . .**201** D8
Garfit's La PE21 . . . .**208** D1
Garford Ct PE6. . . . .**173** C7
Garford La 8 PE9 . . . .**171** D3
Garganey Wk DN36 . . . . . .**185** F5
Garibaldi St 6 DN32 . . . . .**189** B1
Garmston St 8 LN1 . . . . . .**234** B3
Garner's La PE34 . . . .**161** A4
Garner St DN32 . . . .**191** E6
Garnet Gr 6 HU3 . . . .**180** A4
Garnett St DN35 . . . .**192** D8
GARNSGATE PE12. . . . .**159** E5
Garnsgate Rd PE12 . . . . . .**216** A5
Garratt Cl LN4 . . . .**81** E4
Garratt Rd 7 PE9 . . . .**219** B4
Garrick Cl LN5 . . . .**205** C3
Garrick La DN36. . . . .**195** C7
Garrick Wlk PE2 . . . .**231** B7
Garrison Rd HU9 . . . .**181** C6
Garth La DN31 . . . .**191** D8
GARTHORPE
Garthorpe LE14 . . . .**150** A4
Garthorpe and Fockerby DN17. .**7** F6
Garthorpe Rd DN17 . . . .**7** C4
Garth The HU10 . . . .**179** A4
Garthway 7 DN36. . . . .**195** D2
Garton Gr
3 Grimsby DN32. . . . .**192** A5
3 Kingston upon Hull HU5. . .**179** C7
Garton St 7 PE1. . . . .**226** A5
Gascoigne 3 PE4 . . . .**220** E5
Gashouse La 3 DN9 . . . .**28** A3
Gas House La 16 PE12 . . . . .**160** E4
Gas La
7 Navenby/Wellingore
LN5 . . . .**107** A8
Stamford PE9 . . . .**219** C5
5 Thorney PE6 . . . .**176** A3
Gas St 3 Horncastle LN9 . . .**199** C3
19 Stamford PE9. . . . .**219** C5
GATE BURTON DN21. . . . . . .**53** B2
Gated Rd PE22 . . . .**99** C7
Gatehouse Rd Goxhill DN19 .**11** F7
Moortown LN7 . . . .**32** E1
Gate La DN33 . . . .**191** D1
Gateroom La PE22 . . . .**114** E3
Gate Way DN31 . . . .**188** E2
Gateway The 4 NG24 . . . . .**104** A4
Gatewood La DN7 . . . .**14** E1
Gatherums The DN35 . . . . .**192** E5
Gatram Rd PE24. . . . .**90** D6
Gaunt Cl 5 PE12. . . . .**157** B6
Gauntlet Dro PE20 . . . .**134** F6
Gauntlet Rd
3 Bicker PE20. . . . .**135** A4
Grimoldby LN11 . . . .**62** B6
Gaunt St LN5 . . . .**234** A1
GAUTBY LN8 . . . .**84** B7
Gautby Lane LN10 . . . .**84** A6
Gautby Rd LN8 . . . .**83** F7
Gautry La DN9 . . . .**28** B4

Gavel St PE7 . . . .**233** C8
Gayle Rd LN4 . . . .**110** E8
Gaysfield Rd 6 PE21 . . . . .**126** C1
Skegness PE25. . . . .**206** C2
Gayton Ct PE3 . . . .**225** C5
GAYTON ENGINE LN12. . . . . .**63** C6
GAYTON LE MARSH LN13. . . .**62** F3
GAYTON LE WOLD LN11. . . . .**59** E4
Gayton Rd DN35. . . . .**193** A3
Gazeley Gdns PE7 . . . .**231** B2
Geddington Rd PE2 . . . . . .**230** E8
GEDNEY PE12 . . . .**159** D7
GEDNEY BROADGATE
PE12. . . . .**159** D5
Gedney Church End Prim Sch
PE12. . . . .**159** D7
Gedney Cl 13 Bicker PE20. .**135** A4
Grimsby DN37 . . . .**190** C8
GEDNEY DROVE END
PE12. . . . .**149** A4
Gedney Drove End Cty Prim
Sch PE12 . . . .**148** F3
GEDNEY DYKE PE12. . . . . . .**148** B1
GEDNEY HILL PE12 . . . .**168** D2
Gedney Hill CE VC Prim Sch
The PE12. . . . .**168** B2
Gedney Hill Gate PE12. . . .**168** F7
Gedney Rd PE12 . . . .**216** A6
Gee St HU3 . . . .**180** C5
GEESTON PE9 . . . .**171** A2
Geeston Rd PE9. . . . .**171** A2
Geipel Cl DN37 . . . .**194** F5
Gelder Beck Rd DN17. . . . . .**29** C6
Gelder's La PE12 . . . .**158** A1
GELSTON NG32 . . . .**118** F4
Gelston Rd NG32 . . . .**119** A4
Gemsbok Cl 3 HU4 . . . . . .**179** D2
Genesis Way
Great Coates DN37 . . . .**24** B6
Pyewipe DN37 . . . .**188** A3
Geneva Ave LN2. . . . .**202** B6
Geneva St PE1 . . . .**226** A3
Geoff Moulder Leisure
Complex★ PE21. . . . .**209** A4
George Alcock Wy PE7 . . . .**231** D2
George Ave Gedney PE12 . . .**148** F4
4 Keadby DN17 . . . .**17** D5
Skegness PE25. . . . .**206** B3
George Butler Cl DN37. . . . .**23** F1
George Janney Ct 24
DN32 . . . .**189** C1
George Matthews Gdns 27
PE6 . . . .**175** A1
George Mews 2 LN7. . . . . . .**33** B4
George Sh Ctr The NG31 . .**211** A4
George St
2 Barton-upon-Humber
DN18. . . . .**10** F8
20 Beacon Hill NG24 . . . . . .**104** A4
5 Boston PE21 . . . .**208** E4
Bourne PE10 . . . .**213** D5
Broughton DN20 . . . .**19** D3
Cleethorpes DN35 . . . .**192** F5
Gainsborough DN21. . . . . . .**197** B6
Grantham NG31 . . . .**211** B4
Grimsby DN31 . . . .**191** D7
Helpringham NG34. . . . .**133** D7
Kingston upon Hull HU1 . . . .**180** F6
11 Kirton in Lindsey DN21 . . .**30** B1
Lincoln LN5 . . . .**234** C1
Louth LN11. . . . .**198** B5
Mablethorpe/Sutton on Sea
LN12 . . . .**64** B3
7 Market Rasen LN8. . . . . . .**57** D8
Peterborough PE2 . . . .**230** F8
Scunthorpe DN15 . . . .**183** A4
Sleaford NG34 . . . .**212** C3
Georgette Gdns 2 PE11 . . .**214** B5
George Yd 5 HU1. . . . .**181** A6
Georgian Ct
Peterborough PE3 . . . .**225** E1
6 Spalding PE11 . . . .**214** D3
Georgina Ct 2 DN18 . . . . . .**10** E8
Gerald's Cl LN2 . . . .**202** B5
Gerbera Dr 15 NG24 . . . . .**104** B5
German's La PE34 . . . .**161** D2
Gerrard Mews LN4 . . . .**203** D1
Gershwin Ave HU4 . . . .**179** B4
Gershwin La PE11 . . . .**214** A1
Gertrude St DN32 . . . .**191** E5
Gervase St DN15 . . . .**183** A3
Gibbeson St 6 LN5. . . . . . .**205** E8
Gibbet La LN8 . . . .**57** A5
Gibbon La DN8 . . . .**14** F7
Gibbs Cl 8 PE6 . . . .**164** F3
Giblin Cotts DN15 . . . .**182** E5
Gibraltar Hill LN1 . . . .**234** A3
Gibraltar La 2 DN37 . . . . . .**23** F1
Gibraltar Point National
Nature Reserve★ PE24 . .**103** C1
Gibraltar Point Visitor Ctr★
PE24. . . . .**116** D4
Gibraltar Rd Croft PE24. . . .**103** D1
5 Hemswell Cliff DN21 . . . . .**55** A8
Mablethorpe/Sutton on Sea
LN12 . . . .**64** B4
Seacroft PE24 . . . .**116** C5
Gibson Cl Branston LN4. . . . .**81** E2
1 Sleaford NG34. . . . .**212** B6
Gibson Cres 9 NG24 . . . . .**104** B2
Gibson Gn LN6. . . . .**92** E5
Gibson La 4 HU14 . . . .**2** F5
Gibson Pl 5 PE25 . . . .**206** A5
Gibson Rd 2 DN7 . . . .**26** A8
Gibsons Gdn 2 LN11. . . . . .**50** F7

Giddings Cl PE2 . . . .**229** F4
Giddon's Dro PE6 . . . .**174** A7
Gilbert Dr PE21 . . . .**208** A1
Gilberts Gr 4 PE25 . . . .**206** D8
Gilbert Sutcliffe Ct DN35. .**192** A2
Gilbert Wy 28 NG24 . . . . . .**104** C1
Gilbey Rd DN31 . . . .**188** D1
Gildale PE4. . . . .**221** B4
Gildenburgh Ave PE1. . . . .**226** D5
Gilder Way PE21 . . . .**209** F2
Gildesburgh Rd LN4. . . . . .**203** B1
Giles Acad The **14** PE22 . . .**114** A1
Giles Cl 12 PE22 . . . .**114** A1
Giles Rd PE11 . . . .**214** C2
Giles St DN35 . . . .**192** E6
Gillatts Cl 1 DN20 . . . .**196** F7
Gill Cl DN33 . . . .**191** B2
Gillett La DN15 . . . .**180** B4
Gillett St HU3 . . . .**180** B4
Gilliatt St DN15. . . . .**183** A4
Gilmores La 18 NG24 . . . . .**104** C1
Gilmorton Dr PE1 . . . .**226** D7
Gilpin Cl PE10. . . . .**213** E2
Gilpin St PE1 . . . .**225** E6
Gilstrap Cl 3 NG24. . . . . . .**104** B4
Gimmel's Gate PE22. . . . . .**216** C1
GIPSEY BRIDGE PE22 . . . . .**124** F8
Gipsey Bridge Prim Sch
PE22 . . . .**125** A8
Gipsy Dro Friskney PE22 . . .**114** D7
Langriville PE22 . . . .**124** F8
Gipsy La Gedney PE12 . . . .**216** A8
Holton le Moor LN7. . . . .**32** C1
Osgodby LN8 . . . .**45** D3
Owersby LN7 . . . .**44** F8
Owston Ferry DN9 . . . .**40** C8
South Kelsey LN7 . . . .**32** C1
Swineshead PE20 . . . .**124** A1
Tydd St Mary PE13 . . . .**160** A2
Wrangle PE22 . . . .**114** D2
GIPSYVILLE HU4 . . . .**179** E3
Girdlestone Wlk 2 PE6. . . .**166** F1
Girls School La PE22 . . . . .**126** E3
GIRSBY LN8 . . . .**59** C6
Girsby La LN8 . . . .**59** B6
GIRTON NG23 . . . .**78** C1
Girton Cl 3 DN16 . . . .**185** B4
Girton La NG23 . . . .**78** D1
Girton Rd DN37 . . . .**190** F6
Girton Way 3 PE9. . . . .**219** A7
Gisburn Rd HU13. . . . .**178** F2
Glade The
8 Mablethorpe/Sutton on Sea
LN12 . . . .**77** A7
New Waltham DN36 . . . .**195** E7
Gladiator Rd LN11. . . . .**62** B6
Gladstone Cotts DN21 . . . .**197** B8
Gladstone Dr 1 DN16 . . . . .**183** C1
Gladstone Prim Sch PE1. . .**225** F5
Gladstone St Bourne PE10 .**213** C6
Gainsborough DN21. . . . . . .**197** C5
Kingston upon Hull HU3 . . . .**180** C6
Peterborough PE1 . . . .**225** F3
Gladstone Terr 3 NG31 . . .**211** A5
Glaisdale Gdns NG31 . . . . .**211** B8
Glaisdale Rd 2 DN16 . . . . .**185** D5
Glamis Gdns PE3 . . . .**225** B2
Glamis Pl LN11 . . . .**198** B6
Glamis Rd HU13. . . . .**178** F2
Glanford Gr 12 DN19. . . . . .**11** D8
Glanford Pk (Scunthorpe
United FC) DN15 . . . .**182** A2
Glanford Rd Brigg DN20 . . .**196** D3
Scunthorpe DN17 . . . .**184** F3
Glanford Way DN15 . . . . . .**182** B3
Glanville Ave DN17 . . . .**184** F8
Glanville Cres 2 DN17. . . . .**184** F8
Glasgow St HU3 . . . .**180** A5
Glastonbury Cl 20 PE6 . . . .**175** A1
Glatton Dr PE2 . . . .**231** D6
Gleanings The 6 LN5 . . . . .**107** B8
Glebe Ave PE2 . . . .**229** E4
Glebe Cl
Burton upon Stather DN15. . . .**8** A5
3 Donington on Bain LN11 . . .**59** E1
Gorefield PE13. . . . .**169** E3
Holton le Clay DN36 . . . . . .**195** C3
14 Humberston DN36 . . . . . .**36** C8
5 Ingham LN1. . . . .**54** F2
Scopwick LN4. . . . .**95** C1
5 Sibsey PE22 . . . .**113** B1
1 Skegness PE25 . . . .**206** A7
Sleaford NG34 . . . .**212** A2
2 Spalding PE11 . . . .**214** A4
Glebe Ct PE2. . . . .**231** B8
Glebe End LN4 . . . .**81** A4
Glebe Gdns 2 PE6 . . . .**175** B8
Glebe Pk 2 NG24 . . . .**104** B3
Glebe Rd Brigg DN20 . . . . .**196** C4
Cleethorpes DN35 . . . .**192** E6
Grimsby DN33 . . . .**191** E1
Humberston DN36 . . . .**36** C7
Peterborough PE2 . . . .**231** A8
Scunthorpe DN15 . . . .**183** B4
Thorne/Moorends DN8 . . . . .**15** B8
Wymondham LE14 . . . .**150** B1
Glebe Ret Pk DN15 . . . . . .**183** B4
Glebe The
Sturton by Stow LN1. . . . . . .**66** D8
Upton DN21 . . . .**53** D5
Glebe View 1 PE6 . . . .**217** B6
Glebe Way
Barton-upon-Humber DN18 . .**11** A8
5 Sutterton PE20 . . . .**136** A2
Glebe Wlk 3 PE12 . . . .**167** B8
Glede Farm Wy LN7 . . . . . .**33** B3
Gleedale LN6 . . . .**204** F1
Gleed Ave PE11 . . . .**134** E2

Glemsford Rise **2** PE2 . . .230 C7
Glenarm Cres **7** LN5 . . .205 D3
Glen Ave **4** PE11. . . . . . .145 B1
Glenbank Cl LN6 . . . . . . .204 F3
Glen Cl NG33 . . . . .153 A1
Glencoe Cl **2** DN7 . . . . . . .14 D4
Glencoe St HU3 . . . . . . .179 F6
Glencoe Way PE2 . . . . . .229 D3
Glen Cres
  7 Essendine PE9 . . . . . .163 D3
  Stamford PE9. . . . . . . .219 C7
Glendale PE2 . . . . .229 D6
Glendon Cl **5** LN5. . . . . .205 D3
Glendon Gdns PE13 . . . .170 C2
Glen Dr PE21 . . . . .208 B4
Gleneagles
  Grantham NG31 . . . . . .211 D8
  Peterborough PE2 . . . . .229 F6
  10 Waltham DN37 . . . . .194 C4
Gleneagles Cl **5** PE9 . .218 E6
Gleneagles Cres **6** DN19 . . 4 E2
Gleneagles Dr
  Skegness PE25. . . . . . . .206 D6
  1 Sleaford NG34. . . . . .120 F3
  12 Woodhall Spa LN10 . . .97 C5
GLENEAGLES ESTATE
  PE25. . . . . .206 D6
Gleneagles Gr **4** LN4. . .203 D1
Glenfield Rd DN37. . . . . .190 D8
Glengary Wy NG34 . . . . .121 A3
Glen Gdns **2** PE11 . . . . .145 E3
Glengorm Gdns
  Green Hill NG31 . . . . . .210 D6
  Green Hill NG31 . . . . . .210 E6
Glen Hall Rise **10** DN19 . .11 C8
Glenham Dr **4** HU10 . . .178 F7
Glen Ind Est PE9 . . . . . . .163 D3
Glenn Ave **3** PE11 . . . . .214 C4
Glen Rd
  Castle Bytham NG33 . . .152 D1
  Counthorpe & Creeton
   NG33. . . . . .153 A2
  3 Wittering PE8 . . . . . .172 B1
Glenrock Pk HU15. . . . . 2 B6
Glenside NG33 . . . . .152 E1
Glenside N PE11 . . . . . . .156 C5
Glenside S PE11. . . . . . . .156 C8
GLENTHAM LN8 . . . . .43 E1
Glentham Cl LN6 . . . . . . .205 B3
Glentham Ct **6** LN8 . . . . .43 F1
Glentham Rd
  Bishop Norton LN8. . . . . .43 D3
  5 Gainsborough DN21 . . .53 A8
Glen The PE2 . . . . .231 B7
Glenton St PE1. . . . . .226 C7
GLENTWORTH DN21. . . . .54 E7
Glentworth Cres **4** PE25 .206 D4
Glentworth Rd 53 F7
Glenwood Dr **2** HU4 . . .179 B6
Glenwood Gr LN6 . . . . . .201 D1
GLINTON PE6. . . . . .220 D8
Glinton Rd Helpston PE6 .173 C1
  Newborough PE6 . . . . . .221 C8
Global Ctr Ind Est PE1 . .226 E4
Gloria Way DN37 . . . . . . .190 C7
Glossop Rd DN15. . . . . . .182 B2
Gloucester Ave
  Grimsby DN34 . . . . .191 B4
  Scunthorpe DN16. . . . . .185 B7
Gloucester Cl
  Skegness PE25. . . . . . . .206 B2
  1 Sleaford NG34. . . . . .212 C4
Gloucester Ct **1** DN15. .183 A6
Gloucester Rd
  Grantham NG31 . . . . . .210 C5
  Peterborough PE2 . . . . .231 B7
  7 Stamford PE9. . . . . .219 B6
Gloucester St HU4 . . . . .179 E3
Glover Dr PE4. . . . . .221 F3
Glover Rd DN17 . . . . .184 E8
Glovers Ave **8** DN17 . . . .17 C4
Glovers La **17** NG24. . . .104 B2
Glynn Rd LN1 . . . . .201 E8
Glynn View **14** LN1 . . . .201 E8
Gn Acres DN37. . . . . .194 E4
Gndale **45** DN17 . . . . . . .29 D7
Gnfinch Cl **11** NG34. . . .108 E1
Gn La Ludborough DN36 . . .48 E6
  North End LN11 . . . . .62 E6
Gnwich Cl **4** DN15 . . . . .183 A5
Gnwood Rd PE7. . . . . . . .230 B1
Gn Wy Cl **6** HU10 . . . . .178 F7
Goathland Cl HU3 . . . . . .180 A6
Goathland Cl **3** DN37 . .190 E8
Goble Cl **38** DN18. . . . . . .10 F8
Godber Dr PE4. . . . . .205 F3
Goddam's La PE12 . . . . . .146 F1
Goddard Cl **37** DN18. . . . .10 E8
Goddard Cres **12** PE13 . .170 C1
Godfrey Ave **6** PE11 . . .145 C6
Godfrey Cl **7** PE6 . . . . .174 E5
Godfrey Rd **11** DN8 . . . . .15 A8
Godiva Cl **16** PE6 . . . . . .166 F1
Godiva Cres PE10 . . . . . .213 B6
Godman's La HU10 . . . . .178 B8
Godnow Rd DN17 . . . . . . .16 C6
Godric Sq PE2 . . . . .230 D6
Godsey Cres **9** PE6 . . . .217 C5
Godsey's La PE6 . . . . . . .217 B6
Godson Ave **1** NG34 . . .122 D3
Godwin Cl **8** NG34 . . . . .213 B6
Godwin Rd **8** PE13. . . . .170 D1
Goffsmill PE3. . . . . .225 A4
Goldcrest Cl
  2 Birchwood LN6 . . . . .200 E1
  Scunthorpe DN15. . . . . .182 D6
Goldcrest Way PE7 . . . . .233 A8
Golden Cup Way DN17. . .184 C2

Golden Drop **2** PE6 . . . .173 C4
Golden Gr PE20 . . . . .135 C5
Golden Harvest Way **6**
  PE12. . . . . .158 B6
Goldenholme La **4** DN22 . .65 A5
Gold Fen Dike Bank PE22 .114 D2
Goldfinch Cl LN6 . . . . . . .200 A3
Goldgarth DN32. . . . . . . .192 A5
Goldhay Way PE2 . . . . . .229 F2
Goldie La PE2 . . . . .229 F6
Goldings The **10** DN9 . . . .27 D2
Gold La LN13 . . . . .63 A1
Goldsmith Ct **1** LN4. . . .207 A6
Goldsmith Rd
  Grantham NG31 . . . . . .211 D6
  8 Newark-on-Trent NG24 . .104 B3
Goldsmith Wlk LN2. . . . .202 C7
Goldson's La PE22 . . . . . .126 F6
Golf Course La DN37 . . . .194 F2
Golf Ct PE17 . . . . .160 F5
Golf Rd **4** LN12 . . . . .64 A4
Gollands La DN9 . . . . .27 B2
Goltho Hall La LN8 . . . . . .70 B4
Goltho La LN8. . . . . .70 C4
Goltho La LN8. . . . . .70 B3
Gonerby Hill NG31 . . . . .210 E8
GONERBY HILL FOOT
  NG31. . . . . .210 F8
Gonerby Hill Foot CE Prim
  Sch NG31. . . . . .210 E8
Gonerby La NG32. . . . . . .129 A7
Gonerby Rd NG31 . . . . . .210 E8
Goochgate PE12 . . . . . . .169 A7
Goodacre PE2 . . . . .230 A4
Goodens La PE13. . . . . . .170 A5
Goodfellows Rd **7** PE11 .156 E3
Goodhand Cl DN18 . . . . . .11 A8
Good La LN1 . . . . .234 B4
Goodliff Rd NG31. . . . . . .210 E2
Goodman Cl **6** NG31. . . .129 E5
Goodson Cl **3** PE21 . . . .209 B4
Goodwin Cl **1** NG24 . . .104 B4
Goodwin Dr **8** PE24. . . . .90 B7
Goodwin Cl NG34 . . . . . .104 C1
Goodwin Parade **1** HU3 .180 D5
Goodwin Wlk PE4 . . . . . .221 A4
Goodwood DN17 . . . . . . .184 D4
Goodwood Cl LN11 . . . . .198 A7
Goodwood Dr **10** PE10 . .213 D3
Goodwood La **2** DN35. . .192 F1
Goodwood Rd **8** PE25 . . .90 F3
Goodwood Way **19** LN6 .204 C7
Goole Rd DN14 . . . . .6 C8
Goosander Cl **24** DN18 . . .3 E1
Gooseacre **33** DN17. . . . .29 D7
Goosegate La NG32 . . . . .118 A2
Goose Gn **10** PE12 . . . . .160 E4
Goose La PE23 . . . . .87 D2
Goose's La PE14 . . . . .161 A1
Gordon Ave PE2 . . . . . . .230 C7
Gordon Boswell Romany
  Mus★ PE12. . . . . .214 E1
Gordon Fendick Sch The
  PE13. . . . . .170 D2
Gordon Field **8** LN8. . . . .77 D7
Gordon Gdns **1** DN33. . .194 F8
Gordon Rd LN1 . . . . .234 B3
Gordon St
  Gainsborough DN21. . . .197 D2
  4 Kingston upon Hull HU3. .180 B5
Gordon Way PE2 . . . . . . .230 C7
Goredike Bank PE13. . . . .169 C2
GOREFIELD PE13. . . . . . .169 E2
Gorefield Prim Sch PE13. .169 F2
Gorefield Rd PE13. . . . . . .169 F2
Gorehall Dr **10** LN2 . . . . .68 D7
Gorse La **6** PE11 . . . . . . .214 D4
Gorse Bottesford DN16 . .185 C4
  5 Hatfield DN7 . . . . . . .14 C3
  4 Woodhall Spa LN10 . . .97 E6
Gorse Rd NG31. . . . . .211 D5
Gorse Rise NG31 . . . . . . .211 C5
Gorton Rd HU10. . . . . . . .178 E7
Gorton St DN31 . . . . .189 B2
Gorwick La LN1 . . . . .66 B6
GOSBERTON PE11. . . . . .145 E6
Gosberton Bank PE11 . . .145 E6
GOSBERTON CHEAL PE11 .145 A4
GOSBERTON CLOUGH
  PE11. . . . . .144 D4
Gosberton House Acad
  PE11. . . . . .145 B6
Gosberton Prim Sch PE11 .145 B6
Gosberton Rd PE11. . . . . .145 C4
Goshawk Way LN4 . . . . .207 C6
Goslings Cnr Wood Nature
  Reserve★ LN8 . . . . .70 E2
Gospelgate LN11. . . . . . .198 B5
Gospel La LN5 . . . . .106 C3
Gosport Rd DN34 . . . . . . .191 A6
Gosport Wlk HU4 . . . . . .179 A4
Gostwick PE2 . . . . .229 D5
Gote La PE13 . . . . .169 E3
Gothic Cl **12** LN6 . . . . . .204 D7
GOULCEBY LN11 . . . . .72 D6

Goulceby Road LN11 . . . . . .60 D1
Gouldeby La LN11. . . . . . .72 D6
Goulton St HU3 . . . . .180 B3
Gover's Dro PE12 . . . . . . .159 A2
Gower Rd HU4 . . . . .179 B3
Gowt Bank PE22 . . . . . . .114 C2
Gowts La PE12 . . . . .159 E3
GOXHILL DN19. . . . . .12 A8
Goxhill Ave **4** PE11 . . . .134 E2
Goxhill Cl **14** LN6 . . . . . .204 D7
Goxhill Gdns **4** DN34. . .190 F4
Goxhill Gr **18** LN6. . . . . .204 D7
Goxhill Prim Sch DN19. . . .12 A8
Goxhill Rd DN19. . . . . .11 E8
Goxhill Sta DN19 . . . . . . .11 F8
Graburn Wy DN18. . . . . . .10 E7
GRABY NG34 . . . . .142 F4
Grace Ave LN6 . . . . .204 D3
Grace Cl **4** NG34. . . . . . .212 E3
Grace Cres PE24 . . . . .77 C3
Grace St LN5. . . . . .201 F1
Grace Swan Cl
  4 Hundleby PE23 . . . . . .87 F1
  12 Spilsby PE23 . . . . . . .87 F1
Graeme Rd PE5 . . . . .222 F2
Grafham Cl PE2 . . . . .231 E4
Grafton Ave PE3 . . . . . . .225 C3
Grafton St Grimsby DN32. .189 C1
  Lincoln LN2 . . . . .202 B3
Graham Ave HU4 . . . . . . .179 B3
Graham Hill Way **4** PE10 .213 E4
Graham Rd PE25 . . . . . . .206 B4
GRAINSBY DN36 . . . . .35 F2
Grainsby Ave
  Cleethorpes DN35 . . . . .192 D3
  Holton le Clay DN36 . . . .195 E1
Grainsby Cl LN6 . . . . .205 C5
Grainsby La DN36. . . . . . . .35 E1
Grains Gate LN11. . . . . . . .37 E1
GRAINTHORPE LN11. . . . . .50 B8
Grainthorpe Sch LN11. . . . .50 B7
GRAISELOUND DN9 . . . . . .27 C1
Graizelound Fields Rd DN9 27 D1
Grammar Sch Gd DN16 . .196 C6
Grammar Sch Rd DN20 . .196 C4
Grammar Sch Rd S **3**
  DN20. . . . . .196 C3
Grammar Sch Wlk DN16 . .185 C4
Grampian Cl **14** NG34. . .212 B3
Grampian Way
  Gonerby Hill Foot NG31 . .210 D8
  2 Grimsby DN33. . . . . .194 E8
  Thorne/Moorends DN8 . . .15 A7
Granaries The LN4 . . . . . .108 C8
Granary Cl
  22 Metheringham LN4 . . .95 C4
  14 Spilsby PE23 . . . . . . .87 F1
  5 Waddington LN5 . . . . .93 F6
Granary Croft **7** DN9. . . .27 D2
Granary Ct **12** HU15. . . . . .2 C7
Granary La LN4 . . . . .207 A4
Granary Row LN4 . . . . . . .207 A4
Granary The DN21. . . . . . .29 C4
Granary Way LN9 . . . . . . .199 A3
Granby Ave **5** NG24 . . . .104 A3
Granby Dr
  5 Bottesford NG13 . . . .128 A5
  24 Newark-on-Trent NG24 . .104 B2
Granby Rd LN8 . . . . .47 B5
Granby St PE1 . . . . .226 B2
Grand Parade PE25. . . . . .206 D3
Grand Sluice La **1** PE21 .208 F6
Granely Cl LN1. . . . . .201 C6
GRANGE DN34. . . . . .191 F5
Grange Ave
  13 Barton-upon-Humber
   DN18. . . . . .10 E8
  Hatfield DN7 . . . . .14 D4
  24 Laceby DN37 . . . . . .23 F1
  Misterton DN10 . . . . . . .40 A4
  Peterborough PE1 . . . . .226 A6
  1 Scunthorpe DN15 . . . .183 A5
Grange Cl **17** Hatfield DN7. . .14 D4
  1 Ingham LN1. . . . . . . .54 F2
  5 Misterton DN10 . . . . .40 A4
Grange Cres
  Kingston upon Hull HU10 . .178 E6
  Lincoln LN6 . . . . .205 B3
  Peterborough PE2 . . . . .230 A5
Grange Ct **3** LN5 . . . . . . .92 E1
Grange Dr Clinton Park LN4 207 C5
  Lincoln LN6 . . . . .205 B3
  Misterton DN10 . . . . . . .40 A4
  Spalding PE11 . . . . .214 E4
  Stapleford LN6. . . . . . . .105 A7
Grange Farm La DN36 . . .195 D6
Grange Field DN20 . . . . . .20 D8
Grangehill Rd PE11 . . . . .169 B6
Grange Ind Est DN16 . . . .185 E7
Grange La Balderton NG24 .104 A1
  Canwick LN4 . . . . .81 A4
  Covenham St Bartholomew
   LN11. . . . . .49 D6
  Garthorpe LE14 . . . . . . .150 C4
  Heighington LN4 . . . . . . .81 E4
  Hough-on-the-Hill NG32 . .118 E6
  2 Ingham LN1. . . . . . . .54 F2
  Keddington LN11 . . . . . .198 E8
  8 Manby LN11 . . . . . . .62 C6
  Nocton LN4 . . . . .94 F4
  North Cockerington LN11. . .50 A1
  North Kelsey LN7 . . . . . . .32 A3
  Snitterby DN21. . . . . . . .43 A5
  Stixwould & Woodhall LN10 . .97 B6
  Utterby LN11 . . . . .49 A4
  3 Willingham by Stow DN21 .53 E3
Grange La N DN16. . . . . . .185 D7

Grange La S DN16. . . . . . .185 C5
Grange Mdws PE22. . . . . .113 A1
Grange Paddock DN9 . . . .27 A3
Grange Pk **2** Brough HU15. . 2 C5
  17 Kirk Sandall DN3 . . . .14 A3
  Morton DN21 . . . . .40 D3
  Roughton Moor LN10 . . . .98 A7
  8 Swanland HU14. . . . . . .3 B6
Grange Prim Sch DN34 . .190 F5
Grange Prim Sch The
  DN16. . . . . .185 D5
Grange Rd
  Bracebridge Heath LN4 . .205 F2
  Gainsborough DN21. . . . .41 A1
  Garthorpe & Fockerby DN14 . . 7 E8
  14 Mablethorpe/Sutton on Sea
   LN12. . . . . .77 A7
  4 Metheringham LN4 . . .95 D4
  Peterborough PE3 . . . . .225 D4
  8 Ruskington NG34 . . . .108 D1
  Sutton Bridge PE34 . . . .161 B4
  10 Wisbech PE13 . . . . .170 C1
Grange St LN4 . . . . .109 C7
Grange The **1** DN21. . . . .211 A4
Grange Wlk Grimsby DN34 .191 A6
  6 Misterton DN10. . . . . .40 A5
Gransley Rise PE3. . . . . . .225 C5
Granson Way LN4 . . . . . .203 A2
Granta Cres NG31 . . . . . .211 C7
GRANTHAM NG31 . . . . . .211 C3
Grantham Ave DN36 . . . .191 D1
Grantham Canal Nature
  Reserve★ NG31 . . . . . .210 D1
Grantham Coll NG31. . . . .211 B4
Grantham Cricket Gd
  NG31. . . . . .211 B1
Grantham & District Hospl
  NG31. . . . . .211 A6
Grantham Dr **2** PE25. . . .206 B3
Grantham Fun FarmThe★
  NG31. . . . . .210 F4
Grantham House★ NG31. .211 B5
Grantham Mus★ NG31 . . .211 B4
Grantham Prep SchThe
  NG31. . . . . .139 F8
Grantham Rd
  Boothby Graffoe LN5 . . . .94 A2
  Boston PE21. . . . . .208 A3
  Bottesford NG13 . . . . . .128 B5
  Bracebridge Heath LN4 . .205 F2
  Carlton Scroop NG32 . . . .119 C3
  7 Great Gonerby NG31. . .129 D5
  Great Gonerby NG31 . . . .210 D8
  Harmston LN5 . . . . .93 F6
  Hough-on-the-Hill NG32. . .119 A4
  Ingoldsby NG33 . . . . . . .141 C5
  Navenby/Wellingore LN5. . .107 A8
  Old Somerby NG33. . . . . .140 D8
  Ropsley & Humby NG33 . .131 A1
  2 Skillington NG33 . . . . .151 A8
  Sleaford NG34 . . . . .212 B2
Grantham Sandown SchThe
  NG31. . . . . .211 C5
Grantham St LN2. . . . . . . .234 B2
Grantham Sta NG31. . . . . .211 A3
Granthams The **12** LN2 . . .68 E6
Grantham Town FC NG31. .210 D3
Grantley St NG31. . . . . . . .211 A3
Grants La **29** PE21 . . . . .208 F5
Grant St Cleethorpes DN35 .192 E4
  Lincoln LN1 . . . . .189 D1
GRANT THOROLD DN32. . .192 A7
Granville Ave
  12 Boston PE21 . . . . . . .136 D8
  Northborough PE6 . . . . .217 E1
Granville Rd
  3 Scunthorpe DN15 . . . .183 A6
  Scunthorpe DN15. . . . . .183 A6
Granville St Boston PE21. .208 D5
  Grantham NG31 . . . . . .211 C3
  Grimsby DN32 . . . . .191 F6
  1 Kingston upon Hull HU3. .180 A6
  Peterborough PE1 . . . . .226 A4
Granville Terr PE12 . . . . .160 D4
GRASBY DN38. . . . . .32 F7
Grasby All Saints CE Prim Sch
  The DN38. . . . . .32 F7
Grasby Cl **4** DN21. . . . . . .53 A8
Grasby Cres DN37 . . . . . .190 D7
Grasby Rd
  Great Limber DN37 . . . . . .22 C3
  North Kelsey LN7 . . . . . . .32 D5
  Scunthorpe DN17. . . . . .184 E5
Grasby Wold La DN38. . . . .21 F1
Grasmere Ave PE24 . . . . . .90 E6
Grasmere Cl **3** DN21. . . .197 E6
Grasmere Gdns PE4 . . . . .221 B3
Grasmere Gr **5** DN36. . . .192 E1
Grasmere Way LN6. . . . . .200 D5
Grassdale Pk **2** HU15 . . . .2 B5
Grassgate La PE14 . . . . . .170 E3
Grassmoor Cl **2** LN6 . . . .93 B8
Grassmoor Ct **2** DN15. . .182 B2
Gravecoat La PE11. . . . . .144 E6
Gravel Chy **2** PE6 . . . . . .166 D1
Graveley Cl **4** LN6. . . . . .204 B6
Gravelhill Dro LN4 . . . . . .109 E7
Gravelholes La DN10 . . . . .39 F5
Gravel Pit Hill DN20 . . . . . .31 D6
Gravelpit La LN9 . . . . .199 F2
Gravel Pit La
  1 Humberside Airport
   DN39. . . . . .22 A4
  Scunthorpe DN17. . . . . .184 F2
Gravel Pit Rd
  Barton-upon-Humber DN18. . .3 D1
  Scotter DN21 . . . . .29 C4
Gravel Pits La PE24. . . . . .77 C8

Gravel Rd
  Market Deeping PE6. . . . .165 D3
  Revesby PE22. . . . . .99 B4
Gravel Wlk PE1 . . . . .226 A2
Graves Hill LN5 . . . . .106 F5
Gray Ct PE1. . . . . .225 E8
Graye Dr LN11 . . . . .198 C4
GRAYINGHAM DN21. . . . . .42 D7
Grayingham Rd **2** DN21. . .42 E7
Grayling Cl **2** DN37 . . . .190 D7
Graylings The PE21. . . . . .208 B6
Grayling Way PE21 . . . . . .208 E3
Gray Rd DN17. . . . . .184 D6
Gray St LN9 . . . . .190 E8
Gray's Ct **4** LN11. . . . . . .198 B6
Gray's Rd **2** LN11 . . . . . .198 B6
Gray St LN1. . . . . .234 A4
Gr Ct **12** LN10 . . . . .97 D5
GREAT CARLTON LN11. . . . .62 E4
Great Casterton PE9 . . . .171 B8
Great Casterton CE Prim Sch
  PE9 . . . . .171 C8
Great Casterton Road
  PE9 . . . . .163 B2
Great Cl **1** NG33. . . . . . . .151 D2
GREAT COATES DN37. . . . .24 B5
Great Coates Prim Sch
  DN37. . . . . .190 E8
Great Coates Rd
  Grimsby DN37 . . . . .190 C8
  Healing DN41. . . . . .23 F5
Great Coates Sta DN37 . . .24 B5
Great Field La **1** HU9 . . . .5 E8
GREATFORD PE9. . . . . . . .164 B3
Greatford Gdns PE9 . . . . .164 B3
Greatford Lane PE9 . . . . .163 E1
Greatford Rd Baston PE6 . .164 C4
  5 Uffington PE9 . . . . . .172 C6
  Uffington PE9 . . . . .172 C7
GREAT GONERBY NG31 . . .129 E5
GREAT HALE NG34 . . . . . .122 F2
Great Hale Dro NG34 . . . .123 A2
Great Leighs Bourne PE10 .213 B3
  4 Bourne PE10. . . . . . . .213 C3
GREAT LIMBER DN37. . . . . .22 D3
Great Northern Ct **12**
  NG31. . . . . .211 A4
Great Northern Gdns
  PE10. . . . . .213 D4
Great Northern Terr LN5. .234 C1
Great Northern Terr Ind Est
  LN5. . . . . .234 C1
Great N Rd Balderton NG24 .117 C8
  Empingham PE9 . . . . . . .162 B2
  Great Gonerby NG32 . . . .129 C6
  Long Bennington NG23. . .117 D2
  Tinwell PE9 . . . . .218 D5
  Wansford PE8 . . . . .218 D5
Great Passage St **3** HU1. .180 E5
GREAT PONTON NG33. . . .140 A5
Great Ponton CE Sch
  NG33. . . . . .140 A5
Great Stather Cl DN15 . . . .3 A5
GREAT STEEPING PE23 . . .101 E7
Great Steeping Prim Sch
  PE23. . . . . .101 E7
Great Steeping Rd PE23 . .101 D8
GREAT STURTON LN9. . . . .71 F3
Great Thornton St HU3 . .180 D6
GREAT TOWS LN8 . . . . . . .47 D1
Great Union St HU9 . . . . .181 A7
GREBBY PE23 . . . . .88 D3
Grebe Cl **2** LN6. . . . . . . .204 C1
Grebe Mews DN16 . . . . . .185 F5
Greek St HU3 . . . . .179 F5
Greenacre Cl **7** DN7 . . . . .14 C2
Greenacres
  6 Donington on Bain LN11. . .59 E1
  Peterborough PE4 . . . . .220 E4
  5 Swanland HU14. . . . . . .3 C7
Green Acres HU10 . . . . . .178 C6
Greenacres Dr
  Boston PE21. . . . . .208 D3
  5 Bourne PE10 . . . . . . .213 D3
Greenaway Ct LN3 . . . . . .203 E6
Green Bank DN8 . . . . .15 D6
Greenbank Cl PE21. . . . . .208 D3
Greenbank Dr LN6 . . . . . .205 A5
Green Drift The PE9 . . . . .172 B3
Green Dro Billinghay LN4. .109 F6
  Crowland PE6. . . . . .175 D8
  Helpringham NG34. . . . . .133 F7
  Little Hale NG34. . . . . . . .134 A7
  Thorney PE6 . . . . .175 F6
Green Dyke PE2. . . . . .148 D1
Greendyke La PE13. . . . . .160 A2
Green Farm Cl PE5 . . . . . .223 E2
Greenfield Ave HU13 . . . .178 A3
Greenfield Cl **18** DN19 . . .14 A3
Greenfield Dr **9** DN20. . . .31 A5
Greenfield Rd
  Aby with Greenfield LN13. . .75 D4
  Calceby LN13 . . . . .74 F7
Greenfield Rd
  Coningsby LN4 . . . . .207 D5
  3 Sleaford NG34. . . . . .212 D7
Greenfields
  3 Glentham LN8 . . . . . . .43 F1
  Holbeach PE12. . . . . . . .215 F2
  22 Nettleham LN2 . . . . .68 D2
Greenfields Academy
  NG31. . . . . .211 B1
Greenfields La **5** NG34 . .142 D8
Greenfield Way PE7 . . . . .233 E8
Greenfinch Dr DN35. . . . .192 E1

Greengarth DN17 . . . . .184 F2
Greengate **11** DN9 . . . . .27 E6
Green Gate PE22 . . . . .114 D1
Greengate Ct PE1 . . . . .226 C4
Greengate La **14** DN19 . . . .12 A8
Greengate Rd PE23 . . . . . . .88 D3
Greenham PE3 . . . . .225 A4
Greenhill **8** DN20 . . . . .19 D3
GREEN HILL NG31 . . . . . . .210 E5
Green Hill DN35 . . . . .192 D3
Greenhill Dr **1** LN8 . . . . . .43 D3
Greenhill Rd DN9 . . . . .27 C2
Green Hill Rd NG31 . . . . . .210 F5
Greenhoe Rd DN17 . . . . . .184 D3
Green La Algarkirk PE20 . . .136 B3
Aunsby & Dembleby NG34 . . .132 A4
10 Barton-upon-Humber
 DN18 . . . . .10 F8
Beckingham LN5 . . . . .105 C4
Belton DN9 . . . . .16 D2
Belton & Manthorpe NG32 . .130 B7
Boston PE21 . . . . .208 E7
Bottesford DN13 . . . . .128 B5
Bratoft PE24 . . . . .102 C7
Brigsley DN37 . . . . .35 D4
5 Broughton DN20 . . . . . .19 E3
Cherry Willingham LN3 . . . .203 D5
Collingham NG23 . . . . .91 D3
Deeping St Nicholas PE11 . .166 C8
Dunham-on-Trent NG22 . . . .65 B1
Dunston LN4 . . . . .95 D6
Eagle & Swinethorpe LN6 . . .79 C2
Eaton NG32 . . . . .138 A2
Gedney PE12 . . . . .159 A1
Girton NG23 . . . . .78 C1
Gosberton PE11 . . . . .145 C7
Grantham NG31 . . . . .211 D7
Hatfield DN7 . . . . .14 E1
Hemingby LN9 . . . . .72 C3
Heydour NG32 . . . . .131 D5
Hogsthorpe LN13 . . . . .90 A8
Kingston upon Hull HU13 . . .179 A1
Kirton PE20 . . . . .135 E6
Lea DN21 . . . . .52 F5
Leake Commonside PE22 . . .113 F3
Leverington PE13 . . . . . . .169 F2
Lincoln LN6 . . . . .201 D2
Mablethorpe & Sutton LN12 . .63 F4
Marston NG32 . . . . .118 D1
Middle Rasen LN8 . . . . .57 C7
Moulton PE12 . . . . .146 E1
13 North Kelsey LN7 . . . . .32 A4
North Somercotes LN11 . . . .50 F7
Peterborough PE1 . . . . . . .226 A4
Pilham DN21 . . . . .41 D4
Pinchbeck PE11 . . . . .145 C2
3 Skegness PE25 . . . . . .103 E4
Spalding PE11 . . . . .214 C3
Stamford PE9 . . . . .219 B7
Stickney PE22 . . . . .113 A7
Stixwould & Woodhall LN10 . .97 B8
Strubby with Woodthorpe
 LN13 . . . . .63 B1
Sutterton PE20 . . . . .136 A2
Swinderby LN6 . . . . .92 B5
Thimbleby LN9 . . . . .85 C5
Threekingham NG34 . . . . . .132 E3
Wainfleet St Mary PE24 . . .102 A1
18 Welton LN2 . . . . .68 D6
Westborough & Dry Doddington
 NG23 . . . . .117 F5
Wigtoft PE20 . . . . .135 E1
Willoughby with Sloothby
 LN13 . . . . .89 C5
Woodhall Spa LN10 . . . . . . .97 C5
Wyberton PE21 . . . . .136 F8
Yaxley PE7 . . . . .233 D6
Greenlands Ave **10** DN36 . .195 C6
Green Man La LN4 . . . . . . .94 F1
Green Man Rd LN5 . . . . . . .94 C1
Greenock Way LN6 . . . . . .204 B7
Green Pastures **4** PE12 . .158 B7
Green Rd
Aswarby & Swarby NG34 . . .131 F7
Newborough PE6 . . . . .174 F2
Greenrigg Gdns **1** PE11 . .214 B5
Greens Cl DN15 . . . . .183 B3
Green's Rd **4** DN7 . . . . . .14 C3
Green St **1** NG31 . . . . . .129 D5
Greenstiles La HU14 . . . . . .3 C7
Greenstock La PE13 . . . . .170 A6
Green The
3 Allington NG32 . . . . . .128 F7
Bottesford NG13 . . . . .128 C4
8 Brough HU15 . . . . .2 D6
Castor PE5 . . . . .223 E2
Chapel St Leonard PE24 . . . .90 E7
Cherry Willingham/Reepham
 LN3 . . . . .203 F8
1 Coddington NG24 . . . . .104 D5
Collingham NG23 . . . . .91 C4
Corby Glen NG33 . . . . .152 E7
Dunston LN4 . . . . .95 C5
Gainsborough DN21 . . . . . .197 F4
2 Glinton PE6 . . . . .220 C8
6 Leasingham NG34 . . . . .121 B8
6 Mablethorpe/Sutton on Sea
 LN12 . . . . .64 A4
3 Minting LN9 . . . . .84 C8
Morborne PE7 . . . . .232 A3
15 Navenby/Wellingore
 LN5 . . . . .107 A7
Peterborough PE4 . . . . . . .221 A1
3 Reepham LN3 . . . . .82 A8
Revesby PE22 . . . . .99 B4
6 Scothern LN2 . . . . .68 F4
Scotter DN21 . . . . .29 C3
Spalding PE11 . . . . .214 E5
4 Swanland HU14 . . . . . . .3 B7
Thorne/Moorends DN8 . . . . .15 A8
11 Thorney PE6 . . . . . . .176 A3
Thurlby PE10 . . . . .164 C7
Waltham DN37 . . . . .194 F2
Welbourn LN5 . . . . .106 E4
Yaxley PE7 . . . . .233 E5
Greenway
7 Barton-upon-Humber
 DN18 . . . . .3 F1
Waltham DN37 . . . . .194 E3
2 Welton/Dunholme LN2 . . .68 C7
Greenways **1** HU14 . . . . . .3 A5
Greenway The **1** HU4 . . . .179 C6
Greenwich House Sch **8**
 LN11 . . . . .198 C6
Green Wlk PE6 . . . . .217 A5
Greenwood Cl **1** PE12 . . .215 E2
Greenwood Dr PE21 . . . . .208 F6
Greenwood's Row **5**
 NG31 . . . . .211 A4
Greestone Mount LN2 . . . .234 B3
Greestone Pl LN2 . . . . . . .234 B3
Greestone Strs ✱ LN2 . . . .234 B3
GREETHAM LN11 . . . . .86 D5
Greetham Rd LN9 . . . . .86 C7
Greetham's La DN32 . . . . .192 C5
GREETWELL DN20 . . . . . . .30 C7
Greetwell Cl LN2 . . . . . . .202 B5
Greetwell Ct LN2 . . . . . . .203 B8
Greetwellgate LN2 . . . . . .234 C3
Greetwell Hollow Nature
 Reserve ✱ LN2 . . . . . . .202 D5
Greetwell La
1 Lincoln LN2 . . . . .202 F6
Nettleham LN2 . . . . .202 F8
Greetwell Pl LN2 . . . . . . .202 B5
Greetwell Rd LN2 . . . . . . .234 C3
Gregg Hall Cl **2** LN6 . . . .205 E4
Gregg Hall Cres LN6 . . . . .205 E4
Gregg Hall Dr **4** LN6 . . . .205 E4
Gregory Cl **1** NG32 . . . . .139 C7
Gresham Cl **10** NG24 . . . .104 C4
Gresham St LN1 . . . . .201 D4
Gresley Ct **11** NG31 . . . . .210 E2
Gresley Dr Lincoln LN6 . . . .201 D1
4 Stamford PE9 . . . . . . .219 B4
Gresley Rd LN11 . . . . .198 C4
Gresley Way
Immingham DN40 . . . . . . .186 F5
Peterborough PE3 . . . . . . .225 C4
Gresley Wy DN40 . . . . . . .186 E6
Gretton Cl
1 Claypole NG23 . . . . . .117 E8
Peterborough PE2 . . . . . . .230 C7
Grevel Cl **6** PE11 . . . . . .214 B5
Greyfleet Bank **7** LN11 . . .51 C4
Grey Friars
9 Grantham NG31 . . . . .211 A4
Grantham DN37 . . . . .190 D7
Greyfriars Cl DN17 . . . . . .184 E6
Greyfriars La **9** PE21 . . .208 F4
Greyfriars Rd **11** DN20 . . .19 E3
GREY GREEN DN9 . . . . . . .16 E2
Greyling Cl **5** LN1 . . . . . .201 E8
Greyling View **12** LN1 . . .201 E8
Grey St Gainsborough DN21 .197 B6
Kingston upon Hull HU2 . . .180 D7
Greystone Ave HU5 . . . . . .179 E7
Greystones Rd DN21 . . . . .197 B7
Gride Bank PE22 . . . . .126 E8
Gride The PE22 . . . . .113 E1
Griffins Cl **4** PE6 . . . . . .174 E5
Griffiths Ct PE2 . . . . .229 E5
Grime St DN31 . . . . .191 B8
Grimmer's Rd **12** PE13 . . .170 E1
GRIMOLDBY LN11 . . . . .62 B7
Grimoldby Prim Sch LN11 . .62 C6
GRIMSBY DN31 . . . . .191 B8
Grimsby Auditorium
 DN34 . . . . .190 F8
Grimsby Docks Sta DN31 . .189 A1
Grimsby Institute DN31 . . .191 C4
Grimsby Leisure Ctr DN34 .190 F8
Grimsby Maternity Hospl
 DN33 . . . . .191 C3
Grimsby Pool DN33 . . . . . .191 D4
Grimsby Rd **2** Binbrook LN8 .47 C5
Brackenborough with Little
 Grimsby LN11 . . . . .61 A8
Cleethorpes DN35 . . . . . . .192 B8
Fotherby LN11 . . . . .49 A1
Grimsby DN32 . . . . .189 D1
Humberston DN36 . . . . . . .192 E1
Laceby DN37 . . . . .190 A2
Louth LN11 . . . . .198 A6
Swallow LN7 . . . . .34 B6
Waltham DN37 . . . . .194 F5
Grimsby Town Sta DN32 . . .191 D7
Grimshaw Rd PE1 . . . . . . .226 B6
GRIMSTHORPE PE10 . . . . .153 E5
Grimsthorpe Castle ✱
 PE10 . . . . .153 D5
Grimsthorpe Cl
Grantham NG31 . . . . .210 E6
12 Market Deeping PE6 . .217 A5
Grimston Rd **5** HU10 . . . .178 F6
Grindell St HU1 . . . . .181 D8
GRINGLEY ON THE HILL
 DN10 . . . . .39 C1
Gringley Rd DN10 . . . . .39 E4
Grinter Cl **3** LN6 . . . . . . .93 C8
Grocock Cl PE12 . . . . .146 E2
Groose La PE24 . . . . .115 D8
Grosvenor Ave
Birchwood LN6 . . . . .200 D2
Bourne PE10 . . . . .213 E4
Grosvenor Cres
Grimsby DN32 . . . . .191 D6
Louth LN11 . . . . .198 D7
Grosvenor Ct **3** DN7 . . . . .14 D8
Grosvenor Mews **2** LN4 . .203 D1
Grosvenor Rd
9 Billingborough NG34 . . .133 B3
Kirton PE20 . . . . .136 C6
Louth LN11 . . . . .198 D7
24 Mablethorpe/Sutton on Sea
 LN12 . . . . .64 B3
Skegness PE25 . . . . .206 C4
Wisbech PE13 . . . . .170 D1
Grosvenor St N DN15 . . . . .183 A5
Grosvenor St (South) **2**
 DN15 . . . . .183 A4
Grosvenor Sq **17** LN5 . . .107 A7
Grosvenor St
Grimsby DN32 . . . . .191 D6
Kingston upon Hull HU3 . . .180 D8
4 Scunthorpe DN15 . . . . .183 A4
Grove Cl **10** PE11 . . . . . .145 C1
Grove Cres DN32 . . . . . . .192 C6
Grove Ct
3 Gainsborough DN21 . . .197 C6
Woodston PE2 . . . . .230 F8
Grove Dr **9** LN10 . . . . . . .97 D5
Grove End Rd **3** NG31 . . .211 B4
Grovefield La PE22 . . . . . .126 D5
Grove Hill HU13 . . . . .178 E1
Grove La Peterborough PE3 .225 A2
Waltham DN37 . . . . .194 E4
Grove Leisure Ctr NG24 . . .104 B3
Grovenor Ct **5** DN35 . . . .193 A1
Grove Pk DN10 . . . . .39 F5
Grove Rd **1** Fishlake DN7 . .14 D8
Mablethorpe/Sutton on Sea
 LN12 . . . . .64 C1
Theddlethorpe All Saints
 LN12 . . . . .63 D6
Grove St E **5** PE21 . . . . .209 A5
Grove St W **4** PE21 . . . . .209 A5
Grove St **14** Boston PE21 . .209 A5
Heckington NG34 . . . . . . .122 E2
5 Kirton in Lindsey DN21 . . .30 B1
Newark-on-Trent NG24 . . . .104 B3
Peterborough PE2 . . . . . . .230 F8
Groves The HU4 . . . . .179 B2
Grove The
13 Barrow upon Humber
 DN19 . . . . .11 C8
4 Beckingham DN10 . . . . .40 A1
Edlington with Wispington
 LN9 . . . . .85 B6
6 Gainsborough DN21 . . . .53 A5
Grantham NG31 . . . . .210 E3
Lincoln LN2 . . . . .234 C4
Market Deeping PE6 . . . . . .217 B5
Morton PE10 . . . . .154 B6
Newton on Trent LN1 . . . . . .65 D1
5 Spalding PE11 . . . . . . .214 C6
4 Welton/Dunholme LN2 . . .68 D6
Grove Wood Rd DN10 . . . . .39 F5
Grove Wood Terr **16** DN10 .39 F5
Gr St **14** NG24 . . . . .104 A3
Grundale HU10 . . . . .178 C6
Grundy La LN3 . . . . .57 D2
Grundy's La LN9 . . . . .84 C8
Grunnill Cl **10** PE25 . . . . .206 A5
Guanockgate Rd PE12 . . . .169 A2
Guash Way PE9 . . . . .219 D7
Gubbole's Dro PE11 . . . . . .145 A3
Guelder Rd BE7 . . . . .230 D3
Guernsey Gr DN40 . . . . . . .186 C2
Guildford Cl **11** NG31 . . .210 E5
Guildford La LN5 . . . . .105 F5
Guildford St DN32 . . . . . . .192 A8
Guildhall Dr **2** PE11 . . . .156 E8
Guildhall Mus ✱ PE21 . . . .208 F4
Guildhall Rd HU1 . . . . .180 F6
Guildhall St
Grantham NG31 . . . . .211 A4
Lincoln LN1 . . . . .234 A2
Guild Rd PE13 . . . . .170 E1
Guile Carr La DN7 . . . . .14 D5
Guilicarr La LN7 . . . . .31 F4
Guillemot Dr LN11 . . . . . . .198 D8
Guilsborough Rd PE6 . . . . .175 B2
Guisefield Rd **9** DN9 . . . . .27 D6
Gulham Rd LN8 . . . . .44 D5
Gull Bank Whaplode PE12 . .167 F5
Wisbech St Mary PE13 . . . .177 E3
Gull Dro PE13 . . . . .177 D3
Gull La PE13 . . . . .170 A2
Gull Rd PE13 . . . . .177 F2
Gullymore PE3 . . . . .224 F8
GUNBY
Candlesby with Gunby PE23 . .89 B1
Gunby and Stainby NG33 . . .151 C4
Gunby Ave LN6 . . . . .204 F6
Gunby Hall ✱ PE23 . . . . . . .89 A1
Gunby La PE23 . . . . .89 A1
Gunby Pl DN35 . . . . .192 E4
Gunby Rd
Gunby & Stainby NG33 . . . .151 A4
Scunthorpe DN17 . . . . . . .184 E5
Gunby Road PE24 . . . . .89 C2
Gunfleet Cl **18** PE20 . . . .135 B7
GUNNERBY DN37 . . . . .34 F2
Gunnerby Road DN37 . . . . . .34 F2
Gunners Way DN34 . . . . . .190 D4
GUNNESS DN15 . . . . .17 E6
Gunness & Burringham CE
 Prim Sch DN17 . . . . .17 E5
Gunness La Amcotts DN17 . .17 F8
Gunness La continued
Flixborough DN15 . . . . . . .182 A7
GUNTHORPE
Owston Ferry DN9 . . . . .40 D7
Peterborough PE6 . . . . . . .221 D4
Gunthorpe Prim Sch PE4 . .221 C2
Gunthorpe Rd
Newborough PE6 . . . . .221 D4
Owston Ferry DN9 . . . . .40 C8
Peterborough PE4 . . . . . . .221 C2
Sutton Bridge PE14 . . . . . .160 E1
1 Walpole PE14 . . . . . . .170 F8
Gunton's Rd PE6 . . . . .174 E3
Gurnard Leys PE3 . . . . . . .220 E1
Gurnell St DN15 . . . . .183 A4
Gurry Lane DN9 . . . . .17 A1
Gurth Ave **8** DN3 . . . . . . .14 A1
Guthlac Ave **5** PE4 . . . . .221 B1
Guthram Ct **11** NG34 . . . .107 F1
Guthram Gowt PE11 . . . . .155 E5
Guys Head Rd PE12 . . . . . .160 E8
Guy's Head Rd Lutton PE12 .149 C1
Sutton Bridge PE12 . . . . . .160 F8
Gwash Cl PE9 . . . . .163 C1
Gynewell Gr **4** LN2 . . . . .202 D7
Gypsy La Newton PE13 . . . .170 C4
Whaplode PE12 . . . . .167 F3

H

Haalam Bank LN12 . . . . . . .63 C4
Haarlem Ct **5** PE11 . . . . .214 A2
Habbanya Rise LN4 . . . . . . .95 C7
Habblesthorpe Cl **1** DN22 .52 C1
Habblesthorpe Rd DN22 . . .52 C1
HABERTOFT PE24 . . . . .89 E4
HABROUGH DN40 . . . . .22 E8
Habrough La DN39 . . . . . . .22 B6
Habrough Rd
Immingham DN40 . . . . . . .186 A3
South Killingholme DN40 . . . .12 C2
Habrough Sta DN40 . . . . . .22 E8
Hacconby Dro
Dunsby PE10 . . . . .144 A1
Haconby PE10 . . . . .155 A8
Hacconby La PE10 . . . . . . .154 C7
HACEBY NG34 . . . . .131 E3
Hacke Rd **3** PE3 . . . . .225 D3
Hackness Gr **2** HU5 . . . . .179 D8
Hack's Dro PE6 . . . . .164 F6
HACKTHORN LN2 . . . . .55 E1
Hackthorn CE Prim Sch The
 LN2 . . . . .55 F1
Hackthorn Pl **4** LN2 . . . . .201 F8
Hackthorn Rd LN2 . . . . .68 D8
HACONBY PE10 . . . . .154 D8
HADDINGTON LN5 . . . . .92 F6
HADDON PE7 . . . . .232 B6
Haddon Cl Birchwood LN6 . .200 E1
Peterborough PE2 . . . . . . .231 E5
Haddon Dr **21** NG24 . . . . .104 B2
Haddon Rd
Peterborough PE3 . . . . . . .225 E3
Peterborough PE7 . . . . . . .232 C6
Stamford PE9 . . . . .218 F6
Haddon St HU3 . . . . .179 F4
Haddon Way PE7 . . . . .231 B2
Hadfield Rd
Hampton Vale PE7 . . . . . . .230 E2
7 Lincoln LN6 . . . . .205 A5
Hadleigh Cl NG31 . . . . . . .210 F5
Hadleigh Ct DN15 . . . . . . .183 A4
Hadleigh Dr LN6 . . . . .204 F5
Hadleigh Gn **7** DN17 . . . . .17 D4
Hadleigh Rd DN40 . . . . . . .186 D3
Hadley Rd
Peterborough PE4 . . . . . . .221 B1
Sleaford NG34 . . . . .212 E6
Hadrian Dr **10** PE6 . . . . . .164 E5
Hadrians Ct PE2 . . . . .231 B8
Hadrians Rd **9** LN4 . . . . . .81 A1
Hadrians Wk **12** LN6 . . . . .93 A8
Haff Cl **2** PE20 . . . . .135 C2
Haffenden Rd LN2 . . . . . . .202 A6
Hagbeach Dro PE12 . . . . . .168 A5
Hagbeach Gate PE12 . . . . .158 C6
Hagg Cross Roads PE23 . . . .87 A4
Hagg La **1** DN17 . . . . .16 E3
Hagg Rd PE23 . . . . .87 F2
HAGNABY East Kirkby PE23 .100 A5
Hannah cum Hagnaby LN13 . .76 C6
Hagnaby Abbey LN13 . . . . . .76 C7
HAGNABY LOCK PE22 . . . . .99 F2
Hagnaby Rd PE23 . . . . . . .100 A6
HAGWORTHINGHAM PE23 . . .87 A4
Haig Ave DN16 . . . . .183 B1
Haigh Ct DN32 . . . . .191 F5
Haigh St **4** DN35 . . . . . . .193 A5
Haile Rd DN36 . . . . .193 A1
HAINTON LN8 . . . . .58 F3
Hainton Ave DN32 . . . . . . .191 F8
Hainton Cl DN21 . . . . .197 E3
Hainton Lane LN8 . . . . .58 C2
Hainton Rd Hainton LN8 . . . .58 F3
Lincoln LN6 . . . . .205 C5
Haith's La **4** DN36 . . . . . . .36 B1
Haldane St DN21 . . . . .197 B5
Hale Cl **1** LN2 . . . . .202 E7
Hale Hill La Dunsville DN7 . . .14 E1
Hatfield DN7 . . . . .14 E2
Hale House Rd PE10 . . . . . .153 C2
Hale La PE22 . . . . .112 F1
Hale Rd Heckington NG34 . . .122 E2
Helpringham NG34 . . . . . . .133 D7
Horsington LN10 . . . . .84 B2
Hales Cl DN16 . . . . .185 A2
Hales Entry HU9 . . . . .181 C6
HALESGATE PE12 . . . . . . .146 E1
Hales La LN5 . . . . .107 B8
Haley Cl **6** PE13 . . . . .170 C2
Half Acre Wood **3** DN17 . . .17 D4
Halfleet PE6 . . . . .217 A6
Halford Cl **8** NG33 . . . . . .151 D2
Halfpenny Cl **19** LN2 . . . . .68 D7
Halfpenny La LN11 . . . . . . .60 F4
Halfway House La LN6 . . . . .92 C6
Halfway Houses LN6 . . . . . .92 D5
Halifax App DN20 . . . . .21 A8
Halifax Cl
4 Skegness PE25 . . . . . .206 B5
3 Skellingthorpe LN6 . . . .200 A4
Halifax Dr PE6 . . . . .217 C7
Halifax Rd Balderton NG24 .104 C2
13 Spilsby PE23 . . . . . . .101 A8
Halkon Cl DN17 . . . . .7 D3
Hallam Cl **3** Alford LN13 . . .75 C2
Barrow upon Humber DN19 . .11 B8
Hallam Gr LN6 . . . . .205 C7
Hallam Rd **2** HU4 . . . . . . .179 C2
Hallam's Dro PE20 . . . . . . .123 F2
Hallam's La **3** LN4 . . . . . . .96 B1
Hallaton Rd PE1 . . . . .226 D8
Hall Bank **3** PE13 . . . . . . .169 F7
Hallbrook Ct **5** DN16 . . . .185 A1
Hall Cl Heckington NG34 . . .122 E3
Ropsley NG33 . . . . .131 B1
Hallcroft **5** DN39 . . . . . . .12 A1
Hallcroft Rd **1** DN9 . . . . . .27 D2
Halldon Cl DN17 . . . . .7 A3
Hall Dr Canwick LN4 . . . . . .81 A4
Grantham NG31 . . . . .211 C5
Lincoln LN6 . . . . .205 C7
Swineshead PE20 . . . . . . .135 B7
HALL END PE22 . . . . .114 D1
Hall End Rd PE22 . . . . .114 C1
Haller St HU9 . . . . .181 E8
Hall Farm
5 Market Deeping PE6 . . .217 B6
6 Newark-on-Trent NG24 . .104 D5
Hall Farm Pk ✱ LN7 . . . . . .44 D8
Hallfield Cres NG32 . . . . . .119 C2
Hallfields La PE4 . . . . .221 C1
Hall Garden LN4 . . . . .81 A4
Hallgarth DN36 . . . . .37 B2
Hallgarth Ave DN16 . . . . . .183 B2
Hallgate PE12 . . . . .159 E8
Hall Gate Fleet PE12 . . . . .159 B6
Holbeach PE12 . . . . .215 C1
Moulton PE12 . . . . .157 F5
Wainfleet St Mary PE24 . . .102 C1
Weston PE12 . . . . .146 B1
Hall Gate Rd PE12 . . . . . . .168 E2
Hall Gdns **8** DN15 . . . . . . .9 B5
Hall Hill Rd PE12 . . . . .215 D1
HALLINGTON LN11 . . . . . . .60 F4
Halliwell Cl
5 Kingston upon Hull HU9 . . .5 F8
18 Newark-on-Trent NG24 . .104 A6
Hall La Algarkirk PE20 . . . .136 B3
Benington PE22 . . . . .126 F5
Branston & Mere LN4 . . . . . .81 D1
Burgh le Marsh PE24 . . . . .102 E7
Elsham DN20 . . . . .20 F7
Fiskerton LN3 . . . . .82 C7
Frampton PE20 . . . . .136 E6
Gunby & Stainby NG33 . . . .151 B5
Hough-on-the-Hill NG32 . . .118 F2
Lenton Keisby & Osgodby
 NG33 . . . . .141 E3
Moulton PE12 . . . . .146 E2
Nettleham LN2 . . . . .68 B2
Peterborough PE4 . . . . . . .221 A4
Stainforth DN7 . . . . .14 A6
Stenigot LN11 . . . . .72 D7
Stickney PE22 . . . . .112 F7
Welbourn LN5 . . . . .106 E4
West Keal PE23 . . . . .100 C6
Wrangle PE22 . . . . .114 D1
Hall Leas Dr **1** LN12 . . . . .64 C1
Hall Mdw **1** DN20 . . . . . . .10 C2
Hall Mdw Rd PE6 . . . . .217 F7
Hall Orch La **2** LN5 . . . . .106 E5
Hall Pk Heckington NG34 . . .122 F1
Swanland HU14 . . . . .3 C7
Hall Pk Rd DN40 . . . . .186 D5
Hall Pl **7** PE11 . . . . .214 D4
Hall Rd Buckminster NG33 . .150 F6
Haconby PE10 . . . . .154 D8
Heckington NG34 . . . . . . .122 E1
Hough-on-the-Hill NG32 . . .118 E2
Londonthorpe & Harrowby Without
 NG31 . . . . .211 F4
Hall Rise **7** DN17 . . . . . . .29 D7
Halls Ct LN4 . . . . .95 C6
Halls Hill LN11 . . . . .72 D6
Halls La **6** Keelby DN41 . . .23 A4
9 North Kelsey LN7 . . . . .32 A4
Hall's Rd DN10 . . . . .39 D2
Hall St Crowland PE6 . . . . .166 F1
Kingston upon Hull HU2 . . .180 D7
18 Navenby/Wellingore
 LN5 . . . . .107 A7
Hall Wath LN5 . . . . .92 E2
Hall Way DN39 . . . . .21 F5
Hall Wlk **1** HU15 . . . . .2 D6
Hall Yd **2** Collyweston PE9 .171 B1
28 Metheringham LN4 . . . .95 C4
Halmer Gate PE12 . . . . . . .214 E4
Halmer Gdns PE11 . . . . . . .214 F4
Halmer Paddock **6** PE11 . .214 F5
Haltemprice Leisure Ctr
 HU10 . . . . .178 E7
Haltemprice St HU3 . . . . . .179 F5
HALTHAM LN9 . . . . .98 C6

Haltham Gn DN21 . . . . .197 F4
HALTOFT END PE22 . . . . . . .126 C4
Haltoft End Est PE22. . . . . .126 C3
Halton Cl
  5 Birchwood LN6 . . . . . . .204 B8
  4 Kirton in Lindsey DN21 . . .42 F8
HALTON FENSIDE PE23 . . . .101 C6
HALTON HOLEGATE PE23 . . .101 B7
Halton Holegate CE Prim Sch
  PE23 . . . . .101 B7
Halton Pl DN35. . . . . .192 D4
Halton Rd
  Monksthorpe PE23. . . . . . .101 C8
  Spilsby PE23. . . . . .101 A8
Halton Way 3 DN33. . . . . . .191 C2
Halyard Croft 8 HU1. . . . . .180 F5
Halycon Ave 1 HU13 . . . . . .178 E2
Hambleton La LN8 . . . . .57 E8
Hambleton Rd PE9 . . . . .218 E4
HAMERINGHAM LN9. . . . . . . .86 C2
Hameringham Rd LN9 . . . . . .87 B2
Hamerton La 1 LN9 . . . . . . .199 C3
Hamilton Cl
  6 Bourne PE10 . . . . .213 C7
  4 Grimsby DN34. . . . . . . .190 D4
Hamilton Gr LN6 . . . . .200 B3
Hamilton Rd Alford LN13. . . . .75 F2
  Grantham NG31. . . . . . . .211 D6
  4 Lincoln LN6 . . . . .204 D2
  Scunthorpe DN17 . . . . . . .184 F8
Hamilton St DN31 . . . . .189 D1
Hamilton Way PE21 . . . . . . .208 F3
Hamish Wlk 8 DN40 . . . . . . .186 B3
Ham La PE7. . . . . .229 E7
Hamling Way HU4. . . . . . . .179 D2
Hamlyn Ave HU4 . . . . .179 E7
Hamlyn Dr HU4 . . . . .179 E6
Ham Mere Bird Sanctuary★
  PE2 . . . . .229 E7
Hammerfest Ave DN36. . . . . .195 B7
Hammerton Rd DN17 . . . . . .184 E4
Hammond Cl PE8 . . . . .172 C1
Hammond Ct LN12 . . . . .64 B3
Hammonds Dr PE1 . . . . .226 C1
Hamont Rd DN32 . . . . .192 B7
Hampden Cl 1 LN6 . . . . . . .200 A4
Hampden Cres 3 DN7. . . . . . .26 A8
Hampdens Cl 10 NG24 . . . . .104 C5
Hampden Way
  Sleaford NG34 . . . . .121 A2
  8 Waddington LN5 . . . . . . .94 A7
Hampden Wy LN4 . . . . .207 D3
Hampshire St HU4 . . . . .179 E3
Hampson Gdns 18 DN9 . . . . . .14 A2
Hampstead Pk DN33. . . . . . .191 B2
Hampton Ave PE7 . . . . .230 E2
Hampton Cl
  Humberston DN35 . . . . . . .192 F1
  1 Spalding PE11 . . . . . . .214 E2
Hampton Coll PE7. . . . . . . .230 D1
Hampton Ct PE3 . . . . .225 C6
HAMPTON HARGATE PE7 . . .230 D2
Hampton Hargate Prim Sch
  PE7. . . . . .230 C2
Hampton La PE22 . . . . .127 B7
Hampton Rd
  2 Hatfield DN7. . . . . .14 C4
  Scunthorpe DN16. . . . . . .185 C8
Hampton St LN1 . . . . .201 D4
HAMPTON VALE PE7 . . . . . .230 D1
Hampton Vale Prim Sch
  PE7. . . . . .230 C1
Hanbury PE2. . . . . .229 F3
Hanbury Ave NG31 . . . . . . .211 C2
HANBY NG33 . . . . .141 E7
Hanby La 11 Alford LN13 . . . . .75 F2
  Welton le Marsh PE23 . . . . . .89 B4
Hancock Dr 9 LN3. . . . . .83 B4
Handel Ct DN21 . . . . .197 D5
Handel House Prep Sch
  DN21. . . . . .197 D5
Handley Ct Mews 7
  NG34. . . . . .212 D3
Handley St
  Heckington NG34 . . . . . . .122 E3
  8 Sleaford NG34 . . . . . . .212 D3
Hands on History Mus★
  HU1. . . . . .180 F6
Hangar La DN36. . . . . .195 C4
Hangman's Cnr PE6 . . . . . . .175 B7
Hangman's La
  Edenham PE10 . . . . .153 F7
  Haconby PE10 . . . . .154 A7
Hankey St PE1 . . . . .225 F4
Hankinson's Est PE34. . . . . .161 D1
HANNAH LN13. . . . . .76 E6
Hannah Cres LN6 . . . . .92 E5
Hannath Rd PE11 . . . . .170 B8
Hanover Ct HU1. . . . . .180 E5
Hanover Dr 26 HU15 . . . . .2 C5
Hanover Gdns DN16 . . . . . . .185 C6
Hanover Hill DN21 . . . . .54 F6
Hanover Sq 5 HU1. . . . . . . .180 E5
Hansard Cres 3 LN7 . . . . . . .33 B4
Hansards Dr 2 LN8 . . . . .70 D5
Hansard Way 8 PE20. . . . . .136 C5
Hansel Cl PE2. . . . . .230 E8
Hanson Dr 2 LN12 . . . . .76 E8
Hanson Way DN32 . . . . .192 B8
HANTHORPE PE10 . . . . .154 B7
Hanthorpe Rd PE10 . . . . . . .154 B7
Ha'penny Bridge Way
  HU9 . . . . .181 B5
HARBY NG23 . . . . .79 C5
Harby Cl Grantham NG31 . . . .210 E1
  Lincoln LN6 . . . . .205 B3

Harby Cl continued
  30 Newark-on-Trent NG24 . . .104 B2
Harcourt Dr HU9 . . . . .181 C6
HarCt St NG24 . . . . .104 A4
Harden's La LN9 . . . . .73 F1
Hardian Wy LN7. . . . . .33 A4
Harding Cl
  9 Mablethorpe & Sutton
  LN12 . . . . .64 C1
  6 Mablethorpe/Sutton on Sea
  LN12 . . . . .76 F8
Harding House Gall★ LN2 234 B3
Hardings La PE23 . . . . .88 B2
Hardings The 20 LN2. . . . . . .68 D7
Hardiway PE21. . . . . .209 B5
Hards La PE6 . . . . .165 E1
HARDWICK LN1. . . . . .201 B7
Hardwick Cl Louth LN11 . . . .198 A7
  3 Saxilby with Ingleby LN1 . . .66 C2
Hardwick Ct PE3 . . . . .225 B2
Hardwicke Cl 7 NG31 . . . . .211 A3
Hardwick La LN9 . . . . .65 F5
Hardwick Pl 1 LN2 . . . . . . .202 A8
Hardwick Plot La PE20. . . . .124 C1
Hardwick Rd
  5 Kirton PE20. . . . . .136 C5
  1 Stamford PE9 . . . . .218 F6
Hardwick St HU5. . . . . .180 B8
Hardy Rd PE11. . . . . .184 D6
Hardy's Animal Farm★
  PE25 . . . . .90 E5
Hardys Ct DN32 . . . . .192 A6
Hardy's Dro PE10 . . . . .213 F7
Hardy's La PE6. . . . . .167 D4
Harebell Cl PE1 . . . . .221 F1
HAREBY PE23 . . . . .99 F8
Hareby Hill PE23. . . . . .100 A8
Hareby Rd PE23. . . . . .86 F2
Harecroft Rd PE13 . . . . .170 C1
Hare Hill LN7 . . . . .34 A2
Hare St DN32 . . . . .191 F6
Harewood Ave 7 DN3. . . . . . .14 A2
Harewood Cl PE21 . . . . .209 B5
Harewood Cres
  Lincoln LN6 . . . . .205 A3
  Louth LN11. . . . . .198 B7
Harewood Crest 32 HU15 . . . . .2 D5
Harewood Gdns PE23 . . . . . .225 B2
Harewood Gr 1 DN35 . . . . . .192 F1
Harford Gate PE12 . . . . .159 D5
Hargate Cl 1 PE12 . . . . . . .159 C7
Hargate La PE34 . . . . .161 E2
Hargate Way PE7 . . . . .230 D3
Hargon La NG24. . . . . .104 B7
Hargrave St DN31 . . . . .188 D1
Hargreaves Way DN15 . . . . .183 B6
Harland Rd
  8 Brough HU15. . . . . .2 C6
  Lincoln LN2 . . . . .202 A8
Harlaxton CE Prim Sch
  NG32. . . . . .139 C7
HARLAXTON NG32. . . . . . . .139 C7
Harlaxton Cl 2 LN6 . . . . . . .204 C6
Harlaxton College NG32 . . . .139 D7
Harlaxton Dr 4 LN6 . . . . . . .204 C6
Harlaxton Manor & Gdns★
  NG32. . . . . .139 D7
Harlaxton Rd 3 NG31 . . . . .210 F3
Harlaxton Road Ind Est
  NG31 . . . . .210 F2
Harlech Grange PE3. . . . . . .225 B1
Harlech Way DN32 . . . . .191 F8
Harlech Wlk DN40. . . . . . . .186 B3
Harlequin Dr
  10 Mablethorpe/Sutton on Sea
  LN12 . . . . .64 B3
  6 Spalding PE11 . . . . .214 A5
Harlestone Ct DN34 . . . . . . .190 C4
Harley St HU2. . . . . .180 E8
Harlow St DN31 . . . . .188 D1
Harlton Cl PE2. . . . . .231 E5
HARMSTON LN5 . . . . .93 F5
Harmston Cl LN2. . . . . .202 A8
Harmston Pk Ave LN5 . . . . . . .93 F4
Harmston Rd LN5 . . . . .93 A5
Harneis Cres DN37 . . . . .23 F2
Harness Dr LN4 . . . . .207 A5
Harn Rd PE7 . . . . .230 E2
Harold Rd NG32 . . . . .151 D2
Harold's Bank PE13 . . . . . . .169 B2
Harold St DN32 . . . . .192 A8
Harome Gr HU5 . . . . .179 C7
Harpe Cl 10 PE11 . . . . .156 E8
Harpenden Cl 15 DN7. . . . . . .14 D3
Harpendon Dr 16 DN7 . . . . . .14 D3
Harper Garth LN9 . . . . .85 B5
Harpham Cl DN16 . . . . .185 F5
Harpham Rd
  Gate Burton DN21 . . . . .53 A1
  Marshchapel DN36. . . . . . . .37 B2
  Marton DN21 . . . . .65 D8
HARPSWELL DN21 . . . . .54 E8
Harpswell Cl 7 DN21. . . . . . .53 A8
Harpswell La DN21. . . . . .42 C1
Harpswell Rd LN2. . . . . .202 A7
Harrier Ct 3 LN6. . . . . .204 E8
Harrier Rd 3 DN18. . . . . .3 F3
Harrier Way PE6 . . . . .217 B7
Harriet Cl 5 PE12 . . . . .160 E4
HARRINGTON PE23. . . . . .87 F7
Harrington LN11 . . . . .198 E6
Harrington Ave 4 LN6 . . . . .204 E8
Harrington Croft 8 PE12 . . .215 E2
Harrington Dr 7 PE6. . . . . . .175 C8
Harrington Pl DN16 . . . . . . .185 A5

Harrington Rd
  Hagworthingham PE23 . . . . .87 B4
  7 South Witham NG33 . . . . .151 D2
Harrington Rise 13 NG34. . . .107 F1
Harrington St
  Bourne PE10 . . . . .213 D6
  Cleethorpes DN35 . . . . . . .189 D1
Harrington Way 6 PE6 . . . . .175 C8
Harris Bvd 12 LN12 . . . . .64 B3
Harris Cl
  9 Newborough PE6 . . . . . .174 E4
  11 Skegness PE25 . . . . . . .206 A5
Harrison Cl Horncastle LN9 199 C5
  10 Peterborough PE3. . . . . .224 F3
  Winteringham DN15. . . . . . . .9 A8
Harrison Pl Lincoln LN1 . . . . .234 A4
  North Hykeham LN6 . . . . . .204 D5
Harrison's Dro PE20. . . . . . .124 B2
Harrison's La PE24 . . . . .101 F4
Harrison St DN31. . . . . .191 C7
Harris Rd LN6 . . . . .205 B6
Harris St
  3 Kingston upon Hull
  HU3. . . . . .179 B1
  Peterborough PE1 . . . . . . .225 F6
Harris Vw 11 DN9 . . . . .27 D7
Harris Way NG31 . . . . .211 A2
Harrold Dro PE12 . . . . .177 C8
Harrold's Bank PE13 . . . . . . .177 D8
Harrolds Cl 3 PE13 . . . . . . .170 F1
HARROWBY NG31. . . . . .211 C6
Harrowby CE (Aided) Inf Sch
  NG31. . . . . .211 C6
Harrowby Cl Digby LN4 . . . . .108 E5
  Grantham NG31. . . . . .211 C6
Harrowby Cres NG31 . . . . . .211 E1
Harrowby Est NG31. . . . . . . .211 D6
Harrowby La
  Grantham NG31. . . . . .211 D6
  Londonthorpe & Harrowby Without
  NG31. . . . . .130 C3
Harrowby Rd NG31 . . . . .211 C3
Harrow Cl
  Gainsborough DN21 . . . . . .197 F6
  Heighington/Washingborough
  LN4 . . . . .203 C1
Harrow Close 1 NG23 . . . . . .91 D4
Harrow Dr PE25. . . . . .206 B6
Harrowdyke 6 DN18 . . . . . . .10 E8
Harrow Gdns DN17 . . . . .184 F4
Harrow La DN33. . . . . .191 B1
Harrow Rd
  Deeping St Nicholas PE11. . .166 C7
  6 Mablethorpe/Sutton on Sea
  LN12 . . . . .64 B4
Harrow St Grantham NG31 . . .211 B3
  Kingston upon Hull HU3 . . . .180 B4
Harrows The 15 LN2. . . . . . . .68 D6
Harrox Rd 8 PE12. . . . . .157 F7
Harrox Sq 5 PE12 . . . . .157 F7
Harrys Dream 3 DN20. . . . . . .19 E3
HARSTON NG32. . . . . .138 E5
Harston Rd NG32. . . . . .138 E5
Hartford Ct PE2 . . . . .231 D6
Harthill PL HU3 . . . . .180 C5
Hart La LN15 . . . . .9 B5
Hartland Ave
  Hampton Hargate PE7 . . . . .230 E1
  6 Lincoln LN6 . . . . .205 A1
Hartley Bridge HU9 . . . . . . .181 C6
Hartley St Boston PE21 . . . . .208 F6
  3 Lincoln LN2 . . . . .202 C3
Hartshead Ave DN15 . . . . . .182 C3
HARTSHOLME LN6 . . . . .204 E6
Hartsholme Acad LN6 . . . . . .204 F7
Hartsholme Dr LN6. . . . . . . .205 A8
Hartsholme Pk LN6. . . . . . . .204 F7
Hart St DN35. . . . . .192 C8
Hartwell Cl PE3 . . . . .225 C5
Hartwell Way PE3 . . . . .225 B5
Harvard Cl 1 LN4 . . . . .203 D1
Harvest Ave 34 DN18 . . . . . . .10 E8
Harvest Cl
  21 Kirk Sandall DN3 . . . . . .14 A2
  28 Metheringham LN4 . . . . .95 C4
Harvest Cres 2 DN37. . . . . . .194 C4
Harvest Dr NG24 . . . . .104 B6
Harvester Cl 19 DN9 . . . . . . .27 E6
Harvester Way
  Crowland PE6. . . . . .175 B8
  Peterborough PE1 . . . . . . .226 C1
  1 Sibsey PE22 . . . . .113 B1
Harvest Mews 5 PE11. . . . . .166 C6
Harvest Rise 2 DN19 . . . . . . .11 C8
Harvest Way 3 NG34 . . . . . .212 C2
Harvest Wy 15 PE25 . . . . . . .206 A5
Harvey Ave 7 NG24 . . . . . . .104 C5
Harvey Cl Bourne PE10 . . . . .213 B4
  11 Wittering PE8 . . . . .172 B1
Harvey Kent Gdns 4 LN3 . . . .83 C4
Harveys Cl PE11. . . . . .214 F6
Harveys La LN11 . . . . .198 E6
Harvey St 5 LN1 . . . . .201 D3
Harvey Wk DN36. . . . . .195 D7
Harwich Cl 12 LN5. . . . . . . .205 D3
Harwood Ave PE12 . . . . .215 C1
Harwood Dr 1 HU4 . . . . . . .179 B6
Hase Wlk HU13 . . . . .178 E1
Hassall Rd PE25. . . . . .206 A2
Hassock Hill Dro PE13 . . . . .169 D3
HASTHORPE LN13. . . . . .89 C4
Hasthorpe Rd LN13. . . . . . . .89 C5
Hastings Dr 2 PE24 . . . . . . .102 D2
Hastings Gr HU5 . . . . .179 E7
Hastings Rd PE4 . . . . .221 A2
Hatchet's La
  20 Beacon Hill NG24 . . . . .104 A5
  2 Newark-on-Trent NG24. . .104 A6

HATCLIFFE DN37. . . . . .34 F3
Hatcliffe Cl 2 NG31. . . . . . .211 A8
Hatcliffe Gdns 11 LN2 . . . . .202 A8
Hatcliffe Rd LN8 . . . . .47 C8
Hatcliffe Cl 6 DN33 . . . . . . .191 B3
HATFIELD DN7. . . . . .14 D5
Hatfield La DN3 . . . . .14 A4
Hatfield Rd Hatfield DN7 . . . . .14 F6
  Thorne/Moorends DN8 . . . . .15 A7
Hatfield & Stainforth Sta
  DN7. . . . . .14 C5
HATFIELD WOODHOUSE
  DN7. . . . . .15 A3
Hathersage Ave LN6. . . . . . .204 E2
Hathersage Cl NG31. . . . . . .211 A4
Hathersage Ct 3 DN15 . . . . .182 B2
Hatt Cl 2 PE12. . . . . .157 F7
HATTON LN8 . . . . .71 B3
Hatton Cl 3 LN6 . . . . .205 A7
Hatton Gdns 18 NG24 . . . . .104 A4
Hatton Gr 7 DN33 . . . . .191 B3
Hatton Mdws Nature
  Reserve★ LN8 . . . . .71 A2
Hatton Rd LN2 . . . . .75 C5
HAUGH LN13 . . . . .75 B2
HAUGHAM LN11 . . . . .73 F8
Haugham Pastures LN11. . . . .61 E2
Haugham Road LN11 . . . . . . .61 B1
Haugh La LN11 . . . . .75 A3
Hauser Cl 8 NG34. . . . . .212 B2
Havelock Acad DN32 . . . . . .192 C6
Havelock Dr PE2 . . . . .231 E6
Havelock Mews DN32 . . . . . .192 C6
Havelock St
  Kingston upon Hull HU3 . . . .180 A4
  Spalding PE11 . . . . .214 C3
Havelok Cl 4 LN11 . . . . .198 D4
HAVEN BANK LN4 . . . . .111 B3
Haven Bank Boston PE21 . . .208 E5
  6 Skidbrooke with Saltfleet
  Haven LN11. . . . . .51 C4
  Wildmore LN4 . . . . .111 B2
Haven Ct 7 Blyton DN21 . . . . .41 C5
  9 Fleet PE12. . . . . .159 C7
Haven Ctry Pk★ PE21 . . . . .137 C7
Haven Garth 1 HU15 . . . . . . .2 B5
Haven Gdns DN31 . . . . .188 C1
Haven High Acad PE21. . . . .208 F7
Haven House Rd PE24 . . . . .102 F3
Havenmoor Sta PE24 . . . . . .102 F2
Haven Mdws PE21. . . . . . . .208 C7
Haven Rd
  4 Barton-upon-Humber
  DN18. . . . . .3 E1
  North Killingholme DN40 . . . .13 A6
Haven Side 8 PE21 . . . . . . .102 D1
Havenside Nature Reserve★
  PE21 . . . . .137 A8
Haven The★ PE21 . . . . .208 F4
Haven The HU9 . . . . .181 B6
Haven Village 3 PE21 . . . . .208 F3
Haverfield Rd PE11. . . . . . . .214 D3
Haverholme Cl 10 NG34 . . . .108 E1
Haverholme Dro PE12 . . . . . .159 D5
Haverlands The 3 NG31 . . . .210 E8
Haverstoe Pl DN32 . . . . .192 C3
Haveswater Cl 1 PE4 . . . . . .221 C2
Hawerby Rd 3 Laceby DN37 . .23 F1
  Wold Newton LN8. . . . . .47 F8
Hawker Dr LN11. . . . . .198 D4
Hawking Cl 10 NG33. . . . . . .151 D7
Hawkins Dr 20 PE13 . . . . . . .170 E1
Hawkins Gr NG32. . . . . .192 B6
Hawkins Way 7 DN40 . . . . . .12 E3
Hawksbill Wy PE2. . . . . .231 A8
Hawksdale Cl 3 NG31 . . . . . .211 A7
Hawkshead Gr LN2. . . . . . . .202 A8
Hawkshead Way 2 PE4. . . . .221 C3
Hawksmede Way LN11 . . . . .198 B6
Hawksmoor Cl 2 LN6 . . . . . .204 D1
Hawks Way NG34 . . . . .212 B3
Hawksworth St 3 DN21 . . . .197 D4
Haworth Cl DN15 . . . . .182 B4
Haworth Way PE21 . . . . .208 D7
Haw's La PE11 . . . . .134 F1
Hawthorn Ave Brigg DN20 . . .196 C4
  Cherry Willingham LN3. . . . .203 B6
  Gainsborough DN21 . . . . . .197 D6
  Immingham DN40 . . . . . . .186 E5
  Kingston upon Hull HU3 . . . .179 F5
  Waddington LN5. . . . . .205 C1
Hawthorn Bank PE11 . . . . . .214 B1
Hawthorn Chase
  Lincoln LN2 . . . . .202 E7
  1 Moulton PE12 . . . . .157 F6
Hawthorn Cl
  5 Billinghay LN4 . . . . .109 F6
  1 Mablethorpe LN12 . . . . . .64 B3
  Sleaford NG34 . . . . .212 D3
Hawthorn Cres
  Cleethorpes DN35 . . . . . . .192 D8
  3 Grimsby DN33. . . . . . . .194 F8
  9 Hatfield DN7. . . . . .14 C4
Hawthorn Dr
  Louth LN11. . . . . .198 B6
  New Waltham DN36 . . . . . .195 B5

Hawthorne Ave continued
  4 Scunthorpe DN17 . . . . . .184 F8
  4 Wisbech PE13 . . . . .170 D2
Hawthorne Cl
  2 Bracebridge Heath LN4. . . .81 A1
  5 Manby LN11. . . . . .62 C6
  8 Scopwick Heath LN4 . . . .108 A7
  20 Winterton DN15 . . . . .9 A5
  Wootton DN39 . . . . .11 E2
Hawthorne Cres 3 DN17 . . . .184 F8
Hawthorne Ct 4 NG31. . . . . .210 D2
Hawthorne Gdns 8 DN19 . . . .12 A8
Hawt Horne Rd 17 DN36. . . . .36 C8
Hawthorne Rise 11 LN13 . . . . .88 B3
Hawthorne Wlk 1 LN1 . . . . . .66 D7
Hawthorn Gate 26 DN18 . . . . .10 F8
Hawthorn Gr DN21 . . . . .197 D5
HAWTHORN HILL LN4. . . . . .110 F6
Hawthorn Rd Bourne PE10 . . .213 C6
  Cherry Willingham LN3. . . . .203 B7
  4 Old Leake PE22 . . . . . . .114 A1
  Peterborough PE1 . . . . . . .226 C6
  Skegness PE25. . . . . .206 A2
  Yaxley PE7 . . . . .233 F5
Hawthorn Rise 4 DN19. . . . . .11 C8
Hawthorns The
  Allington NG32. . . . . .128 A6
  14 Nettleham LN2 . . . . .68 D2
Hawthorn Way 4 LN5 . . . . . . .92 F3
Hawthorn Wlk 1 LN1 . . . . . . .66 D7
Hawthorn Wy
  Burringham DN17 . . . . .17 D4
  9 Ingoldmells PE25 . . . . . . .90 D3
HAWTHORPE PE10 . . . . .142 A2
Hawthorpe Rd
  Irnham NG33 . . . . .141 E1
  Keisby PE10 . . . . .141 F3
Hawton Cl 8 DN21 . . . . .197 E6
Hawton La NG24 . . . . .104 A2
HAXEY DN9 . . . . .27 C2
HAXEY CARR DN9 . . . . .27 B4
Haxey CE Prim Sch DN9 . . . . .27 D3
Haxey Gate Rd DN10. . . . . . .39 F7
Haxey Grange 9 DN9 . . . . . . .27 D2
Haxey La DN9. . . . . .27 D1
Haxey Rd DN10. . . . . .39 F6
Haxey Turbary Nature
  Reserve★ DN9. . . . . .27 A4
Hay Barn Rd PE11. . . . . .166 C6
Haycroft Ave 4 DN31. . . . . . .191 C8
Haycroft La PE12 . . . . .159 B7
Haycroft St DN31. . . . . .191 C7
Haydock Park Dr
  Bourne PE10 . . . . .213 B3
  Bourne PE10 . . . . .213 C3
Haydock Wy 10 LN8 . . . . .57 E7
Haydon Ave PE25 . . . . .206 A4
Haydon Cl HU10. . . . . .178 D3
Haydor Ave LN2. . . . . .202 A8
Hayes Yd 4 LN1 . . . . .54 F2
Hayfield Cl
  7 Barnby Dun DN3 . . . . . . .14 A4
  6 Haxey DN9 . . . . .27 D2
Hayfields The PE11. . . . . . . .214 B6
Hay Gn Rd PE34 . . . . .161 E1
Hay Gn Rd (North) PE34. . . .161 E2
Hay Gn Rd (South) PE34 . . . .161 D1
HAY GREEN PE34 . . . . .161 E1
Hayling Mere 4 DN35 . . . . . .192 F1
Haynes Cl 3 DN8 . . . . .15 B8
Haynes Gdns 13 DN8 . . . . . . .15 B8
Haynes Gn 6 DN8. . . . . .15 B8
Haynes Gr 1 DN8 . . . . .15 B7
Haynes Rd DN8 . . . . .15 B8
Hays Cl 4 DN36. . . . . .195 C2
Hayside Ave 14 NG24 . . . . . .104 B2
Hayton Cl 2 DN15. . . . . .9 B5
Hayton Gr HU4. . . . . .179 D4
Haytons La 2 LN12. . . . . .9 D1
Haywain Dr 6 PE11 . . . . . . .166 C6
Haywardsfield 4 PE3 . . . . . .225 A1
Haze La LN6 . . . . .204 C1
Hazeland Cl PE10 . . . . .154 C6
Hazeland Steading PE10. . . .154 C6
Hazel Ave 20 DN17 . . . . .16 D8
Hazelbarrow Dr HU10 . . . . . .178 F3
Hazel Cl Messingham DN17 . . .29 C7
  10 North Hykeham LN6 . . . . .93 A8
Hazel Croft
  4 Immingham DN40 . . . . . .186 A4
  Peterborough PE4 . . . . . . .220 E4
Hazel Ct 29 HU15. . . . . .2 C5
Hazel Dr LN9. . . . . .199 B5
Hazel Gr
  4 Bottesford DN16 . . . . . . .185 B2
  2 Kingston upon Hull HU3. . .180 D5
  Louth LN11. . . . . .198 E4
  Sleaford NG34 . . . . .212 D6
  Stamford PE9. . . . . .218 D6
  Welton/Dunholme LN2 . . . . .68 C6
Hazelnut Cl 3 PE22 . . . . .99 A4
Hazelnut Way LN11 . . . . . . .198 E6
Hazel Rd 6 DN17 . . . . .14 C5
Hazel Wk 29 LN13 . . . . .75 F2
Hazelwood Ave LN6 . . . . . . .204 C8
Hazelwood Dr
  Bourne PE10 . . . . .213 B6
  Hessle HU13 . . . . .178 B3
Hazelwood La PE12 . . . . . . .159 A7
Hazelwood Dr LN1. . . . . . . .210 F7
Headingley Ave 4 DN17. . . . .184 E3
Headland Way
  3 Haconby PE10. . . . . . . .154 D8
  7 Navenby LN5. . . . . .107 B8

Headquarters Cres 5 NG34 120 C8
Heads La HU13 178 C1
Headstead Bank DN22 65 B7
Healey Cl 5 NG23 91 D4
Healey La LN12 63 C4
Healey Rd DN16 185 C8
HEALING DN41 23 F5
Healing Moated Settlement★ DN4 23 F5
Healing Prim Sch DN41 23 F5
Healing Rd 5 DN41 23 D6
Healing Science Acad DN41 23 F5
Healing Sta DN41 23 F6
Heanor Ct DN15 182 B3
HEAPHAM DN21 53 E7
Heapham Cres DN21 197 F4
Heapham La DN21 53 F7
Heapham Rd DN21 197 E5
Hearfield Terr HU13 178 E1
Heartsease Way PE10 213 E3
Heath Cl 4 LN2 68 C7
Heathcote Cl HU10 178 F5
Heathcote Rd Bourne PE10 213 E4
Castle Bytham NG33 152 D1
Coningsby LN4 207 E5
Heathcroft LN3 203 E5
Heather Ave PE1 226 A8
Heather Cl 1 Boston PE21 208 D3
7 Woodhall Spa LN10 97 E6
Heather Ct 9 PE11 214 B6
Heatherdale Cl
6 Grimsby DN33 194 E7
Peterborough PE7 231 C5
Heather Gdns LN6 204 E3
Heather Gr DN16 185 E5
Heather Rd PE25 206 B2
Heather Rd Ind Est PE25 206 B2
Heath Farm Cl NG32 119 F3
Heath Farm Rd NG31 130 C2
Heathfield Ave
Branston LN4 81 E2
Spalding PE11 214 F2
Heathfield Cl 9 DN3 14 A3
Heathfield Ct DN34 191 B6
Heathfield Rd NG31 210 C3
Heath La Ancaster NG32 119 F3
Boothby Graffoe LN5 94 B2
Carlton Scroop NG32 119 D4
Great Ponton NG33 139 D4
Honington NG32 119 C2
Leasingham NG34 121 C7
Normanton NG32 119 F6
Syston NG32 130 D8
Wellingore LN5 107 C8
Welton LN1 67 F6
Wilsford NG32 120 B1
Heathland Way DN36 195 E6
Heathlea 11 LN2 68 F4
Heath Rd
Bracebridge Heath LN4 205 F2
Coleby LN5 93 F3
Helpston PE6 173 C2
15 Navenby LN5 107 A8
5 Nettleham LN2 68 C2
Pilsgate PE9 172 C3
Scopwick LN4 108 B8
Scothern LN2 68 D4
Skegness PE25 206 B3
Heath's Mdw Nature Reserve★ PE24 102 C7
Heath The LN5 107 B7
Heaton Cl
2 Beacon Hill NG24 104 B4
Peterborough PE3 225 B3
Heaton St 1 DN21 197 D4
Hebden Moor Way 8 LN6 93 B8
Hebden Rd DN15 182 C4
Hebden Wlk 9 NG31 211 F6
HECKDYKE DN10 40 C7
Heckdyke La DN10 40 C7
HECKINGTON NG34 122 D3
Heckington Rd NG34 122 C1
Heckington St Andrews CE Prim Sch NG34 122 E3
Heckington Sta NG34 122 E2
Heckington Windmill★ NG34 122 E2
Hedda Dr 2 PE7 230 D3
Hedgefield Hurn PE11 144 F4
Hedge Field Rd NG32 210 A4
HEDGEHOG BRIDGE PE20 124 E5
Hedgehog La PE20 124 D4
Hedge La LN6 92 D4
Hedgelands
Peterborough PE4 221 A5
3 Wisbech PE13 170 D2
Hedgerow Cl 5 DN19 11 C8
Hedgerow La 1 DN20 196 D3
Hedgerows The
Collingham NG23 91 D4
10 Sleaford NG34 212 C6
Hedon Rd HU9 181 B6
HEIGHINGTON LN4 81 F4
Heighington Fen LN4 82 A5
Heighington Rd LN4 81 C4
Heimdal Rd DN33 191 C2
Helen Cres 8 DN40 186 A4
Helene Gr DN32 192 B7
Helenship La DN22 65 A4
Hell La NG33 140 C5
Hellyers Ct HU4 179 D2
Helm Dr HU9 181 C6
Helmsdale Gdns PE4 220 F2
Helmsley Ct 1 PE7 231 F5
Helmsley Gr HU5 179 C7
Helmsley Rd
Green Hill NG31 210 D6
Green Hill NG31 210 E6
Helmsley Way PE11 214 F4
HELPRINGHAM NG34 133 E7
Helpringham Rd
Burton Pedwardine NG34 122 B1
Helpringham NG34 133 C8
Helpringham Sch NG34 133 D7
HELPSTON PE6 173 C4
Helpston Rd Castor PE5 223 D2
Etton PE6 220 A8
Helsby Rd LN5 205 D4
HELSEY PE24 89 F7
Helsey La PE24 89 F7
Helston Wlk DN17 184 C8
Heltwate PE3 225 B7
Heltwate Ct PE3 225 B7
Heltwate Sch PE3 225 B7
Helvellyn Way DN33 191 D1
HEMINGBY LN9 72 B1
Hemingby La Fulletby LN9 86 A8
Horncastle LN9 199 C6
Hemingby Rd LN9 72 B1
Hemingby Way LN9 199 C5
Hemingford Cres PE2 231 E6
Hemington Way 1 PE20 136 C5
Hemmingway Wlk HU13 178 E3
Hempdyke Rd DN15 182 E4
Hemplands The 9 NG23 91 D5
Hempstead Rd 2 PE7 230 C1
HEMSWELL DN21 42 D1
Hemswell Ave
4 Kingston upon Hull HU9 5 E8
Lincoln LN6 205 A7
HEMSWELL CLIFF LN8 55 A8
Hemswell Cliff Prim Sch LN8 43 A1
Hemswell Dr DN31 190 F8
Hemswell La DN21 42 D1
Henderson Ave DN15 182 F4
Henderson Avenue Acad DN15 182 F4
Henderson Cres 2 DN15 182 F4
Henderson Way DN15 9 A5
Heneage Rd DN32 191 F6
Hengist Cl 7 NG34 212 B2
Henley Ct
2 Gainsborough DN21 197 C6
Lincoln LN5 205 D8
Henley St LN5 205 D8
Henlow Cl
6 Birchwood LN6 204 B8
3 Kirton in Lindsey DN21 42 F8
Henrietta St 2 PE11 214 C3
Henry Boot Way HU4 179 B1
Henry La LN3 83 D4
Henry St Grimsby DN31 191 C8
Lincoln LN5 201 F1
Peterborough PE1 226 A4
Scunthorpe DN15 182 F3
Henshaw PE1 226 E6
Henshaw Ave 2 LN12 77 A7
Henson Cl
13 Spalding PE11 214 C2
5 Wisbech PE13 170 D2
Henson Dr
13 Navenby/Wellingore LN5 107 A8
6 Peterborough PE7 230 F5
Henton Cl 13 NG24 104 C5
Herald Wy PE6 221 E3
Hercules Dr 7 NG24 104 A4
Hercules Wy 2 PE2 231 E4
Herdgate La PE11 145 D2
Hereford Ave DN34 191 C5
Hereford Cl 2 NG34 212 C7
Hereford Sq PE10 213 B3
Hereford St HU4 179 E3
Hereford Way 8 NG31 210 E5
Heren Pl 9 PE11 214 A2
Hereward Cl 2 PE1 226 B2
Hereward Cross 6 PE1 226 A2
Hereward Pl DN16 185 E7
Hereward Rd
Peterborough PE1 226 B2
Spalding PE11 214 B4
Hereward St
5 Bourne PE10 213 D5
Lincoln LN1 234 B4
Hereward Way
11 Billingborough NG34 133 B1
21 Crowland PE6 166 E1
Market Deeping PE6 217 E4
Herewood Cross Sh Ctr PE1 226 A2
Heritage Pk Prim Sch PE7 231 F5
Herlington PE2 230 B4
Herlyn Cres 8 PE25 90 E3
Hermes Way NG34 212 A3
Hermitage The 6 PE9 219 A5
Hermit St LN5 234 B1
Heron Cl Grimsby DN32 192 B4
6 Scunthorpe DN15 182 C6
Skegness PE25 103 C8
3 Surfleet PE11 145 E3
Heron Ct PE2 231 D6
Heron Dr DN21 197 F5
Heron Gate DN16 185 F5
Heron Holt 3 DN20 19 D4
Heron Pk PE1 226 F6
Heronry Dr PE6 224 E2
Herons Cl PE9 172 F6
Heron St HU3 180 B5
Heron View LN6 204 E8
Heron Way
43 Barton-upon-Humber DN18 10 E8
Holton le Clay DN36 195 C3
Spalding PE11 214 F2
Wyberton PE21 136 F8
Heron Wlk LN6 204 C1
Herrick Cl PE1 225 E8
Herrick Ct 2 LN4 207 A6
Herrick Rd DN17 184 D7
Herring La
1 Pinchbeck PE11 145 B1
4 Spalding PE11 214 D4
Herrington Ave 3 LN2 68 C2
Hersey Rd 16 LN7 33 B4
Hervey Rd NG34 212 C2
Hesketh Cres 11 PE25 103 E4
Hesketh Ct LE15 162 A8
Hesketh Dr 3 DN3 14 A2
HESSLE HU13 178 D1
Hessle Ave PE21 208 D4
Hessle Ct PE21 208 C4
Hessle Dr PE21 208 C3
Hessle High Sch HU13 178 C2
Hessle Mount Sch HU13 178 C3
Hessle Penshurst Prim Sch HU13 178 F3
Hessle Rd HU4 179 D3
Hessle Sta HU13 3 E4
Hessle View 4 DN18 10 E8
Hetley PE2 230 A4
Hever Cl NG31 210 E5
Hewde La DN15 2 A1
Hewitt Cl PE7 233 B7
Hewitt's Ave
Humberston DN36 192 C1
New Waltham DN36 195 D8
Hewitt's Avenue DN36 195 D8
Hewitt's Cir DN36 192 C2
Hewitts Manor
1 Cleethorpes DN35 192 D2
New Waltham DN36 195 F7
Hewitt's Windmill★ DN21 53 E7
Hewson Rd
5 Humberston DN36 36 D8
Lincoln LN1 201 C4
Hewson's La
33 Barton-upon-Humber DN18 3 E1
Collingham NG23 91 D3
Hewson St 23 DN17 29 D7
Hexham Ave PE10 213 B3
Hexham Ct 3 PE1 226 D3
HEYDOUR NG32 131 D6
Heyford Cl PE4 221 D2
Heynings Cl DN21 53 B4
Heysham Cl 8 LN5 205 D3
Hey St DN35 192 F5
Heythrop Rd 3 DN35 192 E3
HIBALDSTOW DN20 31 A5
Hibaldstow Cl
10 Birchwood LN6 204 C7
9 Grimsby DN34 190 F4
Hibaldstow Prim Sch DN20 31 A5
Hibaldstow Rd LN6 204 C7
Hickling Cl
15 Grantham NG31 210 E2
Kingston upon Hull HU10 179 A6
Hickling Wlk PE4 221 C3
Hickman Cres DN21 197 C8
Hickman Ct DN21 197 E4
Hickman Gr 2 Blyton DN21 41 B5
Collingham NG23 91 C5
Hickman St DN21 197 C4
Hickory Rd 5 LN6 200 C1
Hicks La PE7 230 F5
Hidcote Wlk 27 HU15 2 D5
Hide's La Addlethorpe PE24 90 B1
Skegness PE25 103 B8
Higgins Cl LN6 204 E7
Higgins Rd 5 LN13 75 E2
Higham Way 1 HU15 2 D5
High Barn La LN9 87 D3
Highbridge La PE11 145 C6
Highbridge Rd LN11 49 F2
High Bridge Rd DN8 15 C7
High Broadgate PE13 169 F7
High Bunning La NG34 143 A7
High Burgage DN15 2 B1
Highbury Dr PE12 215 E5
Highbury St PE1 226 A5
Highclere Rd PE7 230 D3
Highcliffe 5 LN5 107 A7
Highcliffe Rd NG31 211 B7
Highcliff Gdns DN15 182 E3
High Cliff Rd DN35 193 A6
High Cres PE9 171 C8
High Ct Way PE7 233 D8
Highdales HU10 178 C8
High Dike
Cranwell & Byard's Leap NG34 120 B8
Easton NG33 151 E8
Great Ponton NG33 140 C4
Navenby/Wellingore LN5 94 B1
North Rauceby NG32 120 A5
Old Somerby NG33 130 E2
Waddington LN5 93 F8
Welby NG31 130 E5
Wellingore LN5 107 B6
Wilsford NG32 119 F1
High Dyke Rd 2 NG34 107 C1
High Fen PE11 144 B4
HIGH FERRY PE22 126 A8
High Ferry La PE22 113 A1
Highfield Ave
4 Immingham DN40 186 B3
4 Lincoln LN6 205 B7
Highfield Ave *continued*
4 Mablethorpe/Sutton on Sea LN12 64 C1
Scunthorpe DN15 182 E3
Wellow DN32 191 E5
Highfield Cl
8 Barnby Dun DN3 14 A4
Foston NG32 117 F2
Gainsborough DN21 197 E5
7 Hatfield DN7 14 D5
8 North Thoresby DN36 36 B1
Osbournby NG34 132 C5
Highfield Cres
17 Barton-upon-Humber DN18 10 F8
Croxton Kerrial NG32 138 D3
4 Westwoodside DN9 27 B2
Highfield Dr
2 Kirton in Lindsey DN21 30 B1
Stapleford LN6 105 A6
Highfield Gr DN20 196 C5
Highfield La
Halton Holegate PE23 101 B8
Revesby PE22 99 B5
Highfield Rd Bainton PE9 172 A4
7 Donington PE11 134 F2
North Thoresby DN36 36 B1
14 Saxilby LN1 66 D2
High Field Rd DN20 196 F5
Highfields
6 Barrowby NG32 210 A5
1 Barrow upon Humber DN19 11 C7
17 Crowle DN17 16 D8
2 Nettleham LN2 68 D2
Highfields La DN14 7 D4
High Fields La PE11 156 E8
Highfields Ms 9 NG31 129 D5
Highfields Rise 29 LN4 95 C4
Highfields Sch NG24 104 B3
Highfield Terr
4 Glentham LN8 43 F1
2 Lincoln LN6 205 A2
Highfield Wy 23 HU14 3 A4
High Garth DN17 184 F2
Highgate
6 Cleethorpes DN35 192 F5
Leverton Outgate PE22 127 B7
High Gate
Helpringham NG34 133 D7
Mablethorpe & Sutton LN12 64 C1
Theddlethorpe St Helen LN12 63 D5
Highgate Cl 3 LN12 64 C1
Highgate La
Claxby with Moorby PE22 99 B6
Normanby by Spital LN8 56 B7
Owmby LN8 55 F6
12 Trusthorpe LN12 64 C1
Highgrove
1 Long Sutton PE12 216 B5
4 Messingham DN17 29 D7
Highgrove Cres PE21 209 C6
Highgrove Gdns PE9 218 E5
High Holme Rd LN11 198 B6
High Horse Mus★ PE22 111 D8
High House Rd DN22 52 A2
High La Croft PE24 102 D6
Mareham on the Hill LN9 85 F2
Highlands 1 PE9 163 C1
Highlands Way PE9 218 F5
Highland Tarn DN40 186 B3
High Leas 1 LN2 68 D2
Highlees Prim Sch PE3 225 C6
High Levels Bank DN8 15 F5
High Leys Rd DN17 184 F3
HIGH MARNHAM NG23 78 B5
High Mdw Grantham NG31 210 D4
Heighington/Washingborough LN4 203 C1
Westborough & Dry Doddington NG23 117 F5
High Mdws 1 Fiskerton LN3 82 A7
Kingston upon Hull HU10 178 C8
High or Main Rd PE12 215 A2
High Point Ret Pk DN31 189 A1
High Rd Barrowby NG32 210 A5
Elloughton-cum-Brough HU15 2 D7
Gorefield PE13 169 F2
Grantham NG31 211 C8
Hough-on-the-Hill NG32 119 A5
Londonthorpe & Harrowby Without NG31 130 D4
Moulton PE12 158 A7
Newton PE13 169 F5
Salmonby LN9 86 E8
Weston PE12 157 C7
Wisbech St Mary PE13 177 F2
High Ridge Comp Sch DN15 182 E3
High Ridge Sports Hall DN15 182 E3
HIGH RISBY DN15 9 A1
High St E DN15 183 C3
High St N 16 NG34 108 E2
High St S
3 Ruskington NG34 108 E1
20 Ruskington NG34 108 E2
High St St Martin's PE9 219 C3
High St W DN21 29 B4
High Side PE13 169 D2
High St 8 Alford LN13 75 F3
Alvingham LN11 49 F2
Barrow upon Humber DN19 11 D8
Barton-upon-Humber DN18 3 E1
Bassingham LN5 92 F2
Baumber LN9 85 A8
1 Beckingham DN10 52 B8
Belton DN9 16 E1
High St *continued*
Benniworth LN8 71 F8
Bicker PE20 135 A4
Binbrook LN8 47 C4
Blyton DN21 41 C5
Boston PE21 208 F3
Bottesford NG13 128 A5
Branston LN4 81 E2
Brant Broughton LN5 105 F4
Broughton DN20 19 D3
Burgh le Marsh PE24 102 E8
Burringham DN17 17 D4
Caistor LN7 33 B4
Carlby PE9 163 D4
Carlton-le-Moorland LN5 105 E8
Castle Bytham NG33 152 D1
Castor PE5 223 F2
Caythorpe NG32 119 B7
Cherry Willingham/Reepham LN3 203 D5
Cleethorpes DN35 192 E6
Collingham NG23 91 D4
3 Collyweston PE9 171 B1
Colsterworth NG33 151 D6
Coningsby LN4 207 A4
Corby Glen NG33 152 E8
Corringham DN21 41 E1
9 Crowle DN17 16 D7
Donington PE11 134 E2
Eagle & Swinethorpe LN6 79 B2
East Ferry DN21 28 B2
Eastoft DN17 7 A3
3 Easton on the Hill PE9 171 D3
Elkington LN11 60 E7
Epworth DN9 27 D7
Eye PE6 175 A1
Faldingworth LN8 56 F3
Fillingham DN21 54 F4
3 Fiskerton LN3 82 A7
Flixborough DN15 8 B2
5 Fulbeck NG32 106 C1
Fulletby LN9 86 B8
Gainsborough DN21 197 D3
Garthorpe & Fockerby DN17 7 E5
Gate Burton DN21 53 A1
Girton NG23 78 C1
Glentham LN8 43 F1
Glinton PE6 220 C8
Gosberton PE11 145 B6
Grainthorpe LN11 50 B8
Grantham NG31 211 A4
Great Gonerby NG31 129 D5
Great Limber DN37 22 D3
Gringley on the Hill DN10 39 C1
Hagworthingham PE23 87 A4
Harby NG23 79 C5
Harlaxton NG32 139 C7
Harmston LN5 93 F5
Hatfield DN7 14 C2
Haxey DN9 27 C2
16 Heckington NG34 122 E2
Heighington/Washingborough LN4 203 B2
Helpringham NG34 133 D7
Hogsthorpe PE24 90 B7
Holbeach PE12 215 E2
Horbling NG34 133 B2
Horncastle LN9 199 B4
Humberside Airport DN39 22 A6
Ingham LN1 54 F2
2 Ingoldmells PE25 90 E3
Ketton PE9 171 A3
Kexby DN21 53 E5
Kingston upon Hull HU1 181 A5
18 Kirton in Lindsey DN21 30 B1
Laceby DN37 23 F1
Leadenham LN5 106 D3
Lincoln LN5 234 A1
2 Little Bytham NG33 163 A8
Long Sutton PE12 216 C4
Luddington & Haldenby DN17 7 C4
18 Mablethorpe/Sutton on Sea LN12 64 B4
Market Deeping PE6 217 B4
Market Stainton LN8 72 A6
Martin LN4 96 C2
Marton DN21 65 D8
Maxey PE6 217 A1
Messingham DN17 29 D7
Metheringham LN4 95 C4
Misterton DN10 39 F5
5 Morton PE10 154 C7
Moulton PE12 157 F6
12 Navenby/Wellingore LN5 107 A7
Nettleham LN2 68 C2
Nettleton LN7 33 C2
Newton on Trent LN1 65 D1
North Ferriby HU14 3 A5
8 North Kelsey LN7 32 A4
Northorpe PE10 164 C7
North Scarle LN6 78 E1
North Thoresby DN36 36 A1
Osbournby NG34 132 C5
Owston Ferry DN9 28 B3
Peterborough PE2 231 A6
Pointon & Sempringham NG34 143 B7
Redbourne DN21 30 F2
Reepham LN3 203 F8
Rippingale PE10 142 F2
Ropsley NG33 131 B1
Roxby cum Risby DN15 8 E1
Saxilby LN1 66 D2
Scampton LN1 67 C6
Scotton DN21 29 C1
Scunthorpe DN15 183 A3
Sixhills LN8 59 A7

High St *continued*
Skegness PE25 . . . . .206 C3
Skellingthorpe LN6 . . . . .200 A5
Snitterby DN21 . . . . .43 D5
South Clifton NG23 . . . . .78 C5
South Ferriby DN18 . . . . .10 A7
South Kyme LN4 . . . . .123 B8
South Witham NG33 . . . . .151 D2
Spalding PE11 . . . . .214 E4
7 Spilsby PE23 . . . . .88 A1
Stamford PE9 . . . . .219 C5
Staunton NG13 . . . . .117 A2
Sturton by Stow LN1 . . . . .66 C7
5 Sutton Bridge PE12 . . . . . .160 F4
Swayfield NG33 . . . . .152 D5
Swinderby LN6 . . . . .92 A5
Swineshead PE20 . . . . .135 B7
Swinstead NG33 . . . . .153 A5
Upton DN21 . . . . .53 D5
Waddingham DN21 . . . . .43 D7
Waddington LN5 . . . . .93 F7
Wainfleet All Saints PE24 . . . .102 D1
Walcott LN4 . . . . .109 D7
Walesby LN8 . . . . .46 B5
Walkeringham DN10 . . . . .39 F3
1 Waltham DN37 . . . . .194 E4
Welbourn LN5 . . . . .106 E5
West/East Butterwick DN17 . . .17 D1
Willingham by Stow DN21 . . . . .53 E3
11 Winterton DN15 . . . . .9 A5
Wootton DN39 . . . . .11 E2
Wroot DN9 . . . . .26 D6
Highstock La PE12 . . . . .168 D1
High Thorpe Cres DN35 . . . .192 D3
High Thorpe Rd LN3 . . . . .83 D1
HIGH TOYNTON LN9 . . . . .86 A4
High Wash Dro 2 PE6 . . . . . .166 E1
Highwood Mews DN35 . . . . .192 E5
Higney Rd PE7 . . . . .230 C1
Higson Rd 4 LN1 . . . . .201 D7
Hilary Gr HU4 . . . . .179 B2
Hilary Rd DN33 . . . . .194 F7
Hilda Cl 6 NG34 . . . . .212 B2
Hildas Ave HU5 . . . . .180 A8
Hilda St 4 Boston PE21 . . . .209 A7
Grimsby DN32 . . . . .189 C1
Hildreds Sh Ctr PE25 . . . . . .206 D3
Hildyard Cl 1 HU10 . . . . .178 F6
Hildyard St DN32 . . . . .192 B8
Hiles Ave 6 DN15 . . . . .9 A5
Hill Abbey LN4 . . . . .95 D7
Hillary Cl 8 Spalding PE11 . .214 B2
1 Stamford PE9 . . . . .219 D6
Hillary Rd DN16 . . . . .185 B5
Hillary Way DN37 . . . . .190 E8
Hill Ave NG31 . . . . .211 B5
Hill Brow HU10 . . . . .178 B6
Hill Cl PE1 . . . . .226 D5
Hill Cres DN21 . . . . .197 F5
Hillcrest NG34 . . . . .107 C2
Hillcrest Ave
Kingston upon Hull HU13 . . . . .178 C2
Yaxley PE7 . . . . .233 E5
Hillcrest Dr 2 DN15 . . . . .8 A4
Hillcrest Early Years Acad
DN21 . . . . .197 F4
Hillcrest Gdns 3 PE20 . . . . .135 B7
Hillcroft 1 LN4 . . . . .203 A2
Hill Ct NG31 . . . . .210 D2
HILLDYKE PE22 . . . . .126 A6
Hill Field 3 PE24 . . . . .102 D2
Hillfoot Dr DN17 . . . . .184 E3
Hillgate PE12 . . . . .168 C2
Hillgate St PE34 . . . . .161 F3
Hillingford Way NG31 . . . . . .210 E3
Hill La PE20 . . . . .136 B5
Hillman Cl LN4 . . . . .205 F3
Hillman Rd HU13 . . . . .178 F3
Hill Rd DN21 . . . . .41 E1
Hill Rise 8 Brough HU15 . . . . .2 C6
Coleby LN5 . . . . .93 F3
Louth LN11 . . . . .198 A7
Hill's Ct 9 NG34 . . . . .212 D4
Hills Dr 14 DN36 . . . . .36 D4
Hillside 4 Ancaster NG32 . . .120 A2
Beckingham LN5 . . . . .105 B4
3 Marton DN21 . . . . .65 E8
Hillside App 5 LN2 . . . . .202 C3
Hillside Ave Lincoln LN2 . . . .202 C3
7 Mablethorpe/Sutton on Sea
LN12 .77 A8
Hillside Cl Ufford PE9 . . . . . .172 F2
Ufford PE9 . . . . .172 F2
Hillside Cres
Barnetby le Wold DN38 . . . . . . .21 B5
3 Grantham NG31 . . . . .211 D2
Hillside Dr
5 Barton-upon-Humber
DN18 .10 E8
Grantham NG31 . . . . .211 D2
Hillside Est NG34 . . . . .108 F2
Hillside Gdns 25 PE8 . . . . . .172 B1
Hillside Rd
6 Broughton DN20 . . . . .19 E4
Glentworth DN21 . . . . .54 F7
Woolsthorpe by Belvoir
NG32 . . . . .128 D1
Hillstead Cl 13 DN36 . . . . . . .36 D4
Hillsyde Ave 11 DN10 . . . . . .39 F5
Hill Terr LN11 . . . . .198 C4
Hill The 4 Saltfleet LN11 . . . .51 C4
Skellingthorpe LN6 . . . . .200 A4
Worlaby DN20 . . . . .10 E1
Hill Top 1 LN5 . . . . .93 E5
Hilltop Ave DN15 . . . . .182 D5
Hilltop Cl LN6 . . . . .79 B2
Hilltop Gdns DN17 . . . . .29 C7
Hill Top La 1 DN21 . . . . .41 B5

Hill Top Pl DN34 . . . . .190 D3
Hill View Cl NG31 . . . . .210 E3
Hill View Rd 14 NG33 . . . . . .151 D2
Hillward Cl PE12 . . . . .230 C6
Hilmore Rd DN34 . . . . .190 C4
Hilton Ave DN15 . . . . .182 B3
Hilton Cl 2 DN9 . . . . .16 E2
Hilton Ct DN35 . . . . .193 B1
Hilton's La PE20 . . . . .136 E1
Hinaidi La LN4 . . . . .95 C7
Hinchcliffe PE2 . . . . .229 E2
Hindon Wlk DN17 . . . . .184 C8
Hine Ave NG24 . . . . .104 B4
Hinkler St DN35 . . . . .192 E5
Hinkley Dr DN40 . . . . .186 B5
Hinman Wlk 9 DN15 . . . . . . .183 B3
Hipper La PE20 . . . . .135 D2
Hither Old Gate PE12 . . . . . .158 D6
Hives La LN6 . . . . .78 E2
Hix Cl PE12 . . . . .215 C2
Hix's La PE13 . . . . .160 A1
Hobart Cl 11 LN5 . . . . .93 E8
Hobart Rd NG31 . . . . .211 D7
Hobart St HU3 . . . . .180 D5
Hobb La 4 DN21 . . . . .29 C3
Hobbs Gdns PE9 . . . . .218 E4
Hobhole Bank PE22 . . . . . . .126 D8
Hobhole Bank Nature
Reserve ★ PE21 . . . . .137 C7
Hob La PE12 . . . . .125 D6
Hobson Rd 7 HU15 . . . . .2 C6
Hobsons Gn PE11 . . . . .214 A5
Hobson Way DN41 . . . . .187 E2
Hockland Rd PE13 . . . . .169 F7
Hockle's Gate PE12 . . . . .159 B7
Hockney Hole La PE12 . . . . .158 A7
Hodder Cl 1 NG31 . . . . .210 F3
Hoddesdon Cres 20 DN7 . . .14 D3
Hoddins Wy PE12 . . . . .216 A6
Hod Fen Dro PE7 . . . . .233 F2
Hodge Ct 3 HU9 . . . . .181 C7
Hodgeoft La LN13 . . . . .63 E1
Hodgson Ave PE4 . . . . .220 E6
Hodgson St HU8 . . . . .181 A7
Hodgson Way 3 LN12 . . . . . . .77 A8
Hodney Rd 3 PE6 . . . . .175 A1
Hodson Cl LN6 . . . . .200 B5
Hodson Gn LN9 . . . . .199 C4
Hodsons Marsh PE25 . . . . . .103 A1
Hoe DN **19** LN8 . . . . .57 D8
Hoekman Dr 3 PE11 . . . . . . .214 B2
Hoekman Way PE11 . . . . . . .214 B2
Hoffleet Rd PE20 . . . . .135 C4
HOFFLEET STOW PE20 . . . . .135 C4
Hogens La PE13 . . . . .170 A5
Hoggard La DN14 . . . . .7 E8
Hogg La HU10 . . . . .178 B8
Hog's Gate PE12 . . . . .158 A6
HOGSTHORPE PE24 . . . . .90 B6
Hogsthorpe Com Prim Sch
PE24 .90 B7
Hogsthorpe Rd LN13 . . . . . . .76 F1
HOLBEACH PE12 . . . . .215 C3
HOLBEACH BANK PE12 . . . . .215 C7
Holbeach Bank Acad
PE12 .215 D7
HOLBEACH CLOUGH PE12 . . .215 B7
Holbeach & District Nature
Reserve ★ PE12 . . . . .215 E2
Holbeach Dro Gate PE12 . . .168 C4
HOLBEACH DROVE PE12 . . . .168 B3
Holbeach Hospl PE12 . . . . . .215 B5
HOLBEACH HURN PE12 . . . . .147 F2
Holbeach Prim Sch PE12 . . .215 D3
1 Spalding PE12 . . . . .157 B6
HOLBEACH ST JOHNS
PE12 .158 E1
HOLBEACH ST MARKS
PE12 .147 D6
Holbeach St Marks CE Prim
Sch PE12 . . . . .147 D6
HOLBEACH ST MATTHEW
PE12 .148 A7
Holbeach Tecnology Pk
PE12 .215 B4
Holbeck Pl 2 DN40 . . . . .186 B4
Holborn Rd PE11 . . . . .214 B2
Holborn St HU8 . . . . .181 B7
Holcroft PE2 . . . . .230 B3
Holdan Cl DN36 . . . . .193 A1
Holdenby Cl 3 LN2 . . . . .202 E7
Holden Dr 9 PE24 . . . . .102 E7
Holden Way 7 NG31 . . . . . . .129 E5
Holderness Rd HU9 . . . . .181 C8
Holdfield PE3 . . . . .225 B6
Holdich St PE3 . . . . .225 E2
HOLDINGHAM NG34 . . . . . . .212 C1
Holdingham La NG34 . . . . . .121 E7
Hole Gate PE23 . . . . .101 C8
Holgate La PE4 . . . . .220 F7
Holgate Pl 20 Swanland HU4 .3 B7
18 Swanland HU14 . . . . .3 B7
Holgate Rd DN16 . . . . .185 D6
Holkham Rd PE2 . . . . .229 D3
Holland Ave
18 Crowle DN17 . . . . .16 D8
Peterborough PE4 . . . . .221 B1
Scunthorpe DN15 . . . . .182 E4
Holland Cl 8 Bourne PE10 . . .213 C5
10 Market Deeping PE6 . . . . .217 A6
Peterborough PE4 . . . . .221 B1
Holland Dr 7 Grasby DN38 . . .32 B7
Skegness PE25 . . . . .206 C1
Holland La PE22 . . . . .114 F4
Holland Mkt 16 PE11 . . . . . .214 D4
Holland Rd Horbling NG34 . .133 B3
Spalding PE11 . . . . .214 E4

Holland Rd *continued*
Stamford PE9 . . . . .219 C6
Swaton NG34 . . . . .133 A3
Holland's Chase PE11 . . . . . .156 A6
Holland St HU9 . . . . .181 D8
Holland Way PE12 . . . . .215 B2
Hollengs La 1 LN11 . . . . .59 E1
Holles St 8 DN32 . . . . .191 E8
Hollies Ave 14 NG24 . . . . . . .104 A6
Hollies The PE12 . . . . .215 E3
Hollin Bridge La DN7 . . . . . . .15 A3
Hollingsworth Ave 1
DN40 . . . . .186 B4
Hollingsworth Cl 5 DN35 .192 D2
Hollingsworth La DN9 . . . . . .27 E6
Hollis' Rd NG31 . . . . .210 F2
Hollowbrook Cl 3 NG34 . . . .108 D2
Hollowdyke La NG24 . . . . . . .104 C1
Hollowgate Hill DN21 . . . . . . .42 E4
Hollowgate La NG23 . . . . .78 A5
Hollowside Rd PE7 . . . . .233 B8
Hollows The 4 LN11 . . . . .61 F3
Holly Cl
Cherry Willingham/Reepham
LN3 .203 E5
5 Grantham NG31 . . . . .211 D2
Horncastle LN9 . . . . .199 A5
Lincoln LN5 . . . . .205 D5
2 Newborough PE6 . . . . .174 E5
Scunthorpe DN16 . . . . .185 C4
1 Sleaford NG34 . . . . .212 D2
6 Stallingborough DN41 . . . . .23 E6
Holly Cres LN11 . . . . .198 E3
Holly Dr Bourne PE10 . . . . . .213 C5
Hessle HU13 . . . . .178 D3
Holly Hill 1 HU15 . . . . .2 E6
Holly Rd PE25 . . . . .206 A2
Holly St LN5 . . . . .205 D5
Hollytree Ave 2 HU5 . . . . . . .179 B7
Holly Tree Cl 9 LN8 . . . . .57 D7
Holly Way 2 PE6 . . . . .217 D4
Hollywell Rd LN5 . . . . .205 D1
Hollywell Rd (The Rookery) 23
LN13 .75 F2
Holly Wlk PE7 . . . . .230 D3
Hollywood Dr 8 NG31 . . . . . .210 F7
HOLME Holme DN16 . . . . .19 A1
Holme NG23 . . . . .91 A4
Holme Ave DN36 . . . . .195 C6
Holme Cl Brigg DN20 . . . . . . .196 D4
Castor PE5 . . . . .223 D2
Thorpe on the Hill LN6 . . . . . . .92 F8
Tinwell PE9 . . . . .218 D3
Holme Dene 1 DN9 . . . . .27 C2
Holme Dr
Burton upon Stather DN15 . . . . .8 B5
Sudbrooke LN2 . . . . .68 F2
Holme Gdns 7 DN7 . . . . .14 C7
Holme Hall Ave DN16 . . . . . .185 B3
HOLME HILL DN32 . . . . .191 E6
Holme La Grassthorpe NG23 .78 A2
Holme DN16 . . . . .185 E2
Marnham NG23 . . . . .78 A4
Messingham DN17 . . . . .29 E8
4 Ruskington NG34 . . . . . . .108 E1
Scunthorpe DN16 . . . . .185 B3
Winthorpe NG24 . . . . .104 B8
HOLME RD DN20 . . . . .135 F8
Holme Rd PE7 . . . . .233 E4
Holmes Cl Louth LN11 . . . . . .198 B7
2 Skidbrooke with Saltfleet
Haven LN11 . . . . .51 C4
Holmes Dr 10 DN7 . . . . .171 A3
Holmes Field 6 LN5 . . . . .92 F3
Holmes La
North Somercotes LN11 . . . . . .38 A1
Roxby cum Risby DN15 . . . . . . .9 D5
2 Welton/Dunholme LN2 . . . . .68 E6
Holmes Rd Frampton PE20 . .124 F1
Glinton PE6 . . . . .220 D7
Horsington LN10 . . . . .83 F1
Kirton PE20 . . . . .136 A8
Stickney PE22 . . . . .113 A7
Stixwould & Woodhall LN10 . . .84 A1
Holmes Road DN10 . . . . .40 B2
Holme St DN32 . . . . .191 E7
Holmes Way
Horncastle LN9 . . . . .199 D1
Peterborough PE4 . . . . .221 D2
Wragby LN8 . . . . .70 C5
Holme Valley Prim Sch
DN16 . . . . .185 C3
Holme Wlk 6 DN21 . . . . .197 F5
Holme Wood Ct 5 DN3 . . . . .14 A1
Holme Wood La
Claxby with Moorby LN9 . . . . . .99 B8
Hameringham LN9 . . . . .86 B1
Holmfield LN3 . . . . .82 B7
Holmfirth Rd DN15 . . . . .182 C4
Holm La NG23 . . . . .104 F1
Holm Rd DN9 . . . . .27 B2
Holmshaw Cl 24 DN3 . . . . . . .14 A2
Holstein Dr DN16 . . . . .185 A2
Holt Cl 10 Lincoln LN6 . . . . . . .93 C8
9 Wittering PE8 . . . . .172 B1
Holt La Horncastle LN9 . . . . .199 D4
Mareham le Fen PE22 . . . . . . .99 A3
Holton Cl DN36 . . . . .195 C1
HOLTON CUM BECKERING
LN8 . . . . .70 C8
HOLTON LE CLAY DN36 . . . .195 D2
Holton-le-Clay Inf Sch
DN36 . . . . .195 D2
Holton le Clay Jun Sch
DN36 . . . . .195 E1
HOLTON LE MOOR LN7 . . . . .45 D4
Holton Mount DN36 . . . . . . .195 C2
Holton Rd Nettleton LN7 . . . . .33 A2

Holton Rd *continued*
South Kelsey LN7 . . . . .32 D1
Tetney DN36 . . . . .195 F1
Holt Prim Sch The LN6 . . . . .200 A3
Holt The DN21 . . . . .197 F5
Holy Cross Gdns 12 NG32 .119 B7
Holydyke DN18 . . . . .10 E8
Holy Family Cath Prim Sch
DN7 . . . . .14 C6
Holyoake Rd DN32 . . . . .192 C6
Holyroad Dr DN15 . . . . .182 D7
Holyrood Cl PE20 . . . . .134 E3
Holyrood Wlk PE11 . . . . .214 E2
Holy Trinity CE Prim Sch
LN4 .207 A5
Holywell Cl 1 PE3 . . . . .225 A1
Holy Well La LN11 . . . . .49 A4
Holywell Rd PE9 . . . . .162 E8
Holywell Way PE3 . . . . .224 F2
Home Beat Dr DN20 . . . . .19 C3
Home Cl 7 Bourne PE10 . . . .213 C7
Bracebridge Heath LN4 . . . . . .205 F3
Kingston upon Hull HU4 . . . . .179 C5
8 Lincoln LN5 . . . . .107 A7
Home Farm Cl
Great Casterton PE9 . . . . .218 C8
Laughterton LN1 . . . . .65 D2
Homefarm La NG23 . . . . .79 A7
Homefield Ave DN31 . . . . . . .191 D3
Home Paddock DN37 . . . . . .194 E4
Home Pasture 4 PE4 . . . . . . .220 F5
Home Pk 4 NG34 . . . . .120 F8
Homers La PE22 . . . . .126 D4
Home St DN15 . . . . .183 B4
Homestead Garth 11 DN7 . . .14 D4
Homestead Gdns 17 PE10 .164 E8
Honeyhill PE4 . . . . .221 E1
Honeyhill Rd LN5 . . . . .169 C2
Honeyholes La LN2 . . . . .68 D6
Honey Pot Cl LN2 . . . . .202 E7
Honey Pot La NG33 . . . . .151 F4
Honey Pot Lane Ind Est
LN34 .151 F4
Honeysuckle Cl
4 Lincoln LN5 . . . . .205 C2
14 Mablethorpe & Sutton
LN12 .76 F8
18 Sutton on Sea Ln11 . . . . . .76 F8
Honeysuckle Ct
Humberston DN35 . . . . .192 E1
Peterborough PE2 . . . . .230 D7
3 Scunthorpe DN16 . . . . .185 D4
Honeysuckle La 16 LN8 . . . . .70 D4
Honeysuckle Pl 19 HU15 . . . .2 C5
HONINGTON NG32 . . . . .119 C2
Honington App 5 LN1 . . . . . .201 D7
Honington Cres LN1 . . . . .201 D7
Honington Rd 2 NG32 . . . . . .130 B8
Honningsvaag Cl DN36 . . . . .195 D7
Hood Cl NG34 . . . . .212 A3
Hood Rd DN17 . . . . .184 D6
Hood St
Kingston upon Hull HU8 . . . . .181 A8
8 Lincoln LN5 . . . . .201 F1
Hook's Dro PE13 . . . . .177 C4
Hooks La LN5 . . . . .106 E6
Hoop End DN36 . . . . .36 D4
Hoopers Cl 4 NG13 . . . . .128 A5
Hoop La LN8 . . . . .70 E2
Hope Gdns PE21 . . . . .208 F6
Hope House Sch NG24 . . . . .104 C3
Hope St Cleethorpes DN35 . .193 A5
Grimsby DN32 . . . . .191 F8
Lincoln LN5 . . . . .201 F1
Hopfield DN20 . . . . .31 A5
Hopgardens 1 DN21 . . . . .53 E3
Hopgarth 11 DN9 . . . . .27 D2
Hop Hills La DN7 . . . . .14 D5
Hopkins Ave DN17 . . . . .185 A7
Hoplands Cl DN36 . . . . .195 E7
Hoplands Rd LN4 . . . . .207 D5
Hoplands The 4 DN34 . . . . .212 F4
Hopland's Wood Nature
Reserve ★ LN13 . . . . .88 F6
HOP POLE PE11 . . . . .165 F5
Hopton St LN9 . . . . .199 B3
Hopwood Cl HU3 . . . . .180 D8
Hopyard La Bassingham LN5 .93 B1
Normanton on Trent NG23 . . . .78 A3
Horace St PE21 . . . . .208 E5
HORBLING NG34 . . . . .133 C2
Horbling Fen Dro NG34 . . . . .133 D2
Horbling La PE22 . . . . .113 A7
Horbling Line Nature
Reserve ★ NG34 . . . . .133 B1
Horbury Cl DN15 . . . . .182 D4
HORKSTOW DN18 . . . . .10 A5
Horkstow Rd DN18 . . . . .10 E7
Hornbeam Ave DN16 . . . . . . .185 B4
Hornbeam Cl 17 NG34 . . . . .108 E1
Hornbeam Dr DN41 . . . . .23 C5
Hornbeam Rd PE7 . . . . .230 B2
Hornby Dr 20 LN12 . . . . .77 A7
HORNCASTLE LN9 . . . . .199 D3
Horncastle Cty Prim Sch
LN9 .199 C4
Horncastle Hill PE23 . . . . .87 A1
Horncastle La
Dunholme LN2 . . . . .68 B5
Grange de Lings LN1 . . . . .67 F5
Horncastle Rd Bardney LN3 . .83 C4
Boston PE21 . . . . .208 F8
Fishtoft PE21 . . . . .125 C5
Fulletby LN9 . . . . .86 A7
Goulceby LN11 . . . . .72 C5
Horsington LN10 . . . . .84 D4
Louth LN11 . . . . .198 A4
Mareham le Fen PE22 . . . . .98 F4

Hig–Hub **257**

Horncastle Rd *continued*
Raithby cum Maltby LN11 . . . .60 F2
Roughton LN9 . . . . .85 C2
Tathwell LN11 . . . . .73 A8
West Ashby LN9 . . . . .199 C8
Woodhall Spa LN10 . . . . .97 F6
Wragby LN8 . . . . .70 D4
Horncastle St Lawrence Sch
The LN9 . . . . .199 D4
Horne La 3 NG22 . . . . .65 B1
Horner Cl 1 LN5 . . . . .205 C2
Horn Lane LE15 . . . . .162 A1
Hornsby Cres DN15 . . . . .182 F4
Hornsby Rd NG31 . . . . .210 E2
Hornsea Parade 4 HU9 . . . . .181 C8
Hornsey Hill Rd DN21 . . . . . . .28 D1
Horn The 1 PE25 . . . . .206 A7
Horse Fair Gn 25 DN8 . . . . . .15 A8
Horse Fayre 7 PE11 . . . . .214 A3
Horsegate PE6 . . . . .217 D4
Horsegate Field Rd DN19 . . . .5 B2
Horseham's La PE20 . . . . . . .135 A5
Horse Mkt 24 LN7 . . . . .33 B4
Horsemoor Dro PE12 . . . . . . .159 B1
Horsemoor La LN9 . . . . .72 C2
Horse Pasture La PE22 . . . . . .65 C7
Horsepit La 12 PE11 . . . . . . .145 C1
Horseshoe Cl
7 Grimsby DN33 . . . . .194 D8
12 Ruskington NG34 . . . . . . .108 D2
Horseshoe La PE20 . . . . .136 D5
Horseshoe Rd PE11 . . . . .214 A2
Horseshoe Terr PE13 . . . . . . .170 C1
Horseshoe Way
Hampton Vale PE7 . . . . .230 D1
Yaxley PE7 . . . . .233 D8
Horseshoe Yd 11 PE6 . . . . . .166 E1
Horsewells St LN10 . . . . .39 C1
HORSINGTON LN10 . . . . .84 C3
Horstead Ave DN20 . . . . .196 D5
Horton St LN2 . . . . .202 C3
Horton Wlk PE3 . . . . .225 C5
Hospital Dro PE12 . . . . .160 C3
Hospital La PE21 . . . . .209 A6
Hospital Rd PE12 . . . . .161 A5
Hotchkin Ave LN1 . . . . .66 E2
Hotham Dr HU5 . . . . .179 B8
Hotham Rd HU5 . . . . .179 A8
Hotham Rd S HU5 . . . . .179 B8
Hotham St HU9 . . . . .181 D7
Hotspur Rd DN21 . . . . .197 C6
HOUGHAM NG32 . . . . .118 C3
Hougham Rd
Hougham NG32 . . . . .118 B4
Westborough & Dry Doddington
NG23 . . . . .117 F5
Hough La
Carlton Scroop NG32 . . . . .119 C4
Claypole NG23 . . . . .117 F7
HOUGH-ON-THE-HILL
NG32 . . . . .119 A5
Hough Rd Barkston NG32 . . .130 B8
Carlton Scroop NG32 . . . . .119 A3
Hough-on-the-Hill NG32 . . . . .118 E7
Houghton Ave PE2 . . . . .231 F5
Houghton Rd NG31 . . . . .211 C2
Houghton Road Ind Est
NG31 . . . . .211 C1
Houlden Way 1 NG34 . . . . . .122 E3
Hounsfield Cl
9 Beacon Hill NG24 . . . . . . .104 C4
Newark-on-Trent NG24 . . . . . .104 B5
Houps Rd 8 DN8 . . . . .15 B8
Hourne Ct HU13 . . . . .178 E2
Hourne The HU13 . . . . .178 E2
House Ct DN16 . . . . .185 D4
Househams La LN11 . . . . .61 F3
Howard Cl PE34 . . . . .161 F2
Howard Fields Wy LN11 . . . . .198 A7
Howard Gr DN32 . . . . .192 B6
Howard Rd 10 LN4 . . . . .108 A7
Howard's Gdns 1 NG24 . . . .104 B2
Howard St LN1 . . . . .201 C4
Howdale La NG32 . . . . .119 A3
Howdales LN11 . . . . .50 D1
Howdales Rd LN11 . . . . .50 E1
Howden Croft Hill HU15 . . . . .2 A8
Howe Ct 2 LN2 . . . . .202 D6
Howegate Dr PE7 . . . . .230 B1
Howe La
Ashby with Scremby PE23 . . . .88 C3
Goxhill DN19 . . . . .11 F8
HOWELL NG34 . . . . .122 D5
Howell Fen Dro NG34 . . . . . .122 D5
Howell Rd NG34 . . . . .122 E3
Howgarth La PE22 . . . . .114 F5
Howitts Rd 14 NG13 . . . . . . .128 A5
Howland Rd PE2 . . . . .230 A3
Howlett Rd DN35 . . . . .193 A4
HOWSHAM LN7 . . . . .32 A6
Howsham La 2 DN38 . . . . . . .32 D8
Howsham Lane DN38 . . . . . . .32 C7
Howsham Road LN7 . . . . .31 F6
Howville Ave 2 DN7 . . . . .14 F3
Howville Rd 1 DN7 . . . . .14 F3
Hoylake Cl DN21 . . . . .197 E6
Hoylake Dr
1 Immingham DN40 . . . . . . .186 D5
Peterborough PE7 . . . . .231 C5
Skegness PE25 . . . . .206 D5
Hoylake Rd DN17 . . . . .184 D3
Hubba Cres PE10 . . . . .135 C6
Hubbard Cl 2 NG34 . . . . .122 D3
HUBBERT'S BRIDGE PE20 . . .124 F2
Hubberts Bridge Sta PE20 .124 E2

Hubert's Cl PE12 . . . . .168 C1
Hub The★ NG34 . . . . .212 E4
Huckles Way PE25 . . . . . . .206 B6
Huddleston Rd DN32 . . . .192 B7
Hudson Ave Kirk Ella HU10 .178 D5
  Scunthorpe DN15 . . . . . . .182 E5
Hudson Cl PE23 . . . . .88 B3
Hudson Ct HU13 . . . . .178 D1
Hudson Dr LN4 . . . . .207 E6
Hudson Gr 3 PE7 . . . . . . .230 F5
Hudson Rd 4 PE11 . . . . .214 C2
Hudson's Gdns 5 PE21 . . .209 B4
Hudson St HU3 . . . . .180 D8
Hudson Way
  Grantham NG31 . . . . .211 A3
  12 Skegness PE25 . . . . . .206 A5
Huggin Carr Rd DN7 . . . . . . .14 F1
Hughes Ford Way 20 LN1 . .66 D2
Hugh Hill La DN7 . . . . .14 E5
Hughson Wlk 3 LN2 . . . . . .68 E6
Hulberry Cl 10 DN41 . . . . . .23 A4
Hull Arena★ HU1 . . . . .180 E4
Hull Coll
  Kingston upon Hull HU1 . . . .181 A7
  Kingston upon Hull HU2 . . . .180 D7
Hull Collegiate Sch HU10 .178 D5
Hull & E Riding Mus★
  HU9 . . . . .181 A6
Hull Maritime Mus★ HU1 180 F6
Hull Rd HU13 . . . . .178 F1
Hull Royal Infirmary HU3 . .180 C6
Hull's Dro PE6 . . . . .167 D3
Hull Sta HU1 . . . . .180 E6
Hull Trinity House Acad
  HU1 . . . . .180 E6
Hull Trinity House Sch
  HU1 . . . . .180 F6
Hull Truck Theatre★ HU2 .180 D7
Humber Bank Factories
  DN41 . . . . .187 D4
Humber Bank S DN31 . . . . .189 C2
Humber Bridge Rd DN31 . .189 C1
Humber Cres
  6 Brough HU15 . . . . .2 C5
  Scunthorpe DN17 . . . . .184 F6
Humberdale Cl 5 HU14 . . .3 B6
Humberdale Dr HU14 . . . . .3 C5
Humber Dock St HU1 . . . .180 F5
Humber Dr 8 PE11 . . . . . .214 A4
Humber Rd
  Barton-upon-Humber DN18 . .3 E1
  Immingham DN40 . . . . .186 A8
  North Ferriby HU14 . . . . .3 A4
Humberside DN15 . . . . .1 E3
Humberside Int Airport
  DN38 . . . . .21 F5
Humber St
  3 Cleethorpes DN35 . . . . .192 F5
  Grimsby DN31 . . . . .189 C1
  Kingston upon Hull HU1 . . . .180 F5
HUMBERSTON DN35 . . . . .193 A2
Humberston Acad DN36 . . .36 C8
Humberston Ave DN36 . . . .195 E6
Humberston CE Prim Sch The
  DN36 . . . . .36 D8
Humberston Cloverfields Acad
  DN36 . . . . .36 C8
Humberstone Holt 1 LN11 .50 F7
Humberstone Rd DN32 . . .192 A6
Humberston Fitties★ The 36 F8
Humberston Pk Specl Sch
  DN36 . . . . .36 C8
Humberston Rd
  Cleethorpes DN36 . . . . . . .192 C3
  Tetney DN36 . . . . .36 C6
Humber Terr DN31 . . . . . .191 C8
Humber View
  3 Barton-upon-Humber
    DN18 . . . . .10 E8
  Kingston upon Hull HU13 . . .178 C2
  4 Swanland HU14 . . . . . . .3 B6
Humberville Rd DN40 . . . .186 D4
HUMBY NG33 . . . . .141 C7
Humby Rd NG33 . . . . .141 B8
Hume Brae 6 DN40 . . . . .186 A8
Hume St 5 DN31 . . . . . . .191 C7
Hunchback La PE13 . . . . .170 E2
HUNDLEBY PE23 . . . . .87 F1
Hundlehouse La LN4 . . . . .111 D4
HUNDLE HOUSES LN4 . . . .111 C4
Hundle Houses La LN4 . . . .111 C4
Hund Oak Dr 9 DN7 . . . . . .14 D4
Hundreds La
  Gringley on the Hill DN10 . . . .39 A5
  Little Sutton PE12 . . . . . . .216 F1
Hundreds Rd PE6 . . . . . . .175 C6
Hungarton Ct 3 PE1 . . . . .226 D8
Hungate LN1 . . . . .234 B2
Hun Gate PE11 . . . . .145 D3
Hungate Rd NG32 . . . . . . .139 A7
Hungerdike Gate PE12 . . .215 A2
HUNGERTON NG32 . . . . . .139 B4
Hungram La LN9 . . . . .71 E1
Hungry Hill La LN11 . . . . . .62 C5
Hunsley Cres DN32 . . . . . .192 B4
Hunsley Dr 5 DN41 . . . . . .23 E6
Hunstan La PE22 . . . . .113 F4
Hunston Rd 4 LN10 . . . . . .97 C5
Huntcliff Sch DN21 . . . . . . .30 C1
Hunter Ave LN11 . . . . .62 C6
Hunter Gr 1 HU3 . . . . . . .180 A4
Hunter Pl LN11 . . . . .188 D4
Hunter Rd Brookenby LN8 . .47 A6
  Brough HU15 . . . . .2 C6
Hunters Cl 9 PE12 . . . . . .215 E2

Hunter's Croft 1 DN9 . . . . .27 D3
Hunters Dr 13 LN4 . . . . . . .95 C4
Hunter's Dr 5 DN10 . . . . . .39 C1
Hunters La Baumber LN9 . . . .72 A1
  Tattershall LN4 . . . . .207 C5
Hunters Rd NG24 . . . . . . .104 C2
Hunting Ave PE2 . . . . .230 F7
Huntingdon Cl 2 PE12 . . .215 E3
Huntingdon Cres 8 DN15. . .8 B4
Huntingdon Pl 5 PE10 . . . .213 C3
Huntingdon St HU4 . . . . . .179 B3
Huntingtower Com Prim Acad
  NG31 . . . . .211 A3
Huntingtower Rd NG31 . . .211 A3
Hunt Lea Ave
  Grantham NG31 . . . . .210 F1
  Lincoln LN6 . . . . .205 C8
Huntly Gr PE1 . . . . .226 A4
Huntly Rd PE2 . . . . .230 E7
Hunt Rd DN16 . . . . .185 C5
Hunts Cl 7 DN20 . . . . .19 E4
Huntsgate PE12 . . . . .159 D4
Hunt's Gate PE12 . . . . . . .159 E1
Hunts La 4 DN20 . . . . .30 F5
Huntsman Cl PE21 . . . . . .209 D2
Huntsmans Chase DN36 . .195 B7
Huntsmans Gate PE3 . . . .224 F3
Ingram Cres 9 DN7 . . . . . .14 C4
Hurdletree Bank PE12 . . . .158 E4
Hurdman Way PE25 . . . . . .90 E3
Hurd's Farm DN20 . . . . . . .20 D8
Hurford Pl DN37 . . . . .194 D7
Hurle Cres PE21 . . . . .208 D6
Hurlstone Cl 25 DN3 . . . . . .14 A2
Hurn Bank PE12 . . . . .147 E2
Hurnbridge Rd LN4 . . . . . .111 A4
Hurn Cl 2 Birchwood LN6 .204 B8
  7 Ruskington NG34 . . . . . .108 D1
Hurn Dro LN4 . . . . .110 A8
Hurn La PE22 . . . . .126 A7
Hurn Rd Holbeach PE12 . . .147 E1
  Marholm PE6 . . . . .220 C3
Hurns End PE22 . . . . .127 C7
HURN'S END PE22 . . . . . . .127 C8
Hurn The
  5 Billingborough NG34 . . . .133 B1
  Digby LN4 . . . . .108 E6
Hurricane Cl DN36 . . . . . .195 C4
Hurst Cres NG32 . . . . .210 A4
Hurst La DN17 . . . . .184 E3
Hurstlea Dr DN36 . . . . . . .193 B1
Hurst The 5 PE25 . . . . . . .206 A6
Hurstwood Cl LN2 . . . . . . .202 D8
Hurton's La LN11 . . . . .49 C6
Hussey Cl 3 NG34 . . . . . .212 E4
Hussey Twr★ PE21 . . . . . .209 A4
Husthwaite Rd 18 HU15 . . . .2 D5
Hutchinson Gdns 5 PE12 157 E7
Hutchinson Rd 2 DN35 . . .192 E7
Huteson La DN15 . . . . .8 C8
Hutson Dr LN6 . . . . .204 F2
HUTTOFT LN13 . . . . .76 E3
Huttoft Bank Pit nature
  Reserve★ LN13 . . . . .77 B6
Huttoft Prim Sch LN13 . . . .76 F3
Huttoft Rd
  17 Mablethorpe & Sutton
    LN12 . . . . .76 F8
  Thurlby LN13 . . . . .76 D2
Hutton Cl 3 PE11 . . . . . . .214 F2
Hutton Rd DN31 . . . . .189 B2
Hutt St HU3 . . . . .180 D7
Hyde Gdns PE6 . . . . .164 F3
Hyde Pk Cl 6 Lincoln LN6 .204 F1
  Nunsthorpe DN33 . . . . . . .191 B2
Hyde Way NG34 . . . . .212 C7
Hyholmes PE3 . . . . .224 F7
Hykeham Rd LN6 . . . . .205 B4
Hykeham Sta LN6 . . . . . . .204 D3
Hymers Ave HU3 . . . . .180 B7
Hymers Coll HU3 . . . . .180 B7
Hyperion St HU9 . . . . .181 A7
Hythegate PE4 . . . . .221 B4

I

Ibbott Cl PE2 . . . . .231 E5
Icehouse Rd HU3 . . . . .180 D6
Icelandic Cl HU3 . . . . .180 C5
Icknield Cl 17 LN4 . . . . . . .81 A1
Ickworth Rd NG34 . . . . . . .212 D3
Ida Rd PE25 . . . . .206 C3
Idas Cl HU9 . . . . .181 A5
Iddesleigh Rd 4 LN10 . . . .97 D6
Idle Bank Epworth DN9 . . . .15 F1
  Haxey DN9 . . . . .26 E2
Ihlee Cl PE4 . . . . .221 C1
Ilex Cl PE7 . . . . .230 C3
Iliffe Gate 3 PE4 . . . . . . .221 D2
Ilkeston Ct 2 DN15 . . . . . .182 B3
Illston Pl 4 PE1 . . . . .226 E7
IMMINGHAM DN40 . . . . . .186 E4
Immingham Bsns Units
  DN40 . . . . .186 D3
Immingham Leisure Ctr
  DN40 . . . . .186 C4
Immingham Mus★ DN40. 186 C3
Impala Way HU4 . . . . .179 D2
Imperial Ave DN35 . . . . . .192 C8
Independence Dr 5 PE11 156 F8
Infield La 5 DN22 . . . . .52 C1
Ingamells Dr LN1 . . . . .66 E2
Ingelow Ave PE21 . . . . . . .208 C6
INGHAM LN1 . . . . .54 F2
Ingham Cl LN6 . . . . .205 B3
Ingham Ct LN4 . . . . .207 E6
Ingham Hall Gdns PE13 . .177 D7
Ingham La LN1 . . . . .55 B1

Ingham Prim Sch LN1 . . . . .54 F2
Ingham Rd Coningsby LN4 . .207 E6
  3 Stow LN1 . . . . .66 C8
Inghams La 1 DN36 . . . . . .36 D4
Inghams Rd 3 DN36. . . . . . .36 D4
INGLEBOROUGH PE14 . . . .170 E5
Ingleborough 1 PE1 . . . . .226 A5
INGLEBY LN1 . . . . .66 C4
Ingleby Cres LN2 . . . . .201 F8
Ingleby Ct 2 PE11 . . . . . .214 F4
Ingleby Gr DN37 . . . . .190 F8
Ingleby Rd 2 DN17. . . . . . . .29 D7
Ingle Ct 2 NG33 . . . . .151 D7
Inglew Cl 8 NG34 . . . . . . .122 E2
Inglenook Dr 2 DN8 . . . . . .15 B8
Ingleton Ave HU4 . . . . . . .179 C6
Inglewood Cl 3 NG24 . . . .104 B1
Inglewood Ct DN16. . . . . . .185 A4
Inglewood Dr 4 HU4 . . . . .179 B5
Ingmires 7 HU15 . . . . .2 D6
INGOLDMELLS PE25 . . . . . .90 E4
Ingoldmells Prim Sch
  PE25 . . . . .90 D4
Ingoldmells Rd PE24 . . . . .102 E8
Ingoldsby Prim Sch NG33 141 D5
Ingoldsby Rd NG33 . . . . . .141 B3
Ingoldsby Road NG33. . . . .141 E3
Ingram Cres 9 DN7 . . . . . .14 C4
Ingram Gdns 11 DN8 . . . . .30 E8
Ingram Gr 10 DN7 . . . . . . .14 C4
Ingram La NG23 . . . . .78 A1
Ingram Pl DN35 . . . . .192 D2
Ingram Rd Boston PE21 . . .208 D6
  Hatfield DN7 . . . . .14 C3
Ingram Row LN9 . . . . .199 B3
Ing Rd PE20 . . . . .134 F4
Ings Bank Hilldyke PE22. . .126 B8
  Leverton PE22 . . . . .126 E7
Ings Dro
  Butterwick PE22 . . . . .126 D7
  Leverton PE22 . . . . .113 E1
Ings La Belchford LN9 . . . . .73 B2
  Brackenborough with Little
    Grimsby LN11 . . . . .49 B4
  Bratoft PE24. . . . . .102 C6
  Brough HU15 . . . . .2 C5
  Cumberworth LN13 . . . . . . .89 E7
  Ellerker HU15. . . . . .1 F8
  2 Hibaldstow DN20 . . . . . . .31 A5
  Horsington LN10 . . . . .84 D2
  Immingham DN40 . . . . .186 E3
  1 Kirk Bramwith DN7. . . . . .14 C7
  Leverton PE22 . . . . .126 F7
  Little Steeping PE23. . . . . .101 E5
  North Coates DN36 . . . . . . .37 A3
  North Ferriby HU14 . . . . . . .3 A4
  Saltfleetby LN11 . . . . .62 F8
  Scamblesby LN11. . . . . .73 A4
  Skidbrooke with Saltfleet Haven
    LN11 . . . . .51 A3
  South Cave HU15 . . . . .1 E7
  South Somercotes LN11. . . .50 E3
  Walkerith DN21 . . . . .40 C3
  Waltham DN37 . . . . .194 F4
  6 West Ashby LN9 . . . . . . .85 E7
  West Ashby LN9 . . . . .199 D8
  West Stockwith DN10. . . . . .40 C6
  Winterton DN15 . . . . .9 D7
Ings Rd Benington PE22 . . .126 D8
  Gringley on the Hill DN10 . . . .39 B3
  Kirton in Lindsey DN21. . . . .29 F1
  Mablethorpe & Sutton LN12. .76 E7
INGTHORPE PE9 . . . . .218 A8
Inhams Cl PE13 . . . . .177 D5
Inley Dro PE12 . . . . .169 A8
Inner St NG31 . . . . .211 B3
Innings The 1 NG34. . . . . .212 D3
Innovation Way
  Alwalton PE2 . . . . .229 B5
  Great Coates DN37 . . . . . . .24 B6
Inns Cl LN6 . . . . .204 E3
Inshops Ctr DN32 . . . . . . .189 B1
Intax Mews DN32 . . . . . . .191 F6
Invenio Acad DN15 . . . . . .182 E5
Inverness Rd 14 DN7 . . . . .14 D4
Iona Cl DN21 . . . . .197 E6
Iona Dr DN36 . . . . .36 D8
Ipswich Gdns NG31 . . . . . .210 E5
Iqra Acad PE3 . . . . .225 C8
Irby Cres 9 PE12 . . . . . . .158 B7
Irby Ct DN35 . . . . .192 D3
IRBY IN THE MARSH
  PE24 . . . . .102 B6
Irby Pl PE21 . . . . .208 E5
Irby Rd DN17 . . . . .184 E5
Irby St PE21 . . . . .208 E5
IRBY UPON HUMBER DN37 . .34 D7
Irchester Pl PE3 . . . . .225 D5
Ireland Wlk HU4 . . . . .179 B4
Ireton Ave 2 NG24 . . . . . .104 C4
Iris Dr PE2 . . . . .230 E8
Irish Hill LN11 . . . . .198 A5
IRNHAM NG33 . . . . .141 E1
Irnham Rd
  Corby Glen NG33 . . . . .141 C1
  Osgodby NG33 . . . . .141 E2
  Stamford PE9 . . . . .219 C7
Iron Bar Dro PE11 . . . . . . .155 F4
Ironstone Cl LN2 . . . . .202 C5
Ironmonger St 5 PE9 . . . .219 C5
Ironstone Rd LN7 . . . . .45 D8
Irvine Rd 2 DN16 . . . . . . .185 C5
Irwin Rd DN21 . . . . .41 C6
Isaac Newton Prim Sch The
  NG31 . . . . .210 F3
Isaac Newton Way NG31 . .211 F6
Isaac's Hill DN35 . . . . .192 E6

Isaan Newton Ctr 14
  NG31. . . . . .211 A4
Isham Rd PE3 . . . . .225 D4
Isherwood Cl PE1 . . . . . . .226 A6
Isis Ct HU9 . . . . .181 B5
Isis Wy PE2 . . . . .229 B5
ISLAND CARR DN20 . . . . . .196 B2
Island Carr Rd DN20 . . . . .196 A3
Island Rd DN17 . . . . .7 E6
Isle Cl 3 DN17 . . . . .16 D8
Islip Ct 2 LN9 . . . . .199 D3
Ison Cl 4 NG34 . . . . .120 E8
Itlings La HU13 . . . . .178 F1
Itterby Cres DN35 . . . . . . .192 C3
Itter Cres PE4 . . . . .221 C1
Ivanhoe Rd 4 DN16 . . . . .183 C1
Ivatt Ct 18 NG31 . . . . .210 E2
Ivatt Way PE3 . . . . .225 C6
Ivel Cl 6 LN12 . . . . .64 B5
Ivel Gr 4 LN12 . . . . .64 B5
Ivery La PE22 . . . . .114 D4
Ivesdyke Cl 3 PE13 . . . . .170 B2
Ivy Cl DN7 . . . . .14 E4
Ivy Cres PE21 . . . . .208 D3
Ivy Farm Ct 20 DN41 . . . . .23 F5
Ivy Gr PE4 . . . . .221 B2
Ivy House La PE24 . . . . . . .115 C8
  Graintthorpe LN11 . . . . .37 E1
Ivywood Cl 14 LN6 . . . . . .204 B8
Ixworth Cl 26 PE6 . . . . . .175 C4

J

Jack Fletcher Cl LN4 . . . . . .81 E1
Jack Haws La 3 PE9 . . . . .172 D4
Jack Hunt Sch PE3 . . . . . .225 B3
Jack Hunt Swimming Pool
  PE3 . . . . .225 B3
Jacklin Cl 5 LN11 . . . . . . .50 B8
Jacklin Cres LN12 . . . . .64 A4
Jacklin Dr 3 LN11 . . . . . . .51 C4
Jacklin La DN17 . . . . .7 C3
Jacklins App DN16 . . . . . . .185 A3
Jack Row La DN7. . . . . .14 B8
Jack Simpson Cl 6 LN9 . . .199 B2
Jacks La 6 PE23 . . . . .87 F1
Jackson Dr 3 PE20 . . . . . .136 C5
Jackson Mews 6 DN40. . . .186 A4
Jackson Rd 1 DN15 . . . . . .182 E3
Jackson's Field LN8 . . . . . .57 B7
Jacksons La 6 PE24. . . . . .102 E8
Jackson's Pl DN21 . . . . . . .192 D1
Jackson St Grimsby DN31 . .191 C8
  Kingston upon Hull HU3 . . . .180 D4
Jackson Wy
  8 Stamford PE9 . . . . .218 F6
  Welton HU14 . . . . .2 E4
Jacobean Rd 4 LN6 . . . . . .204 D6
Jacobs Cl LN11 . . . . .48 F4
Jacobs Ct 2 PE11 . . . . . . .214 C6
Jade Gr 1 HU3 . . . . .180 A4
Jaguar Dr LN6 . . . . .204 D1
Jail La PE22 . . . . .126 F2
James Ave
  6 Mablethorpe/Sutton on Sea
    LN12 . . . . .64 C2
  Peterborough PE1 . . . . . . .226 C1
  Skegness PE25 . . . . .206 B6
James Ct
  Gainsborough DN21. . . . . . .197 D5
  Louth LN11 . . . . .198 C6
  12 Market Rasen LN8. . . . . .57 E7
Jameson Bridge St 8 LN8 .57 D8
Jameson Keep HU13 . . . . .178 C2
Jameson Rd LN11 . . . . .48 A4
Jameson St 2 HU1. . . . . . .180 F6
James Pl DN39. . . . . .12 B1
James Rd Crowland PE6 . . .166 F1
  1 Hemswell Cliff DN21. . . . .55 A8
  Peterborough PE6 . . . . . . .175 B7
James St Boston PE21 . . . .208 E5
  Brigg DN20 . . . . .196 B3
  Grimsby DN31 . . . . .191 C8
  Lincoln LN2 . . . . .234 B3
  Louth LN11 . . . . .198 C6
Jameston Cl NG31. . . . . . .210 E3
James Watt Rd NG24 . . . . .104 B6
James Way 9 DN40 . . . . . .186 B3
Jankin La PE34. . . . . .161 F1
Janton Ct DN36 . . . . .195 C7
Japan Rd DN21 . . . . .197 B5
Japonica Hill 3 DN40 . . . .186 C3
Jaque's Bank DN8. . . . . . . .16 A5
Jarratt Hill La HU15 . . . . . .1 D8
Jarratt St HU1 . . . . .180 F7
Jarvis Cl LN6 . . . . .204 F2
Jarvis's Gate PE12 . . . . . .159 C1
Jasmin Cl 9 PE13 . . . . . . .170 E1
Jasmine Cl PE10 . . . . .213 E5
Jasmine Ct 2 Goxhill DN19 .12 A8
  Peterborough PE2 . . . . . . .229 E2
  Spalding PE11 . . . . .214 A2
Jasmine Way
  Immingham DN40 . . . . .186 C3
  Yaxley PE7 . . . . .233 F6
Jasmine Wy 15 LN8. . . . . . .70 D4
Jasmin Rd LN6 . . . . .204 C8
Jason Rd 8 LN6 . . . . .205 A5
Javelin Ave 8 LN8 . . . . . . .47 B6
Javelin Rd 12 LN11 . . . . . .62 C6
Jefferson Cl 24 PE8 . . . . .172 B1
Jefferson Dr 23 HU15. . . . . .2 C6
Jeffery Ave 6 PE13 . . . . . .170 E1
Jeffrey La DN9 . . . . .16 E1
Jekil's Bank Holbeach PE12 158 C1
  Moulton PE12. . . . . .167 F8

Jekil's Bank continued
  Whaplode PE12 . . . . .168 B8
Jekil's Gate PE12 . . . . . . .159 A5
Jellicoe Ave LN2 . . . . .202 D3
Jellicoe Dr DN16 . . . . .183 C1
Jellings Pl PE1 . . . . .226 A4
Jenkins Cl Louth LN11 . . . .198 C5
  5 Skegness PE25 . . . . . . .206 A7
Jenkins' La PE22 . . . . .127 A6
Jenner Ct 2 DN35 . . . . . . .192 B8
Jenner Pl DN35 . . . . .192 B8
Jenning St HU8 . . . . .181 A8
Jenny Brough La HU13 . . .178 B3
Jenny Brough Mdws
  HU13 . . . . .178 B3
Jenny Cl HU13 . . . . .178 B3
Jensen Mews 2 HU4. . . . . .179 E5
Jensen Rd LN4. . . . . .205 F2
Jericho La DN40 . . . . .12 D7
Jericho Rd 1 NG24 . . . . . .104 B1
Jermyn Mews LN4 . . . . . . .203 D1
Jermyn St NG34. . . . . .212 D4
Jerusalem LN6. . . . . .79 F5
Jerusalem Rd LN6. . . . . . . .200 A4
Jesmond Ave 5 DN17 . . . .184 C3
Jesmond View LN11. . . . . .201 E8
Jessop Cl Beacon Hill NG24 104 B5
  Cherry Willingham/Reepham
    LN3 . . . . .203 E5
  Horncastle LN9 . . . . .199 C3
  9 Leasingham NG34 . . . . . .121 B8
Jessop Way NG24 . . . . . . .104 B5
Jiggle's Gate PE12 . . . . . .158 F1
Jill Gr HU13. . . . . .178 F1
Job's La LN6. . . . . .79 C1
Jobson Rd LN9 . . . . .199 D2
Jock Hedge PE24 . . . . .102 E6
Joel Sq 8 NG34 . . . . .107 F1
John Adams Way PE21 . . .208 C3
John Blow Prim Sch 13
  NG23. . . . . .91 D4
John Brown Cl LN9 . . . . . .199 A4
John Clare Prim Sch PE6 .173 B4
John Cornwell Vc Dr
  DN36 . . . . .195 D6
John Coupland Hospl
  DN21. . . . . .197 B7
John Eve Way PE6. . . . . . .217 B6
John Fielding Com Specl Sch
  PE21 . . . . .209 A6
John Foster Cl 9 NG31. . . .211 D7
John Gold Ave 6 NG24 . . .104 A4
John Harrison CE Prim Sch
  DN19 . . . . .11 C8
John Harrison's Cl 3
  DN19 . . . . .11 D8
John Harrison Way PE21 . .215 B2
John Harrox Prim Sch The
  PE12 . . . . .157 F7
John Hunt Primary Sch
  NG24. . . . . .104 B2
John Leggott College
  DN17. . . . . .184 E8
John Pope Wy 17 NG24 . . .104 A6
John Smith Cl LN13 . . . . . .89 A6
Johnson Ave PE11. . . . . . .214 E2
Johnson Cl 8 Belton DN9. . .16 C2
  3 Skegness PE25 . . . . . . .206 A7
Johnson Community Hospl
  PE11 . . . . .214 D3
  Louth LN11 . . . . .207 B6
Johnson Dr
  Bracebridge Heath LN4 . . . .205 F4
  9 Scotter DN21 . . . . .29 C4
Johnson's Dro PE13. . . . . .177 B6
Johnson's La 7 DN17. . . . . .16 C7
Johnsons Rd 6 NG24. . . . .104 C1
Johnson St DN35 . . . . . . .192 B8
Johnson Way 14 PE24 . . . .102 C7
Johnson Wlk PE1 . . . . . . .225 F7
John Spendluffe Tech Coll
  LN13 . . . . .75 F2
John St Lincoln LN2 . . . . . .234 C2
  13 Market Rasen LN8. . . . . .57 D8
John Swain's Way PE12. . .216 C5
John Wake Cl 2 PE6 . . . . .217 B6
John Wesley Rd PE4. . . . . .220 E3
John Whitgift Acad DN37 190 D8
Jolls La LN9 . . . . .86 C5
Jolly Comm La LN13. . . . . .77 B2
Jolly Farmer Bank PE21 . . .126 C3
Jolly Farmer La PE21 . . . . .126 C3
Jonathan Dr PE25 . . . . . . .206 C4
Jonathan Gdns 1 NG34 . . .212 F3
Jones Hill PE7 . . . . .233 A4
Jonquil Ave DN16 . . . . . . .185 D5
Jordan Mews 2 PE1 . . . . .226 B3
Jordan's Cradge Bank Rd
  PE11. . . . . .156 C2
Jorose St 4 PE3. . . . . .225 A3
Jorose Way PE3. . . . . .224 F3
Joseph Ogle Cl DN36 . . . .195 B7
Joseph St DN31 . . . . .191 C8
Joshua Way 4 DN21 . . . . . .43 D7
Joy Paine Cl PE21 . . . . . . .208 C6
Joy's Bank PE12 . . . . .158 E1
Jubilee Ave Boston PE21. . .208 E6
  Faldingworth LN8. . . . . .56 F3
  Grantham NG31 . . . . .211 C5
Jubilee Cl 4 Bardney LN3. . .83 B4
  Cherry Willingham/Reepham
    LN3 . . . . .203 E6
  Coningsby LN4 . . . . .207 D5
  1 Hogsthorpe PE24 . . . . . .90 B7
  17 Kirton PE20 . . . . .136 C5
  Lincoln LN6 . . . . .204 F1
  Long Sutton PE12 . . . . . . .216 C5
  Martin LN4 . . . . .96 C2

Jubilee Cl continued
8 Morton PE10........154 C7
Scotter DN21...........29 B3
1 Spalding PE11.......214 C4
Sutton St James PE12...159 C1
Jubilee Cres
Gainsborough DN21....197 D5
Louth LN11............198 C8
Jubilee Ct 6 NG34....212 E4
Jubilee Dr 3 Bardney LN3..83 C4
Market Deeping PE6....217 C6
10 Wragby LN8.........70 D4
Jubilee Gr NG34.....212 C6
Jubilee Parade PE24..90 D7
Jubilee Pl 45 DN18...10 E8
Jubilee Rd LN11......50 E7
Jubilee St
Peterborough PE2......230 F8
2 Ruskington NG34....108 E1
Jubilee Way Crowland PE6..166 F1
Horncastle LN9........199 B4
Scunthorpe DN15......183 B3
Jude Gate PE22......114 E3
Judge Cl 3 PE21.....209 C4
Judy Cross PE11.....145 B8
Julian Bower LN11...198 B4
Julian Cl HU5.......179 A7
Julian St DN32......192 A7
Julian's Wlk 8 HU10..178 F6
Julia Rd LN4........203 D1
Julia's Mead 12 PE11..214 B5
Julius Wy LN6.......93 B8
Junction Rd 10 DN7...14 C6
Junella Cl HU3......180 A4
Jungle Zoo The★ DN35..193 B3
Junior Cadets Rd NG34..120 B8
Juniper Cl
Flixborough DN15......182 C6
10 Leasingham NG34...121 B7
3 Lincoln LN5.........205 C2
Spalding PE11.........214 F4
Juniper Cres
Peterborough PE3......225 A2
Spalding PE11.........214 F5
Juniper Dr 13 LN2....68 F4
Juniper Way
Gainsborough DN21....197 D5
3 Sleaford NG34......212 D2
Juniper Wy LN6......92 D5
Juno Wy PE2.........231 D4
Jupiter Ave
Peterborough PE7......231 D3
Stanground PE7........231 C4
Jury Rd PE7.........233 E8
Justice Hall La 10 DN17..16 D8
Justice La DN14......7 B8
Justice Wy PE7......233 B8
Justinian Wy 16 LN6..93 B8
Jutland Cl DN36.....195 D7

K

Karelia Ct HU4.......179 B5
Karen Ave 12 DN41....23 A4
Karsons Way LN2......68 D7
Katherine Cres PE25..206 D2
Kathleen Ave
Cleethorpes DN35......192 D8
Scunthorpe DN16......185 B5
Kathleen Gr DN32.....192 C7
Kathleen Rice Cl DN35..192 D8
Kaymile Cl 13 DN36...195 C6
KEADBY DN17.........17 D7
Keadby Cl DN17.......204 F7
Keal Bank PE22.......100 C3
Keal Carr Nature Reserve★
PE23..................100 E7
KEAL COTES PE23......100 C4
Keal Hill PE23.......100 B7
Kealholme Rd DN17....29 D7
Keaton Cl PE25.......206 A5
Keats Ave Grantham NG31..211 E6
Scunthorpe DN17.......184 D7
Keats Cl Lincoln LN2..202 C7
17 Mablethorpe/Sutton on Sea
LN12..................77 A7
Keats Dr NG34........121 E4
Keats Gr 2 PE9.......218 E5
Keats Rd 10 NG24.....104 B3
Keats Way PE1........225 D7
Keb La DN15..........9 D2
Keble Cl 4 PE9.......219 A7
Keble Ct 1 LN4.......207 B5
KEDDINGTON LN11......198 F8
Keddington Ave LN1...201 E8
Keddington Cres 2 LN11..198 D7
Keddington Rd Louth LN11..198 C7
Scunthorpe DN17.......184 F4
Kedlestone Rd NG31....210 F1
Kedleston Rd PE7.....231 F6
Keeble Dr LN4........203 D1
KEELBY DN41..........23 A5
Keelby Prim Sch DN41..23 A5
Keelby Rd
6 Gainsborough DN21...53 A8
Scunthorpe DN17.......184 F5
Stallingborough DN41...23 C6
Keel Dr 9 Bottesford NG13..128 A5
Kirton PE20...........136 D5
Keeling St 7 LN11.....50 F7
Keepers Cl 2 LN2.....68 D7
Keepers Way NG34.....212 C6
Keeper's Way 5 DN9....16 E1
Keeton Rd PE1........225 E7
Keightley Rd PE12.....147 B5
Keir Hardie Wlk DN32..191 D7
KEISBY PE10..........141 F3

Keisby Rd PE10.......142 A3
Keith Cres 15 DN37....23 F1
Kelburn Rd PE2.......229 D4
KELBY NG32...........131 C8
Kelby Rd NG32........120 C1
KELFIELD DN9.........28 C4
Kelham Rd
9 Great Gonerby NG31..129 E5
2 Great Gonerby NG31..210 E8
Grimsby DN32..........192 D6
Kellet Gate PE12.....157 B5
Kells Cl 6 LN5.......205 D3
Kell's Dro PE20......124 E1
Kelly Cl 14 PE11.....156 E8
Kelsey Ave DN15......182 B3
Kelsey La 1 DN17.....17 D4
Kelsey Prim Sch LN7...32 A4
Kelsey Rd LN7........32 C2
Kelsey St LN1........234 A2
Kelso Ct PE4.........221 A1
Kelso Dr PE13........213 C3
KELSTERN LN11........48 A1
Kelstern Cl 1 LN6....204 C6
Kelstern Ct 1 DN34...191 A5
Kelstern Rd LN6......204 C6
Kelston Dr 2 HU13....179 A3
Kelthorpe Cl PE9.....171 A2
Kemble Cl LN6........204 B8
Kemeshame Ct DN37....194 F4
Kemp Rd Grimsby DN31..189 C3
3 Swanland HU14......3 B6
Kemp St PE6..........166 E1
Kempton Cl 3 PE11....156 E3
Kempton Dr 4 DN7.....14 C2
Kempton Rd
12 Bourne PE10.......213 D3
Kingston upon Hull HU3..179 E6
Kempton Vale DN35....192 F1
Kempton Way NG31.....210 F4
Kendal Cl 2 PE4......221 D2
Kendal Ct DN16.......185 C6
Kendale Rd DN16......185 E8
Kendal Rd DN40.......186 E3
Kendal Way HU5.......179 C7
Kendon Gdns DN8......15 B8
Kendrick Cl PE2......231 D6
Kenford St DN36......195 C7
Kenilworth Cl 3 LN1...66 C3
Kenilworth Dr LN6....205 C5
Kenilworth Rd
Cleethorpes DN35......192 D4
Grantham NG31.........211 F5
Scunthorpe DN16.......183 C1
Kenlan Rd 23 PE13.....170 D1
Kenleigh Dr PE21.....209 D4
Kenmare Cres DN35....191 F2
Kenmar Rd 20 DN37....23 F1
Kenmore Dr 10 LN10...97 C6
Kennedy Ave 21 Alford LN13..75 F2
Skegness PE25........206 C2
Kennedy Cl DN20......196 E3
Kennedy Rd
Bracebridge Heath LN4..205 F3
Holbeach PE12........215 C4
Kennedy Way DN40.....186 C4
Kennedy Way Sh Ctr
DN40..................186 C4
Kennel La
Doddington & Whisby LN6..79 E5
Reepham LN3..........203 B3
Kennels Rd PE6.......224 D4
Kennel Wlk LN3.......203 F8
Kenner Cl 4 LN6......205 A6
Kennet Gdns PE4......221 C1
Kenneth Ave
2 Burgh le Marsh PE24..102 E8
8 Hatfield DN7.......14 C2
5 Stainforth DN7.....14 C6
Kenneth Campbell Rd 4
DN36..................37 C5
Kenneth St 1 LN1.....201 F6
Kennington Cl LN2....68 E5
Kennulphs Cl 5 PE6...175 C8
Kensington Cl PE21...215 F3
Kensington Dr 6 PE11..156 E3
Kensington Gdns 7 LN12..64 B3
Kensington Pl DN33...195 A8
Kensington Rd DN15....182 B3
Ken Stimpson Com Sch
PE4...................220 F4
Kent Ave LN12........63 F5
Kent Cl
Kingston upon Hull HU9..181 C7
3 Sutton Bridge PE12..160 E4
Kent Dr 4 DN20.......31 A5
Kentmere Pl 4 PE4....221 D2
Kentra Cl PE13.......170 C2
Kent Rd
9 Binbrook Tech Pk LN8..47 B6
Leake Commonside PE22..113 F3
Peterborough PE3......225 E2
Kent St Grimsby DN32..189 B1
6 Lincoln LN2........202 C3
Kentwell Rd PE7......230 F2
Kenwardly Rd HU10....178 E8
Kenwick Cl LN11......198 D3
Kenwick Dr NG31......211 D4
Kenwick Gdns LN11....198 D3
Kenwick Hill
Legbourne LN11........198 E5
Raithby cum Maltby LN11..61 C3
Kenwick Pastures LN11..198 D3
Kenwick Rd LN11......198 D2
Kenya Dr DN17........184 F2
Kenyon Cl
Heighington/Washingborough
LN4...................81 E4

Kenyon Cl continued
8 Thorne/Moorends DN8..15 A8
Kerries Wlk DN17.....184 C7
Kerrison View 5 LN2...68 D2
Kerr's Cres NG32.....118 D2
Kerry Dr HU10........178 C6
Kerry Pit Way HU10...178 C6
Kesgrave St 1 DN31....189 C1
Kesteven and Sleaford High
Sch Selective Acad
NG34..................212 D4
Kesteven Cl 1 PE6....217 D4
Kesteven Ct
3 Habrough DN40......22 E8
7 Lincoln LN6........204 D2
Kesteven Dr 7 PE6....217 A6
Kesteven Gr 19 DN17...16 D8
Kesteven & Grantham Girls'
Sch NG31............211 B5
Kesteven Rd PE9......219 C7
Kesteven St Lincoln LN5..234 B1
1 Sleaford NG34......212 E4
Kesteven Way 7 PE10..213 C5
Kesteven Wlk 3 PE1....226 B2
Kestrel Ave 10 DN21...197 F5
Kestrel Cl
6 Birchwood LN6......204 D8
Clinton Park LN4......207 C6
2 Sleaford NG34......212 B3
Kestrel Ct Grantham NG31..210 F2
Longthorpe PE3........225 A2
Kestrel Dr Bourne PE10..213 C6
Louth LN11............198 D8
Kestrel Rd
8 Scopwick Heath LN4..108 A7
Scunthorpe DN17.......184 E6
Kestrel Rise LN6.....79 B1
Keswick Cl 2 PE4.....221 D3
Ketco Ave PE9........171 A4
Ketel Cl PE12........216 C3
Ketlock Hill La 1 DN22..52 B1
KETSBY LN11..........74 D3
Ketsby La LN11.......74 C3
Kettering Rd
Scunthorpe DN16.......183 C2
Wothorpe PE9.........219 B2
Kettlebridge La DN40..12 E6
Kettleby La DN20.....20 E3
Kettleby Thorpe La 3 DN20..196 D4
KETTLETHORPE LN1.....65 F3
Kettlethorpe Dr 17 HU15..2 D5
Kettlethorpe Rd LN1...65 E3
Kettlewell St DN32....191 E5
KETTON PE9...........171 A3
Ketton CE Prim Sch PE9..171 A3
Ketton Drift PE9.....171 C3
Ketton Rd PE9........171 B2
Kew Gdns 3 NG24......104 A2
Kew Rd DN35..........192 E6
KEXBY DN21...........53 E5
Kexby La DN21........53 C4
Kexby Mill Cl 5 LN6...93 B8
Kexby Rd DN21........54 D6
Kexby Wlk DN21.......197 F3
Keyholme La DN36.....37 D2
Key Theatre★ PE1.....226 B1
Keyworth Dr 10 LN7...33 B4
Khormaksar Dr LN4....95 C7
Kiddier Ave DN37.....194 D7
Kidd La HU15.........2 D6
Kidgate LN11.........198 B5
Kidgate Mews LN11....198 B5
Kilburn Ave 4 HU2....180 F8
Kilburn Cres 1 LN6...205 A6
Kildare Dr PE3.......225 C4
Kilham PE2...........229 E2
Killarney Cl NG31....211 E7
Killingholme Haven Pits
Nature Reserve★ DN40..13 A6
Killingholme Prim Sch
DN40..................12 E3
Killingholme Rd DN40..12 F2
Kilmister Ct 10 LN8...70 D5
Kiln Ave HU5.........179 F4
Kiln Hill 4 LN8......59 A7
Kiln La DN20.........196 B3
Fulbeck NG32..........106 C1
Immingham DN41.......187 C2
Louth LN11............198 B6
Stallingborough DN41...186 F1
Kiln La Ind Est DN41..187 B3
Kiln La Trading Est DN41..187 C2
Kiln Yd LN11.........198 C5
Kilnwell Rd 12 LN8....57 D8
Kilverstone PE4......220 F6
KILVINGTON NG13......117 A1
Kimberley Ct 7 DN16...185 D4
Kimberley St HU3.....180 C7
Kimberley Terr NG31...210 E2
Kimblewick La PE14....214 A2
Kimbolton Ct PE1.....225 F3
Kime Cl 4 DN34.......142 C8
Kime Ct PE25.........206 C8
Kime Mews PE20.......136 D5
Kime's La 6 PE22.....98 F4
Kinder Ave LN6.......205 A2
Kinderley Prim Sch PE13..169 F6
Kinderley Rd PE13.....170 D2
King Charles Cl HU10..178 E7
King Edward Ave 7 LN10..97 C6
King Edward Cr 8 LN10..97 C6
King Edward Rd
Thorne/Moorends DN8..15 A8
9 Woodhall Spa LN10..97 C6
King Edward St Belton DN9..16 E2
4 Grimsby DN31.......189 A1
3 Kingston upon Hull HU1..180 F6

King Edward St continued
Kirton in Lindsey DN21..30 B1
Scunthorpe DN16.......183 A1
Sleaford NG34.........212 C3
King Edwards Terr 4 HU15..2 B5
King Edward VI Acad 7 PE23..87 F1
King Edward VI Gram Sch The
LN11..................198 A5
KINGERBY LN8.........44 E3
Kingerby Beck Mdws Nature
Reserve★ LN8........44 E5
Kingerby Cl DN21.....197 E3
Kingerby Rd
Bishopbridge LN8......44 F1
Scunthorpe DN17.......184 E5
Kingfisher Cl
25 Barton-upon-Humber
DN18..................3 E1
3 Birchwood LN6......204 D8
Brigg DN20............196 A3
Scunthorpe DN15......182 D5
Yaxley PE7............233 D5
Kingfisher Ct 2 PE11..214 F2
Kingfisher Dr
2 Skegness PE25......206 A7
Skirbeck Quarter PE21..208 E3
4 Surfleet PE11......145 E3
Kingfishers PE2......229 D6
King George Ave 1 LN10..97 B6
King Georges Ct 3 DN7..14 C5
King George V Ave 1
PE12..................215 F3
King George V Stadium
DN32..................192 B5
King Henry Chase PE3...225 A5
King John Bank
2 Sutton Bridge PE14..170 F8
Walpole PE14..........161 A2
King Johns Rd 6 PE20..135 B7
King John St LN4......212 C4
King Oswald Rd 12 DN9..27 C6
King St 8 DN21.......197 D3
King St La LE14.......150 A6
Kings Arms Yd 2 LN2...234 B2
Kings Ave PE25.......206 E8
King's Ave Boston PE21..209 C3
Brigg DN20............196 D3
King's Bench St HU3...180 B5
Kingsbridge Cl 1 PE4..220 E5
Kings Cl PE22........112 C8
King's Cl 15 DN7.....14 D4
Kingscliffe Rd NG31...211 A8
King's Cres Boston PE21..209 C3
Swineshead PE20......135 B8
Kings Croft 1 DN17....16 E6
Kingscroft Dr 31 HU15..2 D5
King's Cross Cl 2 HU3..180 C6
King's Cswy DN14.....6 E8
Kings Ct 19 Kirton PE20..136 C5
Louth LN11............198 E7
Old Bolingbroke PE23..100 A7
9 Scawby DN20........30 F8
Scunthorpe DN15......183 B4
Kingsdale DN17.......184 E2
King's Delph Dro PE7..231 E2
Kingsdown Dr PE9.....218 E5
Kingsdown Rd LN6.....204 B7
Kings Dyke Cl PE2.....231 E6
Kingsfield LN5.......105 B4
Kingsgate
Market Deeping PE6....217 C6
Kings Gate DN32......192 A7
Kings Gdns PE1.......226 A5
Kings Hill 2 NG32.....119 B7
Kings La LN12........120 C8
Kings Leigh 1 HU3....180 C6
Kingsley Ave PE10....213 B6
Kingsley Cl
4 Barnack PE9........172 D3
6 Brough HU15.......2 B1
Kingsley Ct 8 LN4.....82 B1
Kingsley Gr DN33.....191 C4
Kingsley Rd
14 Mablethorpe/Sutton on Sea
LN12..................64 B4
North Hykeham LN6.....204 B5
Peterborough PE1......226 C4
Kingsley St LN1......234 A4
Kingsline Cl 1 PE6....176 A3
Kings Manor LN4......207 D4
Kings Mews DN35......193 C1
Kingsport Cl 1 HU3....180 A7
Kings Rd Holbeach PE12..215 F3
Immingham DN40.......186 E5
Metheringham LN4.....95 C4
Peterborough PE2......231 B6
Stamford PE9..........219 B6
King's Rd
Barnetby le Wold DN38..21 B5
Humberston DN35......193 B3
Spalding PE11.........214 D5
Kings Sch The NG31....211 B5
King's Sch The PE1.....226 A4
Kings Sconce Ave 2
NG24..................104 A5
King St 1 Billinghay LN4..109 F5
Boston PE21...........208 E4
East Halton DN40......12 D7
Gainsborough DN21....197 D3
15 Goxhill DN19.......12 A8
10 Kirton PE20.......136 C5
Lincoln LN5...........234 A1
14 Mablethorpe/Sutton on Sea
LN12..................64 B3
Market Rasen LN8......57 D8
1 Peterborough PE1...226 A2
Scunthorpe DN15......183 B4

King St continued
18 Sutton Bridge PE12..160 E4
Thorne/Moorends DN8..15 A8
Wainfleet All Saints PE24..102 A2
West Deeping PE6......173 A8
Wilsford NG32.........120 A1
Winterton DN15........9 A5
Yarburgh LN11.........49 E4
Kingsthorpe Cres PE25..206 C1
Kingston Ave
Grantham NG31.........210 E4
Grimsby DN34..........191 A6
Kingston upon Hull HU13..178 F1
Kingston Cl 7 DN35....193 A1
Kingston Communications
Stadium (Hull City AFC Hull
RLFC)★ HU3..........180 B7
Kingston Dr PE2......231 E5
Kingston International Bsns
Pk HU9..............5 F8
Kingston Rd
Kingston upon Hull HU10..178 F8
Scunthorpe DN16.......185 A7
Kingston Ret Pk HU1...180 E5
Kingston St
Kingston upon Hull HU1..180 E4
Kingston upon Hull HU1..180 E5
Kingston Terr NG34....212 E5
KINGSTON UPON HULL
HU1...................180 F4
Kingston View 20 DN18..10 F8
Kingston Wharf 4 HU1..180 F5
King Street Ind Est PE6..164 D1
Kingsway Boston PE21...209 B3
Bourne PE10...........213 D6
3 Brigg DN20.........196 A4
Cleethorpes DN35......193 A5
11 Leverington PE13...170 E1
Lincoln LN5...........201 F1
Nettleham LN2.........68 C2
Scunthorpe DN15......182 C3
Stainforth DN7........14 C6
Tealby LN8............46 C1
Kings Way LN2........68 C7
Kingsway Sta DN35.....193 B4
Kings Wlk NG31.......211 A4
KingsWy 3 NG24.......104 B3
KINGTHORPE LN8.......70 C2
Kingthorpe Rd LN8.....70 C1
King William Cl 4 PE34..161 F3
Kinloch Way DN40......186 B2
Kinloss Cl 11 LN6.....204 C6
Kinnears Wlk PE2......229 F2
Kinoulton Ct 16 NG31..210 E2
Kinross Rd NG34......120 F2
Kinsbourne Gn 40 DN7..14 D4
Kinsley Wlk 8 DN15....183 B3
Kintore Dr NG31......211 C4
Kipling Ave
Little London PE11.....214 A1
4 Scunthorpe DN17....184 D7
Kipling Cl
4 Grantham NG31......211 E6
St Giles LN2..........202 B7
3 Stamford PE9.......218 E5
Kipling Ct PE1.......225 E8
Kipling Dr
4 Mablethorpe/Sutton on Sea
LN12..................77 A7
14 Sleaford NG34.....212 F4
Kiplinton Cl 2 HU3....180 A7
Kipling Wlk 1 HU4.....179 D2
Kippings The 8 PE10...164 C8
Kirby Ct 5 PE1.......214 F4
Kirby Wlk 2 PE3......225 C4
KIRK BRAMWITH DN7....14 A6
KIRKBY LN8...........44 F3
Kirkby Bank PE23.....99 E3
KIRKBY FENSIDE PE23...99 E4
Kirkby Gr DN33.......191 A3
Kirkby Gravel Pit Nature
Reserve★ LN8........207 A8
KIRKBY GREEN LN4......108 E8
Kirkby Hill PE23......100 A7
KIRKBY LA THORPE NG34..121 F5
Kirkby la Thorpe CE Prim Sch
NG34..................121 F5
Kirkby Moor Nature Reserve★
LN10..................98 A5
KIRKBY ON BAIN LN10...98 B5
Kirkby on Bain CE Prim Sch
LN10..................98 C5
Kirkby Rd
Ewerby & Evedon NG34..122 B5
Scunthorpe DN17.......184 E4
Kirkby St
7 Kingston upon Hull
HU2...................180 F8
Lincoln LN5...........201 F1
KIRKBY UNDERWOOD
PE10..................142 D2
Kirkby Underwood Rd
PE10..................154 A8
Kirk Cl 4 DN15.......182 E4
Kirkdale Cl 2 NG34....121 B8
Kirkden Paddocks DN9..16 C2
KIRK ELLA HU10.......178 C8
Kirkenes Cl DN36......195 B6
Kirkgate PE13........169 F7
Kirk Gate Waltham DN37..194 E4
6 Whaplode PE12......158 B7
Kirkgate St PE13......170 E1
Kirk Gdns PE21.......208 D7

Kirkham Cl HU13.......178 F2
Kirkhouse Gn Rd DN7....14 A8
Kirklands Rd HU5......179 E8
Kirkmeadow PE3.......225 A8
Kirk Rd LN4..........81 E1
Kirk Rise HU10.......178 C7
Kirkside DN37........194 D4
Kirkstall PE2........230 B3
Kirkstall Cl LN2......202 E6
Kirkstead Bridge LN10...97 B4
Kirkstead Cres DN33...191 B3
Kirkstead St ■ LN10...97 C5
Kirkstone House Sch PE6 164 E4
Kirkton Gate PE3......225 A1
Kirkway HU10.........178 B7
Kirk Way NG34........212 C2
Kirkwood Cl PE3......225 C2
Kirman Cres ⑤ DN17...184 F3
KIRMINGTON DN39.......22 A6
Kirmington CE Prim Sch
DN39................22 A6
Kirmington Cl ⑧ LN6...204 C6
Kirmington Gdns DN34 191 A7
Kirmington Rd DN39....21 F7
KIRMOND LE MIRE LN8...46 F3
Kirmond Rd LN8........47 A4
Kirness Dro LN4......109 C6
KIRTON PE20..........136 D5
Kirton Cl ② NG24.....104 B1
Kirton Distribution Pk
PE20...............136 C5
Kirton Dro LN4.......110 F1
KIRTON END PE20......136 B6
Kirton Holme Rd PE20..124 E1
KIRTON HOLME PE20....135 E8
KIRTON IN LINDSEY DN21..30 C2
Kirton La Hatfield DN8...14 E7
② Long Bennington NG23 117 D4
Stainforth DN7.......14 D6
Kirton Lindsey Prim Sch
DN21................30 B1
Kirton Lindsey Sta DN21..30 B2
Kirton Prim Sch PE20...136 C5
Kirton Rd Blyton DN21...41 D6
Holme DN16...........19 B2
Manton DN21..........30 A3
Messingham DN17.......29 E6
Scawby DN20..........30 C8
Scotter DN21.........29 D3
Waddingham DN21......43 B7
Kisgate ⑩ LN1........66 D7
Kishorn Ct DN40......186 B2
Kisimul Sch LN6.......92 A6
Kit Cat La PE20.......145 F8
Kite Way PE7.........233 A8
Kitty Briggs La NG31...210 E1
Kitwood Cl ④ PE21....209 B4
Kitwood Rd PE21......209 B4
KNAITH DN21..........53 A3
Knaith Hall La DN22....52 E3
Knaith Hill DN21......53 A3
KNAITH PARK DN21......53 B4
Knapton Ct LN7........33 B4
Knarr Fen Rd PE6.....176 E2
Kneeland DN21.........68 D6
Knight Cl Holdingham NG34 212 D7
Market Deeping PE6....217 D5
Knight Ms PE2........231 A6
Knighton Cl PE7......230 D1
Knight Pl ⑧ LN5......205 E8
Knightsbridge ② DN36..195 C6
Knightsbridge Rd ④ DN17 .29 D7
Knights Cl ⑤ Belton DN9..16 E2
⑱ Laceby DN37.......23 F1
Leverington PE13.....170 B2
Knight's Ct DN16.....185 A3
Knight St Grimsby DN32..192 B6
④ Lincoln LN5.......205 E8
② Pinchbeck PE11....145 B1
Knight Terr LN5......205 E8
Knipe Ave PE11.......214 C3
KNIPTON NG32.........138 C6
Knipton CE Prim Sch
NG32...............138 C6
Knipton ⑧ NG24.......104 B2
Knipton La NG32......138 C6
Knipton Rd NG32......138 B4
Knole Wlk PE3........225 B3
Knoll St DN35........192 F6
Knolls The NG32......210 B5
Knoll The NG31.......210 D8
Knowle St ⑳ LN12.....64 B3
Knowles Wy ⑧ LN3.....83 B4
Kohima Cl ③ PE10.....213 E7
Kooreman Ave ⑲ PE13..170 D1
Kristen Turton Cl DN36..195 D2
Kristiansand Cl ⑤ DN36..195 B6
Kyme Rd Boston PE21...208 D6
Heckington NG34......122 E3

L

Labour in Vain Dro LN4..110 A6
Labrador Dr ⑲ DN20....19 E4
Laburnham Ave DN37...194 D4
Laburnham Cl DN37....194 D4
Laburnum Ave
Gainsborough DN21....197 D6
④ Gunness DN15......17 E6
Yaxley PE7...........233 F6
Laburnum Cl
⑧ Bourne PE10.......213 C6
Grantham NG31.......211 D5
Lincoln LN6..........205 A2

Laburnum Cl continued
⑦ Wisbech PE13......170 E1
Laburnum Cres LN11...198 E4
Laburnum Ct
② Cherry Willingham/Reepham
LN3................82 A8
Hessle HU13.........178 E1
Laburnum Dr
Cherry Willingham/Reepham
LN3................203 D5
Grimsby DN34........190 E7
Ingoldmells PE25.....206 D8
③ Kingston upon Hull HU5. 179 B7
Morton PE10.........154 B7
Laburnum Gdns PE20..136 C5
Laburnum Gr
⑧ Burton upon Stather
DN15................8 B5
⑯ Crowle DN17.......16 D7
Peterborough PE1....226 B8
Scunthorpe DN16.....185 B7
Spalding PE11.......214 F5
Laburnum Rd NG34....107 C2
LACEBY DN37..........23 E1
LACEBY ACRES DN34...190 C4
Laceby Acres Academy
DN34...............190 D4
Laceby Rd Grimsby DN34..191 A4
Laceby DN37..........190 C3
Scunthorpe DN17.....184 C5
Laceby St LN2........202 B3
Lacey Gdns LN11.....198 D6
Lacey Gdns Jun Sch LN11 198 D6
Lacey Gr NG24........104 C2
Lacey's Cl PE22......126 F6
Lacey's Dr PE22......126 F6
Lacey's La PE22......126 E6
Lacy Cl ㉑ LN2........68 D2
Ladbroke Cl ⑧ NG34...133 D7
Ladds Cl ⑥ PE21.....209 C4
Ladds La PE6.........217 A1
Ladd's Mill Cl ⑦ LN6...93 B8
LADE BANK PE22.......113 F5
Lade Bank Old Leake PE22. 113 F5
Wrangle PE22........114 B6
Lady Anne Wy ㉙ HU15...2 D5
Lady Bower ⑨ LN6.....205 A2
Ladybower Way PE4...221 C3
Lady Charlotte Rd PE7..230 C3
Lady Fen La LN13......76 B1
Lady Frances Cres DN35. 192 C5
Lady Frances Dr ⑭
PE23...............101 A8
Lady La PE24.........102 A2
Lady Lodge Dr PE2....230 C3
Lady Margaret's Ave PE6 217 C5
Lady Matilda's Dr PE25..206 C8
Lady Meers Rd LN3...203 E6
Lady Romayne Cl PE9..219 C4
Ladysmith Rd DN32...191 F7
Ladysmith Terr NG31..210 E7
Ladywell Gate ④ HU15...2 E6
Ladywood Rd PE11....214 E6
Lafford Ct NG34......212 B5
Lafford Dr ② LN4.....109 F6
Laforey Rd DN31......188 A3
Lagonda Cl LN4.......205 F1
Lagoon Rd DN17......184 B6
Lailey Rd HU13.......178 B2
Laing Cl ② LN3........83 B4
Lake Field Rd PE7....233 B8
Lakeside Anderby PE24...77 C3
Great Coates DN37....24 B6
Peterborough PE4....221 B5
Peterborough PE7....230 C2
Pyewipe DN37........188 A3
Lakeside Dr DN17.....184 C5
Lakeside Gr HU4.....179 D4
Lakeside Leisure Ctr PE24 .230 A5
Lakeside Parkway
Scunthorpe DN16.....185 E4
Scunthorpe DN16.....185 F5
Lakeside Ret Pk DN16..185 F6
Lakeside Sta DN35....193 B2
Lakeside Vw LN3......82 F6
Lakeview LN3 ③ LN6...204 C1
Lakeview Rd LN6.....205 C6
Lakeview Way PE7....230 C2
Lalgrate Pl DN35.....192 F1
Lambert Ave ⑫ HU15...2 C6
Lambert Bank Fleet PE12. 158 D1
Holbeach PE12.......168 D8
Lambert Mews ⑤ PE9..219 C4
Lambert Rd
④ Allington NG32....128 F7
Grimsby DN32........191 D6
Lambes Ct PE4.......220 E4
Lambeth Wlk ③ PE9...219 A6
Lamb Gdns LN2.......202 B6
Lamb La Benington PE22. 127 A4
Newport HU15........1 B8
Lambourn Ct ⑧ DN35..192 F1
Lambourne Rise DN16..185 A4
Lambourne Way ⑤ NG34 122 D2
Lambs Row ⑤ PE21...208 E6
La Milesse Way ■ PE20. 135 C7
Lammas Leas Rd ④ LN8. 57 E7
Lammas Rd PE1......226 A7
Lammin's La ② PE22...99 A4
Lamplight Sq NG31...210 F4
Lamport Cl ⑨ PE6....217 A6
Lampton Gr DN32.....191 D6
Lanark St ② HU5.....180 B8
Lancaster App DN40....12 D4
Lancaster Ave
Grimsby DN31........191 B7
Horncastle LN9......199 C5

Lancaster Ave continued
Skegness PE25.......206 A5
Lancaster Cl
⑧ Great Steeping PE23..101 D7
Long Sutton PE12....216 C4
Stickney PE22........113 A7
⑥ Waddington LN5....94 A7
Lancaster Ct
⑥ Nunsthorpe DN33...191 B2
⑭ Welton/Dunholme LN2..68 D7
Yaxley PE7..........233 F6
Lancaster Dr
⑥ Coningsby LN4....207 D4
Long Sutton PE12....216 C4
⑦ Market Rasen LN8...57 E8
Moorland Prison DN7...26 A8
⑨ Scampton Airfield LN1..67 F5
⑩ South Killingholme DN40..12 E3
Lancaster Gdns ② NG31 211 D2
Lancaster Gn LN21.....54 F8
Lancaster Pl ④ LN5...201 F1
Lancaster Rd
⑪ Beacon Hill NG24...104 C5
③ Binbrook Tech Pk LN8..47 B6
Gringley on the Hill DN10..39 D1
Scunthorpe DN16.....185 A5
⑩ Stamford PE9......219 B6
Lancaster Sch The LN6..204 C8
Lancaster Way
㉕ Brough HU15........2 C5
Market Deeping PE6...217 B7
② Skellingthorpe LN6..200 A4
Yaxley PE7..........233 F6
Lancelot Ct HU9......181 C6
Lancelot Way ⑦ PE11..214 B3
Lancer Ct DN33.......191 A2
Lancewood Gdns ⑧ LN6. 204 C8
Lancia Cres LN4......205 F2
Lancing Cl ⑦ PE4....221 A3
Lancing Way ④ DN18..194 E8
Land Dike LN11........37 A1
Landeck Ave DN34....191 B6
Lander Cr ■ PE7......230 F5
Landings La LN36.....195 C4
Landings La DN36.....195 C4
Landmere Gr LN2.....200 D1
Land of Gn Ginger ⑩
HU1................180 F6
Landor Ave ③ DN17...184 D7
Landsdowne Ct ㉒ LN12..77 A8
Landsdowne Ct PE11...214 F6
Landsdowne Rd ② PE25..206 C4
Landseer Ave DN24....90 D8
LANEHAM DN22.........65 A3
Laneham Rd NG22......65 A1
Laneham St Rampton DN22..65 A5
Scunthorpe DN15.....183 A3
Lanes The ⑩ DN36.....36 D4
Lane The
■ Easton on the Hill PE9. 171 D3
Ruskington NG34.....108 C2
West Deeping PE6....173 B7
Laney Cl LN2........202 C7
Langary Gate Rd PE12..158 E1
Langdale Ave DN33....194 D7
Langdale Cl LN2......202 B8
Langdale Cres NG31..211 A8
Langdyke PE1........226 F6
Langer Cl ⑤ LN6.....204 B6
LANGFORD NG23........91 C1
Langford Gdns NG31..211 B6
Langford La NG23......91 A2
Langford Rd PE2......231 A7
Langford Wlk ■ HU4...179 B7
Langham Rd PE24......90 B7
Langhole Dro PE11...145 B1
LANGHOLME DN9........39 E8
Langholme DN9........27 B1

Langholme Wood Nature
Reserve* DN9........39 D8
Langley Cl PE3.......225 B8
Langley Cl LN11.......198 E4
Langley Dr DN16......185 A2
Langley Pl DN35......193 A4
Langley Rd LN6......204 D2
Langley Wlk DN40....186 D3
LANGRICK PE22.......124 E6
LANGRICK BRIDGE PE22. 124 E4
Langrick Rd Boston PE21. 208 C6
Coningsby LN4........98 C1
Holland Fen with Brothertoft
PE20...............124 E4
Langthwaite Cl ⑳ HU15..2 D5
LANGTOFT PE6........164 F3
Langtoft Drain Rd PE6..165 C4
Langtoft Outgang Rd
PE11...............165 D6
Langtoft Prim Sch PE6.. 164 F3
LANGTON Langton LN9....85 B3
Langton by Spilsby PE23...87 F5
LANGTON BY WRAGBY
LN8................70 F3
Langton Cl Grimsby DN33. 191 A3
Horncastle LN9......199 A3
Lincoln LN2.........202 B7
Langton Cl PE25.....206 C5
Langton Dr Grimsby DN33. 191 A3
Horncastle LN9......199 A3
Langton Hill
Horncastle LN9......199 A3
Kingthorpe LN8.......70 E2
Langton La LN9........85 C4
Langton Rd
Holton le Clay DN36...195 E2
Panton LN8...........71 B6
Peterborough PE1....226 D7

Langwith Dr PE12.....215 C2
Langwith Gdns PE12..215 C1
LANGWORTH LN3........69 B3
Langworthgate LN2...234 C3
Langworth Rd LN2......69 B4
Lannimore Cl LN5.....205 D3
Lansbury Rd ⑫ NG24..104 B2
Lansdall Ave ④ DN35...52 F6
Lansdowne Ave
Grimsby DN32........191 D4
Lincoln LN6..........205 C5
Lansdowne Dr ㉑ LN12...77 A8
Lansdowne Rd
⑧ Navenby/Wellingore
LN5................107 A8
Yaxley PE7..........233 F6
Lansdowne St LN3.....180 C6
Landsown Link ■ DN35..192 E3
Lansdown Rd ④ DN40...186 B4
Lansdown Way LN10....97 C5
Lantern La HU15........1 B5
Laporte Rd DN40.....187 C5
Lapwater La PE12.....147 C6
Lapwing Cl LN6......200 A3
Lapwing Wy
② Barton-upon-Humber
DN18................3 E1
Scunthorpe DN16.....185 F5
Larch Ave Allington NG32. 128 A6
⑯ Nettleham LN2......68 D2
Larch Cl ⑧ Bourne PE10. 213 C7
② Grantham NG31....210 D2
Immingham DN40.....186 E5
Ruskington NG34.....108 D1
Yaxley PE7..........233 F6
Larch Ct ⑨ DN21.....197 E6
Larch Gn NG34.......107 D1
Larch Gr Peterborough PE1. 226 C6
⑧ Scawby DN20.......30 F8
Scunthorpe DN16.....185 B7
Larchmont Cl ⑩ HU15...2 C6
Larch Rd DN35.......192 D2
Larch Way ⑧ NG34...212 D2
Larchwood Cres LN6..200 D1
Larden Ave DN33.....194 E8
Lares Ave PE2.......231 D4
Lark Cl ⑬ LN8.........70 D4
Lark Dr ④ LN5.......107 A7
Larkin Ave LN3......203 D5
Larklands PE3.......225 B1
Lark Rise
⑥ Market Deeping PE6. 217 B7
Scotter DN21.........29 B3
Larkspur Ave ⑥ DN41...23 F5
Larkspur Croft PE21..208 C6
Larkspur Rd LN2......202 D7
Larkspur Wlk PE4....221 B3
Larkspur Wy PE11....214 B6
Larks Rise PE10......154 B7
Larmour Rd DN37....190 D7
Larne Cl ⑫ LN5......205 C2
Larne Rd LN5........205 D2
Larners Fields ⑥ LN1..66 C7
Las End ㉗ DN21.......30 B1
Lashbrook Garth HU4..179 B4
Lastingham ㉚ HU15....2 C6
Latham Ave PE2......230 C7
Latham Ct PE20......124 B8
Latimer Gdns ⑫ NG34.. 122 E3
Lattimers Paddock PE9..172 C4
LAUGHTERTON LN1......65 D2
LAUGHTON DN21........41 C8
Laughton Cres LN2....202 A8
Laughton Dr ⑭ PE9...218 E6
Laughton La DN21.....40 D3
Laughton Rd Blyton DN21..40 F5
Boston PE21.........208 D6
Laughton Way LN2....201 F7
Laughton Way N LN2..201 F8
Launde Gdns ⑤ PE9...218 E4
Launder Terr NG31...211 A3
Laundon Rd NG34....132 E3
Laura Ct ⑤ PE25......90 E3
Laureate Gr PE11....214 B4
Laurel Cl
⑥ Donington PE11...134 E2
⑧ Gainsborough DN21. 197 E6
Kingston upon Hull HU5.. 179 B7
Lincoln LN5.........205 D5
Yaxley PE7..........233 D4
Laurel Dr ⑦ PE6.....176 A3
Laurel Gr LN7........32 A1
Laurel La
Kingston upon Hull HU5..179 D7
Thornton Curtis DN39...11 E4
Laurels Cl ■ DN40....22 E8
Laurel Way DN16.....185 D4
Lauridston Cl ⑨ DN37...23 E1
Laurier St DN35......192 D8
Lauriston Rd NG31...210 F6
Laurold Ave ■ DN7....15 A3
Laval Pl PE21........209 B5
Lavender Cl ⑥ Lincoln LN5 205 C2
⑩ Sleaford NG34......212 D2
② Yaxley PE7.........233 F6
Lavender Cres PE1....226 B8
Lavender Dr PE11....214 A2
Lavender Gr DN36....195 B7
Lavender Way
Bourne PE10........213 C7
㉑ Newark-on-Trent NG24. 104 C5
⑱ Scunthorpe DN15...183 B3
■ Stamford PE9......219 C7
Lavender Wlk ■ HU5..179 C7
Lavenham Ct PE2.....230 C7
Lavenham Gr LN6....205 A5

Lavenham Rd DN33....194 D7
Lavington Grange PE1..226 E6
Law Cl ■ PE11........214 B5
Lawley Cl LN2.......203 B8
Lawn Ave
Peterborough PE1....226 A7
Skegness PE25.......206 D2
Lawn Cres ■ PE25....206 D2
Lawn Ct LN1.........234 A4
Lawn in Lincoln The*
LN1................234 A3
Lawn La NG33........152 F2
Lawns The Collingham NG23 91 D5
④ Grimsby DN31......191 C7
Kingston upon Hull HU10. 178 D7
Peterborough PE4....221 C1
⑱ Wisbech PE13......170 C1
Lawnswood HU13.....178 D2
Lawnswood Ct DN16...185 A4
Lawn Wood Nature Reserve*
NG33...............152 E2
Lawrance Way ⑩ PE10. 164 C8
Lawrence Ave PE7....231 C2
Lawrence Cl ■ LN6....205 B7
Lawrence La ③ NG34..120 C8
Lawrence Rd PE8......172 C1
Lawrence's Dro PE10..164 F8
Lawrence St
㉕ Beacon Hill NG24...104 A5
Grimsby DN31........191 C8
Law's Cl PE6.........174 C5
Lawson Ave Grimsby DN31. 191 B8
Peterborough PE2....231 D6
Lawson Ct ⑮ LN2......68 E3
Lawson Leas ⑤ NG32..210 A5
Lawyers Cl PE12.....215 E2
Laxton Cl PE6........217 F5
Laxton Gdns ⑦ PE11.. 156 E8
Laxton Gr DN16......185 A2
Laxton La NG32......152 E7
Laycock Ave ② DN10...39 C1
Layerthorpe Rd ■ HU4. 179 C2
Laythorpe Ave PE25..206 D1
Laythorpe Gdns ② LN4. 207 C4
LEA DN21.............52 F5
Leaburn Rd DN17......29 D7
Leadenhall Rd PE12..147 C6
LEADENHAM LN5......106 C3
Leadenham CE Prim Sch
LN5................106 D3
Leading Dro PE7.....233 D3
Lea Dr DN32.........191 F5
Leaf Ave PE7........230 D3
Leafbridge Way LN6..204 C3
Leafere Way ■ PE13...170 B2
Lea Garth ⑥ DN17.....29 D7
Leagate Cl LN4......207 F6
Leagate Rd Coningsby LN4. 207 F6
Langriville PE22......124 F8
Thornton le Fen PE22..111 F1
Lea Gdns PE3........225 F1
Lea Gr ② LN3.........83 C4
LEAKE PE22..........127 C8
LEAKE COMMONSIDE
PE22...............113 F3
LEAKE FOLD HILL PE22.. 114 A2
Leakes Row LN11.....198 C7
Leake's Row LN11....198 C7
Lealand Cl ■ LN2.....202 E6
Lealand Way PE21....209 A2
Leame Cl HU3........180 A7
Leamington Cl ② DN16..183 C1
Leamington Ct DN16..183 C1
Leamlands La PE12...149 B1
Lea Pk Home Est PE21. 209 B4
Lea Rd DN21.........197 D2
Lea Rd W DN21.......197 D1
Leas Cl DN37........194 D3
Lease La DN40.........12 D6
LEASINGHAM NG34....121 B8
Leasingham La NG34..108 C1
Leasingham St Andrews CE
Prim Sch NG34......121 B7
Leas Rd NG34........122 F2
Leas The NG32.......119 B1
Lea The NG34........121 B8
Leaver Gate PE24....102 B2
Leaves Lake Dro PE11. 155 E7
Lea View ② PE9......163 C1
Lebanon Dr ③ PE13...170 E1
Lechler Cl LN2........68 D3
Leconfield Cl ⑦ LN6..204 C6
Leconfield Rd ⑱ LN6..204 C7
Ledbury Dr DN36.....195 D7
Ledbury Rd PE3......225 C3
Ledham PE2.........229 D4
Lee Ave
Heighington/Washingborough
LN4................203 D1
Sutterton PE20......136 B2
Leeder Cl PE7.......231 D1
Lee Fair Gdns ■ DN17..184 F2
Leek Hill ⑱ DN15......9 A5
Leeming St ⑧ LN6...204 C6
Lee Rd Lincoln LN2...234 C4
Yaxley PE7..........233 D4
Lee Smith St HU9....181 E7
Lees Rest Houses HU4..179 C6
Lee St LN11.........198 B5
Lees The PE6........217 E5
Lees Wlk HU3........180 A7
Legard Ave DN16.....185 B6
Legard Dr HU10......178 E6
Legarde Ave HU4.....179 C6
LEGBOURNE LN11......61 F3
Legbourne Abbey LN11..61 F3
Legbourne Cl ■ LN1...201 D7
Legbourne Rd LN11...198 E3

Legbourne Road LN11 . . . . . . .62 C4
Legbourne Wood Nature
Reserve★ LN11 . . . . .61 F2
Legends Wy **3** HU4 . . . . . .179 E5
Leggott Way **8** DN41 . . . . . .23 E6
Legion Cl **8** HU15 . . . . .2 C5
LEGSBY LN8 . . . . .58 A4
Legsby Ave DN32 . . . . .191 E5
Legsby Pl DN32 . . . . .191 E4
Legsby Prim Sch LN8 . . . . . . .58 A4
Legsby Rd LN8 . . . . .57 E2
Leicester Cl LN4 . . . . .203 C1
Leicester Gr NG31 . . . . .210 D5
Leicester Mews PE10 . . . . . .213 B3
Leicester Rd PE8 . . . . .222 C4
Leicester St
Kingston upon Hull HU3 . . . .180 D8
1 Sleaford NG34 . . . . .212 D4
Leiden Fields **2** PE11 . . . . .214 B2
Leighton PE2 . . . . .230 C4
Leighton Cres **2** LN6 . . . . .205 B6
Leighton Gr DN33 . . . . .191 C4
Leighton Prim Sch PE2 . . . . .230 C4
Leighton Wlk **4** PE12 . . . . .159 D7
Leinsters Cl PE3 . . . . .225 D3
Leiston Ct **21** PE6 . . . . .175 A1
Lemon Wong La LN5 . . . . . .106 C3
Lenham La HU1 . . . . .180 E6
LENTON NG33 . . . . .141 E5
Lenton Gn LN2 . . . . .202 B7
Lenton's La Friskney PE22 . . .115 A5
Leverton PE22 . . . . .126 F6
Lenton Way **2** PE20 . . . . .136 D6
Leofric Ave PE10 . . . . .213 B5
Leofric Cl **19** PE6 . . . . .166 F1
Leofric Sq PE1 . . . . .226 E3
Leonard Cres DN15 . . . . . . .182 F3
Leonard St **4** HU3 . . . . . . .180 D8
Leopold Cl DN16 . . . . .185 A6
Lerowe Rd PE13 . . . . .170 E1
Leslie Ct **5** DN15 . . . . .183 B3
Leslie Manser Prim Sch
LN6 . . . . .204 B7
Lessingham PE2 . . . . .229 D4
Lestrange St DN35 . . . . .192 C7
Lethbridge Rd PE4 . . . . .221 D2
Lettwell Cres **1** PE25 . . . . .206 D1
Levellers Wy **12** NG24 . . . .104 C4
Levels La Blaxton DN9 . . . . . .26 A4
Misson DN10 . . . . .39 A7
Leven Rd DN16 . . . . .185 D6
Levens Wlk PE3 . . . . .225 B3
Leveret Chase LN6 . . . . .92 D5
Leverett Rd PE21 . . . . .209 B4
LEVERINGTON PE13 . . . . . .170 B3
Leverington Comm PE13 . . . .169 F1
Leverington Prim Acad
PE13 . . . . .170 B2
Leverington Rd PE13 . . . . . .170 C1
Levers Cl PE21 . . . . .209 F5
Leverstock Gn **38** DN7 . . . . .14 D4
LEVERTON PE22 . . . . .126 F6
Leverton CE Acad DN22 . . . . .52 B1
LEVERTON HIGHGATE
PE22 . . . . .127 A6
Leverton Leisure Ctr
PE22 . . . . .127 A7
LEVERTON LUCASGATE
PE22 . . . . .127 B6
LEVERTON OUTGATE
PE22 . . . . .127 B7
Leverton Rd DN22 . . . . .52 B1
Levington St **2** DN31 . . . . .189 C1
Lewes Ave NG31 . . . . .210 D5
Lewes Gdns PE4 . . . . .221 A3
Lewis Ave **13** LN12 . . . . .77 A8
Lewis Ct **15** PE11 . . . . .214 C2
Lewis Rd Cleethorpes DN35 . .192 D8
Coningsby LN4 . . . . .207 D4
Lewis St
Gainsborough DN21 . . . . . . .197 D3
Lincoln LN5 . . . . .234 B1
Lexington Dr HU4 . . . . .179 C5
Leyburn Rd LN6 . . . . .204 F4
Leyden Cl **6** DN40 . . . . . . .186 B4
Leyland Ave DN7 . . . . .14 E4
Leys Cl NG32 . . . . .210 B4
Leys Farm Jun Sch DN17 . . .184 F4
Leys La DN15 . . . . .183 C1
Leys Ln **7** DN10 . . . . .39 C1
Leys The
Cherry Willingham LN3 . . . . .203 E6
Peterborough PE3 . . . . .225 A1
Leytonstone La PE10 . . . . . .213 D2
Libertas Dr **1** PE2 . . . . . . .231 E4
Liberty La HU1 . . . . .181 A6
Liberty Pk **3** HU15 . . . . .2 D5
Lichfield Ave
Peterborough PE4 . . . . .220 F3
Scunthorpe DN17 . . . . .184 C7
Lichfield Cl NG31 . . . . .210 E4
Lichfield Ct DN32 . . . . .192 B6
Lichfield Rd
Bracebridge Heath LN4 . . . . .81 A2
Grimsby DN32 . . . . .192 B6
12 Hatfield DN7 . . . . .14 D4
Liddell St HU2 . . . . .180 E7
Lidgard Rd DN36 . . . . .193 A1
Lidgate Cl PE2 . . . . .230 C7
Lidgett Cl **10** DN20 . . . . . . .30 F8
Lidgett The **7** DN9 . . . . . . .27 D6
Lifeboat Ave PE25 . . . . .206 D1
Lighter-than-Air Rd
NG34 . . . . .107 C1
Lighton Ave **4** PE20 . . . . . .136 C5
Lilac Ave DN16 . . . . .183 C1
Lilac Cl Birchwood LN6 . . . . .204 C8
Bourne PE10 . . . . .213 B6

Lilac Cl continued
Wisbech PE13 . . . . .170 E1
Lilac Ct DN33 . . . . .194 D8
Lilac Rd
9 Elloughton-cum-Brough
HU15 . . . . .2 C5
Peterborough PE1 . . . . .226 C7
Lilac Wlk PE7 . . . . .233 F6
Lilacwood Dr **5** NG31 . . . . .210 F7
Lila Dr **1** PE11 . . . . .145 B7
Liburn Cl **5** NG34 . . . . .121 B8
Liburn Dr PE11 . . . . .214 C6
Lilford Cl **5** LN2 . . . . .202 E7
Lilford Rd LN2 . . . . .202 E7
Lilley St **6** NG23 . . . . .117 D3
Lillicrap Ct **2** LN1 . . . . . . .234 B4
Lilly's Carr Nature Reserve★
PE23 . . . . .100 E6
Lilly's Ct LN2 . . . . .234 B4
Lily La **13** NG24 . . . . .104 B5
Lilywood Rd **12** DN20 . . . . . .19 D3
Lima Wy PE2 . . . . .231 D4
Limber Bridle Road DN37 . . . .23 C2
Limber Cl **2** DN21 . . . . .53 A7
Limber Ct DN34 . . . . .191 A6
Limber Hill Binbrook LN8 . . . . .47 D4
Great Limber DN37 . . . . .22 E2
Limber Rd
Great Limber DN41 . . . . .22 E5
Humberside Airport DN39 . . . .22 A6
Swallow LN7 . . . . .34 A7
Limber Vale DN34 . . . . .191 A6
Limburg Dr **7** PE11 . . . . . .214 A2
Lime Ave Scunthorpe DN16 . . .19 A3
Wisbech PE13 . . . . .170 D1
Limeberry Pl
7 Birchwood LN6 . . . . . . .204 B8
8 Birchwood LN6 . . . . . . .204 B8
Lime Cl
Burgh le Marsh PE24 . . . . . .102 D7
2 Langtoft PE6 . . . . .164 F3
8 Old Leake PE22 . . . . . .114 A1
RAF Cranwell NG34 . . . . . . .107 D1
Ruskington NG34 . . . . .108 D1
Lime Cres Greetwell LN2 . . . .203 B8
Waddington LN5 . . . . .205 C1
Lime Ct PE11 . . . . .214 E3
Limedale View **2** DN3 . . . . .14 A3
Lime Gr Bassingham LN5 . . . .92 F2
2 Boston PE21 . . . . .209 C2
2 Bottesford NG13 . . . . . .128 A5
Caythorpe NG32 . . . . .119 C7
Cherry Willingham/Reepham
LN3 . . . . .203 D5
9 Goxhill DN19 . . . . .12 A8
Grantham NG31 . . . . .211 C6
Holbeach PE12 . . . . .215 D3
Holton le Clay DN36 . . . . . . .36 C7
Humberston DN36 . . . . .36 C7
7 Ingoldmells PE25 . . . . . .90 D3
Louth LN11 . . . . .198 C7
Scunthorpe DN16 . . . . .185 B7
Lime Kiln Cl PE3 . . . . .225 E4
Lime Kiln Way LN2 . . . . . . .202 C4
Limelands **2** LN2 . . . . .234 C3
Lime St Grimsby DN31 . . . . .191 C8
Kingston upon Hull HU8 . . . .181 A8
3 Sutton Bridge PE12 . . . .160 F4
Limes The
7 Beckingham DN10 . . . . .40 A1
Castor PE5 . . . . .223 F1
4 Stallingborough DN41 . . .23 D6
17 Waltham DN37 . . . . . . .172 B1
Limetree Ave DN33 . . . . . . .191 C3
Lime Tree Ave
Gainsborough DN21 . . . . . . .197 D3
Kingston upon Hull HU13 . . .178 F2
2 Market Deeping PE6 . . . .217 A6
20 Metheringham LN4 . . . . .95 C4
Peterborough PE1 . . . . .225 F4
Limetree Cl
13 Sleaford NG34 . . . . . .212 D2
Yaxley PE7 . . . . .233 F7
Lime Tree Cl
1 Collingham NG23 . . . . . .91 D4
6 Fulbeck NG32 . . . . .106 C1
6 Lincoln LN6 . . . . .204 E8
Lime Tree Gr **4** DN8 . . . . . .15 A8
Lime Tree Paddock **2** LN2 . .68 F4
Limetree Wlk **1** NG34 . . . . .122 E1
Limewalk PE12 . . . . .216 C6
Lime Wlk **9** PE22 . . . . .114 A1
Limewood Way **2** LN2 . . . . .202 F6
Linchfield Cl PE6 . . . . .217 E5
Linchfield Com Prim Sch
PE6 . . . . .217 D5
Linchfield Rd PE6 . . . . .217 D6
LINCOLN LN1 . . . . .234 C2
Lincoln Ass Rm★ LN2 . . . . .234 B3
Lincoln Ave LN6 . . . . .205 C8
Lincoln Bishop King CE Prim
Sch The LN5 . . . . .201 F1
Lincoln Bvd DN31 . . . . .191 B7
Lincoln Castle★ LN1 . . . . . .234 A3
Lincoln Castle Acad LN1 . . . .201 E7
Lincoln Castle Way DN19 . . . .4 D2
Lincoln Cath★ LN2 . . . . . . .234 B3
Lincoln Christ's Hospl Sch
LN2 . . . . .202 B6
Lincoln Cl **4** Crowle DN17 . . .16 D7
Grantham NG31 . . . . .210 D4
5 Market Deeping PE6 . . . .217 A6
Lincoln Coll LN2 . . . . .234 C3
Lincoln Cres **2** DN21 . . . . . .42 F8
Lincoln Dr
4 Beacon Hill NG24 . . . . .104 A6
Brumby DN16 . . . . .185 B7
Lincoln Cty Hospl LN2 . . . . .202 C4

Lincoln Dr
27 Barton-upon-Humber
DN16 . . . . .10 F8
30 Caistor LN7 . . . . .33 B4
3 Scampton Airfield LN1 . . .67 F5
5 Waddington LN5 . . . . . . .94 A7
24 Winterton DN15 . . . . . . .9 A5
Lincoln Drill Hall★ LN1 . . . . .234 B2
Lincoln Gate DN36 . . . . .48 D5
Lincoln Gdns DN16 . . . . . . .185 A6
Lincoln Gdns Prim Sch
DN16 . . . . .185 A6
Lincoln Gn
Kingston upon Hull HU4 . . . .179 C7
Skegness PE25 . . . . .206 B5
Holton le Clay DN36 . . . . . .195 C2
Morton DN21 . . . . .197 F6
Lincoln La Boston PE21 . . . . .208 E5
Holbeach PE12 . . . . .147 D5
Kettlethorpe LN1 . . . . .65 F3
Osgodby LN8 . . . . .44 F2
Thorpe on the Hill LN6 . . . . . .92 E8
Lincoln Rd Bassingham LN5 . .92 E7
10 Binbrook Tech Pk LN8 . . .47 B6
Brant Broughton LN5 . . . . . .105 F5
Brant Broughton & Stragglethorpe
LN5 . . . . .106 A5
Canwick LN4 . . . . .81 B3
Caythorpe NG32 . . . . .119 B6
Cleethorpes DN35 . . . . .192 C5
Deeping Gate PE6 . . . . .217 C3
Digby LN4 . . . . .108 D6
Doddington & Whisby LN6 . . .204 A6
Dunholme LN2 . . . . .68 C4
Dunston LN4 . . . . .95 B5
Faldingworth LN8 . . . . .56 F3
Fenton LN1 . . . . .65 E3
Fiskerton LN3 . . . . .203 F4
1 Glinton PE6 . . . . .220 C8
Heighington/Washingborough
LN4 . . . . .203 A2
Holton cum Beckering LN8 . . .70 B7
Honington LN7 . . . . .119 C2
Horncastle LN9 . . . . .199 A4
Ingham LN1 . . . . .54 F2
1 Leasingham NG34 . . . . .121 B8
Lincoln LN6 . . . . .204 F1
Louth LN11 . . . . .61 B8
Metheringham LN4 . . . . .95 C4
Middle Rasen LN8 . . . . .57 B7
Moorland Prison DN7 . . . . . .26 A8
Nettleham LN2 . . . . .68 B1
Newark-on-Trent NG24 . . . .104 A6
Northborough PE6 . . . . .217 D1
Peterborough PE6 . . . . .220 D5
Ruskington NG34 . . . . .108 D2
Saxilby with Ingleby LN1 . . . .66 E1
4 Skegness PE25 . . . . . . .206 C3
Skellingthorpe LN6 . . . . . . .200 B4
Sleaford NG34 . . . . .212 B7
Stamford PE9 . . . . .219 C7
West Barkwith LN8 . . . . .71 A7
Lincoln Rd Bridge NG24 . . . .104 A5
Lincoln Rd Nocton LN4 . . . . . .95 A7
Lincoln St Christopher's Sch
The LN5 . . . . .205 B4
Lincoln St Peter at Gowts CE
Prim Sch The LN5 . . . . . . .201 E4
Lincoln St Peter-in-Eastgate
CE (Cont) Inf Sch The
LN2 . . . . .234 C3
Lincoln's Ave **2** LN4 . . . . . .168 C2
Lincoln Sch of Art and Design
LN2 . . . . .234 B3
Lincolnshire Archives★
LN1 . . . . .234 B3
Lincolnshire Aviation Heritage
Ctr★ PE23 . . . . .99 F5
Lincolnshire Coast Light Rly★
PE25 . . . . .90 D1
Lincolnshire Montessori Sch
LN7 . . . . .33 C4
Lincolnshire Rare Breeds
Poultry★ LN4 . . . . .61 F8
Lincolnshire Rd Transport
Mus★ LN6 . . . . .204 D5
Lincolnshire Showground★
LN1 . . . . .67 E4
Lincolnshire Wolds Rly★
DN36 . . . . .48 F6
Lincoln St
Gainsborough DN21 . . . . . . .197 C5
Kingston upon Hull HU2 . . . .180 F8
Lincoln Sta LN5 . . . . .234 B1
Lincoln Way **1** PE11 . . . . . .214 C5
Linda Cres LN1 . . . . .198 B4
Lindale Gdns DN16 . . . . . . .185 C7
Lindbergh Dr **17** PE11 . . . . .214 C2
Linden Ave **3** Branston LN4 . .81 D2
16 Newark-on-Trent NG24 . .104 A3
Linden Cl **16** DN7 . . . . .14 D4
Linden Ct PE11 . . . . .214 E5
Linden Dene **1** LN6 . . . . . .204 D1
Linden Dr PE24 . . . . .102 D7
Linden Gdns PE2 . . . . .229 C5
Linden Rd LN9 . . . . .199 C4
Linden Rise PE10 . . . . .213 D7
Lindens PE13 . . . . .177 A3
Lindens The NG31 . . . . .211 B2
Linden Terr DN21 . . . . .197 D3
Linden Way Boston PE21 . . . .209 A7
Pinchbeck PE11 . . . . .144 D1
Linden Wlk LN11 . . . . .198 C4
Lindholme **15** 29 C3
Lindholme Bank Rd DN7 . . . . .15 B1
Lindholme Rd LN6 . . . . .204 D5
Lindisfarne Ave DN36 . . . . . .195 B6
Lindisfarne Rd PE6 . . . . .175 A1
Lindisfarne Way NG31 . . . . .210 E5
Lindis Rd PE21 . . . . .209 C5

Lindley St DN16 . . . . .185 A6
Lindrick Cl **4** NG31 . . . . . . .211 D7
Lindrick Cl DN21 . . . . .197 E6
Lindrick Rd **6** DN7 . . . . . . .14 F3
Lindrick Wlk **5** DN37 . . . . . .194 C4
Lindridge Wlk PE3 . . . . .225 A2
Lindsey Ave PE6 . . . . .217 A6
Lindsey Cl **6** Bourne PE10 . .213 C5
Gainsborough DN21 . . . . . . .197 F2
Peterborough PE4 . . . . .221 B1
Lindsey Cl **12** DN9 . . . . . . .27 E6
Lindsey Ctr **4** DN21 . . . . . .197 D4
Lindsey Dr Crowle DN17 . . . . .16 D8
6 Healing DN41 . . . . .24 A5
Lindsey Pl HU4 . . . . .179 D6
Lindsey Rd
Cleethorpes DN35 . . . . .192 F4
Stamford PE9 . . . . .219 C6
4 Uffington PE9 . . . . .172 C6
Lindsey Rise **2** DN33 . . . . .194 F8
Lindsey Rise **2** DN16 . . . . .183 C2
Lindsey Way LN11 . . . . .198 D4
Lindsey Wy PE22 . . . . .125 A8
Lindum Ave
3 Immingham DN40 . . . . .186 B3
Lincoln LN2 . . . . .234 C3
Lindum Cotts PE13 . . . . . . .170 B2
Lindum Cres **5** DN20 . . . . .196 B4
Lindum Gr
Chapel St Leonard PE24 . . . . .90 E7
1 Crowle DN17 . . . . .16 C7
Lindum Mews LN6 . . . . .204 D2
Lindum Rd
Cleethorpes DN35 . . . . .193 A4
Lincoln LN2 . . . . .234 B3
Lindum Sq **5** PE25 . . . . . . .206 B5
Lindum St
12 Beacon Hill NG24 . . . .104 A4
Scunthorpe DN15 . . . . .183 B3
Lindum Terr LN2 . . . . .234 C3
Lindum Way **9** PE11 . . . . . .134 F2
Lindum Wlk **1** LN7 . . . . . . .32 A1
Linecroft La DN10 . . . . .40 B4
Linga La LN5 . . . . .93 A3
Linga St **26** HU15 . . . . .2 D5
Ling Dr **11** DN21 . . . . .197 F5
Lingfield Cl **6** LN1 . . . . .66 D3
Ling Garth PE1 . . . . .226 B8
Linghall La LN4 . . . . .111 E5
Ling House La DN7 . . . . .14 A5
Ling La NG33 . . . . .152 C5
Ling Moor Prim Sch LN6 . . . .204 E3
Lings La LN4 . . . . .14 D3
Lingwood Pk **8** PE3 . . . . . .225 A1
Linkage Coll PE23 . . . . .100 F7
Link Rd PE1 . . . . .225 F3
Links Ave **2** LN12 . . . . .64 B5
Links Cres **4** PE25 . . . . . . .103 E4
Linksde DN36 . . . . .195 E6
Linkside PE3 . . . . .220 F1
Links Rd DN35 . . . . .193 A3
Link The
Bracebridge Heath LN4 . . . . .205 F4
Kingston upon Hull HU4 . . . .179 C5
2 Leasingham NG34 . . . . .121 B8
Louth LN11 . . . . .198 E5
1 Navenby/Wellingore
LN5 . . . . .107 A7
Linkway **7** DN7 . . . . .14 F3
Link Way PE11 . . . . .214 E4
Linley Cl **4** NG23 . . . . .91 D4
Linley Dr PE21 . . . . .208 E2
Linnaeus St HU3 . . . . .180 C6
Linnet PE2 . . . . .229 D6
Linnet Cl Birchwood LN6 . . . .204 D8
7 Market Deeping PE6 . . . .217 C5
Scunthorpe DN15 . . . . .182 D6
Linnet Dr LN10 . . . . .143 A3
Linnet Garth DN16 . . . . .185 F5
Linnet Way **11** NG24 . . . . . .104 A4
Linseed Ave **15** NG24 . . . . .104 A6
Linthorpe Gr HU10 . . . . .178 E8
Linton **21** HU15 . . . . .2 C6
Linton Cl Freiston PE22 . . . . .137 E7
Westwoodside DN9 . . . . .27 A2
Linton Rise **3** DN15 . . . . . . .8 A4
Linton St **5** LN5 . . . . .201 F1
LINWOOD LN8 . . . . .57 D5
Linwood Ave **5** DN33 . . . . .194 F8
Linwood Cl
Gainsborough DN21 . . . . . . .197 F3
5 Sleaford NG34 . . . . . . .212 C6
Linwood Rd Lissington LN8 . . .57 D3
Martin LN4 . . . . .96 A3
Linwood Warren Nature
Reserve★ LN8 . . . . .58 A6
Lions Wy NG34 . . . . .212 F6
Liquorpond St **11** PE21 . . . .208 F4
Lisburn Cl **7** LN5 . . . . .205 D2
Lisburn Gr DN33 . . . . .191 D2
Lisle Marsden CE Mid Sch
DN32 . . . . .191 E4
Lissett Cl **8** LN6 . . . . .204 B6
Lissingly La LN3 . . . . .57 C4
LISSINGTON LN3 . . . . .57 E2
Lissington Cl **2** LN2 . . . . . .201 F7
Lissington Rd
Gainsborough DN21 . . . . . . .197 F3
Wickenby LN3 . . . . .57 C1
Lister Rd Peterborough PE1 . .225 F7
Scunthorpe DN15 . . . . .182 C3
Lister St Grimsby DN31 . . . . .191 B8
Kingston upon Hull HU1 . . . .180 E5
LISTOFT PE24 . . . . .89 F7
Listoft La PE24 . . . . .89 F7
Litchfield Cl PE7 . . . . .233 F5

Little Bargate St LN5 . . . . . .205 E8
Littlebeck Cl HU3 . . . . .180 A7
Littlebeck Rd **3** DN36 . . . . . .36 C8
Little Becks DN37 . . . . .23 F2
Little Belt The DN21 . . . . . . .197 D7
LITTLEBOROUGH DN22 . . . . .52 F1
Littleborough La DN22 . . . . . .52 C2
Littleborough Rd DN22 . . . . . .52 C2
Littlebury Gdns PE12 . . . . . .215 C2
LITTLE BYTHAM NG33 . . . . .163 A8
Little Bytham Rd
Castle Bytham NG33 . . . . . .152 E1
Counthorpe & Creeton
NG33 . . . . .153 A2
LITTLE CARLTON LN11 . . . . .62 C4
LITTLE CASTERTON PE9 . . .171 E8
Little Casterton Rd PE9 . . . .218 F8
Little Casterton Road PE9 . .163 B1
LITTLE CAWTHORPE LN11 . . .61 E2
Littlechild Dr **4** PE13 . . . . .170 B2
Little Cl Edenham PE10 . . . . .153 D5
18 Eye PE6 . . . . .175 A1
LITTLE COATES DN31 . . . . .190 F7
Littlecoates Prim Sch
DN31 . . . . .188 D1
Little Coates Rd DN34 . . . . .190 E4
Little Comm PE12 . . . . .215 B7
LITTLE COMMON PE12 . . . . .215 B8
Littlecote Gr PE4 . . . . .225 E8
Little Dog Dro PE2 . . . . .158 C1
Little Dowgate PE13 . . . . . . .170 B1
Little Dro PE20 . . . . .124 C2
Littlefair Rd **6** HU9 . . . . .5 D8
LITTLEFIELD DN34 . . . . . . .191 B6
Littlefield La
Grimsby DN31 . . . . .191 A6
Marshchapel DN36 . . . . .37 B2
Little Gate La LN4 . . . . .82 A1
Little George St HU8 . . . . . .181 A8
Little Gonerby CE (Aided)
Infant's Sch NG31 . . . . . . .211 B5
LITTLE GRIMSBY LN11 . . . . .49 B2
Little Grimsby La LN11 . . . . . .49 A1
LITTLE HALE NG34 . . . . . . .133 E8
Little Hale Dro NG34 . . . . . .133 F8
Little Hale Rd NG34 . . . . . . .122 E1
Little Holme Rd PE34 . . . . . .161 C2
Little Johns Cl PE3 . . . . .224 F3
Little John St DN34 . . . . . . .191 B6
Little La Broomfleet HU15 . . . .1 C6
6 Collingham NG23 . . . . . .91 C4
Gringley on the Hill DN10 . . . .39 C1
Louth LN11 . . . . .198 C5
Surfleet PE11 . . . . .145 B3
5 Welbourn LN5 . . . . . . .106 E5
Whaplode PE12 . . . . .158 A5
Wrawby DN20 . . . . .196 F6
LITTLE LIMBER DN37 . . . . . .22 C5
LITTLE LONDON Legsby LN8. . .58 A5
Long Sutton PE12 . . . . .216 D5
Spalding PE11 . . . . .214 A1
Tetford LN9 . . . . .73 F2
Little London PE12 . . . . .216 D6
Little London La LN8 . . . . . . .58 C6
Little Marsh La PE22 . . . . . .159 B7
Little Mason St **3** HU1 . . . . .181 A7
Littlemeer PE2 . . . . .229 F4
Little Merebalk La LN9 . . . . . .86 B2
Little Michael St DN31 . . . . .191 B7
Littlemoors La PE22 . . . . . . .113 A3
LITTLE PONTON NG31 . . . . .140 A7
Littleport La **3** PE22 . . . . . .113 A1
Little Ramper PE13 . . . . . . .170 D2
Little Scrubs Wood Nature
Reserve★ LN8 . . . . .70 E1
Little Side Rd PE20 . . . . . . .135 E8
Little S St **16** LN11 . . . . . . .198 B5
LITTLE STEEPING PE23 . . . .101 D5
Little Steeping Mud & Stud
Cottage★ PE23 . . . . .101 D6
LITTLE SUTTON PE12 . . . . .160 C5
Little Tathwell LN11 . . . . .61 B1
Little Thorpe La LN6 . . . . . . .79 F1
LITTLE WELTON LN11 . . . . . .60 F6
LITTLE WISBEACH NG34 . . .143 C6
Little Wlk DN8 . . . . .40 B5
Littlewood Rd DN8 . . . . .15 B8
Littleworth Dro
Deeping St Nicholas PE11 . . .156 D1
Heckington NG34 . . . . .122 F4
Spalding PE11 . . . . .156 D2
Sutton St Edmund PE12 . . . .176 F8
Livermore Gn PE4 . . . . .220 E6
Liverpool Dr LN6 . . . . .200 B2
Liverpool St HU3 . . . . .180 A3
Livesey Rd DN36 . . . . .48 E6
Livingstone Dr PE11 . . . . . . .214 B2
Livingstone Rd Hessle HU13 . .3 F4
3 Yaxley PE7 . . . . .233 D5
Lloyd Pl **10** DN21 . . . . .55 A8
Lloyds Ave DN17 . . . . .184 F8
Lobelia Dr **1** DN17 . . . . . . .185 A1
LOBTHORPE NG33 . . . . .152 A3
Loch Fyne Cl PE2 . . . . .229 B4
Loch Lomond Way PE2 . . . . .229 C4
Locke Way HU13 . . . . .178 B3
Lockham Gate PE22 . . . . . . .114 B2
Lockhill DN31 . . . . .189 A2
Lock Hill **30** DN8 . . . . .15 A8
Locking Cl **17** LN6 . . . . . . .204 C6
Locking Garth LN1 . . . . .49 D5
Lock Keepers Ct HU9 . . . . . .181 C6
Lock Keepers Way LN11 . . . .198 D7
Lock La DN8 . . . . .15 A8

Lock Rd Alvingham LN11 . . . . **49** F2
North Coates DN36 . . . . **37** A3
Locks Cl PE6 . . . . **174** A8
Locksley Christian Sch
LN11 . . . . **62** C6
Locksley Cl
6 Boston PE21 . . . . **208** E7
4 North Somercotes LN11 . . **50** F7
Locksley Way 5 LN11 . . . . . **50** F7
Lockton Cl 2 PE20 . . . . **135** B7
Lockton Ct 10 DN37 . . . . . **190** E8
Lockton Gr 1 HU5 . . . . **179** D8
Lockwood Bank DN9 . . . . . . **27** E6
Lockwood Cl 12 DN18 . . . . . **10** F8
Lockwood Ct 1 DN15 . . . . **182** E4
Lockwood St HU2 . . . . **180** F8
Lockwood Way PE7 . . . . **233** E8
Lode Cl PE7 . . . . **231** C4
Loder Ave PE3 . . . . **224** F2
Lodge Ave 22 DN18 . . . . **10** F8
Lodge Cl 10 Brough HU15 . . . . **2** C7
Kingston upon Hull HU13 . . **178** F1
6 Welton/Dunholme LN2 . . **68** D7
Lodge Ct 37 DN7 . . . . **14** D4
Lodge Cvn Pk LN4 . . . . **207** A4
Lodge Dr LN6 . . . . **105** A8
Lodge Gdns HU13 . . . . **178** C2
Lodge La Flixborough DN15 . . . **8** B2
Kirk Bramwith DN7 . . . . **14** A8
Nettleham LN2 . . . . **68** D1
Upton DN21 . . . . **53** D5
Lodge Rd Bourne PE10 . . . . . **213** C2
4 Coningsby LN4 . . . . **207** A5
Kelby NG32 . . . . **131** D8
Scunthorpe DN15 . . . . **182** C2
Tattershall Thorpe LN10 . . . . **97** E3
Lodge Top Cl LN6 . . . . **204** E5
Lodge Way NG31 . . . . **211** A6
Lodington Ct 5 LN9 . . . . . **199** D3
Loft Ave DN37 . . . . **190** E8
Loganberry Dr HU4 . . . . . . **179** C4
Loire Ct PE3 . . . . **225** E4
Lomax Dr 2 NG34 . . . . . . **212** C6
Lombard St DN34 . . . . **191** A7
Lombardy Dr PE1 . . . . **226** B8
Lomond Gr DN36 . . . . **36** C8
Lomond Rd HU5 . . . . **179** E8
Londesborough St HU3 . . . **180** C7
Londesborough Way 13
LN4 . . . . **95** D4
London Rd Boston PE21 . . . . **208** E1
Bracebridge Heath LN4 . . . . **205** F5
Frampton PE20 . . . . **136** D7
Grantham NG31 . . . . **211** B3
Haugham LN11 . . . . **74** A7
Long Sutton PE12 . . . . **216** C4
Louth LN11 . . . . **198** C3
Newark-on-Trent NG24 . . . . **104** B2
5 Newark-on-Trent NG24 . . **104** B3
Osbournby NG34 . . . . **132** C5
Peterborough PE2 . . . . **226** A1
Sleaford NG34 . . . . **212** C1
Spalding PE11 . . . . **214** C2
Tathwell LN11 . . . . **61** C2
Wansford PE8 . . . . **222** B2
Wothorpe PE9 . . . . **219** C2
Yaxley PE7 . . . . **233** C5
LONDONTHORPE NG31 . . . **130** D4
Londonthorpe La NG31 . . . **211** E8
Londonthorpe Rd NG31 . . **211** F7
Long Acre 1 LN12 . . . . **64** B4
LONG BENNINGTON
NG23 . . . . **117** D3
Long Bennington CE Prim Sch
NG23 . . . . **117** D3
Longcliffe Rd NG31 . . . . . . **211** A8
Long Cl La LN3 . . . . **82** B7
Longcroft Dr 1 NG34 . . . . **107** C1
Long Cswy PE1 . . . . **226** A2
Longdales Pl LN2 . . . . **202** A7
Longdales Rd LN2 . . . . **201** F6
Longden St HU3 . . . . **180** A4
Longdon Cl 6 PE12 . . . . . . **160** E4
Long Dro Bourne PE10 . . . . . **155** B1
Gosberton PE11 . . . . **144** B6
Rippingale PE10 . . . . **143** D3
Thurlby PE10 . . . . **164** E7
Walcott LN4 . . . . **109** E8
Wisbech St Mary PE13 . . . . **177** D4
Long Edge LN11 . . . . **62** E3
Long Farm La DN22 . . . . **52** E2
Longfellow Dr 7 NG24 . . . **104** B3
Long Field Dr 2 DN3 . . . . . **14** A1
Longfield Gate PE2 . . . . . . **230** A6
Longfield Rd DN34 . . . . . . **190** E4
Long Field Rd 23 DN3 . . . . **14** A2
Long Gates LN11 . . . . **51** A1
Longhead La PE14 . . . . **170** D3
Longhedge Dro PE20 . . . . . **134** E5
Long Hedge La
Greetham with Somersby
LN9 . . . . **86** C5
Swaby SN13 . . . . **74** E4
Long Hedges PE22 . . . . . . **126** B6
Long Hollow NG33 . . . . . . **131** C3
Longhorn Cl DN37 . . . . **194** B4
Longhurst Gdns PE21 . . . . **208** D7
Long La
Auburn Haddington & South
Hykeham LN6 . . . . **93** B7
Barnby in the Willows NG24 **104** F4
Fleet PE12 . . . . **168** B3
Ingham LN1 . . . . **54** E2
Leadenham LN5 . . . . **107** A2
Moulton PE12 . . . . **157** E5

Long La continued
Mumby LN13 . . . . **76** E2
Redmile NG32 . . . . **128** A1
2 Westborough & Dry
Doddington NG23 . . . . . . **117** F3
Willoughton DN21 . . . . **42** E3
Longlands LN13 . . . . **63** D3
Longleat Dr LN11 . . . . **198** A7
Long Leys Rd LN1 . . . . **201** C6
Longmeadow Rise 18
DN41 . . . . **23** A4
Longmeadows PE10 . . . . . . **154** B7
Longmeadows Dr DN37 . . . . **23** F2
Long Pasture 5 PE4 . . . . . **220** F5
Long Rd
1 Scunthorpe DN15 . . . . . **182** F4
Terrington St Clement PE34 **161** F5
3 Tydd St Mary PE13 . . . . **170** C8
Longrigg Wlk 17 PE20 . . . **135** B7
Long St 2 Foston NG32 . . . **117** F1
Great Gonerby NG31 . . . . . **129** E5
LONG SUTTON PE12 . . . . . **216** C4
Long Sutton Butterfly Pk★
PE12 . . . . **216** D6
Long Sutton Prim Sch
PE12 . . . . **216** B5
LONGTHORPE PE3 . . . . **225** A2
Longthorpe Ct 3 PE3 . . . . **225** A2
Longthorpe Gn PE3 . . . . . . **225** B1
Longthorpe House Mews 11
PE3 . . . . **224** F2
Longthorpe Parkway PE3 **225** C1
Longthorpe Prim Sch
PE3 . . . . **225** A2
Long Toft Prim School
DN7 . . . . **14** C6
Longton Rd 4 DN3 . . . . **14** A2
Longueville Ct PE2 . . . . . . **230** B5
Longwater PE2 . . . . **230** B6
Long Wood La LN4 . . . . **95** C2
Long Wood Rd DN21 . . . . . . **41** A1
Lonsdale Ct 20 DN36 . . . . . **36** D8
Lonsdale Gr PE10 . . . . **213** E6
Lonsdale Pl 3 LN5 . . . . . . **201** F1
Lonsdale Rd PE9 . . . . **218** E5
Lonsdale St 5 HU3 . . . . . . **180** A6
Loop La 1 PE12 . . . . **157** F7
LOOSEGATE PE12 . . . . **158** A8
Loosegate Rd PE12 . . . . . . **158** A8
Lopham La DN37 . . . . **34** F8
Lord Dr 4 NG31 . . . . **129** E5
Lord Porter Ave 9 DN7 . . . **14** C7
Lords La 19 DN19 . . . . **11** D8
Lord's La 6 NG33 . . . . **151** A8
Lord St Gainsborough DN21 **197** C4
Grimsby DN31 . . . . **191** B8
4 Sleaford NG34 . . . . **212** C3
17 Stainforth DN7 . . . . **14** C6
Lornas Field PE7 . . . . **230** D2
Lorne Cl 1 HU2 . . . . **180** F8
Lorne St LN5 . . . . **234** C1
Losecoat Cl 1 PE9 . . . . . . **219** D7
Lothian NG34 . . . . **120** F2
Lotus Cl 7 LN5 . . . . **93** F7
Lotus Ct LN6 . . . . **204** D1
Loughborough Univ of
Peterborough PE1 . . . . . **226** A3
Lough Rd LN9 . . . . **72** F1
Louisberg Rd DN21 . . . . **54** F8
Louis Dr HU5 . . . . **179** D8
Louis St HU3 . . . . **180** C8
LOUTH LN11 . . . . **198** E6
Louth Academy LN11 . . . . . **198** B7
Louth Cty Hospl LN11 . . . . **198** B6
Louth Kidgate Prim Sch
LN11 . . . . **198** C5
Louth Mus★ LN11 . . . . . . **198** B5
Louth Playgoers Riverhead
Theatre★ LN11 . . . . **198** D7
Louth Rd East Barkwith LN8 . . **58** E1
Fotherby LN11 . . . . **49** A3
Grimsby DN33 . . . . **191** D1
1 Holton le Clay DN36 . . . **195** D2
Horncastle LN9 . . . . **199** C5
LOUTH LN11 . . . . **61** F8
New Waltham DN36 . . . . . . **195** B6
Skidbrooke LN11 . . . . **50** D2
Skidbrooke with Saltfleet Haven
LN11 . . . . **51** C4
2 West Ashby LN9 . . . . . . **85** E7
Wragby LN8 . . . . **70** D5
Louth Sta Est (Ind) LN11 **198** C6
Louth Trading Est LN11 . . **198** C7
Lovat Cl HU3 . . . . **180** D5
Loveden Cl 32 NG24 . . . . . **104** B2
Loveden Ct DN35 . . . . **193** A3
Loveden View 6 NG32 . . . **119** B7
Love La Caythorpe NG32 . . . . **119** C7
Gainsborough DN21 . . . . . . **197** C6
Louth LN11 . . . . **198** A5
Spalding PE11 . . . . **214** E3
5 Sutterton PE20 . . . . **136** A2
Wrangle PE22 . . . . **114** C4
Lovell Rd DN17 . . . . **184** C3
Lovell Way PE34 . . . . **161** F2
Lovers La PE5 . . . . **222** F2
Love's Hill Castor PE5 . . . . **223** F1
Peterborough PE5 . . . . **224** A1
Loves La LE15 . . . . **162** A1
Love's La PE20 . . . . **135** C8
Lovett Rd DN35 . . . . **189** E1
LOW BARLINGS LN3 . . . . . . **82** E8
Lowbridge La 4 PE11 . . . . **145** C6
Low Burgage DN15 . . . . **2** B1
LOW BURNHAM DN9 . . . . . . **27** E5
Low Church Rd 2 LN8 . . . . **57** C8
Low Comm La HU15 . . . . **2** D4
Lowcroft DN9 . . . . **27** D2

Lowcroft Cl 4 DN9 . . . . **27** D2
Low Cross St 6 DN17 . . . . . **16** D8
Low Deeps La DN10 . . . . **26** B1
LOWER BASSINGTHORPE
NG33 . . . . **140** E4
LOWER BITCHFIELD
NG33 . . . . **141** A3
Lower Church Rd LN6 . . . . **200** B5
Lowerdale 27 HU15 . . . . **2** C6
Lower High St 9 LN5 . . . . . **93** F7
Lower Kenyon St 10 DN8 . . **15** A8
Lower Mdws 23 DN18 . . . . . . **3** F1
Lower Rd NG32 . . . . **119** A5
Lower Sow Dale Nature
Reserve★ PE23 . . . . **100** B8
Lower Spring St 1 DN31 . . **189** A1
Low Farm Dr NG34 . . . . . . **142** C8
Low Farm La
Owmby DN38 . . . . **32** B8
Somerby DN38 . . . . **21** B1
Lowfield Cl
4 Barnby Dun DN3 . . . . . . **14** A3
31 Kirton in Lindsey DN21 . . **30** B1
Lowfield Ct HU10 . . . . **178** F6
Lowfield House HU10 . . . . **178** F6
Lowfield La
Balderton NG24 . . . . **104** A1
Belchford LN9 . . . . **73** C2
Low Field La HU15 . . . . **2** E5
Lowfield Rd HU10 . . . . **178** E5
Lowfields LN3 . . . . **83** E5
Low Fields Ave 1 PE11 . . . **214** F4
Lowfields La
Allington NG32 . . . . **128** F7
Butterwick PE22 . . . . **126** E5
Lowfields Rd PE22 . . . . . . **126** E6
LOW FULNEY PE12 . . . . . . **157** B4
Low Fulney Est PE12 . . . . **157** C5
Low Garth DN17 . . . . **184** F2
Lowgate PE12 . . . . **159** C8
Kingston upon Hull HU1 . . . **181** A6
Lutton PE12 . . . . **160** A8
Low Gate Friskney PE22 . . . **115** A6
Gosberton PE11 . . . . **145** C7
Marshchapel DN36 . . . . **37** C1
Moulton PE12 . . . . **146** C1
Surfleet PE11 . . . . **145** C3
Tydd St Mary PE13 . . . . **160** A1
Lowgate Ave 7 PE20 . . . . . **135** A4
Lowgate Cres PE12 . . . . . . **159** E8
Low Gate La 6 PE20 . . . . . **135** A4
Lowgate Rd
Ashby with Scremby PE23 . . . **88** D2
Conisholme LN11 . . . . **50** C5
Hogsthorpe PE24 . . . . **90** B8
Low Holland La DN22 . . . . . **52** C2
Lowick Gdns PE3 . . . . **225** C5
Low La Croft PE24 . . . . **102** D6
Holbeach PE12 . . . . **215** F4
Kirk Bramwith DN7 . . . . **14** A6
Middle Rasen LN8 . . . . **45** C1
Rigsby LN13 . . . . **75** F1
Terrington St Clement PE34 **161** E3
Wrangle PE22 . . . . **114** B3
Low Levels Bank DN8 . . . . . **15** D4
Low Leys Rd 6 DN17 . . . . **184** E3
LOW MARNHAM NG23 . . . . . **78** A4
Low Mill La PE20 . . . . **136** E1
Lowmoor La LN9 . . . . **85** C3
Low Moor Rd LN6 . . . . **204** E5
Low Pk La LN4 . . . . **81** F4
Low Rd Bardney LN3 . . . . **83** E4
Barrowby NG32 . . . . **210** A4
Besthorpe NG23 . . . . **91** C7
Blyborough DN21 . . . . **42** E6
Croft PE24 . . . . **102** F5
Crowland PE6 . . . . **175** A8
Friskney PE22 . . . . **114** F4
Grantham NG31 . . . . **211** C8
Harmston LN5 . . . . **93** D6
Healing DN41 . . . . **23** F5
Holbeach PE12 . . . . **147** F2
Marshchapel DN36 . . . . **37** A1
Osgodby LN8 . . . . **45** B3
South Kyme LN4 . . . . **123** B8
Spalding PE11 . . . . **214** F4
Wainfleet St Mary PE24 . . . **102** C1
Walpole Cross Keys PE34 . . **161** D3
Worlaby DN20 . . . . **20** C8
Wyberton PE21 . . . . **136** E7
LOW RISBY DN15 . . . . **9** A2
Low St
Beckingham DN10 . . . . **40** A1
Billingborough NG34 . . . . . . **133** B1
Collingham NG23 . . . . **91** C4
Dunham-on-Trent NG22 . . . . **65** A1
Harby NG23 . . . . **79** B5
Haxey DN9 . . . . **27** D2
North Ferriby HU14 . . . . **3** A4
5 South Ferriby DN18 . . . . **10** A7
Winterton DN15 . . . . **9** A5
Lowther Gdns PE4 . . . . . . **221** B2
Lowther St HU3 . . . . **180** A7
Low Thorpe Rd LN3 . . . . **83** D1
LOW TOYNTON LN9 . . . . . . **199** F6
Low Toynton Cl LN9 . . . . . **199** D5
Low Toynton Rd LN9 . . . . . **199** D5
Low Wood La LN6 . . . . **91** F8
Loxley PE4 . . . . **220** E4
Loxley Gn HU4 . . . . **179** B7
Loxley Way 6 HU15 . . . . **2** D5
Loyalty La DN18 . . . . **3** E2
Loyd St HU10 . . . . **178** F6
Lucan Ct 13 PE22 . . . . **113** B1
Lucas Ct 4 DN41 . . . . **23** F5
Lucern Ct LN11 . . . . **198** D6
Lucerne Ct 4 PE11 . . . . . . **214** B6
Lucetta Gdns 9 PE11 . . . . **214** B5

Lucian Wlk HU4 . . . . **179** A1
Lucina Dr PE2 . . . . **231** D4
Lucius Cl LN6 . . . . **93** A8
Lucy Twr St LN1 . . . . **234** B4
Luda Terr LN11 . . . . **198** D7
LUDBOROUGH DN36 . . . . . . **48** D6
Ludborough Pk DN36 . . . . . **48** E6
Ludborough Rd
13 North Thoresby DN36 . . . **36** B1
North Thoresby DN36 . . . . . . **48** D8
Ludborough Sta DN36 . . . . **48** F6
Ludborough Way 8 DN35 **192** F3
LUDDINGTON DN17 . . . . **7** D3
Luddington & Garthorpe Prim
Sch DN17 . . . . **7** C3
Luddington Rd
Garthorpe & Fockerby DN17 . . **7** E5
1 Peterborough PE4 . . . . . **221** D1
LUDFORD LN8 . . . . **59** A8
Ludford CE Sch LN8 . . . . . **59** B8
Ludford Cres DN21 . . . . . . **197** E3
Ludford Dr 9 LN6 . . . . **205** A7
Ludford Rd Binbrook LN8 . . . **47** C4
Sixhills LN8 . . . . **58** F6
Ludford St DN32 . . . . **191** E6
Ludgate Ct DN37 . . . . **194** D4
Ludlow Ave DN34 . . . . **191** A7
Ludlow Cl PE10 . . . . **213** C3
Ludlow Gdns
Green Hill NG31 . . . . **210** E6
4 Quadring LN8 . . . . **145** A8
Ludlow Pl DN35 . . . . **192** E5
LUDNEY LN11 . . . . **50** C6
Ludney La LN11 . . . . **50** C5
Luffenham Cl 4 PE9 . . . . . **218** E5
Lulworth Ave HU4 . . . . **179** A3
Lulworth Ct DN17 . . . . **184** C8
Lulworth Wlk DN40 . . . . . . **186** D3
Lumbert Way NG23 . . . . **91** C6
Lumley Ave PE25 . . . . **206** D3
Lumley Cres 3 PE25 . . . . . **206** D4
Lumley Pl 2 LN5 . . . . **201** F1
Lumley Rd PE25 . . . . **206** C3
Lumley Sq 8 PE25 . . . . . . **206** C3
Luna Wy 3 PE2 . . . . **231** D4
Lunds The HU10 . . . . **178** C6
Lundy Cl DN40 . . . . **186** C2
Lunedale Rd DN16 . . . . . . **185** D5
Lunn La 5 NG23 . . . . **91** C4
Lunn's Cres 21 DN18 . . . . . **10** E8
Lupin Rd LN2 . . . . **202** C8
Lurgan Cl LN5 . . . . **205** D3
LUSBY PE23 . . . . **86** F2
Lusher Way DN21 . . . . **41** A1
Luton Cl 1 LN6 . . . . **200** B1
Luton Rd HU5 . . . . **179** F8
LUTTON PE12 . . . . **160** A8
Lutton Bank PE12 . . . . **148** D1
Lutton Garnsgate PE12 . . . **216** A4
Lutton Gate Rd PE12 . . . . **168** E4
LUTTON GOWTS PE12 . . . . **216** D8
Lutton Gowts PE12 . . . . . . **216** D7
Lutton Gr PE3 . . . . **225** C6
Lutton Lodge La PE12 . . . . **149** B2
Lych Gate 10 DN20 . . . . . . **19** D3
Lydbrook Rd DN16 . . . . . . **183** A1
Lydd Cl LN6 . . . . **204** C6
Lydford Rd DN40 . . . . **186** D3
Lydia Ct 3 DN40 . . . . **186** A4
Lygon St DN16 . . . . **183** B1
Lyle Cl 5 LN12 . . . . **64** A4
Lyme Wlk 3 PE3 . . . . **225** C4
Lymington Garth HU4 . . . . **179** A3
Lymn Bank PE24 . . . . **102** C4
Lymn Ct 2 NG31 . . . . **210** E2
Lynchwood PE2 . . . . **229** C5
Lyndale Ave 17 DN3 . . . . . . **14** A1
Lyndale Pk PE2 . . . . **229** C6
Lynden Ave NG31 . . . . **210** E8
Lyndhurst Ave
3 Grimsby DN33 . . . . **191** D3
Skegness PE25 . . . . **206** B5
Lyndhurst Ct 1 PE25 . . . . **206** B5
Lyndis Wlk PE12 . . . . **215** E1
Lyndon Bsns Pk LN6 . . . . **204** B5
Lyndon Cres LN11 . . . . . . **198** D8
Lyndon Way Louth LN11 . . . **198** D8
Stamford PE9 . . . . **218** E5
Lyneham Cl LN6 . . . . **204** B7
Lyn Ellis Cl 2 PE21 . . . . . . **209** C4
Lynmouth Cl 1 LN6 . . . . . . **205** A1
Lynmouth Dr DN17 . . . . . . **184** C8
Lynn Rd
Walpole Cross Keys PE34 . . **161** C3
Walsoken PE13 . . . . **170** E2
Lynnwell Cl PE25 . . . . **206** A6
Lynton Ave HU4 . . . . **179** B3
Lynton Cl DN15 . . . . **182** D4
Lynton Parade DN31 . . . . . **191** B7
Lynton Prep Sch DN15 . . . **183** A4
Lynton Rd PE1 . . . . **225** F6
Lynton Rise DN35 . . . . **192** E4
Lynwood Ave HU10 . . . . . . **178** E6
Lyric Cl 1 HU3 . . . . **180** C5
Lysaghts Way DN15 . . . . **8** C1
Lysander Dr PE6 . . . . **217** B7
Lytham Cl
8 Heighington/
Washingborough LN4 . . . **203** D1
Londonthorpe &
Harrowby Without NG31 . . **211** E7
Lytham Dr DN37 . . . . **194** C3
Lythemere PE2 . . . . **230** C4
Lyttelport Cl PE11 . . . . . . **214** D8
Lytton St LN2 . . . . **234** C2
Lyvelly Gdns PE1 . . . . **226** E6

M

MABLETHORPE LN12 . . . . . . **64** C3
Mablethorpe Prim Acad
LN12 . . . . **64** A4
Mablethorpe Rd
North Coates DN36 . . . . **37** A3
Theddlethorpe St Helen LN12 . **63** F5
Macarthy Cl DN33 . . . . **191** A2
Macaulay Dr Lincoln LN2 . . **202** B6
Newark-on-Trent NG24 . . . . **104** B3
Macaulay Prim Acad
DN31 . . . . **191** B8
Macaulay St DN31 . . . . . . **191** B8
Macaulay Way DN31 . . . . . **191** C8
Mace Rd PE2 . . . . **231** D5
Machray Pl DN35 . . . . **192** D7
Mackender Ct 5 DN40 . . . **185** C6
Mackenzie Pl 5 DN40 . . . . **186** B3
Maclure St DN31 . . . . **189** B2
Macmillan Ave LN6 . . . . . . **204** C2
Macphail Cres LN1 . . . . **66** E2
Maddison La PE23 . . . . **88** B3
Madeley La HU3 . . . . **180** C4
Madely Cl 4 LN9 . . . . **199** D3
Maegan Way DN35 . . . . . . **192** E5
Mafeking Terr PE21 . . . . . **209** A7
Maffit Rd PE5 . . . . **223** D3
Magdalen Cl 4 DN16 . . . . **185** B4
Magdalene Rd DN34 . . . . . **190** F5
Magdalene View NG24 . . . **104** B4
Magdalen Mus★ PE24 . . . **102** D1
Magdalen Rd PE24 . . . . . . **102** D2
Magdellan Ct PE3 . . . . **225** E2
Magee Rd PE4 . . . . **221** B1
Magellan Dr 9 PE23 . . . . . **101** A8
Magellan Way PE11 . . . . . **214** C2
Magistrates Rd PE7 . . . . . **233** D8
Magna Cres 15 NG34 . . . . **122** E2
Magna Mile LN8 . . . . **59** B8
Magnolia Ave PE3 . . . . . . **225** A2
Magnolia Cl LN4 . . . . **81** C2
Magnolia Dr 5 DN36 . . . . **195** D1
Magnolia Rd NG34 . . . . . . **212** D2
Magnolia Rise 4 DN40 . . . **186** C3
Magnolia Way DN16 . . . . . **185** B7
Magnus CE Acad NG24 . . . **104** A3
Magnus Ct 18 LN6 . . . . **93** B8
Magnus St 9 NG24 . . . . . . **104** A4
Magpie Cl LN6 . . . . **200** A3
Magpie La 3 DN22 . . . . **52** C1
Magrath Ct 1 DN20 . . . . . **196** C3
Maiden Cl 1 DN40 . . . . . . **186** A4
Maiden Ct 19 LN1 . . . . **66** D2
Maiden Gr 2 NG34 . . . . . . **212** E3
Maiden La Hogsthorpe PE24 . . **90** B7
11 Stamford PE9 . . . . **219** C5
Maidens Rd 10 PE20 . . . . . **136** A2
MAIDENWELL LN11 . . . . **73** E6
Maiden Well Cl 18 LN5 . . . **107** A8
Maidenwell La 11 LN7 . . . . **32** A4
Maiden Well La 5 LN5 . . . **107** A8
Maidment Dr LN1 . . . . **201** C2
Maidwell Way DN34 . . . . . **190** C4
Main App Rd DN16 . . . . . . **183** C3
Main Ave
Bracebridge Heath LN4 . . . . **205** F3
Scunthorpe DN17 . . . . **184** C6
Maine Ave DN15 . . . . **182** B5
Main Rd Anwick NG34 . . . . **109** A1
Ashby cum Fenby DN37 . . . . **35** D3
Barkston NG32 . . . . **130** B8
Belchford LN9 . . . . **73** A2
Benniworth LN8 . . . . **59** B1
Bourne PE10 . . . . **154** C5
18 Brookenby LN8 . . . . **47** B6
Carrington PE22 . . . . **112** C7
Collyweston PE9 . . . . **171** B1
2 Donington on Bain LN11 . . **59** E1
Dunsby PE10 . . . . **143** B2
East Kirkby PE23 . . . . **99** E5
Etton PE6 . . . . **173** E5
Friskney Eaudike PE22 . . . . **115** C6
Gedney PE12 . . . . **159** D7
Goulceby LN11 . . . . **72** E6
Gunby & Stainby NG33 . . . . **151** B5
Haconby PE10 . . . . **154** C8
Heighington/Washingborough
LN4 . . . . **203** B2
Leadenham LN5 . . . . **106** D3
Little Hale NG34 . . . . **122** E1
Little Steeping PE23 . . . . . . **101** D6
Long Bennington NG23 . . . . **117** D3
Nocton LN4 . . . . **95** B7
North Willingham LN8 . . . . . **58** D7
Parson Drove PE13 . . . . **177** F8
3 Potterhanworth LN4 . . . . **82** B1
Quadring PE11 . . . . **134** F1
Saltfleet LN11 . . . . **51** C4
2 Sibsey PE22 . . . . **113** B1
Sotby LN8 . . . . **71** E5
Spilsby PE23 . . . . **87** B3
Stickford PE22 . . . . **100** B3
Stickney PE22 . . . . **113** B5
Thurlby PE10 . . . . **164** D8
Toynton All Saints PE23 . . . **100** F6
2 Tydd St Mary PE13 . . . . **170** C4
Ulceby with Fordington LN13 . **88** B3
Utterby LN11 . . . . **48** F5
West Keal PE23 . . . . **100** C3
Wigtoft PE20 . . . . **135** D3
Wisbech St Mary PE13 . . . . **177** A2
Withern with Stain LN11 . . . . **62** E1
Main Ridge E PE21 . . . . . . **209** A5
Main Ridge W 9 PE21 . . . . **209** A5
Main St (Southorpe) PE9 . **172** E2
Main St Ailsworth PE5 . . . . **223** D2

Main St continued
Ancaster NG32 . . . . .119 F3
Ashby de la Launde & Bloxholm
  LN4 . . . . .108 B5
Barlings LN3 . . . . .69 C3
Barnack PE9 . . . . .172 B3
Barrowby NG32 . . . . .210 A5
Baston PE6 . . . . .164 E4
4 Bishop Norton LN8 . . . .43 D3
Bonby DN20 . . . . .10 C2
Boothby Graffoe LN5 . . . . . . .94 A2
Boothby Pagnell NG33 . . . . .140 F5
Bottesford NG13 . . . . .128 C4
Broomfleet HU15 . . . . .1 C6
Brough HU15 . . . . .2 C6
Buckminster NG33 . . . . .150 E5
Cadney DN20 . . . . .31 E6
Careby Aunby & Holywell
  PE9 . . . . .163 B7
Carlton Scroop NG32 . . . . . .119 C4
Castor PE5 . . . . .223 D3
Chapel Hill LN4 . . . . .110 E5
Claypole NG23 . . . . .117 F7
Clipsham LE15 . . . . .162 C7
Crowle DN17 . . . . .16 E6
Croxton Kerrial NG32 . . . . . .138 D3
Denton NG32 . . . . .139 A7
Doddington & Whisby LN6 . . .79 D5
Dorrington LN4 . . . . .108 E3
Dunham-on-Trent NG22 . . . . .65 B1
East/West Stockwith DN10 . . .40 C5
Edenham PE10 . . . . .153 F4
Ellerker HU15 . . . . .2 A8
Ewerby & Evedon NG34 . . . .122 C6
Farcet PE7 . . . . .231 C2
Fenton NG23 . . . . .105 C1
Fishlake DN7 . . . . .14 D8
Foston NG32 . . . . .117 F1
Fulstow LN11 . . . . .49 B8
Gedney PE12 . . . . .148 B1
Graiselound DN9 . . . . .27 D1
1 Grasby DN38 . . . . .32 E7
Great Casterton PE9 . . . . . . .218 C8
Greatford PE9 . . . . .164 C2
Gunby & Stainby NG33 . . . . .151 B4
Hackthorn LN2 . . . . .55 E1
Haconby PE10 . . . . .154 D8
Hatfield DN7 . . . . .14 F3
Honington NG32 . . . . .119 C1
Horkstow DN18 . . . . .10 A5
Horsington LN10 . . . . .84 D3
Hougham NG32 . . . . .118 C3
Ingoldsby NG33 . . . . .141 D5
Laneham DN22 . . . . .65 A3
Mablethorpe & Sutton LN12 . .64 B1
Mareham le Fen PE22 . . . . . .98 F3
Marston NG32 . . . . .118 D2
Newark-on-Trent NG24 . . . . .104 C2
Normanby by Spital LN8 . . . . .55 F7
North Carlton LN1 . . . . .67 C4
North Kyme LN4 . . . . .109 F3
North Leverton with
  Habblesthorpe DN22 . . . .52 B1
North Rauceby NG34 . . . . . .120 E5
Norton Disney LN6 . . . . .92 C2
Osgodby LN8 . . . . .45 A3
RAF Cranwell NG34 . . . . . . .120 C8
Ryhall PE9 . . . . .163 D1
Scawby DN20 . . . . .30 F7
Scopwick LN4 . . . . .95 D1
Scothern LN2 . . . . .68 F4
Scredington NG34 . . . . .132 F7
Southorpe PE9 . . . . .172 L1
South Rauceby NG34 . . . . . .120 E4
South Scarle NG23 . . . . .91 E6
Sproxton LE14 . . . . .138 F1
Sutton on Trent NG23 . . . . . . .91 A8
Swanland HU14 . . . . .3 B7
Syston NG32 . . . . .130 A7
Thistleton LE15 . . . . .151 C1
Thorney NG23 . . . . .78 F7
Thornton Curtis DN39 . . . . . . .11 E5
Thorpe on the Hill LN6 . . . . . .92 E8
1 Timberland LN4 . . . . .96 B1
Torksey LN1 . . . . .65 D6
Ufford PE9 . . . . .172 F3
Upton DN21 . . . . .53 D5
Welby NG32 . . . . .130 F5
West Ashby LN9 . . . . .85 E7
Westborough & Dry Doddington
  NG23 . . . . .117 E5
Whitton DN15 . . . . .1 E3
Wilsford NG32 . . . . .120 C2
Worlaby DN20 . . . . .20 D8
1 Wymondham LE14 . . . . .150 C1
Yaxley PE7 . . . . .233 E5
Mainwaring Cl 5 LN2 . . . . .68 E5
Mainwaring Rd LN2 . . . . . .234 C4
Maisdike La PE12 . . . . . . .159 B5
Maize Ct 9 NG34 . . . . . . .212 F3
Malborne Way PE2 . . . . . .230 B4
Malborough Dr 4 LN12 . . . .64 A3
Malcolm Ave NG34 . . . . . .107 C1
Malcolm Rd DN34 . . . . . . .190 F4
Malcolm Sargent Prim Sch
  PE9 . . . . .218 E5
Maldon Dr HU9 . . . . .181 C6
Malham Ave HU4 . . . . .179 C6
Malham Cl LN6 . . . . .200 C1
Malham Dr LN6 . . . . .200 C1
Malim Way 3 NG31 . . . . . .210 F8
Malkinson Cl
  1 West Halton DN15 . . . . .8 E7
  12 Winterton DN15 . . . . . . .9 A5
Mallalieu Ct 2 DN15 . . . . .182 E4
Mallard Ave 6 DN3 . . . . . . .14 A4
Mallard Cl Birchwood LN6 . .200 E1
  5 Essendine PE9 . . . . . . .163 D3

Mallard Cl continued
19 Healing DN41 . . . . .23 F5
  Skellingthorpe LN6 . . . . . . .200 A3
  Spalding PE11 . . . . .214 E2
Mallard Ct
10 Grantham NG31 . . . . . .210 E2
4 North Hykeham LN6 . . . .204 C1
5 Stamford PE9 . . . . .219 B4
Mallard Dr 6 LN7 . . . . .33 B4
Mallard Dro PE11 . . . . .134 B1
Mallard Mews DN32 . . . . .191 E6
Mallard Rd
  Low Fulney PE12 . . . . .157 C5
  Peterborough PE3 . . . . .220 E1
3 Scunthorpe DN16 . . . . .185 D5
Mallards Reach 8 PE11 . . .134 F2
Mallards The 5 PE6 . . . . . .174 A5
Mallard Way Brigg DN20 . . .196 A3
  Skegness PE25 . . . . .103 C3
Malling Wlk DN16 . . . . .185 B2
Mallory Cl 6 LN6 . . . . .204 C7
Mallory Dr
3 Spalding PE11 . . . . .214 C2
  Yaxley PE7 . . . . .233 D3
Mallory La 18 PE9 . . . . . . .219 B5
Mallory Rd
1 Ashby de la Launde &
  Bloxholm LN4 . . . . .108 A7
  Peterborough PE1 . . . . .226 C2
4 Scunthorpe DN16 . . . . .185 D5
Mallowfield 2 LN8 . . . . . . .57 B8
Mallows La PE22 . . . . .113 C2
Mall Sh Ctr The LN1 . . . . . .234 B2
Malmesbury Dr 3 DN34 . . .191 C6
Malm St HU3 . . . . .180 B6
Malpas Ave 4 DN21 . . . . . .197 D5
MALTBY LN11 . . . . .60 F3
Maltby Ave DN37 . . . . .190 C3
Maltby Cl 20 PE8 . . . . .172 B1
Maltby Dr PE6 . . . . .164 D4
Maltby La 12 DN18 . . . . .3 E1
MALTBY LE MARSH LN13 . . .76 A8
Maltby Rd
  Scunthorpe DN17 . . . . .184 E5
  Skegness PE25 . . . . .206 D5
Maltby Way LN9 . . . . .199 D3
Malten La 8 PE12 . . . . . . .158 B7
Malting La PE11 . . . . .134 E2
Maltings La NG31 . . . . .210 E7
Malting Sq PE7 . . . . .233 F6
Maltings The 5 Alford LN13 .75 F3
1 Leasingham NG34 . . . . .121 B7
  Long Sutton PE12 . . . . .216 B5
8 Thorney PE6 . . . . .176 A3
  Wothorpe PE9 . . . . .219 C2
Maltings Way DN32 . . . . . .191 E8
Maltkiln Cl 17 NG34 . . . . . .212 F4
Maltkiln La
1 Beacon Hill NG24 . . . . .104 A5
  Brant Broughton LN5 . . . . .105 F5
2 Elsham DN20 . . . . .20 F7
Malt Kiln La 1 LN5 . . . . . . .93 F6
Maltkiln Rd
  Barton-upon-Humber DN18 . . .3 F1
  Fenton LN1 . . . . .65 E3
Malton Rd LN6 . . . . .204 C1
Malus Cl PE7 . . . . .233 D6
Malvern Ave Grimsby DN33 .191 A3
  Heighington/Washingborough
  LN4 . . . . .203 D2
  Spalding PE11 . . . . .214 E6
Malvern Cl Lincoln LN5 . . . .205 D4
15 Lincoln LN6 . . . . .93 C8
20 Lincoln LN6 . . . . .93 C8
  Sleaford NG34 . . . . .212 B2
  Spalding PE11 . . . . .214 E6
4 Thorne/Moorends DN8 . .15 A7
Malvern Dr 5 NG31 . . . . . .210 E8
Malvern Rd
5 Mablethorpe/Sutton on Sea
  LN12 . . . . .64 B4
  Peterborough PE4 . . . . .221 C4
  Scunthorpe DN17 . . . . .184 F7
Manasty Rd PE2 . . . . .229 C2
MANBY LN11 . . . . .62 D6
Manby Hall Bsns Pk DN40 . .186 C6
Manby Middlegate LN11 . . . .62 D7
Manby Rd
  Immingham DN40 . . . . .186 C6
  Legbourne LN11 . . . . .61 E4
  Scunthorpe DN17 . . . . .184 D6
Manby Rd by Pass DN40 . . .186 D6
Manby Road LN11 . . . . .62 C4
Manby St LN5 . . . . .205 D6
Mancetter Sq PE4 . . . . . . .220 F1
Manchester Rd 11 LN5 . . . .94 A7
Manchester St
  Cleethorpes DN35 . . . . .192 D8
  Kingston upon Hull HU3 . . . .180 A4
Manchester Way
3 Donington PE11 . . . . . .134 F2
  Grantham NG31 . . . . .210 C5
Mandalay Dr 1 PE10 . . . . .213 E7
Mandarin Dr PE21 . . . . . . .208 E3
Mandela Link 1 DN31 . . . .191 C7
Mandeville PE2 . . . . .229 F4
Mandike Rd PE20 . . . . .136 C2
Manifold Rd DN16 . . . . . . .185 E5
Manlake Ave DN15 . . . . .9 A5
Manley Cl DN9 . . . . .27 D6
Manley Ct 1 DN9 . . . . .27 D6
Manley Gdns Brigg DN20 . . .196 B3
1 Cleethorpes DN35 . . . . .192 F3
Manley St 4 DN15 . . . . . . .183 B3
Mannaberg Way
  Scunthorpe DN15 . . . . .183 A6
  Scunthorpe DN15 . . . . .183 B6
Manners Cl 3 PE9 . . . . . . .172 C6

Manners Rd NG24 . . . . . . .104 B2
Manners St NG31 . . . . .211 A6
Manning Rd PE10 . . . . .213 D5
Manningtree Cl DN32 . . . . .191 E6
Mann La DN9 . . . . .16 D2
Manor Ave Grimsby DN32 . .191 D6
  Peterborough PE2 . . . . .231 B7
Manor Cl 6 Bardney LN3 . . .83 C4
11 Baston PE6 . . . . .164 E5
  East Kirkby PE23 . . . . .99 F4
  Farcet PE7 . . . . .231 C2
3 Great Gonerby NG31 . . .129 C5
11 Keelby DN41 . . . . .23 A5
7 Langtoft PE6 . . . . .164 E5
7 Leasingham NG34 . . . . .121 B7
  Lincoln LN2 . . . . .234 B4
14 Metheringham LN4 . . . .95 D4
15 Ruskington NG34 . . . . .108 D2
  Ryhall PE9 . . . . .163 C2
7 Sibsey PE22 . . . . .113 B1
2 Spalding PE11 . . . . .214 C1
6 Welbourn LN5 . . . . .106 E5
13 Wittering PE8 . . . . .172 B1
  Yaxley PE7 . . . . .233 D5
Manor Cliff 1 LN8 . . . . .55 F6
Manor Ct 9 Bourne PE10 . . .213 C5
2 Carlton-le-Moorland LN5 .105 E8
17 Nettleham LN2 . . . . . . .68 C2
  Nocton LN4 . . . . .95 B7
1 Stallingborough DN41 . . .23 E6
2 Sudbrooke LN2 . . . . .68 F3
Manor Ct Rd 7 DN9 . . . . . . .27 E6
Manor Dr 12 Baston PE6 . . .164 E5
2 Binbrook LN8 . . . . .47 C4
3 Bonby DN20 . . . . .10 C2
4 Brough HU15 . . . . .2 C6
5 Great Gonerby NG31 . . .129 C5
1 Great Gonerby NG31 . . .129 C5
  Halton Holegate PE23 . . . . .101 B7
7 Harlaxton NG32 . . . . . . .139 C7
  Holbeach PE12 . . . . .215 D3
1 Long Bennington NG23 . .117 C3
  Peterborough PE6 . . . . .221 E3
8 Scawby DN20 . . . . .30 E8
  Skegness PE25 . . . . .206 B5
8 Skegness PE25 . . . . . . .206 B6
10 Skegness PE25 . . . . . . .206 B6
2 Sudbrooke LN2 . . . . .68 F2
  Waltham DN37 . . . . .194 E5
7 Wragby LN8 . . . . .70 D4
Manor Farm Cl 43 DN17 . . .29 D6
Manor Farm Ct DN33 . . . . .194 F7
Manor Farm Dr 3 LN1 . . . . .66 D7
Manor Farm La Castor PE5 .223 E2
3 Essendine PE9 . . . . .163 D3
Manor Farm Rd DN17 . . . . .184 E6
8 Hatfield DN7 . . . . .14 E4
  Peterborough PE2 . . . . .231 C7
Manor Gdns Boston PE21 . .209 A4
8 Hatfield DN7 . . . . .14 E4
  Peterborough PE2 . . . . .231 C7
Manor Grange PE21 . . . . . .126 C1
Manor Hill LN11 . . . . .60 A1
Manor Hill Cnr PE12 . . . . . .169 D7
Manor House Ct PE6 . . . . . .217 E4
Manor House La
1 Fulletby LN9 . . . . .86 B8
  Westborough & Dry Doddington
  NG33 . . . . .117 E5
Manor House Mus LN13 . . . .75 F3
Manor House Rd PE12 . . . . .146 F2
Manor House St
5 Horncastle LN9 . . . . . . .199 B4
  Peterborough PE1 . . . . .226 A3
Manor La Aisthorpe LN1 . . . .67 C7
4 Barrow upon Humber
  DN19 . . . . .11 D8
  Bourne PE10 . . . . .213 C4
  Broadholme LN6 . . . . .200 A4
5 Carlton-le-Moorland LN5 .105 E8
  Goxhill DN19 . . . . .11 F8
  Grayingham DN21 . . . . .42 E7
  Hougham NG32 . . . . .118 C3
  Threekingham NG34 . . . . . .132 E3
16 Waddington LN5 . . . . . .93 F7
1 Welton/Dunholme LN2 . .68 D6
  Wrangle PE22 . . . . .114 B2
Manor Leas Acad LN6 . . . . .205 B3
Manor Leas Jun Sch LN6 . .205 B3
Manor Paddock 2 DN32 . . .128 F7
Manor Paddocks LN5 . . . . . .92 E2
MANOR PARK DN17 . . . . . . .184 D6
Manor Pk 7 LN11 . . . . .61 F3
Manor Pl NG34 . . . . .212 C5
Manor Rd Barrowby NG32 . .210 A5
  Bottesford NG13 . . . . .128 A5
  Burton Coggles NG33 . . . . .152 C8
  Carlby PE9 . . . . .163 E4
2 Collingham NG23 . . . . . .91 D4
  Coningsby LN4 . . . . .110 E8
1 Crowle DN17 . . . . .16 D7
  East Ella HU5 . . . . .179 B8
  Folksworth PE7 . . . . .232 D1
4 Hagworthingham PE23 . .87 A4
  Hatfield DN7 . . . . .14 E4
  Heighington/Washingborough
  LN4 . . . . .203 B1
  Kingston upon Hull HU5 . . . .179 B8
  Kirton PE20 . . . . .136 B5
  Lincoln LN2 . . . . .234 A4
  Northorpe DN21 . . . . .42 A8
  Saxilby LN1 . . . . .66 D2
  Scunthorpe DN16 . . . . .185 B3
  Sleaford NG34 . . . . .212 B2
5 Stainforth DN7 . . . . .14 C7
  Stretton LE15 . . . . .162 A6
  Swanland HU14 . . . . .3 B6
  Swinderby LN6 . . . . .92 A5
  Twin Rivers DN14 . . . . .7 E7

Manor Rd continued
  Wansford PE5 . . . . .222 F2
Manor Rise LN3 . . . . .203 F8
Manor St
7 Heckington NG34 . . . . .122 E3
4 Kingston upon Hull HU1 .180 F6
  Ruskington NG34 . . . . .108 D2
Manor Stables Craft Ctr★
  NG32 . . . . .106 C1
Manor Way
  Kingston upon Hull HU10 . . .178 F6
6 Langtoft PE6 . . . . .164 F5
  Market Deeping PE6 . . . . . .217 E4
Manrico Dr LN1 . . . . .201 C7
Manse Ave LN5 . . . . .205 D4
Mansell Cl 1 PE11 . . . . . . .214 B3
Mansel St 3 DN32 . . . . . . .189 D1
Mansfield Ct
4 Grimsby DN32 . . . . . . .189 C1
  Peterborough PE1 . . . . .226 C5
Mansfield Rd DN15 . . . . . . .182 B2
Mansgate Hill LN7 . . . . .33 B3
Mansion Ct Gdns DN8 . . . . .15 A8
Manson Cl 11 DN34 . . . . . .190 D4
MANTHORPE
  Grantham NG31 . . . . .211 A8
  Toft with Lound and Manthorpe
  PE10 . . . . .164 A7
Manthorpe Dro PE10 . . . . . .164 F8
Manthorpe Drove PE10 . . . .164 F8
Manthorpe Rd
  Grantham NG31 . . . . .211 B7
  Obthorpe PE9 . . . . .164 B5
Mantle Gn PE22 . . . . .115 B6
MANTON DN21 . . . . .30 B5
Manton PE3 . . . . .225 A3
Manton Cl DN20 . . . . .30 F6
Manton La DN20 . . . . .30 E6
Manton Rd Lincoln LN2 . . . .201 F7
  Manton DN21 . . . . .30 B4
MANTON WARREN DN16 . . . .30 B8
Mantree Cross DN21 . . . . . .41 A8
Manwaring Way 15 PE20 . . .135 B7
Maple Ave 8 Crowle DN17 . .16 D7
  Grimsby DN34 . . . . .190 E7
  Keelby DN41 . . . . .23 A4
  Kingston upon Hull HU10 . . .178 F8
13 Northorpe PE10 . . . . . .164 C8
2 Scunthorpe DN15 . . . . .182 C5
10 Wisbech PE13 . . . . . . .170 D1
  Woodhall Spa LN10 . . . . . . .97 C6
Maple Cl Brigg DN20 . . . . . .196 E3
  Gainsborough DN21 . . . . . .197 B2
9 Keelby DN41 . . . . .23 A4
5 Kingston upon Hull HU5 . .179 C7
  Leasingham NG34 . . . . .121 C7
  Louth LN11 . . . . .198 D7
42 Messingham DN17 . . . . .29 D7
  Thimbleby LN9 . . . . .199 A5
4 Waddington LN5 . . . . . . .93 E8
Maple Ct
  Gainsborough DN21 . . . . . .197 F5
  Yaxley PE7 . . . . .233 F6
Maple Dr
5 Bassingham LN5 . . . . . .92 F3
  Market Rasen LN8 . . . . .45 D1
1 Sudbrooke LN2 . . . . .68 F2
Maple Gdns PE10 . . . . .213 D6
Maple Gr 22 Healing DN41 . .23 F5
12 Heckington NG34 . . . . .122 D3
  Holbeach PE12 . . . . .215 A2
  Immingham DN40 . . . . .186 C5
  New Waltham DN36 . . . . . . .195 B5
3 Scopwick Heath LN4 . . .108 A7
  Spalding PE11 . . . . .214 F4
Maple Rd PE21 . . . . .209 C2
Maple St LN5 . . . . .205 D5
Maples The PE21 . . . . .226 F5
Maple Tree Cl E DN16 . . . .183 A1
Maple Tree Cl W DN16 . . . .183 A1
Maple Tree Way DN16 . . . .183 A1
Maple Walk DN37 . . . . .23 F2
Maple Way 12 PE11 . . . . . .134 E2
Maple Wlk PE7 . . . . .230 C2
Maplewood Ave HU5 . . . . . .179 B7
Maplewood Cl NG31 . . . . . .210 F7
Maple Wy PE5 . . . . .103 C2
Mappleton 14 LN6 . . . . .93 B8
Marbury Cl 26 LN13 . . . . . . .75 F2
March Rd PE13 . . . . .177 F1
March St 13 DN21 . . . . .30 B1
Marconi Dr PE7 . . . . .233 D6
Marcus Cl 13 LN6 . . . . .93 A8
Marcus St DN34 . . . . .191 A6
Mardale Gdns PE4 . . . . . . .221 D2
Marden Hill PE23 . . . . .100 D6
Mareham La
  Aswarby & Swarby NG34 . . .132 E7
  Graby NG34 . . . . .142 F4
  Pointon & Sempringham
  NG34 . . . . .142 F7
  Sleaford NG34 . . . . .212 F2
  Threekingham NG34 . . . . . .132 F3
MAREHAM LE FEN PE22 . . . .99 A3
Mareham le Fen CE Prim Sch
  PE22 . . . . .99 A4
MAREHAM ON THE HILL
  LN9 . . . . .86 A2
Mareham Rd
  Hameringham LN9 . . . . .86 C2
  Horncastle LN9 . . . . .199 D2
MARFLEET HU9 . . . . .5 E8
Marfleet Ave 2 HU9 . . . . . . .5 D8
Marfleet Cnr 9 DN36 . . . . . .36 B1
Marfleet La HU9 . . . . .5 E8
Marfleet Prim Sch HU9 . . . . .5 E8

Margaret Ave 1 DN17 . . . . .17 D5
Margaret Dr PE21 . . . . .209 B6
Margaret Gr 1 HU13 . . . . . .178 F1
Margaret Moxon Wy HU1 . . .180 E6
Margaret Pl DN36 . . . . .195 C6
Margaret St
5 Grimsby DN32 . . . . .191 F7
  Immingham DN40 . . . . .186 C3
Margrave La
  Garthorpe & Fockerby DN17 . .7 E5
  Reedness DN14 . . . . .6 E7
Marham Cl 4 LN6 . . . . .204 B8
MARHOLM PE6 . . . . .220 C1
Marholm Rd
4 Peterborough PE3 . . . . .220 F1
  Peterborough PE6 . . . . .224 B3
  Ufford PE9 . . . . .172 F2
Marian Ave 22 LN12 . . . . . .64 B3
Marian Rd PE21 . . . . .208 F7
Marian Way
6 Skegness PE25 . . . . . . .206 B3
  Waltham DN37 . . . . .194 B4
Mariette Way 5 PE11 . . . . .214 B6
Marigold Cl Lincoln LN2 . . . .202 C8
  Stamford PE9 . . . . .218 C6
Marigolds PE6 . . . . .217 D5
Marigold Wlk
3 Humberston DN35 . . . . .192 E1
5 Sleaford NG34 . . . . . . .212 F3
Marina 28 LN5 . . . . .93 F7
Marina Rd 15 LN12 . . . . . . .64 B3
Marina View
  Chapel Hill LN4 . . . . .110 E5
8 Thorne/Moorends DN8 . .15 A7
Marine Ave
11 Mablethorpe LN12 . . . . .64 B3
8 Mablethorpe/Sutton on Sea
  LN12 . . . . .64 C1
  North Ferriby HU14 . . . . .3 A4
  Skegness PE25 . . . . .206 D1
Marine Ave W 8 LN12 . . . . .76 F8
Mariner Cl PE4 . . . . .221 F2
Mariner Cres LN2 . . . . .202 A6
Mariner Ct LN2 . . . . .202 A6
Marine Rd PE11 . . . . .214 E5
Mariners Arms Flats 2
  DN17 . . . . .17 D6
Mariners Cl HU9 . . . . .181 C6
Marine Wharf 5 HU1 . . . . . .180 F5
Marine Wlk LN6 . . . . .200 B5
Marisco Ct 2 LN2 . . . . .77 A8
Marjorie Ave LN6 . . . . .205 D8
Mark Ave Horncastle LN9 . . .199 A5
  Sleaford NG34 . . . . .212 F4
MARKBY LN13 . . . . .76 C5
Market Cl 3 PE24 . . . . .102 E8
Market Ct 5 Crowle DN17 . . .16 D7
  Long Sutton PE12 . . . . .216 C5
MARKET DEEPING PE6 . . . . .217 E6
Market Deeping Com Prim
  Sch PE6 . . . . .217 C6
Market Hall★ LN11 . . . . . . .198 B5
Market Hill
  Scunthorpe DN15 . . . . .183 B4
  Winteringham DN15 . . . . .2 B1
Market La Old Leake PE22 . .127 C8
  Terrington St Clement PE34 .161 F1
Market Pl 3 Alford LN13 . . . .75 F2
1 Binbrook LN8 . . . . .47 C4
21 Boston PE21 . . . . .208 F5
2 Brigg DN20 . . . . .196 B3
  Coningsby LN4 . . . . .207 A4
2 Epworth DN9 . . . . .27 E6
  Gainsborough DN21 . . . . . .197 C4
2 Grantham NG31 . . . . . .211 A4
4 Horncastle LN9 . . . . . . .199 B4
6 Kingston upon Hull HU1 . .181 A6
38 Kirkby in Lindsey DN21 . .30 B1
  Long Sutton PE12 . . . . .216 C4
9 Louth LN11 . . . . .198 B5
  Market Deeping PE6 . . . . . .217 B4
10 Market Rasen LN8 . . . . .57 D8
  Owston Ferry DN9 . . . . .28 B3
4 Sleaford NG34 . . . . . . .212 D4
5 Spalding PE11 . . . . .214 D4
  Swineshead PE20 . . . . .135 B7
4 Wragby LN8 . . . . .70 D5
MARKET RASEN LN8 . . . . . .57 E8
Market Rasen CE Prim Sch
  The LN8 . . . . .57 D7
Market Rasen Dr PE10 . . . .213 B3
Market Rasen Race Course
  LN8 . . . . .57 F7
Market Rasen Rd
  Dunholme LN2 . . . . .68 E6
  Holton cum Beckering LN8 . . .70 B8
  Lissington LN3 . . . . .57 E1
  Snarford LN8 . . . . .56 E1
  Welton/Dunholme LN2 . . . . .68 E6
Market Rasen Sta LN8 . . . . .57 D7
Market Rasen Way PE12 . . .215 E3
Market Sq 17 PE21 . . . . . . .208 F5
Market St Bottesford NG13 . .128 A5
3 Cleethorpes DN35 . . . . .192 F6
  Gainsborough DN21 . . . . . .197 D4
  Grimsby DN31 . . . . .191 D8
  Long Sutton PE12 . . . . .216 C5
3 Sleaford NG34 . . . . . . .212 D4
11 Spilsby PE23 . . . . .88 A1
31 Winterton DN15 . . . . . . .9 A5
MARKET STAINTON LN8 . . . .72 C8
Market Stainton La LN8 . . . .72 C8
Marketstede PE7 . . . . .230 B2
Market Way PE11 . . . . .214 C8

Markham Mews DN37 . . . .194 F4
Markham Ret Pk PE9 . . . .219 E7
Markhams Orch DN33 . . . .194 F7
Markham Way **2** DN20 . . .196 F7
Markillie La PE12 . . . . .160 A3
Marklew Ave DN34 . . . . . .191 B7
Mark Rise **1** DN21 . . . . . . .41 C5
MARLBOROUGH LN5 . . . . .93 B4
Marlborough Ave
  2 Haxey DN9 . . . . .27 D2
Heighington/Washingborough
  LN4 . . . . .203 C1
Kingston upon Hull HU13 . .178 D2
  2 Spalding PE11 . . . . .214 E2
Marlborough Cl
  21 Grimsby DN32 . . . . . . .189 C1
  5 Lincoln LN2 . . . . .202 C8
Yaxley PE7 . . . . .233 E5
Marlborough Dr **1** DN16 . .185 B8
Marlborough Rd **11** DN8 . . .15 B7
Marlborough St **11** DN21 . .197 D5
Marlborough Terr **3** HU2 .180 E7
Marlborough Way DN35 . .192 F1
Marles Cl **9** NG24 . . . . . . .104 B5
Marleston La NG24 . . . . . .104 A2
Marlowe Dr LN2 . . . . .202 B6
Marlowe Gr PE4 . . . . .225 E8
Marlowe Rd DN17 . . . . . . .184 D7
Marlow Rd DN21 . . . . .197 E6
Marmaduke St **3** HU3 . . .180 C4
Marmion Dr **7** DN15 . . . . .9 A5
Marmion Rd
Coningsby LN4 . . . . .207 E5
  4 Scunthorpe DN16 . . . .185 C8
Marne Ave PE4 . . . . .221 A1
Marne Gdns LN1 . . . . .201 E6
Marne St HU5 . . . . .180 A8
Marnham Road NG23 . . . . .78 A3
Marples Mews DN35 . . . . .192 F5
Marquess Ct **7** PE10 . . . .213 D5
Marquis Ave
  25 Newark-on-Trent
  NG24 . . . . .104 A2
New Waltham DN36 . . . . . .195 D7
Marrat Ct **7** St Giles LN2 . .202 D6
St Giles LN2 . . . . .202 E6
Marratts La NG31 . . . . . . .129 D5
Marriot's Gate **6** PE12 . . .160 A8
Marriott Ct PE1 . . . . .226 E5
Marris Dr **11** DN15 . . . . .9 B5
Marris Wy **9** LN7 . . . . .33 A3
Marr La HU15 . . . . .1 A7
Marron Cl **29** NG24 . . . . . .104 C1
Marsden Dr DN15 . . . . . . .182 D3
Marsden Rd DN31 . . . . . . .189 D1
Marshall Ave
Grimsby DN34 . . . . .191 B4
Kingston upon Hull HU10 . .178 E8
Marshall Cl
  3 Fishtoft PE21 . . . . .126 C1
  6 Laceby DN37 . . . . .23 E1
Marshall Ct **9** NG24 . . . . .104 C2
Marshall's Bank PE13 . . . .177 D8
Marshall's Way PE7 . . . . . .231 C2
Marshalls Yard DN21 . . . . .197 D4
Marshall Way **2** DN21 . . . .53 A8
Marsham PE2 . . . . .229 F3
Marsh Ave PE21 . . . . .209 A2
MARSHCHAPEL DN36 . . . . .37 B2
Marshchapel Cl **2** DN35 . .192 F3
Marshchapel Prim Sch
  DN36 . . . . .37 B2
Marsh Dro PE11 . . . . .146 A5
Marshfield Rd **1** DN16 . . .185 C5
Marshfields Sch PE1 . . . . .226 D7
Marsh La Algarkirk PE20 . .146 B8
Barnetby le Wold DN38 . . . .21 B4
Barrow upon Humber DN19 . . .4 C2
Barton-upon-Humber DN18 . . .3 F1
Boston PE21 . . . . .209 A1
Burgh le Marsh PE24 . . . . .102 E7
Carlton-le-Moorland LN5 . . .106 A7
Cottam DN22 . . . . .65 C6
Dunham-on-Trent NG22 . . . .65 B1
Grainthorpe LN11 . . . . .50 C7
Kettlethorpe LN1 . . . . .65 C2
Middle Rasen LN8 . . . . .57 B8
Misterton DN10 . . . . .40 A5
New Holland DN19 . . . . .4 D2
North Leverton with
  Habblesthorpe DN22 . . . . .52 E1
North Somercotes LN11 . . . .38 C1
Orby PE24 . . . . .89 E2
Saundby DN22 . . . . .52 B7
Skidbrooke with Saltfleet Haven
  LN11 . . . . .51 C5
South Cockerington LN11 . . .62 B8
South Killingholme DN40 . . . .13 B4
Stallingborough DN41 . . . . .23 F6
Tattershall LN4 . . . . .97 D1
Winteringham DN15 . . . . . . .2 A1
Wyberton PE21 . . . . .136 F8
Marshland High Sch PE14 .170 E4
Marshlands Dr PE12 . . . . .215 F3
Marshland St **10** PE14 . . . .161 F3
Marsh Rd **3** Crowle DN17 . .16 C8
Gedney PE12 . . . . .148 C2
Holbeach PE12 . . . . .215 F8
Kirton PE20 . . . . .137 A3
Orby PE24 . . . . .90 B3
Spalding PE12 . . . . .157 B7
Sutterton PE20 . . . . .146 A7
Tydd St Mary PE13 . . . . . .160 C1
Walkeringham DN10 . . . . . .40 B3
Walpole PE14 . . . . .170 F8

Marsh Rd *continued*
Weston PE12 . . . . .145 F1
Marsh The PE14 . . . . .170 E8
Marsh Way **3** DN36 . . . . . .37 C5
MARSTON NG32 . . . . .118 C2
Marston Cl **27** NG24 . . . . .104 B2
Marston Hall & Gdns*
  NG32 . . . . .118 D2
Marston La NG32 . . . . . . .129 A7
Marston Moor Rd NG24 . . .104 C4
MARTIN Martin LN4 . . . . . .96 C3
Roughton LN9 . . . . .85 B1
Martin Cl
  2 Bottesford DN16 . . . . .185 B2
Heighington/Washingborough
  LN4 . . . . .81 E4
Louth LN11 . . . . .198 D8
Skellingthorpe LN6 . . . . . . .200 A3
Martin Ct PE4 . . . . .221 A4
Martin Dales Dro **1** LN10 . .97 B4
Martin N Dro LN4 . . . . .96 D3
Martin Rd LN4 . . . . .96 C2
Martinsbridge PE1 . . . . . . .226 F7
Martin's Cl **5** DN19 . . . . . . .11 D8
Martins Cross Dro PE20 . .124 C3
Martin S Dro LN4 . . . . .96 D3
Martins Rd Crowland PE6 . .167 E4
Ulceby DN39 . . . . .12 B1
Martin St LN5 . . . . .201 F1
Martins Way PE2 . . . . .229 F5
Martins Wlk **11** LN12 . . . . . .77 A8
Martin Way
Ingoldmells PE25 . . . . .206 C8
New Waltham DN36 . . . . . .195 B6
MARTON DN21 . . . . .65 D8
Marton Gr
  3 Grimsby DN33 . . . . . . .191 A3
  35 Hatfield DN7 . . . . .14 D4
Marton Prim Sch DN21 . . . .65 E8
Marton Rd
  10 Newark-on-Trent
  NG24 . . . . .104 A3
Sturton by Stow LN1 . . . . . .66 B7
Willingham DN21 . . . . .53 E2
Martston Thorold's Charity CE
  Sch The NG32 . . . . .118 D2
Martyn Rd DN35 . . . . .192 D7
Marvel St HU9 . . . . .181 B7
Marvis Cres PE7 . . . . .230 C3
Marwald La PE13 . . . . .170 A7
Mary Armyne Rd PE2 . . . . .230 B5
Mary La LE14 . . . . .138 B1
Marylebone Wlk **2** DN33 . .191 B2
Mary Lovell Wy PE22 . . . . .113 A8
Mary St DN15 . . . . .182 F3
Mary Sumner Way **3**
  DN15 . . . . .182 E4
Mary Walsham Cl PE2 . . . .231 E5
Masefield Dr **10** LN12 . . . . .77 A7
Maskew Ave PE1 . . . . .225 E6
Mason Cl LN12 . . . . .77 A7
Mason Dr Scunthorpe DN17 .184 E3
  6 Stamford PE9 . . . . . . .218 F6
Masons Ct DN18 . . . . .10 E8
Mason St HU2 . . . . .180 F7
Masovian La LN6 . . . . .56 C5
Massey Cl **11** Epworth DN9 . .27 D6
Kingston upon Hull HU3 . . . .180 A5
Massey Rd LN2 . . . . .234 C4
Massey St HU3 . . . . .180 A4
Mast Dr HU9 . . . . .181 C6
Masterton Cl **6** PE9 . . . . . .219 D7
Masterton Rd PE9 . . . . . . .219 C7
Mathew Ford Way DN41 . . . .23 C7
Mathews St DN35 . . . . . . .192 C7
Matilda Rd LN6 . . . . .201 D1
Matley PE2 . . . . .229 E5
Matlock Ct DN15 . . . . .182 B2
Matlock Dr Grimsby DN37 . .190 F8
Lincoln LN6 . . . . .204 E2
Matmore Cl PE11 . . . . .214 F3
Matmore Gate PE11 . . . . . .214 F3
Mat Pitts La PE24 . . . . . . .102 C1
Matthew Flinders Way
  PE21 . . . . .208 D3
Matthew Humberstone CE Sch
  DN35 . . . . .192 C5
Mattimore Dr **6** PE12 . . . .215 E2
Maud Foster Mill* PE21 .209 A6
Maud St **2** PE21 . . . . .209 A5
MAVIS ENDERBY PE23 . . . . .87 C1
Mavis Enderby Cross Roads
  PE23 . . . . .87 D1
Mavis Rd **2** DN17 . . . . . . .184 E6
Mawford Cl PE12 . . . . .146 E2
Mawson Gdns **6** PE24 . . . .102 E2
MAWTHORPE LN13 . . . . . . .88 F8
Mawthorpe Hill Rd LN13 . . .88 F8
MAXEY PE6 . . . . .173 C7
Maxey Cl **11** PE6 . . . . .217 A5
Maxey Ct LN11 . . . . .198 B6
Maxey Rd Maxey PE6 . . . . .173 C6
Northborough PE6 . . . . . . .217 C1
Maxey View PE6 . . . . .217 C3
Maxham's Gn Rd PE6 . . . . .173 D3
Maximus Rd LN6 . . . . .93 A8
Maxstead Cl HU13 . . . . . . .178 B3
Maxwell Ave LN6 . . . . .205 C8
Maxwell Ct DN34 . . . . .190 D5
Maxwell Dr **1** LN12 . . . . . . .64 B3
Maxwell Rd PE2 . . . . .230 D6
Mayall Ct **23** LN5 . . . . .93 F7
Maybell Cl **5** DN21 . . . . . . .53 A7
May Blossom Wlk PE11 . . .214 B3
May Cres LN1 . . . . .201 D4
Mayfair Ave LN6 . . . . .205 C7
Mayfair Cres **12** DN37 . . . .194 C4

Mayfair Ct DN35 . . . . .193 A1
Mayfair Dr **4** PE11 . . . . . .214 B1
Mayfair Dr W DN37 . . . . . .190 C8
Mayfair Gdns PE21 . . . . . .209 B7
Mayfield Ave
Gainsborough DN21 . . . . . .197 B7
  3 South Killingholme DN40 . . .12 F2
  6 Stainforth DN7 . . . . . . .14 D6
Mayfield Cl
  3 Grimsby DN33 . . . . . . .194 D8
  15 Pinchbeck PE11 . . . . . .156 E8
Mayfield Cres Louth LN11 . .198 D4
  3 Middle Rasen LN8 . . . . .57 C8
Mayfield Dr **1** PE25 . . . . . .90 D3
Mayfield Gr **5** PE25 . . . . . .206 B3
Mayfield Rd PE1 . . . . .226 A6
Mayfield St HU3 . . . . .180 C8
Mayflower Ave DN40 . . . . .186 C3
Mayflower Cl
  2 Gainsborough DN21 . . . .52 F6
  6 South Killingholme DN40 . . .12 E3
Mayflower Dr **5** LN4 . . . . .122 D2
Mayflower Mews **9**
  NG31 . . . . .211 A3
Mayflower Rd PE21 . . . . . .209 C3
Mayflower Way **2** LN12 . . .64 B3
May Gr HU13 . . . . .178 D2
Mayland Ave HU5 . . . . . . .179 A8
Mayner's Dike PE12 . . . . . .169 F8
Mayor's Wlk PE3 . . . . .225 E3
Maypole House Sch LN13 . .88 E8
Maypole St DN21 . . . . .42 D2
Maysfield Ct **10** DN20 . . . . .31 A5
Maysfield Dr **6** PE13 . . . . .170 B2
Mays La LN1 . . . . .66 E2
May's La PE13 . . . . .170 A2
May St DN35 . . . . .192 D8
Maythorpe Cl **3** HU3 . . . . .180 A7
Maytime Cl **7** PE11 . . . . . .214 A5
Maytree Dr PE12 . . . . .216 D5
McInnes St **4** LN2 . . . . . . .202 C3
McVeigh Ct **13** DN41 . . . . . .23 F5
Mdw Cl **11** LN8 . . . . .57 E7
Mdw Ct DN21 . . . . .42 E7
Mdw Lands DN21 . . . . .40 D3
Mdwlily Ct **14** DN36 . . . . . .195 C6
Mdwsweet La LN6 . . . . .92 D5
Mdw View Allington NG32 . .128 A6
  6 Willingham by Stow DN21 . . .53 E3
Mead Cl **6** Lincoln LN6 . . . .205 A5
Peterborough PE3 . . . . . . .220 F1
Meadenvale PE1 . . . . .226 F5
Mead Garth DN15 . . . . . . .182 B6
Meadow Ave DN9 . . . . .12 A2
Meadowbank **5** DN9 . . . . .16 E1
Meadow Bank PE22 . . . . . .126 F6
Meadow Bank Ave **1** LN3 . .82 B6
Meadowbank Rd HU3 . . . . .179 E7
Meadowbrook
  9 Ancaster NG32 . . . . . .120 A3
  4 Ruskington NG34 . . . . .108 D2
Meadow Cl
  1 Bourne PE10 . . . . .213 D5
  7 Cherry Willingham/Reepham
  LN3 . . . . .82 A8
  1 Colsterworth NG33 . . . .151 E6
  5 Goxhill DN19 . . . . .5 A1
Lincoln LN6 . . . . .93 C8
  3 Louth LN11 . . . . .198 C4
  1 Manby LN11 . . . . .62 C6
  2 Metheringham LN4 . . . . .95 D4
  2 Pinchbeck PE11 . . . . . .145 C1
  4 Scothern LN2 . . . . .68 F4
Spalding PE11 . . . . .214 E6
Meadowcroft **7** LN11 . . . . .59 E1
Meadow Croft
  3 Kirk Sandall DN3 . . . . . .14 A1
Waltham DN37 . . . . .194 E5
Meadow Ct Grimsby DN34 . .190 E7
  15 Hibaldstow DN20 . . . . .30 F5
Meadowdale Cres **3**
  NG31 . . . . .211 A8
Meadow Dr
Barton-upon-Humber DN18 . .10 F8
  4 Binbrook LN8 . . . . .47 C5
Grimsby DN33 . . . . .194 D8
  2 Healing DN41 . . . . .24 A5
  13 Misterton DN10 . . . . . . .39 F5
Meadow Dro PE13 . . . . . . .213 F7
Meadow End NG31 . . . . . . .211 D2
Meadowfield
  4 Middle Rasen LN8 . . . . .57 C8
Sleaford NG34 . . . . .212 C5
Meadowfield Ct **17** LN5 . . . .93 E8
Meadow Field Rd **6** DN3 . . .14 A3
Meadow Gardens **15** NG23 .91 D4
Meadowgate PE9 . . . . .172 F5
Meadow Gate PE10 . . . . . .213 D6
Meadowgate La **3** PE11 . . .214 A3
Meadow La
Auborn Haddington & South
  Hykeham LN6 . . . . .93 B7
Bennworth LN8 . . . . .59 B1
Girton NG23 . . . . .78 C2
Leasingham NG34 . . . . . . .121 B7
  9 Lincoln LN6 . . . . .93 C8
Normanton on Trent NG23 . .78 B3
North Cockerington LN11 . . . .50 A1
North Hykeham LN6 . . . . . . .93 C8
North Scarle LN6 . . . . .78 F1
Pointon & Sempringham
  NG34 . . . . .143 C6
  16 Ryhall PE9 . . . . .163 C1
Meadowlake Cl LN6 . . . . . .200 D1
Meadowlily Ct DN36 . . . . . .195 C6
Meadow Rd Dunston LN4 . . .95 C5
Hessle HU13 . . . . .178 B1
Langtoft PE6 . . . . .217 A8

Meadow Rd *continued*
Newark-on-Trent NG24 . . . .104 B2
Newborough PE6 . . . . .221 B8
Scunthorpe DN17 . . . . .184 C6
Meadow Rise
  5 Barnby Dun DN3 . . . . . .14 A4
Blyton DN21 . . . . .41 C6
  1 Gainsborough DN21 . . . .53 A5
  7 Saxilby LN1 . . . . .66 D2
Meadows Cl **9** DN23 . . . . .117 D3
Meadows La Lincoln LN4 . . .202 E2
Reepham LN3 . . . . .69 A1
Meadows Prim Sch The
  LN5 . . . . .205 C2
Meadows Rise **1** LE14 . . . .150 B1
Meadows The
  2 Beckingham DN10 . . . . .52 B8
Burringham DN17 . . . . .17 D4
  8 Long Bennington NG23 . .117 D3
Mablethorpe/Sutton on Sea
  LN12 . . . . .64 C2
  5 Market Deeping PE6 . . .217 C5
Messingham DN17 . . . . .29 D8
  7 Pinchbeck PE11 . . . . . .145 C1
Skegness PE25 . . . . .206 A4
Westwoodside DN9 . . . . . . .27 A2
Meadowsweet **2** PE9 . . . .218 C7
Meadow The **29** LN7 . . . . .33 B4
Meadow Vale **4** DN20 . . . . .30 F8
Meadow View
Humberston DN35 . . . . . . .192 F1
  6 Morton PE10 . . . . .154 D6
Swinderby LN6 . . . . .92 A5
Meadow View Bsns Units
  PE9 . . . . .219 F6
Meadow Way
Billingham LN4 . . . . .109 E6
Bracebridge Heath LN4 . . . .81 A1
  7 Old Leake PE22 . . . . . .114 A1
Spalding PE11 . . . . .214 A2
  6 Welton/Dunholme LN2 . . .68 D6
Meadow Wlk
  19 Kirk Sandall DN3 . . . . .14 A2
  6 Swanland HU14 . . . . . . .3 B7
Mead The **11** Laceby DN37 . .23 F1
Lincoln LN6 . . . . .205 A5
Peterborough PE4 . . . . . . .221 A1
Meadway
Cherry Willingham/Reepham
  LN3 . . . . .203 E6
  11 Market Deeping PE6 . . .217 A6
  3 Spalding PE11 . . . . . . .214 A4
Mead Wlk HU4 . . . . .179 C6
Meakers Way LN13 . . . . . . .76 F3
Meals Gate PE4 . . . . .221 D2
Mears Ct **6** PE11 . . . . .214 A1
Measham Dr **4** DN7 . . . . . .14 D7
Measures Cl **10** PE10 . . . . .154 D6
Mechanic La HU3 . . . . .180 C5
Medborne Gdns **11** PE1 . . .226 D8
Meden Ave **12** HU15 . . . . . . .2 D5
Medesweel PE2 . . . . .230 C3
Medforth St PE21 . . . . .208 E8
Medieval Village of
  Gainsthorpe* DN21 . . . . .30 D4
Medina Gdns LN12 . . . . . . .64 B2
Medium Section Rd DN16 . . .19 A4
MEDLAM PE22. . . . . .112 D7
Medlam Cl PE22. . . . . .112 C7
Medlam La PE22 . . . . .112 D7
Medlam Rd PE21 . . . . .208 C3
Medlar Dr **4** HU15 . . . . .2 D5
Medlock Cres **5** PE11 . . . . .214 F5
Medway **7** LN4 . . . . .66 D7
Medway Cl **3** PE11 . . . . . . .145 C6
Medway Cres LN6 . . . . .205 B2
Medway Pl **5** DN34 . . . . . .191 A5
Medworth PE2 . . . . .229 F3
Meeres' La PE20 . . . . .136 A5
Meering Cl **12** NG23 . . . . . .91 D5
Meering La NG23 . . . . .91 C7
Meers Bank LN12 . . . . .64 A6
Meeting House La LN5 . . . .105 F5
Meggan Gate PE3 . . . . . . .225 A1
Meggitt La DN15 . . . . .2 A1
Megs La **10** LN5 . . . . .107 A8
Melbourne Ave **4** DN33 . . .191 D3
Melbourne Cl **19** LN6 . . . . .204 D7
Melbourne Dr **4** PE25 . . . .206 A4
Melbourne Rd
Birchwood LN6 . . . . .204 C8
Grantham NG31 . . . . .211 D7
  4 Stamford PE9 . . . . . . .219 D6
Melbourne Way **9** LN5 . . . .93 E8
Melbury Wlk DN17 . . . . . . .184 C8
Meldrum Dr DN21 . . . . . . .197 E1
Melford Cl PE3. . . . . .225 A2
Melford Ct DN16 . . . . .185 E5
Melholme La LN11 . . . . .50 A2
Melior Com Coll DN17 . . . .184 D4
Melior Community Acad
  DN17 . . . . .184 E7
Mellor Wy DN36. . . . . .195 D7
Mellows Cl
Cherry Willingham/Reepham
  LN3 . . . . .203 F8
Peterborough PE1 . . . . . . .226 C3
Mellwood View DN9. . . . . . .28 A3
Mel Marshall Wy PE22 . . . .114 C2
Melrose Cl
  9 Stamford PE9 . . . . . . .218 C4
  6 Woodhall Spa LN10 . . . .97 C6
Melrose Dr PE2 . . . . .231 A7
Melrose La **13** LN6 . . . . . . .204 B8
Melrose Rd DN21 . . . . .197 C6
Melrose St HU3 . . . . .179 F6
Melrose Way DN37 . . . . . . .188 A1
MELTON HU14. . . . . .2 F5

Melton Bottom HU14 . . . . . .2 F6
Melton Fields **4** HU14. . . . . .2 F5
Melton Old Rd HU14. . . . . . .2 F6
Melton Rd North Ferriby HU14 .3 A5
Wrawby DN20 . . . . .20 F4
Wymondham LE14 . . . . . . .150 B1
MELTON ROSS DN38 . . . . . .21 D5
Melton Ross Rd DN39. . . . . .11 C1
Melville Cl **5** LN4 . . . . .81 E2
Melville St
  1 Kingston upon Hull
  HU1 . . . . .180 E5
Lincoln LN5 . . . . .234 B2
Melwood Cl DN9 . . . . .27 F6
Melwood Hill DN9 . . . . .27 F6
Melwood View **18** DN9 . . . .27 E6
Memorial Gdns LN4 . . . . . . .81 C1
Memorial Hall Dr **3** LN5 . .107 A4
Memorial La PE12 . . . . . . .148 B1
Menasha Way DN16 . . . . . .185 E2
Mendip Ave Grimsby DN33 .191 C1
  25 Lincoln LN6 . . . . .93 C8
Mendip Cl
  6 Gonerby Hill Foot
  NG31 . . . . .210 E8
  2 Lincoln LN5 . . . . .205 D3
  2 Spalding PE11 . . . . . . .214 B6
Mendip Gr PE4 . . . . .221 C2
Mendip Rd DN17 . . . . .184 D8
Menson Dr DN7 . . . . .14 D4
Mentmore Gdns PE21 . . . .208 B4
Mercer Dr LN1 . . . . .201 D6
Mercer Rd DN21 . . . . .197 B6
Mercer Row LN11 . . . . .198 B5
Mercia Cl **14** NG34 . . . . . . .212 B2
Mercia Dr **3** NG32 . . . . . . .120 A2
Mercia Gdns **2** PE10 . . . . .213 B5
Mercia Gr **4** PE6 . . . . .164 E5
Mercian Ct PE2 . . . . .231 C4
Mercury Cl PE7 . . . . .231 C4
Mercury Way PE12 . . . . . . .215 D3
Merebalk La LN9 . . . . .86 B2
Mere Balk La LN9 . . . . .85 A7
Mere Booth Rd PE22. . . . . .125 A7
Mere Cres DN16. . . . . .185 D7
Meredith Ave DN17 . . . . . .184 D6
Mere Dro Old Leake PE22. . .113 F4
Yaxley PE7 . . . . .233 F4
Mere La Edenthorpe DN3 . . .14 A1
Heydour NG32 . . . . .131 D6
Winterton DN15 . . . . .9 A7
Merelade Gr **4** PE4 . . . . . .220 E5
Mere Rd
Branston & Mere LN4. . . . . .81 E1
Waddington LN5. . . . . .93 F7
Meres Leisure Ctr &
  Swimming Pool NG31 . . . .210 D3
Meres Rd NG31 . . . . .210 C3
Mereway The NG33. . . . . . .141 A5
Meridian Cl **1** PE21 . . . . . .209 D4
Meridian Leisure Centre
  LN11 . . . . .198 D5
MERIDIAN POINT DN35 . . . .193 B3
Meridian Point Ret Pk
  DN35. . . . . .193 B3
Meridian Rd PE21 . . . . . . .209 C4
Meridian View LN11 . . . . . .198 B4
Meridian Wlk **2** PE12 . . . . .215 B2
Meriton PE2 . . . . .229 F3
Merleswen LN2 . . . . .68 D6
Merlin Cl PE10 . . . . .213 E3
Merlin Dr **2** DN20 . . . . .21 A8
Merlin Rd
  14 Binbrook Tech Pk LN8 . . .47 B6
Scunthorpe DN17 . . . . .184 E6
Merrick Cl **13** NG31 . . . . . .129 E5
Merrick St HU9 . . . . .181 B7
Merriemeade Dr **4** PE25 .206 D1
Merrifield Rd **7** PE24 . . . . .102 E2
Merryweather Ct **7** DN16 .185 B2
Mersey Cl PE11 . . . . .214 B5
Mersey Way DN37 . . . . . . .190 D8
Merton Rd DN16 . . . . .185 A3
MESSINGHAM DN17. . . . . . .29 D7
Messingham La DN20 . . . . . .30 D8
Messingham Nature Reserve*
  DN17. . . . . .29 D7
Messingham Prim Sch
  DN17. . . . . .29 D7
Messingham Rd
East Butterwick DN17 . . . . .28 D3
Scotter DN21 . . . . .29 C4
Scunthorpe DN17. . . . . . . .184 F4
Meteor Rd LN11. . . . . .62 C6
METHERINGHAM LN4. . . . . .95 D4
Metheringham Airfield Visitor
  Ctr* LN4. . . . . .96 A2
Metheringham Cl **1** LN6 .204 D7
Metheringham Delph Nature
  Reserve* LN4 . . . . .96 D7
Metheringham Fen La LN4. .95 E5
Metheringham Heath La
  LN4 . . . . .94 E3
Metheringham Prim Sch
  LN4 . . . . .95 C4
Metheringham Sta LN4. . . . .95 D4
Metro Ctr The PE2. . . . . . . .230 D6
Mewburn PE3. . . . . .220 E1
Mew Gull Dr **27** LN12. . . . . .77 A7
Mews The HU3. . . . . .180 C5
Meynell Ave **3** LN6 . . . . . .205 C8
Meynell Dr DN21 . . . . .40 D8
Meynell St DN9 . . . . .40 D8
Meyrick Rd **18** NG24 . . . . .104 A5
Michael Foale La LN11. . . . .198 C7
Michaelgate LN2. . . . . .234 B3

Michael Moses Wy PE20 . .135 C7
Mickle Gate PE3 . . . . .225 A1
Middle Barn Hill DN20 . . . .10 D1
Middlebridge Rd DN10 . . . .39 D3
Middle Broad Dro PE13 . .169 D5
Middlebrook Cl 10 LN6 . . .205 A5
Middlebrook La 1 DN8 . . .15 A7
Middlebrook Rd 4 LN6 . . .205 A5
Middleburg St HU9 . . . . . .181 D8
Middlecott Cl 2 PE21 . . . .208 F2
Middlecott Sch The PE20 .136 C5
Middle Dro Gedney PE12 . .148 C2
    Holland Fen with Brothertoft
    PE21 . . . . .208 A7
    Kirton PE20 . . . . .124 D2
    Newton PE13 . . . . .169 E4
Middle Fen Dro PE20 . . . .134 D4
Middle Fen La LN4 . . . . . .82 C5
Middlefield 7 PE7 . . . . . .230 D3
Middlefield La
    Gainsborough DN21 . . . .197 E2
  1 Glentham LN8 . . . . . . .43 F1
Middlegate LN5 . . . . .92 F2
Middlegate Cl 12 DN19 . . .11 C8
Middlegate La Bonby DN20 .10 C3
    Elsham DN20 . . . . .21 A7
    Elsham Hill DN20 . . . . . .20 E8
    Orby PE24 . . . . .89 D2
    South Ferriby DN18 . . . . .10 B7
Middlegate Rd PE20 . . . . .136 C6
Middlegate Rd E PE20 . . .136 D5
Middlegate Rd (West) 1
    PE20 . . . . .136 D6
Middleham Cl
  3 Kingston upon Hull
    HU9 . . . . .181 E8
  2 Peterborough PE7 . . . . .231 F5
Middle Holme La 3 NG23 . .91 A8
Middle La Amcotts DN17 . . .7 E1
    Stainton le Vale LN8 . . . . .46 C4
    Sturton le Steeple DN22 . .52 E3
    Thorpe on the Hill LN6 . . .92 F8
Middlemarsh Rd DN32 . . .103 A7
Middle Marsh Rd PE12 . . .146 F2
Middlemere Bank PE22 . . .126 E7
Middlemore Yd 1 NG31 . .211 E6
Middle Pasture 3 PE4 . . .220 F5
Middleplatt Rd DN40 . . . .186 E5
MIDDLE RASEN LN8 . . . . . .57 B8
Middle Rasen Prim Sch The
    LN8 . . . . .57 B8
Middle Rd Crowland PE6 . .166 E1
    Newborough PE6 . . . . . .221 E7
    Terrington St Clement PE34 161 D4
    Tydd St Mary PE13 . . . . .160 B1
  7 Whaplode PE12 . . . . . .158 B7
Middle St Aisthorpe LN1 . . .67 D7
    Cammeringham LN1 . . . . .55 A1
    Corringham DN21 . . . . . .41 E2
    Croxton Kerrial NG32 . . .138 D4
    Dunston LN4 . . . . .95 C5
    Farcet PE7 . . . . .231 C2
    Fillingham DN21 . . . . . . .55 A5
    Gunby & Stainby NG33 . .151 B5
  5 Lincoln LN6 . . . . .93 C8
    Metheringham LN4 . . . . .95 D4
  14 North Kelsey LN7 . . . . .32 A4
  5 Potterhanworth LN4 . . .82 B1
    Rippingale PE10 . . . . . . .142 F2
    Scampton LN1 . . . . .67 D6
    Scotton DN21 . . . . .29 C1
  5 Skillington NG33 . . . . .151 A8
    South Carlton LN1 . . . . . .67 D3
    Willoughton DN21 . . . . . .42 E3
Middlesykes La LN11 . . . . .62 C7
Middlethorpe Prim Sch
    DN35 . . . . .192 D3
Middle Thorpe Rd DN35 . .192 D3
Middleton PE3 . . . . .225 A4
Middleton Cl 9 DN17 . . . .29 D7
Middleton Ct HU5 . . . . . . .180 D8
Middleton Prim Sch PE3 . .225 A4
Middleton Rd
    Newark NG24 . . . . .104 B6
    Scunthorpe DN16 . . . . . .185 B4
Middleton's Field LN2 . . . .234 B4
Middletons La DN38 . . . . . .32 E7
Middletons Rd PE7 . . . . . .233 D5
Middleton St HU3 . . . . . . .180 C8
Middleton Way NG34 . . . .121 C2
Middle Wy LN3 . . . . .203 E5
Midfield Pl 16 DN36 . . . . .36 D8
Midfield Rd DN36 . . . . . . .36 D8
Midfield Way 14 DN41 . . . .23 A4
Midgate PE1 . . . . .226 A2
Mid Gate PE22 . . . . .113 E3
Midgate (East) PE22 . . . .113 E1
Midgate La PE22 . . . . .113 E1
Midgley Cl HU3 . . . . .180 C5
Midholm LN3 . . . . .203 E5
Midia Cl LN1 . . . . .201 C7
Midland Ind Est DN16 . . .185 D8
Midland Rd
    Peterborough PE3 . . . . . .225 E3
    Scunthorpe DN16 . . . . . .183 D1
Midsummer Gdns PE12 . .216 A4
Midthorpe La 3 LN9 . . . . .85 E7
MIDVILLE PE22 . . . . .113 E8
Midville Cl 10 LN1 . . . . . .201 E6
Midville La PE22 . . . . .100 B1
Midville Rd Midville PE22 .113 E7
    Toynton All Saints PE23 . .100 F4
Mid Water Cir 5 PE7 . . . .230 B1
Mid Water Cres PE7 . . . . .233 B8
Midway Ct 3 LN2 . . . . .68 D2
Midway Gr HU4 . . . . .179 E4
Milcroft Cres DN7 . . . . . . .14 D4
Mildenhall Dr LN6 . . . . . .204 B8

Mildmay Rd PE4 . . . . .225 D8
Mildmay St LN1 . . . . .234 A4
Mile Dro PE6 . . . . .173 F5
Mile End Ave 19 DN7 . . . . .14 D3
Mile La LN12 . . . . .64 A2
Miles Bank PE11 . . . . .214 C7
Miles Cross Hill LN13 . . . .75 D1
Milestone La PE11 . . . . . .145 C1
Milfoil La 3 LN12 . . . . . . .167 B8
Milford Ct 3 DN32 . . . . . .189 C1
Milford Ct Bsns Pk LN11 . .198 A8
Milkinghill La PE20 . . . . . .135 A5
Milking Nook Dro PE10 . .154 F3
Milking Nook Rd PE6 . . . .221 C8
Millard Ave DN7 . . . . .14 D4
Millard Nook 30 DN7 . . . .14 D4
Mill Bank PE12 . . . . .159 A5
Mill Bank Rd 3 DN10 . . . . .39 F3
Millbeck Bank HU15 . . . . . .1 E8
Millbeck Dr LN2 . . . . .202 B8
Millbrook Cl 3 LN6 . . . . . .93 B8
Millbrook La LN8 . . . . .70 C4
Millbrook Sch DN16 . . . . .185 B6
Millbrook Way 30 DN18 . . .10 F8
Mill Cl 7 Alford LN13 . . . . .75 F3
    Billinghay LN4 . . . . .109 E5
  5 Brigg DN20 . . . . .196 A3
  4 Croft PE24 . . . . .102 E2
  5 Marshchapel DN36 . . . .37 C2
    Murrow PE13 . . . . .177 D5
  2 North Leverton with
    Habblesthorpe DN22 . . .52 B1
  7 Peakirk PE6 . . . . .174 A5
    Waltham DN37 . . . . .194 E3
  26 Scotter DN21 . . . . .170 D1
Mill Cres Peterborough PE2 229 E4
  20 Scotter DN21 . . . . .29 C3
Mill Croft 3 Scawby DN20 .30 F8
  1 Scunthorpe DN16 . . . . .185 D7
Mill Ct Lincoln LN1 . . . . . .234 A4
  1 Waddingham DN21 . . . .43 D7
Mill Dr NG31 . . . . .211 C2
Mill Drove Bourne PE10 . .213 E7
    Crowland PE6 . . . . .175 A8
    Deeping St Nicholas PE11 .155 D1
Mill Drove North PE12 . . .157 B2
Mill Drove South PE12 . . .157 B1
Millennium Fst Coll PE25 .206 B3
Millennium Way PE34 . . . .160 F3
Miller Ave DN32 . . . . .192 C6
Miller Cl 12 DN8 . . . . .15 B7
Miller La DN8 . . . . .15 B7
Miller Rd DN21 . . . . .41 A1
Millers Brook DN9 . . . . . . .16 E1
Millers Cl
    Heighington/Washingborough
    LN4 . . . . .81 E4
  4 Sleaford NG34 . . . . . . .212 C2
Miller's Cl PE10 . . . . .143 A3
Millers Ct LN11 . . . . .198 C6
Millers Dale 2 LN6 . . . . . .204 F2
Millers' Gate PE22 . . . . . .113 A2
Millers Quay 5 DN20 . . . .196 A3
Millers Rd LN5 . . . . .93 F6
Millers Rest PE12 . . . . . . .158 C7
Millers Way 6 Alford LN13 . .75 F3
  6 Heckington NG34 . . . . .122 E2
Miller Wy PE1 . . . . .226 C1
Mill Farm Est LN4 . . . . . .207 B5
MILLFIELD PE1 . . . . .225 F5
Mill Field 1 LN12 . . . . .64 C2
Millfield Ave
    Grimsby DN33 . . . . .191 D3
  3 Saxilby LN1 . . . . .66 D2
Mill Field Cl 6 PE6 . . . . . .173 C4
Millfield Cres NG32 . . . . .119 B6
Mill Field Ct 11 DN18 . . . . .14 A3
Millfield Gdns 6 PE6 . . . .166 F1
Millfield La E PE20 . . . . . .136 D7
Millfield La W PE20 . . . . .136 D7
Millfield Prim Acad LN4 . .81 F4
Millfield Rd
    Bratoft PE24 . . . . .102 C7
  3 Market Deeping PE6 . . .217 A6
  21 Metheringham LN4 . . . .95 C4
  7 Morton PE10 . . . . .154 D8
    South Somercotes LN11 . . .50 F5
    Thorne/Moorends DN8 . . .15 A8
Mill Field Rd
  8 Donington PE11 . . . . . .134 E2
    Fishlake DN7 . . . . .14 C8
    Scunthorpe DN16 . . . . . .183 E3
Mill Garth
    Cleethorpes DN35 . . . . . .192 D3
    Roughton Moor LN10 . . . .98 A7
Millgate 10 LN5 . . . . .107 A7
Mill Gate PE12 . . . . .158 B1
Mill Gn Rd PE11 . . . . .214 C7
Millgood Cl LN11 . . . . . . .198 D5
MILL HILL PE2 . . . . .229 E3
Mill Hill Ellerker HU15 . . . .2 A8
    Frisney PE22 . . . . .115 C3
    Gringley on the Hill DN10 . .39 B1
    Nettleham LN2 . . . . .68 C2
Mill Hill Cres DN35 . . . . . .192 E5
Mill Hill Dr DN16 . . . . . . .185 C3
Mill Hill La PE20 . . . . .135 B7
Mill Hill Rd DN7 . . . . .14 D3
Mill Hill Way LN11 . . . . . . .62 A8
Mill House La 1 DN15 . . . . .9 B5

Millhouse St Rise 5
    DN40 . . . . .186 A4
Mill House Windmill* DN17 7 C4
Mill La Addlethorpe PE25 . .90 D1
    Ashby with Scremby PE23 . . .88 D3
    Aubourn Haddington & South
    Hykeham LN5 . . . . .92 F5
  8 Barrow upon Humber
    DN19 . . . . .11 C8
    Beesby with Saleby LN13 . . .75 F5
    Bicker PE20 . . . . .135 B4
    Billinghay LN4 . . . . .109 E5
    Boston PE21 . . . . .208 E4
    Brant Broughton & Stragglethorpe
    LN5 . . . . .105 E5
    Bratoft PE24 . . . . .102 C7
    Brigg DN20 . . . . .196 B2
    Brough HU15 . . . . .2 C6
  9 Broughton DN20 . . . . . .19 E3
    Burgh on Bain LN8 . . . . . .59 D5
    Butterwick PE22 . . . . . . .126 E4
    Caistor LN7 . . . . .33 C4
    Castor PE5 . . . . .223 F1
  7 Croxton Kerrial NG32 . .138 D4
    Donington PE11 . . . . . . .134 F2
    Donington on Bain LN11 . . .59 D2
    Eagle & Swinethorpe LN6 . .79 C2
    East Halton DN40 . . . . . . .12 D6
    Firsby PE24 . . . . .102 A7
    Fleet PE12 . . . . .168 C2
    Fosdyke PE20 . . . . .136 D1
    Friskney PE22 . . . . .115 C7
    Gainsborough DN21 . . . .197 B8
    Gorefield PE13 . . . . .169 E1
    Gosberton PE11 . . . . . . .145 C6
  4 Gowxhill DN19 . . . . .5 A1
    Grainthorpe LN11 . . . . . .50 B8
    Great Casterton PE9 . . . .171 B8
    Great Ponton NG33 . . . .140 A5
    Hackthorn LN2 . . . . .56 B1
    Haxey DN9 . . . . .27 B2
    Heighington/Washingborough
    LN4 . . . . .81 E4
    Hemingby LN9 . . . . .72 B1
    Heydour NG32 . . . . .131 B5
    Hogsthorpe PE24 . . . . . . .90 B7
    Holbeach PE12 . . . . .215 B5
    Holton le Clay DN36 . . . . .36 B4
    Horbling NG34 . . . . .133 B3
    Horncastle LN9 . . . . .199 B4
    Huttoft LN13 . . . . .76 E4
    Immingham DN40 . . . . . .186 A4
  8 Keelby DN41 . . . . .23 A4
  5 Ketton PE9 . . . . .171 A3
    Kingston upon Hull HU10 .178 C6
    Kirton PE20 . . . . .136 A7
    Kirton in Lindsey DN21 . . .30 C1
    Legbourne LN11 . . . . .61 F3
    Lincoln LN5 . . . . .201 E1
    Little Steeping LN13 . . . .101 C6
    Louth LN11 . . . . .198 B7
    Maltby le Marsh LN13 . . . .75 F8
    Manby LN11 . . . . .62 C7
  4 Marshchapel DN36 . . . . .37 C2
    Marston NG32 . . . . .118 D2
    Martin LN4 . . . . .96 C2
    Martin LN4 . . . . .96 C3
    Middle Rasen LN8 . . . . . .57 C7
    Minting LN8 . . . . .71 B2
    Mumby LN13 . . . . .76 F1
    Newton NG34 . . . . .133 B8
    North Clifton NG23 . . . . .78 C7
  3 North Kelsey LN7 . . . . .32 A4
    Osgodby LN8 . . . . .45 A3
    Owmby LN8 . . . . .55 E6
    Peterborough PE5 . . . . . .228 F7
    Pickworth NG34 . . . . . . .132 A1
    Roughton Moor LN10 . . . .98 A7
    Saltfleetby LN11 . . . . . . .51 C1
    Saxilby LN1 . . . . .66 D2
    Scamblesby LN11 . . . . . .72 F5
    Scawby DN20 . . . . .30 F8
    Skegness PE25 . . . . .206 A8
    Skidbrooke with Saltfleet Haven
    LN11 . . . . .51 C4
  10 South Ferriby DN18 . . . .10 A7
    South Somercotes LN11 . . .50 D4
    South Witham NG33 . . . .151 C1
    Sturton by Stow LN1 . . . . .66 C6
    Sutterton PE20 . . . . .135 F2
  19 Sutton Bridge PE12 . . .160 E4
    Swineshead PE20 . . . . . .135 A8
    Tallington PE9 . . . . .172 F7
    Tetford LN9 . . . . .73 E1
    Thorney PE8 . . . . .228 B7
    Tinwell PE9 . . . . .218 D3
    Tydd St Mary PE13 . . . . .160 B1
    Wainfleet All Saints PE24 .102 C1
    Walkeringham DN10 . . . . .39 F3
    Welbourn LN5 . . . . .106 F4
    Welton LN2 . . . . .68 E8
    Welton le Marsh PE23 . . . .89 A3
    West Keal PE23 . . . . .100 B4
    West Walton PE14 . . . . . .170 F4
    Whaplode PE12 . . . . .158 B7
    Wigsley NG23 . . . . .78 F4
    Wildmore LN4 . . . . .111 C4
    Willoughby with Sloothby
    LN13 . . . . .89 C6
    Woodhall Spa LN10 . . . . .97 B5
    Wrangle PE22 . . . . .114 D1
    Wrawby DN20 . . . . .20 E3
Mill La Cl PE24 . . . . .90 B7
Mill La W HU15 . . . . .2 B6
Mill Marsh Rd PE12 . . . . .146 D2
Mill Mere Rd
    Corringham DN21 . . . . . . .41 D2
  5 Waddington LN5 . . . . . .93 F7

Mill Moor Way 3 LN6 . . . .204 D1
Millom Way DN32 . . . . . . .191 F8
Mill Pl DN35 . . . . .192 E5
Millport Dr HU4 . . . . .179 B2
Mill Race DN36 . . . . .36 E4
Mill Rd Addlethorpe PE24 . .90 D2
    Boston PE21 . . . . .209 B3
    Claypole NG23 . . . . .117 E7
    Cleethorpes DN35 . . . . . .192 E5
    Crowle DN17 . . . . .16 D8
    Donington on Bain LN11 . . .59 E2
    Hibaldstow DN20 . . . . . . .30 E4
  2 Keadby DN17 . . . . .17 D5
    Lincoln LN1 . . . . .234 A4
    Luddington & Haldenby DN17. .7 C1
    Market Rasen LN8 . . . . . .57 D7
    Maxey PE6 . . . . .173 C2
    Pilsgate PE9 . . . . .172 C3
    Swanland HU14 . . . . .3 A6
    Walpole PE14 . . . . .170 F6
    Wisbech St Mary PE13 . .177 D5
Mill Rise
  6 Navenby/Wellingore
    LN5 . . . . .107 A7
  14 Scothern LN2 . . . . .68 F4
    Swanland HU14 . . . . .3 A6
Mill Row Barrowby NG32 .129 B3
  2 Lincoln LN1 . . . . .234 A4
Mills Cl 15 NG23 . . . . .117 D3
Mills Dr DN7 . . . . .26 A8
Mills Service Rd DN16 . . . .19 A4
Mill St
    Kingston upon Hull HU1 . .180 E6
    Ryhall PE9 . . . . .163 C2
    Scamblesby LN11 . . . . . .73 A4
Millstone Cl
    Horncastle LN9 . . . . .199 A3
  9 Kirton in Lindsey DN21 . .30 B2
Millstone La 3 PE9 . . . . . .172 D3
Millstream Rd LN4 . . . . . .81 E4
MILLTHORPE NG34 . . . . . .143 E5
Millthorpe Dro NG34 . . . .143 E5
Millthorpe La NG34 . . . . .142 F5
Millthorpe Rd NG34 . . . . .143 B5
Mill View
    Peterborough PE7 . . . . . .229 A5
  5 Waltham DN37 . . . . . . .194 E4
Mill View Cl
    Addlethorpe PE24 . . . . . . .90 D4
    Epworth DN9 . . . . .27 D7
Millview Ct LN9 . . . . .199 B4
Mill View Cl 2 LN8 . . . . . . .70 D4
Millview Gdns 3 DN20 . . .20 E3
Millview Rd
  11 Heckington NG34 . . . . .122 E2
    Ruskington NG34 . . . . . .108 D2
Mill View Rd 9 LN8 . . . . . .70 D4
Mill Vw 31 DN18 . . . . .3 E1
Mill Wy LN11 . . . . .49 B7
Milman Rd LN2 . . . . .202 B4
Milne Gn 4 PE20 . . . . .135 B7
Milners Ct 22 PE9 . . . . . . .219 C5
Milner's La 2 PE23 . . . . . .87 F1
Milner St 20 NG24 . . . . . .104 A4
Milnyard Sq PE2 . . . . .229 C2
Milson Cl
  18 Barton-upon-Humber
    DN18 . . . . .10 E8
  3 Broughton DN20 . . . . . .19 D4
    Coningsby LN4 . . . . .207 D4
Milson Rd 17 DN41 . . . . . .23 A4
Milsons La LN13 . . . . .75 B6
Milson Way LN4 . . . . .207 D4
Milton Cl Branston LN4 . . .81 D2
    Cherry Willingham LN3 . .203 E5
  2 Gainsborough DN21 . . .197 E6
Milton Dr PE13 . . . . .170 B1
Milton Rd
    Gainsborough DN21 . . . .197 E6
    Grimsby DN34 . . . . .191 B4
    Peterborough PE2 . . . . . .231 A7
    Scunthorpe DN16 . . . . . .185 B5
Milton St Lincoln LN5 . . . .205 E7
    Newark-on-Trent NG24 . .104 A3
Milton Way
    Kirkby la Thorpe NG34 . .121 E4
    Peterborough PE2 . . . . . .224 E3
  2 Sleaford NG34 . . . . . . .212 F3
Mimosa Cl DN16 . . . . .185 E4
Mina Cl PE2 . . . . .231 D4
Minden Pl 4 DN21 . . . . . . .55 A8
Minerva Cl 13 NG32 . . . . .120 A3
Minerva Wy LN6 . . . . .204 C1
MININGSBY PE22 . . . . .99 D7
Miningsby Rd PE23 . . . . . .99 F8
Minnett's Hill NG32 . . . . .130 B8
Minnow Cl 1 DN37 . . . . . .190 D7
Minshull Rd DN35 . . . . . . .192 F4
Minsmere Cl PE11 . . . . . . .214 B5
Minster Dr
    Cherry Willingham/Reepham
    LN3 . . . . .203 E7
    Louth LN11 . . . . .198 D4
Minster Precincts 9 PE1 .226 A2
Minster Rd
  15 Misterton DN10 . . . . . .39 F5
    Scunthorpe DN15 . . . . . .182 B2
Minster Yd LN2 . . . . .234 B3
MINTING LN9 . . . . .84 D8
Minting Cl 9 LN1 . . . . . . .201 E8
Minting La LN9 . . . . .71 D1
Mint La LN1 . . . . .234 A2
Mint St LN1 . . . . .234 A2
Mirfield Rd Grimsby DN32 .191 F4
    Scunthorpe DN15 . . . . . .182 C4
Misson Bank DN9 . . . . . . .26 C3
MISTERTON DN10 . . . . . . .39 F5
Misterton PE2 . . . . .229 E3

Mic–Moo 265

Misterton Prim Sch DN10 . .39 F4
Mitchell Cl Eastgate PE1 . .226 C2
  3 Hatfield DN7 . . . . .14 D5
  7 Skellingthorpe LN6 . . . .200 A4
Mitchell Dr LN1 . . . . .201 C6
Mitchell Rd LN4 . . . . .207 F6
Mitre La 16 PE21 . . . . .208 F5
Moat House Rd 22 DN21 . . .30 B1
Moat La Bolingbroke PE23 .114 A8
    Old Leake PE22 . . . . .114 B1
  3 South Killingholme DN40. .12 E3
  4 Welbourn LN5 . . . . . . .106 C5
Moat Rd Scunthorpe DN15 . .8 C1
    Terrington St Clement PE34 161 F1
Moat Wlk NG31 . . . . .211 E6
Modder St DN16 . . . . .185 B6
Moggswell La PE2 . . . . . . .230 B4
Moira Cl 5 DN7 . . . . .14 D7
Mole Dro PE12 . . . . .168 C1
Molinari Ave DN36 . . . . . . .36 C4
Mollison Ave DN35 . . . . . .192 F5
Mollison Rd HU4 . . . . .179 A3
Molyneux Sq
  1 Hampton Vale PE7 . . . .230 B1
    Yaxley PE7 . . . . .233 B8
Monaco Way PE10 . . . . . . .213 A4
Monarch Ave PE2 . . . . . . .231 A6
Monarchs Rd PE20 . . . . . .136 A3
Monce Cl LN2 . . . . .68 C7
Monckton Way LN2 . . . . . . .68 D5
Mondemont Rd Cl 4 PE12 .215 E3
Money Bridge La PE11 . . .144 F1
Moneys Yd 7 NG34 . . . . . .212 D4
Monic Ave HU13 . . . . .178 F2
Monkhouse Ct 5 PE11 . . .214 A3
Monks Abbey Prim Sch
    LN2 . . . . .202 B4
Monks Ave LN11 . . . . .198 C6
Monks Cl 4 Hatfield DN7 . .14 D5
    New Quarrington NG34 . .212 A2
Monks Dr 22 PE6 . . . . . . .175 A1
Monks Dyke Rd LN11 . . . .198 D5
Monks' Dyke Tennyson Coll
    LN11 . . . . .198 D5
Monks Gr PE4 . . . . .220 E5
Monks Ho La 12 PE11 . . . .214 A4
Monks House La 5 PE11. .214 A4
Monks Leys Terr LN2 . . . .234 C3
Monks Manor Ct LN2 . . . .202 B5
Monks Manor Dr LN2 . . . .202 B4
Monks Mdw 5 PE6 . . . . . .175 B8
Monks Rd Lincoln LN2 . . .234 B2
    Scunthorpe DN17 . . . . . .184 F6
  8 Swineshead PE20 . . . . .135 B7
MONKSTHORPE PE23 . . . .101 E8
Monksthorpe La PE23 . . . .88 F1
Monks Way LN2 . . . . .202 C3
Monks Way East HU14 . . . .2 F5
Monks Way Ind Est LN2 . .202 D3
Monks Way West HU14 . . . .2 F5
Monks Wlk 4 PE11 . . . . . .214 A4
Monkton 3 HU15 . . . . .2 D6
Monkwood 17 NG23 . . . . .91 D5
Monmouth La PE11 . . . . . .216 E8
Monmouth St HU4 . . . . . .179 E3
Monmouth Way NG31 . . .210 E6
Monsal Dale LN6 . . . . .204 F2
Monson Ct LN5 . . . . .201 E1
Monson Pk LN6 . . . . .200 A4
Monson Rd DN21 . . . . .42 A8
Monson St LN5 . . . . .234 A1
Monson St LN1 . . . . .201 E6
Mons St HU5 . . . . .180 A8
Montague St
    Cleethorpes DN35 . . . . . .189 D1
    Lincoln LN2 . . . . .234 C2
Montague Terr 1 LN2 . . . .234 C2
Montagu Rd PE4 . . . . .225 D8
Montaigne Cl 3 LN2 . . . . .202 D7
Montaigne Cres LN2 . . . . .202 D7
Montaigne Gdn LN2 . . . . .202 D7
Montbretia Dr 2 DN17 . . .185 A1
Monteith Cres PE21 . . . . .209 B5
Montgomery Rd
    Cleethorpes DN35 . . . . . .192 D5
    Skegness PE25 . . . . .206 A3
Montrose Cl
  8 Grantham NG31 . . . . . .211 D7
  1 Lincoln LN6 . . . . .204 E1
  10 Stamford PE9 . . . . . . .218 E6
Montrose Gr NG34 . . . . . .121 A2
Montrose St 5 DN16 . . . . .183 B2
Monument Rd
  5 Bicker PE20 . . . . .135 A4
    Stixwould LN10 . . . . .97 D7
Monument St PE1 . . . . . . .226 A3
Moody La DN31 . . . . .188 C3
Moon's Gn 3 PE12 . . . . . .157 F6
Moor Bank PE22 . . . . .113 C3
Moor Bottom Rd DN17. . . . .6 C1
MOORBY PE22 . . . . .99 B6
Moorby Cl LN1 . . . . .201 E7
Moorby Rd PE22 . . . . .98 F6
Moor Closes Nature Reserve*
    NG32 . . . . .120 A2
Moor Dike Rd DN7 . . . . . . .26 A8
Moore Cl NG33 . . . . .117 F7
Moor Edges Rd DN8 . . . . .15 B8
Moore's La 1 PE6 . . . . . . .175 A1
Moor Farm Nature Reserve*
    LN10 . . . . .98 A6
Moorfield Rd 2 PE3 . . . . .225 D3
Moorfields La DN14 . . . . . .6 F7
Moor Gate PE12 . . . . .159 A4
Moorgate Cl PE10 . . . . . . .154 D7

Moor Gn HU4 . . . . .179 B7
Moorhen Cl
  Skirbeck Quarter PE21. . . . . .208 E3
  Witham St Hughs LN6. . . . . . .92 D4
Moorhouse Rd HU5 . . . . . . .179 B8
MOORHOUSES PE22. . . . . . . .112 A8
Moorhouses Rd PE22. . . . . .111 F8
Moorings The
  Broughton DN20 . . . . .196 A3
  Burton LN1 . . . . .200 D7
Moor La
  Ashby de la Launde & Bloxholm
    LN4. . . . . .108 C3
  Besthorpe NG23. . . . . .91 D7
  Blankney LN4. . . . . .95 E4
  Braceby & Sapperton NG34 .131 E1
  Branston & Mere LN4. . . . . . .81 F2
  Caistor LN7 . . . . .33 A5
  5 Cherry Willingham/Reepham
    LN3. . . . . .82 A8
  Hatfield DN8 . . . . .15 D3
  Horsington LN10 . . . . .84 D2
  Kirkby on Bain LN10 . . . . . . .97 F6
  Laneham DN22. . . . . .65 A3
  Leasingham NG34 . . . . .121 C7
  Lincoln LN6 . . . . .204 C1
  Long Bennington NG23. . . . .117 C3
  Marlborough LN5 . . . . .93 A4
  Martin LN4. . . . . .96 A2
  North Clifton NG23. . . . . .78 D6
  Potter Hanworth LN4. . . . . . .82 B2
  Reepham LN3. . . . . .69 B1
  Roughton LN10. . . . . .98 B7
  South Clifton NG23. . . . . .78 E5
  South Witham NG33. . . . . . .151 B2
  Stapleford LN6. . . . . .105 B8
  Thorpe on the Hill LN6 . . . . . .79 E1
  Thurlby LN6. . . . . .92 E4
  Wroot DN9 . . . . .26 C6
Moorland Ave
  1 Lincoln LN6. . . . . .205 A5
  4 Walkeringham DN10 . . . . .39 F3
Moorland Cl
  8 Carlton-le-Moorland
    LN5. . . . . .105 E8
  5 Walkeringham DN10 . . . . .39 F3
Moorland Cres 5 LN6. . . . .205 B6
Moorland Dr DN36 . . . . . . .195 C7
Moorland Lane 17 B1
Moorlands 9 DN9. . . . . .27 A2
Moorlands The 23 LN4. . . . . .95 D4
Moorland Way
  5 Epworth DN9. . . . . .27 E6
  Lincoln LN6. . . . . .204 F5
Moor Owners Rd DN8 . . . . . .15 D8
Moor Pk 5 NG34. . . . . .108 C7
Moor Pk Dr 9 LN10 . . . . . . .97 C5
Moor Rd Bottesford DN17 . .184 C2
  15 Collingham NG23. . . . . . .91 D5
  Crowle DN17. . . . . .16 C8
  Newborough PE6. . . . . .174 C5
  Owersby LN8 . . . . .45 A5
  Snitterby DN21. . . . . .43 D5
  Thorne DN8. . . . . .15 C7
  Walesby LN8 . . . . .45 E3
Moorside PE22. . . . . .98 E3
MOOR SIDE PE22. . . . . .111 D8
Moor Side PE22. . . . . .111 C8
Moorside Ct LN6. . . . . .204 E1
Moors La LN8. . . . . .59 A2
Moors Rd DN15. . . . . .182 C3
Moor St LN1. . . . . .201 D4
Moorswood Gate PE12. . . .159 D3
MOORTOWN LN7. . . . . .32 C2
Moortown Cl 9 NG31 . . . . .211 D7
Moortown Rd LN7. . . . . .33 A3
Moorwell Bsns Pk DN17 . .184 D3
Moorwell Rd DN17. . . . . . . .184 E2
Moray Cl 5 PE9. . . . . .218 D6
MORBORNE PE7. . . . . .232 B3
Morborne Cl PE2. . . . . .231 D6
Morborne La PE7. . . . . .232 D4
Morborne Rd PE7. . . . . .232 C2
Morborn Rd 4 PE7. . . . . . . .230 C2
Mordaunt Ave DN33. . . . . . .194 D7
Morden Cl 12 LN4 . . . . .95 D4
Moreland Ave 1 LN12. . . . . .77 A8
Moresby Wy PE7. . . . . .231 A5
Morfield Gr 5 DN9. . . . . .27 D6
Morgan Cl PE7. . . . . .233 E6
Morgans Cl 2 NG24. . . . . . .104 D5
Morgan Way 5 DN19. . . . . . . .4 E2
Morkery La
  Castle Bytham NG33 . . . . . .152 B2
  North Witham NG33. . . . . . .151 F2
Morley La 10 PE20. . . . . . . .135 A4
Morley Rd DN17. . . . . .184 F5
Morley's La NG33. . . . . .152 F7
Morley St 2 DN21. . . . . . . .197 C5
Morley Way PE2. . . . . .230 D5
Morningside Dr PE25. . . . . .103 C7
Morpeth Cl PE2. . . . . .230 C6
Morpeth Rd PE3. . . . . .225 C3
Morpeth St HU3. . . . . .180 D7
Morpeth Wlk DN34. . . . . . . .191 A7
Morris Cl 2 LN1. . . . . .68 D6
Morris Ct PE7. . . . . .233 E6
Morris Gdns 2 PE25 . . . . . .206 B5
Morrison Cl 10 LN12. . . . . . .76 F8
Morris Rd HU3 . . . . .179 E7
Morris St PE1. . . . . .226 B3
Mortal Ash Hill DN16 . . . . . .19 C2
Mortimer Dr HU10 . . . . .178 F6
MORTON Morton DN21 . . . . .197 C8

MORTON *continued*
  Morton PE10 . . . . .154 C6
  Thorpe on the Hill LN6 . . . . . .92 C6
Morton Carr DN21. . . . . .40 C4
Morton CE (Controlled) Prim
  Sch PE10 . . . . .154 D7
Morton Cl
  Gainsborough DN21. . . . . . .197 B8
  Immingham DN40 . . . . .186 B5
Morton Dr LN6. . . . . .204 F7
Morton Dro PE10. . . . . .155 A6
Morton Front DN21. . . . . . . .197 B7
Morton La LN6. . . . . .92 C8
Morton N Dro PE10. . . . . . .155 B7
Morton Rd
  Gainsborough DN21. . . . . . .197 C7
  Grimsby DN34. . . . . .191 B7
  Laughton DN21. . . . . .41 B8
  Swinderby LN6. . . . . .92 B7
Morton St HU3. . . . . .180 C8
Morton Terr DN21. . . . . . . .197 B8
Morton Trentside Prim Sch
  DN21. . . . . .197 B8
Morton Way LN9 . . . . .199 C1
Morus Cl PE11. . . . . .214 E2
Mosscroft La DN7. . . . . .14 F3
Mossdale Cl NG31. . . . . . . .129 F5
Moss Dr PE25. . . . . .206 C2
Mossop Dr PE6. . . . . .164 E3
Moss Rd Grimsby DN32. . . . .191 E7
  Kirk Bramwith DN7. . . . . .14 A8
Motherby La LN1. . . . . .234 A2
MOULTON PE12. . . . . .157 F7
MOULTON CHAPEL PE12. . .157 E1
Moulton Chapel Prim Sch
  PE12. . . . . .157 F1
Moulton Chapel Rd PE12 .157 C1
Moulton Cl 1 DN34. . . . . . .190 D4
Moulton Cres 13 NG24. . . .104 B2
MOULTON EAUGATE
  PE12. . . . . .167 F8
Moulton Gr PE3. . . . . .225 C6
Moulton Marsh Nature
  Reserve★ PE12 . . . . .146 F8
Moulton Mere Bank PE12 .157 E3
MOULTON SEAS END
  PE12. . . . . .146 E2
Mount Ave
  14 Barton-upon-Humber
    DN18. . . . . .10 E8
  Kingston upon Hull HU13 . .178 D2
  10 Winterton DN15 . . . . .9 B5
Mountbatten Ave
  11 Pinchbeck PE11. . . . . . .156 E8
  Stamford PE9. . . . . .219 A6
  Yaxley PE7 . . . . .233 D5
Mountbatten Cl 5 DN16. . .185 B4
Mountbatten Dr 2 PE13. . .170 C1
Mountbatten Way
  Bourne PE10 . . . . .213 E7
  Peterborough PE3. . . . . . . .225 B6
Mount Ct 6 NG24 . . . . .104 B2
Mount La
  Burton Pedwardine NG34. . .122 A2
  Kirkby la Thorpe NG34 . . . . .121 F3
  Legsby LN8. . . . . .58 A3
Mountney Pl 9 NG24. . . . . .104 A6
Mount Olivet LN11. . . . . . . .198 A6
Mount Pleasant
  9 Alford LN13. . . . . .75 F2
  Binbrook LN8 . . . . .47 B4
  1 Holton le Clay DN36 . . . .195 D1
  Kingston upon Hull HU9 . . . .181 C8
  Louth LN11. . . . . .198 C5
  8 New Holland DN19 . . . . . . .4 E2
  Peterborough PE2 . . . . .231 C7
  Sleaford NG34 . . . . .212 E5
  6 Wainfleet All Saints
    PE24. . . . . .102 D2
  Waltham DN37. . . . . .194 D5
Mount Pleasant Cl DN21. . . .53 B1
Mount Pleasant Rd PE13. .170 D1
Mount Pleasant Windmill★
  DN21. . . . . .30 B2
Mount Rd
  Bracebridge Heath LN4 . . . .205 F3
  Newark-on-Trent NG24 . . . .104 B2
Mount Royale Cl DN39. . . . .12 A1
Mount St
  9 Grantham NG31 . . . . . . .211 A5
  Lincoln LN1. . . . . .201 E6
Mountsteven Ave PE4. . . . .221 B1
Mount Street Acad LN1. . . .201 E6
Mount The 15 DN3 . . . . .14 A1
Mount Tumbledown Cl 9
  PE12. . . . . .160 E4
Mount View 5 HU14 . . . . .3 A5
Mourne Terr 11 LN5. . . . . . .205 D2
Mowbeck Wy NG31. . . . . . . .210 F3
Mowbray Cl 3 Haxey DN9 . . .27 D3
  16 Skegness PE25. . . . . . . .206 A5
Mowbray Ct 23 DN9. . . . . . . .27 E6
Mowbray Rd
  Bretton PE3 . . . . .220 D1
  14 Thorne/Moorends DN8. . .15 B7
  4 Westwoodside DN9 . . . . . .27 E6
  Gainsborough DN21. . . . . . .197 C6
Moxon's La 13 LN5. . . . . . . .93 F7
Mrs Mary Kings CE
  (Controlled) Prim Sch
  LN4. . . . . .96 B3
Mrs Smith's Cottage★
  LN5. . . . . .107 B8
Much La LN1. . . . . .234 A1
MUCKTON LN11. . . . . .74 D8
Muckton Rd
  Little Cawthorpe LN11 . . . . . .61 E2
  Muckton LN11. . . . . .74 D6

Muckton Wood Nature
  Reserve★ LN11. . . . . .74 E8
Mucky La DN15 . . . . .9 C5
Muirfield Grantham NG31 . .211 D8
  11 Waltham DN37. . . . . . . .194 C4
Muirfield Cl
  Birchwood LN6. . . . . .204 B7
  6 Spalding PE11. . . . . .214 C2
Muirfield Croft DN40. . . . . .186 C4
Muirfield Dr PE25. . . . . .206 D5
Mulberry Ave 3 LN6. . . . . . .204 F2
Mulberry Cl
  5 North Thoresby DN36 . . . .36 B1
  Sleaford NG34 . . . . .212 D2
  Waddington LN5. . . . . .205 D1
Mulberry Ct 6 PE20. . . . . . .135 B6
Mulberry Dr 2 DN17. . . . . . .16 D7
Mulberry Gdns
  Bottesford DN16 . . . . .185 E4
  Paston PE4. . . . . .221 C1
Mulberry La DN37. . . . . .23 F2
Mulberry Rd LN8. . . . . .45 E5
Mulberry Way
  Skegness PE25. . . . . .206 B6
  Spalding PE11. . . . . .214 E3
Mulberry Wlk 11 NG34. . . .122 D3
Mulgrave Cl DN37. . . . . .190 F8
Mulgrave St 5 DN15 . . . . . .183 A4
Mulgrave St HU8. . . . . .181 A8
Mull Way DN40. . . . . .186 C2
Multon Ings La PE20. . . . . .136 B7
MUMBY LN13. . . . . .76 F1
Mumby Cl
  22 Beacon Hill NG24 . . . . . .104 A5
  12 North Thoresby DN36 . . . .36 B1
Mumby Mdws LN13 . . . . .76 F1
Mumby Rd LN13. . . . . .76 F2
Mumby's Bridge Rd PE22 . .98 F2
Munday Way LN13. . . . . .170 B2
Munstead Wy 2 HU15 . . . . . .2 D5
Munster Ct 6 DN31. . . . . . . .189 C1
Munton Fields NG33. . . . . . .131 A1
Murdock Rd LN5. . . . . .205 E6
Murrayfield Ave 3 NG34. . .120 F3
Murray St 2 DN31. . . . . .189 B2
MURROW PE13. . . . . .177 D5
Murrow Bank PE13. . . . . . . .177 D6
Murrow La PE13. . . . . .177 F5
Murrow Primary Acad
  PE13. . . . . .177 D5
Museum of Lincolnshire Life★
  LN1. . . . . .234 A4
Musgraves Orch LN2. . . . . . .68 E7
Muskham PE3 . . . . .224 F4
Musselburgh Way PE10. . . .213 B3
Mussons Cl NG31. . . . . .152 E7
Muster Roll La PE21. . . . . . .209 A3
Musticott Pl 17 PE13. . . . . .170 C1
MUSTON NG13. . . . . .128 C5
Muston La NG13. . . . . .128 B5
Muston Meadows National
  Nature Reserve★ NG13 . .128 B3
Muston Rd NG31. . . . . .210 E2
Muswell Rd PE3. . . . . .225 E4
Mutton La DN10. . . . . .39 F1
Myers Cl NG32. . . . . .120 C1
Myles Way 15 PE13. . . . . . . .170 D2
Myrtle Ave PE1. . . . . .226 C7
Myrtle Ct PE1. . . . . .226 C7
Myrtle Gr PE1. . . . . .226 C7
Myrtle House Cvn Pk PE1 .226 F5
Myrtle Rd 5 DN7 . . . . .14 C4
Myrtle Way 16 HU15 . . . . .2 C5
Myton St HU1 . . . . .180 E6

N

Naam Gr LN1. . . . . .234 A4
Naam Pl LN1. . . . . .234 A4
Nab La DN7. . . . . .14 C8
Nags Head Pas 10 NG34. . .212 D4
Nairn Dr PE2. . . . . .229 D4
Nairn Rd PE9 . . . . .218 E6
Nandike Cl 4 HU10 . . . . .178 F6
Nan Sampson Bank DN9 . . .26 B4
Nansicles Rd PE2. . . . . .230 D6
Napier Pl PE2. . . . . .229 C6
Napier St LN2. . . . . .234 C2
Narrow Boats The 3
  DN20 . . . . .196 A3
Narrow La Belchford LN9. . . .73 B2
  Twin Rivers DN14. . . . . .7 C3
  Whaplode PE12. . . . . .158 C4
Narrow Lane DN9. . . . . .28 A7
Naseby Cl 21
  Hatfield DN7. . . . . .14 D3
  Peterborough PE3 . . . . .225 C5
Naseby Dr DN31. . . . . .191 B8
Naseby Gr DN31. . . . . .191 B7
Nash Cl 18 NG34. . . . . .122 E2
Nash La 2 LN6. . . . . .204 E1
Natal View LN1. . . . . .201 D8
Nathan Cl PE3. . . . . .225 B2
National Ave HU5 . . . . .179 F8
National CE Jun Sch The
  NG31. . . . . .211 B5
National Fishing Heritage
  Ctr★ DN31. . . . . .191 E8
National Parrot Sanctuary
  The★ PE22. . . . . .114 D7
Natural World Ctr★ LN6 . . .79 F1
Natureland Seal Sanctuary★
  PE25. . . . . .206 E4
Natures Way PE7. . . . . .233 A8
NAVENBY LN5. . . . . .107 A8
Navenby CE Prim Sch
  LN5. . . . . .107 B8

Navenby La
  Ashby de la Launde & Bloxholm
    LN4. . . . . .107 F6
  Bassingham LN5 . . . . .93 A1
Navenby Cl DN31. . . . . .188 A2
Navigation House★ **8**
  NG34. . . . . .212 E4
Navigation La 28 LN7. . . . . .33 B4
Navigation Way HU9 . . . . . .181 C6
Naylors Dr 5 LN8. . . . . .57 B8
Naylor's Row 3 HU9 . . . . . .181 B7
Ndola Dr LN9 . . . . .199 C2
Neale Rd 16 LN6 . . . . .93 C8
Neals Cres NG31. . . . . .210 F4
Neal's Gate PE12. . . . . .158 E2
Neap House Rd
  Flixborough DN15 . . . . .182 A7
  Gunness DN15 . . . . .17 E6
Neatgangs La DN19 . . . . .5 A3
Neath Rd DN16. . . . . .183 A1
Neaverson Rd 2 PE6 . . . . . .220 D7
Needham Ct PE7. . . . . .233 E4
Needham Dr PE12. . . . . .159 C1
Needham Rd PE10. . . . . .154 C6
Needles The 8 PE25 . . . . . .206 A7
Neile Cl LN2. . . . . .202 D7
Nelson Cl 5 Crowland PE6 . .166 F1
  4 Skegness PE25. . . . . . . .206 A7
Nelson Dr LN4. . . . . .203 B2
Nelson Gdns 31 PE13. . . . . .170 D1
Nelson Rd Fiskerton LN3. . . . .82 A6
  Kingston upon Hull HU5 . . . .179 B7
  4 Mablethorpe/Sutton on Sea
    LN12. . . . . .64 B3
  1 Newark-on-Trent NG24. . .104 A2
Nelson St
  Gainsborough DN21. . . . . . .197 C6
  Grimsby DN32. . . . . .189 B1
  Kingston upon Hull HU1 . . . .181 A5
  Lincoln LN1. . . . . .201 D3
Nelson Way
  9 Boston PE21. . . . . .208 E4
  5 Grimsby DN34. . . . . .190 D4
Nelthorpe Cl 9 DN39. . . . . . .12 A1
Nelthorpe St LN5. . . . . .201 E1
Nene Cl Bourne PE10 . . . . . .213 A4
  Guyhirn PE13 . . . . .177 F2
  10 Ruskington NG34 . . . . . .108 D2
  Wansford PE8 . . . . .222 A3
  4 Wittering PE8 . . . . .172 B1
Nene Ct 4 Grantham NG31 .210 E2
  3 Spalding PE11. . . . . .214 F5
Nenegate Sch PE1 . . . . .226 C3
Nenelands 8 PE12. . . . . . . .160 F4
Nene Mdws 1 PE12. . . . . . . .160 F4
Nene Parade 9 PE13. . . . . . .170 C1
Nene Park Acad PE2. . . . . . .230 A5
Nene Parkway PE3. . . . . . . .224 F1
Nene Pk 6 LN6. . . . . .204 C1
Nene Rd LN1. . . . . .201 E8
Nene St PE1. . . . . .226 B2
NENE TERRACE PE6. . . . . . .175 D6
Nene Terr PE6 . . . . .175 D7
Nene Valley Prim Sch
  PE2. . . . . .230 D8
Nene Way PE5. . . . . .222 F2
Neptune Cl 2 PE2. . . . . .231 D4
Neptune St
  Cleethorpes DN35 . . . . .192 E7
  Kingston upon Hull HU1 . . . .180 D4
Nero Pl PE2. . . . . .231 F4
Nero Wy LN6. . . . . .93 A8
Neslam Rd NG34. . . . . .143 C2
Ness La LN17 . . . . .7 E6
Netherfield PE12. . . . . .215 B2
Nethergate DN9 . . . . .27 B2
Nether La NG32. . . . . .139 A7
Netherlands Way DN41. . . .187 B3
Netherton Rd HU4. . . . . .179 B4
Nettlecroft La NG32. . . . . . .119 C6
NETTLEHAM LN2. . . . . .68 D2
Nettleham CE VA Jun Sch The
  LN2. . . . . .68 C2
Nettleham Cl LN2. . . . . .202 A6
Nettleham Infant Sch The
  LN2. . . . . .68 C2
Nettleham Rd Lincoln LN2. .234 C4
  Scothern LN2. . . . . .68 E3
Nettleholme 10 DN7. . . . . . .14 D4
NETTLETON LN7. . . . . .33 A3
Nettleton Cl LN4. . . . . .81 C3
Nettleton Com Prim Sch
  LN7. . . . . .33 A3
Nettleton Dr LN6. . . . . .92 E5
Nettleton Rd LN7. . . . . .33 B3
Neustadt Ct 10 LN2. . . . . . .234 B3
Neville Ave PE11. . . . . .214 F4
Neville Cl
  5 Keadby with Althorpe
    DN17. . . . . .17 D4
  Kingston upon Hull HU3 . . . .180 D5
Neville Cres 3 DN15 . . . . .9 A5
Neville La DN7. . . . . .14 A8
Neville Rd DN16. . . . . .183 C2
Neville St DN35. . . . . .192 D8
Neville Turner Way DN37 .194 D4
NEWARK PE1. . . . . .226 E6
Newark Acad The NG24. . . .104 B3
Newark Air Mus★ NG24. . . .104 D6
Newark Ave PE1. . . . . .226 C6
Newark Hill Foston NG23 . . .117 F1
  Great Gonerby NG31. . . . . . .129 D6
Newark Hill Prim Sch
  PE1. . . . . .226 D6

Newark & Nottinghamshire
  Agricultural Society's
  Showground★ NG24 . . . .104 C7
NEWARK-ON-TRENT
  NG24. . . . . .104 B4
Newark Rd
  Barnby in the Willows
    NG24. . . . . .104 E3
  Bassingham LN5 . . . . .92 E2
  Dry Doddington NG23. . . . . .117 A5
  Fenton LN1. . . . . .65 D4
  Leadenham LN5 . . . . .106 C3
  Lincoln LN6 . . . . .204 D3
  Newark-on-Trent NG24 . . . .104 C5
  North Rauceby NG34 . . . . . .120 C7
  Norton Disney LN6 . . . . .91 F2
  Peterborough PE1 . . . . .226 E2
  Stapleford LN6. . . . . .105 B8
  Swinderby LN6. . . . . .92 A4
Newark Rd Ind Est PE1 . . . .226 E4
Newark Vw NG31. . . . . .210 D6
Newark Wlk DN40. . . . . .186 D3
NEW BALDERTON NG24. . . .104 A2
NEWBALL LN3. . . . . .69 D3
NEW BARNETBY DN38. . . . . .21 D5
New Beacon Rd NG31 . . . . .211 C4
Newbey Cl PE3. . . . . .225 B3
Newbey Gr 2 NG34. . . . . . . .190 E4
Newbolt Ave 2 DN17. . . . . . .184 D7
Newbolt Cl 1 LN7. . . . . .33 A3
Newborn Ave DN15. . . . . . . .182 E4
Newborn Cl PE2. . . . . .231 E5
NEWBOROUGH PE6 . . . . .174 E4
Newborough CE Prim Sch
  PE6. . . . . .174 E4
Newborough Rd PE4 . . . . . . .174 E1
Newboults La 2 PE9. . . . . . .219 A5
Newbridge Hill LN11 . . . . . .198 C6
Newbridge La LN11 . . . . .49 E5
New Bridge Rd HU9 . . . . . . .181 C8
Newbury Cl 3
  3 Beacon Hill NG24 . . . . . .104 C4
  15 Newark-on-Trent NG24. .104 C5
Newbury Cres PE10 . . . . . . .213 C2
Newbury Terr DN37 . . . . . . .188 A1
Newby Rd DN31. . . . . .191 C7
New Cartergate Cl 1 DN31 .191 D7
Newcastle Dr PE2. . . . . .230 D6
Newcastle Rd 4 NG31. . . . . .210 D5
New Chapel La 8 DN37. . . . .23 F1
New Cl DN33. . . . . .191 C4
New Clee Sta DN31. . . . . . . .189 D1
New Cleveland St HU8. . . . .181 A8
New College Stamford
  PE9. . . . . .219 C6
New Coll Stamford PE9. . . .219 D8
Newcomb Ct
  2 Sleaford NG34 . . . . .212 B7
  16 Stamford PE9. . . . . .219 B5
Newcombe Way 2 PE2 . . . .229 D2
Newcomen Way DN15 . . . . .183 B6
Newcot La LN4. . . . . .81 F4
New Cres LN3. . . . . .203 D6
Newcroft La LN11. . . . . .50 A8
New Cross Rd 3 PE9. . . . . . .219 C6
New Cut PE6. . . . . .176 D5
Newdike Gate PE12. . . . . . . .158 C5
Newdown Rd DN17. . . . . . . .184 D3
Newell Lane PE9 . . . . .162 F5
New End Hemingby LN9. . . . . .72 B1
  5 Wainfleet All Saints
    PE24. . . . . .102 D2
NEW ENGLAND Croft PE24. .102 E2
  Peterborough PE1. . . . . . . .225 D7
New England Rd NG33. . . . . .141 B7
New Est
  1 Little Bytham NG33 . . . . .163 A8
  Swinstead NG33. . . . . .153 A5
New Fen Dike PE12. . . . . . . .169 A7
New Fen Dro PE12 . . . . .168 B1
Newfield Cl 10 DN3. . . . . . . .14 A4
Newfield Dr LN4. . . . . .109 F3
Newfield Rd NG34. . . . . .212 C5
Newfields PE13. . . . . .169 D1
NEW FLETTON PE2. . . . . . . .231 B8
Newgate La NG31. . . . . .130 D4
Newgate Rd PE13. . . . . .169 F6
Newgates 3 PE9. . . . . .219 C5
New Gdn St 5 HU1. . . . . .180 F7
New George St HU2 . . . . . . .180 F7
New Gn 3 DN7. . . . . .14 C6
Newhall Rd
  13 Kirk Sandall DN3. . . . . . .14 A2
  10 Kirk Sandall DN3. . . . . . .14 A2
NEWHAM PE22. . . . . .112 A1
Newham La PE22. . . . . .112 A1
New Hammond Beck Rd
  PE21. . . . . .208 A3
Newham Rd 2 PE9. . . . . .219 A4
Newhaven Dr LN5. . . . . .205 D3
New Haven Terr DN31. . . . . .188 D1
New Hill NG32. . . . . .119 A5
NEW HOLLAND DN19 . . . . .4 E2
New Holland CE Methodist
  Prim Sch DN19. . . . . .4 E2
New Holland Rd 2 DN19 . . . . .4 E1
New Holland Sta DN19. . . . . . .4 E3
New Ings La PE22. . . . . .52 E3
Newington Ave HU4. . . . . . .179 E5
Newington Prim Sch HU3 .180 A4
Newington St HU3. . . . . .179 F4
New Inn La 3 DN7. . . . . .14 C7
New La Girton NG23. . . . . . . .78 D2
  Great Carlton LN11 . . . . .62 E3

New La *continued*
Leasingham NG34 121 B7
Reedness DN14 6 E8
Tathwell LN11 61 A1
Toynton St Peter PE23 101 A5
Wansford PE8 222 C1
New Lakeside PE7 230 B1
Newland LN1 234 A2
Newland Ave DN15 182 E2
Newland Dr DN15 182 D3
Newlands DN21 197 E5
Newland St W 2 LN1 234 A2
Newlands Ct DN21 197 E5
Newlands Lane DN9 28 A7
Newlands Pk DN36 193 B1
Newlands Rd
2 Haconby PE10 154 D8
Parson Drove PE13 177 D7
Surfleet PE11 145 F4
Newland View 17 DN9 27 E6
Newland Wlk DN15 182 E3
NEW LEAKE PE22 114 A8
New Leake Prim Sch
PE22 113 F7
New Life Chrsitian Acad
HU2 180 F8
Newlyn Cl
4 Kingston upon Hull
HU13 179 A2
New Waltham DN36 195 C7
Newman Cl 19 PE8 172 B1
Newmarch Ct DN33 191 B2
Newmarket LN11 198 C4
Newmarket Ave 13 PE10 213 D3
Newmarket Cl PE1 226 B6
Newmarket St 4 DN32 191 F8
New Marsh Rd PE12 149 B3
New Mdw Dro PE7 231 D1
NEW MEADOW PE7 231 F2
New Michael St 4 HU1 180 E5
New Mill Field Rd DN7 14 E3
Newnham Cres DN16 185 A4
Newnham Rd 17 NG24 104 A5
New Park Pl 3 LN2 202 F6
New Pk Est 1 DN7 14 D7
Newport LN2 234 B4
Newport Ave NG31 210 D4
Newport Cl 4 HU3 180 D5
Newport Cres
2 Waddington LN5 93 F7
1 Waddington LN5 93 F7
Newport Ct 1 LN1 234 B4
Newport Dr DN15 9 A6
Newport St 8 DN18 3 F1
Newport Wlk DN40 186 D3
Newport Wy PE9 172 F2
NEW QUARRINGTON
NG34 212 A2
New Rd Blankney LN10 96 F5
Brantingham HU15 2 C8
Cleethorpes DN35 192 F6
Clipsham LE15 162 B7
1 Collyweston PE9 171 B1
Croft PE24 103 C3
Deeping St Nicholas PE6 166 D5
5 Easton on the Hill PE9 171 D3
9 Eye PE6 175 A1
Folksworth PE7 232 E6
Holbeach St Marks PE12 147 F6
Laceby DN37 35 A8
Langtoft PE6 164 F3
Peterborough PE1 226 B2
Quadring PE11 145 C8
Ryhall PE9 163 C1
Scunthorpe DN17 184 B6
Silk Willoughby NG34 121 A1
Spalding PE11 214 D4
Staunton NG13 117 B2
Sutton Bridge PE12 160 F5
Swinefleet DN14 6 C4
Thistleton LE15 151 D1
Wainfleet All Saints PE24 101 E2
Waltham DN37 194 E4
Worlaby DN20 10 D1
New River Dro
Cowbit PE12 156 F3
3 Spalding PE12 214 C1
New River Gate PE12 168 D8
New Roman Bank PE34 161 D3
New Row
Gonerby Hill Foot NG31 210 E7
3 Market Deeping PE6 217 D4
8 Messingham DN17 29 D7
Newsham Dr DN34 191 A7
Newsham Garth HU4 179 B5
Newsham La DN39 22 B8
New St
Aby with Greenfield LN13 75 B5
14 Beacon Hill NG24 104 A4
7 Brigg DN20 196 C3
Elsham DN20 20 E7
1 Gainsborough DN21 197 C5
Grantham NG31 211 A5
Grimsby DN31 191 E7
5 Heckington NG34 122 E2
Helpringham NG34 133 D7
6 Louth LN11 198 B5
Osbournby NG34 132 D5
Sleaford NG34 212 E4
4 Stamford PE9 219 C6
Newstead Ave
24 Beacon Hill NG24 104 A5
Cherry Willingham/Reepham
LN3 203 E5
Holton le Clay DN36 195 E2
Newstead Cl PE6 175 A2
Newstead Rd
Cleethorpes DN35 192 E4

Newstead Rd *continued*
2 Mablethorpe/Sutton on Sea
LN12 64 C3
Newstead PE9 219 F6
Ryhall PE9 163 D1
Newstead St
Kingston upon Hull HU5 180 A8
Quarrington NG34 212 C2
Newsum Gdns 23 DN41 23 A4
NEWTOFT LN8 56 E5
NEWTON Newton PE13 170 A5
Newton and Haceby NG34 132 A3
Newton Abbot Wy 2
PE10 213 C3
Newton Bar NG34 132 A3
NEWTON BY TOFT LN8 56 E6
Newton Cl
8 Metheringham LN4 95 C4
Swinderby LN6 92 A5
5 Wragby LN8 70 D4
Newton Ct 6 NG33 151 E7
Newton Dr LN3 203 C6
Newton Gr DN33 191 C4
Newton La Binbrook LN8 47 D5
15 Ruskington NG34 108 E2
Newton Marsh La
Tetney DN36 36 F6
Tetney Lock DN36 37 A5
NEWTON ON TRENT LN1 65 D1
Newton-on-Trent CE Prim
Sch LN1 65 C1
Newton Pk 10 NG23 117 D3
Newton Rd DN16 185 E6
Newton St
5 Grantham NG31 211 B4
3 Kingston upon Hull HU3 180 B4
Lincoln LN5 234 B1
Newark-on-Trent NG24 104 A4
Newton Terr LN11 198 C5
Newton Thorpe Cl HU14 3 B7
Newton Way
5 Colsterworth NG33 151 D7
Sleaford NG34 212 D5
Newton Wy PE1 226 D2
Newtown 8 Spilsby PE23 101 A8
Stamford PE9 219 D5
New Town 6 PE9 171 D3
Newtown Ct
Kingston upon Hull HU9 181 E7
Stamford PE9 219 C4
Newtown Sq HU9 181 E7
New Trent St DN17 16 E6
NEW WALTHAM DN36 195 D7
New Waltham Prim Sch
DN36 195 C7
New Wlk HU14 3 A4
NEW YORK LN4 111 C5
New York Prim Sch LN4 111 C4
New York Rd LN4 110 F6
Nicholas Ct 26 DN18 10 E8
Nicholas Taylor Gdns 1
PE3 224 F3
Nicholas Way DN21 41 E2
Nichol Hill 2 LN11 198 B5
Nicholls Ave PE3 225 E3
Nicholson Rd
3 Healing DN41 24 A5
Immingham DN40 12 E4
Nicholson St
17 Beacon Hill NG24 104 A4
8 Cleethorpes DN35 192 F5
Nicholson Way 7 DN9 27 D7
Nickersons Wlk 7 LN7 33 A3
Nicolette Way 10 PE11 214 B5
Nicolgate La DN20 196 D4
Nicolson Dr 18 DN18 10 F8
Nidd's La PE20 136 E4
Nightingale Cl
10 Balderton NG24 104 C2
35 Barton-upon-Humber
DN18 10 F8
Scunthorpe DN15 182 D5
Nightingale Cres 1 LN6 204 E8
Nightingale Ct PE4 221 E2
Nightingale Dr PE7 233 D6
Nightingales 13 PE6 217 C5
Nightleys Rd DN22 65 B5
Nile Dr PE11 214 A5
Ninescores La DN9 26 B4
Ninth Ave
3 Fixborough Ind Est DN15 8 A1
Grantham NG31 211 F5
NINTHORPE PE25 206 D6
Nipcut Rd PE6 175 C2
Nisa Wy DN15 8 C1
NOCTON LN4 95 B7
Nocton Cty Prim Sch LN4 95 C7
Nocton Dr LN2 201 F8
Nocton Fen La LN4 83 A1
Nocton Rd
7 Potterhanworth LN4 82 B1
Potter Hanworth LN4 95 B8
Noel St DN21 197 C6
Nooking La DN37 23 D2
Nookings Dr 3 DN20 31 A5
Nooking The DN9 27 C3
Nookin The 1 LN5 106 E5
Nook The
Croxton Kerrial NG32 138 D3
7 Easton on the Hill PE9 171 D3
4 Helpston PE6 173 C4
Sproxton LE14 150 C7
Norbeck La LN2 68 C6
Norburn
2 Peterborough PE3 220 F1
Peterborough PE3 225 B8
Norfolk Ave DN15 8 B4
Norfolk Bank La HU15 1 F8

Norfolk Cl 1 LN8 47 B6
Norfolk Cres
Bracebridge Heath LN4 205 F4
1 Scampton Airfield LN1 67 E5
Norfolk Ct 19 DN32 189 C1
Norfolk La DN35 192 E7
Norfolk Pl 4 PE21 208 F6
Norfolk St Ind Est PE21 208 F7
Norfolk Sq 5 PE9 219 B6
Norfolk St Boston PE21 208 F6
Kingston upon Hull HU2 180 E7
Lincoln LN1 201 C4
Peterborough PE1 225 F4
Norland Ave HU4 179 C6
Norman Ave
5 Boston PE21 208 F5
11 Newark-on-Trent NG24 104 A6
NORMANBY DN15 8 C3
NORMANBY-BY-SPITAL
LN8 55 E7
NORMANBY BY STOW
DN21 53 E1
Normanby Cliff Rd LN8 55 D7
Normanby Enterprise Pk
DN15 182 F8
Normanby Hall Ctry Pk★
DN15 8 C3
Normanby Hill LN7 45 E7
NORMANBY LE WOLD LN7 45 F5
Normanby Pk Farming Mus★
DN15 8 C3
Normanby Prim Sch LN8 55 E7
Normanby Rd
Burton upon Stather DN15 8 C3
Nettleton LN7 33 B2
3 Owmby LN8 55 F6
Scunthorpe DN15 183 A5
Skegness PE25 206 C7
Stow DN21 53 F1
Normanby Rise LN8 45 E5
Norman Cl
9 Barton-upon-Humber
DN18 10 F8
30 Metheringham LN4 95 C4
NORMAN CORNER DN37 194 C2
Norman Cres 1 DN17 184 F8
NORMAN CROSS PE7 232 F2
Norman Dr Frith Bank PE22 125 D5
7 Hatfield DN7 14 D3
Normandy Cl LN11 198 E6
Normandy Rd DN35 192 D5
Normangate PE5 223 D2
Norman Mews 3 PE10 213 D5
Norman Rd Grimsby DN34 191 B7
Hatfield DN7 14 D3
Peterborough PE1 226 C4
Norman St 1 LN5 234 B1
NORMANTON
Bottesford NG13 128 A7
Normanton NG32 119 D5
Normanton La NG13 128 A6
Normanton Rd
3 Beacon Hill NG24 104 B5
1 Crowland PE6 166 F1
Peterborough PE1 226 D7
Normanton Rise HU4 179 C7
Norman Wy LN3 83 C5
Nornabell St 1 HU8 181 C8
Norris Cl 10 NG34 122 D3
Norris St LN5 201 F1
Norsefield Ave DN37 194 E5
Nortcote Heavy Horse Ctr★
PE23 101 D7
Northam Cl PE6 175 B3
Northampton Rd DN16 183 C1
North Ave PE10 153 D6
North Bank Crowland PE6 166 E1
Thorney PE6 227 D1
North Bank Rd 4 PE1 226 D3
NORTHBECK NG34 132 F8
North Beck La PE23 87 E1
NORTHBOROUGH PE6 217 E2
Northborough Prim Sch
PE6 173 F6
Northborough Rd PE6 174 C5
Northborough Road PE6 221 E8
NORTH CARLTON LN1 67 C4
NORTH CARR DN9 27 C3
North Carr La DN20 9 F3
North Carr Rd
Misterton DN10 39 F7
Scotter DN17 28 E5
West Stockwith DN10 40 B6
North Church Side 12
HU1 180 F6
Northcliffe Rd NG31 211 A7
North Cliff Rd DN21 30 C2
NORTH CLIFTON NG23 78 C7
North Clifton Prim Sch
NG23 78 C6
North Coates Rd DN36 37 A4
NORTH COCKERINGTON
LN11 50 A1
North Cockerington CE Prim
Sch LN11 50 A1
Northcote Heavy Horse Ctr★
PE23 101 D7
NORTH COTES DN36 37 A3
North Cotes CE Prim Sch The
DN36 37 B3
North Cres 7 NG13 128 A5
Northcroft 4 LN1 66 D3
Northcroft La NG23 91 C5
North Cswy LN4 82 D4
North Ct 10 LN2 68 C2
North Cty Prim Sch The
DN21 197 B6
North Dale Ct 4 DN21 30 B2

Northdale Pk 1 HU14 3 B7
North Dales Rd LN4 82 A5
North Dr 2 Ancaster NG32 120 A3
5 Balderton NG24 104 C1
1 Kingston upon Hull HU10 178 F6
RAF Cranwell NG34 107 D1
Swanland HU14 3 B7
North Dro Bicker PE20 134 E6
Deeping St Nicholas PE11 155 F1
Helpringham NG34 133 E7
Lutton PE12 148 D1
Quadring PE11 144 C8
Swaton NG34 133 E4
North Eastern Rd DN8 15 A8
NORTH ELKINGTON LN11 48 D1
North Elkington La LN11 48 E1
NORTH END Alvingham LN11 49 E3
Saltfleetby LN11 62 F8
Swineshead PE20 135 B8
North End 8 Goxhill DN19 12 A8
South Ferriby DN18 10 A8
7 Welbourn LN5 106 E5
Wisbech PE13 170 C1
North End Cres 9 DN36 36 D4
North End La
2 Fulbeck NG32 106 C1
Saltfleetby LN11 62 F8
South Cockerington LN11 50 F1
South Kelsey LN7 32 A2
Sturton le Steeple DN22 52 E4
North End Rd 7 DN36 36 D4
Northern Ave DN20 196 C5
Northern Rd NG24 104 A5
Northern Road Ind Est
NG24 104 A5
Northern's Cl NG33 151 D5
Northey Rd PE6 227 C2
North Farm Rd DN17 184 D3
Northfield Rd DN21 41 B8
North Fen Dro PE20 134 E4
North Fen Rd
3 Glinton PE6 220 C8
Helpringham NG34 133 D7
NORTH FERRIBY HU14 3 B4
North Ferriby CE Prim Sch
HU14 3 A5
Northferry La 2 DN9 16 D1
NORTHFIELD HU13 178 F2
Northfield HU14 3 B7
Northfield Ave
Kingston upon Hull HU13 178 E3
3 Sudbrooke LN2 68 F3
Northfield Cl
Kingston upon Hull HU10 178 D6
19 Ruskington NG34 108 E2
1 Scunthorpe DN16 185 C6
11 Tetney DN36 36 D4
West Butterwick DN17 17 D1
Northfield Industrial Est
PE6 217 C8
Northfield La Amcotts DN17 7 E2
North Clifton NG23 78 D7
Thornton Curtis DN39 11 D5
Willoughton DN21 42 C4
Northfield Rd
Ashby with Scremby PE23 88 D1
Kingston upon Hull HU3 179 F6
Messingham DN17 185 A1
North Leverton with
Habblesthorpe DN22 52 D1
Peterborough PE1 225 F7
4 Ruskington NG34 108 E2
Sleaford NG34 212 A2
Welton LN2 68 D7
North Field Rd PE6 217 B7
Northfield Rise 1 LN1 66 C2
Northfields Bourne PE10 213 D7
Stamford PE9 219 C6
Northfields Ct PE9 219 C6
North Foreland Dr 3
PE25 206 D8
North Forty Foot Bank
PE21 208 A6
NORTHGATE PE11 144 D1
Northgate Crossgate PE11 145 B1
Kingston upon Hull HU13 178 E2
Lincoln LN2 234 B4
Louth LN11 198 B5
North Gate
Gosberton PE11 145 A6
Newark-on-Trent NG24 104 A5
Pinchbeck PE11 144 E1
Sleaford NG34 212 D5
Northgate Ct LN11 198 B6
Northgate La LN11 62 B7
Northgate Sports Hall
NG34 212 D5
NORTH GREETWELL LN2 203 B8
North Halls 1 LN8 47 C5
NORTH HARBY NG23 79 C7
North Heath La NG32 106 D1
North Holme
19 Tetney DN36 36 D4
8 Tetney DN36 36 D4
North Holme Rd LN11 198 B7
NORTH HYKEHAM LN6 204 D2
North Ing Dro PE11 134 C4
Northing La LN2 68 F5
North Ings La LN13 77 A5
North Ings Rd DN7 14 E5
Northings The 1 NG32 210 B4
North Intake La DN9 40 D8
NORTH KELSEY LN7 32 A4
NORTH KELSEY MOOR
LN7 32 D4
North Kelsey Rd LN7 33 A4
North Kesteven Ctr★ LN6 204 D1
North Kesteven Sch LN6 204 D1

NORTH KILLINGHOLME
DN40 12 D3
North Killingholme Ind Est
DN40 12 D4
NORTH KYME LN4 109 F4
North Kyme Cty Prim Sch
LN4 109 E3
North La Coningsby LN4 110 E8
Marshchapel DN36 37 C2
2 Navenby/Wellingore
LN5 107 A8
Reepham LN3 68 F1
Stainton le Vale LN8 46 E5
Swaby LN13 74 E4
NORTHLANDS PE22 113 A4
Northlands Ave 3 DN15 9 A5
Northlands La PE22 113 A4
Northlands Rd
Glentworth DN21 54 E6
Winterton DN15 9 A6
Northlands Rd S 10 DN15 9 A5
NORTH LEVERTON WITH
HABBLESTHORPE DN22 52 B1
North Leys Rd DN22 52 E1
North Lincoln Rd DN16 183 F2
North Lincolnshire Mus★
DN15 183 A2
North Lincolnshire Shopping
Pk DN15 182 B3
North Lindsey Coll DN17 184 E8
North Marsh Rd DN21 197 C6
Northminster PE1 226 A3
North Moor Dr 2 DN10 39 F3
North Moor La Martin LN4 96 B3
Messingham DN17 29 B8
Northmoor Rd DN17 6 C1
North Moor Rd
Scotter DN17 29 C5
Walkeringham DN10 39 F3
North Moss La DN41 187 B1
Northolme
Gainsborough DN21 197 D5
Sutton St Edmund PE12 168 E5
Northolme Circ 2 HU13 178 E2
Northolme Cres
Kingston upon Hull HU13 178 E2
Scunthorpe DN15 182 F3
Northolme Ct LN11 198 C7
Northolme Rd HU13 178 E2
Northon's La PE12 215 C3
NORTH ORMSBY LN11 48 E4
NORTHORPE
Donington PE20 134 E3
Northorpe DN21 42 A8
Thurlby PE10 164 C8
Northorpe Cl LN6 204 F7
Northorpe La PE10 164 C8
Northorpe Rd
Donington PE11 134 D3
Halton Holegate PE23 101 B8
Scotton DN21 29 D1
NORTH OWERSBY LN8 44 E5
North Parade
Gainsborough DN21 197 F4
Grantham NG31 211 A6
Holbeach PE12 215 E3
Lincoln LN1 234 A3
Scunthorpe DN16 185 D6
Skegness PE25 206 D3
4 Sleaford NG34 212 D7
North Parade Extension
PE25 206 E5
North Prom DN35 192 E7
North Quay DN31 189 C3
North Ramper DN21 44 A7
NORTH RAUCEBY NG34 120 E5
North Rd Bourne PE10 213 D8
Bratoft PE24 102 B8
7 Cranwell NG34 107 F1
Gedney Hill PE12 168 D4
1 Keadby with Althorpe
DN17 17 C6
Kingston upon Hull HU4 179 E4
Leadenham LN5 106 D3
Mablethorpe & Sutton LN12 64 B1
Sleaford NG34 212 C5
Sturton le Steeple DN22 52 B4
Tattershall Thorpe LN4 97 F3
Tetford LN9 73 F1
Tydd St Mary PE13 160 B2
NORTH RESTON LN11 62 B2
North Road LN11 60 B3
North Scaffold La NG23 91 D3
NORTH SCARLE LN6 78 F2
North Scarle Miniature
Railway★ LN6 78 F1
North Scarle Prim Sch LN6 78 E2
North Scarle Rd NG23 91 F8
North Sea La DN35 193 A1
North Shore Rd PE25 206 D6
Northside 2 DN9 27 C2
Northside La 2 DN22 52 C1
North's La DN37 34 D8
NORTH SOMERCOTES
LN11 50 F8
North Somercotes CE
(Controlled) Prim Sch
LN11 50 F7
North St
1 Barrow upon Humber
DN19 11 D8
2 Boston PE21 208 F6
Bourne PE10 213 D5
Caistor LN7 33 B4
Cleethorpes DN35 192 F6

North St continued
3 Crowland PE6 . . . . **166** E1
9 Crowle DN17. . . . . **16** D8
Digby LN4. . . . . **108** E6
Folksworth PE7 . . . . **233** A1
Gainsborough DN21 . . . . . . **197** C5
7 Grantham NG31 . . . . . . **211** A5
Horncastle LN9 . . . . **199** C4
Kingston upon Hull HU10 . . **178** E6
Middle Rasen LN8 . . . . **57** B8
Morton DN21 . . . . **197** C8
8 Nettleham LN2 . . . . **68** C2
Osbournby NG34 . . . . **132** C3
Owston Ferry DN9 . . . . **28** B3
Peterborough PE1 . . . . **226** A2
Roxby cum Risby DN15. . . . . . **9** A4
Scunthorpe DN15 . . . . **183** B4
Stamford PE9. . . . . **219** B5
Sturton le Steeple DN22. . . . **52** B3
Thimbleby LN9 . . . . **85** B5
West Butterwick DN17. . . . . **17** D1
West/East Butterwick DN17 . **28** D8
Winterton DN15. . . . . **9** B6
North Terr PE1. . . . . **226** E7
NORTH THORESBY DN36 . . **36** B1
North Thoresby Prim Sch
  DN36. . . . . **36** A1
North Thoresby Sta DN36 . . **36** C1
Northumberland Ave
13 Scampton Airfield LN1. . . **67** E5
2 Stamford PE9 . . . . **219** A4
Northumberland Dr DN34 **191** B6
Northumbria Rd NG34 . . . . **212** B2
North Walls HU1 . . . . **181** A6
North Warren Rd DN21 . . . **197** B6
Northway 3 LN11. . . . . **49** E8
North Way
6 Lincoln LN6 . . . . **204** D2
Marshchapel DN36. . . . . **37** B2
NORTH WILLINGHAM LN8 . . **58** D7
NORTH WITHAM NG33 . . . . **151** D4
North Witham Bank LN1 . . **234** A2
North Witham Rd NG33 . . . **151** D1
Northwood Dr
Hessle HU13 . . . . **178** B3
Sleaford NG34 . . . . **212** C6
NORTON DISNEY LN6. . . . . . **92** C2
Norton Disney Rd LN5 . . . . **92** D1
Norton Gr HU4 . . . . **179** D4
Norton La Bishop Norton LN8 **43** C2
Thurlby LN6. . . . . **92** C4
Norton Rd
Peterborough PE1 . . . . **225** F6
Scunthorpe DN16. . . . . **185** B5
Stapleford LN6. . . . . **105** C8
Norton St NG31 . . . . **211** A3
Norwich Ave DN34 . . . . . . **191** A4
Norwich Cl
Heighington/Washingborough
  LN4 . . . . **203** E1
3 Sleaford NG34. . . . . **212** C7
Norwich Dr LN4. . . . . **81** A2
Norwich Rd PE13. . . . . **170** E1
Norwich Way 7 NG31 . . . . **210** E5
Norwood Ave DN15. . . . . . **182** F2
Norwood Cl 3 HU10. . . . . . **178** E7
Norwood La
Borough Fen PE6 . . . . **174** C1
Peterborough PE4 . . . . **221** F2
Norwood Prim Sch PE4. . . **221** C3
Norwood Rd
7 Hatfield DN7 . . . . **14** C5
4 Skegness PE25 . . . . **103** E4
Norwood St HU3 . . . . **180** C7
Norwood Yd Cl LN4 . . . . **96** C1
Nostell Rd DN16. . . . . **183** D1
Nottingham Rd 1 NG13 . . **128** A5
Nottingham Terr 5 LN2 . . **234** C3
Nottingham Way PE1 . . . . **226** C6
Novello Garth HU4 . . . . . . **179** B4
Nowells La 6 PE10. . . . . . **213** D5
Nuffield Cl 6 DN16. . . . . . **185** B4
Nunburnholme Ave 5 HU14 **3** A4
Nunburnholme Pk HU5 . . . **179** B7
Nunnerley Pl DN37. . . . . . **194** F5
Nuns Cnr DN33. . . . . **191** C4
Nuns Rd DN17 . . . . **184** F6
NUNSTHORPE DN33. . . . . . **191** B4
Nunsthorpe & Bradley Pk
Children's Ctr DN33 . . . . **191** A4
Nunthorpe Cl 36 DN7. . . . . **14** D4
Nurburgring Gdns PE10 . . **213** B3
Nurseries The LN4 . . . . . . **108** E7
Nursery Cl
4 Barton-upon-Humber
  DN18. . . . . **3** F1
2 Collingham NG23 . . . . . . **91** D4
14 Dunholme LN2. . . . . **68** E6
Langworth LN3. . . . . **69** B3
Peterborough PE1 . . . . **226** A4
10 Saxilby LN1 . . . . **66** D2
Scunthorpe DN17. . . . . **184** F3
Nursery Ct 15 Brough HU15. . **2** C5
Sleaford NG34 . . . . **212** D2
Nursery Dr PE13 . . . . **170** E2
Nursery Gdns
25 Alford LN13. . . . . **75** F2
6 Holton le Clay DN36. . . . **195** D2
22 Newark-on-Trent NG24. . . **104** B2
Nursery Gr LN2 . . . . **202** A6
Nursery La Belvoir NG32. . **138** C6
Morton DN21. . . . . **40** D3
Peterborough PE1 . . . . **226** D2
Nursery Rd Boston PE21 . . **209** B2

Nursery Rd continued
Cranwell & Byard's Leap
  NG34. . . . . **120** C8
Nursery St 2 LN8 . . . . **57** D7
Nurses La
Skellingthorpe LN6. . . . . . . **200** A5
4 Wymondham LE14. . . . . **150** C1
Nursey Cl PE12. . . . . **216** D6
Nutfields Gr 7 DN7 . . . . . . **14** C6
Nut La PE22. . . . . **114** C1
Nutwood View 4 DN16. . . **185** D4

O

Oak Ave 13 Brough HU15 . . . . . **2** C6
Grimsby DN32. . . . . **191** E4
Hampton Vale PE7 . . . . **230** B2
2 Scawby DN20 . . . . **30** F8
11 Welton/Dunholme LN2 . . **68** E6
Oak Cl 8 Ingoldmells PE25 . . **90** D3
Louth LN11. . . . . **198** E4
14 Sudbrooke LN2. . . . . **68** F2
5 Woodhall Spa LN10 . . . . . **97** E6
Oak Cres Boston PE21 . . . . **208** E2
Bourne PE10 . . . . **213** B6
Cherry Willingham/Reepham
  LN3 . . . . **203** D5
Oak Ct Lincoln LN6 . . . . **205** A5
1 Spalding PE11. . . . . **214** E3
Oakdale Ave
8 Kingston upon Hull
  HU10. . . . . **178** E8
Peterborough PE2 . . . . **231** D4
Oakdale Cl 4 HU3 . . . . **211** A8
Oakdale Prim Sch PE7. . . . **231** C4
Oakdene Ave 19 LN4. . . . . . **81** A1
Oak Dr
Barton-upon-Humber DN18 . . **10** F8
Kingston upon Hull HU5 . . . **179** B7
44 Messingham DN17 . . . . . . **29** D7
Oak Farm Paddock LN6. . . **204** C1
Oakfield 16 LN1 . . . . **66** D2
Oakfield Cl 2 DN20 . . . . . . **196** E3
Oakfield Prim Sch DN16 . . **185** A5
Oakfield Rd
26 Balderton NG24 . . . . . . **104** C1
Skellingthorpe LN6. . . . . . . **200** B5
Oakfield St LN2 . . . . **202** B3
Oakford Cl DN17 . . . . **184** D8
Oak Gr
13 Barnetby le Wold DN38 . . . **21** B4
3 Barrow upon Humber
  DN19. . . . . **11** C7
6 Market Deeping PE6 . . . . **217** B6
Oakham Ave 5 LN12 . . . . . . **64** A3
Oakham Gr NG31 . . . . **210** E6
Oakham Terr 2 PE21. . . . . **208** F3
Oakham Wlk DN40 . . . . . . **186** E3
Oak Hill 4 LN2 . . . . **203** B2
Oak House La PE22. . . . . . **126** C4
Oakhurst Cl NG31 . . . . **211** D2
Oakland Ave 39 DN7 . . . . . . **14** D4
Oakland Cl 3 LN1. . . . . **201** D7
Oaklands
3 Beckingham DN10. . . . . . . **40** A1
8 Collingham NG23 . . . . . . **91** D4
Eastfield PE1. . . . . **226** B4
5 Woodhall Spa LN10 . . . . . **97** D5
Oaklands Dr
Kingston upon Hull HU13 . . **178** D3
4 Wisbech PE13 . . . . **170** E1
Oaklands Pk LN10. . . . . **98** A7
Oaklands Rd DN40 . . . . . . **186** C5
Oaklands The
1 Branston LN4 . . . . **81** E2
6 Wragby LN8 . . . . **70** D4
Oakland Way 13 PE11. . . . . **145** C1
Oakleaf Rd PE1 . . . . **226** C6
Oakleigh DN16. . . . . **185** C3
Oakleigh Dr Canwick LN1 . . **201** C6
Peterborough PE2 . . . . **230** C3
Oakleigh Rd NG31. . . . . . . **210** C3
Oakleigh Terr LN1. . . . . . . **201** C6
Oakley Dr PE11 . . . . **214** E6
Oakley Pl PE12. . . . . **147** F2
Oak Rd Glinton PE6. . . . . . **220** B8
1 Healing DN41. . . . . **24** A5
Scunthorpe DN16. . . . . **185** B7
Sleaford NG34 . . . . **212** D2
Stamford PE9. . . . . **218** D7
Oakroyd Cres 22 PE13. . . . **170** D1
Oakside Pk Ind Est NG34. . **212** F6
Oaks La DN10 . . . . **39** F2
Oak Sq 9 PE6 . . . . **175** C8
Oaks The Balderton NG24 . . **104** C2
15 Nettleham LN2 . . . . **68** D2
1 Scothern LN2 . . . . **68** F3
Oak Tree Ave DN21. . . . . . **197** F6
Oaktree Cl 3 PE11. . . . . . . **145** B7
Oak Tree Cl
3 Long Bennington
  NG23. . . . . **117** D3
7 Market Rasen LN8. . . . . . . **57** D7
Oak Tree Dr LN6 . . . . **92** D4
Oak Tree Mdw LN9 . . . . . . **199** C5
Oak Tree Wlk 25 DN17 . . . . **16** D7
Oak View 13 Dunholme LN2. . **68** E6
Peterborough PE3 . . . . **224** F2
3 Heckington NG34 . . . . . . **122** D3
Oakwell Cl DN16 . . . . **185** D4
Oakwood Ave 4 LN6. . . . . **204** C8
Oakwood Cl HU10 . . . . **179** A7
Oakwood Dr DN7 . . . . **190** C2
Oakwood Glade PE12. . . . . **215** C4
Oakwood Pk PE12. . . . . . . **146** E2
Oakwood Rise 2 DN16 . . . **185** B4

OASBY NG32 . . . . **131** C6
Oasby Rd NG32. . . . . **131** C7
Oasis Academy DN40 . . . . . **186** C4
Oasis Acad Nunsthorpe
  DN33. . . . . **191** B4
Oasis Acad Parkwood
  DN17. . . . . **184** D8
Oasis Acad Wintringham
  DN32. . . . . **191** E4
Oat Dr NG34 . . . . **212** E3
Oatfield Way NG34 . . . . . . **122** D2
Oban Cl 7 PE9. . . . . **218** E6
Oban Ct 6 DN40 . . . . **186** C3
Oberon Cl LN1 . . . . **201** C6
OBTHORPE PE10. . . . . **164** C6
Obthorpe La PE10. . . . . . . **164** C7
Occupation La
Anderby PE24. . . . . **77** C3
Carrington PE22. . . . . **99** C1
6 North Kelsey LN7 . . . . **32** A4
Swanland HU14 . . . . **3** B8
Occupation Rd
Great Gonerby NG32 . . . . . **129** C6
Lincoln LN1. . . . . **234** A4
Peterborough PE1 . . . . **225** E6
Occupation Road LN11 . . . . **66** B3
Ocean Ave PE25. . . . . **206** D1
Ocean Bvd HU9 . . . . **181** B6
Octagon Dr **14** PE13 . . . . **170** C1
Octavia Cl 23 PE13 . . . . . . **170** E1
Octavian Cres 14 LN6. . . . . . **93** A8
Odecroft PE3 . . . . **225** C7
Odin Ct DN33 . . . . **191** B2
Off Haydons Ave PE25 . . . . **206** A4
Ogilvy Dr DN17. . . . . **184** F3
Ogrey PE10 . . . . **164** C7
O'Hanlon Ave DN20 . . . . . **196** D3
Old Annandale Rd HU10 . . **178** E8
Old Bailey Rd PE7 . . . . **233** C8
Old Bakery Yd 12 PE25. . . . **206** A6
Old Barn Ct
Fleet Hargate PE12 . . . . . . **159** C8
Ludford DN37. . . . . **59** A7
Old Barn La DN15. . . . . **9** A4
Old Barracks The NG31 . . . **211** C4
Old Black Dro NG34 . . . . . **109** D1
OLD BOLINGBROKE PE23. . **100** B8
Old Boston Rd LN4 . . . . . . **207** D3
Old Bowling Gn 4 LN13 . . . **75** F2
Old Brewery La PE12 . . . . . **216** D4
Old Brickkiln La LN5. . . . . . **92** F2
Oldbrook PE3. . . . . **220** E1
Old Brumby St DN16. . . . . **185** A8
Old Carpenter's Yd 1 DN7. **14** B6
Old Chapel Ct 2 DN21. . . . . **43** D7
Old Chapel La
2 Burgh le Marsh PE24. . . . **102** E7
9 Laceby DN37. . . . . **23** F1
Old Chapel Rd LN6 . . . . . . **200** A4
Old Church La 1 PE23. . . . **101** D7
Old Church Rd PE24 . . . . . . **90** D4
OLD CLEE DN32. . . . . **192** C6
Old Clee Prim Sch DN32 . . **192** B6
Old Cobham Orch 18
  NG24 . . . . **104** A3
Old Courts Rd 2 DN20. . . . **196** C3
Old Crosby DN15. . . . . **183** A5
Old Ctyd The 1 DN21. . . . . . **65** D6
Old Dairy 11 DN8 . . . . **11** D8
Old Dairy Cl 32 DN8 . . . . . . **15** A8
Old Dairy Rd 8 LN8. . . . . . . **57** E8
Old Dairy The PE21. . . . . . **209** A1
Olde Curiosity Mus ★ LN12 **64** C3
Olde Farm Ct LN7. . . . . **32** A1
Old Epworth Rd (East) 1
  DN7 . . . . **14** F4
Old Farm Ct 4 DN37. . . . . **194** C4
Old Fen Bank
Wainfleet All Saints PE24. . . **101** F2
Wainfleet St Mary PE24 . . . **102** A1
Old Fen Dike Gedney PE12. **158** F1
Sutton St James PE12 . . . . **169** B8
Old Fendike Rd PE12 . . . . . **157** B3
Old Fen La Coningsby LN4 . . **207** E1
Pinchbeck PE11 . . . . **145** A1
Old Fen Rd PE22 . . . . **115** A8
Oldfield Cl
9 Barnby Dun DN3 . . . . **14** A4
1 Stainforth DN7 . . . . **14** B6
Oldfield Cres 16 DN7 . . . . . **14** C6
Oldfield La PE22 . . . . **127** C6
Old Field La DN7 . . . . **14** A5
Oldfield Rd 20 DN8 . . . . **15** B7
Old Fleet DN37. . . . . **190** C6
OLD FLETTON PE2. . . . . . . **231** A6
Old Fletton Prim Sch PE2 **230** F6
Old Forge Cl 17 DN9. . . . . . **39** F5
Old Forge Rd 7 DN10 . . . . . **39** F5
Old Forty Foot Bank
  NG34 . . . . **123** C1
OLD GATE PE12 . . . . **159** F3
Old Grammar School Wy 8
  LN8 . . . . **70** D5
Old Great N Rd
Stamford PE9. . . . . **218** C8
Thorney PE8. . . . . **228** B7
Wansford PE8 . . . . **222** C2
Old Haddington La LN6 . . . **92** F6
Old Hall Dr HU10 . . . . **178** C8
Old Hall Gdns 5 NG34. . . . **104** C5
Old Hall La 6 PE11. . . . . . . **145** D2
Old Hall Spinney NG32. . . **119** C2
Oldham Dr **8** PE11. . . . . . . **145** C1
Old Hammond Beck Rd
  PE21. . . . . **208** A2
Old Haxey Rd DN10. . . . . . . **39** F6
Old Hill The NG32 . . . . **138** C6
Old Hundred La PE12. . . . . **167** F2

Old Immingham Road
  DN41. . . . . **23** D6
Old Inn La PE12. . . . . **146** E7
Old Ironside Rd DN16. . . . . **183** D3
Old Iron Way PE21 . . . . . . **209** C5
Old Knarr Fen Dro PE6. . . . **176** C2
Old La DN14 . . . . **6** F7
Oldlane Gate DN14 . . . . **6** D4
Old Leicester Rd PE8 . . . . . **222** A3
OLD LEAKE PE22. . . . . **114** A1
Old Leake Prim Sch PE22 . **114** A1
Old Leys La DN21. . . . . **43** A3
Old Lincoln Rd
Caythorpe NG32. . . . . **119** B7
Wragby LN8. . . . . **70** C5
Old Lynn Rd 2 PE13. . . . . . **170** E1
Old Main Rd
1 Barnetby le Beck DN37 . . . **35** B6
East Heckington PE20 . . . . **122** E2
Fleet Hargate PE12 . . . . . . **159** C7
Fosdyke PE20. . . . . **146** D8
Irby DN37. . . . . **34** D7
Old Leake PE22 . . . . **114** B1
Scamblesby LN11 . . . . **72** F5
Old Manor Dr **13** DN20. . . . . **30** E8
Old Mill Cres NG24 . . . . . . **104** A4
Old Mill Dro PE7 . . . . **233** D2
Old Mill La
10 Broughton DN20 . . . . **19** E3
Grimoldby LN11. . . . . **62** B6
Horncastle LN9 . . . . **199** C3
Whitton DN15. . . . . **1** E3
Wrawby DN20 . . . . **196** F7
Old Mill Pk LN11. . . . . **198** C6
Old Mkt Ave PE23 . . . . **100** F8
Old Mkt Pl DN31 . . . . **191** D7
Old Nick Theatre DN21 . . . **197** D4
Old N Rd PE8 . . . . **222** A3
Old Oak Pl PE10. . . . . **213** E4
Old Orch NG32 . . . . **210** A5
Old Paddock Ct
1 Horncastle LN9. . . . . **199** B4
New Waltham DN36 . . . . . . **195** F6
Old Pl 3 NG34 . . . . **212** F4
Old Plumtree La 3 DN36 . . **36** B1
Old Pond Cl 7 LN6. . . . . . . **200** D1
Old Pond La PE5 . . . . **223** E2
Old Pond Pl 20 HU14. . . . . . . **3** A4
Old Post La NG33. . . . . **151** D6
Old Post Office La
8 Barnetby le Wold DN38 . . . **21** B4
Butterwick PE22. . . . . **126** E4
4 South Ferriby DN18. . . . . . **10** A7
Old Priory Farm 6 PE6 . . . **217** F4
Old Quarry The 8 DN38 . . . **32** E7
Old Rd Grimsby DN37 . . . . **190** C8
Healing DN37. . . . . **24** B5
Old Rectory Dr
1 Tallington PE9 . . . . **172** F7
Wansford PE8 . . . . **222** A4
Old Rectory Gdns DN16. . . **185** A6
Old Rectory The ★ DN9 . . . . **27** E6
Old Roman Bank
Skegness PE25 . . . . **206** D6
Terrington St Clement PE34 **161** E3
Old Sch Dr **14** DN20. . . . . . . **30** F5
Old Sch La
4 Billinghay LN4 . . . . **109** F6
6 Cranwell NG34 . . . . **120** F8
Donington on Bain LN11. . . . **59** E2
5 Fishtoft PE21. . . . . **126** C1
2 North Kelsey LN7 . . . . **32** A4
Scunthorpe DN16. . . . . **185** B3
Old Sch Mews 12 PE23. . . . **88** A1
Old School Cl Brigg DN20 . . **196** C4
Thurlby PE10. . . . . **164** C7
Old School La 26 NG24. . . . **104** A4
Old School Rd PE22 . . . . . . **99** E7
Old Sch Yd 17 DN21. . . . . . . **30** B1
Old S Eau Bank PE12 . . . . **168** A1
Old Showfields DN21 . . . . **197** D6
Old Sluice Rd PE12 . . . . . . **215** B8
Old Smithy Ct 1 LN4. . . . . **207** D4
**Old Smithy & Heritage Ctr
The** ★ DN9 . . . . **23** B3
OLD SOMERBY NG33 . . . . . **140** D8
Old Stack Yd La DN21. . . . . **41** E3
Old Stack Yd The
Fenton LN1. . . . . **65** E3
3 Wrawby DN20 . . . . **196** F6
Old Sta Yd Bottesford NG13 **128** B6
Morton PE10 . . . . **154** C0
Old Thorne Rd DN7. . . . . . . **14** E4
Old Train Yd The PE10 . . . **213** D4
Old Trent Rd DN21 . . . . . . **197** A3
Old Upper Ings La DN22. . . **52** D3
Old Vicarage Dr **5** DN15. . . . . **9** D1
Old Vicarage La
12 Lutton PE12. . . . . **160** A8
Lutton PE12 . . . . **216** C8
Old Vicarage Pk 2 DN20. . . **30** E8
Old Village St DN15 . . . . . . **17** E6
Old Wainfleet Rd 11 PE25 **206** B3
Old Warp La 11 DN18 . . . . . **10** A7
Old Wharf Ind Est NG31. . . **210** F3
Old Wharf Rd 9 NG31. . . . **211** A4
Old Wood 1 LN6. . . . . **200** C1
Old Wood Cl LN6. . . . . **200** C1
OLD WOODHALL LN9 . . . . . . **85** A4
Old Woodhall Road LN9 . . . **84** F2
Oliver Cl 5 NG34. . . . . **104** A4
Oliver Ct DN31 . . . . **191** D8
Olive Rd PE1. . . . . **226** C7
Oliver Rd
Hampton Vale PE7 . . . . **230** B1
16 Long Bennington NG23 . . **117** D3
Oliver St DN35 . . . . **192** D8
Olivier Ct HU4 . . . . **179** E3

Ollard Ave PE13. . . . . **170** D1
Olsen Rise LN2. . . . . **202** D6
Omega Bvd DN8 . . . . **14** F8
On Hill 17 HU14 . . . . **3** B7
Onslow St HU10. . . . . **178** F5
Ontario Rd DN17 . . . . **184** E3
Onyx Gr 2 HU3 . . . . **180** A4
Oosterbeek Cl 5 PE10. . . . **213** E4
Opportune Rd 25 PE13. . . . **170** C1
Orangewood Cl 7 NG31 . . **210** F8
Orangeleaf Way DN18 . . . . . **4** A1
ORANGE ROW PE34 . . . . . . **161** F3
Orange Row 3 PE34 . . . . . **161** F3
Orange Row Rd 1 PE34. . . **161** F3
Orb La DN15. . . . . **183** A7
ORBY PE24. . . . . **89** C2
Orby Bank PE24. . . . . **89** D3
Orby Gr DN33 . . . . **191** A3
Orby Holme Field La PE24 . **89** D3
Orby Rd Addlethorpe PE24. . **90** B4
Burgh le Marsh PE24 . . . . . . **89** D1
Orchard Ave 8 DN21. . . . . . **29** C3
Orchard Cl
4 Barrow upon Humber
  DN19. . . . . **11** C7
23 Barton-upon-Humber
  DN18. . . . . **10** F8
Bassingham LN5 . . . . **92** F3
Billinghay LN4 . . . . **109** E6
11 Birchwood LN6 . . . . **204** B8
4 Blyton DN21. . . . . **41** C5
6 Bourne PE10. . . . . **213** C6
4 Burringham DN17. . . . . . . **17** D4
9 Burton upon Stather DN15 . **8** B5
Cherry Willingham/Reepham
  LN3 . . . . **203** D5
11 Donington PE11. . . . . . . **134** F2
4 Gonerby Hill Foot NG31. . **210** E8
Great Hale NG34 . . . . **122** E1
2 Hatfield DN7 . . . . **14** C3
6 Helpringham NG34 . . . . . **133** D7
3 Kingston upon Hull HU10 **178** F7
1 Kirton in Lindsey DN21 . . . **30** B2
Leverington PE13. . . . . **170** E1
Louth LN11. . . . . **198** C7
2 Mablethorpe/Sutton on Sea
  LN12. . . . . **64** A3
4 Market Deeping PE6 . . . . **217** D4
12 Messingham DN17 . . . . . . **29** D7
25 Metheringham LN4 . . . . . **95** C4
2 Morton PE10. . . . . **154** C7
4 Moulton PE12. . . . . **157** F6
Newton on Trent LN1 . . . . . . **65** D1
Peterborough PE3 . . . . **225** D3
9 Pinchbeck PE11. . . . . **156** E8
2 Scothern LN2 . . . . **68** F4
5 Scunthorpe DN16 . . . . . . **185** B6
2 Sleaford NG34. . . . . **212** F4
18 Stamford PE9. . . . . **219** B5
7 Welton/Dunholme LN2 . . . **68** D6
Whaplode PE12 . . . . **215** A7
Orchard Croft
4 Epworth DN9. . . . . **27** C4
6 Grimsby DN33. . . . . **194** E7
Orchard Ct Thorney PE6 . . **175** F3
Waltham DN37. . . . . **194** D4
Orchard Dr
7 Burton upon Stather
  DN15. . . . . **8** B5
3 Gunness DN15 . . . . **17** E6
3 Hatfield DN7 . . . . **14** C3
12 Heckington NG34 . . . . . . **122** E2
5 Kingston upon Hull HU13 . **178** E1
2 Rampton DN22 . . . . **65** A5
Walton Highway PE14 . . . . . **170** F4
Winteringham DN15. . . . . **2** B1
Orchard Garth 18 LN5 . . . . . **93** E8
Orchard Gdns 4 PE13. . . . **170** A1
Orchard Gr Boston PE21 . . **209** B6
1 Hatfield DN7 . . . . **14** D5
Maxey PE6 . . . . **173** C7
Misterton DN10. . . . . **40** A4
Orchard La 12 LN1. . . . . **66** D2
Orchard Mews PE2. . . . . . **230** F8
Orchard Pk
20 Coddington NG24 . . . . . **104** C5
4 Manby LN11. . . . . **62** C6
5 Fiskerton LN3 . . . . **82** A7
Orchard Rd Barnack PE9 . . **172** E3
Kingston upon Hull HU4 . . . **179** B5
4 Stamford PE9 . . . . **219** B5
Orchards CE Prim Sch
  PE14. . . . . **170** D2
Orchard St Boston PE21 . . **208** D6
Lincoln LN1. . . . . **234** A2
Peterborough PE2 . . . . **230** F7
2 Spalding PE11. . . . . **214** D3
22 Thorne/Moorends DN8 . . **15** A8
Orchards The
Harrowby Est NG31 . . . . . . **211** C6
Immingham DN40 . . . . **186** B3
8 Middle Rasen LN8 . . . . . . **57** B8
Peterborough PE2 . . . . **229** F4
Orchard The Etton PE6 . . . **173** E5
Market Deeping PE6. . . . . . **217** B5
New Waltham DN36 . . . . . . **195** C6
Peterborough PE4 . . . . **221** A3
Washingborough LN4. . . . . **203** A2
Orchard Way
5 Coningsby LN4 . . . . **207** C4
5 Cowbit PE12. . . . . **167** C8
Easton on the Hill PE9 . . . . **171** C3
1 Mablethorpe/Sutton on Sea
  LN12. . . . . **64** A3
3 Market Rasen LN8. . . . . . . **57** E8
6 Nettleham LN2 . . . . **68** D2
Orchard Wy 19 NG24 . . . . **104** B2

Orchid Cl
[17] Newark-on-Trent
NG24. . . . . .104 A3
Yaxley PE7 . . . . .233 F7
Orchid Rd LN5 . . . . .205 C2
Orchid Rise DN15 . . . . . .182 F7
Orchid Way PE25 . . . . . .206 A4
Ordoyno Gr [2] NG24. . . .104 C5
Ore Blending Rd DN16. . . 19 A4
Orfeus Dr PE2 . . . . .231 F4
Orford Ms DN33. . . . . . .191 B1
Orford Rd LN8 . . . . 47 B5
Oribi Cl HU4 . . . . .179 C2
Origin Wy DN37 . . . . 24 B6
Oriole Rd DN17 . . . . . . .184 E6
Orion Cl [8] HU3. . . . . . .180 B5
Orion Way [4] DN34. . . .190 D4
Orkney Pl DN40 . . . . . . .186 C2
Orme La LN11. . . . . .198 C6
Orme Rd PE3 . . . . .225 D4
Ormiston Bushfield Acad
PE2 . . . . .229 E3
Ormiston Maritime Acad
DN34. . . . . .191 B5
Ormiston Meadows Acad
PE2 . . . . .229 C5
Ormiston South Parade Acad
DN31. . . . . .191 D8
Ormonde Cl NG31 . . . . .211 A3
Ormsby Cl DN35. . . . . . .192 D3
Ormsby House Dr [7] PE22 . .99 A4
Ormsby Rd
Scunthorpe DN17. . . . . .184 E5
South Ormsby LN9 . . . . . 74 D1
Ormsby Ring LN11 . . . . . 74 C1
Orton Ave PE2 . . . . .230 E7
Orton Brick Works PE7 . .233 B8
ORTON BRIMBLES PE2 . .229 D5
Ortongate Sh Ctr PE2. . .229 E3
ORTON GOLDHAY PE2 . .229 F3
ORTON LONGUEVILLE
PE2 . . . . .230 B5
ORTON MALBOURNE PE2 .230 C4
Orton Mere PE2. . . . . . .230 B7
Orton Parkway PE2. . . . .229 D4
ORTON SOUTHGATE PE2 .229 C2
ORTON WATERVILLE PE2. .229 E4
ORTON WISTOW PE2 . . .229 C5
Orton Wistow Prim Sch
PE2 . . . . .229 C6
Orwell Dr [4] PE11 . . . . .214 A1
Orwell Gr PE4. . . . . .221 D1
Orwell St DN31. . . . . . . .189 C1
Osborne Cl [3] LN1. . . . .201 E6
Osborne Dr DN36 . . . . .195 D1
Osborne Pk [1] PE13 . . . .170 C2
Osborne Rd
Immingham DN41 . . . . . .187 B2
Wisbech PE13 . . . . .170 C2
Osborne St
[1] Cleethorpes DN35. . . .192 F6
Grimsby DN31 . . . . .191 D7
Kingston upon Hull HU1. .180 E6
Osborne Way LN9 . . . . .199 A4
Osborn Way [9] NG34. . .122 D3
OSBOURNBY NG34. . . . .132 C4
Osbournby Prim Sch
NG34. . . . . .132 C5
Osbourne Cl PE4 . . . . . .221 D1
Osbourne Way [7] PE6 . .217 A5
Ose [3] PE25 . . . . .206 B6
Oseby La NG34. . . . . . . .133 A1
OSGODBY
Lenton Keisby and Osgodby
NG33. . . . . .141 E3
Osgodby LN8. . . . . 45 A3
Osgodby Prim Sch LN8 . . 45 A3
Osgodby Rd LN8 . . . . 44 E5
Osier Ave PE7. . . . . .230 D2
Osier Rd PE11. . . . . .214 E5
Oslear Cres DN35 . . . . . .192 E5
Oslear's La LN11. . . . . . . 73 D5
Oslinc Ostrich Farm *
PE22 . . . . .99 B7
Osprey PE2. . . . . .229 F2
Osprey Cl [5] NG34. . . . .212 B3
Osprey Dr Healing DN37 . . 24 B5
Scunthorpe DN16. . . . . .185 F5
Osric Ct PE1 . . . . .226 C5
Ostler Cl [8] NG31 . . . . .210 F8
Ostler Dr PE10. . . . . . . .213 B4
Ostler's La DN18 . . . . . . .10 A5
Oswald Rd
Scunthorpe DN15. . . . . .183 A3
[1] Woodston PE2 . . . . . .230 D7
Oswin Cl [1] NG34 . . . . .212 C2
OTBY LN8. . . . . .46 A4
Otby La LN8. . . . . .46 A3
Ottawa Rd DN17. . . . . . .184 E4
Otter Ave [11] LN1 . . . . . 66 D2
Otterbrook PE2 . . . . . . .229 D5
Otterburn St [4] HU3. . . .180 A5
Otters Cotts LN5 . . . . . .205 D7
Oulton Cl LN6. . . . . .205 C4
Oundle Cl
Heighington/Washingborough
LN4 . . . . .203 C1
Scunthorpe DN16. . . . . .185 C3
Oundle Rd
[5] Mablethorpe/Sutton on Sea
LN12 . . . . .64 C1
Peterborough PE2 . . . . .229 E6
Our Lady of Lincoln Cath Prim
Sch LN2. . . . . .202 A7
Ousemere Cl [14] NG34. .133 B1
Outer Circ Dr LN2. . . . . .202 C7
Outer Circ Gn LN2. . . . . .202 C6

Outer Circ Ind Est LN2 . .202 D5
Outer Circ Rd LN2. . . . . .202 D5
Outfield PE3 . . . . .220 E1
Outfield La PE24 . . . . . . .101 F7
Outgang La DN22 . . . . . . 65 A6
Outgang The
Brantingham HU15. . . . . . 2 B7
Brantingham HU15. . . . . . 2 C8
Outgate Crowle DN17. . . . 16 E7
Leverton Outgate PE22 . .127 B6
Out Holme La DN36. . . . . 36 E3
Outwood Acad Brumby
DN16. . . . . .185 B8
Oval App LN2 . . . . .202 B7
Oval The [5] Brough HU15 . . . 2 C5
Grimsby DN33. . . . . . . .191 C1
[1] Hatfield DN7. . . . . 14 C5
Kingston upon Hull HU10 . .178 E8
Lincoln LN2 . . . . .202 B7
Scopwick LN4. . . . . .108 B7
[2] Scunthorpe DN17. . . .184 E3
Overcoat La DN22 . . . . . . 65 B7
Overgate Rd NG33. . . . . .152 D5
Overstone Ct PE3 . . . . . .225 D6
Overton Ave HU10. . . . . .178 E8
Overton Cl [4] LN5. . . . . .107 B8
Overton Cl [9] DN18. . . . . 3 E1
Overton Rd LN4 . . . . . . .207 D4
Overton Way PE2 . . . . . .229 F4
Owen Ave HU13. . . . . . . .179 A1
Owen Cl [7] PE9 . . . . . . .172 D3
Owe's La LN11. . . . . .51 A5
Owl Cl LN6. . . . . 92 D5
Owl Dr PE20 . . . . .135 B7
Owl End PE7. . . . . .233 D5
Owl End Wlk PE7. . . . . . .233 D5
Owmby Rd
[4] Searby cum Owmby
DN38. . . . . 32 D8
Spridlington LN8 . . . . 55 F7
Owmby Wold La DN38. . . 21 E1
OWSTON FERRY DN9. . . . 28 B3
Owston Ferry Rd DN9. . . . 27 F1
Owston Rd DN10 . . . . 40 B6
Oxburgh Cl
[3] Peterborough PE7. . . .231 F5
[1] Wisbech PE13 . . . . . .170 C1
Oxby Cl [17] NG34. . . . . .122 E2
Oxclose PE3 . . . . .225 A8
OXCOMBE LN9. . . . . 73 D4
Oxcombe Cl DN33 . . . . . .194 D7
Oxcroft Bank Moulton PE12 .157 F1
Whaplode PE12 . . . . . . .158 A2
Oxeney Dr [2] LN3 . . . . . . 69 C3
Oxfield Dr PE13 . . . . . . .169 F3
Oxford Cl LN4. . . . . .203 C1
Oxford Ct [1] NG34. . . . .212 D7
Oxford Gdns PE12. . . . . .215 D1
Oxford Rd
Peterborough PE1 . . . . .225 F5
[2] Stamford PE9 . . . . . .219 A7
Oxford St Boston PE21. . .208 F3
Cleethorpes DN35 . . . . . .192 F5
Grantham NG31. . . . . . .211 B3
Grimsby DN32 . . . . .189 B1
Kingston upon Hull HU2 . .181 A8
[2] Lincoln LN5 . . . . .234 B1
Market Rasen LN8 . . . . . . 57 D8
Scunthorpe DN16. . . . . .185 D6
Oxlands La DN17 . . . . . . .102 B7
Oxmarsh La DN19 . . . . . . 4 E2
Ox Moor Pasture Rd DN17 . . 7 B1
Oxney Rd PE1. . . . . .226 D5
Oxney Rd Ind Est PE1 . . .227 A6
Ox Pasture La DN17 . . . . . 7 C2
Ox Pasture Lane LN9 . . . . 85 B2
Oyster Cl DN35. . . . . . . .192 F5

P

Pacey Cl LN6 . . . . 92 A6
Pach Wy [30] NG24. . . . .104 C1
Packhorse Gdns PE20 . . .135 B6
Packman La HU10. . . . . .178 B8
Paddington Way PE10 . . .154 D7
Paddock Cl
[6] Ancaster NG32 . . . . .120 A2
[13] Bracebridge Heath LN4 . . .81 A1
Ropsley NG33. . . . . .131 B1
Paddock Ct [3] DN40 . . . .186 C3
Paddock Gn [3] PE11. . . .214 D5
Paddock Gr [2] PE21 . . . .208 F4
Paddock La [5] Blyton DN21 . .41 C5
[1] Metheringham LN4 . . . 95 D4
West Butterwick DN17. . . 17 C1
Paddock Lane DN9 . . . . . 28 A7
Paddock Rd NG34. . . . . .120 C8
Paddock Rise
[11] Barrow upon Humber
DN19. . . . . 11 C8
Ingoldsby NG33. . . . . . . .141 C5
Paddocks The
[1] Barnetby le Beck DN37 . . .35 B6
[28] Beacon Hill NG24 . . .104 A4
[5] Beckingham DN10. . . . 40 A1
[6] Bottesford DN16. . . . .128 A5
[7] Burgh le Marsh PE24. .102 E7
Canwick LN4 . . . . 81 A4
Carlton Scroop NG32 . . . .119 C3
[4] Crowle DN17. . . . . . . 16 D7
Gedney PE12 . . . . .159 E7
Great Hale NG34 . . . . . . .122 C5

Paddocks The continued
[1] Holbeach PE12 . . . . . .215 E3
Kingston upon Hull HU10 . .178 B7
[10] Long Bennington NG23 . .117 D4
Newton on Trent LN1 . . . . 65 C1
[2] Peterborough PE4. . . .220 E5
Stapleford LN6. . . . . . . .105 C8
Swayfield NG33. . . . . . . .152 E5
Tinwell PE9 . . . . .218 D3
[12] Wainfleet All Saints
PE24 . . . . .102 D1
[4] Wellingore DN21. . . . . 53 E3
Paddock The
[8] Allington NG32 . . . . . .128 F7
[3] Barkston NG32 . . . . . .130 B8
[2] Burton upon Stather DN15 . . 8 B4
[4] Cherry Willingham LN3 . .203 E6
[10] Collingham NG23 . . . . 91 D4
Kingston upon Hull HU4 . .179 B5
Louth LN11. . . . . .198 A5
Manby LN11. . . . . 62 C5
[1] Market Deeping PE6 . .217 A6
[2] Marton DN21 . . . . 65 D8
[4] Morton PE10. . . . . . . .154 C7
[2] North Ferriby HU14. . . . 3 A5
[7] Owmby LN8. . . . . 55 F6
[16] Ruskington NG34 . . .108 D2
Skellingthorpe LN6. . . . . .200 A4
Sleaford NG34. . . . . .212 C4
[5] Sleaford NG34. . . . . . .212 F4
[5] Stamford PE9 . . . . . . .219 A5
[16] Sudbrooke LN2. . . . . 68 F2
[3] Swanland HU14. . . . . . 3 C7
Paddock View PE22. . . . .100 B2
Paddock Vw DN36. . . . . . 36 C4
Paddock Wy [4] DN7 . . . . 14 F4
Pademoor Terr DN17. . . . . 7 A2
Padholme Rd PE1 . . . . . .226 C3
Padholme Rd E PE1. . . . .226 D3
Padley Rd LN2 . . . . .202 E6
Padleys La PE23. . . . . . . .100 C4
Padmoor La DN21. . . . . . . 53 C5
Padmore Pl [8] PE6 . . . . .164 E4
Pado La LN13. . . . . 74 E4
Padstow Wlk PE7. . . . . . .184 C8
Pagehall Cl DN33 . . . . . .191 D1
Paignton Ct DN33 . . . . . .194 E6
Pailing's Ride NG24. . . . .104 F2
Pain La PE22. . . . . .113 E3
Painshall Cl [11] LN2. . . . . 68 D7
Painters Way [20] LN12 . . 76 F8
Paisley Prim Sch HU3 . . .180 A6
Paisley St HU3 . . . . .180 A7
Palace Theatre * NG24 . .104 A4
Palgrave Way LN1 . . . . . .214 D8
Palma Ct [2] PE24. . . . . . .90 D7
Palm Ct PE1 . . . . .226 B8
Palmer Ave HU10 . . . . . .178 D8
Palmer Cl [3] DN34 . . . . .212 B6
Palmer La [15] DN19 . . . . .11 B8
Palmer Rd
Great Gonerby NG32 . . . .129 C6
Lincoln LN2 . . . . .202 A6
Palmers Rd PE1. . . . . . . .226 F5
Palmerston Rd PE2. . . . . .230 F7
Palm Rd LN5. . . . . .205 C1
Palmwood Cl [3] NG31. . .210 F7
Pamela Cl DN40. . . . . . . .186 D4
Pamela Rd DN40. . . . . . .186 D4
Pandora Dr PE7. . . . . . . .231 C4
Pandyke La PE22. . . . . . .113 F3
Pannel Ct PE6 . . . . .164 E5
PANTON LN8 . . . . 71 B5
Panton Cl [6] PE6. . . . . . .217 D5
Panton Rd East Barkwith LN8 .71 B8
Hatton LN8. . . . . 71 B4
Papermill La
Ewerby & Evedon NG34 . .121 E7
Tealby LN8. . . . . 46 D2
Pape's La PE24. . . . . .101 F4
Papyrus Rd PE4 . . . . .220 D3
Parade The LN3. . . . . . . .203 E6
Northborough PE6. . . . . .173 F7
Paradise La [5] Fulletby LN9 . .86 B8
Horncastle LN9 . . . . .199 C3
Paradise Pl [6] Brigg DN20 .196 B3
Paradise Row LN9. . . . . .199 C4
Paragon St HU1. . . . . . . .180 E6
Parish Church Prim Sch
DN21. . . . . .197 C5
Parishes St The DN15 . . .183 B3
Parish Mews [3] DN21. . . .197 D5
Parish's La PE22. . . . . . . .115 A4
Park Acad PE1 . . . . .208 E6
Park Ave Allington NG32 . .128 F7
[15] Barton-upon-Humber
DN18. . . . . 10 E8
Billinghay LN4 . . . . .109 F5
[17] Crowle DN17. . . . . . . 16 D7
Grimsby DN32 . . . . .191 E4
Heighington/Washingborough
LN4. . . . . .203 D2
Kingston upon Hull HU13 . .178 E3
Lincoln LN6. . . . . .204 F7
Louth LN11. . . . . .198 E6
[21] Mablethorpe/Sutton on Sea
LN12. . . . . 64 B3
Misterton DN10. . . . . 39 E6
Scunthorpe DN17. . . . . . .184 F4
Skegness PE25. . . . . .206 D4
Sleaford NG34. . . . . .212 F4
Spalding PE11 . . . . .214 C5
Sutterton PE20. . . . . . . .136 A2
Park Cl [1] Gosberton PE11 . .145 B6
Immingham DN40 . . . . . .186 C4
Lea DN21. . . . . 52 F5
Spalding PE11 . . . . .214 C5

Park Cl continued
[8] Sudbrooke LN2. . . . . . 68 F2
Thorney PE6. . . . . .176 B3
[7] Westwoodside DN9. . . . 27 A2
Yaxley PE7 . . . . .233 F5
Park Cres
Heighington/Washingborough
LN4. . . . . .203 D1
[16] Metheringham LN4 . . . 95 D4
Newark-on-Trent NG24 . .104 A6
Peterborough PE1 . . . . . .226 A3
Sleaford NG34. . . . . .212 F4
Swinderby LN6. . . . . 92 B6
Thorne/Moorends DN8 . . . 15 A7
Thorney PE6. . . . . .176 B3
Park Ct Scunthorpe DN15 . .183 B4
[2] Weston PE12. . . . . . . .157 E7
Parkdale [44] DN18 . . . . . 10 E8
Park Dr Grimsby DN32 . . .191 E5
Market Deeping PE6. . . . .217 A5
[6] Westwoodside DN9. . . . 27 A2
Parker Ave LN5 . . . . .205 D4
Parker Cl Laceby DN37 . . . 23 E2
Stamford PE9 . . . . .218 E7
Parker Rd Humberston DN36 .36 D3
[23] Wittering PE8 . . . . . .172 B1
Parkers Cl [12] PE24 . . . . .102 E7
Parkers La DN16 . . . . . . .185 C6
Parker St
[16] Beacon Hill NG24 . . .104 A4
Cleethorpes DN35 . . . . . .192 F5
Parkes Cl [4] NG24. . . . . .104 D5
Park Est PE6 . . . . .217 E4
Park Farm Cres PE7 . . . . .231 F5
Park Farm Rd
Peterborough PE6 . . . . . .224 E5
Scunthorpe DN15. . . . . . .182 F7
Park Farm Way PE7. . . . .231 F6
Parkfield Ave [14] HU14. . . 3 A4
Parkfield Dr East Ella HU3. .179 F7
Kingston upon Hull HU3 . .179 F6
Parkfield Rd
[7] Ruskington NG34 . . . .108 E2
[13] Ryhall PE9. . . . . .163 C1
Park Gate [7] PE21. . . . . .208 F5
Park Gdns PE12. . . . . . . .215 E3
Park Hill
Cherry Willingham/Reepham
LN3. . . . . .203 C5
[28] Kirton in Lindsey DN21 . . 30 B1
Parkhill Cres [3] DN3 . . . . 14 A4
Parkhill Rd [2] DN3 . . . . . 14 A4
Parkhill Rise [7] DN15. . . . . 9 B5
Park Home Ave PE7 . . . . .230 D1
Park Home Rd PE7 . . . . . .230 D1
Parkin Rd [7] Cowbit PE12 . .167 B8
Scunthorpe DN17. . . . . . .184 F4
Parkinson Ave [1] DN15 . .183 A3
Parkinson's Way [1] LN12 . .64 C2
Park La [12] Alford LN13. . . 75 F3
[10] Billinghay LN4 . . . . . .109 F5
Billinghay LN4 . . . . .109 F5
[5] Boston PE21. . . . . . . .208 F6
Bracebridge LN5 . . . . . . .205 D6
Burton LN1. . . . . .200 D4
Coningsby LN4 . . . . .207 C4
Denton NG32 . . . . .139 A7
[2] Donington PE11 . . . . .134 E2
East Kirkby PE23 . . . . 99 E5
Ewerby & Evedon NG34 . .122 B7
Freiston PE22. . . . . .126 D3
Gorefield PE13. . . . . .169 F3
Heighington/Washingborough
LN4. . . . . .203 C2
Holbeach PE12. . . . . . . .215 E3
Humberston DN35. . . . . .192 F1
Leverington PE13. . . . . . .170 A3
Long Sutton PE12. . . . . . .216 C5
Manby LN11 . . . . 62 C5
Peterborough PE1 . . . . . .226 C4
Pinchbeck PE11 . . . . . . .145 D3
Redbourne DN21 . . . . 30 F3
Saxby All Saints DN20 . . . 10 A3
[1] Scawby DN20 . . . . 30 F8
[1] Skillington NG33. . . . . .151 A8
Spalding PE11 . . . . .214 C5
Stamford PE9 . . . . .219 C4
[5] Surfleet PE11 . . . . . . .145 D2
Swineshead PE20. . . . . . .135 A7
Westwoodside DN9. . . . . . 27 A2
Wigsley NG23 . . . . 78 F5
Park La Cl [6] DN7 . . . . . . 14 C2
Park La E HU4. . . . . .179 C5
Parklands
[2] Fleet Hargate PE12 . . .159 C7
Mablethorpe/Sutton on Sea
LN12. . . . . 64 B3
[1] Mumby LN13 . . . . 76 F1
[4] West/East Butterwick
DN17. . . . . 28 D8
Parklands Ave
New Waltham DN36 . . . . .195 E6
Nocton LN4 . . . . 95 B7
Parklands Cl [4] NG24. . . .104 C5
Parklands Cres [11] HU14 . . 3 A5
Parklands Dr
[4] Harlaxton NG32 . . . . .139 C7
[10] North Ferriby HU14. . . . 3 A5
Parklands Mews HU13. . . . 3 E4
Parkland Way LN8 . . . . . . 70 C4
Park La Rd [11] DN7. . . . . 14 C2
Park La W HU4. . . . . .179 C5
Park-Lea [6] NG34. . . . . .108 E2
Park Rd [1] Alford LN13. . . 75 F3
[1] Allington NG32 . . . . . .128 F7
Boston PE21. . . . . .208 F4
[5] Brough HU15. . . . . 2 E6
Claxby LN8 . . . . 45 E4

Park Rd continued
Grantham NG31 . . . . . . .211 B5
Holbeach PE12 . . . . .215 D2
[1] Horncastle LN9 . . . . . .199 C4
Long Sutton PE12 . . . . . .216 C5
Mablethorpe/Sutton on Sea
LN12 . . . . .64 C1
Market Deeping PE6 . . . .217 D4
Peterborough PE1 . . . . . .226 A3
Spalding PE11 . . . . .214 C4
Swinstead NG33. . . . . . .153 A5
[1] Weston PE12. . . . . . . .157 E7
[5] Willingham DN21. . . . . 53 E3
Park Rd E LN12. . . . . 64 C1
Park Rd W LN12. . . . . 64 C1
Park Road LN9. . . . . 85 F1
Park Row
Kingston upon Hull HU3 . .180 D7
Louth LN11. . . . . .198 E7
Northfield HU13. . . . . . . .178 E2
Parks Cl LN39. . . . . 12 A1
Parksgate Ave LN6 . . . . .204 F5
Parkside [17] Nettleham LN2 . .68 C2
Peterborough PE2 . . . . . .230 B6
Parkside Cres PE1 . . . . . .214 C5
Parkside Dr [13] PE24 . . . . 90 D7
Parkside The [4] NG33. . .151 D2
Park Springs Rd DN21 . . .197 F2
Park Sq SN15 . . . . .183 A2
Parks Rd [8] DN7 . . . . 14 C4
Park St Cleethorpes DN35 . .189 D1
Grimsby DN32 . . . . .192 B8
Kingston upon Hull HU3 . .180 D6
Lincoln LN1 . . . . .234 A2
[11] Messingham DN17 . . . 29 D7
Peterborough PE2 . . . . . .230 F7
Swinefleet DN14 . . . . 6 D8
Winterton DN15. . . . . 9 B5
PARKS THE PE7 . . . . 14 C4
Parkstone Gr [28] DN7 . . . 14 D4
Park Terr [2] PE1 . . . . . . .226 A6
Park The
[24] Beacon Hill NG24 . . .104 A4
Coningsby LN4 . . . . .207 D5
Lincoln LN1 . . . . .234 A2
Potter Hanworth LN4 . . . . 95 B8
Park View
[25] Barton-upon-Humber
DN18. . . . . 10 F8
Cleethorpes DN35 . . . . . .192 C8
Crowle DN17 . . . . 16 D6
Kingston upon Hull HU4 . .179 E4
Mablethorpe/Sutton on Sea
LN12. . . . . 64 C1
[10] Messingham DN17 . . . 29 D7
[15] Northorpe PE10 . . . . .164 C8
[13] Thorne/Moorends DN8 . .15 A7
Park View Ave LN4 . . . . . . 81 D2
Park View Cl [7] DN19. . . . 11 C7
Park View Terr DN17. . . . . 28 C8
Parkway The
Kingston upon Hull HU10 . .178 E8
Spalding PE11 . . . . .214 A2
Park Wlk
Easton on the Hill PE9 . . .171 D3
Kingston upon Hull HU4 . .179 B5
Parkwood Rise [14] DN3 . . 14 A3
Parliament Cl [11] PE25. .206 B4
Parliament St
[3] Brough HU15. . . . . 2 D6
[7] Kingston upon Hull HU1. .180 F6
Peterborough PE1 . . . . . .225 F5
Parnell St [3] DN21. . . . . .197 C5
Parnwell Prim Sch PE1 . .226 F7
Parnwell Way PE1. . . . . .226 F6
Parris Pl DN35 . . . . .192 D7
Parry Rd [22] LN12 . . . . . 64 B3
Parslins The PE6. . . . . . . .217 F5
Parsonage La PE12. . . . . .159 F1
Parson Dro Billinghay LN4. .109 F7
Parson Dro La PE13. . . . . .170 B2
PARSON DROVE PE13. . . .177 D7
Parson La LN5 . . . . .106 C8
Parson's Dr [3] PE21. . . . .208 E7
Parson's Dro
Holland Fen with Brothertoft
PE20 . . . . .124 A8
Swaton NG34. . . . . .133 D4
Parsons Halt [2] LN11. . . .198 C6
Parsons La [18] LN13. . . . . 75 F2
Parson's La PE12. . . . . . .168 B4
Parthian Ave PE21 . . . . . .136 D8
PARTNEY PE23 . . . . 88 A3
Partney CE (Aided) Prim Sch
PE23. . . . . 88 B3
Partney Rd PE23 . . . . 87 C4
Partridge Cl [4] Caistor LN7 . .33 B4
[4] Scunthorpe DN16. . . . .184 E6
Yaxley PE7 . . . . .233 D6
Partridge Dr LN7. . . . . . . 33 F2
Partridge Gn LN6 . . . . 92 D5
Partridge Gr PE4. . . . . . . .220 E5
Pashley Rd DN8 . . . . 15 B7
PASTON PE4 . . . . .221 D1
Paston Farm Adventure Ctr *
PE4. . . . . .221 C2
Paston La PE4. . . . . .221 B1
Paston Parkway PE4 . . . .221 C4
Paston Ridings PE4 . . . . .221 C1
Paston Ridings Prim Sch
PE4. . . . . .221 D1
Pasture Ave [9] DN17 . . . . 17 D4
Pasture Cl
[7] Colsterworth NG33. . . .151 E7

Pasture Cl *continued*
Grantham NG31 . . . . **211** D1
Pasture Dr
Hampton Vale PE7 . . . . **230** B2
4 Hampton Vale PE7 . . . . . **230** C1
Louth LN11 . . . . **198** D4
Pasture Dro PE10 . . . . **154** F7
Pasture Grove 17 NG23 . . . . **91** D4
Pasture La Amcotts DN17 . . . **7** D1
Bassingham LN5 . . . . **93** B2
Belvoir NG32 . . . . **138** C6
Garthorpe & Fockerby DN17 . . **7** D6
Market Rasen LN8 . . . . **57** E8
Northborough PE6 . . . . **173** F6
Nunsthorpe DN33 . . . . **191** B1
Pasture Rd DN18 . . . . **197** F4
Pasture Rd N DN18 . . . . **3** F1
Pasture Rd S DN18 . . . . **4** A1
Pastures Ct 36 DN17 . . . . **29** D7
Pastures Rd NG32 . . . . **210** A5
Pasture St DN32 . . . . **191** E7
Pastures The
12 Cowbit PE12 . . . . **167** B8
12 Long Bennington NG23 . . **117** D3
Old Somerby NG33 . . . . **140** E8
1 Rampton DN22 . . . . **65** A5
12 Welton LN2 . . . . **68** D6
Pasture The PE6 . . . . **217** C6
Pasture Wharf Nature
Reserve★ DN18 . . . . **4** A2
Patchett Cl DN33 . . . . **191** B2
Patch Rd LN6 . . . . **92** D4
Pateley Moor Cl 13 LN6 . . . . **93** C8
Patman's La PE22 . . . . **114** E4
Patricks Cl 5 LN7 . . . . **32** A4
Patrick St DN32 . . . . **191** E5
Patriot Cl PE11 . . . . **214** C4
Patten Ave 2 PE24 . . . . **102** D1
Patterdale Rd
Kingston upon Hull HU5 . . . **179** E8
3 Peterborough PE4 . . . . . **221** E2
Paul Cres 4 DN36 . . . . **36** C8
Paulette Ct 11 PE11 . . . . . . **214** B5
Pauleys Ct 29 PE9 . . . . **219** C5
Paul La 1 DN15 . . . . **9** D1
Paulsgrove PE2 . . . . **229** D5
Paul's La LN4 . . . . **207** C2
Paul's Wlk DN17 . . . . **184** B7
Pavilion Gdns
3 Scunthorpe DN17 . . . . . . **182** F2
5 Sleaford NG34 . . . . **212** D3
Pavilion Way DN36 . . . . **195** C7
Pavillion Gdns LN6 . . . . **205** A4
Paving Way LN6 . . . . **204** C4
Pawlett Cl PE6 . . . . **217** D5
Paxton Dr PE2 . . . . **229** D4
Payne Ave PE13 . . . . **170** D1
Paynell 23 LN2 . . . . **68** D6
Paynells PE2 . . . . **230** A3
Paynesholm PE4 . . . . **221** E1
Paynter Wlk DN33 . . . . **191** A2
Peace Haven 2 DN37 . . . . . **194** C5
Peach La NG32 . . . . **128** F6
Peach Tree Cl 5 DN16 . . . . . **185** D4
Peach Tree Ct 5 HU3 . . . . . **180** D5
Peachwood Cl 4 NG31 . . . . **210** F8
Peacock Cl 5 NG34 . . . . **212** E3
Peacock Pl 8 DN21 . . . . **197** F5
Peacocks Launde NG23 . . . **117** E7
Peacock's Rd PE22 . . . . **112** B1
Peacock St DN17 . . . . **184** F5
Peacocks The 5 NG23 . . . . **117** D3
Peacock Way PE3 . . . . **224** F2
Peak Dale LN6 . . . . **204** E2
Peake Cl Holdingham NG34 . **212** C7
Peterborough PE2 . . . . **230** F6
PEAKIRK PE6 . . . . **174** A5
Peakirk-cum-Glinton CE Prim
Sch PE6 . . . . **220** C8
Peakirk Rd
Deeping Gate PE6 . . . . **217** F3
Glinton PE6 . . . . **220** D8
Northborough PE6 . . . . **174** A7
Peaks Ave DN36 . . . . **195** C7
Peaksfield Ave DN32 . . . . . . **191** F5
Peaks La Grimsby DN36 . . . . **191** F2
New Waltham DN36 . . . . . . **195** F3
Peaks Parkway
Grimsby DN32 . . . . **191** F5
New Waltham DN36 . . . . . . **192** A1
Pearces La 3 PE10 . . . . **154** C7
Pearces Rd PE6 . . . . **227** B5
Pearl Cl 8 PE25 . . . . **206** C4
Pearl Ct PE12 . . . . **215** D3
Pea Rm Craft Ctr &
Heckington Village Trust Sta
Mus★ NG34 . . . . **122** F2
Pearson Prim Sch HU3 . . . . **180** D8
Pearson Rd DN35 . . . . **192** F3
Pearson St 5 HU2 . . . . **180** E7
Peartree Cl 5 LN6 . . . . **200** D1
Pear Tree Cl
4 Epworth DN9 . . . . **27** C4
Horncastle LN9 . . . . **199** C5
Sleaford NG34 . . . . **212** D2
Waltham DN37 . . . . **194** D4
Pear Tree Cres 2 PE13 . . . . **170** B1
Peartree Hill Rd PE12 . . . . . **168** B8
Peartree House Rd PE12 . . . **215** F7
Pear Tree La
Covenham St Bartholomew
LN11 . . . . **49** B6
Kirk Bramwith DN7 . . . . **14** A8
Utterby DN36 . . . . **48** E5
Pear Tree Rd PE20 . . . . **136** D5

Peascliffe Dr NG31 . . . . **211** A8
Peaseholme HU13 . . . . **178** C1
Peasgate La
Toynton All Saints PE23 . . . **100** F6
Toynton St Peter PE23 . . . . **101** A7
Peashill La NG32 . . . . **139** B8
Peat Carr Bank DN9 . . . . . . **26** C3
Peatlings La PE13 . . . . **170** C1
Pebble Cl 4 PE12 . . . . **160** E4
Peck Ave PE21 . . . . **208** D4
Peck Hill NG33 . . . . **131** B1
Peckover Cl 4 PE7 . . . . **231** F5
Peckover Prim Sch PE13 . . **170** C1
Pecks Dro W 4 PE11 . . . . . . **214** F2
Peddars Ct 16 LN4 . . . . **81** A1
Peddars Way PE3 . . . . **225** A2
Pedlar La LN11 . . . . **62** A7
Pedley La 15 PE13 . . . . **170** C1
Peel Castle Rd Old DN8 . . . . **15** B7
Peele Sch The PE12 . . . . . . **216** D6
Peel Hill Rd 9 DN8 . . . . **15** B7
Peel St
Kingston upon Hull HU3 . . . **180** D8
Lincoln LN5 . . . . **201** E1
Pegasus Gr 6 PE10 . . . . **213** E7
Pegasus Rd DN20 . . . . **21** A8
Pegasus Wy DN37 . . . . **24** B6
Pelham Ave DN33 . . . . **191** C1
Pelham Cl
20 Barton-upon-Humber
DN18 . . . . **10** E8
Peterborough PE3 . . . . **224** F2
7 Sudbrooke LN2 . . . . **68** F2
Pelham Cres 1 DN41 . . . . . . **23** A4
Pelham Dr 1 HU9 . . . . **181** C7
Pelham Ind Est DN40 . . . . . **186** B6
Pelham La Canwick LN4 . . . . **81** A4
North Owersby LN8 . . . . . . **45** B7
Pelham Pl DN33 . . . . **191** C1
Pelham Rd
Claxby LN8 . . . . **45** D6
Cleethorpes DN35 . . . . **192** D7
Grimsby DN31 . . . . **191** C7
2 Holton le Clay DN36 . . . . **195** C2
Immingham DN40 . . . . **186** B3
1 Skegness PE25 . . . . **206** C4
Pelham Sq 4 DN35 . . . . **192** E7
Pelham St LN5 . . . . **234** B1
Pelham View 1 DN20 . . . . . . **30** F5
Pell Pl 7 PE21 . . . . **209** C4
Pell's Dr 5 PE20 . . . . **136** D5
Pemberton Dr DN36 . . . . . . **195** B6
Pemberton St 1 HU8 . . . . . **181** B7
Pembrey Cl 11 LN6 . . . . **204** C7
Pembroke Ave
Green Hill NG31 . . . . **210** D6
Green Hill NG31 . . . . **210** E6
Peterborough PE2 . . . . **229** F5
Scunthorpe DN16 . . . . **185** A3
Yarborough DN34 . . . . **191** A7
Pembroke Gr 1 PE6 . . . . . . **220** D8
Pembroke Rd
Grimsby DN34 . . . . **191** A5
Stamford PE9 . . . . **219** A4
Pendeen Cl
6 Gainsborough DN21 . . . . **197** E6
New Waltham DN36 . . . . . . **195** C7
Pendine Cres LN6 . . . . **205** A1
Pendlebury Dr 4 PE6 . . . . . **217** D5
Pendleton PE3 . . . . **225** B6
Pendred Ave LN6 . . . . **92** D4
Pendreth Pl DN35 . . . . **192** D7
Pendula Rd PE13 . . . . **170** E1
Penelope Gr PE2 . . . . **231** F4
Penfold La 1 LN4 . . . . **203** C2
Pengleton Cl 18 NG33 . . . . . **151** D2
Penistone Ct 2 HU9 . . . . . . **181** D7
Pennell St LN5 . . . . **201** E1
Pennine Cl 9 DN40 . . . . **186** A4
Pennine Rd 7 DN8 . . . . **15** A7
Pennine Way
Gonerby Hill Foot NG31 . . . **210** E7
Peterborough PE4 . . . . **221** B2
Spalding PE11 . . . . **214** E6
Pennington PE2 . . . . **229** E3
Pennington St HU8 . . . . **181** B7
Pennistone Pl DN33 . . . . . . **191** A2
Pennycress Cl LN2 . . . . **202** C8
Pennyfield 16 PE11 . . . . **156** E8
Pennygate PE11 . . . . **214** A4
Penny Gdns 6 PE20 . . . . . . **136** C5
PENNY HILL PE12 . . . . **215** D6
Pennyhill Cl PE11 . . . . **214** E6
Penny Hill Rd PE12 . . . . **215** E3
Penny La LN4 . . . . **96** C2
Penny Toft La PE11 . . . . **214** B8
Penrith Gr 2 PE4 . . . . **221** E2
Penrose Cl 19 LN6 . . . . **93** C8
Penshurst Ave HU13 . . . . . . **178** F3
Penshurst Mews HU13 . . . . **178** F3
Penshurst Rd DN35 . . . . **192** D4
Pen St PE21 . . . . **209** A5
Penswick Gr 6 NG24 . . . . . **104** A5
Pentelow Cl PE13 . . . . **177** D5
Pentland Dr
23 North Hykeham LN6 . . . . **93** C8
Sleaford NG34 . . . . **121** A2
Pentlands The 2 PE4 . . . . . **221** C2
Pentney Cl PE2 . . . . **231** C7
Penwald Cl 7 PE6 . . . . **175** B8
Penwald Ct 6 PE6 . . . . **174** A5
Penway Dr PE11 . . . . **214** B8
Penwith Dr 2 HU10 . . . . **178** F7
Peploe Cres 10 DN19 . . . . . . **4** E2
Peploe La 9 DN19 . . . . **4** E2
Peppercorn Cl
3 Lincoln LN6 . . . . **201** D1

Peterborough PE1 . . . . **225** E6
Peppercorn Wlk
5 Grimsby DN33 . . . . **191** E7
8 Holton le Clay DN36 . . . . **195** D2
Peppermint Gr 7 PE25 . . . . **206** D2
Peppermint Way PE12 . . . . **215** B4
Pepper's La NG34 . . . . **133** C4
Peppin La LN11 . . . . **49** A2
Percheron Dr 4 PE11 . . . . . **214** A2
Percival St
Peterborough PE3 . . . . **225** E2
Scunthorpe DN15 . . . . **183** A4
Percy St
8 Kingston upon Hull
HU2 . . . . **180** E7
6 Lincoln LN2 . . . . **202** B3
3 Scunthorpe DN16 . . . . . **183** B2
Peregrine Cl
Kingston upon Hull HU4 . . . **179** D2
6 Sleaford NG34 . . . . **212** B3
Peregrine Pl PE10 . . . . **213** E3
Peregrine St PE7 . . . . **230** D1
Peregrine Way LN11 . . . . . . **198** D8
Periwinkle Way 3 PE10 . . . . **213** D3
Perkin Field PE34 . . . . **161** F2
Perkins Cl 2 DN37 . . . . **190** F8
Perkins La PE6 . . . . **173** C6
Permain Cl DN33 . . . . **191** E1
Perney Cres 17 LN6 . . . . **93** C8
Pernys Cl PE7 . . . . **230** D3
Perrin Ave 6 PE25 . . . . **206** A5
Perry Cl 7 PE11 . . . . **214** A4
Perry La LN4 . . . . **205** F4
Perry La NG23 . . . . **91** A7
Perry Rd PE13 . . . . **170** B2
Perry St HU3 . . . . **180** A6
Pershore Ave DN34 . . . . **190** D4
Pershore Way
Birchwood LN6 . . . . **204** C6
Eye PE6 . . . . **175** B2
Perth Cl Bourne PE10 . . . . . **213** C3
7 Skegness PE25 . . . . **206** A4
Perth Rd PE9 . . . . **218** E6
Perth St W HU5 . . . . **180** A8
Perth St HU5 . . . . **179** F8
Perth Way DN40 . . . . **186** B2
Pescod Sq 27 PE21 . . . . . . **208** F5
Petchell Way 2 DN32 . . . . . **191** F8
PETERBOROUGH PE1 . . . . **225** D5
Peterborough Cath★ PE1 **226** A2
Peterborough City Hospl
PE3 . . . . **225** B4
Peterborough Coll of Adult Ed
PE1 . . . . **226** B3
Peterborough Dr 7 PE6 . . . **224** E2
Peterborough Her Ctr★
PE3 . . . . **225** A1
Peterborough High Sch
PE3 . . . . **225** D2
Peterborough Mus & Art
Gall★ PE3 . . . . **225** A2
Peterborough NV Sta PE2 **225** F1
Peterborough Rd
Castor PE5 . . . . **223** E1
19 Collingham NG23 . . . . . . **91** D5
23 Eye PE6 . . . . **175** A1
Langtoft PE6 . . . . **217** A8
Newborough PE6 . . . . **174** E4
Peterborough PE7 . . . . **231** C3
Scunthorpe DN16 . . . . **185** B7
Wansford PE8 . . . . **222** A4
Peterborough Rd South
PE6 . . . . **175** B7
Peterborough Regional Coll
PE1 . . . . **226** B3
Peterborough Sch The
PE9 . . . . **225** E2
Peterborough Sta PE3 . . . . **225** F2
Peterborough Way NG34 **212** C7
Peter Chambers Way 9
LN12 . . . . **64** A4
Peterfield Rd 7 PE7 . . . . . . **230** B1
Petergate 1 PE9 . . . . **219** B4
Peterhouse Cl
Peterborough PE3 . . . . **225** E3
1 Stamford PE9 . . . . **219** B7
Peterhouse Ct DN16 . . . . . . **185** A4
Peterhouse Rd DN34 . . . . . . **190** F6
Peter Paine Ct PE22 . . . . . . **126** F4
Peter Paine Sports Ctr
PE21 . . . . **208** B5
Peter Seadike La PE11 . . . . **145** D5
Petersfield Cl LN6 . . . . **204** B7
Peter's La LN13 . . . . **63** B2
Peterson Dr
New Waltham DN36 . . . . . . **195** D7
New Waltham DN36 . . . . . . **195** D7
Peterspoint PE12 . . . . **160** D3
Petfield Dr HU10 . . . . **178** F5
Pethley La NG34 . . . . **143** A6
Petticoat La 15 PE21 . . . . . **208** F5
Pettit Way 5 PE21 . . . . **209** C4
Petts Cl 5 PE13 . . . . **170** E1
Petts La PE22 . . . . **160** F5
Petuaria Cl HU15 . . . . **2** B6
Petworth Cl 2 PE6 . . . . **217** A5
Petworth La 6 HU3 . . . . **179** F5
Peveril Ave DN17 . . . . **184** F4
Peveril Pl NG31 . . . . **210** D5
Peveril Rd PE1 . . . . **225** F6
Pheasant Cl DN17 . . . . **184** E6
Pheasant Ct 5 LN7 . . . . **33** B4
Pheasant Gr PE4 . . . . **220** E5
Pheasant Way PE7 . . . . **233** D5
Phelps Pl DN32 . . . . **192** C5
Phelps St DN35 . . . . **189** D1
Pheonix Ave DN15 . . . . **182** F6

Philip Ave
Cleethorpes DN35 . . . . **192** D4
Waltham DN37 . . . . **194** E5
Philip Ct 4 LN6 . . . . **204** F1
Philip Gr Cleethorpes DN35 **192** D4
Skegness PE25 . . . . **206** B4
Philips Cres DN15 . . . . **182** F3
Phillipot Cl 8 NG24 . . . . . . **104** B5
Phillips Ct 6 PE9 . . . . **219** C4
Phillips La 8 DN37 . . . . **23** F1
Phoenix Cl PE2 . . . . **231** B6
Phoenix Clayton Sch PE2 **230** B4
Phoenix St LN2 . . . . **197** F3
Phoenix La
20 Balderton NG24 . . . . . . **104** C1
Balderton NG24 . . . . **104** C2
10 Crowland PE6 . . . . **175** B8
Phoenix Parkway DN15 . . . **182** E7
Phoenix Sch The PE2 . . . . . **230** C3
Phoenix St 6 DN32 . . . . . . **191** D7
Phorpres Cl PE7 . . . . **230** D3
Phorpres Houses PE7 . . . . **230** F4
Phorpres Way PE7 . . . . **230** E3
Photinia Cl 8 LN4 . . . . **81** E2
Phyllis Ave DN34 . . . . **191** B7
Phyllis Taylor Gdns DN32 **191** D7
Piccadilly 4 DN36 . . . . **195** C6
Piccadilly Way 1 PE10 . . . . **154** D6
Pickards Way LN5 . . . . **170** C1
Pickathorpe La LN11 . . . . . . **50** E6
Pickering Ct DN37 . . . . **190** E8
Pickering Gr 15 DN8 . . . . . . **15** A7
Pickering Grange 33 HU15 . **2** D5
Pickering Rd HU4 . . . . **179** C3
Pickering's Mdw Nature
Reserve★ LN2 . . . . **68** F6
Pickerings The 19 HU14 . . . . **3** A4
Pick Hill La Grimoldby LN11 **142** E8
South Cockerington LN11 . . **50** C1
Picksley Cres DN36 . . . . . . **195** D1
PICKWORTH
Pickworth NG34 . . . . **142** A8
Pickworth PE9 . . . . **162** E4
Pickworth Lane PE9 . . . . . . **162** C3
Pickworth Rd PE9 . . . . **162** F2
Pickworth's Dro PE10 . . . . **155** A3
Pidgeon Cote La 20 DN19 . . **12** A8
Pied Bull Cl 8 PE9 . . . . **171** A3
Pier St 9 HU1 . . . . **180** F5
Pietermaritz St 4 LN1 . . . . **201** E8
Pieter Maritz View 15
LN1 . . . . **201** E8
Pigot Wy 5 LN2 . . . . **202** D6
Pike Dam La PE12 . . . . **159** A6
Pilgrim Ave DN40 . . . . **186** D3
Pilgrim Gr PE4 . . . . **221** F2
Pilgrim Hospl PE21 . . . . . . **209** A8
Pilgrims App DN21 . . . . **197** F2
Pilgrim Sch The PE20 . . . . **124** B6
Pilgrim's Cl 5 DN40 . . . . . . **12** E3
Pilgrims Way DN40 . . . . . . **186** A4
Pilgrim's Way PE11 . . . . . . **214** A4
Pilgrims Wy PE7 . . . . **197** F2
PILHAM DN21 . . . . **41** C4
Pilham Ct DN21 . . . . **197** F3
Pilham La DN21 . . . . **41** C4
Pilley's La PE21 . . . . **125** F5
Pilmore La PE12 . . . . **157** B6
Pilots View DN18 . . . . **3** E2
Pilots Way HU9 . . . . **181** B5
PILSGATE PE9 . . . . **172** C4
Pilton Cl PE4 . . . . **221** D1
Pimpernel Way 2 DN16 . . . **185** D4
PINCHBECK PE11 . . . . **156** E8
Pinchbeck Ave 4 DN16 . . . **183** C2
Pinchbeck East CE Prim Sch
The PE11 . . . . **156** E8
Pinchbeck Engine Mus★
PE11 . . . . **145** E1
Pinchbeck Fen Slipe Nature
Reserve★ PE11 . . . . **156** A6
Pinchbeck La PE24 . . . . **102** F4
Pinchbeck Rd
5 Butterwick PE22 . . . . . . **126** E3
Spalding PE11 . . . . **214** D5
PINCHBECK WEST PE11 . . . **156** A7
Pinder Ave
Peterborough PE4 . . . . **221** E3
Peterborough PE4 . . . . **221** E3
Pinder La 10 PE11 . . . . **134** F2
Pinder's Dro PE22 . . . . **114** B5
Pine Cl 14 Balderton NG24 . **104** C1
Grimsby DN37 . . . . **188** A1
Holbeach PE12 . . . . **215** C3
Lincoln LN1 . . . . **201** E8
12 Newark-on-Trent NG24 . **104** A6
4 Sleaford NG34 . . . . **212** D3
Stamford PE9 . . . . **218** D6
7 Waddington LN5 . . . . **93** E8
Pine Ct
3 Cleethorpes DN35 . . . . . **192** D2
Spalding PE11 . . . . **214** F4
Pinefield Ave 7 DN3 . . . . . . **14** A3
Pinefield Rd 8 DN3 . . . . **14** A3
Pine Hall Rd DN3 . . . . **14** A3
Pine Mdws HU10 . . . . **178** B8
Pine Pk 3 DN18 . . . . **3** E1
Pines The DN21 . . . . **197** F2
Pinetree Ave 11 DN36 . . . . **29** C3
Pinetree Cl 5 DN20 . . . . **19** E4
Pine Tree Cl
Peterborough PE1 . . . . **226** B8
Woodside DN9 . . . . **26** D6
Pinetrees Ct 4 NG34 . . . . . **212** E4
Pine Wlk 5 Brough HU15 . . . . **2** C6
4 Healing DN41 . . . . **24** A5
Pinewood Ave PE8 . . . . **172** B1

Pinewood Cl
Bottesford DN16 . . . . **185** A4
5 Bourne PE10 . . . . **213** B5
Pinewood Cr 8 LN6 . . . . . . **204** B8
Pinewood Cres DN33 . . . . . **190** F3
Pinewood Dr NG31 . . . . **210** F8
Pinewood Gr 2 HU5 . . . . . . **179** C7
Pinfold 15 DN9 . . . . **27** E6
Pinfold Cl
7 Bassingham LN5 . . . . . . **92** F3
6 Bottesford NG13 . . . . . **128** A6
8 Collingham NG23 . . . . . **91** D5
11 Northorpe PE10 . . . . . . **164** C8
Osbournby NG34 . . . . **132** D5
Pointon & Sempringham
NG34 . . . . **143** B6
Rippingale PE10 . . . . **142** F2
Pinfold Gdns 4 DN36 . . . . . **195** D1
Pinfold La Anderby PE24 . . . . **77** B3
Beesby with Saleby LN13 . . **76** A6
11 Bottesford NG13 . . . . . **128** A6
Fishlake DN7 . . . . **14** D8
Fishtoft PE21 . . . . **137** C8
Great Steeping PE23 . . . . . **101** E6
Grimsby DN33 . . . . **191** D1
Halton Holegate PE22 . . . . **101** C6
8 Holton le Clay DN36 . . . . **195** D1
Irby in the Marsh PE24 . . . **102** B6
Legbourne LN11 . . . . **61** E3
Marston NG32 . . . . **118** D2
Minting LN9 . . . . **71** C1
1 Misterton DN10 . . . . **39** F5
18 Newark-on-Trent NG24 . **104** B2
Pointon & Sempringham
NG34 . . . . **143** B6
8 Ruskington NG34 . . . . . **108** E2
South Rauceby NG34 . . . . . **120** E4
2 Stallingborough DN41 . . . **23** D6
Stamford PE9 . . . . **219** C3
Stickney PE22 . . . . **113** A6
Swaby LN13 . . . . **74** E4
Walcott LN4 . . . . **109** C7
Weston PE12 . . . . **157** D8
Pinfold Rd Bourne PE10 . . . **213** D5
Castle Bytham NG33 . . . . . **152** D1
Pinfold The LN4 . . . . **108** D5
Pinfold Way 1 NG34 . . . . . . **108** E2
Pingle Cl DN21 . . . . **197** E4
Pingle La Bishop Norton LN8 **43** D3
Northborough PE6 . . . . **173** F6
20 Wellingore LN5 . . . . **107** A7
Pingle Leys 6 LN8 . . . . **43** D3
Pingle Nature Reserve The★
LN4 . . . . **207** D5
Pingles The 9 PE10 . . . . . . **164** C8
Pingle The
2 Billingborough NG34 . . . **133** B1
Northborough PE6 . . . . **173** F6
Peterborough PE6 . . . . **217** F1
Pingley La DN20 . . . . **196** D2
Pingley Mdw DN20 . . . . **196** D2
Pinnacle Cl 11 PE6 . . . . **175** B8
Pinney's Ct 21 DN41 . . . . . . **23** F5
Pinnings La DN21 . . . . **43** D6
Pinstock La 10 PE12 . . . . . . **159** C7
Pintail Cl DN16 . . . . **185** F5
Pintail Gdns PE7 . . . . **233** B8
Pinter La DN21 . . . . **197** F2
Pioneer Way LN6 . . . . **204** E4
Pioneer Wy PE6 . . . . **175** B1
Piper La PE4 . . . . **221** F3
Pipistrelle Ct 4 PE4 . . . . . . **221** A3
Pippin Cl Louth LN11 . . . . . **198** C5
Misterton DN10 . . . . **40** A4
Pippin Ct
10 Beacon Hill NG24 . . . . **104** A5
3 Scunthorpe DN15 . . . . . **182** C5
Pippin Dr PE16 . . . . **185** B2
Pippin Gdns PE14 . . . . **170** F1
Pippin Way DN7 . . . . **14** D3
Pipwell Gate PE12 . . . . **146** E1
Pitcairn Ave 1 LN2 . . . . **202** D6
Pitcher Row La PE20 . . . . . **136** B1
Pit La Gedney PE12 . . . . **149** A4
Great Ponton NG33 . . . . . . **140** B4
Ketton PE9 . . . . **171** A4
Pitman Ave 23 DN18 . . . . . . **10** E8
Pitmoor La DN39 . . . . **12** A1
Pitomy Dr NG23 . . . . **91** C5
Pitt La DN10 . . . . **39** C2
Pittneys PE4 . . . . **221** D1
Pitts Rd LN4 . . . . **203** C1
Pitt St HU3 . . . . **179** F7
Pk House Sch PE6 . . . . **176** A3
Pk Prim Sch PE21 . . . . **208** E7
Plains La DN8 . . . . **15** F3
Plains The PE9 . . . . **162** D4
Plane St HU3 . . . . **180** A5
Planet Ice★ PE1 . . . . **220** E1
Plank Dro PE6 . . . . **175** B8
Plantain Cl 1 DN16 . . . . **185** D4
Plantation Dr 5 HU14 . . . . . . **2** F5
Plantation Dr E HU4 . . . . . . **179** C6
Plantation Dr W HU4 . . . . . **179** C6
Plantation Rd
Cranwell & Byard's Leap
NG34 . . . . **107** C1
29 Thorne/Moorends DN8 . . **15** A8
Planting Rd NG33 . . . . **140** B1
Plash Dro PE13 . . . . **177** F4
Plassey Rd 6 DN21 . . . . **55** A8
Platform Dr PE12 . . . . **216** A4
Platts Cl PE11 . . . . **157** A8
Platts La Bucknall LN10 . . . . **84** B4
Tetford LN9 . . . . **73** E1
Platt's La NG32 . . . . **118** B4
Playgarth Est LN4 . . . . **108** E4
Playhouse The★ NG34 . . . . **212** D4

Playhouse Yd **2** NG34 . . . . . .212 D4
Playing Field La **2** LN8 . . . .59 A7
Playtowers★ DN35 . . . . . .193 B3
Pleasance Way LN11 . . . . .62 C6
Pleasant Ave LN11 . . . . . . .198 D5
Pleasant PI **6** LN11 . . . . . . .198 C6
Pleasant Terr **18** LN5 . . . . .205 E8
Pleasure Island Theme Pk★
 DN35 . . . . .193 C2
Plimsoll Way HU9 . . . . . . .181 B6
Plot La NG23 . . . . .91 E6
Plough Dr **18** LN8 . . . . .57 D8
Plough Hill **23** LN7 . . . . . . .33 B4
Plough La
 1 Cherry Willingham/Reepham
  LN3 . . . . .82 A8
 6 Fiskerton LN3 . . . . .82 A7
 6 Newborough PE6 . . . . . .174 E5
Ploughmans Ct **3** LN2 . . . .202 E6
Ploughmans La **4** LN2 . . . .202 E6
Plover Ct **18** DN18 . . . . .3 E1
Plover Dr **15** HU15 . . . . .2 C6
Plover Gr Birchwood LN6 . .204 E8
 Louth LN11 . . . . .198 C8
Ploverly **2** PE4 . . . . .221 A5
Plover Rd **1** PE9 . . . . .163 D3
Plover Sq **3** LN7 . . . . .33 B4
Plover Wy DN16 . . . . .185 F5
Plowden Rd HU3 . . . . .179 F5
Plowright Theatre★
 DN15 . . . . .183 A2
Plumpton Chase PE10 . . . .213 C3
Plum Tree Dr **3** DN36 . . . . .37 C2
Plumtree Hill Rd DN7 . . . . .14 C7
Plumtree La **2** DN36 . . . . .36 B1
Plum Tree Way DN16 . . . . .183 A1
Plymouth Cl
 Gainsborough DN21 . . . . .197 F2
 23 Winterton DN15 . . . . . .9 A5
Plymouth Rd DN17 . . . . . . .182 C1
Poachers Brook LN6 . . . . . .200 A5
Poacher's Croft **3** DN9 . . .16 E1
Poachers Ct **23** LN1 . . . . . . .66 D2
Poachers Gate **4** PE11 . . .145 C1
Poachers Hide **2** PE11 . . .145 B7
Poachers La LN2 . . . . .68 F3
Poachers Mdw **20** LN2 . . . .68 D2
Poachers Rest **3** LN2 . . . . .68 D7
Pocklington Cres **3**
 NG24 . . . . .104 B7
Pocklington Rd **24** NG23 . . .91 D5
Pocklington Way **10** NG34 .108 E2
PODE HOLE PE11 . . . . .156 C5
Pode La PE22 . . . . .197 F2
Poffinder Wood Rd DN7 . . .14 E7
POINTON NG34 . . . . .143 B7
Pointon Rd NG34 . . . . .143 B8
Point Rd PE25 . . . . .90 F3
Poke Holes Lane LN11 . . . . .60 A6
Poles Bank DN9 . . . . .26 E6
Policemans La **2** LN4 . . . .203 C2
Pollards The PE10 . . . . .213 D2
Pollyplatt La LN1 . . . . .67 E5
Pollyplatt Prim Sch LN1 . . .67 F5
Polton Cl **3** DN7 . . . . .14 D7
Polton Toft **2** DN7 . . . . . . .14 D7
Polyanthus Dr **4** NG34 . . .212 F3
Polygon Wlk **4** NG31 . . . . .211 F6
Pomona Wy PE2 . . . . .231 D4
Pond Cl **19** LN2 . . . . .68 D6
Pond La **4** PE10 . . . . .213 E2
Pond Side DN39 . . . . .11 E3
Ponds La HU15 . . . . .1 A6
Pond St
 Great Gonerby NG31 . . . . .129 D5
 8 Harlaxton NG32 . . . . .139 C7
Ponds Way **10** DN18 . . . . . . .3 E1
Ponds Wy **28** DN18 . . . . .3 E1
Ponsonby Dr PE2 . . . . .230 D8
Ponton Ave NG31 . . . . .211 E2
Ponton Rd NG33 . . . . .140 D5
Poolbank La HU15 . . . . .2 E5
Pool Cl **4** PE11 . . . . .214 C6
Pool Dr DN17 . . . . .184 F4
Poole's La **8** PE23 . . . . .87 F1
Pooley Way PE7 . . . . .233 D6
Poolham Lane LN10 . . . . . . .84 D1
Pools La **8** PE20 . . . . .136 A2
Poor Gdn Rd NG34 . . . . . . .132 F6
Poor Plat La LN13 . . . . .62 F3
Poor's End LN11 . . . . .50 B8
Pope's La Leverington PE13 .170 A4
 Terrington St Clement PE34 .161 E2
Pope Way PE1 . . . . .225 E8
Poplar Ave Lincoln LN6 . . . .201 C3
 Mablethorpe/Sutton on Sea
  LN12 . . . . .64 A5
 Peterborough PE1 . . . . . . .226 A8
Poplar Cl
 Anlaby with Anlaby Common
  HU4 . . . . .179 A5
 Boston PE21 . . . . .208 D2
 Ruskington NG34 . . . . . . .108 E2
 Burringham DN17 . . . . . . .17 D4
Poplar Cres Bourne PE10 . . .213 B6
Poplar Ct Lincoln LN6 . . . . . .205 B4
 Spalding PE11 . . . . .214 B4
 Welbourn LN5 . . . . .106 E4
Poplar Dr Brigg DN20 . . . . .196 C5
 6 Broughton DN20 . . . . .19 D3
 2 Gosberton PE11 . . . . .145 C6
 Humberston DN36 . . . . . .193 B1
Poplar Farm Sch NG31 . . . .210 D6
Poplar Gdns DN16 . . . . . . .185 B7
Poplar Gr
 5 Cleethorpes DN35 . . . . .192 E7
 3 Scotter DN21 . . . . .29 C3

Poplar La Corringham DN21 .41 D2
 Gedney Dyke PE12 . . . . . .148 D1
Poplar Rd Bucknall LN10 . . . .84 A3
 Cleethorpes DN35 . . . . . .192 E7
 6 Hatfield DN7 . . . . .14 C4
 2 Healing DN41 . . . . .23 F5
Poplar Rd Bsns Units
 DN35 . . . . .192 E7
Poplars Mobile Homes
 DN15 . . . . .182 B5
Poplar St LN5 . . . . .205 D5
Poplar Wy PE25 . . . . .103 C2
Popple Dro PE13 . . . . .169 D1
Popple St HU9 . . . . .181 B6
Popplewell Cl **3** DN9 . . . . .16 E2
 1 Scunthorpe DN15 . . . .182 C6
Popplewell Terr **18** DN9 . . .27 C6
Poppy Cl Boston PE21 . . . . .208 B4
 Spalding PE11 . . . . .214 B6
Poppyfields The **14** NG23 . .91 D4
Poppyfield Way DN20 . . . . .196 B4
Poppy Mews **27** DN41 . . . . .23 F5
Poppy PI **6** PE10 . . . . .213 D3
Poppy Rd LN6 . . . . .92 D5
Porcher Way PE21 . . . . .208 C6
Portal Gn **8** PE25 . . . . .206 A5
Portchester Cl PE2 . . . . . . .231 F5
Porter Ave PE4 . . . . .221 F2
Porter's La **4** PE21 . . . . . . .171 D3
Porter St
 Kingston upon Hull HU3 . . .180 E5
 Scunthorpe DN15 . . . . . . .183 A4
Porthcawl Cl **12** NG31 . . . .211 D7
Port La PE5 . . . . .223 E1
Portland Ave
 Grimsby DN32 . . . . .191 E4
 Peterborough PE1 . . . . . .225 F7
Portland Dr **6** PE25 . . . . . .206 A7
Portland Manor DN32 . . . . .191 E4
Portland PI Grimsby DN32 . .191 E4
 9 Kingston upon Hull HU2 .180 E7
Portland St Boston PE21 . . .208 E5
 Kingston upon Hull HU2 . . .180 D7
 Lincoln LN5 . . . . .234 B1
Portland Terr **5** DN21 . . . . .197 D3
Portman CI PE3 . . . . .225 C4
Portman Rd DN16 . . . . .182 E6
Portsmouth Cl **1** NG31 . . .210 F5
Portsmouth Wlk HU4 . . . . .179 B4
PORT SUTTON BRIDGE
 PE12 . . . . .160 F4
Postgate HU1 . . . . .180 F6
Postland Rd PE6 . . . . .166 F1
Post Mill Cl LN6 . . . . .204 C1
Post Office Hill NG33 . . . . .151 B5
Post Office La
 Ashby cum Fenby DN37 . . . .35 D3
 Burton Coggles NG33 . . . .152 C8
 Chapel Hill LN4 . . . . .110 E5
 2 Humberside Airport DN39 22 A6
 South Scarle NG23 . . . . . . .91 E7
 5 Spilsby PE23 . . . . .88 A1
 3 Sutterton PE20 . . . . . .136 A2
 Whitton DN15 . . . . .1 E3
Posts The NG32 . . . . .129 B3
Potesgrave Way **8** NG34 . .122 D3
Pot La PE20 . . . . .146 E8
Pottergate LN2 . . . . .234 B3
Pottergate Rd
 Ancaster NG32 . . . . .120 A3
 Caythorpe NG32 . . . . .119 D7
 Fulbeck NG32 . . . . .106 E1
 Normanton NG32 . . . . . . .119 E5
 Welbourn LN5 . . . . .106 F4
POTTERHANWORTH LN4 . .82 B1
POTTERHANWORTH BOOTHS
 LN4 . . . . .82 C2
Potterhanworth CE Prim Sch
 The LN4 . . . . .82 B1
Potterhanworth Rd
 Branston & Mere LN4 . . . . . .82 A1
 Heighington LN4 . . . . .81 F3
 Potter Hanworth LN4 . . . . .95 B8
Potter Hill Road NG23 . . . . .91 E3
Potters Cl **2** PE10 . . . . . . .213 E4
Potter's Lodge Meadows
 Nature Reserve★ NG33 .152 B2
Potters Way PE1 . . . . .226 B1
Pottinger Gdns **5** LN7 . . . .33 A3
Potts La DN17 . . . . .16 D7
Poulter Ave PE2 . . . . .231 D5
Pound Rd LN4 . . . . .96 C2
Poverty La LN11 . . . . .61 B2
Powells Cres DN16 . . . . . . .185 B6
Powell St PE21 . . . . .209 C2
Pratt Ave PE4 . . . . .221 D2
Prebend La LN2 . . . . .68 C7
Precinct Cres
 5 Skegness PE25 . . . . . .103 E4
 2 Skegness PE25 . . . . . .103 E4
Precincts The **5** PE6 . . . . .217 B5
Precinct The DN17 . . . . . . .184 D7
Premier Ct **6** NG31 . . . . . .211 A5
Prenton Cl **3** LN6 . . . . . . .205 A5
Prescott Ave **11** HU15 . . . .2 C5
Prescott Gr **3** DN7 . . . . . . .14 D4
Prestland PE6 . . . . .217 A6
Preston Dr DN20 . . . . .196 C4
Prestongate HU13 . . . . . . .178 E1
Preston La **15** DN18 . . . . . . .10 F8
Prestwick Cl
 2 Birchwood LN6 . . . . . .200 B1
 Londonthorpe & Harrowby Without
  NG31 . . . . .211 E7
Pretoria St LN12 . . . . .210 E7
Pretoria St HU3 . . . . .179 F5
Pretymen Cres DN36 . . . . . .195 C5
Prial Ave LN6 . . . . .205 B6

Prial CI LN6 . . . . .205 C6
Pride Parkway NG34 . . . . . .212 F7
Pridmore Rd NG33 . . . . . . .152 E8
Priestfield Dro **1** PE12 . . . .159 D7
Priestgate
 3 Barton-upon-Humber
  DN18 . . . . .10 F8
 4 Peterborough PE1 . . . .226 A2
Priest Hill La PE23 . . . . .87 A5
Priestley Cl **7** PE20 . . . . . .136 C5
Priest's House★ PE9 . . . . .171 C3
Primitive Chapel La **1**
 DN40 . . . . .12 F2
Primrose Ave **13** NG24 . . . .104 A6
Primrose Cl
 8 Healing DN41 . . . . .23 F5
 6 Lincoln LN5 . . . . .205 C2
 7 Morton PE10 . . . . .154 D6
 11 North Hykeham LN6 . . .93 A8
 Peterborough PE1 . . . . . . .226 A8
 9 Skegness PE25 . . . . . .206 A5
Primrose Cres
 Boston PE21 . . . . .208 B4
 4 Pinchbeck PE11 . . . . .156 E8
Primrose Dr
 1 Kingston upon Hull
  HU5 . . . . .179 C8
 Yaxley PE7 . . . . .233 F7
Primrose La **4** NG34 . . . . . .107 C1
Primroses **1** PE6 . . . . .217 D5
Primrose St DN21 . . . . .197 D3
Primrose Way
 6 Grantham NG31 . . . . . .211 D2
 Humberston DN35 . . . . . .192 E1
 2 Scunthorpe DN15 . . . .182 C6
 2 Spalding PE11 . . . . . . .214 A2
 2 Stamford PE9 . . . . . . .218 C7
Prince Albert Gdns **2**
 DN32 . . . . .189 A1
Prince Alfred Ave **1**
 PE25 . . . . .206 D3
Prince Ave **8** PE25 . . . . . . .90 D7
Prince Charles Ave **11** LN8 .70 D4
Prince Charles Dr **32** DN18 .10 F8
Prince Edward Dr DN40 . . . .187 A4
Prince George Rd PE10 . . . .213 B4
Prince George St PE25 . . . .206 C3
Prince Henry Dr DN40 . . . . .187 A4
Prince of Wales Cl **12**
 PE13 . . . . .170 D2
Prince Philip Dr **37** DN18 . . .10 F8
Princes Ave Grimsby DN31 . .191 C7
 Kingston upon Hull HU13 . .178 E1
Princes Ct **3** PE20 . . . . . . .213 D6
Prince's Dock St **16** HU1 . .180 F6
Princes Gate PE1 . . . . .226 B4
Princes Gdns PE1 . . . . .226 B4
Princes Parade PE25 . . . . . .206 C3
Princes Quay Sh Ctr HU1 . .180 F6
Princes Rd
 Peterborough PE2 . . . . . . .231 A7
 1 Stamford PE9 . . . . . . .219 C4
Prince's Rd DN35 . . . . .192 E6
Princess Alexandra Ct **1**
 DN17 . . . . .184 F3
Princess Anne Rd PE21 . . . .209 C6
Princess Ave DN7 . . . . .14 C6
Princess Dr
 34 Barton-upon-Humber
  DN18 . . . . .10 F8
 Grantham NG31 . . . . .211 D7
Princess Gr PE6 . . . . .217 C6
Princess Margaret Ave **28**
 LN4 . . . . .95 C4
Princess Rd PE20 . . . . .136 C4
Princess Royal Cl **4** LN2 . .234 C3
Princess Sq LN4 . . . . .109 E6
Princess St Boston PE21 . . .208 D5
 1 Immingham DN40 . . . .186 C3
 Lincoln LN5 . . . . .201 E1
Princes St Brigg DN20 . . . . .196 C3
 Holbeach PE12 . . . . .159 A7
Princess Wlk DN17 . . . . . . .197 F4
Prince St **13** HU1 . . . . .180 F6
Prince William Dr **8**
 PE22 . . . . .126 E3
Prince William Rd **3** LN8 . .56 D5
Pringle Cl LN4 . . . . .207 D5
Pringles The PE22 . . . . .98 F4
Prins Ave PE13 . . . . .170 D1
Prins Ct **16** PE13 . . . . .170 D1
Printing Office La **14** DN17 .16 D8
Priors Cl DN36 . . . . .195 D5
Priors Gate PE4 . . . . .220 E4
Prior St LN5 . . . . .201 E1
Priory Acad LSST The
 LN5 . . . . .205 E6
Priory City of Lincoln Acad
 The LN5 . . . . .205 A8
Priory Cl
 Gainsborough DN21 . . . . .197 F4
 Louth LN11 . . . . .198 C5
 Market Deeping PE6 . . . . .217 F4
 35 Newark-on-Trent NG24 .104 B2
 12 Northorpe PE10 . . . . .164 C8
 11 Ruskington NG34 . . . .108 E1
 12 Swanland HU14 . . . . . . .3 B7
Priory Cres
 Scunthorpe DN17 . . . . . . .185 A6
 Ulceby DN39 . . . . .12 A2
Priory Ct Boston PE21 . . . . .209 F5
 10 Grantham NG31 . . . . .211 A4
 11 South Witham NG33 . .151 D2
 Stamford PE9 . . . . .219 D5

Priory Dr **5** LN3 . . . . .82 B6
Priory Farm Dr **4** HU4 . . . .179 D2
Priory Gdns PE7 . . . . .228 F3
Priory Gr HU4 . . . . .179 D3
Priory La
 6 Barrow upon Humber
  DN19 . . . . .11 D8
 Dunston LN4 . . . . .95 D5
 Manby LN11 . . . . .62 C6
 Scunthorpe DN17 . . . . . . .184 F6
Priory La Jun Sch DN17 . . . .184 E6
Priory Lane Community Sch
 DN17 . . . . .184 F6
Priory Pk HU4 . . . . .179 B1
Priory Rd Boston PE21 . . . . .209 F5
 Fishtoft PE21 . . . . .126 C2
 Grimsby DN37 . . . . .190 D6
 Louth LN11 . . . . .198 C6
 Peterborough PE3 . . . . . . .225 E3
 Ruskington NG34 . . . . . . .108 E1
 Scunthorpe DN17 . . . . . . .185 A6
 Spalding PE11 . . . . .214 D3
 Stamford PE9 . . . . .219 D5
Priory Ruskin Acad The
 NG31 . . . . .211 A7
Priory Sch The PE11 . . . . . .214 F4
Priory Way
 2 Gainsborough DN21 . . .53 A5
 Kingston upon Hull HU4 . . .179 A1
 Sleaford NG34 . . . . .212 A2
Priory Witham Acad The
 LN6 . . . . .205 B5
Private La LN8 . . . . .55 F7
Proby CI PE7 . . . . .233 D5
Procters Cl DN23 . . . . .78 C1
Proctors Cl **6** PE12 . . . . . .159 C7
Proctors Rd LN2 . . . . .202 D5
Proctor's Way **6** DN20 . . . .31 A5
Progress Way NG31 . . . . . . .211 A6
Promenade
 Chapel St Leonard PE24 . . . .90 E5
 Cleethorpes DN35 . . . . . .192 F7
 Mablethorpe/Sutton on Sea
  LN12 . . . . .64 D1
Prospect Ctr **12** HU2 . . . . .180 E7
Prospect La **2** DN15 . . . . . . .8 C8
Prospect PI
 1 Grantham NG31 . . . . . .211 A5
 Kingston upon Hull HU9 . . .181 B7
 2 Market Rasen LN8 . . . . .57 E7
Prospect St Horncastle LN9 .199 B5
 Kingston upon Hull HU2 . . .180 E7
Prospect Terr **8** DN21 . . . . .197 D3
Prospero Ct **2** PE20 . . . . . .230 F6
Proudfoot La PE12 . . . . . . .159 B6
Providence Cres
 17 Barton-upon-Humber
  DN18 . . . . .10 E8
 Kingston upon Hull HU5 . . .179 D7
Providence PI **3** LN4 . . . . .207 C4
Providence Row **3** HU3 . .180 E8
Provost Rd **11** LN11 . . . . . . .62 C6
Prunus Ave HU10 . . . . .178 F8
Pryme Rd DN16 . . . . .185 C8
Pryme St HU10 . . . . .178 F6
Prystie PI PE20 . . . . .192 D2
Psalter Rd LN13 . . . . .88 E6
Puddiners La PE24 . . . . .6 E7
Pudding and Dip La
 8 Hatfield DN7 . . . . .14 D4
 Hatfield DN7 . . . . .14 D5
Pudding Bag La PE9 . . . . . .172 C4
Pudding La PE11 . . . . .214 E8
Puddingpoke La **8** PE12 . .160 A8
Puffin La PE7 . . . . .233 D8
Pulcroft Rd HU13 . . . . .178 D2
Pullan Cl **9** LN5 . . . . .205 D3
Pullinger Way LN4 . . . . .81 E1
Pullman Cl **11** LN4 . . . . .95 D4
Pullover La PE20 . . . . .146 E7
Pullover The PE24 . . . . .90 E7
Pulman St HU3 . . . . .180 A7
Pulvertoft La **12** PE21 . . . .208 F4
Pump Hill DN20 . . . . .31 D6
Pump La Fenton NG23 . . . . .105 C1
 5 Skidbrooke with Saltfleet
  Haven LN11 . . . . .51 C4
Pump Sq **18** PE21 . . . . . . .208 F5
Punchbowl La
 Boston PE21 . . . . .208 B7
 Holland Fen with Brothertoft
  PE20 . . . . .125 B4
Purbeck Rd
 5 Grimsby DN33 . . . . . . .194 E8
 Scunthorpe DN17 . . . . . . .182 C1
Purcell Cl **1** NG31 . . . . . . .211 D6
Puritan Way PE21 . . . . .208 C2
Puttock Gate PE20 . . . . . . .146 D7
Pyecroft PE1 . . . . .226 B6
PYEWIPE DN31 . . . . .188 C4
Pyewipe Bglws DN31 . . . . . .188 E1
Pyewipe Rd DN31 . . . . .188 E1
Pyhill PE3 . . . . .225 B7
Pyke Rd LN6 . . . . .204 D5
Pymoor La PE22 . . . . .113 B2
Pynder Cl LN4 . . . . .203 A2
Pyruss Dr HU4 . . . . .179 B2
Pytchley Wlk DN35 . . . . . . .192 E2

Q

QUADRING PE11 . . . . .145 A8
Quadring Bank PE11 . . . . . .144 E6
Quadring Cowley & Browns
 Prim Sch PE11 . . . . .135 A1
QUADRING EAUDIKE
 PE11 . . . . .145 C8

Quadring Rd
 Donington PE11 . . . . .134 F2
 Quadring PE11 . . . . .145 B7
Quaker La **7** Boston PE21 . .208 F4
 Spalding PE11 . . . . .214 A3
Quantock Cl
 7 Kingston upon Hull
  HU3 . . . . .180 D5
 1 Scunthorpe DN17 . . . .184 D8
 3 Thorne/Moorends DN8 . .15 A7
Quantock Ct **9** NG34 . . . . .212 B3
Quantock Gdns DN41 . . . . .23 E5
Quantock Rd DN33 . . . . . . .194 E8
QUARRINGTON NG34 . . . . .212 B1
Quarry La PE6 . . . . .173 C7
Quarry Rd LN11 . . . . .198 C4
Quarryside LN11 . . . . .198 B4
Quart La DN14 . . . . .6 D6
Quay La DN14 . . . . .6 C7
Quayside Ctr★ NG34 . . . . .212 E4
Quayside E **6** PE10 . . . . . . .213 E2
Quayside W **7** PE10 . . . . . .213 E2
Quays The DN21 . . . . .197 B5
Quebec Rd
 Mablethorpe/Sutton on Sea
  LN12 . . . . .64 B4
 Scunthorpe DN17 . . . . . . .184 E3
Queen Charlotte Ms **1**
 PE1 . . . . .226 A6
Queen Eleanor Ave NG31 . .210 C5
Queen Eleanor Prim Sch
 NG23 . . . . .79 B6
Queen Elizabeth Ave **3**
 DN18 . . . . .10 A7
Queen Elizabeth Gram Sch
 LN9 . . . . .199 A4
Queen Elizabeth Rd
 6 Humberston DN36 . . . . .36 C8
 Lincoln LN1 . . . . .201 D8
Queen Elizabeth's Grammar
 Alford LN13 . . . . .75 E2
Queen Elizabeth's High Sch
 The DN21 . . . . .197 C7
Queen Elizabeth St **1** LN8 .70 D5
Queen Elizabeth Way **33**
 DN18 . . . . .10 F8
Queen Headland La LN5 . . . .92 F1
Queen Mary Ave DN35 . . . . .192 C7
Queen Mary Ave Inf Sch
 DN32 . . . . .192 C7
Queen Mary Rd LN1 . . . . . .201 D8
Queen St PI **1** LN11 . . . . . .198 C5
Queen's Ave
 5 Barton-upon-Humber
  DN18 . . . . .3 F1
 Market Deeping PE6 . . . . .217 C6
 2 Spalding PE11 . . . . . . .157 B6
Queen's Bank PE12 . . . . . . .167 C5
Queensbury Way **2** HU14 . . .3 B6
Queens Cres DN17 . . . . .17 D6
Queen's Cres Lincoln LN1 . .201 D5
 15 Stainforth DN7 . . . . . .14 C6
Queens Ct **3** LN11 . . . . . . .198 D4
Queen's Ct **18** DN8 . . . . . . .15 A8
Queens Dock Ave **4** HU1 . .180 F6
Queens Dr **24** DN17 . . . . . . .16 D7
Queen's Dr PE25 . . . . .206 E8
Queen's Drive Infant Sch
 PE1 . . . . .226 A5
Queen's Dr W PE1 . . . . . . .226 A5
Queen's Est PE24 . . . . .102 C1
Queensfield
 Gainsborough DN21 . . . . .197 B7
 South Kelsey LN7 . . . . . . .32 A1
Queensgate Ctr PE1 . . . . . .226 A2
Queen's Gate St HU3 . . . . .180 B5
Queen's Gdns PE1 . . . . .226 A5
Queens Parade DN31 . . . . . .191 C7
Queen's Parade DN35 . . . . .192 F5
Queens Pk Cl **1** LN12 . . . . .64 C3
Queens Rd
 Immingham DN40 . . . . . . .187 A4
 8 Mablethorpe/Sutton on Sea
  LN12 . . . . .77 A8
 Peterborough PE2 . . . . . . .231 B7
 Skegness PE25 . . . . .206 B4
 Spalding PE11 . . . . .214 F5
Queen's Rd
 9 Barnetby le Wold DN38 . .21 B4
 1 Boston PE21 . . . . .209 A5
 Bourne PE10 . . . . .213 D6
 14 Heckington NG34 . . . .122 E2
 Newark-on-Trent NG24 . . .104 A5
Queen's Royal Lancers Mus
 The★ NG32 . . . . .138 C3
Queens St PE9 . . . . .219 B6
Queen St **6** Bardney LN3 . . .83 B4
 5 Bardney LN3 . . . . .83 C4
 Barton-upon-Humber DN18 . . .3 F1
 Boston PE21 . . . . .208 E5
 Bottesford NG13 . . . . . . .128 A6
 Brigg DN20 . . . . .196 C3
 4 Collingham NG23 . . . . .91 D5
 Epworth DN9 . . . . .27 E6
 Gainsborough DN21 . . . . .197 D3
 4 Grantham NG31 . . . . . .211 A3
 5 Grimsby DN32 . . . . . . .191 E8
 Horncastle LN9 . . . . .199 C3
 Kingston upon Hull HU1 . . .181 A5
 Kirton in Lindsey DN21 . . . .30 B1
 Lincoln LN5 . . . . .201 E1
 Louth LN11 . . . . .198 B5
 9 Market Rasen LN8 . . . . .57 D8
 2 Peterborough PE1 . . . .226 A2
 3 Scunthorpe DN16 . . . .183 C2

Queen St continued
Sleaford NG34 . . . . .212 C3
6 Spilsby PE23 . . . . .88 A1
17 Sutton Bridge PE12 . . . .160 E4
Thorne/Moorends DN8 . . .15 A8
15 Winterton DN15 . . . . .9 A5
20 Wisbech PE13 . . . . .170 D1
Yaxley PE7 . . . . .233 F6
Queen's View Cres DN16 . .185 D7
Queensway
Gainsborough DN21 . . . . .197 F4
1 Grantham NG31 . . . . . .211 E6
Grimsby DN37 . . . . .190 F8
1 Ingoldmells PE25 . . . . . .90 E3
Lincoln LN2 . . . . .202 E5
Long Sutton PE12 . . . . . .216 C6
Louth LN11 . . . . .198 E5
8 Mablethorpe/Sutton on Sea
LN12 . . . . .64 B4
Pointon & Sempringham
NG34 . . . . .143 B6
2 Potterhanworth LN4 . . . .82 B1
18 Ruskington NG34 . . . . .108 D2
21 Saxilby LN1 . . . . .66 D2
Scunthorpe DN16 . . . . . .185 C7
Skellingthorpe LN6 . . . . .200 A3
Sturton by Stow LN1 . . . . .66 C6
Queensway Ind Est DN17 .185 E6
Queens Wlk PE2 . . . . . . .230 E8
Queen's Wlk PE4 . . . . . . .219 A5
Queenswood Rd DN16 . . . .185 C3
Queen Victoria Sq HU1 . . .180 F6
Quibell Rd 8 NG24 . . . . . .104 A3
Quibell's La NG24 . . . . . . .104 A6
Quick La PE12 . . . . .168 A7
Quicksrt Drove PE7 . . . . .233 F3
Quilter Ave HU4 . . . . .179 B5
Quintin Cl LN4 . . . . .205 F1
Quinton Rd DN32 . . . . . . .191 E4
Quintus Pl LN6 . . . . .93 B8
Quorn Cl 7 PE6 . . . . .174 E4
Quorn Dr 5 LN6 . . . . .205 C8
Quorn Gdns 1 LN11 . . . . .198 D4
Quorn Mews 4 DN35 . . . . .192 E3
Quorum The HU4 . . . . . . .179 D3

R

Rabbithill La NG23 . . . . . . .78 D3
Racecourse Rd PE9 . . . . . .171 E3
Racecourse The
Bourne PE11 . . . . .214 A1
2 Spalding PE11 . . . . . . .156 E3
Race La DN39 . . . . .11 C3
Race Lane DN38 . . . . .21 C5
Rachel Cl DN21 . . . . .197 C7
Radcliffe Cl 5 PE9 . . . . . .219 B5
Radcliffe Ct PE25 . . . . . . .185 D8
Radcliffe Rd
7 Healing DN41 . . . . .24 A5
3 Stamford PE9 . . . . . . .219 B5
Raddle Way 8 NG24 . . . . .104 A2
Radford Cl PE8 . . . . .172 C1
RAF Digby Ops Mus ★
LN4 . . . . .108 A7
Ragdale Cl 2 PE1 . . . . . . .226 E7
RAGNALL NG22 . . . . .78 A8
Railway St 17 NG33 . . . . .151 D1
Railway La PE12 . . . . .160 E3
Railway Pk Cl 1 LN6 . . . . .201 D1
Railway Pk Mews LN6 . . . .201 D1
Railway Pl 4 DN31 . . . . . .189 B2
Railway St
Barnetby le Wold DN38 . . .21 B4
Grimsby DN32 . . . . .189 B1
Kingston upon Hull HU1 . .180 F5
Railway Terr
3 Grantham NG31 . . . . . .211 A3
5 Grimsby DN32 . . . . . . .191 D7
Railworld ★ PE3 . . . . . . .225 F1
RailWy Cl PE11 . . . . .214 D6
Rainsbutt Rd DN17 . . . . . . .6 C1
Rainton Ct 3 PE11 . . . . . .214 F4
Rainwall Ct 2 PE20 . . . . .136 A2
Rainwall's La PE20 . . . . . .136 A3
RAITHBY LN11 . . . . .60 F3
Raithby Ave 20 DN41 . . . . .23 A4
RAITHBY BY SPILSBY
PE23 . . . . .87 D2
Raithby Cross Roads PE23 .87 C2
Raithby Gr 6 DN33 . . . . . .191 A3
Raithby Hill PE23 . . . . .87 D1
Raithby Rd PE23 . . . . .87 D1
Raithby Road LN11 . . . . . . .61 A2
Rake Bridge Bank DN7 . . . .14 D2
Raleigh Ct 2 PE11 . . . . . .214 C2
Raleigh Dr HU9 . . . . .181 D6
Raleigh Way PE25 . . . . . . .225 B6
Ralph Brown Way 5 LN9 . .199 B2
Ralphs La PE20 . . . . .136 C7
Ramblers La DN18 . . . . . . .3 E1
Ram Bvd DN15 . . . . .182 E7
Ramper La LN1 . . . . .65 E4
Ramper Rd DN22 . . . . .52 B7
Ramper The 6 PE11 . . . . .156 E3
RAMPTON DN22 . . . . .65 A4
Rampton Rd DN22 . . . . . . .65 A4
Ramsay Cl PE25 . . . . .206 C1
Ramsden Ave 8 DN18 . . . . .10 E8
Ramsey Way PE2 . . . . . . .231 F6
Ramsgate LN11 . . . . .198 C6
Ramsgate Rd LN11 . . . . . .198 C6
Ramskir La DN7 . . . . .14 C7
RANBY LN8 . . . . .72 B5

Ranby Rd DN17 . . . . .184 E5
RAND LN8 . . . . .70 A5
Randall Bank PE12 . . . . . . .70 A5
Rand Farm Pk ★ LN8 . . . . .70 A5
Rand La LN8 . . . . .70 A5
Randolph Rd PE20 . . . . . .146 D7
Randsfield Ave 20 HU15 . . . .2 C5
Rangefield PE2 . . . . .229 E4
Rangell Gate PE12 . . . . . .157 B5
Range Rd LN11 . . . . .211 C5
Rangoon Way 4 PE10 . . . .213 E7
Ransom Ct 8 DN29 . . . . . .22 A6
Ransome Cl 7 NG24 . . . . .104 B4
Ransome Way 17 HU15 . . . .2 C6
Ranters Row 8 LN13 . . . . .75 F2
Ranville Cl 11 PE11 . . . . . .145 C1
Ranworth Rd 1 PE25 . . . . .206 D7
Ranyard La LN11 . . . . .72 E5
Rase La 5 LN8 . . . . .57 D8
Rasen Cl 3 LN8 . . . . .57 B8
Rasen Ct 2 PE1 . . . . .226 D3
Rasen La LN1 . . . . .234 A4
Rasen Rd Tealby LN8 . . . . .46 B1
Walesby LN8 . . . . .45 F1
Rasen Road LN7 . . . . .32 B1
Rason's Ct 8 PE21 . . . . . .209 A5
Rasper Rd Pools Nature
Reserve ★ DN40 . . . . . .186 A8
Rat Abbey DN40 . . . . .9 C4
Ratcliffe Ct 1 PE1 . . . . . .226 D7
Rathbone Cres PE3 . . . . . .225 E2
Rathkenny Cl PE12 . . . . . .215 E2
Rats Pen La LN11 . . . . .62 C1
Ratten Row PE22 . . . . . . .127 A5
Rauceby CE Sch NG34 . . . .120 E5
Rauceby Dro NG34 . . . . . .120 E7
Rauceby La NG34 . . . . . . .120 E7
Rauceby Sta NG34 . . . . . .120 F3
Rauceby Terr LN1 . . . . . . .234 A2
Ravel Cl PE9 . . . . .218 F6
Raven Cl 1 LN20 . . . . .19 D4
Ravencroft La 6 DN10 . . . . .40 A1
Ravendale 31 DN18 . . . . . . .10 F8
Ravendale Cl
Gonerby Hill Foot NG31 . . .211 A8
Holton le Clay DN36 . . . . .195 E1
Ravendale Dr LN2 . . . . . . .202 A7
Ravendale Rd
Cleethorpes DN35 . . . . . .193 A3
Gainsborough DN21 . . . . .197 E3
Ravendale St N 3 DN15 . . .183 B3
Ravendale St S DN15 . . . . .183 B3
Ravenhill DN35 . . . . .192 D3
Ravens Bank PE12 . . . . . .158 B2
Ravenscar Rd 5 DN37 . . . .188 A1
Raven's Dro PE12 . . . . . . .159 A3
Ravensfleet Rd DN21 . . . . . .40 C6
Raven's Gate Fleet PE12 . . .159 A3
Holbeach PE12 . . . . .158 E2
Ravensmoor Cl 4 LN6 . . . .204 E1
Ravenspurn Way DN31 . . . .191 D8
Raven St HU9 . . . . .181 D7
RAVENSTHORPE PE3 . . . . .225 C6
Ravensthorpe Prim Sch
PE3 . . . . .225 C7
Ravens View LN6 . . . . .92 A4
Ravenwood LN4 . . . . .203 A4
Rawcliffe Gr HU4 . . . . . . .179 D5
Rawling Way HU3 . . . . . . .180 C5
Rawlinson Ave 27 LN7 . . . .33 B3
Rawnsley Cl 18 LN13 . . . . .75 F2
Rawsons La PE21 . . . . . . .125 E5
Raybrook Cl 5 PE21 . . . . .208 E7
Raymond Mays Way PE10 . .213 D2
Raymond Rd DN16 . . . . . .185 C7
Rayner Ave PE2 . . . . .231 E5
Raysor's La PE22 . . . . . . .114 A2
Rayton Cl LN4 . . . . .203 A2
Raywell Cl 1 HU10 . . . . . .178 F7
Raywell Lane HU14 . . . . . . .3 B8
Raywell St HU2 . . . . .180 E7
Reaches The PE6 . . . . . . .175 C3
Read Cl 2 NG24 . . . . .104 C1
Reading Cl LN4 . . . . .203 E1
Reading Gate DN14 . . . . . . .6 C4
Reading Rm Yd 2 HU14 . . . .3 A4
Reads La 4 NG33 . . . . . . .151 D7
Read Way LN4 . . . . .207 D5
Reams Cl 4 PE21 . . . . . . .209 D4
Reapers Cl 1 PE12 . . . . . .215 B2
Reaper's Rise 20 DN9 . . . . .27 E6
Reaper's Way 8 DN9 . . . . . .27 D2
REASBY LN3 . . . . .69 C6
Reasby Rd LN3 . . . . .69 C7
Reckitt Dr HU14 . . . . .3 B6
Recreation Gd Rd DN7 . . . .219 B6
Recreation Rd 2 PE10 . . . .213 D5
Recto Ave DN32 . . . . .191 F5
Rectors Way 8 PE4 . . . . . .221 D2
Rectory Cl
1 Barrowby NG32 . . . . . .210 A5
2 Binbrook LN8 . . . . .47 C5
2 Fishtoft PE21 . . . . .126 C1
Potter Hanworth LN4 . . . . .95 B8
Rectory Gdns
2 Beckingham DN10 . . . . .40 A1
2 Glinton PE6 . . . . .220 C8
Peterborough PE7 . . . . . .233 F6
Rectory La Addlethorpe PE24 .90 C4
Barrowby NG32 . . . . .210 A5
Bottesford NG13 . . . . . . .128 A6
Claypole NG23 . . . . .117 F8
Etton PE6 . . . . .173 D5
3 Fulbeck NG32 . . . . . . .106 C1
Gainsborough DN21 . . . . . .52 F5
2 Gedney PE12 . . . . .159 D7

Rectory La continued
Glinton PE6 . . . . .220 C8
Harlaxton NG32 . . . . . . .139 C7
Leadenham LN5 . . . . . . .106 C2
2 Mareham le Fen PE22 . . .98 F4
North Witham NG33 . . . . .151 D4
4 Owmby LN8 . . . . .55 F6
2 Peakirk PE6 . . . . .174 A5
Stainton le Vale LN8 . . . . .46 D5
24 Waddington LN5 . . . . . .93 F7
Woolsthorpe by Belvoir
NG32 . . . . .138 D8
Rectory Lea DN21 . . . . .54 F4
Rectory Rd Anderby PE24 . . .76 F2
Boston PE21 . . . . .209 B3
Coleby LN5 . . . . .93 F3
Newton PE13 . . . . .170 B5
Ruskington NG34 . . . . . .108 D1
Tydd St Mary PE13 . . . . .160 B1
Rectory Road LN9 . . . . .85 D1
Rectory St Beckingham LN5 .105 B4
Epworth DN9 . . . . .27 E6
Red Barn La PE20 . . . . . . .136 B3
Redbourn Cl 2 DN16 . . . . .183 B1
REDBOURNE DN21 . . . . . . .30 F3
Redbourne Dr LN2 . . . . . . .202 A8
Redbourne Mere DN21 . . . . .30 E2
Redbourne Rd
Grimsby DN33 . . . . .191 B3
Hibaldstow DN20 . . . . . . .30 F4
Waddingham DN21 . . . . . .43 C7
Redbourn E Rd DN16 . . . . . .19 A6
Redbourne St
Kingston upon Hull HU3 . . .180 B5
1 Scunthorpe DN16 . . . . .183 C2
Redbourn Terr 4 PE21 . . . .208 F3
Redbourn Way DN16 . . . . .183 B2
Redbridge PE4 . . . . .220 E6
Red Cap La PE21 . . . . . . .208 E8
Redcar Cl LN6 . . . . .204 F4
Redcar Gr DN32 . . . . .192 A5
Redcliff Dr 22 HU14 . . . . . .3 A4
Redcliffe Rd NG31 . . . . . . .211 B7
Redcliff Rd
Kingston upon Hull HU13 . . .3 E4
Melton HU14 . . . . .2 F5
Redcombe La DN20 . . . . . .196 B4
Redcote Dr LN6 . . . . .204 F4
Redcot Gdns PE9 . . . . . . .219 B6
Redcross St NG31 . . . . . . .211 B5
Redfern Cl HU3 . . . . .180 D5
Redgate Ct 5 PE1 . . . . . . .226 E7
Redgate Rd LN2 . . . . .170 C8
Redhall Cl 9 DN3 . . . . .14 A2
Redhall Dr LN4 . . . . .205 F4
Red Hall Farm La LN4 . . . .205 F4
Redhill La LN8 . . . . .59 A8
Red Hill Nature Reserve ★
LN11 . . . . .72 E7
Red House Gdns 9 NG32 . .128 F7
Red La South Ferriby DN18 . . .9 F7
Welby NG32 . . . . .130 F5
Redland Cres 3 DN8 . . . . . .15 B8
Red Leas La LN11 . . . . .62 A8
Red Lion Sq 19 PE9 . . . . .219 B5
Red Lion St 3 Bicker PE20 .135 A4
6 Boston PE21 . . . . .208 F5
3 Spalding PE11 . . . . . . .214 D4
8 Stamford PE9 . . . . . . .219 B5
Redman Cl DN21 . . . . . . .197 E5
Redmile Cl Bourne PE10 . . .154 D5
Pinchbeck PE11 . . . . . . .214 C8
Red Mile La PE11 . . . . . . .214 C8
Redmile's La 2 PE9 . . . . . .171 A3
Redmile Wlk 5 PE1 . . . . . .226 D7
Red Rd LN8 . . . . .84 B8
Redshank Dr DN16 . . . . . .185 F5
Redshank Way PE7 . . . . . .230 C1
Redstone Ind Est PE21 . . . .208 E3
Redstone Rd PE21 . . . . . . .208 E3
Redthorne Cl 2 PE11 . . . . .214 F5
Redthorn Way NG23 . . . . . .117 F7
Redwing Cl
Peterborough PE2 . . . . . .231 E7
Skellingthorpe LN6 . . . . . .200 A3
Redwing Gr 1 LN6 . . . . . . .204 D8
Redwood Ave 11 NG34 . . . .212 D2
Redwood Ct DN16 . . . . . . .185 D3
Redwood Dr
Cleethorpes DN35 . . . . . .192 D2
Waddington LN5 . . . . . . .205 D1
Reedbush Ave 4 LN2 . . . . .202 F6
Reed Cl PE7 . . . . .230 C2
REEDHAM LN4 . . . . .111 C7
Reedham Garth HU4 . . . . .179 A3
Reedham La LN4 . . . . .207 F2
Reedings Cl NG32 . . . . . . .210 B5
Reedings Rd NG32 . . . . . . .210 B5
Reedland Way PE7 . . . . . . .230 C1
Reedmace Cl 8 PE6 . . . . . .174 E4
Reedmans Cl 5 PE6 . . . . . .164 F3
REED POINT LN4 . . . . .110 E2
Reed St 7 HU2 . . . . .180 E7
REEPHAM LN3 . . . . .203 F8
Reepham PE2 . . . . .229 D4
Reepham CE (Controlled)
Prim Sch LN3 . . . . .203 F8
Reepham Rd LN3 . . . . .82 A7
Reet 2 DN31 . . . . .189 B1
Reeves Way PE1 . . . . .226 B5
Refinery Rd DN16 . . . . . . .183 F2
Reform Pl 2 NG34 . . . . . . .212 C4
Reform St
9 Crowland PE6 . . . . . . .166 E1
Kingston upon Hull HU2 . . .180 F7

Reform St continued
Stamford PE9 . . . . .218 F5
Regal Gdns 2 NG33 . . . . . .162 E8
Regal Pl PE2 . . . . .231 A8
Regency Ct 13 DN18 . . . . . .3 E1
Regency Gdns NG31 . . . . .211 D5
Regency Way PE3 . . . . . . .225 E1
Regent Ave LN6 . . . . .200 C1
Regent Dr 18 DN17 . . . . . . .16 D7
Regent Gdns DN31 . . . . . .191 C5
Regent Rd LN12 . . . . .64 B4
Regent St Sh Arc DN32 . . .191 D7
Regents Cl
2 Collingham NG23 . . . . . .91 D4
3 Scunthorpe DN15 . . . . .183 A5
4 Skegness PE25 . . . . . .206 C1
Regents Pk Cl 7 LN6 . . . . .204 F1
Regent St PE11 . . . . .214 C3
Reginald Rd DN35 . . . . . . .182 F5
Regina Wlk 10 PE24 . . . . . .90 D7
Reindeer Cl LN9 . . . . .199 A4
Rein The DN9 . . . . .27 A2
Reldene Dr HU5 . . . . .179 B7
Rembrandt Way PE11 . . . . .214 B3
Remigius Gr LN2 . . . . .202 C7
Remple Ave 2 DN7 . . . . . . .15 A3
Remple Comm Rd DN7 . . . . .14 F2
Remple La 3 DN7 . . . . .15 A3
Renault Dr LN4 . . . . .205 F1
Rendel St DN31 . . . . .188 F1
Renew's Dro PE6 . . . . . . .166 D3
Renfrew Cl 2 LN5 . . . . . . .205 C2
Renfrew Dr NG34 . . . . . . .121 A2
Renfrew Rd LN5 . . . . .205 C2
Renton Cl HU5 . . . . .178 F5
Reporto Ave DN32 . . . . . . .191 F5
Repton Cl LN4 . . . . .203 D1
Repton Dr 2 DN16 . . . . . . .185 B3
Repton Rd 2 LN12 . . . . . . .64 B4
Repton St 7 LN12 . . . . .64 B4
Reservation NG34 . . . . . . .212 F7
Reservoir Rd PE11 . . . . . .145 F4
Reservoir St LN1 . . . . .234 A4
Resolute Cl 6 PE23 . . . . . .101 A8
Resolution Cl PE21 . . . . . .208 A4
Responso Ave DN32 . . . . . .191 F5
Reston Ct DN35 . . . . .193 A3
Reston Gr 4 DN33 . . . . . . .191 B4
Retief Cl LN1 . . . . .201 D8
Retief View LN1 . . . . .201 D8
Retreat The
Easton on the Hill PE9 . . . .171 C3
6 Maxey PE6 . . . . .173 C6
REVESBY PE22 . . . . .99 C3
Revesby Abbey PE22 . . . . . .99 C5
Revesby Ave Boston PE21 . .208 D4
Grimsby DN34 . . . . .190 F4
Scunthorpe DN16 . . . . . .185 A7
Revesby Bank
Carrington PE22 . . . . .99 B1
Revesby PE22 . . . . .112 B8
REVESBY BRIDGE PE22 . . . .99 C3
Revesby Cl Boston PE21 . . .208 D4
Lincoln LN6 . . . . .204 F6
Revesby Cnr 5 PE22 . . . . . .99 A4
Revesby Ct DN16 . . . . . . .185 A8
Revesby Dr PE25 . . . . .206 A4
Revigo Ave DN32 . . . . . . .191 F5
Revill Cl 5 Claypole NG23 . .117 E8
17 Scotter DN21 . . . . .29 C3
Reynard Ct DN21 . . . . .53 E3
Reynard St 3 PE23 . . . . . . .88 A1
Reynolds Cl 2 HU14 . . . . . . .2 F5
Reynolds Dr 1 LN6 . . . . . .205 B6
Reynolds Gdns 6 PE12 . . . .157 F7
Reynold's Paddock 2 LN5 . .93 A5
Reynolds Prim Sch DN35 . .192 D7
Reynolds St DN35 . . . . . . .192 D7
Rhine Ave 6 PE2 . . . . .230 E8
Rhodes Ave 2 NG34 . . . . . .212 C3
Rhodes St HU3 . . . . .179 F5
Rialto Ave DN32 . . . . .191 F5
Ribble St 4 HU3 . . . . .180 B4
Ribbon Pond Dr NG24 . . . .104 A2
Riber Cl 2 LN5 . . . . .210 E5
Ribes Cl 1 PE7 . . . . .230 D3
Ribston Cl 7 DN16 . . . . . . .185 A2
RIBY DN37 . . . . .23 C2
Riby Cl 3 DN21 . . . . .53 A7
Riby Cross Roads DN37 . . . .23 C3
Riby Ct DN36 . . . . .195 E2
Riby Rd Cabourne LN7 . . . . .33 D6
Keelby DN41 . . . . .23 A4
Scunthorpe DN17 . . . . . .184 E5
Stallingborough DN41 . . . .23 C4
Swallow LN7 . . . . .34 A7
Riby Sq DN31 . . . . .189 B1
Riby St DN31 . . . . .189 B1
Richard Busby Way 14
PE12 . . . . .160 A8
Richards Ave LN6 . . . . . . .204 F4
Richards Ct 13 NG34 . . . . .122 D3
Richardson Cl
Bourne PE10 . . . . .213 D7
18 Humberston DN36 . . . . .36 D8
Richardson Rise DN21 . . . .197 F3
Richard St DN31 . . . . .191 C8
Richard Young Cl 4
PE13 . . . . .170 D2
Richdale Ave 1 DN21 . . . . .30 B2
Richmond Ave PE4 . . . . . . .221 A2
Richmond Cl Boston PE21 . .209 A5
Caythorpe NG32 . . . . . . .119 B6
2 Newark-on-Trent NG24 . .104 A2
2 Sleaford NG34 . . . . . . .212 B2
Richmond Ct 1 PE25 . . . . .206 C2
Richmond Dr
Green Hill NG31 . . . . . . .210 E5
Lincoln LN6 . . . . .204 F3

Richmond Dr continued
Scunthorpe DN16 . . . . . . .185 C4
Skegness PE25 . . . . .206 C1
Richmond Leisure Complex
PE25 . . . . .206 B1
Richmond Rd
Cleethorpes DN35 . . . . . .192 C5
Gainsborough DN21 . . . . .197 F4
Grimsby DN34 . . . . .191 A6
Kingston upon Hull HU13 . .178 E2
Lincoln LN1 . . . . .201 D4
Louth LN11 . . . . .61 B8
10 Trusthorpe LN12 . . . . . .64 C1
Richmond Sch The PE25 . . .206 C2
Richmond Way PE13 . . . . . .170 B2
RIDDINGS DN17 . . . . .184 F4
Rider Gdns PE21 . . . . . . .209 D2
Rides The 7 PE6 . . . . .164 F3
Ridge Cl 14 LN2 . . . . .68 D6
Ridge View 2 Brigg DN20 . .196 D4
Ermine LN1 . . . . .201 D8
Fillingham DN21 . . . . .54 F4
Harmston LN5 . . . . .93 F4
Ridge View Rd LN4 . . . . . .205 F4
Ridgeway 13 LN2 . . . . .68 D2
Ridge Way
Peterborough PE2 . . . . . .231 B8
Scunthorpe DN17 . . . . . .182 E1
Ridgeway Rd HU5 . . . . . . .179 B7
Ridgeway The DN34 . . . . . .190 D3
Ridgewell Cl 10 LN6 . . . . .204 D8
Ridgewood Ave 14 DN3 . . . .14 A1
Ridgewood Dr 5 DN15 . . . . .8 A4
Ridings The Bourne PE10 . .213 C3
Kingston upon Hull HU5 . . .179 A8
Market Rasen LN8 . . . . . . .57 F7
17 North Ferriby HU14 . . . . .3 A4
Ridley Ave PE25 . . . . .206 D2
Rightwell E PE3 . . . . .225 A5
Rightwell E PE3 . . . . .225 A5
Rightwell W PE3 . . . . .225 A5
RIGSBY LN13 . . . . .75 D2
Rigsby Wood Nature
Reserve ★ LN13 . . . . . . .75 C3
Rigsmoor Cl 2 LN6 . . . . . . .93 C8
Rileston Pl DN16 . . . . .185 B2
Riley Cl
Bracebridge Heath LN4 . . .205 F1
Yaxley PE7 . . . . .233 D6
Riley Wy HU3 . . . . .179 F7
Rimac Rd LN11 . . . . .51 D2
Rimes La DN22 . . . . .65 A7
Rime's La LN10 . . . . .98 C6
Rimington Rd 4 PE21 . . . . .126 C1
Ringers La PE13 . . . . .170 B2
Ring Beck La HU15 . . . . . . .2 A8
Ring Moor Cl 7 LN4 . . . . . .109 F5
Ringrose La HU10 . . . . . . .178 E6
Ringrose St HU3 . . . . .179 F5
Ringstead Rd PE4 . . . . . . .221 D1
Ringstone Chase PE10 . . . .142 F1
Ringwood Rd PE3 . . . . .224 F3
Ringwood Cl
4 Birchwood LN6 . . . . . .200 D1
1 Scunthorpe DN16 . . . . .185 B4
Rinks La LN5 . . . . .92 E1
Rinovia Dr DN33 . . . . .191 A3
Rio Dr NG23 . . . . .91 D5
Ripley Cl DN15 . . . . .182 B2
Ripley Dr LN6 . . . . .205 A3
Riplingham Rd HU10 . . . . .178 A8
Ripon Cl
1 Bracebridge Heath LN4 . . .81 A7
Grantham NG31 . . . . . . .210 F3
Peterborough PE2 . . . . . .220 F3
Scunthorpe DN17 . . . . . .184 C7
11 Skegness PE25 . . . . . .206 D7
Ripon Dr NG34 . . . . .212 C6
Ripon Pl 17 LN12 . . . . .64 B3
Ripon St Grimsby DN31 . . .191 C8
Lincoln LN5 . . . . .201 F1
Ripon Way HU9 . . . . .181 C8
RIPPINGALE PE10 . . . . . . .142 F2
Rippingale Rd PE10 . . . . . .142 D2
Rippons Dro PE6 . . . . .217 E2
RISBY LN8 . . . . .46 B3
Risby Dr PE3 . . . . .225 B8
Risby Gn LN6 . . . . .204 F7
Risby Rd DN15 . . . . .9 A1
Risdale 28 LN7 . . . . .33 B4
RISEGATE PE11 . . . . .144 F4
Risegate Rd PE11 . . . . . . .144 F4
RISEHOLME PE2 . . . . .229 E3
Riseholme Cl LN2 . . . . .68 A2
Riseholme Coll LN1 . . . . . . .67 E4
Riseholme La LN2 . . . . .67 F2
Riseholme Rd
Gainsborough DN21 . . . . .197 F3
Lincoln LN2 . . . . .201 D4
Rise The
16 Navenby/Wellingore
LN5 . . . . .107 A8
8 North Ferriby HU14 . . . . .3 A5
Scunthorpe DN17 . . . . . .184 E3
South Ferriby DN18 . . . . . .10 A8
Risewood La NG33 . . . . . .130 F5
Riston St HU3 . . . . .180 C5
Rivan Gr DN33 . . . . .194 D7
Rivehall Ave 7 LN2 . . . . . . .68 D2
Rivelin Cres DN16 . . . . . . .185 A8
Rivelin Pl DN16 . . . . .185 A8
Rivelin Rd DN16 . . . . .185 A7
Rivendale PE4 . . . . .220 F2
River Bain Rd LN8 . . . . .72 C8
River Bank PE12 . . . . .214 C1
Riverbank Cl Althorpe DN17 .17 D5
Chapel Hill LN4 . . . . .110 C5
Guyhirn PE13 . . . . .177 F2

Riverbank Cl continued
Market Deeping PE6......217 E3
Riverbank Rise 17 DN18.....3 E1
Riverbank Studios ★ PE11 214 E4
River Ct 20 PE11.........214 D4
Riverdale 8 LN2..........68 D2
Riverdale Rd DN16.......185 A7
Rivergate
3 Peterborough PE1.....226 A1
5 Spalding PE11.........214 D2
Rivergate Sh Ctr PE1....226 A1
River Gr HU4............179 E3
Riverhead LN11..........198 D7
Riverhead Rd LN11.......198 D6
Riverhead Terr LN11.....198 D7
River La Anwick NG34....109 B1
Deeping St James PE6...174 B7
Keddington LN11.........198 D7
Moulton PE12............158 A8
Peterborough PE3........225 F2
River Mdw DN20..........196 A2
Rivermead LN6...........205 C4
Rivermead Cl LN6........205 C4
River Rd West Burton DN22..52 D4
West Walton PE14........170 C4
Riverside 2 Brigg DN20...196 A3
Grantham NG31...........211 B4
Market Deeping PE6......217 D4
5 Scotter DN21..........29 C4
2 Spalding PE11.........214 B5
Riverside App DN21......197 C5
Riverside Cl
14 Bottesford DN13......128 A6
12 Sleaford NG34........212 D4
Riverside Ct Louth LN11..198 D6
South Field HU13........3 E4
Riverside Dr
Humberston DN35........193 C2
Lincoln LN5.............234 A1
Riverside Gdns
Parson Drove PE13.......177 C7
Peterborough PE3........225 D1
Riverside Ind Est PE21...209 A2
Riverside Mead PE2......231 B8
Riverside Pk
Grantham NG31...........211 B6
Spalding PE11...........214 E2
Riverside Pk Homes PE11 208 E4
Riverside Rise LN11......198 D7
Riverside Spinney PE8....222 A4
Riverside The 11 NG34....212 D4
Riverside Wlk
8 Bottesford DN13.......128 A6
Grantham NG31...........211 B4
River Terr 4 PE13........170 C1
Riverton Cl LN1..........201 D8
Riverton View LN1.......201 D8
Riverview
Church Laneham DN22....65 B4
Long Bennington NG23...117 D4
River View
21 Barton-upon-Humber
DN18..................10 F1
Northfield HU13.........178 F1
Riverview Ave HU14.......3 A4
River Way PE21..........209 C2
Roadwood La NG23........78 F8
Robden Ct PE2...........225 E1
Roberta Cl 10 PE25......206 A4
Robert Ave PE1..........225 F8
Robert Barnett Cl 6
HU13...................178 E2
Robert Cl DN40..........186 B4
Robert Dukeson Ave
NG24...................104 A6
Robert Rayner Cl PE2....230 D6
Robert's Field Nature
Reserve ★ PE9..........162 F5
Robert's Gr PE25........206 D7
Robertson Ave 6 NG34...121 B8
Robertson Cl 14 LN5.....93 F7
Robertson Dr NG34.......212 D5
Robertson Rd
3 Grantham NG31........210 F5
Lincoln LN6.............204 E1
Roberts St DN32.........192 A8
Robert St DN15..........183 A3
Robert Tressell Wlk 2
LN2....................202 C7
Robey St LN5............205 E8
Robin Cl Bottesford DN16 185 B2
8 Market Deeping PE6...217 F4
12 Sleaford NG34........212 B3
Robin Hood Cl PE3.......224 F2
Robin Hood Cres 13 DN3...14 A1
Robin Hood Rd
11 Kirk Sandall DN3.....14 A1
Skegness PE25...........206 C3
Robin Hood's Wlak PE21..208 F2
Robin Hood's Wlk PE21...208 F6
Robins Cl PE2...........230 E8
Robins Cres LN6.........92 D5
Robins Field PE8........222 A4
Robinson Ave 4 LN13.....75 E2
Robinson Cl DN15........182 E4
Robinson La
Grimsby DN31............189 C2
Louth LN11..............198 C5
Robinson Pl LN5.........105 F5
Robinson Rd DN40........186 F6
Robinson St E DN32......191 E7
Robinson's Gr 8 DN20....31 A5
Robinson's La 1 DN36....36 B1
Robins Wood PE8.........222 A4
Robin Wlk DN37..........24 B5
Robson Rd DN35..........192 D7
Rochdale Rd DN16........185 A5
Rochester Ave HU4.......179 B3

Rochester Cl
8 Bracebridge Heath LN4...81 A2
2 Scunthorpe DN17.......184 C7
Rochester Ct
2 Bourne PE10...........213 C7
Humberston DN35.........193 A1
Rochester Dr
Birchwood LN6...........200 D2
9 Grantham NG31.........210 E5
Rochford Cres PE21......209 B5
Rochford Twr ★ PE21.....209 E5
Rochford Twr La PE21....209 D6
Rockbourne Pl PE4.......225 E8
Rocket La DN9...........27 C4
Rockingham Cl 8 PE6.....217 A6
Rockingham Cres DN34...190 D4
Rockingham Ct 9 DN34...190 D4
Rockingham Gr PE4......221 A2
Rockingham Rd 4 PE9....218 A5
Rockley Ct HU10.........178 F6
Rock Rd Peterborough PE1 225 F6
Stamford PE9............219 B5
Rock The NG32...........138 B4
Roden Wy 2 PE7..........230 F5
Rod Mill Rd DN16........183 E1
Rodney Cl 9 HU2.........180 E8
Roeburn Wy PE11.........214 A4
Roegate La PE12.........159 F1
Roeze Cl 14 LN10........97 C5
Rogues Alley PE13.......177 C4
Rokeby Ave HU4..........179 B5
Rokeby Cl HU4...........179 B5
Rokeby Mews HU4........179 B5
Rokeby Pk HU4...........179 B5
Rokeby Pk Prim Sch HU4..179 B5
Rolleston Cl 3 LN2......201 F7
Rolleston Garth PE1.....226 C8
Rollitt Cl HU10.........178 F5
Rolls Cl PE7............233 E7
Roman Bank Bourne PE10..213 E4
Chapel St Leonards PE24..90 E8
Holbeach PE12...........215 D8
Huttoft PE24............77 C4
1 Ingoldmells PE25......206 D8
Moulton PE12............146 E2
Newton PE13.............170 B4
6 Skegness PE25.........206 C3
Spalding PE11...........214 F6
Stamford PE9............219 A5
Roman Cl
9 Metheringham LN4.....95 D4
Navenby LN5.............107 B8
Roman Dr PE8............222 D2
Roman Pavement LN2.....202 C4
Roman Rd Moulton PE12...157 D1
Panton LN8..............71 B5
Scawby DN20.............30 D8
Roman Way
7 Ancaster NG32.........120 A2
Auborn Haddington & South
Hykeham LN5............93 A4
Horncastle LN9..........199 D3
Riddings DN17...........184 F6
Roman Wharf LN1.........201 C3
Roman Wy LN7............33 A3
Romany Gdns PE2.........231 D5
Roma Rd PE7.............231 C4
Romney Cl 3 LN6.........205 B6
Romney Ct 6 NG34.....212 D5
Romney Dr LN6...........205 B5
Romsey Ct DN34..........190 D5
Romulus Way 13 LN6......93 B8
Ronald Cl 3 PE25........206 C4
Rood's La PE12..........157 C8
Rookery Ave
2 Grimsby DN33..........191 D3
Sleaford NG34...........212 B3
Rookery Cl LN11.........198 D8
Rookery Croft 14 DN9....27 E6
Rookery La Ancaster NG32 119 F2
13 Leasingham NG34.....121 B7
Lincoln LN6.............205 C6
Wildmore LN4............111 E2
Wymondham LE14.........150 B1
Rookery Rd 2 Bicker PE20 135 A4
16 Healing DN41.........23 F5
Sutton Bridge PE12......160 D7
Rookery The
14 Collingham NG23......91 D5
Peterborough PE2........229 C7
2 Scawby DN20..........30 F8
Yaxley PE7..............233 D5
Rooklands 10 DN21.......29 C3
Rook's La LN10..........39 F6
Roosdyke La PE22........137 D7
Roper's Bridge La PE20..136 A4
2 Lutton PE12...........160 A8
Roper's La PE12.........159 D1
Ropery La PE12.........159 D1
Ropery Rd DN21..........197 B7
Ropery St Grimsby DN32..191 F7
Kingston upon Hull HU3...180 D4
Ropery The LN1..........234 A3
Ropewalk 6 LN8..........70 D5
Ropewalk Gall ★ DN18....3 F1
Ropewalk The
1 Caistor LN7...........33 B4
2 Colsterworth NG33.....151 E6
Rope Wlk Lincoln LN6....234 A2
15 Thorne/Moorends DN8..15 A8
ROPSLEY NG33............131 B1
Ropsley CE Prim Sch
NG33...................131 A1
Ropsley Rd NG33.........140 E8
Rosaire Pl DN33.........195 A8
Rosalind Ave DN34.......191 B7
Rosamond St 7 HU3.......180 B4

Rose Ave PE2............231 C7
Rosebank DN21...........197 B7
Roseberry Ave
26 Hatfield DN7.........14 D4
Skegness PE25...........206 D1
Rosebery Ave Boston PE21 208 C5
Lincoln LN1.............201 D4
Rose Cottage Gdn Ctr &
Tropical Forest ★ LN1...156 D8
Rose Cottage La LN5.....94 A3
Rose Cres PE12..........158 D3
Rosedale Scunthorpe DN17 184 E2
Waltham DN37............194 C5
Rosedale Cl
Cherry Willingham LN3...203 E5
4 Lincoln LN6..........204 F3
Rosedale Dr NG31........211 B8
Rosedale Gr HU5.........179 D7
Rosefield Cl 27 NG24....104 C1
Rosefields DN21.........197 B5
Rosegar Ave PE20........135 F2
Rosegarth St 4 PE21.....208 F4
Rose Gdns DN40..........186 C4
Rose Gr 1 PE25..........206 D5
Rosehill Cl 6 LN1.......66 D2
Rosehip Rd 8 PE10.......154 D2
Rose La
Beesby with Saleby LN13..75 F5
Pinchbeck PE11..........156 E8
4 Westwoodside DN9.....27 A2
Rose Leigh Way PE11.....214 C2
Rosemary Ave
Grimsby DN34............190 F6
11 Market Deeping PE6...217 C5
Rosemary Cres NG31.....210 E1
Rosemary Gdns
12 Bourne PE10..........213 C6
Peterborough PE1........225 F8
Rosemary La LN2.........234 B2
Rosemary Rise NG33.....141 D5
Rosemary Way DN35......192 E1
Rose Mdws.............208 B4
Rosemount Dr DN16......185 B6
Rosemount Grange HU13..178 C3
Rosemount La 5 DN21....43 D7
Rose Pl PE21............209 A3
Roseum Cl LN6..........204 E5
Roseveare Ave DN31......191 A7
Roseway 6 DN21.........197 D5
Rose Wlk Scunthorpe DN15 183 C3
Upton DN21.............53 D5
11 Wisbech PE13........170 C1
Wittering PE9...........172 B1
Rosewood Cl
12 Beacon Hill NG24....104 A5
2 Birchwood LN6........204 C8
4 Rosewood DN16........179 B7
Rosewood Dr 5 NG34.....212 D2
Rosewood Way
Hampton Hargate PE7....230 F2
1 Scunthorpe DN16......185 B3
Rosey Row 4 HU9.........181 C7
Rosina Gr N 2 DN32......192 B6
Rosina Gr S 4 DN32......192 B6
Roslyn Rd HU3...........179 E7
Rosmead St HU9..........181 D8
Rosner Dr HU13..........178 B2
Rosper Rd DN40..........186 A8
Rosper Road Pools Nature
Reserve ★ DN40.........186 A8
Rossall Cl
9 Mablethorpe/Sutton on Sea
LN12..................77 A7
Scunthorpe DN16.........185 C3
Rossa Rd LN13...........76 D7
Ross Cl
5 Coddington NG24......104 D5
St Giles LN2............202 D6
Ross Dr PE9.............218 E2
Rossetti St LN11........211 E5
Rossington Cl
18 Metheringham LN4....95 C4
28 Sandilands LN12......77 A8
Ross La 6 DN15..........9 B5
Ross Rd DN31............189 D1
Rostrop Rd LN4..........95 C7
Rosyth Ave PE7..........229 D3
Rothbart Way PE7........230 C3
Rothbury Rd DN17........184 F7
Rotherby Gr 3 PE3.......226 E7
Rotherham Cl PE21.......208 B4
Rothschild Cl PE21......208 B4
Rothwell Ave 8 DN33....191 B3
Rothwell Cl DN21........197 E4
Rothwell Lane LN7.......34 B1
Rothwell Rd Cabourne LN7..33 C3
4 Lincoln LN2..........201 F7
Scunthorpe DN15.........182 D4
Rothwell Road LN7.......34 A3
Rothwell Way PE2........230 C3
Rotten Row
Pinchbeck PE11..........156 E8
Theddlethorpe St Helen LN12 63 E5
Rotton Sykes La DN15....1 F2
Rotunda The 8 DN10......52 B8
ROUGHTON LN10...........98 B7
Roughton Ct 5 LN2.......202 A8
ROUGHTON MOOR LN10.....98 A7
Roughton Moor Wood Nature
Reserve ★ LN10.........97 F6
Roughton Rd LN10........98 B6
Roundhouse Cl PE1.......226 D3
Roundlands PE20.........136 D2
Roundway Grimsby DN34...191 B4
2 Immingham DN40.......186 C3
Roundway The HU4........179 C5

Rous Ct PE6.............164 E5
Routland Cl 8 LN8.......70 D4
Roval Dr DN40...........186 A4
Rowan Ave
Peterborough PE1........226 C6
Spalding PE11...........214 E5
Rowan Cl
6 Barrow upon Humber
DN19..................11 C8
7 Keelby DN41..........23 A4
10 Wisbech PE13........170 E1
Rowan Cres DN16.........185 C3
Rowan Ct
34 Chapel St Leonard PE24..90 D7
5 Goxhill DN19.........12 A8
11 Heighington/Washingborough
LN4...................203 D1
Rowan Dr
5 Healing DN41.........23 F5
Humberston DN36.........36 D8
Silk Willoughby NG34....121 B2
Rowan Rd Lincoln LN6....204 F3
Waddington LN5..........205 D1
Rowans The
Gainsborough DN21.......197 F5
Holbeach PE12...........159 A7
9 Nettleham LN2........68 C2
New Waltham DN36........195 E6
4 Westwoodside DN9.....27 A2
Rowan Way
1 Boston PE21..........209 A7
Bourne PE10.............213 A6
6 Metheringham LN4.....95 C4
Rowanwood Dr 7 NG31....210 F7
Rowan Wy NG24..........104 A3
Rowdyke Rd PE21.........136 F7
Rowe Ave PE2............230 D7
Rowgate Rd LN11.........73 A5
Rowland Ct 1 PE4.......220 F5
Rowland Rd DN16.........183 B2
Rowland St 3 DN31......189 B2
Rowlandson St 3 DN31...189 B2
Rowland Way PE25........206 A4
Rowledge Ct PE4.........221 A1
Rowley Rd PE21..........209 A4
Rowmills Rd 2 DN16......185 C8
Rowston Cl LN2..........201 C6
Rowston St DN35.........193 A5
Roxborough Cl LN6.......200 E2
Roxburgh Dr NG34........121 A3
Roxburgh Rd PE9.........218 F6
Roxburgh St 1 HU5......180 B8
Roxby Cl LN6............204 F6
Roxby Csway DN15.......9 C4
Roxby Rd DN15...........8 F4
Roxholm Cl 2 NG34......108 D1
Roxholme Rd
Leasingham NG34........121 B8
Ruskington NG34.........108 C2
Roxton Ave DN41.........23 A5
Roxton Hall Dr 15 HU14...3 A5
Roxton La DN40..........23 A6
Roxton Rd DN40..........23 A7
Royal Air Force Coll The
NG34...................120 B8
Royal Arthur Cl 5 PE25..206 C1
Royal Cl 16 PE12........160 E4
Royal Ct DN35...........193 B1
Royal Mews PE11.........180 C6
Royal Oak Ct
13 Heckington NG34.....122 E3
19 Louth LN11..........198 B5
Royal Oak La
1 Auborn Haddington & South
Hykeham LN5............93 A5
Martin LN4..............96 C2
Royal St DN31...........189 A2
Royal Standard Ct PE12..216 D3
Royalty Bank PE22.......101 B3
Royal Way PE21..........209 F2
Royce Cl PE7............233 E6
Royce Rd
Peterborough PE1........226 D3
2 Spalding PE11........214 F6
Roydon Gr LN6..........205 B6
Royle Cl PE2............230 C5
Royston Ave PE2.........230 C6
Ruards La DN19..........5 A1
RUCKLAND LN11...........73 F5
Ruckland Ave LN1........201 E7
Rudd Cl PE1.............226 C1
Rudgard Ave LN3.........203 E6
Rudgard La LN1..........234 A3
Rudham Ave DN32........191 E4
Rudkin Dr 5 NG34.......212 D6
Rudyard Cl 7 LN12......77 A7
Rudyard Gr PE4..........221 C3
Rue de L'yonne 1 NG23...91 D5
Rue de Nozay 3 DN20....19 E4
Rufford Gn 2 LN6........205 C8
Rufford Rd DN35.........192 E4
Rugby Ct 1 NG31........211 B3
Rugby Rd
4 Mablethorpe/Sutton on Sea
LN12..................64 B4
Scunthorpe DN16.........185 A8
Rugby St 5 HU3.........180 B4
Rumbold La 3 PE21......102 D1
Runcorn Garth HU4......179 B3
Runcorn Rd LN6.........204 B5
Running Post La PE20....135 C4
Runswick Cl LN6.........205 A3
Runswick Ct DN32........192 B6
Runswick Rd DN32........192 B6
Runway La DN36..........195 C4
Rupert Rd 1 DN33.......191 D3

Rural Ave PE11..........144 D1
Rushcliffe Rd NG31......211 A7
Rushes The 18 DN18......3 F1
Rush Furlong Nature
Reserve ★ DN9..........27 E3
Rushmere PE2............229 F6
Rushmoor Ctry Pk ★ LN11..61 F8
Rushton Ave PE4.........220 E4
Rushtons Way 12 DN20....30 F5
Rushy Dro PE1...........145 C8
Rushy La DN7............14 B8
Ruskin Ave LN2..........202 B6
Ruskin Gn LN2...........202 B6
RUSKINGTON NG34.........108 E2
Ruskington Cl DN37......188 A2
Ruskington Sta NG34.....108 E1
Ruskin Rd 13 LN12......64 B4
Ruskin St
2 Gainsborough DN21....197 D2
Kingston upon Hull HU3...180 B6
Russell Ave Lincoln LN6..93 C8
Newark-on-Trent NG24....104 A2
Russell Cl
8 Scunthorpe DN15......183 A5
12 Thorney PE6.........176 A3
Russell Cres NG34.......212 F4
Russell Ct DN35.........193 A1
Russell Dr 2 PE12......167 B8
Russell Hill PE8........222 A6
Russell Rd 7 NG34......121 B8
Russell Read Almshouses 13
NG31...................211 A4
Russell St
Kingston upon Hull HU2...180 E7
Lincoln LN5.............205 D6
Peterborough PE1........225 F3
32 Wisbech PE13........170 C1
Russell Wlk 2 DN17......29 D7
Russet Cl 4 DN15........182 C5
Russet Dr LN11..........198 C4
Russet La DN20..........196 F6
Rustic Ave PE7..........233 B8
Rustic La DN31..........41 C6
Ruston Rd NG31..........211 F7
Ruston Way LN6..........201 D3
Ruther Cl 2 PE2........230 F8
Rutland Ave
3 Newark-on-Trent
NG24...................104 A3
Waddington LN5..........93 E8
Rutland Cl 13 NG33......151 E2
Rutland Dr DN36.........195 C5
Rutland La 14 LN15......128 A5
Rutland Rd
Kingston upon Hull HU5...179 E8
25 Mablethorpe/Sutton on Sea
LN12..................63 B3
Scunthorpe DN16.........185 D7
Skegness PE25...........206 D3
Stamford PE9............219 D7
Rutland St 2 DN32......189 D1
Rutland Terr PE9........219 A4
Rutland Way Ryhall PE9...163 C1
15 Scampton Airfield LN1..67 E5
Rycroft Ave PE6.........217 F5
Rycroft Cl
1 Deeping St James PE6..217 F4
5 Market Deeping PE6...217 F4
Rycroft St NG31.........211 B3
Rydal Ave DN33..........194 D7
Rydal Cl LN6............200 D2
Rydal Ct PE4............221 C3
Ryde Ave NG31..........210 A4
Rye Cl NG34.............212 E3
Rye Cres 3 HU15........2 D5
Ryecroft LN5............205 D2
Rye Ct DN33............191 B1
Rydale 6 HU15..........2 D6
Rydale Ave 1 DN15......9 A6
Rydale Cl NG31..........211 B8
Ryefield PE6............164 E3
Ryefield La PE12........159 B3
Rye La LN13.............75 D5
RYHALL PE9..............163 C1
Ryhall CE Prim Sch PE9..163 C1
Ryhall Rd
Great Casterton PE9.....171 C8
Stamford PE9............219 D5
Ryhall Rd Ind Est PE9...219 D8
Ryland Bridge LN2.......68 E6
Ryland Gdns 10 LN2......68 D6
Ryland Rd LN2...........68 D6
Rymac Cres PE25.........90 E4
Rymer Pl DN35...........193 A4
Ryton Rd PE21...........208 B3

S

Sable Cl HU4............179 C2
Sabre Way PE1...........226 F4
Sackville Cl DN40.......186 D4
Sackville Rd DN40.......186 D4
Sackville St 2 DN31.....171 C7
Sacred Heart RC Prim Sch
PE3....................225 A5
Sacrewell Farm & Ctry Ctr ★
PE8....................222 C5
Sacrewell Lodge Sch
Wansford PE8............222 A6
Wansford PE8............222 A6
Saddleback Rd
Skidbrooke with Saltfleet Haven
LN11..................51 A3

Saddleback Rd continued
South Cockerington LN11.....50 E1
Saddle Ct PE4...........225 E8
Saddle Dr PE10..........154 C6
Saddle Row NG34........120 B8
Saddlers Cl Glinton PE6....220 D8
Osbournby NG34............132 D5
Saddler's Cl 11 LN4........95 C4
Saddlers Mead 10 PE11....214 A2
Saddlers Way
Fishtoft PE21.............209 C2
5 Long Sutton PE12.....216 B5
9 Middle Rasen LN8.......57 E7
Saddler's Way 2 DN9.....27 D3
Saddlers Wy 13 LN8........57 E7
Sadler Cl 9 PE25........206 C1
Sadler Rd LN6...........204 B5
Saffrondale HU10........178 E2
Saffron Dr PE7...........233 B8
Saffron Wlk 12 PE10......213 C5
Sage Ct Boultham LN6.....205 D8
Lincoln LN5.............205 D8
Sagefield Cl 5 DN33......194 D8
Sage's La PE2...........225 C8
Sail Cl PE21............208 C4
Sailors Wharf HU9.......181 C6
Sainsbury Way HU4.......179 A1
St Abbs Cl 3 HU9........181 A5
St Aiden's Rd 5 LN6......204 E2
St Albans Ave DN31......191 A8
St Albans Cl
5 Grantham NG31.......210 D5
16 Hibaldstow DN20......30 F5
3 Scunthorpe DN17......184 C7
St Alban's Dr 16 PE6......175 A1
St Andrews NG31........211 D7
St Andrews Ave 2 DN17...184 F2
St Andrews CE Prim Sch
LN10..................97 C6
St Andrews Cl LN5.......201 F1
St Andrew's Cl
4 Helpringham NG34....133 D7
Redbourne DN21..........30 F3
St Andrew's Com Prim Sch
HU10.................178 C7
St Andrew's Cres 6 NG34 121 B7
St Andrews Ct
Immingham DN40........186 A4
4 Timberland LN4.......96 C1
St Andrews Dr
6 Saxilby LN1...........66 C2
4 Woodhall Spa LN10....97 D6
St Andrew's Dr
1 Burton upon Stather
DN15..................8 B4
Grimsby DN32...........192 B4
Lincoln LN6............205 C8
Skegness PE25..........206 D5
St Andrew's Gdns LN6....205 C8
St Andrews Gr 33 DN7.....14 D4
St Andrews La DN40......186 B5
St Andrew's Mount HU10..178 C8
St Andrew's Pl 3 LN5.....234 B1
St Andrews Rd
2 Mablethorpe/Sutton on Sea
LN12..................64 B4
Northborough PE6.......217 E1
St Andrew's Rd
6 Butterwick PE22......126 E3
Spalding PE11...........214 C1
St Andrew's St
8 Heckington NG34......122 E3
16 Kirton in Lindsey DN21...30 B1
4 Lincoln LN5..........234 B1
St Andrew's Way
8 Barnby Dun DN3........14 A3
Epworth DN9.............27 E7
4 RAF Cranwell NG34...120 C8
St Andrews Wlk 5 LN10....97 C5
St Annes Ave 8 LN11......50 F7
St Anne's CE (Cont) Prim Sch
NG31.................211 C3
St Annes Cl Lincoln LN2...202 B4
Skegness PE25..........206 C6
3 Sleaford NG34........212 C6
4 Spalding PE11........214 C4
St Anne's Com Specl Sch
HU15..................2 E5
St Anne's Rd
9 Keelby DN41..........23 A5
Lincoln LN2............202 B4
St Anne's St NG31.......211 C3
St Annes Way PE25.......214 C6
St Anne's Wlk 13 HU15....2 D6
St Ann's Ave DN34.......191 B6
St Ann's La PE21.........208 F3
St Anns Wharf 1 PE21....208 F3
St Aubins Cres LN4.......81 F4
St Audrey Cl PE2........231 D6
St Augustine Ave DN32....191 E5
St Augustine Cres DN16...185 B5
St Augustine Rd LN2......202 F6
**Saint Augustine's Cath Vol
Acad The** PE9..........219 C7
St Augustines CE Jun Sch
PE2...................230 F8
St Augustine's CE Sch
PE13.................170 D2
St Augustine's Wlk PE2....230 E8
**St Augustine Webster Cath
Vol Acad** DN15.........182 D4
St Augustin Way NG31....211 A4
St Barbara's Cres 7 DN15..8 B4
St Barnabas CE Prim Sch
DN38..................21 B4

St Barnabas Ct 4 HU3....180 C4
St Barnabas Dr 1 HU14....3 C7
St Barnabas Rd DN38......21 B4
St Bartholomews CE Prim Sch
PE11.................156 A8
St Bartholomew's Cl 4
DN41..................23 A4
St Bede Ct HU4..........179 E5
St Bedes Cath Vol Acad
DN16.................185 B6
St Bee's Dr 19 PE6.......175 A1
St Benedict Cl 18 PE6.....166 F1
St Benedict's Cl 2 PE6....220 D8
St Benedict's Ct 2 LN6....204 D2
St Benedicts Sq LN5......234 A2
St Benet's Gdns 2 PE6....175 A1
**St Bernadettes Cath Prim Vol
Acad** DN16............185 C6
St Bernards Ave LN11......198 D6
St Bernards Cl LN11.......198 E6
St Bernard's Cl 13 DN20....19 E4
St Bernard's La LN11......198 E5
St Botolph La PE2........230 C6
St Botolphs CE Prim Sch
Peterborough PE2.......230 B6
Sleaford NG34..........212 B3
St Botolphs Cl 2 LN1......66 D3
St Botolph's Cres 5 LN5...205 E8
St Botolphs Ct 16 LN5.....205 E8
St Botolphs Gate LN1......66 D3
St Botolphs Infants Sch
LN5...................205 D8
St Botolphs Mews 31
PE21.................208 F5
St Botolphs Rd 7 NG34....212 C6
St Botolph's Rd DN16......185 C7
St Botolph's Way PE6.....176 A2
St Catherine Ct PE12......215 F3
St Catherines 15 LN5......205 E8
St Catherines Cres DN16..185 A4
St Catherines Ct
Ashby DN16............185 D6
Grimsby DN34..........190 F6
St Catherine's Ct LN5.....205 D7
St Catherine's Dr 3 DN7...14 C2
St Catherine's Gr LN5.....205 D7
St Catherine's Rd
Grantham NG31.........211 B3
Lincoln LN5............205 E7
St Chads Ct 8 LN2........68 E6
St Chads Gate DN37......188 A1
St Chad's Rd DN16........185 D7
St Chads Wlk S 20 DN37...190 E8
St Charles RC Prim Sch
HU2.................180 E8
St Christophers Cl 1
NG34................107 F1
St Christopher's Rd 11
DN36..................36 C8
St Claire's Ct 6 LN6......204 C8
St Clares Wlk DN20.......196 C2
St Clement's Cl 9 PE9.....219 A5
St Clements Ct 2 LN12....77 A8
St Clement's Ct 3 LN1.....234 B4
St Clement's Dr 4 LN3.....82 B6
St Clements Gn PE25......206 B4
St Clements Rd 17 NG34...108 D2
St Clement's Rd
1 Lincoln LN6..........204 E2
2 Skegness PE25.......206 B4
St Clements Way DN36....195 C7
St Crispins Cl 2 DN40....12 E4
St Crispin's Cl 3 LN6......204 D2
St Cuthberts Ct 14 LN1....234 B4
St Davids Cl 2 PE25......206 D6
St David's Cl 2 LN3.......203 E7
St Davids Cres DN17......184 E3
St David's Rd LN6........204 D2
St David's Sq PE1........226 D1
St David's St 13 LN8......47 B6
St Denys Ave NG34.......212 B6
St Deny's Ct 2 DN40......12 E3
St Edith Gate 6 LN11.....62 C6
St Edmonds Cl PE24......115 D8
St Edmunds Cl 3 NG31....210 D5
St Edmunds Ct DN34......190 F6
St Edmunds Rd NG34......212 C3
St Edmunds Walk PE7.....230 D2
St Edmunds Wy 5 PE1.....230 D2
St Edward's Dr 15 LN2....68 F2
St Edwins Cl 18 DN7......14 D4
St Edwins Dr 19 DN7......14 D4
**St Faith & St Martin CE Jun
Sch The** LN1..........201 D4
St Faiths CE Inf Sch LN1...201 D4
St Faith's St 6 LN1.......201 D4
St Firmin's Way PE10.....164 D7
St Frances Cl PE25.......206 B6
St Francis Ave DN31......191 A8
St Francis Ct 5 LN6......204 D2
St Francis Gdns 23 LN12...77 A7
St Francis Gr 1 DN37......23 E1
St Francis Specl Sch The
LN1...................201 E7
St George Ave PE2........231 E6
St George's Acad NG34....212 C4
St Georges Ave 3 PE9.....219 D6
St George's Ave 5 DN7....14 C2
St George's CE Com Prim Sch
DN21.................197 F2
St George's CE Prim Sch
PE9...................219 C7
St Georges Cl
4 Cranwell NG34.......107 F1
22 Thorne/Moorends DN8...15 B7
St George's Cl DN21.......30 F3
St Georges Dr 3 LN10.....97 C5

St George's Hill DN21......54 F7
St Georges La LN2........67 F1
St Georges Prim Sch HU3..180 A6
St Georges Rd 21 DN8.....15 B7
St George's Rd
Kingston upon Hull HU3...180 A5
17 Wittering PE8........172 B1
St George's St 6 PE9......219 C5
St Georges Way 11 NG31..211 D7
**St Gilbert of Sempringham CE
Prim Sch The** NG34.....143 B7
St Gilberts CE Prim Sch
PE9...................219 A5
St Gilbert's Cl NG34.......143 B6
St Gilbert's Rd PE10......213 C6
ST GILES LN2............202 C7
St Giles Ave Lincoln LN2...234 C4
1 Sleaford NG34........212 F4
St Giles' Ave DN33........191 D1
St Guthlac Ave 1 PE6.....217 B5
St Guthlac's Cl 2 PE6.....166 F1
St Guthlac's Way 1 PE21..126 C1
St Helenas CE Prim Sch
LN13..................89 A7
St Helens Ave DN33.......191 D3
St Helen's Ave LN6.......205 B7
St Helen's Cl NG31........210 D4
St Helen's Cres DN7.......194 D1
St Helen's Dr 14 HU15......2 D6
St Helen's Rd Brigg DN20..196 D3
7 Lea DN21.............53 A5
St Helens Way DN21.......42 E2
St Helier's Rd DN34.......192 E7
St Hilary's Cl 1 LN6......204 D2
St Hilda's Ave DN34......191 B6
St Huberts Dr PE25.......206 B6
St Hughes Cl PE1.........226 C4
St Hugh's Ave DN35......192 E6
St Hugh's Cath Prim Sch The
LN6...................204 B7
St Hugh's Cl 7 LN3.......203 E7
**St Hugh's Communication and
Interaction Coll** 5
DN16.................183 B1
St Hugh's Cres DN16......185 C8
St Hugh's Dr
3 Barlings LN3..........69 C3
Lincoln LN6............204 D2
St Hughs Hospl DN32......191 F4
St Hugh's Terr 3 LN1......66 C7
St Hybald's Gr 2 DN20....30 F7
St Ives Cres DN34........190 E5
St James Ave
Grimsby DN34..........191 A6
7 Hatfield DN7..........14 C3
Peterborough PE1.......225 F7
St James Cl
19 Crowle DN17........16 D7
Kingston upon Hull HU13..179 A7
Newton PE13...........170 A5
St James Ct
2 Scunthorpe DN15.....183 A3
11 Trusthorpe LN12.....64 C1
St James' Ct 2 DN34.....191 C6
St James Pl
North Hykeham LN6......204 E3
Scunthorpe DN16.......185 D4
St James Rd Brigg DN20...196 D3
Long Sutton PE12.......216 A1
1 Welton HU14...........2 F5
St James' Sch DN34.......191 C6
St James Rd 5 DN20......30 E8
St James St HU3.........180 D5
St James's Way 5 PE11...214 D2
St James View LN11.......198 B4
St James Way 2 PE12.....157 E1
St Joan's Dr 5 DN20......30 E8
St John Fisher Cath High Sch
PE1...................226 C4
St John's Ave
6 Cherry Willingham/Reepham
LN3...................203 E7
1 Lincoln LN6..........204 E2
St Johns CE Prim Sch
PE2...................231 C7
St Johns Church Sch PE2..229 F3
St Johns Cl 2 Baston PE6..164 E5
Brigg DN20.............196 D3
21 Goxhill DN19.........12 A8
Scampton LN1...........67 C6
St John's Cl
11 Leasingham NG34....121 B7
6 Morton PE10.........154 C7
6 Ryhall PE9...........163 C1
St Johns Ct Grange PE11...191 A5
6 Grantham NG31.......211 A3
St John's Dr
Corby Glen NG33.......152 F7
Ingoldmells PE25.......90 E4
6 Spalding PE11........214 B3
St Johns Mews PE12.......215 E2
St John's Prim Sch LN4....205 F4
St Johns Rd PE2..........231 B7
St John's Rd Boston PE21..209 A3
Bracebridge Heath LN4...205 F2
7 Humberston DN36......36 C8
Lincoln LN2............201 F6
Scunthorpe DN16.......185 C6
Spalding PE11..........214 C3
Weston PE12............157 C2
19 Wittering PE8........172 B1
St John's St
3 Holbeach PE12.......215 E2
Peterborough PE1.......226 B2

St John's St continued
21 Stamford PE9........219 B5
St John St 1 PE24.......102 D1
St John's Terr 13 DN21....197 D3
St John's Wlk HU13.......178 F2
St Joseph Dr HU4........179 C5
**St Joseph's Cath Prim
Voluntary Acad** DN35...192 D4
St Judes Cl PE3..........225 C4
St Julian's Wells HU10....178 B8
St Katherines Ms 3 PE7...230 C2
St Kyneburgha Cl PE5.....223 E2
St Lamberts Gr 4 PE12....157 D7
St Lawrence Acad The
DN15.................182 E3
**St Lawrence CE (Controlled)
Prim Sch** LN6.........200 B4
St Lawrence Dr 9 LN3.....83 C4
St Lawrence Rd DN7.......14 C4
St Lawrence's Pl DN16....185 D7
St Lawrence Rd DN16......185 D6
St Lawrence St 3 LN9.....199 B4
St Lawrence Way 3 PE9...172 F7
St Leodegar's Cl PE20....136 D7
St Leonard Cl PE21.......209 A6
St Leonard's Ave DN31....191 A8
St Leonards Dr PE24......90 D7
St Leonard's Dr
4 Woodhall Spa LN10....97 D5
11 Woodhall Spa LN10...97 D5
St Leonard's La
Lincoln LN2............234 C3
South Cockerington LN11...62 B7
St Leonard's Rd 2 PE13...170 B2
St Leonard's St 8 PE9.....219 C5
St Luke's Cl
Cherry Willingham/Reepham
LN3...................203 F7
1 Hatfield DN7..........14 C2
St Luke's Cl 3 DN36.......36 C8
St Lukes Ct HU10.........178 F8
St Luke's Ct 7 DN32......191 F8
St Luke's Prim Sch DN16..185 D8
St Luke's St HU3.........180 D6
St Margaret's Ave PE25...206 A6
St Margaret's CE Sch The
LN13..................63 A1
St Margarets Cl LN13......76 F3
St Margaret's Cl
17 Laceby DN37.........23 F1
6 Lincoln LN6..........205 B4
St Margaret's Cres 6
DN40..................22 E8
St Margaret's Dr PE22.....113 A2
St Margaret's Gdns LN6...205 A4
St Margarets Mews DN34..190 F6
St Margarets Pl 2 PE2....230 F6
St Margarets Rd 1 PE2....230 F6
St Margaret's Wlk
Scunthorpe DN16.......185 C5
5 Scunthorpe DN16.....185 D6
St Mark's Ave 3 LN3......203 E7
St Mark's Cl
North Hykeham LN6......204 E3
Skegness PE25..........206 D5
St Mark's Ct 3 PE1.......226 A3
St Marks Dr 6 PE6........166 E1
St Marks Rd PE13.........169 E3
St Mark's Rd
Holbeach PE12..........147 D6
10 Humberston DN36.....36 C8
St Marks Sh Ctr LN5......234 A1
St Mark's Sq
Kingston upon Hull HU3...180 A1
Lincoln LN5............234 A1
St Marks St PE1..........226 A3
St Mark St
Kingston upon Hull HU8...181 A8
Lincoln LN5............234 A1
St Marks Terr 25 PE21....208 F5
St Martins NG31.........152 E1
St Martins Ave 2 HU4.....179 E6
St Martins CE Prim Sch
DN9...................28 A3
St Martins Cl 2 NG34.....107 F1
St Martin's Cl
8 Blyton DN21..........41 C5
4 Stamford PE9........219 C4
Stubton NG23...........118 B7
St Martin's Cres DN33....191 C3
St Martin's La LN1........234 B3
St Martins Park 7 DN9....28 A3
St Martin's Pl 5 DN41.....23 A4
St Martins Prep Sch
DN32.................191 D5
St Martin's Rd
Newborough PE6........221 F8
4 Scawby DN20.........30 E8
1 Wisbech PE13........170 E2
St Martin's St Lincoln LN2..234 B3
Peterborough PE1.......225 F5
St Martin's Way 4 NG32..120 A3
St Mary Cl 12 PE6........166 F1
St Mary's Abbey (Cistercian) ★
PE20.................135 C2
St Mary's Ave
4 Barnetby le Wold DN38...21 A4
4 Pinchbeck PE11......156 A4
12 Welton/Dunholme LN2...68 F2
Wittering PE8..........172 C1
St Mary's Cath Prim Vol Acad
DN20.................196 C5
St Marys Cl South Field HU13..3 E4
5 Weston PE12.........157 D7
St Mary's Cl Bainton PE9..172 F5
18 Bottesford NG13.....128 A6
2 Brough HU15...........2 C7

St Mary's Cl continued
Farcet PE7.............231 C2
Grimsby DN32...........192 C6
Peterborough PE1.......226 B4
Thorney PE6............176 A2
Wilsford NG32..........120 C1
St Mary's Cres
9 Manby LN11..........62 C6
5 Stow LN1.............66 C8
Swineshead PE20.......135 B6
St Marys Ct 6 PE1........226 B2
St Mary's Ct 5 DN15.....182 C6
St Marys Dr
5 Sleaford NG34.......212 C6
13 Sutterton PE20......136 C4
St Mary's Dr 2 Hatfield DN7 14 C2
Peterborough PE2.......229 F4
St Mary's First & Middle Sch
DN32.................191 F8
St Mary's Gdns
6 Cowbit PE12..........167 B8
Long Sutton PE12......216 C5
3 Whaplode PE12......158 B2
St Mary's Hill 17 PE9......219 C5
St Mary's La
4 Barton-upon-Humber
DN18...................10 F8
Binbrook LN8...........47 C4
Claxby LN8.............45 E5
Louth LN11.............198 A5
St Mary's Mdws 2 PE12...159 D7
St Mary's Pk LN11.......198 A6
St Mary's Pl 14 PE9......219 C5
St Mary's RC High Sch
DN33.................191 A3
St Mary's Rd Hatfield DN7...14 C3
2 Lincoln LN6..........204 E2
Skegness PE25.........206 B6
West Walton PE14......170 E4
St Marys Sch LN2........234 C3
St Marys Sq LN9.........199 B4
St Mary's St Farcet PE7...231 C2
Lincoln LN5............234 A1
12 Stamford PE9.......219 C5
St Mary's Way 2 PE22....114 A1
St Marys Wlk 21 HU14.....3 B7
St Mathews Cl 2 LN6......201 D1
St Matthews Cl 11 PE25...206 A4
St Matthew's Cl
5 Cherry Willingham/Reepham
LN3...................203 C7
4 Holbeach PE12........215 D2
St Matthew's Dr 13 PE12..160 E4
St Matthew's Rd 12 DN36..36 C8
St Matthew St HU3.......180 B5
St Mawes Cres DN34......191 A7
St Mawes Way NG31......210 D5
St Mellion Dr NG31.......211 E7
St Michael CE Prim Sch
PE7...................231 E4
St Michael Ct 25 LN5.....93 F7
St Michael's Ave PE13.....170 D1
St Michael's CE Prim Sch
Thorpe on the Hill LN6....92 E8
Thorpe on the Hill LN6....92 E8
St Michael's CE Sch LN11 198 D5
St Michaels Cl 8 LN4.....109 F5
St Michaels Ct 16 DN8....15 B7
St Michael's Cres 5
DN16.................185 C8
St Michael's Ct 22 DN19...12 A8
St Michael's Dr 15 DN8....15 B7
St Michael's Gate PE2.....226 F7
St Michael's La
11 Wainfleet St Mary
PE24.................102 D1
Wainfleet St Mary PE24...115 D8
St Michael's Mount 18 HU14 3 B7
St Michael's Rd
Grimsby DN34..........190 D4
3 Louth LN11..........198 C5
16 Wittering PE8.......172 B1
St Michaels Terr 7 LN1....234 B3
St Michael's Way 1 NG34 120 C8
St Michaels Wlk 8 NG34..212 C6
St Nectan Cl 9 HU3.......180 A4
St Nicholas Ave HU4......179 C2
**St Nicholas CE (Controlled)
Prim Sch** PE21.........209 B4
St Nicholas CE Prim Sch
DN39..................12 A1
St Nicholas Cl
4 Barkston NG32.......130 B8
Boston PE21............209 B3
St Nicholas Ct DN16......185 E4
St Nicholas Cty Prim Sch
PE12.................160 A4
St Nicholas Dr DN37......190 C6
St Nicholas Gdns HU4.....179 C2
St Nicholas Rd
Boston PE21............209 B3
Thorne/Moorends DN8...15 A8
St Nicholas St LN1.......234 A4
St Nicholas Way
10 Lutton PE12.........160 A8
5 Spalding PE11........214 A4
St Norbert's Cath Prim Sch
DN17..................16 D7
St Norbett's Cath Prim Sch
PE11.................214 C4
St Olaf's Dr DN32.........191 D6
St Olave's Dr 17 PE6......175 A1
St Paul Rd DN21..........197 B7
St Paul's Ave 4 LN3.......203 E7
St Pauls Cl PE24.........102 D7
St Paul's Cl PE13.........169 E2
St Pauls Com Prim Sch
PE11.................214 F6

St Pauls Gdns DN16 . . . . . .185 B5
St Paul's Gdns PE10 . . . . . .213 D4
St Paul's La **2** LN1 . . . . . .234 B3
St Paul's Rd
 Gainsborough DN21 . . . . . .197 B7
 Peterborough PE1 . . . . . . .225 F7
 Scunthorpe DN16 . . . . . . .185 B6
 Spalding PE11 . . . . .214 F5
St Pauls St HU2 . . . . .180 E8
St Paul's St PE9 . . . . .219 C5
St Paul St **1** HU2 . . . . .180 E8
St Pega Cl **17** PE6 . . . . . . .166 F1
St Pega's Rd PE6 . . . . .220 D7
St Peter and St Paul Cath Vol
 Acad LN6 . . . . .205 B7
St Peter at Arches **6** LN2 234 B2
St Peter & St Paul CE Prim
 Sch
 Burgh le Marsh PE24 . . . . .102 D7
 Scunthorpe DN17 . . . . . . .185 B5
St Peter's Ave
 8 Cherry Willingham/Reepham
 LN3 . . . . .203 E7
 Cleethorpes DN35 . . . . . . .192 E6
 Kingston upon Hull HU10 . .178 E6
 Lincoln LN6 . . . . .204 D2
 Scunthorpe DN16 . . . . . . .185 B4
St Peters CE Aided Jun Sch
 PE13 . . . . .170 E1
St Peters CE Prim Sch
 Cleethorpes DN35 . . . . . . .192 E6
 Dunston LN4 . . . . .95 C6
St Peter's CE Prim Sch
 Gringley on the Hill DN10 . . .39 B1
 Wymondham LE14 . . . . . .150 B1
St Peters Cl DN21 . . . . .40 B5
St Peter's Cl
 Burgh le Marsh PE24 . . . . .102 D8
 4 Holton le Clay DN36 . . .36 C8
St Peter's Cres DN36 . . . . . .36 C8
St Peters Ct **9** PE9 . . . . . .219 B4
St Peter's Ct **36** DN18 . . . . .3 E1
St Peter's Dr **4** LN10 . . . . .97 D5
St Peters Gr **2** DN37 . . . . .23 E1
St Peter's Gr **14** DN21 . . . .29 C3
St Peter's Hill
 4 Grantham NG31 . . . . . .211 A4
 14 Stamford PE9 . . . . . .219 B5
St Peter's La **7** LN12 . . . . .64 C2
St Peters Rd
 11 Bourne PE10 . . . . . . .213 C5
 Peterborough PE1 . . . . . . .226 A2
St Peter's Rd **12** DN21 . . . .29 C3
St Peter's St PE9 . . . . .219 B4
St Peter's Way PE6 . . . . . . .176 A2
St Pierre Ave NG31 . . . . . . .211 E7
St Polycarp's Dr PE12 . . . . .168 B3
St Quintins Cl **5** HU9 . . . . .181 C8
St Rumbold's St LN2 . . . . . .234 B2
St Sebastians CE (Aided) Prim
 Sch NG31 . . . . .129 E5
St Simon's Dr **9** LN3 . . . . .203 E7
St Stephen's Sh Ctr HU1 . . .180 D6
St Stephens St HU1 . . . . . . .180 D6
St Swithins Cl **1** PE20 . . . .135 A4
St Swithuns Sq LN2 . . . . . .234 B2
St Thomas' CE Prim Sch
 PE21 . . . . .208 F1
St Thomas Ct Boston PE21 208 F2
 Long Sutton PE12 . . . . . . .216 B5
St Thomas Dr PE21 . . . . . . .208 E2
St Thomas Moore RC Prim
 Sch PE1 . . . . .226 D4
St Thomas Moore Rd
 HU4 . . . . .179 A4
St Thomas More RC Prim Sch
 HU4 . . . . .179 A4
St Thomas Rd **2** PE11 . . . .214 D2
St Thomas' Rd **13** DN36 . . .36 C8
St Tibba Way **12** PE9 . . . . .163 C1
St Valentines Way PE25 . . . .206 B6
ST VINCENT 211 D3
St Vincent Cl **2** PE25 . . . . .206 A6
St Vincent's Ave DN15 . . . . .183 A6
St Vincent's Rd NG31 . . . . . .211 C3
St Wilfrid's Cl **18** LN4 . . . . .95 D4
St William Ct PE12 . . . . . . .215 F3
Salacon Way **16** DN32 . . . .189 C1
Saladine Ct **24** DN41 . . . . .23 F5
Salamander Cl DN31 . . . . . .191 B8
SALEBY LN13 . . . . .75 F6
Salem St **5** PE11 . . . . .145 B6
Salisbury Ave **2** LN8 . . . . .47 B6
Salisbury Cl
 1 Grantham NG31 . . . . .210 D5
 Morton DN21 . . . . .40 D3
 1 Saxilby with Ingleby LN1 . .66 D2
 2 Scunthorpe DN17 . . . .184 C7
Salisbury Dr
 2 Canwick LN4 . . . . .81 A2
 Waltham DN37 . . . . .194 D4
Salisbury Rd PE4 . . . . .220 F3
Salisbury St
 Gainsborough DN21 . . . . . .197 C7
 Kingston upon Hull HU13 . .178 D1
Salix App **1** LN6 . . . . .204 C8
Sallie Bank La LN1 . . . . .65 D2
Sallows Rd PE1 . . . . .226 B6
SALMONBY LN9 . . . . .86 E8
Salmonby Rd Salmonby LN9 . 86 F2
 Scunthorpe DN17 . . . . . . .184 E4
Salsbury Ave DN34 . . . . . . .191 B6
Saltash Rd HU4 . . . . .179 A2
Saltburn Gr **5** DN32 . . . . .192 A5
SALTBY LE14 . . . . .138 F1
Saltby Rd
 Croxton Kerrial NG32 . . . . .138 D3
 Sproxton LE14 . . . . .150 C7

Saltergate Lincoln LN2 . . . . .234 B2
 Peterborough PE1 . . . . . . .226 E7
 The Willows DN37 . . . . . . .188 A1
Salter Gate LN11 . . . . .51 A1
Saltergate Rd **28** DN17 . . . .29 D7
 Spalding PE11 . . . . .214 B5
Salters Cl **18** LN4 . . . . .81 A1
Saltersford Gr NG31 . . . . . . .211 D1
Saltersford Rd NG31 . . . . . .211 D2
Saltersgate PE1 . . . . .226 F7
Salters' La LN11 . . . . .48 B4
Salters Lane PE9 . . . . .163 A1
Salters Way NG34 . . . . .132 F3
Salters Way
 14 Donington PE11 . . . . .134 E2
 Gayton le Marsh LN11 . . . . .62 E3
SALTFLEET LN11 . . . . .51 B4
SALTFLEETBY ALL SAINTS
 LN12 . . . . .51 C1
Saltfleetby CE Prim Sch
 LN11 . . . . .63 A8
SALTFLEETBY ST CLEMENT
 LN11 . . . . .51 C2
SALTFLEETBY ST PETER
 LN11 . . . . .63 B8
Saltfleetby-Theddlethorpe
 Dunes National Nature
 Reserve ★ LN11 . . . . .51 E3
Saltfleet La PE11 . . . . .145 B4
Saltfleet Rd Saltfleetby LN12 51 D1
 Theddlethorpe All Saints
 LN12 . . . . .63 B8
Saltford Ave **2** HU9 . . . . . . .5 F8
Saltgrounds Rd HU15 . . . . . . .2 B5
Salthouse La HU1 . . . . .181 A6
Saltings The **6** PE34 . . . . . .161 F3
Saltmarsh PE2 . . . . .230 C4
Saltmarsh Ct **4** HU4 . . . . .179 D2
Saltney Gate PE12 . . . . .215 A6
Salts Rd PE14 . . . . .170 F4
Salvesen Rd DN35 . . . . .189 D1
Salvesen Way HU3 . . . . . . .180 A3
Samman Cl HU10 . . . . .178 D6
Sampey Way **13** NG34 . . . .133 B1
Samphire Cl DN36 . . . . .37 C5
Sampson St PE7 . . . . .230 C4
Sam Scorer Gall ★ LN1 . . . .234 B3
Samuel Ave DN32 . . . . .192 B6
Samuel John Wy **12** PE25 206 A5
Samworths Cl PE5 . . . . .223 F2
Sanbeds La DN9 . . . . .27 B2
Sanctuary Way DN37 . . . . . .190 C6
Sandars Cl DN9 . . . . .28 B3
Sandars Rd DN21 . . . . .53 A8
Sandbeck Arc PE25 . . . . . . .206 D3
Sandbeck Ave PE25 . . . . . . .206 C2
Sandbeck La DN21 . . . . .41 B6
SANDBRAES LN7 . . . . .33 A4
Sandcliffe Rd NG31 . . . . . . .211 A7
Sanders Cl Lincoln LN1 . . . . .201 D8
 12 Mablethorpe & Sutton
 LN12 . . . . .77 A7
Sanderson Cl **1** DN16 . . . .183 B1
Sanderson's Bank DN10 . . . .26 C2
Sanders View LN1 . . . . .201 D8
Sandfield Cl DN17 . . . . .184 D5
Sandfield Dr **3** HU15 . . . . . .2 C5
Sandford PE3 . . . . .225 B5
Sandford St **8** DN31 . . . . .188 D1
Sandgate Cl DN33 . . . . .191 B1
Sandhayes La LN8 . . . . .43 F4
Sandhill La **1** LN22 . . . . . . .52 B3
Sandhill Rd LN4 . . . . .7 B6
SANDHOLME PE20 . . . . . . .136 F4
Sandholme La PE20 . . . . . . .136 E6
Sandhouse Cres
 3 Scunthorpe DN16 . . . .183 C1
 Scunthorpe DN16 . . . . . . .185 C8
Sandhurst Cres **5** NG34 . . .212 B2
Sandhurst La DN21 . . . . .77 A7
Sandhurst Rd
 3 Hampton Vale PE7 . . . .230 D1
 5 Mablethorpe/Sutton on Sea
 LN12 . . . . .77 A7
SANDILANDS LN12 . . . . .77 A8
Sandilands Cl **12** LN12 . . . .77 A7
Sandilands Pit Nature
 Reserve ★ LN12 . . . . .77 A7
Sand La Barkston NG32 . . . .129 F8
 Besthorpe NG23 . . . . .91 C8
 Broadholme LN6 . . . . .66 D1
 4 Broughton DN20 . . . . .19 D3
 Caistor LN7 . . . . .32 E4
 Fenton LN1 . . . . .65 D3
 Great Steeping PE23 . . . . .101 C7
 Hougham NG32 . . . . .118 C5
 Manton DN21 . . . . .30 A5
 Marston NG32 . . . . .118 E1
 Messingham DN17 . . . . . . .29 A7
 Osgodby LN8 . . . . .45 B3
 Spalford NG23 . . . . .78 D4
 Thorney NG23 . . . . .79 B8
 Torksey LN1 . . . . .65 E5
 Wroot DN9 . . . . .26 C6
Sandlees La NG34 . . . . .123 B4
Sandlemere Cl **3** HU3 . . . .180 A5
Sandon Cl NG31 . . . . .211 C5
Sandon Rd NG31 . . . . .211 B5
Sandown Cl **5** PE11 . . . . . .156 E3
Sandpiper Dr PE10 . . . . . . .213 D4
Sandpiper Dr
 Kingston upon Hull HU4 . . .179 B1
 Peterborough PE2 . . . . . . .231 E6

Sandpiper Wy **21** DN18 . . . . .3 E1
Sand Pit La DN15 . . . . .1 C1
Sandpit Rd LN4 PE6 . . . . . . .176 A3
Sandra Cres LN4 . . . . .203 D1
Sand Rd DN17 . . . . .28 B8
Sandringham Ave **29**
 PE13 . . . . .170 D1
Sandringham Cl
 5 Stamford PE9 . . . . . . .219 B7
 3 Whaplode PE12 . . . . .158 B6
Sandringham Cres DN17 . . . .184 F3
Sandringham Ct **4** PE12 . . .215 F3
Sandringham Dr
 Londonthorpe & Harrowby
 Without NG31 . . . . .211 E5
 Louth LN11 . . . . .198 B7
 13 Mablethorpe & Sutton
 LN12 . . . . .76 D2
 Wragby LN8 . . . . .70 D4
Sandringham Gdns PE21 . . .209 C6
Sandringham Rd
 32 Brough HU15 . . . . . . .2 C5
 Cleethorpes DN35 . . . . . . .192 D4
 2 Peterborough PE4 . . . .225 C8
Sandringham St HU3 . . . . . .180 A6
Sandringham Way **3** PE6 217 A5
Sandringham Wlk **6**
 PE11 . . . . .214 D2
Sandringham Wy **8** NG34 212 C2
Sands Cl **3** DN17 . . . . .17 D5
Sands Ct
 1 North Ferriby HU14 . . . . .3 A4
 Rippingale PE10 . . . . .143 A3
Sandsfield La DN21 . . . . . . .197 D2
Sands La Brantingham HU15 . . .1 F7
 Brough HU15 . . . . .2 C6
 Carlton-le-Moorland LN5 . . .92 E1
 Ellerker HU15 . . . . .2 A4
 Scotter DN21 . . . . .29 B3
 2 Scunthorpe DN18 . . . . .10 A7
SANDTOFT DN8 . . . . .16 A3
Sandtoft Cl LN6 . . . . .204 D6
Sandtoft Ind Est DN8 . . . . . .16 A3
Sandtoft Rd Hatfield DN7 . . . .15 A4
 Sandtoft DN9 . . . . .16 B3
Sandtone Gdns PE11 . . . . . .214 D5
Sandwell Dr LN6 . . . . .200 D1
SANDY BANK LN4 . . . . .111 E6
Sandy Bank Coningsby PE22 98 C1
 Sandy Bank LN4 . . . . .111 E6
Sandy Bank Rd LN4 . . . . . . .111 D6
Sandy Cl **1** DN36 . . . . .37 C5
Sandyford La PE22 . . . . .113 E3
Sandy Gate Quadring PE11 . .144 F7
 Sutton St James PE12 . . . .169 A7
Sandygate Cl NG34 . . . . . . .133 C1
Sandygate Cres PE22 . . . . . .113 E3
Sandygate La NG34 . . . . . . .133 B2
Sandygate La NG34 . . . . . . .133 C2
Sandy La Anderby PE24 . . . . .77 C3
 Belchford LN9 . . . . .73 A2
 Calceby LN13 . . . . .74 F2
 Candlesby with Gunby PE23 . 88 F1
 Chapel St Leonard PE24 . . . .90 E7
 Great Steeping PE23 . . . . .101 D7
 Lusby with Winceby PE23 . . .86 F1
 North Willingham LN8 . . . . .58 C8
 Tealby LN8 . . . . .46 C1
 Tydd St Giles PE13 . . . . . . .170 A7
 5 West Ashby LN9 . . . . . .85 E7
 Woodhall Spa LN10 . . . . . . .97 E7
Saner St HU3 . . . . .180 B6
Sansford St **5** LN6 . . . . . . .205 A6
Santolina Wy HU4 . . . . .179 C2
SANTON DN15 . . . . .19 B7
Santon Lane DN15 . . . . .19 C7
Sapling Cl **3** NG24 . . . . . . .104 B3
SAPPERTON NG34 . . . . .141 E8
Sapperton PE4 . . . . .220 F6
Sapphire Cl PE24 . . . . .89 C2
Sapphire Gr **7** HU3 . . . . . .180 A4
Saracen Cl DN21 . . . . .197 F2
SARACEN'S HEAD PE12 . . . .215 A7
Sarah Gate PE11 . . . . .145 B8
Sarah's Wlk DN37 . . . . .184 B6
Sargeants Cl **9** PE22 . . . . .113 B1
Sargent Cl **4** LN4 . . . . .95 C4
Sargent's Ct **5** PE9 . . . . . .219 A6
Sargent's Way **15** DN20 . . .31 A5
Sargon Way **3** DN31 . . . . .188 A3
Sarthe Cl **5** PE20 . . . . .135 B7
Sassaby Cl HU4 . . . . .179 C3
Satinwood Cl **10** LN6 . . . . .200 C1
Satterley Cl LN6 . . . . .92 D4
Saturn Dr PE2 . . . . .231 D4
Saunby Gr DN35 . . . . .192 E7
Saundby Rd DN22 . . . . .52 B7
Saundergate La PE21 . . . . . .136 D8
Saunders Cl **7** PE2 . . . . . .230 E8
Saunders St **3** DN31 . . . . .191 C8
SAUSTHORPE PE23 . . . . .87 C4
Sausthorpe Rd
 Partney PE23 . . . . .88 A3
 Sausthorpe PE23 . . . . .87 F3
Sausthorpe St **9** LN5 . . . . .201 F1
Savile St HU1 . . . . .180 F6
Saville Rd Ind Est PE3 . . . . .225 D5
Saville Rd PE3 . . . . .225 D4
Saville St LN5 . . . . .205 D7
Savory Rd **1** PE13 . . . . . . .170 D1
Savoy Ct **7** DN36 . . . . . . .195 C6
Sawcliffe Ind Est DN15 . . . . .183 B5
Sawmill La LN4 . . . . .70 C6
Sawyers Cl **28** NG24 . . . . .104 A4
SAXBY LN8 . . . . .55 F5
SAXBY ALL SAINTS DN20 . . .10 A3

Saxby Ave PE25 . . . . .206 D2
Saxby Cl DN40 . . . . .186 A4
Saxby Cliff Rd LN8 . . . . .55 D4
Saxby Gdns PE1 . . . . .226 C5
Saxby Gr DN33 . . . . .191 A3
Saxby Hill DN20 . . . . .10 B4
Saxby Rd Bonby DN20 . . . . . .10 B4
 Horkstow Wolds DN18 . . . . .10 C5
 Scunthorpe DN17 . . . . . . .184 E5
SAXILBY LN1 . . . . .66 D3
Saxilby CE Prim Sch LN1 . . . .66 E2
Saxilby Rd Lincoln LN1 . . . . .201 A7
 Skellingthorpe LN6 . . . . . . .200 A6
 Sturton by Stow LN1 . . . . . .66 D6
Saxilby Road LN1 . . . . .67 A1
Saxilby Sta LN1 . . . . .66 D2
Saxon Cl
 7 Barton-upon-Humber
 DN18 . . . . .10 F8
 10 Metheringham LN4 . . . .95 D4
 Spalding PE11 . . . . .214 F2
Saxon Cres DN35 . . . . .192 E6
Saxon Ct **2** Blyton DN21 . . .41 C5
 Grimsby DN31 . . . . .188 D2
 Scunthorpe DN16 . . . . . . .185 B3
Saxondale HU4 . . . . .179 B7
Saxonfield LN7 . . . . .33 A4
Saxon Gate **15** PE20 . . . . .136 C5
Saxon Rd **8** Barnack PE9 . .172 D3
 Peterborough PE1 . . . . . . .226 C3
Saxon St **4** LN1 . . . . .234 A4
Saxon Way
 2 Ancaster NG32 . . . . . .120 A2
 Bourne PE10 . . . . .213 C6
 17 Caistor LN7 . . . . .33 B4
 3 Horncastle LN9 . . . . . .199 D3
 6 Ingham LN1 . . . . .54 F2
 Kingston upon Hull HU13 . .178 F1
 Louth LN11 . . . . .198 B4
Saxon Wlk **16** PE20 . . . . . .136 C5
Saxon Wy LN3 . . . . .83 C5
Saxony Way **6** PE11 . . . . . .134 C2
Saxton Cl **2** DN17 . . . . . . .184 E6
Sayer Ct PE2 . . . . .229 F2
Scalby Gr HU5 . . . . .179 D8
Scald Gate PE22 . . . . .115 B8
Scale Cl **1** LN4 . . . . .181 A6
Scale La Staith **9** HU1 . . . .181 A6
Scalesgate Rd PE12 . . . . . . .159 B1
Scalford Dr PE1 . . . . .226 C8
Scallow La DN17 . . . . .29 D6
Scalp Rd PE21 . . . . .137 B7
SCAMBLESBY LN11 . . . . .72 F5
Scamblesby CE Prim Sch
 LN11 . . . . .72 F5
Scamblesby Hill LN9 . . . . . . .72 E4
SCAMPTON LN1 . . . . .67 D6
Scampton Airfield LN1 . . . . . .67 E6
Scampton Ave LN6 . . . . .204 F6
Scampton CE Prim Sch
 LN1 . . . . .67 D6
Scampton Cl **3** DN34 . . . . .191 A5
Scampton Way
 Gainsborough DN21 . . . . . .197 E3
 Scampton LN1 . . . . .67 F5
 Skegness PE25 . . . . .206 A5
Scandinavian Way DN41 . . . .187 B3
Scanlan Cl LN4 . . . . .207 F6
Scarborough Bank PE22 . . . .100 B1
Scarborough Cl
 Green Hill NG31 . . . . .210 E6
 Rippingale PE10 . . . . .142 F2
Scarborough La LN4 . . . . . . .111 B2
Scarborough Rd LN11 . . . . . .61 B8
Scarborough St HU3 . . . . . .180 A4
Scarbrough Ave PE25 . . . . . .206 D4
Scarbrough Espl PE25 . . . . . .206 E3
Scargate La LN4 . . . . .108 F8
Scarle Cl **1** LN6 . . . . .205 A2
Scarle La LN6 . . . . .79 B2
Scarrington Cres HU4 . . . . . .179 B6
Scarrow Cl HU3 . . . . .180 A7
Scarsdale Wy NG31 . . . . . . .211 A1
SCARTHO DN33 . . . . .194 E8
Scartho Junior Acad
 DN33 . . . . .191 D2
Scartho Pk DN33 . . . . .191 B2
Scartho Rd DN33 . . . . .191 D2
SCAWBY DN20 . . . . .30 E8
Scawby Acad DN20 . . . . .30 E8
Scawby Cres LN6 . . . . .204 F7
Scawby Rd Brigg DN20 . . . . .196 A2
 Broughton DN20 . . . . .19 E2
 Grimsby DN33 . . . . .191 A3
 Scawby DN20 . . . . .31 A7
 Scunthorpe DN17 . . . . . . .184 E5
Sch NG31 . . . . .129 F4
Schiphol Way DN39 . . . . .21 E5
Schofield Cl **7** DN19 . . . . . .11 C8
School Cl **1** Maxey PE6 . . . .173 C7
 Peterborough PE4 . . . . . . .225 A5
School Cres Anwick NG34 . . .109 B1
 1 Surfleet LN2 . . . . .68 F4
 5 Surfleet PE11 . . . . . . .145 E3
School Croft DN9 . . . . .27 B2
School Dr
 27 Messingham DN17 . . . .29 D7
 6 Welton/Dunholme LN2 . .68 C6
School Hill LN4 . . . . .150 C7
Schoolhouse La **11** LN11 . . .198 B5
School House La B DN10 . . . .39 F3
School Houses **9** DN20 . . . .19 E4
School La Aby LN13 . . . . .75 D3
 Addlethorpe PE24 . . . . .90 D3
 Appleby DN15 . . . . .9 D1
 1 Baston PE6 . . . . .164 E4
 Beckingham LN5 . . . . .105 B4
 8 Bicker PE20 . . . . .135 A4

St P-Sco 275

School La continued
 Binbrook LN8 . . . . .47 B5
 5 Bonby DN20 . . . . .10 C2
 Boothby Pagnell NG33 . . . .140 F5
 Brattleby LN1 . . . . .67 C8
 Buckminster NG33 . . . . . . .150 F5
 Butterwick PE22 . . . . .126 E3
 Cabourne LN7 . . . . .33 D5
 Canwick LN4 . . . . .81 A4
 Claypole NG23 . . . . .117 E8
 7 Colsterworth NG33 . . . .151 D7
 1 Coningsby LN4 . . . . . . .207 C4
 5 Croxton Kerrial NG32 . . .138 D4
 4 Donington PE11 . . . . . .134 F2
 East Keal PE23 . . . . .100 E6
 Edenham PE10 . . . . .153 F4
 Fulletby LN9 . . . . .86 B8
 4 Glinton PE6 . . . . .220 C8
 18 Goxhill DN19 . . . . .12 A8
 Grayingham DN21 . . . . .42 E7
 Great Steeping PE23 . . . . .101 E7
 Hainton LN8 . . . . .58 E3
 3 Harmston LN5 . . . . .93 F5
 Heighington/Washingborough
 LN4 . . . . .203 C2
 5 Helpringham NG34 . . . .133 D7
 2 Irby LN37 . . . . .34 D7
 Kingston upon Hull HU10 . .178 C8
 9 Lincoln LN6 . . . . .204 F1
 5 Lutton PE12 . . . . .160 A8
 Maltby le Marsh LN13 . . . . .76 A8
 4 Mareham le Fen PE22 . . .99 A4
 Marston NG32 . . . . .118 D2
 3 Maxey PE6 . . . . .173 C7
 12 New Holland DN19 . . . . .4 E2
 1 New Holland DN19 . . . . .4 E2
 North Cockerington LN11 . . .49 F1
 3 North Ferriby HU14 . . . . .3 A4
 4 North Kelsey LN7 . . . . . .32 A4
 North Scarle LN6 . . . . .78 E1
 North Somercotes LN11 . . . .50 F7
 Old Leake PE22 . . . . .114 A1
 Old Somerby NG33 . . . . . .140 E8
 Raithby PE23 . . . . .87 D2
 Redbourne DN21 . . . . .30 F3
 Ropsley NG33 . . . . .131 B1
 Rothwell LN7 . . . . .33 E2
 1 Scampton Airfield LN1 . . .67 F5
 Sedgebrook NG32 . . . . . . .128 F4
 Silk Willoughby NG34 . . . . .121 A1
 Snitterby DN21 . . . . .43 D5
 South Carlton LN1 . . . . .67 D3
 7 South Ferriby DN18 . . . .10 A7
 Springthorpe DN21 . . . . . . .53 E8
 2 Sturton by Stow LN1 . . . .66 C7
 17 Tetney DN36 . . . . .36 D4
 Thistleton LE15 . . . . .151 C1
 Thorpe on the Hill LN6 . . . . .92 E8
 6 Uffington PE9 . . . . .172 C6
 Walcott LN4 . . . . .109 C7
 3 West/East Butterwick
 DN17 . . . . .28 D8
 2 Willingham by Stow DN21 .53 E3
 Wilsford NG32 . . . . .120 C1
School Rd **1** Barnack PE9 . .172 C6
 Newborough PE6 . . . . .174 E5
 10 RAF Cranwell NG34 . . .120 C8
 Scunthorpe DN16 . . . . . . .185 B6
 8 South Killingholme DN40 . 12 E3
 West Walton PE14 . . . . . . .170 E4
 Winteringham DN15 . . . . . . .2 A1
School View NG13 . . . . .128 A5
School Wlk DN35 . . . . .192 C5
School Yd Mews DN20 . . . . .196 C4
Schooner Ct HU4 . . . . .179 B3
Schrimshaw Ct **6** PE25 . . . .206 C4
Schrimshire's Rd PE22 . . . . . .52 A1
Scoggins Way **4** NG34 . . . .122 D3
Scoldall La PE11 . . . . .145 E4
Scolding Dro PE6 . . . . .176 E5
SCOPWICK LN4 . . . . .95 D1
Scopwick Pl **3** LN2 . . . . . . .201 F8
Scorer St LN5 . . . . .201 F1
Scotenoon PE2 . . . . .229 E3
Scotgate PE9 . . . . .219 A5
SCOTHERN LN2 . . . . .68 D5
Scothern La **4** Barlings LN3 69 C3
 Dunholme LN2 . . . . .68 E5
 Stainton by Langworth LN2 . .68 E4
 10 Welton/Dunholme LN2 . .68 B4
Scothern Rd LN2 . . . . .68 D3
Scotia Rd PE21 . . . . .209 F2
Scotia Way PE21 . . . . .209 F2
SCOTLAND NG33 . . . . .141 C5
Scotland La NG33 . . . . .141 B5
Scotney Dr NG31 . . . . .211 F5
Scotney St PE1 . . . . .225 E7
Scott Ave DN17 . . . . .184 C6
Scott Cl **6** Claypole NG23 . .117 E8
 Grimsby DN37 . . . . .190 F8
 Peterborough PE2 . . . . . . .231 E6
Scott Dr **18** Spalding PE11 . .214 C2
 1 Yaxley PE7 . . . . .233 D1
Scotten Dike Dro PE10 . . . . .154 E6
SCOTTER DN21 . . . . .29 B3
Scotter Prim Sch DN21 . . . . . .29 C3
Scotter Rd Laughton DN21 . . .41 C8
 Messingham DN17 . . . . .29 C5
 Scunthorpe DN17 . . . . . . .182 C1
Scotter Rd S DN17 . . . . .184 C3
SCOTTERTHORPE DN21 . . . . .29 B5
Scotterthorpe Rd DN21 . . . . .29 B4
Scott Gdns LN2 . . . . .202 C6
Scottlethorpe PE10 . . . . . . .153 E4
Scottlethorpe Rd PE10 . . . . .153 D3

SCOTTON DN21 . . . . .29 C2
Scotton Comm Nature
Reserve★ DN9 . . . . .27 B1
Scotton Dr 7 LN6 . . . . .205 A7
Scotton Rd DN21 . . . . .29 C3
Scott's Cl PE6 . . . . .164 E3
Scott's Hill 4 NG32 . . . . . . .106 C1
Scotts Rd DN35 . . . . .220 D8
Scott St
  Gainsborough DN21 . . . . . . .197 C5
  Kingston upon Hull HU2 . . . .180 F7
SCOTT WILLOUGHBY
  NG34 . . . . .132 B4
SCRAFIELD LN9 . . . . .86 C3
SCRANE END PE22 . . . . .137 F8
Scrane End East PE22 . . . . . .137 E8
Scrap Bay Rd DN16 . . . . .19 A3
SCREDINGTON NG34 . . . . . .132 E7
Scredington Rd
  Burton Pedwardine NG34 . . .122 B1
  Helpringham NG34 . . . . .133 C7
SCREMBY PE23 . . . . .88 E2
Scremby Rd PE23 . . . . .88 C1
SCRIVELSBY LN9 . . . . .98 E8
Scrivelsby Ct DN35 . . . . .193 A3
SCRUB HILL LN4 . . . . .111 B6
Scrub La Authorpe LN11 . . . . .75 A8
  East Halton DN40 . . . . .12 E5
  Withern with Stain LN11 . . . . .62 D1
Scullery La NG33 . . . . .141 A5
SCUNTHORPE DN15 . . . . . . .183 B5
Scunthorpe CE Prim Sch
  DN15 . . . . .183 A4
Scunthorpe General Hospl
  DN15 . . . . .182 E2
Scunthorpe Leisure Ctr
  DN15 . . . . .183 B3
Scunthorpe Sta DN16 . . . . . .183 A2
Sea Bank PE20 . . . . .145 F8
Seabank Rd 22 PE13 . . . . . . .170 C1
Sea Bank Rd PE24 . . . . .90 E7
Seabrook Dr DN16 . . . . .185 A2
SEACROFT PE25 . . . . .103 E4
Seacroft Cl 18 NG31 . . . . . . .211 D7
Seacroft Dr 10 PE25 . . . . . . .206 C1
Seacroft Espl PE25 . . . . .103 E4
Seacroft Rd
  Cleethorpes DN35 . . . . .193 A5
  Mablethorpe/Sutton on Sea
  LN12 . . . . .64 B3
Seacroft Sq
  10 Skegness PE25 . . . . .103 E4
  11 Skegness PE25 . . . . .116 E8
SEADYKE PE20 . . . . .136 E3
Sea Dyke PE22 . . . . .114 B2
Seadyke Rd Kirton PE20 . . . .136 E3
  Wisbech St Mary PE13 . . . . .177 F6
Sea Dyke Way 1 DN36 . . . . . .37 C2
Sea End Rd PE22 . . . . .127 A4
Seafield Rd 5 PE13 . . . . .170 B2
Seaford Rd DN35 . . . . .193 B1
Sea Front Rd
  10 Skegness PE25 . . . . .103 E4
  9 Skegness PE25 . . . . .103 E4
Seagate Rd PE12 . . . . .216 D2
Seagate Terr PE12 . . . . .216 D4
Seagran Ave
  Kingston upon Hull HU13 . . .178 F3
  7 Kingston upon Hull HU4 . .179 A3
Seagull Cl HU4 . . . . .179 E2
Seaholme Rd LN12 . . . . .64 B2
Sea La Benington PE22 . . . . .127 B4
  Butterwick PE22 . . . . .126 F3
  Friskney PE22 . . . . .115 C5
  Hogsthorpe PE24 . . . . .90 C7
  Huttoft LN13 . . . . .77 A4
  Ingoldmells PE25 . . . . .90 E3
  Leverton PE22 . . . . .127 B6
  Mablethorpe/Sutton on Sea
  LN12 . . . . .77 A7
  North Coates DN36 . . . . .37 B4
  Old Leake PE22 . . . . .114 C1
  Saltfleet LN11 . . . . .51 C5
  Theddlethorpe St Helen LN12 . .63 E7
  Wrangle PE22 . . . . .114 C1
Seal Cr DN36 . . . . .195 D7
Sealey's La PE13 . . . . .177 D8
Seal Sanctuary & Nature Ctr
  The★ LN12 . . . . .64 B5
Seamer Gr 1 DN32 . . . . .192 A5
SEARBY DN38 . . . . .32 C8
Searby Hill DN38 . . . . .32 B8
Searby Rd Lincoln LN2 . . . . .202 B8
  Scunthorpe DN17 . . . . .184 E4
Searby Wold La DN38 . . . . . . .21 E1
Sea Rd Anderby PE24 . . . . .77 B2
  18 Chapel St Leonard PE24 . . .90 D7
  Cleethorpes DN35 . . . . .192 F6
Seargeants Cl 1 PE6 . . . . . .174 E4
Searjeant St PE1 . . . . .225 E5
Searson Cl PE9 . . . . .172 F7
Seascale Wlk DN32 . . . . .191 F8
Seas End Rd Moulton PE12 . .146 D1
  Surfleet PE11 . . . . .145 E3
SEATHORNE PE25 . . . . .206 E8
Seathorne Cres PE25 . . . . . . .90 F1
Seathorne Prim Sch PE25 . . .206 D7
Seaton Cl PE7 . . . . .233 D6
Seaton Gr Grimsby DN32 . . .192 A5
  Kingston upon Hull HU4 . . . .179 E5
Seaton Rd
  Kingston upon Hull HU4 . . . .178 F2
  Scunthorpe DN17 . . . . .184 D8
  6 Stamford PE9 . . . . .219 B4
Sea View LN11 . . . . .51 D3

Sea View Rd PE25 . . . . .206 D5
Sea View St DN35 . . . . .192 F5
Seawall La DN36 . . . . .37 C5
Sebrights Way PE3 . . . . .224 F3
Second Ave Brookenby LN8. . .47 A6
  Fixborough Ind Est DN15 . . . . .7 F1
  Grantham NG31 . . . . .211 F6
  Grimsby DN33 . . . . .191 B4
  5 Scampton Airfield LN1 . . . . .67 E5
  3 Scunthorpe DN17 . . . . . . .184 C6
  Spalding PE11 . . . . .214 A4
Second Dro Crowland PE6. . .166 E3
  Gosberton PE11 . . . . .144 C3
  Peterborough PE1 . . . . .226 D1
Second Dro Ind Est PE1. . . .226 D1
Second Marsh Rd PE14 . . . . .170 C3
Secret Gdns 10 LN7 . . . . .33 A3
SEDGEBROOK NG32 . . . . . . .128 F5
Sedgebrook Cl 1 LN2 . . . . .201 F8
Sedgebrook Rd NG32 . . . . . .128 F6
Sedge Cl
  6 Barton-upon-Humber
  DN18. . . . . .3 F1
  Leasingham NG34 . . . . .121 C7
Sedgefield Ct PE10 . . . . .213 B3
Sedge Hole Cl Nature
  Reserve★ DN9 . . . . .27 F2
Sedgemoor Cl 3 LN6. . . . . . .204 E1
Sedge Pl 9 PE12 . . . . .167 B8
Sedgewood Way DN15. . . . . .182 C6
Seed Cl La 4 DN37 . . . . .23 F1
Seedlands Cl PE21 . . . . .209 B7
Sefton Ave PE13 . . . . .170 E1
Sefton St 2 HU3 . . . . .180 B4
Segmere St 3 DN35 . . . . . . .193 A5
Segrave Gr HU5. . . . . .179 D8
Selbourne Rd 4 DN34. . . . . .190 E4
Selby Cl LN6 . . . . .205 A3
Selby Ct DN17. . . . . .184 D7
Selby Rd DN8 . . . . .14 F8
Selby St HU3 . . . . .180 A5
Selemba Wy NG34 . . . . .121 A2
Selge Way DN33 . . . . .190 F3
Selkirk St HU5 . . . . .180 A8
Sellers Grange PE2. . . . . . . .230 B4
Sellwood Ct NG34 . . . . .212 F7
Sellwood Gdns LN9 . . . . . . .199 B3
Selmeston Ct DN34. . . . . . . .191 C6
Selwyn Ave 16 HU14 . . . . .3 A4
Selwyn Ct DN34 . . . . .190 F6
Selwyn Rd PE9. . . . . .219 A7
Sempers Cl LN6 . . . . .92 E8
Sennefleet Rd DN21 . . . . .29 B4
Sense Coll PE7 . . . . .230 E3
Sentance Cres PE20 . . . . . . .136 C6
Sequana Ct HU9 . . . . .181 B6
Seraphim App Rd DN16 . . . .183 E1
Seraphim Rd DN16 . . . . .183 F1
Serena Rd 5 PE25 . . . . .206 D2
Serlby Gdns PE2 . . . . .225 B3
Serpentine Gn Sh Ctr
  PE7 . . . . .230 D3
Serpentine St 1 LN8 . . . . . . .57 D7
Serpentine The PE7 . . . . . . .230 D3
Service Rd DN37 . . . . .190 D8
Service Rd 10 6 DN37. . . . . .188 A1
Service Rd 1 18 DN37. . . . . .190 E8
Service Rd 12 2 DN37. . . . . .188 A1
Service Rd 13 4 DN37. . . . . .188 A1
Service Rd 14 3 DN37. . . . . .188 A1
Service Rd 15 16 DN37. . . . . .190 E8
Service Rd 16 DN37 . . . . . . .190 E8
Service Rd 17 DN37 . . . . . . .190 F8
Service Rd 18 DN37 . . . . . . .190 F8
Service Rd 19 4 DN37. . . . . .190 F8
Service Rd 20 19 DN37. . . . . .190 E8
Service Rd 2 17 DN37 . . . . . .190 E8
Service Rd 21 1 DN37. . . . . .190 E8
Service Rd 22 3 DN37. . . . . .190 E8
Service Rd 23 DN37 . . . . . . .190 E8
Service Rd 25 11 DN37. . . . . .190 E8
Service Rd 26 9 DN37. . . . . .188 A1
Service Rd 3 15 DN37 . . . . . .190 E8
Service Rd 4 8 DN37 . . . . . . .190 E8
Service Rd 5 13 DN37 . . . . . .190 E8
Service Rd 6 14 DN37 . . . . . .190 E8
Service Rd 7 3 DN37 . . . . . . .190 F8
Service Rd 8 8 DN37 . . . . . . .188 A1
Service Rd 9 9 DN37 . . . . . . .188 A1
Service Rd No 1 3 DN32. . . .189 B1
Service Rd No 2 4 DN32. . . .189 B1
Services Rd DN16 . . . . .183 E2
Setchfield Pl PE2 . . . . .230 F7
Setterwood Garth 2
  HU10 . . . . .178 E8
Setts Cl PE10 . . . . .213 C2
Sevayn's Dr 12 NG34. . . . . . .107 F1
Sevenacres PE2. . . . . .229 E5
Seven Quay Rd DN40 . . . . . .186 E7
Seventh Ave 3 NG31. . . . . . .211 F6
Seventy Acre La DN37 . . . . . .33 F8
Severn Ct PE4. . . . . .220 E2
Severn Rd PE11 . . . . .214 F5
Severn St LN1. . . . . .201 C4
Severn Way 2 DN37 . . . . . . .190 E8
Sewell Cl PE6. . . . . .217 E5
Sewell Rd LN2 . . . . .234 C3
Sewell's Wlk LN5 . . . . .201 E1
Sewell Wy 1 PE11 . . . . .214 A1
Sewer La 3 HU1. . . . . .180 F5
SEWSTERN NG33 . . . . .150 F4
Sewstern Cl 15 LN4. . . . . .81 A1
Sewstern La
  Allington NG32. . . . . .128 E7
  Long Bennington NG23. . . . . .117 A1
  Sedgebrook NG32 . . . . .128 D4
Sewstern Rd
  Gunby & Stainby NG33 . . . . .151 B4

Sewstern Rd continued
  Wymondham LE14 . . . . .150 D2
Seymour La LN11 . . . . .198 C4
Seymour La 14 LN13 . . . . .75 C7
Seymour Pl PE4 . . . . .221 F2
Seymour St HU3 . . . . .179 F5
Sezanne Wlk 10 PE11 . . . . . .214 C6
Shackleton Cl
  Market Deeping PE6. . . . . . . .217 B7
  10 Spalding PE11 . . . . .214 C2
Shackleton Wy PE7 . . . . .233 D5
Shaddys Wlk LN13 . . . . .88 E6
Shadows La LN8 . . . . .43 D1
Shadwell Rise 29 DN18 . . . . . .3 E1
Shaftesbury Ave
  Birchwood LN6. . . . . .200 D2
  Grimsby DN34 . . . . .191 B7
Shaftesbury Mews 6
  DN36. . . . . .195 C6
Shaftesbury Way 2 NG23. . .91 D5
Shakespeare Ave
  Grantham NG31 . . . . .211 E6
  Peterborough PE1 . . . . .225 F7
  4 Lincoln LN5 . . . . .205 E8
Shakespeare Cl 6 HU3 . . . . .180 D8
Shakespeare St
  5 Gainsborough DN21 . . . . .197 D2
  5 Lincoln LN5 . . . . .205 E8
  13 Newark-on-Trent NG24. . .104 A3
Shakespeare Way PE11 . . . . .214 A1
Shamfields Rd 3 PE23 . . . . .101 A8
Shamrock Cl PE2 . . . . .231 C7
Shamrock Cl LN5 . . . . .205 E6
Shanklin Dr NG31 . . . . .210 E4
Shannon Ave LN6 . . . . .205 A5
Shannon Cl 2 Lincoln LN6 .205 A5
  11 Spalding PE11. . . . . .214 A4
Shannon Rd 8 LN4. . . . . . . .207 D4
Shardloes LN4 . . . . .81 E2
Shardloes Rd 9 PE25 . . . . . .103 E4
Sharma Leas PE4 . . . . .220 E3
Sharmans Cl 11 LN12 . . . . . . .77 A7
Sharman Way PE11. . . . . . . .214 B5
Sharnbrook Ave 1 PE7. . . . .230 C1
Sharpe Cl 35 DN18 . . . . .10 E8
Sharpe Rd NG31 . . . . .211 C6
Sharpe's Rd PE6 . . . . .165 C3
Sharp's Cl PE10 . . . . .213 B6
Sharp's La PE22. . . . . .127 A6
Sharp Wlk LN6 . . . . .93 C8
Shaw Ave 35 HU15. . . . . .2 D5
Shawbury Cl 10 LN6 . . . . . . .204 C6
Shaw Dr DN33 . . . . .191 E1
Shawfield Cl 10 DN3. . . . . . . .14 A3
Shaw Rd Boston PE21 . . . . . .208 C7
  Grantham NG31 . . . . .210 D2
  Gringley on the Hill DN10 . . . .39 C2
Shaws La Hilldyke PE22 . . . . .126 C5
  Little Sutton PE12. . . . . .160 B3
  Old Leake PE22 . . . . .127 B8
Shaws Mews LN11 . . . . .198 B5
Shaw St HU9. . . . . .181 B7
Shaw Way 4 LN2 . . . . .68 C2
Shays Dr 1 LN6. . . . . .205 A7
Shearers Dr 12 PE11. . . . . . .214 A2
Shearman's Wath
  Thimbleby LN9 . . . . .85 C6
  West Ashby LN9 . . . . .199 A8
Shears Ct DN37 . . . . .194 F4
Shearwater Cl
  3 Birchwood LN6. . . . . .200 E1
  Louth LN11. . . . . .198 D8
Shearwater Rd LN6. . . . . . . .200 E1
Sheep Cote La DN7 . . . . .14 D2
Sheep Dip La DN7. . . . . .14 D4
Sheepdyke La
  2 Bonby DN20 . . . . .10 C2
  4 Careby Aunby & Holywell
  PE9. . . . . .163 A8
Sheepfold St DN32 . . . . .191 E7
Sheepgate PE2 . . . . .127 A6
Sheep Marsh La DN36 . . . . . .37 B3
Sheep Mkt
  2 Spalding PE11. . . . . .214 D4
  11 Stamford PE9. . . . . .219 B5
Sheepwalk
  Aubourn Haddington & South
  Hykeham LN5 . . . . .92 E5
  Peterborough PE4 . . . . .221 E1
Sheepwash La LN4 . . . . .81 E4
Sheep Wash Lane LN3. . . . . .211 B1
Sheffield Pk Ave DN15. . . . . .182 F5
Sheffield St (East) 1
  DN15 . . . . .183 A4
Sheffield St (West) 4
  DN15 . . . . .182 F4
Sheffield St DN15 . . . . .183 A4
Sheila Cres 4 PE11 . . . . .214 A3
Sheldon Gdns HU13 . . . . . . .178 A3
Sheldon Rd
  Nunsthorpe DN33 . . . . .191 A4
  Nunsthorpe DN33 . . . . .191 A2
Sheldrake Rd 1 NG34 . . . . . .212 B3
Shelford St DN15. . . . . .183 A3
Shelley Ave
  Grantham NG31 . . . . .211 D6
  Grimsby DN33 . . . . .191 B4
Shelley Cl
  3 Mablethorpe/Sutton on Sea
  LN12 . . . . .77 A7
  New England PE1 . . . . .225 F8
  12 Stamford PE9 . . . . .218 E6
Shelley Dr Lincoln LN2 . . . . .202 B6
  7 Sleaford NG34. . . . . .212 F4
Shelroy Cl DN15. . . . . .182 C5
Shelton Rd PE2 . . . . .231 D6
Shenley Cl 11 DN7. . . . . .14 D3

SHEPEAU STOW PE12 . . . . . .167 F3
Shepeau Stow Prim Sch
  PE12. . . . . .167 F3
Shepherds Cl PE4 . . . . .221 A4
Shepherd's Croft 1 DN9 . . . .27 D7
Shepherd's La NG34. . . . . . .133 E7
Shepherd's Wlk PE9 . . . . . . .163 D1
Sheppard's Cl
  Heighington/Washingborough
  LN4 .81 E4
  Heighington/Washingborough
  LN4. . . . . .81 E4
Sheppard's Dro PE6. . . . . . . .167 B1
Shepperson's Ave PE11. . . . .144 F5
Shepton La NG34. . . . . .142 A8
Sheraton Cl 15 LN6. . . . . . . .204 D7
Sheraton Dr 13 DN36 . . . . . . .36 D8
Sherborne Rd PE1 . . . . .226 D6
Sherbourne Cl 10 PE20 . . . .135 B7
Sherbrooke St 2 LN2 . . . . . .202 D4
Sherburn Cres DN15. . . . . . .182 D5
Sherburn St
  Cleethorpes DN35 . . . . .192 F4
  Kingston upon Hull HU9 . . . .181 D8
Sheridan Cl 1 Lincoln LN2 .202 C7
  16 Newark-on-Trent NG24. . .104 B2
Sheridan Rd PE1 . . . . .225 F8
Sheriff Way PE21 . . . . .208 E7
Sheringham Way PE2 . . . . . .230 C6
Sherwood Ave
  Boston PE21 . . . . .208 E7
  Newark-on-Trent NG24 . . . . .104 A4
  4 Peterborough PE2. . . . . . . .230 F7
  7 Wisbech PE13 . . . . .170 D1
Sherwood Cl
  1 Louth LN11 . . . . .198 C4
  Stamford PE9 . . . . .218 F5
Sherwood Dr
  Kingston upon Hull HU4 . . . .179 A4
  Spalding PE11 . . . . .214 D6
  Waddington LN5. . . . . .205 D1
Sherwood Rd
  10 Coningsby LN4 . . . . .207 D4
  Grimsby DN34 . . . . .190 F6
  3 Mablethorpe/Sutton on Sea
  LN12 . . . . .64 B4
Sherwood Rise 7 NG32 . . . . .119 B7
Sherwood Vale DN15 . . . . . .182 C3
Shetland Way DN40 . . . . . . .186 C2
Shillaker Ct PE10. . . . . .213 D4
Shipton Rd DN16 . . . . .185 C5
Shire Ave PE11. . . . . .214 A5
Shire Cl 6 LN4. . . . . .109 F6
Shiregate 12 LN4. . . . . .95 C4
Shire Gr PE21 . . . . .226 C5
Shire La NG23. . . . . .117 D8
Shires Orch 6 NG32. . . . . . .138 D4
Shirewood La PE22. . . . . .99 A5
Shirley Cres DN16 . . . . .185 B8
Shivean Gate 5 PE12. . . . . . .157 F7
Shodfriars La 4 PE21 . . . . . .208 F4
Shoe La LN9 . . . . .72 C5
Shoemaker's La DN21 . . . . . .29 E5
Shoff Dro PE11. . . . . .134 D1
Shoff Rd PE11. . . . . .134 D1
Sholt's Gate PE12 . . . . .158 C7
Shop Hill 7 PE22 . . . . .98 F4
Shop La Goulceby LN11 . . . . . .72 D6
  New Barnetby DN38. . . . . .21 D5
Shore Rd Freiston PE22. . . . .126 F1
  Garthorpe & Fockerby DN17 . . .7 F5
Shore View PE7 . . . . .230 B2
Shortacres Rd PE2 . . . . .230 F7
Short Dro Gosberton PE11. . .144 C5
  Pointon & Sempringham
  NG34. . . . . .143 F4
  Thurlby PE10 . . . . .164 B8
Shortfen PE2 . . . . .230 C4
Short Ferry Rd LN3. . . . . .82 F6
Shortfield La PE21. . . . . .209 E8
Short Furrow 9 LN5 . . . . . . .107 B8
Short Hollow NG33 . . . . .131 C1
Short La Fotherby LN11 . . . . . .49 A2
  Ingham LN1 . . . . .54 F3
  Lincoln LN1 . . . . .234 A2
  1 West Halton DN15. . . . . .8 E8
  3 Wisbech PE13 . . . . .170 A1
Shortleys Rd DN22 . . . . .65 B5
Short's Cnr PE22 . . . . .112 D3
Short St
  2 Cleethorpes DN35. . . . . . .192 F6
  6 Spalding PE11. . . . . .214 C4
Short Wheatley La NG23. . . .91 D3
Shortwood La
  Bullington LN8 . . . . .69 F4
  Friesthorpe LN3. . . . . .57 A2
Shorwell Cl 3 NG31. . . . . . . .210 E4
Shotbolt La PE11. . . . . .214 F8
Shrewsbury Ave PE2 . . . . . . .230 D5
Shropshire Rd 9 LN1 . . . . . . .67 E5
Shrubberies Nature Reserve
  The★ PE12 . . . . .216 B5
Shrub Rd PE7 . . . . .230 C1
Shrubwood Cl 3 NG34 . . . . .122 E2
Shuttlefield La PE20. . . . . . . .135 F4
Shuttleworth Ct 12 LN6. . . . . .93 C8
Sibcy La NG24 . . . . .104 B2
Sibelius Rd HU4. . . . . .179 B4
SIBSEY PE22 . . . . .113 B2
Sibsey Ct DN37. . . . . .188 A2
Sibsey Drain Bank PE22 . . . .126 A3
Sibsey Free Prim Sch The
  PE22. . . . . .113 A2
Sibsey La 3 PE21 . . . . .208 F4
Sibsey Rd Boston PE21 . . . . .209 B8
  Fishtoft PE21. . . . . .125 F5
Sibsey Trader Windmill★
  PE22 . . . . .113 A2

Sibthorpe Dr LN2 . . . . .68 F2
Sibthorp Gdns LN4 . . . . .81 A4
Sibthorp St LN5 . . . . .201 E1
Sickling Gate Rd PE2 . . . . . .115 B7
Sidebar La NG34 . . . . .123 C4
Side La DN33 . . . . .195 A7
Side Row NG24 . . . . .104 A4
Side St 2 NG32 . . . . .128 F7
Sidings Ct 3 HU15 . . . . .2 B5
Sidings Rd DN31 . . . . .191 A8
Sidings The Cranwell NG34 120 E8
  Holbeach PE12. . . . . .215 D1
  Horncastle LN9 . . . . .199 A3
  Lincoln LN6 . . . . .234 A1
  Long Sutton PE12 . . . . .216 B4
  2 Louth LN11 . . . . .198 C5
  23 Mablethorpe/Sutton on Sea
  LN12 . . . . .77 A8
  6 Morton PE10 . . . . .154 D6
  8 Moulton PE12 . . . . .157 F6
  9 Ruskington NG34 . . . . . . .108 E1
  25 Saxilby LN1 . . . . .66 D2
Sidlaw Gr LN5 . . . . .205 C2
Sidney Chase LN1 . . . . .54 F1
Sidney Cl PE24 . . . . .90 D6
Sidney Ct 1 DN35. . . . . .192 B8
Sidney Pl DN35 . . . . .192 B8
Sidney Rd Grimsby DN34 . . .191 B7
  5 Scunthorpe DN17 . . . . . . .184 C6
Sidney St
  4 Cleethorpes DN35. . . . . . .189 D1
  Cleethorpes DN35 . . . . .192 B8
  Grantham NG31 . . . . .211 A6
  Lincoln LN5 . . . . .205 E8
Sidney Terr 17 LN5 . . . . .205 E8
Sidney Way DN35 . . . . .192 B8
Signal Rd NG31 . . . . .211 C5
Signhills Ave DN35 . . . . .193 A4
Signhills Infant Acad
  DN35. . . . . .193 A4
Silica Cres DN17 . . . . .184 C5
SILK WILLOUGHBY NG34. . .121 C1
Silt La PE20 . . . . .136 E3
Silt Pit La PE21. . . . . .137 A7
Siltside PE11 . . . . .144 D4
Silverbell DN16 . . . . .185 E4
Silver Birch Rise DN16. . . . . .185 B3
Silvergarth DN32. . . . . .192 B5
Silver Hill PE7 . . . . .230 D3
Silverines Mdws Nature
  Reserve★ LN11 . . . . .72 E5
Silver La 20 PE9 . . . . .219 B5
Silversides La DN20 . . . . . . .196 A2
Silversides La Cvn Site
  DN20 . . . . .196 A2
Silver's La PE13. . . . . .177 E7
Silver St Bardney LN3. . . . . . . .83 C4
  Barnetby le Wold DN38. . . . . .21 B4
  Barrow upon Humber DN19 . .11 C7
  Baumber LN9 . . . . .72 A1
  Benniworth LN8. . . . . .71 F8
  Branston LN4 . . . . .81 E2
  Coningsby LN4 . . . . .207 C4
  Gainsborough DN21. . . . . . . .197 C4
  Holton le Clay DN36 . . . . . . .195 D4
  11 Kingston upon Hull HU1. . .180 F6
  Lincoln LN2 . . . . .234 B2
  Minting LN9 . . . . .84 C8
  North Clifton NG23 . . . . .78 C7
  Owston Ferry DN9 . . . . .28 B2
  Peterborough PE2. . . . . .230 F7
  1 Ruskington NG34 . . . . . . .108 E1
  Stainforth DN7 . . . . .14 C6
  3 Waddingham DN21. . . . . . . .43 D7
  6 Wainfleet All Saints
  PE24 . . . . .102 D1
  Winteringham DN15. . . . . .2 B1
  Wisbech PE13 . . . . .170 D1
  3 Wragby LN8 . . . . .70 D5
Silverstone Rd
  17 Birchwood LN6 . . . . .204 C7
  6 Bourne PE10 . . . . .213 C5
Silvertoft La PE20 . . . . .136 B8
Silverwood Rd
  8 Bottesford NG13 . . . . .128 A5
  Peterborough PE2. . . . . .225 F5
Silvester Rd PE5 . . . . .223 E2
Silvester St HU2 . . . . .180 F7
Simons Cl
  4 Donington on Bain LN11 . .59 E1
  5 Louth LN11 . . . . .198 C4
Simon's Gn LN6 . . . . .205 C6
Simons Pl DN35 . . . . .192 D7
Simon Weir La PE20 . . . . . . .135 D8
Simpson Cl
  5 Balderton NG24. . . . . .104 C2
  17 Barrow upon Humber
  DN19. . . . . .11 D8
  Chapel St Leonard PE24 . . . . .90 D6
Simpson's Fold DN36 . . . . . .195 B6
Simpson St 16 PE23. . . . . . . .88 A1
Sincil Bank LN5 . . . . .234 B1
Sincil Bank (Lincoln City FC)
  LN5 . . . . .201 E1
Sincil Sch The LN5 . . . . .205 E8
Sincil St LN5 . . . . .234 B2
Sinclair Cl PE21 . . . . .208 E8
Sinderson Rd DN36 . . . . .36 D8
Singerfire Rd PE5 . . . . .223 D2
Sir Francis Hill Com Prim Sch
  LN6 . . . . .205 C8
Sir Isaac Newton Cl 3
  PE12. . . . . .215 E3
Sir Isaac Newton Dr 3
  PE21. . . . . .208 F1
Sirius Acad HU4. . . . . .179 B4
Sirius Cl 3 HU3. . . . . .180 B5

Sir John Nelthorpe Sch
DN20 . . . . .196 C3
Sir Robert Pattinson Acad
LN6 . . . . .204 E2
Sir William Robertson High
Sch The LN5 . . . . .106 E4
Siskin Cl PE10 . . . . .143 A3
Siskin Cres DN16 . . . . . . .185 B2
Sissley PE2 . . . . .229 E2
Sitwell St HU8 . . . . .181 A8
Sixfields Cl LN6 . . . . .205 A7
SIXHILLS LN8 . . . . .58 E6
Sixhills La Little London LN8 . 58 B5
  Ludford LN8 . . . . .59 A7
Sixhills Rd LN8 . . . . .58 D6
Sixhills St DN32 . . . . .191 E7
Six House Bank PE11 . . . . .123 E3
Six Hundreds Dro PE20 . .123 E3
Sixth Ave Brookenby LN8 . . .47 B6
  Fixborough Ind Est DN15 . . . .8 A1
  [2] Grantham NG31 . . . . .211 F6
  Scunthorpe DN17 . . . . .184 B6
Skaters Way PE4 . . . . .221 A4
Skayman Fields [7] LN6 . . . .105 E8
Skegger Beck Rd DN38 . . . .21 A4
SKEGNESS PE25 . . . . .206 C4
Skegness Bsns Ctr PE25 .206 B3
Skegness Coll of Vocational
  Ed PE25 . . . . .206 C2
Skegness & District Hospl
  PE25 . . . . .206 B3
Skegness Gram Sch PE25 206 C4
Skegness Infant Acad
  PE25 . . . . .206 C4
Skegness (Ingoldmells)
  Aerodrome PE25 . . . . .90 D1
Skegness Jun Sch PE25 . .206 C4
Skegness Motor Racing
  Stadium PE24 . . . . .90 A2
Skegness Rd
  Burgh le Marsh PE24 . . . . .103 A7
  Chapel St Leonard PE24 . . . .90 D6
  Ingoldmells PE25 . . . . .90 E3
  Partney PE23 . . . . .88 B3
  Skegness PE25 . . . . .103 C8
  [5] Wainfleet All Saints
  PE24 . . . . .103 A7
Skegness Ret Pk PE25 . . .206 A3
Skegness Sports Ctr PE25 206 B5
Skegness Sta PE25 . . . . . .206 C4
Skegness Wr Leisure Pk★
  PE25 . . . . .90 E1
SKELDYKE PE20 . . . . .136 F4
Skeldyke Rd PE20 . . . . . . .136 D5
SKELLINGTHORPE LN6 . . . .200 B4
Skellingthorpe Rd LN6 . . .200 D2
Skells Ct PE9 . . . . .219 D5
Skelton Cl [14] NG34 . . . . . .122 D3
Skelton Dr PE12 . . . . .216 C3
Skelton Rd DN17 . . . . .184 C7
SKENDLEBY PE23 . . . . .88 D4
Skendleby Nature Reserve★
  LN13 . . . . .88 B6
Skerries Cl [5] LN6 . . . . . . .205 A1
Skerry La NG13 . . . . .128 C5
SKIDBROOKE LN11 . . . . .51 B3
Skillings La HU15 . . . . .2 C5
SKILLINGTON NG33 . . . . . . .151 B8
Skillington Rd
  Gunby & Stainby NG33 . . . .151 B6
  Stroxton NG33 . . . . .139 F4
SKINNAND LN5 . . . . .106 C8
Skinnand La LN5 . . . . .106 D7
Skinners La
  [6] South Ferriby DN18 . . . . . .10 A7
  Waltham DN37 . . . . .194 E4
Skinner's La
  Middle Rasen LN8 . . . . .45 C1
  South Kyme LN4 . . . . .110 B1
Skipmarsh La
  Leverton PE22 . . . . .126 E8
  Old Leake PE22 . . . . .113 C1
Skippingdale Ind Pk
  DN15 . . . . .182 C7
Skippingdale Rd DN15 . . .182 F6
Skipwith Cres [20] LN4 . . . . .95 D4
Skipworth Way PE25 . . . . .206 C8
SKIRBECK PE21 . . . . .209 B3
Skirbeck Dr [15] LN1 . . . . . . .66 D2
Skirbeck Gdns PE21 . . . . .209 B3
SKIRBECK QUARTER
  PE21 . . . . .208 D2
Skirbeck Rd PE21 . . . . . . .209 A3
Skirmore Rd PE22 . . . . . . .114 C5
Skirth Rd LN4 . . . . .109 F6
Skitter Rd DN40 . . . . .5 D1
Skye Cl PE2 . . . . .229 C5
Skylark Dr DN16 . . . . .185 B2
Skylarks Cl [6] PE7 . . . . . . .230 D3
Slack The [4] DN17 . . . . .16 D8
Slash La LN9 . . . . .86 D3
Slate Drift [2] PE9 . . . . . . .171 C2
Slate Farm Cl [7] LN8 . . . . . .43 D3
Slate Mill Pl NG31 . . . . . . .211 B5
Slate Mill The NG31 . . . . .211 B5
Slay Pit Cl [3] DN7 . . . . .14 F4
Slay Pit La DN7 . . . . .14 F3
Slea Cotts [15] NG34 . . . . . .212 D4
SLEAFORD NG34 . . . . .212 B4
Sleaford (Aided) RC Prim Sch
  NG34 . . . . .212 C2
Sleaford Art Studio★
  NG34 . . . . .212 D5
Sleaford Coll NG34 . . . . . .212 E4
Sleaford Enterprise Pk
  NG34 . . . . .212 F6
Sleaford Leisure Ctr
  NG34 . . . . .212 E4

Sleaford Lollycocks Field
  Nature Reserve★ NG34 .212 E4
Sleaford Mareham Nature
  Reserve★ NG34 . . . . .212 E2
Sleaford Rd Ancaster NG32 120 A2
  Barnby in the Willows NG24 104 F5
  Boston PE21 . . . . .208 B4
  Bracebridge Heath LN4 . . . .81 A1
  Coningsby LN4 . . . . .207 A4
  Cranwell NG34 . . . . .120 F8
  East Kirkby PE23 . . . . .99 E4
  Folkingham NG34 . . . . . . .142 D8
  Heckington NG34 . . . . . . .122 D3
  Honington NG32 . . . . .119 C2
  Leadenham LN5 . . . . .106 D2
  [14] Leasingham NG34 . . . . .121 B7
  Metheringham LN4 . . . . . . .95 B4
  [18] Navenby/Wellingore
  LN5 . . . . .107 A7
  Newark-on-Trent NG24 . . .104 A5
  North Kyme LN4 . . . . .109 C2
  Ruskington NG34 . . . . . . .108 E1
  Tattershall LN4 . . . . .110 D7
  Walcot near Folkingham
  NG34 . . . . .132 D2
Sleaford Sta NG34 . . . . . . .212 D3
Sleaford Virtual Mus★ [7]
  NG34 . . . . .212 C4
Sledge La LN8 . . . . .59 B8
Sledmere Gr HU4 . . . . .179 E5
Sleepers Cl [1] PE12 . . . . . .216 B4
Sleights Cl HU3 . . . . .180 A7
Sleights Dr [2] PE14 . . . . . .170 F1
Sleights La HU15 . . . . .1 B6
Slessor St [2] LN5 . . . . .94 A7
Slipe Dro PE10 . . . . .155 F5
Slipe The PE10 . . . . .213 F4
Slippery Gowt La PE21 . . .136 F8
Slipway DN35 . . . . .193 A6
SLOOTHBY LN13 . . . . .89 D5
Sloothby High La
  Hogsthorpe PE24 . . . . .90 A6
  Willoughby with Sloothby
  PE24 . . . . .89 F6
Sluice La DN18 . . . . .9 E8
Sluice Rd Holbeach PE12 .215 B8
  South Ferriby DN18 . . . . .9 F8
  Sutton Bridge PE12 . . . . . .161 A6
  Whaplode PE12 . . . . .147 B4
Small Dro PE12 . . . . .157 E7
Small Dro La PE11 . . . . . . .144 E1
Small End Rd PE22 . . . . . . .114 E6
Smalley Rd PE21 . . . . .209 D4
Smallwood PE3 . . . . .225 B5
Smeeton Ct [6] NG34 . . . . . .212 D6
Smeeton's La PE20 . . . . . . .146 C7
Smithdale Cl [9] PE11 . . . . .214 C6
Smith Field [10] DN36 . . . . . .36 B1
Smithfield PE6 . . . . .176 B3
Smithfield Rd DN16 . . . . . .185 D6
Smithson Cl [11] NG24 . . . . .104 B2
Smith St Beacon Hill NG24 . 104 A4
  Lincoln LN5 . . . . .201 C1
  Scunthorpe DN15 . . . . .182 F4
Smithy La
  [7] Barnetby le Wold DN38 . . .21 B4
  Friskney PE22 . . . . .115 A6
Smooting La [4] LN3 . . . . . . .82 A8
Smooting The LN8 . . . . .46 C1
Smoots The [19] LN5 . . . . . .107 A8
Smythe La DN22 . . . . .52 D1
Snaffer's La PE12 . . . . .158 C5
Snainton Gr [4] HU5 . . . . . .179 D8
Snaith Ave PE20 . . . . .146 D7
Snaith Cl [3] LN6 . . . . .204 B6
SNARFORD LN2 . . . . .56 D1
Snarford Rd LN3 . . . . .69 D8
SNELLAND LN3 . . . . .69 E6
Snelland La LN3 . . . . .69 E6
Snelland Rd LN3 . . . . .69 E8
Snetterton Cl [1] LN6 . . . . .204 C7
Snipe Dales Ctry Pk★ PE23 86 F3
Snipe Dales Nature Reserve★
  LN9 . . . . .86 E3
SNITTERBY DN21 . . . . .43 D5
Snitterby Carr La DN21 . . . .43 F5
Snitterby Rd DN21 . . . . .43 E5
Snowberry Gdns [5] LN6 . .204 C8
Snow Cl NG34 . . . . .212 C7
Snowden Cl [1] PE6 . . . . . . .175 C8
Snowdon Cl [4] LN5 . . . . . . .205 D3
Snowdonia Ave DN15 . . . .182 D7
Snowdon Rd [3] NG23 . . . . . .91 D4
Snowdrop Ave [22] NG24 . . .104 C5
Snowdrop Cl [10] DN41 . . . . . .23 F5
Snowdrop La LN11 . . . . .198 A6
Snowdrop Pl [8] PE11 . . . . . .214 A5
Snowhills PE7 . . . . .233 E6
Sobrite Wy PE4 . . . . .220 F7
Sods La PE11 . . . . .145 D5
Soff La DN19 . . . . .12 A6
Soggin La LN5 . . . . .106 F5
Soke Parkway PE1 . . . . . . .221 E1
Soke Rd PE6 . . . . .174 D5
Solent Dr PE11 . . . . .214 B5
Solhem Ave [13] PE21 . . . . .136 D8
Solomon Ct DN35 . . . . .192 D5
Solway Ave PE21 . . . . .136 E8
Solway St [5] DN37 . . . . . . .190 E8
SOMERBY DN38 . . . . .21 B1
Somerby Cl
  [8] Moulton PE12 . . . . .157 F7
  [3] Stamford PE9 . . . . .219 B7
Somerby Dr [6] DN9 . . . . . . .28 A3
Somerby Garth [4] PE21 . . .136 D8
Somerby Gr NG31 . . . . .211 D2
Somerby Hill NG31 . . . . . . .211 C2
Somerby Pl NG31 . . . . .211 E1

Somerby Rd
  Gainsborough DN21 . . . . . .197 F5
  Ropsley & Humby NG33 . . .141 A8
  Scunthorpe DN17 . . . . .184 D5
Somerby Wold La DN38 . . . .21 C1
Somerby Wy DN21 . . . . .53 A8
Somercotes Rd LN11 . . . . . .51 A3
Somerden N PE21 . . . . .5 F8
Somerfield Dr [9] LN11 . . . . .50 F7
SOMERSBY PE23 . . . . .87 A7
Somersby Ave [9] LN12 . . . .64 B8
Somersby Cl LN6 . . . . .205 C4
Somersby Ct
  [15] Louth LN11 . . . . .198 B5
  North Carlton LN1 . . . . .67 C4
Somersby Gn PE21 . . . . . . .209 B7
Somersby Gr [2] PE25 . . . .206 D1
Somersby Rd LN9 . . . . .86 F6
Somersby St DN31 . . . . . . .191 D8
Somersby Way PE21 . . . . .209 B7
Somersby Wy LN11 . . . . . . .198 E6
Somerscales St [2] LN3 . . .180 E8
Somerset Dr [4] DN15 . . . . . . .8 A4
Somerset St HU3 . . . . .180 A5
Somerton Cl NG34 . . . . . . .212 C3
Somerton Dr [3] DN7 . . . . . . .14 F3
Somerton Gate La LN5 . . . . .93 D7
Somerton Rd DN40 . . . . . . .186 D3
Somervell Rd DN16 . . . . . .185 C4
Somerville PE4 . . . . .220 E5
Somerville Cl [11] LN5 . . . . . .93 E8
Somerville Ct [14] LN5 . . . . . .93 E8
Somerville Rd [1] PE9 . . . . .219 A6
Somes Cl [1] PE9 . . . . .172 C6
Somme Cl LN1 . . . . .201 E7
Sonia Crest DN40 . . . . .186 B4
Sophia Ave DN33 . . . . .191 C1
Sorbus Cl [3] PE7 . . . . .230 D3
Sorbus Cl [5] HU3 . . . . .180 D6
Sorbus View [4] HU5 . . . . . .179 C7
Sorby Cl PE25 . . . . .206 E8
Sorrel Cl [3] Binbrook LN8 . . .47 C5
  [1] Market Deeping PE6 . . . . .217 D6
  [4] Stamford PE9 . . . . .218 D6
  Yaxley PE7 . . . . .233 B8
Sorrel Ct LN6 . . . . .204 C8
Sorrel Dr PE11 . . . . .214 A5
Sorrel Way Hessle HU13 . . .178 B1
  Scunthorpe DN15 . . . . .182 C6
Soss La DN10 . . . . .40 A5
SOTBY LN8 . . . . .71 E5
Sotby Mdws Nature Reserve★
  LN8 . . . . .71 E5
SOTS HOLE LN4 . . . . .96 C7
Soulby La PE22 . . . . .114 C2
Sour La DN7 . . . . .14 E8
Soutergate [13] DN18 . . . . . . .3 F1
South Airfield Rd NG34 . . .120 C8
South Axholme Com Sch
  DN9 . . . . .27 D6
South Bank [3] DN17 . . . . . . .17 D6
Southbank La DN22 . . . . . . .65 A8
SOUTH BRAMWITH DN7 . . . . .14 A6
South Brick Lines NG34 . . .120 B8
South Bridge Rd [2] HU9 . .181 A5
Southburn Ave HU5 . . . . . .179 E7
SOUTH CARLTON LN1 . . . . . .67 D3
South Carr Rd DN20 . . . . . . .31 A4
South Church Side [14]
  HU1 . . . . .180 F6
Southcliffe Rd [19] DN21 . . . .29 C3
South Cliff Rd [27] DN21 . . . .30 B1
SOUTH CLIFTON NG23 . . . . . .78 B5
Southcoates La HU9 . . . . . .181 E8
SOUTH COCKERINGTON
  LN11 . . . . .62 A8
South Cres
  [11] Bottesford NG13 . . . . . .128 A5
  [1] Chapel St Leonard PE24 . . .90 D7
South Cross Moors Road
  DN17 . . . . .17 A6
South Dale LN7 . . . . .33 B4
South Dale Cl [3] DN21 . . . . .30 B2
Southdown LN5 . . . . .205 D1
Southdown Rd PE7 . . . . . . .233 F5
South Dr
  [12] Balderton NG24 . . . . . . .104 C1
  [4] Stow LN1 . . . . .66 C8
South Dro Bicker PE20 . . . .134 E4
  Helpringham NG34 . . . . . . .133 D4
  Lutton PE12 . . . . .149 A1
  Quadring PE11 . . . . .144 A8
  Spalding PE11 . . . . .156 E2
SOUTH ELKINGTON LN11 . . . .60 E7
South Ella Dr HU10 . . . . . . .178 D7
South Ella Farm Ct HU10 . .178 D6
South Ella Way HU10 . . . . .178 D7
SOUTH END DN19 . . . . .12 B7
South End Boston PE21 . . .208 F4
  Collingham NG23 . . . . .91 C4
  Hogsthorpe PE24 . . . . .90 B6
  South Ferriby DN18 . . . . . . .10 A7
  Thorne/Moorends DN8 . . . . .15 A7
South End La DN22 . . . . .52 E3
Southern Dr HU4 . . . . .179 C5
Southern La LN6 . . . . .92 B7
Southern Lane LN5 . . . . . . .105 E4
Southern Rd DN40 . . . . .186 D7
Southern Way DN40 . . . . . .186 C7
Southern Wlk DN33 . . . . . . .194 F7
South Fen Rd Bourne PE10 213 F4
  Helpringham NG34 . . . . . . .133 D6
SOUTH FERRIBY DN18 . . . . . .10 B8
South Ferriby Prim Sch
  DN18 . . . . .10 A7
Southfield
  [7] Balderton NG24 . . . . .104 C2
  [7] Belton DN9 . . . . .16 E1

Southfield continued
  [4] Kingston upon Hull HU13 . . .3 E4
SOUTH FIELD HU13 . . . . .3 E4
Southfield Ave DN33 . . . . .194 F7
Southfield Cl
  [18] Thorne/Moorends DN8 . . .15 B7
  Ulceby DN39 . . . . .12 B1
Southfield Dr
  [10] Epworth DN9 . . . . .27 D6
  [2] Louth LN11 . . . . .198 C4
  [21] North Ferriby HU14 . . . . . . .3 A4
Southfield La
  Beckingham DN10 . . . . .52 B8
  Fishtoft PE21 . . . . .137 C8
  [6] Old Leake PE22 . . . . .114 A1
  Old Leake PE22 . . . . .127 A8
  Willoughton DN21 . . . . .42 D3
Southfield Pl LN9 . . . . .199 C3
Southfield Rd
  [1] Broughton DN20 . . . . .19 D3
  [13] Crowle DN17 . . . . .16 D7
  Grimsby DN33 . . . . .194 F7
  Holton le Clay DN36 . . . . . .195 D1
  North Kelsey LN7 . . . . .31 E8
  Scunthorpe DN16 . . . . .185 C5
  Thorne/Moorends DN8 . . . . .15 B7
  [1] Winterton DN15 . . . . .8 F5
Southfields [7] Binbrook LN8 47 C4
  Bourne PE10 . . . . .213 D4
  [3] Sleaford NG34 . . . . .212 D3
Southfields Ave PE2 . . . . .231 D5
Southfields Dr [10] PE13 . . .170 D2
Southfields Dr PE2 . . . . . . .231 D5
Southfields Prim Sch PE2 231 D5
South Furlong Croft [22]
  DN9 . . . . .27 E6
Southgate
  Kingston upon Hull HU13 . . .178 E1
  [12] Pinchbeck PE11 . . . . . . .156 E8
  Scunthorpe DN15 . . . . .183 B3
South Gate NG34 . . . . .212 D4
Southgate Spinneys [3]
  NG34 . . . . .120 E4
Southgate Way PE2 . . . . . .229 C2
South Gn DN34 . . . . .161 F2
SOUTH GREEN DN34 . . . . . . .161 E2
South Heath La NG32 . . . . .106 D1
South Ing Dro PE11 . . . . . .134 E1
South Ings La PE24 . . . . . . .90 B5
South Intake La DN9 . . . . . . .40 C7
SOUTH KELSEY LN7 . . . . .32 A1
South Kesteven Works
  NG31 . . . . .210 F3
SOUTH KILLINGHOLME
  DN40 . . . . .12 E3
SOUTH KYME LN4 . . . . .123 B8
South La
  Kingston upon Hull HU13 . . .178 E1
  Stainton le Vale LN8 . . . . . .46 E4
  Willingham DN21 . . . . .54 A3
Southland Ct DN37 . . . . . . .188 A1
Southland Dr [5] LN6 . . . . .205 B4
Southlands Ave
  Gainsborough DN21 . . . . . .197 B8
  Louth LN11 . . . . .198 D3
  Peterborough PE1 . . . . . . .226 A6
Southlands Dr
  Grantham NG31 . . . . .211 C4
  Morton DN21 . . . . .197 B8
Southlands Gdns DN21 . . .197 B8
South Lawn Wy HU14 . . . . . .2 F5
South Lincs Con Ctr
  NG31 . . . . .211 A1
South Marsh Rd
  Immingham Power St
  DN41 . . . . .187 F1
  Stallingborough DN41 . . . . .23 F7
South Marsh Rd Ind Est
  DN41 . . . . .187 F2
South Mkt Pl [7] LN13 . . . . .75 F2
Southmoor La
  Newton on Trent LN1 . . . . . .78 D8
  Snitterby DN21 . . . . .43 E5
Southmoor Rd Crowle DN17 16 C8
  Newton on Trent LN1 . . . . . .78 D8
South Moor Rd DN10 . . . . . .39 F3
Southoe Rd PE7 . . . . .231 D2
Southolme DN21 . . . . .197 D4
SOUTH ORMSBY LN11 . . . . . .74 D2
SOUTHORPE PE9 . . . . .172 E2
Southorpe La DN21 . . . . . . .42 A7
Southorpe Paddock Nature
  Reserve★ PE9 . . . . .172 E1
South Osbourne Wy
  DN40 . . . . .186 D6
SOUTH OWERSBY LN8 . . . . . .44 E4
South Parade Boston PE21 208 C4
  [1] Caythorpe NG32 . . . . .119 B7
  Gainsborough DN21 . . . . . .197 F3
  Grantham NG31 . . . . .211 B2
  Grimsby DN31 . . . . .191 D8
  [7] Lincoln LN1 . . . . .201 D4
  Peterborough PE3 . . . . . . .225 E3
  [5] Saxilby LN1 . . . . .66 D2
  Skegness PE25 . . . . .206 D2
  South Kyme LN4 . . . . .123 B8
  Spalding PE11 . . . . .214 C3
  Thorne/Moorends DN8 . . . . .15 A7
South Pk LN5 . . . . .205 F8

South Pk Ave
  Bracebridge Heath LN5 . . .205 F8
  Lincoln LN5 . . . . .201 F1
South Pk Enterprise Coll
  DN17 . . . . .184 D3
South Pk Ind Est DN17 . . .184 D3
South Pk Rd DN17 . . . . . . .184 D3
South Ramper
  Bishop Norton LN8 . . . . .44 A5
  North Owersby DN21 . . . . . .44 A6
SOUTH RAUCEBY NG34 . . . .120 E4
South Rd Bourne PE10 . . . .213 D4
  Chapel St Leonard PE24 . . . .90 E6
  [5] Keadby with Althorpe
  DN17 . . . . .17 C6
  Mablethorpe/Sutton on Sea
  LN12 . . . . .64 C1
  North Somercotes LN11 . . . .50 E7
  Sturton le Steeple DN22 . . . .52 C4
  Tetford LN9 . . . . .73 F1
SOUTH RESTON LN11 . . . . . . .62 D1
SOUTHREY LN3 . . . . .83 D1
South Ridge Cres [2]
  DN17 . . . . .184 F3
South Rise [6] LN8 . . . . .47 C4
South St Mary's Gate [4]
  DN31 . . . . .191 D7
South Scaffold La NG23 . . .91 E3
South Scarle La LN6 . . . . . . .78 E1
South Scarle Rd NG23 . . . . .91 E6
South Sea La DN36 . . . . .36 D7
South Side DN15 . . . . .2 A1
SOUTH SOMERCOTES
  LN11 . . . . .50 E5
South St [12] Alford LN13 . . . .75 F2
  [17] Alford LN13 . . . . .75 F2
  [10] Barnetby le Wold DN38 . . .21 B4
  Bole DN22 . . . . .52 C5
  Boston PE21 . . . . .208 F4
  Bourne PE10 . . . . .213 D4
  Caistor LN7 . . . . .33 B4
  [1] Cleethorpes DN35 . . . . . .193 A5
  [20] Crowland PE6 . . . . .166 F1
  Drayton PE20 . . . . .135 C6
  Horncastle LN9 . . . . .199 B3
  Keelby DN41 . . . . .23 A5
  Louth LN11 . . . . .198 B5
  Morton DN21 . . . . .197 C8
  [15] North Kelsey LN7 . . . . . . .32 A4
  Owston Ferry DN9 . . . . .28 B2
  Peterborough PE1 . . . . . . .226 B2
  Roxby cum Risby DN15 . . . . .8 F3
  Scamblesby LN11 . . . . .72 F5
  Swineshead PE20 . . . . .135 B7
  West Butterwick DN17 . . . . .28 D8
  [17] Winterton DN15 . . . . .9 A5
South Terr Boston PE21 . . .208 F3
  [4] Louth LN11 . . . . .198 C5
SOUTH THORESBY LN13 . . . .75 A3
South Thoresby Rd LN13 . . .75 A4
South View Anlaby HU4 . . .179 B6
  Broughton DN20 . . . . .19 D4
  Holton le Clay DN36 . . . . . .195 E1
  Humberston DN36 . . . . . . .193 A1
  Peterborough PE2 . . . . . . .230 F7
  Yarborough DN34 . . . . .191 A6
South View Ave
  Brigg DN20 . . . . .196 C5
  Burringham DN17 . . . . .17 D4
South View Cl [4] PE25 . . . .206 D2
South View Com Prim Sch
  PE6 . . . . .166 E1
Southview Gdns LN9 . . . . . .73 F1
South View La LN11 . . . . . . .62 A7
Southview Leisure Ctr
  PE25 . . . . .103 C8
South View Rd PE4 . . . . . . .225 D8
South View [16] LN2 . . . . .68 C6
Southview Ave
  [3] Kingston upon Hull HU9 . . . .5 F8
  Peterborough PE4 . . . . . . .220 C4
Southwell Cl
  Barrowby NG31 . . . . .210 C5
  [11] Caistor LN7 . . . . .33 A3
Southwell Dr
  [3] Skegness PE25 . . . . .206 D7
  [9] Skegness PE25 . . . . .206 D7
Southwell Rd [2] PE13 . . . .170 D1
Southwell's La [1] LN9 . . . .199 C4
Southwell Way PE10 . . . . .213 B3
Southwick Cl PE4 . . . . .221 C1
SOUTH WILLINGHAM LN8 . . . .59 A2
SOUTH WITHAM NG33 . . . . .151 E2
South Witham Acad
  NG33 . . . . .151 E3
South Witham Nature
  Reserve★ NG33 . . . . .151 F2
Southwold Cres DN33 . . . .194 E8
South Wood Dr [10] DN8 . . .15 A7
Sovereign Cl
  [12] Grimsby DN34 . . . . .190 D4
  [12] Wisbech PE13 . . . . .170 C1
Sovereign Pl PE3 . . . . .225 C2
Sovereign St [4] NG34 . . . .142 E4
Sow Dale Nature Reserve★
  PE23 . . . . .87 A1
Sowers La DN15 . . . . .9 A5
Spa Bldgs LN2 . . . . .234 B2
Spafford Cl [7] DN21 . . . . . . .65 E3
Spa Hill [9] DN21 . . . . .30 B1
Spain Ct [7] PE21 . . . . .208 F4
Spain La [5] PE21 . . . . .208 F4
Spain Pl PE21 . . . . .209 A4
SPALDING PE11 . . . . .214 E6

Spalding Acad PE11 . . . . . . **214** F4
Spalding Bulb Mus★
PE11 . . . . **145** C1
Spalding Comm **6** PE11 . **214** B1
Spalding Dro Cowbit PE12 .**157** A3
Spalding PE12 . . . . **214** E1
Spalding FE Ctr PE11 . . . . . **214** D4
Spalding Gate PE12 . . . . . . **158** B8
Spalding Gram Sch PE11 .**214** D3
Spalding High Sch PE11 . .**214** F3
Spalding Monkhouse Prim
Sch The PE11 . . . .**214** A3
Spalding Parish CE Day Sch
PE11 . . . .**214** E2
Spalding Prim Sch PE11 . .**214** B5
Spalding Rd Algakirk PE20 .**136** B2
Boston PE21 . . . .**208** E3
Bourne PE10 . . . .**213** E5
Crowland PE6 . . . .**167** B3
Deeping St James PE6 . . . .**165** D1
Gosberton PE11 . . . .**145** C5
Holbeach PE12 . . . .**215** A2
Market Deeping PE6. . . . . . **217** E5
Pinchbeck PE11 . . . .**214** C8
Scunthorpe DN16 . . . .**185** B8
Wigtoft PE20 . . . .**135** E1
Spalding Rd Bsns Pk
PE10 . . . .**213** F5
Spalding St John the Baptist
Prim Sch The PE11 . . . . .**214** C2
Spalding Sta PE11. . . . .**214** C4
SPALFORD **78** D4
Spalford La LN6. . . . .**78** E2
Spalford Rd LN6 . . . .**78** E3
Spalford Warren Nature
Reserve★ NG23 . . . .**78** D2
Spall Cl DN33 . . . .**191** A2
SPANBY NG34 . . . .**132** F4
Spanby Dr **5** LN6 . . . .**205** A7
Spanby La NG34. . . . .**132** F5
Spanning Dr **22** LN13 . . . . .**75** F2
Spa Rd Lincoln LN5. . . . .**234** C2
1 Woodhall Spa LN10 . . . . **97** D6
Spark's La PE12 . . . .**158** A4
Spark St DN34 . . . .**191** A7
Sparrowgate Rd PE14 . . . .**170** F1
Sparrow La
2 Long Bennington
NG23. . . . .**117** D3
Marnham NG23 . . . .**78** A3
Newball LN8. . . . .**69** F2
Sparrow Rd **1** PE7 . . . . . .**230** D1
Spa St LN2. . . . .**202** B3
Spaw La **5** LN11 . . . .**198** B6
Spayne Rd PE21. . . . .**209** A4
Speechley Rd PE7 . . . .**233** F6
Speechley's Dro PE6 . . . . .**174** F7
Speedwell Cl **23** NG24 . . . .**104** C5
Speedwell Cres DN15. . . . .**182** C6
Speedwell Ct PE7. . . . .**217** D6
Speedwell Dr **16** PE10 . . . .**213** D3
Speeton Gr HU5. . . . .**179** D7
Speight Cl **5** NG24. . . . . . .**104** B7
Spencer Ave
Peterborough PE2 . . . .**231** D5
Scunthorpe DN15. . . . .**182** E4
Spencer Cl
3 Long Sutton PE12 . . . . .**216** B5
West Walton PE14 . . . .**170** E4
Spencer Gdns
7 Butterwick PE22 . . . . . .**126** E3
Holbeach PE12. . . . .**215** F3
Spencer St Grimsby DN31. .**189** D1
6 Kingston upon Hull HU2. .**180** E7
9 Lincoln LN5 . . . .**205** E8
Spence St **10** PE23. . . . .**87** F1
Spendla's La PE12. . . . .**159** F3
Spendluffe Ave **3** LN13. . . .**75** F3
Spennymoor Cl **1** LN6 . . . . .**93** B8
Sperrin Cl **5** LN5 . . . .**205** D2
Speyer Ave PE11 . . . .**214** C5
Speyside Ct **1** PE2. . . . . . .**229** D4
Spice Ave PE21 . . . .**136** D8
Spicer's La PE22 . . . .**127** B5
Spilby Mdws **12** PE23 . . . . .**101** A8
SPILSBY PE23 . . . .**101** A8
Spilsby Cl **8** LN6. . . . .**204** D8
Spilsby Hill PE23 . . . .**100** B8
Spilsby Prim Sch PE23. . . . .**88** A1
Spilsby Rd Boston PE21. . . .**209** A6
Eastville PE22 . . . .**101** A1
High Toynton LN9 . . . .**86** B4
Horncastle LN9 . . . .**199** E4
Scunthorpe DN17. . . . .**184** E5
Spilsby PE23. . . . .**101** A8
Thorpe St Peter PE24. . . . . .**102** B4
Spindelwood Dr **8** PE10 .**213** D3
Spindles The PE10 . . . .**213** D7
Spindlewood **1** HU15. . . . . . .**2** C7
Spinnaker Cl HU9 . . . .**181** C6
Spinners Cl **3** NG34. . . . . .**212** E3
Spinney Cl
Immingham DN40 . . . .**186** A6
7 Manby LN11 . . . .**62** C6
5 Ryhall PE9 . . . .**163** C1
Spinney Croft Cl **14** HU14 . . .**3** A5
Spinney La **10** Ryhall PE9 .**163** C1
2 Scopwick Heath LN4 . . .**108** A7
Spinneys The **5** LN2 . . . . . .**68** D7
Spinney The
1 Barnby Dun DN3 . . . .**14** A3
13 Barrow upon Humber
DN19. . . . .**11** D8
Brigg DN20. . . . .**196** D2
3 Gainsborough DN21 . . . .**197** F5

3 Grimsby DN31 . . . .**191** C7
Cherry Willingham/Reepham
LN3 . . . .**203** F8
2 Market Deeping PE6 . . . .**217** B5
7 Swanland HU14. . . . .**3** B7
7 Winthorpe NG24 . . . .**104** B7
Spinney Wlk
Kingston upon Hull HU4 . . . .**179** C6
Longthorpe PE3 . . . .**225** B2
Spion Kop La PE20 . . . .**135** E3
Spirea App LN6 . . . .**204** C8
Spire Cl LN1 . . . .**201** E7
Spire Gdns **5** NG24 . . . . . .**104** A6
Spire Hull & East Riding Hospl
HU10. . . . .**178** E5
Spires The **19** PE20 . . . . . .**136** A2
Spire View
1 Bottesford NG13 . . . . . .**128** A6
14 Grantham NG31 . . . .**211** A5
1 Kingston upon Hull HU13 .**178** E1
Sleaford NG34. . . . .**212** A2
Spire View Rd LN11 . . . . . .**198** C5
Spirewic Ave PE25 . . . .**206** D8
Spiros Rd **3** PE2 . . . .**231** E4
Spital Hill
Gainsborough DN21. . . . . . .**197** E5
18 Louth LN11 . . . .**198** B5
SPITAL IN THE STREET
LN8 . . . .**43** B1
Spital La LN8 . . . .**55** B8
Spital St LN1. . . . .**234** B4
Spital Terr DN21 . . . .**197** D4
Spitfire Ave LN11 . . . .**62** B6
Spitfire La DN36 . . . .**195** C4
Spittal Hill Rd PE22. . . . . . .**126** C4
SPITTLEGATE NG31 . . . .**211** A3
Spotfield La PE20 . . . .**136** C7
Spout Hill HU15. . . . .**2** C8
Spout Yd **6** LN11 . . . .**198** B6
Spratt Cl LN9 . . . .**199** D1
Spratton Ct DN34 . . . .**190** C4
SPRIDLINGTON LN8 . . . .**55** F3
Spriggs Cl NG34. . . . .**212** C3
Sprignall PE3 . . . .**224** F4
Sprigs Rd
Hampton Vale PE7 . . . .**230** B2
Hampton Vale PE7 . . . .**230** B2
Springbank DN20 . . . .**196** C5
Spring Bank
5 Binbrook LN8 . . . .**47** C4
Grimsby DN34 . . . .**191** A7
Kingston upon Hull HU3 . . . .**180** D7
Spring Bank W HU5. . . . . . .**179** D2
Springbank Cl HU4 . . . .**179** D2
Springburn St HU3 . . . .**180** A5
Spring Cl **9** LN2 . . . .**68** E6
Spring Ct Dunston LN4 . . . . .**95** C5
Louth LN11. . . . .**198** C5
13 Welton/Dunholme LN2 . . .**68** D7
Springdale Cl
Kingston upon Hull HU10 . . .**178** F8
2 Kingston upon Hull HU9. . . .**5** D8
Spring Dr
22 Balderton NG24 . . . . . .**104** C1
9 Balderton NG24 . . . .**104** C1
Farcet PE7 . . . .**231** B2
Spring End **3** NG31 . . . . . .**129** D5
Stagsden PE2. . . . .**229** F4
STAINBY NG33 . . . .**151** C5
Staindale Rd DN16 . . . .**185** D5
Stainesway LN11. . . . .**198** E7
STAINFIELD Haconby PE10 .**154** A8
Stainfield LN8. . . . .**83** B8
Stainfield Rd Kingthorpe LN8 **70** B1
Kirkby Underwood PE10. . . .**142** D1
Morton PE10 . . . .**154** B7
STAINFORTH DN7. . . . .**14** C6
Stainforth Inf Sch DN7. . . . .**14** C6
Stainforth Kirton La Prim Sch
DN7. . . . .**14** C6
Stainforth Moor Rd DN7. . . .**15** C3
Stainforth Rd DN7. . . . .**14** A5
Stain La LN12 . . . .**63** E3
STAINSBY LN9. . . . .**86** F6
Stainton Ave **6** DN21. . . . . .**43** D7
STAINTON BY LANGWORTH
LN3 . . . .**69** C4
Stainton Cl **5** DN21 . . . .**53** E5
Stainton Dr Grimsby DN33 .**191** A3
8 Immingham DN40 . . . . . .**186** B4
Scunthorpe DN17. . . . .**184** E4
Stainton Gdns LN1 . . . .**201** E2
Stainton La LN2. . . . .**69** B4
STAINTON LE VALE LN8 . . . . .**46** E5
Stallebrass Cl PE2. . . . .**231** E5
STALLINGBOROUGH DN41. . . .**23** E6
Stallingborough CE Prim Sch
DN41. . . . .**23** E6
Stallingborough Rd
Immingham DN40 . . . .**186** B2
Keelby DN41 . . . .**23** A3
Stallingborough Sta DN41 . .**23** E6
STAMFORD PE9. . . . .**219** D4
Stamford Bsns Pk PE9 . . . .**219** E6
Stamford Cl
4 Market Deeping PE6 . . . .**217** B5
Sleaford NG34. . . . .**212** C4
Stamford High Sch PE9. . . .**219** C4
Stamford Jun Sch PE9. . . . .**219** B3
Stamford Leisure Ctr PE9 . .**219** D6
Stamford Lodge Rd PE6 . . .**224** C5
Stamford Mus★ PE9. . . . . .**219** C5
Stamford Rd Barnack PE9. .**172** C4
Buckminster NG33. . . . .**151** A4

Stamford Rd continued
Collyweston PE9 . . . .**171** C2
Colsterworth NG33 . . . .**151** E5
Easton on the Hill PE9 . . . . .**219** A1
Essendine PE9 . . . .**163** D2
Helpston PE6 . . . .**173** C1
Ketton PE9 . . . .**218** A2
Marholm PE6 . . . .**220** A1
Market Deeping PE6. . . . . . .**217** A4
Tinwell PE9 . . . .**218** A6
West Deeping PE9 . . . .**173** A7
Stamford Ret Pk PE9 . . . . .**219** D6
Stamford & Rutland Hospl
PE9 . . . .**219** D6
Stamfords Art Ctr★ PE9. . .**219** C5
Stamford Sch PE9. . . . .**219** C5
Stamford St NG31 . . . .**211** B2
Stamford Sta PE9 . . . .**219** C4
Stamford Theatre★ **28**
PE9. . . . .**219** C5
Stamford Welland Acad
PE9 . . . .**219** B7
Stamford Wlk **25** PE9 . . . . .**219** C5
Stamp End LN2 . . . .**234** C2
Stamper St **2** PE3 . . . .**224** F3
Standard La LN5 . . . .**93** A2
Standish Ct **4** PE2 . . . .**230** D8
Standish Gr PE21 . . . .**209** B7
Standish La DN40 . . . .**186** B5
Stane Dr **12** LN4. . . . .**81** A1
Stanfield Rd **2** DN9 . . . .**27** D6
Stanford Cl **1** DN37 . . . .**23** F1
Stanford Jun & Inf Sch
DN37. . . . .**23** E1
Stanford Wlk **4** PE3. . . . . .**225** C4
STANGROUND PE2 . . . .**231** C5
Stanground Acad PE7 . . . .**231** C5
Stanholme La DN36 . . . .**36** A1
Stanhope Ave **7** LN10 . . . . .**97** D6
Stanhope Gdns **1** PE21. . .**209** C4
Stanhope Pl DN35 . . . .**192** C7
Stanhope Rd LN9 . . . .**199** C4
Stanhope Terr **3** LN9 . . . . .**199** C5
Stanhurst La DN7 . . . .**15** A5
Staniland Acad DN21 . . . . .**208** D4
Staniland Rd PE21. . . . .**208** D3
Staniland Way
1 Humberston DN36 . . . . . .**36** D6
Peterborough PE4 . . . .**221** A5
Staniwell Rise DN17 . . . . . .**184** D7
Staniwells Dr **11** DN20 . . . .**19** D3
Stanley Ave **5** LN12 . . . . . .**64** B3
Stanley Cl **2** PE24. . . . .**102** C2
Stanley Cres LN4. . . . .**205** F4
Stanley Dr
11 Sutterton PE20 . . . .**136** A2
Sutton Bridge PE12 . . . .**160** E4
Stanley Gdns **18** DN7 . . . . .**14** C6
Stanley Jackson Wy **24**
HU15 . . . .**2** D5
Stanley Pl **1** LN5 . . . .**201** F1
Stanley Rd
Peterborough PE1 . . . .**226** A3
Scunthorpe DN15. . . . .**182** C3
Stanley St
14 Beacon Hill NG24 . . . . .**104** A5
Bourne PE10 . . . .**213** C6
Gainsborough DN21. . . . . . .**197** D2
Grimsby DN32 . . . .**189** C1
Kingston upon Hull HU3 . . . .**180** C7
Lincoln LN5 . . . .**205** D7
1 Stamford PE9 . . . .**219** C5
Stan Rowing Ct PE2. . . . . . .**231** C7
Stansfield Gdns DN40 . . . . .**186** A5
Stansted St **5** DN31. . . . . .**188** D1
Stanthaket Ct **12** LN1 . . . . .**234** B3
Stanton Cl **2** PE10 . . . .**213** E5
Stanton Rd **4** LN12. . . . .**77** A8
Stanton's Pit Nature Reserve★
PE10 . . . .**163** C8
Stanton Sq PE7 . . . .**230** D2
Stanton St **7** NG31 . . . .**211** A4
Stanwick Ct PE3 . . . .**225** F2
Stapes Garth **1** LN11. . . . . .**50** B8
Stapledon Rd PE2 . . . .**229** D2
Staplee Way PE1 . . . .**226** F7
STAPLEFORD LN6. . . . .**105** B3
Stapleford Ave LN2. . . . .**201** F8
Stapleford La
Coddington NG24 . . . .**104** A6
Collingham NG23 . . . .**91** E1
Staple La NG24. . . . .**104** B1
Staple Rd DN40 . . . .**12** F3
Staples La **12** LN5 . . . .**93** F7
Stapleton Wy PE11 . . . .**214** D8
Star Carr La DN20 . . . .**196** D8
Star Cl PE1 . . . .**226** C3
Starella Gr HU3. . . . .**180** A4
Star Fen Dro NG34 . . . .**123** A4
Starham Rd LN7 . . . .**31** C4
Starks La LN8. . . . .**58** D7
Stark Wy **3** LN2. . . . .**202** D6
Star La Holbeach PE12. . . . .**215** C7
4 Stamford PE9 . . . .**219** C5
Star La Mews **26** PE9 . . . . .**219** C5
Star Lode Dro PE11. . . . . . .**144** B1
Star Mews PE1. . . . .**226** C2
Star Rd PE1. . . . .**226** D7
Stathern Rd PE1 . . . .**226** D7
Stathern Wlk NG31 . . . .**210** E2
Stather Rd DN15 . . . .**8** A1
Stathers Wlk **3** HU10. . . . .**178** F6
Station App
6 Ancaster NG32 . . . .**120** A3
Boston PE21. . . . .**208** E4
Cleethorpes DN35 . . . .**192** F7
11 Donington PE11 . . . . . .**134** E2

Station App continued
Louth LN11. . . . .**198** C6
Station Ave
New Waltham DN36 . . . .**195** D6
16 South Witham NG33 . . . .**151** D2
Wisbech St Mary PE13. . . . .**177** C5
Station Cl **9** NG23 . . . .**91** D4
Station Ct **33** Canal Side DN8 **15** A8
7 Hatfield DN7 . . . .**14** D4
Station Field LN6 . . . .**200** B3
Station La Horncastle LN9 . .**199** A3
Searby cum Owmby DN38 . . .**32** D7
Station Mews
New Waltham DN36 . . . .**195** C6
17 Wragby LN8 . . . .**70** D4
Station Rd
Ailsworth PE5. . . . .**223** C1
Alford LN13 . . . .**75** D4
Algarkirk PE20 . . . .**146** B8
Bardney LN3. . . . .**83** B4
Barkston NG32. . . . .**129** F8
Barlings LN3 . . . .**69** B3
Barnack PE9. . . . .**172** E4
Beckingham DN10 . . . .**52** B8
1 Billingborough NG34 . . . .**133** B1
Blyton DN21. . . . .**41** C5
Bottesford NG13 . . . .**128** A6
Bourne PE10 . . . .**155** C3
Branston LN4. . . . .**81** E2
Brough HU15 . . . .**2** B5
Burgh le Marsh PE24 . . . . .**102** C8
Burringham DN17 . . . .**17** E4
Candlesby with Gunby PE24. . .**89** B1
Careby Aunby & Holywell
PE9 . . . .**163** A8
Castle Bytham NG33 . . . . . .**152** D1
6 Cherry Willingham/Reepham
LN3 . . . .**82** A8
Cherry Willingham/Reepham
LN3 . . . .**203** F8
Cleethorpes DN35 . . . .**192** F5
Collingham NG23 . . . .**91** D4
Corby Glen NG33 . . . .**152** D7
Deeping St James PE6 . . . .**174** B7
Digby LN4. . . . .**108** E5
Donington on Bain LN11 . . . .**59** E1
East Halton DN40. . . . .**12** D7
Epworth DN9 . . . .**27** D7
6 Essendine PE9 . . . .**163** D3
Fulstow LN11. . . . .**49** A7
Garthorpe & Fockerby DN17 . .**7** E6
Gedney Hill PE12 . . . .**168** C1
Gosberton PE11. . . . .**145** A5
Grantham NG31 . . . .**211** B3
Grasby DN38 . . . .**32** E6
Great Steeping PE23 . . . . . .**101** F6
Grimsby DN37 . . . .**190** D4
Gunness DN15 . . . .**17** E5
Habrough DN40 . . . .**12** F1
Halton Holegate PE23 . . . . .**101** B8
Harby NG23 . . . .**79** B5
Harmston LN5 . . . .**93** E5
Hatfield DN7 . . . .**14** D4
Haxey DN9 . . . .**27** D1
Healing DN41 . . . .**23** F5
Heckington NG34. . . . .**122** E2
Heighington LN4 . . . .**81** E4
Helpringham NG34. . . . .**133** D7
9 Hibaldstow DN20 . . . .**30** F5
Holbeach PE12. . . . .**215** D2
Holton le Clay DN36 . . . .**36** B4
Hubbert's Bridge PE20. . . . .**124** E1
Keadby with Althorpe DN17 . .**17** D6
6 Ketton PE9 . . . .**171** A3
Kingston upon Hull HU13 . . .**178** E1
Kirton PE20 . . . .**136** C5
Kirton in Lindsey DN21. . . . . .**30** B2
Knaith DN21. . . . .**53** A4
Legbourne LN11. . . . .**61** E3
Lincoln LN6 . . . .**204** D3
Little Steeping PE23 . . . . . .**101** D5
5 Long Sutton PE12 . . . . .**216** B4
Ludborough DN36 . . . .**48** E6
16 Mablethorpe & Sutton
LN12 . . . .**76** F8
20 Mablethorpe/Sutton on Sea
LN12 . . . .**64** B4
Metheringham LN4. . . . .**95** D4
Midville PE22 . . . .**113** E8
Midville PE22 . . . .**113** E8
1 Misterton DN10. . . . .**40** A5
Misterton LN13 . . . .**89** A6
Morton PE10 . . . .**154** D6
Moulton PE12. . . . .**157** F6
Mumby LN13 . . . .**76** F1
North Kelsey LN7 . . . .**32** B4
Northorpe PE10 . . . .**164** C7
North Thoresby DN36. . . . . .**36** B3
Owston Ferry DN9 . . . .**28** A2
Peterborough PE3 . . . .**225** F2
Potter Hanworth LN4 . . . . . .**82** A1
Ruskington NG34. . . . .**108** E1
Scawby DN20. . . . .**30** F7
Scredington NG34 . . . .**132** F7
Scunthorpe DN15. . . . .**183** A2
Sibsey PE22 . . . .**113** C1
Sleaford NG34. . . . .**212** D3
South Kelsey LN7 . . . .**32** D2
South Killingholme DN40 . . . .**13** A5
South Witham LN8 . . . .**59** A1
Stallingborough DN41 . . . . . .**23** E6
Stamford PE9. . . . .**219** B4
Stixwould & Woodhall LN10 . .**97** A8
Sturton le Steeple DN22. . . . .**52** B3
Surfleet PE11. . . . .**145** E3
Sutterton PE20. . . . .**136** A1
Swinderby LN6. . . . .**92** A6
Swineshead PE20. . . . .**123** F1

Station Rd *continued*
Theddlethorpe All Saints
LN12 . . . . .63 D7
Thorney PE6 . . . . .176 A3
Thornton Curtis DN39 . . .11 F5
Thorpe on the Hill LN6 . . .79 E1
Thorpe St Peter PE24 . . .102 B3
Timberland LN4 . . . . .96 B1
Torksey LN1 . . . . .65 D6
Tumby Woodside PE22 . . .98 F1
Tydd St Mary PE13 . . . . .170 C8
Ulceby DN39 . . . . .12 B1
Waddington LN5 . . . . .93 F7
Wainfleet All Saints PE24 .102 D1
Walkeringham DN10 . . . . .40 A3
Waltham DN36 . . . . .195 A6
Waltham LE14 . . . . .138 A1
Whitton HN15 . . . . .1 D1
Wickenby LN3 . . . . .57 B1
Woodhall Spa LN10 . . . . . .97 D6
Station Rd Ind Est PE20 .135 A8
Station Rd N PE34 . . . . .161 C2
Station Rd S PE34 . . . . .161 C1
Station Rd (West) LN1 . .211 A3
Station St Boston PE21 . .208 E5
Donington PE11 . . . . . . .134 E2
Lincoln LN5 . . . . .234 A1
Rippingale PE10 . . . . . . .143 A3
1 Spalding PE11 . . . . . .214 D4
Station Terr LN5 . . . . . .106 D3
Staunton Ct LN1 . . . . . .201 D3
STAUNTON IN THE VALE
NG13 . . . . .117 A2
Staunton Rd 9 NG24 . . .104 A3
Staunton St 3 LN1 . . . . .201 D3
Staunt Rd PE22 . . . . . . .112 E2
Stavanger Cl DN36 . . . .195 B6
Staveley Rd LN13 . . . . . . .75 E2
Staverton Cres LN6 . . . .200 B1
Staverton Rd PE4 . . . . . .220 E3
Staves Ct 5 DN36 . . . . . .36 C4
Staxton Cl PE6 . . . . .220 A1
Staxton Ct HU9 . . . . . . .181 D8
Steadfold La PE9 . . . . . .218 A3
Steadings The
Flixborough DN15 . . . . . . .8 B2
North Scarle LN6 . . . . . . .78 F2
Stealgoose La DN9 . . . . .16 F3
Steamer Point Rd LN4 . . .95 C7
Steapas Cl PE23 . . . . . . .101 D7
Steeles Dr NG24 . . . . . .104 C2
Steepers The 4 LN2 . . . . .68 D2
Steep Hill LN2 . . . . .234 B3
Steeping Ct LN1 . . . . . . .201 E8
Steeping Dr DN40 . . . . .186 A3
Steeping Rd
Halton Holegate PE23 . . .101 C6
Thorpe Fendykes PE24 . . .101 F3
Steeple Leas 15 NG31 . . .211 A5
Steeple Vw PE11 . . . . . .214 A1
Stells La PE21 . . . . .208 F3
STENIGOT LN11 . . . . .72 B8
Stenigot Cl 3 LN6 . . . . .204 C6
Stenigot Gr LN6 . . . . . . .204 D6
Stenigot Rd 1 LN6 . . . . .204 D6
Stenner Rd LN4 . . . . . . .207 F6
Stennett Ave 1 PE11 . . .156 E2
STENWITH NG33 . . . . . .128 D3
Stephen Cl 3 DN39 . . . . .12 A1
Stephen Cres
16 Barton-upon-Humber
DN18 . . . . .10 F8
Grimsby DN34 . . . . .190 E4
Humberston DN36 . . . . . .36 C8
Stephen Rd DN34 . . . . . .104 A6
Stephenson Ave
Gonerby Hill Foot NG31 . .210 F8
Pinchbeck PE11 . . . . . . .214 E8
Stephenson Cl
9 Alford LN13 . . . . .75 E2
4 Boston PE21 . . . . . . .208 F1
14 Colsterworth NG33 . . .151 D7
Heighington/Washingborough
LN4 . . . . .81 E4
Yaxley PE7 . . . . .233 D4
Stephenson Ct 5 PE1 . . .226 B2
Stephenson Rd LN6 . . . .204 D4
Stephenson Way PE10 . .213 D7
Stephenson Wy NG24 . . .104 B6
Stephens Way 4 PE6 . . .217 F4
Stephen's Way NG34 . . .212 F3
Sterling Cres DN37 . . . .194 C4
Sterling Pl 8 LN10 . . . . . .97 E6
Sterne Ave 9 DN20 . . . . .19 D3
Steve Newton Ave LN9 . .199 B2
Stevenson Pl 1 DN35 . . .192 D5
Stevenson's Way 33 DN18 . .10 E8
Stevern Way PE1 . . . . . .226 F4
Steward Wy 5 PE4 . . . . .221 E2
STEWTON LN11 . . . . .61 E5
Stewton Gdns LN11 . . . .198 D4
Stewton La LN11 . . . . . .198 E4
Steyning La PE7 . . . . . . .135 A7
Steynings The PE4 . . . . .221 A3
STIBBINGTON PE8 . . . . .222 C2
STICKFORD PE22 . . . . . .100 B2
STICKNEY PE22 . . . . . . .113 A8
Stickney CE (Aided) Prim Sch
PE22 . . . . .113 A8
Stickney Farm Pk★ PE22 .113 D7
Stickney La 1 PE22 . . . .112 D7
Still Cl PE6 . . . . .217 B5
Still The PE13 . . . . .170 B1
Stirling Cl 4 DN21 . . . . .197 E6
Stirling Ct
14 Grantham NG31 . . . .210 E2
Heckington NG34 . . . . . .122 D2
Stirling Dr 12 NG24 . . . .104 C5

Stirling Rd PE9 . . . . . . .218 F5
Stirling St Grimsby DN31 .189 D1
Kingston upon Hull HU3 . .179 F6
Stirling Way
Market Deeping PE6 . . . .217 C2
Peterborough PE3 . . . . . .220 E1
4 Skellingthorpe LN6 . .200 A4
STIXWOULD LN10 . . . . . . .97 B8
Stixwould Rd LN10 . . . . . .97 C7
Stixwould Road LN10 . . . .84 C1
Stockbridge Pk 3 HU15 . . .2 C7
Stockbridge Rd HU15 . . . .2 C7
Stocken Hall Mews LE15 .152 A1
Stocken Hall Road LE15 .162 A7
Stockham Ct DN33 . . . . .191 A2
STOCKHOLES TURBARY
DN9 . . . . .16 B2
Stockholes Turbary Rd
DN9 . . . . .16 C2
Stockhouse La PE11 . . . .145 B3
Stocking Way LN2 . . . . .202 F6
Stockman's Ave 2 PE12 .215 F3
Stockmoor La LN8 . . . . . .57 A8
Stocknail 5 Belton DN9 . .16 E1
Castor PE5 . . . . .223 F1
Ludborough DN36 . . . . . .48 E6
Stockshill Rd DN16 . . . . .185 C6
Stocks La LN8 . . . . .56 F3
Stockwell Gate PE12 . . .215 A4
Stockwell Gr 6 HU9 . . . . .5 F8
Stockwell Prim Sch HU9 . . .5 F8
Stockwith Mill★ PE23 . . . .87 B5
Stockwith Rd Haxey DN9 . .27 E1
Walkeringham DN10 . . . . .40 A3
STOKE ROCHFORD NG33 .139 F2
Stoke Rochford Hall Con &
Leisure Ctr★ NG33 . . . .139 F2
Stokesay Ct 8 PE3 . . . . .225 B2
Stokes Dr NG34 . . . . . . .212 B6
Stoke St 4 HU2 . . . . .180 E4
Stoksley Wlk DN37 . . . . .190 F8
Stonebow Ctr LN2 . . . . .234 B2
Stonebridge PE2 . . . . . .230 C5
Stonebridge Lea PE2 . . .230 C5
Stonebridge Rd NG31 . . .211 B4
Stonecross Rd NG34 . . .107 E1
Stone Dr LE15 . . . . .152 A1
Stonefield Ave LN2 . . . .234 B4
Stonefield Pk LN2 . . . . . .68 C7
Stonegate Gedney PE12 .159 D6
Spalding PE11 . . . . .214 E3
28 Thorne/Moorends DN8 . .15 A8
Stone Gate Cowbit PE12 .157 B1
Weston PE12 . . . . .145 F2
STONE HILL DN7 . . . . . . .14 F4
Stone Hill DN7 . . . . .15 A4
Stone Hill Rd DN7 . . . . . .15 A4
Stonehouse Rd PE7 . . . .233 E5
Stone La
Aubourn Haddington & South
Hykeham LN5 . . . . .92 E6
Burringham DN17 . . . . . .17 E4
Humby NG33 . . . . .141 C8
Peterborough PE1 . . . . . .225 F5
Sutterton PE20 . . . . . . .135 F1
6 Waddington LN5 . . . . .93 F7
Stoneleigh Ct PE3 . . . . .225 B2
Stonemasons Ct 4 NG31 .211 B4
Stone Moor Rd LN6 . . . . .93 B8
Stonepit La Marston NG32 .118 C2
8 Skillington NG33 . . . .118 B5
Stone Pit La Skendleby PE23 .88 D4
Willingham DN21 . . . . . . .53 F3
Stone Pit Lane DN41 . . . .23 A3
Stonepit Rd HU14 . . . . . . .2 E6
Stonesby Rd LE14 . . . . .138 E1
Stone's Cl 4 PE24 . . . . . .90 B7
Stones La 13 Spilsby PE23 . .88 A1
West Keal PE23 . . . . . . .100 C5
Stone's La PE24 . . . . . . .77 C1
Stones Pl 1 LN6 . . . . . . .200 E1
Stone Way NG34 . . . . . .212 B6
Stonewell Row LN9 . . . .199 C4
Stonewort Ave
2 Hampton Vale PE7 . . .230 B1
Yaxley PE7 . . . . .233 B8
Stoney La DN21 . . . . .54 F7
Stoney Track NG32 . . . .139 B6
Stoney Way 15 DN36 . . . .36 C4
Stoney Yd LN12 . . . . . . .200 A5
Stony Cl 10 DN7 . . . . . . .14 C7
Stonyford Dr 9 DN7 . . . . .14 C5
Stool Cl Rd 2 DN9 . . . . . .16 E1
Storbeck Rd 15 PE13 . . .170 D1
Storey's Bar Rd PE6 . . . .227 A3
Storey's La PE24 . . . . . .102 E7
Storrington Way PE4 . . . .221 A3
Stortford St 7 DN31 . . . .188 D1
Story St 11 HU1 . . . . . . .180 E7
Stothards La 7 DN19 . . . .12 A8
Stothard's Gate PE12 . . .158 E2
Stour Ct 7 NG31 . . . . . . .210 E2
Stourton Pl LN9 . . . . . . .199 B4
Stove Ct LE15 . . . . .162 A8
Stovin Cres DN15 . . . . . . .9 A5
STOW LN1 . . . . .66 C8
Stow Cl DN37 . . . . .190 D8
Stowehill Rd PE21 . . . . .221 D2
Stowe Rd PE6 . . . . .164 E2
Stowgarth 36 DN18 . . . . .10 F8
Stowgate Rd PE6 . . . . . .174 A8
Stow Hill LN9 . . . . .150 C7
Stow La NG34 . . . . .133 A1
Stow Pk Rd Marton DN21 . .65 E8
Stow LN1 . . . . .66 B8

Stow Rd Scunthorpe DN16 .185 B7
Sturton by Stow LN1 . . . . .66 C8
Willingham DN21 . . . . . . .53 E2
Wisbech PE13 . . . . .170 E1
St. Peters Orchard 2 DN18 . .3 F1
Strafford St DN21 . . . . . .197 D2
STRAGGLETHORPE LN5 . .105 E3
Stragglethorpe La
Caythorpe NG32 . . . . . . .118 E8
Fulbeck NG32 . . . . .105 E2
Strahane Cl LN5 . . . . . . .205 C3
Straight Dro PE7 . . . . . . .231 E1
Strait Bargate 26 PE21 . .208 F5
Strait The LN2 . . . . .234 B3
Strand Cl
Kingston upon Hull HU2 . .180 E3
7 Kingston upon Hull HU2 .180 E8
8 Mablethorpe/Sutton on Sea
LN12 . . . . .64 B3
Strand Community Sch
DN32 . . . . .189 B1
Strand St DN32 . . . . . . .189 B1
Strand The LN12 . . . . . . .64 B3
Stratford Ave DN34 . . . .191 A4
Stratford Dr 5 DN16 . . . .183 C1
Stratford Pl 7 PE1 . . . . .213 C3
Stratten Cl 5 NG34 . . . .107 C1
Stratton Pk 1 HU14 . . . . .3 C6
Strawberry Ave PE3 . . . .225 A5
Strawberry Cl 13 PE13 . .170 C1
Strawberry Fields Dr
PE12 . . . . .147 D6
Strawberry Gdns HU9 . . .181 B7
Strawberry Hall La 4
NG24 . . . . .104 A5
Strawberry Hill DN37 . . .194 B4
Strawberry St HU9 . . . . .181 B7
Strayfleets La PE22 . . . .126 D5
Stray Gn 12 NG34 . . . . .108 E2
Street La North Kelsey LN7 . .32 B4
North Leverton with
Habblesthorpe DN22 . . . .65 A8
Street Life Mus of Transport★
HU9 . . . . .181 A6
Streetway PE21 . . . . . . .136 E2
Stretham Way 5 PE10 . . .213 C2
Stretton Cl 4 LN1 . . . . . .66 C7
Stretton Rd LE15 . . . . . .162 B6
Strickland Rd DN17 . . . . . .7 A3
Stricklands Dr 4 PE6 . . .175 C8
Strickland St HU3 . . . . . .180 C4
Stromberg St HU10 . . . .178 F5
Strong's Bank PE12 . . . .158 F4
Strong's Gate PE12 . . . .158 F3
Strood Cl NG32 . . . . . . .139 C8
Stroud Cl 8 PE10 . . . . . .213 D5
STROXTON NG33 . . . . . .139 E5
Stroxton La NG33 . . . . . .139 F5
Stroykins Cl DN34 . . . . .190 F6
STRUBBY LN13 . . . . .63 C1
Strubby Airfield LN13 . . . .75 E8
Strubby Cl
9 Birchwood LN6 . . . . .204 D8
Cleethorpes DN35 . . . . .193 A4
Strugg's Hill La PE20 . . .136 B3
Stuart Cl Peterborough PE2 .231 C6
Scunthorpe DN17 . . . . . .184 F2
Stuart Ct PE1 . . . . .226 B4
Stuart St NG31 . . . . . . .211 C3
Stuart Wortley St 1
DN31 . . . . .189 B2
Stubbs Cl 21 HU15 . . . . . .2 D5
STUBTON NG23 . . . . . . .118 B7
Stubton Lodge Rd NG23 .118 C8
Stubton Rd NG23 . . . . . .117 F7
Studcross DN9 . . . . .27 D6
Studio Cl SN12 . . . . .77 A8
Studley St HU8 . . . . . . .181 B8
Stukeley Cl Lincoln LN2 . .202 E6
Peterborough PE2 . . . . . .231 D5
Stukeley Gdns 2 PE12 . .215 C2
Stukeley Hall Dr
9 Holbeach PE12 . . . . .215 D2
Holbeach PE12 . . . . . . .215 D2
Stukeley Rd PE12 . . . . . .215 D2
Stumpacre PE3 . . . . . . .225 A8
Stump Cross Hill NG34 . .212 C1
Stumpcross La PE20 . . . .135 B6
Stumps La PE12 . . . . . . .157 B7
Sturdy Hill LN11 . . . . . . .62 E4
STURGATE DN21 . . . . . . .53 F8
Sturgate Airfield DN21 . . .53 E6
Sturgate Rd LN8 . . . . . .204 C7
Sturgate Wlk DN21 . . . .197 F3
Sturmer Ct 1 DN16 . . . .185 B2
Sturrock Ct 12 NG31 . . .210 E2
Sturrock Way PE3 . . . . .225 C8
STURTON DN20 . . . . .30 F7
STURTON BY STOW LN1 . .66 C7
Sturton by Stow Prim Sch
LN1 . . . . .66 D8
Sturton CE Prim Sch DN20 .52 C2
Sturton Cl 1 LN2 . . . . . .201 F7
Sturton Gr 2 DN33 . . . . .191 B4
Sturton La Hatton LN9 . . .71 C3
Scawby DN20 . . . . .30 E7
Sturton Way PE1 . . . . . .216 B5
Stutte Cl LN11 . . . . .198 E3
Styles Croft 6 HU14 . . . . .3 C6
Subway St HU3 . . . . . . .180 B3

Subway The DN16 . . . . . .19 A4
Sudbeck La 17 LN2 . . . . . .68 D6
SUDBROOK NG32 . . . . . .119 E3
SUDBROOKE LN2 . . . . . . .68 F7
Sudbrooke Dr LN2 . . . . .202 A7
Sudbrooke La LN2 . . . . . .68 C2
Sudbrooke Rd LN2 . . . . . .68 E5
Sudbrook Rd NG32 . . . . .119 D4
Sudbury Cl LN6 . . . . . . .205 A5
Sudbury Ct PE7 . . . . . . .231 F5
Sudbury Pl LN11 . . . . . .198 B4
Suddle Way 19 DN41 . . . .23 A4
SUDTHORPE NG32 . . . . .119 C8
Sudthorpe Hill 8 NG32 . .106 C1
Suffolk Acre LN4 . . . . . .207 C4
Suffolk Cl PE3 . . . . .225 B2
Suffolk Ct DN32 . . . . . . .189 C1
Suffolk Rd 10 LN1 . . . . . .67 E5
Sugar Way PE2 . . . . . . .230 D8
Suggitt's Ct DN35 . . . . .192 D8
Suggitt's La DN35 . . . . .192 B8
Suggitt's Orch DN35 . . . .192 D8
Sullivan Rd HU4 . . . . . . .179 B4
Summerdale 28 DN18 . . .10 E8
Summerdale Ave DN37 . .194 E5
Summerfield Cl
Waltham DN37 . . . . .194 E5
16 Wisbech PE13 . . . . .170 C1
Summerfield Ct 3 NG34 .212 D6
Summerfield Dr 4 NG34 .212 D6
Summerfield Rd PE1 . . . .225 F4
Summerfields PE22 . . . .114 B1
Summergangs La DN21 . .197 D1
Summergates La PE24 . .102 C7
Summergroves Way HU4 .179 B2
Summer Hill LN11 . . . . . .197 E5
Summer Hill Cl PE4 . . . .221 C2
Summer La PE12 . . . . . .216 D2
Summer Lesure La PE12 .159 F2
Summer's Rd 15 NG24 . .104 A5
Sunbeam Ave LN6 . . . . .204 D1
Sunbeam Rd HU4 . . . . . .179 D5
Suncastle★ PE25 . . . . . .206 E4
Sunderfleet La LN11 . . . . .51 A5
Sunderland Cl LN6 . . . . .200 A4
Sunfield Cres LN6 . . . . .200 D1
Sunfields Cl PE12 . . . . .157 C3
Sunflower Cl PE21 . . . . .214 B3
Sunflower Way PE21 . . .208 B4
Sunningdale
Grantham NG31 . . . . . . .211 C8
Peterborough PE2 . . . . . .229 E6
8 Waltham DN37 . . . . .194 C4
Sunningdale Ave
Brigg DN20 . . . . .196 C5
Spalding PE11 . . . . .214 C2
Sunningdale Cl
Chapel St Leonard PE24 . .90 E7
1 Skegness PE25 . . . . .206 D4
6 Woodhall Spa LN10 . . .97 C5
Sunningdale Cres 2
PE25 . . . . .206 D4
Sunningdale Dr
Boston PE21 . . . . .208 C6
Chapel St Leonard PE24 . .90 E7
4 Immingham DN40 . . .186 D5
Lincoln LN5 . . . . .205 D8
Skegness PE25 . . . . . . .206 D4
Sunningdale Gr LN4 . . . .203 D1
Sunningdale Rd
5 Hatfield DN7 . . . . . . .14 F3
Kingston upon Hull HU13 .178 F2
Scunthorpe DN17 . . . . . .184 D4
Yaddlethorpe DN17 . . . . .184 D3
Sunningdale Way DN21 . .197 F2
Sunnybank 11 DN18 . . . .10 E8
Sunny Bank HU3 . . . . . .180 B7
Sunny Bank Gdns DN10 . .39 C2
Sunny Cnr DN33 . . . . . . .191 D1
Sunny Hill Cl 1 PE11 . . .145 D2
Sunny Hill 3 DN21 . . . . . .30 B1
Sunnymead PE4 . . . . . . .220 E6
Sunway Dr DN16 . . . . . .185 B5
SURFLEET PE11 . . . . . . .145 C3
Surfleet Bank PE11 . . . .145 D2
Surfleet Lows Nature
Reserve★ PE11 . . . . . .145 D3
Surfleet Prim Sch PE11 . .145 D3
Surfleet Rd 5 PE11 . . . .145 D2
SURFLEET SEAS END
PE11 . . . . .145 F3
Surfside 5 LN12 . . . . . . .77 A8
Surrey Ct 20 DN32 . . . . .189 C1
Surrey Garth HU4 . . . . . .179 B4
Surtees St DN31 . . . . . . .189 B2
Sussex Ave PE21 . . . . . .208 B4
Sussex Cl 7 LN8 . . . . . . .47 B6
Sussex Ct DN32 . . . . . . .189 C1
Sussex Gdns LN1 . . . . . . .67 E5
Sussex Rd PE9 . . . . .219 B6
Sussex St DN35 . . . . . . .192 B8
SUSWORTH DN17 . . . . . .28 D5
Susworth Rd DN17 . . . . . .28 E4
Sutcliffe Ave DN33 . . . . .191 A3
Sutherland Way PE9 . . . .218 F5
Suthers Sch DN24 . . . . .104 C1
SUTTERBY PE23 . . . . .87 E7
Sutterby La PE23 . . . . . . .87 F8
SUTTERTON PE20 . . . . . .136 A3
SUTTERTON DOWDYKE
PE20 . . . . .146 A8
Sutterton Dro LN4 . . . . .110 E1
Sutterton Enterprise Pk
PE20 . . . . .136 A2
Suttling Dales La PE22 . .126 E2
SUTTON
Beckingham LN5 . . . . . .105 B3
Sutton PE5 . . . . .222 F2

Sutton Branch Line Walkway
& Conservation Area★
LN12 . . . . .76 F6
SUTTON BRIDGE PE12 . . .160 D4
Sutton Cl
Heighington/Washingborough
LN4 . . . . .203 A1
15 Nettleham LN2 . . . . .68 C2
SUTTON CROSSES PE12 . .216 C1
Sutton Ct 2 PE25 . . . . . .206 C3
Sutton Gate PE12 . . . . . .159 D1
Sutton Heath Rd 222 D7
Sutton La LN5 . . . . .105 F5
Sutton Mdws PE12 . . . . .170 C2
SUTTON ON SEA LN12 . . .76 F8
Sutton on Sea Prim Sch
LN12 . . . . .77 A8
SUTTON ON TRENT NG23 . .91 A8
Sutton Pl Kirk Ella HU10 . .178 D5
4 Scawby DN20 . . . . . . .30 F7
Sutton Rd Beckingham LN5 .105 B4
Bilsby LN13 . . . . .76 C4
16 Kirk Sandall DN3 . . . .14 A3
Mablethorpe/Sutton on Sea
LN12 . . . . .64 C2
Newton PE13 . . . . .170 B6
Sutton St James PE12 . . .159 D2
Terrington St Clement PE34 .161 F2
SUTTON ST EDMUND
PE12 . . . . .168 F4
SUTTON ST JAMES PE12 . .159 C1
Sutton St James Com Primary
School PE12 . . . . .159 C1
Sutton's La PE6 . . . . . . .217 D4
Svenskaby PE2 . . . . . . .229 B6
SWABY LN13 . . . . .74 E4
Marshchapel DN36 . . . . . .37 B2
Swaby Cl Lincoln LN2 . . .202 A8
Swaby Cres 4 PE25 . . . .206 B4
Swaby Dr DN35 . . . . . . .192 D3
Swaby Valley Nature
Reserve★ LN13 . . . . . .74 F4
Swadales Cl 11 NG31 . . .129 E5
Swain Ct PE2 . . . . .230 F8
Swain's Dro PE13 . . . . . .170 C2
Swale Ave PE4 . . . . .221 C1
Swale Bank PE11 . . . . . .144 D5
Swaledale 10 HU15 . . . . .2 D6
Swaledale Pl 2 DN16 . . .185 E6
Swale Dr DN37 . . . . .197 F6
Swale Rd 14 HU15 . . . . . .2 D5
Swales Rd 12 DN36 . . . . .36 D8
SWALLOW LN7 . . . . .34 B5
Swallow Ave LN6 . . . . . .200 A3
SWALLOW BECK LN6 . . . .205 B5
Swallowbeck Ave LN6 . . .205 A4
Swallow Cl
5 Chapel St Leonard PE24 . .90 D7
6 Gainsborough DN21 . . .53 A7
1 Sleaford NG34 . . . . .212 C3
Swallow Ct 5 DN9 . . . . . .27 D7
Swallow Dr
3 Claypole NG23 . . . . .117 E8
15 Healing DN41 . . . . . .23 F5
Louth LN11 . . . . .198 D8
Wragby LN8 . . . . .70 D4
Swallowfield PE4 . . . . . .220 E4
Swallowfield Dr HU4 . . . .179 B2
Swallowfields Ct 2 PE25 .206 A4
Swallow Gate Rd LN11 . . .51 B2
Swallow Hill PE10 . . . . . .164 B7
Swallow La
Tydd St Giles PE13 . . . . .170 B8
Wootton DN39 . . . . .11 E2
Swallow Rd DN37 . . . . . . .47 B8
Swallow Road DN37 . . . . .34 C2
Swallow's Cl NG31 . . . . .210 E2
Swallow Vale LN7 . . . . . .34 B7
Swallow Wlk 3 PE6 . . . . .217 D5
Swanage Wlk HU4 . . . . .179 B4
Swan Cl PE11 . . . . .214 F2
Swan Ct 7 DN21 . . . . . . .197 F5
Swan Dr Skegness PE25 . .103 C7
6 Sturton by Stow LN1 . .66 D7
Swanella Gr HU3 . . . . . .180 A4
Swan Gdns Newark PE1 . .226 E6
Parson Drove PE13 . . . . .177 C7
Swanhill PE8 . . . . .222 A4
Swanhole La PE22 . . . . .126 D4
Swanholme Cl LN6 . . . . .204 E5
SWANLAND HU14 . . . . . . .3 A7
Swanland Butts Cl HU10 .178 C6
Swanland Cl 25 DN8 . . . .15 B7
Swanland Ct 24 DN8 . . . .15 B7
Swanland Dale HU14 . . . .3 B8
Swanland Garth 6 HU14 . .3 A5
Swanland Hill HU14 . . . . .3 A8
Swanland Prim Sch Acad
HU14 . . . . .3 B6
Swanland Rd HU13 . . . . .178 C2
Swan Moor Bank PE22 . .114 C3
Swannacks View 3 DN20 . .30 F7
Swann St 5 HU2 . . . . . . .180 F8
Swan's La LN5 . . . . .105 F5
Swanspool 8 PE25 . . . . .225 B6
Swan St 1 Lincoln LN2 . .234 B2
Spalding PE11 . . . . .214 D4
Swapcoat La PE12 . . . . .216 B5
Swapcoat Mews PE12 . . .216 B5
SWARBY NG34 . . . . .132 A7
Swarby La NG34 . . . . . . .132 A7
SWATON NG34 . . . . .133 D4
Swaton La NG34 . . . . . . .133 C3
SWAYFIELD NG33 . . . . . .152 D5
Swayne Cl LN2 . . . . .202 D7

Swaythling Cl LN6........204 E5
Sweetbriar 3 PE9........218 C7
Sweet Briar Cl 6 DN37...194 C5
Sweetbriar La PE4.......220 F6
Sweet Cl 2 PE6...........217 D5
Sweet Dews Gr HU9......181 D8
Sweetlands Way PE11....145 B5
Swen Cl 17 LN2............68 D7
Swift Ave LN11............62 C6
Swift Cl
Market Deeping PE6.......217 D4
Yaxley PE7..............233 A8
Swift Ct 1 PE11..........214 F2
Swift Dr DN20............196 A3
Swift Gdns LN2..........202 C7
Swift Gn LN2.............202 B7
Swift Rd DN17...........184 D6
Swiftsure Cres DN34.....190 D4
Swift Way PE10..........164 B7
Swinburne Cl 9 NG24....104 B3
Swinburne La DN17......184 D7
Swinburne Rd DN17......184 D7
Swin Cl PE20.............135 C6
SWINDERBY LN6............92 A5
Swinderby Cl 1 NG24....104 B5
Swinderby Gdns 2 DN34 .191 A5
Swinderby Rd
Collingham NG23..........91 E4
Eagle & Swinethorpe LN6....79 B1
North Scarle LN6...........78 F1
Norton Disney LN6.........92 C2
South Scarle NG23.........91 F7
Swinderby Sta LN6........92 B7
Swindler's Dro PE12......157 C6
Swinefleet Rd DN14.........6 B8
Swinegate Grantham NG31 211 A5
Kingston upon Hull HU13....178 E1
Swine Hill NG32..........139 C7
SWINESHEAD PE20........135 B7
SWINESHEAD BRIDGE
PE20....................123 F1
Swineshead Rd
Boston PE21.............208 A3
Frampton PE20..........124 E1
Swineshead St Marys CE Prim Sch PE20................135 C7
Swineshead Sta PE20.....123 F1
Swine's Mdw Rd PE6.....217 D8
SWINETHORPE LN6........79 B4
Swingbridge Rd NG31....210 D2
SWINHOPE LN8.............47 C7
Swinhope Hill LN8........47 C5
Swinhope Rd
Binbrook Tech Pk LN8.......47 B6
Thorganby LN8.............47 C8
SWINSTEAD NG33.........153 A5
Swinstead CE Prim Sch NG33...................153 A5
Swinstead Rd
Corby Glen NG33.........152 F7
Counthorpe & Creeton NG33...................153 A3
Irnham NG33.............141 E1
Swinster La DN40.........12 E6
Swinthorpe La LN3........69 C7
Switchback LN8............47 C2
Swithin Cl HU13..........179 A2
Swynford Cl LN1...........65 D2
Sybil Rd 18 PE13.........170 D1
Sycamore Ave
Grimsby DN33............191 C3
Peterborough PE1........226 C6
Sycamore Cl
1 Barnetby le Wold DN38...21 B4
4 Birchwood LN6........204 E8
Bourne PE10..............213 A5
Branston LN4...............81 D3
2 Broughton DN20.........19 D3
Cherry Willingham/Reepham LN3....................203 D5
Croft PE24................102 E4
Hessle HU13..............178 C3
Kingston upon Hull HU5....179 C7
5 Scopwick Heath LN4....108 A7
Sycamore Cres
5 Birchwood LN6........204 E8
Scunthorpe DN16.........185 E4
Sycamore Ct 3 NG31.....210 D2
Sycamore Dr
7 Gainsborough DN21....197 E6
Louth LN11................198 E5
Sleaford NG34............212 D6
3 Waddington LN5.........93 E8
Sycamore Gr LN4...........81 A1
Sycamore La 2 LE14.....150 B1
Sycamore Rd
Fordington LN13...........88 B6
16 Ruskington NG34......108 E1
Sycamores The 5 PE11...214 B1
Sycamore View PE12.....168 C2
Sycamore Way 16 DN36....36 C8
Sydney Dr 3 PE25........206 A4
Sydney Rd PE2............231 D5
Sydney St
23 Beacon Hill NG24......104 A5
Boston PE21...............208 D5
Sydney Terr 23 NG24.....104 A4
Syd Wilson Ct LN1........201 D7
Syerston Way 5 NG24....104 B5
Syfer Cl 8 LN7..............33 A3
Sykemouth Dro PE20.....124 C1
Sykes Cl
6 Kingston upon Hull HU10.....................178 F6
15 Swanland HU14...........3 B7
Sykes La Goxhill DN19........5 A2
Newark-on-Trent NG24....104 B2
Saxilby with Ingleby LN1....66 C3
Sykes St 2 HU2...........180 F7
Sylvan Ave 5 LN10.........97 D6
Sylvden Dr 24 PE13.......170 E1
Sylvester St 12 DN21.......30 B1
Symmington Cl PE2......230 F8
Symons Cl 8 HU2.........180 E8
Sympson Cl LN2..........202 E6
Syne Ave 5 PE25.........206 D1
Syringa Gn LN6...........200 C1
SYSTON NG32.............130 A7
Syston Gr LN5............205 D4
Sywell Cl 16 LN6.........204 C6

T

Tabor Ct PE7.............230 D2
Tacitus Wy LN6............93 B8
Tadman St HU3...........180 D4
Taggs Dr 7 PE25.........206 A6
Taining La DN7.............14 C8
Tait Cl PE1................226 C5
Talbot Ave PE2...........230 D6
Talbot Cl
20 Navenby/Wellingore LN5.....................107 A8
4 Spilsby PE23...........101 A8
Talbot Rd
Immingham DN40.........186 D3
Skegness PE25...........206 C4
Talbot Wlk DN16.........183 B2
Talisman Dr DN16........185 A2
Tallert Way DN33.........190 F3
Tall Gables 2 NG22.......65 B1
TALLINGTON PE9.........172 E7
Tallington Dry Ski Ctr★ PE9....................172 F7
Tallington Lakes Leisure Pk★ PE9....................173 A8
Tallington Rd PE9........172 F6
Tall Trees HU13...........178 C3
Tamar Ct 5 NG31.........210 E2
Tamar Dr DN36...........195 D7
Tamarisk Way DN16......185 D5
Tamar Way 3 LN6........205 A2
Tamar Wlk DN17.........184 C8
Tame Ct 4 NG34.........212 D5
Tamson Way 5 NG34.....212 D5
Tamworth Cl NG31.......210 D5
TAMWORTH GREEN PE22..126 E1
Tanglewood PE4..........220 F6
Tanglewood Cedar Falls 3 PE11....................214 B1
Tanhouse PE2............230 C5
Tanners Ct LN5...........234 A1
Tanners' La NG33........152 E8
Tanner's La LN5..........234 A1
Tannery Cl Boston PE21...208 E4
7 Bourne PE10...........213 E4
7 Waltham DN37.........194 E4
Tannery La 3 NG34......142 D8
Tansley Ct 1 DN15.......182 B2
Tansor Garth PE3.........225 C5
Tansy Wy PE11...........214 B6
Tantallon Ct 6 PE3.......225 B1
Tapin Cl LN1..............201 C6
Tarleton Ave 1 LN10......97 E6
Tarleton Cl 2 DN3.........14 A2
Tarragon Way PE10.......213 C6
Tarrant PE4...............220 E6
Tarran Way PE25.........206 B5
Tasburgh St DN32........191 F6
Tasman Cl 7 PE11.......214 B2
Tasman Rd 5 PE23.......101 A8
TATHWELL LN11............61 B2
Tattersall Cl DN17.......184 D5
TATTERSHALL LN4........207 A5
Tattershall Ave DN34....190 F4
TATTERSHALL BRIDGE LN4......................110 D7
Tattershall Castle★ LN4..207 A4
Tattershall Cl 3 NG31....210 E5
Tattershall Coll Bldgs★ LN4......................207 A4
Tattershall Dr 10 PE6.....217 A5
Tattershall Lakes Ctry Pk★ LN4......................207 A3
Tattershall Prim Sch LN4 .207 A5
Tattershall Rd
Billinghay LN4............109 F5
Boston PE21..............208 D7
Fishtoft PE21.............125 C5
Kirkby on Bain LN10.......98 B4
Woodhall Spa LN10........97 D5
Tattershall Sta Gall & Pottery★ LN4.........110 E7
TATTERSHALL THORPE LN4......................207 B8
Tattershall Way LN11....198 A8
Tatwin Dr 8 PE6.........175 B8
Taunton Cl 2 NG34......212 D7
Taunton Rd
6 Bourne PE10...........213 C3
Kingston upon Hull HU4....179 A3
Taunton Way DN33.......194 E8
Tavella Ct 1 DN9..........27 B2
Tavern Cl LN13.............89 A6
Taverner Rd PE21........208 D6
Taverners Ct LN11........198 C6
Taverners Rd PE1.........225 F4
Tavern La 7 PE24..........90 B7
Tavistock Cl 15 PE6......176 A3
Tavistock Rd PE11........214 B2
Tawney St PE21..........208 F6
Tawny Owl Cl 22 DN36.....36 D8
Taylor Cl 6 Belton DN9.....16 E2
5 Boston PE21...........209 D4
Branston LN4...............81 E1
Taylor's Ave DN35........192 E4
Taylor's Dro PE12........159 C1
Taylors Gdn LN11........198 D5
Taylor St DN35...........189 D1
TEALBY LN8................46 C1
Tealby Cl
1 Gainsborough DN21.....53 A7
Immingham DN40.........186 A4
Tealby Gr DN33...........191 B3
Tealby Rd
Middle Rasen LN8..........57 E8
Scunthorpe DN17.........184 D5
Tealby Sch LN8............46 D1
Tealby St 11 LN5..........205 E8
Teal Cl 4 Brigg DN20......196 A3
Caistor LN7.................33 A4
3 Skegness PE25.........206 A6
Teal Dr
Barton-upon-Humber DN18..10 E8
Yaxley PE7................233 B8
Teale St DN15............183 A4
Teal Gr 10 PE12..........167 B8
Teal Park Rd LN6.........204 A3
Teal Pl LN7.................33 A4
Teal Rd LN4...............110 E8
Team Gate DN37..........190 C6
Teanby Ct 5 PE3..........224 F3
Teanby Dr 8 DN15...........9 A5
Teasel Dr 7 PE10.........213 D3
Teasles 6 PE6.............217 D6
Tedder Dr 3 LN5...........93 F7
Teddy's Farm★ LN5.....105 C4
Tee La DN15.................8 B5
Tees Ct DN37.............190 E8
Teesdale Cl LN6..........200 C2
Teesdale Rd NG31........211 A7
Telford Dr Newark NG24...104 B6
Yaxley PE7................233 D6
Telford Pl DN34...........191 A7
Telford Wy 12 NG33......151 D7
Temperance Ave 5 DN17..29 D7
Temperance La 2 NG23....91 C4
Temper Rd DN16..........185 F8
Temperton's La 5 DN9....28 A3
Tempestes Wy 1 PE7.....231 D3
Tempest St LN2...........202 B3
Templar Ct DN16..........185 B3
Templars Way 2 NG33...151 D2
Temple Bruer Templar Preceptory★ LN5......107 C4
Temple Cl 2 Alford LN13...75 E2
4 Belton DN9...............16 E2
3 Brough HU15..............2 E6
Templefield Rd DN21......42 D4
Temple Gdns LN2.........234 B3
Temple Goring 1 LN5....107 B8
Temple Grange PE4.......220 F6
Temple La Aylesby DN37...23 E1
6 Welton HU15..............2 E6
Templeman Dr PE9........163 E5
Templemans La DN36......36 A1
Templemeads Cl 3 PE10 .154 D6
Temple Rd
Aslackby & Laughton NG34...................142 E5
Welbourn LN5.............107 A4
Westcliffe DN17...........184 F6
Temples Ct 3 PE6.........173 B4
Temple Terr LN11.........198 B6
Templeway Cl 5 NG32....119 B7
Templeway Sq 8 NG32...119 B7
Temple Wlk 2 HU15........2 E6
Ten Acre Dro PE11........135 C1
Ten Acre La
Pinchbeck PE11...........145 C1
Wyville cum Hungerton NG32...................139 B5
Tendley Ave HU3..........179 F5
Tenens Way PE21.........209 A1
Tennyson Ave
Grantham NG31..........211 E5
16 Mablethorpe/Sutton on Sea LN12.....................64 B4
Sleaford NG34............212 D5
4 Thorne/Moorends DN8...15 B8
Tennyson Cl Benniworth LN8 59 B1
Brigg DN20...............196 D2
2 Caistor LN7..............33 A3
12 Mablethorpe/Sutton on Sea LN12.....................77 A7
14 Metheringham LN4......95 C4
Tennyson Dr Bourne PE10 .213 D3
22 Welton/Dunholme LN2...68 D6
Tennyson Gdns LN9.......199 D2
Tennyson Gn 3 PE25.....206 C2
Tennyson High Sch The LN12.....................64 C3
Tennyson Rd
Cleethorpes DN35........192 E7
Louth LN11................198 C4
17 Mablethorpe/Sutton on Sea LN12.....................64 B4
Newark-on-Trent NG24....104 B2
Peterborough PE1.........225 F7
2 Ruskington NG34.......108 E2
Scunthorpe DN16.........185 D7
Tennyson St
Gainsborough DN21.......197 D5
Grimsby DN31.............191 D8
1 Lincoln LN1..............201 D4
Tennyson Way 1 PE9....218 E5
Tennyson Wlk LN3........203 C6
Tennyson Wy 17 PE23....101 A8
Tensing Rd DN16..........185 C5
Tentercroft St LN5........234 A1
Tenter La
6 Navenby/Wellingore LN5.....................107 A8
13 Stamford PE9..........219 C5
Tenters The PE12.........215 E2
Tern Rd PE7...............230 C2
Terrace La PE22............99 C5
Terrace The
Great Ponton NG33.......140 A5
Louth LN11................198 D4
10 Spilsby PE23............88 A1
Terrington Pl DN35.......192 D4
TERRINGTON ST CLEMENT PE34.....................161 E3
Terry Ave 21 NG24........104 A6
Terry O'Toole Theatre★ LN6.....................204 D1
TETFORD LN9..............73 F1
Tetford Hill LN9............73 E3
Tetford Rd LN9.............86 A5
Tethering La DN10.........39 A2
TETLEY DN17...............16 D6
Tetley Rd DN16...........185 C7
Tetley View 3 DN17.......16 E6
TETNEY DN36..............36 D4
Tetney Blow Wells Nature Reserve★ DN36..........36 E3
Tetney Cl 6 LN1..........201 E8
Tetney La DN36...........195 E2
TETNEY LOCK DN36........37 A4
Tetney Lock Rd DN36......36 E4
Tetney Marshes Nature Reserve★ DN36..........37 C7
Tetney Prim Sch DN36.....36 D4
Tetney Rd DN36............36 C7
Tewkesbury Dr 4 DN34..191 C6
Thackeray Ct DN37.......190 E8
Thacker Bank
Great Carlton LN12........63 B7
Three Bridges LN11........62 F6
Thacker La DN7............14 C8
Thackers Cl PE8..........222 A4
Thackers La LN4............81 D2
Thacker's Rd PE22........112 B2
Thackers Way PE6........217 D5
Thames Cl 3 PE24.........90 B7
Thames Cres 5 PE24......90 B7
Thames Ct DN37..........190 E8
Thames Mdw Dr 2 PE24...90 B7
Thames Rd Grantham NG31 210 E2
Spalding PE11.............214 F5
Thames St Hogsthorpe PE24 .90 B7
Louth LN11................198 D6
Thary La PE21.............145 E4
Thatch Carr Bank DN9......26 D4
Thatchers Wlk PE22.......113 B2
Theaker Ave DN21.........197 F5
THEALBY DN15...............8 D4
Thealby La DN15............8 E5
Thealby Rd DN15............8 C3
Theatre Royal★ LN2.....234 B2
THEDDLETHORPE ALL SAINTS LN12.....................63 D7
Theddlethorpe Prim Sch LN12.....................63 D6
Theddlethorpe Rd LN12....63 F4
THEDDLETHORPE ST HELEN LN12.....................63 E8
Theodore Rd DN15........182 E4
Theodore St LN1..........234 A4
Theresa Cl 8 PE25........206 A4
Therm Rd HU8.............181 A8
Thesiger St
2 Grimsby DN32..........189 B1
Lincoln LN5...............201 F1
Thesiger Wlk 8 DN31.....189 B1
THETFORD PE6............164 E5
Thetford Ave 5 PE6.......164 E5
THIMBLEBY LN9............85 B5
Thimbleby Hill LN9.........85 C5
Thinholme La DN9..........27 A1
Third Ave 20 Brookenby LN8 .47 B6
1 Fixborough Ind Est DN15 ..8 A1
Grantham NG31...........211 F7
4 Scampton Airfield LN1....67 E5
2 Scunthorpe DN17.......184 C6
Spalding PE11.............214 A4
Third Dro Gosberton PE11..144 B4
Moulton PE12.............146 F7
Peterborough PE1.........226 E2
Third Hill Rd LN4...........81 F3
Third La DN37..............35 D3
Third Marsh Rd PE14......170 C3
Thirkleby Cres DN32......192 B4
Thirlmere Ave DN33.......194 E7
Thirlmere Cl 8 LN6.......205 A2
Thirlmere Gdns 3 PE4....221 C3
Thirlmere Way 1 LN6....200 D1
Thirsk Dr LN6.............204 F4
Thisle Gdns PE11.........214 C4
Thistle Cl LN2.............202 C8
Thistle Dr PE2............231 C7
Thistlemoor Rd PE1.......225 E7
Thistleton La LE15........151 D1
Thomas Cl 7 PE3..........224 F3
Thomas Cowley High Sch The PE11.....................134 F2
Thomas Ct 13 NG34.......212 D4
Thomas Deacon Acad PE1......................226 B5
Thomas Gibson Dr LN9...199 D3
Thomas Kitching Way 8 LN3.......................83 C4
Thomas Mid Cott Dr 20 PE20.....................136 C5
Thomas Rd
10 Balderton NG24........104 C1
Scunthorpe DN17.........184 F8
Thomas St Grimsby DN32..191 F7
Kingston upon Hull HU9....181 B7
Lincoln LN2...............234 C2
Sleaford NG34............212 D4
Thomas Sully Cl LN9.....199 A4
Thompson Cl
19 Coddington NG24......104 C5
Skegness PE25...........206 C5
3 Spalding PE11..........214 C3
Thompson Dr 25 DN7......14 D4
Thompson Rd DN36.......195 D7
Thompsons Gd PE7.......230 D3
Thompson's La
Fosdyke PE20.............146 E8
Hough-on-the-Hill NG32....119 A5
Thompson St 10 DN15....183 B3
Thonock Cl LN2...........201 F7
Thonock Dr 7 LN1..........66 C2
Thonock Rd DN21.........197 D8
Thoresby Pl DN35.........192 E4
Thoresby Prim Sch HU5...180 B8
Thoresby Rd Fulstow LN11..49 A8
Scunthorpe DN17.........184 D5
Tetney DN36................36 D3
Thoresby St HU5..........180 B8
THORESTHORPE LN13......75 F4
THORESWAY LN8...........46 D7
Thoresway Dr LN2........202 A7
Thoresway Gr 5 DN33....191 A3
Thoresway Rd LN8..........46 C8
Thorgam Ct DN31.........191 C7
THORGANBY DN37..........47 B8
Thorganby Rd
Cleethorpes DN35........193 A3
Swinhope LN8..............47 C7
Thorlby Haven 12 PE20...135 A4
Thorley Cres PE2..........230 D8
Thorn Bank DN9............26 E4
Thornbury Dr DN33.......191 B1
Thornbury Rd DN40.......186 D3
Thorndales La PE22.......113 A5
Thorndike Way DN21......197 E3
Thorndyke Mews 7 DN21.....................197 D3
THORNE DN8...............15 B8
Thorne Brooke Prim Sch DN8......................15 B7
Thorne Green Top Prim Sch DN8......................15 A7
Thorne King Edward Pri Sch DN8......................15 B8
Thorne N Sta DN8..........14 F8
Thorne Rd Edenthorpe DN3..14 A2
Sandtoft DN8...............16 A3
8 Stainforth DN7...........14 C7
Thorne S Sta DN8..........15 B7
Thorne Swimming Baths DN8......................15 B8
Thorne Waste Drain Rd DN8......................15 E8
Thorne Way PE20.........136 C4
THORNEY Thorney NG23.....78 F8
Thorney PE6...............176 A3
Thorney Heritage Mus★ PE6.......................176 A3
Thorney Rd
2 Crowland PE6...........175 C8
Newborough PE6..........174 D5
Wisbech St Mary PE13....177 C2
Thorney Rd South PE6....175 C8
THORNEY TOLL PE13......177 A2
Thorngarth La 9 DN19.....11 D8
Thorngate LN5.............234 B2
Thornham's Way 8 HU15...2 C7
Thornhill Cres 4 DN17....184 F3
Thornhill Gdns DN34.....191 A7
Thornhill La DN22..........52 E1
Thornholme Dr DN16......185 A3
Thorniman La PE20........136 E6
Thorn La DN19..............12 A8
Thorn Leigh 3 HU3........180 C6
Thornleigh Dr PE2.........230 C6
Thornmead PE4............221 B4
Thorn Rd PE7..............230 C2
Thorns La NG32...........210 A8
THORNTON LN9.............85 C2
Thornton 20 HU15...........2 C6
Thornton Abbey★ DN39....12 B5
Thornton Abbey Sta DN39 .12 A5
Thornton Ave Boston PE21 208 D3
Scunthorpe DN16.........185 A7
Thornton Cl
3 Heighington/Washingborough LN4......203 A2
Kingston upon Hull HU13...178 D1
Langriville PE22...........124 F8
6 Lincoln LN6..............205 A7
Peterborough PE4.........221 C3
Thornton Cres
Cleethorpes DN35........192 E4
Horncastle LN9............199 C2
Thornton Ct DN36.........195 D8
THORNTON CURTIS DN39...11 E4
Thornton Curtis Rd DN18..11 A3
Thornton Gdns 21 DN41....23 A4
Thornton Gr 5 DN34......190 E4
THORNTON LE MOOR LN7...44 E7
Thornton Pl DN40.........186 B3
Thornton Rd
Barrow upon Humber DN19..11 D6
7 Collingham NG23.........91 D4
Goxhill DN19................11 F6
Owersby LN7...............44 E7
South Kelsey LN7...........32 A1
Spalding PE11.............214 F3
Thornton Curtis DN39......11 E4
Thornton St
Barrow upon Humber DN19..11 C7

Thornton St continued
6 Gainsborough DN21 . . . . . **197** D3
Thornton Way LN3 . . . . . . **203** E6
Thornwell La **2** PE23. . . . . . .**87** A4
Thornwick Ave HU10 . . . . . **178** E8
Thornwick Cl **2** HU3 . . . . . **180** C5
Thorold Ave
5 Cranwell NG34 . . . . **120** E8
Cranwell & Byard's Leap
NG34. . . . . **107** E1
Thorold Gdns **1** NG32 . . . . **130** B8
Thorold Pl **1** DN3. . . . .**14** A2
Thorold Rd NG32. . . . . **210** A4
Thorold St Boston PE21 . . . **208** F6
Grimsby DN31 . . . . **189** C1
Thorolds Way PE5. . . . . . . **223** D2
Thorold Way LN5. . . . .**93** F4
Thoroton Ave NG34 . . . . . . **104** B2
Thoroughfare DN37 . . . .**35** D3
Thoroughfare La NG24 . . . . **104** B8
THORPE LN12 . . . .**64** A1
Thorpe Ave Lincoln LN1 . . . **201** D8
Moulton PE12. . . . . **157** E2
Peterborough PE3 . . . . . . **225** C2
Thorpe Bank PE22. . . . . . . **101** B3
Thorpe Camp Visitor Ctr ★
LN4 . . . . **207** B8
Thorpe Cl **3** NG24 . . . . . . **104** D5
THORPE CULVERT PE24. . . **102** A3
Thorpe Culvert Sta PE24. . . **102** A3
Thorpe Dr NG34 . . . . **120** E2
Thorpe Dro NG34 . . . . **120** E3
Thorpe Fen PE24 . . . . **101** E3
THORPE FENDYKES PE24. . . **101** F3
Thorpehall Rd **12** DN3 . . . . .**14** A2
Thorpe La
Aubourn Haddington & South
Hykeham LN6 . . . .**93** A8
Brattleby LN1. . . . .**67** B7
Eagle & Swinethorpe LN6. . .**79** C1
Tealby LN8. . . . .**46** B1
THORPE LATIMER NG34. . . **133** C6
Thorpe Lea Rd PE3. . . . . . . **225** E2
THORPE LE VALE LN8. . . . . .**47** B1
Thorpe Mdws PE3. . . . . . . **225** C2
Thorpe Pk Rd PE3. . . . . **225** C3
Thorpe Pl LN4 . . . . **207** B6
Thorpe Prim Sch PE3. . . . . **225** B3
Thorpe Rd
Doddington & Whisby LN6 . . .**79** E2
Ewerby & Evedon NG34 . . . **122** C6
Peterborough PE3 . . . . . . **225** B1
Tattershall LN4 . . . . **207** C6
THORPE ST PETER PE24. . . **102** B3
Thorpes La **3** NG32 . . . . . **138** D4
Thorpe's La PE12. . . . . **158** B6
THORPE TILNEY LN4. . . . . . **109** C8
Thorpe Tilney Dro
Timberland LN4 . . . .**97** A1
Walcott LN4 . . . . **109** C8
Thorpe Wood PE3. . . . . . . **224** F1
Thorsby Cl LN5. . . . . **205** D1
Thorseby Cl **3** PE3. . . . . . . **225** B3
Threadneedle St **9** PE21 . . **208** F5
Threave Ct
Orton Longueville PE3 . . . . **230** A8
Peterborough PE3 . . . . . . **225** A1
Three Bridge La LN11 . . . . . .**63** A7
THREE BRIDGES LN11 . . . . . .**63** A7
Threekingham NG34 . . . . . . **132** E3
Three Leys La DN22 . . . .**52** B2
THROCKENHOLT PE12 . . . . **177** B8
Throstlenest PE7 . . . . **231** C3
Thrumber Marsh La LN13 . . .**76** F1
Thrunscoe Prim Acad
DN35. . . . . **192** E5
Thrunscoe Rd **7** DN35. . . . **192** F5
Thrush Cl LN6 . . . . **212** B3
Thurlaston Cl PE3. . . . . **225** B2
THURLBY Bilsby LN13 . . . . . .**76** D2
Thurlby LN5. . . . .**92** E4
Thurlby PE10 . . . . **164** C8
Thurlby Cl **4** LN4 . . . . **203** A2
Thurlby Com Prim Sch
PE10. . . . . **164** C8
Thurlby Cres LN2 . . . . **202** B8
Thurlby Fen Nature Reserve★
PE10. . . . . **164** F7
Thurlby Rd Bassingham LN5 . .**92** F3
Bilsby LN13 . . . .**76** B3
Gainsborough DN21 . . . . . **197** E4
Thurlow Ct **1** LN2. . . . . . . **202** E7
Thuro Gr PE2 . . . . **230** A3
Thursfield PE4. . . . . **221** A4
Thurstan Cl PE10. . . . . **213** B6
Thurston Gate **2** PE3 . . . . **225** A1
Thyme Ave Bourne PE10 . . . **213** C5
12 Market Deeping PE6 . . . **217** C5
Thyme Ct LN6. . . . . **205** D8
Tiber Cl **13** PE11 . . . . **214** A4
Tiber Rd LN6. . . . . **204** C1
Tichbourne Cl **3** HU3 . . . . **180** C5
TICKENCOTE PE9 . . . . **171** A8
Ticklepenny Wlk LN11. . . . . **198** E7
Tideswell Ct DN15. . . . . . . **182** B2
Tigers Wy HU4 . . . . **179** E5
Tilbury Rd HU4. . . . . **179** B3
Tilebarn La PE20 . . . . **134** F7
Tilgate Rd PE7 . . . . **233** E8
Tilia Cl
Kingston upon Hull HU4 . . . **179** B2
Scunthorpe DN16 . . . . **185** D4
Tilia Gr **10** PE22 . . . . **114** A1
Tilia Way **5** PE10 . . . . **213** E2
Till Bridge La Marton LN1 . . .**65** F8

Till Bridge La continued
Scampton LN1. . . . .**67** A6
Stow LN1 . . . .**66** A8
Tillbridge Rd LN1 . . . .**66** D7
Tilley Gate LN11 . . . .**51** B3
Tilling Ct NG31. . . . . **211** A2
Tilman Dr PE7 . . . . **230** F5
Tilney Ave PE21 . . . . **208** D6
Tilney The **10** PE12 . . . . . . **158** B7
Tilton Ct PE1. . . . . **226** C8
Timber Hill NG33. . . . . **151** A4
TIMBERLAND LN4. . . . .**96** C1
Timberland DN16 . . . . **185** C4
Timberland Dro LN4. . . . . . .**96** E2
Timberland Rd LN4. . . . .**96** C2
Timberley Dr DN37. . . . . . . **190** C7
Timm's La **18** LN5 . . . .**93** F7
Timms's Dro PE20. . . . . . . **134** E8
Timson Ct **5** DN10 . . . .**52** B8
Tindale Bank Rd DN9 . . . . . .**39** C8
Tindall Cl **2** PE13 . . . . **170** D2
Tindall Way PE24 . . . . **102** D1
Tinkermere Cl **3** LN2 . . . . . .**68** D6
Tinker's Dro PE13. . . . . **170** D1
Tinker's La Girton NG23 . . . .**91** C8
2 Waddington LN5 . . . .**93** F6
Tinkle St LN11 . . . .**62** C7
Tin La PE10. . . . . **213** C5
Tinsley Cl NG23 . . . . **117** F7
Tintagel Ct **7** PE3. . . . . . . **225** B1
Tintagel Way DN36. . . . . . . **195** C7
Tintern Rise **4** PE6 . . . . . . **175** A1
Tintern Wlk DN37. . . . . **188** A1
Tinus Ave PE7 . . . . **230** C1
Tiverton Rd PE3. . . . . **225** C3
Tiverton St DN35. . . . . **189** E1
Tivoli Gdns DN32. . . . . **191** F8
Tobias Gr **4** PE9 . . . . **218** C7
Tobruk Cl **1** LN6 . . . . **201** D2
Todd La DN21. . . . .**41** C4
Todds Cl **1** Swanland HU14 . . .**3** C6
18 Tetney DN36 . . . .**36** D4
Todds Ct **26** DN17 . . . .**29** D7
Todds La **1** DN15 . . . .**8** A4
Todd's La HU15 . . . .**2** A8
Todkill's La **7** PE12 . . . . . . **160** F4
TOFT PE10. . . . . **163** F8
Toft Cl PE24 . . . . **115** D8
Toft Field La PE22. . . . . **114** A3
TOFT HILL PE22. . . . .**98** D5
Toft Hurn **1** PE22 . . . .**98** F4
Toft La **17** Sleaford NG34 . . **212** D4
Toft Newton LN8. . . . .**56** F7
Toftland PE2. . . . . **230** C5
TOFT NEXT NEWTON LN8 . . .**56** C7
Tofts Rd **10** DN18. . . . .**10** E8
Toft Tunnel Nature Reserve★
PE10 . . . . **154** A1
Tolethorpe Sq **6** PE9. . . . . **219** B6
TOLL BAR DN35 . . . . **195** A5
Toll Bar PE9 . . . . **218** C8
Toll Bar Ave
6 Bottesford NG13 . . . . . . **128** A6
New Waltham DN36. . . . . . **195** B6
Tollbar Rd
Great Gonerby NG32 . . . . . **129** B8
Marston NG32 . . . . **118** C1
Toll Bar Rd Croft PE24 . . . . **103** C3
Grantham NG31 . . . . **211** C3
Tollemache Fields **9**
NG33. . . . . **151** D2
Tollemach Rd (North)
NG31 . . . . **139** F8
Tollemach Rd (South)
NG31. . . . . **139** F8
Tollesby La **34** DN7. . . . .**14** D4
Tollfield Rd PE21. . . . . **209** B7
Tollgate Peterborough PE3 . **225** A5
Spalding PE11 . . . . **214** C4
Toll House Rd PE2 . . . . **230** C7
Toll's La PE12. . . . . **215** E5
Tom La NG34 . . . . **120** C5
Tomline Rd **5** DN41. . . . . . .**23** A5
Tomline St DN31. . . . . **189** B1
Tomlinson Ave **4** DN15. . . **182** E3
Tomlinson Cl **3** LN4 . . . . . **207** A5
Tomlinson Dr LN18 . . . .**10** E7
Tomlinson Way **5** NG34 . . **108** E2
Tom Otter's La **3** LN1. . . . . .**66** B1
Tom Potts Row HU15 . . . .**2** E8
Tonbridge **1** DN33 . . . . . . **194** E8
Tonbridge Wlk DN33 . . . . . **194** E8
Toneham La PE7. . . . . **175** F2
Tonglet Cl **3** PE25 . . . . . . **206** C1
Tonnant Way DN34 . . . . . . **190** D5
Toogood St **6** HU2. . . . . . **180** F8
Tooley La PE22. . . . . **114** C2
Tooley St Boston PE21. . . . . **209** A3
Gainsborough DN21. . . . . . **197** D3
Toothill Gdns DN34. . . . . . **190** F6
Toot La PE21. . . . . **209** D4
Topaz Gr **3** HU3 . . . . **180** A4
Topham Cres **13** PE6 . . . . . **176** A3

Top La Goulceby LN11. . . . . . .**72** C6
Kirk Bramwith DN7. . . . .**14** A6
Top Lodge LN6 . . . . **200** B4
Topmoor Way PE4 . . . . **221** D1
Top Rd
4 Croxton Kerrial NG32 . . . **138** D4
Little Cawthorpe LN11 . . . . .**61** C4
Osgodby LN8 . . . .**45** A2
South Killingholme DN40 . . .**12** E3
Thoresway LN7 . . . .**46** A7
Thorney NG23 . . . .**78** F7
Winterton DN15 . . . .**8** F6
Worlaby DN20 . . . .**10** D1
Top Rd The LN9 . . . .**99** C8
Topsgate PE12. . . . . **159** C7
Torbay Dr DN33. . . . . **194** E6
Torchil Cl HU10 . . . . **178** C6
Torfrida Dr PE10. . . . . **213** B6
Torfrid **14** PE6 . . . . **166** F1
Torgate Ave LN5 . . . .**92** F2
Torgate La LN5 . . . .**93** A2
Torkington Gdns **9** PE9 . . **219** B5
Torkington St PE9. . . . . **219** A5
TORKSEY LN1 . . . .**65** E5
Torksey Ave LN1 . . . .**66** C2
Torksey Dr DN33. . . . . **191** B3
Torksey Ferry Rd DN22 . . . . .**65** B5
TORKSEY LOCK LN1 . . . .**65** E5
Torksey Pl **3** DN33. . . . . . . **191** B3
Torksey St
14 Kirton in Lindsey DN21 . . .**30** B1
Rampton DN22. . . . .**65** A5
Torold Dr PE7. . . . . **230** D2
Tor-o-Moor Gdns **2** LN10 . .**97** E6
Tor-o-Moor Rd **9** LN10 . . . .**97** E6
Toronto St **2** LN2 . . . . **202** C3
Torpel Way **5** PE6 . . . . **173** C7
Torrington La
East Barkwith LN8 . . . .**71** A8
Fleet PE12 . . . . **159** B5
Legsby LN8. . . . .**58** C1
Torrington Rd Lincoln LN2 . . **201** F8
Scunthorpe DN17 . . . . **184** C8
Torrington St DN32 . . . . . . **191** F5
Torr St DN21. . . . . **197** D4
Torskey Castle ★ LN1 . . . . .**65** D5
*Tortoiseshell Wood Nature
Reserve* ★ NG33 . . . . **152** B2
Tossey La LN11 . . . .**50** B2
Tothby Cl **1** LN13. . . . .**75** E3
Tothby La LN13 . . . .**75** E2
Tothby Mdws LN13 . . . .**75** E3
TOTHILL LN11 . . . .**62** E1
Tothill Cl LN6 . . . . **204** F7
Totnes Pl Green Hill NG31 . . **210** E6
Green Hill NG31. . . . . **210** E6
Totney St DN33 . . . . **194** E6
Tottermire La **5** DN9 . . . . . .**27** D7
Touthill Cl PE1. . . . . **226** A2
Towell Rd PE21. . . . . **209** B3
Tower Ave
Bracebridge Heath LN4 . . . **205** F3
Lincoln LN2. . . . . **202** D4
Tower Cl
9 Mablethorpe & Sutton
LN12 . . . .**64** B3
Woodhall Spa LN10 . . . .**97** F7
Tower Cres LN2 . . . . **202** D4
Tower Ct PE2 . . . . **230** F8
Tower Dr Lincoln LN2. . . . . **202** D4
Woodhall Spa LN10 . . . .**97** F7
Tower Espl PE25 . . . . **206** D3
Tower Flats LN2 . . . . **202** D4
Tower Gdns Boston PE21. . . **209** A4
23 Dunscroft DN7 . . . .**14** D3
1 Lincoln LN2 . . . . **202** D4
Tower Hill
Kingston upon Hull HU13 . . **178** E1
Westwoodside DN9 . . . .**27** B2
Tower Hill Dr HU13 . . . . . . **178** E1
Tower Hill Mews **2** HU13 . **178** E1
Tower House La **7** HU12. . . . .**5** F8
Tower La Harmston LN4. . . . .**94** B4
Spalding PE11 . . . . **214** D3
Tower Rd PE21. . . . . **209** A5
Tower Rd Acad PE21. . . . . . **209** A6
Tower St **14** Boston PE21. . . **208** F5
1 Kingston Dock Village
HU9. . . . . **181** A5
Towers The **2** PE25. . . . . . **206** D5
Tower View
Kingston upon Hull HU10 . . **178** C5
Sleaford NG34 . . . . **212** B3
Towgood Cl **7** PE6. . . . . . . **173** C4
Tow La **5** NG32 . . . . **117** F1
Towler St PE1. . . . . **226** A3
Town Bridge **22** PE21 . . . . **208** F5
Town Dam Dro PE11. . . . . . **144** F8
Town Dam La PE11 . . . . . . **134** F2
Town Dro PE11 . . . . **144** F8
Town End NG32 . . . . **120** B2
Town Farm Cl **1** PE11. . . . **156** F8
Townfield La **5** PE20. . . . . **135** C7
TOWNGATE PE6 . . . . **164** F1
Towngate E PE6 . . . . **217** C7
Towngate W PE6. . . . . **217** A6
Town Hall Sq DN31. . . . . . . **191** E7
Town Hall St **4** DN31. . . . . **191** E7
Town Hill DN20 . . . .**19** E4
Town Hill Dr DN20. . . . .**19** E4
Townhill Sq **24** NG24 . . . . **104** C1
Towning Cl **9** PE6 . . . . **217** D6
Townley Cl LN9 . . . . **199** D1
Town Rd Sleaford NG34 . . . **212** B5
Tetney DN36. . . . .**36** D4
Townsend Cl
Humberston DN36 . . . . **193** C1

Townsend Cl continued
4 Peterborough PE1. . . . . **226** A3
Townsend Rd **6** PE8 . . . . . **172** B1
Townsend Way LN4 . . . .**95** C4
Townside DN40 . . . .**12** D6
Town St Cottam DN22 . . . . . .**65** B6
Immingham DN40 . . . .**12** E4
South Somercotes LN11 . . . .**50** E4
Westborough & Dry Doddington
NG23. . . . . **117** F3
TOYNTON ALL SAINTS
PE23. . . . . **100** F6
Toynton All Saints Prim Sch
PE23. . . . . **100** F6
Toynton Cl **3** LN6. . . . . . . **205** B4
TOYNTON FEN SIDE PE23 . **100** F6
Toynton La PE23 . . . . **101** B6
Toynton Rd DN33 . . . . **191** B3
TOYNTON ST PETER
PE23. . . . . **101** A6
Trader Bank Frithville PE22 **125** F8
Sibsey PE22 . . . . **113** A2
Trafalgar Ave
Grimsby DN34 . . . . **190** D5
Skegness PE25. . . . . **206** D4
Trafalgar Ct
2 Heighington/
Washingborough LN4 . . . **203** B2
2 Scunthorpe DN15 . . . . . **183** A6
Trafalgar Pk DN36 . . . . **195** D7
Trafalgar Pl **3** PE21 . . . . . **208** E4
Trafalgar Sq
Long Sutton PE12. . . . . . . **216** B4
4 Sutton on Trent NG23 . . . .**91** A8
Trafalgar St **5** HU3 . . . . . . **180** D7
Trafford Est PE14 . . . . **170** F4
Trafford Pk **25** PE13 . . . . . **170** E1
Trafford Rd
Kingston upon Hull HU10 . . **178** E8
13 Wisbech PE13 . . . . **170** E1
Trafford St DN15 . . . . **183** B4
Traffords Way DN20. . . . . . .**30** F6
Train Gate **23** DN21 . . . .**30** B1
Tramway Dr **21** LN12. . . . . .**76** F8
Tranby Ave HU13 . . . . **178** D2
Tranby Croft HU13 . . . . . . **178** C5
Tranby Dr DN32. . . . . **192** B4
Tranby La
Anlaby with Anlaby Common
HU10. . . . . **178** B5
Swanland HU14 . . . .**3** C6
Tranby Lodge Gdns HU13 . **178** C1
Tranby Mdws Pk HU13. . . . **178** C3
Tranby Ride HU10 . . . . **178** C5
Tranmere Ct HU3 . . . . **180** B5
Transport Rd DN16 . . . . . . **183** E2
Travellers Rest Cvn Site
NG31 . . . . **211** B1
Travis Dr **10** DN8 . . . .**15** B8
Travis Cl **14** DN8 . . . .**15** B8
Travis St **15** DN8 . . . .**15** B8
*Travis St Lawrence CE Prim
Sch* DN7. . . . .**14** E4
Traviss Cl **2** DN16. . . . . . . **185** B8
Treadgold Ave **10** NG31 . . . **129** E5
Treading Bank PE13 . . . . . . **169** C4
Treasure La LN11 . . . .**49** F5
Treece Gdns **10** DN18. . . . . .**3** F1
Tree Cl PE25 . . . . **206** A5
Trefoil Dr PE25 . . . . **103** C6
Trehampton Dr **4** DN21 . . . .**53** A5
Trelawney Cres **2** LN1. . . . **201** E8
Trelowen Wy **7** PE2 . . . . . **230** F5
Tremayne Ave **1** HU15 . . . . .**2** C5
Trenchard Cl DN40. . . . . . . **186** E5
Trenchard Rd
9 Ashby de la Launde &
Bloxholm LN4 . . . . **108** A7
Cranwell & Byard's Leap
NG34. . . . . **120** D8
3 Mablethorpe/Sutton on Sea
LN12 . . . .**64** B3
Trenchard Sq
2 Scampton Airfield LN1. . . .**67** F5
1 Waddington LN5 . . . .**94** A7
Trent Ct **6** DN37 . . . . **190** E8
Trentholme Dr **37** DN17. . . .**29** D7
Trent La Beacon Hill NG24 . . **104** A5
Besthorpe NG23. . . . .**91** B7
Girton NG23 . . . .**78** B1
Newton on Trent LN1 . . . . . .**65** C1
South Clifton NG23. . . . .**78** B5
Trenton Ave HU4. . . . . **179** B6
Trent Port Rd DN21. . . . . . .**65** D8
Trent Rd Grantham NG31. . . **210** D2
Keadby with Althorpe DN17 . .**17** D6
Trentside
Gainsborough DN21. . . . . . **197** B8
Keadby with Althorpe DN17 . .**17** C3
Trent Side DN17. . . . .**7** F1
Trent St
Gainsborough DN21. . . . . . **197** D3
Scunthorpe DN16 . . . . **183** B2
Trentvale Ave DN21. . . . . . **197** F6
Trentvale Prep Sch DN17 . . .**17** D6
Trent View Ermine LN1 . . . **201** D8
Keadby DN17. . . . .**17** D5
5 Marton DN21 . . . .**65** E8
Trent Wlk **13** HU15. . . . .**2** D5
Trent Wy **5** NG24 . . . . **104** A5
Tresham Rd PE2 . . . . **229** D3
Trevitt Cl **1** NG34. . . . . . . **212** B7
Trevor Cl **2** DN37 . . . .**23** F1
Trevose Dr **2** LN6. . . . . . . **205** A1
Triangle Dr **9** DN31 . . . . . **188** F1
Triangle The **13** HU14. . . . . .**3** A4
Trienna PE2 . . . . **230** B5
Trinity Acad DN8. . . . .**15** B8

Trinity Cl **10** Crowland PE6 . **166** E1
10 Goxhill DN19. . . . .**12** A8
Trinity Ct **9** DN20 . . . .**19** C4
Trinity Gr HU13 . . . . **178** E2
Trinity House La **12** HU1 . . **180** F6
Trinity La LN11 . . . . **198** D6
Trinity Rd
Cleethorpes DN35 . . . . **192** E5
Newark-on-Trent NG24 . . . **104** A2
Scunthorpe DN16 . . . . **185** A4
Stamford PE9. . . . . **219** A6
Wisbech PE13 . . . . **170** E1
Trinity St Boston PE21. . . . **208** E4
Gainsborough DN21. . . . . . **197** D3
14 Grimsby DN31. . . . . . . **189** C1
Kingston upon Hull HU3 . . . **180** C7
3 Peterborough PE1. . . . . **226** A2
Trinity Wharf **8** HU1. . . . . **181** A6
Trinity Wlk **1** DN18 . . . .**3** F1
Tritton Rd LN6 . . . . **201** D2
Trollope St LN6 . . . . **234** B1
**Trollybus Mus at Sandtoft
The** ★ DN8 . . . .**16** A3
Tromso Cl DN36. . . . . **195** B6
Trondheim Cl DN36 . . . . . . **195** B6
Trondheim Way DN41 . . . . **187** A2
Troon Cl
Grantham NG31 . . . . **211** D8
7 Heighington/Washingborough
LN4 . . . . **203** D1
11 Stamford PE9 . . . . **218** E6
3 Woodhall Spa LN10 . . . . .**97** C6
Troon Ct **2** NG34 . . . . **120** F3
Troon Rd DN7. . . . .**14** D4
Trotters La **2** NG32 . . . . . . **139** C7
Troughton Way **10** PE13 . . **170** B2
Troutbeck Cl
6 Lincoln LN2 . . . . **202** A8
1 Peterborough PE4 . . . . **221** D3
Troutsdale Gr HU9 . . . . **181** F8
Truesdale Gdns PE6. . . . . . **164** E3
Truman Cl LN8 . . . .**56** F3
Trunch La PE24 . . . .**90** D5
Trundle La **2** DN7. . . . .**14** D8
Trunkass La DN34 . . . .**34** D7
Truro Cl 6 Grantham NG31 **210** F5
7 Skegness PE25 . . . . **206** D7
5 Sleaford NG34. . . . . . . **212** C5
Truro Dr LN6 . . . . **204** B8
Truro Way 2 PE11 . . . . . . **214** C4
TRUSTHORPE LN12 . . . .**64** B2
Trusthorpe Rd **2** LN12 . . . . .**64** C1
Tuckers Nook PE6. . . . . **173** C7
Tucker's Yd PE2 . . . . **231** C7
Tudor Ave PE7 . . . . **230** C1
Tudor Cl Beacon Hill NG24 . **104** A4
23 Brough HU15. . . . .**2** C5
24 Humberston DN36 . . . . . .**36** D8
Northorpe PE10 . . . . **164** C7
Peterborough PE4 . . . . . . **221** C2
4 Sutterton PE20 . . . . **136** A2
1 West Newton LN8 . . . .**56** C7
Tudor Cl (Doglands) LN8 . . . .**56** C5
Tudor Dr **4** Boston PE21. . . **208** E7
Louth LN11. . . . . **198** C4
Tudor La **2** HU15 . . . .**2** C5
Tudor Pk LN9 . . . . **199** D4
Tudor Pl
Market Deeping PE6. . . . . . **217** E5
Market Deeping PE6. . . . . . **217** F5
Tudor Rd LN6. . . . . **204** B8
Tudor Way PE15 . . . . **215** D1
Tudworth Field Rd DN7. . . . .**15** B5
Tudworth Rd DN7. . . . .**15** A5
Tulip Fields PE12. . . . . **158** C7
Tulip Rd DN15 . . . . **183** C3
Tulipwood Ave **11** LN6 . . . **200** C1
Tumby Cl PE22. . . . .**98** D2
Tumby La PE22. . . . . **100** A6
Tumby Rd LN4 . . . . **207** E6
TUMBY WOODSIDE PE22 . . **111** B8
Tummel Ct DN40 . . . . **186** B2
Tunnard St Boston PE21. . . **208** F5
Grimsby DN32 . . . . **192** B8
Tunnel Bank PE10 . . . . **213** F3
Tunnel Rd DN20. . . . . **196** F7
Tupcroft Road DN10 . . . .**39** F4
Tuplin Road **10** LN12. . . . . .**64** A4
Turbary Rd DN9. . . . .**27** B6
Turf Moor Rd **4** DN7 . . . . . .**15** A3
Turnberry App DN37 . . . . . **194** C4
Turnberry Cl
1 Grantham NG31 . . . . . . **211** D7
Heighington/Washingborough
LN4 . . . .**81** E4
4 Sleaford NG34. . . . . . . **120** F3
Turnberry Dr **4** LN10 . . . . . .**97** C6
Turnberry Ms **19** DN7 . . . . .**14** C6
Turnbury Cl LN6 . . . . **204** B7
Turner Ave **3** LN6. . . . . . . **205** A6
Turner Cl **2** LN5 . . . . **107** B8
Turner Ct LN6. . . . . **204** B8
Turner Rd PE4 . . . . **221** F2
Turner's La **17** HU14 . . . .**3** A5
Turner St
18 Kirton in Lindsey DN21 . . .**30** B1
Lincoln LN1 . . . . **234** A4
Turnor Cl
5 Colsterworth NG33. . . . . **151** E6
1 Wragby LN8 . . . .**70** D5
Turnor Cres NG31 . . . . **211** C5
Turnor Rd NG31 . . . . **211** F4
Turnpike Cl
Great Gonerby NG31 . . . . . **210** D1
14 Wisbech PE13 . . . . **170** E1

Turnpike Rd
  Hampton Vale PE7 . . . . **230** B1
  Ryhall PE9 . . . . **163** C2
Turnpole Cl 2 PE9 . . . . **219** D7
Turnstone Way PE2 . . . . **231** D7
Turpin Cl DN21 . . . . **197** F5
Turves Rd PE6 . . . . **175** A2
Tut Hole PE23 . . . . **100** F7
Tuxhill Rd PE34 . . . . **161** E1
Tweed St Horncastle LN9 . . **199** D2
  10 Spalding PE11 . . . . **214** A4
Twelve Foot Bank LN4 . . . . . **109** F5
Twelvetree Ave PE4 . . . . **220** E5
TWENTY PE10 . . . . **155** C3
Twenty Dro PE10 . . . . **155** C3
Twenty Foot Bank LN4 . . . . **110** C6
Twigmoor Side Road DN17 **29** F7
Twitchell 4 LN1 . . . . **66** D7
Two Plank La PE11 . . . . **214** B6
Two Pole Dro PE7 . . . . **231** F1
Two Sisters Cl 3 PE12 . . . . **160** E4
Twyford Cl 2 NG33 . . . . **151** E6
Twyford Gdns
  3 Dogsthorpe PE1 . . . . . . **226** D7
  Grantham NG31 . . . . **211** C4
Twyning Pl DN35 . . . . **192** D7
Tydd Low Rd
  Long Sutton PE12 . . . . **160** A3
  Sutton Cross PE12 . . . . . . **216** B1
Tydd Rd Pinchbeck PE11 . . . **156** C6
  Sutton Bridge PE12 . . . . . . **160** E2
TYDD ST GILES PE13 . . . . . . **169** F7
TYDD ST MARY PE13 . . . . . . **160** A1
Tydd St Mary CE (Aided) Prim
  Sch PE13 . . . . **160** A1
Tydeman Cl DN16 . . . . **185** A2
Tyesdale PE3 . . . . **225** A4
Tyghes Cl PE6 . . . . **217** F5
Tyler Ave DN31 . . . . **191** A7
Tyler Cres 2 PE22 . . . . **126** E3
Tylers 30 PE24 . . . . **90** D7
Tylers Mews PE4 . . . . **220** F3
Tyndal Rd NG31 . . . . **210** F5
Tyne Cl 4 Lincoln LN6 . . . . **205** A2
  Spalding PE11 . . . . **214** A4
Tyne St HU3 . . . . **180** B4
Tyne Way 7 DN37 . . . . **190** E8
Tyrrell Pk PE1 . . . . **226** D2
Tyson Cl
  21 Barton-upon-Humber
    DN18 . . . . **3** F1
  Grantham NG31 . . . . **211** C6
Tytton Cl 2 PE21 . . . . **136** D8
Tytton La E PE21 . . . . **136** D8
Tytton La W PE21 . . . . **136** D8

U

UFFINGTON PE9 . . . . **172** C6
Uffington Ave LN6 . . . . **205** A6
Uffington CE Prim Sch
  PE9 . . . . **172** C6
Uffington Cl 10 LN6 . . . . . . **205** A7
Uffington Rd Barholm PE9 **164** B1
  2 Barnack PE9 . . . . **172** D4
  Stamford PE9 . . . . **219** E6
UFFORD PE9 . . . . **172** F3
UK Coll DN31 . . . . **191** B8
ULCEBY Ulceby DN39 . . . . . . **12** B1
  Ulceby with Fordington LN13 **88** C7
Ulceby Cross LN13 . . . . **88** B8
Ulceby Rd
  Scunthorpe DN17 . . . . **184** D5
  South Killingholme DN39 . . **12** C2
  Wootton DN39 . . . . **11** F3
ULCEBY SKITTER DN39 . . . . **12** C2
Ulceby Sta DN39 . . . . **12** C2
Uldale Cl LN6 . . . . **200** C2
Uldale Way PE4 . . . . **221** D2
Ullswater Ave PE4 . . . . **221** B2
Ullswater Cl 6 LN6 . . . . **205** A2
Ullyatt's Dro PE20 . . . . **124** B3
Ulster Ave DN33 . . . . **191** D6
Ulster Rd DN21 . . . . **197** D6
Ulverston Cl PE1 . . . . **221** F1
Ulverston Rd HU4 . . . . **179** A3
Ulyett La DN17 . . . . **28** C8
Unicorn Row 10 DN21 . . . . . **30** B1
Union Pl 1 PE21 . . . . **208** F5
Union Rd Lincoln LN1 . . . . **234** A3
  Thorne/Moorends DN8 . . . . **15** A8
Union St 2 Boston PE21 . . **208** F5
  Grantham NG31 . . . . **211** A5
  Holbeach PE12 . . . . **159** A7
  Louth LN11 . . . . **198** B6
  14 Market Rasen LN8 . . . . **57** D8
Unity Ave HU13 . . . . **178** F1
Unity Gdns PE12 . . . . **216** E3
Unity Rd DN32 . . . . **192** C6
Unity Sq 5 LN2 . . . . **234** B2
Unity Way DN7 . . . . **14** D5
University Acad Holbeach
  PE12 . . . . **215** D3
University Ct 2 NG31 . . . . . **211** B3
University of Lincoln Brayford
  (Main Campus) LN6 . . . **234** A2
University of Lincoln
  Holbeach Campus PE12 **215** D4
University of Lincoln
  Riseholme Campus LN2 . . **68** A2
Upgate LN11 . . . . **198** B5
Upland Cl LN9 . . . . **199** A5
Uplands PE4 . . . . **221** A5

Uplands Dr NG31 . . . . **211** D6
Upper Burgess St 2
  DN31 . . . . **191** E8
Upper Cl The 8 LN1 . . . . **66** D7
Upper Ings La DN22 . . . . **52** D2
Upper Kenyon St 9 DN8 . . **15** A8
Upper Lindum St LN2 . . . . **234** C3
Upper Long Leys Rd LN1 . **234** A4
Upper Row NG22 . . . . **65** A1
Upper Saxon St LN1 . . . . . **234** A4
UPPERTHORPE DN9 . . . . **27** B3
Upperthorpe Hill DN9 . . . . . **27** A2
Uppingham Rd 6 LN12 . . . . **64** C1
Upsall Rd 9 PE22 . . . . **126** E3
UPTON Upton DN21 . . . . **53** E5
  Upton PE6 . . . . **223** B6
Upton Cl Peterborough PE2 **231** E5
  Peterborough PE3 . . . . **225** A2
Upton Rd Knaith DN21 . . . . . **53** B4
  Upton PE6 . . . . **223** A3
Upton Wlk DN21 . . . . **197** F3
Urban St LN5 . . . . **205** D6
Uredale Pl DN16 . . . . **185** E5
Usher Gall * LN2 . . . . **234** B3
Usher Gn 4 Lincoln LN6 . . **205** B6
  3 Lincoln LN6 . . . . **205** B7
USSELBY LN8 . . . . **45** C4
Utgard Way 4 DN33 . . . . . . **191** B2
UTTERBY LN11 . . . . **48** F4
Utterby Dr DN34 . . . . **191** C5
Utterby Prim Sch The
  DN36 . . . . **48** E5
Uttoxeter Cl PE10 . . . . **213** B3

V

Vacherie La LN4 . . . . **109** F3
Vagarth Cl 15 DN18 . . . . **3** E1
Valda Vale DN40 . . . . **186** A4
Vale Acad The DN20 . . . . . . **196** B4
Vale Ct PE23 . . . . **101** A8
Vale Dr Hampton Vale PE7 . **230** C1
  Yaxley PE7 . . . . **233** D8
Valence Rd PE2 . . . . **229** F4
Valentine Cl Boston PE21 . **209** C3
  1 Kingston upon Hull HU4 . **179** A2
Valentine Rd LN6 . . . . **201** C1
Vale Rd
  Gonerby Hill Foot NG31 . . **210** F8
  10 Spilsby PE23 . . . . **101** A8
Valerian Cl 7 LN6 . . . . **93** B8
Vale The HU10 . . . . **178** B7
Vale View NG23 . . . . **117** F5
Vale Wood DN35 . . . . **185** C3
Valiant Rd
  8 Coddington NG24 . . . . . **104** C5
  Manby LN11 . . . . **62** C5
Valletta St HU9 . . . . **5** E8
Valley Dr HU10 . . . . **178** B7
Valley La
  Long Bennington NG23 . . . **117** B4
  Swaby LN13 . . . . **74** E4
Valley Pk View PE2 . . . . **230** D8
Valley Rd Grantham NG31 **210** C4
  1 Waddington LN5 . . . . . . **93** E8
Valley View 8 NG24 . . . . . **104** D5
Valley View Dr DN16 . . . . . **185** A2
Valliant St 7 LN5 . . . . **94** A7
Vampire Rd LN11 . . . . **62** C5
Vancouver Cres DN37 . . . . **184** E4
Vanderbank Terr 2 PE9 . . **218** E4
Vanessa Dr DN21 . . . . **197** C7
Vanessa Rd LN11 . . . . **198** A4
Vane St HU3 . . . . **180** D7
Van Gogh Dr 8 PE11 . . . . . **214** B3
Vanguard Ct 4 NG34 . . . . . **212** A3
Vanwall Dr 8 LN5 . . . . **93** F7
Varah Cl 39 DN18 . . . . **10** D1
Varlow Rd 1 LN7 . . . . **33** B4
Varsity Cl 4 DN7 . . . . **26** A8
Vars Rd PE7 . . . . **230** B2
Vasey Cl 1 LN6 . . . . **66** E2
Vaughan Ave
  Bottesford NG13 . . . . **128** B6
  Grimsby DN36 . . . . **192** B4
Vaughan Rd 1 HU13 . . . . **3** F4
Vauxhall Rd
  12 Boston PE21 . . . . **209** A5
  Bracebridge Heath LN4 . . **205** F2
Veall Ct LN4 . . . . **207** C4
Veal St DN31 . . . . **191** C7
Velden Way 5 LN8 . . . . **57** D7
Venables Cl 18 PE24 . . . . . . **102** E7
Venables Way LN2 . . . . **202** D6
Vence Cl 1 PE9 . . . . **219** A5
Venom Rd LN11 . . . . **62** C5
Ventnor Ave NG31 . . . . **210** E4
Ventura Bsns Pk DN31 . . . **188** D2
Venture Ct PE11 . . . . **157** A8
Venture Way NG31 . . . . **210** D2
Venus Wy
  Peterborough PE2 . . . . **231** D4
  Peterborough PE2 . . . . **231** D4
Verde Cl PE6 . . . . **175** A2
Verdun Cl LN1 . . . . **201** E7
Vere Rd PE1 . . . . **225** F7
Vere St LN1 . . . . **201** F6
Vere Terr DN31 . . . . **191** C8
Vergette Rd PE6 . . . . **220** D8
Vergette St PE1 . . . . **226** B3
Vermont Gr PE3 . . . . **225** E1
Vermuyden Villas DN8 . . . . **16** A3
Vernatts Gn PE11 . . . . **214** C7
Vernon Ave NG31 . . . . **210** F8
Vernon Rd PE25 . . . . **206** C4
Vernon St LN5 . . . . **201** D1
Veronica Cl 9 PE25 . . . . . . **206** A7

Vessey Cl 7 NG24 . . . . **104** B2
Vesta Cl 4 PE2 . . . . **231** D4
Viaduct Ave 2 DN20 . . . . . **196** F6
Vicarage Cl
  5 Collingham NG23 . . . . . . **91** D5
  4 Cowbit PE12 . . . . **167** B8
  Holbeach PE12 . . . . **158** D1
Vicarage Cres 4 DN15 . . . . . **8** B5
Vicarage Ct 18 NG34 . . . . . **212** D4
Vicarage Dr LN6 . . . . **200** B3
Vicarage Dro PE20 . . . . **134** D5
Vicarage Farm Rd 5 PE1 **226** D3
Vicarage Gdns
  2 Brough HU15 . . . . **2** C6
  1 Elloughton HU15 . . . . **2** C7
  5 Littlefield DN34 . . . . . . **191** C6
  6 Old Leake PE22 . . . . . . **114** A1
  Scunthorpe DN15 . . . . **182** F2
  1 Wrawby DN20 . . . . **20** E3
Vicarage La
  Beckingham DN10 . . . . **40** B1
  Broughton DN20 . . . . **19** E1
  Cadney DN20 . . . . **31** D6
  3 Carlton-le-Moorland LN5 **105** E8
  Dunston LN4 . . . . **95** C6
  Elsham DN20 . . . . **20** F7
  Grasby DN38 . . . . **32** E7
  Harmston LN5 . . . . **93** F5
  1 Helpringham NG34 . . . **133** D7
  1 Immingham DN40 . . . . . **12** E4
  1 Kingston upon Hull HU13 **178** E1
  4 Long Bennington NG23 **117** D3
  Long Sutton PE12 . . . . **216** D2
  11 Lutton PE12 . . . . **160** A8
  21 Nettleham LN2 . . . . **68** C2
  1 Scawby DN20 . . . . **30** E8
  Scopwick LN4 . . . . **95** C1
  6 Scothern LN2 . . . . **68** F4
  4 Sibsey PE22 . . . . **113** B1
  South Clifton NG23 . . . . . . **78** C5
  Wainfleet All Saints PE24 **102** D1
  19 Wellingore LN5 . . . . . . **107** A7
  Wootton DN39 . . . . **11** E3
Vicarage Lawn DN34 . . . . . **191** C6
Vicarage Pk 4 DN15 . . . . **9** D1
Vicarage Rd
  Great Carlton LN11 . . . . . . **62** E4
  4 Heckington NG34 . . . . . **122** E3
  Willoughton DN21 . . . . **42** E4
  Wrawby DN20 . . . . **196** F6
Vicarage View DN37 . . . . . . **22** D3
Vicarage Way 4 PE7 . . . . . **233** D5
Vicar La 2 HU1 . . . . **180** F5
Vicars Ct LN2 . . . . **234** B3
Vicar's Wlk 6 DN17 . . . . **16** D7
Viceroy Cl 2 HU2 . . . . **180** F8
Viceroy Dr PE11 . . . . **156** F8
Vickers La 4 LN11 . . . . **198** B5
Victor Dr 1 LN6 . . . . **204** C1
Victoria Ave 1 Hatfield DN7 **14** E4
  Sleaford NG34 . . . . **212** C3
  1 Woodhall Spa LN10 . . . . **97** D5
Victoria Bank NG34 . . . . . . **133** B1
Victoria Cl
  Gainsborough DN21 . . . . . **197** F2
  2 Marshchapel DN36 . . . . **37** C2
  2 Stainforth DN7 . . . . **14** C5
  Wike Well End DN8 . . . . . . **15** B7
Victoria Ct 5 DN15 . . . . **8** B5
Victoria Dock Prim Sch
  HU9 . . . . **181** B6
VICTORIA DOCK VILLAGE
  HU9 . . . . **181** C5
Victoria Dr 5 DN18 . . . . **3** E1
Victoria Gdns 11 NG24 . . . **104** A4
Victoria Gr
  Heighington/Washingborough
    LN4 . . . . **203** D1
  Morton PE10 . . . . **154** D7
Victoria Mews 18 PE11 . . . **214** D4
Victoria Pas LN1 . . . . **234** A3
Victoria Pier * HU1 . . . . . . **181** A5
Victoria Pl 1 Boston PE21 **208** F4
  3 Bourne PE10 . . . . **213** E4
  Peterborough PE1 . . . . **225** F4
Victoria Rd
  Barnetby le Wold DN38 . . . **21** B4
  10 Keelby DN41 . . . . **23** A5
  Louth LN11 . . . . **198** C7
  Mablethorpe/Sutton on Sea
    LN12 . . . . **64** B3
  2 Market Rasen LN8 . . . . . **57** E8
  Scunthorpe DN16 . . . . **185** A5
  Skegness PE25 . . . . **206** B3
  Stamford PE9 . . . . **219** B6
Victoria Ret Pk DN31 . . . . . **189** A1
Victoria St N DN31 . . . . **189** A1
Victoria St S 4 DN31 . . . . . **191** E7
Victoria St W DN31 . . . . **191** E7
Victoria St
  Billingham NG34 . . . . **133** B1
  3 Billinghay LN4 . . . . **109** F6
  Grantham NG31 . . . . **211** A2
  4 Holbeach PE12 . . . . . . **215** E2
  Kingston upon Hull HU13 . **179** A1
  Lincoln LN1 . . . . **234** A3
  Peterborough PE1 . . . . **226** A5
  Peterborough PE2 . . . . **230** F6
  10 Spalding PE11 . . . . . . **214** D4
  3 Wragby LN8 . . . . **70** D5
Victoria Stables PE10 . . . . **213** D4
Victoria Terr LN1 . . . . **234** A3
Victoria Way DN31 . . . . **188** D2
Victor St Grimsby DN32 . . **189** C1
  Kingston upon Hull HU9 . . **181** C8
Victor Way Bourne PE10 . . **213** E3
  10 Waddington LN5 . . . . . **94** A7
Victory Cl 6 PE12 . . . . **157** F6

Victory Ct 1 PE11 . . . . **214** C3
Victory Gdns 23 PE6 . . . . . **166** F1
Victory Way
  2 Barton-upon-Humber
    DN18 . . . . **3** F1
  8 Grimsby DN34 . . . . **190** D4
  6 Sleaford NG34 . . . . **212** A3
Viersen Platz PE1 . . . . **226** A1
Vigo Cl LN1 . . . . **201** C7
Viking Cl 8 Bourne PE10 . . **213** C6
  Immingham DN40 . . . . **186** A4
  7 Swineshead PE20 . . . . **135** B7
  11 Waddington LN5 . . . . . . **93** F7
Viking Sch The PE25 . . . . . **206** B4
Viking Way
  32 Metheringham LN4 . . . . **95** C3
  7 Northorpe PE10 . . . . . . **164** C8
  Spalding PE11 . . . . **214** F2
Villa Cl 3 Branston LN4 . . . . **81** E2
  Long Sutton PE12 . . . . **216** A5
Villa Ct DN35 . . . . **192** C4
Village Farm LN5 . . . . **92** F3
Village Farm Dr 5 LN1 . . . . **66** C7
Village St
  Burton Coggles NG33 . . . **152** C8
  Easton NG33 . . . . **139** F2
  Pickworth NG34 . . . . **142** A8
  Sedgebrook NG32 . . . . . . **128** F4
  Walcot NG34 . . . . **132** C2
  Woolsthorpe by Belvoir
    NG32 . . . . **128** D1
Village The PE2 . . . . **230** B5
Villa La PE20 . . . . **135** B7
Ville Rd DN16 . . . . **185** D6
Vincent Cl 3 HU4 . . . . **179** A2
Vincent Rd DN33 . . . . **191** B2
Vine Cl 13 NG13 . . . . **128** A5
Vine Cres 8 PE21 . . . . **136** D8
Vine Ct 3 NG34 . . . . **133** B1
Vinegarth 3 DN9 . . . . **27** E6
Vinehall Rd 3 DN9 . . . . **27** C2
Vine Rd
  Chapel St Leonard PE24 . . **90** E7
  1 Skegness PE25 . . . . **103** E4
Vine St Billingborough NG34 **133** C1
  12 Grantham NG31 . . . . . **211** A5
  Lincoln LN2 . . . . **234** C2
  Spalding PE11 . . . . **214** D4
  Stamford PE9 . . . . **219** C5
Vine Wlk PE3 . . . . **225** B4
Vineyard Rd PE1 . . . . **226** B2
Viney Cl PE1 . . . . **226** D5
Vinters Way PE22 . . . . **126** E3
Vintners Cl PE3 . . . . **225** D3
Violeta Wy 5 PE2 . . . . **231** E4
Violet Cl
  4 Humberston DN35 . . . . **192** E1
  9 Morton PE10 . . . . **154** D6
Virginia Cl
  1 Peterborough PE3 . . . . . **225** A2
  Willoughby LN13 . . . . **89** A7
Virginia Dr LN11 . . . . **198** E5
Viscount Cl 17 PE11 . . . . . . **156** E8
Viscount Rd PE2 . . . . **231** A6
Viscount Way 6 DN36 . . . . . **36** D8
Vista The 3 DN32 . . . . **192** B5
Visual Arts Ctr * DN15 . . . **183** C3
Vivian Ave DN32 . . . . **192** B5
Vivian Cl 1 NG31 . . . . **210** F8
Vixen Cl PE7 . . . . **233** F6
Voases Cl HU10 . . . . **178** E6
Voases La HU10 . . . . **178** E6
Vokes St PE2 . . . . **230** D8
Voyager Acad The PE4 . . . **221** A1
Vulcan Cres LN6 . . . . **204** C2
Vulcan Dr
  Market Deeping PE6 . . . . . **217** B7
  4 Scampton Airfield LN1 . . **67** F5
Vulcan St 9 LN5 . . . . **94** A4
Vulcan Way DN7 . . . . **15** A1
Vyner Cl 18 LN12 . . . . **64** B3

W

Waby Cl DN37 . . . . **190** D7
WADDINGHAM DN21 . . . . . . **43** D7
Waddingham Pl
  5 Habrough DN40 . . . . . . **22** E8
  New Waltham DN36 . . . . . **195** D5
Waddingham Prim Sch
  DN21 . . . . **43** D7
Waddingham Rd LN7 . . . . . . **31** F1
WADDINGTON LN5 . . . . **93** F7
Waddington Dr 1 DN17 . . **184** E3
Waddington La NG23 . . . . . **91** C7
Waddington Pl 4 DN34 . . . **191** A5
Waddington Rd NG34 . . . . **212** C2
Waddington Redwood Cty
  Prim Sch LN5 . . . . **93** E8
WADDINGWORTH LN10 . . . . **84** C6
Waddingworth Gr LN2 . . . . **202** A8
Waddingworth Road LN10 **84** C5
Wade Pk Ave PE6 . . . . **217** C4
Waggoners Cl 11 DN21 . . . **29** C4
Waggoners Way PE10 . . . . **154** C6
Waggoners Wlk PE22 . . . . **113** B1
Waggons Way 4 DN7 . . . . . **14** C5
Wagoners Wlk 14 PE25 . . . **206** A5
Waincroft Cl PE24 . . . . **102** E2
Wainer Cl LN6 . . . . **204** C2
WAINFLEET ALL SAINTS
  PE24 . . . . **102** D2
WAINFLEET BANK PE24 . . . **102** B1
Wainfleet Magdalen CE/
  Methodist Sch PE24 . . . **102** D2
Wainfleet Rd Boston PE21 **209** D7
  Croft PE24 . . . . **102** D7

Wainfleet Rd continued
  Firsby PE23 . . . . **101** F6
  Fishtoft PE21 . . . . **209** D7
  Grimsby DN33 . . . . **191** B4
  Irby in the Marsh PE24. . . **102** B6
  Skegness PE25 . . . . **206** A3
  Thorpe St Peter PE24 . . . . **102** C3
Wainfleet Rd Industrial Est
  PE25 . . . . **206** A2
WAINFLEET ST MARY
  PE24 . . . . **115** E8
Wainfleet Sta PE24 . . . . . . **102** D1
WAINFLEET TOFTS PE24 . . **115** C8
Wainman Rd PE2 . . . . **230** D5
Wainwell Mews 3 LN2 . . . **234** C3
Wainwright PE4 . . . . **220** E5
WAITHE DN36 . . . . **36** A3
Waithe La DN37 . . . . **35** E4
Wakefield Ave DN21 . . . . . . **29** D4
Wakefield Cl
  Barrowby NG31 . . . . **210** C4
  10 Bracebridge Heath LN4 . **81** A2
Wakehurst Rd PE7 . . . . **230** F2
Wake Rd PE1 . . . . **226** B2
Wakerley Dr PE2 . . . . **230** C7
Wakerley Rd 6 DN21 . . . . . . **29** C3
Wakes Cl 1 PE10 . . . . **213** E4
Wake St LN1 . . . . **234** A4
Walbury Cl 4 LN5 . . . . **205** D2
WALCOT Alkborough DN15 . . **8** B8
  Walcot Near Folkingham
    NG34 . . . . **132** C1
Walcot Bar NG34 . . . . **132** D2
Walcot Cl LN6 . . . . **204** C5
Walcot La NG34 . . . . **142** C8
Walcot Rd Alkborough DN15 . **8** B8
  Ufford PE9 . . . . **172** F3
WALCOTT LN4 . . . . **109** D7
Walcott Prim Sch LN4 . . . . **109** C7
Walcott Rd LN4 . . . . **109** E6
Walcott St HU3 . . . . **180** C4
Walcot Way 2 PE9 . . . . **218** E6
Walcot Wlk PE3 . . . . **225** B3
Waldeck St LN1 . . . . **234** A4
Walden Gdns 1 PE21 . . . . **208** E4
Waldo Rd LN4 . . . . **205** F5
Waldorf Rd DN15 . . . . **193** A1
Waldo Way DN15 . . . . **8** C1
WALESBY LN8 . . . . **46** A3
Walesby DN33 . . . . **194** D8
Walesby Hill LN8 . . . . **46** B3
Walesby La LN8 . . . . **46** B2
Walesby Rd
  Market Rasen LN8 . . . . **57** E8
  Middle Rasen LN8 . . . . **45** E1
  Scunthorpe DN17 . . . . **184** E4
Walford Cl 2 NG13 . . . . **128** A5
Walford Dr LN6 . . . . **205** A6
Walgrave PE2 . . . . **230** B4
Walker Ave DN33 . . . . **194** F8
Walker Cl 3 DN15 . . . . **8** E7
Walker Dr 4 DN15 . . . . **9** A5
Walkergate 14 LN11 . . . . . **198** B5
WALKERINGHAM DN10 . . . . **39** E3
Walkeringham Nature
  Reserve * DN10 . . . . **39** E3
Walkeringham Prim Sch
  DN10 . . . . **39** F3
Walkeringham Rd
  Beckingham DN10 . . . . **40** A2
  Gringley on the Hill DN10 . . **39** D2
WALKERITH DN21 . . . . **40** B4
Walkerith Rd
  East Stockwith DN21 . . . . . **40** B5
  Gainsborough DN21 . . . . . **197** B8
  Morton DN21 . . . . **40** D3
Walker Rd PE6 . . . . **220** D7
Walkers Cl
  4 Bottesford NG13 . . . . . **128** B5
  Scunthorpe DN15 . . . . **183** B3
Walker's Cl 5 DN38 . . . . **21** B4
Walkers Ct 20 DN17 . . . . . . **29** D7
Walker St HU3 . . . . **180** C5
Walkers Way
  Barrowby NG32 . . . . **210** A3
  Peterborough PE3 . . . . **224** F3
  Ulceby DN39 . . . . **12** B2
Walkington Way 18 LN12 . . **77** A4
Walk La Humberston DN36. . **36** C7
  Irby DN37 . . . . **34** D7
  Langton by Wragby LN8 . . . **70** F4
Walks Rd DN15 . . . . **120** F1
Walks The 4 PE9 . . . . **171** B1
Walk The DN21 . . . . **197** F3
Wallace's Dro PE6 . . . . **176** D4
Wallace St 1 PE11 . . . . **214** A1
Wallace Way 3 PE21 . . . . . **136** E3
Walled Gdn The 5 LN5 . . . . **93** F5
Waller St HU9 . . . . **181** C8
Walliker St HU3 . . . . **180** A6
Wallingfen La HU15 . . . . **1** B8
Wallis Ave LN6 . . . . **205** B4
Wallis Ct DN33 . . . . **191** B2
Wallisgate PE12 . . . . **158** C2
Wallis Rd LN11 . . . . **198** D5
Wallnutt Dr 7 DN9 . . . . **16** D1
Walls Ave 5 PE24 . . . . **102** E7
Wall's La PE25 . . . . **90** E2
Wall St Gainsborough DN21 **197** D3
  Grimsby DN36 . . . . **191** A7
Wallworks Mews NG31 . . . **211** B4
Walmer St 1 LN2 . . . . **202** C3
WALMSGATE LN11 . . . . **74** C5
Walmsgate DN34 . . . . **191** B4
Walmsgate Gdns 3 DN33 . **191** B4
Walmsgate Pl 3 DN33 . . . . **191** B4
Walmsgate Wlk DN33 . . . . **191** B4
Walmsley St HU3 . . . . **180** D7

Walnut Cl Louth LN11. . . . . .198 E6
5 Newborough PE6 . . . . . .174 E4
14 Ruskington NG34 . . . . .108 E2
2 Waddington LN5 . . . . . . .93 E8
Walnut Cres DN35. . . . . . . .192 D2
Walnut Dr 1 DN20 . . . . .30 F7
Walnutgarth 6 NG34. . . . . .212 F3
Walnut Gr
3 Colsterworth NG33. . . . .151 E7
Peterborough PE4 . . . . . . .221 B2
Walnut La DN37. . . . . .23 F2
Walnut Mews PE3. . . . . . . .225 E2
Walnut Pl LN5 . . . . .234 B1
Walnut Rd
3 Bottesford NG13. . . . . .128 A5
Kirton PE20 . . . . .136 C6
Walnut Tree Wy HU4 . . . . .179 D3
Walnut Way PE14. . . . . . . .170 F7
Walpole Bank PE14. . . . . . .170 F7
Walpole Cl PE11 . . . . .214 D8
WALPOLE CROSS KEYS
PE34. . . . . .161 C3
Walpole Cross Keys Com Prim
Sch PE34 . . . . .161 D2
WALPOLE MARSH PE14. . . .170 F4
Walsall Garth HU4 . . . . . . .179 B4
Walsham Rd PE7 . . . . .233 D8
Walshaw Cl LN4. . . . . .81 E1
Walsh Gdns 7 DN33. . . . . . .191 B2
Walsingham Ct 3 PE13. . . .170 C1
Walsingham Dr NG32. . . . . .152 F7
Walsingham Way 13 PE6. . .175 A1
WALSOKEN PE13. . . . . .170 E1
WALTHAM DN37. . . . . .194 D5
Waltham Cl
9 Birchwood LN6 . . . . . . .204 C6
2 Dogsthorpe PE1 . . . . . .226 D8
33 Newark-on-Trent NG24. .104 B8
Waltham Grange 5 DN35 192 E3
Waltham Leas Prim Sch
DN37. . . . . .194 E5
Waltham Mus of Rural Life★
DN37. . . . . .194 D3
Waltham Rd
Barnoldby le Beck DN37. . .194 A3
Birchwood LN6. . . . . .204 B6
Brigsley DN37 . . . . .194 C1
Croxton Kerrial NG32. . . . . .138 A4
Grimsby DN33 . . . . .194 F8
Waltham St 1 HU1. . . . . . . .180 E7
Waltham Windmill★
DN37. . . . . .194 E3
WALTON PE4. . . . . .221 A1
Walton Gdns NG31. . . . . . . .211 A4
Walton Girls High Sch The
NG31. . . . . .210 F1
Walton Gr DN33. . . . . .191 C4
Walton Heath Cl 2 NG31 211 D7
WALTON HIGHWAY PE14. . .170 F3
Walton Pk PE4. . . . . .221 A1
Walton Rd
7 Leverington PE13 . . . . .170 B2
Marholm PE6 . . . . .220 C1
Wisbech PE13. . . . . .170 E1
Walton St Leisure Ctr
HU3. . . . . .180 A6
Walton St HU3. . . . . .180 A7
Walton Way 3 NG32. . . . . .139 C7
Wandell's View HU15. . . . . . .2 C8
Wansbeck Rd 8 NG34. . . . .121 B7
WANSFORD PE8. . . . . .222 A4
Wansford Rd PE8. . . . . .222 A3
Wanton La PE34. . . . . .161 F3
Wanton's Cross Gate
PE12. . . . . .159 D2
Wanton's La PE12. . . . . . . .159 E2
Wapping La 8 DN21 . . . . . . .65 E8
Warblers Cl 22 DN18. . . . . . . .3 E1
Warbon Ave PE1 . . . . .225 F7
Warburton Ct DN32 . . . . . . .191 F7
Warburton St 19 NG24. . . . .104 A5
Wardall St DN35. . . . . .192 F6
Ward Cl PE1 . . . . .226 B3
Ward Cres PE21 . . . . .209 E4
Wardentree La PE11. . . . . .157 A8
Wardentree Pk PE11 . . . . . .157 A8
Wardour Dr NG31 . . . . .211 F5
Ward's La PE22 . . . . .114 A3
Ward St DN35. . . . . .192 C8
Wareley Rd PE2. . . . . .225 F1
Wares Way DN15. . . . . .182 B3
WARGATE PE11. . . . . .145 B5
Wargate Field La PE11. . . .145 C5
Wargate Way PE11. . . . . . .145 B6
Waring St LN9. . . . . .199 B3
Warley Ave 1 DN16 . . . . . .185 C8
Warley Dr DN16. . . . . .185 C8
Warley Rd DN16. . . . . .185 C7
Warneford Gdns HU5. . . . . .180 A8
Warneford Rd DN35. . . . . . .192 D8
Warping Way DN15. . . . . . . .182 B3
Warren Cl DN21. . . . . .197 B6
Warren Ct
Hampton Hargate PE7 . . . .230 C2
5 St Giles PE1. . . . . .202 D6
Warrendale 12 DN18. . . . . . .10 E8
Warren Farm Cl DN40 . . . . .12 D7
Warren La Wellingore LN5. .107 C6
Witham St Hughs LN6. . . . . .92 D4
Warrenne Cl 21 DN7. . . . . . .14 D4
Warrenne Keep 8 PE9 . . . . .219 B4
Warrenne Rd DN7. . . . . .14 D4
Warren Rd
North Somercotes LN11. . . .51 A4
Scunthorpe DN15. . . . . . . .183 B5
5 Thorne/Moorends DN8. . .15 B7
Wothorpe PE9 . . . . .219 C1
Warren Way NG31. . . . . . . .211 F7

Warren Wood Com Sch
DN21. . . . . .197 E2
Warth La PE25 . . . . .206 A5
Warwick Ave DN33 . . . . . . .191 A4
Warwick Cl Bourne PE10. . .213 C2
9 Grantham NG31 . . . . . . .210 D5
1 Hatfield DN7 . . . . .14 F3
2 Saxilby with Ingleby LN1. .66 C2
Warwick Dr 24 DN18. . . . . . .10 E8
Warwick Rd
7 Chapel St Leonard PE24. .90 D7
Cleethorpes DN35 . . . . . . .192 D4
Louth LN11. . . . . .198 B8
Newark-on-Trent NG24. . . .104 B2
Peterborough PE4 . . . . . . .221 A2
Scunthorpe DN16. . . . . . . .183 C1
Warwick St HU9 . . . . .181 B7
Wascana Cl HU4 . . . . .179 B3
Wasdale Cl 1 LN6. . . . . . . .200 C1
Wasdale Gdns 1 PE4. . . . . .221 E2
Washbeck Rd PE12 . . . . . . .167 A5
Washdike Dro PE11 . . . . . . .135 C1
Washdike La
Donington PE11. . . . . .135 A1
Stoke Rochford NG33. . . . .140 A3
Toynton St Peter PE23 . . . .101 B6
Wainfleet St Mary PE24 . . .102 C1
Wash Dike La PE22 . . . . . . .115 A6
Washdike Rd
Algarkirk PE20 . . . . .136 B1
Kirton PE20 . . . . .136 A6
Washdyke La
Belton & Manthorpe NG32. .130 A6
Boston PE21. . . . . .208 B7
Cumberworth LN13 . . . . . . .89 E8
Elsham DN20 . . . . .20 D6
Immingham DN40 . . . . . . .186 B5
Leasingham NG34 . . . . . . .121 C7
Mumby LN13 . . . . .76 F1
Nettleham LN2. . . . . .68 B2
Old Leake PE22 . . . . .113 F4
Osgodby LN8 . . . . .45 A3
Washdyke Rd 7 NG32. . . . .106 C1
Washdyke Ret Pk DN40 . . .186 C4
WASHINGBOROUGH LN4. . .203 D2
Washingborough Acad
LN4. . . . . .203 C2
Washingborough Rd
Heighington/Washingborough
LN4. . . . . .81 E4
Lincoln LN4. . . . . .202 D1
Washinghall La DN17. . . . . . .7 A2
Washington Cl 6 LN4. . . . . .207 C4
Washington Dr 5 LN8. . . . . .56 D5
Washington St 4 DN21. . . . .197 D4
Wash National Nature Reserve
The★ PE12 . . . . .149 C2
Wash Rd Fosdyke PE20 . . . .146 D7
Kirton PE20 . . . . .136 D4
Washtub La NG23 . . . . .91 E6
Washway Rd Fleet PE12 . . .159 B8
Holbeach PE12. . . . . .215 C6
Moulton PE12. . . . . .146 F4
WASPS NEST LN4. . . . . .95 E7
Wassand St HU3 . . . . .180 C4
Wass La LN8. . . . . .71 E5
Waste Gn La PE20 . . . . .146 C7
Water Bank DN9 . . . . .26 E5
Waterbelly La PE20. . . . . . . .13 B1
Water End Marholm PE6 . . .220 B1
Peterborough PE7 . . . . . . .229 A5
Waterfall Gdns 2 PE6 . . . . .174 E4
Waterford La LN3. . . . . .203 D5
Waterfront The PE21 . . . . . .208 F3
Waterfurlong PE9. . . . . .219 A4
Watergall 1 PE3. . . . . .220 F1
Watergall Prim Sch 2 PE3 .225 B8
Watergate
11 Grantham NG31 . . . . . .211 A5
10 Stamford PE9 . . . . .219 C5
Water Gate Quadring PE11 .145 B8
Sleaford NG34 . . . . .212 D4
Water Hill LN4. . . . . .82 B7
Waterhills Ct 81 LN7. . . . . . .33 B4
Waterhouse La HU1. . . . . . .180 E5
Waterhouse Way PE7. . . . . .230 F2
Watering Dyke Houses LN2 67 F4
Water La
1 Ancaster NG32. . . . . . . .120 A2
Bourne PE10. . . . . .213 D2
Castle Bytham NG33 . . . . .152 D1
Castor PE5 . . . . .223 C1
6 Colsterworth NG33. . . . .151 D7
Elloughton-cum-Brough HU15. 2 D6
Gunby & Stainby NG33 . . . .151 B5
5 Hagworthingham PE23 . . .87 A4
Lincoln LN1. . . . . .234 A2
4 Lincoln LN6. . . . . .93 C8
1 Long Bennington NG23. .117 D4
12 South Witham NG33 . . .151 D2
4 Spalding PE11. . . . . . . .214 D2
Threekingham NG34 . . . . . .132 F3
Thurlby LN5 . . . . .92 E3
Thurlby PE10. . . . . .164 C8
Tinwell PE9 . . . . .218 B6
2 West Halton DN15. . . . . . .8 E7
Waterlees Rd PE13 . . . . . . .170 D1
Water Lily Way 4 PE10. . . .213 D3
Waterloo Cl 1 NG32 . . . . . .119 B7
Waterloo Dr
4 Grimsby DN33. . . . . . . .191 B2
2 Morton PE10. . . . . .154 D6
Waterloo La LN6. . . . . .200 B3
Waterloo Paddock LN5 . . .106 D3
Waterloo Rd
Mablethorpe/Sutton on Sea
LN12. . . . . .64 B4

Waterloo Rd continued
Peterborough PE1 . . . . . . .226 A5
Waterloo St
6 Kingston upon Hull
HU2. . . . . .180 E8
Kingston upon Hull HU2. . .180 E8
Lincoln LN6 . . . . .201 D2
4 Market Rasen LN8. . . . . .57 D8
Waterlow Dr 22 DN15. . . . . . .9 A5
Watermill La 12 LN2. . . . . . .68 C2
Water Mill La PE23 . . . . . . .100 F6
Water Mill Rd LN9. . . . . . . .199 B4
WATER NEWTON PE8. . . . . .228 C7
Waters Edge DN20 . . . . . . .196 A3
Waters' Edge Ctry Pk★
DN18. . . . . .3 F2
WATERSIDE DN8. . . . . .14 E8
Waterside
5 Billinghay LN4. . . . . . . .109 F5
4 Louth LN11. . . . . .198 D7
3 Ryhall PE9. . . . . .163 C1
Thorne DN8. . . . . .14 E8
Water Side DN15. . . . . .2 B1
Waterside Bsns Pk HU13. . . .3 F4
Waterside Cl 10 PE10. . . . . .213 C7
Waterside Dr 3 DN31. . . . . .191 D8
Waterside Gdns 5 PE12. . . .215 E2
Waterside N LN5. . . . . .234 B2
Waterside Rd DN18. . . . . . . .3 C2
Waterside S LN5. . . . . .234 B2
Waterside Sh Ctr LN2. . . . .234 B2
Waterside Wy 32 PE24. . . . . .90 D7
Waterslade Rd PE7. . . . . . . .233 C4
Water St PE9 . . . . .219 C4
Waterton Cl 2 PE6. . . . . . . .217 E4
Waterton La DN7. . . . . .14 C2
Waterton Wy 9 PE7. . . . . . .230 B1
Waterwell La NG32. . . . . . . .120 C4
Waterwheel La LN4. . . . . . . .81 D2
Waterworks La PE6 . . . . . . .220 B6
Waterworks St
1 Gainsborough DN21. . . .197 D2
Immingham DN40 . . . . . . .186 D5
Waterworth Rd PE2. . . . . . .229 E1
Watery La Asterby LN11. . . . .72 F5
Butterwick PE22. . . . . .126 F3
Goulceby LN11. . . . . .72 D6
Lissington LN3. . . . . .57 D1
Little Cawthorpe LN11 . . . . .61 E2
Mareham le Fen PE22. . . . . .98 F4
Swaby LN13. . . . . .74 E4
4 Welton/Dunholme LN2. . .68 E6
1 West Ashby LN9. . . . . . . .85 E7
Wickenby LN3. . . . . .70 A8
Watford Ave DN34. . . . . . . .190 F4
Watkin St N DN31. . . . . .188 F1
Watkin St S 2 DN31. . . . . . .188 F1
Watkins La 2 DN22. . . . . . . .52 B3
Watling Cl 7 Bourne PE10. .213 C6
8 Bracebridge Heath LN4. . .81 A1
Watson Pk 4 DN10. . . . . .52 B8
Watsons Croft 5 DN7 . . . . . .14 D6
Watt Ave 11 NG33. . . . . . . .151 D7
Watt Cl PE4. . . . . .221 C2
Watts La LN11. . . . . .198 C4
Waudby Cl HU13. . . . . .178 B3
Wauldby Cl 4 HU10. . . . . . .178 E7
Wauldby Road HU15. . . . . . .2 E7
Wauldby View 2 HU14. . . . . .3 B7
Waumsley Way 1 LN13. . . . .75 E2
Wavell Dr LN2. . . . . .202 E4
Waveney Cl 1 DN15. . . . . . . .8 B5
Waveney Gr PE4 . . . . .221 C2
Waverley Ave LN6. . . . . .204 F3
Waverley Gdns
3 Leverington PE13. . . . . .170 B1
Stamford PE9 . . . . .218 F6
Waverley Pl 3 PE9. . . . . . . .218 F6
Waverley St HU1. . . . . .180 E5
Waverly Cl PE10. . . . . .154 D7
Waxwing Wy DN37 . . . . .24 B5
Wayet Rd 8 PE11. . . . . .156 E8
Wayford Cl PE13 . . . . .225 A2
Wayside
5 Holton le Clay DN36 . . . .195 D2
Scunthorpe DN16. . . . . . . .185 A3
Wayside Dr DN36. . . . . .195 C7
Weatherthorn PE2. . . . . . . .230 C5
Weaver Rd LN6. . . . . .204 B5
Weavers Croft 11 DN9. . . . . .27 A2
Webb Cl 38 DN10. . . . . .10 E8
Webster Ave DN15. . . . . . . .182 E3
Webster Cl 3 LN6. . . . . .205 A5
Websters Cl PE6 . . . . .220 D8
Webster Way NG31. . . . . . .210 E7
Wedgewood Cl 10 LN6. . . . .204 D7
Wedgewood Dr 4 PE11. . . .214 B5
Wedgewood Gr 9 LN6. . . . .204 D7
Wedgewood Rd LN6. . . . . . .204 D7
Wedland La PE24 . . . . .102 D3
WEECAR NG23. . . . . .78 D1
Weedon Cl PE4 . . . . .221 D2
Weekes Rd DN35. . . . . .192 F4
WEELSBY DN32. . . . . .192 A5
Weelsby Ave DN32. . . . . . . .191 F4
Weelsby Gr DN32. . . . . .191 E6
Weelsby Prim Sch DN32. . .192 A8
Weelsby Rd DN32. . . . . .191 D5
Weelsby St S DN32. . . . . . . .192 A7
Weelsby St
15 Grimsby DN31. . . . . . . .189 C1
Grimsby DN32. . . . . .192 A8
Weelsby View DN36. . . . . . .195 D8
Weelsby Way HU13. . . . . . .178 C2
Weeping Elm Way 6
DN16. . . . . .185 D4
Weeton Way 5 HU10. . . . . .178 E7
Wegberg Rd LN4. . . . . .95 C7

Weir Cl 3 DN9. . . . . .27 A2
Weir Farm 3 LN2. . . . . .68 F4
Weir Rd DN9. . . . . .27 A2
Weirs La PE22 . . . . .126 C2
Weir St LN5. . . . . .205 D8
Welbeck Ave NG24 . . . . . . .104 A5
Welbeck Dr PE11. . . . . .214 C5
Welbeck Pl 3 DN34. . . . . . .190 E4
Welbeck Rd DN35. . . . . .192 C5
Welbeck St HU5. . . . . .180 B8
Welbeck Way Louth LN11. . .198 B6
Peterborough PE4 . . . . . . .230 D7
WELBOURN LN5 . . . . .106 F5
Welbourn Cl NG34 . . . . .212 C3
Welbourne PE4 . . . . .221 A4
Welbourne CE Prim Sch
LN5 . . . . .106 E5
Welbourne La PE12. . . . . . .215 C4
Welbourne La E PE12. . . . . .215 C4
Welbourne Lane South
PE12. . . . . .215 B3
Welbourn Gdns 9 LN2. . . . .202 A8
Welbourn Prim Sch PE4 . . .221 A4
Welbourn Rd LN5 . . . . .106 A5
Welbourn Wlk HU4. . . . . . . .179 B6
WELBY NG32. . . . . .130 F5
Welby Cl NG34 . . . . .212 B4
Welby Dr 3 PE11 . . . . .145 B6
Welby Gdns
Grantham NG31 . . . . .211 A6
Holbeach PE12. . . . . .215 B2
Welby St 6 NG31 . . . . .211 A4
Welby-Everard Ct NG31 . . .211 B4
WELDON RD DN21. . . . . .42 E1
Weldon Rd PE2. . . . . .229 E1
Wel Fen La NG23 . . . . .117 E8
Welfen Road South NG31. . .211 B4
Welham Acad DN32 . . . . . . .191 F6
Welholme Ave DN32. . . . . . .191 E5
Welholme Rd DN32. . . . . . . .191 E6
WELL LN13. . . . . .88 C3
Welland Acad PE1. . . . . .226 C8
Welland Ave DN34 . . . . .190 F4
Welland Bank PE6 . . . . .166 C1
Welland Cl
8 Beacon Hill NG24 . . . . .104 A5
Peterborough PE1 . . . . . . .226 A7
9 Ruskington NG34 . . . . . .108 D2
1 Spalding PE11. . . . . . . .214 C2
Welland Ct 3 DN31. . . . . . . .210 E2
Welland Dr Bourne PE10. . .213 A4
2 Burton upon Stather DN15 . .8 B5
Welland Hospl PE11 . . . . . . .214 F6
Welland Mews PE9. . . . . . . .219 C4
Welland Rd
Borough Fen PE1. . . . . . . .174 E1
Boston PE21. . . . . .208 B3
Lincoln LN1 . . . . .201 D8
Peterborough PE1 . . . . . . .226 B8
Spalding PE11. . . . . .214 D3
2 Wittering PE8 . . . . .172 B1
Welland Way PE6 . . . . .217 E4
Wellbeck Cl 4 DN20 . . . . . .196 D4
Wellesley Ct 3 LN8 . . . . . . .57 D8
Wellesley Way NG34. . . . . .120 B8
Wellfield Cl 6 NG33. . . . . . .151 D2
Wellgarth DN32 . . . . .192 B5
Wellhead La LN4. . . . . .95 B7
Well High La LN13. . . . . .75 D1
WELLINGORE LN5. . . . . .107 A7
Wellingore Rd 5 LN2. . . . . .201 F8
Wellington Ave
Coningsby LN4. . . . . .207 D2
11 Mablethorpe/Sutton on Sea
LN12. . . . . .64 B4
Wellington Cl
7 Heckington NG34 . . . . .122 E2
Skellingthorpe LN6. . . . . . . .79 F6
9 South Killingholme DN40. .12 E3
Wellington Ct
Grant Thorold DN32 . . . . . .192 A8
Holton le Clay DN36 . . . . . .195 C4
Wellington Dr 1 NG31 . . . . .211 D2
Wellingtonia Park 4
PE21. . . . . .208 E1
Wellington La HU3. . . . . . . .180 D8
Wellington Rd
2 Beacon Hill NG24 . . . . .104 A4
Boston PE21. . . . . .209 B4
Mablethorpe/Sutton on Sea
LN12. . . . . .64 B4
Wellington St Wes HU1. . . .180 E5
Wellington Sq 12 LN5. . . . . .94 A7
Wellington St
12 Gainsborough DN21 . . .197 D3
Grimsby DN32. . . . . .191 F8
Kingston upon Hull HU1. . .180 F5
Lincoln LN1. . . . . .201 D4
4 Louth LN11. . . . . .198 C6
Peterborough PE1 . . . . . . .226 B2
7 Scampton Airfield LN1. . .67 E5
Wellington Way
1 Elsham Wold Ind Est
DN20. . . . . .21 A8
Market Deeping PE6. . . . . .217 B2
1 Skegness PE25 . . . . . . .206 A5
Wellington Yd 4 PE23. . . . . .88 A1
Well La LN2. . . . . .234 B3
WELLOW DN32. . . . . .191 E5
Wellowgate DN32. . . . . .191 D7
Wellowgate Mews DN32. . .191 D6
Wellow Rd 5 NG23. . . . . . . .117 D4

Wal–Wes 283

Wells Cl continued
5 Skegness PE25 . . . . . . .206 D7
Wells Cres DN35 . . . . .192 E2
Wells Ct PE2 . . . . .231 D6
Wells Dr
Bracebridge Heath LN4 . . . .81 A2
4 Market Rasen LN8. . . . . .57 E7
Wells La DN22. . . . . .65 B7
Wells Pl PE21. . . . . .136 E1
Wells Rd DN37. . . . . .23 D4
Wells St Grimsby DN31. . . .191 B7
Kingston upon Hull HU3. . .180 A5
Scunthorpe DN15. . . . . . . .183 B4
Well St
5 Bishop Norton LN8 . . . . .43 D3
Messingham DN17. . . . . . . .29 C7
Wellsted St HU3. . . . . .180 C5
Wells The 13 LN2. . . . . .68 D6
Wellsyke La LN10 . . . . .98 A6
Wellsykes Lane LN4 . . . . . . .81 D4
Well Turn LN13 . . . . .75 F1
Well Vale 2 DN33. . . . . .194 D8
Well Vale Cl 29 PE24. . . . . . .90 D7
Well Vale Ct PE24 . . . . .90 D6
Welmore Rd PE6. . . . . .220 D8
Welsdale Rd LN11. . . . . .59 E2
WELTON Welton HU15. . . . . .2 E6
Welton LN2. . . . . .68 C6
Welton Cl 32 DN18. . . . . . . .10 E8
Welton Cliff LN2. . . . . .68 B7
Welton Gdns LN2. . . . . .201 F8
WELTON HILL LN2. . . . . .69 A8
WELTON LE MARSH PE23 . . .89 B3
WELTON LE WOLD LN11. . . .60 C6
Welton-le-Wold Nature
Reserve★ LN11. . . . . .60 D7
Welton Low Rd HU15 . . . . . . .2 C6
Welton Old Rd HU15. . . . . . . .2 E6
Welton Prim Sch HU15 . . . . .2 D5
Welton Rd Brough HU15 . . . .2 C5
Nettleham LN2. . . . . .68 C3
Welton Road LN11. . . . . .68 C6
Welton St Mary's CE Prim Sch
LN2. . . . . .68 C6
Welton Wold View 9 HU14. . 3 B7
Welwyn Cl NG31 . . . . .210 L1
Wembley Rd LN11. . . . . .50 F7
Wembley St DN21. . . . . .197 C4
Wendan Rd 9 DN8. . . . . .15 A7
Wende The PE11. . . . . .214 A3
Wendover Cl
19 Humberston DN36. . . . .36 D8
Messingham DN17. . . . . . . .29 D7
Rippingale PE10. . . . . .142 F2
Wendover Mews 3 PE10. . .213 E5
Wendover Rd 13 DN17. . . . . .29 D7
Wendover Rise DN35 . . . . . .192 E5
Wenlock St HU3 . . . . .180 C6
Wensleydale Cl 1 NG31. . . .211 A8
Wensleydale Rd DN16. . . . .185 E6
Wensum Cl 4 PE11 . . . . . . .214 C1
Wentworth Cl
Gainsborough DN21. . . . . .197 E6
Heighington LN4. . . . . .203 E1
4 Skegness PE25 . . . . . . .206 D6
1 Spalding PE11. . . . . . . .214 C1
Willerby HU10. . . . . .178 F8
Wentworth Cres 2 DN19 . . . 4 E2
Wentworth Dr
Dunholme LN2. . . . . .68 E5
Grantham NG31 . . . . .211 D8
28 Messingham DN17 . . . . .29 D7
2 Saxilby with Ingleby LN1. .66 D2
Tydd St Giles PE13 . . . . . . .170 A7
Wentworth Rd
Grimsby DN34. . . . . .191 B7
Scunthorpe DN17. . . . . . . .184 D2
Wentworth St 1 PE1. . . . . .226 A1
Wentworths The PE12. . . . .216 A4
Wentworth Way
Kingston upon Hull HU9. . .181 C7
7 Woodhall Spa LN10 . . . . .97 C5
Werneth Rd DN32 . . . . .191 F8
WERRINGTON PE4. . . . . . . .220 F4
Werrington Bridge Rd
PE6. . . . . .221 B6
Werrington Centre PE4. . . .221 A5
Werrington Ctr PE4. . . . . . .221 A5
Werrington Gr PE4. . . . . . . .220 F2
Werrington Gr Cvn Pk
PE4. . . . . .220 F2
Werrington Mews 5 PE4. . .221 A3
Werrington Parkway PE6. . .220 C5
Werrington Pk Ave 2
PE4. . . . . .221 A3
Werrington Prim Sch
Peterborough PE4. . . . . . . .221 A5
Werrington PE4 . . . . .221 A5
Werrington Sports Ctr
PE4. . . . . .220 F4
Werry's La 4 PE10 . . . . .213 C5
Wesleyan Ct LN2. . . . . .234 B2
Wesleyan Rd PE1. . . . . .226 A7
Wesley Ave 5 PE34. . . . . . .161 F3
Wesley Cl 4 Epworth DN9 . . .27 E1
15 Metheringham LN4 . . . . .95 C4
Sleaford NG34 . . . . .212 C2
1 Terrington St Clement
PE34. . . . . .161 F3
2 Winterton DN15. . . . . .9 A5
Wesley Cres 2 DN35. . . . . .192 C4
Wesley Ct
8 Grimsby DN31. . . . . . . .189 C1
4 Kingston upon Hull HU3. .180 C5
Wesley Rd Brigg DN20. . . . .196 C3

Wesley Rd *continued*
Cherry Willingham LN3. . . . .**203** B6
Scunthorpe DN16. . . . .**185** E7
9 Terrington St Clement
PE34. . . . .**161** F3
Whaplode PE12 . . . .**158** C7
Wesley St 19 DN21 . . . .**30** B1
Wesley Way LN9 . . . .**199** D3
Wesley Wy LN6 . . . .**78** F2
Wesselow Rd LN4 . . . .**207** F6
Wessex Cl
Peterborough PE2 . . . .**231** D7
Sleaford NG34 . . . .**212** B1
West Acridge 16 DN18 . . . . . .**3** E1
WEST ASHBY LN9 . . . .**85** E7
West Ave
Cranwell & Byard's Leap
NG34. . . . .**120** B8
Grantham NG31 . . . .**210** D3
6 Stainforth DN7 . . . .**14** C6
West Bank Crowland PE6. . .**166** E1
Saxilby with Ingleby LN1 . . . .**66** C2
Stainforth DN7 . . . .**14** B7
West Bank Rd PE12. . . . .**161** A8
West Banks NG34 . . . .**212** C4
WEST BARKWITH LN8 . . . . . .**70** F7
Westbeck 2 NG34 . . . .**108** D2
Westbeck La DN21 . . . .**42** C5
West Bight 1 LN1. . . . .**234** B3
WESTBOROUGH NG23 . . . . . .**117** E3
Westborough La NG23. . . . .**117** D4
Westborough Way HU4. . . .**179** B6
Westbourne Ave 3 HU13 . .**178** E2
Westbourne Dr
22 Crowle DN17. . . . .**16** D7
6 Glinton PE6. . . . .**220** C8
Westbourne Gdns 5
PE11. . . . .**214** A1
Westbourne Gr
6 Grimsby DN33. . . . .**194** F8
Kingston upon Hull HU13 . . .**178** D2
6 Lincoln LN1 . . . .**201** D3
Westbourne Pk PE10 . . . . . .**213** B5
Westbourne Pl 2 NG31. . .**210** E4
Westbourne St 5 HU3. . . . .**180** A4
Westbrecks La DN22 . . . .**65** A7
Westbrick Ave 5 HU3 . . . . .**179** F5
Westbridge Rd PE21. . . . . .**208** A3
Westbrook Ave 1 PE2. . . . .**230** F7
Westbrooke Cl LN6. . . . .**205** B8
Westbrooke Gr 32 LN7. . . .**33** B4
Westbrooke Rd LN6. . . . . . .**205** B8
West Brook La NG23. . . . . . .**117** D4
Westbrook Pk Cl 2 PE2 . . .**230** F7
Westbrook Pk Rd PE2 . . . . .**230** E7
Westburn Ave 4 DN19 . . . . .**4** E2
Westbury Dr PE7. . . . .**230** F2
Westbury Pk 3 DN35. . . . . .**193** A1
Westbury Rd DN35. . . . .**193** A1
WEST BUTTERWICK DN17 . .**28** D8
West Butterwick CE Prim Sch
DN17. . . . .**28** D8
West Butterwick Rd DN17. .**17** C3
WESTBY NG33. . . . .**140** F3
Westby Rd
Bitchfield & Bassingthorpe
NG33. . . . .**140** F2
Burton Coggles NG33. . . . . .**152** C8
WESTCLIFF DN17. . . . .**184** E7
Westcliffe NG34. . . . .**108** B2
Westcliffe Prim Sch
DN17. . . . .**184** D6
Westcliffe Rd
Ruskington NG34 . . . .**108** C2
21 Scotter DN21. . . . .**29** C3
Westcliffe St LN1. . . . .**201** D6
Westcliff Gdns DN17 . . . . . .**184** F7
West Coates Rd DN31 . . . . .**188** D2
West Cob Gate PE12 . . . . . .**157** F6
Westcombe Sq PE1 . . . .**226** D4
West Comm Cres DN17 . . . .**184** F8
West Comm Gdns DN17. . . .**184** F7
West Comm La DN17 . . . . . .**184** E7
West Comm N Rd DN17 . . . .**29** A8
West Comm Sports Hall
DN17. . . . .**184** E8
Westcroft Dr 3 LN1. . . . .**66** D3
West Cross St 24 DN21. . . . .**30** B1
West Ct 14 DN8 . . . .**15** A7
Westdale Cres 2 DN21. . . . .**30** B2
Westdale Dro PE11. . . . .**134** C2
WEST DEEPING PE6 . . . .**173** B8
West Dock Ave HU3 . . . .**180** B4
West Dock St HU3. . . . .**180** B3
West Dr Coningsby LN4 . . . .**110** E8
Sudbrooke LN2. . . . .**68** F3
West Dro PE12. . . . .**168** C2
West Dro N PE12 . . . .**168** C3
West Dro S PE12 . . . .**168** C1
WEST ELLA HU10 . . . .**178** A8
West Ella Rd
Kingston upon Hull HU10 . . .**178** C7
Swanland HU14 . . . .**3** C7
West Ella Way HU10. . . . . . .**178** C7
West Elloe Ave PE11. . . . . . .**214** E6
WEST END PE22 . . . .**126** E6
West End
Burgh le Marsh PE24 . . . . . .**102** D8
Garthorpe & Fockerby DN17 . . .**7** E5
Gorefield PE13. . . . .**169** E3
Harlaxton NG32 . . . .**139** B7
Hogsthorpe PE24 . . . .**90** B7
Holbeach PE12. . . . .**215** D2
Ingham LN1. . . . .**54** F2
Langtoft PE6. . . . .**164** E3

West End *continued*
7 Spilsby PE23 . . . .**87** F1
Swanland HU14 . . . .**3** B6
Walcott LN4. . . . .**109** C7
Winteringham DN15. . . . .**2** A1
Yaxley PE7. . . . .**233** D4
West End Cl
9 Bottesford NG13. . . . . . .**128** A6
Laughton DN21 . . . .**41** B8
West End Cres 9 PE23 . . . . .**87** F1
West End La DN36. . . . .**37** B1
West End Rd Boston PE21. .**136** D8
Epworth DN9. . . . .**27** C8
2 Habrough DN40 . . . .**22** E8
Kirton PE20 . . . .**136** B7
Maxey PE6 . . . .**217** A1
Ulceby DN39 . . . .**11** F1
Wyberton PE21. . . . .**208** B2
West End Villas 11 PE9 . . . .**219** A5
Westerby Ct LN7 . . . .**32** A1
Westerdale 5 HU14. . . . .**3** B7
Westerdale Gr HU9. . . . .**181** E8
Westerdale Rd
2 Grantham NG31 . . . .**211** A7
Scunthorpe DN16. . . . .**185** D5
Westerdale Way DN37 . . . .**190** E8
Westerley Cl PE3. . . . .**225** C4
Westerly Way 1 PE11 . . . . .**214** A5
Western App 6 NG34 . . . . .**120** D8
Western Ave Brigg DN20. . .**196** C5
Easton on the Hill PE9 . . . . .**171** C3
Holbeach PE12. . . . .**215** C2
Lincoln LN6 . . . .**205** C7
Peterborough PE1 . . . .**226** B7
8 Saxilby LN1 . . . .**66** C2
Western Cres LN6. . . . .**205** C8
Western Dr
Balderton NG24 . . . .**104** C1
11 Barton-upon-Humber DN18 .**3** E1
9 RAF Cranwell NG34. . . . .**120** C8
Western Gn DN15 . . . .**2** A1
Western Outway DN34. . . . .**191** A4
Western Prim Sch DN34 . . .**190** B5
West Fen Drain Bank
PE22. . . . .**112** D1
West Fen Drainside PE22 . .**112** F7
West Fen La PE22 . . . .**100** A1
Westfield DN21. . . . .**29** C1
WEST FIELD DN40. . . . .**12** C6
Westfield App LN2 . . . .**203** A8
Westfield Ave Boston PE21 **208** D4
Greetwell LN2 . . . .**203** B8
Grimsby DN33 . . . .**191** C3
Westfield Cl
8 Metheringham LN4 . . . . . .**95** D4
2 Yaxley PE7. . . . .**233** D5
Westfield Dr
Greetwell LN2 . . . .**203** A8
22 Messingham DN17 . . . . . .**29** D7
1 Pinchbeck PE11. . . . .**156** E8
3 Skegness PE25 . . . .**206** B4
11 Swineshead PE20 . . . . . .**135** B7
Westfield Garth 2 DN17. . . .**16** E6
Westfield Gr DN35 . . . .**192** D6
Westfield La
Collingham NG23 . . . .**91** B4
Cumberworth LN13 . . . .**89** D8
Kirk Bramwith DN7 . . . .**14** B8
North Greetwell LN3 . . . . . .**203** C7
West Field La
1 Swanland HU14. . . . .**3** B6
Thorpe on the Hill LN6 . . . . . .**92** E8
Westfield Pk 11 NG15. . . . . . .**2** C6
Westfield Rd Bardney LN3 . .**83** D1
Barton-upon-Humber DN18 . . .**3** C1
Fishlake DN7 . . . .**14** B8
13 Goxhill DN19 . . . .**12** A8
8 Hatfield DN7 . . . .**14** E4
Kingston upon Hull HU4 . . . .**179** D5
Newton PE13 . . . .**169** F5
Peterborough PE3 . . . .**225** E4
Scunthorpe DN17. . . . .**184** B6
Waltham DN37. . . . .**194** C4
2 Wisbech PE13 . . . .**170** E2
Yarburgh LN11. . . . .**49** D3
Yaxley PE7. . . . .**233** D5
Westfield Rise HU13. . . . . .**178** D2
Westfields 1 Alford LN13. . .**75** F2
Easton on the Hill PE9 . . . . .**171** C3
Westfield St 4 LN1. . . . . . .**201** D3
Westfield Villas DN7. . . . . .**14** E4
Westfield Way PE6 . . . .**164** E2
WESTGATE DN9 . . . .**16** D2
Westgate Grantham NG31. .**211** A4
Grimsby DN31 . . . .**188** F1
Kexby DN21 . . . .**53** E4
Lincoln LN1 . . . .**234** A3
Louth LN11. . . . .**198** A5
Peterborough PE1 . . . .**225** F2
Scotton DN21. . . . .**29** C1
Sleaford NG34 . . . .**212** C4
West Gate
9 Ruskington NG34 . . . .**108** C2
Wainfleet All Saints PE24. . .**101** E2
Weston PE12 . . . .**157** D2
Westgate Acad LN1. . . . . . .**234** A4
Westgate House ★ LN11 . . .**198** A5
Westgate Pk 3 NG34. . . . . .**212** C4
Westgate Pl 7 LN11. . . . . . .**198** B5
Westgate Rd DN9 . . . .**16** D2
West Gn
Kingston upon Hull HU10 . . . .**3** C8
29 Messingham DN17 . . . . . .**29** D7
West Gr
7 Colsterworth NG33 . . . . .**151** E6
Kingston upon Hull HU4 . . . .**179** D7
West Grantham Acad St
Hugh's The NG31. . . . .**210** E3

West Grantham Acad St
John's The NG31. . . . .**210** D3
Westhall Cl 1 LN5 . . . .**92** E1
Westhall Rd 16 LN2. . . . .**68** D7
WEST HALTON DN15 . . . .**8** E8
West Halton Hill DN15 . . . . . .**8** F7
West Halton La DN15. . . . . . .**8** C8
West Hann La DN19 . . . .**4** C1
Westhaven 2 PE9. . . . .**171** D3
West Haven Way DN40. . . . .**186** B8
Westhawe PE3. . . . .**224** F7
West Hill 1 HU13 . . . .**3** E4
Westhill Rd DN34 . . . .**191** A5
Westholm 2 LN3 . . . .**203** E5
Westholm Cl LN2. . . . .**202** D8
Westholme Cl 11 DN15 . . . . .**8** B4
Westholme La DN38. . . . .**21** C5
WESTHORPE PE11. . . . .**144** F5
Westhorpe Rd PE11 . . . .**144** F5
Westhouses PE22 . . . .**112** F5
WEST KEAL PE23. . . . .**100** C6
West Keal Rd
East Keal PE23. . . . .**100** D8
Mavis Enderby PE23. . . . .**87** C1
Westkirke Ave DN33. . . . . . .**191** D1
West La Baumber LN9 . . . . . .**72** A1
Girton NG23 . . . .**78** C1
Haltham LN9 . . . .**98** C6
7 Keelby DN41. . . . .**23** A4
Skidbrooke with Saltfleet Haven
LN11. . . . .**51** A2
5 Winterton DN15 . . . .**9** B5
Westlaby La LN3 . . . .**69** E8
Westlake Ave PE7. . . . .**230** C1
West Lake Ave PE7 . . . .**230** B1
Westland Rd
Kingston upon Hull HU10 . . .**178** B7
5 Westwoodside DN9. . . . . .**27** B2
Westlands Ave
Grimsby DN34 . . . .**191** C5
4 Tetney DN36 . . . .**36** D4
Westlands Rd HU5 . . . .**179** B8
West Lea DN33. . . . .**194** F7
West Leys Pk 7 HU14 . . . . . .**3** B6
West Leys Rd HU14 . . . .**3** B6
Westlode St PE11 . . . .**214** D4
WEST MARSH DN31 . . . .**188** F1
West Marsh Ind Est DN31 .**188** F1
West Marsh La
Barrow upon Humber DN19. . . .**4** B1
Goxhill DN19 . . . .**5** A3
West Marsh Rd
Pinchbeck PE11 . . . .**145** E1
Spalding PE11 . . . .**214** F6
Westmere Com Prim Sch
PE12 . . . .**157** E7
West Mid Mere Rd DN40. . . .**12** D3
West Mill 1 PE9 . . . .**171** C2
West Mill Gate 2 LN3 . . . . .**203** E6
Westminster Way 2
NG31 . . . .**210** F5
Westminster Cl DN21. . . . . .**40** D3
Westminster Dr
Grimsby DN34 . . . .**191** C6
14 Hatfield DN7 . . . .**14** C2
1 Spalding PE11. . . . .**214** B1
Westminster Gdns 24 PE6 **175** A1
Westminster Ind Est LN6. .**204** D4
Westminster La 6 PE10 . . .**213** B5
Westminster Pl PE1 . . . . . .**226** F5
Westminster Rd
5 Broughton DN20 . . . .**19** D4
Lincoln LN6 . . . .**204** D4
Westmoor La LN1. . . . .**65** E2
West Moor Rd LN10 . . . .**39** F3
Westmoreland Ave 12 LN1 .**67** E5
Westmoreland Cl 7 DN9 . . .**27** A2
Westmoreland Gdns 4
PE1 . . . .**226** B2
Westmoreland Rd 2
PE12. . . . .**157** F6
Westoby La DN19 . . . .**11** C7
WESTON PE12 . . . .**157** D7
Weston Bypass PE12 . . . . . .**157** D7
Weston Gr DN40 . . . .**186** B5
WESTON HILLS PE12. . . . . . .**157** C3
Weston Hills CE Prim Sch
PE12. . . . .**157** D2
Weston Hills Rd PE12. . . . . .**157** B4
Weston Miller Dr 8 PE13 . .**170** D1
Weston St Mary CE Prim Sch
PE12 . . . .**157** E7
Westonville 6 PE9. . . . .**171** B1
Westover Dr 4 DN15. . . . . . .**8** A4
West Parade
Grimsby DN31 . . . .**191** C7
Kingston upon Hull HU3 . . . .**180** C7
Lincoln LN1 . . . .**234** A3
Peterborough PE3 . . . .**225** D3
Spalding PE11 . . . .**214** B4
Wisbech PE13 . . . .**170** C1
West Parklands Dr 9 HU14. .**3** A5
Westport Rd 11 DN35. . . . . .**193** A1
WEST RASEN LN8. . . . .**56** E8
WEST RAVENDALE DN37. . . . .**35** A4
West Rd
Billingborough NG34 . . . . . .**133** B1
Bourne PE10 . . . .**213** B4
Deeping St Nicholas PE11 . . .**156** D3
Haconby PE10 . . . .**154** C8
2 Keadby with Althorpe
DN17. . . . .**17** C6
Pointon & Sempringham
NG34. . . . .**143** A6
3 Ruskington NG34 . . . . . .**108** D1
2 Tallington PE9 . . . .**172** F7
Tetford LN9 . . . .**73** E1
Thorney NG23 . . . .**78** F8

West Rd *continued*
1 Tydd St Mary PE13. . . . . .**170** C8
West Riverside DN40 . . . . . .**186** E8
West Row 4 PE21. . . . .**208** E4
WESTRUM DN20 . . . .**196** C1
Westrum La DN20 . . . .**196** D2
Westry Cl Barrowby NG32 . .**210** A3
1 Leverington PE13 . . . . . .**170** F1
Westry Cnr NG32 . . . .**210** A4
West St Gdns 8 PE9. . . . . . .**219** A5
West St Mary's Gate 3
DN31 . . . .**191** D7
Westside PE11 . . . .**214** A1
Westside NG31. . . . .**139** E8
Westside Rd
Cranwell & Byard's Leap
NG34. . . . .**107** E1
Grimsby DN31 . . . .**188** F2
West Sq Brigg DN20 . . . .**196** C4
Brigg DN20 . . . .**196** C4
West St Alford LN13 . . . .**75** E2
Barkston NG32. . . . .**130** A8
Barnetby le Wold DN38. . . . . .**21** B4
Billinghay LN4 . . . .**109** F6
Boston PE21. . . . .**208** E4
Bourne PE10 . . . .**213** C5
Cleethorpes DN35 . . . .**192** F6
Clipsham LE15. . . . .**162** B7
7 Crowland PE6 . . . .**166** E1
Easton on the Hill PE9 . . . . .**171** C3
Folkingham NG34 . . . .**142** C8
Gainsborough DN21. . . . . . .**197** B8
Hagworthingham PE23 . . . . . .**87** A4
Helpston PE6 . . . .**173** B4
Hibaldstow DN20 . . . .**30** F5
Horncastle LN9 . . . .**199** A3
Kingston upon Hull HU1 . . . .**180** E6
Long Sutton PE12 . . . .**216** B4
11 Navenby/Wellingore
LN5. . . . .**107** A7
North Kelsey LN7 . . . .**32** A4
Osbournby NG34 . . . .**132** C5
1 Roxby cum Risby DN15 . . .**8** F3
Scawby DN20. . . . .**30** E8
Scunthorpe DN15. . . . .**183** A3
Stamford PE9. . . . .**219** A4
Swaton NG34 . . . .**133** C4
Thorne/Moorends DN8 . . . . .**15** A7
2 Timberland LN4. . . . .**96** B1
West/East Butterwick DN17 . .**28** C8
West Halton DN15 . . . .**8** E7
Winterton DN15. . . . .**9** A5
WEST STOCKWITH DN10 . . . .**40** C6
West Stonebridge PE2. . . .**230** C5
West Syke La LN1 . . . .**66** B7
West Terr DN20 . . . .**196** B3
West Terr St 10 DN17. . . . . .**16** D7
WEST TORRINGTON LN8 . . . .**58** A1
West Torrington Rd LN8 . . .**57** E3
West View
3 Ancaster NG32 . . . .**120** A3
5 Bardney LN3 . . . .**83** B4
Messingham DN17 . . . .**29** C7
15 North Ferriby HU14. . . . . . .**3** A4
Scunthorpe DN17. . . . .**184** E3
West View Cl 8 DN41 . . . . . .**23** A5
West View Cres 25 PE24. . . .**90** D7
Westville Rd PE22 . . . .**112** B2
WEST WALTON PE14 . . . . . .**170** E4
Westward Cl DN34 . . . .**191** C5
Westward Ho DN34. . . . . . .**191** C5
Westward Row LN4 . . . .**207** A5
Westway 18 LN2 . . . .**68** D2
West Way PE25 . . . .**206** D7
West Wells La 4 DN10 . . . . .**39** C1
Westwick Dr LN6. . . . .**205** B7
Westwick Gdns LN6. . . . . . .**205** B6
WEST WILLOUGHBY
NG32 . . . .**119** E2
Westwinds Gdns 19 DN15 . .**9** A5
Westwold Rd 25 LN7. . . . . . .**33** B4
WESTWOOD PE3. . . . .**225** B4
Westwood
6 Broughton DN20 . . . .**19** D4
5 Peterborough PE3. . . . . .**225** C4
Westwood Cl LN6 . . . .**205** A8
Westwood Dr
Bourne PE10 . . . .**213** B4
3 Kingston upon Hull HU4. .**179** B6
Lincoln LN6 . . . .**205** A8
Westwood Ind Est PE3. . . . .**225** D7
Westwood Pk Cl PE3 . . . . . .**225** C3
Westwood Pk Rd PE3. . . . . .**225** D2
Westwood Rd 1 DN41. . . . . .**23** F5
WESTWOODSIDE DN9 . . . . . .**27** A2
Westwoodside CE Prim Sch
DN9. . . . .**27** B2
West Wr Crescen PE7 . . . . .**230** C1
West Wy NG32 . . . .**128** A4
Wetherby Cl
3 Bourne PE10 . . . .**213** C7
6 Market Rasen LN8. . . . . . .**57** E7
Wetherby Cres LN6. . . . . . .**204** F4
Wetherby Way 1 PE1 . . . . .**226** D3
Wetmoor La LN2 . . . .**56** C1
Wetsyke La 4 NG24 . . . . . .**104** C2
Wexford Cl 9 PE10. . . . .**213** E4
Weydike Bank PE12 . . . .**159** A4
Weyford Rd 4 DN35. . . . . . .**193** A1
Weymouth Cl 10 LN5 . . . . . .**205** D3
Weymouth Cres DN17 . . . . .**182** C1
Weymouth Way PE1. . . . . . .**226** D6
Whalebone La NG31. . . . . . .**140** B7
Whale Dro Holbeach PE12. .**168** A1
Whaplode PE6 . . . .**167** E1
Whalley St PE1. . . . .**226** B3
WHAPLODE PE12. . . . .**158** A7

Whaplode CE Prim Sch
PE12. . . . .**158** C7
WHAPLODE DROVE PE12. . . .**168** B4
WHAPLODE ST CATHERINE
PE12. . . . .**158** C2
Wharfdale Cl 6 DN15 . . . . . .**17** E6
Wharfedale Dr 2 LN6 . . . . .**204** F3
Wharfedale Pl 1 DN16 . . . . .**185** E6
Wharfe La
Kirkby on Bain LN10 . . . .**98** C5
Tattershall LN4. . . . .**207** D3
Wharf Rd
Crowle DN17 . . . .**16** D7
Grantham NG31 . . . .**211** A4
12 Horncastle LN9 . . . .**199** B4
12 Misterton DN10. . . . .**39** F5
Peterborough PE2 . . . .**230** E8
Stamford PE9. . . . .**219** C4
Wharfside Mews 6 NG34 .**212** D4
Wharf St 20 NG34 . . . .**160** E4
Wharf The DN36 . . . .**37** A5
Wharncliffe Rd DN31 . . . . . .**189** C3
Wharncliffe Rd N DN31. . . . .**189** B3
Wharncliffe St HU5. . . . .**180** A8
WHARTON DN21. . . . .**41** B4
Wharton Rd DN21. . . . .**41** A5
Wharton St DN31 . . . .**191** B7
Whattoff Way PE6. . . . .**164** D4
Whatton's Cl NG32 . . . .**128** F5
Wheatdole PE2 . . . .**230** A3
Wheatfield Cl
5 Barnby Dun DN3 . . . .**14** A3
Epworth DN9 . . . .**27** F6
2 Kingston upon Hull HU4. .**179** D2
Wheatfield Dr 7 DN37. . . . .**194** C5
Wheatfield Rd LN6. . . . .**200** C1
Wheatfields 1 PE12. . . . . . .**158** B7
Wheatfields Rd PE6 . . . .**164** E2
Wheat Gr 8 NG34 . . . .**212** F3
Wheatgrass La NG32 . . . . . .**119** B7
Wheatholme La NG23 . . . . . .**78** D6
Wheatley Bank PE14 . . . . . .**170** F1
Wheatley La
1 Carlton-le-Moorland
LN5. . . . .**105** E8
Collingham NG23 . . . .**91** D2
Wheatley Lane LN5. . . . .**105** E8
Wheatley Rd DN22 . . . .**52** A3
Wheatmere Dro PE12. . . . . .**157** B5
Wheatsheaf Ave 1 NG24 .**104** A4
Wheatsheaf Cl
3 Holbeach PE12 . . . .**215** B2
Sibsey PE22 . . . .**113** B2
Wheatsheaf Ct 5 PE11 . . . .**166** C6
Wheatsheaf La 4 NG23. . . .**117** D4
Wheatsheaf Way PE9 . . . . .**218** E5
WHEELBRIDGE PE24 . . . .**103** A2
PE24 . . . .**116** A6
Wheeldon St 9 DN21. . . . . .**197** D3
Wheeler Cl PE21 . . . .**209** A4
Wheeler Dr 2 PE21 . . . .**208** E1
Wheeler Prim Sch 9
HU3. . . . .**179** F5
Wheeler St HU3 . . . .**179** F6
Wheelwright Cl PE10 . . . . . .**154** C6
Wheelwrights Ct NG34 . . . .**109** B1
Wheel Yd PE1. . . . .**226** A2
Whelpton Cl LN9 . . . .**199** D3
Whetstone Ct 1 PE1 . . . . . .**226** E7
Whichcote Rd PE6 . . . .**174** C7
Whimbrel Chase DN16. . . . .**185** F5
Whimbrel Way
6 Long Sutton PE12 . . . . . .**216** B4
New Waltham DN36. . . . . . .**195** D7
Whin Moor La HU15 . . . .**2** A7
Whins Gate DN17 . . . .**7** A4
WHISBY LN6 . . . .**79** E2
Whisby Ct DN36. . . . .**195** E2
Whisby Nature Pk ★ LN6 . . .**79** F1
Whisby Rd LN6. . . . .**204** A4
Whisby Way LN6 . . . .**204** C5
Whiston Cl 5 PE4. . . . .**221** D2
Whiston Way 9 DN18 . . . . . .**3** F1
Whitacre PE1. . . . .**226** E6
Whitby Ave PE6 . . . .**175** B1
Whitby Dr DN32 . . . .**192** A5
Whitby St HU8 . . . .**181** B8
Whiteacres 3 PE12. . . . . . .**216** B4
Whitebeam Cl
4 Hampton Hargate PE7. . .**230** D3
Kingston upon Hull HU3 . . . .**180** D5
Whitebread Rd PE20. . . . . . .**136** A7
White Bridges 1 PE21. . . . .**208** E1
White Croft PE3. . . . .**225** B6
Whitecross Gate PE20. . . . .**146** D8
Whitecross La NG34. . . . . . .**121** F1
White Cross La 4 PE11. . . . .**145** D2
Whitecross St 12 DN18 . . . . .**10** F8
Whitefriargate HU1. . . . . . .**180** F6
Whitefriars St 7 LN2. . . . . .**202** E6
Whitefriars Rd LN2. . . . .**202** F6
White Gate LN9 . . . .**73** E2
Whitegate Hill LN7. . . . .**33** C3
Whitehall 5 PE11. . . . .**145** C6
Whitehall Cres LN4. . . . .**205** F4
Whitehall Ctry Cotts
DN35. . . . .**192** A1
Whitehall Gr LN1. . . . .**234** A3
Whitehall Rd 6 DN35. . . . . .**193** A1
Whitehall Terr 1 LN1 . . . . .**234** A3
White Hart La 1 NG23. . . . . .**91** C4
Whitehead Cl 5 LN12 . . . . . .**64** B5
Whitehorse La 10 PE21. . . .**208** F4
White House Cl
29 Hatfield DN7 . . . .**14** C4
4 Stainforth DN7 . . . .**14** C7
White House Garth 19
HU14 . . . .**3** A5

White House La
Boston PE21 . . . . **209** D3
3 West Halton DN15 . . . . **8** E8
White House Mews 16 HU14. **3** A5
Whitehouse Rd 1 NG34 . . . **108** E2
White La Harmston LN5 . . . . . **93** F5
Thorne DN8 . . . . **15** A8
White Leather Sq NG34 . . . **133** C1
Whitemoor La NG23 . . . . . . **91** C3
WHITE PIT LN13 . . . . **74** D4
Whitepit Way LN13 . . . . **74** D4
White Pit Way LN13 . . . . **75** E3
Whitepost Rd PE6 . . . . **174** F3
White Rd DN36 . . . . **48** C8
White Row La LN12 . . . . **64** C1
Whites La LN5 . . . . **92** E2
White's Rd DN35 . . . . **192** F5
White St HU3 . . . . **179** F5
Whitestone Rd PE14 . . . . . . **184** C6
White's Wood Acad DN21 **197** F4
White's Wood La
1 Corringham DN21 . . . . **53** A8
Gainsborough DN21 . . . . . . **197** F4
Whitethorn Gr 7 LN6 . . . . **200** C1
Whitewater PE2 . . . . **229** D6
Whiteways PE2 . . . . **229** D6
Whitewell Cl 4 DN21 . . . . . . **30** B1
White Wlk LN6 . . . . **178** C6
Whitfield Rd DN17 . . . . **184** C6
Whitfield St NG24 . . . . **104** A4
Whitgift Cl DN37 . . . . **23** F1
Whitgift Way DN37 . . . . . . **190** E8
Whiting Sq PE21 . . . . **208** F6
Whitley Cl 5 LN6 . . . . **200** A4
Whitley St 11 LN1 . . . . **67** E5
Whitley Way PE6 . . . . **217** B7
Whitman Cl 9 PE9 . . . . **172** D3
Whitman Rd DN17 . . . . **184** C6
Whitsed Rd 8 PE6 . . . . **174** E5
Whitsed St PE1 . . . . **226** B3
Whittington PE1 . . . . **226** E7
Whittle Cl
11 Beacon Hill NG24 . . . . . **104** A5
2 Boston PE21 . . . . **208** F1
Whittle Rd NG34 . . . . **212** C7
Whittlesey Rd
Peterborough PE2 . . . . **231** B7
Thorney PE6 . . . . **175** F1
WHITTON DN15 . . . . **1** E2
Whitton Rd Alkborough DN15 . **1** C1
Whitton DN15 . . . . **1** E2
Whitwell PE4 . . . . **221** E2
Whitworth Way 12 LN8 . . . **57** D7
Whomsley Cl 4 NG24 . . . . **104** B4
Whoofer La DN21 . . . . **40** E8
Whyalla Cl 2 LN11 . . . . **50** B8
Whyche The LN4 . . . . **109** E5
WICKENBY LN3 . . . . **69** F8
Wickenby Airport LN3 . . . . . **69** F8
Wickenby Cl
6 Grimsby DN34 . . . . **190** F4
Lincoln LN6 . . . . **205** A3
Wickenby Cres LN1 . . . . . . **201** E7
Wickenby Rd LN3 . . . . **57** C1
Wickenby Wy PE25 . . . . **206** B6
Wicken La PE22 . . . . **113** F3
Wicken Way PE3 . . . . **225** C6
Wickham Rd DN31 . . . . **189** C2
Wicklow Ave DN33 . . . . **194** E8
Wick Rd PE7 . . . . **230** B2
Wide Bargate 8 PE21 . . . . **208** F5
Widford Gn 8 DN7 . . . . **14** D3
Widow Fen La LN13 . . . . **76** C3
Wigeon Cl 14 PE12 . . . . . . **167** B8
Wigeon Wk DN16 . . . . **185** F5
Wigford Way LN5 . . . . **234** A2
Wigg La PE24 . . . . **90** D8
Wigmore Dr PE7 . . . . **231** F5
Wignal's Gate PE12 . . . . . . **215** A2
WIGSLEY NG23 . . . . **78** F5
Wigsley Cl 7 LN6 . . . . **204** D6
Wigsley Rd
6 Birchwood LN6 . . . . **204** D6
Harby NG23 . . . . **79** B5
North Scarle LN6 . . . . **78** E3
Wigsley Road NG23 . . . . . . **79** A6
WIGTOFT PE20 . . . . **135** E3
Wigtoft Bank Wigtoft PE20 **135** C3
Wigtoft PE20 . . . . **135** D1
Wigtoft Rd PE20 . . . . **135** F2
Wigtoft Way PE20 . . . . **135** E2
Wike Gate Cl 3 DN8 . . . . . . **15** B7
Wike Gate Gr 2 DN8 . . . . . . **15** B7
Wike Gate Rd DN8 . . . . **15** B8
WIKE WELL END DN8 . . . . . . **15** B7
Wilberforce Dr 6 HU1 . . . **180** F7
Wilberforce House ★ HU1 **181** A6
Wilberforce Rd PE1 . . . . . . **225** E7
Wilberforce St HU3 . . . . . . **180** B6
Wildfowlers Way PE12 . . . . **148** F4
Wildlake PE24 . . . . **230** C5
Wildmore Cl LN4 . . . . **111** C6
Wildmore Cres PE22 . . . . . **114** F6
Wildshed La PE24 . . . . **102** D7
WILDSWORTH DN21 . . . . **40** E8
Wiles Ave 5 PE12 . . . . **157** E1
Wiles's La PE20 . . . . **135** B4
Wilford Gr PE25 . . . . **206** C1
Wilfred Ave NG24 . . . . **104** B2
Wilkie Cl DN15 . . . . **182** C3
Wilkie Dr NG34 . . . . **142** C8
Wilkinson Dr 9 LN8 . . . . **57** B8
Wilkinson Rd 7 NG32 . . . . **117** F1
WILKSBY PE22 . . . . **99** A5
Wilksby La PE22 . . . . **99** A6
Wilks Rd NG31 . . . . **211** A4
Willan Ct PE22 . . . . **230** F8
Willders Garth PE15 . . . . . **215** F2

Willerby Rd HU5 . . . . **179** C8
Willerton Rd 3 LN11 . . . . . . **50** F7
Willesby Rd PE11 . . . . **214** E5
Willesden Ave PE4 . . . . **225** D8
Willey's La PE24 . . . . **90** B8
William Alvey CE Sch
NG34 . . . . **212** E5
William Barcroft Jun Sch
DN32 . . . . **192** C7
William de Yaxley CE Aided
Junior Sch The PE7 . . . . **233** E6
William Farr CE Comp Sch
LN2 . . . . **68** D6
William Gn Cl 9 LN12 . . . . . **76** F8
William Hildyard CE (Aided)
Prim Sch PE6 . . . . **217** B5
William Law CE Prim Sch
PE4 . . . . **220** F5
William Lovell CE Sch
PE22 . . . . **113** A7
William Mews DN37 . . . . . . **194** F5
Williams Cl 1 PE6 . . . . **174** E5
Williams Dr DN39 . . . . **12** B1
Williams La 3 NG34 . . . . . . **104** C1
Williamson Ave PE3 . . . . . . **225** E3
Williamson's Dro LN4 . . . . **110** A3
Williamson St
Kingston upon Hull HU9 . . . **181** C7
Lincoln LN2 . . . . **234** B4
William St
15 Beacon Hill NG24 . . . . . **104** A4
Cleethorpes DN35 . . . . . . **192** E5
2 Grantham NG31 . . . . . . **211** A3
Kingston upon Hull HU1 . . . **180** C5
24 Saxilby LN1 . . . . **66** D2
1 Scunthorpe DN16 . . . . . **183** B2
William Stukeley CE Prim Sch
PE12 . . . . **215** D2
William Tow Cl 7 LN12 . . . . **76** F8
William Way PE25 . . . . **206** B2
William Wright Dock HU3 **180** C3
Williamson La LN2 . . . . **201** F8
WILLINGHAM BY STOW
DN21 . . . . **53** F3
Willingham Hill LN8 . . . . . . **58** E7
Willingham La LN8 . . . . **57** F6
Willingham Rd
East Barkwith LN8 . . . . **58** E1
Fillingham DN21 . . . . **54** D4
Lea DN21 . . . . **53** A5
Market Rasen LN8 . . . . **57** E7
Marton DN21 . . . . **53** B1
Tealby LN8 . . . . **58** A7
Willingham St DN32 . . . . . . **191** E6
Willington Rd PE20 . . . . . . **136** A7
Willoughby DN32 . . . . **191** F8
Willis Cl LN1 . . . . **234** A4
Willis Terr LN1 . . . . **234** A4
Willonholt PE3 . . . . **225** C7
Willoughby Mdw Nature
Reserve ★ LN13 . . . . **89** B6
WILLOUGHBY LN13 . . . . **89** B7
Willoughby Ave 2 PE6 . . . **217** C5
Willoughby Branch Line
Nature Reserve ★ LN13 . **89** A7
Willoughby Chase DN21 . . **197** E1
Willoughby Cl
Corby Glen NG33 . . . . **152** F7
Helpringham NG34 . . . . . . **133** E7
Silk Willoughby NG34 . . . . **121** B1
Willoughby Ct PE1 . . . . **226** E8
Willoughby Dr 1 PE23 . . . . **88** A1
Willoughby Gall The ★
NG33 . . . . **152** F8
Willoughby Gr 5 DN34 . . . **190** F4
WILLOUGHBY HILLS PE21 . . **209** E7
Willoughby La
Authorpe LN11 . . . . **74** F8
Muckton LN11 . . . . **62** C1
Waddington LN5 . . . . **205** C1
Willoughby Mdw Nature
Reserve ★ LN13 . . . . **89** B6
Willoughby Mem Trust Gall ★
NG33 . . . . **152** F7
WILLOUGHBY MOOR
NG32 . . . . **119** F2
Willoughby Rd
16 Alford LN13 . . . . **75** F2
Ancaster NG32 . . . . **119** D7
Aunsby & Dembleby NG34 . **132** B4
Boston PE21 . . . . **209** A7
Bourne PE10 . . . . **213** E4
Claxby St Andrew LN13 . . . . **88** F6
Cumberworth LN13 . . . . . . **89** E8
14 Hibaldstow DN20 . . . . . . **31** A5
Mablethorpe/Sutton on Sea
LN12 . . . . **64** C1
Scunthorpe DN17 . . . . **184** E5
Sleaford NG34 . . . . **120** F4
Stamford PE9 . . . . **219** C7
Willoughby Road Prim Acad
DN17 . . . . **184** F4
Willoughby Sch DN17 . . . . **213** D3
Willoughby St 1 DN21 . . . **197** D3
WILLOUGHTON DN21 . . . . . . **42** D4
Willoughton Prim Sch
DN21 . . . . **42** D4
Willoughton Rd 3 PE25 . . **206** D2
Willow Ave
4 Misterton DN10 . . . . **39** F5
Peterborough PE1 . . . . **226** B7
Willow Bank Lane DN21 . . . **40** C4
Willowbrook Dr DN20 . . . . **196** A4
Willow Cl 12 Barnetby DN38 . **21** B4
Gainsborough DN21 . . . . . **197** B7
10 Heckington NG34 . . . . . **122** E3
Horncastle LN9 . . . . **199** A5
6 Laceby DN37 . . . . **23** E1

Willow Cl continued
Ruskington NG34 . . . . **108** D1
17 West Saxilby LN1 . . . . . . **66** D2
Scopwick LN4 . . . . **95** D1
Skellingthorpe LN6 . . . . . . **200** B3
Willow Ct
3 Bracebridge Heath LN4 . . **81** A1
Heighington/Washingborough
LN4 . . . . **203** C2
18 Long Bennington NG23 . **117** D3
1 Sleaford NG34 . . . . **212** B1
14 Wragby LN8 . . . . **70** D4
Willow Dr
14 Barton-upon-Humber
DN18 . . . . **3** F1
9 Bourne PE10 . . . . **213** C7
27 Brough HU15 . . . . **2** C5
2 Coningsby LN4 . . . . **207** D4
Kingston upon Hull HU10 . . **178** D8
Louth LN11 . . . . **198** C8
35 Messingham DN17 . . . . . **29** D7
Willow Dro PE6 . . . . **174** E6
Willowfield Ave 12 LN2 . . . . **68** D2
Willow Gdns 2 DN19 . . . . . . **11** D8
Willow Gr
1 Keadby with Althorpe
DN17 . . . . **17** D6
7 Scawby DN20 . . . . **30** F8
Scunthorpe DN16 . . . . **185** C2
Willow Hall La PE6 . . . . **227** D6
Willow Holt PE7 . . . . **230** C3
Willow La Billinghay LN4 . . . **109** E6
3 Cranwell NG34 . . . . **120** F8
Dunston LN4 . . . . **95** C6
3 Goxhill DN19 . . . . **5** A1
Grantham NG31 . . . . **210** F2
Ruskington LN4 . . . . **109** B3
Willowmead Cl DN15 . . . . . **182** C6
Willow Pk DN37 . . . . **194** B4
Willow Rd 1 Branston LN4 . . **81** D2
Lincoln LN6 . . . . **204** F2
5 Newark-on-Trent NG24 . . **104** B3
Stamford PE9 . . . . **218** D7
Willow Row PE11 . . . . **214** E5
Willow Row Bank LN11 . . . . **62** F6
Willows Cl PE13 . . . . **160** A1
Willows Ct LN4 . . . . **207** A4
Willows La PE22 . . . . **125** F7
Willows Prim Acad DN37 . **190** E8
WILLOWS THE DN37 . . . . . . **190** E7
Willows The
6 Cranwell NG34 . . . . **107** F1
5 Crowland PE6 . . . . **166** E1
Glinton PE6 . . . . **220** D8
Kingston upon Hull HU13 . . **178** E4
Willow Tree Cl DN40 . . . . . **186** D5
Willow Tree Gdns LN6 . . . . **204** C8
Willow Wlk PE11 . . . . **214** E5
Willow Wy NG32 . . . . **128** A6
WILL ROW LN12 . . . . **63** C5
Will Row LN12 . . . . **63** C5
Wilmington Dr 18 LN12 . . . . **77** A8
Wilmore La DN38 . . . . **32** E7
WILSFORD NG32 . . . . **120** C1
Wilsford La NG32 . . . . **120** A2
Wilson Cl
Ingoldmells PE25 . . . . **90** C3
8 North Ferriby HU14 . . . . . . **3** A4
Wilson Ct LE15 . . . . **162** A8
Wilsons Cl DN15 . . . . **183** B3
Wilson St
Cleethorpes DN35 . . . . . . **192** D8
Gainsborough DN21 . . . . . **197** B5
2 Kingston upon Hull HU10 **178** E6
Kingston upon Hull HU10 . . **178** E6
4 Kingston upon Hull HU9 . **181** B7
Lincoln LN1 . . . . **234** A4
WILSTHORPE PE9 . . . . **164** C4
Wilsthorpe Rd PE10 . . . . . . **164** C6
Wilton Ave 14 PE24 . . . . . . **90** D7
Wilton Ct PE3 . . . . **225** C4
Wilton Dr PE3 . . . . **225** C4
Wilton Rd DN16 . . . . **192** D1
Wilton Rd Ind Est DN36 . . **195** F8
Wilton Road Ind Est
DN36 . . . . **192** D1
Wilton St HU8 . . . . **181** B8
Wiltshire Ave DN15 . . . . **8** B4
Wiltshire Rd HU4 . . . . **179** E2
Wilyman Cl 21 LN12 . . . . . . **77** A7
Wimberley Cl 3 PE12 . . . . **157** D7
Wimberley Way
8 Boston PE11 . . . . **156** E8
3 South Witham NG33 . . . **151** D2
Wimbishthorpe Cl 3
NG13 . . . . **128** A6
Wimborn Ave DN34 . . . . . . **191** B6
Wimborne Dr 7 PE1 . . . . . **226** E7
WINCEBY PE23 . . . . **86** E3
Winceby Ave DN31 . . . . **191** B8
Winceby Gdns LN9 . . . . **199** D4
Winceby Rd LN9 . . . . **86** D2
Winchcombe Ave DN34 . . . **190** E4
Winchelsea Prim Sch
Ruskington NG34 . . . . **108** D1
Winchelsea Rd 14 NG34 . . **108** E1
Winchester Ave DN33 . . . . **191** A3
Winchester Cl
3 Bracebridge Heath LN4 . . **81** A2
6 Skegness PE25 . . . . **206** D7
Winchester Ct 9 LN6 . . . . . . **93** B8
Winchester Dr
Bottesford DN16 . . . . **185** C3
Heighington/Washingborough
LN4 . . . . **203** C1
6 Mablethorpe/Sutton on Sea
LN12 . . . . **64** A3

Winchester Rd
Grantham NG31 . . . . **210** E4
13 Hatfield DN7 . . . . **14** C4
8 Wainfleet All Saints
PE24 . . . . **102** D2
Winchester Way
Peterborough PE3 . . . . **225** E1
Sleaford NG34 . . . . **212** C7
Winchilsea Ave 18 NG24 . . **104** A4
Wincolmlee HU2 . . . . **181** A7
Windass Ct HU13 . . . . **178** E1
Windermere Ave
4 Grimsby DN33 . . . . **194** E7
Lincoln LN6 . . . . **205** A2
Windermere Cres DN36 . . . **192** E1
Windermere Rd LN2 . . . . . . **202** D8
Windermere Way PE4 . . . . **221** C3
Windgate Way PE8 . . . . **222** A6
Windlass Cl 6 DN8 . . . . **15** A8
Windle Dr PE10 . . . . **213** E2
Windlesham Ave DN33 . . . . **194** D7
Windmill Cl Holbeach PE12 **215** B2
Market Deeping PE6 . . . . . **217** D5
4 Waddington LN5 . . . . **93** F6
Windmill Dr
Burgh le Marsh PE24 . . . . . **102** D8
3 Heckington NG34 . . . . . **122** E2
Windmill Gdns 3 PE13 . . . **170** E2
Windmill La 5 Alford LN13 . **75** F2
Gosberton PE11 . . . . **144** F6
Windmill St PE1 . . . . **225** F5
Windmill View 3 LN1 . . . . **234** A4
Windmill Way HU13 . . . . . . **178** F1
Windrush Dr PE4 . . . . **221** D1
Windsmoor Rd 13 LN8 . . . . **47** B6
Windsor Ave
Holbeach PE12 . . . . **215** F2
1 Kingston upon Hull HU10 **178** E7
3 Peterborough PE4 . . . . . **225** C8
Windsor Bank PE21 . . . . . . **209** A3
Windsor Cl Collingham NG23 **91** D4
6 Keelby DN41 . . . . **23** A5
1 Sleaford NG34 . . . . **212** B2
4 Stamford PE9 . . . . **219** B7
6 Sudbrooke LN2 . . . . **68** F2
Windsor Cr 4 PE7 . . . . **230** B1
Windsor Cres Boston PE21 **209** A4
1 Crowle DN17 . . . . **16** C7
4 Ingoldmells PE25 . . . . . . **90** D3
Scunthorpe DN17 . . . . **184** F2
Yaxley PE7 . . . . **233** F2
Windsor Ct
3 Bourne PE10 . . . . **213** C3
1 Grimsby DN31 . . . . **189** C1
12 Hatfield DN7 . . . . **14** C2
Windsor Dr 19 Caistor LN7 . **33** B4
Grantham NG31 . . . . **211** E5
Peterborough PE2 . . . . **231** D6
Spalding PE11 . . . . **214** D2
Wisbech PE13 . . . . **170** D2
Windsor Gdns DN15 . . . . . . **216** C5
Windsor Gr 1 DN19 . . . . **5** A1
Windsor La DN17 . . . . **16** C7
Windsor Mews LN11 . . . . . **198** C5
Windsor Pk Cl 5 LN6 . . . . . **204** F1
Windsor Rd
Cleethorpes DN35 . . . . . . **192** C5
Crowle DN17 . . . . **16** C7
Louth LN11 . . . . **198** B8
Yaxley PE7 . . . . **233** F6
Windsor Terr 11 PE21 . . . . **209** A5
Windsor Way
Barnetby le Wold DN38 . . . **21** B5
Broughton DN20 . . . . **19** E4
Wine Hill La LN11 . . . . **51** B5
Winfrey Ave PE11 . . . . **214** D4
Wingate Parade DN37 . . . . **190** E8
Wingate Rd DN37 . . . . **190** D8
Wingate Way PE10 . . . . . . **213** E7
Wing Dr PE21 . . . . **209** C4
Wingfield PE2 . . . . **229** F3
Wingfield Ct NG31 . . . . **210** F1
Winn Ct DN35 . . . . **192** E5
Winniffe Gdns LN2 . . . . **202** D7
Winn La 4 LN9 . . . . **86** B8
Winnowsty La LN2 . . . . **234** C3
Winn St Lincoln LN2 . . . . . . **234** C2
2 Scunthorpe DN16 . . . . . **183** B2
Winship Cl 4 HU3 . . . . **180** C5
Winslow Dr DN40 . . . . **186** B5
Winslow Gate PE12 . . . . . . **159** B8
Winslow Gr 2 DN34 . . . . . . **190** F4
Winslow Rd
4 Boston PE21 . . . . **209** C4
Peterborough PE3 . . . . **225** C3
Winsover Rd PE11 . . . . **214** B3
Winston Ave DN34 . . . . **191** B6
Winston Dr PE25 . . . . **206** B6
Winston Gdns PE21 . . . . . . **209** A7
Winston Rd PE23 . . . . **100** F8
Winston Way
5 Brigg DN20 . . . . **196** D4
Farcet PE7 . . . . **231** C2
Winterbeck Cl 5 NG13 . . . **128** A6
Winterdale Cl 7 NG24 . . . . **104** B5
Wintergold Ave PE11 . . . . . **214** A5
WINTERINGHAM DN15 . . . . . . **2** A1
Winteringham Foreshore
Nature Reserve ★ DN15 . . **2** B1
Winteringham La DN15 . . . . **2** A1
Winteringham Prim Sch
DN15 . . . . **2** A1
Winteringham Rd DN15 . . . . **9** B6
Winter Ct DN21 . . . . **197** D2
Winter's La
9 Long Bennington
NG23 . . . . **117** D4
Long Sutton PE12 . . . . **160** A3

WINTERTON DN15 . . . . **9** A5
Winterton PE1 . . . . **221** E1
Winterton CE Inf Sch DN15 . **9** A5
Winterton Cl 7 PE9 . . . . . . **218** F6
Winterton Com Acad DN15. **9** A6
Winterton Rd
Roxby cum Risby DN15 . . . . **8** F2
Scunthorpe DN15 . . . . **183** B4
Winteringham DN15 . . . . . . **9** B8
WINTHORPE
Langford NG23 . . . . **104** B8
Skegness PE25 . . . . **206** C8
Winthorpe Ave PE25 . . . . . **206** D8
Winthorpe Cl 17 LN6 . . . . **204** D7
Winthorpe Gr 16 LN6 . . . . **204** D7
Winthorpe Prim Sch
NG23 . . . . **104** C8
Winthorpe Rd
Birchwood LN6 . . . . **204** D7
Grimsby DN33 . . . . **191** B3
Kingston upon Hull HU13 . . **178** F3
4 Kingston upon Hull
HU13 . . . . **179** A3
8 Newark NG24 . . . . **104** B7
Winthorpe Way
Ingoldmells PE25 . . . . **206** D8
Skegness PE25 . . . . **90** E1
Winton Gdns 17 LN5 . . . . . **107** A8
Winton Rd 11 LN5 . . . . **107** A8
Wintringham 28 HU15 . . . . . **2** C6
Wintringham Rd DN32 . . . . **191** E6
Winwick Pl PE3 . . . . **225** C5
Winyates PE2 . . . . **229** F3
Winyates Prim Sch PE2 . . **230** A3
Wire Hill La LN8 . . . . **70** E5
Wirral Ave 7 DN34 . . . . . . **190** F4
WISBECH PE13 . . . . **170** B1
Wisbech Rd
Long Sutton PE12 . . . . **216** C1
Thorney PE6 . . . . **176** A3
Walpole PE14 . . . . **161** C1
Walsoken PE14 . . . . **170** C2
Wisbech St Mary PE13 . . . . **177** A2
Wisdom Cl 23 NG24 . . . . . **104** C1
Wiseholme Rd LN6 . . . . **200** B2
Wiseman's Gate 1 PE12 . . **157** D7
Wiske Ave 3 HU15 . . . . **2** D5
WISPINGTON LN9 . . . . **84** E6
Wispington Road LN9 . . . . . **84** E7
Wistaria Cl PE13 . . . . **170** E1
Wisteria Ave LN4 . . . . **81** D2
Wisteria Dr DN41 . . . . **23** F5
Wisteria Rd PE7 . . . . **233** D4
Wisteria Way Bourne PE10 **213** B7
Scunthorpe DN16 . . . . **185** E4
Werrington PE4 . . . . **221** B3
Wistow Gr HU4 . . . . **179** D5
Wistow Way PE2 . . . . **229** D6
Witchford Cl 2 LN6 . . . . . . **204** B6
Witchford Rd 3 LN6 . . . . . **204** B6
Witham HU9 . . . . **181** B7
Witham Ave PE22 . . . . **125** D5
Witham Bank Dogdyke LN4 **110** D8
Timberland LN10 . . . . **97** C3
Witham Bank E 4 PE21 . . . **208** E6
Witham Bank W PE21 . . . . **208** E6
Withambrook Pk NG31 . . . . **211** F7
Witham Cl
7 Beacon Hill NG24 . . . . . **104** A5
Lincoln LN6 . . . . **205** D5
11 Ruskington NG34 . . . . . **108** D2
Stamford PE9 . . . . **219** C6
Witham Cres PE10 . . . . **213** A4
Witham Ct 2 Boston PE21 . **208** E6
Lincoln LN6 . . . . **201** D2
Witham Dr
6 Burton upon Stather
DN15 . . . . **8** B5
Chapel Hill LN4 . . . . **110** E5
Witham Gdns PE21 . . . . . . **208** E6
Witham Gn PE21 . . . . **208** E6
Witham Hall Prep Sch
PE10 . . . . **163** D7
Witham/Haven Mouth Nature
Reserve ★ PE22 . . . . **137** F6
Witham Mews LN4 . . . . **234** A1
WITHAM ON THE HILL
PE10 . . . . **163** D7
Witham Pl Boston PE21 . . . **208** E5
Grantham NG31 . . . . **211** C2
Witham Prospect Sch LN6 . **92** B2
Witham Rd
Gunby & Stainby NG33 . . . **151** C4
5 Long Bennington NG23 . **117** D4
Spalding PE11 . . . . **214** A4
Thistleton LE15 . . . . **151** C1
Woodhall Spa LN10 . . . . . . **97** B5
WITHAM ST HUGHS LN6 . . . **92** D5
Witham St PE21 . . . . **208** F5
Witham Town PE21 . . . . . . **208** E6
Witham View LN4 . . . . **203** A2
Witham Vw LN3 . . . . **82** F4
Witham Way
Peterborough PE4 . . . . **221** D1
Westborough NG23 . . . . . . **117** F3
WITHCALL LN11 . . . . **60** C2
WITHERN LN13 . . . . **63** A1
Withern Rd DN33 . . . . **191** A3
Withington St 1 PE12 . . . . **160** E4
WITTERING PE8 . . . . **172** B1
Wittering Airfield PE8 . . . . **171** F1
Wittering Cl 5 LN6 . . . . . . **204** D6
Wittering Ford Rd PE8 . . . **172** C1
Wittering Prim Sch PE8 . . **172** B1
Wittering Rd PE9 . . . . **172** D3

Witty St HU3. . . . . .180 A3
Wivell Dr **1** DN41 . . . . .23 A5
Wlker Cl **22** NG24 . . . . .104 A4
Woad Farm Rd PE21 . . . . .209 B4
Woad La Fishtoft PE22 . . . .137 C7
Grimsby DN31 . . . . .188 A2
Long Sutton PE12 . . . . .216 E5
Woburn Ave LN1 . . . . .201 E6
Woburn Cl Lincoln LN1 . . . .198 B7
4 Market Deeping PE6 . . .217 A5
Peterborough PE3 . . . . . . .225 A1
Woburn Dr Grantham NG31 .211 F5
Thorney PE6 . . . . .176 A2
Woburn Gr **1** LN10 . . . . . . .97 C5
Woburn St HU3 . . . . .179 F4
Woffindin Cl **12** NG31 . . . . .97 E5
Woldcarr Rd East Ella HU3 .179 F7
Kingston upon Hull HU3 . . .179 F6
WOLD NEWTON LN8 . . . . . .47 F7
Wold Rd
Barrow upon Humber DN19 . .11 D7
Burnham DN18 . . . . .10 F4
Kingston upon Hull HU5 . . .179 C8
Wootton DN39 . . . . .11 C2
Worlaby DN20 . . . . .10 E1
Wolds Cl **5** DN17 . . . . .16 D7
Wolds Leisure-De Aston
Sports Ctr LN8 . . . . .57 E7
Wolds The DN21 . . . . .43 D6
Wold The DN38 . . . . .21 E3
Wold View **1** Brigg DN20 . .196 D4
25 Brough HU15. . . . . .2 C6
Caistor LN7 . . . . .33 C4
Fotherby LN11 . . . . .49 A2
Holton le Clay DN36 . . . . .195 C2
3 Nettleham LN2 . . . . . . .68 D2
Rothwell LN7 . . . . .33 F2
Wolf La PE13 . . . . .169 F1
Wolfreton Ct
3 Anlaby HU10 . . . . .178 E6
Anlaby HU10 . . . . .178 E6
Wolfreton Dr HU10 . . . . . .178 F6
Wolfreton Garth HU10 . . . .178 D8
Wolfreton La HU10 . . . . . .178 F8
Wolfreton Mews HU10 . . . .178 F7
Wolfreton Rd HU10 . . . . . .178 F7
Wolfreton Sch HU10 . . . . .178 C7
Wolfreton Villas **5** HU10 .178 F7
Wolla Bank Nature Reserves★
PE24 . . . . .77 D1
Wollaston Rd
Cleethorpes DN35 . . . . . . .192 E6
Peterborough PE3 . . . . . . .225 C6
Wolseley Cl PE7 . . . . .233 D6
Wolsey Dr **6** DN19 . . . . . . .11 C7
Wolsey Rd NG24 . . . . .104 A6
Wolsey Way LN2 . . . . .202 D8
Womersley Rd DN31 . . . . .189 C2
Wong Gdns NG32 . . . . . . .210 A4
Wong Row NG31. . . . . .211 A5
Wongs La PE24 . . . . .102 B7
Wong The LN9 . . . . .199 B3
Woodale Cl DN15 . . . . . . .182 C6
Woodapple Ct **4** DN41 . . . .23 E6
Woodbank
1 Deeping St Nicholas
PE11 . . . . .166 C6
Skellingthorpe LN6 . . . . . .200 A3
Woodbine Ave DN20 . . . . .196 C4
Woodbine Contemporary
Arts★ PE12 . . . . .168 A3
Woodbine St PE2 . . . . . . .231 A8
Woodbridge Rd NG34 . . . .212 E6
Woodbridge Rd Ind Est
NG34 . . . . .272 E6
Woodbridge Way **15** LN10. .97 C5
Woodburn Cl LN1 . . . . . . .201 E8
Woodburn View **13** LN1 . . .201 E8
Woodbyth Rd PE1 . . . . . . .226 A6
Wood Carr La DN9 . . . . . . .16 C2
Wood Cl DN33 . . . . .194 F7
Woodclose Rd DN17 . . . . .184 D6
Woodcock La LN1 . . . . . . .200 C8
Woodcock St HU3. . . . . . . .180 A4
Woodcote Cl PE1 . . . . . . .226 A7
Woodcroft Cl **9** PE6 . . . . .217 A5
Woodcroft Rd
Marholm PE6 . . . . .220 A3
4 Saxilby LN1 . . . . .66 C2
Woodcross Ave DN16 . . . .185 D4
Wood Dr **4** HU14 . . . . .3 A5
Wooden Beck Hill DN10 . . .39 E2
Wood End NG33. . . . . .131 A1
WOOD ENDERBY PE22 . . . . .98 F6
Wood Enderby La LN9 . . . . .98 D6
Wood Farm Cl **12** LN7. . . . .33 A3
Woodfield **7** PE9 . . . . . . .171 B1
Woodfield Ave LN6 . . . . . .200 C1
Woodfield Cl
9 Birchwood LN6 . . . . . .200 C1
15 Humberston DN36 . . . . .36 D8
Spalding PE11 . . . . .214 F2
Woodfield La HU13 . . . . . .178 C1
Woodfield Rd
Gainsborough DN21 . . . . . .197 F5
Peterborough PE3 . . . . . . .225 D3
Woodford Gdns DN15 . . . .169 E3
Woodgarr Ave **4** DN17 . . . .17 D6
Woodgate PE6 . . . . .173 C4
Woodgate La
Beckingham LN5 . . . . .105 C4
Kingston upon Hull HU5 . . .179 F8
Maxey PE6 . . . . .173 D6

Woodgate La continued
Maxey PE6 . . . . .217 A1
Woodgate Rd
Kingston upon Hull HU5 . . .179 F7
Leverington PE13 . . . . .170 A2
7 Moulton PE12 . . . . . . .157 E1
Woodgates Cl **15** HU14 . . . .3 A5
Woodgates La HU14 . . . . . .3 A6
Woodgates Mount **3** HU14 .3 A5
Woodhall Cl PE21 . . . . . . .208 C5
Woodhall Cres **9** LN1 . . . .66 C2
Woodhall Dr Lincoln LN2. . .201 F8
Waltham DN37. . . . . .194 C4
Woodhall Rd
Horncastle LN9 . . . . .199 A3
Roughton LN9. . . . . .85 C3
Stixwould LN10 . . . . .97 C7
Woodhall Rise PE4 . . . . . .220 F6
WOODHALL SPA LN10 . . . . .97 E5
Woodhall Spa Cottage Mus★
LN10. . . . . .97 D6
Woodhead Cl **4** PE9 . . . . .219 D7
Woodhill Ave DN21 . . . . . .197 E6
Woodhill Cl **2** HU10. . . . . .178 E7
Wood Hill Rd DN21 . . . . . . .29 B3
Woodhill Rise HU13 . . . . . .178 C2
WOODHOUSE DN9 . . . . .16 E3
Woodhouse Gn Rd DN7 . . . .14 B8
Woodhouse La
2 Belton DN9 . . . . .16 E3
Hatfield DN7 . . . . .14 D2
Holbeach PE12. . . . . .159 A8
Moulton PE12. . . . . .159 A8
Woodhouse Prim Sch DN7 .15 A4
Woodhouse Rd DN16 . . . . .185 E8
Woodhouse St HU9 . . . . . .181 D7
Woodhurst Rd PE2 . . . . . .231 D6
Wood La Bardney LN3 . . . . .83 B4
Beckingham DN10 . . . . .52 A8
Croxton Kerrial NG32 . . . . .138 A6
Fishlake DN7 . . . . .14 D8
Gringley on the Hill DN10 . . .39 C2
1 Lincoln LN6 . . . . .93 A8
Little Cawthorpe LN11 . . . . .61 F2
Louth LN11. . . . . .198 D4
Norton Disney LN6 . . . . . . .92 B3
Quadring PE11 . . . . .135 C1
South Kyme LN4 . . . . .109 F1
South Kyme LN4 . . . . .123 B8
South Scarle SG23 . . . . . . .91 F7
Sturton le Steeple DN22 . . . .52 A3
Thurlby PE10 . . . . .213 C1
Woodland Ave
1 Bourne PE10 . . . . . . .213 B5
22 Brough HU15. . . . . .2 C6
15 Crowle DN17. . . . . . . .16 D8
Gainsborough DN21. . . . . .197 B7
Skellingthorpe LN6 . . . . . .200 B2
Woodland Chase DN21 . . .197 E5
Woodland Cl **13** PE22 . . . .114 A1
Woodland Dr
8 Broughton DN20 . . . . . .19 D4
5 Elsham DN20. . . . . . . .20 F7
Grantham NG31. . . . . .211 F7
Kingston upon Hull HU10 . .178 C6
6 Woodhall Spa LN10 . . . .97 E6
Woodland End HU4 . . . . . .179 C5
Woodland Lea **2** PE6 . . . .173 B4
Woodland Park HU13 . . . . .178 B1
Woodland Rise LN11 . . . . .198 A6
Woodlands Langford NG24 .104 B8
Long Sutton PE12 . . . . . . .216 D4
5 Louth LN11 . . . . .198 C6
Woodlands Acad PE23 . . . . .87 F1
Woodlands Ave
Immingham DN40 . . . . . . .186 C5
15 Keelby DN41 . . . . .23 A4
6 Spilsby PE23 . . . . .87 F1
Woodlands Cl
5 Barrow upon Humber
DN19 . . . . .11 C7
Potter Hanworth LN4 . . . . . .95 B8
Woodlands Dr
1 Colsterworth NG33 . . .151 E7
Grantham NG31. . . . . .211 C4
Woodlands Inf Sch LN6. . . .200 C1
Woodlands La **14** HU15 . . . .2 C6
Woodlands Prim Sch
DN33 . . . . .191 A2
Woodlands Rd HU5 . . . . . .179 B7
Woodlands Rise **7** HU14 . . .3 A5
Woodlands The
11 Beacon Hill NG24 . . . .104 C4
3 Market Deeping PE6 . . .217 B5
Peterborough PE1 . . . . . . .226 E5
1 Stallingborough DN41. . .23 D6
Woodland View
2 Barnetby le Wold DN38 . .21 B4
Lincoln LN4 . . . . .234 C3
Scunthorpe DN15 . . . . . . .182 C3
15 Spilsby PE23 . . . . . . .101 A8
Woodland Way **16** DN9 . . . .27 E6
Woodland Wlk **1** DN35. . . .192 E1
Woodlea Cl **2** DN17 . . . . . .14 D2
Woodmans Cl **15** NG34. . . .122 D3
Woodman's Ct **4** PE22 . . . .98 F4
Woodmill Bank PE12 . . . . .159 F2
WOODNOOK NG33 . . . . . . .140 C7
Woodpecker Cl LN6 . . . . . .200 A3
Woodpecker Ct PE6 . . . . . .221 E2
Woodpecker Way DN21. . . . .42 E8
Wood Rd **24** LN13 . . . . .75 F2
Woodrow Pk DN33 . . . . . . .191 D1
Woodrow Pl PE11 . . . . . . .214 B4

Woodrush Rd **6** LN2 . . . . .202 C8
Woods Cl **14** NG23 . . . . . . .117 D3
WOODSIDE DN9 . . . . .26 D6
Woodside Boston PE21 . . . .208 E1
Branston & Mere LN4. . . . . .81 D2
Kingston upon Hull HU13 . .178 D1
8 Swanland HU14. . . . . . . .3 C7
Woodside Ave NG34. . . . . .212 D6
Woodside Cl **1** PE10 . . . . .164 C8
Woodside Ct NG34 . . . . . .212 D7
Woodside Dr DN17 . . . . . .184 C5
Woodside E PE10 . . . . . . .164 D8
Woodside Falconry &
Conservation Ctr★ LN3. . .69 D3
Woodside La DN9 . . . . .26 D6
Woodside Rd PE20 . . . . . .136 B5
Woods La Drayton PE20 . . .136 B5
2 South Killingholme DN40. .12 F2
Wood's La
Kingston upon Hull HU1 . . .180 E5
3 Pinchbeck PE11. . . . . .145 D2
Woodsley Ave DN35 . . . . .192 E5
Woods Mdw **1** DN20 . . . . .30 F6
Wood St **3** DN32. . . . . . . .191 F8
Woods Terr DN21 . . . . . . .197 C5
Woodstock **27** NG24 . . . . .104 A4
Woodstock Rd DN16. . . . . .183 D1
Woodstock St LN1 . . . . . . .201 D4
WOODSTON PE2 . . . . .230 E7
Woodstone Gate PE2. . . . .230 D6
Woodston Ind Est PE2 . . . .230 E6
Woodston Prim Sch PE2. . .230 D7
Woods Way DN36 . . . . .36 C4
WOODTHORPE LN13 . . . . . . .75 D7
Woodthorpe Ave PE21 . . . .209 C4
Woodvale Ave LN6 . . . . . .204 C6
Woodvale Cl **14** LN6 . . . . .204 C6
Wood View Bourne PE10 . .213 C5
1 Messingham DN17 . . . . .29 C7
3 Swanland HU14 . . . . . . .3 B7
Woodville Gdns E **3**
PE21. . . . . .208 D3
Woodville Gdns W **2**
PE21. . . . . .208 D3
Woodville Rd PE21 . . . . . .208 D4
Woodward Dr **6** PE4. . . . .221 E2
Woodward's La
Little Sutton PE12 . . . . . . .160 B3
Long Sutton PE12. . . . . . . .216 F1
Woodwards The **1** NG24 . .104 B3
Wood Way LN11 . . . . .198 E5
Woodyard The **4** NG32. . . .119 B7
Woolcroft Cl **2** PE13 . . . . .170 A1
Woolfellhill Rd PE6 . . . . . .174 F1
Woolgard PE3 . . . . .225 A3
Woolley's La
Castle Bytham NG33 . . . . .152 A4
North Witham NG33 . . . . . .151 F4
Woollin Ave DN17 . . . . . . .185 A6
Woolpack Mdws LN11 . . . . .50 F7
Woolram Wygate PE11 . . . .214 C5
WOOLSTHORPE BY BELVOIR
NG32 . . . . .128 D1
WOOLSTHORPE-BY-
COLSTERWORTH NG33. . .151 D7
Woolsthorpe La
Belvoir NG32 . . . . .138 D7
Bottesford NG13 . . . . .128 C4
Woolsthorpe Manor★
NG33. . . . . .151 D7
Woolsthorpe Rd **3** NG33 . .151 D7
Woolwich Dr **2** HU4 . . . . .179 B2
WOOTTON DN39 . . . . .11 F3
Wootton Ave PE2 . . . . . . .231 A6
Wootton Ct DN17 . . . . . . .184 C8
Wootton Dr PE2. . . . . .230 F6
Wootton Rd Grimsby DN33 .191 A3
Wootton DN39 . . . . .11 F2
Worlaby DN20 . . . . .10 F1
Wootton St Andrews CE Prim
Sch DN39. . . . . .11 E3
Worcester Ave DN34 . . . . .191 A4
Worcester Cl
11 Birchwood LN6 . . . . . .204 D7
7 Bracebridge Heath LN4. .81 A2
5 Louth LN11 . . . . .198 C5
Scunthorpe DN16 . . . . . . .185 A2
Worcester Cres **4** PE9 . . .219 B6
Worcester Rd
Grantham NG31. . . . . .210 D4
4 Wisbech PE13 . . . . . . .170 D1
Wordsworth Cl
3 Grantham NG31 . . . . .211 E6
Peterborough PE4 . . . . . . .225 E8
Wordsworth Ct
5 Grimsby DN31. . . . . . .189 C1
13 Sleaford NG34. . . . . .212 F4
Wordsworth Dr NG24. . . . .104 B3
Wordsworth Gr **2** PE10 . .213 D3
Wordsworth Rd
North Greetwell LN3 . . . . .203 C6
Scunthorpe DN17 . . . . . . .184 D6
Wordsworth St **6** LN2. . . .234 B3
Workhouse La
Algarkirk PE20 . . . . .136 B1
Hogsthorpe PE24 . . . . .90 C7
Workington Ave **8** HU4 . . .179 B6
Works La NG23 . . . . .117 A3
Worlaby Acad DN20 . . . . . .20 D8
Worlaby Rd DN33 . . . . . . .191 B1
World's End Rd PE13 . . . . .160 A1
Worldwide Way DN41 . . . . .187 C2
Wormgate PE21. . . . . .208 F5
Worship St HU2. . . . . .180 F7
Worsley PE2 . . . . .230 A4

Worsley Cl
1 Holton le Clay DN36. . .195 C2
Immingham DN40 . . . . . . .186 D4
Worsley Rd DN40. . . . . . . .186 D4
Worthington La NG32 . . . .128 D1
Worthington Rd **6** NG24 . .104 C2
Wortley's La PE21 . . . . . . .208 A2
Wortley St DN16 . . . . .183 A4
WOTHORPE PE9 . . . . .219 B2
Wothorpe Hill PE9 . . . . . .219 A1
Wothorpe Mews **3** PE9 . . .219 B4
Wothorpe Rd PE9 . . . . . . .219 B4
WRAGBY LN8. . . . . .70 E5
Wragby Prim Sch LN8 . . . . .70 D5
Wragby Rd Bardney LN3. . . .83 C4
Holton cum Beckering LN8. .70 C7
Lincoln LN2 . . . . .234 C3
Lissington LN3 . . . . .57 C2
Reepham LN3 . . . . .68 F1
Scunthorpe DN17 . . . . . . .184 D5
Stainfield LN8. . . . . .83 B6
Wragby Rd E
Greetwell LN2 . . . . .203 A8
Reepham LN3 . . . . .68 E1
Wragby St **3** DN32. . . . . .191 F7
WRAGHOLME LN11 . . . . . . .50 A8
Wragholme La LN11 . . . . . .50 A8
Wragholme Rd LN11 . . . . . .50 A8
WRANGLE PE22. . . . . .114 C1
WRANGLE BANK PE22. . . . .114 B4
Wrangle Bank PE22 . . . . . .114 B4
WRANGLE LOWGATE
PE22. . . . . .114 D2
Wrangle Prim Sch PE22 . . .114 C2
WRANGLE LOW GROUND
PE22. . . . . .114 D4
Wrangle Prim Sch PE22 . . .114 C2
WRAWBY DN20 . . . . .20 E4
Wrawby Rd Brigg DN20 . . .196 D4
Scunthorpe DN17 . . . . . . .184 C5
Wrawby St Mary's CE Prim
Sch DN20. . . . . .20 E4
Wrawby St DN20 . . . . .196 C3
Wray Cl **9** DN37 . . . . .194 C5
Wray St **20** DN21 . . . . .30 B1
Wren Cl
Deeping St Nicholas PE11 . .166 B6
11 Healing DN41 . . . . .23 F5
15 Market Deeping PE6 . . .217 C5
4 Sleaford NG34. . . . . . .212 B3
Wren Cres DN33 . . . . .191 B2
WRESSLE DN20. . . . . .19 F4
Wressle Rd DN20. . . . . .19 E3
Wright Ave PE2 . . . . .231 D5
Wright's Dro PE6 . . . . . . .175 B7
Wrights Gdns DN10 . . . . . .40 A3
Wrights La **5** LE14 . . . . . .150 C1
Wright's La Friskney PE22. .115 A5
Sutton Bridge PE12 . . . . . .160 E4
Wright St HU2 . . . . .180 E7
Wrightsway LN2 . . . . .202 D5
WROOT DN9 . . . . .26 C5
Wroot Rd DN9 . . . . .26 A3
Wroot Road DN9. . . . . .27 A6
Wroot Travis Charity Prim Sch
DN9. . . . . .26 D5
Wroxall Dr NG31 . . . . .210 E4
Wroxham Ave DN34 . . . . . .190 E5
Wroxham Cl **7** LN6 . . . . . .205 A2
Wrygarth Ave **7** HU15. . . . .2 C5
Wulfram Dr NG31 . . . . . . .211 E2
Wulfric Sq PE3. . . . . .225 C8
Wyatt Ave **13** DN20 . . . . . .19 D3
Wyatt Cl LN4. . . . . .96 B2
Wyatt Rd LN5 . . . . .205 D7
Wybeck Rd DN15 . . . . . . .183 A6
Wybers Way DN37. . . . . . .190 D7
WYBERS WOOD DN37 . . . . .190 C6
Wybers Wood Prim Sch
DN37 . . . . .190 C8
Wybert Cres **6** PE21 . . . . .136 D8
Wybert La PE21 . . . . .136 D8
WYBERTON PE21 . . . . .136 D8
Wyberton Low Rd **1**
PE21. . . . . .208 F2
Wyberton Prim Sch PE21. .136 E7
Wyberton Roads PE20 . . . .137 A7
Wyberton W Rd PE21 . . . .208 C2
Wyche Ave **13** PE6. . . . . . .166 F1
Wycliffe Gr PE4. . . . . .220 E5
Wydham Pk PE2 . . . . .229 D6
Wye Pl PE4 . . . . .221 C1
Wye Valley Rd **3** PE2. . . . .230 E8
Wygate Mdws LN11 . . . . . .214 B5
Wygate Park Acad PE11 . . .214 B4
Wygate Park Academy
PE11. . . . . .214 A4
Wygate Pk PE11. . . . . .214 A5
Wygate Rd PE11 . . . . .214 B4
Wyggeston Ave **22** NG13 . .128 A6
Wyggeston Rd **21** NG13 . . .128 A6
WYKEHAM PE12 . . . . .145 F1
Wykeham La
Burgh on Bain LN8 . . . . . . .59 C6
Weston PE12 . . . . .145 F1
Wykes La PE11 . . . . .135 A2
Wykes Rd Donington PE11. .135 B1
Yaxley PE7. . . . . .233 D4
Wyke St HU9. . . . . .181 D7
Wyke The **8** PE11. . . . . . .214 A3
Wyke Wy HU15. . . . . .2 E5
Wylson Cl **5** NG34 . . . . . .120 F8
Wyman Way PE2 . . . . .229 D5
Wymark View DN33 . . . . . .190 F3
Wymersley Rd HU5 . . . . . .179 A8
WYMONDHAM LE14 . . . . . .150 B1

Wymondham Drift LE14. . .150 D1
Wyndham Cl NG31 . . . . . . .211 C5
Wyndham Rd **9** DN36 . . . .195 C6
Wyndham St HU3 . . . . . . .180 C7
Wynmoor Rd DN17 . . . . . .184 F7
Wyredale Dr DN16. . . . . . .185 D5
Wyside Cres PE7 . . . . .230 B1
Wythes La PE21. . . . . .126 C2
Wyton Cl **8** LN6 . . . . .204 B6
Wyvern Cl **3** DN17. . . . . . .16 D8
WYVILLE NG32 . . . . .139 C4
Wyville Rd Grantham NG31 .210 E1
Hungerton NG32 . . . . .139 B4
Little Ponton & Stroxton
NG31. . . . . .139 E8
Wyville Wlk LN6. . . . . .204 F7

Y

YADDLETHORPE DN17 . . . .184 E3
Yale Cl LN4. . . . . .203 D1
YARBOROUGH DN34 . . . . . .191 A7
Yarborough Cl **3** DN36. . . .195 C2
Yarborough Cres
17 Broughton DN20 . . . . . .19 E4
Lincoln LN1 . . . . .201 E6
Yarborough Ct DN15 . . . . .182 B2
Yarborough Dr **3** DN31 . . .191 D8
Yarborough Leisure Ctr
LN1. . . . . .201 E6
Yarborough Prim Sch
DN34. . . . . .190 F7
Yarborough Rd
Boston PE21 . . . . .136 E8
Brigg DN20. . . . . .196 B3
Grimsby DN34 . . . . .190 F6
Keelby DN41 . . . . .23 A5
1 Lincoln LN1 . . . . .234 A4
Scunthorpe DN16. . . . . . . .19 A4
9 Skegness PE25 . . . . . .206 A6
Yarborough Rise LN7. . . . . .33 C4
Yarborough Terr LN1. . . . .234 A4
YARBURGH LN11. . . . . .49 E4
Yarburgh Rd LN11. . . . . . . .49 E2
Yarde The **2** PE10 . . . . . .213 E2
Yardley Way **2** DN34 . . . .190 D4
Yards End La PE7 . . . . . . .233 A1
Yarmouth Ave
Grantham NG31. . . . . .210 D4
3 Kingston upon Hull HU4. .179 A3
Yarnsworth Rd **6** NG24. . .104 A2
Yarra Rd DN35 . . . . .192 F6
Yarrow Rd DN34 . . . . .190 F7
Yarwell Cl PE2 . . . . .230 D7
Yarwell Rd PE8 . . . . .222 A3
Yawling Gate Rd PE22. . . .114 F5
YAWTHORPE DN21 . . . . . . .42 A2
YAXLEY PE7. . . . . .233 E6
Yaxley Infant Sch PE7. . . .233 F4
Yew Cl HU13. . . . . .178 D3
Yew Dr DN16. . . . . .185 B2
Yew Gro **19** DN36. . . . . . . .36 C8
Yews La **4** DN37 . . . . .23 E1
Yew Tree Cl **1** PE10. . . . . .213 C6
Yewtree Dr HU5. . . . . .179 B7
Yew Tree Gr **1** PE21 . . . . .209 C2
Yew Tree Way **1** NG24. . . .104 C5
Yew Tree Wlk PE3. . . . . . . .225 A2
York Ave Lincoln LN1. . . . .201 D4
Scunthorpe DN16. . . . . . . .185 B4
York Cl LN4. . . . . .203 D1
York Dr **33** HU15 . . . . .2 C5
Yorke Dr NG24. . . . . .104 A5
York Gdns
2 Gosberton PE11 . . . . .145 B6
30 Wisbech PE13 . . . . . . .170 D1
York House Rd NG34. . . . .120 C8
York Pl DN35 . . . . .192 C4
York Rd
5 Binbrook Tech Pk LN8 . .47 B5
Bourne PE10 . . . . .213 C3
Brigg DN20. . . . . .196 B4
Hatfield DN7 . . . . .14 D4
Kirton in Lindsey DN21 . . . .30 C1
Mablethorpe/Sutton on Sea
LN12 . . . . .64 D1
Peterborough PE1 . . . . . . .225 F6
RAF Cranwell NG34 . . . . . .107 C1
Sleaford NG34 . . . . .212 C6
9 Stamford PE9 . . . . . . .219 B6
Wisbech PE13 . . . . .170 D1
York Ride **4** PE12 . . . . . . .216 B3
York St (Boston United FC)
PE21. . . . . .209 A5
Yorkshire Moors Bottom Road
DN17 . . . . .16 B8
Yorkshireside DN17 . . . . . . .7 A3
York St Boston PE21. . . . . .209 A4
Grimsby DN31 . . . . .191 C8
York Terr **3** DN10. . . . . . . .40 A5
York Way
5 Bracebridge Heath LN4. .81 A2
Grantham NG31. . . . . .210 C5
York Wy **4** PE25 . . . . .206 D7
Youlgrave Ave **6** LN12 . . . .77 A8
Younger's La PE24 . . . . . .103 A8
Young Pl DN35 . . . . .192 B7
Youngs Ave **9** NG24. . . . .104 C1
Youngs Cl **18** NG24 . . . . . .104 C5

Z

Zara Cl PE21 . . . . .209 A4
Zetland St HU3. . . . . .180 A5